NAB Broadcast Engineering and IT Conference (BEITC 2025)

AA005530

Las Vegas, Nevada, USA
5-9 April 2025

ISBN: 979-8-3313-1938-0

Printed from e-media with permission by:

Curran Associates, Inc.
57 Morehouse Lane
Red Hook, NY 12571

CURRAN ASSOCIATES INC. proceedings.com

Some format issues inherent in the e-media version may also appear in this print version.

National Association of Broadcasters (NAB)
1 M Street SE
Washington, D.C. 20003

Phone: (202) 429 5300

www.nab.org

Additional copies of this publication are available from:

Curran Associates, Inc.
57 Morehouse Lane
Red Hook, NY 12571 USA
Phone: 845-758-0400
Fax: 845-758-2633
Email: curran@proceedings.com
Web: www.proceedings.com

NATIONAL ASSOCIATION OF BROADCASTERS

Proceedings of the
2025 NAB Broadcast Engineering and IT Conference
Table of Contents

Proceedings of the
2025 NAB Broadcast Engineering and IT Conference
Table of Contents

NATIONAL ASSOCIATION OF BROADCASTERS

Proceedings of the
2025 NAB Broadcast Engineering and IT Conference
Table of Contents

Proceedings of the

2025 NAB Broadcast Engineering and IT Conference

Table of Contents

Proceedings of the
2025 NAB Broadcast Engineering and IT Conference
Table of Contents

NAB®

NAB Broadcast Engineering and Information Technology Conference

PROCEEDINGS 2025

A collection of papers from the 2025 NAB Broadcast Engineering and Information Technology (BEIT) Conference

These Proceedings contain technical papers presented at the 2025 NAB Broadcast Engineering and Information Technology (BEIT) Conference, April 5 – 9, 2025.

Published by the NAB Technology Department.

NATIONAL ASSOCIATION OF BROADCASTERS

Foreword

In 2025, we celebrate the 79th annual NAB Broadcast Engineering and Information Technology (BEIT) Conference. Throughout BEIT's history, we have witnessed the continued evolution of broadcast and media technology. Technical topics like AI, 5G, streaming and cloud are as impactful as AM and FM radio and TV that made up the first Broadcast Engineering Conference many decades ago. ATSC 3.0 continues its march toward deployment and is enabling emerging services like the Broadcast Positioning System (BPS™).

This year the NAB BEIT Conference Proceedings serve as both a reminder of and an inspiration for this technical evolution and documents the many applications of innovative technologies to broadcasting and media. Papers on cloud technologies, media workflows, artificial intelligence, BPS™, ATSC 3.0 and other timely topics are all solidly represented. We hope that this informative collection of over 45 technical papers will serve as an important reference for you.

The NAB BEIT Conference was developed under the guidance of the NAB BEIT Conference Committee. This committee had the difficult task of selecting the papers to present among the many qualified proposals, and their hard work has resulted in an exceptional conference lineup and an equally worthy Proceedings publication.

We would also like to thank our producing partner organizations for their support, ideas and initiative - the Society of Broadcast Engineers (SBE), Institute of Electrical and Electronics Engineers Broadcast Technology Society (IEEE-BTS), the North American Broadcasters Association (NABA), Public Media Venture Group (PMVG) and the Society of Cable Telecommunications Engineers (SCTE).

Thank you for participating in the NAB BEIT Conference, and we welcome any feedback you may have on ways to improve the Proceedings.

Sincerely,

Sun Sachs
2025 NAB BEIT Conference Committee Chair
Townsquare Media

Sam Matheny
Executive Vice President, Technology, and Chief Technology Officer
National Association of Broadcasters

1 M Street SE
Washington DC 20003 3512
Phone 202 429 5300
nab.org

NATIONAL ASSOCIATION OF BROADCASTERS

2025 NAB Broadcast Engineering and IT Conference

Program Committee

Sun Sachs (Chair)
Senior Vice President, Product, Digital & Engineering
Townsquare Media
Purchase, N.Y.

Rick Ackermans
Director, RF and Transmissions Engineering
CBS Operations and Engineering
New York, N.Y.

Harvey Arnold
Senior Vice President, Engineering
Sinclair Broadcast Group
Hunt Valley, Md.

Cindy Hutter Cavell
Director, Cavell-Mertz Spectrum Division
Capitol Airspace Group
Haymarket, Va.

Felipe Chavez
Chief Operating Officer
Bustos Media
Tucson, Az.

David Kolesar
Senior Broadcast Engineer
Hubbard Broadcasting
College Park, Md.

Sarah Foss
Chief Technology Officer
Audacy, Inc.
Philadelphia, Pa.

Chris Homer
Director of Engineering
KGUN TV
Tucson, Az.

Jason Ornellas
Regional Director of Technology
Bonneville International Corporation
Sacramento, Calif.

Anthony Plosz
Chief Technology Officer
Graham Media Group
Chicago, Ill.

David Burke
Chief Technology Officer
Gray Television
Atlanta, Ga.

Thomas Edwards
Senior Manager, Product, Solutions Architecture
Amazon Web Services
Los Angeles, Calif.

Joe Seccia
Regional Director, RF Transmission
TelevisaUnivision, Inc.
Miami, Fla.

Marisabel Rodriguez
Global Services Manager
Google Cloud
Buenos Aires, Argentina

Partner Organization Representatives

NABA:
Rebecca Hanson
Director-General
North American Broadcasters Association
Toronto, Ontario, Canada

SBE:
Stan Moote
Chief Technology Officer
International Association of Broadcasters and Media
Toronto, Ontario, Canada.

SCTE:
Dean Stoneback
Senior Director, Engineering and Standards
SCTE
Exton, Pa.

IEEE-BTS:
Terry Douds
IEEE Broadcast Technology Society
Lancaster, Ohio

Digital-Only Boosters for HD Radio Single-Frequency Networks

Alan Jurison
Independent Consultant
Syracuse, New York, United States
ajurison@storm.net

Jeff Baird, Mike Raide
Xperi
Columbia, Maryland, United States

Abstract – While analog FM and hybrid HD Radio boosters in Single Frequency Networks (SFNs) have been widely studied, deployed, and discussed, this paper will explore experimental observations of the first fielded high-power IBOC digital-only booster using off-the-shelf Gen4 HD Radio™ hardware. What makes this different from existing installations is that the booster transmits a digital-only MP1 signal with no host analog FM component. Topics include potential applications, appropriate timing of implementations, and impact on analog and digital signal performance in the field.

Summary of FM Single Frequency Networks (Boosters) in the United States

In the United States, the Federal Communications Commission has authorized FM boosters under 47 C.F.R. Part 74 for decades. Many broadcasters have implemented these systems in the analog FM-only domain with varying degrees of success. Generically and historically speaking, the most successful implementations have traditionally been deployed in areas with severe terrain blockages. The general opinion regarding boosters deemed successful in this category was that the terrain caused enough isolation between the two signals that the synchronization (or lack thereof comparing yesterday's technology with today's modern precision methods) were only secondary improvement factors.

In areas with little to no terrain shielding, FM boosters have historically been unsuccessful because there has been no reliable way to deliver the identical FM stereo composite multiplex signal from the main transmission site to the individual booster nodes in a single frequency network. Other factors include using outdated booster node siting methods, incorrect assumptions using outdated propagation models, as well as booster antenna selection, directional patterns and orientation.

Coverage in areas without significant terrain isolation between the main and booster signal(s) has been plagued for decades due to a variety of factors. Most notably, challenges existed within the broadcast transmission ecosystem on how to reliably deliver a synchronized copy of the primary FM analog stereo composite multiplexed signal to the booster site(s) and to have precision delay controls of these systems to offset the propagation delay of the two arriving signals in mutual interference areas. These deployments historically used isolated off-the-air reception, Studio-to-Transmitter (STL) links via legacy analog microwave, equalized phone lines, and in later iterations, moved to digital AES audio transport at either 32 kHz, 44.1 kHz, or 48 kHz linear Pulse Code Modulation (PCM) encoded audio over Time

Division Multiplexed (TDM) based T1/E1 lines once commonly used by telecommunications providers, or digital radio systems that emulated the T1/E1 environment in a Point-to-Point (P2P) digital link via microwave.

While much work was performed on these systems to make them the best available for synchronization, given the resources and technology at the time, the signals delivered to the modulator stage in exciters located at the main transmitter and booster node(s) were never truly identical. Even with the introduction and migration to digital audio, distribution, and precision timing delay methods yielded improvement over previous designs, analog-only booster networks often still had mixed successes.

Perhaps the most common mistake noticed in large, competitive markets is when the main transmitter site is using the latest modern digital audio processor with an internal stereo generator and transmitter, but the booster site is using an integrated stereo generator inside the exciter at the booster site. Even if dual-matched digital audio processors were employed, they would never truly be synchronized. As demonstrated in the research and development phases of NRSC-G203, *NRSC IBOC Time and Level Alignment Guideline* [1], separate audio processors and stereo generators available even today are essentially "time machines" and do not uniformly treat precisely time-aligned incoming audio signals in a deterministic manner to their output to the main and booster exciters.

Other booster implementations often used different exciter manufacturers or models from the main and booster sites, which have their own throughput delay characteristics from audio input to RF output, which most broadcasters do not have the knowledge or toolsets to measure. This became particularly important as exciters evolved from analog designs and implemented Digital Signal Processing (DSP) and later Field Programmable Gate Arrays (FPGA) systems. Very rarely was the exciter the same make and model for both the main and booster stations, and even if they were so, firmware versions and configuration settings were often not known or coordinated, causing dissimilarities in the analog FM modulation waveforms emitted from each site.

Finally, until recently, exciters did not have direct-on-board GPS discipline for time aligning the incoming signals, nor did they have any mechanisms to synchronize the modulated output using GPS reference. Some older exciters offered 10 MHz and 1 PPS inputs, but as discovered in the NRSC-G203 NRSC IBOC Time and Level Alignment Guideline research, different reference oscillator output and input sections on exciters were never identically matched and often suffered from clocking errors over time due to dissimilar electrical interfaces, sampling techniques within the exciters, and external factors such as cable quality, length, and termination. In essence, the industry was going down the right path; however, moving from external reference sources to direct-on-board GPS references in the HD Radio Exporter, exciters, and IP transport encoder/decoder has proven to be far more reliable. Now all the components in the system have consistent, reliable, and identical clocking.

Thus, historically speaking, prior to 2018, the main and booster nodes often had varying differences in FM modulation envelopes in multiple domains (timing, frequency) that broadcasters tried to control to the best of their ability, given the equipment that was available. However, this was far from the level of precision required to implement a successful analog FM booster or SFN network with minimal mutual interference in areas without terrain isolation.

As the FM IBOC HD Radio system became widely adopted in North America, stations with boosters desired to add hybrid digital to these single frequency network/booster nodes to gain the benefits of audio quality and signal robustness of the digital system in both the main and booster coverage areas. HD Radio employs a digital modulation scheme known as Orthogonal Frequency-Division Multiplexing (OFDM). However, the Gen3 and prior transmission architectures of HD Radio offered no means to deterministically synchronize the Layer 1 OFDM timing. Therefore, while it was possible to outfit a network of hybrid FM+HD main and boosters, the signal processing throughput of these different exciters, and even the HD carrier generation was never synchronized at the Layer 1 OFDM frame to the degree of accuracy needed to yield acceptable results in mutual interference areas, causing destructive mutual interference within the digital domain.

Similarly, because of this lack of deterministic capabilities, the time-aligned analog FM and HD1 content could depart from each other, and the coherence of these two dissimilar signals at both the main and or booster sites simultaneously was impossible to achieve, yielding a poor listener/consumer experience. Typically, broadcasters would synchronize FM / HD1 audio on the main signal due to its larger geographical footprint and typically larger population coverage. The boosters, with smaller coverage areas, would have FM/HD1 synchronization errors and continuous alignment drifting patterns far exceeding the NRSC-5-E specification of ±68 microseconds (μs). This is equivalent to ±3 audio samples at a sampling rate of 44.1 kHz [2]. This provided poor listener experience during blends on any Gen3-fielded FM+HD booster. Also, since the Layer 1 OFDM frames were never synchronized, the mutual interference areas received destructive digital interference, and the radios blended more frequently to impaired, unaligned analog audio.

Present-day Solutions

In the mid-2010s, industry technologists came together to work on designs and overcome many of these early implementation issues. Today, broadcasters are finally able to achieve what they had hoped for decades ago. Xperi and various transmission and IP codec manufacturers started developing and later implementing the Generation 4 (Gen4) transmission architecture in new transmitters, and that offered for the first time the technical capabilities to synchronize the HD Radio IBOC OFDM Layer 1 physical layer with precision between multiple exciters with a high degree of accuracy (within 1 μs).

Audio processors have moved to "single-box" FM+HD integrated designs, where FM and HD1 audio are processed identically. Newer IP transport solutions that can digitally encode and decode the analog FM stereo composite multiplex signal alongside the HD Radio Exporter to Exciter (E2X) transport protocol have proven to be key technologies we did not have before. The analog FM stereo composite baseband can be either encoded directly by the processor AES 192 kHz format, or some SFN transport systems can encode an analog baseband input into AES 132 kHz – 192 kHz for SFN synchronization and transport. The confluence of having hybrid analog FM+HD digital transmissions linked together in the current Gen4 iteration of SFN-enabled systems has allowed broadcasters to achieve a degree of accuracy never realized in earlier iterations of hardware or previous system designs.

Now with the proper hardware, firmware/software, configuration, and implementation of best practices, commercialized solutions allow the arrival of these signals to be distributed to the main and any number of booster nodes over IP Networks. Because the analog FM frequency domain is now an exact identical copy at the main and booster exciter(s), and the HD Radio E2X data network is also replicated, this information can be assembled by the modulator of the exciter and combined with GPS synchronization, precisely and deterministically transmitted at the main transmitter site as well as the booster site(s), proving very ideal for SFNs. Because the copies of these signals are digital streams, they can now be easily and identically replicated, allowing support for multiple FM boosters or nodes of an SFN and geographically distributed without much additional effort.

With new commercialized solutions available for broadcasters to procure and implement, there has been a notable increase in successful and sustainable FM+HD booster deployments across North America [3]. An example of FM+HD SFN testing in Canada is shown in Figure 1. These are not only successful in areas with severe terrain challenges, but the industry is also seeing some positive impacts from boosters in areas that may have little to no terrain isolation.

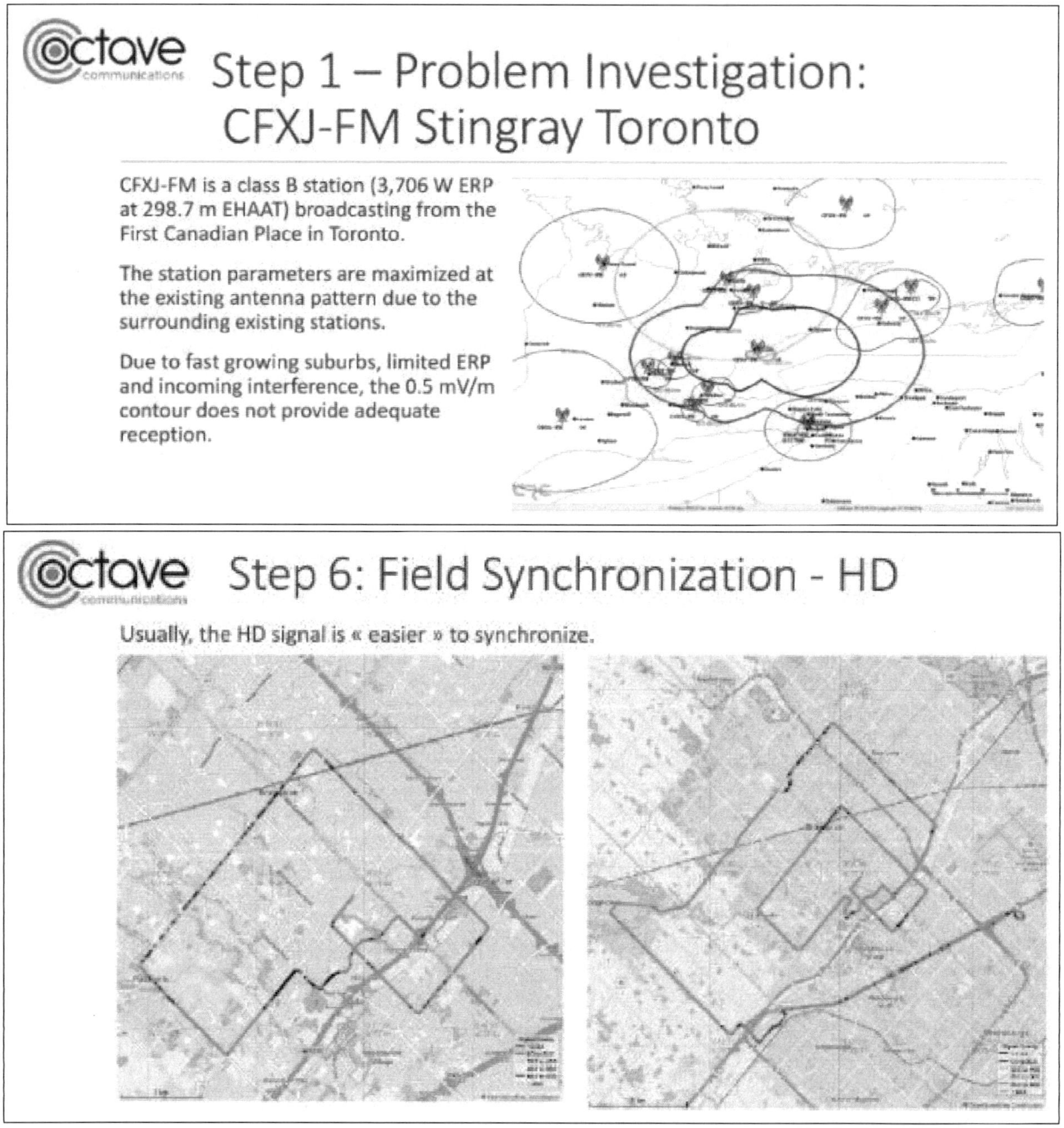

FIGURE 1: FM+HD BOOSTER EXPERIMENTAL TESTING CFXJ, TORONTO, CANADA [3].
COURTESY FRANCOIS GAUTHIER (USED WITH PERMISSION).

Absent Terrain, Modern Day Analog Caveats Still Exist

Consider the simple form of a single main primary station and single booster/SFN station, (i.e., a 1:1 relationship). It is now possible to constrain the main and booster signals to have identical signals, and an engineer can easily adjust the timing of the signal in a graphical user interface (GUI) to reduce mutual interference areas, but one can still run into trouble.

Even with these new tools, the analog portion of FM booster/SFN networks is still incredibly challenging if stringent engineering and design principles are not met. The transmission systems are now accurate within 1 μs at a single point location (for modern sited systems, this is generally at or near the booster site). As the signal is amplified to higher powers and the signal departs the booster's antenna system, the laws of physics and propagation still prevail. The signal propagates one kilometer in 3.33 μs, or at one mile 5.37 μs (1.61 km). The mixing of these two identical signals may perfectly be aligned and arrive in an optimized area, but as you depart from that area, in its simplest form, it is possible that an analog FM-only receiver will receive the two signals and create a multipath-like effect as they arrive at the receiver at slightly offset times. Other factors, including true multipath and Raleigh-fading of the incident signals, can still compound and create undesired effects in the analog domain.

Absent no severe terrain blockages, if the analog FM coverage footprint of a booster site causes a delay spread larger than 10 - 15 μs in geography, there is enough propagation delay between the main and booster signals to create mutual interference that some may find listening to be concerning or objectionable. ITU-R BS.412-9 [4] and ITU-R BS.1284-1 [5] help inform us of the strict signal ratios and time of arrival requirements to produce a high-quality analog FM booster/SFN.

The analog FM ITU recommendations were later affirmed in laboratory testing by Philipp Schmid of Nautel in 2009 [6] as shown in Figure 2 as well as joint lab research and field testing in 2016 conducted by Mr. Schmid of Nautel [7] and John Kean, then of Kean Consultants, LLC [8] as shown in Figure 3.

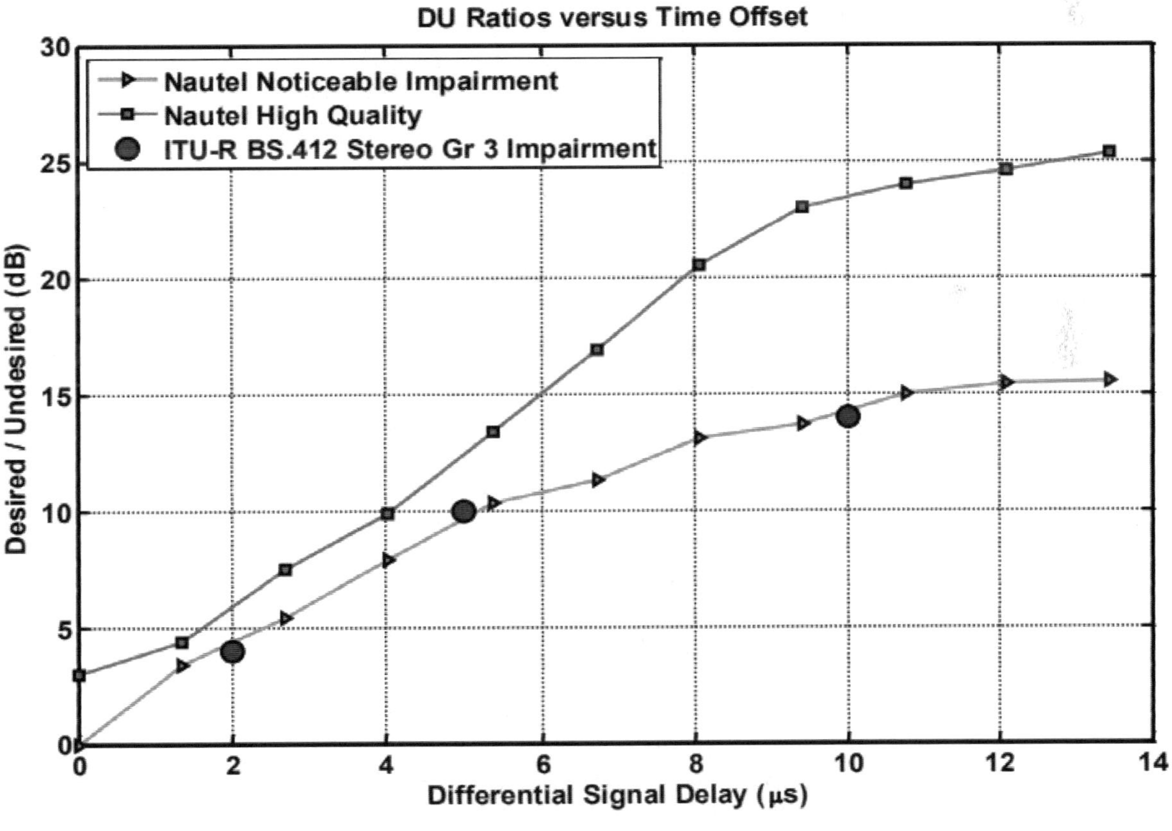

FIGURE 2: STEREO FM SFN AUDIO IMPAIRMENT TESTS [6], [7].
COURTESY NAUTEL (USED WITH PERMISSION).

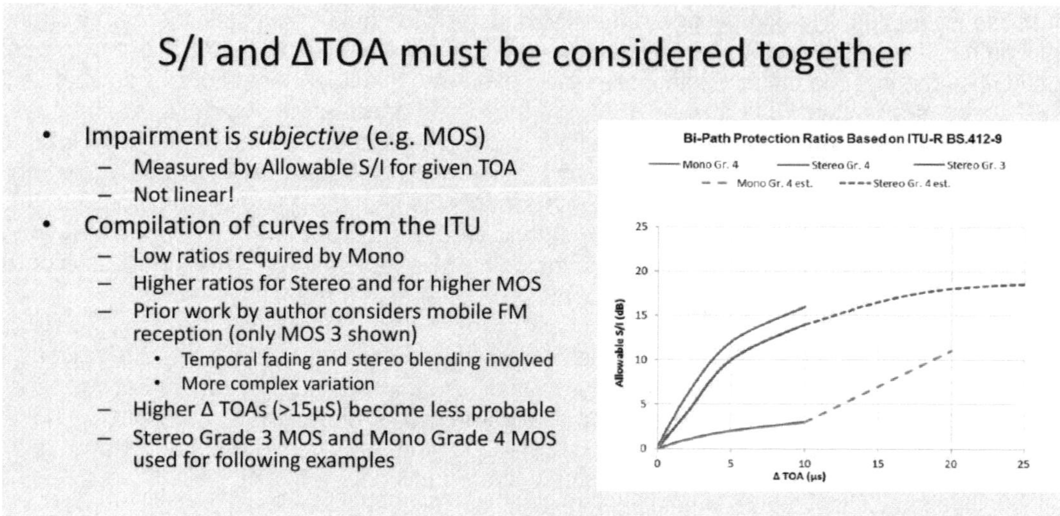

FIGURE 3: 2016 KPCC/KUSC FIELD TESTING ANALYSIS [8].
COURTESY JOHN KEAN (USED WITH PERMISSION).

In general terms, engineers designing and siting modern analog FM booster systems have been adapting by creating additional booster/SFN sites that cover smaller areas to reduce analog mutual interference zones. Tools available involve using lower Effective Radiated Power (ERP) and employing tighter directional patterns to limit the arrival delay of the main and booster signals in the desired improvement area within the analog domain as much as possible. The authors of this paper acknowledge that it may be an effective design response to mitigate mutual interference in the analog FM domain.

However, we note that constructing, operating, and maintaining booster sites is an expensive proposition. The equipment to achieve this is not inexpensive, and other operating cost factors such as tower/site leases, electrical utilities, generators, redundant high-bandwidth and high-quality IP delivery via fiber, point-to-point microwave, or satellite networks are needed to support these SFNs. Monitoring, maintenance, and engineering human resource factors are also to be considered. As such, the more boosters that are employed, the higher the capital and operating costs are for a station. This cost structure is something that readers should be aware of and factor in their business decisions.

Also, adding additional boosters/SFN nodes (1:2+) can create even more complex interference scenarios if three or more signals are mixing and creating mutual interference at a given location. Caution should be used in these situations.

Digital Coverage Benefits

While the analog domain can remain challenging, implementing a properly configured and synchronized HD Radio SFN has a host of major benefits. The HD Radio OFDM Layer 1 transport layer uses a robust modulation and coding system that supports booster/SFN use in its underlying design principles. Over the last two decades, as this system was deployed, it was theorized that HD Radio SFNs would be much more robust than analog SFNs because of a design implementation feature in OFDM systems known as a guard interval.

In simplest terms, the beginning of each symbol is preceded by a guard interval. If the echoes fall within this interval, they will not affect the receiver's ability to safely decode the actual data, as data is only interpreted outside the guard interval [9].

The HD Radio FM transmission systems specifications specify a guard interval of 75 μs [10]. While the system designers, transmission manufacturers, and interested broadcasters knew this specification, it was unknown how well this would directly translate into measurable field coverage. For example, what is the maximum difference in arrival times of a main and booster signal, considering factors such as propagation phenomena, Rayleigh fading, multipath, environmental noise, and other effects?

Xperi, transmitter manufacturers, and engineering consulting firms created lab simulations to test the limits of the 75 μs specification limit. The prevailing wisdom gained from the lab simulations was that broadcasters could safely divide that number in half, to 30 - 35 μs and not be concerned about destructive digital interference from the main and booster, so long as all incident signals or rays of the main FM and booster(s) arrived at the receiver within that 30 - 35 μs.

The number is effectively halved due to real-world environmental impacts we find in the field, including issues like broadband noise within the FM band, incoming first adjacent channel interference, Rayleigh fading, multipath, nearby terrain or man-made obstructions (like buildings, overpasses, retaining walls, etc.) that cause signal blockage or reflections, doppler shift in moving vehicles and other factors. As illustrated in Figure 4, ITU-R BS.2214-6 Table 91 Terrain Obstructed Fast Rayleigh Multipath (TORM) channel model can introduce up to 16 μs of delay in the most severe conditions [11].

Terrain Obstructed Fast Rayleigh Multipath (TORM) channel model

Ray	Delay (μs)	Attenuation (dB)	Doppler frequency (Hz)
1	0.0	10.0	5.231 (reflects ~60 km/h
2	1.0	4.0	
3	2.5	2.0	
4	3.5	3.0	
5	5.0	4.0	
6	8.0	5.0	
7	12.0	2.0	
8	14.0	8.0	
9	16.0	5.0	

FIGURE 4: ITU-R BS.2214-6 TABLE 91 [11], DESCRIBING THE TERRAIN OBSTRUCTED FAST RAYLEIGH MULTIPATH (TORM) CHANNEL MODEL.

These items impact the coding redundancies and cumulatively subtract from the "link budget" of the theoretical lab 75 μs value.

Early Digital Field Tests

While it was thought that 30 - 35 μs was a safe value to design an HD Radio SFN, these numbers were assumed based on theoretical and laboratory studies. To confirm this, Russ Mundschenk, Field Test Manager and Senior Manager of Broadcasting Engineering *(now retired)* at Xperi *(then iBiquity Digital)* with funding from NAB FASTROAD, performed low-power HD Radio Booster/SFN tests in 2009 - 2011 on stations WD2XAB / WD2XAB-FM1 Baltimore and WKLB-FM / WKLB-FM1 Boston with experimental transmission hardware and firmware [12]. The primary conclusions from these field tests were:

- SFNs using digital-only boosters selectively expand HD Radio signal coverage;
- Digital time delays between main and booster signals need to be adjusted to account for propagation delays in the overlap regions to minimize inter-symbol interference;

- Digital coverage is enhanced within the station's protected contour when using a SFN with a digital-only booster;
- Two overlapping, properly aligned, and synchronized digital signals ***do not degrade*** HD Radio performance; *(emphasis added)*
- A Delphi automotive receiver with attributes of a well-designed, modern FM receiver experienced little interference to the main station's host analog signal near an all-digital booster station;

Many of these findings were later independently affirmed by joint field testing in 2016 conducted by Philipp Schmid of Nautel, John Kean then of Kean Consultants, LLC, Ron Thompson and Tom King of The University of Southern California on KUSC / KUSC-FM1 in Los Angeles (see Figure 5) [7] [8] [13]. Field tests were performed with special test equipment, software, and firmware on the Generation 3 (Gen3) HD Radio technology ecosystem. However, SFN abilities were not native to the Gen3 core, so this solution was not commercialized beyond the KUSC test, as Gen4 was where future development was being invested in.

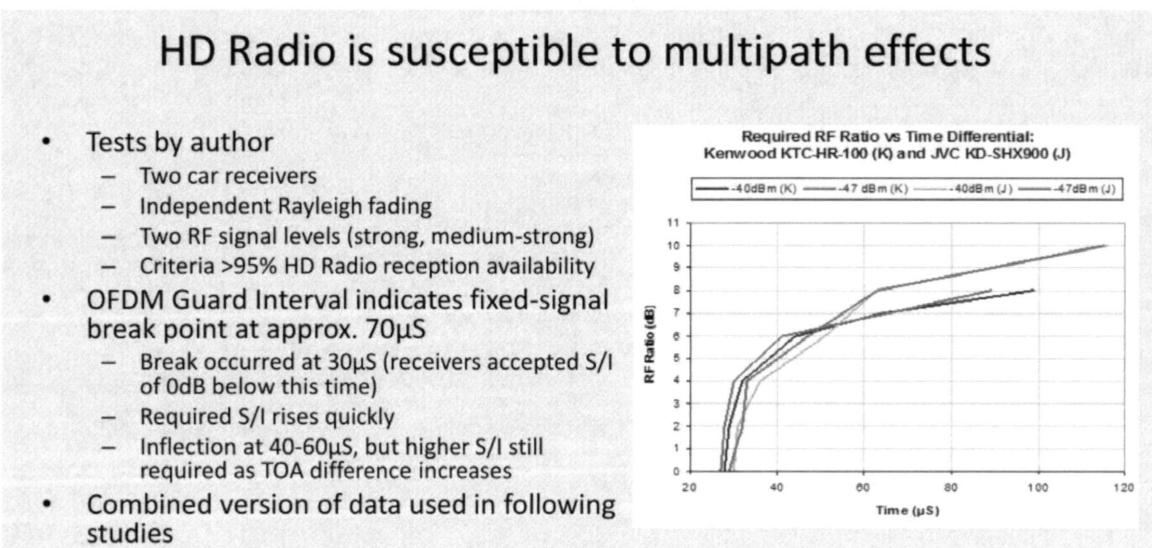

FIGURE 5: 2016 KUSC FIELD TESTING ANALYSIS [8].
COURTESY JOHN KEAN (USED WITH PERMISSION).

2023 Gen4 Commercialized FM+HD SFN Testing: San Francisco

Previous testing was conducted with specialized test equipment, firmware, and software distributions that were not available to the general broadcasting community. With the Gen4 HD Radio ecosystem which fundamentally supports HD Radio SFNs, broadcasters are now able to purchase equipment and systems to design and implement these systems with "off-the-shelf" hardware. While this does not minimize the need to properly geographically place booster or SFN sites, it is far easier now to implement these systems once a booster site or sites have been identified.

Once commercialized systems became available, the authors of this paper were more recently able to affirm the previous findings referenced above, now on Gen4 commercialized solutions. The initial test stations were:

- **KMEL / KMEL-FM2 San Francisco** (Xperi, GatesAir, iHeartMedia Joint Testing, July 2023)
- **KSAN / KSAN-FM1 San Francisco** (Xperi, GatesAir, Cumulus Media Joint Testing, July 2023)

In the San Francisco tests, the parties were able to positively establish both analog and digital transmission synchronization within the measurement accuracy of 1 μs using special receiver test equipment provided by Xperi. The teams were also able to make delay changes within the Gen4 system with 1 μs accuracy and track those manual changes needed to establish the proper offset of booster transmissions in the field. Small-scale and large-scale delay changes were made. The San Francisco implementations are significant because they have been in continuous operation and completely synchronized for several years. The parties worked together to harden the Gen4 analog and digital SFN implementation alongside the GatesAir Intraplex SynchroCast™ system selected for the IP transport of the signals from the main transmitter sites to the booster sites to move it from proof-of-concept to a production-quality commercialized product.

The authors acknowledge that other consultants, engineering firms and broadcasters have performed similar field testing and implementation of FM+HD boosters using Gen4 commercialized solutions. However, we are not aware of a body of technical results from these efforts that have been widely publicized or shared in a public forum, such as the NAB BEITC Proceedings or other venues.

2023-2024 Gen4 Commercialized FM+HD SFN Testing: Atlanta

While teams iteratively learned on the two San Francisco tests, the most telling system studied to date by the authors later came in 2023-2024 in Atlanta.

The Atlanta tests have proven the benefits of boosters in FM+HD Radio SFNs, which can produce dramatic increases in coverage and significant benefits for the public listening audience. What has made the Atlanta tests a substantial milestone in FM+HD Radio booster research was the significant amount of power of the booster site in both the analog domain (18 kW ERP) [14] and in the FM IBOC domain operating at -10 dBc 1.8 kW ERP [15]. The authors are unaware of any FM+HD IBOC booster running at power levels of this significant magnitude.

Here are some details on these facilities:

WWPW / WWPW-FM1 Atlanta (Xperi, iHeartMedia Joint Testing, July 2024 – December 2024)

- Main Facility:
    - WWPW 105.3 MHz FCC ID 63406
    - Class C1
    - Analog: 61 kW ERP @ 367m HAAT
    - Digital: 0.61 kW (610 Watts) ERP IBOC at -20 dBc Service Mode MP1
- Booster Facility:
    - WWPW-FM1 105.3 MHz FCC ID 777236
    - Analog: 18 kW ERP @ 121m HAAT
    - Digital:1.8 kW (1,800 Watts) ERP IBOC at -10 dBc Service Mode MP1

Figure 6 illustrates the relationship of these two facilities on a single contour study map. As shown, WWPW is what would be commonly considered a "rimshot" FM signal into the major Atlanta market [16]. While a Class C1 facility at 61 kW ERP, the main transmitter facility is approximately 34 miles from the urbanized downtown core of Atlanta. The 18 kW booster was located approximately 13 miles from downtown. The booster site was positioned with the incoming wavefront from the main FM site to align with key urbanized areas and desired target audience locations. The booster was optimized with a directional pattern maxima at 53 degrees true North.

After extensive FM+HD combined field coverage data had been collected, the results corroborated earlier experiences in prior studies outside of Atlanta. With FM analog operating 18 kW ERP at the booster location, in analog coverage in areas that had a Desired/Undesired ratio (D/U) of 6 dB or less and an arrival time differential of the main and booster signals of beyond 10 μs, analog interference was noticed on a variety of automotive OEM receivers.

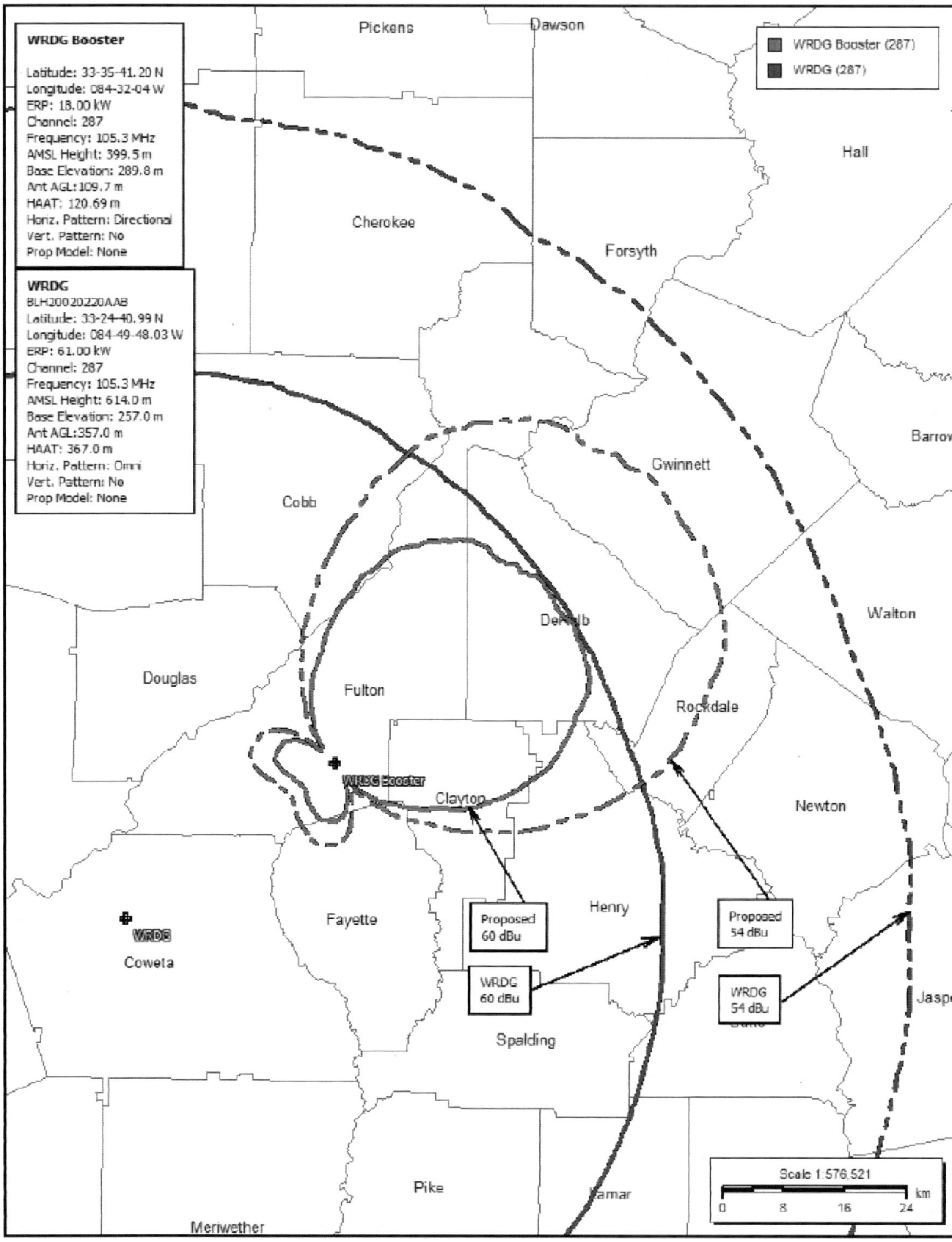

FIGURE 6: CONTOUR SHOWING OF 105.3 MHz WWPW / WWPW-FM1 *(FORMERLY WRDG)* [14].

It should be noted that the extent of impairment or annoyance varied greatly from vehicle to vehicle, and the authors attribute this to different vehicle receive antenna systems designs as well as internal receiver multipath mitigation techniques. While there was not a scientific study in this regard, one positive observation the team made is that most of the modern OEM receiver designs observed tend to manage the analog mutual interference caused by the main and booster with precise synchronization much better than older receivers. Since multipath is now better defined with the Terrain Obstructed Fast Rayleigh Multipath (TORM) channel model with 16 µs of delay [11] it seems some receiver designs *may* be masking mutual analog interference caused by boosters as multipath. That may be worthy of its own study in the future.

2024 Gen4 Commercialized Digital-Only Booster SFN Testing: Atlanta

While the analog domain provided mixed successes, since the initial booster sign-on, it was immediately noticed that significant digital gains were noticed in the Atlanta urbanized downtown core of the market. The booster's IBOC carriers directly synchronized with the main facility, providing seamless transitions between main-to-booster and booster-to-main. In areas with a D/U of 6 dB or less, because the arrival time of the two digital signals were never different by more than 30 µs though the entire extent of the coverage area, the transitions were completely transparent to the end-user (listener) in every vehicle examined and on every piece of test equipment used in our evaluations. The two synchronized digital signals were confirmed to be complementary to each other (constructively combining as opposed to destructively interfering). Observations were made on the HD1 (MPS) audio stream, as well as the data channels providing Program Service Data (PSD), album art/station logos (Artist Experience), and additional automotive telematics data being broadcast on the station. Special receiver test equipment provided by Xperi also definitively confirmed this.

Because of its closer proximity and higher ERP, the HD Radio signal in the urbanized Atlanta downtown core was mostly provided by the booster. It was noted that in most vehicles, the IBOC signal contributed by the booster survived the effects of blanketing interference and Receiver Induced Third Order Intermodulation Effects (RITOIE) caused by the in-town Class C and other combined FM signals emanating and mixing in the urbanized Atlanta core. For perspective, the area includes approximately 27 FM stations ranging from C0, C1, C2, A, and at least a dozen FM translators, almost 1.2 megawatts (MW) of nearby in-band FM RF. These signals are all positioned near the heavily congested concurrent sections of Interstate 75 with Interstate 85 and the interchange with Interstate 20. Traffic is extremely heavy in this area for most of the day. Essentially any audio impairments in the analog domain were completely erased with HD Radio receivers, and the receivers stayed locked in digital in a very hostile RF environment.

At the time, with over 1.6 million, or 35-40% of registered automobiles in the Atlanta DMA with HD Radio, the test team wanted to evaluate the use of the booster in an IBOC-only mode. The goal was to transmit no analog FM signal component from the booster site to minimize or eliminate any interference in the analog domain. However, there was a desire to continue to provide a robust HD Radio experience in the modern automobile.

Currently, "All Digital" FM IBOC operations are not authorized under 47 C.F.R. Part 73 or Part 74 of the Federal Communications Commission rules applicable to FM and FM booster stations. However, in interest in exploring the viability of HD Radio digital-only boosters, the licensee requested Experimental Special Temporary Authority to allow the WWPW-FM1 booster to run up to 1.8 kW ERP in "IBOC (digital) only" in Service Mode MP1 without an analog center carrier, synchronized with the main station WWPW. The Commission granted the application and issued Experimental Authority on July 10, 2024 [17]. Field testing began two weeks after the grant.

To inform our digital-only booster SFN testing, we reviewed Section 9 regarding digital-only booster testing [12]. The team's initial and primary concerns were to examine what effects there would be for analog-only FM receivers near the booster site (if any). The team was concerned that the digital-only booster running at the effective power of -10 dBc 1.8 kW could cause blanketing interference to analog FM-only radios in a heavily traveled area. The booster site was only a few miles from a major Interstate interchange between I-85 and I-285, and the Hartsfield–Jackson Atlanta International Airport (IATA: ATL, ICAO: KATL), the busiest airport in the world. The team was specifically concerned about some of the elevated highway flyovers of the interchange, where hundreds of thousands of vehicles traverse daily, and there are frequent traffic backups and delays in this area of concern during peak congestion times.

Before the booster went live, we performed laboratory tests with a variety of OEM radios and used Longley-Rice signal propagation to estimate the D/U ratios at this very heavily traveled corridor near the booster site. Lab tests indicated little concern about modern OEM receivers that were manufactured and installed in vehicles as OEM equipment in the past decade.

To inform our laboratory tests, using V-Soft Probe4™, we adjusted the booster analog ERP from 18 kW (analog FM-only) to 1.8 kW (HD IBOC digital only). Figure 7 demonstrates a 2 meter Above Ground Level (AGL) Longley Rice D/U propagation estimation of the "blanketing" area of concern, the fly-over ramps interconnecting the highways is emphasized by a red circle.

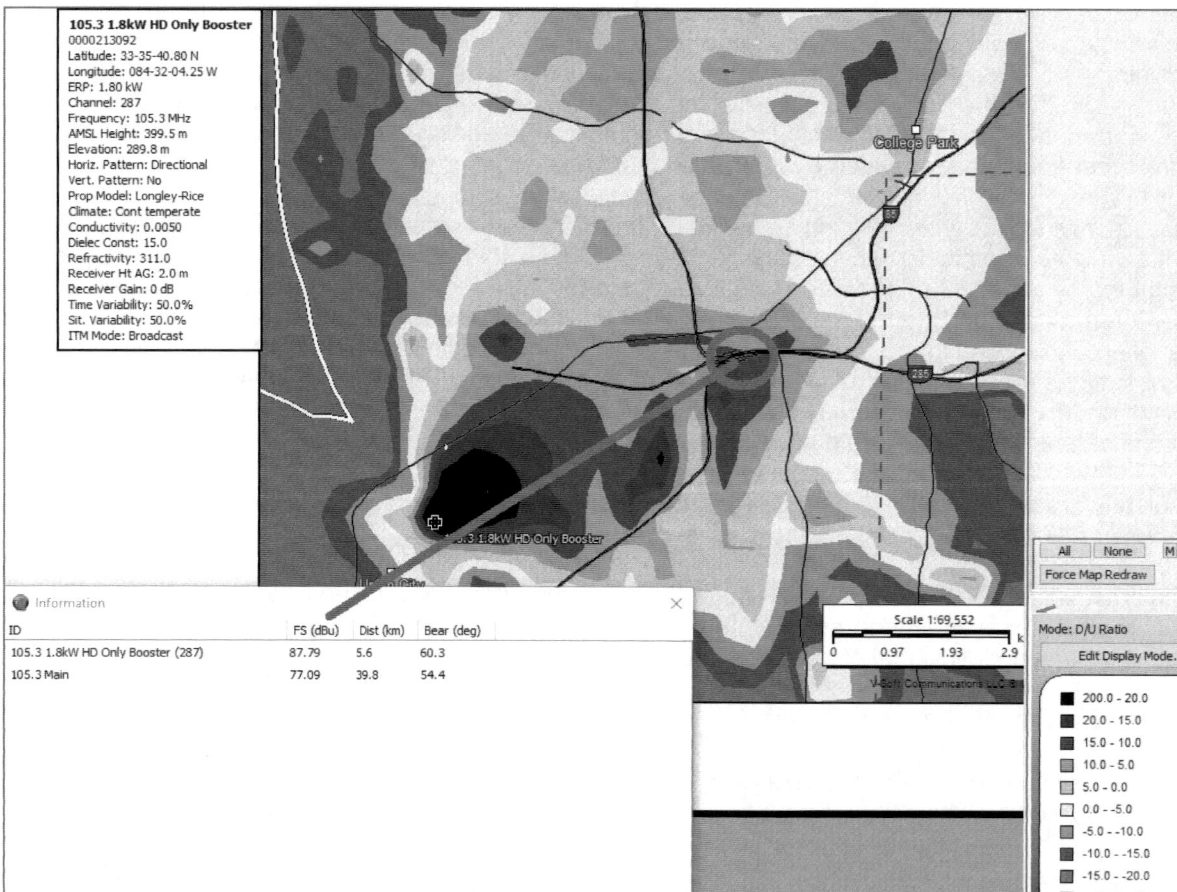

FIGURE 7: DIGITAL-ONLY BOOSTER BLANKETING ANALYSIS OF WWPW / WWPW-FM1, +10.7 DBC PREDICTED.

Figure 8 is a photograph taken during the lab simulation testing receiver compatibility. In the field, reviewing the estimated signal strength of the digital only booster versus analog component coming from the main analog site shown in Figure 9, the estimated ratio of digital signal 87.79 dBu – analog FM signal 77.09 dBu = +10.7 dB difference. The predictive mapping estimating the digital-only carriers could be +11 dBc compared to the analog. For perspective, the digital-only booster was only approximately 3.5 miles (5.6 km) from this study location. In contrast, the analog FM signal from the main site is traveling approximately 24.7 miles (39.8 km) to arrive at this location.

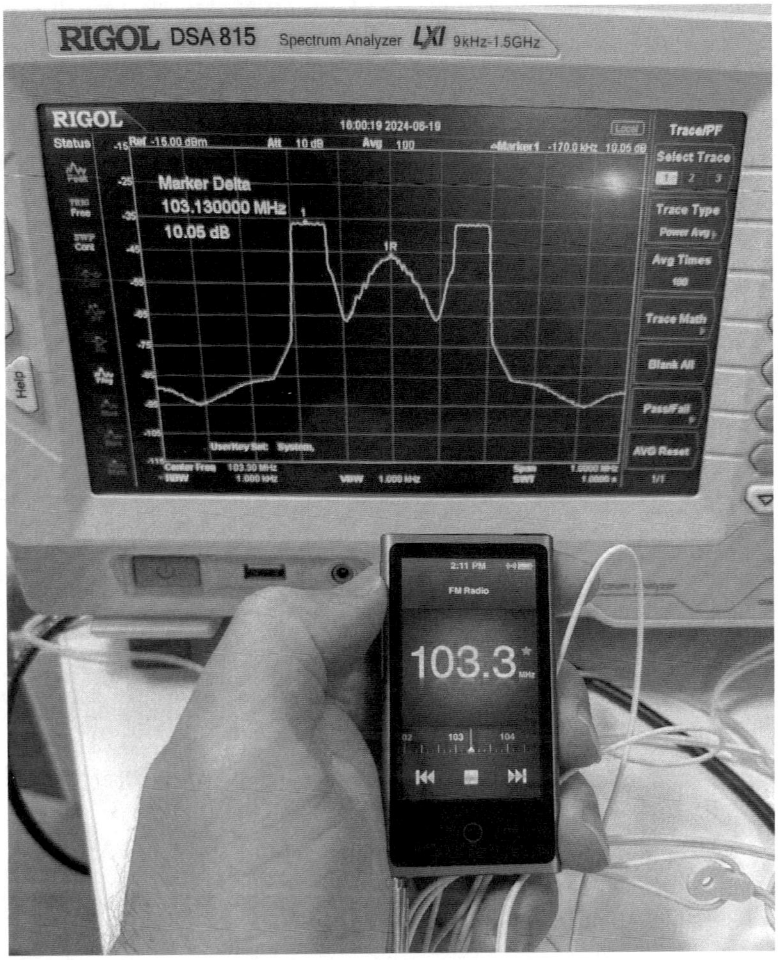

FIGURE 8: LAB TESTING DIGITAL-ONLY BOOSTER BLANKETING OF VARIOUS RECEIVERS, +10 DBC TESTED.

Once the digital-only booster went live, we suspected we might need to select a power level below 1.8 kW ERP digital (-10 dBc equivalent) to balance the digital coverage needs with host compatibility with analog FM-only receivers. It was much to our surprise that this was never necessary. We were able to locate several test vehicles near the predicted Longley Rice location at the I-85 / I-285 Interchange. We achieved comparable results spectrally, validating our predictive modeling and laboratory testing methodologies were accurate within 0.37 dB. (predicted +10.7 dBc – measured +10.33 dBc = 0.37 dB).

The teams used a wide range of OEM receivers installed in vehicles for testing in the areas of concern for potential blanketing interference caused by the digital-only booster, but none was ever found. In all, the team worked with 19 different test vehicles. The vehicles tested are listed in Table 1 and Table 2 below. Furthermore, over 5 months of digital-only booster operation, not a single interference inquiry or complaint was reported by the listening public. In fact, while performing digital on/off testing for the underlying testing supporting this paper, the station and team received multiple complaints that the digital-only booster was off, and inquiries were made about when the digital would be turned back on because of the dramatic listening improvements provided.

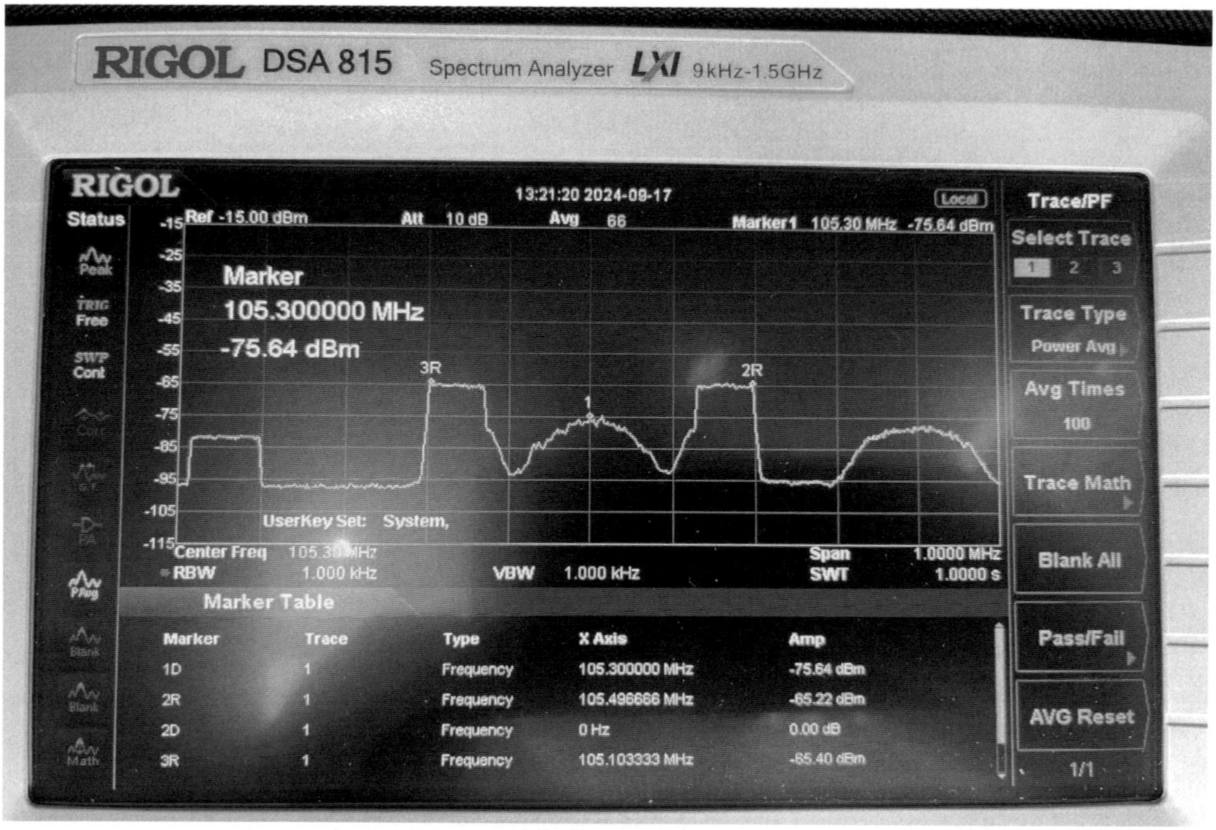

FIGURE 9: FIELD MEASUREMENT: DIGITAL-ONLY BOOSTER BLANKETING FIELD TESTING, +10.33 DBC MEASURED NEAR I-85/I-285/ ATLANTA AIRPORT.

Therefore, the teams feel very confident that digital-only boosters are viable. The need for them will grow in importance as OEM factory-installed HD Radio penetration rates in automobiles continue to accelerate, improving the listening and visual experience in the dash.

Table 1 lists the vehicles used in drive testing. Specifically with the Chrysler Pacifica, 2022, 2023, and 2024 models were used and logged thousands of miles, with and without factory-installed HD Radio. In addition, several gasolene Internal Combustion Engine (ICE) models and plug-in hybrid electric vehicle (PHEV) models were used during testing.

Chrysler Pacifica (2022-2024)	Chevrolet Colorado Z71 (2021)
Jeep Grand Cherokee	Hyundai Tucson
Jeep Wagoneer	Ford F-150 (2019)

TABLE 1: VEHICLES DRIVEN THROUGHOUT THE COVERAGE AREA, ALL 2023 OR 2024 MODELS EXCEPT WHERE NOTED.

Vehicles used in fixed-location test are listed in Table 2. Note that all HD-capable radios were forced into analog FM for analog host compatibility testing. HD digital-only booster off/on testing was performed, and no degradation in analog FM reception was noticed.

Ford Escape	Mazda CX5
Ford Explorer	Mercedes CLA-250 Coupe
GMC Terrain	Mini Cooper
Honda CRV	Toyota Equinox
Hyundai Sonata	Toyota RAV4
Hyundai Tucson	Toyota Tacoma (2022)
Kia Sportage	

TABLE 2: FIXED-LOCATION TESTS AT ATL AIRPORT RENTAL CAR LOT. ALL 2023 OR 2024 MODELS EXCEPT WHERE NOTED.

Main vs Booster HD Radio Predictive Coverage Mapping

Predictive measurements of the gain of the digital-only booster are shown overlayed on a Google Earth map, shown in Figure 10. A closer view of the urbanized Atlanta metropolitan area is shown in Figure 11. The estimated population gains from the digital only booster are shown in Table 3.

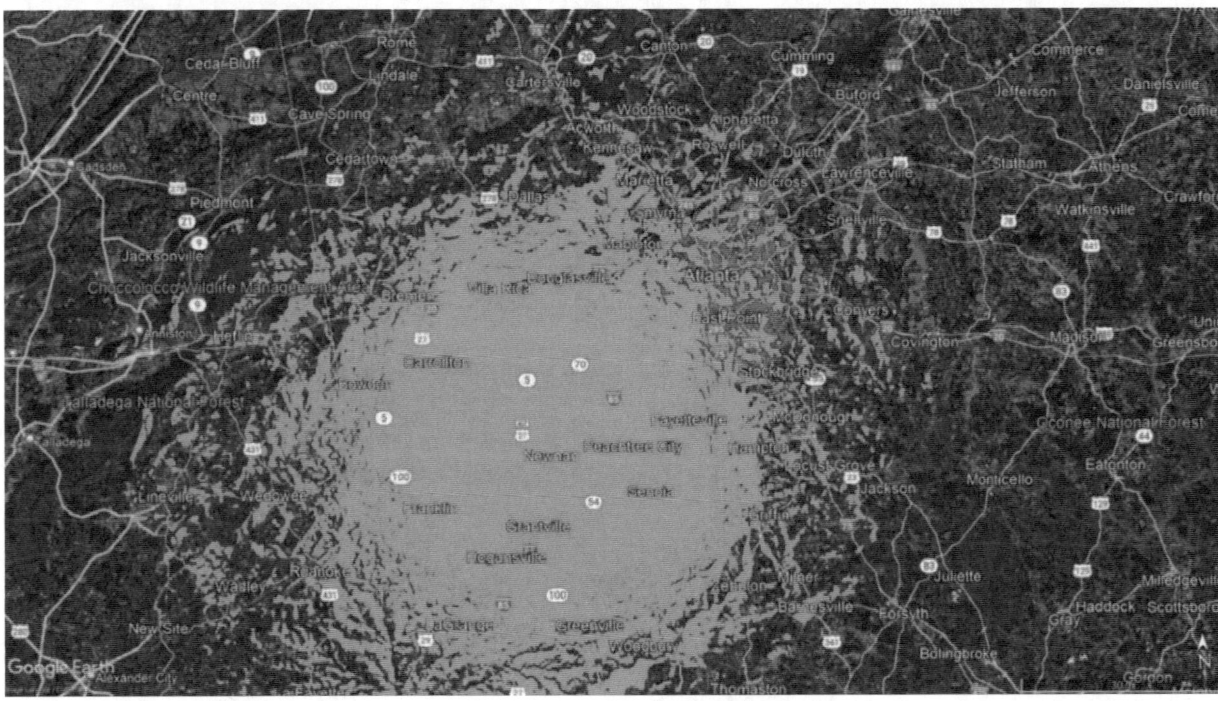

FIGURE 10: HD RADIO REGIONAL COVERAGE PREDICTIVE STUDIES FOR WWPW DIGITAL (GREEN) AND WWPW-FM1 DIGITAL-ONLY BOOSTER (RED).

FIGURE 11: DIGITAL COVERAGE PREDICTIVE STUDIES FOR WWPW DIGITAL (GREEN) AND WWPW-FM1 DIGITAL-ONLY BOOSTER (RED), URBANIZED ATLANTA ZOOM-IN.

Configuration	**HD Service Population**
Main HD -20 dBc + -10 dBc Digital Only Booster	3,231,161
Main Only -20 dBc	2,208,936
Net Population Gain of Digital Coverage from Digital Only Booster	**+1,022,225**

TABLE 3: DIGITAL COVERAGE PREDICTIVE POPULATION STUDIES, ESTIMATED NET GAIN OF DIGITAL COVERAGE FROM BOOSTER.

Main vs. Booster HD Radio Measured Coverage Mapping

Figure 12 demonstrates that the HD reception from the main site only has significant impairments in the downtown urbanized area of Atlanta. The grey trail shows the effects of blanketing interference and Receiver Induced Third Order Intermodulation Effects (RITOIE) caused by the in-town Class C and other combined FM signals emanating and mixing in the urbanized Atlanta core. You will note the same route, depicted in Figure 13 with the digital-only booster shows digital reception was dramatically improved in these areas. The predictive measurements of the gain of the digital-only booster were confirmed with field measurements using a test and measurement solution from Octave Communications Nomad [18], shown in Figure 14. Additional field tests and measurements were performed with special test receivers from Xperi, which corroborated the results shown below.

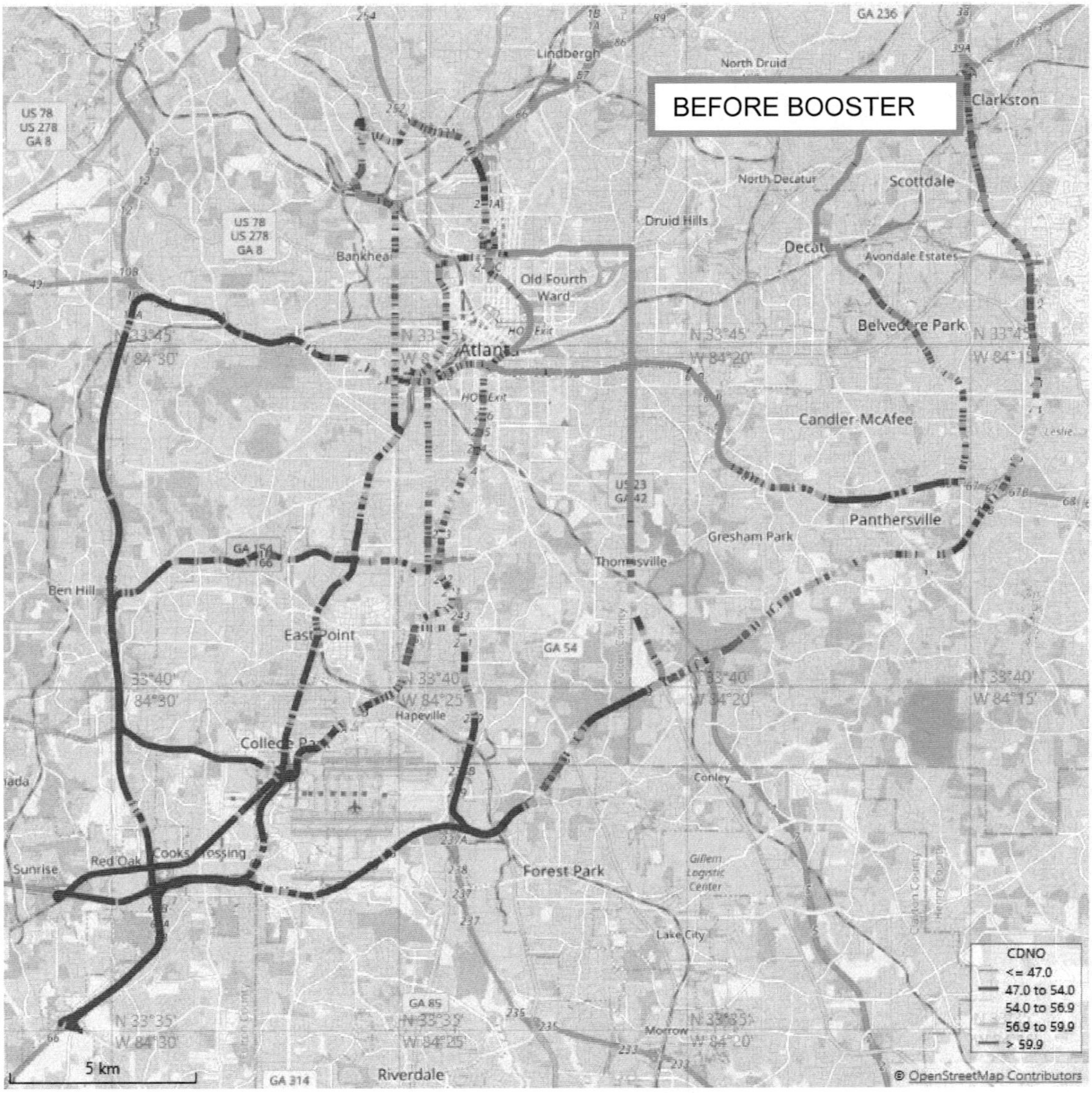

FIGURE 12: MEASURED HD SIGNAL CD/NO FM+ HD MAIN SITE ONLY (NO BOOSTER), REGIONAL COVERAGE SHOWN.

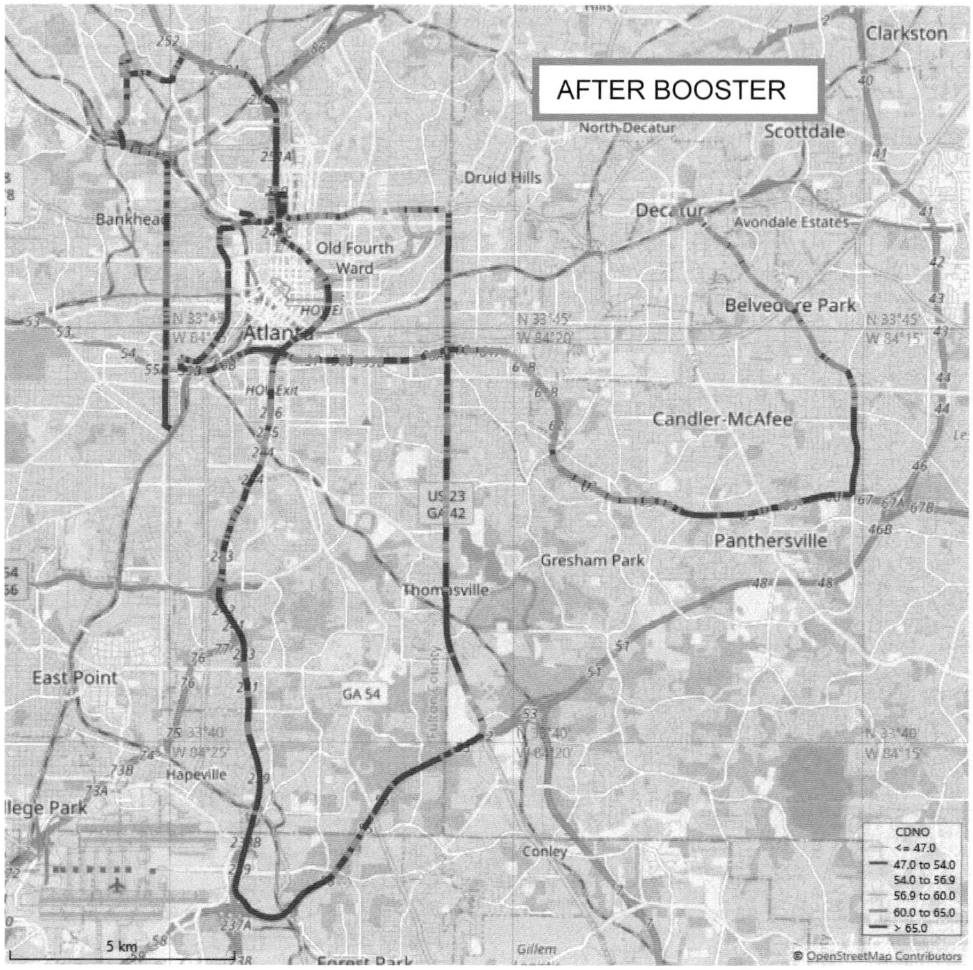

FIGURE 13: MEASURED HD CD/NO WITH MAIN FM+HD AND DIGITAL-ONLY BOOSTER COVERAGE, SHORTER URBANIZED ATLANTA TEST ROUTE.

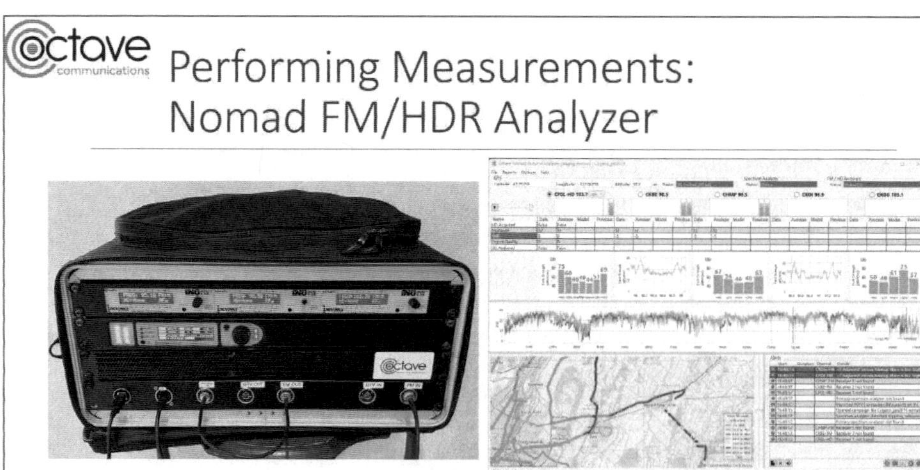

FIGURE 14: OCTAVE COMMUNICATIONS NOMAD TEST AND MEASUREMENT EQUIPMENT [3] [18].

Gen4 SFN Architecture Topology Diagrams and Implementation Photos

The equipment and signal flow of the two stations is shown in Figure 15 and Figure 16.

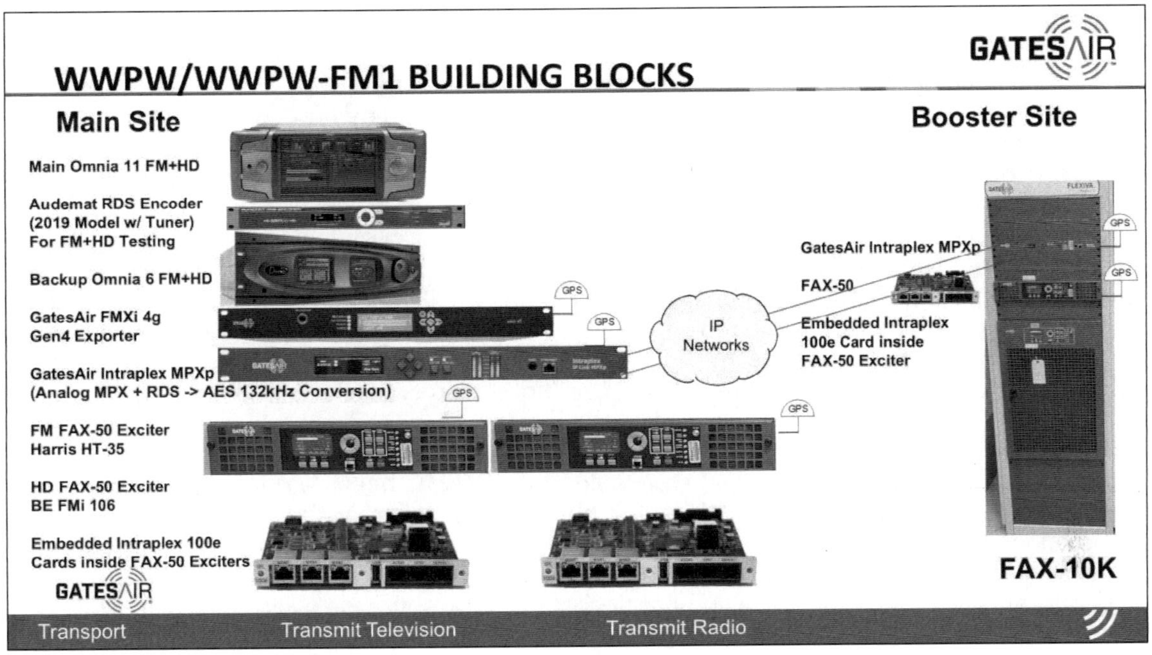

FIGURE 15: GEN4 SFN LAYOUT WWPW / WWPW-FM1.
(COURTESY GATESAIR, USED WITH PERMISSION).

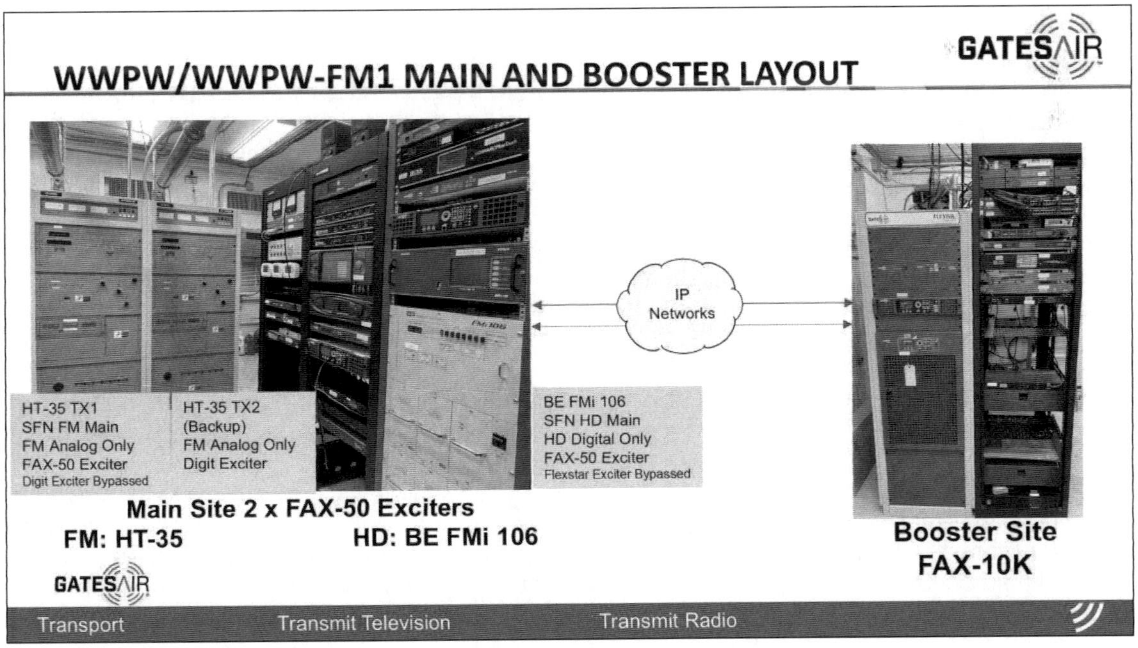

FIGURE 16: GEN4 SFN DESIGN – PHYSICAL SITE LAYOUTS WWPW / WWPW-FM1.
(COURTESY GATESAIR, USED WITH PERMISSION).

Future Digital-Only Booster SFN Considerations (-10 dBc to +10 dBc)

Since these tests indicate that modern automotive receivers effectively mitigate potential interference from digital-only boosters to the primary station's analog host signal, future experiments measuring digital coverage with hybrid booster digital signal injections above -10 dBc may be warranted. Although not permitted under current FCC rules, since boosters are always located within the protected service contour of the primary station, digital interference to co-channel and adjacent-channel stations is expected to be negligible. The host analog ERP of the booster would be reduced while maintaining the maximum authorized digital ERP. This would reduce interference from the analog signal while still providing very robust digital coverage.

In this context, the booster's analog ERP would still be used to establish the limits of maximum analog and digital power from a specific site to be compatible with the existing booster application, contour protection and licensing scheme. The center analog FM carrier ERP could potentially be reduced (on the booster only) while maintaining the maximum digital ERP authorized for that site. While the analog to digital hybrid injection ratio changes in this potential scenario, even at +10 dBc, the booster would never exceed the total digital ERP originally authorized for the specific site.

Given an effective analog FM booster/SFN coverage in areas without significant terrain is geographically limited to about 10 – 15 µs, HD Radio FM IBOC has been demonstrated to perform well at more than twice that distance to 30 – 35 µs. Future experimentation of an FM+HD booster to allow digital operation adjustments at -5 dBc, 0 dBc, +5 dBc, or +10 dBc intervals should be considered. This could effectively enable broadcasters to reduce the analog footprint of the booster/SFN to mitigate analog interference while maintaining a very large, robust digital coverage system.

This concept can be visualized on the map below in Figure 17. Keeping in mind that there is no destructive interference in the HD Radio system throughout this station's geography, the 60 dBu contour is the 1.8 kW ERP effective -10 dBc maximum digital power available for this site and loosely defines the large extent of the digital coverage from the booster site.

The underlying red indicates areas of predicted analog interference that were undesirable at 18 kW ERP analog FM from this site. Using the V-Soft Probe 4 variable threshold time delay propagation module. If the analog ERP could be reduced by 10 dB from 18 kW ERP to 1.8 kW ERP, that would loosely be defined as the 70 dBu contour on the same map. Note that nearly all the red underlay predicting interference is mitigated at this analog power level. If digital power remained at 1.8 kW ERP, this would effectively be a booster where the FM and HD power are equal, or 0 dBc.

Expanding this concept further, reducing the analog carrier by another 10 dB to +10 dBc (or -20 dB from where we started), and we end up with the 80 dBu contour being the effective analog FM coverage area of the booster. Note the red underlay predicting analog interference is almost non-existent at this power level, which would be 0.18 kW or 180 Watts Analog FM ERP. If the HD digital power remained at 1.8 kW, the 60 dBu contour remains the effective digital coverage area of the booster. This would effectively illustrate a booster where the HD power is +10 dBc. The digital power remains high while the analog power is reduced to mitigate analog interference. A spectral visualization of these varying injection ratios is demonstrated in Figure 18.

This type of implementation could have some very interesting and compelling applications, particularly in urbanized areas, as HD Radio penetration increases in the dashboard. The injection of a small bit of analog could also potentially help with the small population of legacy radios that may not tolerate a digital-only booster nearby [12].

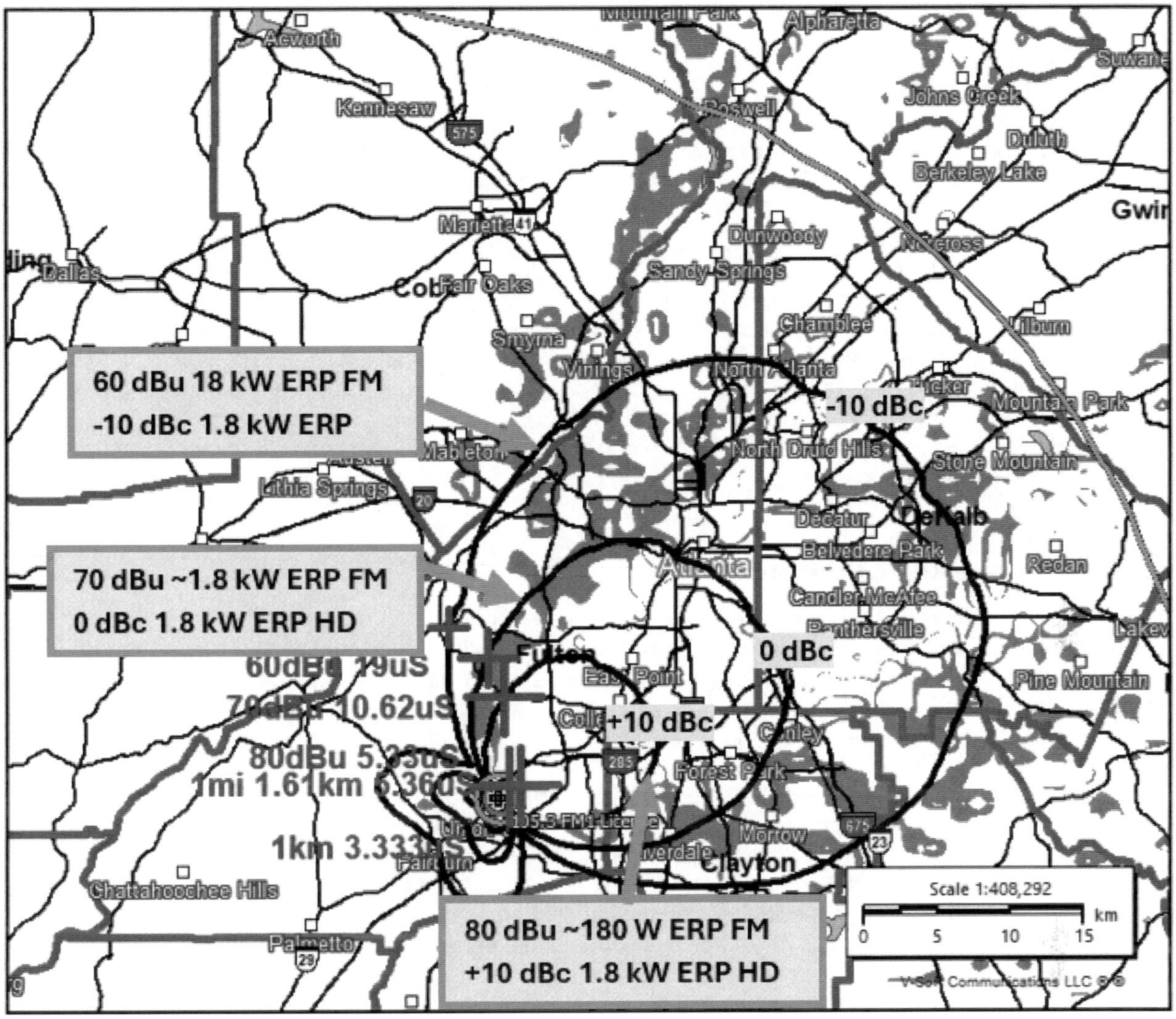

FIGURE 17: ANALOG FM INTERFERENCE PREDICTED AT 18 KW BETWEEN WWPW / WWPW-FM1. DIGITAL-ONLY BOOSTER PREDICTED BENEFITS AT -10 DBC, 0 DBC, AND +10 DBC.

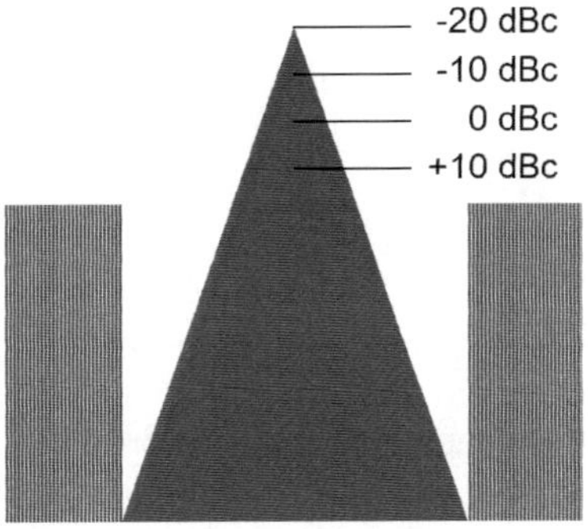

FIGURE 18: GRAPHICAL SPECTRAL DEPICTION OF -20 DBC, -10 DBC, 0 DBC, +10 DBC INJECTION RATIO FOR FUTURE HD RADIO SFN DIGITAL-ONLY TESTING. COURTESY XPERI (USED WITH PERMISSION)

Monitoring Benefits of Hybrid FM+HD Booster Operations

Deserving a paper of its own, having embarked on several high-profile, large-scale booster projects, the authors have found implementing a hybrid FM+HD booster SFN provides a level of confidence and monitoring that you are unable to obtain with just an analog-only FM SFN. By employing a hybrid FM+HD SFN, you can use the more precisely controlled HD signal to cross-reference and validate that the analog FM is also aligned at all times. It is a check and balance system.

When a station employs a hybrid FM+HD main/booster SFN, common existing "off the shelf" broadcast monitoring solutions can be used to measure the correlation between the FM and HD1. These receiver-based solutions can provide an alarm when the analog, digital, or both depart from their normal timing routines and can be used for external confidence monitoring that your booster network is working within some degree of precision when nobody is present in the booster coverage area [19]. As more FM+HD hybrid boosters are deployed, the authors hope that additional test, measurement and monitoring tools will become available to broadcasters to ensure the proper signal quality, synchronization, and alignment in both the FM and HD domains. Additionally, the industry may consider a best practices implementation guide for boosters.

Industry Transport Standards

Commercialized solutions on the air today have been developed within single transmission vendor ecosystems, and some proprietary methodologies have been developed to achieve these results. As we look forward to the future, industry technology leaders are working towards open, interoperable standards of transporting the combined analog FM stereo multiplex signal alongside the HD Radio Exporter to Exciter (E2X) data stream via IP networks.

Efforts are underway within the United States in the National Radio Systems Committee (NRSC) IBOC Standards Development Working Group (ISDWG), and internationally within the Institute of Electrical and Electronics Engineers (IEEE) Broadcast Technology Standards Committee (BTSC) Aggregated Content Delivery Link (ACDL) Working Group to develop global standards that could apply to use cases outside of North America. We hope that with these efforts, once open standards are defined, manufacturers could work towards developing a robust marketplace of interoperable products for these signals to be transported between equipment from multiple manufacturers. Allowing broadcasters to have a broad set of solutions available to them.

While SFNs prove to be the most stringent design constraint for these transport standards, they are important because they will also improve the FM/HD1 time alignment and coherency of standalone stations without SFNs. Having a deterministic startup will dramatically improve the listener experience for all stations while also reducing the engineering human resources needed to maintain and monitor the time alignment of the FM/HD1 audio.

Acknowledgments

The authors would like to recognize the following individuals and organizations who have contributed to the success of these studies and enabled the industry to better comprehend HD Radio SFNs:

WWPW Atlanta: Jeff Littlejohn, Steve George, Troy Langham, Ben Brinitzer, James Gay, Randy Mullinax, Jim Ganter, Oscar Franco, Charlie Harrell with iHeartMedia

KMEL San Francisco: Jeff Littlejohn, Jeff White, Anna Mookerjee, Horace Wong, Steven Garaventa, David Williams *(retired)*, Chuck Waltman *(retired)* with iHeartMedia

KSAN San Francisco: Conrad Trautmann, Shaun Sandoval, Andrew Stern, David Alvarado with Cumulus Media

Gen4 transmission and transport: Keyur Parikh, Brad Thomson, Ted Lantz, Kevin Haider, Dave Kroeger, Jeffrey Merrow, Hema Subramanian, Gavin Gundler, Toby Miller with GatesAir

Ashruf El-Dinary, Jeff Detwiler, Paul Peyla, Russ Mundschenk *(retired)*, Russ Iannuzzelli *(retired)* with Xperi

John Kean with Cavell, Mertz, a division of Capitol Airspace Group

Philipp Schmid with Nautel

François O. Gauthier and Eric Juteau with Octave Communications

John Gray with V-Soft Communications

KUSC Los Angeles: Ron Thompson and Tom King with The University of Southern California

Co-author Alan Jurison is Chair of the IBOC Standards Development Working Group (ISDWG) which reports to the Digital Radio Broadcasting (DRB) Subcommittee within the National Radio Systems Committee (NRSC). At the time of the San Francisco and Atlanta tests, he was employed by iHeartMedia. He presently is an independent consultant.

References

[1] NRSC-G203-A: NRSC IBOC Time and Level Alignment Guideline, https://nrscstandards.org/standards-and-guidelines/documents/guidelines/nrsc-g203-a.pdf

[2] NRSC-5-E: HD Radio™ FM Transmission System Specifications, SY_SSS_1026s, Section 4.3.1 https://nrscstandards.org/standards-and-guidelines/documents/standards/nrsc-5-e/NRSC-5-E_reference_documents.pdf

[3] Gauthier, F. "Octave Communications presentation on FM-SFN in Canada," Central Canada Broadcast Engineers, Technologists & Technicians, 2023 Conference https://www.octavecom.ca/CCBE2023SFNGauthier.pdf

[4] ITU-R BS.412-9, Annex 3: "Protection ratio for FM sound broadcasting in the case of the same programme and synchronized signals."

[5] ITU-R BS.1284-1, "General methods for the subjective assessment of sound quality"

[6] Schmid, P., "FM+IBOC Broadcast Systems Architecture Considerations for Single Frequency Networks", 2009 NAB Broadcast Engineering Conference Proceedings

[7] Schmid, P., "Single Frequency Networks for HD Radio", 2017 NAB Broadcast Engineering and Information Technology Conference Proceedings https://www.nautel.com/content/user_files/2018/08/Single-Frequency-Networks-for-HD-Radio-2018.pdf

[8] Kean, J. "Developing HD Radio SFN (Booster) Standards" 2016 NAB Broadcast Engineering Conference Presentation *(presentation session only)*

[9] OFDM Guard Interval definitions - https://en.wikipedia.org/wiki/Guard_interval, https://en.wikipedia.org/wiki/Orthogonal_frequency-division_multiplexing#Guard_interval_for_elimination_of_intersymbol_interference

[10] NRSC-5-E: HD Radio™ FM Transmission System Specifications, SY_SSS_1026s, Section 4.3.4 https://nrscstandards.org/standards-and-guidelines/documents/standards/nrsc-5-e/NRSC-5-E_reference_documents.pdf

[11] ITU-R BS.2214-6, Table 91 Terrain Obstructed Fast Rayleigh Multipath (TORM) channel model

[12] TX_FTR_2758 - HD Radio™ SFN Field Test Results - WD2XAB Baltimore & WKLB Boston – Revision 01.14, https://cache.nabpilot.org/wp-content/uploads/2018/02/fastroad/SFN Field Test Results - WD2XAB & WKLB.pdf

[13] Schmid, P., "SFNs for HD Radio: Synchronizing the IBOC Signal" https://www.nautel.com/content/user_files/2018/07/HD-SFN-Field-Trials-slides.pdf

[14] New FM Booster Station Construction Permit Application, WRDG-FM1 *(now WWPW-FM1)*, Facility ID 777236, https://enterpriseefiling.fcc.gov/dataentry/views/public/fmDraftCopy?displayType=html&appKey=25076ff386be5a130186cbba231f0614&id=25076ff386be5a130186cbba231f0614

[15] FM Booster Engineering STA Application for -10 dBc operation, WWPW-FM1, Facility ID 777236 https://enterpriseefiling.fcc.gov/dataentry/views/public/fmDraftCopy?displayType=html&appKey=25076ff38b63e0c4018b875e83980f3f&id=25076ff38b63e0c4018b875e83980f3f

[16] Rimshot (broadcasting) definition - https://en.wikipedia.org/wiki/Rimshot_(broadcasting)

[17] FM Booster Experimental STA Application for -10 dBc IBOC Only Operation, WWPW-FM1, Facility ID 777236 https://enterpriseefiling.fcc.gov/dataentry/views/public/fmDraftCopy?displayType=html&appKey=25076f9190547d8301908334b9730f61&id=25076f9190547d8301908334b9730f61

[18] Octave Communications HDR/FM Analyzer v3, Eric Juteau, François O. Gauthier https://www.octavecom.ca/nomad_fm.html

[19] Inovonics 551/552 FM & HD Radio Modulation Monitors with FM/HD1 alignment monitoring Inovonics JUSTIN 808 HD Radio Alignment Processor *(not installed in air chain, monitor only)*
https://www.inovonicsbroadcast.com/product/551
https://www.inovonicsbroadcast.com/product/552
https://www.inovonicsbroadcast.com/product/808

Creating a High-Quality, Efficient Visual Radio System Without Breaking the Bank

Fabio Gattari, Alex Gattari
Etere
Singapore
office@etere.com

Abstract – The evolution of radio broadcasting has been remarkable, with significant technological advancements shaping the way we consume media. From its humble beginnings as an audio-only medium, radio has transformed into a dynamic and interactive platform, incorporating visual elements to enhance the listener experience. The integration of video into radio broadcasts, commonly known as "visual radio" has created new opportunities for broadcasters to engage audiences. However, building a high-quality visual radio system need not come with a prohibitive price tag. With thoughtful planning and the right technology, it's entirely possible to create a cost-effective visual radio system that delivers professional results.

The Radio Yesterday and Radio Today

In the past, radio was exclusively an audio medium. The primary focus was on delivering clear, high-quality sound to listeners. Equipment was relatively simple: microphones, transmitters, and audio mixers were the core tools used in producing and broadcasting shows. While radio stations invested in high-quality audio equipment, the overall production process was straightforward, with a clear emphasis on sound quality.

However, the radio industry today has adapted to the demands of a more visually-oriented audience [1]. As digital technology has advanced, the incorporation of video into radio broadcasts has become the norm. Visual radio systems allow broadcasters to offer more interactive and engaging content, combining video with the traditional audio format [2]. This shift has opened the door for live-streaming radio shows, podcasting with a visual component, and even broadcasting live events with both audio and video.

Connection of Video Devices

A key challenge in creating a visual radio system is ensuring that the video devices, such as cameras, video mixers, and graphics systems, can communicate seamlessly. Traditionally, setting up a professional video system involved complex wiring and expensive equipment. However, modern video systems can be simplified by using more affordable and flexible solutions (see Figure 1).

One visual radio solution provider, Etere, tackled this problem by instead of using the traditional serial digital interface (SDI) cables, using a fully network device interface (NDI) setup (see Figure 2). That makes it so that Etere is able to control every device through a virtual router, and those things include also the virtual video-mixer.

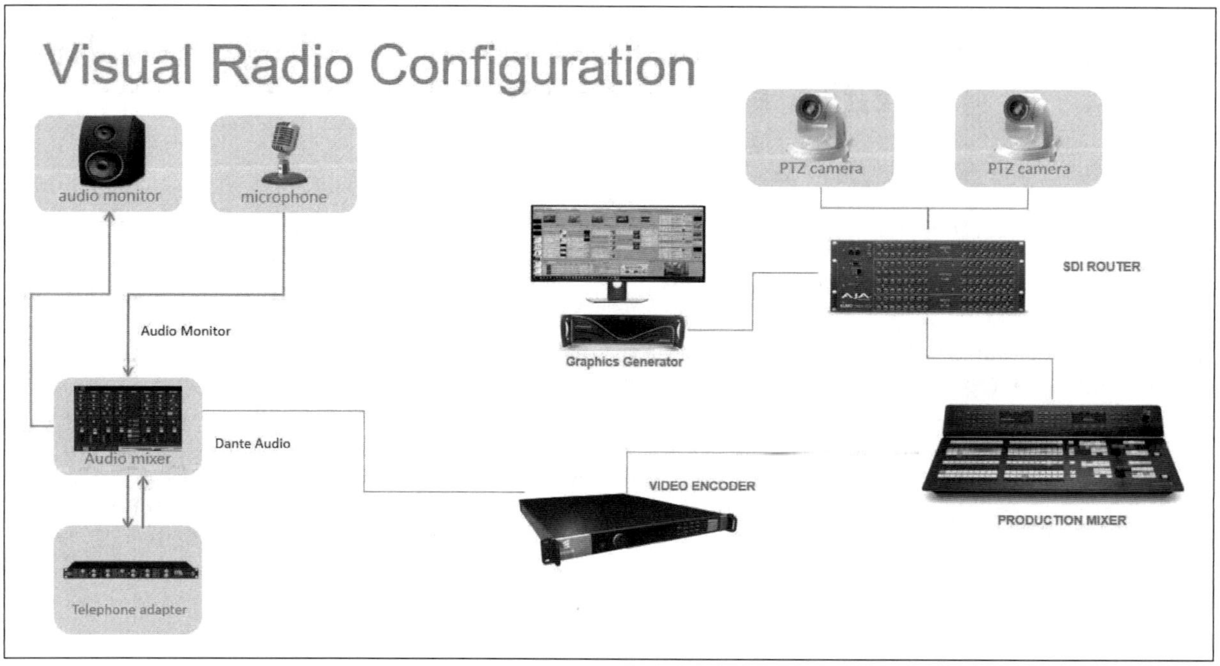

FIGURE 1: VISUAL RADIO CONFIGURATION. (SOURCE: ETERE)

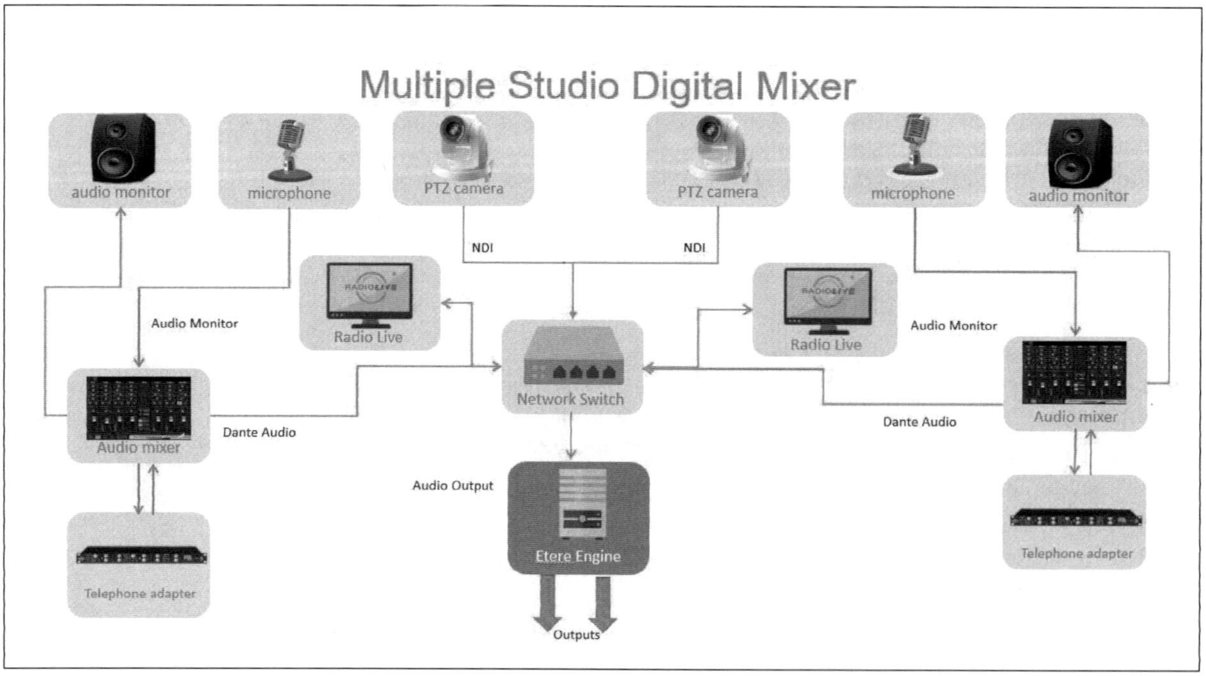

FIGURE 2: MULTIPLE STUDIO DIGITAL MIXER.

Reducing the Components

Using a traditional TV broadcasting component is an expensive exercise, video is not the core business of a radio and it does not require the extreme attention to details used by TV broadcasters. Today most of the video devices are based on software, so instead of traditional devices, a software platform that includes video mixers, effects, character generators, camera controls, etc. is recommended. In addition, lighting can be included using the standard and inexpensive general-purpose interface (GPI) protocol to control light scenes.

Effective Management of Visual Radio Components

Once the video devices are connected, the next challenge is managing them effectively to ensure a smooth and professional broadcast. One key aspect of managing a visual radio system is selecting the appropriate camera based on the microphone that is currently open. This can be automated, ensuring the camera switches to the person speaking without requiring manual intervention.

Graphics also play a significant role in visual radio production [4]. Setting up graphics according to the mixer setup allows broadcasters to display relevant information (such as lower thirds, titles, logos or advertisements) on the screen as part of the broadcast (as shown in Figure 3). This process can be automated to a degree, with the system using predefined settings to determine when graphics should be added based on the content being shown.

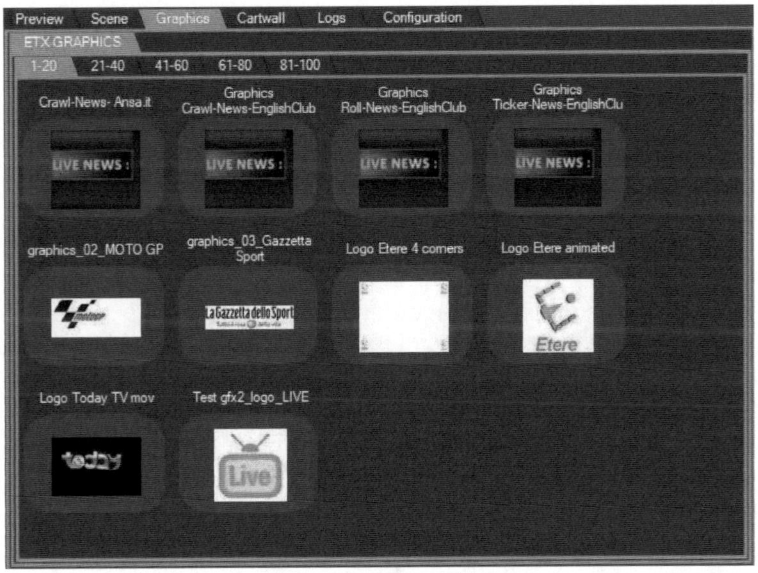

FIGURE 3: GRAPHICS EDITOR.

Another important feature of modern visual radio systems is auto-graphics, such as news tickers or live event overlays. These graphics can be triggered automatically based on predefined rules or events, saving time and allowing the production team to focus on content creation. Additionally, as previously mentioned, lighting control can be integrated into the system using the GPI, which can trigger lighting changes in sync with intro and outro videos, further enhancing the overall broadcast experience.

Video and Audio Management

In a visual radio system, the management of both video and audio paths is crucial for maintaining high-quality production standards. Audio will typically be routed through an audio mixer, where various sound sources, such as microphones, music, and sound effects, are mixed and balanced. Video, on the other hand, will go through a video mixer, which allows the operator to switch between different video sources, such as live cameras, pre-recorded videos, and graphics.

The ability to manage both video and audio paths effectively ensures that the broadcast flows seamlessly. Crossfades between video sources and audio tracks are essential for smooth transitions during the show. For example, a video mixer might crossfade from one camera to another, while the audio mixer performs a similar crossfade between different audio tracks. These transitions help maintain a professional production, ensuring that the audience experiences a polished, engaging broadcast.

Additionally, integrating auto-adding graphics onto the video feed using an internal programmable Character Generator (CG) (as shown in Figure 4) can streamline the process of adding on-screen text, titles, or other graphics. This reduces the workload for the production team and ensures that graphics appear automatically when needed.

FIGURE 4: CONTROL THE CG APPEARANCE WITH THE GRAPHICS PANEL.

Integrated Platform for Media Management

As visual radio systems grow in complexity, managing large video files becomes a critical challenge. An integrated media management platform is necessary to handle large video files, allowing for efficient storage, retrieval, and editing of content (as shown in Figure 5). This platform should also offer integrated video trimming capabilities, enabling producers to quickly edit and trim video files for broadcast.

In addition to video management, content management becomes essential. This includes managing not just video content but also music scheduling. By integrating video and audio content management into a single platform, broadcasters can streamline the production process and ensure that both media types are synchronized and ready for broadcast.

Director Interface

The director interface acts as a streamlined management hub, providing real-time access to vital information such as intros, outros, cluster data, durations, dates, thumbnails, descriptions, artists, and precise timings (as shown in Figure 6). This powerful interface not only centralizes key operational details but also elevates the multimedia experience, making broadcast operations more intuitive, efficient, and seamless. By offering immediate visibility and control over all aspects of the broadcast, it empowers directors to enhance content delivery while simplifying the overall workflow. Ideally a visual radio system will give you a complete multimedia experience with an interface that makes your broadcaster operations smoother and more accessible.

FIGURE 5: INTEGRATED PLATFORM FOR RADIO AND MEDIA MANAGEMENT.

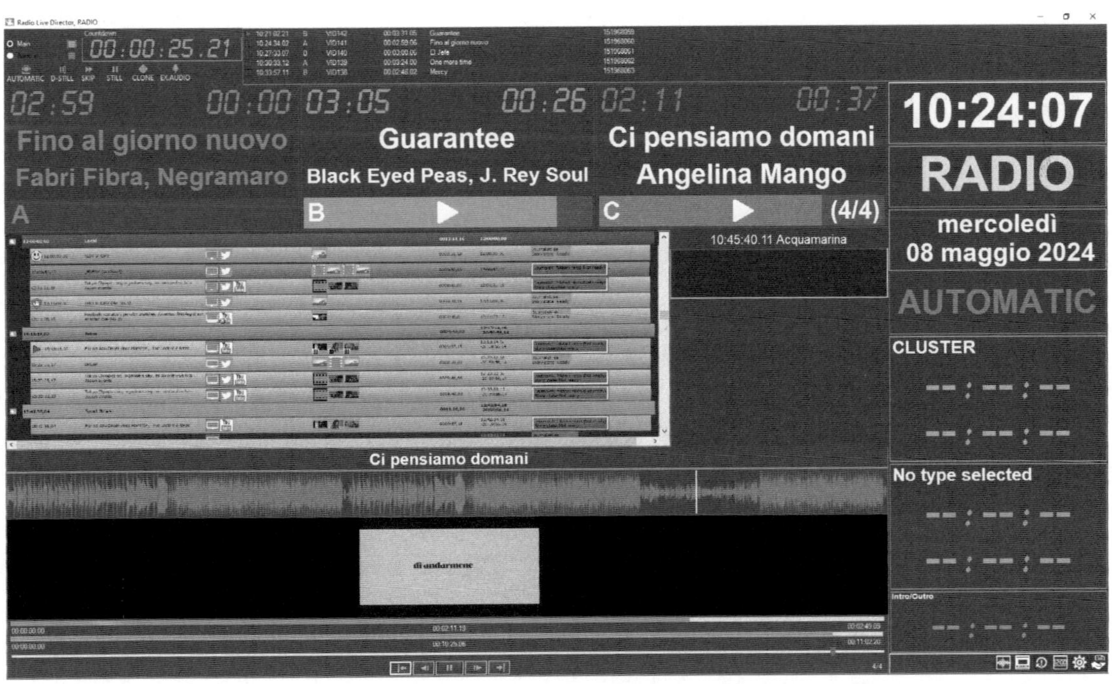

FIGURE 6: DIRECTOR INTERFACE.

Media Asset Management Integration

Furthermore, integration with Media Asset Management (MAM) systems significantly enhances the organization of audio assets, offering advanced metadata fields that enable more precise sorting and retrieval across scheduling and logging applications. This streamlined approach makes it easier to locate and leverage media quickly and efficiently. The integrated MAM system simplifies the processes of ingesting, indexing, storing, and retrieving media, resulting in improved operational efficiency and ensuring that assets are always accessible when needed. This seamless integration optimizes workflow, reduces time spent searching for assets, and enhances overall productivity in broadcast operations.

Social Media Integration

Social media integration empowers broadcasters to seamlessly publish assets or playlist items directly to social platforms, expanding their reach and visibility. Additionally, the metadata associated with these assets can be enriched before publishing, allowing for more targeted, engaging, and relevant content [5]. This capability not only enhances audience interaction but also drives greater engagement by providing context and valuable information that resonates with viewers across social media channels.

User Rights Management

Given the vast array of features in visual radio software, effectively managing user access rights is crucial for maintaining security and operational efficiency. A seamlessly integrated Active Directory user rights management ensures real-time synchronization of user profiles, enabling broadcasters to effortlessly manage complex user permissions. This integration allows for secure, streamlined access control across multiple platforms, ensuring that the right individuals have the appropriate levels of access while safeguarding sensitive information and maintaining smooth workflow across the organization.

Moving Radio to MOS Standard for the News

For news broadcasts, it's important to move radio systems toward the MOS (Media Object Server) standard. This ensures that video content can be easily integrated into the news process (as shown in Figure 7), allowing for a seamless transition between radio and TV formats. If a station has a shared radio and TV newsroom platform, this integration becomes even more critical, enabling content to be easily shared between radio and TV producers.

Redundant Without Breaking the Bank

Redundancy is also a critical consideration when designing a visual radio system. To ensure reliability, the system must be active-active, meaning that there is a backup for every critical component, but with a software-only approach, this can be achieved using inexpensive virtualisation of the resources, so moving to virtual is mandatory to have a cost-effective redundancy.

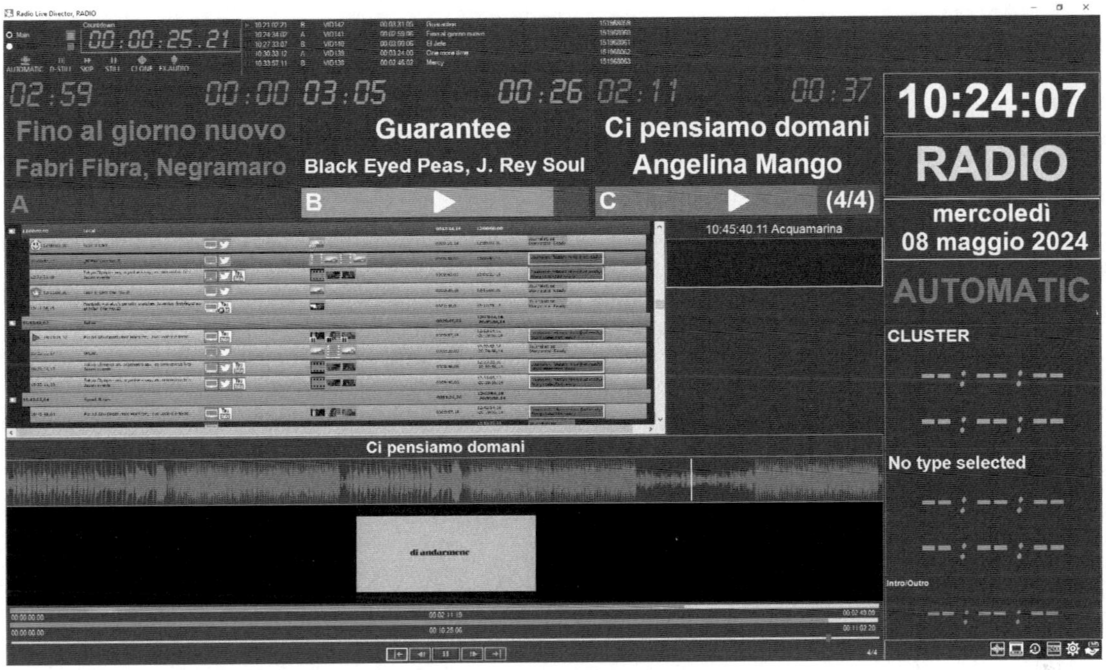

FIGURE 7: RADIO NEWS RUNDOWN.

Additional Features

Some additional features to improve your workflow are:

- An automated control of lights. The system can automatically change preset lighting scenes based on which microphone is open, closed or even by what point you are in the playlist.
- Virtual video-mixer. With a fully virtual mixer, you can do everything a physical mixer is able to do, yet you don't have to pay for another box as it's fully integrated, and with the possibility of using the integrated or external graphics, you're able to show multiple video feeds with quality while being cost-effective.
- Having a music and ads scheduling system which is fully integrated with a visual radio. This allows you to have conditional advertising based on whether the system is broadcasting on radio or TV, as TV ads and radio ads are very different.

Conclusion

Building a high-quality visual radio system without significantly increasing costs is entirely feasible with the right approach [3]. Radio stations can create engaging, professional broadcasts without breaking the bank by leveraging modern technologies like virtualization, automating key functions like camera selection and graphics management, and integrating platforms for media management and redundancy. With thoughtful planning and the right investment in scalable technology, broadcasters can offer an enhanced multimedia experience to their audience while maintaining cost efficiency. The future of visual radio is bright, and with the right tools, it's within reach for any station looking to stay ahead of the curve.

References

[1] "White Paper of the future of radio", Arcom, https://www.arcom.fr/sites/default/files/2024-06/arcom-Livre-blanc-radio-summary-english-version.pdf

[2] "Key Trends: Where is the Radio Industry headed in 2023?," Rgb Broadcasting, https://www.rgbbroadcasting.com/blog/key-trends-where-is-the-radio-industry-headed-in-2023/

[3] "The Evolution of Radio: From Golden Age to Digital Renaissance," fastforward, https://fastforward.com.cy/educational/evolution-radio-golden-age-digital-renaissance

[4] "360 Radio Experience: Connecting Live Listening with User Interaction and Visual Radio," VRT innovation, https://zenodo.org/record/2850792/files/TVX_WS_Marconi19_v4.pdf

[5] "The Use of Social Media (Instagram) for the Radio Industry (Content and Marketing Strategies to Increase Audience Loyalty)," E3S Web if Conferences, https://www.e3s-conferences.org/articles/e3sconf/pdf/2023/63/e3sconf_icobar23_02031.pdf

Beyond the Cloud: Native Broadcasting with ATSC 3.0

Jay Willis
ONE Media Technologies
Hunt Valley, Maryland, United States
jwillis@sbgtv.com

Abstract – The broadcast industry is undergoing a major shift as broadcasters increasingly integrate cloud-based solutions to enhance the efficiency, reliability, and scalability of their operations. The advent of ATSC 3.0—a next-generation broadcast standard—enables the entire broadcast operations chain to become 'cloud-native,' opening unprecedented opportunities for flexible and resilient deployment strategies. This paper proposes a unified approach to cloud-to-terrestrial broadcasting, examining how ATSC 3.0's capabilities can support such a fully integrated broadcast infrastructure. By analyzing current and potential implementations, we highlight the transformative potential of cloud-based broadcasting for optimizing playout, signal distribution, and emission. The goal is to provide a blueprint for broadcasters navigating the shift to a future-ready, cloud-centric operational paradigm.

Introduction

I joined ONE Media in 2019 with the expectation of deploying ATSC 3.0 across many Sinclair stations. The prospect of traveling to each site, installing equipment alongside local engineers, and providing high-level training was exciting. As we approached the deployment of ATSC 3.0 in Las Vegas in 2020, our team worked closely with vendors to ensure that the equipment and software met the new standard.

Then, COVID-19 disrupted everything. The Las Vegas deployment was originally scheduled around NAB 2020, but with travel completely shut down, we had to devise a new plan. Instead of on-site installations, the team pre-configured as much of the equipment as possible, shipped it to local stations, and remotely guided local engineers through the setup process.

Broadcast technology has continuously evolved—and continues to change rapidly. We've moved from FPGA-based encoding to software-based encoding, from the ATSC 1.0 standard to the enhanced ATSC 3.0 standard, and from SDI cabling to IP-based solutions like SMPTE 2110 and NDI. Now, the industry is undergoing another major shift: migration from on-premises infrastructure hardware to the cloud.

Sinclair has been at the forefront of this transition, consolidating traditional master control operations into a centralized cloud-based playout model. However, cloud migration isn't just about reducing local station operations, it's about enhancing flexibility, improving efficiency, strengthening IT security, and replacing aging hardware. The next step is to build on our early cloud playout work and extend the cloud's capabilities into the ATSC 3.0 transmission chain. This will allow us to deliver the final master control output to a cloud-based ATSC 3.0 air chain and eliminate multiple encoding and re-encoding steps.

This paper presents a unified approach to cloud-based broadcasting, detailing the transition from cloud-based playout to ATSC 3.0 studio to transmitter link transport protocol (STLTP) emission. It also serves as a reflection on the joint 2024 NAB Show demonstration conducted by AWS, Ateme, and Enensys, showcasing the potential of end-to-end cloud workflows in broadcasting.

ATSC 1.0 vs. ATSC 3.0

ATSC 1.0 is a fully constrained “last century” standard that offers truly little flexibility. It relies on the MPEG-2 codec and transport, standards that are now over 30 years old. The transmission's bitrate is fixed at 19.39 Mbps. Additionally, 8-VSB modulation suffers from multipath interference, which occurs when a signal arrives at a receiver at different time intervals due to reflections, dispersion, and other terrestrial path anomalies. Unlike analog TV, where multipath interference might result in a ghosting or fuzzy picture, in ATSC 1.0, it leads to complete signal loss, preventing any decoding.

ATSC 3.0 addresses these issues by utilizing Orthogonal Frequency Division Multiplexing (OFDM), bootstrap-enabled variable framing structures, and IP transport (to name a few). By incorporating OFDM along with guard intervals, the standard effectively mitigates multipath interference, transforming it from a problem into an advantage. This approach allows broadcasters to deploy multiple synchronized transmitters within a market, improving coverage and reception.

ATSC 3.0 – A Flexible, IP-Based Future

ATSC 3.0 is a revolutionary shift, providing unmatched flexibility and futureproofing for emerging codecs and technologies. Unlike its predecessor, ATSC 3.0 is entirely IP-based, meaning it uses the same packetized data structures as modern internet communications. This design enables NextGen TV services to be delivered seamlessly to televisions, set-top boxes, home gateways, and a wide variety of other connected and unconnected portable and mobile devices.

Since ATSC 3.0 is fully IP-based, it unlocks numerous new capabilities beyond traditional broadcasting. One key advantage is efficient one-to-many data delivery, which has applications far beyond television. For example, broadcasters can transmit enhanced GPS signals for precision agriculture, autonomous vehicles, and even robotic lawnmowers, offering location accuracy beyond traditional GPS capabilities. The standard also enables geo-targeted emergency alerts, allowing broadcasters to send alerts to specific users rather than an entire designated market area (DMA).

ATSC 3.0 also provides unprecedented flexibility in encoding parameters. Broadcasters can dynamically adjust bitrate and resolution based on content requirements, optimizing transmission quality in real time. Additionally, the standard supports the creation of new Broadcast Enabled Streaming TV channels (BEST) for breaking news or live events without requiring viewers to rescan their TVs.

Another significant advancement is the integration of interactive content. Think of ATSC 3.0’s A/344 standard as a ”browser,” defining the framework for broadcasting HTML-based overlays within broadcaster applications, effectively extending web-like experiences to television screens. This feature allows for enhanced viewer engagement, such as interactive news updates, sports statistics, or personalized content recommendations.

Harnessing the Cloud

The cloud is nothing new—AWS, Microsoft Azure, and Google Cloud have been around for years, and broadcast technology can now modernize itself by leveraging cloud-based infrastructures. There are significant efficiency gains with a cloud-based playout. Previously, each station had to receive a file, transcode it, and ingest it into a playout system manually. Operators then had to mark the segment in/out points before adding the content to a playlist. Now, with cloud-based workflows, we transcode the file once, segment it once for all stations, and make it instantly available for playback—eliminating redundant processing. For example, a syndicated show like Jeopardy or Wheel of Fortune, which aired across multiple markets, previously required separate processing for each station. Cloud playout solves this inefficiency.

Since we now operate from a unified cloud source, we can ensure consistent quality across all markets. We have full visibility into the transcode quality of every stream, as well as the reliability of the underlying infrastructure. Well-designed cloud environments inherently offer built-in redundancy, with hardware and data centers designed for high availability. Additionally, cloud infrastructure allows for dynamic scaling—resources can be increased or reduced as needed, optimizing costs by avoiding unnecessary CPU and memory expenses.

Bringing ATSC 3.0 to the cloud will accelerate air chain deployment. No longer will engineers need to manually install drivers on servers or ensure BIOS versions are up to date. Instead of waiting for limited engineering resources to install hardware, we can provision EC2 instances in the cloud almost instantly with Infrastructure as code (IaC).

Cloud adoption, however, presents challenges. Key concerns include how to transport video into the cloud while ensuring sufficient bandwidth and network redundancy, and training operations teams to support this modern technology. This shift requires a fundamental change in how technical teams operate. We must consider how we architect cloud-based workflows optimally, provide support, and staff for this transformation.

Figure 1 outlines departments impacted by cloud-based playout. As shown, there are significant shifts not only in engineering and operations but also in areas like traffic and promotions, which must adapt their processes to the new workflow.

The Playbook

Sinclair began its cloud transition in 2022, and while the process has been gradual, considerable progress has been made. As of February 2025, we have successfully migrated over 100 services.

At a basic level, cloud playout is simple—a file is placed on a playlist and played to an output. However, as we integrate master control functions, such as handling live news, network feeds, and breaking news, the complexity increases. The high-level diagram in figure 2 illustrates this workflow. On the left side, live-to-air video is transmitted from the TV station (the "ground") to the cloud. Examples of live-to-air video include news control room feeds for the daily newscast, network feeds from each market, and local programming feeds that go directly on-air.

At most sites, we use Ateme Titan Edge to encode a transport stream, which is then sent over Zixi to AWS. This is our transport into the cloud, but any transport stream encoder will work. Transport streams are typically carried over UDP (User Datagram Protocol). UDP is susceptible to packet loss, jitter, and out-of-order delivery because it lacks built in error correction. To mitigate this we utilize protected streaming protocols such as SRT, Zixi and RIST. Each protocol improves on basic UDP transport streams by providing error recovery, retransmission, and adaptive bitrate control [2].

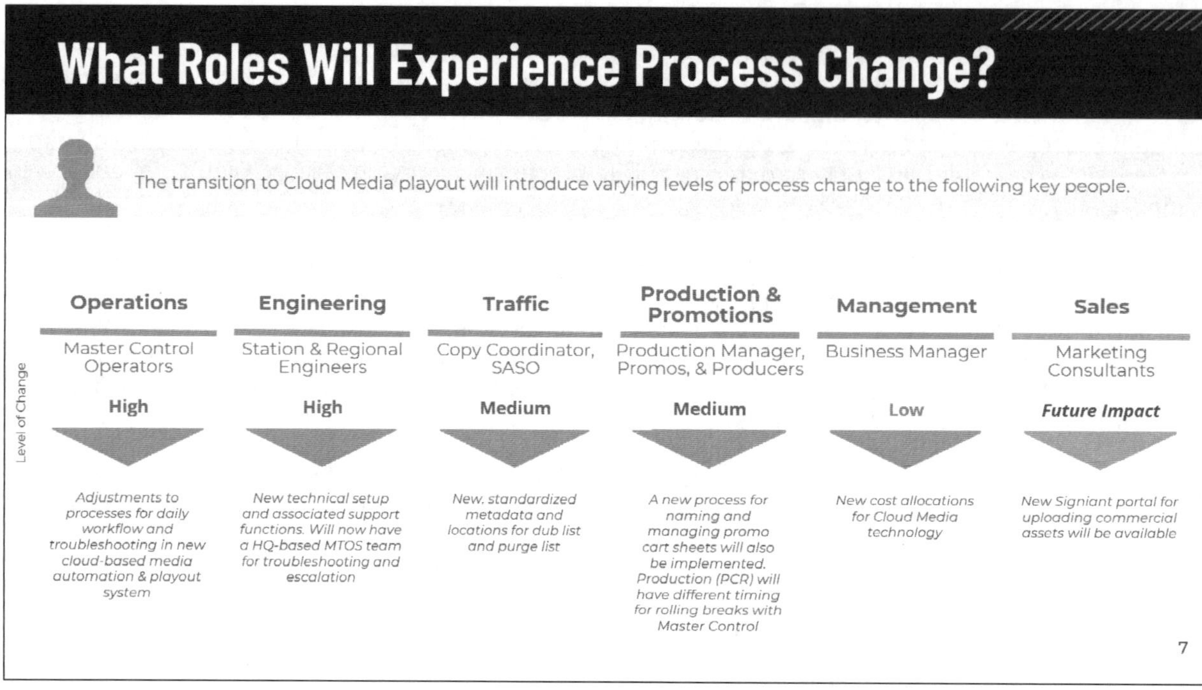

FIGURE 1: PROCESS CHANGES BY DEPARTMENT [1].

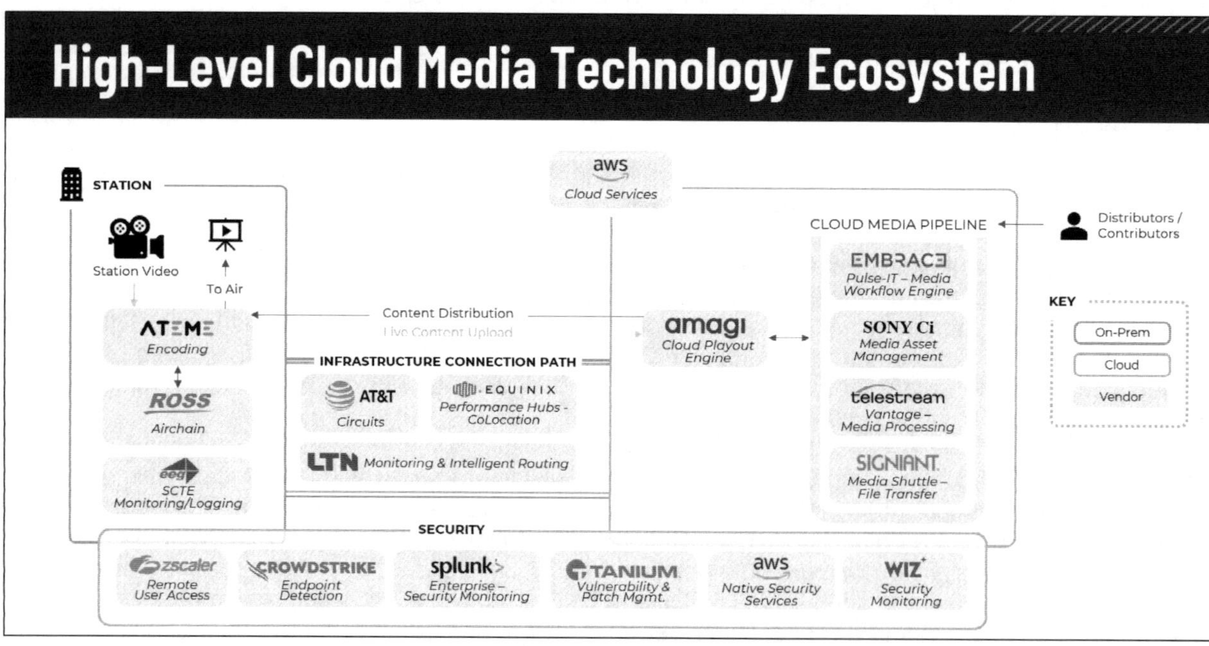

FIGURE 2: CLOUD PLAYOUT WORKFLOW [1].

Once the live video arrives in AWS, the transport stream feeds the Amagi cloud playout system, which serves as our cloud-based master control (see Figure 3). Amagi's centralized architecture allows for significant optimization when it comes to Media asset and live ingests. It also provides a cross-region cloud redundancy where infrastructure has been spun up on AWS us-east-1 and us-west-2 regions for a full geo redundant architecture.

On the right side of the AWS workflow, we see the Cloud Media Pipeline, which handles media file imports. The majority of our stations' playlists comprise of content delivered as a file. For example, when the Maury show is delivered as a file, we configure the linear playlist to insert ad spots after each segment.

Network affiliation determines each station's resolution. Our ABC, Fox, CW, and MyTV affiliates broadcast in 720p, while CBS and NBC broadcast in 1080i. We transcode all media into these two resolutions to match the broadcast chain.

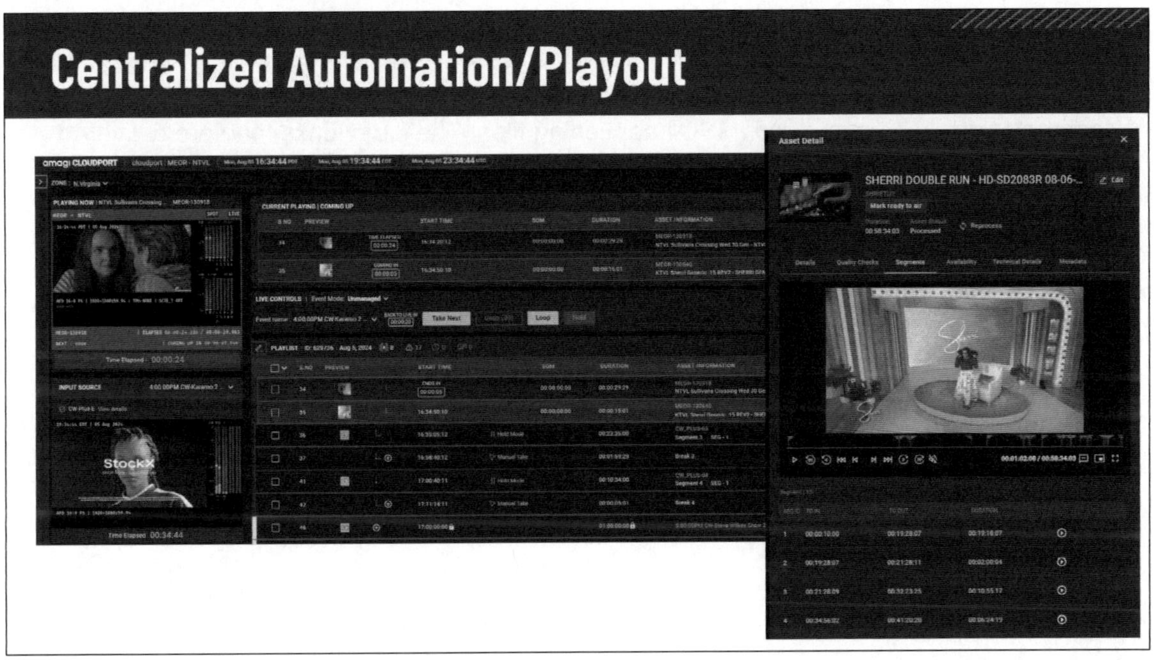

FIGURE 3: AMAGI CLOUD PLAYOUT INTERFACE [1].

Cloud-Based ATSC 3.0 Air Chain

The output of Amagi playout feeds directly into the ATSC 3.0 air chain—eliminating the need to send content back to a station for additional encoding. This "stay-in-the-cloud" approach improves efficiency and reduces latency.

At the 2024 NAB Show, Ateme, AWS, and Enensys demonstrated the feasibility of running an ATSC 3.0 air chain entirely in the cloud (see Figure 4). Since then, the cloud ecosystem for ATSC 3.0 has grown, with DigiCAP and other vendors now offering cloud-ready solutions.

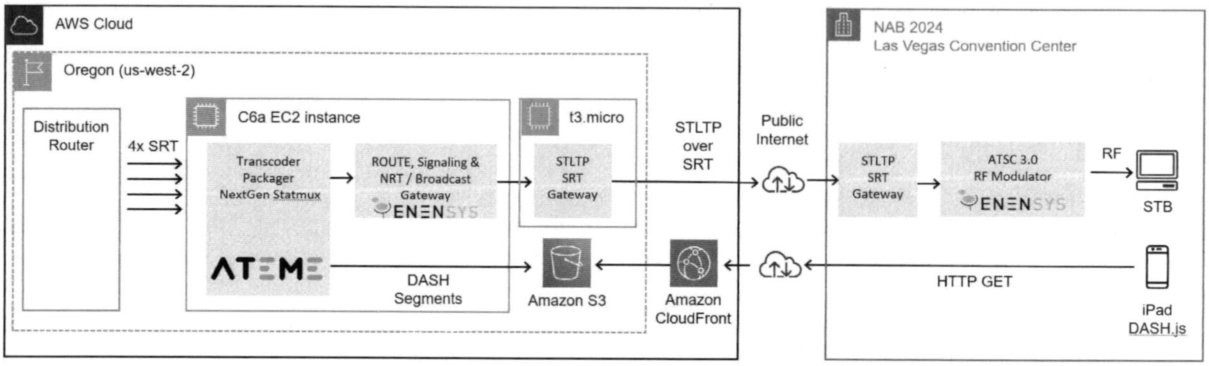

FIGURE 4: CLOUD BASED ATSC 3.0 AIR CHAIN WORKFLOW AT THE 2024 NAB SHOW [3].

Key ATSC 3.0 Cloud Components

The encoder receives a transport stream from master control. The encoder produces the stream into DASH segments with AC-4 audio and IMSC1 captioning files. The file chunks then are delivered via unicast WEBDAV delivery to the Route, signaling & Broadcast Gateway. The encoder is built on a separate EC2 compute instance on AWS. C6A instances are powered by an AMD EPYC processor. Sizing can range from 2 vCPU all the way up to 192 vCPU as illustrated in Figure 5.

Product Details

Amazon EC2 C6a instances are powered by 3rd generation AMD EPYC processors and are designed for compute-intensive workloads.

Instance Size	vCPU	Memory (GiB)	Instance Storage (GB)	Network Bandwidth (Gbps)	EBS Bandwidth (Gbps)
c6a.large	2	4	EBS-Only	Up to 12.5	Up to 10
c6a.xlarge	4	8	EBS-Only	Up to 12.5	Up to 10
c6a.2xlarge	8	16	EBS-Only	Up to 12.5	Up to 10
c6a.4xlarge	16	32	EBS-Only	Up to 12.5	Up to 10
c6a.8xlarge	32	64	EBS-Only	12.5	10
c6a.12xlarge	48	96	EBS-Only	18.75	15
c6a.16xlarge	64	128	EBS-Only	25	20
c6a.24xlarge	96	192	EBS-Only	37.5	30
c6a.32xlarge	128	256	EBS-Only	50	40
c6a.48xlarge	192	384	EBS-Only	50	40
c6a.metal	192	384	EBS-Only	50	40

FIGURE 5: AMAZON EC2 C6A SIZING OPTIONS [4].

The ATSC 3 Packager receives the DASH segments and assembles them into a multicast stream. The packager injects signaling data into the stream, including Low Level Signaling (LLS), Service List Table (SLT), and Service Layer Signaling (SLS) tables (ATSC 3.0's equivalent of PSIP in ATSC 1.0). SLT Defines the service's name, virtual channel and where the decoder can find the SLS. The SLS is a table that defines where the video, audio and CC components multicast are located. These tables provide crucial metadata that allows end-user devices to locate and decode services.

The broadcast gateway manages the physical layer parameters for transmission. It defines Physical Layer Pipes (PLPs)—e.g., PLP 0 as a robust 16-QAM layer for mobile reception, while PLP 1 carries HD services. Ensures correct sequencing of IP packets before compiling them into STLTP (Studio-to-Transmitter Link Transport Protocol).

STLTP is a UDP-based transport protocol, with FEC added to the UDP flow. To ensure reliability over public IP networking, the 2024 NAB Show demo encapsulated STLTP within a protected transport protocol. Various protection mechanisms are available, including RIST, SRT, and Zixi. In the demo, SRT was selected due to its bi-directional TCP handshake, which creates a reliable tunnel for UDP packet transport. On the receiving end, the SRT tunnel is unwrapped, restoring the raw UDP stream for transmission. Once the STLTP is in UDP form, it is ready to be sent to the ATSC 3 transmitter.

Hybrid Offerings – Ensuring Reliability in the Cloud

"The cloud never fails!" While this statement reflects the cloud's resilience, failures—whether in cloud infrastructure or network connectivity—are always a possibility.

To mitigate risk, each station is equipped with a Disaster Recovery (DR) server that mirrors the cloud playout system. This server provides a baseband output on-premises, enabling the integration of a standby air chain. This hybrid approach includes an ATSC 3.0 encoder, packager, and gateway.

Both the cloud-based SRT feed and the on-prem standby air chain are routed to a redundancy failover device as shown in Figure 6. This device continuously probes the STLTP feed to ensure valid payload data is present. If the primary cloud feed encounters issues, the system automatically switches to the on-prem backup.

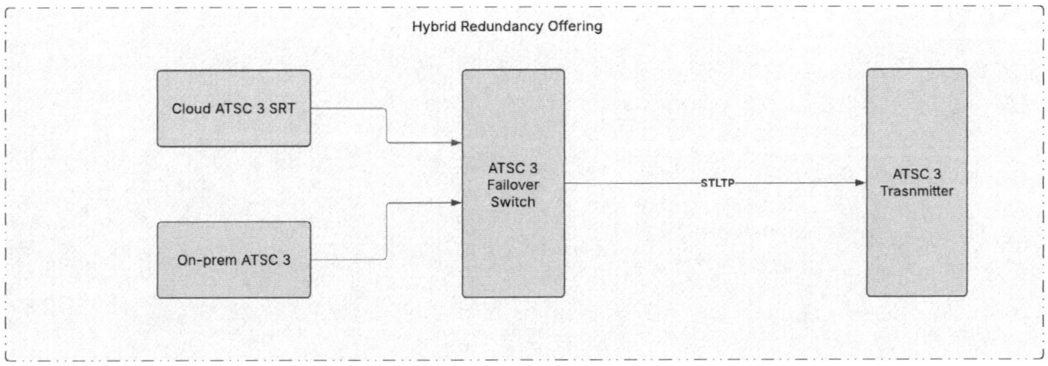

FIGURE 6: HYBRID REDUNDANCY OFFERINGS.

Conclusion

In the early days of ATSC 3.0 deployment, the various technologies and implementations were largely unproven. Like any new standard, time and industry adoption have led to maturity. Today, we have seasoned encoders, packagers, and gateways that fully support the evolving ATSC 3.0 ecosystem.

As the ATSC 3.0 standard matures, so does vendor support. A few years ago, deploying an ATSC 3.0 air chain in the cloud would have been impractical—neither the technology nor vendor infrastructure were ready. Now, cloud-based broadcasting is not only viable but also strategically advantageous and large-scale implementations are underway.

Leveraging the cloud as the primary infrastructure accelerates station deployments. By eliminating the need for on-site physical server installations, complex cabling, and manual network configuration, cloud-based deployment significantly reduces the time required for station setup.

As our industry gears up to meet an anticipated sunsetting of ATSC 1.0, the agility of these approaches will become more important, and our industry will rapidly need to transition stations to ATSC 3.0. Sinclair has deployed 35 host stations and 12 hosted sites over the past four years. However, a mandated transition would require much faster, planned, and organized deployment. By leveraging the cloud, broadcasters can scale and streamline this process dramatically.

We have reached a turning point where technology has matured, and we can finally harness the cloud's full potential in the broadcast industry.

References

[1] Hamri, Walid (2024). Transforming Master Control to the Cloud [Unpublished PowerPoint slides], Sinclair Broadcast Group

[2] AVW Group (undated), *Internet video protocols: Zixi, SRT and RIST comparison*. Retrieved January 31, 2025 from https://www.avw.com.au/images/wellav/Internet_Video_Protocols.pdf

[3] Kauffman, Boris (2024). NAB 2024 ATSC 3 Demo [Unpublished PowerPoint slides], Amazon Web Services

[4] Amazon Web Services. (2025). Amazon EC2 C6a instances. AWS. https://aws.amazon.com/ec2/instance-types/c6a/

ATSC 3.0 and TV 3.0 in the Cloud

Boris Kauffmann
Amazon Web Services
São Paulo, SP, Brazil
boriskff@amazon.com

Abstract – The transition to ATSC 3.0 and TV 3.0 enables broadcasters to leverage cloud infrastructure for traditional broadcast workflow. This paper presents a comprehensive reference architecture for implementing ATSC 3.0 and TV 3.0 systems on Amazon Web Services (AWS). The architecture addresses key challenges in networking and high availability requirements for broadcast operations. We demonstrate solutions for multicast routing in Virtual Private Clouds using AWS Transit Gateway, reliable Studio-to-Transmitter Link Transport Protocol (STLTP) delivery over public internet using Automatic Repeat reQuest (ARQ) protocols, and hybrid delivery optimization using Content Delivery Networks. Our implementation achieved zero packet loss during multiple tests ranging from 5 to 13 days between different AWS regions using Secure Reliable Transport (SRT) and Reliable Internet Stream Transport (RIST) protocols. Maximum round-trip times averaged 153 ms across continental distances. The architecture supported the continuous operation of commercial broadcast software, including encoders, ROUTE servers, and ATSC 3.0 gateways, while maintaining broadcast-grade reliability. Results from field testing validate the feasibility of cloud-based ATSC 3.0 implementations, providing broadcasters a blueprint for migration from traditional infrastructure while optimizing operational costs and maintaining security compliance for 24/7 broadcast operations.

Introduction

Broadcasting is undergoing a fundamental transformation from traditional on-premises infrastructure to cloud-based architectures [1]. The Advanced Television Systems Committee (ATSC) 3.0 standard enables this transition by introducing an IP-based transport layer that utilizes cloud computing capabilities [2]. This convergence of broadcast and broadband technologies presents unique challenges and opportunities for infrastructure design and implementation in the cloud. Brazil has selected ATSC 3.0 technologies as the foundation for its next-generation digital television system, TV 3.0 (DTV+). Initial experimental deployments are scheduled for 2025, with full deployment planned for 2026 [3].

Traditional broadcast architectures demand substantial investment in on-premises equipment while facing inherent limitations in scalability and flexibility. Cloud-based ATSC 3.0 implementations address these challenges but introduce new networking, reliability, and security considerations—particularly for the Studio-to-Transmitter Link (STL) connecting cloud infrastructure to on-premises transmission sites [4].

TV 3.0 builds upon ATSC 3.0's transport and physical layer specifications while introducing additional requirements for hybrid broadcast-broadband delivery and enhanced Over-the-Air (OTA) content regionalization. The Brazilian system's planned rollout in 2026, with experimental emissions beginning in 2025, provides an opportunity to validate cloud-based broadcast architectures in real-world deployments. This convergence of broadcast and broadband technologies requires careful infrastructure design and implementation consideration.

This paper presents a reference architecture for implementing ATSC 3.0 and TV 3.0 workflows on Amazon Web Services (AWS). We examine infrastructure design patterns for broadcast-grade reliability, network optimization for critical protocols, including ROUTE and Studio-to-Transmitter Link Transport (STLTP) [5], high availability architectures for 24/7 operations, and security considerations for public-facing broadcast services. Our implementation validates this approach through real-world testing with commercial broadcast software providers, demonstrating how cloud services can be architected to support ATSC 3.0 and TV 3.0 requirements while maintaining traditional broadcast systems' performance and reliability expectations.

Cloud Reference Architecture for ATSC 3.0

Implementing ATSC 3.0 and TV 3.0 in cloud infrastructure requires careful consideration of three key elements: component placement, networking architecture, and instance sizing. All components—except the RF exciter and transmitter—can be virtualized, enabling flexible deployment models while maintaining broadcast-grade reliability requirements.

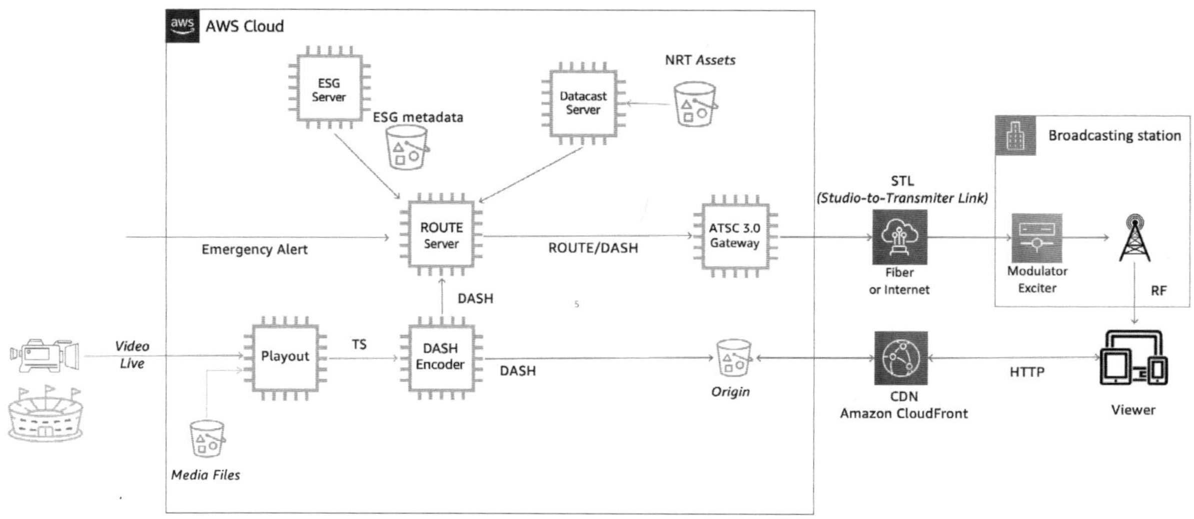

FIGURE 1: REFERENCE ARCHITECTURE DIAGRAM SHOWING THE COMPLETE WORKFLOW FROM PLAYOUT TO TRANSMISSION SITE.

The architecture (Figure 1) consists of three main processing stages: encoding, packaging, and delivery. In our proof of concept, the encoding stage employs compute-optimized Amazon EC2 c6i.8xlarge instances running Ateme's Titan Live DASH (Dynamic Adaptive Streaming over HTTP) encoder. These instances process incoming transport stream feeds from playout systems. While ATSC 3.0 implementations utilize HEVC encoding, TV 3.0 deployments require support for Versatile Video Coding (VVC), which may necessitate different instance sizing based on specific encoding requirements and content complexity. These reference instances, featuring 32 vCPUs and 64 GiB of memory, demonstrated sufficient performance for HD and UHD workflows in our testing environment.

The packaging stage employs ROUTE servers hosted on general-purpose instances (t3.2xlarge) running Enensys' MediaCast, processing DASH segments into ROUTE sessions, and generating Low-Level Signaling (LLS) tables. While this stage requires less computational resources than encoding, it demands stable network performance for handling multiple ROUTE sessions. Our implementation utilized similar instance types for the ROUTE Gateway, running Enensys' SmartGate and being responsible for creating Physical Layer Pipe (PLP) and STLTP generation. These instance sizes should be considered reference points, with actual deployments requiring sizing based on specific channel count, bitrate requirements, and redundancy needs.

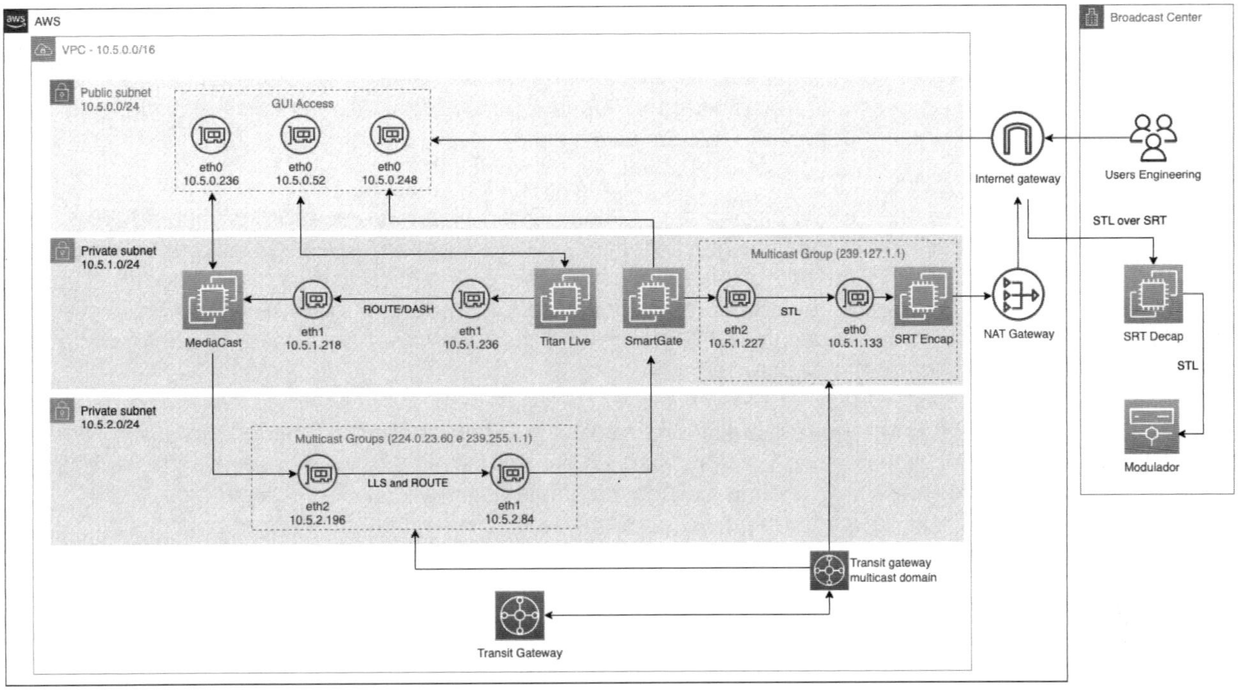

FIGURE 2: VPC ARCHITECTURE DIAGRAM SHOWING SUBNET LAYOUT, TRANSIT GATEWAY CONFIGURATION, AND MULTICAST ROUTING.

Network design centers around an AWS Transit Gateway implementation that enables multicast routing inside VPC (Virtual Private Cloud) subnets. This configuration supports the ROUTE protocol's multicast requirements while maintaining isolation between processing stages. Each component has its Elastic Network Interfaces (ENIs) operating in dedicated subnets with specific security group configurations, ensuring controlled traffic flow and maintaining broadcast chain integrity.

Hybrid Delivery Capabilities

The cloud architecture leverages the DASH encoder to support multiple delivery workflows simultaneously. While traditional broadcast implementations require separate encoding chains for OTA and OTT (Over-the-Top) delivery, our cloud-based architecture enables a unified approach. The encoder generates two distinct outputs from the same source: an Adaptive Bit Rate (ABR) DASH stream optimized for OTT delivery via Content Delivery Networks (CDNs) and a Constant Bit Rate (CBR) DASH stream for broadcast distribution.

This unified encoding approach provides several advantages. For OTT delivery, the ABR DASH streams are distributed through Amazon CloudFront, utilizing its global edge network to optimize content delivery to streaming viewers. The same encoder simultaneously provides CBR DASH streams to the ROUTE server for traditional broadcast delivery. This architecture enables hybrid scenarios where viewers can receive content through either broadcast or broadband paths, with the ability to seamlessly switch between delivery methods based on reception conditions [6].

The hybrid delivery capability becomes particularly relevant for ATSC 3.0 implementations, where broadcasters can leverage cloud infrastructure to provide enhanced services and fallback options. During broadcast reception issues, whether due to poor RF conditions or STLTP transport interruptions, receivers could automatically switch to broadband delivery, ensuring continuous service to viewers. This approach maximizes the benefits of cloud infrastructure while maintaining the reliability expected of broadcast services.

Network Architecture

Reliable transport of broadcast signals in cloud infrastructure requires specialized networking configurations to support traditional broadcast protocols and modern streaming delivery methods. A key challenge lies in supporting multicast traffic within VPCs, supporting ROUTE session transport, and ensuring reliable STLTP unicast delivery to transmission sites.

Multicast Support in AWS

Traditional ATSC 3.0 components rely heavily on multicast internal communication, particularly for ROUTE sessions and Low-Level Signaling (LLS) delivery. While standard VPCs do not natively support multicast routing, AWS Transit Gateway provides the necessary functionality through multicast domains. Our implementation utilizes dedicated multicast-enabled subnets for ROUTE server to ATSC 3.0 gateway communication, with specific IGMP (Internet Group Management Protocol) configurations to support session discovery and management [7].

AWS multicast implementation requires specific infrastructure components to function correctly. Nitro-based instances are mandatory for multicast support on the sender side, as they provide the necessary hardware virtualization features for handling multicast traffic efficiently. On the receiver side, Nitro-based instances are not mandatory but highly recommended. This requirement affects instance selection across all components that participate in multicast communication, including ROUTE servers and ATSC 3.0 gateways.

The Transit Gateway multicast implementation supports dynamic member registration through IGMPv2, allowing for flexible scaling of broadcast components. When configuring multicast domains, each subnet association requires proper IGMP configuration to support group membership discovery. Additionally, EC2 instances must be configured to enable IGMPv2 explicitly.

Multicast Group Configuration

AWS Transit Gateway multicast domains require explicitly configuring ENIs as multicast sources or group members. There are two methods to manage these group memberships:

1. **IGMPv2 Support**: When enabled, hosts can dynamically join or leave multicast groups using IGMP JOIN and LEAVE messages. Any ENI in subnets associated with the multicast domain can send and receive multicast traffic. This provides automatic group membership management without manual intervention.
2. **Static Configuration**: When IGMPv2 support is disabled, administrators must explicitly register ENIs as sources or group members through the AWS API or Console. Only designated sources can send multicast traffic in this mode, and only registered members can receive it.

It's important to note that a subnet can only be associated with one multicast domain, and IGMPv2 and static source support cannot be enabled simultaneously in the same domain. This configuration model enables precise traffic management and simplifies troubleshooting. Figure 3 shows the multicast domain configuration of two multicast groups for LLS and ROUTE sessions and their respective ENI IDs.

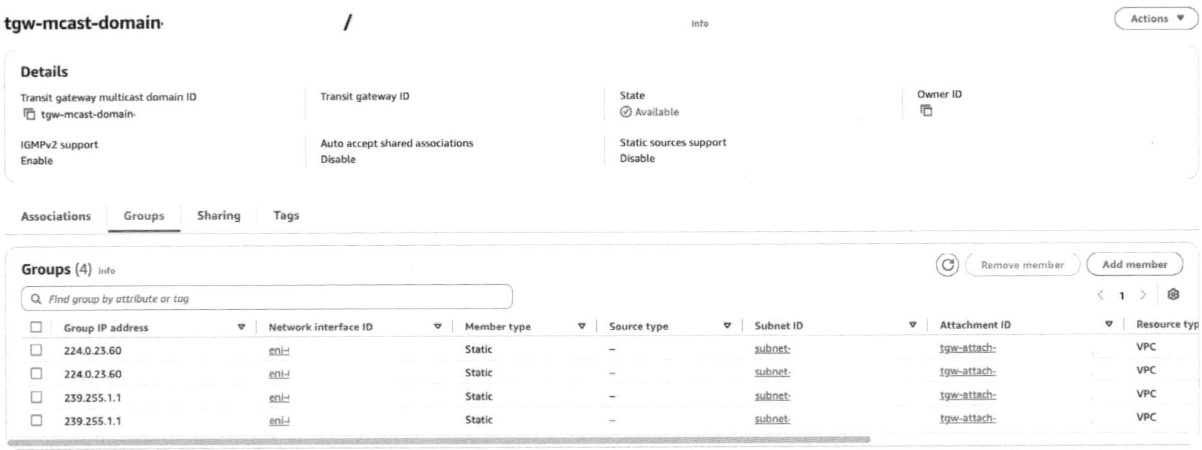

FIGURE 3: TRANSIT GATEWAY MULTICAST ARCHITECTURE SHOWING GROUPS CONFIGURATION.

STLTP Transport Optimization

The delivery of STLTP from cloud infrastructure to on-premises transmission sites presents unique challenges. To validate reliability and performance, extensive testing was conducted between multiple AWS regions and transmission sites. Tests were performed between AWS's Oregon and São Paulo regions, connecting to transmission facilities in Las Vegas, France, and São Paulo.

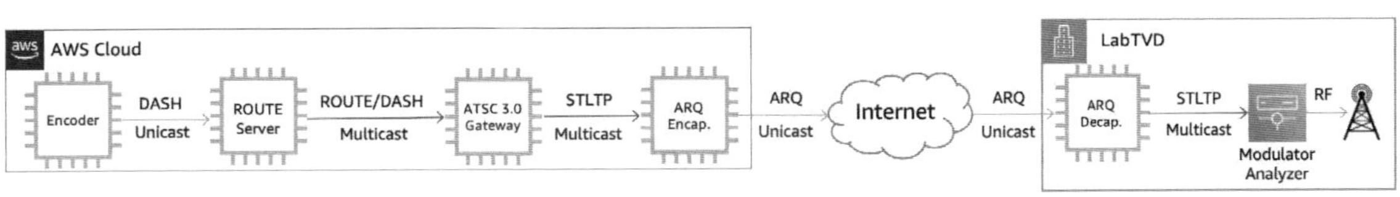

FIGURE 4: END-TO-END TEST SETUP.

The validation environments were configured with an STLTP bitrate of 32 Mbps and an ARQ latency buffer set to four times the measured Round-Trip Time (RTT) to accommodate network jitter, and round-trip times varied significantly based on geographic distance, ranging from 33ms for Oregon-Las Vegas connections to 153ms for Oregon-Rennes paths. Test durations ranged from 4.8 to 12.9 days to ensure statistical significance.

Testing demonstrated that properly configured ARQ protocols, like SRT [8] and RIST [9], could achieve broadcast-grade reliability for STLTP transport over the public internet. The SRT protocol configuration proved crucial for optimal performance. Setting SRT latency to four times the round-trip time provided consistent packet recovery. At the same time, FEC with ARQ in "Always" mode offered by SRT protocol demonstrated superior recovery compared to "On Request" mode. Implementing 800 STLTP packet buffer sizes at the modulator achieved stable delivery across all test scenarios.

Transport integrity validation was conducted through a comprehensive chain of professional broadcast equipment. The KaiMedia KMR-U4K and Avateq AVQ-1040 STLTP stream analyzers provided detailed metrics on transport integrity. Modulation testing utilized ProTelevision Technologies PT3063 and Enensys Vortex II and Rohde & Schwarz modulators, with final validation through ATSC 3.0 set-top box demodulation using the ZapperBox M1.

A series of six long-duration tests were conducted with various combinations of FEC and ARQ configurations. Tests employing FEC with ARQ in "Always" mode demonstrated the highest performance, achieving zero packet loss over multiple days of continuous operation. The combined use of FEC matrix configurations (10/5 and 15/5) with ARQ provided sufficient recovery, enhancing overall system reliability. In contrast, tests conducted without FEC showed increased susceptibility to network impairments, though still maintaining acceptable performance levels for broadcast operations.

The testing results conclusively demonstrated that STLTP transport over public internet using properly configured ARQ protocols can achieve reliability levels suitable for broadcast operations. This approach offers significant cost advantages over traditional dedicated circuits while maintaining the necessary quality of service for broadcast applications.

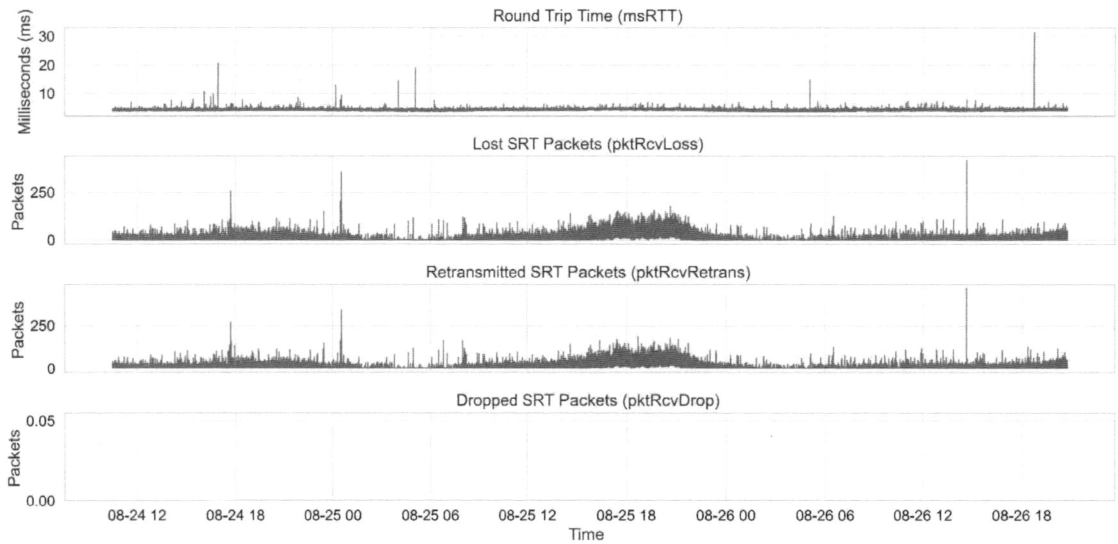

FIGURE 5: SRT STATISTICS FROM ONE OF THE TESTS.

High Availability and Management

Broadcasting operations demand exceptional reliability, with expected uptimes approaching five nines (99.999%). Achieving this level of availability in cloud infrastructure requires careful architectural design and comprehensive monitoring strategies.

Multi-AZ and Region High Availability Design

High availability in cloud-based ATSC 3.0 implementations relies on redundant deployments across multiple Availability Zones (AZs) and/or Regions. Our reference architecture implements active-active configurations for encoding and packaging components, with automated failover mechanisms on the transmitter sites. For STLTP delivery, redundancy is achieved through parallel transport paths originating from different AWS regions or AZs, following the outer tunneling approach specified in [5] Annex D. The primary STLTP stream is generated from the closest AWS region to minimize latency. In contrast, a secondary stream is maintained from a geographically distant region to ensure path diversity.

Timing synchronization presents unique challenges in cloud environments where only Network Time Protocol (NTP) is available as a reference. The ATSC 3.0 gateway implements specialized algorithms to compute nanosecond precision timing according to epoch measurements, providing sufficient accuracy for ATSC 3.0 physical layer requirements. This enables accurate timestamp generation requirements specified in [5] without relying on Precision Time Protocol (PTP).

When implementing redundant paths from different AWS regions, the variation in RTT requires careful consideration of buffer configurations. Our testing between a transmitter site in São Paulo and multiple AWS regions revealed significant RTT variations: 12ms to São Paulo (sa-east-1), 120ms to North Virginia (us-east-1), and 176ms to Oregon (us-west-2). These varying latencies demonstrate the importance of flexible buffer management in maintaining synchronized delivery. The ATSC 3.0 gateway accommodates these variations by signaling the Maximum Network Delay (MND) parameter, ensuring consistent stream delivery across all paths.

The MND configuration serves as an upper bound for network delay compensation, ensuring that all modulators in the network generate identical emissions simultaneously despite experiencing different path latencies in the STLTP reception. For instance, with an MND setting of 100ms, the system might accommodate an 80ms delay for a path with higher latency while having a 40ms for a lower latency path. This differential buffering enables synchronized emission across all transmission sites.

The STLTP redundancy could also be implemented by enabling the redundancy field in the Common Tunnel Protocol (CTP) header, allowing multiple RTP/UDP/IP (Real-time Transport Protocol/User Datagram Protocol/Internet Protocol) unicast streams to be delivered to the transmitter via diverse network paths. Each stream carries identical sequence numbers in its RTP headers, enabling the transmitter to perform packet-level selection and reconstruction of the STLTP stream before physical layer processing. This redundancy approach protects against regional cloud outages and internet path disruptions while maintaining compliance with the [5] specification for reliable STLTP delivery over public networks. The modulator's ability to aggregate packets from multiple streams provides seamless operation even during partial path failures.

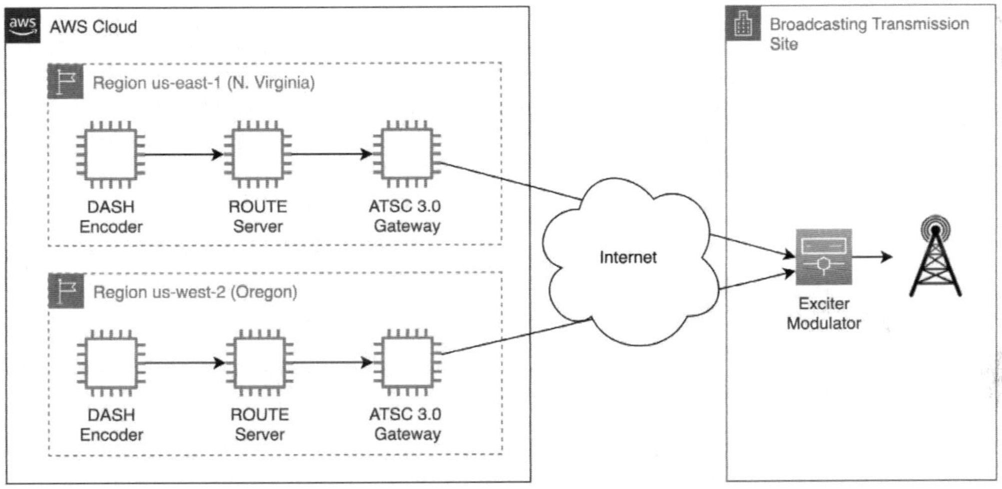

FIGURE 6: MULTI-REGION DEPLOYMENT ARCHITECTURE WITH ACTIVE-ACTIVE CONFIGURATION.

These mechanisms work together to ensure that the system maintains the required five nines (99.999%) availability while operating within the constraints of cloud infrastructure. The architecture's ability to maintain precise timing and seamless failover across geographically distributed regions demonstrates the viability of cloud-based ATSC 3.0 implementations for mission-critical broadcast operations.

Conclusion

The transition of broadcasting infrastructure to cloud platforms represents a significant evolution in television delivery systems. Through extensive testing and implementation, this study has demonstrated that cloud-based ATSC 3.0 and TV 3.0 systems can achieve the reliability and performance requirements traditionally associated with dedicated broadcast hardware. Successfully implementing critical broadcast functions in cloud infrastructure while maintaining broadcast-grade reliability establishes a viable path forward for broadcasters considering migration to cloud-based operations.

Our research revealed that ARQ protocols, specifically SRT and RIST, can effectively transport Studio-to-Transmitter Link Transport Protocol streams over public internet infrastructure with zero packet loss over extended operational periods. This finding challenges the traditional assumption that dedicated circuits are necessary for reliable broadcast transport. The implementation of AWS Transit Gateway proved capable of supporting the complex multicast requirements of ATSC 3.0 systems, effectively replicating traditional broadcast networking capabilities in cloud infrastructure.

The architecture's multi-region deployment strategy demonstrated robust redundancy capabilities, which are crucial for maintaining broadcast operations during regional outages or network disruptions. Through careful configuration of timing synchronization and buffer management, the system maintained precise timing requirements across geographically distributed transmission sites. These results validate that properly configured cloud infrastructure can meet the demanding reliability requirements of broadcast operations.

As broadcasters continue to evaluate cloud migration strategies, several areas warrant further investigation. Future research should optimize failover automation mechanisms and explore advanced hybrid delivery scenarios that leverage broadcast and broadband capabilities. The evolution of ATSC 3.0 and TV 3.0 standards and implementation requirements will likely drive additional innovations in cloud-based broadcast architectures.

This research provides a foundation for future cloud-based broadcast implementations, demonstrating that converging traditional broadcasting with cloud infrastructure can deliver the reliability and performance required for next-generation television systems. The successful validation of this architecture offers broadcasters a practical blueprint for modernizing their infrastructure while maintaining the high standards of broadcast television delivery.

References

[1] Lee, J. -y. et al., "IP-Based cooperative services using ATSC 3.0 broadcast and broadband," IEEE Transactions on Broadcasting, vol. 66, no. 2, pp. 440-448, June 2020.

[2] Advanced Television Systems Committee, "ATSC Standard: Physical Layer Protocol (A/322:2024-04)," Washington, DC, USA, Apr. 2024.

[3] SBTVD Forum, "TV 3.0 Project - Testing and Evaluation Report," São Paulo, Brazil, 2023.

[4] Kauffmann, B., "Arquitetura de Referência ATSC 3.0 em Nuvem Pública," Dissertação de Mestrado, Universidade Presbiteriana Mackenzie, São Paulo, 2024.

[5] Advanced Television Systems Committee, "ATSC Standard: Scheduler / Studio to Transmitter Link (A/324:2024-04)," Washington, DC, USA, Apr. 2024.

[6] Advanced Television Systems Committee, "ATSC Standard: Signaling, Delivery, Synchronization, and Error Protection", (A/331:2024-04)," Washington, DC, USA, Apr. 2024.

[7] AWS Documentation, "Working with multicast in Transit Gateway," Amazon Web Services, 2024. Available: https://docs.aws.amazon.com/vpc/latest/tgw/working-with-multicast.html

[8] Sharabayko, M. P., Sharabayko, M. A., Dube, J., Kim, JS., Kim, JW., "draft-sharabayko-srt-latest: The SRT Protocol," Internet Draft, IETF, Work in Progress.

[9] Video Services Forum, "VSF TR-06-2 RIST Protocol Specification – Main Profile," Alexandria, VA, USA, 2022.

Optimizing ATSC 3.0 Spectrum Utilization with Dynamic Resource Allocation and Management

Nick Hottinger
ONE Media Technologies
Hunt Valley, Maryland, United States
njhottinger@sbgtv.com

Abstract – The spectrum allocated to broadcasters is our most valuable resource, making it essential to find methods and technologies to optimize its use. Modern standards like ATSC 3.0 include technologies that enhance spectrum efficiency, such as advanced video codecs, an adaptable physical layer, and support for diverse data transmission. However, fully realizing the potential of these innovations remains an ongoing challenge. This paper examines the infrastructure, implementation techniques, and additional technology necessary to most efficiently utilize broadcast spectrum. Key use cases will be considered, including complete channel utilization to avoid unused (null) packets, dynamic data transfer adjustment to support critical short-term events, and scheduled physical layer adaptation to fit different applications. Additionally, an analysis will compare the spectral efficiency of typical ATSC 3.0 deployments with optimized configurations, highlighting potential improvements in spectral efficiency that can lead to improved channel monetization through increased service adaptability.

Introduction

Spectral resources are becoming increasingly limited due to the increasing demand from mobile networks and other technologies. The recent incentive auctions saw a major portion of spectrum sold to mobile operators [1]. Broadcasters' options are also limited by laws that restrict local and national ownership percentages, along with the obligations and responsibilities that station owners must fulfill [2]. Despite these limitations, the unique services broadcasters deliver remain crucial to the communities they serve. It is therefore essential for broadcasters to utilize their allocated channels as efficiently as possible.

Broadcasters can take advantage of the opportunities of ATSC 3.0 to improve encoding efficiency, physical layer flexibility, and modulation performance. However, even with these benefits, it is not enough to simply upgrade. During the early phase of the transition to 3.0, broadcasters need to maintain their ATSC 1.0 signal. To meet this requirement, broadcasters have set up lighthouse stations to host the primary services in the market [3]. This has resulted in crowded channels with multiple participants, and limits what a station can implement. Therefore, it is essential to explore methods and tools that maximize the efficient use of available spectrum.

Efficiency Improvement of US Broadcast Standards

From the NTSC standard that first enabled black and white TV in 1941, to the ATSC1.0 digital transition in 2009 [4], broadcast in the US has continuously improved efficiency and capability. Today, we have an

This paper is excerpted from the Proceedings of the 2025 NAB Broadcast Engineering and Information Technology (BEIT) Conference, © 2025, National Association of Broadcasters, 1 M Street SE, Washington, DC 20003 USA.

opportunity for further improvement with ATSC 3.0. By comparing the new standard to the widely deployed ATSC 1.0, we can see the significant improvements in spectrum efficiency enabled by upgrading.

ATSC 1.0 has limitations in areas like physical layer, codec usage, and delivery types. The older standard uses 8VSB modulation that offers a fixed 19.39 Mbps capacity and does not perform well in multipath environments. In contrast, ATSC 3.0 uses OFDM modulation, which offers improved spectral efficiency. As represented in Figure 1, ATSC 3.0 modulation operates closely to the Shannon Limit, the theoretical maximum efficiency of a communication channel. It has a ~3.7dB signal-to noise ratio (SNR) requirement reduction for a similar capacity to ATSC 1.0, represented by the A/53 tag in the figure [5].

ATSC 3.0 also offers flexible physical layer configuration options like Physical Layer Pipes (PLPs), which allows a broadcaster to customize their channel design for different applications, such as mobile reception or high-capacity service delivery. ATSC 3.0 also upgrades from the outdated MPEG-2 codec to HEVC, which provides up to 200% encoding efficiency improvement, and shifts from MPEG-TS to IP-based technology, enabling new business opportunities and faster adoption of new technologies.

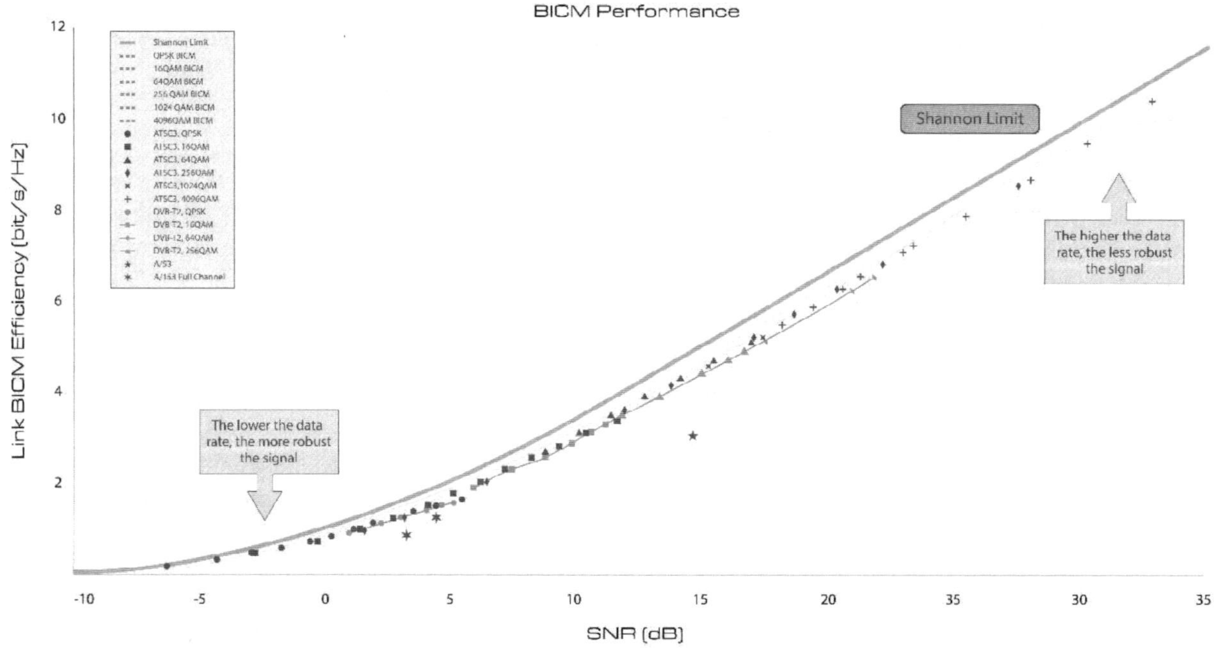

FIGURE 1: MODULATION PERFORMANCE COMPARISON [5].

While the advantages of ATSC 3.0 are clear, finding and implementing methods to make the most of its capabilities is imperative. To realize the dream of new business opportunities and improve critical services, broadcasters need to examine the infrastructure and implementation techniques required to enable ATSC 3.0's full potential.

Efficiency Techniques

Typical ATSC 3.0 Infrastructure

Modern infrastructure for ATSC 3.0 includes a relatively standard set of equipment. Typically, a station will use an encoder to accept distribution feeds, which arrive in various delivery formats with different parameters. The encoder will transcode the distribution feeds to be ATSC 3.0 compliant, implementing the HEVC video codec and the AC4 audio codec, then package the streams into either DASH or MPU segments.

These streams are then delivered to a Packager, where they are packaged into ROUTE or MMTP format and assigned Service Level Signaling (SLS), allowing individual service discovery and component listing. The Packager also builds the Service List Table (SLT), providing a basic service list for the ATSC 3.0 channel, and includes ancillary data such as ESG services or data distribution streams.

The output data is then ingested by a Scheduler, which builds the physical layer parameters and creates a multiplexed ATSC 3.0 channel in the form of a Studio to Transmitter Link Protocol (STLTP) . The STL signal is sent to a transmitter to modulate and create the over-the-air signal. An example of this system is shown in Figure 2.

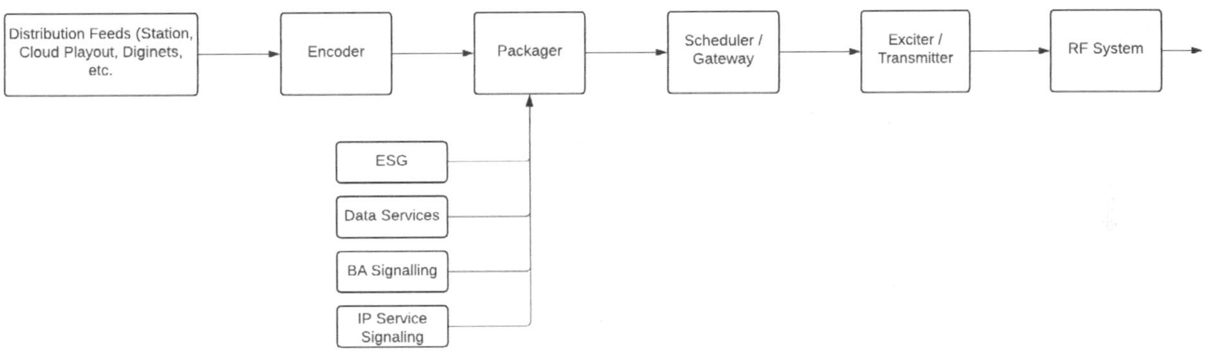

FIGURE 2: TYPICAL ATSC 3.0 INFRASTRUCTURE

ATSC 3.0 Statmux

A statistical multiplexer (statmux) is a device that dynamically allocates bandwidth among multiple data streams based on stream complexity, optimizing the overall use of available capacity. This maintains capacity utilization consistency while ensuring the necessary resources are available for each stream, improving video quality while reducing the need for spectral padding. A statmux can improve spectral efficiency by up to 20% and provides stable and predictable data utilization [6].

A statmux should be designed to fit the available capacity of a PLP exactly to guarantee complete bandwidth utilization and reduce or eliminate null packets. Figure 3 illustrates an example of total service bitrate utilization with and without a statmux. As shown, without a statmux in place, real time bitrate utilization is less predictable, and may require padding to prevent overflow, resulting in null packets when the bandwidth goes unused.

The statmux also makes the implementation of the advanced use cases enabled by ATSC 3.0 simpler by providing a single point of control for consistent and predictable bandwidth utilization. Individual stream parameters such as minimum bitrate or relative priority can be defined within the statmux. Any adjustment to the statmux pool size ensures real-time resource allocation based on complexity, while respecting individual service requirements. This simplifies channel control by reducing the need for individual service adjustment to utilize the total capacity.

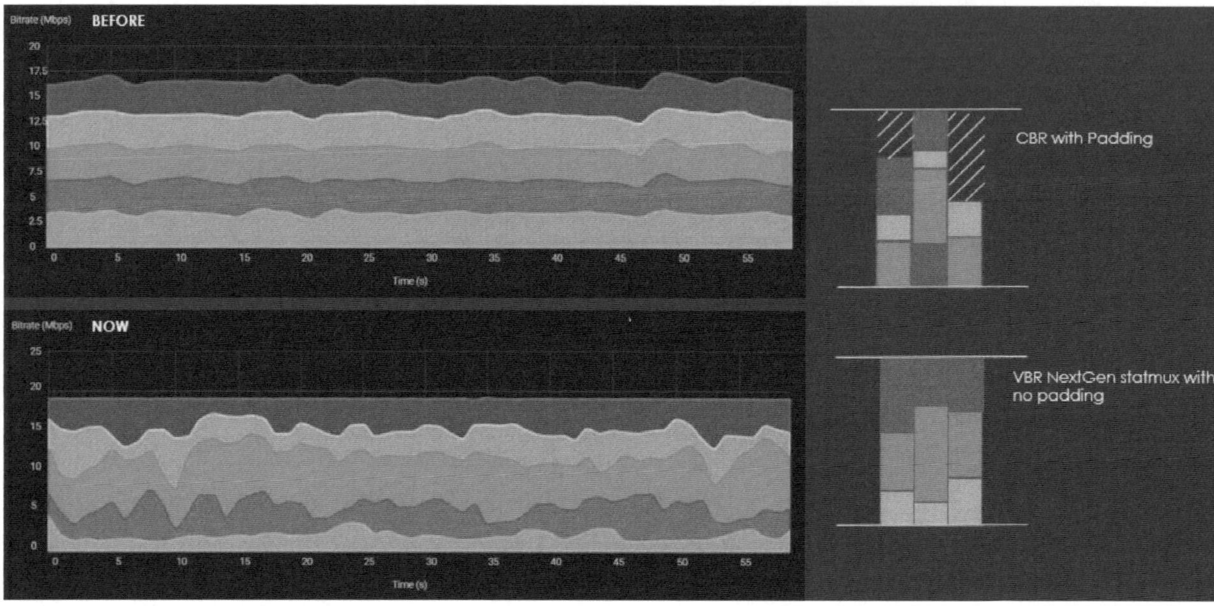

FIGURE 3: BANDWIDTH UTILIZATION WITH AND WITHOUT STATMUX. TOP GRAPH SHOWS BIT UTILIZATION WITH CONSTANT BIT RATE (CBR) WITH PADDING; LOWER GRAPH IS PERFORMANCE OF VARIABLE BIT RATE (VBR) ATSC 3.0 STATMUX WITH NO PADDING.

ATSC 3.0 expands broadcasting capabilities beyond typical audio and video services to include file delivery, enhanced advanced emergency information (AEI) messages, and other use cases which may require dedicated bandwidth. ATSC 3.0 statmux allows for adjustments in real time to enable these options.

System Manager

To efficiently implement the advanced features of ATSC 3.0 requires an orchestration platform with access to and control over the station. To provide software updates via data delivery or allow enriched data with AEI requires either an automated implementation or a real-time adjustment to channel resources.

ATSC has introduced a solution based on a broadcast core network (BCN) and System Manager. The BCN is a control layer that coordinates activities across multiple stations. The BCN would allow user interaction to negotiate channel resources for different applications and interfaces with the System Manager to implement the application at individual stations. The System Manager controls all devices and related resources in the ATSC 3.0 air chain. It modifies channel resources based on time-based or authorized external triggers to implement actions received from the BCN.

Figure 4 shows the architecture of an orchestration platform. As shown, the platform allows user interaction directly to the BCN. The BCN then provides instruction to the System Manager which implements the request through direct control of the broadcast air chain. The platform will also interact with TELCO platforms to diversify delivery options. An ATSC 3.0 receiver is the end device which receives the delivery from the broadcast station and has a feedback loop to the BCN.

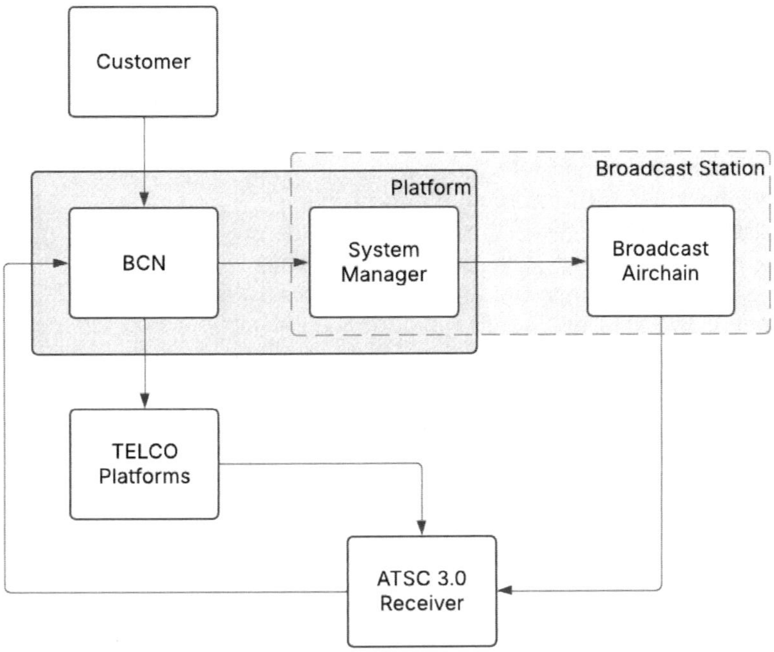

FIGURE 4: BROADCAST PLATFORM ARCHITECTURE.

The platform is capable of implementing the advanced features of ATSC 3.0 including file distribution, CDN offload, Event or Flash channel addition, and AEI Enriched Data distribution. These features all require temporary capacity within a channel. The System Manager produces this capacity by one of the following methods:

- Instruct encoders to lower the A/V quality of certain programs;
- Update/adjust parameters of PLPs to allow for higher throughputs;
- Update/adjust parameters of the statmux, reducing the bitrate pool size.

The statmux parameter adjustment is the most straightforward way to increase capacity as it is a single point of control. It also ensures continued service delivery, without negatively impacting service.

The physical layer adjustment makes the most fundamental change but also has the highest potential to impact service availability as receivers may need to relock a channel after the change. However, there are several instances where a significant channel modification may be necessary. These could include adjustments to allow for a new service delivery type, such as a mobile service, or a PLP adjustment to prioritize high-capacity delivery such as 4k upscaled service. The System Manager takes advantage of the precise timing and automation to schedule the physical layer adjustments to occur during lower viewership periods.

Specific Use Cases

Advanced features enabled by ATSC 3.0 such as file distribution, CDN Offload, or AEI messaging require temporary capacity within a channel. These features can be enabled by combining statmux, System Manager, and the other necessary ATSC 3.0 infrastructure. This implementation maintains near 100% channel efficiency, even while adding temporary services by dynamically adjusting the capacity. One such use case is enabling delivery of enriched data and media with AEI.

ATSC 3.0 allows broadcasters to associate media and enriched data to emergency alerts, surpassing the capabilities of today's mandatory EAS messages. AEI messages can include videos, real-time updates, and other potentially lifesaving information.

An efficiently designed channel will not have the capacity for short-term events like AEI. To address this, the statmux and System Manager allocate the channel capacity by the process below:

1. An Emergency Alerting System detects an emergency message and sends the triggering mechanism to a broadcaster's backend platform.
2. The broadcaster's system receives the alert and sends out the initial AEI messages.
3. The backend system associates relevant additional data or media.
4. The backend system determines the necessary bitrate to deliver content in a reasonable time. This is determined by the data type. For instance, a live stream's capacity is equal to the service bitrate, but a file's capacity is based on the acceptable time of transmission.
5. The backend system triggers a reduction in statmux capacity to reduce the PLP utilization while maintaining all active services.
6. The System Manager begins transfer of critical AEI data for the necessary duration.
7. Once the delivery and AEI event is completed, the backend system stops the AEI Content data transfer and readjusts the statmux to fill the PLP.
8. System returns to normal operation.

Spectral Efficiency and Monetization Analysis

ATSC 3.0 Spectral Efficiency

As discussed, ATSC 3.0 offers substantial improvement to areas such as physical layer performance and encoding efficiency. As a point of illustration, Table 1 shows a comparison between the channel utilization percentage of an HD service using HEVC in ATSC 3.0 and MPEG-2 in ATSC 1.0. A full HD program encoded with MPEG-2 has a typical bitrate of ~10Mbps. That same program could be encoded with HEVC at ~3Mbps. As shown, an HD service provided at identical quality on a channel with similar receivability requires 52% of spectral resources in ATSC 1.0 while requiring only 12% of spectral resources in ATSC 3.0.

	ATSC 1.0	**ATSC 3.0**
Typical HD service bitrate requirement (Mbps)	10	3
Channel Bandwidth (Mbps), assuming 1 PLP and SNR threshold of ~15dB	19.39	25.5
Channel Utilization %	52%	12%

TABLE 1: HD SERVICE RESOURCE UTILIZATION COMPARISON

Monetization with Spectrum Utilization

The described infrastructure improves efficiency by up to 20% and reduces or eliminates null packets in a PLP, providing new monetization opportunities. Applications like automotive connectivity to provide software updates and other upgrades, CDN offload offering improvement to real-time content delivery, and enhanced GPS using ATSC 3.0 to improve GPS accuracy have the potential for a significant total addressable market [7].

The spectrum utilization of different applications must be considered when implementing these new business opportunities. Within a channel, there are several factors that influence total spectral utilization, so spectral utilization can be specifically considered for the portion of spectrum dedicated to usable bandwidth. The usable bandwidth can typically be determined by the PLP design. Separate PLPs may require different spectral resources to achieve a targeted capacity. The intended receiver and necessary rate of transfer will have a large impact on the spectral resources required to deliver a service.

For example, consider the spectral utilization of a large file transfer requiring 3 Mbps of capacity where the transfer rate was calculated by the BCN to deliver the order in a given time period. Table 2 compares this service with different PLP modulation parameters. As shown, the more robust the PLP is, the larger the impact is to spectrum utilization. The single 3 Mbps service requires nearly half of a channel's spectral resources in the most robust example shown in the table.

Payload Requirement (Mbps)	Modulation Parameters (Constellation-Code Rate)	Receivability Threshold (dB)	PLP Capacity (Mbps)	Spectral Utilization %
3	256QAM-9/15	15.55	25.5	12%
3	64QAM-9/15	11.55	19.12	16%
3	16QAM-9/15	7.32	12.75	24%
3	QPSK-9/15	1.97	6.37	47%

TABLE 2: SPECTRAL RESOURCE UTILIZATION COMPARED TO DIFFERENT MODULATION PARAMETERS.

When considering monetization, not all bits are created equal. Broadcasters should determine a value for their spectrum based on the percentage of spectrum utilization and time ($/Hz-s). This value should be determined based on a variety of factors, such as the existing service delivery and monetary requirements to offer a competitive service. Using this model, services that require higher spectral resources will necessitate larger service costs.

Future Efficiency Enhancements

For the future, further efficiency improvements enabled by the standard are ongoing. On the physical layer, ATSC 3.0 allows for the use of MIMO (multiple in, multiple out) broadcasting, where orthogonal polarities can be used to double the potential capacity of a PLP. Based purely on bitrate availability, this would also effectively double the efficiency of a 6 MHz channel.

Additionally, ATSC 3.0 is positioned to include emerging technologies that can be deployed once they mature and are approved by the standards committee. As an example, versatile video coding (VVC), a codec currently under consideration for inclusion in the standard, could improve encoding efficiency by up to 40 % compared to HEVC [8]. Due to the nature of the IP-based standard, ATSC 3.0 can implement and accept these new technologies without breaking the signal.

Improvements can also be expected to resource adjustment management. For instance, proper scheduling, signaling, and standardization can adjust physical layer parameters less impactful to service availability. This would allow significant capacity adjustment for different reception scenarios to be enabled.

Conclusion

ATSC 3.0 offers broadcasters new ways to improve service offerings and maximize spectral efficiency, but key technologies and implementations need to be considered to realize the opportunities enabled by the 3.0 upgrade. As shown, the ATSC 3.0 statmux, System Manager and controlling platform can maximize efficiency, improve service quality, and enable new use cases such as enriched data with AEI. By improving spectral efficiency and resource management, station monetization can be significantly increased due to the newly available opportunities.

References

[1] "Broadcast Incentive Auction and Post-Auction Transition", May 2017, https://www.fcc.gov/about-fcc/fcc-initiatives/incentive-auctions#:~:text=Auction%20Results,U.S.%20Treasury%20for%20deficit%20reduction.

[2] "FCC Broadcast Ownership Rules", January 2020, https://www.fcc.gov/consumers/guides/fccs-review-broadcast-ownership-rules

[3] The National Association of Broadcasters, "Next Generation Television (ATSC 3.0) Station Transition Guide", April 2019, https://nabpilot.org/projects/atsc-3-0/nab-next-generation-television-atsc-3-0-station-transition-guide/

[4] "TV Standards in North America", https://www.eai.org/webpages/1202

[5] Rossiter, Steven, "Implications and Optimization of Coverage and Payload for ATSC 3.0", April 2017, https://www.gatesair.com/documents/papers/Rossiter_-_Implications_and_Optimization_of_Coverage_and_Payload_for_ATSC_3.0.pdf

[6] "Ateme Launches NextGen Statmux Bringing 20% Efficiency Gains in NextGenTV", March 2023, https://www.ateme.com/press/ateme-launches-nextgen-statmux-bringing-20-efficiency-gains-in-nextgen-tv/

[7] "Local Broadcasters Form Joint Venture to Provide High-Speed Data Transmission Services to Clients Across the United States", January 2025, https://sbgi.net/local-broadcasters-form-joint-venture-to-provide-high-speed-data-transmission-services-to-clients-across-the-united-states/

[8] Siqueira et al, "Rate-Distortion and Complexity Comparison of HEVC and VVC Video Encoders", February 2020, https://www.researchgate.net/publication/340689145_Rate-Distortion_and_Complexity_Comparison_of_HEVC_and_VVC_Video_Encoders

NEXTGEN Incident Response Communication System – Using ATSC 3.0

Fred Engel
Device Solutions Inc
Morrisville, North Carolina, United States
fengel@device-solutions.com

Tim Bagnall
Mosaic ATM
Leesburg, Virginia, United States
tbagnall@mosaicatm.com

Mark Corl
Triveni Digital
Princeton, New Jersey, United States
mcorl@trivenidigital.com

Chris Pandich, Don Smith
PBS North Carolina
Research Triangle Park, North Carolina, United States
cpandich@pbsnc.org; dsmith@pbsnc.org

Jim Stenberg
Over The Air RF Consulting, LLC
Portland, Maine, United States
jim@otarf.com

Dan Wesely
Mosaic ATM
Leesburg, Virginia, United States
dwesely@mosaicatm.com

Tony Sammarco, Chris Lamb
Device Solutions Inc
Morrisville, North Carolina, United States
tsammarco@device-solutions.com; clamb@device-solutions.com

Abstract – This paper provides a timely description of a National Aeronautics and Space Administration (NASA) research project investigating the use of a mobile ATSC 3.0 datacasting station to help support wildland fire management operations. We will discuss a proposed innovation called the NextGen Incident Response Communication System (NIRCS). NIRCS is a rapidly deployable, mobile, long-range broadcast communications system using ATSC 3.0 technology – the digital terrestrial broadcast system built on the internet protocol (IP) – to enable one-way datacasting of IP-compatible data, including ultra-high-definition video, high-fidelity audio, and other types of data packets (e.g., aircraft position messages).

The Problem – Applications of Uncrewed Aircraft Systems (UAS) in Wildland Firefighting Efforts Are Limited Due to Poor Situational Awareness

Over the last few years, the NASA Aeronautics Research Mission Directorate (ARMD) has successfully investigated capabilities that help support management of wildfires. One ARMD project in particular, the Advanced Capabilities for Emergency Response Operations (ACERO), focuses on the use of uncrewed aircraft systems (UASs) and other advanced aviation technologies to improve wildland fire coordination and operations. With many valuable applications that remove humans from harm's way, UASs are

increasingly being used in wildland firefighting. Applications range from real-time intelligence gathering, including photography, video, and thermal mapping to aerial ignition (Figure 1 [1]). In aerial ignition, UASs safely start prescribed burns without having to overly endanger front-line personnel.

FIGURE 1. UAS AERIAL IGNITION OPERATION.

Although UASs show great promise to significantly improve wildland firefighting operations, they have not yet reached their full potential. A significant roadblock impeding their more widespread application is the lack of situational awareness about the real-time position of UASs by airborne pilots operating nearby in crewed wildland firefighting aircraft. Airborne pilots simply do not know enough about the active location of UAS. Without precise and continuous UAS location data, the many aircraft supporting the operation must maintain a high degree of separation, forcing UASs to operate in areas displaced from the nexus of the firefight where they have less impact. The ATSC 3.0 innovation proposed here aims to remedy this issue, improving crewed aircraft situational awareness of UAS positioning and helping to expand the applications of UASs in the wildland firefight.

Proposed Innovation – The NextGen Incident Response Communication System

The proposed innovation – the **NextGen Incident Response Communication System (NIRCS)** – is a rapidly deployable, mobile, long-range ATSC 3.0 datacasting communications system, as envisioned in Figure 2. The innovation directly addresses one of the NASA ACERO project's critical technological needs: a reliable, resilient, and secure data communication system for quick data dissemination to support effective decision-making. By addressing this ACERO need, NIRCS solves the problem of wildland firefighting pilots not knowing the real-time location of UASs.

FIGURE 2. A RENDERING OF THE NEXTGEN INCIDENT RESPONSE COMMUNICATION SYSTEM DATACAST STATION.

Mosaic ATM and Device Solutions Inc researched and refined the NIRCS concept during a six-month Phase I Small Business Innovation Research project for the NASA Langley Research Center in support of the NASA ACERO project. The first phase of the project concluded in early February 2025. The team hopes to continue the project in a second phase beginning in the Summer of 2025 to produce a prototype NIRCS system and demonstrate the technology in a formal flight test program.

NIRCS uses ATSC 3.0 technology, a digital terrestrial broadcast system using the internet protocol (IP) that enables one-way communication of IP-compatible data, including ultra-high-definition video, high-fidelity audio, and other types of data packets (e.g., real-time aircraft position messages). Table 1 lists the key features of NIRCS.

NIRCS, as a general-purpose digital datacasting system, can send a variety of data to suit many aviation purposes:

- Vehicle position and operational volume data
- Temporary flight restrictions (TFRs)
- Notices to Airmen (NOTAMs)
- Airspace procedures, structure, and adaptation
- Weather information
- UAS surveillance video
- High-fidelity audio

Feature	Description
Protocol	Internet Protocol
Radio Freq.	Ultra-High Frequency (UHF) broadcast 470 to 608 MHz
Throughput	Bit rates vary from 1 to 10 MB/s depending on broadcast settings.
Direction	One-way
Range	• Up to 60 nm for simple data packets (e.g., aircraft position reports) • Less for high-definition video and high-fidelity audio data packets
Encryption	Compatible with standard IP encryption protocols, like IPsec
Distributable Content	Compatible with any content that can be sent over IP (e.g., text messages, documents, audio, and video)
Benefits	**General** • Expands broadcast coverage area • Reduces data dissemination latency • Allows for encryption to protect proprietary and sensitive information • Interoperates with existing devices **Wildland Firefighting Specific** • Facilitates coordination of airspace operations • Significantly reduces the voice communication burden currently placed on aircraft operators • Allows for expansion of UAS operations in the firefighting effort, day and night • Allows wildfire incident aircraft to operate more efficiently and effectively

TABLE 1. NIRCS KEY FEATURES.

Illustration of the NIRCS Wildland Firefighting Use Case

Though NIRCS, as a general ATSC 3.0 datacasting solution, has numerous applications, in this section we focus on a wildland firefighting use case to illustrate its potential.

Figure 3 shows an operational view of this NIRCS wildland firefighting use case where NIRCS broadcasts the UAS's position data, operational volume data, and surveillance video to crewed aircraft at long ranges as well as fire line personnel on the ground. Source datacast content originates with a UAS operating near and over the fire. The UAS continuously relays its 3D position and velocity information (i.e., latitude, longitude, altitude, speed, and heading) and surveillance video to a linked ground control station where the remote pilot is stationed. Collocated with the UAS ground control station is the NIRCS mobile datacast station which rapidly ingests and broadcasts this stream of UAS data throughout the coverage area. Crewed aircraft and other users within range and equipped with a compatible NIRCS receiver and tablet, hosting an end user software application, are then able to receive and review important and timely mission information.

Figure 4 shows a typical NIRCS cockpit configuration with a NIRCS receiver affixed to the cockpit's interior windshield and a tablet positioned approximately where it would sit strapped to a pilot's knee. These pieces of technology, coupled with the tablet's software application, provide the two crewed firefighting aircraft – the air tanker and helitack – significantly enhanced situational awareness. Not only do they each have access to surveillance videos about the state of the fire, but each also knows the real-time location of the UAS, allowing the crewed aircraft to operate more safely and efficiently to the UAS.

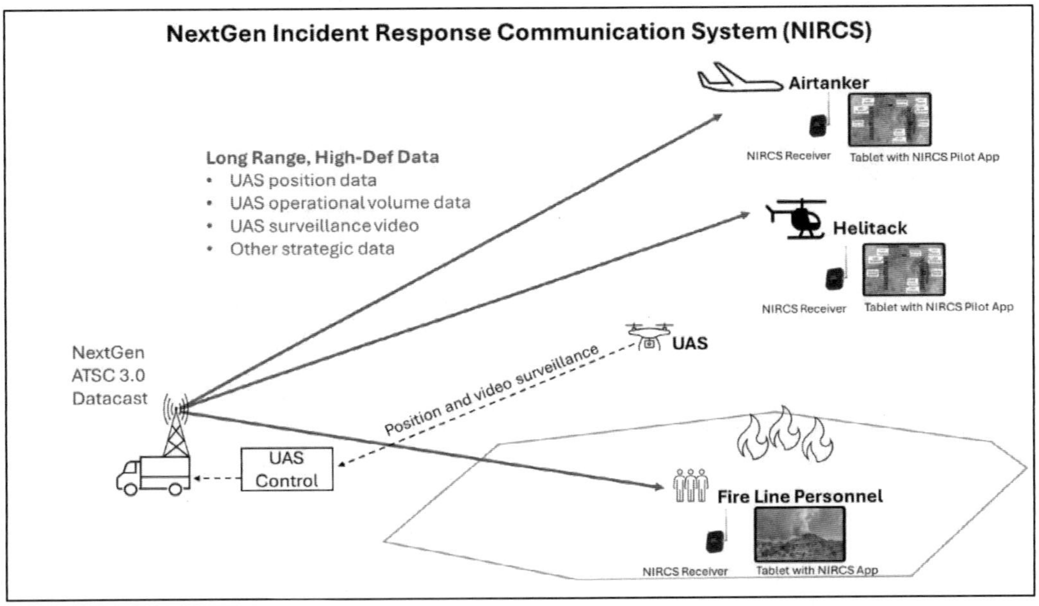

FIGURE 3. NIRCS ENABLES LONG-RANGE BROADCAST OF UAS POSITIONS, UAS OPERATIONAL VOLUMES, AND UAS SURVEILLANCE VIDEO.

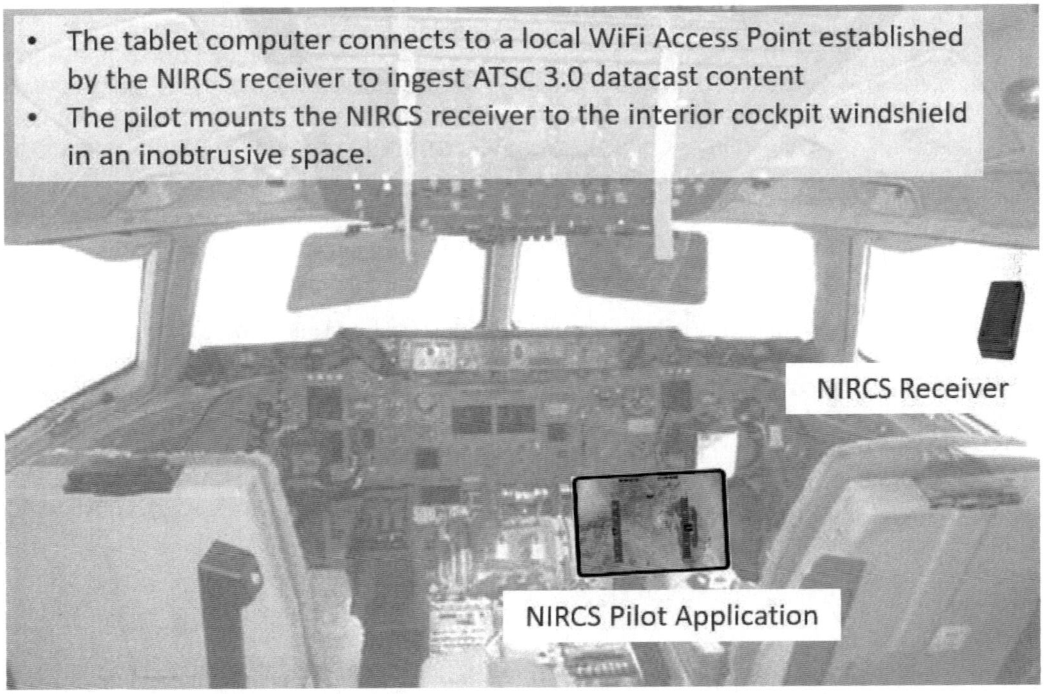

FIGURE 4. NIRCS COCKPIT CONFIGURATION.

The figures below further illustrate the NIRCS wildland firefighting use case, showing screenshots from conceptual end user software applications which enhance the user's situational awareness of the operation and fire. One figure shows a display specifically for pilots and the other shows a more general display applicable to many NIRCS end users participating in the firefight.

NIRCS Pilot Application

Figure 5, a screenshot adapted from an existing Mosaic ATM software application, shows a concept for the NIRCS pilot application. Mosaic ATM developed the application during a previous NASA research effort called the small UAS Collision Avoidance System (sUCAS). As the name implies, sUCAS helps pilots avoid collisions with UASs. The sUCAS leverages the NASA Langley Research Center's DAIDALUS software, a reference implementation of RTCA's DO-365 Detect and Avoid standard [2]. The application serves a number of aviation purposes, including flight planning, tracking, and scenario simulation to support education and training.

In the flight tracking mode, the application dynamically follows the pilot's aircraft as it travels through airspace. The user may select from several different backgrounds, including aerial imagery, VFR charts, streets, and terrain. Aerial imagery background is shown in Figure 5. The application also conveys the real-time location of other nearby air traffic in a display commonly known as a cockpit display of traffic information (CDTI). Though Figure 5 is a snapshot, in practice, it looks more like a video as aircraft move throughout the airspace.

To describe the NIRCS pilot application, we use the California York fire that occurred in the summer of 2023 in the Mojave Desert. The underlying aerial imagery seen is near Hart, CA. The scenario features four aircraft consisting of an air tanker and three UAS all performing wildland firefighting operations. The NIRCS software application is explained from the perspective of the air tanker pilot.

The position of the air tanker – termed "ownship" – is denoted by the blue chevron at the center of the figure. At this moment in the scenario, ownship is traveling at a speed of 105 knots with a heading of 0 degrees and at an altitude of 4600 feet. Three UASs, shown with white chevrons, are operating in the vicinity of ownship: "Drn01," "Drn02," and "Drn03." The concentric circles around ownship and the numbers above each UAS symbol allow the pilot to quickly ascertain the relative horizontal and vertical distances from ownship. The first, second, and third concentric circles around ownship, respectively, are 1.25, 2.50, and 5.00 nautical miles away from ownship horizontally. The numbers above each UAS symbol reveal the relative vertical distance to ownship, in hundreds of feet (e.g., +06 means the aircraft is 600 feet above ownship, -03 means the aircraft is 300 feet below ownship). Besides denoting the location of aircraft, the chevrons also reveal the compass direction the aircraft is travelling (e.g., "Drn02" is traveling due east). The magenta hexagons convey the operational volume for each UAS, letting the pilot know their potential operational ranges.

The display can also convey collision risk to the pilot and suggestive guidance on how to reduce that risk. In the notional scenario of Figure 5, of the three UAS, "Drn03" presents the largest risk to ownship at approximately 1.25 nautical miles away from and only 200 feet above ownership. A small yellow band along the heading compass – stretching from 55 to 90 degrees – indicates headings that ownship should avoid to remain a safe distance from "Drn03." Suggestive guidance bands like this one on the heading compass are also shown on the speed and altitude tapes when the dynamics of the encounter call for it. Band coloring changes depending on the associated risk level, with red coloring indicating higher relative risk to yellow coloring (no red banding is shown in the figure).

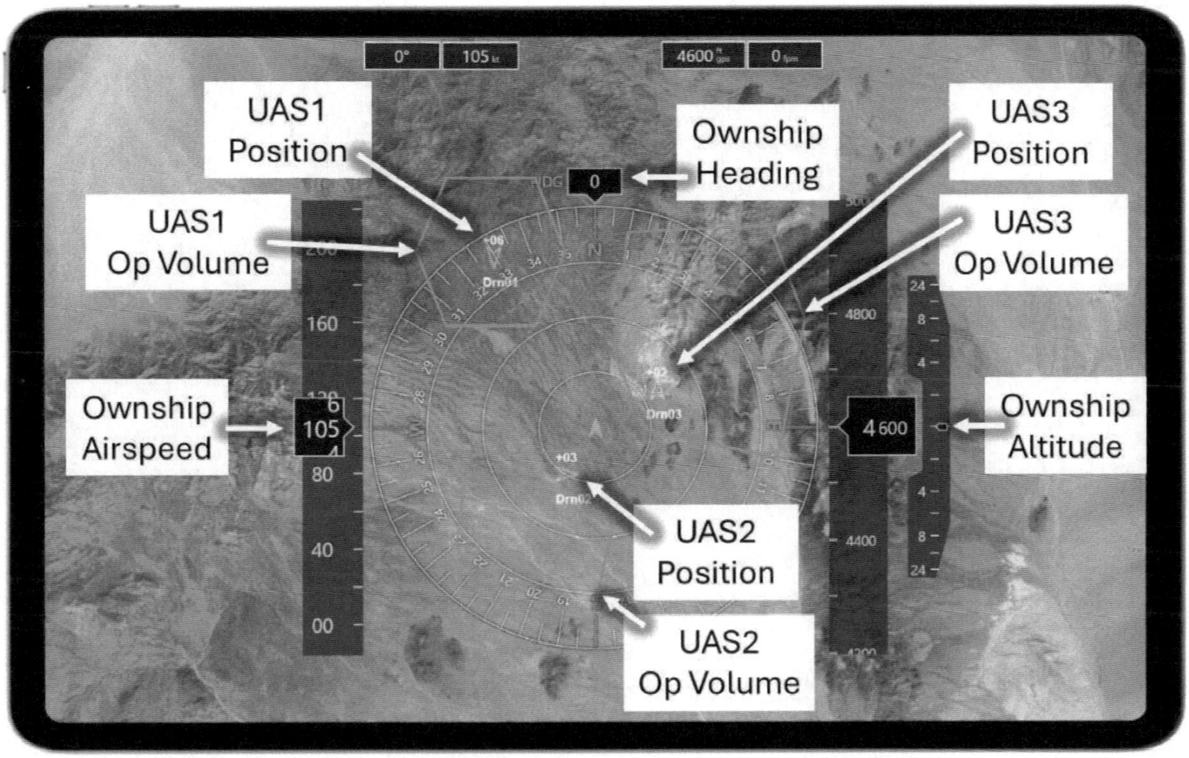

FIGURE 5. NIRCS PILOT APP. THE NIRCS PILOT APP ALLOWS PILOTS TO SEE NEARBY UAS POSITIONS, OPERATIONAL VOLUMES, AND UAS SURVEILLANCE VIDEO.

NIRCS Video Application

Figure 6 shows a more general-purpose software application. Here, the NIRCS video application functions like a typical video viewer application with capabilities to watch live video, pause live or recorded video, and rewind and replay recorded video. Embedded within the application is a channel guide so the user can review information about available ATSC 3.0 broadcasts and tune to the most appropriate channel. Figure 6 assumes that the user has selected "DRN01" from the same York fire scenario and is watching live surveillance video captured by the UAS.

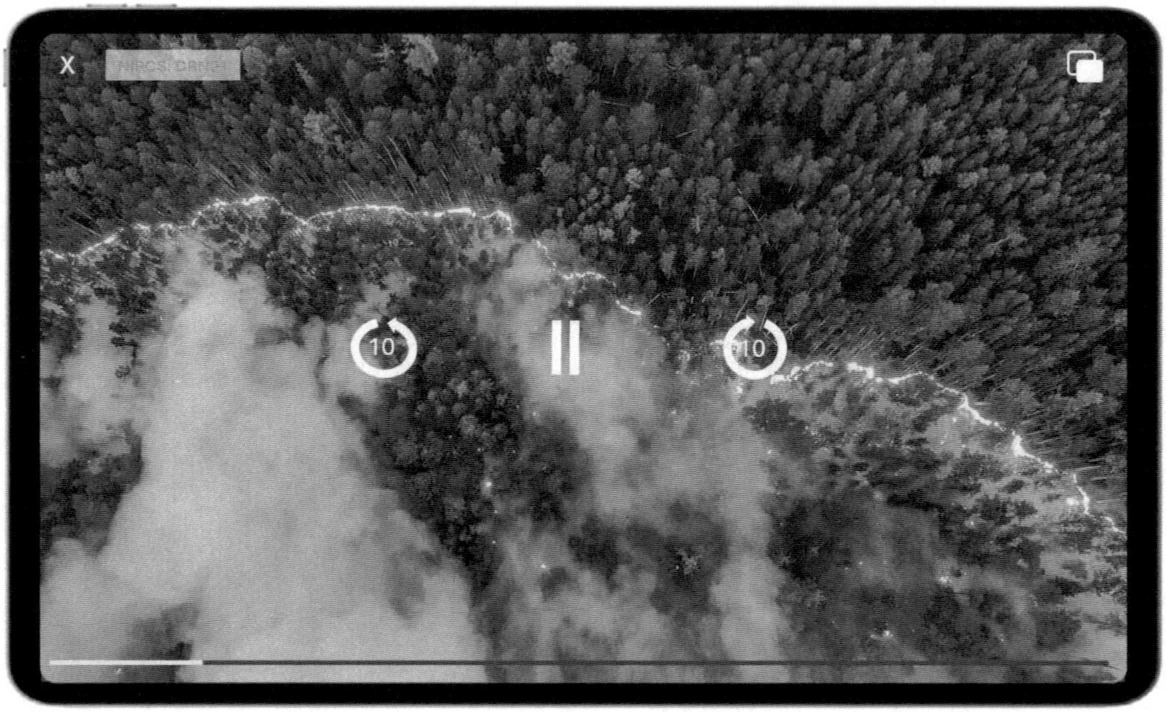

FIGURE 6. NIRCS VIDEO APP. THE NIRCS VIDEO APP ALLOWS PILOTS AND OTHER USERS TO WATCH HIGH-DEFINITION ATSC 3.0 VIDEO IN REAL TIME OR ON DELAY.

Regarding the Collision Between a Civilian Drone and a Canadian Air Tanker During Los Angeles Firefighting Operations in January 2025

On January 9th, 2025, during firefighting operations on the Palisades fire in Los Angeles, a Canadair CL-415 Super Scooper air tanker collided with a civilian drone. Fortunately, the air tanker landed safely after the incident but was taken out of service for several days, depleting the available firefighting resources that were already stretched thin.

FIGURE 7. WING DAMAGE SUFFERED BY A CANADAIR CL-415 SUPER SCOOPER AFTER COLLISION WITH CIVILIAN DRONE DURING LOS ANGELES FIREFIGHTING OPERATIONS IN JANUARY 2025.

By the time of the incident, the Federal Aviation Administration (FAA) had imposed a temporary flight restriction (TFR) for the area which prohibited civilian drone operations. While the FAA investigation is ongoing and it is still too early to say definitively whether NIRCS could have helped prevent the incident, it is this team's expert opinion that it had the potential to help. In a relatively new rule known as Remote Identification (aka Remote ID, or RID), the FAA now requires most civilian drones to continuously broadcast their identity and real-time position and velocity information. Though not depicted explicitly in Figure 3, the NIRCS datacast station design includes RID receivers to collect nearby drone RID broadcasts and include them in the NIRCS broadcast. Consequently, the pilot display shown in Figure 5 would not only have conveyed real-time positioning of official UAS participating in the firefight but also civilian drones complying with the FAA's RID rule.

It is important to note that there have been reports that the civilian drone involved in the incident was below the FAA's RID weight threshold of 0.55 pounds, meaning the drone may not have had to broadcast RID. If the drone was not broadcasting RID or outside the range of NIRCS's RID receiver, NIRCS would have been unable to help prevent the incident. Unofficial and prohibited drone operations near firefighting operations continue to adversely impact wildland firefighting, sightings of which force authorities to temporarily ground firefighting aircraft. The authors urge all civilian drone operators to use their drones responsibly and in accordance with federal regulations.

ATSC 3.0 Background

ATSC 3.0, also known as NEXTGEN TV, is the next generation of digital television, a system that utilizes advanced modulation technologies within the traditional 6 MHz television channel. Developed by the Advanced Television Systems Committee (ATSC) and approved for voluntary use in the United States by the FCC in 2017, ATSC 3.0 has been introduced into over 80 markets in the US and internationally in South Korea, Jamaica, Trinidad and Tobago, and, most recently, Brazil.

ATSC 3.0 is built utilizing Internet Protocol (IP) and can merge the best of over-the-air broadcasting with internet delivered content and applications on connected "smart" TVs. For viewers, whether internet connected or not, it provides better video quality, immersive sound, advanced emergency alerting and informing, and is easily adaptable for future technologies [3].

ATSC 1.0, the current broadcast technology in the US, South Korea, and Canada, was developed in the 1990s and is based on an 8-level vestigial sideband (8VSB) modulation scheme [4] with MPEG 2 video encoding and has fixed capacity of 19.3Mbits/sec [4]. An example of a typical broadcast configuration is shown in Figure 8.

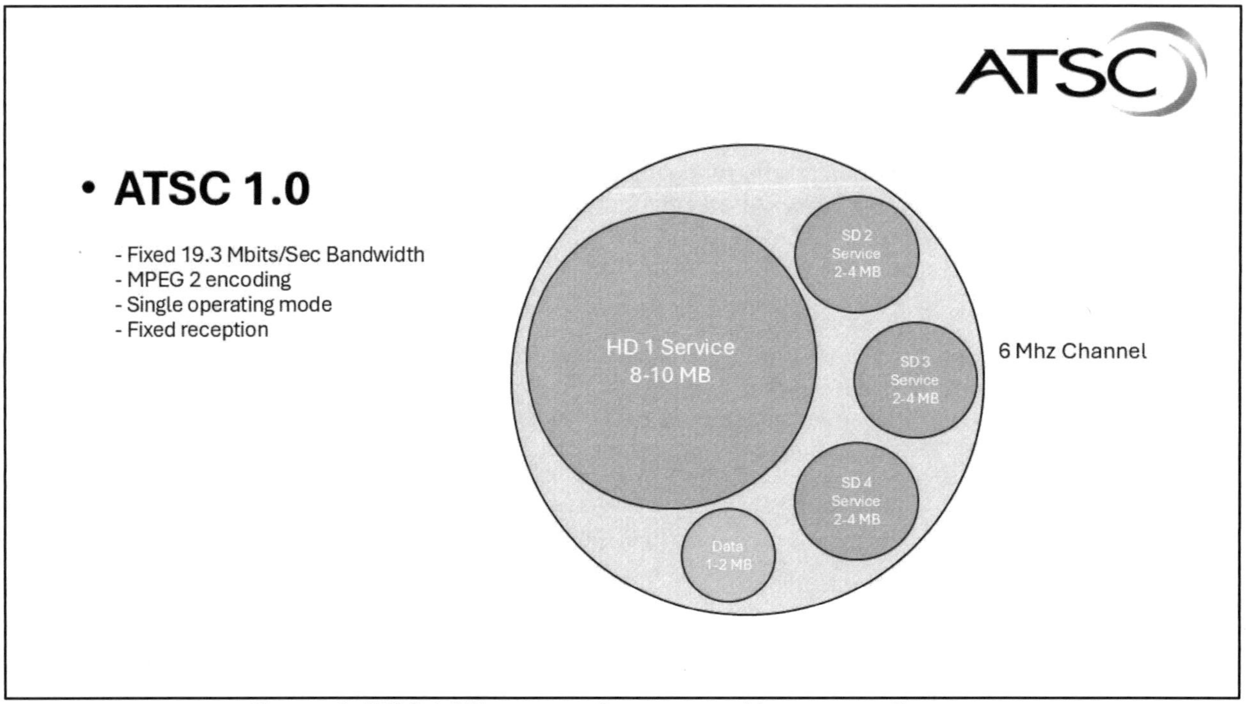

FIGURE 8. ATSC 1.0 TRANSPORT STREAM WITH MULTIPLEXED SERVICES

In this configuration, one high-definition channel service and three standard definition channel services consume most of the bandwidth. Leftover or unused "null bits" are made available for other purposes, in this case for datacasting services shown in orange.

The single carrier used in the 8VSB transmission system makes ATSC 1.0 susceptible to multi-path reception issues where reflections from objects (buildings, water towers, etc.) arriving at a later time than the primary signal, causing significant receiver challenges. For fixed location receivers, buffers within the receiver can be implemented to compensate for multipath interference. However, reliable mobile reception is not possible.

ATSC 3.0 utilizes a very different modulation scheme, Orthogonal Frequency-Division Multiplexing (OFDM) [5][5]. OFDM utilizes a large number of mathematically related low bandwidth subcarriers. As a result, a more spectrum-efficient signal with a higher overall data rate can be achieved. An OFDM signal is also better at compensating for multipath than an 8VSB signal since some subcarriers can be lost and the signal still recovered. Properly configured, the ATSC 3.0 system results in very reliable mobile reception.

The ATSC 3.0 signal can be configured with multiple physical layer pipes (PLPs). Each PLP can be configured with different modulation schemes and data capacities depending on the use case for that PLP. In Figure 9, PLP 1 can be configured to carry video program services and have a similar overage area to an 8VSB signal while PLP 0 can be configured to carry emergency responder or NIRCS data and be more robust, making reception with mobile devices easier and more reliable.

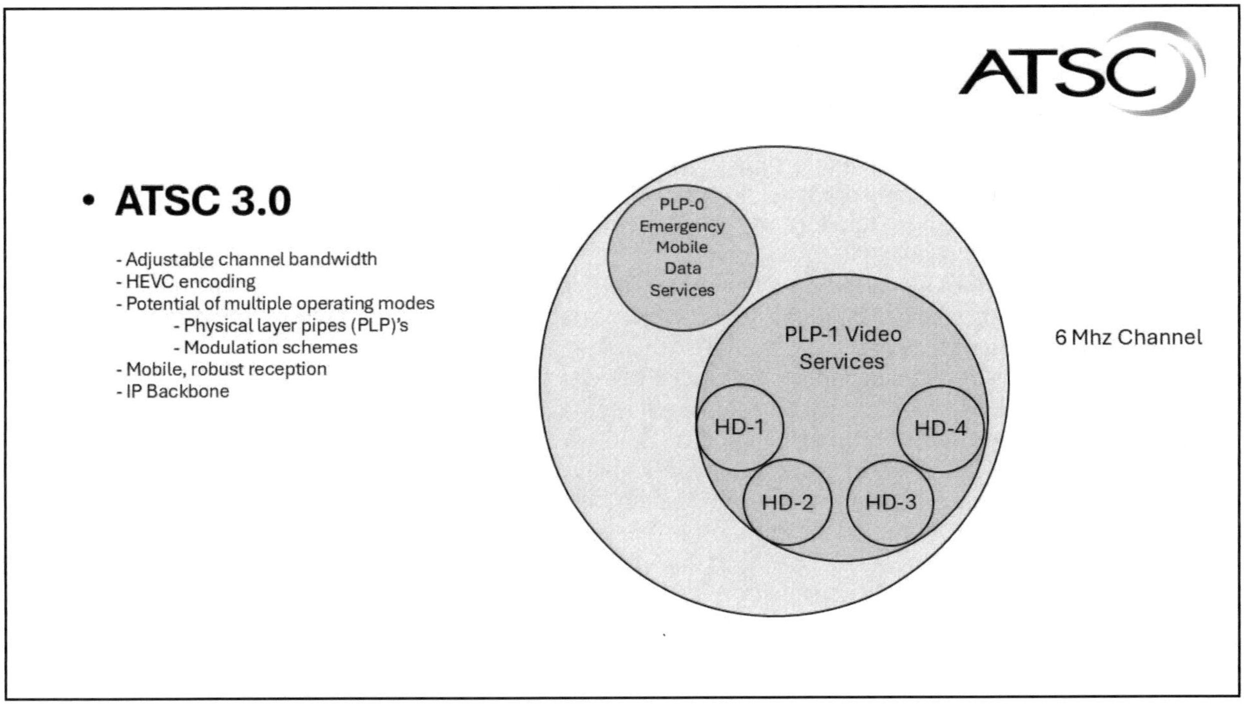

FIGURE 9. ATSC 3.0 PHYSICAL LAYER PIPE CONCEPTUAL DIAGRAM.

ATSC 3.0 and Video Encoding

ATSC 3.0 offers enhanced video and audio quality, improved signal reception, and new interactive services. One of the key features of ATSC 3.0 is its use of H.265 HEVC (High-Efficiency Video Coding) [6] video compression [6]. HEVC provides significant improvements over previous codecs, allowing broadcasters to transmit higher resolution video and HDR (High Dynamic Range) content while using less bandwidth. This coding efficiency creates capacity within the broadcast spectrum, making it possible to deliver other data services without impacting video quality.

As a living standard, the ATSC 3.0 standard can also be amended to implement new technologies as they are developed. In addition to HEVC, the recent approval of H.266 VVC (Versatile Video Coding) encoding by the ATSC [7] holds promise for even more efficient compression, further optimizing bandwidth usage. In the future when this codec is used more widely, improved video compression will allow broadcasters to deliver even higher-quality video or use its freed-up data capacity for additional services. The adoption of ATSC 3.0 with its improved codecs and efficient compression, paves the way for a more versatile and robust broadcasting ecosystem.

ATSC 3.0 and Datacasting

Wireless data broadcasting, or datacasting, is how many types of communications are transmitted. Cellular communications, wi-fi, Bluetooth, broadcast television and many other wireless delivery systems deliver digital data. ATSC 3.0 is an ideal platform for data delivery beyond the audio and video streams used by viewers. Due to its multiple customizable PLPs and highly effective error correction, large volumes of data can be delivered robustly.

A prime example of this is described in the paper submitted by PBS North Carolina, Device Solutions Inc, and Triveni Digital at the 2022 National Association of Broadcasters, Broadcast, Engineering and IT Conference - "ATSC 3.0 as a Use Case for Public Safety Communications – Development Milestones" [8]. The paper discusses the problems associated with existing emergency paging services and how ATSC 3.0 broadcast can provide a cost-effective solution with higher reliability, greater collaboration across jurisdictions, more cost-efficient pagers, and reduced response times.

Many fire and EMS services across the United States still rely on analog VHF paging technology to communicate emergency incident information to first responders. The infrastructure for these paging systems is typically owned, operated, and maintained by the local government or agency to ensure coverage includes as close to 100% of the jurisdiction as possible.

In their paper, Device Solutions Inc and Triveni Digital prove how ATSC 3.0 IP datacasting is well-suited to address the current challenges found within existing analog voice emergency paging. Because TV infrastructure already exists - the transmitter equipment, towers, antennas, power, and spectrum are already in use supporting broadcast television – ATSC 3.0 can be easily adopted and integrated into public safety paging as a redundant method for critical data communication. The footprint of this Public Safety Datacast Paging system would be far greater than current paging systems, which would increase interoperability, reliability, and dependability. Similarly, many Public Safety Answering Points (PSAPs), which provide the information needed by public safety responders, already support the export of such information to their existing paging system. Having a centralized paging system available to several PSAPs in the same geographic area will also increase the ease of providing backup dispatch services between jurisdictions.

Through the support of a DHS SBIR funded Phase II contract, Device Solutions Inc, PBS-NC, and Triveni Digital collaborated to build an end-to-end working prototype emergency paging system. Device Solutions Inc developed a prototype ATSC 3.0 emergency paging receiver. A new dedicated PLP was defined for emergency service for use on PBS-NC's public ATSC 3.0 broadcast infrastructure, and new APIs were defined for use by Triveni Digital's Transport Encoder.

Phase II proved that ATSC 3.0 IP Datacasting provides an opportunity to advance public safety paging to a new level. IP Datacasting provides a redundant method for critical data distribution over a wider area to serve the paging needs of public safety. The ability to alert multiple responders will only take milliseconds using a datacast digital format, which is considerably faster than today's analog paging format. Unlike a cellular service which can only support a limited number of devices in a given area, IP Datacasting is a one-to-many broadcast; the number of simultaneous receivers is unlimited. By delivering the emergency dispatch information in a digital format over datacasting, the technology can support over 2000 dispatches at the same time it would take an analog system to perform a single dispatch.

This demonstrates how IP Datacasting via ATSC 3.0 can provide solutions to unique problems with clear advantages in cost, speed, and public safety.

Technology and Regulatory Considerations

Receiving any large bandwidth data signal with an airborne receiver isn't without challenges. Most airborne communications and data systems utilize low bandwidths and rely on transmission systems designed for reception at high speed, low and high altitude, over long distances. On the other hand, current ATSC 3.0 broadcast infrastructure deployments are optimized for terrestrial ground-based reception where the intended user is stationary with an outdoor antenna or is using a handheld receiver inside a building or in a relatively slow-moving vehicle. While ATSC 3.0 airborne reception in aircraft exceeding 200mph and up to 5000 ft above ground level is certainly possible, fresh thinking about optimizing the transmission variables is required for NIRCS implementation. Utilizing existing broadcast infrastructure presents both technical and regulatory challenges. This section presents some ideas on what is needed and possible to optimize NIRCS for its intended mission.

Reception at High Speed

The NIRCS mission requires reception in both slow- and fast-moving vehicles. Fixed wing aircraft operate in an envelope of speed from roughly 100mph (160kph) (87knots) to 250mph (402kph) (217knots) while rotorcraft typically operate from hovering to 150mph (241kph) (130knots). This defines the primary challenge for the ATSC 3.0 system and sets upper limits on the available capacity of the transmission channel since higher speeds require much more significant coding overhead to ensure they are received properly. The ATSC 3.0 A/322 physical layer specification document [9] describes the various features of modulation and coding within the standard and the A/327 recommended practice document [10] gives information on typical settings and their effects. A dizzying array of variables are available to provide decoding of the signal in a multitude of user scenarios from high capacity/low robustness to low capacity/high robustness on channels with multipath, doppler effects, burst noise, and fading to both fixed and mobile receivers.

The primary physical layer variables in the standard that influence mobile reception are:

1. Formatting of the "bootstrap" signaling
2. Modulation rate and constellation
3. Number and configuration of PLPs
4. Error correction settings including:
    1. Channel estimation
    2. Code length and depth
    3. Echo and doppler protection
    4. Data interleaving type and depth

While numerous drive tests have shown that an ATSC 3.0 signal can be received while traveling over 65mph (105kph), few have looked at speeds significantly above this level. Detailed mathematical simulations and laboratory tests were, however, conducted to understand the performance of various ATSC 3.0 signal combinations and reported in reference [11]. This report gives us an excellent base upon which to build and configure NIRCS although the testing only examined speeds up to 300kph (186mph) (162knots) since this was envisioned as a top speed for ground-based trains.

To obtain robust reception at these high speeds, heavy amounts of error coding must be used along with reduced modulation rates, deeper interleaving, and careful echo cancellation settings. The authors also point out that further optimization of other features may be beneficial to high-speed operations. They found that reception at 300kph was possible for data rates below approximately 3.5MB. One tested combination which was capable of 300kph resulting in 2.14MB data capacity, consisted of Quadrature Phase Shift Keying (QPSK) modulation with 4/15 code rate, 3/2 pilots, 64k code length, 16k frame and preamble FFT lengths, and resulted in a signal to noise ratio of approximately 2.2dB. While this is excellent performance, we hope with further testing that the performance can be further optimized at even higher speeds. To date, we are not aware of any real-world tests at these types of speed.

Transmit System Considerations

The NIRCS vehicle is assumed to be located close to and either above or at the elevation of the theater of operation to provide the highest signal levels to the aircraft and be able to collect local UAS information. This location presents conditions which are quite different from a typical television transmission system.

The resulting recommendations for an optimum vehicle mounted transmission system include:

1. Omnidirectional or configurable sector azimuth coverage. Most locations would likely use an omnidirectional configuration, but it would be advantageous to allow the antenna pattern to be varied at each site dependent on the vehicle's location relative to the operation. For instance, if the vehicle has tall mountains directly behind it, a directional pattern to the front would be advantageous.
2. Coverage from slightly below the horizon to directly above the vehicle with the highest signal levels required in the first 10 degrees of elevation above the horizon (corresponding to greater than 5.5 miles for an aircraft at 5000ft AGL) since the aircraft will be approaching and receding from the theater of operations at these angles and the lowest signal levels when directly overhead since they will be quite close to the vehicle. These values correspond to a relatively moderate elevation gain antenna pointed at the horizon but with reduced values below the horizon as compared to above the horizon in a typical broadcast TV antenna.
3. Vertical polarization to deliver the highest signal levels to short whip antennas located in or on the aircraft. Most whip antennas can be easily mounted to receive vertical polarization and are the de facto standard in vehicles instead of horizontal polarization used on most TV broadcast transmit antennas.
4. Frequency agile operation on any unused UHF TV channel (14 to 36) in the location of the vehicle. This also needs to include ensuring mask compliance for the transmitter on all channels since there will frequently be high power stations on directly adjacent channels.
5. Variable effective radiated power (ERP) levels to allow for expansion and reduction of the total covered area based on; the scale of the fire, the particular interference criteria on the channel of operation at the location, the safety of ground personnel from radiation exposure, and the configuration of the antenna pattern.

Using Existing TV Transmission Systems

Current television broadcast facilities are designed for reception by terrestrial ground-based receivers and typically utilize high elevation gain antennas to focus the signal on the horizon and reduce the output power needed from the transmitter. Gain is achieved by making the antenna longer and by reducing the amount of signal transmitted above the horizon. This is at odds with the recommendations above.

A hypothetical full power station operates on channel 25 at 200 kW ERP using a 28-bay slotted UHF pylon type antenna with an antenna height of 1000 feet. Its elevation pattern shown in Figure 10 is skewed toward the ground so the most powerful portion of the signal is focused below the horizon, not above it. In this case the antenna has 1 degree of downward beam tilt built into the antenna. Figure 10 shows the resulting nulls in the elevation pattern at -1.3, -3.0, and -5.7 degrees.

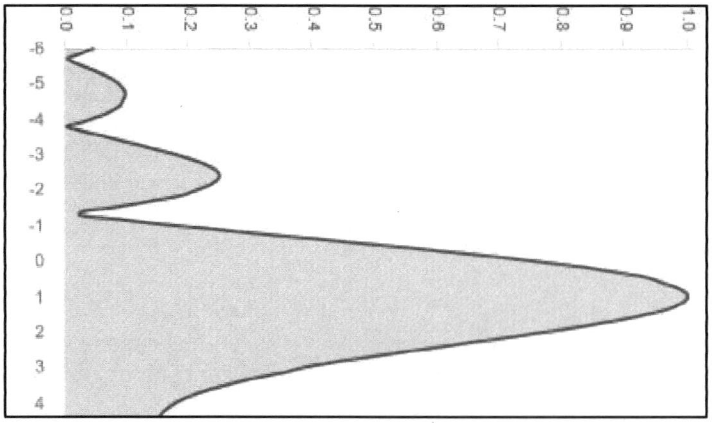

FIGURE 10. TYPICAL 28-BAY UHF SLOTTED PYLON ANTENNA ELEVATION PATTERN.

Low Power (LPTV) and Class A television stations are limited to 15 kW ERP on UHF and tend to use lower gain antennas. A hypothetical low power station operates on channel 25 at 15 kW ERP with an 8-bay slotted pylon antenna with an antenna height of 400 feet. The antenna has 1.75 degree of downward beam tilt built into it since the pattern is much wider than the high gain antenna above. Figure 11 shows a null in the elevation pattern at -5.5 degrees.

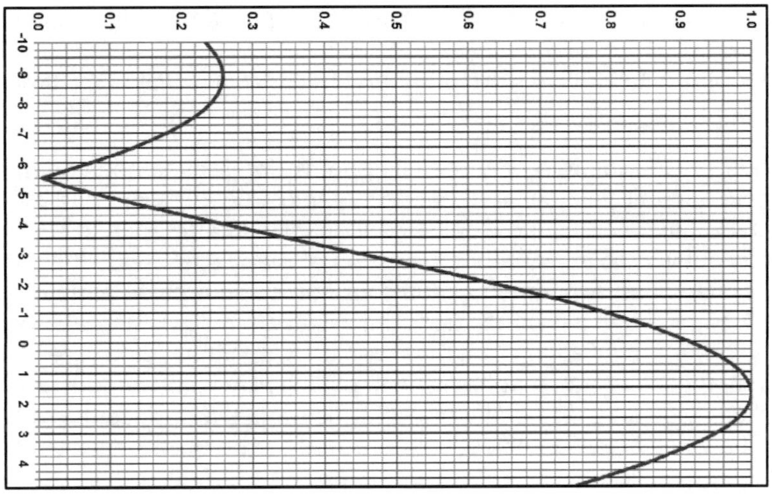

FIGURE 11. 8-BAY SLOTTED PYLON UHF ANTENNA ELEVATION PATTERN.

Taking these typical patterns and calculating the resulting ERPs, Table 2 below shows values toward an aircraft flying at 4600 feet above ground level at certain distances from a transmitter site (Based on a flat earth model). Note that negative angles refer to degrees ABOVE the horizon.

Distance (mi)	Full Power Station			Low Power Station		
	Angle	Field Ratio	ERP (kw)	Angle	Field Ratio	ERP (kW)
6.8	-5.7	0.003	0.002	-6.7	0.158	0.375
8.3	-4.7	0.097	1.882	-5.5	0.006	0.001
10.0	-3.4	0.021	0.088	-4.5	0.160	0.384
30.0	-1.3	0.022	0.077	-1.5	0.712	7.600

TABLE 2. ERP TOWARD AIRCRAFT AT CERTAIN DISTANCES.

The values in Table 2 demonstrate that typical TV systems offer very little capability to provide meaningful signal levels to aircraft without modification.

Regulatory Considerations

We foresee at least these three potential implementations of NIRCS transmission systems:

1. A stand-alone remote operation from a self-contained vehicle that includes a mast with an antenna(s) and a transmitter-like Figure 2 above that operates on an unused UHF channel at a given site.
2. The stand-alone vehicle above operating as an SFN type node within the coverage area of an existing UHF TV station.
3. NIRCS data sent from a modified main antenna of an existing UHF TV station as an ancillary PLP.

The first implementation would require a new licensing/permitting regime and cooperation from the FCC to allow its use. We note that utilizing unused channels, vertical polarization, and minimizing the signal below the horizon as recommended above would help minimize interference to existing TV operations. We see this as an excellent way to implement the system at many sites since they are often rural and in terrain sheltered areas. Use of an experimental authorization could provide a methodology for operation on unused channels. A blanket use allowance from the FCC within some agreed upon parameters would of course be the preferred arrangement. This would require that some level of study be done before each operation and could mean a potential lack of flexibility in movement options. The second and third implementations would be less ominous as far as regulations since they could be covered under existing rules. The SFN operation would be more likely to be quickly approved since the hosting station would be accepting the potential interference upfront to serve the public good. Where the theater of operation is in an urban area (i.e., Los Angeles) this may be the only available option since finding an unused channel may be very difficult. Since the NIRCS operation is only temporary and no ground disturbance is required, there should be very few limitations on potential locations of the vehicle and we do not foresee issues with other permits. The third implementation, using an existing broadcaster's main facility, has the issues discussed above regarding signal levels. However, where those do not present an issue (i.e., stations that are on very tall mountains and the theater of operations is below that horizon), NIRCS could be quickly and easily implemented as an ancillary stream. Each of these implementations requires further study and coordination with the FCC and other stakeholders.

Conclusion

With wildfires and other natural disasters causing increased fatalities, infrastructure damage, and recovery costs, it is imperative to continue investigating new and improved means of communication to support first responders and the public. ATSC 3.0 broadcast technology has been proven to provide wide area and robust data delivery to address these needs. While questions still need to be answered regarding RF propagation patterns, high-speed mobile reception quality, and FCC authorization, the initial work of Mosaic ATM and its technology partners, Device Solutions Inc, Triveni Digital, and other consultants shows NIRCS is a worthy effort to continue to explore and fund.

References

[1] National Interagency Fire Center, "Fire mission photos," [Online]. Available: https://uas.nifc.gov/fire-mission-photos. [Accessed: Feb. 1, 2025].

[2] NASA LARC DAIDALUS, “daidalus,” [Online]. Available: https://nasa.github.io/daidalus/. [Accessed: Jan. 22, 2025].

[3] Advanced Television Systems Committee, "NextGen TV," [Online]. Available: https://www.atsc.org/nextgen-tv/. [Accessed: Feb. 1, 2025].

[4] "ATSC Digital Television Standard, Part 1 – Digital Television System", Doc. A/53 Part 1:2013 7 August 2013.

[5] Chang, R. W. (1966). "Synthesis of Band-Limited Orthogonal Signals for Multi-Channel Data Transmission", *Bell System Technical Journal,* December 1966.

[6] International Telecommunications Union, ITU-T H.265 High Efficiency Video Coding, July 7, 2013.

[7] Advanced Television Systems Committee, A/345 VVC Video Candidate Standard, November 25, 2024.

[8] PBS North Carolina, Device Solutions Inc, and Triveni Digital, "ATSC 3.0 as a Use Case for Public Safety Communications – Development Milestones," NAB BEIT Proceedings April 2022.

[9] Advanced Television Systems Committee, A/322:2024-09, "Physical Layer Protocol" September 13, 2024.

[10] Advanced Television Systems Committee, A/327:2024-12, "Guidelines for the Physical Layer Protocol" December 3, 2024.

[11] Sungjun Ahn, Sung-Ik Park, Jae-Young Lee, Bo-Mi Lim, Sunhyoung Kwon, Namho Hur, Yiyan Wu, Liang Zhang, Wei Li, and Jeonchang Kim, "Mobile performance evaluation for ATSC 3.0 physical layer modulation and code combinations under TU-6 channel", IEEE Transactions on Broadcasting, Vol. 66 #4, December 2020.

Acknowledgement

The authors and contributors to this paper would like to thank Kyrsten Mougey, Executive Assistant at Device Solutions Inc, for her assistance in editing this document.

Media Campaign Workflow Using AI Agents

Matt Ferris
Decentrix Inc.
Denver, Colorado, United States
mferris@decentrix.com

Abstract – The design and implementation of a multi-platform and multi-target advertising campaign currently requires many steps performed by experienced media staff. This paper proposes to provide media knowledge to an AI agent so that a partnership between the campaign planner and the AI agent can efficiently and flexibly create and adjust complex advertising campaigns. The AI agent can be provided with the arriving RFP documents by the planner, and then it can validate attributes and assign missing values to enable efficient and validated campaign creation. The AI agent is provided with OpenAPI documentation of the API into a production campaign repository to create campaigns, validate attributes, and manage the campaigns with attribute updates. Campaign analysis and graphical reporting can be flexibly requested to monitor the detailed campaign assignments. What-if analysis can be requested by the planner to model the campaign outcome metrics so that attributes can be selected that optimize the campaign. This partnership between the user and the AI agent brings the user's industry experience together with the modelling and analysis capability of the AI agent to efficiently perform the workflow necessary for a valid and optimized campaign.

Introduction

Recent advances in artificial intelligence (AI) tools support a productive partnership between campaign managers and AI tools to manage and optimize advertising campaigns through their many phases of implementation and delivery. In order to realize this capability, AI tools should be provided with knowledge files that contain the relevant media industry terms and concepts. These include campaign data relationships with the steps required for implementation and optimization of basic advertising workflows.

Decentrix has implemented a system which supports the following functionality to assist in the goal of delivering an optimum campaign:

- Advanced interaction with the user/planner during the optimization process.
- Guidance from the planner for optimization analysis and constraints.
- Presentation to the planner of analysis and modelling results.
- Direct integration with a operations system for the implementation of the advertising campaign.
- Advanced modelling of campaign outcomes for different parameters.
- Selection of optimum campaign parameters maximizing campaign outcomes such as ROI.
- OAuth security to control access and updates of campaign information.

This paper is excerpted from the Proceedings of the 2025 NAB Broadcast Engineering and Information Technology (BEIT) Conference, © 2025, National Association of Broadcasters, 1 M Street SE, Washington, DC 20003 USA.

Functionality Goals

Planner-AI Interaction

Many aspects of advertising campaign planning rely upon the judgement and experience of the planner. Fundamental aspects such as the forecasting of audiences, their content viewing behavior, and their response to advertising messages needs to be estimated. A system that can analyze and model the campaign outcome as part of a conversation with a planner allows for the experience and judgement of the planner to be incorporated into a final campaign. The back and forth between the planner and the AI system providing changes, requesting analysis and modelling, and viewing the consequential results can produce campaigns that incorporate the best of the planner's experience and the AI's recommendations.

Planner Guidance

Such a system should accept input from the planner in the following categories:

- General campaign attributes
- Audience metrics for the target audience segments over the delivery platforms
- Sales effectiveness functions of the targeted messages
- Requests for campaign generation
- Flexible requests for campaign modelling and what-if calculations
- Requests for campaign analysis, reporting, and charting
- Validation of campaign attributes against database attributes
- Storage of the campaign details in the production database
- Updating of campaign attributes in the campaign database

Reporting and Charting

A user should be able to request flexible presentation of reports and charts for iterative analysis and modelling. With the goal of selecting an optimum campaign, charts that show the campaign outcome as a function of changing parameters are invaluable. The system should generate rich charting analysis with minimal prompting.

Production Integration

The system should directly interface with an operationally live campaign management system so that optimized campaigns can be directly activated. Existing campaigns in the database should be quickly retrievable for analysis or modification by the planner.

Campaign Modelling

By providing media relationships of input metrics to campaign outcomes, the system is therefore not only configured to the business, but localized policies and business language can be readily implemented. This enables the system to accept and deliver requests for complex campaign modelling. By extension, *what-if analysis* enables the planner to adjust media parameters to iterate upon the results of a new campaign modelling process. All of this results in an intelligent interface that supports incremental adjustments to the modelling context for efficient communication and results.

Campaign Optimization

The system should model campaign outcome metrics that can be selected for maximization. The Return on Investment (ROI) metric uses the product profit from sales outcomes against the cost of the campaign insertions to quantify the effectiveness of the campaign investment. This is one of the metrics that can be used to find the optimum allocation of campaign investment. This extends beyond any optimization capabilities of the live campaign management system.

System Security

Current AI implementations sometimes experience hallucinations and provide misinformation when questioned over broad test repositories. To mitigate that issue, our application retrieves campaign facts directly from the database through the secured API and these facts are directly communicated to the user. Also, any data either derived by the AI or supplied by the user that is passed through the API for updates, is extensively validated before updating a campaign.

The architecture for this AI service obtains data through database web services that are secured by OAuth for each user that implements a security policy over the data that can be retrieved, and also the data that can be updated. Separately, the data that is retrieved for a user and referenced in the AI chat conversation is configured explicitly within the AI Service to not be used in any way for training or related activities for use for other user's questions or conversations. Also, the System Prompts and Knowledge files that guide the AI System cannot be observed or retrieved by the User to configure an alternative AI System.

System Overview

To achieve the goals of the system, it consists of the following components:

- An AI System with a user interface and a System Prompt to define the AI role and goals
- An API library to access the campaign operations system for database attribute validation and campaign storage. It requires a security and authentication system together with OpenAPI documentation of the API for the AI system
- Media knowledge files such as a Media Dictionary, a Campaign Management instruction document, and Media Modelling instructions
- Media Data such as Media Audience Metrics, Advertiser sales/outcome metrics, Memory loss parameters for use in modelling and optimizing campaigns
- Campaign Source document such as a campaign Request for Proposal (RFP)

System Diagram

The following diagram illustrates the functional components of the AI powered system and its interface to a live campaign planning and management system.

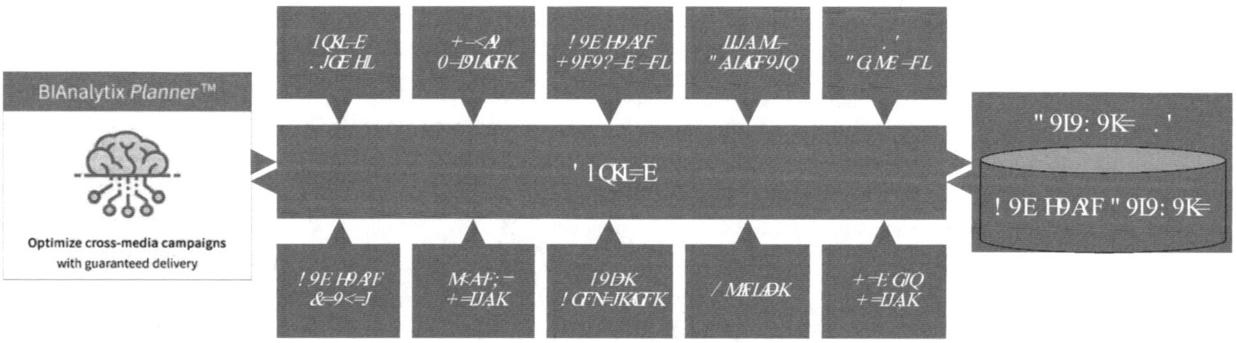

FIGURE 1: AI4MEDIA™ SYSTEM COMPONENTS

AI Component

This AI component is the core of the system to provide an intelligent assistant to the planner to achieve optimized campaigns. The functionality that it supports includes:

- Uses voice or text conversations with the planner to perform tasks to incrementally construct optimized campaigns
- Use API functions when appropriate to perform these tasks.
- Use the required authentication and security
- Use the OpenAPI documentation of all API functions and parameters to enable reliable calls when required by the requested tasks
- Use Knowledge documents to guide the campaign optimization tasks
- A Media Relationships knowledge document to enable media campaign modelling
- A campaign validation knowledge document to validate, apportion and save a campaign
- A System Prompt to set up the AI conversation purpose.

The AI component should be able to operate on a web browser or mobile environment and with a voice or text conversation with the planner. It performs its tasks for campaign management and optimization primarily by writing and executing python code.

The System Prompt for the AI component is used to define the role for the AI as an assistant to the media planner. It also describes all the knowledge files available for use in responding to user requests for advice and user task requests.

Operations System API

To enable planned campaigns to execute and deliver advertising, an API (Application Programming Interface) is used for access to an operations campaign management system. This API provides a range of data exchange functions for the AI components to get and place data into the Operations System database:

- Retrieve lists of valid codes for each attribute in the database
- Retrieve lists of filtered campaigns
- Retrieve full campaign details
- Create new campaigns with orders and lines
- Update campaign attributes

An extremely important part of the API is an authentication and security structure to ensure that users are securely identified and that they have the authority to read or modify the production campaign database. The oAuth security standard is used by a range of AI systems and thus is recommended for the API library. An operational implementation of the system requires that users be securely identified and their authority to perform different functions detected and enforced. The AI component uses the oAuth security standard to obtain an oAuth token for any user and provide it to the API calls. The API layer uses standard security infrastructure to discover the authority of that user to access production campaign data and control the reading and modification of such data.

The recommended technical structure of the API is to use web services that can be documented by the OpenAPI standard. This description of all the functions and their parameters in the API can be read by AI components to ensure they can make valid function calls as part of achieving their task. As part of the implementation of the API, the functions and parameters can be annotated with detailed documentation that is automatically extracted into the OpenAPI documentation. All of this documentation is thus passed to the AI component to ensure appropriate and accurate calls to the API when required.

The API component is necessary to enable to AI component to work with the actual campaign data that will actually insert advertisements. To enable the AI system to reliably use the API to achieve its requested tasks, detailed documentation of the functions and parameters needs to be provided to the AI system. The OpenAPI standard is widely used to document web services, and this document is generated automatically from the implementation of the web services and provided to the AI component.

As part of implementation of the web services, detailed documentation can be annotated onto the functions and parameters, and this is automatically included in the OpenAPI document. This is important to give the AI component full descriptions of the usage and meaning of the functions and parameters to ensure highly reliability of its implementation of requested tasks.

Media Knowledge Files

The Media Dictionary Knowledge file describes each campaign attribute and gives the explanation for the campaign behavior for each of the values for this attribute. This is used by the AI to recommend attribute values that will achieve the stated user requirements for the campaign.

The Campaign Management Knowledge file holds the instruction steps for the different campaign management tasks.

- Initial Campaign Validation and apportionment
- Saving a new Campaign
- Finding and selecting a Campaign
- Updating a campaign attribute

The Media Modelling Knowledge file is an important component of the system for forecasting and optimization. It defines the relationships between the key terms and concepts of modelling a media campaign. It expresses these relationships in both descriptive and formular styles for the AI system to ingest. It documents these relationships as a series of calculation steps to describe the dependencies between each calculation and its prerequisite calculations.

The AI component can take a requested task from the planner and use these Knowledge files to derive and present the campaign outcome metrics over a range of parameters such as campaign size, frequency caps, or length of campaign. Also, the planner can ask for what-if calculations by providing override values for media metrics and asking for the modelled campaign outcome.

Media Data

To support media campaign modelling, Media data is provided to the AI system.

- Audience Metrics
- Sales Conversion Metrics
- Quintile Metrics
- Memory Loss Metrics

Basic Audience Metrics must be provided for each available platform and campaign target alias. For each Platform and Target Alias, these audience metrics support the ability to perform campaign modelling and apportionment:

- the Weekly Capacity Reach,
- the Universe Estimate,
- the Weekly Impression Capacity,
- the Value per Thousand (VPM),
- the Weekly Number of Slots,
- and the Weekly Number of Breaks

The Sales Probabilities are the probability of a product sale for a viewer who has seen F instances of the ad. The Net Revenue earned on each product sale resulting from the campaign is provided to quantify the campaign outcome in terms of money. By providing the Net Revenue per Sale and the Sales Probabilities, the audience campaign metrics of the number of viewers who see the ad F times can be converted to sales and then to money.

The quintile metrics are provided for each target alias and consist of the five proportions of viewing time per quintile. The quintiles are defined by ranking the viewers by their viewing hours and then grouping them into 5 equal sets of viewers from light viewers to heavy viewers.

The memory metrics are the proportion of Viewers who forget K ads after 1 week. These metrics are provided for each target alias and consist of proportions of viewers for K = 0 to 4 ads. For example, if the proportion for forgetting 2 ads is 10%, then 10% of the viewers will forget 2 of the ads that they saw after a week.

Campaign Source Document

As an alternative to manually specifying all the campaign header attributes needed for campaign creation, these values can be supplied as a text document that was externally sourced to the planner. Alternatives are supported such as a screenshot or photo file of the external campaign header data. The AI system can validate the values supplied against the valid database attribute values and also request any additional required missing values.

Media Workflows

Media workflows for an advertising campaign manage processes from the proposal through to delivery, to the post analysis, and billing. These workflows can be grouped into broad categories reflecting the departmental interfaces and handoffs within the organization.

- **Pricing & Planning**– Budget Management, Inventory Evaluation, Audience Research, Data & Estimates.
- **Order Management** – Proposal Planning, Campaign Yield Optimization
- **Ad Operations** – Order Execution, Performance Analysis, Stewardship
- **Business Analysis** – Post Campaign Analysis, Billing

These are depicted in the following diagram.

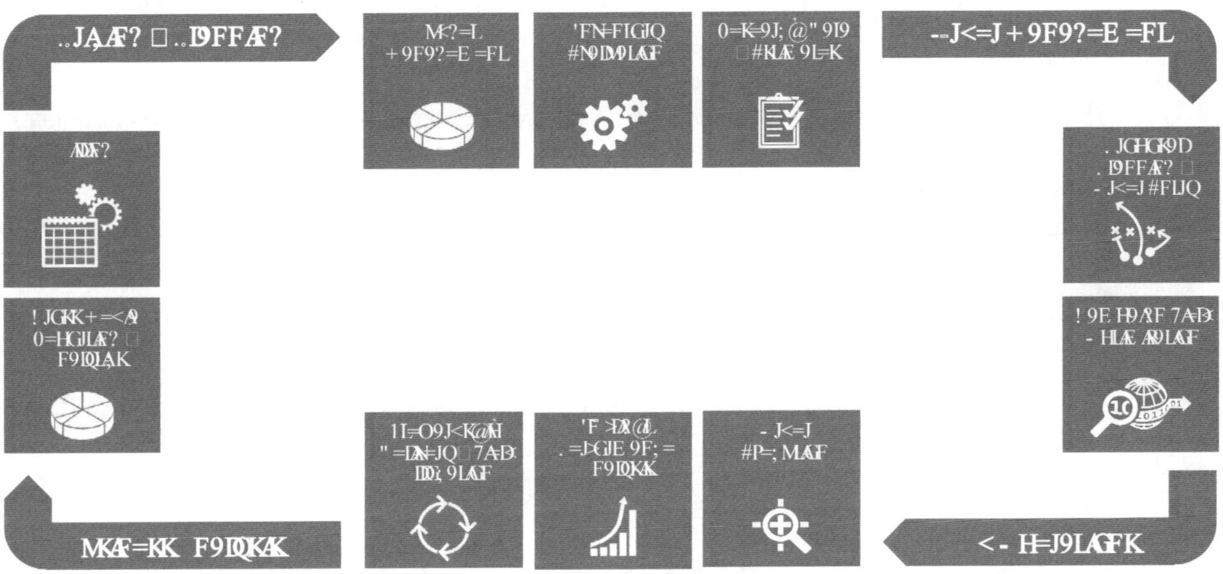

FIGURE 2: MEDIA WORKFLOW – CANDIDATE FUNCTIONALITY FOR AI AGENTS

Although the system has been used to provide AI agents for all of the above workflow items, we will limit our demonstration of capabilities to use cases that manage the operational campaign data. The AI interface can support conversations with the campaign planner to:

- Accept campaign header attributes
- Recommend campaign detail allocation
- Analyze campaign metrics
- Guide mapping of campaign attributes to database values
- Modify campaign parameters at the campaign, order, line or fee level
- Model the campaign over a range of possible attributes
- Analyze the campaign results over those attribute ranges
- Recommend the campaign attributes that maximize campaign outcomes
- Explain the results of modelling campaign options

Defining Campaign Attributes

First steps in campaign management are the supply of Campaign Header Attributes. They can be partially supplied from a file. Any missing attributes will be detected and requested. The values supplied will be validated against the list of valid values from the database. An example conversation follows:

Media Planner:
Validate this campaign RFP.

AI Response:
*The validation for the RFP titled **Generative AI Campaign 20240726** has been completed. Here are the results: Required Campaign Header Attributes:*

- ***Account Executive**: John Smith (Validated)*
- ***Advertiser**: Ford (Validated)*
- ***Agency**: Group M (Validated)*
- ***Sales Planner**: Mary Jones (Validated)*
- ***Campaign Name**: Generative AI Campaign 20240726 (Provided)*
- ***Gross Budget**: $802,116 (Provided)*
- ***CPM**: $19.14 (Provided)*
- ***Start Date**: 10/7/2024 (Provided)*
- ***End Date**: 12/29/2024 (Provided)*
- ***Deal Type**: DSP (Validated)*
- ***Guarantee Type**: Deal (Validated)*
- ***Marketplace**: Scatter (Validated)*
- ***Billing Method**: (Missing) - The billing method was not provided, and this is a required field. The available options are "Campaign" or "Order".*

Requesting Allocations

The first step in the allocations is to distribute the campaign over the weeks of the campaign and then distribute the budget over the platforms and target aliases. Here is an example conversation:

Media Planner:
Frontload the campaign with a weight of 1.5 for the first 4 weeks

AI Response:
*I have frontloaded the campaign with a weight of **1.5** for the first 4 weeks, and the remaining weeks have been assigned a weight of **1.0**. The weekly budget has been recalculated accordingly.*

Media Planner:
Increase the weight for all records with platform ADDRESSABLE by 20%

AI Response:
*I have updated the **TargetPlatformWeight** by increasing it by 20% for all records with the platform "ADDRESSABLE." The updated data has been displayed.*

Media Planner:
Now apportion the detailed campaign.

AI Response:
*The campaign has been successfully apportioned based on the updated target platform weights and universe estimates. The budget and impressions have been calculated for each combination of **TargetAlias** and **Platform**, and the results are displayed.*

Campaign Charting

The user can request the metrics of the detailed campaign to be charted for analysis and review. Here is an example conversation:

Media Planner:
Do a side-by-side bar-chart of the impressions delivered each week by all combinations of platform and target alias.

AI Response:

Impressions By Week For All Combination...

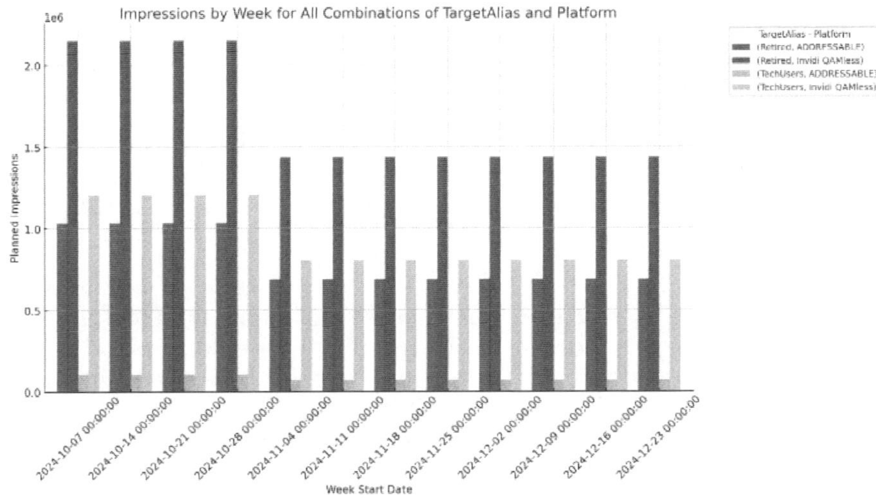

FIGURE 3: IMPRESSIONS BY WEEK.

Media Planner:
Do a pie diagram for the impressions planned for the first week of the campaign by all combinations of platform and target alias.
AI Response:

Impressions For The First Week By Platfor...

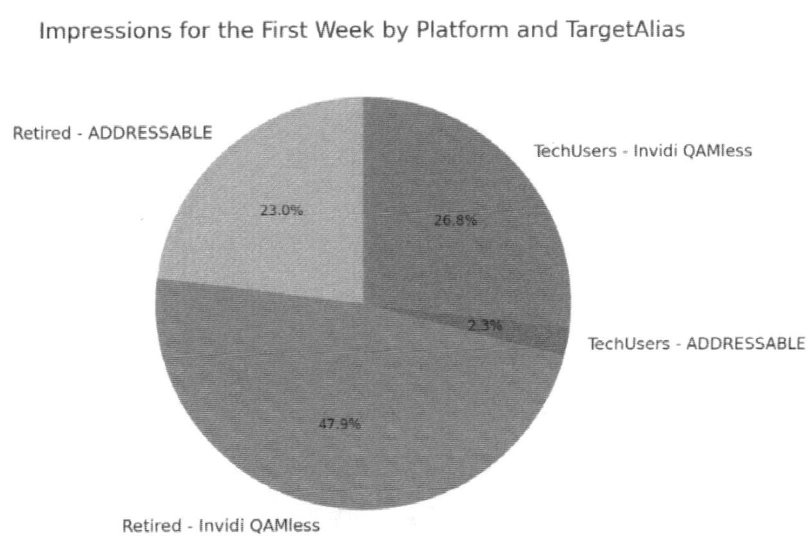

FIGURE 4: IMPRESSIONS FOR THE FIRST WEEK

Attribute Validation

The user can request the list of valid values for an attribute and also request the business results from setting the attribute to each of the possible values. Also, the planner can describe the business behavior desired for the campaign, and the AI system will communicate the attribute to be set and the value that will result in the desired behavior. Here is an example conversation:

Media Planner:
I want a campaign that gives a separate invoice for each platform and target within the campaign. How do I do I do that?
AI Response:
To create a campaign that issues separate invoices for each platform and target, you should set the Billing Method attribute to "Order" rather than "Campaign." This ensures that each order within the campaign (associated with specific platforms and target audiences) generates its own invoice, detailing delivery and costs separately.

Attribute Modification

After the initial campaign creation, there will be many updates to attributes to prepare the campaign for execution and delivery. This process supports the retrieval of the correct campaign from the database and the update of an attribute to the desired validated value. Here is an example conversation:

Media Planner:
Get me the campaign headers that overlap the first week in December and show those with advertiser "Ford".
AI Response:
Here are the campaigns overlapping the first week of December with the advertiser "Ford":

Generative AI Campaign
Campaign ID: DECENTRIX257441
Dates: Oct 07, 2024 - Dec 29, 2024
Account Executive: John Smith
Agency: Group M
Generative AI Campaign
Campaign ID: DECENTRIX257444
Dates: Oct 07, 2024 - Dec 29, 2024
Account Executive: John Smith
Agency: Group M
Generative AI Campaign
Campaign ID: DECENTRIX257445
Dates: Oct 07, 2024 - Dec 29, 2024
Account Executive: John Smith
Agency: Group M
Generative AI Campaign
Campaign ID: DECENTRIX257442
Dates: Oct 07, 2024 - Dec 29, 2024
Account Executive: David Pruitt
Agency: Group M

Media Planner:
Take campaign 3 and show me valid account executives called David
AI Response:
The valid account executives named "David" include:
David Pruitt
If you'd like to update Campaign 3 to assign David Pruitt as the account executive, or if there's another action you'd like, please let me know.
Media Planner:
Yes - update the account executive to David Pruitt
AI Response:

*The account executive for Campaign 3 has been successfully updated to **David Pruitt**. Let me know if there's anything else you'd like to modify or further details you need on this campaign.*

Viewer Frequency Histogram Modelling

The calculation of the Viewer Frequency Histogram can be requested for the week for a specified Platform and Target Alias and for a specified number of insertions N. This uses the viewing probability and the number of insertions in a binomial distribution and then scales n=back to the weekly universe of viewers. Note that this calculation can be performed with or without the quintile breakout. Here is an example conversation:

Media Planner:

When I show 10 ads (N=10), bar chart the viewer histogram of viewers vs frequency up to F=10 for the Retired target and the ADDRESSABLE platform.

AI Response:

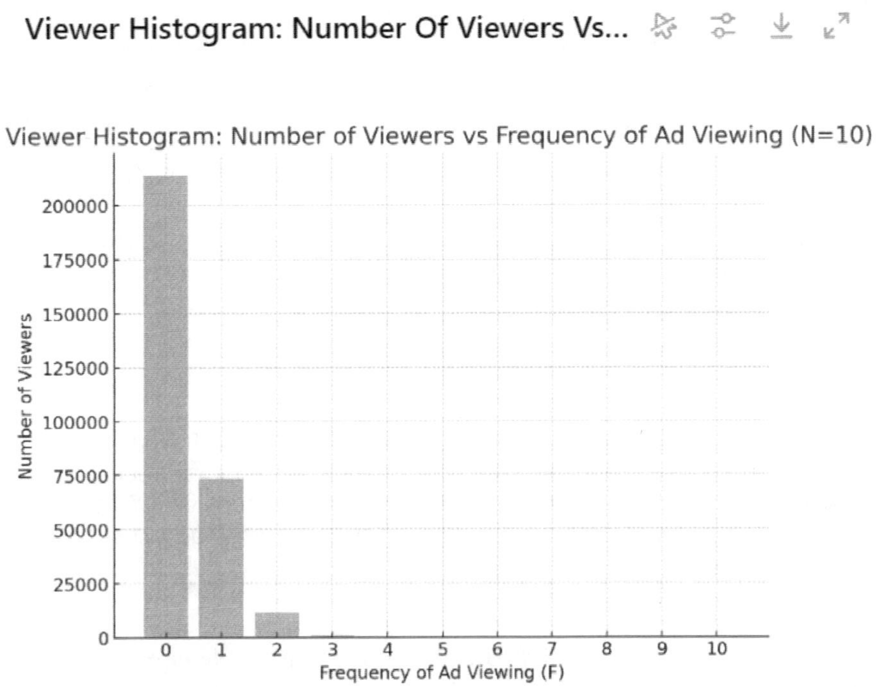

FIGURE 5: VIEWER HISTOGRAM

Sales Histogram Modelling

Given the viewer frequency histogram for a platform, target alias and number of insertions, the sales probabilities can be used to convert to the number of sales that will occur for each frequency. Note that the number of sales for low frequencies can be zero or lower than the higher frequencies.

Media Planner:

Now calculate the Sales for each frequency and plot it.

AI Response:

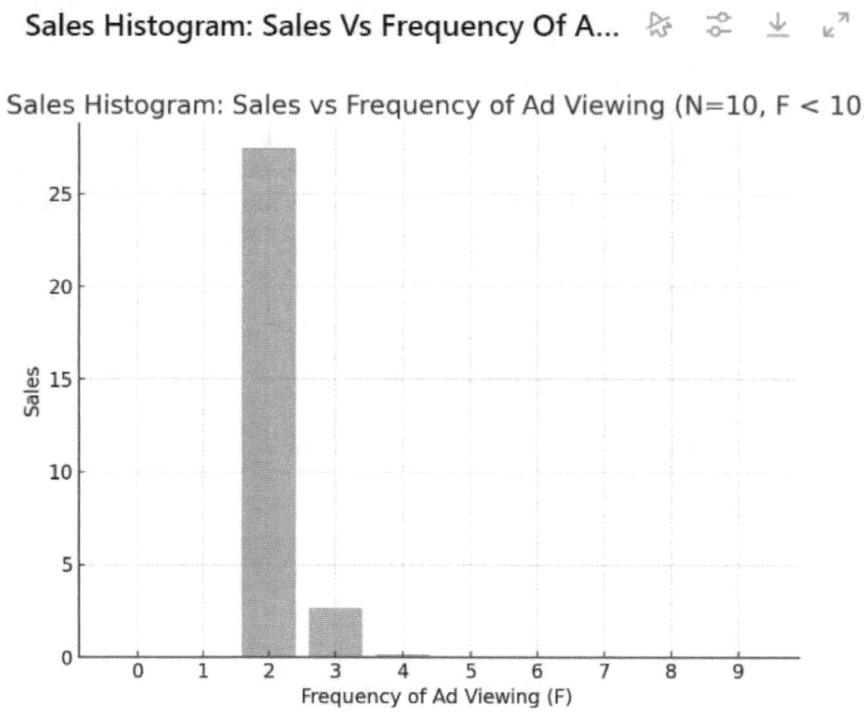

FIGURE 6: SALES HISTOGRAM

Quintile Modelling
Given the quintile proportions for a target alias, then the modelling can be divided into five calculations – one for each quintile group. The Reach and Universe metrics are apportioned by 20% while the impressions and audience is apportioned by the quintile proportions provided. The results of the five models are added together to form the overall modelled result. The change in the modelled results can be requested and reviewed to understand the value of including the quintile breakout as part of the modelling. Here is an example conversation:

Media Planner:
Plot the ROI vs Insertions N for modelling with and without Quintile breakouts
AI Response:

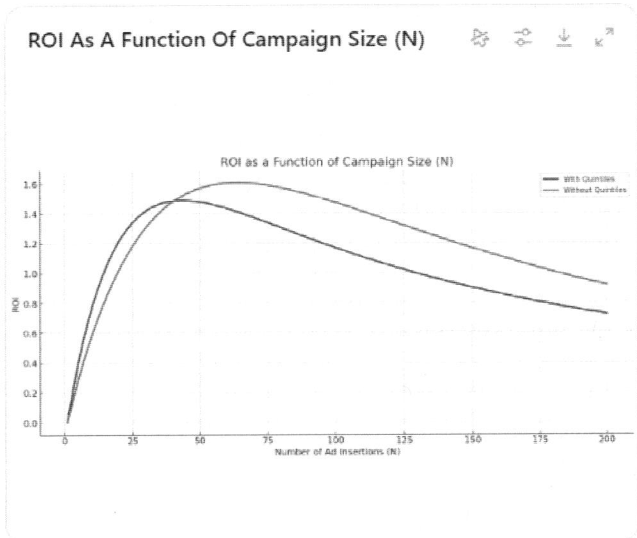

Here is the ROI curve as a function of the campaign size (N) for both models — with and without quintile breakouts. The chart highlights how ROI changes as the number of ad insertions increases, with the peaks indicating the optimal campaign size for each model.

FIGURE 7: ROI BY CAMPAIGN SIZE

ROI Calculation Modelling

By quantifying the Sales and then the revenue returned from those sales, the return on investment ROI can be calculated where the cost of the campaign is given by the impressions purchased times the VPM (Value Per Thousand). The AI system can be requested to provide the details of the calculation to explain the steps used to both inform the user and to allow for verification of the calculation correctness.

Media Planner:

Now show me the steps to derive the ROI for these sales.

AI Response:

To derive the ***Return on Investment (ROI)*** *for the sales based on the campaign, we will follow these steps sequentially:*

Step 1: Derive Total Sales Revenue (R)

The total sales revenue is calculated by summing up the product of the number of sales for each frequency and the net revenue generated from each sale.

- **Sales (S(F))**: This is the total number of sales generated from viewers who saw the ad FFF times, which we already calculated in the previous steps.
- **Net Dollars per Sale (ND)**: From the **Sales Probability** data, for the "Retired" target, the net revenue for each sale is provided as **$45.56**.

Thus, the total sales revenue is:

$$R = \sum_F S(F) \times ND \quad (1)$$

Where S(F) is the sales for each frequency F, and ND is $45.56.

Step 2: Derive Total Campaign Cost (C)

The total campaign cost is derived from the impressions generated by the ad insertions and the value per thousand impressions (VPM).

- **Impressions (I(F))**: This is the total number of impressions generated by the campaign, which we can calculate from the viewer distribution.

- **Value Per Thousand (VPM)**: For the "Retired" target on the **Invidi QAMless** platform, the VPM is given as **$18.25** from the **Target Universes** data.

The total cost of the campaign is calculated by:

$$C = (I_{total} / 1000) \times VPM \tag{2}$$

Where I_{total} is the total number of impressions, and VPM is $18.25.

Step 3: Calculate ROI

*Finally, the **Return on Investment (ROI)** is calculated as:*

$$ROI = R / C \tag{3}$$

Where:

- R is the total sales revenue.
- C is the total cost of the campaign.

Here are the calculated results:

- Total Sales Revenue (R): $1,377.87
- Total Campaign Cost (C): $1,825.00
- Return on Investment (ROI): 0.755 (or 75.5%)

This means that for every dollar spent, the campaign returns approximately $0.755 in sales revenue.

ROI vs N

The ROI metric can be calculated over a range of campaign attributes to observe where the campaign has the highest ROI. This forms the basis of being able to optimize the campaign by selecting the campaign attributes that result in the maximum. Here is an example conversation:

Media Planner:

Now vary N from 1 to 200 and plot the ROI vs Impressions where N derives impressions by multiplying by average audience. Plot the plan impressions as a vertical line.

AI Response:

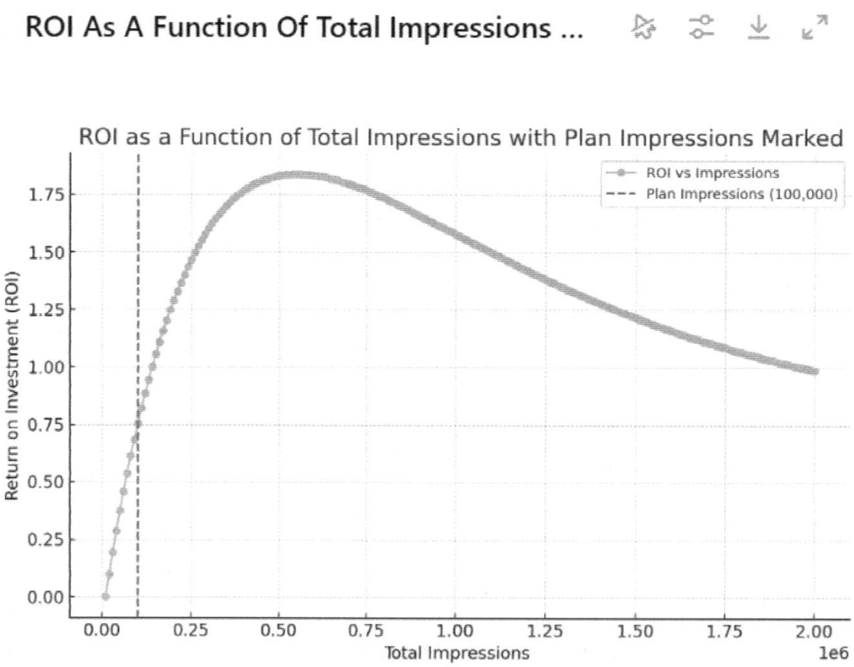

FIGURE 8: ROI BY IMPRESSIONS

Media Planner:

Now plot the ROI vs Insertions for one week for all platforms and targets

AI Response:

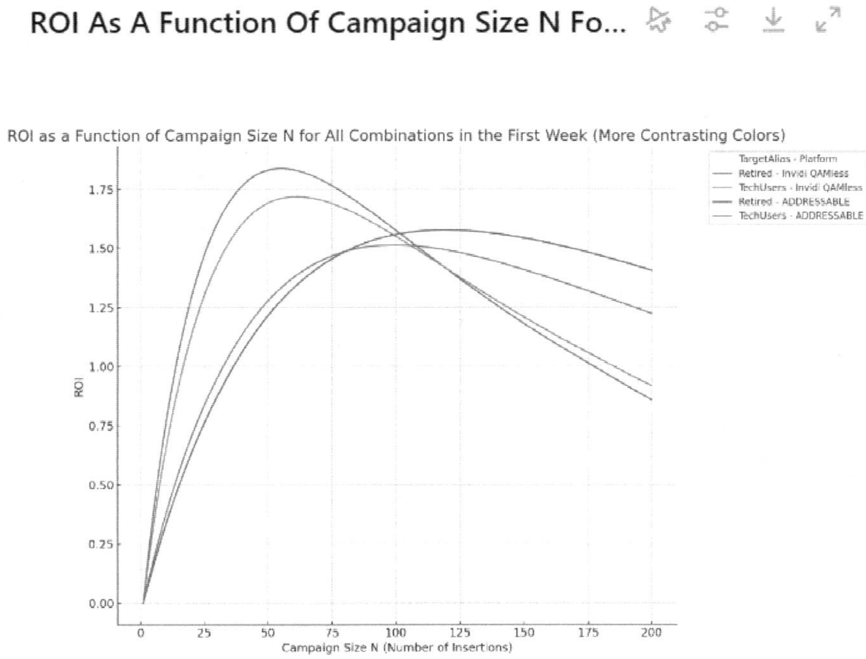

FIGURE 9: ROI BY PLATFORM AND TARGET

Multi Week Histograms

The AI system has been provided with the knowledge file that contains the steps to derive the campaign metrics for a multi-week campaign from the results for a single week. It involves converting the one-week results from a single week universe WCR to the overall multi-week universe estimate UE. Then the probabilities of the frequency distribution for the first week is convoluted with the frequency distribution for the second week to provide the overall frequency distribution (and then the viewer histogram) for the 2-week campaign. Further weeks can be added by the additional convolution of the single week viewer probability distribution.

Having derived the viewer histogram for multiple weeks, then the sales and the ROI can be derived as a function of the length of the campaign. Here is an example conversation:

Media Planner:

Now derive the viewer probability histogram for N = 10 per week for a 2 week campaign. Plot this probability histogram for 2 weeks together with the histogram for 1 week for frequencies up to F=10.

AI Response:

Viewer Probability Histogram For 1 Week ...

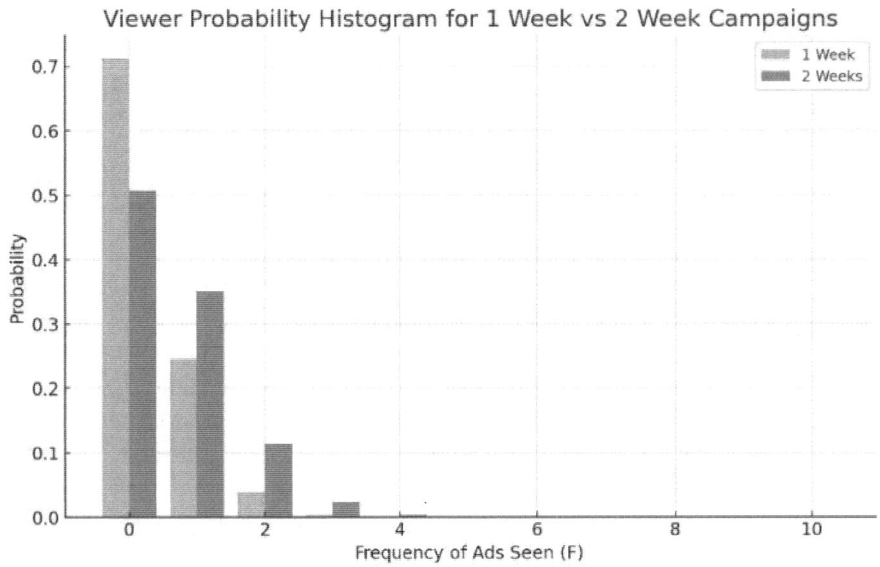

FIGURE 10: – VIEWER HISTOGRAM BY WEEK

Media Planner:
For N= 10 insertions, platform InvidiQAMless, and target Retired, plot the ROI for each campaign length from Weeks = 1 to 10
AI Response:

ROI For Campaign Lengths W=1 To W=12 ...

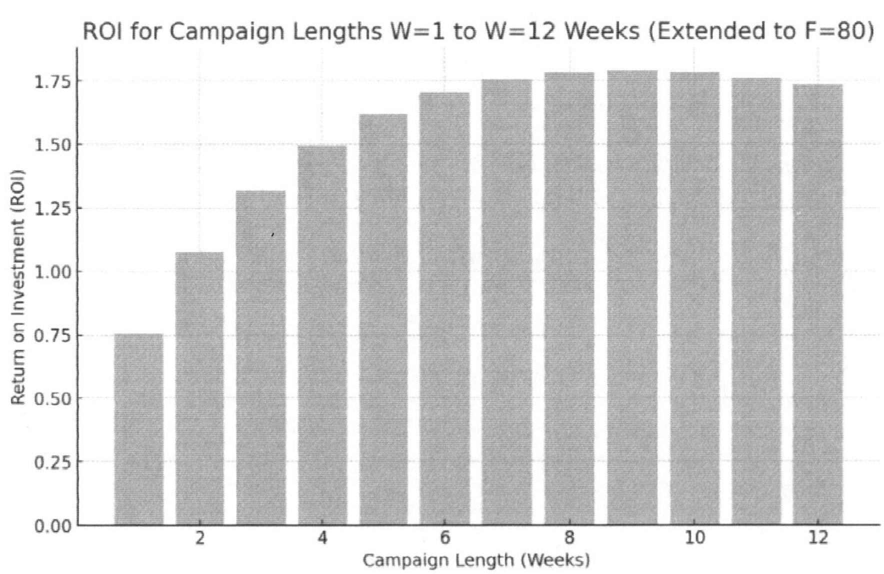

FIGURE 11: ROI BY CAMPAIGN LENGTH

Modelling Presentation

At any point in the modelling, the user can request the results to be presented either as tables of charts. This can be used to understand the efficiency of different campaign options and to observe which campaign attribute would maximize the ROI. Multiple attributes can be part of the modelling presentation to enable overall campaign maximization by selecting values for each of the attributes that result in the most efficient campaign.

Media Planner:

Now repeat this calculation for each frequency cap of FCAP = 2 to 6 and plot a 3D surface.

AI Response:

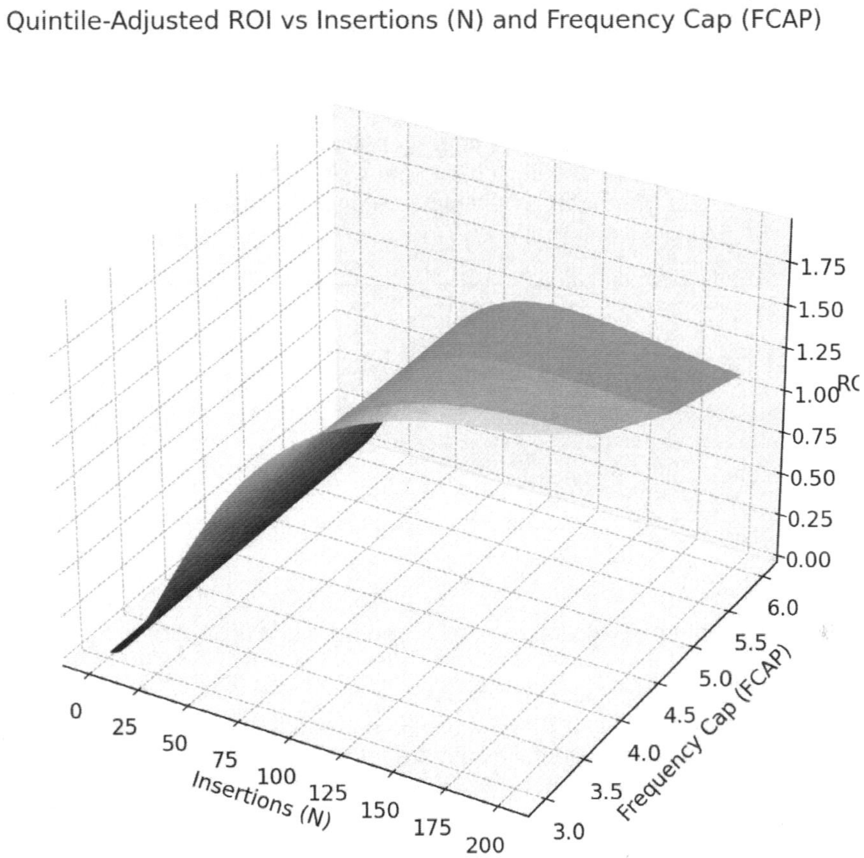

FIGURE 12: ROI BY INSERTIONS AND FREQUENCY

Result Explanation

The user can request the AI system to explain any of the results and to describe the steps it takes as part of calculations. This can give the user insight into the effect of campaign attributes on metrics like ROI and improve the campaign attributes selected. Here is an example conversation:

Media Planner:

I would have thought that the campaign had lower ROI for many weeks as later impressions were wasted. But the ROI grows larger for the first 4 weeks. Why does this ROI grow?

AI Response:

The **ROI** growth for the first few weeks is driven by how the campaign accumulates impressions and sales over time. Here's why the **ROI** might increase for the first few weeks:

Cumulative Effect of Ad Exposures:

- As the campaign continues into more weeks, new viewers who haven't seen the ads in the earlier weeks may now start seeing them. This increases the viewer exposure frequency for both new and existing viewers, leading to higher cumulative sales in the first few weeks.
- The first few weeks are when the majority of viewers are exposed to the ad, which results in increasing returns from higher exposure frequencies.

Sales Probabilities:

- The sales probabilities, although small, are cumulative across the campaign. In the first few weeks, the frequency of ad exposures may stay within the optimal range where sales probabilities remain relevant (between 1 and 10 exposures).
- As more viewers see the ad multiple times, the number of conversions (sales) increases at a faster rate than the cost initially, because the initial set of impressions is efficiently used.

Cost Behavior:

- The cost of the campaign grows linearly based on the number of insertions (ad exposures), but the sales return can grow more quickly in the early weeks, as the cumulative effect of reaching new viewers and increasing ad frequency kicks in.
- The model assumes that in the first few weeks, the same audience continues to be reached efficiently.

Optimizing a Campaign

The media modelling can explore campaign outcomes such as ROI as a function of changing a number of parameters:

- Weekly impressions
- Frequency cap values
- Campaign length in weeks
- Platform-Target selection

Also, the result of different advertiser product metrics can be modelled together with any different media audience metric changes.

The size of the campaign is defined by the number of insertions in a week. Campaign metrics such as ROI can be modelled and charted as a function of campaign size. This chart can be used to compare a proposed campaign size against the campaign size that maximizes the ROI. The AI system can be asked to modify the proposed campaign to adopt the campaign size that maximizes the ROI.

The effect of modifying a frequency cap can be included in the modelling so that parameter can be optimized to find a more efficient campaign with a higher ROI. Note that if sales do not occur for lower frequencies but flatten off for the higher frequencies, then introducing a frequency cap can avoid wasting impressions on viewers that already have a higher frequency of viewing the ad.

By modelling the ROI as the campaign length increases, the effect of additional weeks of impressions on the viewer histogram can be calculated. The resulting calculation of ROI as a function of the campaign length can be used to derive the campaign length that maximized this ROI metric. Here is an example conversation:

Media Planner:
Find the campaigns that overlap the second week of December and have advertiser Ford
Media Planner:
Get the first campaign and show me the orders with the Order Id, Order Name, Target Alias, the Platform, and the frequency cap.
Media Planner:
Show me the third order with the Weekly impressions Goal list.

Media Planner:
Now model this order by extracting the parameters required for the campaign modelling Action function from either the order or the supplied files as instructed, and model it with no quintiles, no memory loss factor = 0.0, and sales factor = 1.0. Retrieve the ROI Final, ROI Total, and ROI Final Total, returned for each campaign length in weeks and plot all the ROIs against the incremental campaign length.
Media Planner:
Now model a range of impressions scale values from 1.0 to 2.0 in steps of 0.2 and a range of frequency caps from [2, 3,4, 0]. Retrieve every one of the 24 results – do not just plot a subset of the results. Plot the resulting ROI Total against the imps final for each frequency cap value. Add a vertical line for the impression scale of 1.0. Recommend the impression scale and frequency cap that maximizes the ROI Total.
AI Response:

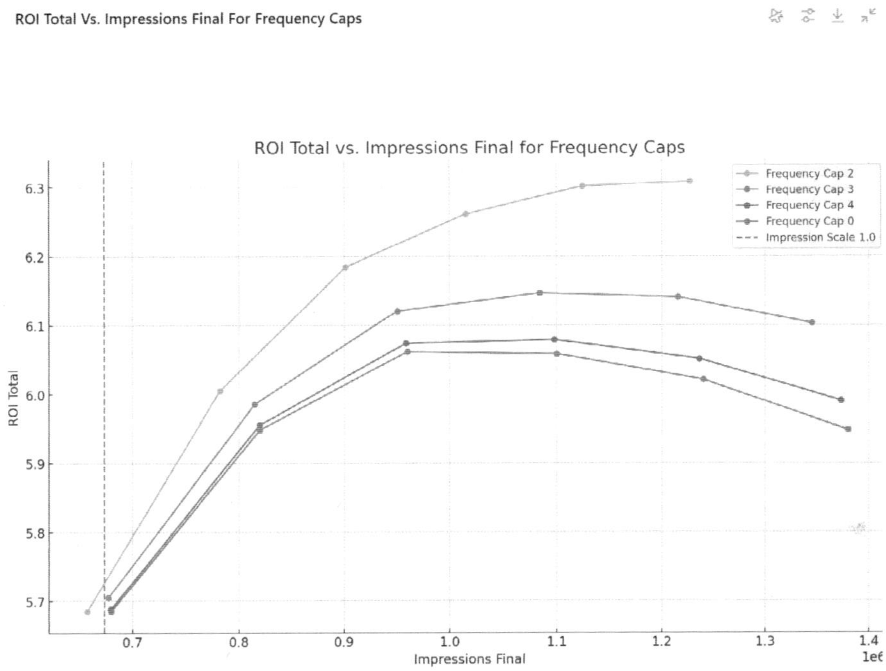

FIGURE 13: ROI TOTAL BY IMPRESSIONS FOR FREQUENCY CAPS

The plot above shows the relationship between ROI Total and Impressions Final for all frequency cap values across the range of impression scales. A vertical line marks the average Impressions Final for an impression scale of 1.0.
Recommendation:

- *Optimal Impression Scale: 2.0*
- *Optimal Frequency Cap: 2*
- *Maximum ROI Total: 6.308*
- *Impressions Final at Optimal Combination: 1,227,140*

This combination achieves the highest ROI Total. Let me know if further analysis or additional details are needed!

AI System Types

LLM Types

The AI system component dictates the capability of the system. Among the leading AI systems there are two types applicable to this system.

- Direct LLM (Large Language Model)
- Tree of Reasoning LLM

A Tree of Reasoning AI system looks at a problem and first constructs a plan of attack. It then considers alternative solutions and develops a tree of reasoning down the different alternatives. All the resulting solutions are then evaluated, and the best solution presented to the User. This approach can solve more difficult questions and score higher on tests using difficult problems. However, it takes more time before responding to a question.

The direct LLM system uses its training and knowledge files to directly generate the answer to the question. It is thus faster in its response.

The requirements of the AI component for the system in this paper is that it is able to follow exactly the steps in the instructions and correctly write and execute python programs to derive the requested data. In practice, the direct LLM type of models are better suited to these requirements. The Reasoning LLM can often try to find solutions outside of the instructions and as a result not correctly derive an accurate solution to the data request. Sometimes they do not have the ability to write and execute programs which hampers their ability to derive data results. Also, the long delay before responding is an impediment to a conversational partnership in finding an optimum campaign. The voice conversation option is sometimes not available for Reasoning LLMs.

AI Strength

AI systems vary significantly in their ability to understand and solve problems. Some difficult questions for the use case in this paper require many steps to be followed exactly, incrementally calculating interim data sets. Other simpler questions only require a few steps in the instructions to be followed. A difficult question might be to ask for the optimum ROI campaign across multiple weeks, impression weights, frequency caps, and platforms using quintiles and memory weighting. A simpler question might be to just derive the Sales for an impression weight within a week for a platform and target alias.

A more powerful LLM is needed to directly answer the more difficult questions accurately. A weaker smaller LLM can skip instruction steps or pick incorrect data from previous steps. Complex results can often be derived using smaller LLMs by asking a series of simpler questions that iteratively lead to the complex answer. But this requires that the user be familiar with the steps necessary to lead to the answer of the more complex problem.

Conclusion

The system provides a powerful assistant for a media planner to derive an optimized advertising campaign through conversational interaction with an AI component tightly coupled to a campaign delivery production system. This paper has detailed the knowledge files and audience metrics supplied to the AI system to enable both detailed modelling but also a flexible interactive analysis of the campaign options. Example conversations have been provided to show the scope of the conversations and the insights provided by the partnership of the planner and an AI system for campaign planning and optimization.

The approach to campaign optimization in this paper proposes a partnership between the planner and the AI system. In this partnership the rich experience of the planner can be blended with the fast modelling and management of the campaign design. Through a series of questions and results from the AI system, the planner can balance the modelled campaign optimum against their past experience of successful campaigns. This partnership can support the planning of a better campaign than either the first choice of the planner or a mechanical optimum of a model.

Role of AI in Quality Checking of Captions

Manik Gupta, Sana Afsar, Jeff Ross
Interra Systems
Cupertino, California, United States
manik@in.interrasystems.com, safsar@in.interrasystems.com, jeff@interrasystems.com

Abstract – In today's ultra-competitive media and entertainment industry, captioning demands exceptional precision. However, when quality control (QC) is conducted manually, it is very labor-intensive and prone to errors, which can lead to compromises in quality. For example, the QC process of ensuring adherence to Federal Communications Commission (FCC) guidelines — specifically, those relating to sync, accuracy, and completeness — requires multiple reviews. Furthermore, it involves verification of segmentation, reading speed, display duration, and layout metrics like row and column count. Caption placement also needs careful adjustment to avoid obstructing important visual elements, while global deliveries necessitate multilingual quality checks to meet diverse audience standards. Additionally, profanity censoring is critical. With all these requirements, performing general checks — such as ensuring captions aren't delayed during critical or suspenseful moments in a scene — can often be overlooked. This paper will explore how Artificial Intelligence (AI) is streamlining these complex QC tasks and freeing up human resources, enabling media companies to focus on the more creative aspects of their workflows.

Introduction

In audio-visual media, captioning demands exceptional precision. However, performing manual quality control (QC) is a labor-intensive process that is prone to errors and can compromise the high quality media service providers strive to deliver. For example, ensuring FCC guidelines of sync, accuracy, and completeness with captions QC not only requires multiple reviews but also involves verifying statistical details such as reading speed, display duration, break at clause boundary, and layout metrics like row and column count. FCC guidelines for caption placement also require careful adjustment to avoid obstructing important visual elements, while global deliveries necessitate multilingual quality checks to meet diverse audience standards. Likewise, profanity censoring needs to be kept in mind as well. With all these rules, more subtle and creative elements of the workflow are often left behind, such as checking if captions are delayed during a suspenseful scene.

The sheer volume of media produced today would demand an enormous human effort to ensure consistent quality. However, Artificial Intelligence (AI) has the potential to simplify these complex QC processes, allowing humans to focus more on creative enhancements instead. In the following sections, this paper explores how AI can be integrated to optimize and enhance the QC workflow for captions, highlighting the role of automation in improving both quality and efficiency in modern media production.

Automatic Speech Recognition

While a manual captioner will need to listen to audio multiple times to get frame-accurate timings for every dialog, an AI tool can use Automatic Speech Recognition (ASR) to generate the timed transcript of audio much faster than in real time. Then, an alignment algorithm can use this transcript to assign frame-accurate time to the dialog in the caption file. It can also flag portions of the caption file where text is missing or inaccurate and supply the correct text.

This process works for any language and just needs an accurate transcript of audio. Today's ASR systems have made remarkable progress with advancements in deep learning, self-supervised models, and large-scale datasets. Multilingual ASR models now support low-resource languages, breaking barriers in accessibility. Moreover, modern ASR engines leverage transformers and end-to-end neural networks, significantly improving accuracy even in noisy environments and across multiple languages. Overall, the shift from rule-based to AI-driven ASR has enabled real-time transcription, accent adaptation, speaker diarization, and punctuation correction.

Computer Vision

It is essential that captions elevate a viewer's experience, and that their placement does not hinder the quality of the video. Captions usually obstruct the actor's faces if displayed on the top of the video, and, if displayed on the bottom, they may hide relevant details such as match scores, forced narratives, or other burnt-in text. A manual reviewer will need to inspect every frame to ensure captions don't overlap with any of these visual elements, which takes considerable time and effort. However, an AI employing Computer Vision (CV) can easily find any such element in video and report an overlap issue. After locating all the visual elements in the frame, AI can correct the overlap using a deterministic algorithm to find the optimal position of captions on screen. These models can detect lip movements and identify speakers — further aiding in optimal positioning near the speaking character.

Deep learning models like YOLO, Mask R-CNN, and Vision Transformers (ViTs) provide reliable accuracy in real-time detection. These models can now learn without labeled data, making them more scalable and adaptable.

Machine Translation

Global deliveries generally consist of subtitles in 30+ languages. To have in-house linguistic experts in so many languages is practically impossible and costly. Instead, modern Machine Translation (MT) models can use contextual embeddings to ensure subtitles match the tone, formality, and nuance of the original dialogue. Traditional MT systems have struggled with context, leading to word-by-word literal translations that may not fit the scene's intent. However, modern MT systems — combined with Large Language Models (LLMs) — not only spot grammatical errors, unnatural phrasing, or inconsistent terminology in subtitles, but also adjust the translation to fit in the desired audio interval and number of words.

Traditional metrics like BLEU and METEOR are now being replaced by AI-driven quality evaluation models (e.g., COMET, chrF++, TransQuest). These models assess translation fluency, accuracy, and cultural appropriateness, making them more reliable for subtitle QC. Researchers are developing specialized MT models for subtitles, trained specifically on subtitling datasets (e.g., OpenSubtitles, MuST-C) to improve dialogue-style translations. With the rise of AI-driven machine translation, the future of subtitle quality checking is set to become faster, more context-aware, and automated.

Natural Language Processing (NLP)

Good-quality subtitles are not just accurately timed and worded; they are also properly segmented and laid out well. Captions should not cover too much of the screen, and must be presented with appropriate reading speed while having adequate display duration. Additionally, captions should be readable by grouping linguistically coherent information and not separating dependent words from each other with a line break. Well-segmented text with breaks on clause boundaries and natural pauses preserves the flow of the dialog and aids in comprehension.

This can be done without human intervention using NLP libraries, which can assign dependency tags to each word. Dependency tags show syntactic dependency, a relation between two words in a sentence where one word is the governor and the other is the dependent of the relation. NLP can assign head information for each word to form a dependency tree. Now, words in one branch will be closer to each other than the words in another branch. The words in a branch form a linguistic unit, and an in-order traversal of the dependency tree will automatically give linguistic units of varying sizes.

For example, suppose that the following sentence needs to be segmented: "This technique can be considered as the simplest way to perform segmentation." Users can leverage NLP to create the following dependency tree in Figure 1:

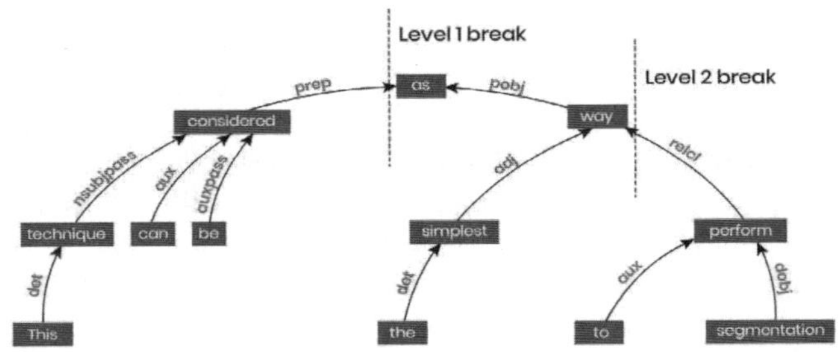

FIGURE 1: DEPENDENCY TREE ILLUSTRATING THE SYNTACTIC SEGMENTATION OF THE SENTENCE "THIS TECHNIQUE CAN BE CONSIDERED AS THE SIMPLEST WAY TO PERFORM SEGMENTATION."

Then, users can leverage dynamic programming (DP) algorithms to choose optimal units that ensure the character limit is satisfied, the number of line breaks is minimal, and the segments have proportional length (i.e., the created segments should not have one small segment and another, much larger segment.) Returning to the previous example, a DP algorithm could consider a limit of 42 characters in a row and a maximum two rows per caption segment to create the following segmentation:

This technique can be considered
as the simplest way to perform segmentation.

The whole process is lightning fast and does away with the need to understand nuances of different languages and complex captioning rules.

Multi-Modal AI

Different AI technologies, including those discussed above, now work in tandem to achieve unprecedented accuracy. ASR can generate text from audio, but ASR coupled with a lip-reading AI helps further align subtitles more precisely with spoken words for even better synchronization. ASR coupled with scene-change information from CV can further align captions' timing to avoid cross scene-change boundaries. It can also improve sole reliance on ASR by providing QC and correct speaker diarization, even in overlapping dialog situations.

Multimodal AI models (e.g., Flamingo, CLIP, VideoBERT) use both text and video context to improve subtitle translation accuracy. These models consider visual elements (e.g. scenes, facial expressions) to locate misinterpretations caused by literal translations and adjust subtitle wording accordingly.

With this contextual understanding from video and audio, these AI models can also help with quality checking of forced narratives more easily, which has been uncharted territory until now. Traditional subtitle systems relied mainly on speech-to-text (namely, ASR), which often fails to capture non-verbal events and background noises. Multi-modal AI identifies important non-speech sounds like laughter, applause, sirens, gunshots, or background music. For example, if a loud car horn interrupts a conversation, the AI can check and insert the missing audio description *[Car honks loudly]* into the captions to improve scene understanding. If a character nods instead of speaking, AI can add *[Character nods]* instead of a blank caption. This helps in silent storytelling, where gestures convey important meaning.

Furthermore, Sentiment Analysis + Vision AI helps captions and subtitles reflect tone, mood, and expressions. For example, it can detect where a flat caption like *"Okay."* should be replaced with *"Okay..." [hesitant tone]* when a worried facial expression is present in video.

Conclusion

The possibilities for improving the quality of captions and subtitles with AI, specifically multi-modal AI, are endless. Ground-breaking advancements in each of the AI domains discussed in this paper, which are combined to create superior multi-model AI systems, have presented unique opportunities to leverage AI in quality checking of captions. Besides, with modern AI chips allowing on-device processing, reliance on cloud computing is also reduced. Now, the comfort, safety, and privacy of on-premise environments are also achievable while using AI in media workflows. Intelligent systems have already started exploiting these technologies, and companies are coming up with advanced tools that will make the future of media absolutely inclusive and captioned.

Enhancing Instream Shoppable Brand and Product Detection in Broadcast, OTT, and VOD Content through Multi-Model Object Detection and Real-Time SCTE-35/SEI/VMAP Integration

Chaitanya Mahanthi
Google, YouTube
New York, New York, United States

Abstract – The increasing adoption of shoppable video content in Broadcast, OTT, and VOD has transformed how consumers engage with digital media. Traditional advertising models struggle to create seamless, interactive, and real-time brand engagement, leading to a need for AI-driven solutions. Emerging technologies now enable real-time product detection, metadata embedding, and interactive instream commerce integration, making video content viewable and instantly shoppable. The paper introduces an AI-based platform that instantly detects brands and products in video streams before implementing metadata structures for interactive shopping platforms. By leveraging deep learning-based object detection models and metadata signaling protocols, the framework ensures synchronized, real-time engagement between consumers and brands, unlocking new monetization opportunities for advertisers.

Multiple AI detection engines under this framework based on YOLO, Mask R-CNN, ResNet, and MobileNet SSD precisely identify products and brand placements inside real-time and pre-recorded content. The detections from the system link up with SCTE-35 (live streams), SEI (compressed video streams), and VMAP (VOD-based ad scheduling), which enable precise frame-level interactivity for product engagement. Based on AI technology, the system allows moment-by-moment brand interactions and stream-based e-commerce capabilities, and advertisers can use it for content monetization. The framework enhances content creator and advertiser success while delivering improved consumer engagement since it automates product detection combined with advertisement synchronization features. This framework redefines media commerce by combining AI-based detection, metadata injection, and HTML-based interactivity, allowing for scalable, real-time, and seamless brand engagement in video content.

Keywords
AI-powered product detection, Broadcast, SCTE-35, SEI, VMAP, OTT, VOD, interactive shopping, and shoppable media.

Introduction

Users have drastically changed their attitudes toward digital media consumption because of developments in the digital space. Audiences today choose over-the-top (OTT) platforms and video-on-demand (VOD) services due to their rising popularity, which turns viewers from passive consumers into active participants in their viewing experience. Viewers can now interact with brands alongside products because of this new trend in video content [1]. The survey found that 60% of OTT video viewers prefer interactive content features showing them products and brands they watch. Scientific progress in artificial intelligence (AI), real-time data analytics, and e-commerce integration capabilities are the primary sources of interactive streamer participation's rising popularity [2].

This paper is excerpted from the Proceedings of the 2025 NAB Broadcast Engineering and Information Technology (BEIT) Conference, © 2025, National Association of Broadcasters, 1 M Street SE, Washington, DC 20003 USA.

Two large technology companies, Amazon Prime and YouTube, have initiated live commerce experiments as industry leaders. Research shows that video-based shopping and live commerce continue to expand at a 40% rate each year after the previous period because customers want instant purchasing options in their streaming content. Through Amazon Live, brands and influencers can display their products in live streams while users can make purchases directly through the streaming platform interface [3]. YouTube Shopping provides creators with a tag system through partnerships with significant e-commerce providers such as Shopify, enabling users to purchase goods without stepping outside the platform. The patterns demonstrate that consumers want content-commerce unification, which unifies streaming content with buying interactions.

The changes in viewer behavior have made traditional online promotion methods fall behind current market demands. Viewers block advertisements through software programs because such placements generate annoyance, yet they fail to provide dynamic interactions. The business need for shoppable video platforms based on AI technology becomes increasingly essential since these systems deliver remarkable benefits to brands regarding consumer engagement and product exposure while streamlining video transaction processes [4].

The substantial changes digital advertising has undergone over the past few years remain insufficient to overcome essential hurdles affecting customer interaction levels and purchase conversions. The current ad industry framework uses pre-roll, mid-roll, and post-roll ads to show commercials, although these interruptions damage instead of improve user satisfaction. [4][5]. The traditional ad interruptive format makes viewers suffer from ad fatigue, leading them to either opt out of watching ads, block them, or change content viewing platforms altogether.

The main drawback of current advertising approaches is that products become visible late. Viewers can observe branded products during movies or sports broadcasts, but they cannot immediately find ways to interact with those products. When viewers observe a smartwatch on an actor in a film, they must perform independent searches online, which leads many of them to abandon their product discovery process [5]. Active links between product placements in media content and real-time viewer interest produce many lost opportunities for brand marketing campaigns.

Brand placements face significant difficulties when timing does not match e-commerce system operations. Most streaming platforms continue displaying static ads across their content through non-algorithmic product detection systems. Persons engaging with content often find advertisements irrelevant to what they wish to watch, thus reducing advertisement effectiveness [6]. Programmatic advertising systems try to find suitable ads based on user behavior patterns but cannot detect genuine product items in live video sequences at runtime. The current market shortfall creates a significant business opportunity to develop AI-based interactive commerce systems enabled by metadata, connecting online videos with product ads and robust purchasing abilities [7].

The current advertising models have insufficient capabilities, so engineers must develop a new system powered by AI detection of objects and metadata plus real-time connectivity to establish video content that can be shopped seamlessly. This investigation aims to establish an AI-based system that identifies products and brands within OTT, broadcast, and VOD content in real time. Various AI detection engines inside the integrated system use metadata standards, including SCTE-35, SEI, and VMAP, to provide seamless access to shoppable products in video streams. The system allows viewers to explore products seamlessly through its embedded e-commerce platform that operates without interrupting their streaming performance.

Research has defined three essential objectives which will help to reach its goal. Real-time shoppable media product detection through AI technology constitutes the core focus of the first main objective. The detection of brands and products in different video content becomes precise because deep learning object detection models, including YOLO, Mask R-CNN, ResNet, and MobileNet SSD, are utilized to achieve this performance. A multi-model method applies to detection systems because it improves accuracy rates and system scalability, allowing it to process various product categories. The framework operates with minimal delay, but detection-triggered delays will eventually become negligible due to continuous improvements in cloud hardware and infrastructure technology. AI detection functions effectively in real-time for both pre-analysed videos and live broadcasts.

The system enhances interactivity using metadata integration through SCTE-35 and SEI signaling for live stream real-time metadata injection. The system integrates interactive elements, including product clickable overlays, QR codes, and pop-ups that appear on-screen when it detects a product. When implementing VOD workflows, the research uses VMAP (Video Multiple Ad Playlist) metadata, which ensures that the products detected by the system match the pre-defined ad cues exactly. The system uses an HTML-based interactive user interface to deliver non-disruptive in-video product interactivity, which lets users browse and buy products from their video viewing position. The method strengthens the streaming environment brand and product visibility; thus, it brings about better viewer involvement, more sales conversions, and greater advertising profits.

System Architecture

The system architecture lets users have AI-enabled shopping interactions within video content through live broadcasts and VOD by detecting products and brands for immediate product metadata input [8]. The system design lets brands and advertisers provide customers with instant interactive buying experiences right from their video content. The system accurately locates brand names as they appear in real-time through YOLO ResNet and Mask R-CNN AI models. Identified products automatically appear at the right times as metadata processing matches their positions in each video timeline segment.

This architecture works with all media systems, including OTT platforms, digital broadcasts, CDN and IPTV networks, to provide easy upgrades for different media environments. The system performs video functions through two main processes: Live Content Workflow handles live streaming, and VOD Content Workflow manages analyzed video content. The workflow processes improve all AI processing plus meta-data insertion and UI updates, so viewers receive uninterrupted shopping experiences during their videos.

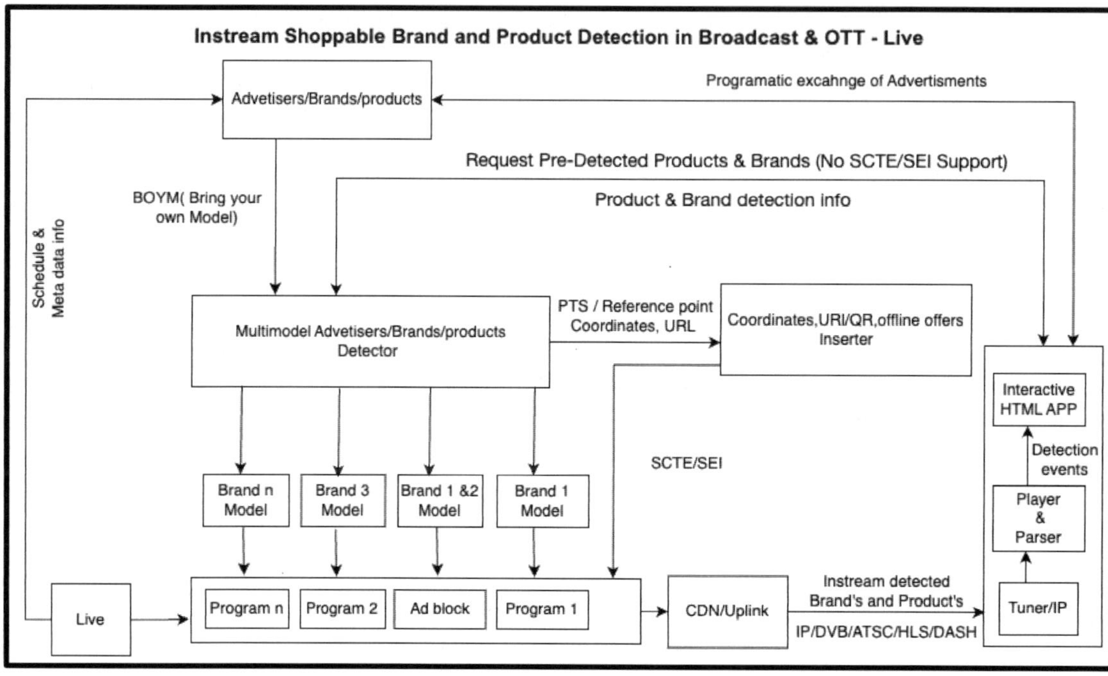

FIGURE 1: SYSTEM ARCHITECTURE

Live Content Workflow

Live streaming puts specific hurdles before shoppable integration since everything constantly changes in real time. The system needs to track products immediately while syncing data and updating the user interface fast enough for comfortable use [4]. The Live Content Workflow lets you detect products instantly, plus it inserts metadata using SCTE-35 or SEI while keeping the UI template ready for commerce interaction throughout live broadcasts.

Real-Time Brand/Product Detection

According to GPU-accelerated benchmark tests, the system requires the detection of products and brands during live broadcasts at delays below 50 milliseconds. Live events achieve fast and precise product detection through NVIDIA Tesla V100 GPUs, which operate on YOLO and ResNet detection models that demonstrate real-time capability with the help of high-speed cloud infrastructure [9].

YOLO performs robust real-time object detection because its speed and response time remain low. It also performs one-time event detection at high speed to identify logos and product locations in images precisely and faster than standard models. YOLO excels at detecting objects during streaming events because it operates at record-breaking speed. YOLO works best on GPU platforms because it allows us to expand video screening capacity quickly [9].

The Residual Neural Network (ResNet) model carries out precise product categorization of detected objects. It correctly recognizes branded items from any angle where part of the product is visible or hidden. Although YOLO detects objects rapidly, ResNet chooses between similar product types to improve its classification results. Our system finds product detections before delivering them to the Metadata Processing Engine, which places SCTE-35 and SEI signaling into the live stream.

Metadata Injection (SCTE-35, SEI)

Users must experience synchronized product information with what they see in the media video. The system delivers accurate metadata placement at the correct video frame using SCTE-35 and SEI signaling systems.

SCTE-35 lets media providers inject product details and adverts into live-streaming content. The technology automatically displays shoppable product features at specific moments with clickable buttons and picture-in-picture eye candy.

SEI adds product data to video files through the H.264/H.265 video format. Compared to SCTE-35, which runs alongside video content, SEI puts its metadata inside the video data stream, preserving metadata through all levels of video compression, especially for OTT and adaptive bitrate content.

```
import json
import binascii
import struct

def create_scte35_packet(detection_info):
    """
    Generates an SCTE-35 packet embedding JSON metadata.
    """
    json_str = json.dumps(detection_info)
    json_hex = binascii.hexlify(json_str.encode()).decode()
    scte35_packet = struct.pack(">B", 0x05) + binascii.unhexlify(json_hex)
    return scte35_packet
```

CODE EXAMPLE FOR SCTE-35 METADATA INJECTION.

The detected product information remains synchronized throughout the broadcast by sending this data in real time.

Real-Time HTML UI Updates

The HTML-based user interface independently does not process either SCTE-35 or SEI events with its current design. The video player reads communication signals from SCTE-35 and SEI to update the HTML display. The player detects the SCTE-35 and SEI signals/markers in the broadcast or OTT stream and triggers an ad request. The player or ad engine then calls a VAST-compliant ad server, which responds with metadata such as creative type (shoppable QR code, interactive banner, or product overlay), duration, and purchase links. If the internet is unavailable, preloaded static QR codes are used, allowing viewers to scan and redirect to shoppable websites or apps. When online, real-time product ads are fetched dynamically, enabling direct access to e-commerce platforms without disrupting the viewing experience.

Once the VAST response is received, the HTML and CSS templates update the player UI with shoppable overlays, not just clickable but fully interactive. These non-linear ad elements allow users to browse product details, add items to their cart, or make a purchase all being done while the video continues playing. This server-guided Ad, Product, and brand Insertion approach ensures seamless broadcast and OTT integration, maximizing ad revenue while providing a frictionless shopping experience [10].

VOD Content Workflow

The availability of offline preparation lets VOD workflows match product names and other data more reliably during processing. Product-related data can be added to content before viewers start watching, allowing them to view items while watching at the ideal moment.

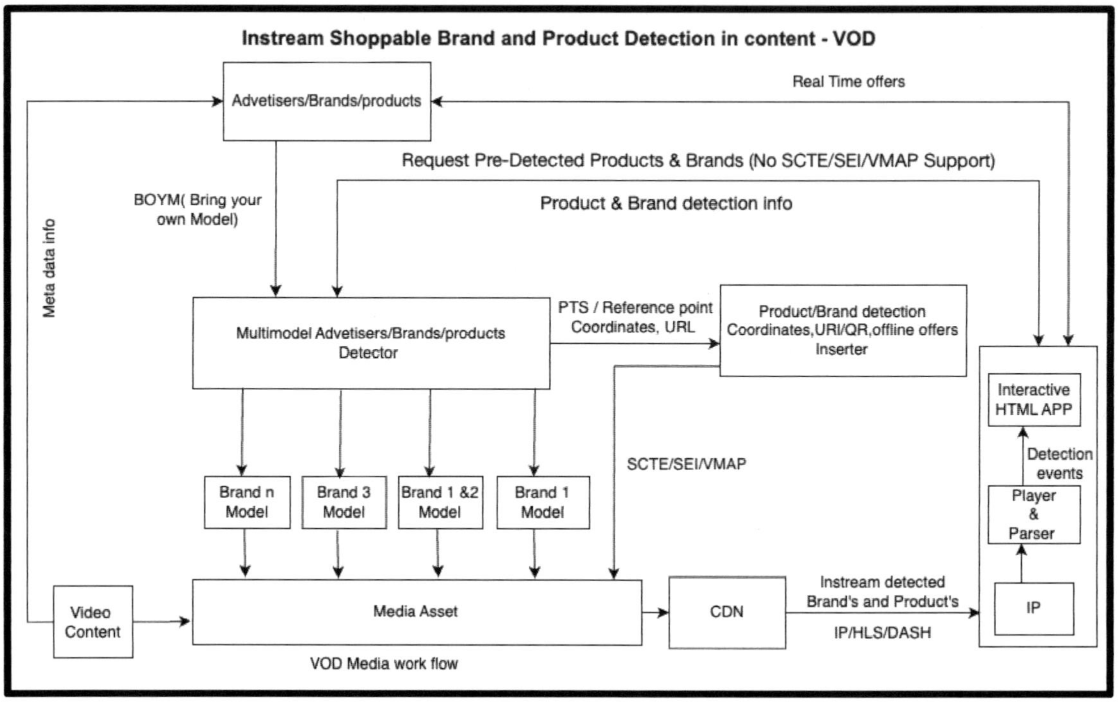

FIGURE 2: VOD (BRAND AND PRODUCT DETECTION)

The diagram outlines the workflow for Instream shoppable brand and product detection in VOD. Video content passes through a multimodal detector using various brand models (BOYM-supported). Detected products/brands generate metadata, coordinates, and URLs, which are inserted via SCTE/SEI/VMAP. The content is then distributed via CDN (IP/HLS/DASH). An interactive HTML app, supported by a player/parser, handles detection events, enabling real-time offers and product interactions.

Offline Frame Analysis

When processing VOD videos in advance, the system can measure the video frames better to find products. The following AI systems performed the needed analysis:

Mask R-CNN helps find exact object boundaries better than other methods, so it works well for detecting complex product placements in pre-recorded content. Instead of finding complete objects, Mask R-CNN can recognize and isolate multiple product elements to provide better object identification. Mask R-CNN works with YOLO to help make quick object detection work, resulting in better metadata labelling in various video frames.

Metadata Pre-Insertion (VMAP Cues for Ad Alignment)

The system must insert technical information on VOD videos before they become available for interaction. VMAP helps provide the reference to the product data into specific points of the videos using this service.

```
<vmap:AdBreak timeOffset="00:02:15.453">
    <Detection class="headphones" confidence="0.98">
        <VASTURL>https://example.com/vast-ad.xml</VASTURL>
    </Detection>
</vmap:AdBreak>
```

EXAMPLE OF VMAP METADATA EMBEDDING

The proper timing of these advertisements and product placements helps involve viewers better and increases advertising income.

Comparison of Live vs. VOD Workflows

Feature	Live Workflow	VOD Workflow
Detection	Real-time AI (low latency)	Pre-analysed AI (high accuracy)
Metadata	SCTE-35, SEI	VMAP (easy integration, supports more detection info), SCTE-35, and SEI
User Interaction	Dynamic overlays, QR codes	Timed product previews, CTA links

TABLE 1: COMPARISON OF LIVE VS. VOD WORKFLOWS [11]

Live streams work best with YOLO because they handle inputs quickly, while Mask R-CNN catches product details perfectly for VOD content after processing. This part shows how to build a technical system that uses AI video object detection combined with metadata addition in streaming environments. We will now study the strengths and faults of AI systems used for product discovery and their accuracy levels.

AI-Based Brand and Product Detection

AI-based brand and product detection technology forms the core of shoppable media services in all broadcast, OTT, and VOD video platforms. Multiple deep-learning systems process data in real time to recognize products and strengthen their vision accuracy before adding metadata for product interaction [12]. This part describes our AI system's strategy, which uses multiple deep learning models to find and divide products on live and recorded videos. It tests each model to measure accuracy plus speed, along with handling conflicts between accurate results and fast processing to select an optimal model arrangement for running media at a real-time scale.

Multi-Model AI Approach

The **Multi-Model AI Approach** integrates multiple AI models, each optimized for specific tasks based on the content type (live streaming or VOD) and operational requirements. This framework connects multiple AI models for high-speed, task-specific detection. The system utilizes YOLO for real-time object detection, Mask R-CNN and MobileNet SSD for object segmentation, and ResNet for product logo analysis. Additionally, the Multi-Model system supports BYOM (Bring Your Own Model), allowing advertisers to provide custom-trained models for more accurate brand detection, provided they follow a supported model format. This modular approach enhances reliability and ensures rapid product and brand detection across various media formats.

YOLO proves to be the premier deep-learning system that performs swift real-time object detection. YOLO operates differently from typical object detection systems that measure images multiple times by quickly handling a whole image during its single forward pass [13]. YOLO offers strong benefits for live streaming usage because it processes information quickly. YOLO delivers 60 FPS capacity to detect logos, brand placements, and consumer products within milliseconds. YOLO performs best when the system needs to identify and tag product details at high speeds in live sports events and other fast-paced broadcasts [14]. Sports broadcasters can apply YOLO to spot which sneakers athletes wear during soccer matches, as the system provides live results. The system recognizes sneaker data to embed metadata with SCTE-35, which activates prompt buying options on-screen.

Mask R-CNN (**Region-Based Convolutional Neural Network**) performs exact object segmentation perfectly in tasks that demand close analysis of video files before distribution [15]. Mask R-CNN offers superior performance because it can trace the outline of individual items and recognize them even if multiple objects overlap or only show part of their surface. The tool brings superior results to fashion content alongside furniture and home decor segments because it detects items with the exactness that products need [16]. The video-on-demand platform runs Mask R-CNN before a cooking show starts to locate branded kitchen tools and ingredients. The system links the identified items to VMAP metadata positions so product recommendations appear at precise times to boost viewer connection and advertising value.

ResNet (**Residual Neural Network**) ResNet meets high standards in classification accuracy. The system works best with logo and brand recognition because it extracts deep features to detect brand information accurately [17]. YOLO and Mask R-CNN find products, while ResNet confirms their correct classification before embedding metadata. ResNet performs better when identifying many brand logos in one visual scene [18]. Also, the system supports advertiser–custom models, thus enabling brands to incorporate their own detection algorithms. It also helps to ensure better recognition precision concerning some particular brands and logos that will assist advertisers in addressing how their brands show in certain videos. These models can be trained on provided datasets from advertisers or any other source and can be easily incorporated into the existing consumable multi-model system for both live and on-demand content.

MobileNet SSD (**Single Shot MultiBox Detector**) delivers fast, shoppable content performance on devices with minimum power requirements and belongs to low-end AI devices for multiplatform applications. The model differs from YOLO and Mask R-CNN since MobileNet SSD operates as a streamlined on-device solution with less GPU power than these alternatives [19]. Technical designers choose this model for smart TVs and streaming equipment with minimum processing power. The technology delivers fast AI functionality directly to smartphones and smart TVs, meaning users can stay connected to AI services while data networks are slow or weak [20]. The mobile shopping app on smart TVs can find fashion brand names of clothes worn by TV actors through MobileNet SSD. Users can click on exposed clothing items during shopping and buy them immediately from the same application window.

FIGURE 3: MULTI-MODEL AI APPROACHES

Performance Evaluation

AI models undergo performance testing that assesses their accuracy levels and speeds up while using minimal resources. The effectiveness of AI-based product detection is measured using Mean Average Precision (mAP) and Precision-Recall Curves [21]. Mean Average Precision evaluates object detection model precision through accurate positive rate tests to confirm that the system correctly finds and labels products. Precision-Recall Curves confirm that the system considers most brand placements by testing the balance between precise product identification and missed opportunities. YOLO v5 performs real-time product detection with an accuracy between 78% and 85%, yet Mask R-CNN reaches 91% accuracy when working on previously analyzed frames. The ResNet system consistently detects brands with 95% success in its logo recognition function [22].

Effective time delays must be maintained to run AI systems smoothly during live-stream broadcasts. Product scanning and metadata attachment fit directly into live viewer streams due to simultaneous real-time performance and excellent detection precision. The YOLO method supports detection speeds of 60+ frames per second, meaning it is the top selection for live video broadcasts [23]. Mask R-CNN delivers highly accurate product detection, making it appropriate for video-on-demand use. ResNet runs at 50 FPS to provide exact brand recognition, while MobileNet SSD works on mobile devices at 80 FPS with an acceptable accuracy level. TensorRT acceleration helps the system run AI inference tasks quickly on significant video streams. Cloud-based systems handle much traffic, which prevents delays in the AI inference process. Model compression methods that convert FP32 numbers to INT8 format make AI models work better on less power-hungry devices, allowing mobile viewing services to benefit from local processing.

The system uses multiple AI models to find products instantly and correctly across every TV broadcast, internet, and video-on-demand platform. The system uses YOLO, Mask R-CNN, ResNet, and MobileNet SSD to provide easily scalable and fast AI-based shopping experiences that deliver high-quality results. YOLO works best for live streaming because of its real-time detection speed, while Mask R-CNN deals with detailed product segmentation of pre-analyzed VOD materials. The ResNet system gives precise results when finding logos and brands, while the MobileNet SSD works well on portable devices by doing tasks quickly.

The paper enhances AI-driven shoppable media with this framework by efficiently evaluating mAP, inference speed, and precision recall to create a scalable and effective solution. The following section studies how SCTE-35 SEI and VMAP metadata injection techniques give users better interaction with AI-driven commerce applications on video.

Metadata Injection and Interaction

A platform must effectively use metadata injection to enable viewers to shop during live and on-demand content streaming. Structured product information acts as an AI intermediary that links detected items to interactive buttons on-screen and allows viewers to interact with products instantly [24]. The article explains how SCTE-35 and SEI signaling work for live streams while VMAP fits video-on-demand processes. Live video streams benefit from SEC-35 and SEI protocols that automatically tag products the instant they show up in real time. VMAP integration gives users scheduled ad break service in VOD content to interact with products at specific times according to their product metadata.

```
{
    'class': 'sofa',
    'type': 'asproduct',
    'vast_url': 'https://example.com/vast-ad.xml',
    'coordinates': {
        'x': 100,
        'y': 150,
        'height': 300,
        'width': 350
    }
}
```

SCTE-35 AND SEI FOR LIVE STREAMS

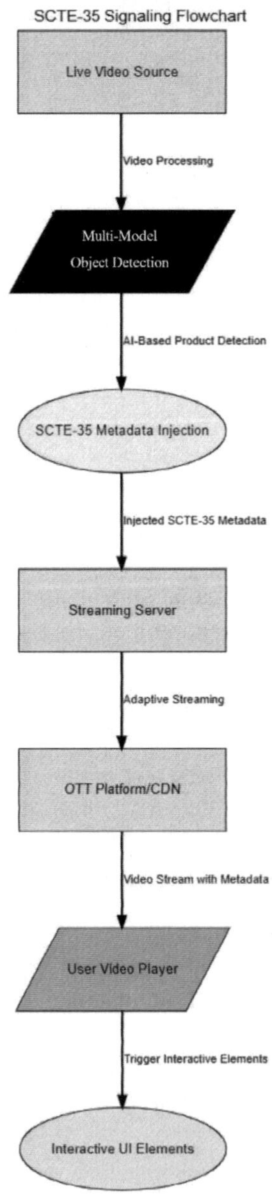

FIGURE 4: SCTE-35 AND SEI FOR LIVE STREAMS

Broadcast and OTT industries use SCTE-35 as their standard way to send cue points and advertisement metadata. Broadcasters can input events to make specific products appear during live streaming at predetermined times. SCTE-35 technology lets live-streaming users respond instantly to video product displays by linking them to buying options.

Within broadcast video, SCTE-35 embeds metadata that triggers interactive items such as clickable areas or pop-ups precisely when a product shows on screen. The product display spots in videos are marked precisely by Splice Inserts during metadata synchronization. LNK-35 segments provide complementary product data that shows brand names, selling prices, and shopping link settings. Live-streaming platforms can create more enjoyable viewer experiences by inserting interactive shopping features when they detect specific content through SCTE-35 technology.

```
def create_scte35_packet(detection_info):
    """
    Create a custom SCTE-35 packet embedding JSON metadata for private data.
    """
    # Convert the detection_info to a JSON string and encode it as hex
    json_str = json.dumps(detection_info)
    json_hex = binascii.hexlify(json_str.encode()).decode()
    protocol_version = 0x00
    encrypted_packet = 0x00
    pts_adjustment = 0x00000000
    cw_index = 0x00
    tier = 0x0FFF
    splice_command_type = 0x05
    # Creating private data for embedding
    private_data_length = len(json_hex) // 2  # Length in bytes
    private_data = binascii.unhexlify(json_hex)
    # Construct the SCTE-35 packet (header + private data)
    scte35_header = struct.pack(
        ">BBQBH",
        protocol_version,
        encrypted_packet,
        pts_adjustment,
        cw_index,
        tier
    )
    scte35_packet = scte35_header + struct.pack(
        ">B", splice_command_type
    ) + private_data
    return scte35_packet
```

SEI (Supplemental Enhancement Information) in Live Streams

The SEI system improves SCTE-35 by placing additional product metadata within H.264/H.265 video encoding data to keep it intact throughout video compression. SCTE-35 has limited use for ad signals and cue point activities, but SEI enables product metadata integration into real-time video streams. The connection of SEI metadata to video content works at the exact frame level to ensure that product data matches what viewers see on screen [25]. SEI metadata sticks with the video stream no matter how the video is sent through different adaptive streaming methods such as HLS, DASH, and MPEG-DASH. The system works without interruptions on various networks and devices. The combined usage of SCTE-35 for signaling and SEI for metadata allows streaming services to set up durable interactive content that matches product information to what viewers see on screen.

Real-Time Shoppable Elements Triggered by SCTE-35

The interactive HTML UI detects SCTE-35 signals to show shopping options on the screen automatically. When viewers click on a detected product, the platform adds product details with purchase options to what they see on the screen. Users who scan the product link using smartphone cameras gain instant access to an online store. The live broadcasts can connect to social commerce actions like voting, polls, and promotions to improve viewer participation with products on display. These interactive purchasing features blend smoothly with regular viewing without bothering viewers.

Code Example: SCTE-35 Metadata Injection

This Python function shows how to insert SCTE-35 metadata into live video content, which links detected products to interactive buying options.

```
import json
import binascii
import struct

def create_scte35_packet(detection_info):
    """
    Generates an SCTE-35 packet embedding JSON metadata.
    """
    json_str = json.dumps(detection_info)
    json_hex = binascii.hexlify(json_str.encode()).decode()
    scte35_packet = struct.pack(">B", 0x05) + binascii.unhexlify(json_hex)
    return scte35_packet
```

The code function arranges product metadata to be sent through SCTE-35 with real-time commerce options. NAB's research confirms that SCTE-35 works well for real-time ad and metadata signaling during live streaming and serves as the foundation in shoppable video work processes today.

VMAP Integration for VOD

The Video on Demand (VOD) structure enables placing merchandise tags at exact playback times before content starts playing. IAB Tech Lab introduced VMAP as a format to define placement times for commercials and shopping content during videos. VMAP best fits VOD systems because it lets platforms set up non-obtrusive product engagement before content streaming starts [26].

VMAP creates a specific way to place ad start and stop points throughout streaming video content like VOD. The ad space marks provide tools to add product information precisely during video playback for easy online shopping experiences. The video setup tool lets advertisers show product shopping options at the right time during each product appearance in their campaigns. VMAP joins forces with VAST to present targeted product ads when they reach their most effective position in videos.

Predefined Product-Based Ad Break Scheduling

The significant advantage of VMAP metadata integration is that it lets you place ads during specified product moments in videos. The system shows product pop-ups that match the content when viewers watch a particular video part. Shoppable overlays automatically show you items to buy and the purchase choices when needed. The VMAP system helps businesses show customized product suggestions to viewers based on what they click and watch.

Code Example: VMAP Metadata Embedding

```xml
<?xml version="1.0" encoding="UTF-8"?>
<vmap:VMAP xmlns:vmap="http://www.iab.net/videosuite/vmap" version="1.0">
  <!-- Nonlinear Pre-roll Ad Break -->
  <vmap:AdBreak timeOffset="00:02:15.453" breakType="nonlinear" breakId="adbreak-1">
    <vmap:AdSource id="adsource-1" allowMultipleAds="false" followRedirects="true">
      <vmap:AdTagURI templateType="vast3">
        <![CDATA[https://example.com/vast-preroll.xml]]>
      </vmap:AdTagURI>
      <!-- Detection Metadata -->
      <DetectionMetadata>
        <Detection class="sofa" confidence="0.95" type="asproduct">
          <Coordinates xmin="100" ymin="150" xmax="300" ymax="350" />
          <VASTURL>https://example.com/vast-ad.xml</VASTURL>
        </Detection>
      </DetectionMetadata>
    </vmap:AdSource>
  </vmap:AdBreak>

  <!-- Nonlinear Mid-roll Ad Break -->
  <vmap:AdBreak timeOffset="00:05:42.782" breakType="nonlinear" breakId="adbreak-2">
    <vmap:AdSource id="adsource-2" allowMultipleAds="false" followRedirects="true">
      <vmap:AdTagURI templateType="vast3">
        <![CDATA[https://example.com/vast-midroll.xml]]>
      </vmap:AdTagURI>
      <!-- Detection Metadata -->
      <DetectionMetadata>
```

```xml
      <!-- Detection Metadata -->
      <DetectionMetadata>
        <Detection class="Tesla" confidence="0.88" type="brand">
          <Coordinates xmin="200" ymin="250" xmax="400" ymax="500" />
          <VASTURL>https://example.com/vast-ad2.xml</VASTURL>
        </Detection>
      </DetectionMetadata>
    </vmap:AdSource>
  </vmap:AdBreak>

  <!-- Nonlinear Post-roll Ad Break -->
  <vmap:AdBreak timeOffset="00:08:19.673" breakType="nonlinear" breakId="adbreak-3">
    <vmap:AdSource id="adsource-3" allowMultipleAds="false" followRedirects="true">
      <vmap:AdTagURI templateType="vast3">
        <![CDATA[https://example.com/vast-postroll.xml]]>
      </vmap:AdTagURI>
      <!-- Detection Metadata -->
      <DetectionMetadata>
        <Detection class="Laptop" confidence="0.92" type="asproduct">
          <Coordinates xmin="150" ymin="100" xmax="350" ymax="300" />
```

The following XML snippet demonstrates how product detection metadata is embedded into a VMAP structure:

```
<vmap:AdBreak timeOffset="00:02:15.453">
    <Detection class="sofa" confidence="0.95">
        <VASTURL>https://example.com/vast-ad.xml</VASTURL>
    </Detection>
</vmap:AdBreak>
```

The specified information helps product ads display during specific times to boost user engagement and increase profits. Research from IAB Tech Lab shows that VMAP helps create video ad metadata formats, making it fundamental for businesses to profit from interactive commercial content.

This block described ways to add product metadata interactivity in streaming and on-demand content. Broadcast audiences can shop interactively during live shows because SCTE-35 and SEI send product-related information directly into television feeds. The VMAP system adds systematic data to VOD processes so that marked shopping points match the main video content [27]. Broadcasters can offer better shopping interactivity to viewers thanks to metadata tech, which helps both digital platforms and advertisers increase their sales potential. The following part will demonstrate how advertisers use real-time targeting and customized item advice to generate profits from AI-detected product identification.

Advertiser Integration and Programmatic Advertising

Streaming interfaces will change to automatically embed ads directly into content delivery using AI technology to spot objects in videos. Digital ads use predetermined spaces online, which may show brands to the incorrect user at incorrect times. Organizations that use AI technology to find streaming targets and add ads automatically will create better viewer experiences that boost sales and make their ads more successful.

This section studies advertisers' connections to programmatic platforms for selling AI-detected items in streaming media through Real-Time Bidding, Demand-Side Platforms, and Supply-Side Platforms.

FIGURE 5: SHOPPABLE ELEMENTS WITH PRODUCT DETECTION, INGESTION AND ADVERTISER INTEGRATION

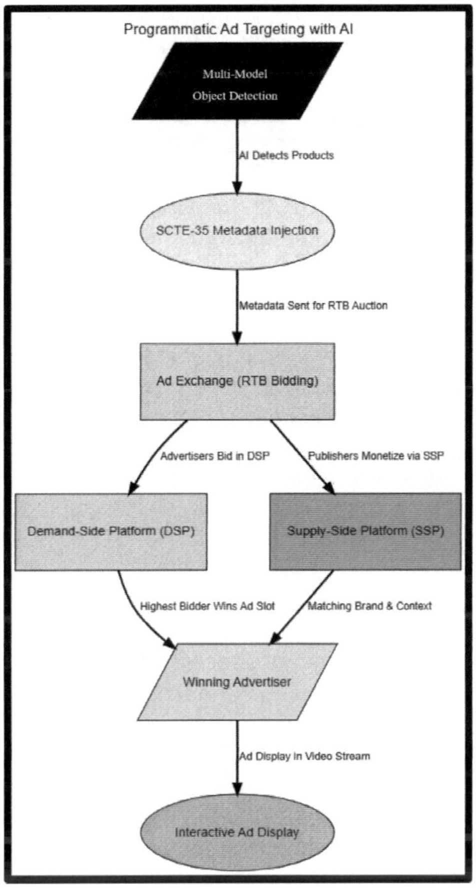

FIGURE 6: ADVERTISER INTEGRATION AND PROGRAMMATIC ADVERTISING

Real-Time Bidding (RTB) for Detected Brands & Products

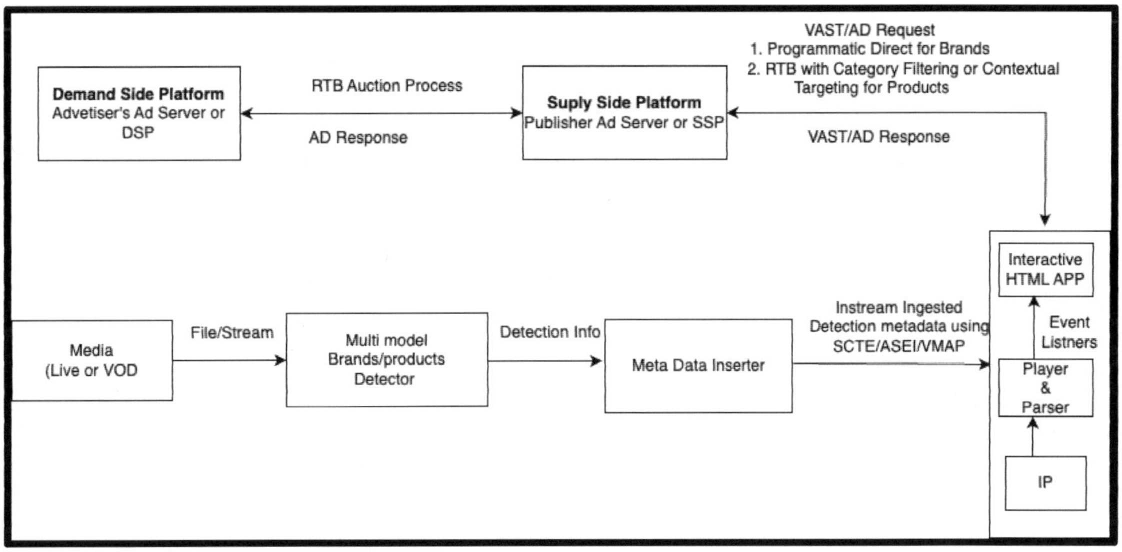

FIGURE 7: REAL-TIME BIDDING (RTB) FOR DETECTED BRANDS & PRODUCTS

The Real-Time Bidding (**RTB**) model enables advertisers to bid for display positions each second as ads become available. After AI-powered object detection finds a product in streaming video, RTB technology selects brands that match what it sees and arranges their ads for display. YOLO and Mask R-CNN's video recognition technology and ResNet can detect branded items in video content. SCTE-35 data injection begins when video feed monitoring detects the signal, while VMAP-based advertising triggers run only on video-on-demand platforms. When a product appears in the list and the user clicks on it, Real Time Bidding (RTB) takes place between advertisers and publishers, allowing the highest bidder to serve linear or non-linear commercials, along with shoppable and clickable video inserts and display units for enhanced engagement

AI technology can spot branded sports shoes on players during an active football match [29]. When metadata reaches RTB's exchange servers, advertisers place immediate bids to acquire access to it. The winning online shopping platform, Nike, Adidas, or Puma, displays a purchasable ad to viewers, which lets them buy the shoes directly through a clickable interface. Advertisers get better ad matching because they show targeted videos at real-time events. The strategy helps publishers draw more money from advertisements by showing them exclusively to the highest bidders. RTB makes online shopping easier because viewers can engage with available products without stopping their video content [30].

DSP & SSP Integration Using Metadata

Demand-side platforms (DSPs) enable advertisers to automatically purchase and show targeted ads across digital platforms in real time. Ad buyers increase efficiency when AI tags products when streaming videos through DSPs. These systems purchase ad opportunities based on content review findings and deliver ads at suitable moments to boost results. AI identifies branded products in a video and creates the necessary metadata simultaneously. The DSP system compares this metadata to available purchase campaigns for an advertiser. The DSP enters a live bid during RTB auctions to give winning placement rights to the most related advertiser. The chosen advertiser delivers the promoted advertisement to keep the product placement relevant to what was found [31].

Company owners partner with publishing Supply-Side Platforms to set up their available advertisement spots for instant sale. Streaming platforms benefit from SSPs in two ways: they automate placing product ads during videos while AI detects products and matches them to suitable advertisements for sale to multiple bidders. Using Mask R-CNN, the VOD platform can recognize and distinguish the endorsed blender during cooking show analysis. The SSP runs a live market auction to help kitchen appliance advertisers find success with their bids. Their clickable promotion appears when the blender is used during the video, making it more appropriate and attracting viewer attention.

Scalability, Challenges, and Performance Evaluation

Brand and product detection systems need flexible characteristics to operate properly across broadcast platforms and OTT and VOD viewing sectors. Metadata detection occurs only at the origin, followed by a one-time injection propagating through CDNs to uphold system efficiency. The system needs to scale its operations for faster detection without compromising accuracy in real-time settings. Software must perform rapid AI analysis to process metadata data in real-time and handle increasing customer requirements. All users must experience fluid viewing despite expanding system capabilities because the UI remains uninterrupted.

The section highlights primary scalability issues affecting Cloud AI and Edge AI systems during video processing tasks. The research examines performance-enhancing measures for metadata injection while establishing AI-based server distribution techniques for streaming environments.

Conclusion

The development of AI systems helps people shop directly from broadcast and streaming videos through real-time interactions. This research develops and demonstrates a combined AI model using YOLO, Mask R-CNN, ResNet, and MobileNet SSD to spot real-time items. Video playback now matches available product data through SCTE-35, SEI, and VMAP standards to create an impactful way for viewers to shop during their TV experience.

The framework helps advertisers effectively engage viewers while gaining new money-making tools that let ads be shown instantly to viewers through the RTB and programmatic ad system. The system maintains high performance by optimizing AI processing and insertion at the cloud and overlaying shoppable ads at the edge, minimizing latency and maximizing ad relevance. This scalable, AI-driven solution transforms the way brands connect with consumers, bridging the gap between content and commerce in real time.

Summary of Findings

Using AI to find products has become essential for quick shopping solutions through streaming media. The system makes deep learning technology work better at recognizing logos, merchandise, and products. The system adds product metadata exactly when product elements appear on the screen to give users a seamless shopping experience. The platform lets users tag products during live events and pre-recorded videos anytime. AI automation turns viewers into buyers directly from their content viewing experience without needing people to search and buy products better.

By incorporating SCTE-35, SEI and VMAP metadata, everyone can easily switch between watching and interacting with the system. In real-time, the SCTE-35 system adds live broadcast metadata to fire interactive features that show product tags, QR codes, and call-to-action elements. SEI keeps interactive functions available by placing video metadata directly into the video compression system. VMAP acts as a product breakdown tool for VOD content, allowing exact ad placements at product moments on-screen. Each metadata standard collaborates to blend the purchasing opportunities into the user's normal viewing routine.

RTB and programmatic ads perform better for advertisers because artificial intelligence helps them deliver appropriate ads that match detected content in real time. The automated RTB system shows advertisements to users based on their interests so they have higher chances of making purchases. DSP tools connect advertisers to product placement chances in video content, while SSP systems let publishers pick optimal ad spots for greater user response and better earnings. The model shows an essential adjustment for digital advertising because ads blend automatically with viewer preferences to generate better response and interest.

Future Work

Improved Latency and Real-Time Responsiveness

Reducing latency is critical, especially for live streaming environments where real-time product detection and metadata injection are essential. Future enhancements should aim to:

- **Optimise AI Models for Edge Computing:** To perform real-time analysis, computer algorithms need to be optimized for running on edge devices.
- **Leverage Low-Latency Streaming Protocols:** Use WebRTC, LL-HLS, etc., to achieve fast metadata synchronization with less buffering.
- **Enhanced Orchestration:** The Multi-Model framework should incorporate advanced rules to dynamically determine which models to use and when, based on content type, detection complexity, and real-time processing needs. It should efficiently orchestrate both parallel and sequential model executions for optimized product and brand detection. Additionally, the system should adhere to advertiser preferences, ensuring that specific models run on designated programs, aligning with brand requirements and campaign strategies

- **Adaptive Workload Distribution:** Employ dynamic load management across the servers to ensure the distribution of many possible workloads, leading to low system-wide latencies during periods of high loads.

Comprehensive Testing and Performance Evaluation

A primary strategy is to conduct comprehensive tests that will help to maintain the system's stability in various media settings. The future roadmap should include:

- **Stress Testing:** Deploy load over the system to evaluate real-time traffic by applying stress to the AI inference and injecting metadata.
- **Benchmarking AI Models:** Assess the detection models to determine their effectiveness on commonly defined measurements, including accuracy, performance density, and resource utilization.
- **User Experience Testing:** Use a few methods and tools, such as A/B Testing, to assess the effectiveness of the interactive aspect and how well it draws the viewers' attention, along with the click-through rates and conversion rates.

Development of Highly Accurate AI Models

The availability of more accurate models for detecting the products and the brands will help increase the user confidence and the satisfaction of the advertisers. Strategies include:

- **Model Fine-Tuning with Diverse Datasets:** For increased model recognition rates, use a large number of diverse data sets, including the identified products, brands, and video environment.
- **Hybrid Model Approaches:** The system's efficiency of YOLO, the accuracy of Mask R-CNN, the familiarity of ResNet, and the effective use of resources of MobileNet SSD to make an amalgamation model.
- **Context-Aware AI:** Apply contextual look-up to distinguish between similar-appearing objects within the video based on their contextual location, lowering the possibility of errors.

Enhanced Product and Brand Recognition Capabilities

Increasing product detail and brand awareness will ensure consumers have a close-to-perfect match shopping experience. Key developments include:

- **Multi-Label Detection:** This allows the system to "see" multiple products in a single snapshot, including those that might be partially or completely overlapping.
- **Dynamic Object Tracking:** Develop tracking techniques that would help sustain the identification of moving objects within different frames of the video, enabling interactive layers.
- **Brand Sentiment Analysis:** We included opinion mining mechanisms to establish the perception of brands/products from the target audience's perspective, which benefits advertisers.

Improving System Scalability

Maintaining adequate performance becomes an issue as the system user base increases, which must be achieved with incremental costs. Future improvements should focus on:

- **Microservices Architecture:** The development of a modular structure to support the provision of new, scalable microservices, including the modularisation of AI detection and processing and the user interface.
- **Distributed AI Inference:** Federated learning and distributed AI inference can be used to process data in a distributed manner with less load on the central server.
- **Auto-Scaling Cloud Infrastructure:** Use auto-scaling techniques to efficiently scale resources according to real-time requirements and demands.

Increased Integration with Advertisers

Enhanced cooperation with advertisers will increase the organization's revenue and improve advertisement targeting. Future developments include:

- **Real-Time Advertiser Dashboards**: Enhance advertiser dashboards to provide real-time updates on views, CTR (click-through rate), and engagement metrics, enabling instant adjustments for campaign optimization.

- **Advanced Dynamic Ad Insertion (DAI)**: Improve integration with programmatic advertising to access a broader range of shoppable ad templates, allowing for more engaging and contextually relevant ad placements based on product identification.
- **Personalized Ad Targeting**: Refine AI-driven targeting by leveraging viewer data and behavioral insights, ensuring that advertisements align with individual preferences for a more personalized shopping experience.

- **Personalized Ad Targeting:** Enable the system to showcase alternative brands or similar products detected within content, offering viewers multiple purchase options while they watch TV.
- **Seamless & Easy Payment Options**: Integrate frictionless payment solutions that allow users to complete purchases effortlessly, improving the overall shopping experience within video content.
- **Enhanced SSP/DSP Integration:** Strengthen connectivity with Supply-Side Platforms (SSPs) and Demand-Side Platforms (DSPs) to enhance ad inventory accessibility, bidding strategies, and automated ad placements, ensuring a more sophisticated and efficient ad delivery system

References

[1] Suominen R. CONSUMER ATTITUDE TOWARD COMMERCIALIZED ENTERTAINMENT BASED ON VIDEO ON DEMAND.

[2] Statista. (2023). *Global trends in interactive video content and OTT engagement.* Retrieved from https://www.statista.com

[3] Wang Y, Lu Z, Cao P, Chu J, Wang H, Wattenhofer R. How live streaming changes shopping decisions in E-commerce: A study of live streaming commerce. Computer Supported Cooperative Work (CSCW). 2022 Dec;31(4):701-29.

[4] Hendrawan SA, Chatra A, Iman N, Hidayatullah S, Suprayitno D. Digital transformation in MSMEs: Challenges and opportunities in technology management. Jurnal Informasi dan Teknologi. 2024 Jun 20:141-9.

[5] Heller B, Bar-Zeev A. The problems with immersive advertising: in AR/VR, nobody knows you are an ad. Journal of Online Trust and Safety. 2021 Oct 28;1(1).

[6] Gunduzyeli B. Programmatic Advertising in E-Commerce: Trends, Challenges, and Strategic Opportunities. InAvoiding Ad Fraud and Supporting Brand Safety: Programmatic Advertising Solutions 2025 (pp. 145-174). IGI Global Scientific Publishing.

[7] Zhang S. The role of Artificial Intelligence in enhancing online sales and the customer experience. https://urn.fi/URN:NBN:fi:amk-2024052415634

[8] Zahra FT, Bostanci YS, Tokgozlu O, Turkoglu M, Soyturk M. Big Data Streaming and Data Analytics Infrastructure for Efficient AI-Based Processing. InRecent Advances in Microelectronics Reliability: Contributions from the European ECSEL JU project iRel40 2024 Apr 22 (pp. 213-249). Cham: Springer International Publishing.

[9] Farhadi A, Redmon J. Yolov3: An incremental improvement. InComputer vision and pattern recognition 2018 Jun 18 (Vol. 1804, pp. 1-6). Berlin/Heidelberg, Germany: Springer.

[10] Dolby.https://www.theoplayer.com/product/theoads?utm_source=google&utm_medium=cpc&utm_campaign=theo-ads&utm_term=sgai&utm_campaign=THEOads+-+Search&utm_source=adwords&utm_medium=ppc&hsa_acc=9981496222&hsa_cam=21787478348&hsa_grp=172414808070&hsa_ad=716187677953&hsa_src=g&hsa_tgt=kwd-2433036202517&hsa_kw=sgai&hsa_mt=p&hsa_net=adwords&hsa_ver=3&gad_source=1&gclid=CjwKCAiAh6y9BhBREiwApBLHC4n_GbQrzwqRabY6LDVRobuy0CyvrAsJG2hmiR0iYB9tplzatQxEihoC1tMQAvD_BwE

[11] AWS Media Services. (2023). Live Streaming vs. VOD Processing: Cloud-Based AI and Metadata Integration. Retrieved from https://aws.amazon.com

[12] IAB Tech Lab. (2023). *Video Multiple Ad Playlist (VMAP) Implementation Guidelines.* Retrieved from https://www.iabtechlab.com

[13] Ross TY, Dollár GK. Focal loss for dense object detection. Inproceedings of the IEEE conference on computer vision and pattern recognition 2017 Jul (pp. 2980-2988).

[14] Parham JR. Animal detection for photographic censusing. Rensselaer Polytechnic Institute; 2021.

[15] Rawat A, Deb D, Upadhyay J. Recent Trends In Peripheral Security Systems. Springer Singapore, Imprint: Springer; 2021 May 6.

[16] Seth A, Jaiswal A, Garg P, Kanji R. Video Segmentation using Deep Learning.

[17] Rajjak SS, Kureshi AK. Multiple-object detection and segmentation based on deep learning in high-resolution video using Mask-RCNN. International Journal of Pattern Recognition and Artificial Intelligence. 2021 Oct 15;35(13):2150038.

[18] Hussain M, Thaher T, Almourad MB, Mafarja M. Optimizing VGG16 deep learning model with enhanced hunger games search for logo classification. Scientific Reports. 2024 Dec 30;14(1):31759.

[19] Ling J, Chen X, Luo Y. Improving the transferability of adversarial samples with channel switching. Applied Intelligence. 2023 Dec;53(24):30580-92.

[20] Aminiyeganeh K. *Performance Evaluation of the Object Detection Algorithms on Embedded Devices* (Doctoral dissertation, Concordia University).

[21] Canepa A. Application-aware optimization of Artificial Intelligence for deployment on resource constrained devices.

[22] Bochkovskiy A, Wang CY, Liao HY. Yolov4: Optimal speed and accuracy of object detection. arXiv preprint arXiv:2004.10934. 2020 Apr 23.

[23] Okokpujie K, Okokpujie IP, Ayomikun OI, Orimogunje AM, Ogundipe AT. Development of a Web and Mobile Applications-Based Cassava Disease Classification Interface Using Convolutional Neural Network. Mathematical Modelling of Engineering Problems. 2023 Feb 1;10(1).

[24] SCTE (Society of Cable Telecommunications Engineers). (2023). *SCTE-35 Digital Program Insertion Cueing Message Standard.* Retrieved from https://www.scte.org

[25] HLS and DASH Specification Committee. (2022). *Supplemental Enhancement Information (SEI) for Adaptive Streaming Protocols.* Retrieved from https://developer.apple.com

[26] IAB Tech Lab. (2023). *VMAP Implementation and Best Practices for Video Streaming Platforms.* Retrieved from https://www.iabtechlab.com

[27] MPEG Working Group. (2022). *H.264/MPEG-4 AVC and HEVC SEI Metadata Processing for Streaming Video.* Retrieved from https://www.iso.org

[28] Interactive Advertising Bureau (IAB). (2023). *Real-Time Bidding (RTB) Protocol Standards.* Retrieved from https://www.iab.com

[29] Google Ads Team. (2023). *How DSPs leverage AI-powered ad targeting in OTT and programmatic video.* Retrieved from https://ads.google.com

[30] The Trade Desk. (2022). *AI-driven programmatic advertising: Enhancing audience targeting and engagement.* Retrieved from https://www.thetradedesk.com

[31] NAB & Digital Advertising Alliance. (2023). *Supply-Side Platforms (SSP) and Real-Time Advertising in Connected TV and OTT.* Retrieved from https://www.nab.org

BPS Mesh Network Initial Deployment Report

Mark T. Corl
Triveni Digital, Inc.
Princeton, New Jersey, United States
mcorl@trivenidigital.com

Vladimir Anishchenko, Ph.D.
Avateq Corp.
Markham, Ontario, Canada
vlad_a@avateq.com

Tariq Mondal
National Association of Broadcasters
Washington, District of Columbia, United States
tmondal@nab.org

Abstract – The BEIT 2024 paper, ATSC 3.0 Broadcast Positioning System (BPS) Mesh Network [3], provided a description of a notional mesh network intended to manage and monitor a collection of ATSC 3.0 television transmissions intended to provide high precision traceable time. A preliminary network of these Broadcast Positioning System (BPS) transmissions has been constructed in the Baltimore and Washington DC region using two transmitters and a third simulated transmitter in the NAB 1M laboratory. Another BPS transmitter has been deployed in the Denver area to reach the NIST facility in Boulder, Colorado where the signal is being analyzed.

This paper describes the actual systems deployed, how they are operating, and the results of the various experiments being carried out using the first installation of a BPS leader / follower architecture in preparation for a fully operational network deployment.

In addition, the paper describes the initial implementation of a network operating software system which has been developed with the intention of supporting a large, perhaps nation-wide deployment of the BPS Mesh Network.

Background

The BEIT 2024 paper, ATSC 3.0 Broadcast Positioning System (BPS) Mesh Network [3], provided a description of a notional mesh network intended to manage and monitor a collection of ATSC 3.0 television transmissions intended to provide high precision traceable time. This section provides a brief overview of the contents of that paper to supply background information.

Broadcast Positioning System

BPS relies on the preamble of an ATSC 3.0 frame to carry a bootstrap emission timestamp. If this timestamp is accurate, a receiver can synchronize its clock using the ATSC 3.0 signal. Moreover, since the ATSC 3.0 signal can easily carry data because of its IP-based transport, the location of the transmission antenna can be sent with the signal. Armed with the precise bootstrap emission time and the location of the antenna, a receiver at a known location can maintain a very accurate clock.

Previous NAB BEIT conference papers [1] and [3] described prototype systems deployed that achieved accuracy and precision meeting critical infrastructure requirements of the United States. Another BEIT conference paper [2] discussed the potential coverage of a BPS signal at various antenna heights and broadcast robustness. That paper posited that within the continental United States, an antenna mounted on each transmission tower at a height of 50m, would be able to receive as many as 70 transmissions at a broad range of frequencies given the target BPS PLP configuration if all high power transmitters were equipped with the BPS technology.

The new synchronization system along with the potential for receiving the signal from so many neighboring transmitters leads to an opportunity to build an extremely robust time transfer system of multiple transmitters, using multiple disparate frequencies and traceable time sources known as a BPS Mesh Network [3].

Receiver / Synchronizer Overview

The Phase II receiver / synchronizer developed by Avateq Corp. is branded "AVQ1050". It operates in two modes: as a synchronizer, which is used to optimize the local broadcast time transmission or as a receiver to monitor and analyze the BPS signal of neighbor transmitters. The AVQ1050 is based on the Avateq RF front-end with an FPGA-based DSP chain contained within a 1RU box and a second unit for post-processing. Additional development of the FPGA-based DSP core was required to meet the Phase II project objectives. The intention of the AVQ1050 design was:

a) to meet the Phase II project technical requirements in full;
b) to provide more flexibility for development, verification and debugging the synchronization chain and its components at all levels;
c) to introduce a set of standard interfaces for off-the-shelf available instrumental hardware. These were realized as PCIe cards for additional NICs, PTP, I/O, Timing, GPS (if required), etc.; and
d) to deliver a versatile platform suitable for potential applications related to the BPS and not limited to the time synchronization task.

Figure 1 provides a diagram of a notional BPS transmission system that was operated during the proof-of-concept Phase II trials. A description of the various blocks is provided after the figure.

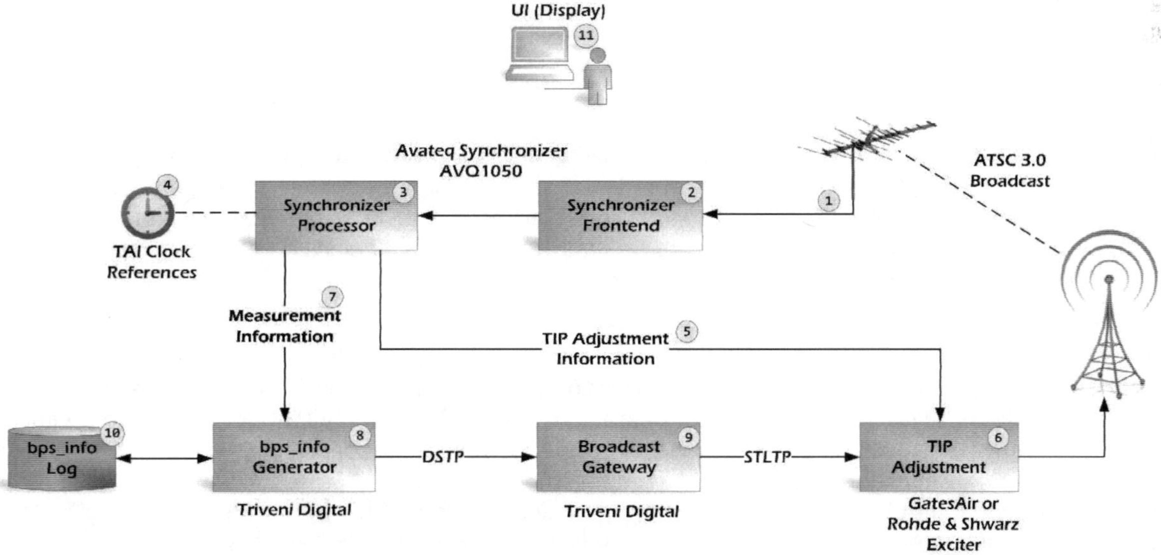

FIGURE 1: BPS TRANSMISSION SYSTEM DIAGRAM.

① The ATSC 3.0 transmission. Compliant transmissions include a time stamp based on the current International Atomic Time (TAI) in the detailed preamble (L1D) according to A/322 [4]. The time represented by the L1D timestamp is referred to as the "Time Information Position" or "TIP" which describes the instant in time at the center of the leading edge of the first sample of the first symbol of the bootstrap when the wave form was emitted from the transmitter antenna.
② The Avateq AVQ1050 ATSC 3.0 BPS Synchronizer Front End. This is a physically separate component that performs the RF signal processing to measure and extract the time signal.
③ The Avateq AVQ1050 ATSC 3.0 BPS Synchronizer Processor is a high-performance computing engine that allows further experimentation to be carried out without constraint. It allows external interfaces through PCIe to high-precision clocks or other devices that may prove useful as the project moves through additional phases in the future.
④ Use of the dedicated processor enables many types of interfaces to reference clocks that were not previously available. Since this system was developed as an experimental platform for the BPS concept, the general-purpose CPU provides more precision clock interface options.
⑤ An adjustment signal is generated by the synchronizer and forwarded back to the exciter to "close the feedback loop". The TIP adjustment interface allows the feedback to be as close as possible to the next emitted frame.
⑥ The TIP adjustment is applied by the exciter to the next available preamble after it receives the TIP adjustment information.
⑦ The Measurement Information is provided to the bps_info Generator function. This information is distinctly different from the information sent to the exciter in step ⑤ above. The information can be a more comprehensive set of data to allow the bps_info structure to carry history and other information helpful to receivers.
⑧ The bps_info Generator uses the latest time differential information along with preset location values to create a bps_info data structure. This data structure is logged and sent to the Broadcast Gateway as a separate data table in a robust PLP.
For Phase II, the bps_info structure was designed as three distinct sections to support different transmission requirements. The timing measurement was separated from the transmitter details and the timing source details to allow higher frequency, dynamic information to be distributed separately from more static data. [3]
⑨ The Broadcast Gateway can operate without knowledge that it is part of the BPS synchronization loop; however, a time adjustment is still available as a lower performance backup.
⑩ The bps_info log function is part of the bps_info Generator. It collects received bps_info structures into a log for post-processing.
⑪ A user interface (UI) is provided via a web interface (HTTP) to allow logging information to be displayed as well as to allow the system to be controlled. Control connections are not shown to reduce diagram complexity. Of particular interest will be a user interface that provides a graph of the time differential value over time to verify that the system is operating correctly. An example of this graphical display is shown in Figure 2.

System Performance

The proof-of-concept developed by the partner companies demonstrated that a feedback control loop can increase the accuracy of the transmitted timestamps of an existing ATSC 3.0 transmission chain. While the Phase I synchronization provided an instantaneous time delay of the stabilized system at less than 300 ns, the Phase II system reduced that number to typically under 10 ns. It was learned that the different exciters had different time response characteristics, meaning they had different transfer functions. It was discovered that the optimal PI controller settings were different in each case.

The Phase II systems included the previous broadcast gateway software used in Phase I but also introduced new firmware into the exciter to allow the synchronizer to control the emitted time directly at its insertion point. The higher performance of the synchronizer / receiver combined with the tighter control loop resulted in an order-of-magnitude improvement in system performance.

The solution demonstrated remains 100% compliant with the ATSC 3.0 standard as was the Phase I system. No change in the standard was necessary for this phase of the BPS project. The solution was demonstrated with transmission equipment from multiple ATSC 3.0 vendors, reinforcing the standard compliance.

Synchronizer Performance

The yellow and blue curves exemplified in Figure 2 correspond to raw measurements of the Bootstrap arrival delay and the filtered and PID-processed TIP adjustment, respectively, provided by the Phase II synchronizer. Note that the scale on the y axis of the graph ranges between ± 0.004 µsec, that is, 4 ns.

It should be noted that the blue line in the graph in Figure 2 shows the variation after PID filtering. This value typically remains below 1 ns.

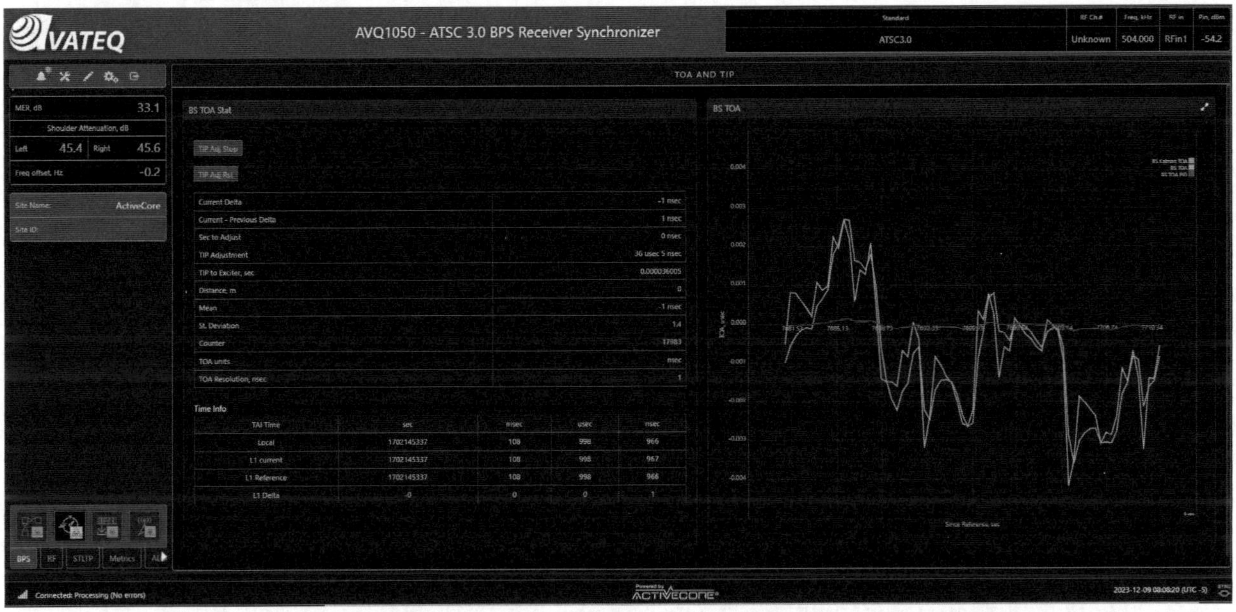

FIGURE 2: EXAMPLE PHASE II SYNCHRONIZER BPS TIME ARRIVAL GRAPH.

Transmitter "Node" Description

In a nationwide deployment of the BPS network, it is expected that the functionality at each node, that is, each transmitter, would be essentially the same with some "leader" transmitters having time traceable to TAI. It is also expected that by adding additional time-keeping equipment, transmitters can move from "followers" to "leaders" and vice versa. This document assumes that all transmitters within receiving range are on separate frequencies, that is, form a multiple frequency network (MFN).

Figure 3 provides a diagram of an exemplary BPS network using four transmitters. The detailed diagram shown associated with one of the transmitters would apply to all the transmitter nodes in the BPS network. In this case, the node would be designated as a "Leader" since it would have a source of traceable time. Figure 3 provides a logical diagram of the systems and functions developed. The numbered paragraphs that follow the diagram correspond to the callouts in the diagram.

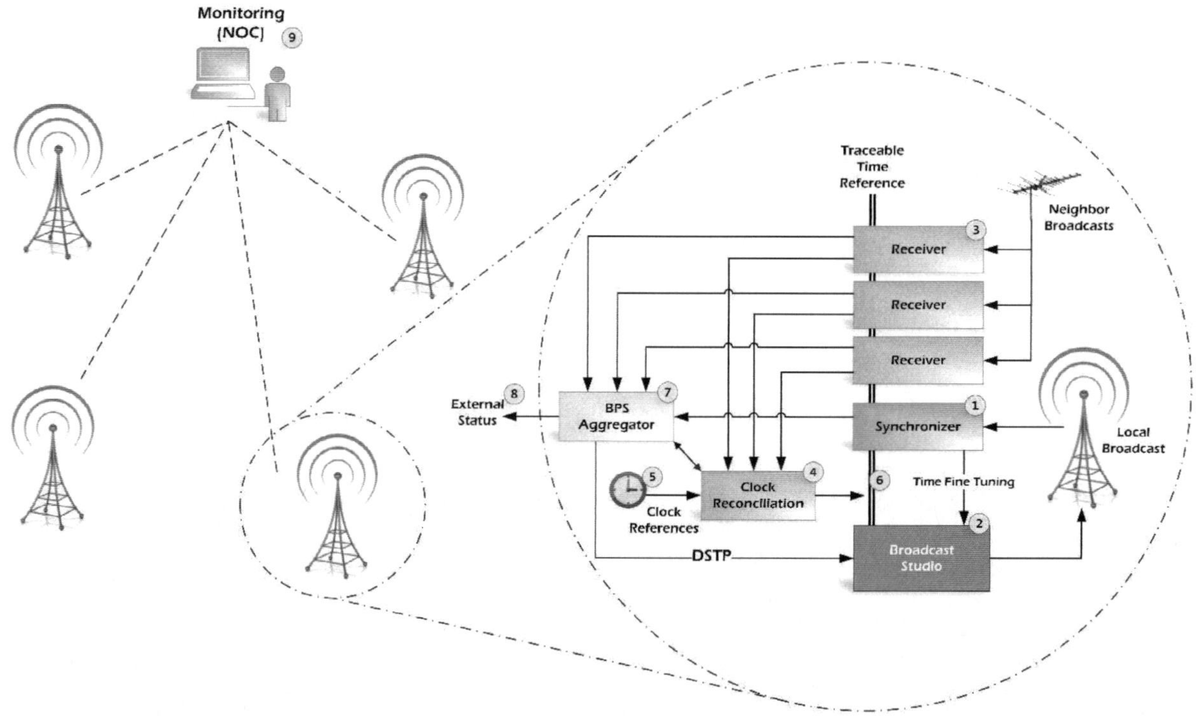

FIGURE 3: BPS TRANSMISSION NODE DIAGRAM.

① This block represents the Avateq AVQ1050 ATSC 3.0 BPS Receiver and Synchronizer described in previous sections. This device, configured to operate as a Synchronizer, receives the local broadcast, measures the bootstrap emission time with the time signaled in the L1D preamble and reports differences. The time difference is passed to the Broadcast Studio air chain ②, specifically, the exciter modified to accept the fine-tuning protocol provided by the synchronizer. Both GatesAir Maxiva XTE and Rohde & Schwarz SDE900/TCE901 exciters provide support for this protocol. All information about the basic processing of the time information is forwarded to the BPS Aggregator ⑦.

② The Broadcast Studio represents an ATSC 3.0 air chain. Internal components of the air chain of primary interest to this document are the Broadcast Gateway and the exciter. The BPS Aggregator function ⑦ provides a multicast or DSTP stream containing bps_info data structure that is formed into a dedicated PLP by the gateway. The output of the gateway is fed, via STLTP, to the exciter which generates the ATSC 3.0 wave form. In addition, the exciter receives fine-tuning information from the Synchronizer to make small adjustments to the emission time of each frame to more accurately generate the time carried in the L1D preamble of each frame.

③ The Avateq AVQ1050 ATSC 3.0 BPS Receiver and Synchronizer can also be used to obtain timing information from neighboring transmitters. In this case, the device is configured to operate as a "Receiver". For this example, three separate devices are required to receive the broadcast from three neighbor transmitters. The number of receivers deployed at any transmitter is limited only by cost since the number of transmissions visible to an ATSC 3.0 transmission tower are likely in the dozens once ATSC 3.0 is fully deployed. The robustness and resiliency of the network increases every time a receiver is added. Like the local synchronizer, these receivers will send all timing information including extracted bps_info to the BPS Aggregator ⑦ function for processing. The clock signals emitted by the receivers are 1PPS and 10MHz reference signals, and date/time info in IRIG-B126 (IRIG-B AM) format. This information is provided to the Clock Reconciliation function ④ for use in determining the best traceable time source.

④ The Clock Reconciliation function will be provided by multiple vendors including Safran, Microchip, and Adtran. This function takes input from each receiver and one or more clock references using them as Input References.

⑤ The Clock Reconciliation function ④ can use multiple clock references to determine the best time reference. The clock icon represents one local clock reference and is backed up by the Input References that can be configured on a priority basis. Additionally, different holdover oscillator options are available.

⑥ The double line represents station synchronized time. This time is sourced from the Clock Reconciliation function ④ and used by all devices as a reference traceable time source.

⑦ The BPS Aggregator function is an extension of the bps_info generator developed in previous phases. It receives information regarding the bps_info from each receiver, the synchronizer and the clock reconciliation system and combines them into a single data stream. There are two types of data reported by the receivers: detailed time information, specifically how each transmitter is varying from the correct time, and static information about each transmitter location and type. The combined bps_info stream along with the detailed timing information are merged into a single multicast IP stream fed into the Broadcast Gateway. This forms the complete data source of a dedicated BPS PLP. This data requires very little bandwidth so the PLP can use a very robust modulation / coding (ModCod) setting.

⑧ In addition to providing bps_info streams to the broadcast gateway, the BPS Aggregator function ⑦ also provides status via an external network connection. This is intended to be accumulated by a central management system which would be used to monitor the entire BPS network operation ⑨. Each device in the diagram also provides a local, web-based command, control, and status user interface as is typically provided by each of these devices today which the NOC can use to configure and control each discrete device if desired if some aberration is detected.

⑨ Ultimately, the entire network will require one or more centralized "Network Operations Center(s)" (NOCs) to monitor the overall behavior of the BPS network. The NOC would identify outages and issues with the various devices across the network. There would likely be multiple NOCs separated geographically perhaps monitoring selected regions of BPS systems. Further, the NOC could manage the various devices in the BPS system by accessing their command-and-control websites. This would likely be done over a dedicated VPN, but these details can be determined once the system becomes operational. For a live market trial, an example interface can be provided to demonstrate the basic NOC functionality.

2024 Development and Implementation

The AVQ 1050 Synchronizer / Receiver exceeded all target performance requirements of Phase II development so that system could be deployed as the core synchronization device in a BPS mesh network, as described in the 2024 BEIT paper "ATSC 3.0 Broadcast Positioning System (BPS) Mesh Network" [3]. The synchronizer and the TIP adjustment protocol connecting it to the local exciter allowed ATSC 3.0 transmitters to be stabilized to the accuracy and precision described in the Synchronizer Performance section above. This synchronization process has become known as the "Local Loop". Since there are currently no receivers aside from the AVQ1050 relying on the bps_info to determine the location of the stabilized ATSC 3.0 transmitters, the Local Loop alone is sufficient to transfer traceable time. This has been demonstrated using the KWGN transmitter in the Denver area to transfer time to the NIST facilities in Boulder and their WWVB radio time transmitter in Fort Collins.

While precise broadcast time is the underpinning of the BPS concept, the bps_info data transmission to support simple BPS receivers and managing the overall network are key features as well. The development efforts over the last year have been focused on enabling that functionality to ultimately support the deployment of a large-scale network comprising hundreds of BPS transmitters. To accomplish this, the BPS Aggregator software needed to be expanded significantly, and a network of these aggregators needed to be developed to allow control and management system concepts to be explored. In addition, the AVQ1050 required extensions and modifications to accommodate the various features needed as the network is being developed.

BPS Aggregator

The initial Phase I and Phase II bps_info generation software took information from the Avateq AVQ1050 and its precursor system and formed the bps_info data structures described in [3]. It also read information from the Safran SecureSync 2400 clock reconciliation system to determine which reference clock source was currently active. This clock source information is used to create a portion of the bps_info data structure. The generation software also logged the information as it was received from the various devices in the local loop.

To enable the functionality envisioned in the BPS Mesh network, the bps_info generation software was extended to enable interfaces to the AVQ1050 operating as a receiver to monitor neighbor transmissions. The information supplied by the AVQ1050 in Receiver mode is slightly different compared to the data supplied by Synchronizer mode. One of the primary differences is the bps_info forwarded from the neighbor transmission. The BPS Aggregator allows selection of the various fragments found in the bps_info data to be forwarded on from the local system. This is expected to be valuable to future receivers since the reception characteristics of the AVQ1050 measurement of the neighbor can be compared to the actual signal if both are received.

The primary function of receiving data from the AVQ1050 receiver is to monitor the performance of the neighbor transmitter from a BPS standpoint. As the mesh network grows, multiple monitoring sites for each transmitter will provide confirmation of the transmission at various points throughout the network, assuming receivers are dispersed. Broad dispersion is highly likely since the preamble and BPS PLP will be receivable much farther from the transmitter than is normally the case because of the highly robust modulation configuration well beyond the normal DMA constraints. The BPS Aggregator was developed to monitor both physical communications with the AVQ1050 as well as the next level functions including reception of the bps_info and validation that the time meets configured criteria. Simple graphs are provided that show when the time of arrival of the frames (as depicted in Figure 2) does not exceed configured limits. The BPS Aggregator logs all information from the connected AVQ1050s whether operating in a Synchronizer or Receiver mode.

Figure 4 provides a snapshot of the user interface of the BPS Aggregator operating in the NAB 1M Washington, D.C. laboratory. This user interface was intentionally developed to correspond to the BPS transmission node diagram shown in Figure 3 above. The user interface is a web site that can be accessed locally or through the BPS VPN as described in the BPS Network section below. The user interface diagram is dynamic, changing as status changes within the monitored network node. For example, the "spark line" above the synchronizer is a live graph of the time-of-arrival of each frame reflecting the information shown in the graph in Figure 2. Data from the AVQ1050 is used as the source of this graph. The lines between the elements in the diagram are active and indicate if communication with a particular element is lost or not performing correctly. Each element also contains a redirect icon which is a link to the user interface of that device. For example, clicking on the Synchronizer redirect launches a separate browser tab containing the interface shown in Figure 2. Using this user interface, a user can conveniently see the status of the local BPS functions on one display and gain access to component user interfaces for troubleshooting purposes.

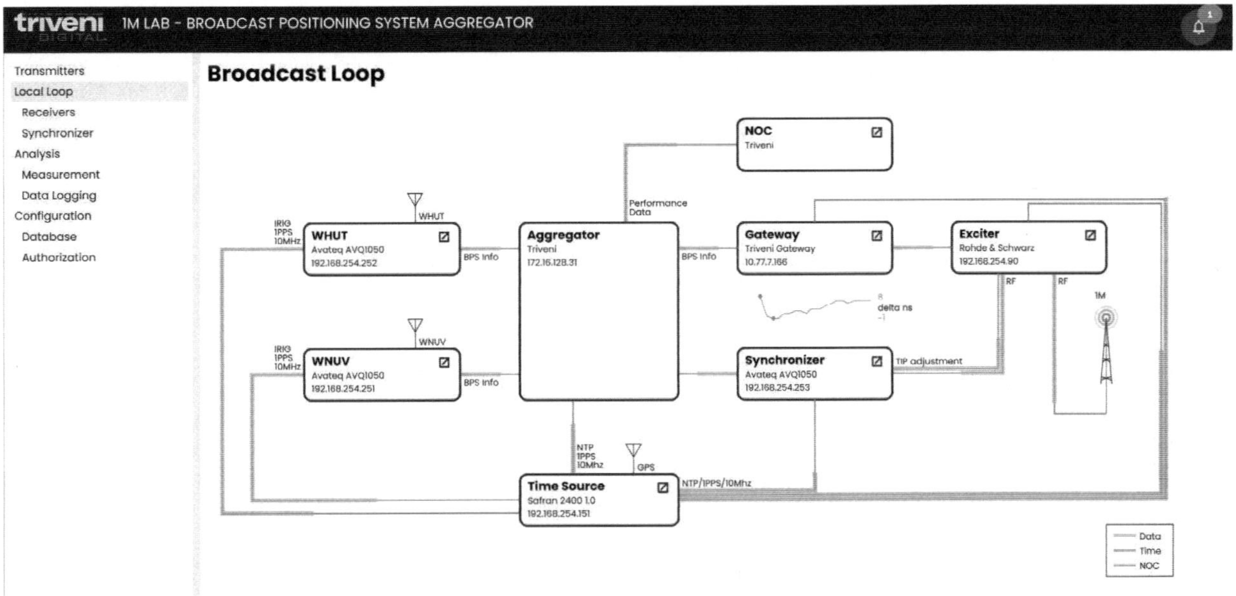

FIGURE 4: BPS AGGREGATOR BROADCAST LOOP USER INTERFACE.

On the left side of the user interface shown in Figure 4 are a list of other pages that the user can access to accomplish particular tasks and see detailed information about monitored functions. For example, the Receivers page, shown in Figure 5, allows the user to add or remove connections to receivers and see detailed information about their connection. Note the panel on the right that shows the BPS Info fragments being received. These are updated when received, typically every second. The user can select which fragments are forwarded to the local broadcast by using the checkbox associated with each fragment. In this case, the fragments from WHUT are being forwarded to the local test broadcast within the 1M lab.

In addition, receivers that cannot be reached are shown with error indicators as is the case with the receiver labeled "Local 1M Receiver" in Figure 5. For this example, the receiver had not been enabled but had been added to the BPS Aggregator to test the failure scenario. The local receiver had also not yet been added to the local broadcast loop diagram. However, the notification that there is a problem can be seen on both Broadcast Loop and Receivers pages as the alarm condition in the upper right corner.

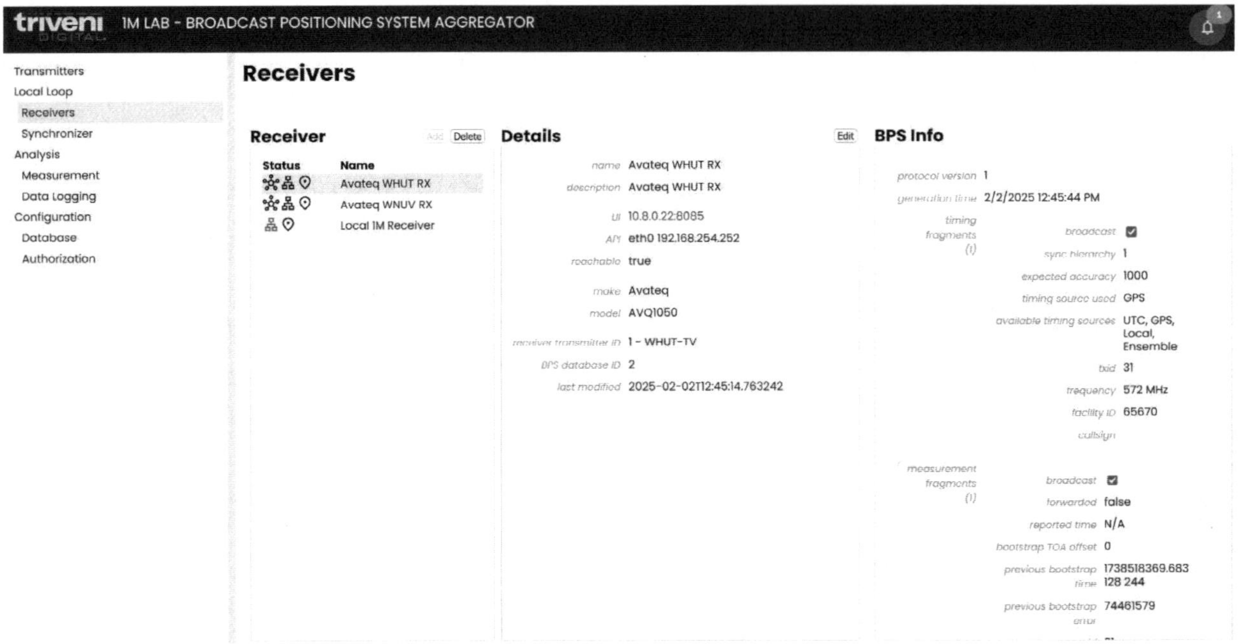

FIGURE 5: BPS AGGREGATOR RECEIVERS USER INTERFACE.

Another key feature of the BPS Aggregator is the ability to log information for export. This capability is found under the "Analysis" section of the menu in the left panel of the user interface. The Measurement page in Figure 6 provides a comparison view of the time of arrival graphs from the local synchronizer and the receivers. This allows comparison between the performance of the local transmission system and the BPS transmissions received with respect to the local reference time.

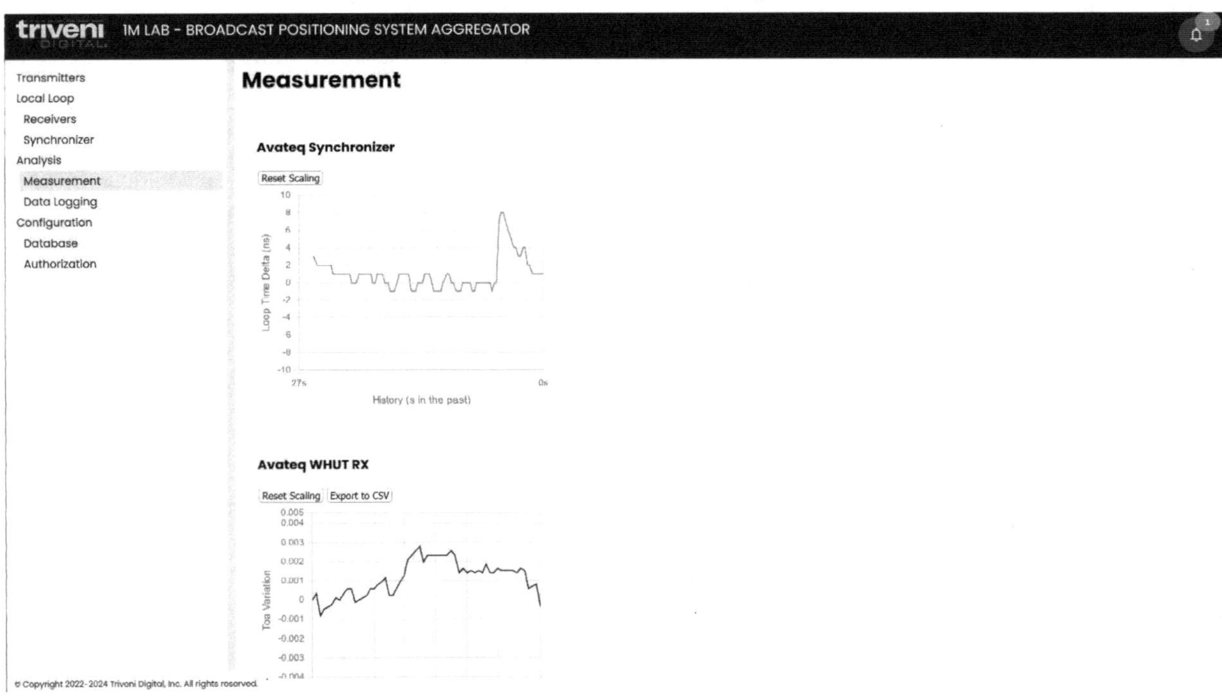

FIGURE 6: BPS AGGREGATOR MEASUREMENT USER INTERFACE.

The data logging page shown in Figure 7 provides a means for a user to export selected data logs for specific times of day. The data is exported as a CSV file that can then be imported into external analysis tools.

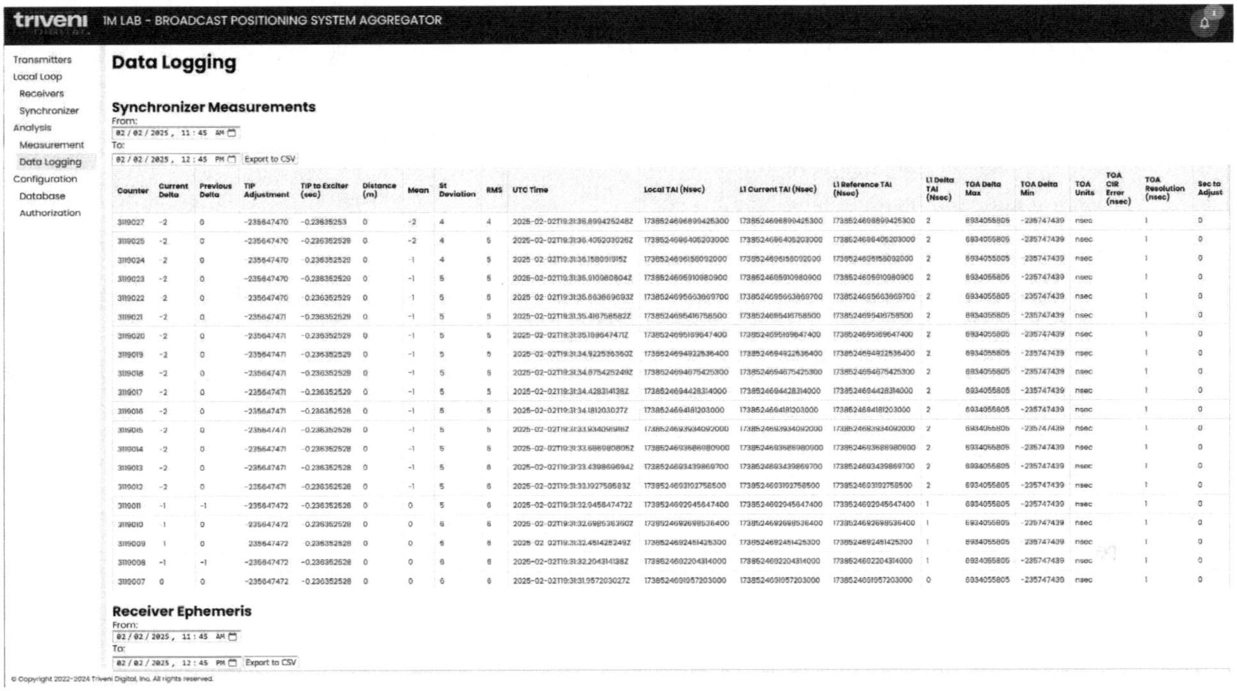

Counter	Current Delta	Previous Delta	TIP Adjustment	TIP to Exciter (sec)	Distance (m)	Mean	St Deviation	RMS	UTC Time	Local TAI (Nsec)	L1 Current TAI (Nsec)	L1 Reference TAI (Nsec)	L1 Delta TAI (Nsec)	TOA Delta Max	TOA Delta Min	TOA Units	TOA CIR Error (nsec)	TOA Resolution (nsec)	Sec to Adjust
3119027	-2	0	-235647470	-0.23635253	0	-2	4	4	2025-02-02T19:31:36.899425248Z	1738524696899425300	1738524696899425300	1738524696899425300	2	6934055805	-235747439	nsec		1	0
3119025	-2	0	-235647470	-0.236352529	0	-2	4	5	2025-02-02T19:31:36.405203026Z	1738524696405203000	1738524696405203000	1738524696405203000	2	6934055805	-235747439	nsec		1	0
3119024	-2	0	-235647470	-0.236352529	0	-1	4	5	2025-02-02T19:31:36.158091915Z	1738524696158092000	1738524696158092000	1738524696158092000	2	6934055805	-235747439	nsec		1	0
3119023	-2	0	-235647470	-0.236352529	0	-1	5	5	2025-02-02T19:31:35.910980804Z	1738524695910980900	1738524695910980900	1738524695910980900	2	6934055805	-235747439	nsec		1	0
3119022	-2	0	-235647470	-0.236352529	0	-1	5	5	2025-02-02T19:31:35.663869693Z	1738524695663869700	1738524695663869700	1738524695663869700	2	6934055805	-235747439	nsec		1	0
3119021	-2	0	-235647471	-0.236352529	0	-1	5	5	2025-02-02T19:31:35.416758582Z	1738524695416758500	1738524695416758500	1738524695416758500	2	6934055805	-235747439	nsec		1	0
3119020	-2	0	-235647471	-0.236352529	0	-1	5	5	2025-02-02T19:31:35.169647471Z	1738524695169647400	1738524695169647400	1738524695169647400	2	6934055805	-235747439	nsec		1	0
3119019	-2	0	-235647471	-0.236352529	0	-1	5	5	2025-02-02T19:31:34.922536360Z	1738524694922536400	1738524694922536400	1738524694922536400	2	6934055805	-235747439	nsec		1	0
3119018	-2	0	-235647471	-0.236352529	0	-1	5	5	2025-02-02T19:31:34.675425249Z	1738524694675425300	1738524694675425300	1738524694675425300	2	6934055805	-235747439	nsec		1	0
3119017	-2	0	-235647471	-0.236352529	0	-1	5	5	2025-02-02T19:31:34.428314138Z	1738524694428314000	1738524694428314000	1738524694428314000	2	6934055805	-235747439	nsec		1	0
3119016	-2	0	-235647471	-0.236352528	0	-1	5	5	2025-02-02T19:31:34.181203027Z	1738524694181203000	1738524694181203000	1738524694181203000	2	6934055805	-235747439	nsec		1	0
3119015	-2	0	-235647471	-0.236352528	0	-1	5	5	2025-02-02T19:31:33.934091916Z	1738524693934092000	1738524693934092000	1738524693934092000	2	6934055805	-235747439	nsec		1	0
3119014	-2	0	-235647471	-0.236352528	0	-1	5	5	2025-02-02T19:31:33.686980805Z	1738524693686980900	1738524693686980900	1738524693686980900	2	6934055805	-235747439	nsec		1	0
3119013	-2	0	-235647471	-0.236352528	0	-1	5	6	2025-02-02T19:31:33.439869694Z	1738524693439869700	1738524693439869700	1738524693439869700	2	6934055805	-235747439	nsec		1	0
3119012	-2	0	-235647471	-0.236352528	0	-1	5	6	2025-02-02T19:31:33.192758583Z	1738524693192758500	1738524693192758500	1738524693192758500	2	6934055805	-235747439	nsec		1	0
3119011	-1	-1	-235647472	-0.236352528	0	0	5	6	2025-02-02T19:31:32.945647472Z	1738524692945647400	1738524692945647400	1738524692945647400	1	6934055805	-235747439	nsec		1	0
3119010	-1	0	-235647472	-0.236352528	0	0	6	6	2025-02-02T19:31:32.698536360Z	1738524692698536400	1738524692698536400	1738524692698536400	1	6934055805	-235747439	nsec		1	0
3119009	1	0	235647472	0.236352528	0	0	6	6	2025-02-02T19:31:32.451425249Z	1738524692451425300	1738524692451425300	1738524692451425300	1	6934055805	235747439	nsec		1	0
3119008	-1	-1	-235647472	-0.236352528	0	0	6	6	2025-02-02T19:31:32.204314138Z	1738524692204314000	1738524692204314000	1738524692204314000	1	6934055805	-235747439	nsec		1	0
3119007	0	0	-235647472	-0.236352528	0	0	6	6	2025-02-02T19:31:31.957203027Z	1738524691957203000	1738524691957203000	1738524691957203000	0	6934055805	-235747439	nsec		1	0

FIGURE 7: BPS AGGREGATOR DATA LOGGING USER INTERFACE.

Another key feature of the BPS Aggregator is to accumulate and filter performance data on how the local system and its neighbors are operating. This performance data is then forwarded to a module referred to as a "performance data collector" or PDC. This functionality is described in more detail in the BPS Network section below.

Since the BPS technology is still undergoing significant efficacy testing and science, the details of how a local transmission system will operate over time are still being explored. A significant amount of experience with the behavior of the monitored systems has been gathered over the last year but as more BPS transmissions are enabled, more data on potential system failures and failure modes will be accumulated. The BPS Aggregator is architected in a way that allows straightforward expansion and monitoring extensions. This flexibility will be necessary when the BPS network expands and becomes fully operational.

Receiver / Synchronizer Improvements

Based on experimental results obtained during Phase I and Phase II tests, initial implementation of the AVQ1050 Receiver and Synchronizer has been significantly improved thanks to additionally introduced metrics, enhanced accuracy and an integrated set of tools for the BPS signal quality analysis and troubleshooting. A newly introduced BPS Ephemeris© data structure provides real-time estimation of the BPS signal reception and allows integrating the Receiver with the BPS Aggregator.

Figure 8 below presents one channel of the enhanced AVQ1050 BPS Receiver multi-channel architecture. The following numbered paragraphs correspond to callouts in the architectural blocks and provide more details on the supporting functionality.

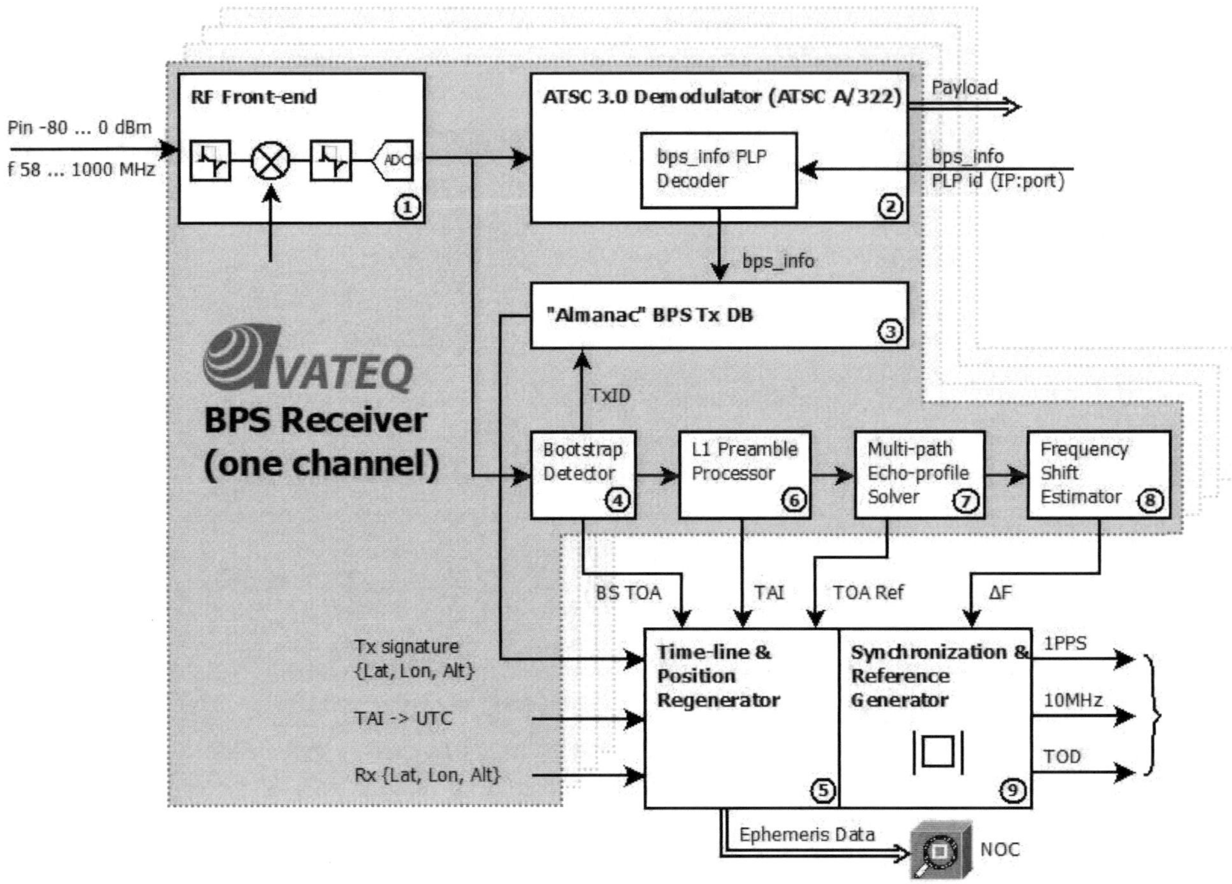

FIGURE 8: AVQ1050 MULTICHANNEL BPS RECEIVER FUNCTIONAL DIAGRAM.

① The AVQ1050 BPS Receiver's RF front-end provides signal amplification, filtering, and sampling. It supports RF signal reception in the frequency range of 50 to 1000MHz with signal levels from -80 to 0dBm.

② The signal is demodulated according to the ATSC A/322 Physical Layer Protocol [4], and the payload, including the BPS-specific "bps_info," is extracted.

③ The Transmitter Identification (TxID) can be obtained from the signal by the Bootstrap Detector or from a global BPS ATSC 3.0 Transmitter Database, similar to the GPS Almanac. Based on the TxID and data from the bps_info, a Transmitter Signature can be defined which includes geolocation and other characteristics to assist in accurate calculation of the time of signal arrival and the receiver's position.

④ The Accuracy of Bootstrap Time-Of-Arrival (BS TOA) detection directly impacts the signal propagation delay calculation. As the signal-delivered TAI timestamp has a nanosecond resolution, detection of the BS TOA with accuracy comparable to the TAI timestamp resolution is critical for the BPS system performance.

The implemented approach to the BS TOA estimation has been extensively tested and verified over different levels of the signal SNR, modulation and coding schemes creating a basis for the further development of the signal timing information restoration. To improve the BS TOA estimation accuracy for the signals with low SNR, an optimization technique based on the signal statistical characterization over time has been designed and integrated into the algorithm. As the experimental results indicate the design provides the BS TOA estimation accuracy within the units of single-digit nanoseconds.

⑤ The Transmitter Signature is used by the Timeline & Position Regenerator as an initial time point for restoring a whole timeline at the Receiver. The timeline is used for tuning and maintaining the receiver internal clock.

⑥ The Receiver internal clock is synchronized with the TAI timestamp extracted from the ATSC 3.0 signal by the L1 Preamble Processor.

⑦ Another critical characteristic of the Receiver performance is its ability to provide accurate timing information in a multipath operational environment. The multipath propagation environment is a well-known and "hard to fight" real-life phenomena causing multiple signal peaks to appear at the receiver input. Each signal peak (or the main signal echo) can be individually characterized by its time-of-arrival and amplitude. It is critical to detect the earliest peak and use it as a reference for the estimation of the signal propagation delay.

Multiple peaks which are dispersed in a short time interval with small relative delays, i.e. the peaks arriving at the receiver input with small relative delays in their TOAs make the reference peak selection a non-trivial task – several echoes can be seen as a single peak.

The Multipath Echo-profile Solver core is based on an iterative technique for the TOA of the earliest multipath component selection as a time reference for ATSC 3.0-based BPS signals. The technique is based on Channel Impulse Response (CIR) signal processing as the primary source for presentation of a dispersed-in-time received signal. The designed processing provides a signal peak arrival time resolution in a range of 1 to 5 nanoseconds.

Figure 9 provides an example of multiple echoes and automatic selection of a reference peak for the specific Transmitter ID.

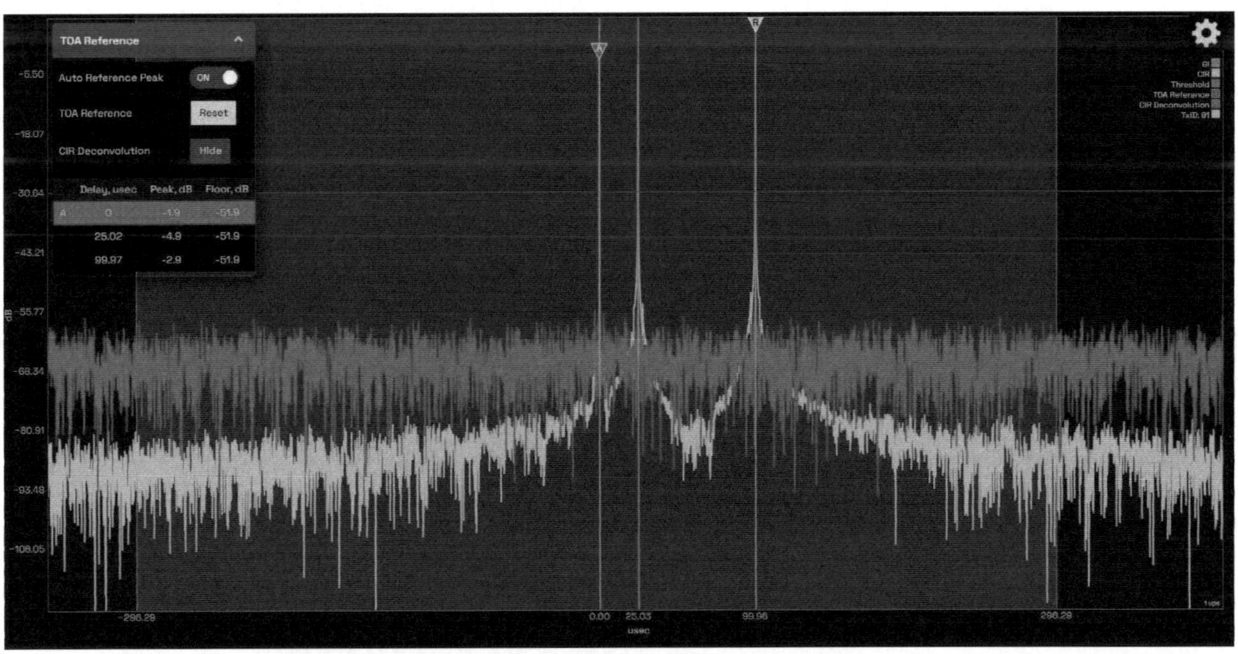

FIGURE 9: AVQ1050 MULTIPATH REFERENCE PEAK SELECTION.

⑧ Frequency Shift Estimator outputs the signal frequency offset for fine-tuning the Synch and Reference Generator core.

⑨ The Synch and Reference Generator is a source of 1PPS and 10MHz references, which are standard signals used for applications and equipment requiring time and frequency synchronization.

The next steps of further improving the Receiver performance include experimental research on the vulnerability of BPS signals to spoofing and jamming, developing methodologies and processing techniques for detection and mitigation of such attacks, and increasing the accuracy and reliability of timing information, especially under dynamic reception conditions.

BPS Network

The BPS network is envisioned to provide a centralized mechanism of monitoring and managing a large number of deployed BPS transmission systems. At the highest level, this is conceptualized in Figure 3 where each transmission node is connected to a centralized, cloud-based Network Operating Center (NOC). This concept requires each transmission node, specifically, the BPS Aggregator in each node, to be connected, in some fashion, with the network management system.

To accomplish this, a BPS virtual private network (VPN) has been deployed. BPS Aggregators connected to this system can deliver performance data to the central management system and can be controlled through that system, if allowed. However, since the BPS local loop involves equipment directly producing the transmission, connecting to an external network, even a secure VPN, is not allowed by many broadcasters. Thus, it has become clear that many modalities of communication from the BPS Aggregator into the BPS network will need to be developed.

Another feature of the mesh network is that each transmission may be monitored not only by the local synchronizer with the local loop but by neighbors, and perhaps multiple neighbors. All this information would be reported to the central system and would need to be presented to the operator monitoring the network in a clear way that could easily identify anomalies and problems.

Current Deployment

The initial deployment of a BPS network was undertaken in 2024. This network involved three transmissions and two laboratories along with a cloud-based server. Figure 10 provides a current connection diagram of these deployed systems across the United States. At present, only the 1M and Triveni Digital labs along with WHUT at Howard University are connected directly to the BPS VPN. Though not currently connected, the KWGN BPS Aggregator will soon be sending performance data through an HTTPS connection to the Cloud Node which is operating as the network center. The numbers within the diagram are described in paragraphs following Figure 10.

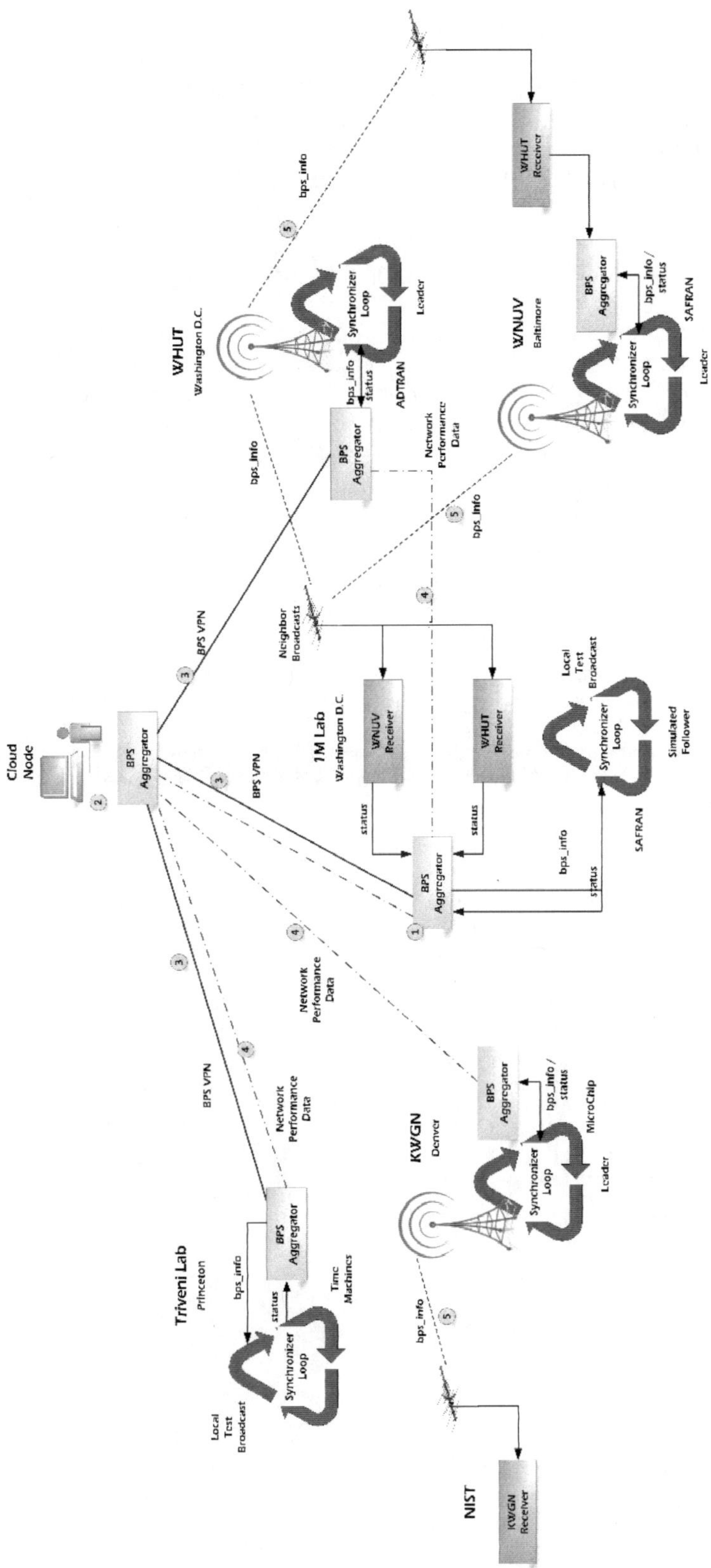

FIGURE 10: BPS NETWORK ACTIVE TEST DEPLOYMENT.

① The BPS Aggregator exists at every node within the network performing multiple functions, sometimes simultaneously.

② The Cloud Node is a single BPS Aggregator configured to operate solely as a performance data collector. It receives data from the 1M Lab and the Triveni Lab over the BPS VPN. It receives data from WHUT through the 1M Lab which is also operating as a PDC. It receives data from KWGN through a one-way HTTPS connection through their firewall. There is no communication allowed back to the KWGN BPS Aggregator. The user interface of the cloud node does not have a local loop or receivers but instead has only transmitters and network monitoring user interface pages. See Figure 11 for an example of the Transmitters user interface page on the Cloud Node.

③ The BPS VPN provides complete access to the various BPS functions within transmission systems. The user can access the BPS Aggregator interface, the interfaces of the Synchronizer and Receivers, and other equipment if enabled. Note that the interfaces of the other equipment are only available if VPN tunneling has been configured on the BPS Aggregator system. This is not required for the system to operate since the BPS Aggregator can communicate with those systems via local networking.

④ The network performance data can be sent to any PDC accessible within the network. In the current deployment, most systems are sending their data directly to the Cloud Node ②. However, the BPS Aggregator at WHUT is sending its performance data to the BPS Aggregator in the 1M Lab which, in turn, is forwarding it on to the cloud node. This confirms that the system can operate in a hierarchy of nodes.

⑤ The bps_info signal as described in [3]. Note that bps_info is intended to be consumed by all BPS receivers deployed while the performance data is only relevant to the BPS network operation.

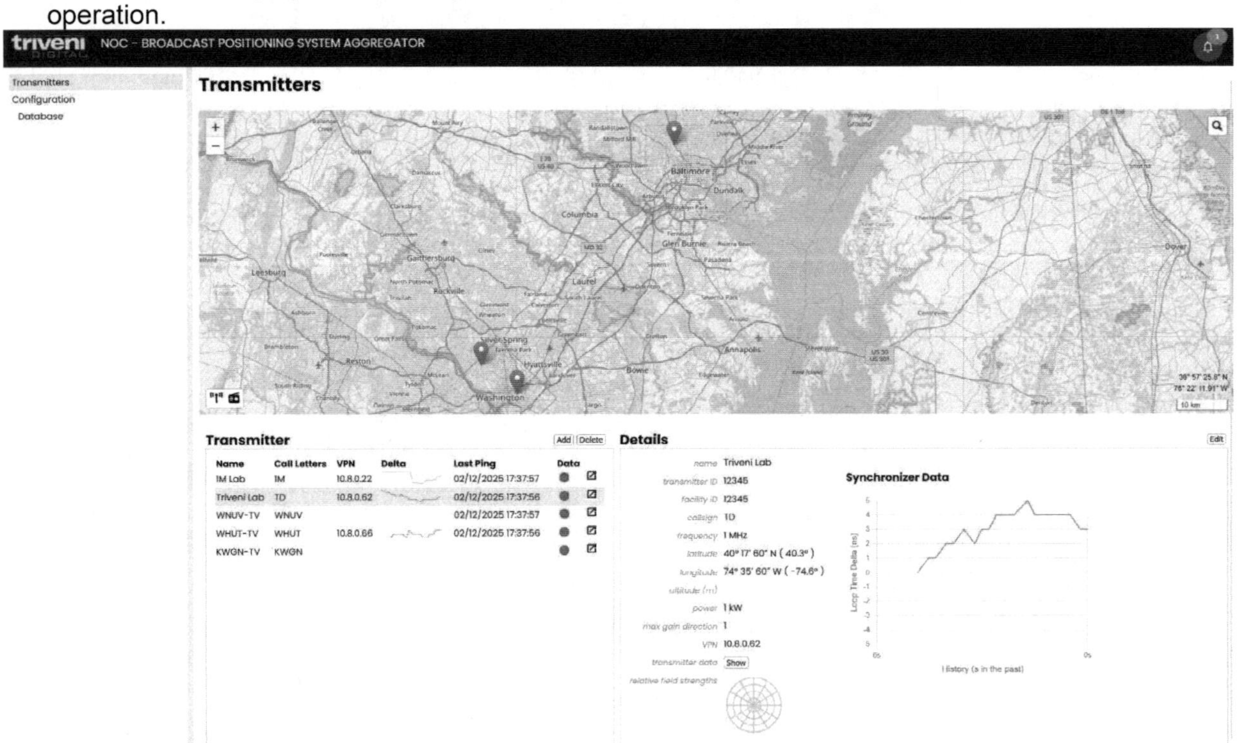

FIGURE 11: BPS AGGREGATOR TRANSMITTERS USER INTERFACE.

Future Development

Because of the limited number of BPS transmissions on air at the current time, there is a limited need for a fully operational network management system. This provides an opportunity to experiment and discover new ways of communicating with the BPS Aggregator and other BPS equipment in anticipation of scaling to an operational network. There are many different network topologies deployed by broadcasters and different nodes may need to be deployed to integrate with those topologies. For example, it may be necessary to establish an intermediate network node within a DMZ that can communicate with the BPS network while also communicating with the BPS equipment in the local transmitter air chain.

The BPS Aggregator will also need to be upgraded to enable certificate management and signing of the bps_info data structure to make it more secure. The bps_info structure will need to be modified slightly to allow a signature to be added. In addition, a notification mechanism will need to be created that will allow the systems to operate in an unattended fashion and notify operators when error conditions occur. Currently, only obvious faults are detected such as device communication failure, channel off-air, BS TOA exceeding thresholds, and missing bps_info. However, as more operational experience is gathered, it is expected that more failure modes will be discovered. It is anticipated that notifications will be either email, SMS messages or even SNMP traps.

Finally, it is expected that additional user interface pages will need to be developed as more transmitters are added to the network. One can envision a display similar to Figure 10 that indicates performance of individual nodes and the relationship of each transmitter node to the network. Also, the user interface pages as currently constructed will not scale well if hundreds or thousands of transmitters are added to the network. New methods of visualizing many transmitters will need to be developed. These will likely be driven by failure modes since only misbehaving systems will demand operator attention.

References

[1] Corl, M., et al, "BPS ATSC 3.0 Broadcast Emission Time Stabilization System Proof-of-concept," Proceedings of the 2023 NAB Broadcast Engineering and Information Technology (BEIT) Conference.

[2] Diamond, P., et al, "Delivering Traceable Reference Time for ATSC 3.0-based Broadcast Positioning System (BPS)," Proceedings of the 2023 NAB Broadcast Engineering and Information Technology (BEIT) Conference.

[3] Corl, M., et al, "ATSC 3.0 Broadcast Positioning System (BPS) Mesh Network," Proceedings of the 2024 NAB Broadcast Engineering and Information Technology (BEIT) Conference. https://nabpilot.org/product/atsc-3-0-broadcast-positioning-system-bps-mesh-network/

[4] ATSC: "ATSC Standard: Physical Layer Protocol," Doc. A/322:2022-11, Advanced Television Systems Committee, Washington, DC, 14 November 2022.

Field Test of ATSC 3.0/BPS Precise Time Distribution

Jeff A. Sherman, David A. Howe
Time and Frequency Division, National Institute of Standards and Technology (NIST)
Boulder, Colorado, United States
jeff.sherman@nist.gov, david.howe@nist.gov

Abstract – The Broadcast Positioning System (BPS™) is a protocol for high-resolution time transfer between a reference clock at a ATSC 3.0 transmitter and a BPS receiver's disciplined-clock output. Time transfer is a prerequisite for (and useful by-product of) positioning/navigation systems such as Global Navigation Satellite Systems (GNSS); for example, the Global Positioning System (GPS). In principle, BPS may address potential vulnerabilities in critical applications with GNSS dependence, mostly due to relatively weak GNSS signal levels at Earth's surface. In 2024, BPS was added to the ATSC 3.0 transmission of the station KWGN in the Denver, Colorado metropolitan area. To measure BPS time transfer stability, BPS receivers were installed at two NIST campuses (the furthest: 106 km away) and compared against independent local atomic clock timescales. As an example, over one 50-day period and a non-line-of-sight (NLOS) transmission path of 30 km that includes terrain obstruction, we observed peak-to-peak time deviations on the order of tens of nanoseconds (including all variation of the reference time scales), a stability roughly comparable with ubiquitously deployed, single-band GPS receivers.

Overview and Motivation

GNSS, as a Positioning, Navigation, and Timing (PNT) utility, supports billions of dollars daily in economic activity [1]. Time synchronization (approximately at the level of one microsecond or better) by GNSS supports critical infrastructure sectors such as telecommunications, transportation, financial markets, and electric power transmission. However, GNSS signals are relatively weak at Earth's surface, making receivers vulnerable to accidental or purposeful interference. GNSS constellations are vulnerable to space weather phenomena or other disruptions. Therefore, we recognize motivation for other PNT or nation-scale time synchronization approaches as alternatives to (or augmentation of) GNSS usage: for example, terrestrial beacon sources, Low Earth Orbit (LEO) constellations (which share only some of the same risks as GNSS), or point-to-point one-way or two-way time transfer links.

The Broadcast Positioning System (BPS) protocol, compatible within ATSC 3.0, is described elsewhere [2–5]. Briefly, the time of transmission of each ATSC 3.0 frame's Bootstrap word is encoded within the Preamble portion of the ATSC 3.0 data frame. A BPS synchronizer device, connected to a local reference clock, observes the ATSC 3.0 transmission close to the transmitter and encodes additional data for a distinct Physical Layer Pipe (PLP) within the frame relating the transmitted timestamps accurately to the reference clock, the transmitter's spatial coordinates, and other metadata describing a local timing network. The design of BPS allows it to augment an existing ATSC 3.0 transmission chain with minimal modification. TV transmitters operate with up to 1 MW equivalent radiated power (ERP) over a wide range of allocated frequency bands. Collectively, TV transmitters constitute pre-existing infrastructure with nearly-universal national coverage of the United States, including borders and coastal regions. Finally, BPS takes advantage of a feature in ATSC 3.0 which allows portions of the

This paper is excerpted from the Proceedings of the 2025 NAB Broadcast Engineering and Information Technology (BEIT) Conference, © 2025, National Association of Broadcasters, 1 M Street SE, Washington, DC 20003 USA.

transmission to be more robustly detected than the encapsulated TV data. Typically, the TV PLP service is configured to require 15 dB signal-to-noise ratio (SNR) for decoding; the BPS PLP requires only -5 dB SNR.

Experimental Setup and Prior Results

Initial observations of BPS time transfer measured against NIST atomic clock time scales were presented recently [6]. For context, we re-summarize the experimental setup and prior findings.

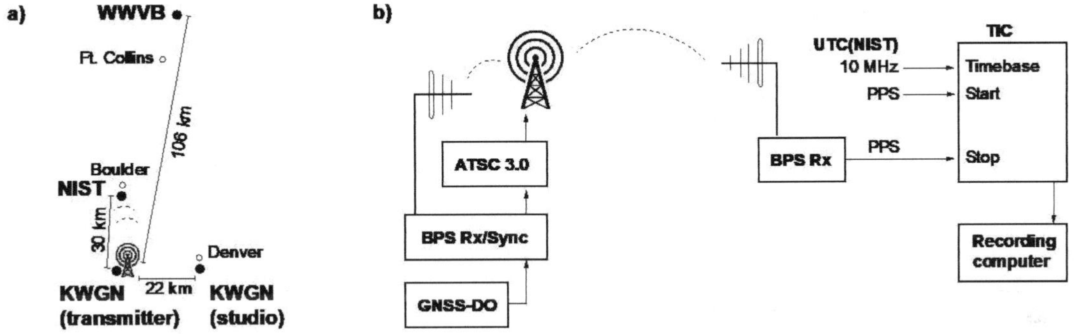

FIGURE 1: EXPERIMENTAL SETUP. A) GEOGRAPHIC LOCATIONS OF THE KWGN TRANSMITTER AND THREE BPS RECEIVER SITES (SEE TEXT). B) A BPS RECEIVER OUTPUTS A PULSE-PER-SECOND (PPS) SIGNAL, DERIVED FROM A QUARTZ OSCILLATOR DISCIPLINED BY BPS WHENEVER THE BPS SIGNAL CAN BE TRACKED. A TIME INTERVAL COUNTER (TIC) MEASURES THE TIME DELAY BETWEEN EACH PPS FROM THE LOCAL ATOMIC TIMESCALE AND BPS. AT THE NI+ST BOULDER FACILITY, THE LOCAL ATOMIC TIME SCALE IS UTC(NIST), NIST'S REALIZATION OF COORDINATED UNIVERSAL TIME. THE TIC ACCURACY AND LINEARITY ARE SUPPORTED BY A 10 MHZ REFERENCE SIGNAL COHERENT WITH UTC(NIST); THE TIC INSTABILITY IS APPROXIMATELY 50 PS PER SINGLE-SHOT MEASUREMENT, DECREASING TO 1 PS OVER AVERAGING INTERVALS LONGER THAN 1 HOUR.

Figure 1 illustrates the deployment and test of BPS in the Denver metropolitan area. Television station KWGN (Nexstar Media Group, Inc.) transmits ATSC 3.0 / BPS (channel 34, UHF 593 MHz) from a mountain-top tower west of Denver, Colorado. For convenience, the transmitter's reference clock is a GNSS-disciplined oscillator (GNSS-DO; Microchip TP4500) but independent atomic clocks have referenced BPS transmissions in separate studies. BPS receivers were installed at three locations, the KWGN studio (22 km east; clear line of sight [LOS]), the NIST campus in Boulder (30 km north; terrain obstructed non-line-of-sight [NLOS]), and the NIST WWVB radio station near Ft. Collins (106 km north; clear LOS). Each receiver (Avateq 1050) is paired with a roof-mounted, commercial-off-the-shelf (COTS) UHF TV directional antenna with no additional filters or amplifiers.

In the prior study [6], spanning 22 days from September 3, 2024, BPS was continuously observed and measured against atomic time scales at the NIST Boulder and WWVB facilities. Peak-to-peak variation (of about 55 ns) in these observations was highly correlated. We subtracted the NIST and WWVB observation records to remove variation due to the BPS transmitter's reference clock (a GNSS-DO, at the time configured to use L1 and E1 GPS and Galileo signals only). The remaining variation, about 30 ns peak-to-peak with a random-walk character, was highly correlated with an independent measurement of the difference between the atomic time scales, UTC(NIST) – UTC(NIST@WWVB), afforded by NIST measurements of GPS (L1 and L2 bands) in "common view" at both campuses. By subtracting this measurement of UTC(NIST) – UTC(NIST@WWVB), we obtained a residual series representing several irreducible elements related to BPS propagation and reception in typical deployments: two non-common paths (106 nm LOS and 30 km NLOS), two uncorrelated BPS receivers, noise in two time interval counters (TICs), and intra-facility signal distribution. Noise (of order 1 ns) due to the GPS common-view technique is also present in this "double-difference" signal, so analysis that follows overestimates the noise in BPS time transfer somewhat.

The peak-to-peak residual variation was approximately 22 ns, but over all possible averaging intervals the time deviation (TDEV) statistic remained below 2 ns. For context, over the same test period, the TDEV of UTC(NIST) – GPS(L1 only) remained below 4 ns. TDEV of UTC(NIST) – GPS(L1 and L2) remained below 0.8 ns. While the TDEV statistic does not fully characterize time transfer accuracy, it remains a useful measure when high-quality local clocks can be leveraged as holdover oscillators at both ends of a time transfer link, enabling optimal averaging of time-difference measurements to discern the state of clock rate and time offsets.

A separate finding in the prior stability study involved measurement of BPS at the KWGN studio, which employed an identically-configured GNSS-DO as a reference clock. These measurements, though not continuous, exhibited a maximum TDEV below 600 ps and TDEV below 300 ps for averaging intervals of several hours suggesting excellent time-transfer performance over a LOS propagation path.

New Results with an Additional 50 Days of Observation

In November, 2024, the KWGN BPS transmitter's GNSS-DO reference clock was reconfigured to use dual-band GNSS signals (L1/L2 GPS and the corresponding E1/E6 for Galileo) as originally intended. Thereafter, the direct observation of UTC(NIST) - BPS improved in stability significantly, reducing the need for "common-view" observations involving both UTC(NIST) and UTC(NIST@WWVB) atomic timescales to tease out performance limits.

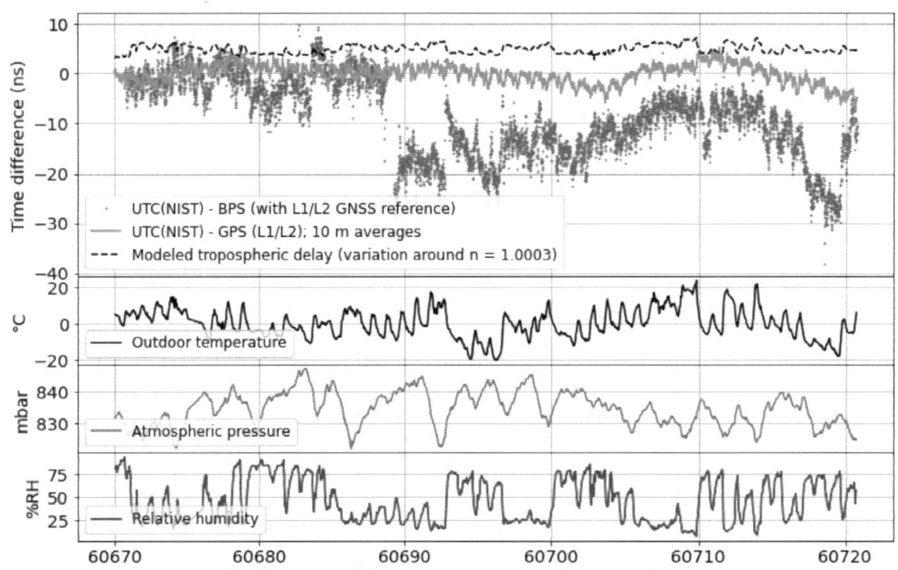

FIGURE 2: FROM 50 DAYS OF MEASUREMENT, WE PLOT TEN-MINUTE AVERAGES OF UTC(NIST) – BPS (BLUE) AND UTC(NIST) – GPS (ORANGE). INITIAL OFFSETS ARE SUBTRACTED FROM EACH SERIES SINCE SEVERAL FIXED OFFSETS (SUCH AS CABLE DELAYS) ARE NOT OTHERWISE COMPENSATED. OUTLIER POINTS ARE VERY RARE; THEY ARE DETERMINED AND REMOVED WHEN > 300 NS FROM THE MEDIAN. THE LOWER INSET PLOTS SHOW OUTDOOR MEASUREMENTS OF TEMPERATURE, ATMOSPHERIC PRESSURE, AND RELATIVE HUMIDITY AT THE NIST BOULDER FACILITY. WE NOTE POSITIVE CORRELATION WITH TEMPERATURE. SEE TEXT FOR DISCUSSION.

Figure 2 shows the measurement of UTC(NIST) - BPS compared with a NIST measurement of UTC(NIST) – GPS(L1 and L2). Strong positive correlation is observed between UTC(NIST) – BPS and the measured outdoor temperature at NIST Boulder; correlation is especially visible with fast temperature changes. The black dashed line in the top plot of Figure 2 is a computation of the expected BPS delay variation due changes in index of refraction according to temperature, pressure, and humidity variation [7]. The estimate is based on sensor data recorded on the NIST Boulder rooftop, includes no account of refractive effects or variation with elevation along the path and does not explain a significant amount of the variation in UTC(NIST) – BPS. Further study is merited, especially comparing NLOS and LOS propagation.

A sudden step of about -25 ns observed in the BPS data near Modified Julian Date (MJD) 60689 (2025-Jan-14) is likely related to known operator maintenance activity that involved lower transmitter power and/or a possible change to undetermined interference in the NLOS propagation of KWGN to NIST Boulder. Figure 3, below, examines this interval closely with BPS observations from both NIST Boulder and NIST WWVB facilities. Besides the apparent time step, the NLOS BPS receiver in Boulder lost lock for approximately 10 hours (during which no data are plotted). However, the LOS BPS measurement near Ft. Collins of UTC(NIST@WWVB) – BPS was uninterrupted and continuous throughout. From this we gather a single inconclusive anecdote about the sensitivity of BPS time transfer to NLOS path or other interference and its fluctuations.

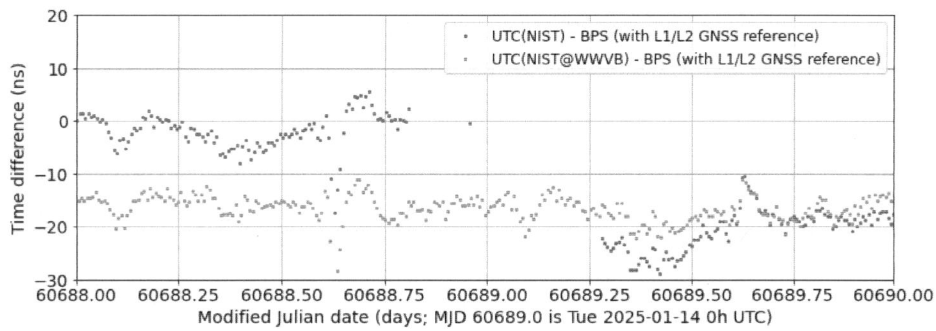

FIGURE 3: DURING A PERIOD WHERE KWGN TRANSMITTER POWER WAS ADJUSTED LOWER, THE BOULDER BPS RECEIVER LOST LOCK FOR ABOUT 10 HOURS (GAP IN BLUE SERIES) AND EXHIBITED AN APPARENT TIME STEP OF ABOUT -25 NS. OBSERVATION OF THE KWGN BPS SIGNAL AT THE NIST WWVB FACILITY SHOWS NO INTERRUPTION OR CHANGE.

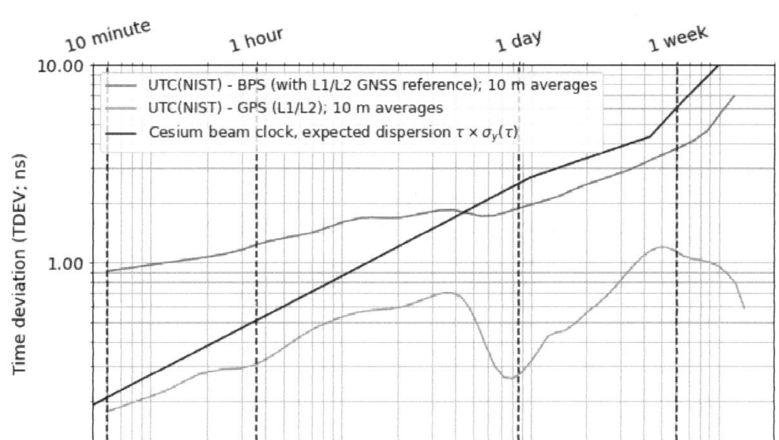

FIGURE 4: THE TIME DEVIATION (TDEV) TIME-DOMAIN NOISE STATISTIC IS A MEASURE OF AVERAGED TIME-DIFFERENCE FLUCTUATION AS A FUNCTION OF AVERAGING INTERVAL. TDEV IS INSENSITIVE TO TIME AND RATE OFFSETS. TDEV IS PLOTTED FOR THE DATA IN FIGURE 2 (BLUE AND ORANGE). FOR CONTEXT, WE ALSO PLOT THE EXPECTED TIME DISPERSION OF A COMMERCIAL CESIUM BEAM ATOMIC CLOCK (BLACK) BASED ON ITS SPECIFIED ALLAN DEVIATION $\sigma_y(\tau)$.

Figure 4 summarizes the variations observed in Figure 2 using the common Time Deviation (TDEV) statistic: a measure of expected fluctuations after averaging as a function of averaging interval. The fluctuations of UTC(NIST) – BPS are approximately within a factor of three or four from measured UTC(NIST) – GPS (L1 and L2); despite the impairments from NLOS propagation and no compensation of tropospheric index-of-refraction variations. For context, the expected time deviation of a rate-corrected COTS cesium beam atomic clock is also shown.

Outlook

Results presented here and in [6] suggest that in its tested state, BPS appears promising for high-resolution, GNSS-independent time transfer between fixed stations where initial offsets can be calibrated externally (e.g., by a one-time use of GNSS, traveling clock, etc.). Impairments due to reduced transmitter power, NLOS propagation, or tropospheric variation are observed on the order of ten nanoseconds over 30 km (and one instance of loss of lock); such effects are expected to depend on geographic details unique to each deployment. In general deployment, BPS receivers must compute (and remove) the signaling delay from transmitter to receiver accurately, either by using known or derived spatial coordinates.

Disclaimer

Certain equipment, products, or proprietary methods are identified in this paper in order to specify the experimental procedure adequately. Such identification is not intended to imply recommendation or endorsement of any product or service by NIST, nor is it intended to imply that the materials or equipment identified are necessarily the best available for the purpose. This paper is intended to accompany a presentation of the most-recent BPS time transfer observations and has not been subject to independent peer-review.

Acknowledgement

The authors thank Tariq Mondal, VP of Advanced Technology at National Association of Broadcasters (NAB), Brett Jenkins, EVP, Chief Technology & Digital Officer at Nexstar Media Group, Inc. and Dave Stromberg, VP Technology at KDVR Fox31/KWGN CW2/Denver HUB Engineering for deploying BPS at KWGN and transmitting BPS signal for our testing. The authors also thank Dr. Judah Levine for insight and substantial contributions to the NIST and WWVB time scale including their synchronization, and WWV/B operators for support: Matt Deutch, Glenn Nelson, Jim Spicer, Kyle Kniegge, and Bill Yates. The authors are grateful for the technical support provided by RJ Russell, President of Technical Broadcast Solutions Incorporated (for operations at WHUT) and Vladimir Anishchenko, CTO and co-founder of Avateq Corp. Finally, we thank Sam Matheny, EVP and CTO at NAB, for providing resources to conduct the study.

References

[1] O'Connor, A. C., et al., "Economic benefits of the global positioning system (GPS)," RTI Report Number 0215471, June 2019. https://www.rti.org/sites/default/files/gps_finalreport618.pdf

[2] Mondal, T., et al., "Broadcast Positioning System (BPS) using ATSC 3.0," *Proceedings of the 2021 NAB Broadcast Engineering and Information Technology (BEIT) Conference.* https://nab.org/bps/Broadcast_Positioning_System_Using_ATSC30.pdf

[3] Diamond, P., et al., "Delivering traceable reference time for ATSC 3.0-based Broadcast Positioning System (BPS)," *Proceedings of the 2023 NAB Broadcast Engineering and Information Technology (BEIT) Conference*. https://nab.org/bps/Delivering_Traceable_Reference.pdf

[4] Corl, M., et al., "BPS ATSC 3.0 broadcast emission time stabilization proof-of-concept," *Proceedings of the 2023 NAB Broadcast Engineering and Information Technology (BEIT) Conference*. https://nab.org/bps/BPS_ATSC_3_0_Broadcast_Emission.pdf

[5] Corl, M., et al., "ATSC 3.0 Broadcast Positioning System (BPS) mesh network," *Proceedings of the 2024 NAB Broadcast Engineering and Information Technology (BEIT) Conference.* https://nab.org/bps/ATSC_3_0_BPS_Mesh_Network.pdf

[6] Sherman, J.A., et al., "Time transfer performance of the Broadcast Positioning System™ (BPS™)," Proceedings of the 2025 International Technical Meeting (ITM), Institute of Navigation (ION), ION ITM 2025, Jan. 27-30, 2025.

[7] International Telecommunications Union, "Recommendation ITU-R P.453-11. The radio refractive index: its formula and refractivity data," July 2015. https://www.itu.int/dms_pubrec/itu-r/rec/p/R-REC-P.453-11-201507-S!!PDF-E.pdf

Transferring Traceable Time to BPS-Enabled ATSC 3.0 Station

Francisco Girela Lopez
Safran Electronics & Defense
Rochester, New York, United States
Francisco.girela@nav-timing.safrangroup.com

Ramki Ramakrishnan
Safran Electronics & Defense
Rochester, New York, United States
ramki.ramakrishnan@nav-timing.safrangroup.com

Abstract – Broadcast Positioning System (BPS) necessitates precise time synchronization across TV stations, utilizing a shared time reference and their fixed locations for triangulation and reliable positioning, with time over fiber solutions connected to trusted timing sources serving as a viable method for maintaining accurate synchronization. In this paper, we present a concept to link BPS leader stations to timescales maintained by National Metrology Institutes (NMIs) using High Accuracy White Rabbit synchronization through optical networks.

Timekeeping and Traceability

Timekeeping refers to the process of recording and managing time, ensuring that activities and events occur at the correct times. It encompasses various methods and technologies used to measure, track, and synchronize time accurately. Timekeeping is crucial in many aspects of daily life, including work schedules, transportation, scientific research, and communication systems. Accurate timekeeping ensures punctuality, coordination, and efficiency in both personal and professional settings.

Time traceability refers to the ability to relate time measurements to a recognized standard, typically Coordinated Universal Time (UTC), through an unbroken chain of comparisons. This ensures that timekeeping systems and devices are synchronized and accurate, allowing for consistent and reliable time references across different locations and applications. Traceability is crucial in various fields, such as telecommunications, finance, and scientific research, where precise time synchronization is essential. By maintaining traceability, organizations can ensure that their time measurements are accurate, comparable, and compliant with international standards.

The UTC time scale is maintained and distributed by the Bureau International des Poids et Mesures (BIPM), or in English, the International Bureau of Weights and Measures, which is located near Paris, France in an area considered to be international territory. Therefore, the BIPM maintains neutrality as an intergovernmental organization that is not controlled by any country. Its mandate is to provide a single, coherent system of measurements based on an International System of Units (SI).

The SI is built upon seven base units of measurement. One of the base units is the second, which serves as the standard unit for time interval and the foundation for world timekeeping. Since 1967, the SI second has been an "atomic" second. It's defined as "The duration of 9,192,631,770 periods of the

This paper is excerpted from the Proceedings of the 2025 NAB Broadcast Engineering and Information Technology (BEIT) Conference, © 2023, National Association of Broadcasters, 1 M Street SE, Washington, DC 20003 USA.

radiation corresponding to the transition between two hyperfine levels of the ground state of the cesium-133 atom", and its duration is precisely determined by cesium atomic clocks.

UTC is created not with just one atomic clock, but rather by using an "ensemble" of atomic clocks. The time produced by UTC time scales ensembles is obtained by averaging the time produced by individual clocks. A weighted average, rather than a simple arithmetic average, is used. This means that some clocks – specifically the clocks with the best frequency stability – are given more "weight" and contribute more to the average than others.

UTC is a global time scale with a large clock ensemble. The UTC ensemble is spread around the world; with more than 400 clocks residing in more than 80 laboratories in more than 60 nations.

The National Institute of Standards and Technology (NIST) maintains its own version of Coordinated Universal Time, known as UTC(NIST), which serves as the official time for the United States. This was established by the America COMPETES Act of 2007, which designates Coordinated Universal Time (UTC) as the official time for the U.S., as "interpreted or modified by the Secretary of Commerce, in coordination with the Secretary of the Navy." The Secretary of Commerce assigns the timekeeping duties to NIST, an agency within the Department of Commerce, while the Secretary of the Navy assigns these responsibilities to the United States Naval Observatory (USNO) within the Department of Defense. Both NIST and USNO act as the official timekeepers for the United States.

UTC (NIST) is a local time scale, with an ensemble typically consisting of 10 to 15 clocks, all of which reside in the NIST laboratories in Boulder, Colorado. NIST operates two secondary UTC(NIST) time scales at locations outside of its Boulder, Colorado campus. The first is located in Fort Collins, Colorado and the second is located at the NIST headquarters in Gaithersburg, Maryland.

Each NIST clock is also a member of the UTC ensemble, so UTC(NIST) can be thought of as a subset of UTC. The most important distinction between UTC and UTC(NIST), however, is that UTC is a virtual or "paper" time scale that does not produce any physical signals, and that UTC(NIST) does produce physical signals. The signals produced by UTC(NIST) are in the form of electrical pulses or sine waves, and these signals are distributed to users and then used to synchronize or calibrate other clocks.

Time Synchronization Background

In different sectors, typical deployments involve a stable time reference to synchronizing local time resources across different locations. Global Navigation Satellite Systems (GNSS) are the primary source of time due to their affordability, precision, ease of deployment, and global reach. This technology provides time and frequency references with accuracy in the tens of nanoseconds and is related to Coordinated Universal Time (UTC). However, GNSS signals are susceptible to accidental or intentional signal disruptions, natural interferences from weather conditions, and urban constraints affecting signal coverage and integrity. This is the main reason why BPS has been proposed; to complement or replace GNSS based positioning and synchronization due to its vulnerabilities.

Network-based protocols have emerged as a complementary solution to distribute time and frequency signals at a lower cost using a primary time reference. These protocols enable the distribution of time information to nodes without satellite coverage through a reliable physical infrastructure, enhancing accuracy. The extensive reach of wired communications supports the scalability and feasibility of this approach, offering a solution with increased capillarity and availability.

The most commonly used protocols are NTP and IEEE 1588-2008, also known as PTP. Under well-controlled conditions, NTP can achieve microsecond-level accuracy using a software-based solution, while PTP can provide accuracy up to tens of nanoseconds using hardware timestamps and well-controlled scenarios with time-aware switches and nodes.

Although these technologies are well-supported with commodity solutions for their respective industries, challenges arise when accuracy requirements fall below 100 nanoseconds. Different factors can prevent these protocols from being accurate enough and maintain traceability to their source. These factors can be categorized in three different ways depending on their origin:

A. Internal Factors

- **Timestamping Precision**: Time synchronization protocols timestamp the Start of Frame (SoF) of transmitted and received packets to calculate the latency of the transmission and infer the clock offset between different devices. The precision of those timestamps and the resolution of the capture directly affect the achievable accuracy.
- **Latency Consistency**: In order to properly calculate the offset using the captured timestamp, there is a need for consistent latency during regular operation and between reconnections. This might change due to buffers, clock recovery mechanisms in transceivers, and other electronics. Latency changes have a direct impact on the achievable accuracy.
- **Delay Calibration**: There are different delays in the transmission and reception of packets since they are timestamped in the devices. Those delays need to be calibrated to be removed from the final offset calculation.
- **Time base resolution:** Analogously to the timestamp resolution, this is the time base update period that keeps track of time. In this case, if the time base is updated using an internal counter increased each clock cycle, the uncertainty will be equal to the clock period.
- **Clock drift between corrections:** This is produced by the frequency difference between the local oscillators in different devices during the elapsed time between corrections. This will affect the precision of the synchronization between corrections.
- **Clock phase offset:** In those cases where time synchronization accuracy is very relevant, there is a limitation on the achievable accuracy in logic due to its maximum operating frequency. IF that limitation wants to be overcome, there is a need for further corrections using the phase relationship between the clocks from different devices as the reference.

B. External Factors

- **Optical Transfer Technique**: The network architecture and chosen optical transfer technique significantly impact latency, determinism, and stability. The most accurate distribution is typically deployed in point-to-point connections between endpoints for synchronization. However, in long-distance scenarios reusing existing telecom infrastructure, the elements and technologies in use must be considered. Long-distance deployments often use Wavelength Division Multiplexing (WDM), allowing timing channels to be multiplexed with other channels or inserted as alien wavelengths, sharing the medium and associated costs. The main challenge is that most telecom WDM circuits follow a bi-fiber unidirectional architecture, which does not guarantee symmetry between transmission and reception paths. WDM distribution in long-distance scenarios is typically performed through high-capacity core networks, terminating on endpoints for optical distribution that support various technologies like Ethernet, Optical Transport Network (OTN), Synchronous Optical Networking (SONET), Synchronous Digital Hierarchy (SDH), Multi-Protocol Label Switching (MPLS), Segment Routing, or Time Sensitive Networking (TSN). Most endpoints will affect the time synchronization due to noise, buffering, and retiming of signals. However, Synchronous Ethernet (SyncE)-compliant transponders might be used to establish time synchronization links. Time synchronization jitter is affected by optical transfer elements and accumulated noise in each element used to transport the optical signal.
- **Optics Accuracy and Determinism**: The optical transfer technique directly impacts propagation delay asymmetry and time synchronization accuracy. The conversion from electrical signals to optical signals by the Small Form-factor Pluggable (SFP) module affects synchronization accuracy. Any variance in emitted wavelength or internal transmission and reception delays in SFPs between power cycles or different SFP batches results in semi-static time synchronization inaccuracy. Similar effects are observed in Dispersion Compensation Modules (DCM), Optical Multiplexers and Demultiplexers (MUX/DEMUX), optical filters, circulators, or amplifiers.

- **Asymmetry Calibration**: In single-fiber bidirectional links, asymmetry is created by using different wavelengths over a symmetric optical path. In bi-fiber unidirectional links, asymmetry is linked to physical asymmetries in the optical path. Calibration is needed to account for physical asymmetry, performed using techniques like loopback-based, GNSS-assisted, or network-effect calibrations. Asymmetry is considered a static source of inaccuracy, measured and removed similarly to endogenous delay calibration.

C. Common Factors

- Dynamic effects equally affect both internal and external factors, typically originating from environmental aspects like temperature, humidity, airflow, the Sagnac effect, or vibration, and hardware factors like aging of SFPs or oscillators, or changes in infrastructure like optical fiber movement or signal attenuation. Temperature significantly influences accuracy, affecting internal delays in hardware, oscillator frequencies, and transmitted wavelength in SFPs. SFP wavelength stability has an increasing effect with longer link distances, becoming a significant error source. Received optical signal power also significantly influences accuracy, associated with optical pulse dispersion and detection threshold at the SFP photoreceiver. Attenuation in the link and potential aging of optics must be considered when designing long-distance networks.

Broadcast Positioning System Background

At the NAB BEIT 2024, two papers covered the mesh network architecture for a BPS deployment [1] and how traditional GNSS time servers could be used to reconcile the timing information required to retransmit, timestamp and coordinate the different base stations [2]. The new synchronization system along with the potential for receiving the signal from many neighboring towers leads to an opportunity to build an extremely robust system of multiple transmitters, using multiple disparate frequencies and traceable time sources.

In a nationwide deployment of the BPS network, it is expected that the functionality at each node would be essentially the same with some "leader" transmitters having traceable time. It is also expected that by adding additional time-keeping equipment, transmitters can move from "Followers" to "Leaders" and vice versa. It is noteworthy that the overall performance of BPS systems will greatly depend on the accuracy of the time synchronization references received by the “Leader” stations from traceable sources and how well they are able to distribute it to “Follower” stations and end users. Moreover, the received time information must be traceable to an official source of timing in the territory if this system aspires to become an alternative to GNSS based synchronization.

As a reference, Figure 1 provides a diagram of an exemplary BPS network using four transmitters. The detailed diagram shown associated with one of the transmitters would apply to all the transmitter nodes in the BPS network. In this case, the node could be designated as a “Leader” or a “follower” depending on the clock references available in such location.

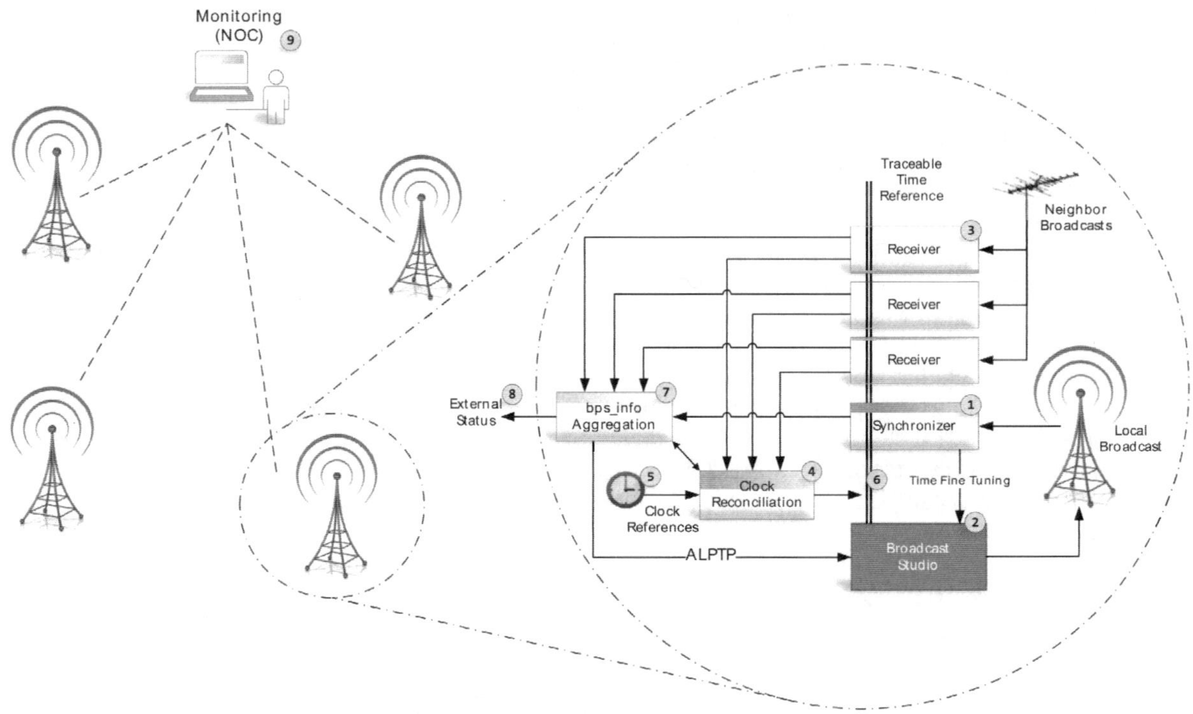

FIGURE 1 – BPS TRANSMISSION NODE DIAGRAM

For the topic of this paper, the relevant building blocks within BPS transmission node are the Clock Reconciliation, the Clock References and the internal time distribution within the station.

The Clock Reconciliation takes input from each receiver and one or more clock references using them as Input References. As proposed in [1] and [2] this function is performed by a Safran SecureSync 2400 which can be synchronized to different time and frequency sources that are referred to as Input References, or just References. References can be a GNSS receiver, or other sources delivered into the SecureSync 2400 unit via dedicated (mostly optional) inputs. It is also possible to enter a system time manually, which SecureSync 2400 can then synchronize to. For SecureSync 2400 to declare synchronization, it needs both a valid 1PPS, and Time reference.

The concept of Reference Priority in the SecureSync 2400 allows the ranking of multiple references for redundancy purposes. This allows SecureSync 2400 to gracefully fall back upon a lower ranking Time reference without transitioning into Holdover in case a reference becomes unavailable or invalid. The priority order assigned to the available references typically is a function of their accuracy and reliability.

The SecureSync 2400 accepts up to six option cards that can be used for additional Input or Output references. These signals might come from the Synchronizer or from the external clock references to synchronize the node or can be distributed to the other elements to share a common time reference.

Providing Traceability and High Accuracy References to BPS

To enhance synchronization accuracy beyond what previous protocols offer, higher accuracy alternatives were developed to deliver sub-nanosecond time synchronization accuracy in Ethernet networks to thousands of nodes with high reliability and determinism.

This technology is known as White Rabbit (WR) and has been standardized as the High Accuracy profile in the IEEE 1588 (PTP) standard. WR is a synchronization technology developed as an open-source project in 2009.

The primary feature of WR technology is its ability to achieve sub-nanosecond time synchronization accuracy in standard optical fiber networks. It utilizes standard technologies like Ethernet, PTP, and Layer 1 syntonization, similar to Synchronous Ethernet (SyncE). This capability to enhance timing performance without overhauling the fiber infrastructure has led to its adoption in numerous scientific and industrial applications.

Another significant aspect of WR technology is its frequency distribution precision, which is specified to be better than 50 picoseconds. A typical WR link operates on a master/slave model, where the master distributes time information to the slave node. WR devices can also function as grandmasters to distribute stable external time references, using analog 1 Pulse Per Second (1PPS) and 10 MHz clock signals for time reference and NTP for Time of Day (ToD) information.

In its initial version, WR supports 1 Gigabit (G) Ethernet connections and maintains time synchronization accuracy even when data packets are combined with WR packets.

The main mechanisms of WR technology include:

- **Layer 1 Syntonization**: Similar to SyncE, the clock reference from the master is distributed to the slave. A Clock Data Recovery (CDR) retrieves the transmission clock from the received data stream, which is then used to adjust the local transmission clock, creating an internal copy of the reference clock.
- **Network Time Packets Exchange**: WR extends standard PTPv2 packets for time synchronization, including specific signaling messages to establish the WR link and aggregate calibration parameters. This packet exchange generates hardware timestamps for both transmission and reception, which are used to compute the clock offset between the master and the slave.
- **Phase Measurement**: To overcome the resolution limitations of hardware timestamps, WR uses syntonization to perform phase measurements with picosecond resolution between the received and transmission clocks in the master and slave. This enhances timestamp information and improves clock offset calculation accuracy.

A key feature of WR technology is its ability to compensate for fiber asymmetry and fixed delays. This is achieved through a calibration process based on a bidirectional link scheme, where two different wavelengths are used to transmit information between both ends using the same fiber. By default, this link distance is limited to 10 km due to the pre-calibrated Small Form-factor Pluggables (SFP) used in research facilities.

Local area deployments are straightforward, but calibration has been a recurring topic for deploying long-distance links or using different optics, facilitating WR integration into existing infrastructures. This has been approached following different techniques:

- **Precalibration in Dedicated Links**: The distance limitation for WR links is due to the SFP transmission power. Long-distance SFPs supporting up to 120 km links can be calibrated using the standard calibration procedure for a specific fiber type. This distance can be extended by using multiple WR nodes or bidirectional amplification, although the latter requires calibration for each amplifier. Absolute calibration has been studied to simplify the deployment of network components.
- **Precalibration in Shared WDM Links**: WDM technology can be used to deploy bidirectional links, reducing asymmetries. This technique allows the introduction of various optical equipment, such as Dispersion Compensation Modules (DCM), optical multiplexers, or optical amplifiers, while sharing the physical medium with other applications. The maturity of this approach has been demonstrated, and it is now fully supported by leading WR companies. The temperature impact on WR WDM links has also been studied.
- **GNSS-Based Calibration**: Once the link is deployed, on-site calibration can be performed using GNSS receivers at each end. The accuracy depends on the instantaneous offset between both receivers, which can be affected by factors such as antenna position or internal delays.

Calibrated GNSS receivers can achieve accuracy close to the nanosecond level, making this method a viable alternative due to WR synchronization stability.

- **Swapping-Based Calibration**: Depending on the deployment, swapping-based methods can measure link asymmetries using a stable time reference. This technique allows for sub-nanosecond accuracy in bi-fiber links where distance asymmetry cannot be compensated. However, it requires access to both ends and no unidirectional equipment can be installed in the link.
- **Network Effect Calibration**: In extensive WR networks with redundant topologies, several loopbacks formed by multiple links can be closed, measuring the offset at each location with different configurations. This procedure allows for the calculation and compensation of asymmetry in each deployed link when a minimum of three locations are connected. This methodology, first introduced in the literature, is used by other timing techniques and can also be applied to WR calibration. Although WR has typically been approached from a point-to-point perspective, there is no reason not to extend this concept to more general approaches.

The combination of the high accuracy and determinism design for WR together with the ability to calibrate the synchronization links are the basic conditions to maintain the levels of traceability and accuracy required by “Leader” nodes in BPS.

Moreover, one of the primary challenges in monitoring time synchronization in real-world environments is the lack of measurement equipment capable of performing distributed measurements across different network locations that cannot be connected to a local measurement unit like an oscilloscope or time counter. This issue, combined with the fact that most time synchronization devices report their statistics based on their own software calculations, creates a scenario where achieving traceability and assessing the health of the time synchronization network is difficult without deploying loop-backs or complex timestamping comparisons, which would require additional bandwidth or computational resources to ensure performance.

However, WR devices can be used as a ground-truth reference to monitor the timing distribution network while also distributing time synchronization. This approach leverages the sub-nanosecond time synchronization accuracy in conventional optical fiber networks with support for multiple time sources, interoperability with various inputs, and the ability to measure the offset from passive references not used to discipline the WR device. This allows WR devices to use multiple time references for redundant time distribution or to monitor other nodes in the production BPS network. WR probes can be strategically deployed to measure the timing performance network in real-time, achieving picosecond-level accuracy. In distributed scenarios, the minimal accuracy degradation of WR can be used to interconnect WR probes, compare their data, and respond to unexpected behaviors.

Consequently, the WR devices can select more than just a single reference clock. Additional backup references, which can be used if the active reference is lost, and "survey" references, which are only configured to be measured, can be set up. Following this configuration, the WR will measure the offset against the active local reference and the backup and "survey" references, storing their metrics in an internal database that can be exported and visualized by the user.

WR capabilities can be added to the SecureSync 2400 clock combiner which is proposed as one of the center pieces in the BPS node design. In that case, the data comparing the synchronizer inputs, the GNSS references and the time over fiber synchronization would be plotted in a graph in real-time. The plot also allows historic data to be displayed and can zoom in on any data range or on a specific reference. A data set can be exported or deleted.

When comparing the multiple Input sources coming from the neighboring transmitters against traceable Input sources (i.e., GNSS or Time over Fiber systems), this graph will show the timing performance of the different elements in the system and will be able to provide traceability to UTC time. The active

Input reference in the SecureSync 2400 will be used to synchronize all the equipment used in the broadcast and BPS systems.

This technology distributes an UTC(NIST) reference sourced directly from the NIST timescale using dedicated terrestrial optical fiber links. The terrestrial time distribution network interconnects NIST time reference with multiple nodes in the contiguous US situated in key critical infrastructure locations with resiliency and precision. The WR infrastructure combines diverse fiber paths, redundant GNSS time servers with hardened and calibrated RF deployments and miniaturized atomic clocks for supporting holdover periods. The failover and recovery arbitration are fully automated and executed seamlessly to eliminate the impact on the BPS nodes and remove the need for expensive and hard to manage Cesium clocks. This technology provides secure WR, PTP, NTP, PPS, IRIG and 10 MHz frequency references in multiple stations in different metro areas where the "Leader" or "Follower" BPS nodes are deployed.

The system design is done in collaboration with NIST to ensure that the NIST time reference transferred over the terrestrial optical fiber links is 100% traceable and it is completely GNSS independent, fully removing the dependency on wireless information transferred via satellite (GNSS) or ground stations during its regular operation. This guarantees that the proposed time distribution is a resilient, precise, secure and sovereign solution, which is deployed and managed on US national soil. The network architecture design, which is based on redundant and diverse optical paths, makes it extremely hard to tamper, attack or degrade the performance of this service. Although the system is fully independent from GNSS, it benefits from existing GNSS constellations and potentially other available CPNT technologies to further improve its resiliency and to offer distributed GNSS reception monitoring capabilities.

Conclusion

White Rabbit (WR) technology enhances synchronization accuracy beyond previous protocols by delivering sub-nanosecond time synchronization accuracy in Ethernet networks to thousands of nodes with high reliability and determinism. Standardized as the High Accuracy profile in the IEEE 1588 (PTP) standard, it improves timing performance without overhauling the fiber infrastructure and can be calibrated to maintain traceability.

WR devices can monitor timing distribution networks in real-time, using multiple time references for redundant distribution or monitoring other nodes. They can select more than one reference clock, with backup and "survey" references configured. WR capabilities can be integrated into the SecureSync 2400 clock combiner, providing real-time data comparison and traceability to UTC time to BPS "Leader" and "Follower" nodes.

The system design, in collaboration with NIST, ensures the NIST time reference is 100% traceable and GNSS-independent, offering a resilient, precise, secure, and sovereign solution deployed on US soil. The network architecture, based on redundant and diverse optical paths, enhances security and performance, benefiting from existing GNSS constellations and other Complementary PNT technologies for improved resiliency and distributed GNSS reception monitoring.

References

[1] Corl, M., et al, "ATSC 3.0 Broadcast Positioning System (BPS) Mesh Network" Proceedings of the 2024 NAB Broadcast Engineering and Information Technology (BEIT) Conference.

[2] Girela-Lopez, F., et al, "Leveraging traditional GNSS time servers for resiliency and interoperability in Broadcast Positioning Systems (BPS)" Proceedings of the 2024 NAB Broadcast Engineering and Information Technology (BEIT) Conference.

Broadcast and Digital Out of Home (DOOH) A Convergence Thru Datacasting

Ted Korte
USSI Global
Melbourne, Florida, United States
ted.korte@ussiglobal.com

Abstract – The digital advertising landscape is evolving, and with it, the lines between broadcast TV and DOOH are blurring as both platforms are experiencing similar needs and similar challenges. Even though broadcast is a "Lean Back" experience and DOOH is a "Passing By" experience, both need to effectively communicate their messages with minimal disruption to a person's day. Delivering the right message to the right person at the right time is timeless and the technology available today is making this easier to do than ever before.

This paper examines the integration of dynamic content delivery via datacasting to enhance audience engagement in Digital Out of Home (DOOH) advertising. Our approach involved preloading a diverse array of content onto edge devices using datacasting technology, which was then tailored to real-time audience presence using computer vision analytics (CVA). We mixed DOOH ads with broadcast content to create a more engaging viewer experience, focusing on contextually relevant messaging based on second- and third-party data like location analytics and behavioral science insights.
Key methods included the use of multi-zone presentations, conditional content playout based on audience demographics, and the measurement of engagement through metrics like Gaze Through Rate, Session Time, and Attention Time. Trials were conducted at various high-traffic events from 2023 to 2025, where we observed the impact of content type, format, and relevance on audience interaction. Results indicated that content that was daily updated or event-specific significantly increased audience capture and engagement. However, challenges included managing content frequency to avoid fatigue and ensuring relevance without infringing on privacy or trust. The paper discusses the potential of datacasting in not only improving DOOH but also in transforming traditional linear TV into a Connected TV (CTV) platform, suggesting a convergence that could benefit both advertising platforms.
We conclude that while datacasting provides a promising method for enhancing DOOH effectiveness, further research is needed in areas like privacy protection, content optimization, and the integration of generative AI for ad personalization. The study paves the way for future explorations into more efficient, audience-centric advertising strategies in public spaces.

Introduction

This paper explores our initiatives to boost audience interaction with Digital Out of Home (DOOH) advertising by blending broadcast content with targeted ads, and by employing edge computing to customize content based on the audience present. We utilized datacasting to preload a variety of content onto edge devices, informed by second- and third-party data like location analytics and behavioral insights. After preloading with a comprehensive set of media, we employed Computer Vision Analytics (CVA) to select the most appropriate content for the specific audience in real-time. This method allowed us to process and utilize data directly at the edge, bypassing the need for additional server interactions for ad placement.

Our study on datacasting centers on the delivery of file-based media to digital signage, particularly in DOOH environments. These include public spaces like streets, university campuses, commercial complexes, and other high-traffic zones ideal for advertising. Historically, DOOH advertising was centrally managed with limited adaptability to local conditions, akin to a traditional TV broadcast schedule, Figure 1. Our objective was to revolutionize this approach by pushing a broader range of media choices, decision-making, and playlist management to the edge, enabling content playout conditioned on real-time local data, Figure 2.

NOTE that this is not a formal research paper, and these were not scientific trials with representative samples in controlled environments.

FIGURE 1: DOOH CENTRALLY MANAGED AND CONTROLLED.

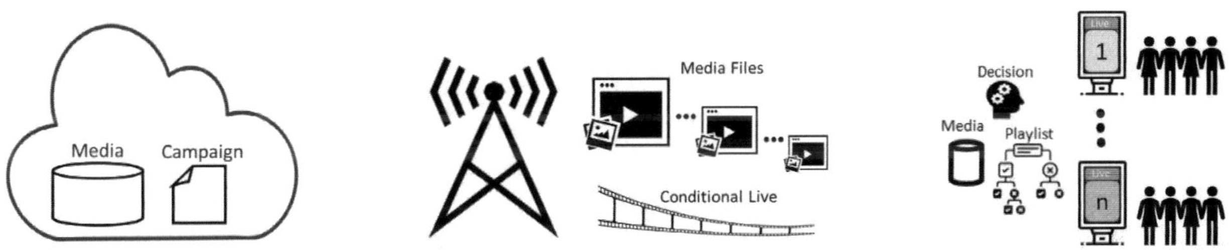

FIGURE 2: DOOH CENTRALLY ORCHESTRATED, LOCALLY MANAGED AND CONTROLLED.

Methods

We conducted experiments using various content formats and sources, combining both broadcast and DOOH materials. We also employed computer vision analytics to test conditional content playout based on the observed audience.

The initial two images in Figure 3 featured a multi-zone layout with a title zone, a 16x9 video zone, and a lower graphic zone. The strategy involved a static header displaying the company name alongside a lower graphic that complemented the video. In some instances, as seen in these images, we rotated 2-3 graphics every 7 seconds. We applied this approach to previously aired broadcast videos (without audio or subtitles) to assess if the visual content alone was engaging enough. The first experiment included directional audio, with the idea that if viewers moved closer, they would be further engaged by the sound. A QR code was implemented for tracking the call to action. The third image shows a standard full-screen DOOH advertisement in a 9x16 aspect ratio, which studies suggest can outperform 16x9 formats by up to 2:1 [1], making it important to test the effectiveness of reusing broadcast content directly. DOOH ads are typically designed to be concise and easy to read for people passing by whereas broadcast ads anticipate a more captive audience.

FIGURE 3: EXAMPLE MULTI-ZONE PRESENTATION ALONGSIDE TRADITIONAL DOOH.

We chose to focus on three key metrics for evaluating the effectiveness of the decision-making process depicted in Figure 4:

- **Gaze Through Rate** is a type of measurement for audience capture. It is the percentage of people who had the opportunity to view the display (distance, angle, and direction of travel) who actually did view the display. It is meant to visualize how effective the content is at attracting attention from passersby.
- **Session time** is the total duration a person stayed in the area of opportunity to view.
- **Attention time** is a type of measurement for audience engagement. It is the duration of time a person in the area of opportunity to view is continuously viewing the display.

Together, session and attention times indicate how much time viewers dedicated to the content.

System inputs: Included a large, contextually relevant pool of both advertising and non-advertising content, tailored to the time, place, activity, and expected audience. This comprised typical broadcast and DOOH materials, plus live public safety and communication messages, alongside behavioral and audience data.

System outputs: Quantified audience reactions to the displayed media.

To set our trials apart from traditional DOOH, we started with familiar local broadcast content to engage viewers, then transitioned to contextually relevant ads stored locally. If engagement continued, a call-to-action was presented; if engagement dropped, the content was changed, similar to the YouTube skippable Ad timeline [2].

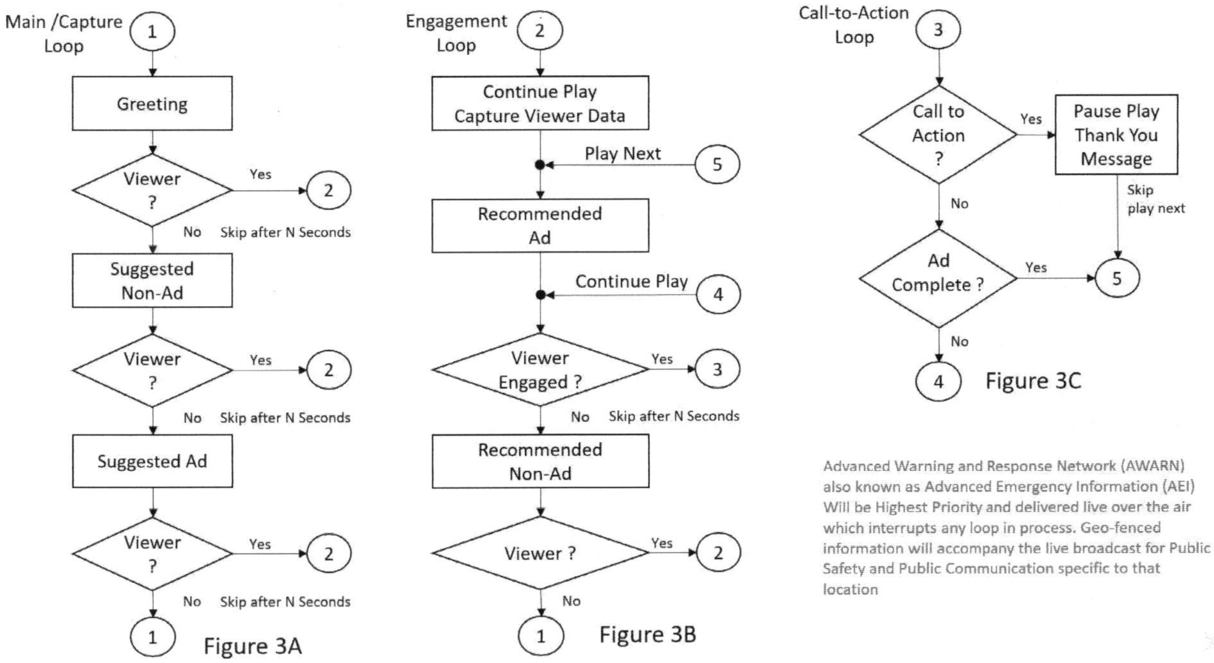

FIGURE 4: DECISION FLOW.

Our trials were all event based which provided a uniform environment for collecting comparison data:

- 2023 – CES show, NAB show, Smart City Connect show
- 2024 – NAB show, Woodward Dream Cruise, DSE show
- 2025 – CES show, (NAB show TBD)

Long-term trials at fixed locations, coupled with a clear strategy for campaigns and content, would better simulate a Digital Out-of-Home (DOOH) environment. This effort is still ongoing.

The trials utilized outdoor-rated 55-inch kiosks equipped with:

- Components for receiving over-the-air datacasting,
- Storage for file-based media,
- Computer vision analytics capabilities,
- AI processing capabilities,
- and a content management system (CMS) digital signage player.

Results

Table 1 represents data averaged during each individual event. Three key metrics were used to illustrate the incremental changes in audience capture and engagement from event to event.

Event Date	Gaze Through	Session Time (Seconds)	Attention Time (Seconds)	Budgeted Time
CES 2023 - Jan 5-8	42%	7.5	3.4	45%
NAB 2023 - Apr 15-19	26%	8.2	2.1	26%
WDC 2024 – Aug 17 outside	64%	4.2	1.9	45%
WDC 2024 – Aug 17 inside	71%	10	3.7	37%
CES 2025 – Jan 7-10	85%	7.1	5.6	79%

TABLE 1: EVENT COMPARISON METRICS.

Table 2 represents the DOOH content performance based on type, format and source averaged across all events.

DOOH	Aspect Ratio	Media Duration (seconds)	Dwell Time (seconds)	Media % Viewed	Average Audience Present
Explainer Indoor	16x9	36	11.6	32%	1.8
Explainer Outdoor	16x9	36	8.4	23%	2.6
MLK Day Greeting	9x16	7	3.9	56%	1.8
Christmas Greeting	9x16	7	4.6	66%	2.6
Super Bowl Poll	9x16	7	4.7	67%	1.7
DOOH Ad	9x16	30	7.1	24%	2.4
DOOH Ad	9x16	15	7.3	49%	2.4
DOOH Ad	9x16	10	4.3	43%	2.0
DOOH Ad	9x16	7	5.3	76%	2.0
DOOH Ad	9x16	5	3.1	62%	1.5

TABLE 2: DOOH CONTENT AND ADVERTISING METRICS.

Table 3 represents the Television content performance based on type, format and source averaged across all events.

TV	Aspect Ratio	Media Duration (seconds)	Dwell Time (seconds)	Media % Viewed	Average Audience Present
TV News Full	16x9	30	10.7	36%	3.4
TV News Short	16x9	15	6.9	46%	2.2
TV Weather Full	16x9	65	12.9	20%	4.2
TV Weather Short	16x9	25	9.8	39%	2.7
TV Ad	16x9	15	7.3	49%	2.1
TV Ad	16x9	10	5.8	58%	1.9

TABLE 3: TV CONTENT AND ADVERTISING METRICS.

Table 4 represents the Public Safety and Public Communications (PSPC) content performance based on type, format and source averaged across all events.

PSPC	Aspect Ratio	Media Duration (seconds)	Dwell Time (seconds)	Media % Viewed	Average Audience Present
Active Shooter	9x16	20	10.5	53%	1.9
Tornado Warning	9x16	20	11.3	57%	1.5
Missing Person	9x16	15	9.9	66%	2.1
Silver Alert	9x16	15	6.3	42%	1.8

TABLE 4: PSPC CONTENT METRICS.

Discussion

Trials:

In Table 1, we were highly satisfied with our debut at CES 2023. We invested significant effort into developing content that effectively boosted gaze-through rates. Achieving engagement with the audience for approximately half the duration they were within view was deemed a success.

At NAB 2023, we experienced a setback because of the increased complexity in conditional content playback for testing purposes. Rather than creating fresh content, we recycled the material from CES 2023 and put more focus on conditional play, which ended up disengaging the audience. Despite having more of their physical presence (session time), we captured less of their attention on our display (attention time).

The Woodward Dream Cruise (WDC) 2024, a significant event for car enthusiasts, provided a genuine outdoor test scenario. We deployed two dual-sided kiosks—one indoors and one outdoors. The broadcaster we collaborated with was instrumental in producing high-resolution, contextually fitting content and delivering daily updates, which was reflected in the gaze-through rates. However, our attention times were lower than expected. Being a single-day event, it was challenging to capture the attention of visitors primarily there to admire the thousands of classic cars parading along Woodward Avenue in Detroit.

For CES 2025, we benefited from exceptional content support, featuring daily updates which directly contributed to higher gaze-through rates. We achieved our highest average engagement to date and were particularly impressed with the ratio of Session Time to Attention Time. This indicated that the majority of the time visitors spent at the location was dedicated to viewing our content.

In Table 2, we delved deeper into the DOOH audience analytics. We extracted how much of the full clip duration was viewed and the average number of people concurrently viewing. An animated explainer video was used to introduce datacasting. Although it garnered decent dwell times due to its engaging content, its longer length and the lack of audio were drawbacks.

We also evaluated brief greetings and a sports poll, which were static, full-screen visuals designed for quick readability. We assumed that the full 7-second duration wasn't necessary for viewers to grasp the content. Yet, given the unpredictable timing of viewer engagement, this length was still deemed suitable. This content was presented in the traditional portrait orientation for DOOH, but instead of commercial ads, it was used to engage and capture the audience's attention.

We tested four different ad durations, with the 7-second and 15-second ads showing the best performance. Static ads were most effective when under 7 seconds; however, ads shorter than this often led to viewers switching contexts before fully absorbing the message, warranting further exploration. Video ads, on the other hand, were most effective when lasting between 10 and 15 seconds, with engagement dropping off as duration exceeded 15 seconds.

To account for multiple viewings by different individuals, DOOH networks employ an "impression multiplier" to estimate total reach, considering factors like foot traffic and dwell time. We measured average audience counts between 1.5 and 2.5 concurrent viewers for this purpose, highlighting the value of real-time measurement for more accurate data.

In Table 3, we examined metrics from content and ads originally produced for television, directly repurposed for DOOH. Displaying 16x9 video on a portrait screen reduced the visual to less than a third of the screen size. These were shown without sound or subtitles to fit the DOOH context better. Despite these adaptations, the performance was surprisingly good, with higher average audience counts than typical DOOH content, suggesting the content attracted larger crowds. However, the low view percentage indicated a potential loss of attention and inefficient use of screen time.

In Table 4, we present metrics for Public Safety and Public Communications (PSPC) messages that interrupt regular programming. PSPC was a focal point at all events and customer meetings, generating significant interest and prompting considerations for integrating more IoT sensors for tasks like air quality monitoring in California or gunshot detection at large venues and campuses. These messages consistently had high dwell times relative to their length, leading to a high viewing percentage. This suggests the duration was adequate for viewers to engage with the alert content potentially leading to further action on their mobile devices.

Next, the key elements of the system will be discussed to better frame the results from the trials. Specifically, why it is important to push more media than required to the edge, the second- and third-party data used, and capabilities of the datacasting system in the scope of supporting a Digital Out of Home network. We'll also discuss how we arrived at the concept of convergence in this context.

Advertising

The advertising industry is on the brink of reaching a one trillion-dollar global valuation [3]. The challenge of delivering the right message to the right person at the optimal moment is exacerbated by ever-shortening audience attention spans and an array of competing platforms. Tech giants like search engines and social media are capturing a significant portion of this market through the use of first-party data, offering a tailored, interactive experience. However, these platforms are not without their flaws, particularly concerning security, privacy, and trust. The proliferation of AI-generated "Deep Fakes" further undermines trust. While first-party data reveals consumer wants, it often misses needs or unknown interests, reinforcing the necessity for trusted sources to initiate information dissemination. A "First Mover" of information from a trusted source.

Out-of-Home (OOH) Advertising is growing but mostly due to digital out-of-home (DOOH) [4]. TV advertising is also growing but mostly due to Connected TV (CTV) [5]. Connected TV (CTV) is a term for any television that can connect to the internet and stream digital content. CTVs can be smart TVs or devices that connect to a TV, like streaming sticks, consoles, or set-top boxes. Within this realm, Free Ad-Supported Streaming TV (FAST) services, enabled by CTV, are the focus here due to their similarities with traditional ad-supported linear TV. Table 5 below illustrates the numerous parallels and notable benefits of these modern DOOH and CTV platforms.

Benefits	Traditional OOH	Digital OOH	Traditional TV	Connected TV
Broad Reach	X	X	X	X
Increased Brand Trust	X	X	X	X
Cost Effective	X	X	X	X
Large High Resolution	X	X	X	X
Data Driven Targeting		X		X
Enhanced Engagement		X		X
Interactivity		X		X
Improved Measurement		X		X
Dynamic Creatives		X		X
Higher Ad Completion Rates				X
Higher Recall Rate		X		
Real-Time Optimization		X		TBD
Contextual Advertising		WIP		WIP
Perceived Relevance		WIP		WIP

TABLE 5: OUT-OF-HOME AND IN-THE-HOME ADVERTISING COMPARISON

These platforms support the need for a trusted source for "first mover" information, but these platforms are not perfect either. Ad completion rates are higher on CTV due to having a captive audience, whereas DOOH achieves higher recall rates [6] and benefits from better real-time optimization due to its edge computing capabilities. Programmatic advertising is quickly becoming the most popular type of advertising, but the real time bidding (RTB) and server-side delivery of Ads seem more fitting for the one-to-one interactions common to online environments.

A unique feature shared by both DOOH and CTV is their focus on small groups, usually fewer than ten people. These groups are often similar in terms of location, time, and activity, but they can differ in age, gender, and viewpoints. This presents a unique challenge in targeting a diverse yet small collective, contrasting with the approach of targeting a single individual, like someone looking for an airline flight and car rental.

FIGURE 5: OUT-OF-HOME AND IN-THE-HOME SMALL AUDIENCE COMPARISON.

Throughout the trials, we showcased and evaluated both 9x16 "portrait" Digital Out of Home (DOOH) ads and 16x9 "landscape" television ads.

Content:

Connected TV (CTV) is experiencing better success with 30 second ads and higher completion rates than DOOH [7-10]. CTV 30-second spots exhibit high completion rates primarily due to the captive nature of the viewing environment, but it may also be attributed to the mix with informational content. A key objective of our study was to explore whether this success could be replicated in DOOH by creating a similar experience.

Content consumption differs between in-home and out-of-home environments. In-home viewing is a "lean-back" experience, while DOOH is a "passing-by" experience. However, both share commonalities—most notably, their reliance on advertising for revenue generation, marketing, and audience influence. CTV benefits from content that is viewer-selected, leading to higher ad completion rates. DOOH can adopt a similar approach by integrating relevant, engaging content to capture audience attention, but in smaller doses.

Our trials have also shown interest in News, Weather, Traffic and Sports updates. This provides leading content, a branding opportunity for the local affiliate, and sponsorship opportunities for their advertisers. In locations where Placed-Based DOOH Ads are effective, it may also be useful to surprise, inspire, educate or give your audience something they didn't know to associate the platform with being a first mover of information. One example of this is a local broadcast affiliate in Florida aired a "myth buster" segment about lighting strikes using a True/False interactive format. Given Florida's status as the lightning capital of the U.S., the segment was captivating, educational, and highly engaging. This type of content not only informs but also primes viewers emotionally, making them more receptive to advertising messages on both CTV and DOOH platforms.

Feedback from datacasting trials indicated widespread interest in Public Safety and Public Communications (PSPC) messaging across nearly every digital signage platform and venue. These messages play a critical role in informing, warning, assisting, and protecting the public. Broadcasters excel in this area, serving as trusted sources of information—particularly in emergencies—when cellular networks may become overwhelmed. The same technology and strategies developed for TV and the Broadcast App to provide specific geo fenced public safety information can be leveraged effectively in DOOH environments.

Figure 6 illustrates examples of PSPC content used during trials, including Active Shooter Instructions, Tornado Warnings with timing and safety guidelines, and Missing Person alerts with essential details and instructions. These types of messages enhance the value of DOOH platforms, reinforcing their role as a vital source of real-time, actionable information.

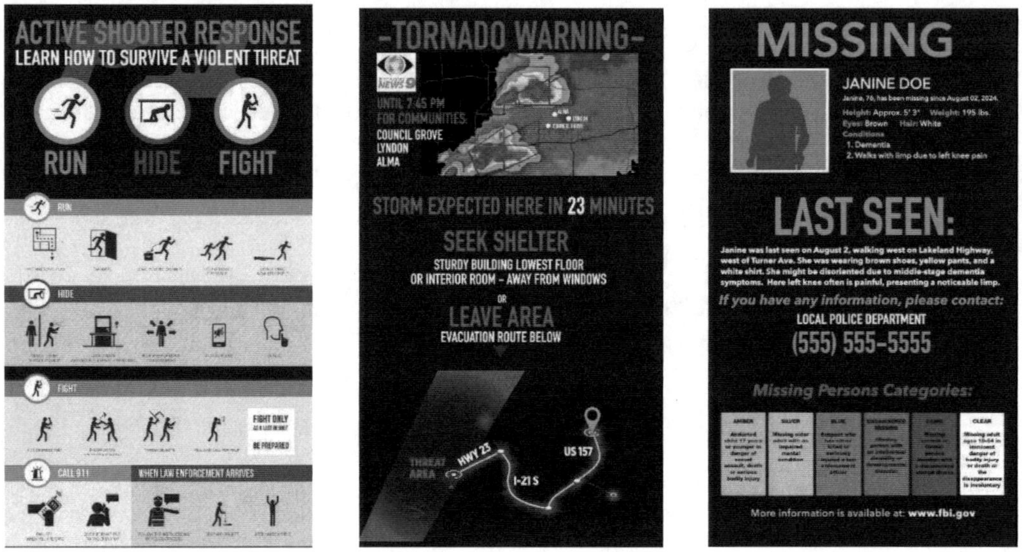

FIGURE 6: EXAMPLE ACTIVE SHOOTER, TORNADO WARNING, AND SILVER ALERT.

Content is still king. FAST CTV is becoming preferred by an increasing number of people because the advertisements are only present when enjoying chosen content vs. paying a fixed fee regardless of usage. Aligning high quality, interesting, and engaging content with contextually relevant advertising will create the best experience for everyone involved. The same should apply to DOOH. Keeping content contextually relevant requires frequent updates which requires the delivery of even more content, further strengthening the case for datacasting to efficiently pre-load media.

Contextual Relevance:

Research indicates that contextually relevant messaging in DOOH boosts effectiveness by an average of 17%, even in its early stages [11]. As seen in Table 5, comparing CTV and DOOH features, both contextual advertising and perceived relevance are marked as works-in-progress (WIP), highlighting their emerging role in the advertising industry. This area holds immense potential for enhancing audience capture, engagement, and conversion rates.

To maximize impact, advertisers have explored various ad formats, interactive methods, and even augmented reality (AR). Simple yet effective content like stock tickers and time & temperature displays have consistently demonstrated strong audience capture, particularly in locations with high visitor return rates.

Additionally, news-driven content can dynamically tailor ads based on trending headlines, transforming signage from background noise into a valuable source of quick, relevant information that seamlessly transitions to a smartphone experience.

While creative production costs have traditionally been a barrier, Generative AI now enables the automatic creation of advertising and content variations. These can be adapted based on season, location, time of day, weather, events, news, traffic, sports, markets, and countless other conditions—making dynamic, highly relevant advertising more accessible and cost-effective than ever.

Figure 7 is a GenAI example using Grok from X.ai [12], of a cruise line advertising campaign targeting young professionals and retirees in Detroit. It only took a few seconds to create several variations for two demographics during two different weather conditions.

FIGURE 7: CRUISE LINE AD TARGETING YOUNG PROFESSIONALS AND RETIREES.

Generative AI has faced scrutiny over copyright concerns, authenticity issues, and overall limitations. However, it continues to demonstrate its potential—especially in terms of automation and content scalability.

Trust remains a critical factor in media. Local journalists, deeply connected to their communities, serve as trusted sources of information. Their work is essential for raising awareness and combating misinformation and disinformation online. Both CTV and DOOH can leverage their content effectively by delivering it in platform-optimized formats.

Audience preferences for advertising vary—some prefer ads tailored to their interests, while others prefer relevance to their current activities. CTV has an advantage in this regard, as first-party data allows for precise targeting based on viewing behavior. For DOOH, audience analytics must be built over time using second- and third-party data to refine targeting and improve contextual relevance.

To engage younger, "Digital First" and "Digital Native" audiences, DOOH may need to incorporate more interactive elements, portrait-mode content, and social media integration. The 9x16 portrait format aligns with the way younger generations consume content on mobile devices, making it a natural and familiar viewing experience [13]. Additionally, integrating social media feeds can showcase trending "User-Generated Content," further enhancing engagement and relevance.

Data

A widely used and trusted data source goes by several names—Geo, Mobile, or Foot Traffic analytics. This location data is collected through smartphone apps, where users, knowingly or unknowingly, agree to share their location information. Aggregators then purchase this data, analyze it alongside millions of other data points from hundreds of apps, and generate insights. This is an example of second-party data.

AI-driven analytics help these companies determine visit patterns, including the number of visits to a location, visitor origins, dwell time, next destinations, and visit frequency Figure 8. With enough data, they can even infer where someone lives, works, where their children go to school, and when soccer practice ends based on recurring location patterns. Many ad networks rely exclusively on this data to power their programmatic advertising strategies.

However, the biggest limitation of this data is its lack of real-time capabilities. While it can reveal how many soccer parents visited a facility last month, it cannot identify who is present at any given moment. For advertisers running 10-30 second ads, this means there's no way to ensure their target audience is actually seeing the message when it airs.

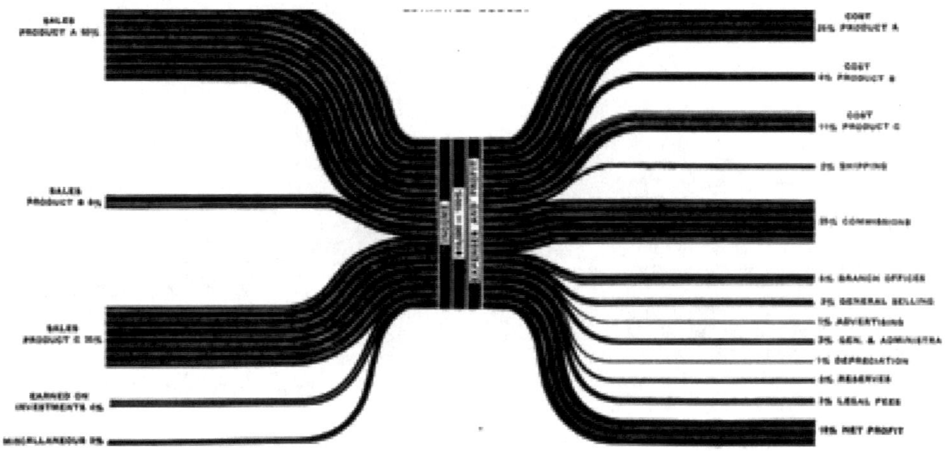

FIGURE 8: AUDIENCE JOURNEY EXTERNAL TO LOCATION.

Presence, Wi-Fi, and Bluetooth location tracking of personal smart devices, along with positioning analytics, were also valuable third-party data sources used in these trials. While their primary function was capturing unique visitors, visit frequency, dwell times, and heat maps (Figure 9) in near real-time, they also played a crucial role in validating computer vision analytics as an additional data source. This multi-layered approach helped ensure greater accuracy and reliability in audience measurement and engagement insights.

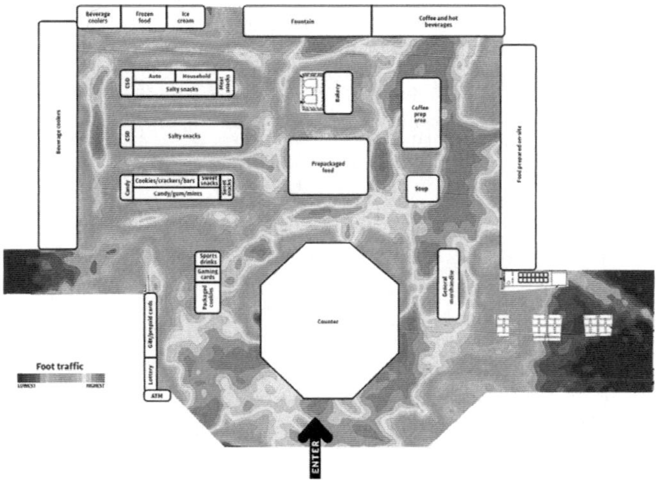

FIGURE 9: AUDIENCE JOURNEYS INTERNAL TO LOCATION.

Computer Vision Analytics (CVA) is a reliable solution for real-time audience insights. It can anonymously capture key demographic data such as age, gender, and emotion, along with dwell times, attention duration, and audience count. When integrated with a content management system (CMS), CVA enables conditional content playback in real time, ensuring that targeted audiences receive relevant messaging. This approach was selected for our testing and trials due to its effectiveness in optimizing engagement.

However, a significant drawback of CVA is the regulatory and privacy concerns surrounding the use of cameras. Some companies and local governments prohibit their use, even when compliant with GDPR, ADPPA, and similar regulations. While CVA is highly effective, its implementation is not always guaranteed, making it essential to consider alternative audience measurement solutions where necessary.

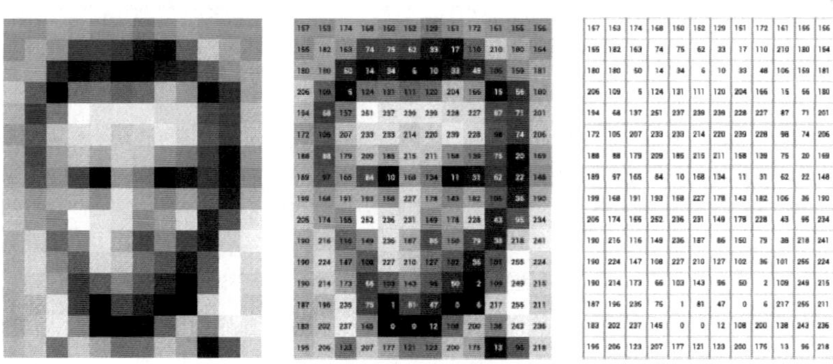

FIGURE 10: COMPUTER VISION ANALYTICS

While these three data sources provided valuable audience insights, they offered little information about general behavior, intentions, or interests. To effectively preload contextually relevant content and ads, it's essential to start each day with as much available knowledge as possible.
Looking into behavioral sciences provided intriguing insights into creating more contextual and engaging experiences. For example, research shows that people tend to be more health-conscious on Mondays, are more likely to make impulse purchases on sunny days and are willing to spend more after 6 PM. Many other behavioral patterns align with specific products or services, offering opportunities for strategic content placement.

Additionally, when people are drawn to a screen, their engagement often triggers curiosity in others, creating a ripple effect. Interactive content amplifies this effect, as the "fear of missing out" (FOMO) drives further participation and attention, making DOOH even more impactful.

FIGURE 11: BEHAVIORAL SCIENCE ON PURCHASE BEHAVIOR.

Even if behavioral science cannot directly influence an audience's actions, it can still serve as a powerful tool for "priming"—using subtle cues to align content and ads with audience tendencies. By strategically integrating these insights, advertisers can create experiences that feel more relevant and engaging.

As Maya Angelou famously said, *"People will forget what you said and forget what you did, but they will never forget how you made them feel"* [14]. Emotional connection is one of the most powerful drivers in advertising. When content resonates on a personal level, it becomes more memorable, increasing the likelihood of audience engagement and action.

Datacasting

DOOH content distribution networks experience four major challenges: Reliability/uptime, security/isolation from other networks, hidden cost, and complexity of management. Low data costs are typically nullified by the cost of managing hundreds of ISPs or IT departments. Lower management costs such as cellular networks are typically nullified by high data costs. Datacasting as a managed service by USSI Global can mitigate all four challenges.

The DOOH use case discussed so far highlights the growing need for delivering more file-based content to the edge than is immediately required. This ensures a broad selection of media for contextual relevance. ATSC 3.0 shows significant potential in supporting this demand, but key questions remain regarding how much, how fast, and how efficiently it can be utilized.

Available bandwidth varies by market, but as a reference point, assuming **25 Mbps per RF channel**, potential ATSC 3.0 capacity per market includes:

- 5 Low band VHF Channels per market (Channels 2-6)
- 7 High band VHF Channels per market (Channels 7-13)
- 23 UHF Channels per market (Channel 14-36)
- 30 Total ATSC 3.0 channels per market (excluding low band VHF)
- 750 Mbps total bandwidth
- 8,100 GB (8TB) of data per day

However, U.S. broadcasters are still fulfilling linear channel obligations, and ATSC 3.0 currently operates under a lighthouse channel-sharing model, limiting available datacasting bandwidth. During trials, available bitrates ranged from **1 Mbps to 4 Mbps**, which translates to:

- 2 - 8 seconds to transfer a MB of data
- 33 - 133 minutes to transfer a GB of data
- 10.8 - 43.2 GB total per day

One key discovery from the trials was that the carousel mechanism in the non-real-time (NRT) service repeatedly retransmitted the same files in a loop, leading to significant bandwidth waste. To mitigate this, we agreed on 4X retransmission, but this further reduced the available bandwidth to approximately 2-10 GB per day.

Despite this limitation, the total test media collection per trial was approximately 1GB, allowing us to successfully meet the preloading goal while still retaining bandwidth for content and ad updates throughout the day. This approach ensured efficient data utilization while maintaining flexibility for real-time adjustments.

Datacasting is not a guaranteed delivery system, so necessary protections need to be in place including the appropriate forward error correction (FEC), file sizes, checksums, parity recovery files, retransmission, applications that support User Datagram Protocol (UDP) reliability and use of a backhaul network for corner cases. The FEC for our trials was also more conservative, which took up usable bandwidth. This work is still in progress.

Ad Network providers set a minimum requirement for DOOH programmatic advertising: delivering a 25MB file within 15 seconds. However, due to lighthouse operation and datacasting bandwidth limitations, this goal was not met. Achieving this requirement would necessitate a bitrate of at least 14 Mbps, which exceeded the available capacity during trials.

Additionally, traditional programmatic advertising delivers ads on a one-to-one basis to each kiosk, which is inefficient for datacasting. To address this, we proposed an alternative approach which leverages datacasting: By preloading a sufficient inventory of relevant ads at the edge, we enabled client-side ad insertion instead of server-side delivery. Local intelligence at the edge determined which available ads to play based on predefined conditions, creating a personalized and context-aware experience. This method closely mirrors the programmatic workflow but in a way that is optimized for datacasting. This approach is also a more sustainable ("greener") approach, significantly reducing the need for high-speed communications to each individual kiosk. To refine this system, stimulus-response data was captured and analyzed, with ongoing work focused on improving targeting, efficiency, and adaptability. This work is still in progress.

Convergence:

Our exploration of datacasting for DOOH and the successful integration of a CMS player on an ATSC 3.0 receiver revealed a path toward more efficient in-home broadcasting. By pre-caching most programming and advertising as file-based content at the edge (Figure 13), we can significantly reduce redundant bandwidth consumption compared to an everything live-linear model (Figure 12). This strategy prioritizes bandwidth for truly live events, such as sports, while delivering a compelling CTV experience. Just as the shift to 16x9 TVs drove ATSC 1.0 adoption, the transition to a Connected TV experience could likely be a key driver for ATSC 3.0 adoption.

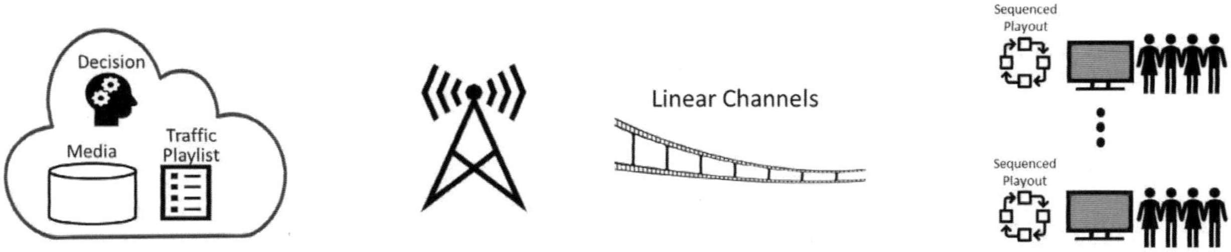

FIGURE 12: TRADITIONAL LINEAR BROADCAST.

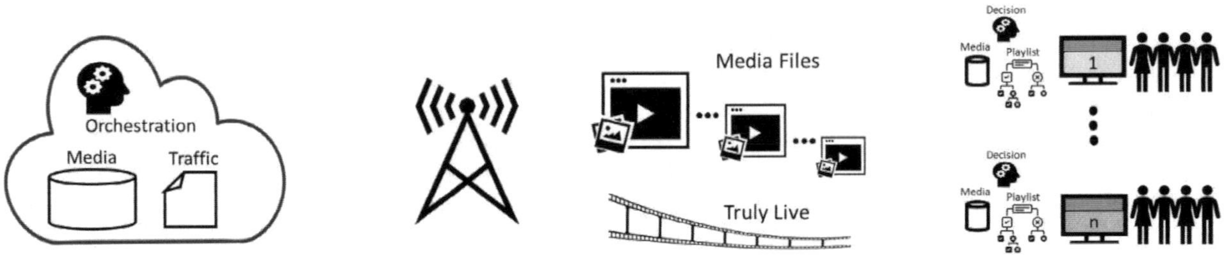

FIGURE 13: DATACASTING FILES TO SMALL GROUPS OF PEOPLE IN-THE-HOME.

By leveraging local intelligence at the edge, we can create personalized recommendations and playlists for each household, enabling more targeted content and advertising delivery. This transforms traditional linear broadcast into a Connected TV FAST experience with enhanced selection and features to compete with internet-based CTV. Key CTV advantages like on-demand playback and personalized program guides can realized. Pre-caching programming and advertising allows for targeted delivery, benefiting viewers, advertisers, and broadcasters. Our tests demonstrate that ATSC 3.0 receivers can store media and capturing viewer data, providing broadcasters with valuable insights exceeding DOOH capabilities. By pre-caching Diginet and much of the main channel programming, we can optimize bandwidth utilization and reduce redundant linear transmission. This frees up bandwidth for prioritized delivery for file-based content or bandwidth for live events.

Sharing the same datacasting content between DOOH and CTV will further optimize bandwidth efficiency while providing cohesion and ad frequency to an omnichannel strategy. This dual platform approach could further strengthen brand credibility and trust.

Historically, traditional broadcast did not have access to the edge until Connected TVs became popular. Broadcasters should take control of the edge, learn from and partner with DOOH operators and receiver manufacturers, and become a CTV competitor. This would level the field in terms of audience measurement and targeting both content and advertising. Let us shift our focus from Mbps of streamed channels to MB of delivered files, taking ownership of the edge, and delivering a superior user experience.

Conclusion

Key Takeaways:

- Content is king. Location matters. Know your audience. The core best practices of DOOH remain essential.
- Datacasting has proven to be an effective method for precaching media on digital signage.
- Programmatic workflows can integrate with datacasting but requires client-side ad insertion. This approach is more efficient, reliable, and environmentally friendly than traditional delivery methods like cellular networks.
- For time-sensitive alerts, switching to live broadcasts is recommended. PSPC alerts such as weather and traffic updates, school closings, or missing persons can be shared across platforms along with supplemental geofenced actionable information.
- Contextual and relevant content enhances audience capture and engagement. Frequent content updates, combined with CVA and conditional play, improve effectiveness.
- DOOH is also gaining traction for community messaging beyond commercial advertising.
- In high return visit locations, fresh, surprising, or thought-provoking content sustains interest in viewing. People expect ads but may ignore static signage over time, so giving them a reason to engage repeatedly is crucial.
- Blending ads with engaging content boosts performance. If done well, the content can prime audiences for upcoming ads, building trust and credibility for the brand and signage. Interactive experiences require more than simple QR Codes.

- Ad recall improves with repetition, but balance is key to avoid fatigue. Content iteration based on real time audience measurement at the edge can enhance recall without overloading viewers.
- Using upper titles and lower graphics to support primary 16x9 video content also proved effective.
- Optimizing precached content requires behavioral science and audience journey analysis to determine what, how often and how much content to store locally.

Challenges

- Bandwidth optimization and high-speed delivery need further improvements.
- Ad format effectiveness—while research suggests 9x16 portrait ads should outperform 16x9 landscape formats [1], this was not confirmed in our trials and requires further study.
- Content innovation is essential for emotional engagement. Generative AI could automate ad variations, but balancing novelty, authenticity, and investment remains a challenge.
- Trust and privacy can be competitive advantages over online platforms. As data privacy concerns grow, compliance and transparency will be critical.
- Directional audio showed mixed results—effective in controlled environments but inconsistent in ad-hoc settings, warranting further investigation.
- Measuring long-term impact beyond immediate metrics (engagement, recall, conversion rates) remains an area for further exploration.

Next Steps

- For DOOH, broaden trials related to precaching of content across various environments and use cases to refine strategies based on real-world feedback.
- For Linear TV, investigate DOOH media cache and edge intelligence operations to determine feasibility of transitioning towards a CTV model, enhancing content delivery and audience engagement.

The ultimate goal is to evolve a new approach to create, deliver, measure, and monetize content effectively in this new converged space.

References

[1] Unknown, "Experiment Four (October 2020): 16x9 vs 9x16 Aspect Ratio", *Marpipe*, October 29, 2020. www.marpipe.com/blog/experiment-four-october-2020

[2] Henke, C., "YouTube's triple threat: Mastering Feed, Shorts and Skippable ads", *Search Engine Land*, October 16, 2024. www.searchengineland.com/youtube-feed-shorts-skippable-ads-447528

[3] Flynn, K. and Fischer, S., "Global ad market to surpass $1 trillion for first time", *Axios*, December 9, 2024. www.axios.com/2024/12/09/ad-revenue-growth-2024

[4] Ritchie, M., "Understanding Digital Out-of-Home (DOOH) Ads and How They Work', *StackAdapt,* July 31, 2024. www.stackadapt.com/resources/blog/digital-out-of-home

[5] Bundle, R., "Is Linear TV Dead? Shifting Budgets To Connected TV", *adlucent*, n.d. www.adlucent.com/resources/blog/is-linear-tv-dead-shifting-budgets-to-connected-tv/

[6] Filyakov, R., "Broadcast advertising vs. DOOH ads: What to choose?", *Look*, February 9, 2024. www.lookdigitalsignage.com/blog/broadcast-advertising-vs-dooh-ads

[7] "How DOOH, streaming audio and CTV connect the cookieless, multi-device world", *Ad Age*, December 2022. www.csbimpact.com/wp-content/uploads/2023/02/20221212_viant_streaming_wp_final.pdf

[8] "Video Completion Rate Analysis", *Unbrex*, 2024. www.umbrex.com/resources/ultimate-guide-to-company-analysis/ultimate-guide-to-marketing-analysis/video-completion-rate-analysis/

[9] "How Did Video Ad Completion Rates Fare Last Year?", *marketing charts*, April 16, 2024. www.marketingcharts.com/digital/video-232642

[10] "Understanding DOOH Ad Performance Metrics: Measuring Success in the Digital Out-of-Home Space", Confirm, August 7, 2024. www.confirm.media/dooh-ad-performance-metrics/

[11] Board, W., "The Moments of Truth – Clear Channel, JCDecaux and Posterscope," *OOH Today,* March 4, 2020. www.oohtoday.com/the-moments-of-truth-clear-channel-jcdecaux-and-posterscope/

[12] Grok, *xAI*, https://x.ai/

[13] Barbush, J., "The Real Reason People Skip Ads", *LinkedIn*, October 20, 2023. www.linkedin.com/pulse/real-reason-people-skip-ads-j-barbush/

[14] Pragasam, R., "How You Made Them Feel", *Compass Group*, June 10, 2014. www.compass-usa.com/how-you-made-them-feel/

Asynchronous Sharing of Media Essence Data in Software Defined Workflows

Gareth Sylvester-Bradley
NVIDIA Development UK Ltd
Reading, United Kingdom
garethsb@nvidia.com

Pravin Sethia
NVIDIA Graphics Pvt Ltd
Pune, Maharashtra, India
pravins@nvidia.com

Thomas True
NVIDIA Corporation
Santa Clara, California, United States
ttrue@nvidia.com

Abstract – As media workflows migrate to open-source software-defined frameworks consisting of a collection of containerized applications running as processing nodes on a cluster of commercial-off-the-shelf (COTS) servers, there is a need for these distributed application processes to asynchronously share media essence data in the most efficient and secure way possible without going back to the baseband transport. This sharing of media essence data is complicated by the fact that some applications perform graphics processing unit (GPU) processing requiring the essence data to be in GPU memory while others perform media processing on the central processing unit (CPU) requiring the essence data to be in system memory. Several technologies exist for such sharing of media essence data between processes on different compute nodes of a cluster so the ultimate solution needs to support multiple transports with an application layer API that support initiating and terminating communications. We compare the various techniques and demonstrate how they can be used within a platform available today for the easy development and deployment of distributed media process pipelines for transcoding and AI applications.

Introduction

The desire for media producers to deploy scalable software-based systems composed of applications from diverse vendors on Commercial Off-The-Shelf (COTS) hardware has led to the evolution of Software Defined Workflows. These Software Defined Workflows implement a collection of Software Media Functions (SMFs) within the European Broadcasting Union's (EBU's) vision for a Dynamic Media Facility [1] shown in Figure 1.

These container-based SMFs, shown in Figure 2, implement media processing operations such as transcoding, color correction, switching, audio and video monitoring as well as AI operations utilizing the software and hardware functionalities of the underlying compute platform based upon industry standard IT principles. The input and output of these media processing functions includes the media essence data to be processed, associated metadata that describes the media essence data as well as control data that provides application controllable parameters to the media function.

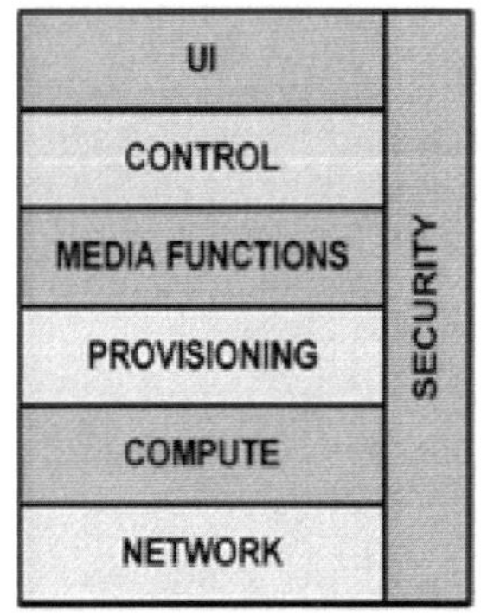

FIGURE 1: EBU DYNAMIC MEDIA FACILITY.

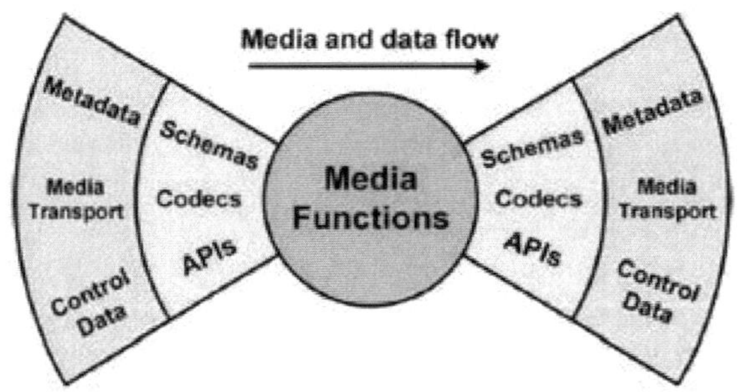

FIGURE 2: SOFTWARE MEDIA FUNCTIONS.

A software-defined workflow subsequently chains together a collection of these media processing functions to create a complete media processing pipeline deployed across multiple cluster compute nodes. Optimal implementation of the pipeline requires that the media essence data be asynchronously shared between the media processing nodes operating on different compute nodes in the most efficient and secure way possible. This sharing of media essence data is complicated by the fact that some applications perform GPU processing requiring the media essence to be in GPU memory while others perform processing on the CPU requiring the essence data to by in system memory.

Several technologies exist for such sharing of media essence data between processes on different compute nodes of a cluster. We compare the various techniques and demonstrate how they can be utilized within our platform [2] constructed for the processing of media essence that combines COTS hardware with a Kubernetes-based module software architecture [3].

Media Processing Platform

Hardware

The hardware platform consists of three COTS servers each consisting of two non-uniform memory access (NUMA) nodes connected via Intel Ultra Path Interconnect (UPI) [4] or AMD Infinity Interconnect [5]. In addition to the two Intel Xeon Gold 6448Y Sapphire-Rapids [6] or AMD EPYC 9354 "Zen 4" Genoa [7] CPUs (Central Processing Units), each server has two, four or eight NVIDIA L40S [8] GPUs

(Graphics Processing Units) for video transcoding and Artificial Intelligence (AI) processing as well as three Network Interface Controllers (NICs), that is two NVIDIA ConnectX-7 NICs [9] for north-south traffic and a single NVIDIA BlueField-3 [10] Data Processing Unit (DPU) for east-west traffic. The basic server configuration is illustrated in Figure 3.

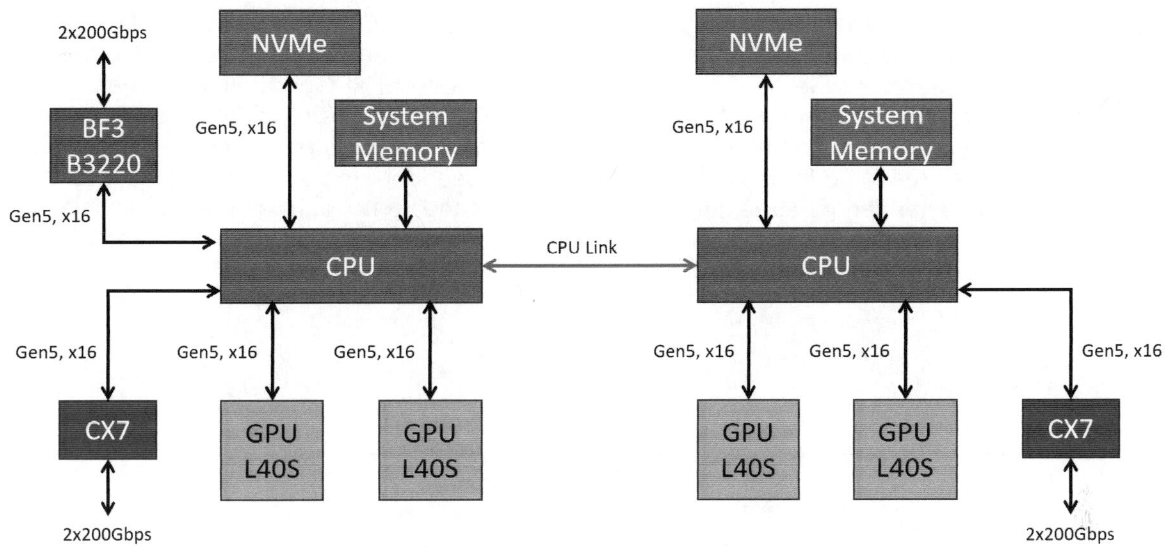

FIGURE 3. COTS SERVER ARCHITECTURE.

In this system, Direct Data Transfer peer-to-peer Direct Memory Access (DMA) transactions are permitted between GPUs and NICs connected to the same NUMA node. For redundancy and scale out, three servers are connected in a cluster configuration as illustrated in Figure 4. Transmission of media essence data between media functions running on different nodes is achieved via redundant 200 Gb/sec high-speed network connections.

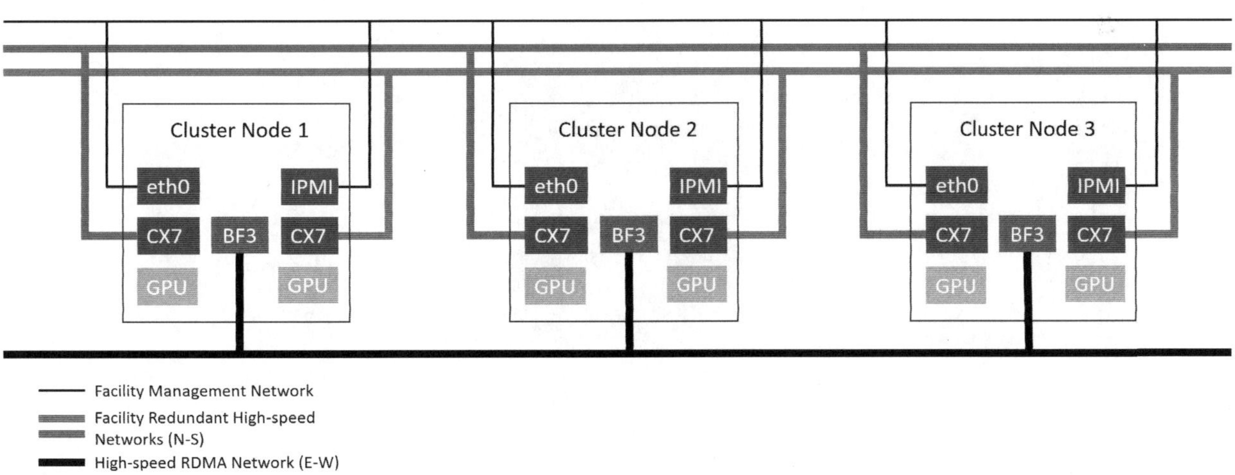

FIGURE 4. HARDWARE PLATFORM.

Software

The software stack is built upon the Red Hat OpenShift enterprise Kubernetes container platform [11] as shown in Figure 5. For a compact production system, Kubernetes is deployed on the three-node hardware cluster such that each server functions as both a master node for Kubernetes control plane functions and worker node for the deployment of the containerized media processing applications. Utilizing a cluster of three servers in this way provides redundancy protection. A standard cluster configuration starting with three control plane nodes and two worker nodes can scale out the media processing capability simply by adding more worker nodes.

The Kubernetes scheduler is responsible for allocating workloads to nodes in the cluster. It finds and scores feasible nodes considering resource requirements, affinity and anti-affinity specifications, etc. It then ensures the application is allocated to the highest scoring node. The OpenShift Kubernetes worker nodes are performance optimized to ensure that every workload or stream is unaffected by other workloads running on the same node. As part of optimization/tuning, worker nodes are configured to (a) isolate CPU cores reserved for the system versus those used for media-processing applications, (b) reserve huge-pages needed for streaming applications, (c) tune kernel parameters, (d) disable redundant services, etc. During this stage, network time protocol (NTP) also gets disabled so that the platform consistently uses precision time protocol (PTP).

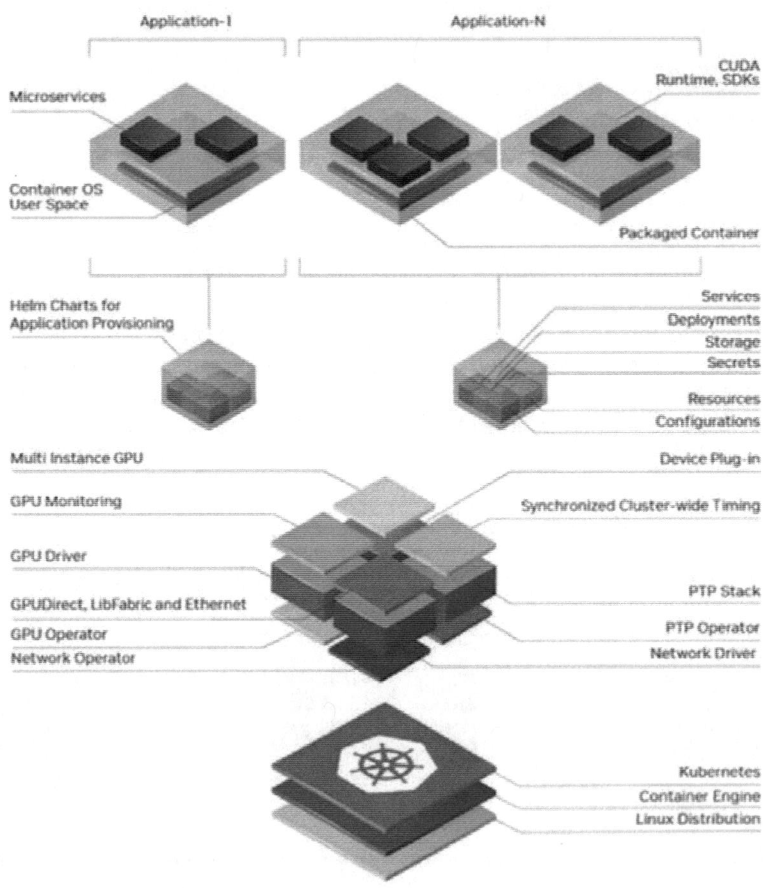

FIGURE 5. SOFTWARE STACK.

Data Transfer Technologies

Several technologies exist for the asynchronous transfer and sharing of media essence data between software media function processes executing on the compute nodes of a cluster. Each of these methods comes with advantages as well as disadvantages. In this section we summarize each of these technologies.

Shared Memory

Shared memory is a method whereby multiple computing processing running on the same compute node can directly read from and write to a common block of memory allowing for rapid data exchange without utilizing traditional inter-process communication (IPC) methods such as message passing. While this technique can be optimal for CPU-based software media functions, this method is not optimal for GPU-based processes as it requires an additional copy between the GPU device memory and the shared system memory. In the case that both software media functions are running on the same GPU, these processes can share GPU-device memory through CUDA [12]. An issue with shared memory is that Kubernetes does not permit the use of shared memory due to the fact that there are no shared namespaces. As a result, shared memory can work across containers in the same pod but not across pods.

RDMA over Converged Ethernet (RoCE)

Remote Direct Memory Access (RDMA) is the direct memory access (DMA) by a computing process executing on a compute node into the memory of another compute node without the direct involvement of the operating system or CPU of either system. RDMA over Converged Ethernet (RoCE) is a network protocol which allows RDMA operations between compute nodes over an Ethernet network [13]. RoCE v1 is an Ethernet link layer protocol that permits RDMA between any two hosts in the same Ethernet broadcast domain while RoCE v2 is an internet layer protocol on top of user datagram protocol (UDP) which allows for packets to be routed.

GPU Direct RDMA

GPU Direct RDMA permits RDMA operations between GPU device memory and the device memory of other hardware devices such as Network Interface Controllers (NICs) without the involvement of the CPU or operating system. GPU Direct RDMA is supported in Rivermax [14], the NVIDIA SDK that leverages the hardware UDP streaming acceleration technology found in NVIDIA NICs/DPUs to provide high throughput low latency video processing for ST 2110 as well as secure reliable transport (SRT), reliable internet stream transport (RIST) and network device interface (NDI).

Application Frameworks

Media Communications Mesh

Media Communications Mesh (MCM) [15] is a framework that enables efficient, low-latency media transport between microservices by creating a secure, standards-based media data plane. MCM also adds the required control-plane communications infrastructure to implement any media control protocol in order to initiate and terminate data exchange between software media functions.

OpenUCX

Unified Communication X (UCX) [16] is a framework for high-bandwidth low-latency communication between compute processes. UCX exposes a set of communication primitives that abstracts the underlying communication technology such that the best available hardware and method (RoCE, GPU accelerators, shared memory, etc.) is utilized. The architecture of UCX is illustrated in Figure 6.

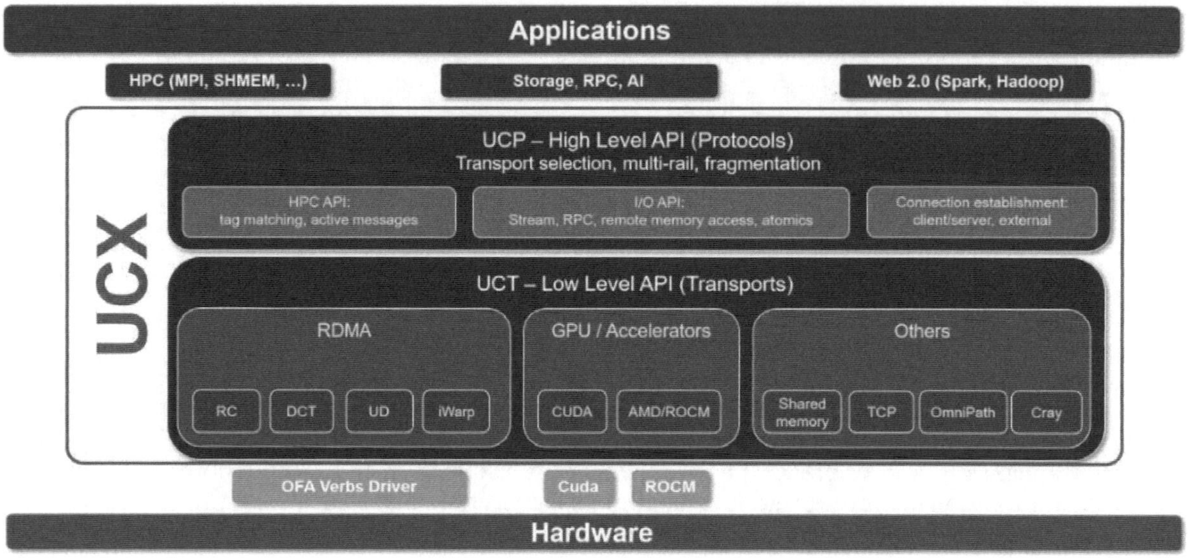

FIGURE 6. UCX ARCHITECTURE.

Libfabric

Libfrabric, also referred to as Open Fabrics Interfaces (OFI) [17] is a framework that defines an API for communication between high-performance parallel and distributed applications. Developed by the OFI working group, Libfabric is a low-level API that abstracts the underlying diverse networking technologies such as transmission control protocol (TCP) sockets, UDP datagram sockets and RoCE.

Results

Our results demonstrate that peer-to-peer transfers between GPUs and between GPUs and NICs result in lower peripheral component interconnect express (PCIe) bus usage, lower CPU usage by eliminating memory copy operations and reduced host memory utilization from the elimination of the need for staging buffers. This leads to reduced stream latency while allowing for an increased stream density. Higher level transfer protocols such as RoCE that leverage kernel bypass permit transfers to achieve line rate while using less CPU cycles than traditional lower-level socket-based transfer protocols. Asynchronous transfers permit compute operations on essence data to proceed while other essence data is copied between DANZ monitoring fabrics (DMFs).

Conclusions

The ultimate solution for the efficient transfer of media essence between DMFs running on the same or different processing nodes needs to be topology-aware and support multiple transport methodologies in order to take full advantage of the underlying hardware. Media essence transfers should utilize a minimal number of CPU cores, host memory and PCIe bus transactions. This is achieved by leveraging RDMA technologies that permit peer-to-peer operations such as GPU Direct RDMA and RoCE.

Acknowledgements

The authors would like to specifically thank their NVIDIA colleague Kartikey Agrawal for his significant contribution to the project testing the achievable bandwidth of the various data transfer technologies as well as their other NVIDIA colleague for their contributions to this project.

References

[1] European Broadcasting Union, "The Dynamic Media Facility – Media Value Chain Transformation," https://tech.ebu.ch/docs/white_papers/White%20Paper%20-%20EBU%20Media%20Factory%20Software%20-%20Media%20Functions.pdf

[2] Sylvester-Bradley, G, Sethia, P, Hastie, R, and True, T, "A Platform for the Development and Deployment of Software-Defined Media Processing Pipelines, "*Proceedings of the 2024 NAB Broadcast Engineering and Information Technology (BEIT) Conference,* April 2024

[3] Kubernetes, https://kubernetes.io/

[4] Intel, "Intel Xeon Process Scalable Family Technical Overview," https://www.intel.com/content/www/us/en/developer/articles/technical/xeon-processor-scalable-family-technical-overview.html.

[5] AMD, "Infinity Architecture," https://www.amd.com/en/technologies/infinity-architecture.

[6] Intel, "Intel Xeo Gold 6448Y Processor," https://www.intel.com/content/www/us/en/products/sku/232384/intel-xeon-gold-6448y-processor-60m-cache-2-10-ghz/specifications.html.

[7] AMD, "4th Generation AMD EPYC Processors," https://www.amd.com/en/products/processors/server/epyc/4th-generation-9004-and-8004-series.html.

[8] NVIDIA, "NVIDIA L40S, Unparalleled AI and Graphics Performance for the Data Center," https://www.nvidia.com/en-us/data-center/l40s/.

[9] NVIDIA, "ConnectX-7 400G Adapters: Accelerated Networking for Modern Data Center Infrastructures," https://resources.nvidia.com/en-us-accelerated-networking-resource-library/connectx-7-datasheet.

[10] NVIDIA, "NVIDIA Bluefield-3 DPU: Programmable Data Center Infrastructure On-a-Chip," https://www.nvidia.com/content/dam/en-zz/Solutions/Data-Center/documents/datasheet-nvidia-bluefield-3-dpu.pdf.

[11] Red Hat OpenShift, https://www.redhat.com/en/technologies/cloud-computing/openshift.

[12] CUDA, https://developer.nvidia.com/cuda-toolkit.

[13] Nvidia, RDMA over Converged Ethernet (RoCE), https://docs.nvidia.com/networking/display/winofv55054000/rdma+over+converged+ethernet+(roce)

[14] Media Communications Mesh, https://openvisualcloud.github.io/Media-Communications-Mesh/docs/README.html#introduction.

[15] NVIDIA, "NVIDIA Rivermax: Optimized Networking SDK for Media and Data Streaming Applications," https://developer.nvidia.com/networking/Rivermax.

[16] Open UCX, https://openucx.org/documentation/.

[17] Libfabric, https://ofiwg.github.io/libfabric/.

Broadcasting Without Boundaries: Seamlessly Integrating EAS into Virtualized Air-Chains

Bill Robertson, Ed Czarnecki PhD
Digital Alert Systems
Lyndonville, New York, United States
bill.robertson@digitalalertsystems.com, ed.czarnecki@digitalalertsystems.com

Abstract –The integration of IP-based workflows in broadcasting has revolutionized traditional radio and television air chains, enhancing flexibility, cost efficiency, and resilience. However, adapting legacy systems, such as the Emergency Alert System (EAS), to modern digital workflows presents technical and regulatory challenges. This paper explores the evolution of EAS implementation, from analog switch-based systems to IP-based architectures, addressing insertion points, signal processing, and compliance requirements. By leveraging networked technologies, broadcasters can streamline EAS integration, enabling centralized and cloud-based operations while maintaining compliance with FCC and FEMA standards. The proposed solutions enhance scalability, reliability, and geo-targeted alert distribution without requiring regulatory modifications, ensuring that EAS remains effective in the evolving broadcast landscape.

Introduction

The implementation of IP-based workflows for radio and television has grown exponentially just over the past few years. These workflows include various traditional hardware-based elements such as mixing and production consoles, routers, and more. The IP world enables the virtualization of several of these elements, providing flexibility, cost savings, and resiliency over the complexity of legacy broadcast air chains.

Virtualization is the creation of virtual versions of physical resources, such as servers, storage, or networks, allowing multiple virtual environments to run on a single physical machine. This technology enhances resource utilization, flexibility, and scalability while isolating workloads for improved efficiency and management. The promise of virtualization is compelling and offers many benefits, but real-world applications introduce real boundaries. Some physical resources obviously don't lend themselves to being wholly virtualized — a microphone, camera, or transmission tower, for example. There are compelling reasons why some resources should remain physically separate — such as reliability, isolation, and security.

Other defining boundaries have nothing to do with signals but are regulatory constraints that are not easily moved or modified. As we outline in this paper, this is the case with the Emergency Alert System (EAS). As broadcasters or Multiple Video Program Distributors (MPVD) such as traditional cable and IPTV systems, we still need to insert critical emergency messages whenever necessary under these rules.

But how do we do this? How can we adapt a system designed in the 1990s to work in a 21st-century transmission system?

For this to work, we must be aware of the type of signal or air chain being used and determine the appropriate insertion points within that air chain. This challenge is further complicated by the fact that the insertion points are no longer as well-defined as they were in baseband when EAS was first introduced.

This paper explores a simplified version of the evolution of radio and television air chains to understand better how virtualization has been achieved to eliminate a number of boundaries and how it can continue to serve as a solution for today and well into the future.

Understanding the Past to Build the Future

The current Emergency Alert System (EAS) has been part of the broadcast and cable infrastructure in the U.S. for nearly three decades, since its adoption by the FCC in 1997. Its long history goes back to an even lengthier implementation of the Emergency Broadcast System (EBS) that EAS replaced.

The graphic in Figure 1 shows the long history of public warnings by broadcasters, beginning with AM radio in the 1950s and continuing through the current EAS/IPAWS system.

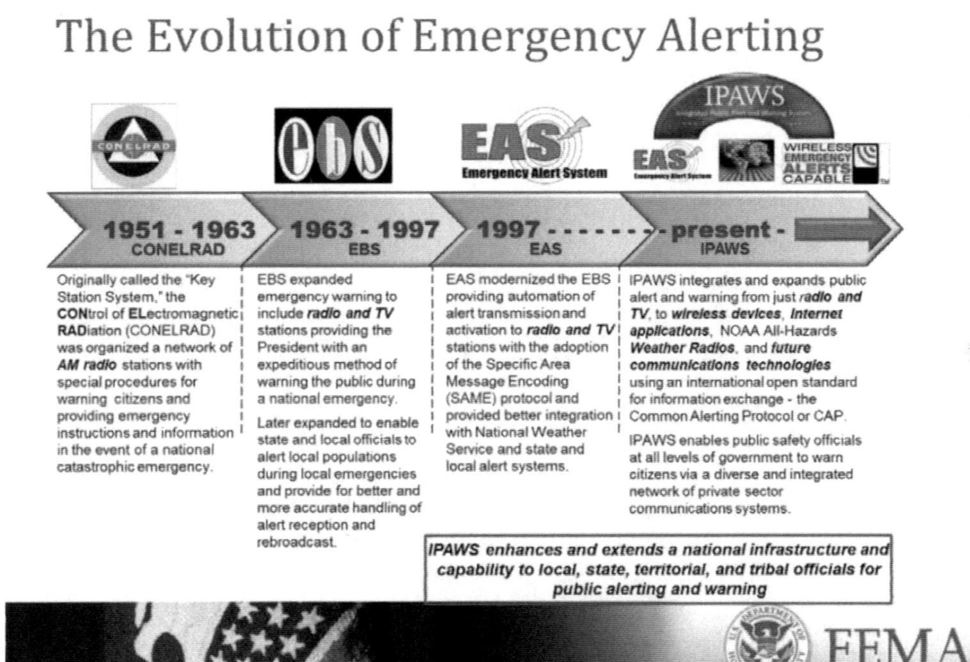

FIGURE 1: HISTORY OF EMERGENCY NOTIFICATION METHODS IN THE U.S. (SOURCE: FEMA IPAWS),

Over this period, the familiar radio daisy chain has remained essential to the system's resiliency and operational continuity during disaster. During this time, the most significant change was the addition of the Common Alert Protocol (CAP) to the Federal Emergency Management Agency (FEMA) Integrated Public Alert and Warning System (IPAWS) monitoring requirement in 2012 — over 13 years ago.

In simple terms, the FCC requires all U.S. broadcasters and MPVDs to carry the required EAS signal. For radio, this is simple: replace the audio. Video providers must place the alert text on the screen — either as full-screen text or a crawl in the upper third — and include the associated audio. As we will see, this added complexity for TV broadcasters spurred more creative implementations.

Since the introduction of the EAS, modern broadcast chains have experienced significant technological changes regarding the signals transported from ingest to transmission. Over nearly three decades, the industry has transitioned from analog to digital and into compressed digital formats. However, the design philosophies of some EAS devices appear to remain stuck in the mid-1990s. Many outdated practices are still in place, becoming the antithesis of modern signal management. Other EAS platforms adopted a more flexible approach, but we'll address that shortly.

When first envisioned, the EAS encoder/decoder was meant to be the last program switch in the air chain. Figure 2 shows examples, and since the signals were mainly analog, this switch was very easy to implement.

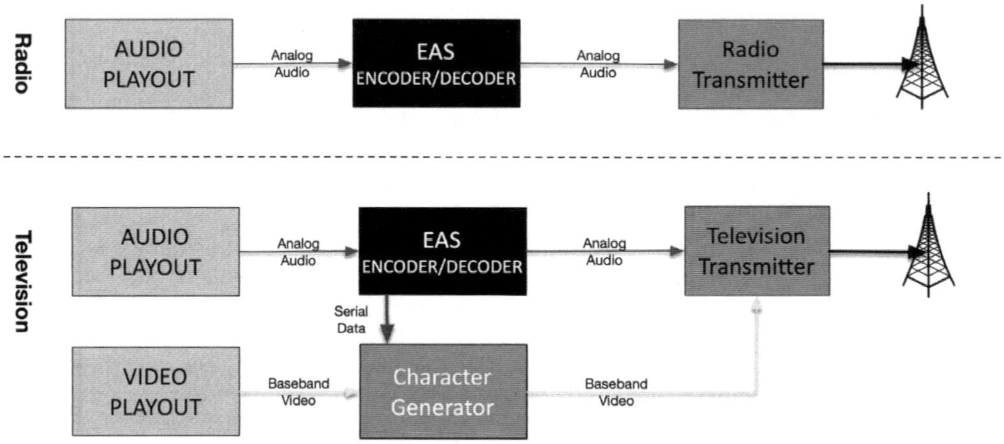

FIGURE 2: SIMPLIFIED EXAMPLES OF RADIO AND TELEVISION AIR CHAINS WITH EAS INSERTION.

Moving into the Digital Realm

Over the past twenty-five years, the digital revolution has fundamentally transformed the manner in which program signals are transmitted. A significant initial step in this transition involved the progression from baseband to quantized digital audio in the AES/EBU format. Despite variations in the signal type, the EAS device has consistently been positioned as the final program switch within the air chain.

Here is where the radio and television realms began to diverge. TV broadcasters quickly adopted digital implementations associated with the visual part of the transmission by quantizing the NTSC or PAL signal into a Serial Digital Interface (SDI). The later extension of the SMPTE standard allows for multiple audio channels to be interleaved within the same transmission. This combined video and embedded audio is made easy using a single coax or fiber connection. Still, it introduced issues with having to de-embed and re-embed the audio signal to accommodate the concept of EAS being the "last program switch."

Other TV equipment manufacturers began creating alternative methods to implement EAS's visual and aural requirements using media keyers. These media keyers combined a character generator with the necessary audio switching in a single device. Adopting media keyers made it much simpler for the EAS device to send text information for character generation, visual display elements, and audio to the media keyer. The media keyer would then typically display the text as a crawl over the program. This fundamentally changed where the audio was switched, marking a significant shift away from relying on the EAS device for audio switching.

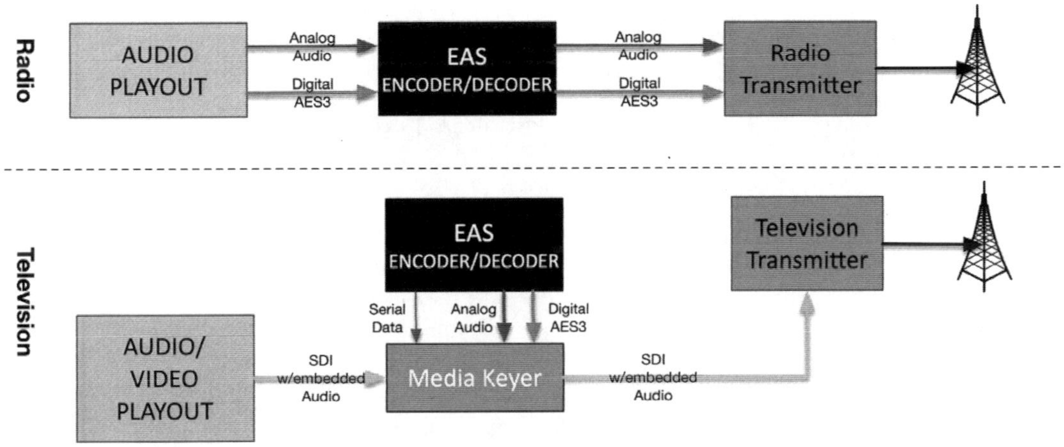

FIGURE 3: TELEVISION MOVES TO MEDIA KEYERS, COMBINING CHARACTER GENERATION AND AUDIO SWITCHING.

The early implementations used serial data and connections with baseband audio. However, as time passed, communications with media keyers became network-based, where we could send text and audio as a data file or in a streaming audio format. This combination of EAS data and audio over a single IP connection lends itself to more efficiently managing EAS insertion with a single connection.

One of the big leaps in television became apparent here. Using an IP interface, the EAS device did not have to reside in close physical proximity to the media keyer. Using a standard network connection allows for implementations such as central casting, with a remote device able to talk to the specific media keyer to align with the channels being sent to the location. Figure 4 illustrates this input change.

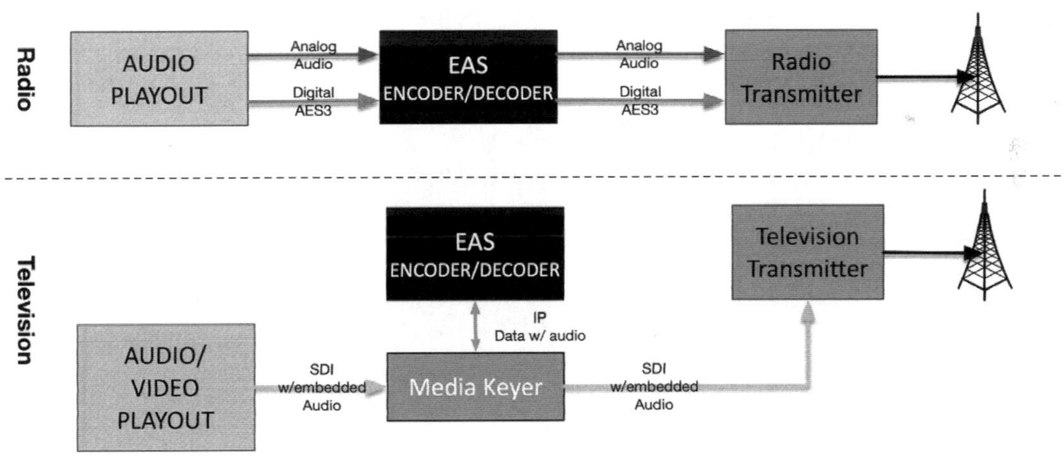

FIGURE 4: MEDIA KEYERS WITH IP CONNECTIONS FOR DATA (TEXT) AND AUDIO.

Television also moved from single channel offerings to multiple subchannels. However, the burden of EAS remains for each stream — main and all subchannels. The management of inserting EAS on each stream compounds the number of devices, connections, and controls. Using an IP connection to multiple media keyers avoids a complex nightmare of serial data, multiple audio distribution amps to feed each playout.

Radio had a digital renaissance at nearly the same time with the advent of HD Radio adding more sources. Still, the signals and switching remained closely associated with baseband audio as analog or AES3 signals as shown in Figure 5.

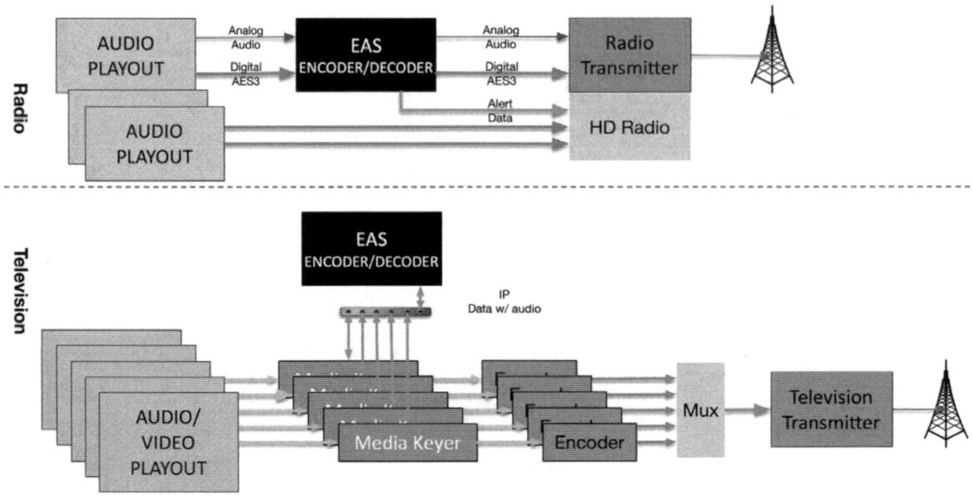

FIGURE 5: EVOLUTION OF RADIO AND TELEVISION AIR CHAINS.

Television quickly adopted MPEG-2 as a compressed digital transport for cable television or multiple-channel transmissions with digital television as ATSC 1.0 or DVB for standard over-the-air and Quadrature Amplitude Modulation (QAM) used in CATV. While content production remained uncompressed, the final transmissions were encoded and multiplexed as the last leg in the chain. These changes required a different methodology to insert EAS, as the streams are no longer accessible or have any means to control one program individually.

It is essential to understand what this implies. What was once the domain of the EAS device to switch the signal has now changed, creating a “virtual switch” with the switch’s action controlled by the EAS device, meaning the actual signal change is no longer performed within the EAS device. We will revisit this premise later.

Currently, we use digital signals in the television sector for compressed digital transport streaming. The primary challenge is accommodating isochronous data transmission within a packetized TCP/IP format. To address this issue, the EAS message is generated as a full-screen display of the alert data along with the associated audio and is presented as an alternative MPEG transport stream. When necessary, a signal is sent to prompt the program multiplexer to switch to this alternate transport stream, as illustrated in the television section of Figure 6.

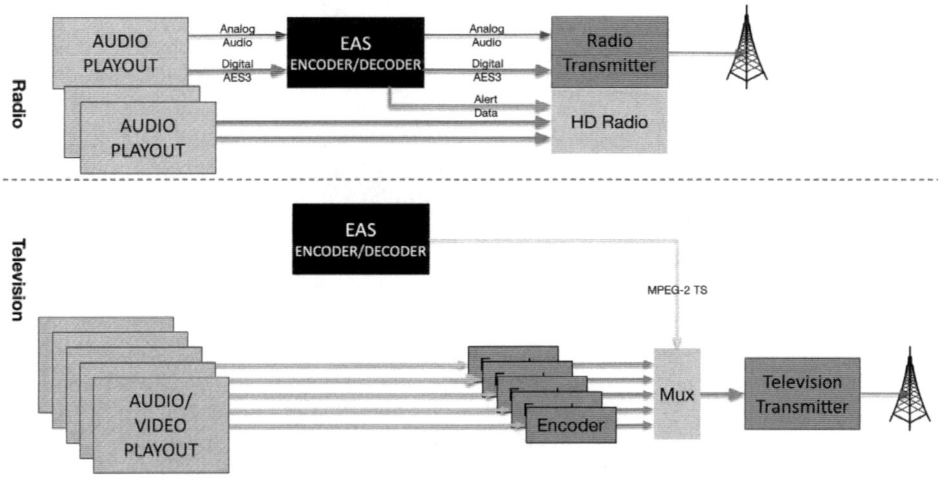

FIGURE 6: INSERTING EAS VIDEO/AUDIO INTO A COMPRESSED DIGITAL AIR CHAIN.

Presenting the EAS signal as a transport stream allows it to be spliced into an encoded signal. Some multiplexers can utilize the presence or absence of the MPEG-2 TS from the EAS device to trigger program switching, thus eliminating the need for a separate mechanism or signal, such as contact closure or a signaling protocol DVS644 (SCTE-18). MVPDs employ a similar method: They force-tune to a "virtual channel" while the alert is played and then switch back to regular programming after the event.

After several more years of product development, television program encoders now integrate many functions from earlier media keyers. This integration allows EAS text and audio to be transmitted over IP to these advanced encoders, eliminating the need for separate and costly media keyers for each program stream. Figure 7 illustrates this configuration, showing the EAS device connecting via IP directly to the video encoders linked to that specific station's output.

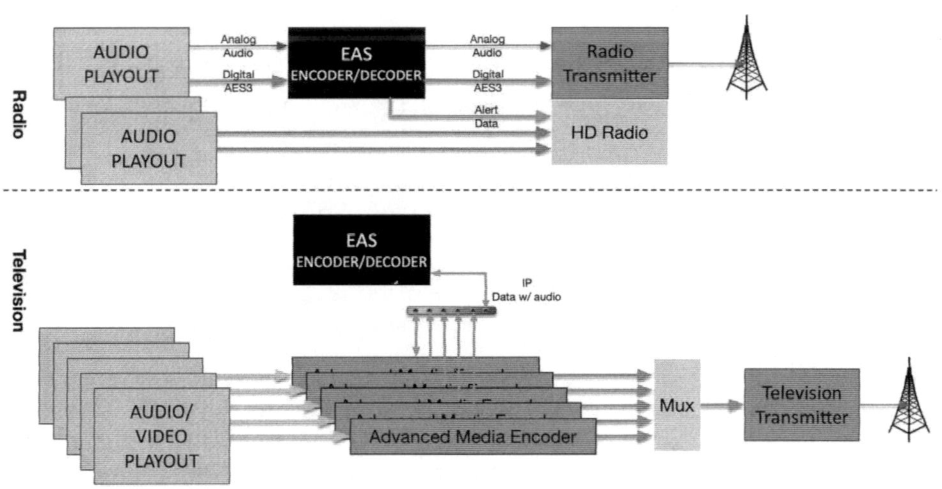

FIGURE 7: TELEVISION AIRCHAIN WITH ADVANCED ENCODERS SUPPORTING EAS OVER IP INPUTS.

Unfortunately, radio broadcasters have not progressed as quickly as their television counterparts. Part of the issue may arise from isolated information. There has been insufficient exchange of ideas and information between the two broadcasting sectors, and the radio industry may not be fully aware of what television has achieved and how it could be applied to radio.

One reason is that, unlike television, which was forced to move to a digital transmission standard, radio broadcasters have not been mandated to change their transmissions. Until recently, there have been few significant incentives to change the overall air chain.

The radio industry has begun to catch up by introducing IP-compatible audio transmission systems like AES67. Adopting IP transport for uncompressed audio offers many benefits and provides a well-supported and consistent method for transporting audio between devices.

However, the AES67 signal presents a major challenge to some traditional EAS devices that only support baseband audio. With this limitation, the air chain requires additional equipment to convert the audio to insert the EAS message, as shown in Figure 8 below.

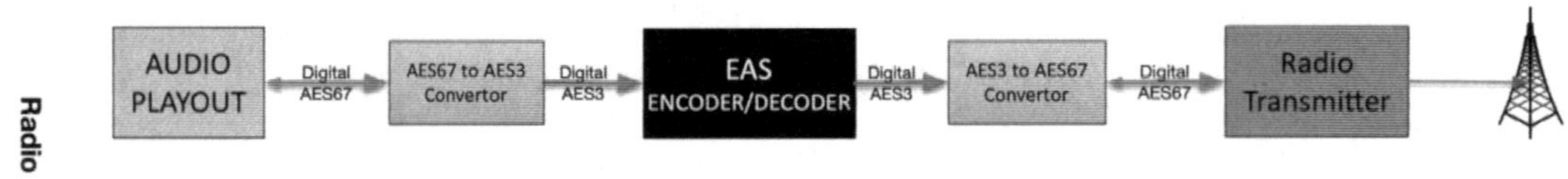

FIGURE 8: RADIO AIRCHAIN REQUIRING UP/DOWN CONVERSION FOR EAS BASEBAND SWITCHING.

With a focus on using the EAS device to enable switching and considering its limitations, the opportunity for improvement is lost. This further restricts the configuration since the EAS device must physically remain in the air chain as it is the final switching device figuratively and literally. This represents little change since EAS was defined almost 30 years ago.

To eliminate this boundary, it is essential to unify around the AES67 air chain and establish a method for switching these signals within the same digital domain. By integrating an AES67 output in the EAS device and providing proper routing control, this IP-based signal can be modified virtually anywhere. Figure 9 below illustrates this concept, where the AES67 signal and IP control of the AES67 switch create a much more streamlined air chain.

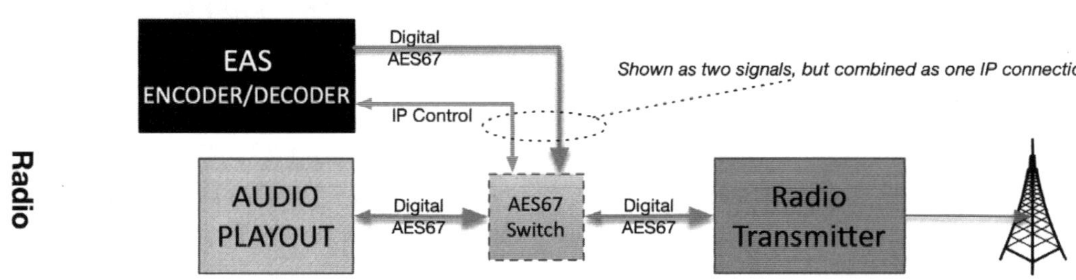

FIGURE 9: RADIO AIRCHAIN USING AES67 AND ROUTING CONTROL TO A VIRTUAL SWITCH.

Note that the AES67 and IP control signals in Figure 9 are depicted as separate lines; however, they constitute a single IP connection. Implementing this type of signal switching allows the EAS device to be positioned anywhere within the network, provided it can detect the AES67 switch.

A crucial aspect of this implementation is ensuring that the EAS device maintains priority control of the switch. It is inadequate to simply install an AES3 to AES67 converter on the EAS device, as there must be a way to ensure the EAS audio takes over when necessary. This involves incorporating a method to control the airchain and override any other programming during an EAS event. In this way, the EAS device continues to act as the final switch in the air chain, albeit virtually.

It is important to understand that the AES67 switch shown in Figure 9 is already integrated into other components of the air chain, typically as part of another device. In some cases, it is a signal router, a converter, perhaps an audio processor, or, more recently, part of the radio transmitter itself. Leveraging this existing capability to present a virtual switch enables significant streamlining of the signal and associated cost savings without introducing complexity.

Using the methods outlined above, it's easy to see how efficient and cost-effective this configuration can be. It does not require multiple conversion levels or separate devices to achieve what is essentially just a signal switch.

Changing the Landscape

Previously, an extra bounding box required positioning the EAS device near the playout equipment due to its reliance on baseband signals. In many remote markets, this often meant installing remote radio receivers to send the necessary monitoring signals back to the EAS device for decoding. While this method is functional, it necessitates additional equipment, connections, and audio streaming support with various encoders and decoders for operation. Additionally, the timing parameters for the EAS tones are not suited for processing lags; hence, capturing the audio, encoding it in a lossy format as a stream, and then decoding it again is susceptible to decoding errors, which could inevitably lead to missing critical alerts.

Broadcasters can eliminate these limitations by standardizing around IP-based audio transport and incorporating controllable switching. Like many television broadcasters arrange for central casting, EAS devices can be positioned remotely, reducing equipment redundancy and streamlining operations. The configurations illustrated in Figure 10 show that this is accessible to both radio and television broadcasters.

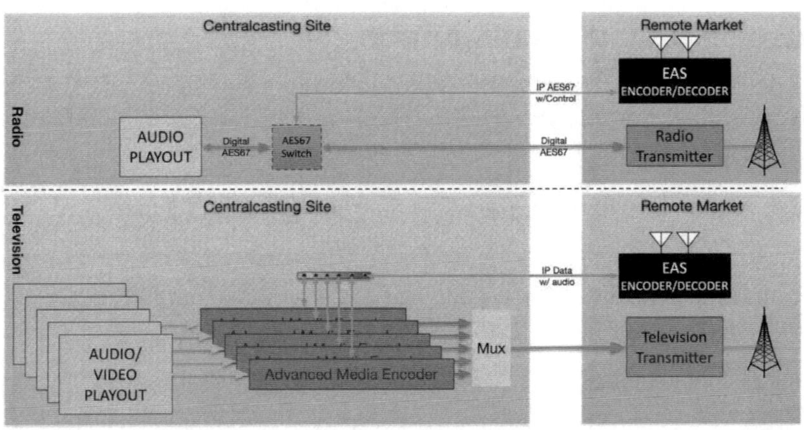

FIGURE 10: RADIO AND TELEVISION AIR CHAINS USING IP INTERFACES TO SUPPORT CENTRALIZATION.

The ongoing evolution of both production and content is rapidly transforming the central casting concept into a cloud-based content delivery system. A significant advantage of this approach is that, as long as the cloud content delivery maintains the same functionality as previous systems, we can keep the EAS device at the remote site and use the same communication over IP to the cloud. This representation in Figure 11 illustrates the shift from central casting to cloud casting.

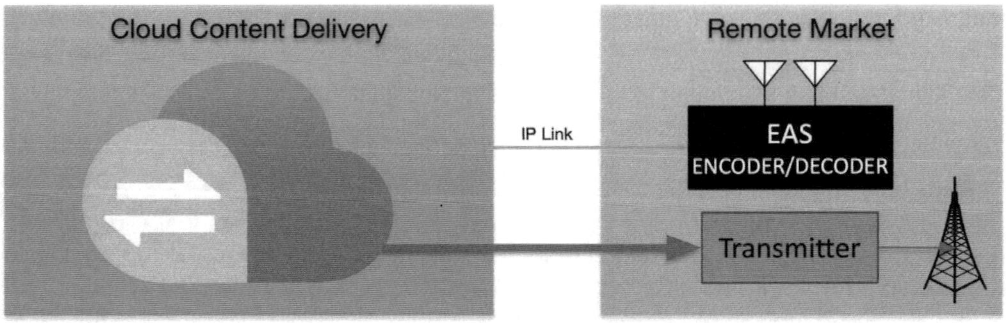

FIGURE 11. CENTRAL CASTING IS BECOMING CLOUD CASTING, WITH CONTENT DELIVERED FROM CLOUD SOURCES, AND APPLIES TO RADIO AND TV.

It is important to note that the representation in Figure 11 is identical for both radio and television. Essentially, only two hardware devices are needed: 1) the EAS device and 2) the transmitter. Additionally, the content may consist of audio for radio or both audio and video for television. The only distinction lies in the IP protocol being used. Moreover, a single EAS device can support multiple protocols, so stations offering both radio and television services only need one EAS device to manage signaling for both air chains.

Benefits of EAS Networked Architectures

Positioning the EAS device in the market, within the monitoring area, as an edge device lessens reliance on the network for initial signal processing. This, in turn, decreases potential failure points, improves reliability, and leads to faster system response times and more efficient integration of EAS functionality into existing systems. Now, a single network connection links the EAS system to encoding/transmission equipment, shrinks the equipment footprint, and significantly streamlines system design.

The redundancy of separating the EAS device and its functionality within the air chain can be recognized by its ability to provide backup during worst-case scenarios, such as losing connectivity to the studio or transmission source.

Resilient to a temporary loss of connectivity to the Internet or the delivery network, the remote market EAS device continues to function, performing critical monitoring and message-decoding tasks. This ensures that essential services remain available even when the network is unreliable or temporarily unavailable and can immediately respond when connectivity is restored, thereby enhancing overall system reliability. Moreover, maintaining the EAS device with its legacy outputs provides a backup air chain and critical redundancy to the transmitter—either radio or television, as depicted in Figure 12.

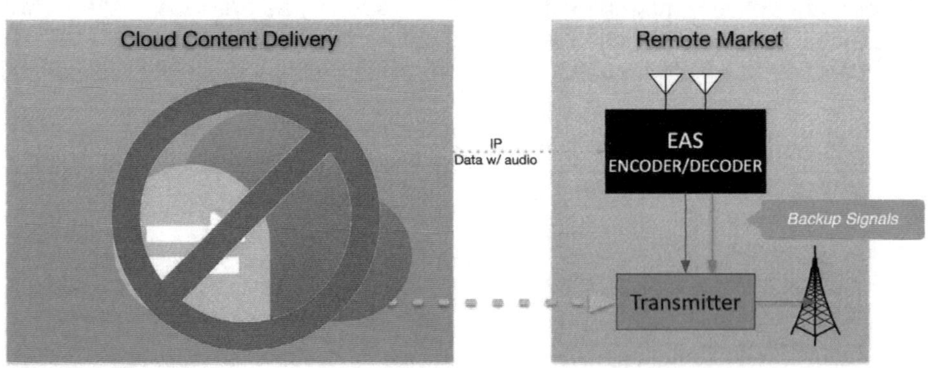

FIGURE 12: LOSS OF NETWORK DOESN'T MEAN LOSS OF EAS MESSAGES WHEN USING STANDARD OUTPUTS.

By processing and filtering data at the edge — at the remote site — only relevant or aggregated alert and system data is transmitted through the network, reducing traffic and conserving overall data bandwidth. This improvement enhances network efficiency and reliability, especially in situations with limited bandwidth, large data volumes, or unstable availability during emergencies.

Removing Boundaries

Federal regulation outlines the required operations of EAS, including the specific attributes and functions of the physical EAS equipment. This equipment is subject to a rigorous FCC Certification process. In addition to the FCC, FEMA also plays a role in device requirements, as EAS devices must demonstrate product adherence through the FEMA Integrated Public Alert and Warning System (IPAWS) Conformity Assessment (CA) Program.

Transitioning to IP-enabled EAS amplifies the benefits of virtualization in distributed edge environments, such as isolation, mobility, and ease of management, while ensuring all essential elements of EAS operation and compliance are upheld. This implementation replaces cascading hardware layers and multiple devices with an intelligent, one-to-many strategy, positioning mission-critical equipment at the edges of the air chain to manage and deliver emergency messages that can be geotargeted for specific alert distribution.

Implementing this architecture offers a comprehensive approach to modern station operations. It achieves the primary mission without necessitating any additional regulatory or substantive changes to the structure or presentation of the EAS messages. Furthermore, many television broadcasters can attest to the adaptability of IP-based systems that have been successfully deployed for years.

Conclusion

Boundaries—both technical and regulatory—have historically constrained EAS implementation. However, modern equipment and properly configured IP-based workflows eliminate these barriers. Transitioning EAS to an IP-based architecture enables broadcasters to position devices in optimal locations, leveraging network connectivity for enhanced efficiency. With virtualized monitoring and compliance reporting, EAS can seamlessly integrate into any air chain without changing FCC regulations.

This approach modernizes EAS without sacrificing compliance or functionality. By leveraging intelligent, network-connected workflows, broadcasters can improve efficiency, scalability, and reliability — ensuring that emergency alerts reach the public quickly and effectively. With more advanced implementations, we can meet both objectives — this is broadcasting without limits.

Cloud-Based Advanced Emergency Information (AEI) System for ATSC 3.0, MVPDs, and IP Delivery

Jason Kim
ONE Media Technologies
Hunt Valley, Maryland, United States
jkim@sbgtv.com

Abstract – This paper proposes a cloud-based Advanced Emergency Information (AEI) System designed to enhance public safety by seamlessly integrating alerts from the Integrated Public Alert and Warning System (IPAWS) with service operators. The AEI System captures emergency alerts in real time, processes them within the cloud, and enables synchronized delivery via ATSC 3.0 broadcast, MVPDs, and internet service operators. The proposed AEI System addresses key interoperability challenges across diverse broadcast and service platforms while ensuring efficiency and flexibility in alert dissemination. Built on a robust system architecture, it utilizes real-time alert processing workflows and advanced delivery mechanisms to improve the reliability of emergency communications. This paper examines these components in detail, highlighting the ability of the AEI System to ensure the widespread, synchronized distribution of critical emergency information to diverse audiences across ATSC 3.0 broadcast and modern communication networks.

Introduction

Recent hurricanes and wildfires have emphasized the importance of a timely and reliable emergency alert system. AEI system is a capability within ATSC 3.0 for transmitting urgent notices related to emergency information [1]. Broadcasters have long been at the forefront of delivering emergency information, but new broadcast technology, the widespread adoption of the internet, and the growth of IP-based services have reshaped the landscape of emergency communication. To keep pace with these developments, a more versatile and interoperable emergency communication system is essential.

The proposed Advanced Emergency Information (AEI) System addresses this need by integrating cloud computing with the ATSC 3.0 standard and IP networks. The System bridges the gap between traditional broadcast methods and modern IP-based delivery platforms, ensuring timely, reliable, and efficient delivery of emergency alerts. This paper focuses on the System's architecture, real-time alert processing workflow, and multi-platform delivery mechanisms.

Challenge

Traditional Emergency Alert System (EAS) and Wireless Emergency Alerts (WEA) encounter significant difficulties disseminating effective emergency alerts. EAS relies heavily on radio and television broadcasts, which only reach individuals who are actively engaged [2]. Additionally, as audiences increasingly shift toward mobile devices and IP-based platforms, the declining reach of traditional broadcasting is making it harder to connect with mobile-first users.

This paper is excerpted from the Proceedings of the 2025 NAB Broadcast Engineering and Information Technology (BEIT) Conference, © 2025, National Association of Broadcasters, 1 M Street SE, Washington, DC 20003 USA.

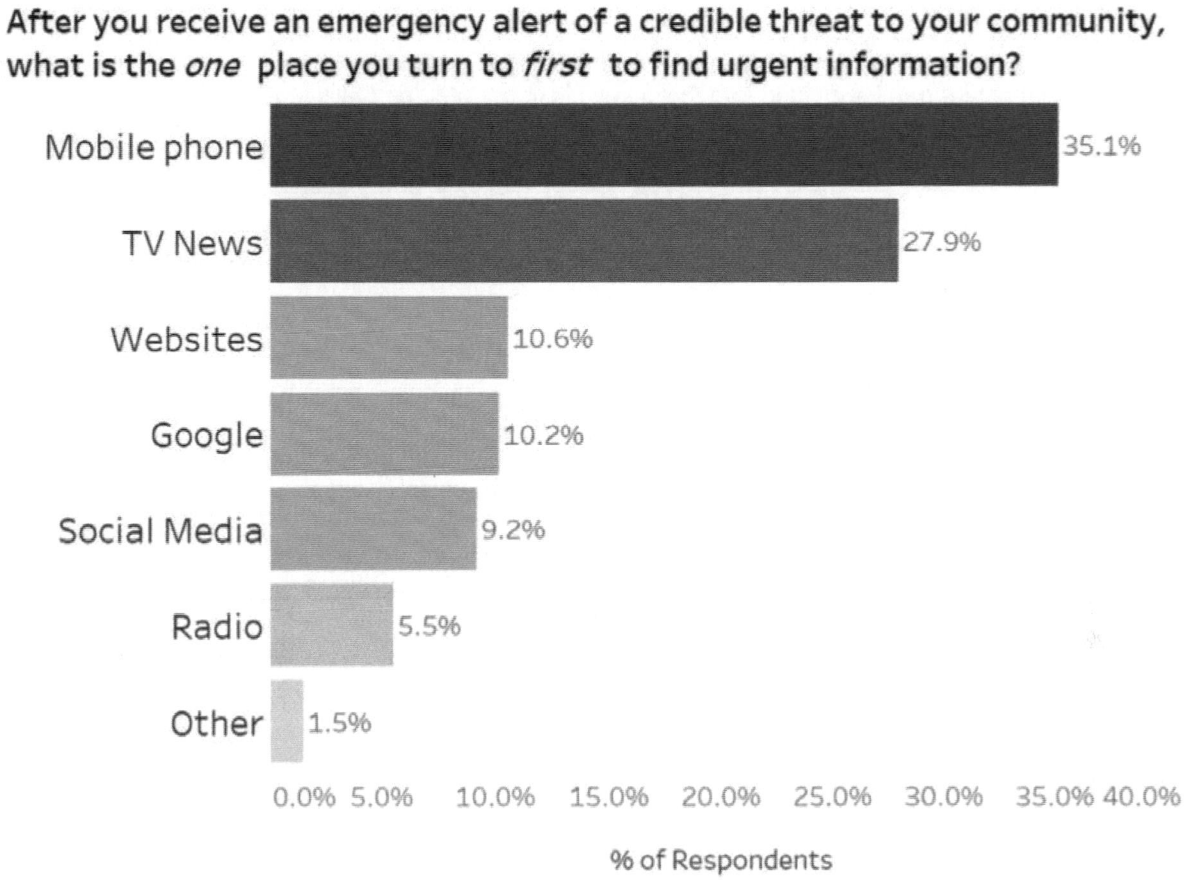

FIGURE 1: CHANGING TRENDS IN VIEWER HABITS HAVE MADE IT HARDER FOR BROADCASTERS TO REACH AUDIENCES IN EMERGENCY SITUATIONS [3].

WEAs, on the other hand, struggle with limited message lengths, accessibility challenges, and inaccuracies in geographic targeting [4]. This results in alerts being sent to unintended areas or failing to reach those who need them most. For example, the entire city of Los Angeles recently received an evacuation warning due to the wildfires, despite only being intended for the residents of a single neighborhood [5]. A significant portion of the population also opts out of notifications, further reducing their effectiveness. Furthermore, WEAs rely on mobile and internet networks, which may delay or even fail to deliver essential alerts under heavy network loads.

A lack of synchronization across multiple platforms further compounds these issues. Traditional broadcast systems often operate independently of contemporary platforms like news websites, social media, and mobile apps, resulting in fragmented and inconsistent messaging. Moreover, EAS and WEA are unable to receive real-time updates, integrate with modern technologies, or provide two-way communication, further impeding their ability to adapt to rapidly evolving emergency situations.

Finally, outdated infrastructure and limited support for enhanced alert content, such as multimedia or interactive instructions, hinder public understanding and responsiveness during crises. Addressing these challenges requires adopting advanced technologies to modernize emergency communication systems that are adaptable to diverse audiences and evolving situations.

System Architecture

The proposed AEI System is designed to ensure scalability, redundancy, and real-time responsiveness. The System architecture can be divided into three key components: the Data Ingestion Module, the Alert Processing Component, and the Distribution System. Each component plays a crucial role in ensuring efficient and reliable alert management.

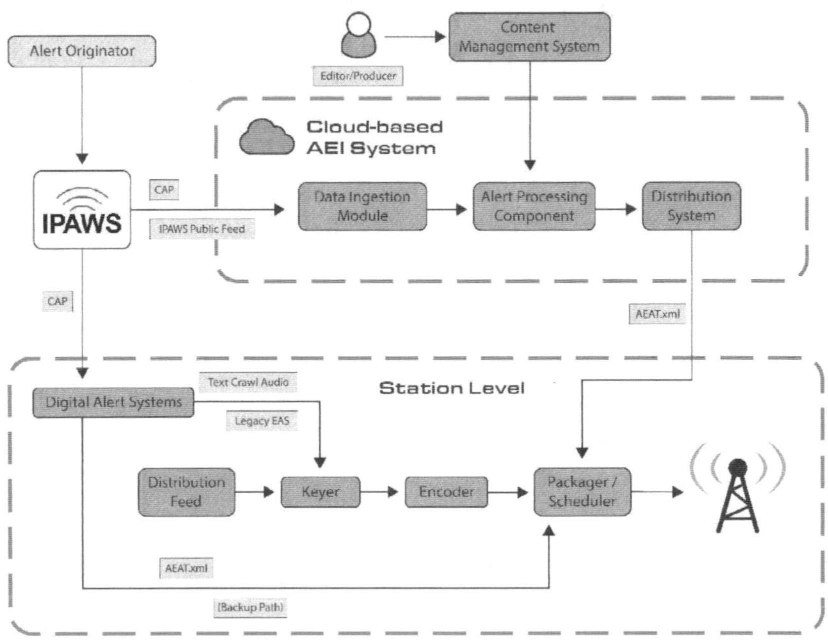

FIGURE 2: CLOUD-BASED AEI SYSTEM ARCHITECTURE.

Data Ingestion Module

The Data Ingestion Module interfaces with the IPAWS CAP (Common Alerting Protocol) Public Feed. The IPAWS CAP receives real-time alerts from multiple emergency channels, including NOAA Weather Radio, EAS, and WEA [6]. Utilizing the IPAWS CAP Public Feed ensures a standardized and reliable method to aggregate alerts from multiple sources, and enables seamless integration, accurate data processing, and efficient transmission.

The Data Ingestion Module retrieves incoming alerts using Amazon EventBridge, a serverless event bus service that enables seamless event routing [7]. The Data Ingestion Module parses the alert types, identifies severity levels, and categorizes messages based on the type of emergency. Once the data is ingested and validated, it is passed to the Alert Processing Component.

Alert Processing Component

The Alert Processing Component transforms CAP messages to formats compatible with multiple delivery platforms. For IP-based systems, like news websites and mobile applications, the messages are converted to JSON or XML. For broadcast, the AEI System converts alerts to the Advanced Emergency Alert Table (AEAT) format used by ATSC 3.0 [8].

Both CAP and AEAT are formatted in XML, so the Alert Processing Component must map the essential CAP elements with the corresponding AEAT elements. This conversion ensures that emergency messages can be effectively transmitted over the air while maintaining all critical information.
The key conversion processes are listed below:

- **Alert Identification:** Each alert in the AEAT format requires a unique identifier, derived from the "identifier" field in the CAP message. This ensures traceability and prevents duplication in the alert Distribution System.
- **Geographical Information:** The AEI System extracts FIPS (Federal Information Processing System) codes from the CAP message and maps them to the corresponding broadcast Designated Market Areas (DMAs). This ensures that the Distribution System can target the impacted regions, allowing for precise and effective emergency alert distribution.
- **Event and Priority Code Mapping:** CAP messages contain event codes that specify the type of emergency. The Alert Processing Component extracts CAP event codes and maps them to the corresponding AEAT priority codes. The mapping allows the broadcaster to further customize alerts. For example, the Sinclair Broadcaster Application color codes the user facing alerts based on the severity of the emergency.
- **Message Content Adaptation:** The textual alert content from the CAP message is mapped to the AEAT message structure. This includes the alert description, instructions, and any available multimedia content.

Distribution System

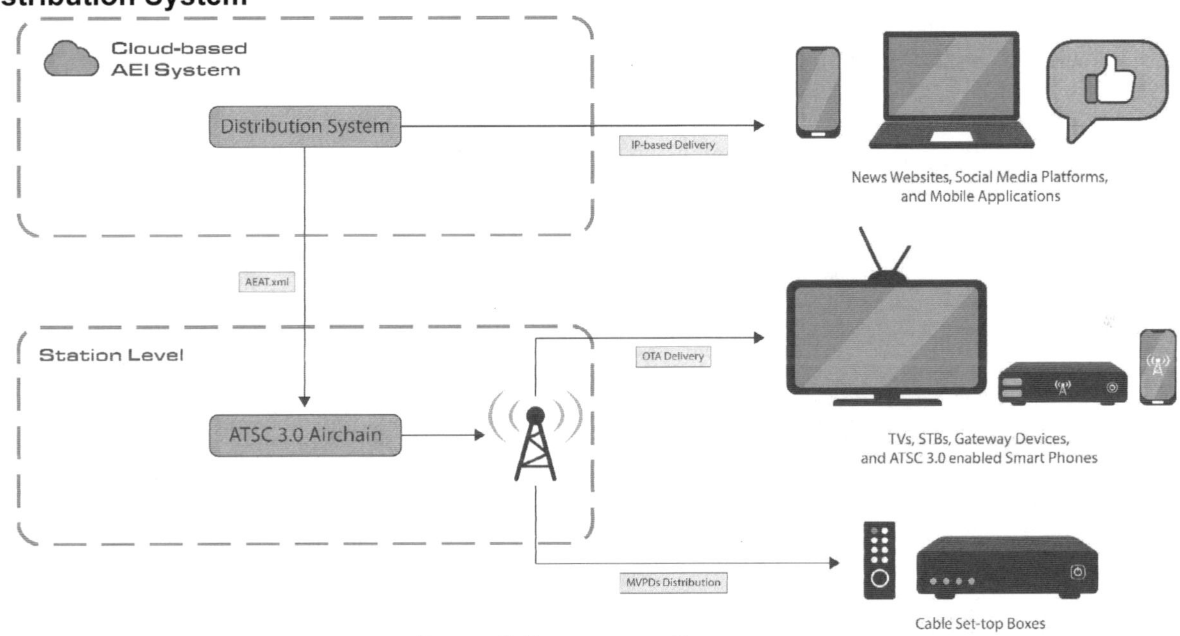

FIGURE 3: DISTRIBUTION SYSTEM.

The Distribution System transmits the formatted alerts through multiple delivery channels to reach the widest possible user base. The alerts are sent out simultaneously via OTA transmission, IP-based platforms, multichannel video programming distributors (MVPDs), and other service providers.

- **Over-the-air (OTA) Delivery:** The AEI System interfaces with the ATSC 3.0 broadcast airchain through APIs. Nextgen TV-compatible devices, including televisions, set-top boxes, gateway devices, and mobile devices equipped with ATSC 3.0 receiver chips, can receive these emergency alerts. WEA messages can be delivered to both wireless devices and over-the-air television with the AEI System.
- **IP-based Platforms:** To reach audiences beyond traditional television, the AEI System delivers emergency alerts to IP-based platforms such as news websites, social media platforms, and mobile applications. This multi-platform strategy guarantees that users relying on mobile or

internet-connected devices can receive real-time alerts, even if they are not viewing a broadcast service. Furthermore, the System provides geotargeting capabilities to allow alerts to be customized based on specific geographic regions using user location.

- **MVPD Providers:** The AEI System expands the distribution of emergency alerts to MVPDs. By integrating with the MVPD infrastructure, the System ensures the seamless delivery of emergency alerts to subscribers via set-top boxes, IPTV services, and other managed video platforms. Service providers can now incorporate alert metadata to improve the delivery of emergency messages, allowing for features such as forced tuning to emergency broadcasts, on-screen alert overlays, and the dynamic insertion of alert banners within video streams.

Newsroom Workflow

The AEI System is built as a plug-in to Sinclair's Content Management System (CMS), Storyline [9]. Integrating the system into Sinclair's CMS avoids increasing the workload of producers by creating a single platform to manage alerts, updates, and information efficiently within the existing infrastructure. The System's Broadcast Newsroom Flash (BNF) feature automatically sends high-severity alerts to the affected areas to avoid delay. Newsroom producers can then review the low-severity alerts and decide whether they need to be broadcast. This prevents alert jamming or unnecessary disruptions to the broadcast. Crucially, the BNF can also update distributed alerts with the latest information, and include images, maps, or video feeds.

In addition, the AEI System's Broadcast News Advisory (BNA) feature allows newsrooms to distribute locally targeted information, such as road closures, school delays, or other community-focused updates.

With the AEI System, newsrooms can provide continuous updates and evolving emergency coverage, keeping communities informed as the situation unfolds.

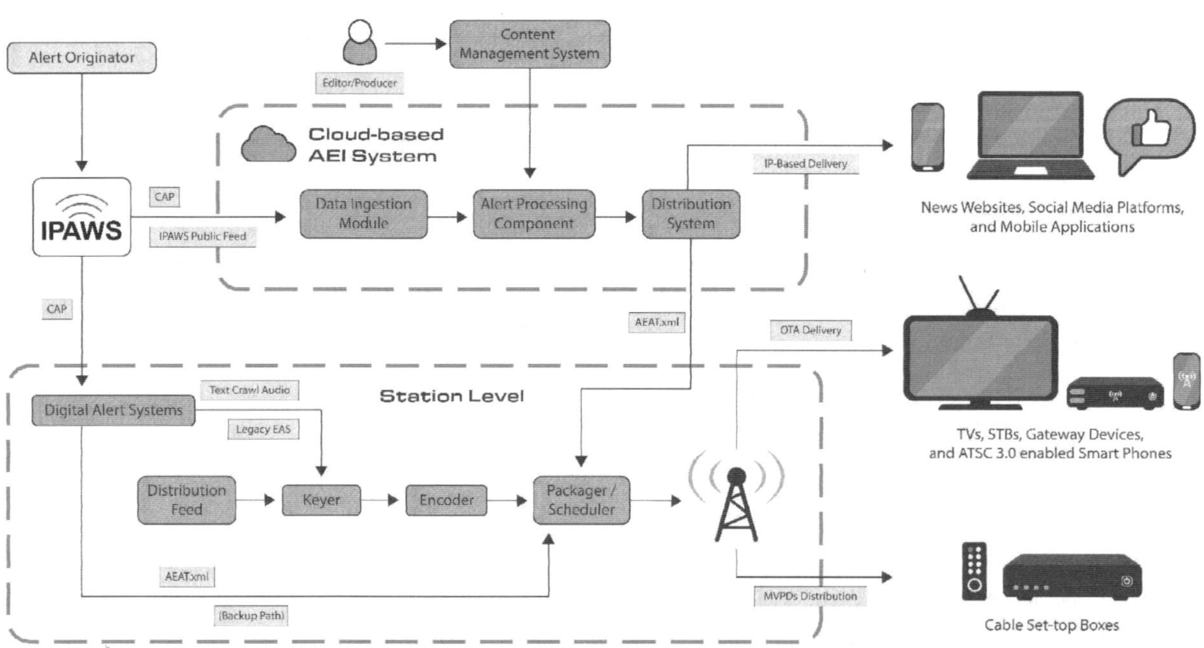

FIGURE 4: END-TO-END SYSTEM DIAGRAM.

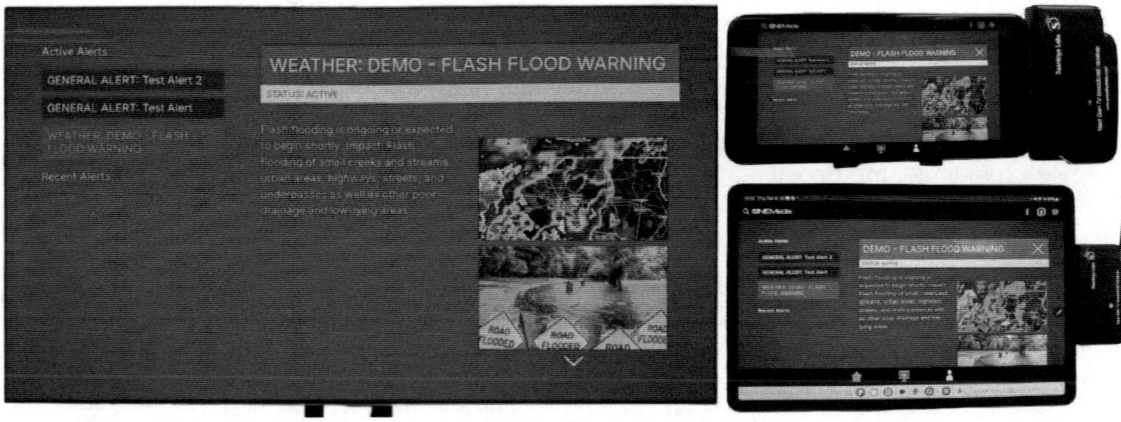

FIGURE 5: EMERGENCY ALERTS ON ATSC 3.0 RECEIVER PLATFORMS.

The AEI System has been tested and demonstrated to industry stakeholders at the ONE Media Technologies Lab in Hunt Valley, Maryland with support from the Federal Emergency Management Agency (FEMA).

Benefits of a Cloud-Based AEI System

A cloud-based system offers several benefits that enhance the efficiency, flexibility, and reach of emergency communications. These benefits are crucial for improving the distribution of emergency alerts across both traditional broadcast and IP-based platforms. The key benefits of the cloud-based AEI system are listed below:

- **Scalability and Flexibility:** Cloud infrastructure can dynamically allocate resources based on the volume of emergency alerts without being constrained by physical infrastructure. In addition, the flexibility of cloud infrastructure makes it easier for the system to integrate with new technologies as they emerge.
- **Cost Efficiency:** By utilizing cloud infrastructure, broadcasters can significantly reduce the expense of dedicated on-premises servers and hardware. Cloud service providers often offer pay-as-you-go pricing models to allow organizations to scale operations based on demand. This strategy guarantees that emergency alert systems stay cost-effective while maintaining high availability during emergencies.
- **Reliability and Redundancy:** Cloud service providers offer their services through an extensive network of redundant data centers. Key features such as automatic failover, traffic rerouting, and load balancing are designed to reduce service disruptions caused by technical failures or natural disasters.
- **Analytics and Monitoring:** Past alerts are stored in an internal database to track dissemination and engagement. Analytics and monitoring tools provide data-driven insights to help broadcasters refine emergency communication strategies and identify patterns in public responses.

Future Applications

The AEI System has the potential to evolve and expand beyond its current capabilities. Future advancements include:

- **Multi-Language Support:** AI-driven translation and text-to-speech capabilities could enable real-time translation of emergency alerts to ensure that critical information effectively reaches diverse audiences and individuals with accessibility needs.

- **American Sign Language (ASL):** The System could integrate with ASL solution providers to convert emergency messages into sign language to enhance the accessibility of emergency alerts for the deaf and hard-of-hearing community.
- **Internet of Things (IoT) Devices:** Emergency alerts can also be delivered to IoT devices. Public displays such as digital signage and public transportation information systems can provide real-time emergency alerts for widespread communication.

Conclusion

The cloud-based Advanced Emergency Information (AEI) System proposed in this paper offers a scalable, flexible, and reliable solution for modern emergency communication. The paper addresses key challenges across diverse broadcast and IP-based service platforms and provides ONE Media's implementation for enhancing public safety in the digital age. By integrating with the IPAWS CAP public feed and leveraging the capabilities of both ATSC 3.0 and cloud infrastructure, the AEI System ensures a standardized and reliable method for aggregating alerts from multiple sources and reaching a broad and diverse audience.

Ongoing and future work is focused on testing the System in real-world scenarios, refining its scalability, and exploring additional features to address accessibility needs.

References

[1] ATSC 3.0 Advanced Emergency Information System Implementation Guide

[2] https://www.fcc.gov/emergency-alert-system

[3] https://www.atsc3advocate.com/_files/ugd/713d71_383b0e6b00ae4e369e4bf75f914694ea.pdf

[4] https://www.fcc.gov/consumers/guides/wireless-emergency-alerts-wea

[5] https://www.nytimes.com/2025/01/10/us/los-angeles-false-evacuation-alert.html

[6] https://www.fema.gov/emergency-managers/practitioners/integrated-public-alert-warning-system

[7] https://aws.amazon.com/eventbridge

[8] ATSC 3.0 Standard. A/331:2024-04, "Signaling, Delivery, Synchronization, and Error Protection"

[9] https://sinclairdigital.com/storyline-product-pg

VVC Broadcast Deployment Update

Justin Ridge
Nokia
Dallas, Texas, United States

Łukasz Litwic
Ericsson
Warsaw, Poland

Abstract – The VVC video coding standard was finalized in July 2020, and is thus almost five years old. In light of this approaching anniversary, VVC's deployment status is reviewed. Major milestones in VVC deployment are detailed, and a comparison with the preceding HEVC codec are provided at an equivalent point in time.

Background

The VVC (Versatile Video Coding) standard [1] was developed jointly by ITU-T and ISO/IEC JTC1, and finalized in July 2020. These two organizations have been developing successful video codecs together for over 25 years, with VVC's forerunners including H.264/AVC and H.265/HEVC. Each of these two codecs have seen broad market adoption in many different industries, with H.264/AVC becoming essentially ubiquitous.

This joint effort between ITU-T and ISO/IEC JTC1 is currently called the Joint Video Experts Team (JVET), and the success of its codecs can be attributed to several factors. Organizationally, JVET brings together many of the best minds in the field of video coding from across the world and spanning a range of industries. This helps ensure that codecs developed will be suitable for use in those industries, and the number of people working on the codec helps ensure that bugs are detected and resolved. Corner-cases are further considered by a rigorous testing and conformance process. Codecs developed openly under the umbrella of internationally-recognized standards bodies enables them to be referenced and gives an assurance that the technology can be licensed on FRAND (fair, reasonable and non-discriminatory) terms.

The codecs themselves have proved to be well-designed and have met market needs – after all, the ultimate test of a codec is whether it is needed. Both H.264/AVC and H.265/HEVC not only delivered the obligatory benefits in terms of coding efficiency, but also involved reasonably successful predictions of appropriate video formats (resolutions) and bit rates, and struck a reasonable balance of performance versus complexity/implementability. They also benefitted from design choices that weren't clearly recognized at the time, such as the ability to efficiently handle high dynamic range (HDR) video.

All this leads us to VVC. As we're often reminded, past performance is no guarantee of future results. While VVC was developed jointly by ITU-T and ISO/IEC JTC1 and inherits the organizational benefits of its forebears, the codec landscape now is quite different from ten years ago. Software-based codecs are more practical, some parties who previously participated in standards development have stepped

This paper is excerpted from the Proceedings of the 2025 NAB Broadcast Engineering and Information Technology (BEIT) Conference, © 2025, National Association of Broadcasters, 1 M Street SE, Washington, DC 20003 USA.

away and been replaced by others, video is even more pervasive, the economics of 'legacy' deployments weigh heavily, there's a different competitive landscape, and even geopolitics plays a role. Added to this, it can be questioned whether VVC's coding efficiency alone will see it deployed, or is some specific use case driving uptake?

In this paper, we put aside these speculative factors and review the current deployment status of VVC, in hardware, software, and services. At the outset, it is acknowledged that this is not an exhaustive list by any means, rather significant highlights which serve as pointers to where VVC deployment is headed. A more comprehensive list can be found, for example, in [2]. We further note that this paper only covers publicly-covered deployments, not those which are known to have occurred in closed ecosystems and remain unreported. We finally compare VVC to H.265/HEVC at the corresponding time after finalization. While this is not a gauge in and of itself, it can provide context for those forming an opinion about VVC's progress.

A Quick VVC Primer

The basic architecture of VVC is similar to its predecessor, H.265/HEVC. New technologies have been included that improve coding efficiency. As a generalization, VVC can encode content using around 50% fewer bits than HEVC for the same subjective quality. Almost every aspect of HEVC has been improved in some way – prediction is improved through combined intra- and inter-prediction, there's new affine motion compensation, a new adaptive loop filter, and many other features. A description of these technologies can be found in [3]. The performance gain derives from the cumulative effect of these new technologies.

As the 'Versatile' in its name suggests, VVC is intended to code a wide range of video content. For 2D video, this includes user-generated content, screen content, and professionally produced 8K HDR. VVC is also designed to handle immersive use cases. The basic premise of a versatile codec is to facilitate interoperability. A device such as a television might not only receive broadcast television, but also be able to play video from connected storage or stream OTT video. Rather than implementing a specialized video codec tailored to each use case, a single versatile codec can be used, resulting in cost and other savings.

VVC achieves this by including tools designed for particular use cases, which an encoder can dynamically choose to utilize or not depending on the type of content it encounters. For example, VVC incorporates palette-mode coding, which is beneficial in coding screen and other computer-generated content. It includes reference picture wraparound, which can be useful in immersive content where 360-degree video is projected onto a 2D grid prior to encoding.

Deployment Considerations

Although VVC has been clearly shown to outperform previous codecs [4][5], that by itself neither justifies nor guarantees adoption. A codec is one component of an overall system architecture, and a number of questions need to be answered. Is there encoded content – do encoders exist, has the codec been incorporated into production workflows? Is it enabled in the operating system and/or capture pipeline? Have delivery mechanisms, ranging from CDNs to broadcast standards, been updated to provide for it? Is there a means of playing back the received video, e.g. in a browser, app, consumer electronics device? Beyond these architectural questions, there are business issues – given that an upgrade to H.265/HEVC may have occurred only recently, does the incremental performance gain of VVC justify new investment? What are the uncertainties & risks, including licensing and the competitive landscape? What is the time horizon for investment return?

All these issues can act as headwinds slowing down the deployment of a codec, counterbalancing the efficiency gains and new use cases that might be enabled. Every situation is unique, and this paper intends to highlight the complexity of the overall ecosystem rather than delving into the calculus involved. Instead, it focuses on the current deployments status of VVC, dividing that topic into software and hardware for convenience.

VVC Software Deployments

Software-based players often bridge the gap between the release of a new codec and deeper integration into device chipsets. VVC software decoders started emerging within about six months of the standard being finalized, with Tencent reporting good results on mobile devices, e.g. 4K UHD bitstream decoding at 30 fps on an Apple A14 processor [6] in January 2021. VVC software decoders from other mobile video service providers, including ByteDance [7] and Kwai [8] were also announced.

Questions are often asked about the latency and power/battery requirements of software decoders, and with good reason. More recent demonstrations, including Ericsson's low-latency mobile gaming demo showcased at NAB in 2024, showed that a software decoder can run at native resolution on an 8-year old mobile device with battery life exceeding 5 hours and latency under 100 msec [9]. In general, it appears fair to say that software codecs on modern devices are a more feasible proposition than for past generations of codecs.

A more general-purpose software implementation, VVenC/VVdeC [10], was initially released by Fraunhofer HHI in September 2020, merely three months after finalization of the standard, and notably includes an encoder with reasonable performance in addition to a decoder. This software has been refined over time, ported to various platforms, and can be used for VVC playback in web browsers [11].

The implementations mentioned to date have been clearly identified as proof-of-concept decoders rather than production-grade mass deployments. But VVC is not just 'lab-ware', and software-based VVC codecs have started to be deployed commercially or in large-scale trials.

MX Player, an OTT platform based in India with around 350 million subscribers, deployed VVC in 2021 [12] using their namesake app. MX Player was subsequently acquired by Amazon [13].

Alibaba have been very active in producing software encoders and decoders, particularly for ARM-based platforms and have demonstrated performance of running 4Kp60 decode with 30% CPU utilization. VVC content encoded using their encoder has been commercially distributed via their Youku streaming service to recent TV models with devices numbering in the tens of thousands [14].

Spin Digital and Intel deployed VVC on one of the biggest stages of all, streaming the 2024 Paris Olympics in 8K UHD to a select audience, using Spin Digital's VVC software decoder for playback [15].

A common theme with these deployments is unicast streaming, which makes it easier to stage deployments by device model or content characteristics, giving VVC a toehold in the market.

In this category, it is also worth mentioning FFmpeg. As of version 7.1 (released in September 2024), FFmpeg's built-in VVC decoder has been deemed 'stable' [16][17] and this version also incorporates VVenC as a VVC encoder option [18]. FFmpeg is not a product in and of itself, but is incorporated into other notable projects such as OBS Studio [19]. This status as an 'enabler' means that popular software can incorporate VVC with relatively minor retooling, and may result in 'grassroots' uptake of VVC. The degree to which this occurs and any flow-on effect on demand for VVC deployment more generally is yet to be seen.

VVC Hardware Deployments

Hardware deployments tend to follow software, so perhaps unsurprisingly VVC-enabled hardware has not made great market inroads at this stage. Hardware deployment in consumer electronics starts with component vendors including it in their respective products, and this we have started to see. MediaTek announced the Pentonic 2000 back in November 2021, and since then VVC support has been progressively added to other TV chipsets in the Pentonic range, including the Pentonic 1000 and Pentonic 800. The latter was announced in mid-2024 and is expected to ship in products from Hisense [20] and Xiaomi [21] (amongst others) in 2025, at list prices as low as US$300 [22]. More generally, Pentonic chips are found in televisions from a large number of major vendors, including Philips, Sony, and various China-based manufacturers including Hisense and TCL. It is known that some chipsets in LG televisions also support VVC hardware playback [23].

From such announcements and reviewing public specs, it is reasonable to say that the number of televisions incorporating VVC-capable chipsets is increasing, and that they are extending downwards from flagship models to mid-range models. However, we also note that manufacturers are shipping televisions with VVC disabled even though it is supported in the underlying chipset. The reasons for this may include content (and therefore demand) – particularly 8K content, for which VVC would provide the greatest benefit; licensing; or engineering reasons. Ultimately these are decisions made by the manufacturer, but it is expected that many of these devices already in the market could have VVC enabled via a firmware update, so that if VVC uptake does accelerate, the number of capable devices could increase rapidly. We note that in [14], Youku claim to have collaborated “closely with TV manufacturers” to deliver VVC streams “on more than 30 latest TV models”, implying that VVC has been enabled to some degree on televisions, e.g. on limited models or in a limited geography.

A number of events may drive further ‘lighting up’ of VVC capabilities in televisions. One is the use of VVC in broadcast television. VVC was added to DVB’s codec ‘toolbox’ in [24], and in February 2025 ATSC published their VVC standard as part of the ATSC 3.0 suite [25]. These are relatively recent events, and engineering & regulatory complexities mean we won’t see VVC broadcasts overnight. On the other hand, Brazil is planning to commence VVC broadcasts later this year (2025) [26]. Thus consumers in Brazil who wish to view TV 3.0 content will need a compatible device – television or converter. In Brazil, this is highly likely to see television models with VVC enabled. Whether this will serve as a ‘proving ground’ that manufacturers assess before enabling VVC elsewhere, or whether it will otherwise spur VVC usage, remains to be seen.

At least one DVB-S2/OTT box is already on the market in Brazil with VVC enabled – the Vivensis VX Smart uses the Realtek RTD1319D chipset [27]. Beyond televisions and streaming boxes, the Valerion VisionMaster is a currently-available, self-described cinematic-grade RGB laser projector that incorporates VVC hardware decoding via a MediaTek SoC [28].

Intel made a significant announcement in September 2024 when they unveiled VVC hardware decode support in their Xe2 graphics chips that form part of the ‘Lunar Lake’ architecture. They are the first of the major graphics chipset manufacturers to announce PC support, and products including Xe2 started shipping in September 2024 from Acer, Asus, Dell, HP, Lenovo, LG, MSI and Samsung [29]. Having VVC hardware already present in laptops means it can be more easily leveraged by software vendors and service providers. To this end, Intel also their video acceleration API (VAAPI) to support VVC [30], which makes it easier for software applications to use hardware accelerators. An example is FFmpeg, with the ‘Cartwheel’ release in mid-2024 incorporating VVC hardware acceleration via VAAPI [31]. Ericsson’s test showed the chipset to allow decoding speed of 1200 FPS for 1080p video [9].

Service Deployment

Availability of implementations contributes to commercial readiness of video codecs, yet it is down to actually deployed services which really tells the story of market take up. It is worth noting it is a typical chicken-and-egg situation where services can't be deployed unless codec implementations are not only available but also incorporated into a sufficient footprint of accessible devices. At the same time there may be less incentive to deploy implementations if there are no prospective services that would benefit from the technology.

After the rapid uptake of AVC due to HD services roll-out, deployment of any subsequent codec technology may appear underwhelming. Looking back at HEVC deployment, hardware availability in particular was fairly advanced before major service roll-out. A key use case for HEVC has been UHD (with 4K resolution) deployment. The initial drive for 4K resolution was augmented with HDR and it is now widely agreed that the term UHDTV captures both 4K resolution as well as HDR with both 4K as well as Full-HD. Data from the UHD Forum's UHD service tracker reports the number of UHD channels deployed since 2014 is shown in FIGURE 1. It can be seen that the deployment accelerated between 2017 and 2020, as well as recently in 2024 with over 50 new reported services, mainly in the US. It can be assumed that majority of the services are deployed with HEVC.

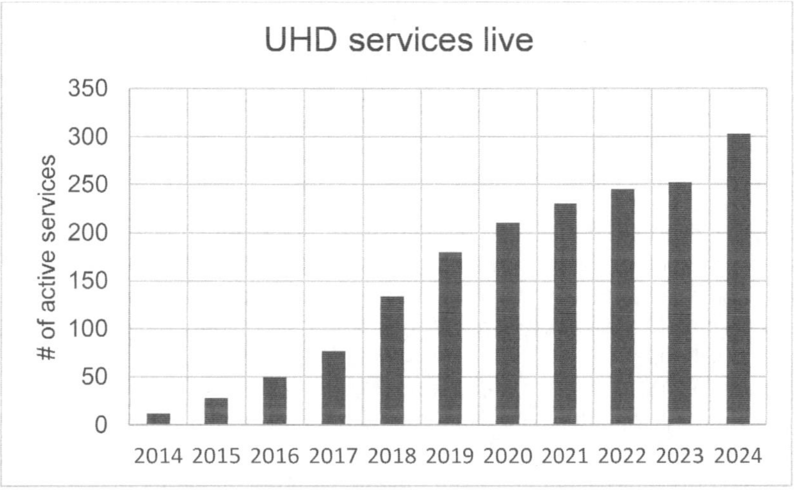

FIGURE 1: NUMBER OF ACTIVE UHD SERVICES AFTER UHD FORUM SERVICE TRACKER.

FIGURE 2 shows data from two industry surveys by Bitmovin [32] and Haivision [33]. We put together the data from all available surveys: for Bitmovin this is from 2017-2024, and for Haivision it is 2021-2024. We see that in 2017, 4 years after HEVC was finalized, use of HEVC was reported by 30% of respondents (as far as we understand there is no qualification on the type and reach of service). Removing year-to-year fluctuations, we observe the general trend for HEVC has been increasing penetration and in the 2024 report HEVC was reported to be used by 50% of respondents. At the same time, AVC's dominance has been slowly eroding from 95% reported usage in 2017 to just under 80% in 2024. The other report, which focuses more on the contribution market, reports higher usage of HEVC; just under 70% of respondents reported HEVC usage in 2024. At the same time AVC's usage is reported at 79%, coincidentally the same level as in Bitmovin report.

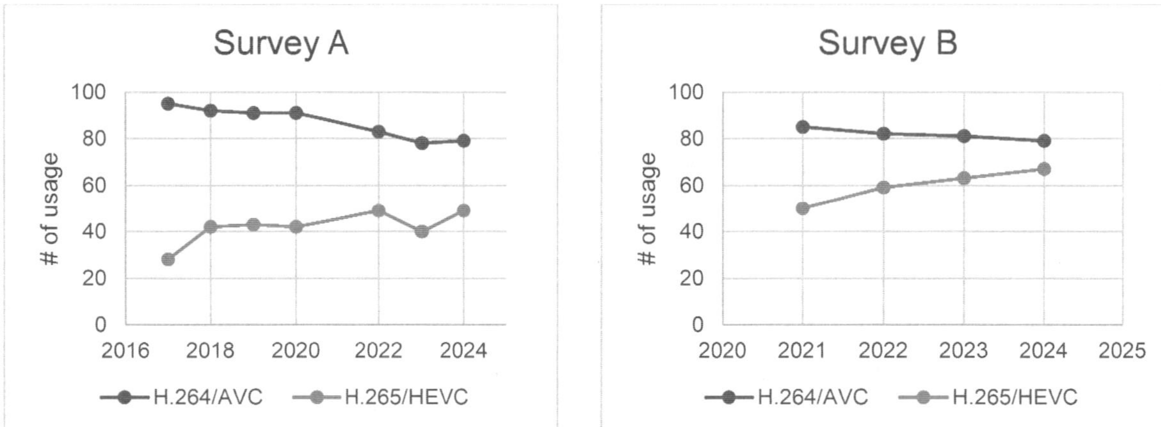

FIGURE 2 COMPARISON OF REPORTED USE OF H.264/AVC AND H.265/HEVC IN SURVEYS FROM BITMOVIN (SURVEY A) AND HAIVISION (SURVEY B).

What may this mean for VVC? One observation could be that VVC lacks the same driving use case as HD was for AVC and UHD/HDR for HEVC. One such application would be 8K. While 8K trials at the Paris Olympics by Intel and OBS demonstrated successful transmission to several locations across the globe with a stringent latency constraint using VVC, wide-spread deployment of 8K services is yet to be seen. Interest in VR 360 video, another potential application that could drive VVC, has slowed while other immersive formats emerged, such as stereoscopic 3D video with the use of MV-HEVC, the multiview extension of HEVC.

On the other hand, high use of AVC/H.264 poses an opportunity. As VVC deployment and footprint increases, those service providers which have not moved to HEVC may consider move directly to VVC as this offers maximum bitrate savings as well as a substantial step change in bitrates. In such a scenario, what could drive VVC deployment would not necessarily mean high resolution formats but extra performance gains for HD and sub-HD resolutions. The fact that VVC offers the lowest bitrates for a given quality across all available codecs plays interestingly into industry's growing interest in using software decoding, since the performance of software decoding is highly dependent on bitrates. In this context we view VVC software decoder deployment as already quite advanced in comparison to HEVC at the same time after standard release. The next section looks closer at comparing the status.

Deployment Milestone Comparison

In this section, we summarize some key deployment milestones and compare them to those of H.265/HEVC. The story for VVC is not yet complete, so this should be viewed more as a snapshot of progress. The circumstances and business environment are different now compared to ten years ago. As mentioned earlier, the software implementations tend to be much more feasible, reducing the urgency for hardware implementations on some platforms, so it would not be appropriate to scan the table and conclude that VVC is doing 'better' or 'worse' than H.265/HEVC at the same point. But we feel it can, in a very coarse way, help to calibrate expectations for VVC uptake.

Milestone	H.265/HEVC date	VVC date
Finalization	January 2013	July 2020
Patent pool formed	+20 months (09/2014)	+12 months (07/2021)
DVB blue book approved	+18 months (07/2014)	+19 months (02/2022)
ATSC standard published	+73 months (02/2019)	+56 months (02/2025)
TV SoC support announced	+24 months (01/2015)	+16 months (11/2021)
GPU support	+24 months (01/2015)	+47 months (06/2024)
Mobile SoC support	+16 months (05/2014)	n/a
DVB broadcast begins	+49 months (03/2017)	n/a

TABLE 1 TIMELINE OF KEY CODEC DEPLOYMENT MILESTONES.

From this very high-level comparison, it can be seen VVC is on par or earlier than H.265/HEVC in several areas relative to finalization of the standard, but behind in some others. Patent pools were formed relatively earlier for VVC, which ought to give some clarity regarding licensing, and incorporation into major standards has occurred in a timely manner. Hardware, particularly for mobile chipsets, has been somewhat slower to eventuate.

Our contention is that, at a high level, VVC is neither dramatically ahead of nor behind H.265/HEVC at a similar post-finalization stage, when taking a global view. This conclusion may be different when restricting consideration to a particular ecosystem or geography.

We have deliberately excluded software milestones, in-browser video, and trial deployments & demonstrations from the comparison, because these can be more subjective. For example, a buggy implementation that takes several steps to install in a browser can't be directly compared to a seamless experience, and a trial limited to a small number of select consumers is quite different from an open beta involving millions. Nonetheless, we see that VVC software implementations have appeared quite quickly on a variety of platforms (including phones, browsers, and smart televisions) so we would claim there is nothing to shrink away from, and in all likelihood an extension of the table to software would be to VVC's advantage.

Conclusion

This paper has reviewed the current deployment status of the VVC video codec in software, hardware and services. It has also provided a comparison with H.265/HEVC in terms of time since standard finalization. In general, we conclude that VVC deployment is not in a drastically different state than H.265/HEVC at a similar point in time post-finalization. There are some areas where VVC is slightly ahead, but others where it is lagging, notably in terms of mobile chipsets.

However, there are key differences in the circumstances that make a direct comparison difficult. In particular, the capability of software decoders has improved markedly over the past ten years, and VVC software codecs already provide superior compression efficiency compared to older codecs and perform well in terms of complexity (power usage), so that the time-to-market of hardware VVC decoders is less critical.

We also see that an increasing number of televisions and other living room devices have underlying support for VVC, so that it is possible for uptake to occur reasonably quickly. However, it cannot be inferred from the current deployment situation when that might occur. It is also noted that the situation varies regionally, with VVC a reasonable near-term prospect in some places such as Brazil.

Certainly the next few years will give us a better indication of where VVC is headed, and how it is tracking toward widespread adoption.

References

[1] ITU-T | ISO/IEC, Rec. ITU-T H.266 | ISO/IEC 23090-3 “Information technology: Coded representation of immersive media – Part 3: Versatile Video Coding”, 2022.

[2] Sullivan, G.J.S. “Deployment status of the VVC standard”, doc. JVET-AJ0021 of ITU-T/ISO/IEC Joint Video Experts Team (JVET), 36th meeting: November 2024.

[3] Bross, B., et. al., “Overview of the Versatile Video Coding (VVC) Standard and its Applications”. IEEE Transactions on Circuits and Systems for Video Technology, 2021, 31 (10), pp. 3736-3764.

[4] Wien, M., et. al., “VVC Verification Test Report for Ultra High Definition (UHD) Standard Dynamic Range (SDR) Video Content”, doc. JVET-T2020 of ITU-T/ISO/IEC Joint Video Experts Team (JVET), 20th meeting: October 2020.

[5] 3GPP, “5G Video Codec Characteristics (Rel. 17)”, TR 26.955 v.2.0.0, July 2022.

[6] Li, Y., et. al., “Performance of a VVC Software Decoder on Mobile Platform”, doc. JVET-U0071 of ITU-T/ISO/IEC Joint Video Experts Team (JVET), 21st meeting: January 2021.

[7] He, Y., et. al., “Performance of a VVC software decoder – BVC”, doc. JVET-V0128 of ITU-T/ISO/IEC Joint Video Experts Team (JVET), 22nd meeting: April 2021.

[8] Feng, W.-L., et. al., “VVC Software Decoder for Mobile Platforms”, doc. JVET-V0070 of ITU-T/ISO/IEC Joint Video Experts Team (JVET), 22nd meeting: April 2021.

[9] Litwic, L, et.al, “Optimizing cloud gaming applications with VVC”, ACM Proceedings of the 4th Mile-High Video Conference, MHV '25, February 18–20, 2025, Denver, CO, USA.

[10] Fraunhofer HHI VVenC software repository. URL: https://github.com/fraunhoferhhi/vvenc.

[11] Wieckowski, A., et. al., “Update on open, optimized VVC implementations VVenC and VVdeC”, doc. JVET-Y0136 of ITU-T/ISO/IEC Joint Video Experts Team (JVET), 25th meeting: January 2022.

[12] “MX Player becomes first OTT to deploy H.266, cuts down video streaming data consumption into half”, Best Media Info, 16 June 2021. URL: https://bestmediainfo.com/2021/06/mx-player-becomes-first-ott-to-deploy-h-266-cuts-down-video-streaming-data-consumption-into-half.

[13] “Amazon and MX Player join forces to accelerate premium free entertainment for 250 million users in India”, Amazon, 7 October 2024. URL: https://www.aboutamazon.in/news/entertainment/amazon-minitv-mx-player-merger.

[14] Fang, S., et. al., “Latest update on Ali266: performance and deployment status”, doc. JVET-AF0211 of ITU-T/ISO/IEC Joint Video Experts Team (JVET), 32nd meeting: October 2023.

[15] “8K live streaming presented by Intel at Paris Olympics”, Spin Digital, 15 August 2024. URL: https://spin-digital.com/events/8k-live-streaming-paris-olympic-games/.

[16] Nestor, M., “FFmpeg 7.1 “Péter” Released with Full Native VVC Decoder, Vulkan Hardware Encoding”, 9to5Linux, 30 September 2024.

[17] Plowman, F., et. al., “lav/vvc: Remove experimental flag”, Github.com, 6 September 2024.

[18] Eesmaa, M., "FFmpeg VVC En/decoder & xHE-AAC installation (Windows, Mac OS and Linux)" Github.com, 18 October 2024.

[19] "OBS Studio". URL: https://obsproject.com/

[20] Richards, D., "Hisense 2025 TV's to get new processor & 4 HDMI 2.1 ports", ChannelNews, 15 January 2025. URL: https://www.channelnews.com.au/hisense-2025-tvs-to-get-new-processor-4-hdmi-2-1-ports/

[21] "Xiaomi launches 4K 144Hz Redmi Smart TV X 2025 with Dolby Vision, VRR, MEMC, HyperOS & more", Gizmochina, 24 October 2024. URL: https://www.gizmochina.com/2024/10/24/xiaomi-redmi-smart-tv-x-2025-series-launch-specs-price/

[22] Schmidt, B., "Xiaomi Redmi Smart TV X 2025: AI, 240Hz, and Wi-Fi 6 Starting at $300", TechForBrains, 25 November 2024. URL: https://www.techforbrains.com/tv/xiaomi-redmi-smart-tv-x-2025-ai-240hz-and-wi-fi-6-starting-at-300/

[23] "LG webOS TV – Supported Video Playback". URL retrieved 14 February 2025: https://www.lg.com/ca_en/support/product-support/troubleshoot/help-library/cs-CT20098005-1437128842789/

[24] ETSI. "Digital Video Broadcasting (DVB); Specification for the use of Video and Audio Coding in Broadcast and Broadcast Applications", ETSI TS 101 154 V2.8.1, 2023.

[25] ATSC. "VVC Video", ATSC A/345. 10 February 2025.

[26] Fórum SBTVD, "TV 3.0 Project". URL retrieved 14 February 2025: https://forumsbtvd.org.br/tv3_0/

[27] "Vivensis VX Smart". URL retrieved 14 February 2025: https://www.androidtv-guide.com/pay-tv-provider/vivensis-vx-smart/

[28] "Valerion VisionMaster". URL retrieved 14 February 2025: https://www.valerion.com/global/visionMaster

[29] Larsen, R., "Next-gen VVC (H.266) video codec debuts in Intel's Lunar Lake chips", FlatPanelsHD, 4 September 2024.

[30] Larabel, M., "Intel's VA-API 2.22 Library Adds VVC/H.266 Video Decode Interface", Phoronix, 2 July 2024.

[31] Larabel, M., "Intel FFmpeg 2024Q2 Update Enables GPU-Accelerated VVC Decoding", Phoronix, 16 July 2024.

[32] The Annual Bitmovin Video Developer Report, 2017-2024, URL retrieved 14 February 2025,https://bitmovin.com/video-developer-report/

[33] Haivision Broadcast Transformation Report, 2021-2024, URL retrieved 14 February 2025, https://www.haivision.com/white-papers/broadcast-ip-transformation-reports/

Why Do You Need Proactive Video Delivery Network Observability?

Adi Rozenberg
AlvaLinks, Ltd
Neve Yamin, Israel
Adi.rozenberg@alvalinks.com

Abstract – The rapid adaptation of IP workflows in production, contribution, cloud, and distribution is always challenging. Organizations spend millions of dollars training the workforce, deploying monitoring solutions and troubleshooting "network issues," which takes an enormous portion of their tasks. Time and effort are wasted on old techniques that were suitable for standard file delivery versus today's high throughput and low latency demands of live production.

In this paper we would like to draw your attention to a different way of thinking, observing and gaining in-depth understanding of the lifeline of the broadcast industry: the network. The traditional reactive way of monitoring events and alarms must evolve to use proactive observability. Unlike standard observability that just collects data from elements and passive probes, proactive observability involves injecting small amounts of traffic into the network to discover the network routes and to support the continuous measurement of the performance of the traffic to gain valuable insights into the experience of the traffic.

History

Ten years ago, once an organization decided to switch to an IP-based workflow, it came with a struggle and a learning curve. Suddenly broadcast teams needed to be on top of recent IP technologies, workflow changes, and often needed to troubleshoot events that are beyond what they can directly observe. The IT team faced strict requirements regarding stability, quality-of-service (QOS), timing and much more.

Now, ten years later, IP delivery is still challenging to master: ST2110 production, remote secure reliable transport (SRT) streams, SMPTE2022-7 multi-path, network device interface (NDI), JPEGXs connection to cloud resources, cloud production and much more. The timing requirements are more strenuous these days due to single frame delay requirements, low latency streaming, and live production in the cloud. The days of a few seconds of delay are gone now - this is a complete headache for both the broadcast and IT teams.

Over the last 25 years the IT industry has been putting out great solutions to monitor network element health, status, traffic statistics and more. Proprietary protocols include Netflow for Cisco, Jflow for Juniper Networks, NetStream for 3Com/HP, NetStream for Huawei Technologies, Cflowd for Nokia, Rflow for Ericsson, AppFlow for Citrix as well as vast industry support for sampled flow (sFlow). The industry has also adopted an IETF protocol, Internet protocol flow information export (IPFIX) with RFC

This paper is excerpted from the Proceedings of the 2025 NAB Broadcast Engineering and Information Technology (BEIT) Conference, © 2025, National Association of Broadcasters, 1 M Street SE, Washington, DC 20003 USA.

5101 (obsoleted by RFC 7011), RFC 5102 (obsoleted by RFC 7012), etc. which were published in 2008.[1] In addition, several companies offers advanced management and monitoring solution to configure and maintain network routers. These are exceptionally good solutions to gain an understanding of the network and the health of specific routing elements.

One major drawback of these solutions is the sampling time: it can range from tens of seconds to minutes. Slow sampling means that transient events which are quite common with network but have a high impact on media feeds may not be detectable and missed completely. Figure 1 is an example of slow sampling illustration showing how poor low sampling will lead to missing out on events.

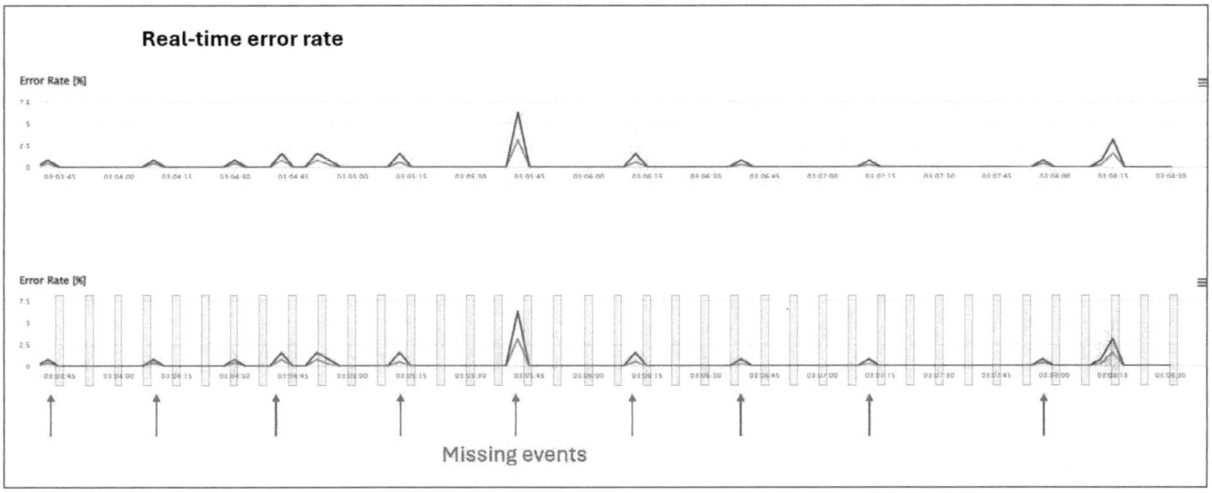

FIGURE 1: LOW SAMPLING PERIOD VS HIGH TRANSIENT EVENTS. SHADED BARS REPRESENT SAMPLING TIMES WHILE THE RED ARROWS SHOW ERROR RATE EVENTS THAT WERE NOT CAPTURED BY THIS SAMPLING.

Figure 1 shows a reference example of error rate versus time (top chart), while the bottom chart shows the same error rate sampled at a low frequency. The red arrows indicate where events are not sampled and may show a wrong network awareness.

What is required today is observability. Observability focuses on collecting data from wherever possible to gain a better understanding of events, trends and more. When coupled with event/alarm logging it becomes an immensely powerful tool to gain visibility. But even with this power in hand the observability solutions in the market suffer from the same slow sampling frequency and no reference data.

Proactive observability addresses this limitation by injecting reference traffic and capturing the traffic across the network – it provides a deeper insight into the network behavior, its transient impact (packet loss, jitter, latency, round trip time or RTT) on the data – to get a more complete view of the health of the network. Today's modern monitoring and observability solutions are based on visualization by way of a dashboard, an example is shown in Figure 2.

Figure 2 shows an example of a dashboard showing multiple charts with time synchronization. In this example (top to bottom) the following are shown (all versus time); Error rate, HOP change (signaling route length changes), max RTT (ms), buffer emulation (ms), Cloud Rider packet rate (pkt/s, a

[1] See https://datatracker.ietf.org/doc/html/rfc7012.

processed data based on error rate vs jitter/RTT/Latency), Jitter (ms), packet loss, and latency (ms). The user can view realtime and historical information.

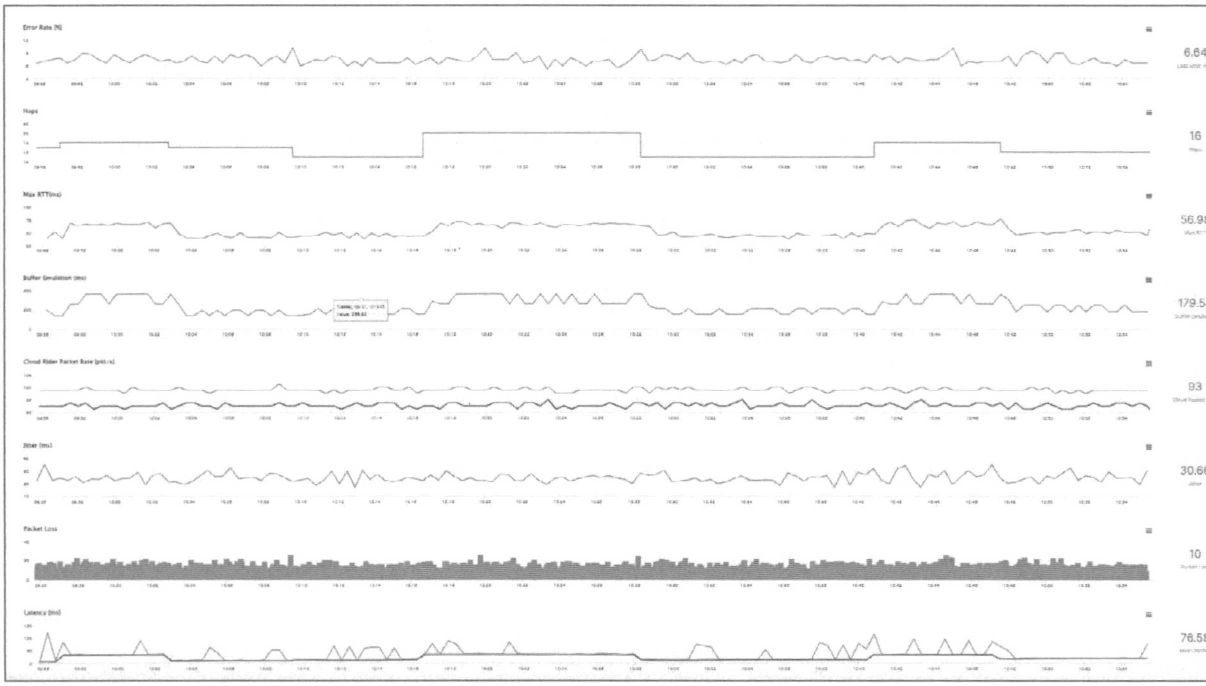

FIGURE 2. EXAMPLE OF REAL-TIME DATA DASHBOARD. (SOURCE: ALVALINKS)

Proactive injected traffic can be used to discover new routes, heavily congested hops, and be a reference for measurements between source to destination regardless of the protocols in use by the organization.

Reactive vs Proactive

The prevailing strategy today is reactive; most equipment manufacturers have alarm/event notification capability, so we can capture and gather these and identify problems. This is still the prevailing approach for many years; get an alarm or event indication (for example, ETSI TR 101 290 transport error, multiviewer flagging, and traditional IT monitoring) and from that try to gather data to find the issue. This approach is based on event replication that may be recurring in hours or days from the original event (after the event has ended). One thing remains; You are still challenged with the question; what caused this problem? Is that my source? Is that my equipment? Is that my local network? Is that the destination? Time is of the essence to live sports and events and so is for distribution.

What do you do next? Most may wait for a repetition of the problem, which may escalate and cause service interruptions. Others will decide to activate a backup system to reduce the service impact. Now comes the tedious task of figuring out the problem. Find probing points, bring experts, call the vendor for support, call the network service provider. At this point DATA is king! The following questions must be answered: what has happened? How did the system behave before the incident? How do I detect additional events and how to avoid this issue properly next time?

This paper focuses on why you need to use proactive video delivery observability and presents a single-panel solution based on real-time and historical data. Data is king in the observability world. If we had real time and historical data that can assist us to identify what may cause the alarm/event – we could save time on detection the event, apply a fix, and monitor if the fix solves the problem.

This is where proactive observability comes into play; proactive means that a small amount of synthetic traffic is injected to run through the network. This traffic is then received by a waiting probe on the other end to extract network performance measurements. The injected traffic is also used for the route discovery process and response time measurement (like the traceroute operation), but this is done continuously – giving far more information, and with time correlation to other measurements. All information is gathered into a time base database for easy display and correlation.

Under the Hood

Proactive observability is all about injecting packets into the network for discovering the available paths from source to destination and continuously testing the network impact on the packets traveling across these paths (Figure 3). The injecting is done continuously to be on top of the route changes and response slow-down and to identify which hop may be causing issues. In parallel, packet-by-packet relationship information is collected: delay variation, latency from the source, reordering, loss of packets and more.

Observability starts with creating synthetic packets. These packets use user datagram protocol/real time transport protocol (UDP/RTP) headers with an additional timestamp reference and unique ID. The timestamp is used for measurements of the origination time and reception time.

Path Discovery

The sending probe starts by trying to reach a receiver probe IP address. The probe sends packets with an increasing Time To Live (TTL) value in a technique which is based on Dublin Trace route.[2] The probe monitors every returned packet with ICMP time exceeded.[3] This way, every change of hop IP address is recorded, as well as the ordering of the responses. Next, we extract the RTT by comparing the internal timestamp with the time the packet was received. This process continuously keeps track of the network changes. In some cases, multiple responses with the same TTL can come back to indicate route diversity.

Link Probing and Testing

Once a path is identified, the sending probe injects packets at a constant rate - this sets the desired sampling time. On the receiving end, the probe captures the synthetic packets and extracts the embedded timestamp plus the network received time information to calculate packet rate, bitrate, packet by packet jitter information, variation between original jitter to received jitter, latency, RTT and more.

[2] See https://github.com/insomniacslk/dublin-traceroute.
[3] See https://en.wikipedia.org/wiki/Internet_Control_Message_Protocol.

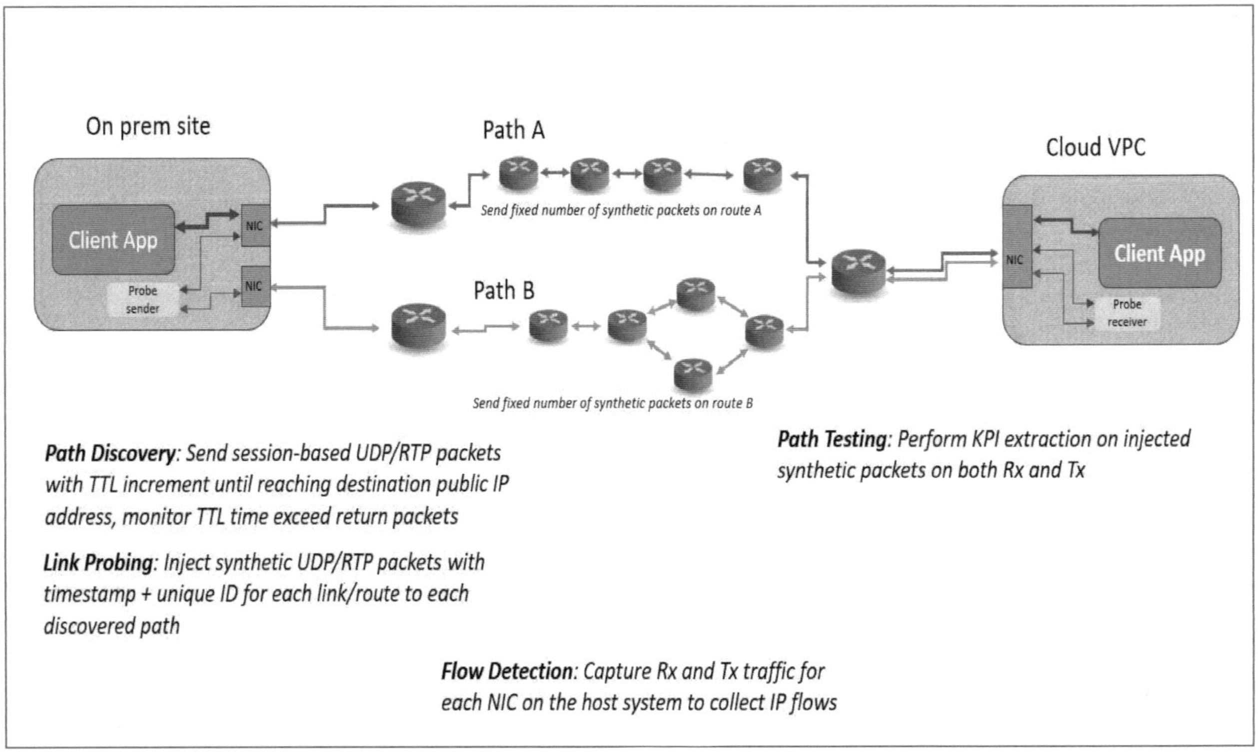

FIGURE 3: DIAGRAM ILLUSTRATING THE INTRODUCTION OF SYNTHETIC PACKETS INTO A NETWORK. (SOURCE: ALVALINKS)

Flow Detection

Both the sender and receiver track the traffic on the network interface they are attached to in order to provide identify various IP flows and if they may be causing an overload on the Network interface (for example high burst of data sent out may take priority of data streams, the same is true on the receiving end).

All the above information is sent to a shared time-based database for additional processing and analytic tasks.

Benefits of Proactive Observability

Proactive observability can help 24/7 operations achieve the following goals:

1. 24/7 continuously discovering and registering the paths that the media is traveling through.
2. 24/7 high precision of gathering and storing information from probed locations.
3. Common time-based database for real time and historical information.
4. Collection of packet-by-packet information:
    a. Packet loss
    b. Jitter
    c. Latency
    d. RTT
    e. Routing hops
    f. Detectable IP flows
    g. User selectable IP flows

5. Every measurement to include min, max, mean, average and more, using sliding windows.
6. Alarming and integration with third party tools.
7. Support for dashboard to present various real time and historical Key Performance Indicator (KPI) in a single panel with time correlation of events.

Now once an event is reported, all you need to do is to look at the information on the dashboard. Event correlation and root cause analysis becomes much easier and faster. No more guessing, no more long captures of traffic – it is already available and waiting for the operator.

Once coupled with Machine Learning (ML) and Large Language Models (LLM), the operator or management system may draw more insights from the information to save time and money for his organization.

Real Use Case

A production studio connected to cloud service (depicted in Figure 4) was taking on occasional hits. Was it the source equipment? Local production network? Gateway to cloud service provider? Dedicated access networks to public cloud? Maybe the cloud can't handle the load. The Software receiver at fault? It was unclear.

The only information available to the operations team was in the form of alarms on the receiving side. All attempts to capture network information using a Wireshark sniffer failed to find the root cause as it was very short-lived. Going for continuous 24-hour live captures of a network events showed a decrease of bitrate with no explanation or correlation. The IT team tried to run traceroute and the outcome was a flat point-to-point route made of fixed hops.[4] An automated script to run traceroute after an alarm showed no different information.

The customer deployed a proactive observability to help identify the problem. The outcome was very surprising: proactive observability found a parallel path in the local production network. The new route only existed for a few minutes, it had no QOS or any provisioning in the gateway heading to cloud service over a cloud access network.

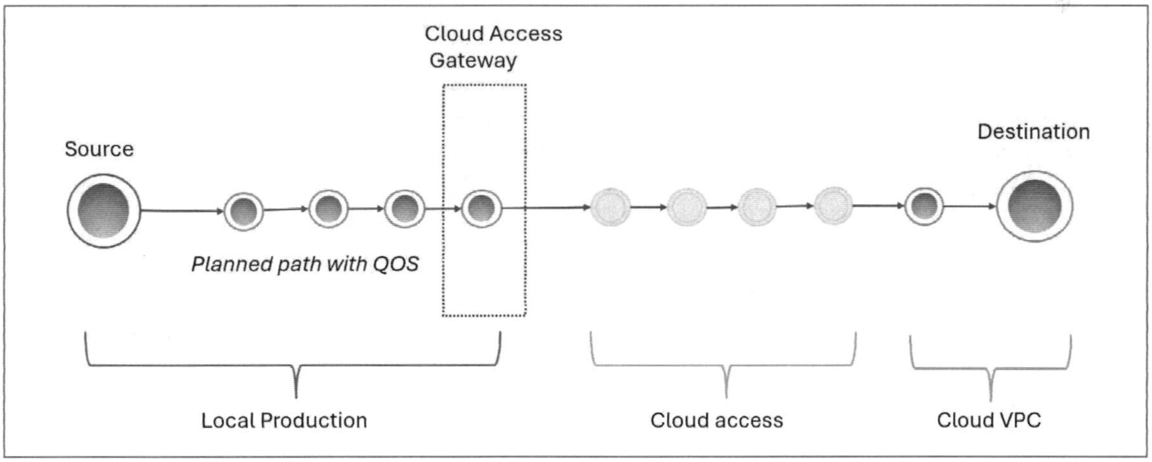

FIGURE 4: NETWORK SCHEMATIC OF A PRODUCTION STUDIO CONNECTED TO A CLOUD SERVICE.

[4] See https://en.wikipedia.org/wiki/Traceroute.

Figure 4 shows the conceptual design of the system as was planned: a local production network (purple) going to a cloud Access Gateway, the network then goes through a cloud access circuit and reaches to a virtual private cloud (VPC) where the receiver software awaits.

Figure 5 shows the network discovered by precise observability. The Local Production network showed an unplanned path to the Cloud Access Gateway.

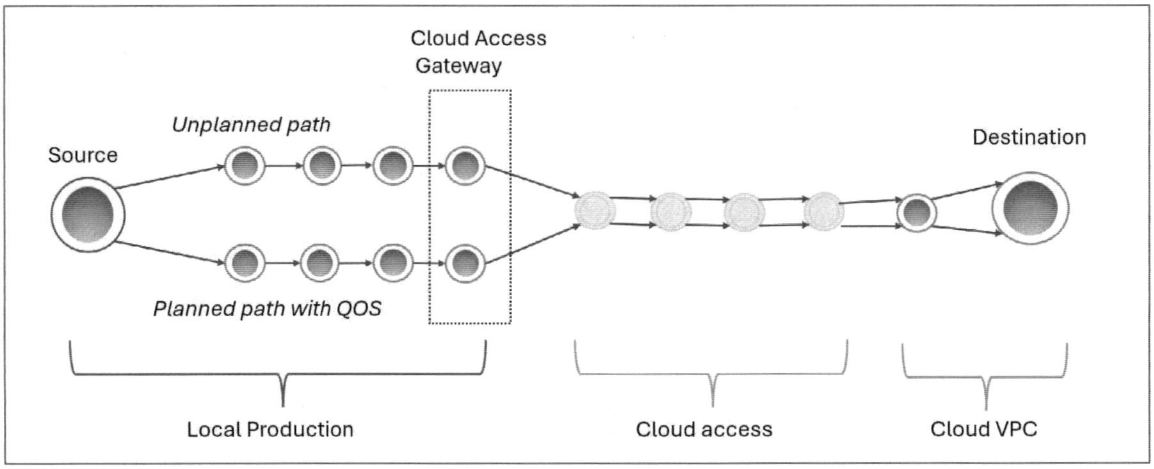

FIGURE 5: DISCOVERED NETWORK BY OBSERVABILITY.

Figure 6 shows a dashboard of real time and historical KPI. The error rate chart (second from the top) shows 3 major events over time: 1) in purple highlight, an 80% packet loss event; 2) in blue highlight, an 80% packet loss event; and 3) in green highlight marked as 3 a 30% packet loss event. The "Cloud Rider Packet rate" chart (at bottom of Figure 6) shows the synthetic traffic and an event that indicates a spike (normally associated with a sudden burst).

It was found that the alarm notifications were correlated to the appearance and disappearance of this new path (see hop 3 in Figure 7). The production data was routed over this short-lived path causing large number of in-flight packets to be lost in a few milliseconds.

Referring to Figure 7 dashboard of HOPS indexes (second chart from the bottom):

- Event 1: shows the first appearance of the hop and route
- Event 2: shows congestion event on this hop
- Event 3: shows the end of the route through the new hop

The dashboard information is clearly visible for the operator or any Machine Learning (ML) to clearly identify the packet loss events to a specific hop in this route and the correlation of the hop appearance and disappearance to the local production network. Weeks of guessing faded into one clear reality. Now the IT team had found the "smoking gun" and could eliminate this route and return to pristine service once more.

Conclusion

With proactive observability, the IT and broadcast teams can attend to more pressing tasks, as the proactive observability will provide continuous data collection when the network is within the acceptable performance criteria and signal exceptions to the operator in real time.

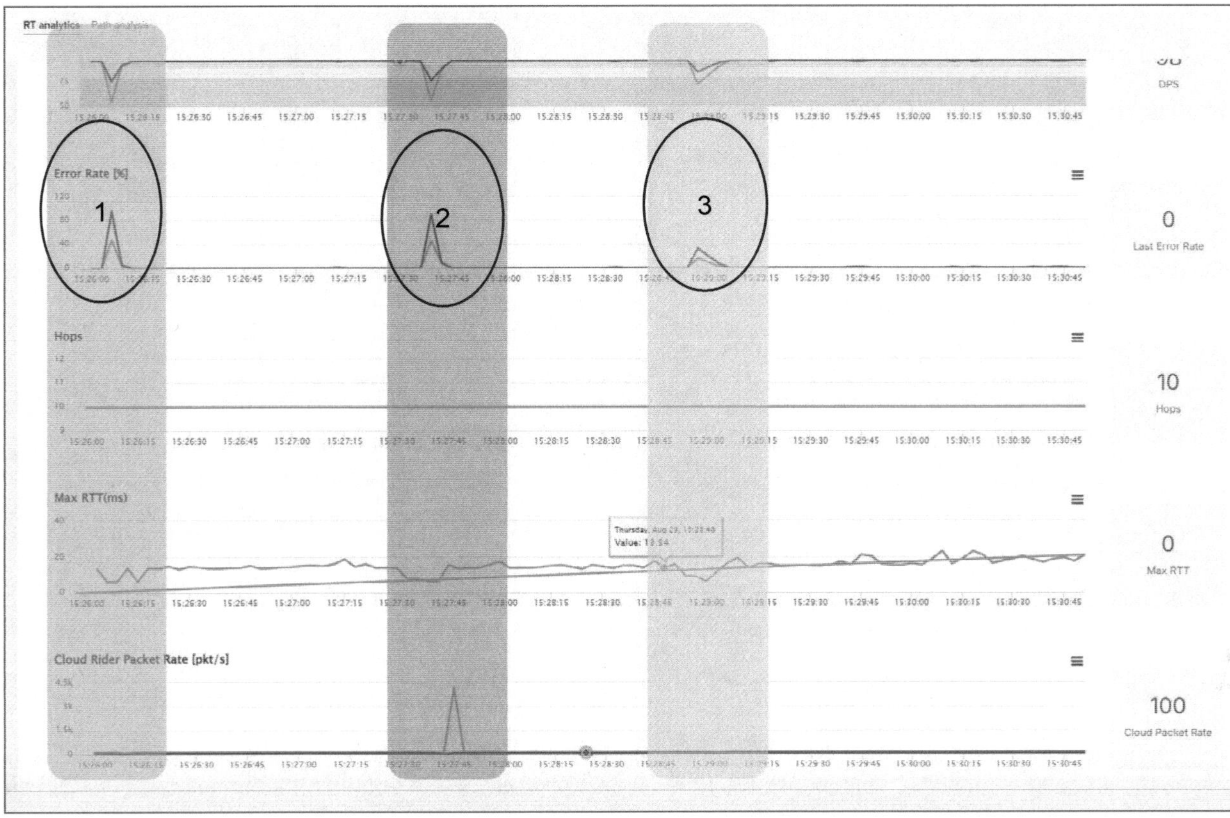

FIGURE 6. THREE EVENTS OF HIGH PACKET LOSS.

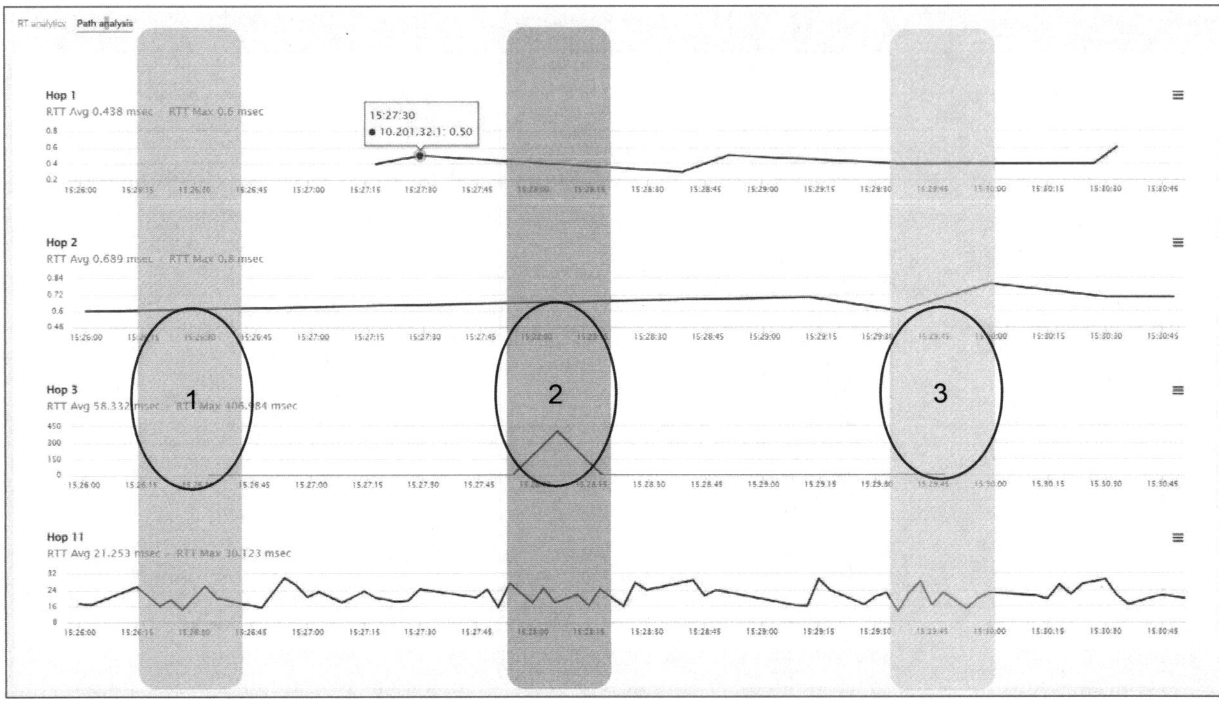

FIGURE 7: HOP3 APPEARANCE (SECOND CHART FROM THE BOTTOM) IS CORRELATED TO LOSS EVENTS.

B2B Content Distribution Over CDN for OTT and Broadcast Services

David Eisenbacher
EZDRM
Rye Brook, New York, United States

Khaled Jerbi
ATEME
Vélizy-Villacoublay, France

Abstract – The evolution of content delivery technologies for OTT and broadcast services has transformed how media is distributed, shifting from satellite-based models to CDN-based frameworks. This paper introduces "B2B Content Distribution over CDN," a modern approach leveraging CDNs and industry-standard DRM technologies—Widevine, PlayReady, and FairPlay. This method ensures cost-efficient, scalable, and secure content delivery across diverse platforms. Core components, including the Common Encryption Scheme (CENC) and the Content Protection Information Exchange (CPIX) protocol, streamline secure key management and distributor access. Advanced features like channel-based access control, real-time content revocation, and blackout enforcement enhance content management while complying with regulatory requirements [1] [2]. By reducing reliance on traditional satellite systems, B2B Content Distribution offers broadcasters and Over-the-Top (OTT) providers with a robust alternative for modernized content delivery.

Introduction

The progress of media consumption has been profoundly influenced by technological advancements in content delivery systems. For decades, traditional broadcast and satellite-based distribution methods, exemplified by technologies like the Basic Interoperable Scrambling System-Conditional Access (BISS-CA), have dominated the industry. These systems provide secure transmission but often come with significant cost and scalability challenges [3].

In recent years, the rise of OTT platforms has disrupted traditional models, demanding more flexible and cost-effective solutions. Content delivery networks (CDNs) have emerged as a transformative alternative, offering scalability and compatibility with diverse consumer devices. Integrating CDNs with industry-standard digital rights management (DRM) technologies—such as Widevine, PlayReady, and FairPlay—has further enhanced content security and control.

This paper introduces "B2B Content Distribution over CDN," a modernized framework that addresses the limitations of traditional systems while meeting the demands of contemporary OTT and broadcast services. By utilizing the Common Encryption Scheme (CENC) and the Content Protection Information Exchange (CPIX) protocol, B2B Content Distribution provides a secure, flexible, and cost-efficient solution for live and on-demand content delivery. This approach also supports advanced features like channel-based access control, real-time revocation, and blackout management, ensuring compliance with licensing and regulatory requirements.

The following sections explore the evolution of content distribution technologies, the architecture of B2B Content Distribution, and its implications for broadcasters and OTT providers seeking to modernize their operations.

From Satellite-Based Models to CDN

The development of content distribution has been a fascinating journey, marked by significant technological advancements that have transformed how media is delivered and consumed. From the reliance on satellite-based models for broadcasting content to the revolutionary impact of OTT platforms and the rise of modern CDNs, each stage reflects a leap in efficiency, scalability, and audience reach. This section delves into the progression of these distribution methods, exploring their core principles, strengths, and the pivotal moments that reshaped the video delivery landscape.

Traditional Models: Satellite-Based Content Distribution

Satellite-based content distribution, such as BISS-CA (Basic Interoperable Scrambling System-Conditional Access), has long been the backbone of broadcasting. These systems use direct encryption to secure content transmission, ensuring that only authorized receivers can access the content. While effective in guaranteeing content security, these models face significant challenges, including:

- High costs: Satellite links and proprietary encryption systems require substantial investment in infrastructure and operational expenses.
- Limited flexibility: Satellite systems are less adaptable to dynamic user demands and cannot easily scale to support variable content delivery needs.
- Regional constraints: Satellite beams cover predefined geographical areas, limiting the ability to tailor content delivery for localized requirements.

Despite these limitations, satellite-based models have set foundational standards for secure content transmission, which newer approaches like CDN-based systems build upon.

OTT: The Video Delivery Game Changer

OTT streaming is more versatile and modern than the linear MPEG-2 Transport Stream (TS) format because it leverages advanced technologies designed for the dynamic and interactive nature of internet-based delivery. Unlike MPEG-2 TS, which is optimized for traditional broadcast environments with fixed schedules and limited interactivity, OTT streaming supports adaptive bitrate streaming (e.g., HLS, DASH to deliver seamless playback across various devices and network conditions [4] [5].

OTT platforms enable personalized content recommendations, on-demand viewing, and multi-device accessibility, catering to modern consumer habits. Furthermore, OTT utilizes more efficient codecs like H.264, H.265, and AV1, enabling higher quality video at lower bitrates compared to MPEG-2 TS. This versatility aligns with the shift toward internet-first media consumption, providing greater scalability and monetization opportunities for content providers. Moreover, the transmission is TCP based which resolves all issues related to error transmission and bypasses the complex error correction algorithms.

This modern approach is further enhanced by CDNs which play a crucial role in optimizing the delivery of OTT content, by reducing latency and ensuring a smooth user experience across diverse geographies.

Modern CDN-Based Distribution

The advent of CDNs has revolutionized how media is distributed, especially for OTT platforms. CDNs comprise geographically distributed servers that store and deliver content efficiently, offering advantages over traditional satellite models:

- **Scalability:** CDNs handle increased traffic without significant infrastructure changes.
- **Cost efficiency:** Using CDNs eliminates the need for expensive satellite links. Along with CDN egress cost to the end distributor can lower the TCO.

- **Flexibility:** CDNs allow dynamic content delivery tailored to user preferences and device compatibility.
- **Pull vs push:** Traditional satellite distribution uses a push of a single level of content over a fixed bandwidth. B2B Content Distribution via CDN allows for a pull of content for only the required content and quality.
- **High availability:** With traditional satellite distribution, signals can be lost or even deliberately jammed during times of political turbulence. In contrast, B2B content distribution via a CDN offers highly scalable and reliable access. Furthermore, leveraging a multi-CDN topology enhances the resilience of the distribution.

To ensure content protection, CDN-based distribution incorporates robust DRM technologies. Widely adopted standards such as Widevine, PlayReady, and FairPlay offer cross-platform compatibility while safeguarding against unauthorized access. This integration of CDNs and DRM technologies forms the foundation of B2B Content Distribution.

B2B Content Distribution: Framework, Applications, and Advantages
The B2B Content Distribution framework represents a modernized approach to delivering secure and scalable content through CDN-based systems (Figure 1). This approach integrates advanced encryption, key management, and DRM technologies to meet the demands of contemporary OTT and broadcast services while addressing the limitations of traditional satellite-based systems.

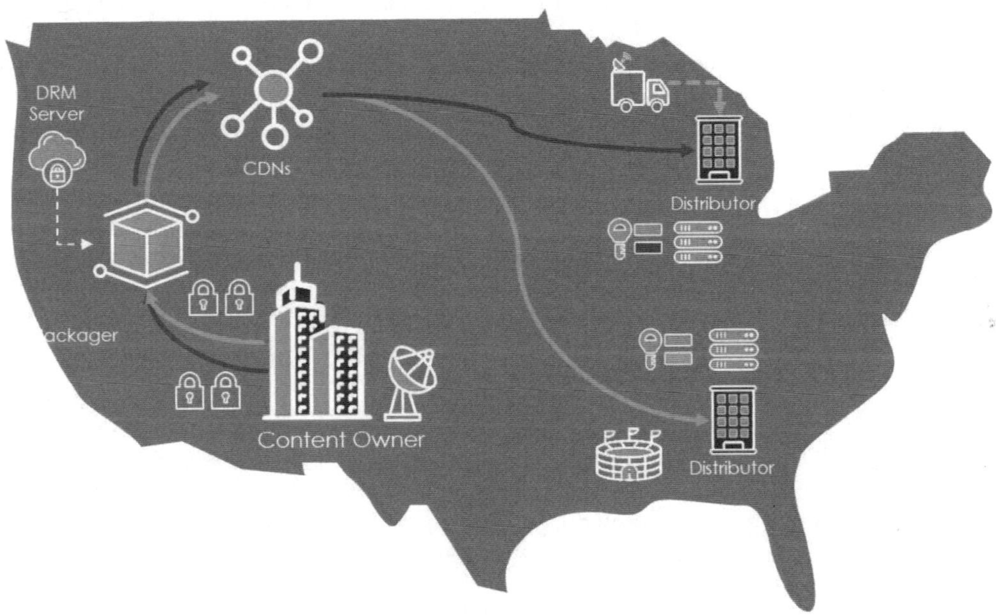

FIGURE 1: SIMPLIFIED ARCHITECTURE OF DESIGN.

At its core, B2B Content Distribution leverages a combination of industry-standard technologies and protocols to ensure secure, efficient, and flexible content delivery. Here is a list of the most iconic involved technologies:

- **Common Encryption Scheme (CENC):** CENC standardizes the encryption process across multiple DRM systems, allowing seamless playback across platforms. This avoids the need for separate encryption for each DRM, significantly simplifying operations while maintaining robust security.
- **Cipher Block Chaining Subsample Pattern (CBCS):** CBCS refers to a specific encryption mode used in the Common Encryption standard (CENC) for protecting digital content within Digital Rights Management (DRM) systems; essentially, it's a way to encrypt video data using a

block cipher mode called Cipher Block Chaining with a specific pattern for better security and compatibility across different DRM platforms.
- **Content Protection Information Exchange (CPIX):** CPIX protocol streamlines secure key management by enabling authorized distributors to access encryption and decryption keys efficiently. This ensures that content remains protected during distribution while providing granular control over distributor access.
- **X.509 Certificates in Secure Communications:** X.509 certificates play a pivotal role in establishing secure communication by providing a framework for authentication and data encryption. These certificates enable entities to verify identities and exchange encryption keys securely, ensuring data integrity and confidentiality while supporting scalable, trusted interactions across networks.
- **End-To-End Encryption:** Unlike traditional satellite distribution, which typically encrypts only the transport layer, B2B Content Distribution employs CBCS with CMAF to secure both video and audio segments [6] [7].

These technologies, gathered, can ensure some advanced functionalities such as:
- **Increase monetization abilities:** Allows not only single top-quality monetization, but the granularity of monetizing specific adaptation sets for distribution models.
- **Out-of-band management:** Allows for entitlement controls separate from the content feeds for individualized messages and controls.
- **Channel-based access control:** Limits access to content based on user roles, subscriptions, or other predefined criteria.
- **Sub-channel-based access control:** Limits access to specify adaptation sets such as video quality level, audio versions
- **Real-time content revocation:** Offers the ability to immediately revoke access to content for unauthorized or non-compliant users.
- **Real-time content enablement:** Offers the ability to immediately allow access to a content stream for affiliate use.
- **Blackout management:** Enforces regional or content-specific blackout periods in compliance with licensing agreements, providing centralized control for broadcasters.
- **Manifest manipulation:** Allows for the HLS/MPEG-DASH manifest to be controlled to allow for switching of video, audio and Advertising changes in real time.

Applications in OTT, Broadcast Services and Beyond

B2B Content Distribution's versatility makes it highly applicable for various media distribution scenarios:
- **OTT services:** OTT platforms benefit greatly from B2B Content Distribution's CDN-based architecture. Features like real-time content revocation ensure the protection of premium content, while channel-based access control enhances the user experience by tailoring content delivery to individual needs. This framework is ideal for live streaming, on-demand libraries, and hybrid models combining both.
- **Broadcast services transitioning from satellite:** Broadcasters looking to move away from expensive satellite systems can adopt B2B Content Distribution to reduce costs and increase flexibility. The integration of DRM systems and advanced management tools allows broadcasters to maintain robust content protection while scaling their operations to meet new demands.
- **Future services:** As innovative experiences such as second-screen engagement, view evoked multi-camera switching, virtual reality, and online gambling continue to emerge in the content space, the B2B distribution model offers the flexibility to securely and reliably deliver source content to these evolving markets.

Advantages of B2B Content Distribution

The framework provides several significant benefits over traditional satellite-based and other proprietary models:

- **Cost efficiency:** By utilizing CDN infrastructure, B2B Content Distribution eliminates the need for expensive satellite links and equipment. This shift significantly reduces operational expenses, making it an attractive option for broadcasters and OTT providers alike.
- **Scalability and flexibility:** CDNs are inherently scalable, supporting increased demand without the need for substantial infrastructure upgrades. This flexibility allows content distributors to adapt to fluctuating audience sizes and deliver content to a global user base efficiently.
- **Enhanced security and content protection:** The combination of CENC, CPIX, and industry-standard DRM technologies ensures that content remains secure across all stages of distribution. Real-time revocation and blackout management further enhance control over content access and compliance.
- **Cross-platform compatibility:** The use of standardized DRM systems ensures that content can be securely accessed across a wide range of devices and platforms, enhancing the user experience while maintaining robust security.
- **Regulatory compliance:** Blackout management and other advanced features enable content providers to meet regional licensing and regulatory requirements with ease, avoiding legal and financial penalties.

By integrating these technologies and features, B2B Content Distribution offers a comprehensive solution tailored to the needs of modern broadcasters and OTT providers. It bridges the gap between traditional satellite-based models and the demands of today's dynamic, multi-platform media landscape.

Implemented Architecture

Figure 2 is a diagram of the flow of the system. The input signal is processed through the encoder, where it is integrated with the Conditional Access (CA) management system and the Key Management System (KMS). During this stage, CPIX packaging policies are configured to define parameters such as key rotation, adaptation sets, and receiver access permissions.

The resulting outputs are distributed via a CDN, enabling end receivers to securely retrieve the content. Each receiver's access is centrally managed through the CA management system. This system uses an encrypted, entitlement-based CPIX document to enforce rights management and control access permissions for each receiver.

Finally, the content is further processed to generate a customized output that meets the specific requirements of distributors.

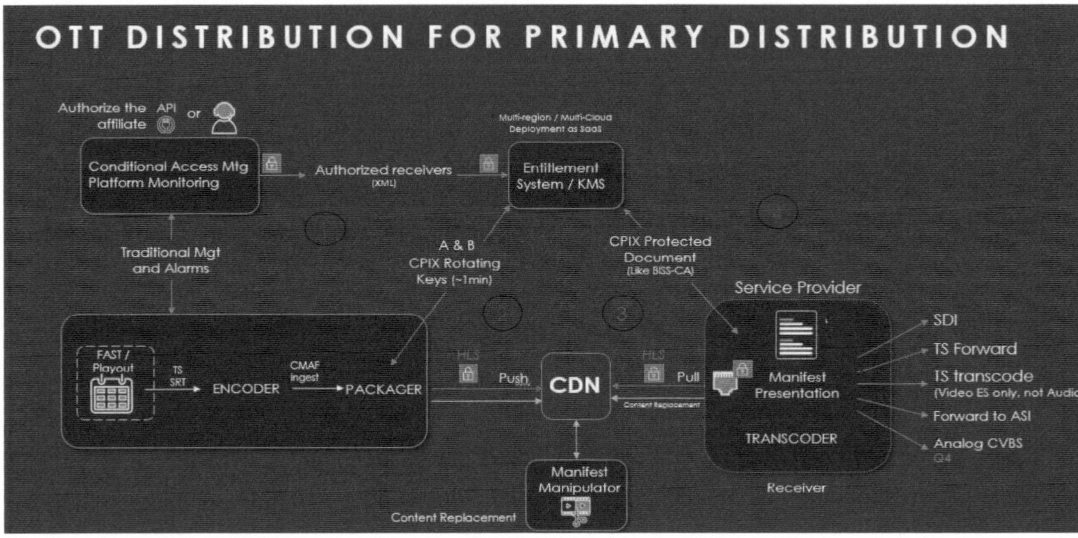

FIGURE 2: COMPLETE ARCHITECTURE.

Conclusion

The evolution of content delivery technologies has ushered in a new era of media distribution, with CDN-based approaches like B2B Content Distribution leading the way. By combining the scalability and flexibility of CDNs with advanced DRM technologies, this framework addresses the limitations of traditional satellite-based models while meeting the demands of modern OTT and broadcast services.

B2B Content Distribution's robust security features, including CENC and CPIX, ensure secure and compliant content delivery. Its support for advanced functionalities like real-time content revocation and blackout management further enhances its utility for broadcasters and OTT providers.

As the media industry continues to evolve, the adoption of innovative solutions like B2B Content Distribution will be essential for staying competitive. By offering a cost-effective and secure alternative to satellite systems, this approach sets a new standard for content distribution, paving the way for a more connected and dynamic future.

References

[1] DASH-IF, CPIX Documentation. Available at: https://dashif.org/docs/CPIX2.1/HTML/Index.html

[2] MPEG Common Encryption (CENC). Available at: https://en.wikipedia.org/wiki/MPEG_Common_Encryption

[3] Basic Interoperable Scrambling System (BISS-CA). Available at: https://tech.ebu.ch/docs/tech/tech3292.pdf

[4] DASH-IF Live Media Ingest Protocol Technical Specification, 26 February 2021, https://dashif.org/Ingest/

[5] SCTE 214-7: MPEG DASH for IP-Based Cable Services Part 4: SCTE Common Intermediate Format (CIF/TS)

[6] ISO/IEC 23000-19:2018 Information technology, Multimedia application format (MPEG-A) Part 19: Common media application format (CMAF) for segmented media.

[7] ISO/IEC 23001-7:2023 Information technology — MPEG systems technologies — Part 7: Common encryption in ISO base media file format files

Optimizing Satellite/Internet Hybrid Content Delivery Using Program Selection

Ciro A. Noronha, Ph.D.
Cobalt Digital Inc.
Champaign, Illinois, United States
ciro.noronha@cobaltdigital.com

Abstract – The Reliable Internet Stream Transport (RIST) Activity Group in the Video Services Forum has been working on a common industry specification for methods to augment satellite delivery using the Internet. The satellite is used for the "heavy lifting", and the Internet is used to "fill in the gaps". Such a system can be further augmented by allowing the receivers to select which programs they require. If this can be achieved, further internet bandwidth optimization is possible, since the headend does not need to "fill in the gaps" for the programs that are not required for that receiver. This method can be designed in a manner that is general enough to apply to other internet transport scenarios in addition to hybrid satellite delivery. The RIST Activity Group has created a backward-compatible extension to RIST Main [1] and Advanced [2] Profiles to allow a receiver to communicate to the sender its content requirements. Once the sender is made aware of these requirements, it can optimize the bandwidth without losing timing compliance by using the NULL Packet Deletion functionality defined in RIST Main Profile. This extension has been published by the Video Services Forum as TR-06-4 Part 6 [3]. This paper is a detailed overview of the technical details of TR-06-4 Part 6, with some application examples derived from existing broadcast feeds. It also includes practical data on bandwidth savings from actual off-air ATSC-1 content.

Problem Definition

In [4], we discussed possible solutions to the problem of augmenting satellite delivery with the internet to recover from signal corruption and/or rain fade. In the general case, what is going over the satellite is a full network feed, and individual sites typically do not need all the programs contained in this network feed. Internet bandwidth can be further optimized if the receiving sites are able to indicate to the headend site which program(s) they require, so only these programs are eligible for packet recovery.

Such a mechanism can be designed in a general way so that it is applicable to any contribution feed that is transmitting multiple programs to multiple receivers; it is not limited to satellite delivery. The problem can be divided into two parts:

1. How does a receiver inform the sender which content it requires?
2. How does the sender transmit a compliant stream with just the content required by the receiver, in an efficient manner that does not require an excessive amount of processing?

Content Selection Protocol

Protocol Requirements

The Content Selection Protocol has the following specific requirements:

- Receivers must be able to select individual programs by program number, to avoid the need for a-priori knowledge of the makeup of the program.

- Receivers must be able to drop individual components of a program. One example would be dropping unneeded audio services.
- RIST Main and Advanced Profiles have the concept of a tunnel that can be carrying multiple transport streams; receivers must be able to make independent selections per transport stream in a RIST tunnel.
- Receivers must be able to request additional PIDs that are not specifically associated with a program. One example would be the tables carrying program names or program guides.
- The protocol must support selection by ranges or programs and PIDs.

Protocol Specification

RIST Main Profile [1] includes a per-tunnel Keep-Alive message that is sent periodically. The message interval is between 1 and 10 seconds. The Keep-Alive message has an optional JSON payload.

TR-06-4 Part 6 [3] makes the JSON payload mandatory and defines extensions to it to implement the content selection function. Adding this functionality to the JSON payload is intrinsically backward compatible, since legacy devices simply ignore unknown JSON entries. The location of the message is illustrated in Figure 1.

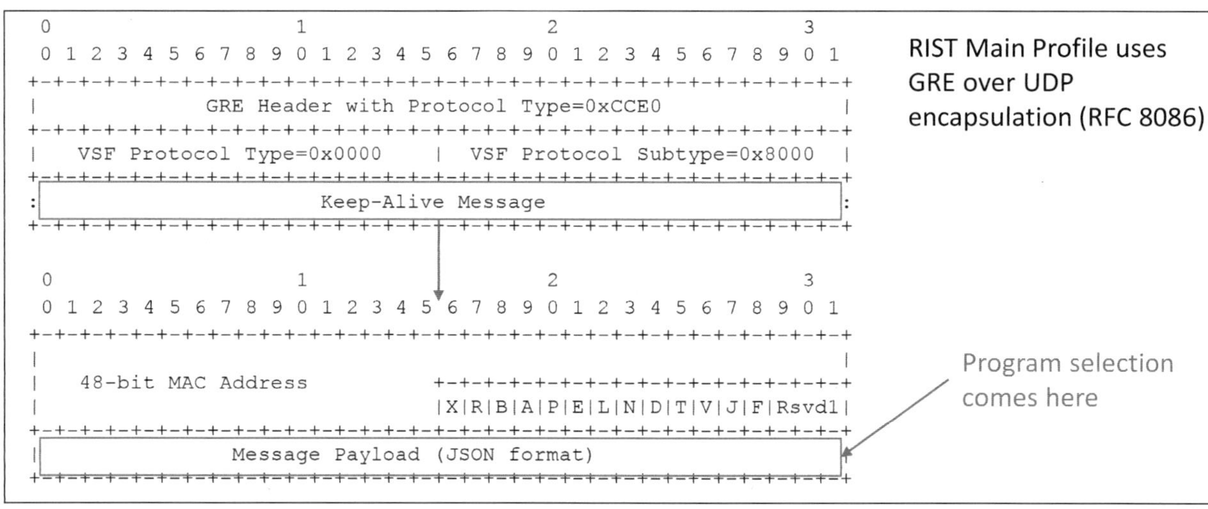

FIGURE 1: PROGRAM SELECTION PROTOCOL IN THE KEEP-ALIVE MESSAGE.

As noted above, RIST Main and Advanced Profile tunnels may be carrying multiple transport streams. These transport streams represent multiple IP flows encapsulated using GRE over UDP in the tunnel and thus can be identified by their individual destination UDP ports. If the Full Datagram mode is used, the source and destination IP addresses can be optionally used as additional selection criteria. This process is illustrated in Figure 2.

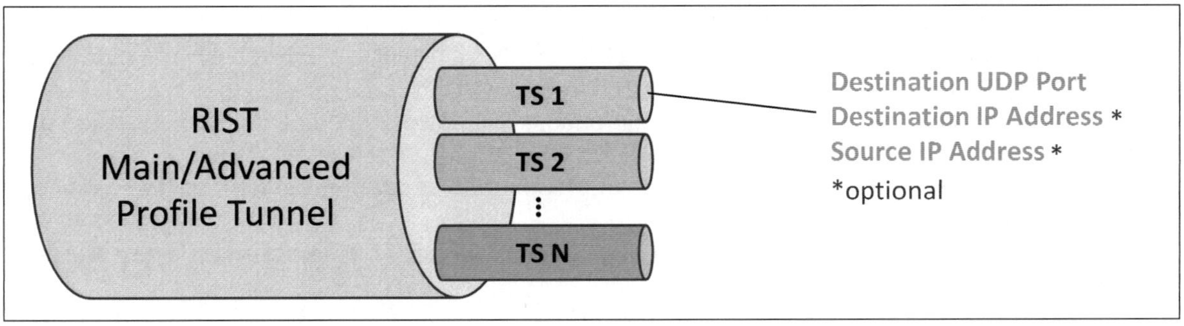

FIGURE 2: SELECTING MULTIPLE TRANSPORT STREAMS ON A TUNNEL.

The JSON fragment for content selection is added as a top-level key value called **contentSelection** and includes one or more sections for each of the desired transport streams. Each section includes the following parameters:

- **UDPPort:** selects the transport stream by destination UDP port, as illustrated in Figure 2 (required).
- **DestinationIP** and **Source IP:** further selects the transport stream by source and/or destination IP address, as illustrated in Figure 2 (optional). These are only available for Full Datagram encapsulation.
- **requestedPrograms:** this is a list of the program numbers requested by the receiver (optional). If not present, all programs in the transport are being requested.
- **requestedPIDs:** this is a list of additional PIDs being requested, with range support (optional). Both decimal and hexadecimal entries are allowed.
- **blockedPrograms:** this is a list of program numbers that the receiver does not require (optional).
- **blockedPIDs:** this is a list of PIDs that the receiver does not require (optional). It is used to block unneeded program elements, such as audio services.

Figure 3 (adapted from [3]) shows an example of the JSON message.

```
"contentSelection": [
  {
    "UDPPort": 5000,
    "DestinationIP": "239.1.1.1",
    "SourceIP": "192.168.1.1",
    "requestedPrograms": [1, 2, 3],
    "requestedPIDs": ["0x110-0x11F", "0x200"],
    "blockedPrograms": [4, 5, 6],
    "blockedPIDs": ["0x300-0x30F", "0x400", "0x500"]
  },
  {
    "UDPPort": 6000,
    "DestinationIP": "239.1.1.2",
    "SourceIP": "192.168.1.2",
    "requestedPrograms": [11, 12, 13],
    "requestedPIDs": ["0x210-0x21F", "0x300"],
    "blockedPrograms": [14, 15, 16],
    "blockedPIDs": ["0x400-0x40F", "0x500", "0x600"]
  }
]
```

Destination UDP port in the tunnel
Optional destination IP address*
Optional source IP address*
List of selected programs, by program number
List of selected PIDs, with range support
Blocked Programs
Blocked PIDS
*Not available for Reduced Overhead flows
Another flow in the same tunnel

FIGURE 3: JSON SYNTAX EXAMPLE.

When sending the message, the following rules apply:

- The receiver must include the content selection JSON fragment in the Keep-Alive message until it detects that the sender has complied with the selection.
- The receiver can stop sending the selection once it has detected compliance but must re-send at least once every 30 seconds.
- If the content selection JSON fragment is not present, the sender interprets it as "keep doing what you are doing now".
- In case of disconnection, the receiver must go back to sending the selection on every Keep-Alive.

The sender uses the following rules to determine which PIDs to send and which PIDs to block (see [5] for a definition of the acronyms):

- PIDs 0 (PAT) and 1 (CAT) are always included.
- All the PMT PIDs listed in the PAT are always included.
- All the EMM PIDs listed in the CAT are always included.
- If a program is selected, all the elements of that program listed in the PMT are included, as well as the PCR PID and any ECM PIDs listed in the relevant descriptors.
- At the program and PID levels, if a program or PID is listed both in the selection list and in the blocked list, it **is** included in the transmission (selection takes priority).
- If a PID is present in the PMT of a selected program, but explicitly blocked in a PID list, it **is not** included in the transmission (the more granular choice takes priority).

The reason why the PAT and all the PMTs are included in the transmission is to give the receiver a full picture of what is available in the transport stream. Additionally, if the stream is encrypted, including the EMMs and ECMs will let an entitled receiver to immediately decrypt the content as soon as it is selected.

RIST Advanced Profile [2] includes a control channel with an encapsulation defined for the Main Profile Keep-Alive messages, which are mandatory for the profile. Therefore, it can use the same protocol described here for content selection.

Operation at the Sender

Once the sender processes the receiver selection using the rules described in the previous section, it will have a list of PIDs to include in the transmission, and a list of PIDs that are not requested by the receiver. The next question is how it should create a **compliant** transport stream based on these lists.

ISO/IEC 13818-1 [5] has the following requirements:

- A transport stream with a single PCR PID (typically a Single Program Transport Stream - SPTS) is allowed to be variable bit rate. It does not need to include NULL packets for timing compliance. For such streams, packets can be removed, and the result is still compliant.
- A transport stream with more than one PCR PID (typically a Multiple Program Transport Stream – MPTS) must be CBR. For such streams, packets can be replaced but not removed.

For transport streams with a single PCR PID, the sender can simply remove the unneeded PIDs and transmit what is left. This is the simplest case.

For transport streams with multiple PCR PIDs, the sender replaces the unneeded PIDs with NULL packets, so the stream is still CBR. Then it can use the NULL Packet Deletion (NPD) feature in RIST Main Profile to regain the bandwidth from these NULL packets. When using NPD, the sender removes the NULL packets but adds a header that indicates where these NULL packets were originally located. The receiver can then re-add the NULL packets, thus reconstructing the original CBR stream and maintaining timing compliance, without the need for transmitting these NULL packets.

The NPD feature is also available in RIST Advanced Profile in the following modes (see [2] for more detail regarding the encapsulation types):

- Encapsulated Main Profile Packets (Type 8)
- Direct encapsulation of Reduced Overhead Packets (Type 3)
- Direct Payload (Type 5) with RTP headers and NPD

Alternatively, RIST Advanced Profile can use Direct Payload (Type 5) with no wrappers and payload compression – the presence of NULL packets will allow for some compression gain. This mode is generally less efficient than NPD.

Bandwidth Overhead Analysis

When a transport stream is carried over IP, it is customary to combine 7 transport packets per IP packet to reduce overhead, as recommended by [6]. The per-packet RIST Main Profile [1] overhead, starting at layer 2 Ethernet, is:

- 14 bytes for layer 2 Ethernet
- 20 bytes for the IP layer (no IP options are usually present)
- 8 bytes for the UDP layer
- 4 bytes for the GRE layer (assuming no sequence numbers or key fields)
- 4 bytes for the VSF protocol layer
- 4 bytes for the Reduced Overhead header (or 28 bytes for Full Datagram)
- 12 bytes for the RTP header
- 8 bytes for the NULL Packet Deletion extension header

Assuming Reduced Overhead operation, the overhead to transmit 7 transport packets is 66 bytes without the NPD extension header, or 74 bytes with it. Since each transport packet is 188 bytes, the overhead without NPD is $66/((188 * 7)) = \mathbf{5.01}\%$, and with NPD is $74/((188 * 7)) = \mathbf{5.62}\%.$

TR-06-4 Part 6 requires that the PAT and all PMTs be always included in the transmission. These tables are typically small and fit into one single 188-byte transport packet, and [5] requires that they be transmitted 10 times per second, resulting in 15.04 kb/s per table. Therefore, the minimum overhead *R* in bits/sec to transmit a transport stream of *B* bits/second with *N* programs, with no content, is:

$$R = B(1 + 0.0562) + 15040(N + 1) \tag{1}$$

Notes:

- A transport stream with *N* programs has one PAT and *N* PMTs,[1] thus the $(N + 1)$ factor in (1).
- The overhead to transport all the PIDs in the transport stream is already included in the 5.62% value, so the bit rate to transport additional individual PIDs can be simply added to (1).

Example Application Scenarios

Application Scenario: Audio Selection

In this application scenario, the sender has a single program transport stream with two audio services with the same content: one is encoded in AAC, and the other in Dolby. A particular receiver only needs the AAC audio selection. The layout for this transport stream is shown in Figure 4.

[1] It is technically possible to section-pack all the PMTs in a single PID, but some standards such as ATSC prohibit this. We elected to assume the more common approach of a separate PID per PMT.

Transport Stream	
PID 0: PAT Program 1: PMT is at 0x100	
PID 0x11: SDT Program 1 Name is *"Music Channel"*	
PID 0x100: Program 1 PMT	PID 0x200: H.264 Video
	PID 0x210: AAC audio, ENG
	PID 0x211: Dolby audio, ENG
	PID 0x21F: SCTE-35 Cue

FIGURE 4: AUDIO SELECTION APPLICATION SCENARIO.

The receiver will send the following JSON selection to the sender:

```
"contentSelection": [
  {
    "UDPPort": 5000,
    "requestedPrograms": [1],
    "requestedPIDs": ["0x11"],
    "blockedPIDs": ["0x211"]
  }
]
```

The sender will take the following actions:

- Transmit PIDs **0x0, 0x11, 0x100, 0x200, 0x210, 0x21F**
- Replace PID 0x211 with NULL packets (or remove it since this is an SPTS)

Application Scenario: Network Feed

In this application scenario, a network feed with content for both East and West Headends is received from satellite and transmitted over the Internet. Each headend only requires their specific programming. However, there is also a Special Events channel that is required by both headends. The scenario and corresponding JSON selection fragments are shown in Figure 5.

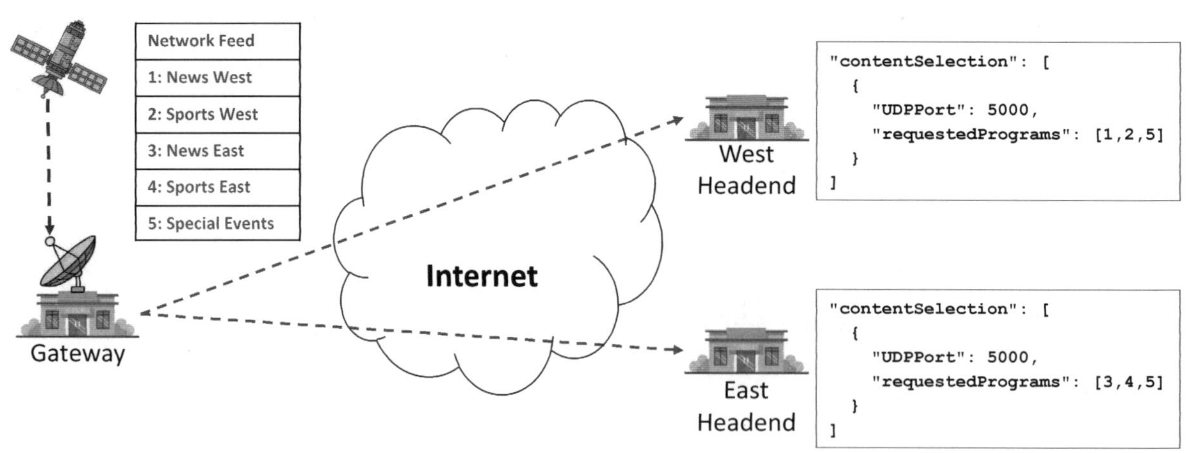

FIGURE 5: NETWORK FEED APPLICATION SCENARIO.

Application Scenario: Limited Bandwidth

In this application scenario, the receiver has limited bandwidth and may not be able to receive the full transport. In addition, it has no knowledge of the contents of the transport, nor its bit rate. When it establishes the RIST Main Profile connection, it needs to block everything at first, so it starts with the following JSON:

```
"contentSelection": [
  {
    "UDPPort": 5000,
    "requestedPIDs": ["0x11"],
    "blockedPIDs": ["0x0-0x1FFF"]
  }
]
```

This will give the receiver the PAT and all the PMTs, which are always included. It will also provide the Service Description Table (PID 0x11 – see [7]) for service names and will allow the receiver to compute the exact transport bit rate, since all the TS packets in the stream will be signaled, and the stream sent to the receiver will have a bit rate on the order of what is indicated in (1). Once the receiver identifies the program it requires, it can change the content selection JSON to request it:

```
"contentSelection": [
  {
    "UDPPort": 5000,
    "requestedPIDs": ["0x11"],
    "requestedPrograms": [1]
  }
]
```

Measurement Results Using Off-Air ATSC Feeds

To test how this process works with actual transport streams, we captured 10 minutes each of ATSC-1 RF channels 27 and 34 in Champaign, Illinois, in the middle of a weekday. The RF signal was good, and the captures had no errors or drops. These RF channels have 5 programs each, using a conventional MPEG-2 statistical multiplexer. Channel 27 has five SD programs, each with a single stereo audio service. Channel 34 has two HD programs, each with two audio PIDs in the usual 5.1+2 audio, and three SD programs with a single stereo audio service.

The Channel 27 measurement details can be found in Table 1. In this test, 7,736,442 packets were captured, corresponding to the usual ATSC-1 bit rate of 19.393 Mb/s. Each row of the table corresponds to a set of transport packets and may include multiple PIDS. The columns in the table are as follows:

- **Program:** PMT program number, if applicable.
- **Content:** Description of the set of transport packets. For programs, we indicate the channel name and number. Programs include the video PID and all the audio PIDs, but no tables.
- **Packets:** Number of transport stream packets received during the 10-minute test for the category of this row.
- **TS Rate (b/s):** Average transport stream rate for this set of PIDs over the 10-minute test.
- **IP Rate (b/s):** For the programs, this would be the IP bit rate to transport this program by itself, using a RIST Main Profile Reduced Overhead tunnel, all the tables required by TR-06-4 Part 6, and the NULL Packet Deletion headers. The value under PAT+PMTs is the baseline overhead if no channels are selected. The rate listed in the Totals row does not include the NPD overhead, since this header would not be necessary if the whole transport is sent.

- **BW Savings:** This column indicates how much bandwidth is saved if the receiver requires just the indicated program, as compared to transmitting the whole transport. The baseline for this percentage is the IP Rate in the Totals row.

Note that if a receiver requires the PSIP tables as well, the additional bit rate required is simply the TS Rate for that row, namely 67,680 bits/sec, since the headers are already accounted for.

Program	Content	Packets	TS Rate (b/s)	IP Rate (b/s)	BW Savings	Note
3	39.1: W27EL-D	1,832,628	4,593,788	5,751,937	71.76%	
4	39.2: QVC	1,041,678	2,611,140	3,769,289	81.49%	
5	39.3: HSN2	1,741,722	4,365,916	5,524,066	72.88%	
6	39.4: QVC2	1,042,166	2,612,363	3,770,513	81.49%	
7	39.5: QVC3	1,738,811	4,358,620	5,516,769	72.91%	
	PAT+PMTs	27,000	67,680	1,158,150		*
	PSIP	35,721	89,541			
	NULL	276,716	693,635			
	Totals	**7,736,442**	**19,392,681**	**20,365,263**		**

* The IP Rate listed here is the minimum as per (1), but with actual table rates
** The IP Rate listed here does not include the NPD header

TABLE 1: RF CHANNEL 27 DETAILS.

Similar measurements are shown in Table 2 for Channel 34.

Program	Content	Packets	TS Rate (b/s)	IP Rate (b/s)	BW Savings	Note
3	3.1: WCIA-HD	2,664,312	6,678,542	7,812,879	61.64%	
4	3.2: WCIX-HD	2,684,364	6,728,806	7,863,142	61.39%	
5	3.3: Bounce	720,239	1,805,399	2,939,736	85.56%	
6	3.4: Grit	655,075	1,642,055	2,776,391	86.37%	
7	27.2: TrueCri	723,021	1,812,373	2,946,709	85.53%	
	PAT+PMTs	17,500	43,867	1,134,337		*
	PSIP	48,193	120,804			
	NULL	223,738	560,837			
	Totals	**7,736,442**	**19,392,681**	**20,365,263**		**

* The IP Rate listed here is the minimum as per (1), but with actual table rates
** The IP Rate listed here does not include the NPD header

TABLE 2: RF CHANNEL 34 DETAILS.

Conclusions

VSF TR-06-4 Part 6 specifies a method for a receiver to communicate its program requirements to a sender, using existing RIST Main Profile mechanisms in a backward compatible way. This method can augment the Satellite Hybrid operation described in [4], but it can also stand on its own.

The current alternatives to this are transcoding (to re-do the MPTS while keeping compliance – requires significant amount of processing power) and SPTS splitting, which only works if the receiver requires a single program. The method presented here imposes minimal burden on the sender (simply requires demultiplexing, which can be implemented very efficiently with a look-up table), while keeping the timing compliance of the stream. The signaling method is also very simple, using standard JSON.

When using RIST Main Profile Reduced Overhead, the “cost” of this method is on the order of 5% of the transport bandwidth, and once this is in place, additional PIDs/services/components can be added with no additional overhead.

Acknowledgements

The author wishes to acknowledge the technical work done by the members of the RIST Activity Group in the Video Services Forum, which was the foundation for this paper.

References

[1] Video Services Forum, “Reliable Internet Stream Transport (RIST) Protocol Specification – Main Profile”, *VSF TR-06*-2, 2024-06-12, <https://static.vsf.tv/download/technical_recommendations/VSF_TR-06-2_2024_06_12.pdf>.

[2] Video Services Forum, “Reliable Internet Stream Transport (RIST) Protocol Specification – Advanced Profile”, *VSF TR-06-3*, 2024-06-12, <https://static.vsf.tv/download/technical_recommendations/VSF_TR-06-3_2024_06_12.pdf>.

[3] Video Services Forum, “Reliable Internet Stream Transport (RIST) – RIST Transport Stream Program Selection”, *VSF TR-06-4 Part 6*, 2024-07-22, <https://static.vsf.tv/download/technical_recommendations/VSF_TR-06-4-Part-6_2024-07-22.pdf>.

[4] Noronha, C., “Satellite/Internet Hybrid Content Delivery (Ku-Band without rain fade!)”, *Proceedings of the 2024 NAB Broadcast Engineering and Information Technology (BEIT) Conference*, 2024-04-16.

[5] International Organization for Standardization, “Information technology — Generic coding of moving pictures and associated audio information: Systems”, *ISO/IEC 13818-1:2023.*

[6] Society of Motion Picture and Television Engineers, “Unidirectional Transport of Constant Bit Rate MPEG-2 Transport Streams on IP Networks”, *SMPTE 2022-2-2007.*

[7] European Telecommunications Standards Institute, “Digital Video Broadcasting (DVB); Specification for Service Information (SI) in DVB Systems”, *ETSI EN 300 468 V1.18.1*, 2023-12, <https://www.etsi.org/deliver/etsi_en/300400_300499/300468/01.18.01_60/en_300468v011801p.pdf>

Enhancing Fantasy League Engagement Through Efficient Hyper-Personalized Highlights

Tony Jones
MediaKind
Southampton, Hampshire, United Kingdom
tony.jones@mediakind.com

Abstract – Hyper-personalization offers the fan the opportunity to view content tailored very specifically for them. That requires fine-grained information about the user and about the content, plus an architecture that brings those together and a suitable base platform that can enable such capabilities. In this paper, the key enablers of making hyper-personalization possible are outlined, including the architectural impact of direct-to-consumer streaming, AI highlights creation and personalization technology. Its use is illustrated by means of an example, using a fantasy team to create a specifically customized on-demand highlights package involving players in the fan's teams in a scalable, cost-effective manner.

Context

Sports content is the most valuable content delivered by both traditional and streaming paths. Sports teams have a high level of personal connection from the fan base, and keeping those fans engaged is important for brand, subscription, sponsorship and advertising revenues.

Highlights and replays are important components of any sports coverage, allowing viewers to never miss the key action and offer multiple angles and slow-motion replays of relevant components. As such, these are well-established additions to the content value. Today's highlights are prepared once for all audiences, and while that is efficient, newer architectures lead to the potential to better engage audiences through hyper-personalization.

At the same time, fantasy teams are another significant component of fan engagement, creating a unique, personal interest in the performance of virtual teams consisting of real sports players.

Fantasy teams are typically tracked on interactive devices – tablets, laptops, etc. – making a good fit with streaming delivery.

Bringing these significant enablers together, as illustrated in Figure 1, can provide a further step in fan engagement.

This paper is excerpted from the Proceedings of the 2025 NAB Broadcast Engineering and Information Technology (BEIT) Conference, © 2025, National Association of Broadcasters, 1 M Street SE, Washington, DC 20003 USA.

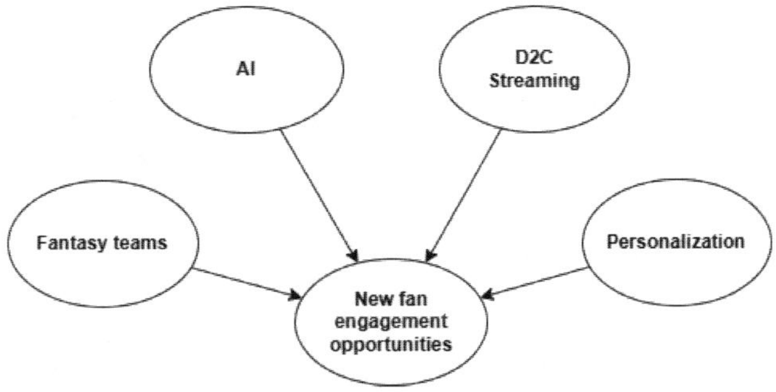

FIGURE 1: NEW FAN ENGAGEMENT OPPORTUNITIES

Existing Solutions

Live Production for Broadcast

In conventional TV systems, there is typically a single production for a live event. All operations related to that production are normally carried out by the production team, either in an Outside Broadcast (OB) truck or via remote production.

The production is operationally disconnected from broadcast channel creation, often with the only connection being a video feed from the production output into the channel's Master Control Room (MCR) switcher – just one among a number of potentially available live feeds for that channel.

The production and channel operations are separate, reflecting the different lifecycles and needs (i.e. event duration for the production and typically 24/7 for the channel).

A typical architecture for a broadcast channel that has live events is illustrated in Figure 2 below:

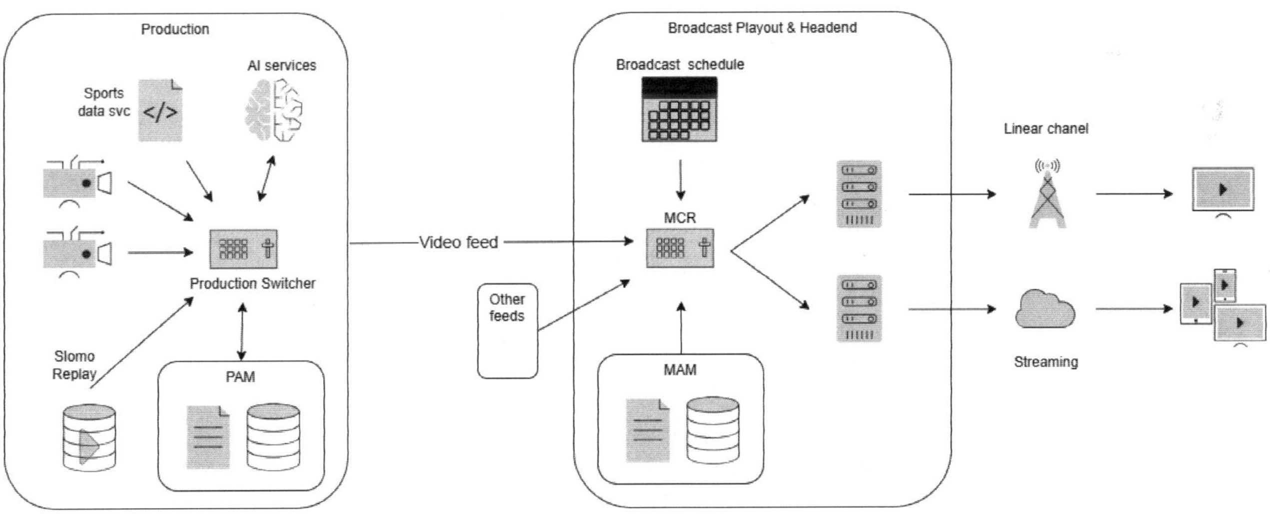

FIGURE 2: TRADITIONAL BROADCAST CHANNEL WITH LIVE PRODUCTION

Production Highlights

Decisions are made by the production team about which replays and highlights are to be made available, meaning everyone sees the same highlights and replays. The result is excellent quality, with an experienced team performing that production, but the cost means that it is not scalable to other scenarios.

Modern asset management during production relies on metadata to locate content for playback. The ability to quickly locate scenes of interest is important for creating those production highlights, and even for publishing to players' social media, however the access to that metadata is generally limited to the production team and is normally stored in the Production Asset Management system.

Sports Data and Metadata

Sports data is an important component of any live sports production, feeding live production graphics as part of the produced program. In addition, sports data is useful for identifying important action within the content, helping generate possible locations for highlights.

External data sources are not the only source for metadata that can be used for highlights, the overall set may include:

- Manual entry during production (including sports data service providers)
- Player transponder tracking
- AI

Each has its pros and cons in terms of cost and accuracy, but AI allows the industrialization of metadata generation. It requires skill to configure the query to the AI processor in order to identify the content that contains important action, but, for a given sport, this is a one-time initial configuration, perhaps with improvements added over time. It may be possible to eventually have a generic approach, however at the time of writing, that appears to be beyond the scope of existing models.

AI processing can use multiple parts of the content:

- Video content
- Audio tracks
- Sports data feeds

Large language models (LLMs) can be used to identify information from the speech in the audio tracks, along with mood and other information. Significant events in the content can often be identified effectively from the audio, with players' names frequently featuring and events being identified by verbal cues.

Any or all of the above sources can be used to create metadata to support content selection.

AI-Created Production Highlights

Over the last few years, AI has begun to have an increasing role in production highlight creation, reducing the manual effort needed and helping to create highlights more quickly. This process is typically a hybrid AI and manual process, with the initial proposals for likely highlights being made by AI, but then refined and filtered by production staff. It is reasonable to expect AI highlights will become more accurate over time, as additional training is applied to the models.

The resulting highlights are often made into a highlights package, combining the top moments of the overall event. This then becomes a new asset and is made available to all consumers by encoding as a discrete VoD asset for subsequent streaming.

It is sometimes also the case that player-specific highlights are created and posted on social media through the players' own accounts. This approach is appropriate for shared assets, where the same highlight content is relevant to many people.

Limitations with Existing Solutions

When considering fantasy team highlights, the number of permutations of content that need to be provided in order to provide a highlights reel for each user becomes very high. To create fantasy league highlights reels, a different approach is needed, because the cost of creating, encoding, storing and delivering a different asset for each different fantasy team would be excessive and the production capability would need to scale to support the number of individual fantasy team permutations. Scaling has multiple sub-requirements: encoding, storage, personalization and delivery.

Technology Enablers for Hyper-Personalization

Direct-to-Consumer Streaming

The move to D2C streaming has several impacts on the overall content flow.

- Coverage for more games can be delivered concurrently because of the effectively unlimited nature of streaming capacity
- For every game, more productions are possible, including guest commentators or specific viewpoints

Since most of the capabilities are needed only for the duration of the live event, the infrastructure can be made more cost-effective by being instantiated and torn down according to the event schedule. This makes it very suitable to deploy the capabilities into public cloud, since they are not permanent costs.

D2C streaming architectures cause fundamental changes to the media supply chain, with the overall chain being both shortened and better interconnected. This is illustrated in Figure 3, below.

Here, the lifecycle of production and streaming are the same: both being based on the event schedule. The video, data and operations are managed together and often instantiated only for the event, ideally with lifecycles managed from automation based on the event schedule.

This shortening of the media supply chain, combined with dynamic instantiation and the capacity flexibility of internet streaming, means that it is possible to further expand coverage also include:

- Access to all original ISOs
- Access to all slow-motion content
- Access to data by and for client applications

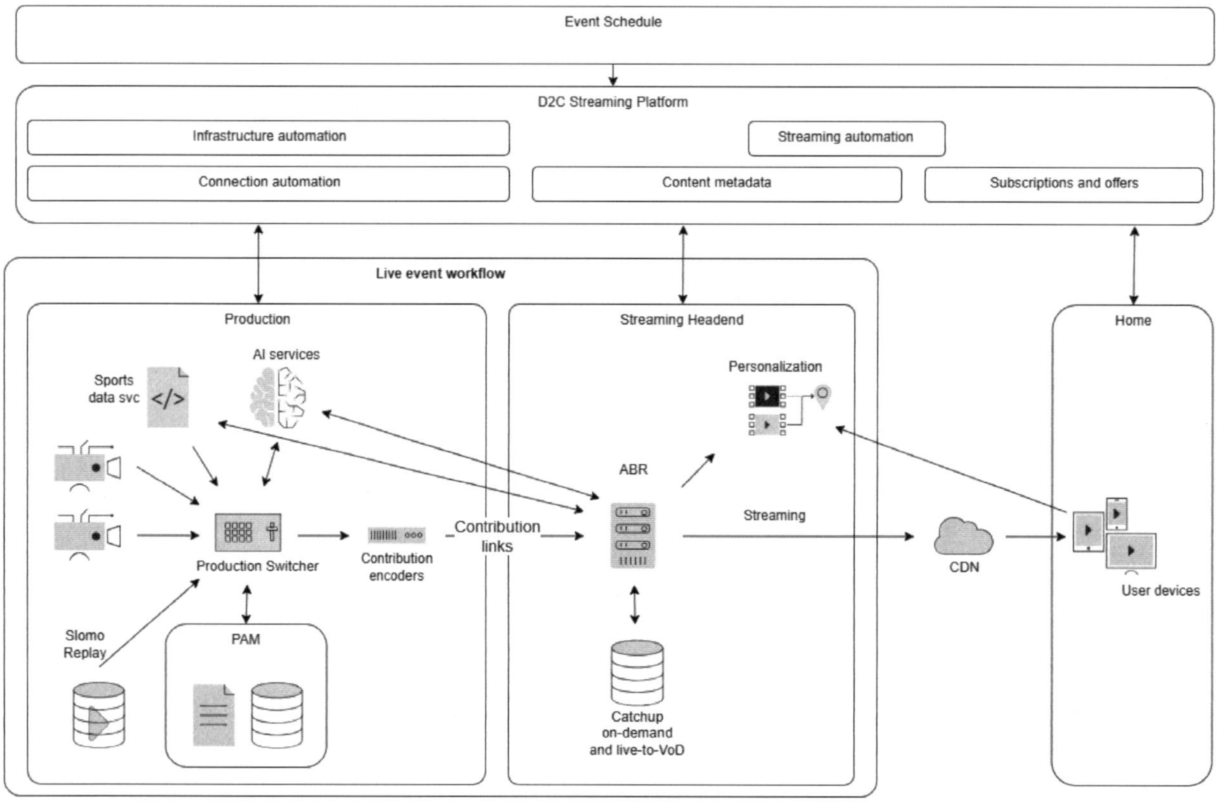

FIGURE 3: DIRECT-TO-CONSUMER (D2C) ARCHITECTURE

Direct-to-consumer streaming means consumers can be connected closer to the source of content and data, and that means that new architectures can be envisaged, taking advantage of the simplification of content processing that comes as a result of the single management of the entire processing chain. This means it is possible to leverage data that exists in one part of the chain to benefit other parts of the chain.

Sports streaming services already make some limited use of this closer data connection, for example by propagating score data through the system and allowing D2C streaming apps to provide data information at the client, for example scores, player metrics, etc. This gives more choice to the consumer.

Personalization

Personalization is well established within streaming services as a means for creating alternative versions of content, whether that be for targeted advertising (via VMAP [1] or VAST [2] interfaces) or for content replacement (for example in support of blackout restrictions). Typically, this uses location, device or identity-based data to modify what is delivered, for example blacking out content for devices in certain areas – most typically to prohibit sports viewing in locations near a venue that is hosting a live sports event. The next step towards hyper-personalization is to connect the content metadata to more detailed information specific to the user.

Figure 4 illustrates how metadata can be made available to support consumer delivery of content.

This increased data capability offers a path to better fan engagement through personalization. Making it available for consumption by the end user, however, can be a challenge that requires specific consideration.

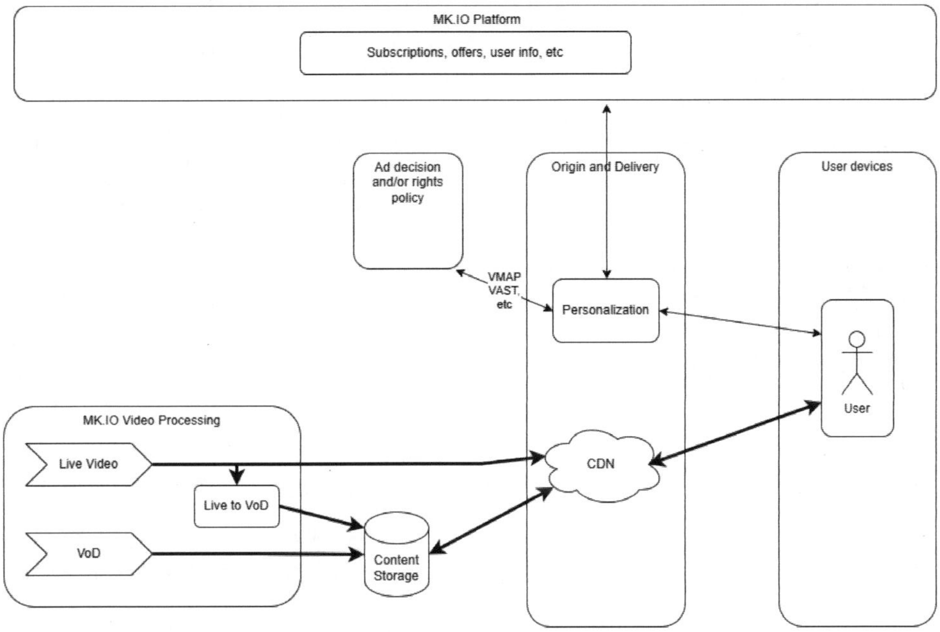

FIGURE 4: STREAMING PERSONALIZATION FOR D2C

An Architecture for Hyper-Personalized Content

Hyper-personalization expands on the basic personalization workflow above to utilize metadata with more yet context for the content and with finer granularity of data from the end user. The ability to create personalized manifests/playlists on request enables new experiences and forms the basis for the hyper-personalization architecture described here. Figure 5 shows how such a personalized architecture can be built by connecting additional metadata to the personalization process.

In such an architecture, the metadata database is key provider of metadata for personalization when clients make requests.

At the same time, the video essence for use in highlights is created by a live-to-VoD capture of the live video, which is recorded for the event and available during and after the event. Since this video content will have already been encoded for live delivery, it simply needs to be recorded under the control of the streaming automation – which can be driven by the live event schedule.

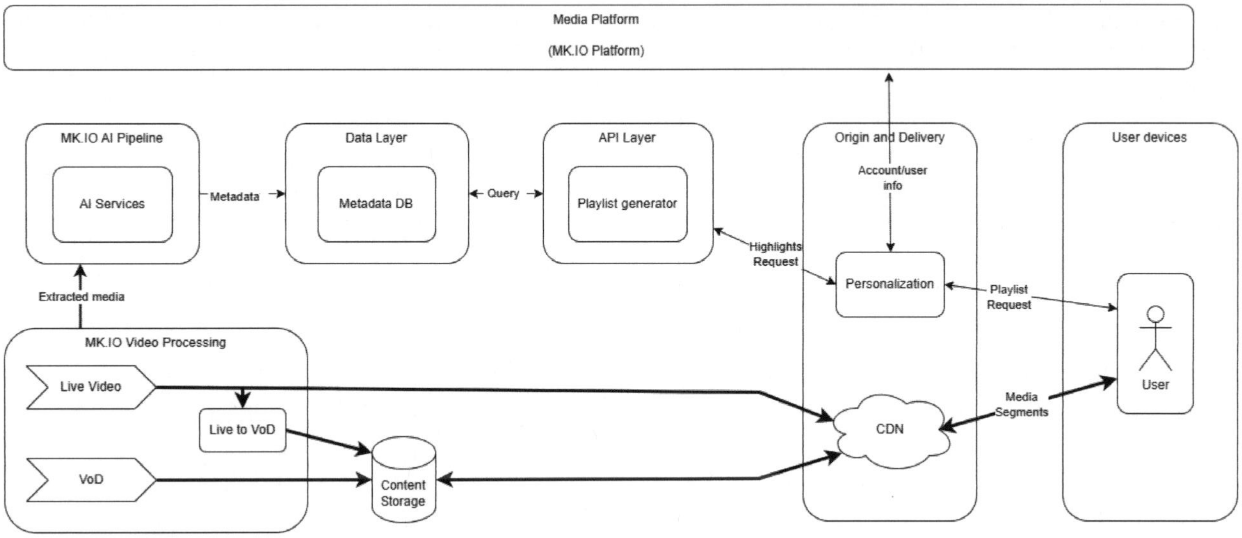

FIGURE 5: CONTENT METADATA CREATION AND FLOW FOR D2C

This architecture offers a new means to personalize the content: a playlist generator that can match a complex user request with fine granularity and respond with the hyper-personalized playlist.

Metadata Database

Key to enabling hyper-personalization is the availability of a metadata database (DB). Data sources for the metadata DB can include external sports data services and manual production data, but increasingly it can take advantage of AI services, such as Microsoft Azure AI Services [3]. These services return a digest of the video content, offering one source that can be used to populate the metadata DB.

Since AI capabilities are evolving rapidly, the ability to easily change the AI processing service becomes important in order to take advantage improved models.

For AI processing, in order to be cost-effective, not all of the source video data is passed to the AI pipeline. The ability to tap into internal stages of processing within the video encoding workflow means that it is possible to extract just the appropriate subset and format of data, reducing the processing required and data transferred to the AI pipeline.

An example of such an AI pipeline is shown in Figure 6, with a combination of AI services for image, audio and transcript analysis, the outputs of which are combined and interpreted to generate metadata to populate the Metadata DB. Any manual sources of metadata can also be used at this point to refine the metadata.

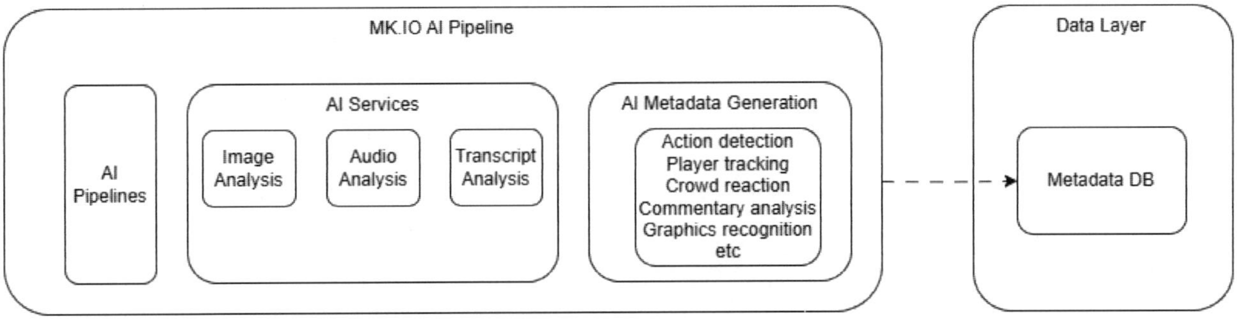

FIGURE 6: AI ARCHITECTURE FOR METADATA CREATION

An example metadata entry created by such an AI pipeline is shown in Figure 7 below:


```
{
    "id": 165,
    "startTimeMs": 4566000,
    "endTimeMs": 4582000,
    "description": "Fulham's Lukic fouls Nottingham Forest's Jota Silva, resulting in a yellow card.",
    "scene_id": 319,
    "importance_score": 7,
    "category": "Momentum-Shift"
},
```


FIGURE 7: METADATA DATABASE CONTENT EXAMPLE

The metadata includes contextual information, including player identities, and the time offsets for start and end within the source asset.

Examples Of Hyper-Personalization

Figure 8 illustrates the sequence of interactions starting when the client requests such a hyper-personalized playlist. The requesting client makes a request, either supplying directly the information on what is wanted by means of query parameters from the client, or by using data known by the video platform back office about the client's preferences (for example, the players in their fantasy team). The result of the flow is a personalized, generated playlist that contains the subset of clips that match the items of interest. This can, of course, be used to create a generic highlights package of clips, however it is also possible to use that to create much more specifically personalized content, as illustrated below by means of two examples, as described below.

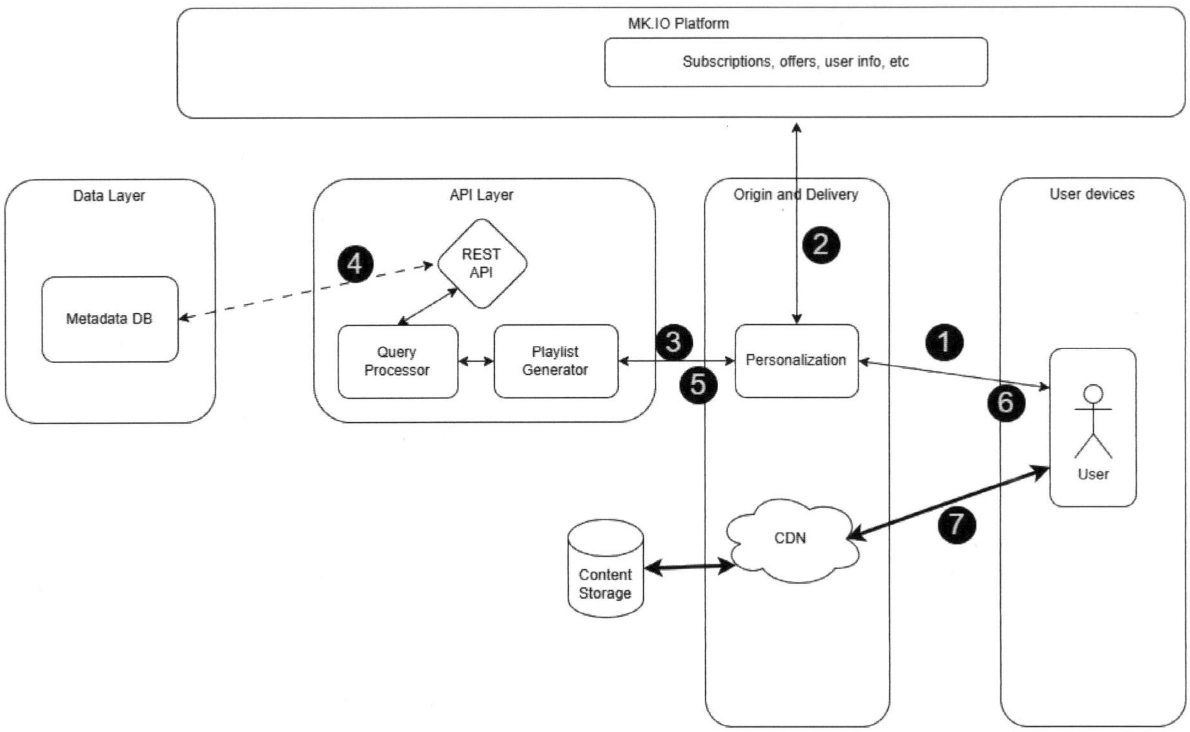

FIGURE 8: INTERACTIONS FOR CREATION OF HYPER-PERSONALIZED CONTENT

Fantasy Team Highlights Example of Hyper-Personalization

Fantasy teams and leagues are a well-established means for increasing fan engagement. Fantasy teams, of course, can contain any permutation of eligible players from an entire league, thus creating the scope for highly personal choices when building the team. Fans who have fantasy teams are commonly interested in the performance of their players and already use real-world sports data to define how well (or otherwise) their team has performed over a weekend or week of fixtures.

This is appealing for fans, but an even better experience would be to be able to show the fan the highlights of all players in their fantasy team. This would previously have been difficult and expensive to achieve because there are a very large number of permutations, so creating a highlight reel for each fantasy team would be difficult and expensive. However, a metadata database means it is now feasible and cost-effective to offer this form of hyper-personalization to fans at the point of delivery. Integrating such a highlights reel in a client application is straight forward, an example is shown in Figure 9.

The detailed flow for a hyper-personalized highlights reel is:

1. Client requests a playback of the highlights for the team, possibly including the players' identities
2. The user's authentication is verified, and potentially the fantasy team players provided from here (if not in the original user request)
3. Personalization makes a request to the API layer
4. The API layer queries the Metadata DB, providing the player info as part of the query
5. The Metadata DB replies with the locations of the content pertaining to the requested players, which is then used by the playlist generator to build a composite playlist
6. The playlist is returned to the client as a manifest
7. The client requests the clips with offsets from the original streamed content, allowing full cache efficiency to be applied

Using the same original streamed content for all personalized highlights means efficiency for scale in terms of encoding, storage and CDN caching.

FIGURE 9: EXAMPLE FANTASY HIGHLIGHTS USER INTERFACE

When a fan wishes to view their fantasy team highlights reel, the app can pass the defined team members as query parameters when making a request for a highlights reel. The request for a playlist is handled by the same form of personalization engine that is used to create personalized advertising. In this case, however, the functionality in response to the request is to build a custom playlist using the supplied metadata, by performing queries into the metadata database.

The metadata database can return time offset values for start and end into the Live-to-VoD clips, allowing the personalization engine to return a composite playlist containing all the highlights from the players in the fantasy team. These are combined into a single playlist and simply reuse the content that was stored as part of the Live-to-VoD workflow – meaning no additional video processing and not degradation of the quality of the video content. The client simply plays back the hyper-personalized playlist.

An example of the resulting highlights content is shown in Figure 9 below. Note that the players are from different real teams and the content may be from different games, but together form one fantasy team.

Player 9 scores	Player 2 prevents score	Player 5 is booked	Goalkeeper makes save	Player 8 offside	Player 10 penalty

FIGURE 10: ILLUSTRATIVE FANTASY HIGHLIGHTS PACKAGE

An example of such a hyper-personalized HLS playlist (with example content) is shown below. Note the variation in source assets and segments, with duration variations to accurately cut the content. A client can simply play through the entire playlist.

```
#EXTM3U
#EXT-X-VERSION:3
#EXT-X-TARGETDURATION:12
#EXT-X-MEDIA-SEQUENCE:0
#EXT-X-PLAYLIST-TYPE:VOD
#EXT-X-START:TIME-OFFSET=0
#EXTINF:5.0
http://cdn.example.com/ads/preroll1.ts
#EXTINF:5.0
http://cdn.example.com/ads/preroll2.ts
#EXTINF:10.0
http://cdn.example.com/vod1/segment1.ts
#EXTINF:10.0
http://cdn.example.com/vod1/segment2.ts
#EXTINF:3.0
http://cdn.example.com/bumpers/bumper1.ts
#EXTINF:8.0
http://cdn.example.com/vod2/segment1.ts
#EXTINF:8.0
http://cdn.example.com/vod2/segment2.ts
#EXTINF:3.0
http://cdn.example.com/bumpers/bumper2.ts
#EXTINF:12.0
http://cdn.example.com/vod3/segment1.ts
#EXTINF:12.0
http://cdn.example.com/vod3/segment2.ts
#EXT-X-ENDLIST
```

Personal Slow-Motion Replays

The approach of using metadata to index content for consumers can be applied to more than just the main production. One of the great advantages of streaming is the ability to offer more options to consumers – those can include guest commentator or alternative productions, right through to making all of the isolated camera feeds available. This means that the consumer can see all of the footage relating to their fantasy team members, regardless of whether the footage was used in the main production.

As a second example, hyper-personalization is applied to slow motion replays. As noted above, not all content is used in main productions, however it can potentially be available for other uses. This second example follows a similar approach to the first example, but in this case, the viewer makes a request to see a slow-motion replay of action that has just happened – regardless of whether or not the main production showed a slow-motion replay at that point. Of course it would be possible to simply play back the normal frame-rate content at less than full speed, however that results in jerky motion with no additional information compared to the full speed playback. It also requires the user to direct the player play back at a slower speed.

Slow-motion cameras operate at a higher frame rate, very often 4x the normal frame rate (so 4x 59.94 frames/sec), with multiple video outputs, each at the standard frame rate, but offset by 1/4th of the time interval – these are known as phases. A single phase is the same format as a standard video signal. When slow-motion cameras are available, one novel approach is to interleave the phases back into the correct sequence (so high frame rate), but then signal the recording of the high-speed result as the standard frame rate. This, of course means the recorded asset will grow in terms of duration at 4x real time, however the advantage is that when played back at the standard frames-per-second rate, the effect is a high-quality slow-motion. The complication is that the time offset from the start of the recording is different from real-time, so in this case the hyper-personalization needs to perform an additional step: converting the requested consumer time offset to the recording's offset (in order to correct for the 4x number of frames). The personalized playlist can then be played back on any player, with no need for the user to configure playback speeds and with full slow-motion quality.

The ability to create such new experiences is made easier by the shortened media supply chain and the associated ability to control the entirety of both the media workflow and the metadata path.

Re-using existing streaming content makes all of the above processes more cost effective, and the use of hyper-personalization and metadata databases allows the consumer to see exactly what they want to see – without creating processing bottlenecks or degrading the content.

Conclusions

Hyper-personalization can bring real consumer value, by enhancing engagement and making content more relevant for the specific user, leveraging direct-to-consumer streaming's ability to connect consumers closer to the content. The flexibility offered by streaming enables the possibility of adding much finer granularity. With previous approaches, including those that use AI to create highlights packages directly, it would have been very costly to achieve per-consumer levels of personalization. Combining metadata (from either AI or manually entered) with streaming personalization means that hyper-personalized playlists can be created efficiently and at scale, making hyper-personalization a reality and leveraging content that is already available.

- D2C streaming impacts the media supply chain, making it shorter, more connected and enabling more content
- The closer connection between production and streaming allows richer metadata use for personalization of consumer delivery, when a suitable core platform is used
- AI processing can form an important part of the availability of such metadata
- Fully connected D2C architectures can use AI to enable fan engaging capabilities, such as fantasy team highlights packages on request, at a sustainable cost.

References

[1] IAB, Video Multiple Ad Playlist (VMAP), version 1.0.1, July 2014

[2] IAB, Video Ad Serving Template (VAST), version 4.0, January 21, 2016

[3] Microsoft, Azure AI services, https://azure.microsoft.com/en-gb/products/ai-services

Integrated Newsroom with Generative AI Efficiency, Accuracy, and Beyond

Maheshwaran G, Punyabrota Dasgupta
Amazon Web Services India
Mumbai, Maharashtra, India
mheshwg@amazon.com, punyabr@amazon.com

Abstract – The rapid evolution of generative AI is transforming the media industry, particularly in news production, distribution, and content value chain management. This paper explores a strategic approach to integrating generative AI technologies across newsroom operations, focusing on purpose-specific, lightweight models tailored to specific tasks. We examine how these targeted AI solutions can enable more efficient, agile, and audience-centric news operations while addressing critical considerations such as infrastructure demands, cost optimization, and implementation challenges.

Our research examines the core components of an integrated newsroom model, demonstrating how purposefully designed generative AI enhances production, quality assurance, engagement, and content reach through advanced techniques including translation, dubbing, and semantic search. By advocating for a judicious and frugal methodology, we aim to empower media organizations to harness the transformative potential of generative AI while mitigating risks and ensuring seamless integration into existing workflows.

The paper further explores the agentic AI approach that can be adopted to optimally orchestrate the newsroom workflow end to end.

Introduction

Traditional newsrooms often operate in silos, with separate teams for print, broadcast, and digital platforms. This fragmented approach leads to inefficiencies, inconsistent storytelling, and limited audience engagement. An integrated newsroom model aims to streamline these processes by fostering seamless collaboration across departments. Central to this model is the use of generative AI, which enhances content creation, automates workflows, and personalizes news delivery.

Traditional Newsroom Challenges

In regions or organizations where integrated newsrooms do not exist, the absence of a unified and collaborative media structure leads to several challenges that hinder the efficiency, quality, and competitiveness of news production. These challenges can have far-reaching impacts on how news is gathered, produced, and distributed, ultimately affecting the speed, reach, and engagement with audiences. Below are the key challenges faced in such environments:

Siloed Operations - In traditional newsrooms, departments for print, broadcast, and digital platforms often operate in isolation, each with its own teams, workflows, and decision-making processes. This

This paper is excerpted from the Proceedings of the 2025 NAB Broadcast Engineering and Information Technology (BEIT) Conference, © 2025, National Association of Broadcasters, 1 M Street SE, Washington, DC 20003 USA.

leads to inefficient communication and collaboration, causing duplication of work and a lack of synergy across platforms. Reporters, editors, and producers might be working on the same story but without coordination, resulting in inconsistencies in how the news is presented on different platforms. Without integration, each department may focus solely on its medium, missing opportunities to cross-promote stories or adapt content for different audiences. This siloed structure also limits the newsroom's ability to quickly adapt to breaking news or rapidly evolving stories across multiple platforms.

Delayed News Distribution - In a fragmented newsroom, the speed of news delivery is often slower due to the lack of coordinated efforts. When teams are not working together, it can take longer to produce and distribute content. For example, print teams may be focused on the next day's newspaper edition, while digital teams are working on immediate online updates, creating a time lag between platforms. Additionally, the absence of a streamlined process can result in delays in adapting news stories for different formats. Without a unified system, stories might not be quickly repackaged for social media, video, or online news outlets, causing missed opportunities to reach audiences in real time, especially in a competitive, fast-paced news environment.

Inconsistent Storytelling - When newsrooms lack integration, each platform—whether print, television, or digital—may offer a different narrative or presentation of the same story. This inconsistency can confuse audiences and diminish trust in the news organization. Print, TV, and online newsrooms may have different priorities or angles, and without collaboration, they risk delivering disjointed versions of the same event. Furthermore, each medium may require different storytelling approaches—visuals for television, detailed analysis for print, or short-form content for digital platforms. Without an integrated strategy, these different needs are often not met cohesively, leading to fragmented content across channels.

Limited Audience Engagement - The rise of social media and digital platforms has changed the way audiences consume news. In a non-integrated newsroom, the ability to engage audiences across different platforms is limited. News organizations that fail to deliver a consistent, cross-platform experience often struggle to build a loyal following. The lack of real-time interaction with audiences, a common feature of integrated newsrooms, results in missed opportunities to gather feedback and adjust content accordingly. For instance, digital-first audiences expect instant updates and real-time coverage on platforms like Twitter, Facebook, or Instagram. Without a coordinated effort to engage these audiences, newsrooms risk losing relevance in a media landscape that increasingly values immediacy and interaction.

Increased Costs and Resource Duplication - In news organizations that do not have an integrated newsroom, each platform—be it print, broadcast, or digital—often has its own dedicated teams and infrastructure. This duplication of resources, including personnel, equipment, and content management systems, leads to higher operational costs. Each department may need separate reporters, editors, and producers, which increases staffing requirements and limits the ability to share resources efficiently. Moreover, the lack of a shared workflow means that stories are often created from scratch multiple times for different platforms, increasing both the time and cost of producing news. In a competitive and financially constrained industry, this inefficiency can be a significant disadvantage.

Inflexibility in Handling Breaking News - Traditional, non-integrated newsrooms often lack the flexibility to respond quickly to breaking news. Different teams working in isolation may not have the agility to pivot quickly and allocate resources effectively to cover urgent stories. In contrast, integrated newsrooms can more easily reassign reporters and editors from across platforms to handle breaking stories, ensuring that coverage is immediate and coordinated. Without integration, news organizations are slower to adapt to the real-time demands of modern audiences, leading to delays in delivering important updates or failing to provide comprehensive coverage in the crucial first hours of a breaking story.

Difficulty Adapting to New Technologies - Newsrooms without integration often face challenges in adopting new technologies that enhance production and distribution capabilities. A fragmented newsroom may have different systems for print, broadcast, and online operations, making it difficult to adopt and implement new tools that can streamline workflows and improve collaboration.

In contrast, integrated newsrooms typically use unified content management systems, cloud-based tools, and collaborative technologies that allow teams to work more efficiently. The absence of such systems in traditional newsrooms hinders the ability to innovate and respond to changing technological trends.

Core Components of Integrated Newsroom

In an era of rapid technological advancement, newsrooms are undergoing a profound transformation. The traditional model of news production is being reimagined through innovative digital technologies, generative AI, and data-driven strategies. Modern newsrooms are no longer just content creators, but dynamic, interconnected ecosystems that prioritize efficiency, collaboration, and personalized audience engagement. The diagram below provides a high level solution architecture of an integrated newsroom.

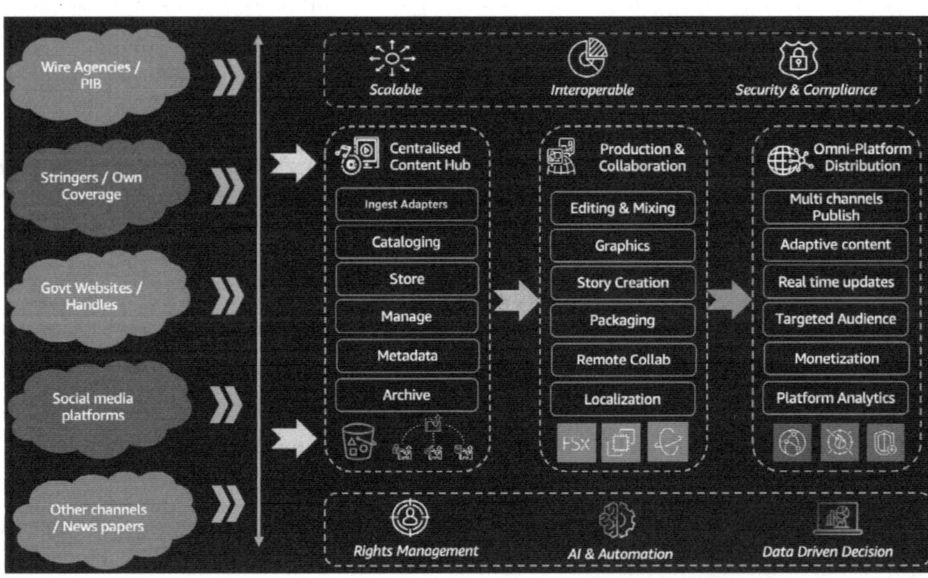

FIGURE 1: REFERENCE ARCHITECTURE OF INTEGRATED NEWSROOM

Centralized Content Hub - A centralized content hub in an integrated newsroom acts as a unified repository where all media assets, such as video clips, text, audio, images, and other resources, are stored and easily accessible to different departments. This centralized approach eliminates the need for separate repositories for each platform, ensuring that all teams—whether working on TV, digital, or print—can access the same content simultaneously. By housing all assets in one location, it streamlines workflows and reduces redundancy. Reporters, editors, and producers can pull content from the hub, modify it for their respective platforms, and push it out in real time. It also simplifies version control, ensuring consistency and accuracy across various news outputs.

AI & Automation - Artificial intelligence (AI) and automation have become essential tools in modern newsrooms to enhance efficiency and content personalization. AI can assist in various stages of news production, from generating story suggestions based on trending topics and audience preferences to automating routine editing tasks like transcription and translation. In an integrated newsroom, AI also plays a role in optimizing content distribution by analyzing audience behavior and recommending the best platforms, time slots, and formats for delivering news. Automation can streamline distribution workflows, ensuring that once a piece of content is ready, it's automatically disseminated across all platforms—television, web, social media, and mobile apps—without manual intervention, freeing up staff to focus on more complex tasks. Generative AI further empowers newsrooms by generating written content, video summaries, or even synthetic media, helping teams produce more content faster and with fewer resources.

Real-Time Collaboration - Real-time collaboration is a hallmark of an integrated newsroom, enabled by shared workspaces and digital tools that allow reporters, editors, and producers to work together from different locations. Tools like cloud-based content management systems, shared editing platforms, and communication apps such as Slack or Microsoft Teams facilitate smooth, continuous collaboration. Editorial decisions, fact-checking, and content creation happen in real-time, making the news production cycle faster and more flexible. This real-time collaboration allows for immediate input from multiple team members, improving the overall quality and speed of the news output. In an integrated newsroom, journalists can work on a story for TV while simultaneously collaborating with a digital team to prepare the same story for social media or the website.

Omni-Platform Distribution - Omni-platform distribution refers to the ability of an integrated newsroom to simultaneously publish content across multiple platforms—TV, websites, social media, mobile apps, and more. Rather than treating each platform separately, the newsroom operates with the understanding that different audiences consume news on different platforms at different times. An integrated system ensures that content is formatted appropriately for each platform and distributed concurrently. This omni-platform approach maximizes audience reach and engagement, allowing the same core story to be customized for each platform's unique needs—whether it's a full-length article for the website, a 2-minute video for social media, or a TV broadcast segment. It ensures that no platform is left behind and that the news organization remains relevant across all channels.

Data-Driven Decision Making - Data-driven decision-making is central to the integrated newsroom model. Audience insights, derived from web analytics, social media interactions, and viewership metrics, allow editorial teams to tailor content more effectively. By analyzing this data, news organizations can identify which stories resonate most with their audience, what times of day content performs best, and which platforms are most effective for particular types of content. This feedback loop allows for continuous optimization of news production and distribution, making the newsroom more responsive to audience needs. Moreover, data-driven decisions help to personalize content, offering audiences a more engaging experience by presenting them with the stories, topics, and formats that they are most interested in.

Benefits of Generative AI in Integrated Newsrooms

Generative AI transforms newsroom operations through five key advantages:

1. **Operational Excellence**
   - Automates routine tasks (article drafting, headline generation, content summaries)
   - Accelerates workflows through intelligent process automation
   - Enables journalists to focus on high-value investigative work
   - Streamlines complex tasks like transcription, video editing, and metadata tagging
2. **Quality and Accuracy Enhancement**
   - Implements real-time fact-checking and verification systems

- Reduces human error through automated cross-referencing
- Maintains consistency across multiple platforms
- Provides systematic content validation before publication

3. **Audience-Centric Content Delivery**
    - Delivers personalized content experiences based on audience analytics
    - Enables dynamic content adaptation across platforms
    - Creates targeted recommendations using behavioural patterns
    - Transforms passive consumption into interactive engagement
4. **Resource Optimization**
    - Reduces operational costs through automated content processing
    - Enables scalable content production without proportional resource increase
    - Maximizes team efficiency through intelligent task distribution
    - Creates a more flexible and responsive operational model
5. **Editorial Integrity**
    - Strengthens journalistic standards through automated bias detection
    - Ensures balanced reporting through content moderation
    - Maintains ethical guidelines across all content
    - Supports editorial decision-making with data-driven insights

Reimagining Integrated Newsroom with Agentic AI

The next-generation integrated newsroom harnesses the power of agentic AI to deliver a seamless and highly efficient content creation process. Agentic AI is a type of AI that can operate independently with minimal human supervision. While generative AI forms the foundational layer, agentic AI elevates the workflow by incorporating iterative refinement through reasoning and reinforcement learning. This synergy not only enhances the reliability of the content but also ensures that each piece is meticulously crafted to meet the highest standards of journalism.

The following diagram and detailed narrative provide a comprehensive overview of the intricate components and workflows that constitute this modern newsroom. Each element is meticulously designed to contribute to the overall efficiency and effectiveness of news production, ensuring that the final output is not only timely but also engaging and accurate.

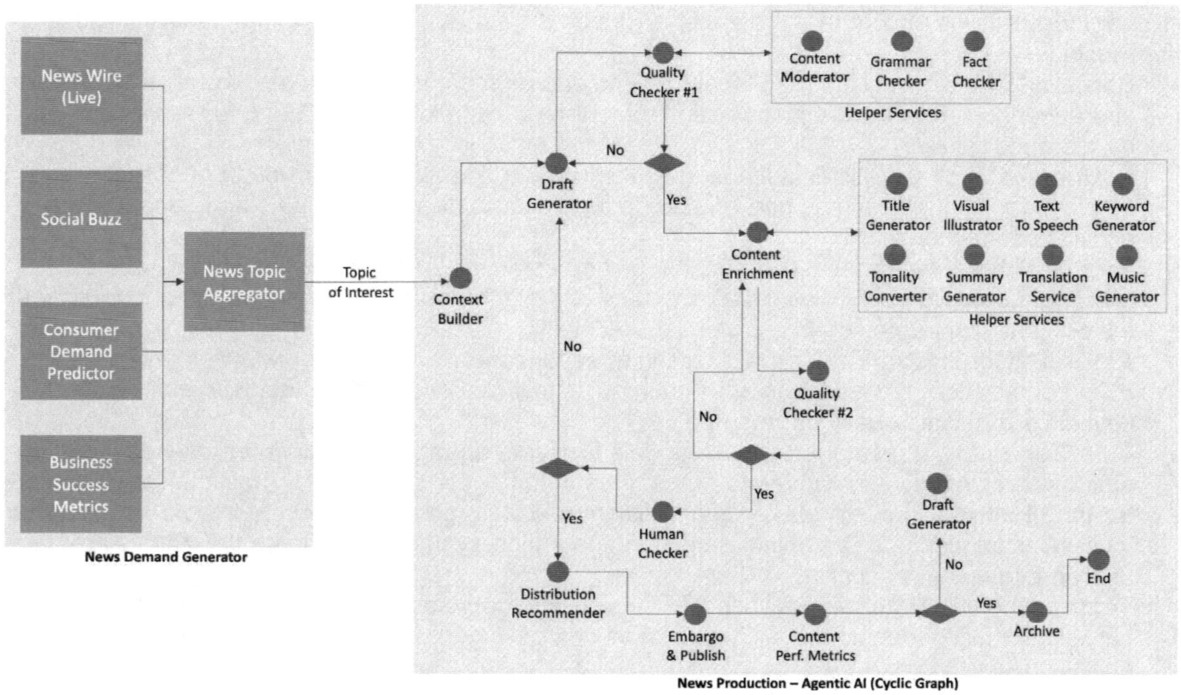

FIGURE 2: EDITORIAL WORKFLOW REIMAGINED WITH AGENTIC AI APPROACH

News Demand Generator: The News Demand Generator integrates multiple data sources to identify trending topics and consumer interests. It employs machine learning algorithms to analyse real-time data from live news wires, social media platforms, and consumer demand predictors. This component uses natural language processing (NLP) techniques to extract relevant keywords and sentiments, providing a comprehensive view of current news trends. The Topic Aggregator utilizes advanced clustering algorithms to categorize the identified topics. It employs techniques such as Latent Dirichlet Allocation (LDA) or Non-negative Matrix Factorization (NMF) to group similar topics together. This component ensures that the newsroom focuses on the most relevant and high-impact subjects, thereby optimizing resource allocation.

Context Builder: The Context Builder enriches the aggregated topics using a knowledge graph. This graph is populated with structured data from various sources, including databases, APIs, and web scraping tools. The component employs graph traversal algorithms to fetch related information, ensuring that the context is comprehensive and up-to-date. This enriched context is crucial for creating well-informed and detailed news articles.

Draft Generator: The Draft Generator leverages generative AI models to create initial drafts of news articles. These models are fine-tuned on a dataset of high-quality news articles to ensure that the generated content is coherent, grammatically correct, and aligned with journalistic standards. The draft generator significantly reduces the time required for initial content creation, allowing human journalists to focus on more complex tasks.

Quality Checker #1: The first Quality Checker employs agentic AI to evaluate the draft generated by the Draft Generator. This component uses a combination of rule-based systems and machine learning models to assess various quality metrics, such as grammatical accuracy, factual correctness, and coherence. If the draft does not meet the predefined standards, the agentic AI system identifies specific issues and suggests revisions, ensuring continuous improvement of the draft.

Helper Services: This encompass a suite of AI-driven tools that assist in refining the draft. These services include:

- **Content Moderator**: Uses NLP techniques to ensure the content adheres to ethical guidelines and editorial standards. It employs sentiment analysis and keyword filtering to identify potentially problematic content.
- **Grammar Checker**: Utilizes advanced NLP models to identify and correct grammatical errors. It employs techniques such as part-of-speech tagging and dependency parsing to ensure accurate corrections.
- **Fact Checker**: Leverages a combination of web scraping, API integrations, and machine learning models to verify the factual accuracy of the information presented. It cross-references the content with trusted sources to ensure reliability.
- **Keyword Generator**: Employs NLP techniques to identify and suggest relevant keywords for SEO optimization. It uses techniques such as TF-IDF and word embeddings to ensure the keywords are contextually appropriate.
- **Title Generator**: Uses generative AI models to create engaging and click-worthy headlines. It employs techniques such as reinforcement learning to optimize titles for maximum engagement.
- **Visual Illustrator**: Leverages computer vision models to generate relevant images or graphics. It uses techniques such as object detection and image synthesis to ensure the visuals are appropriate and high-quality.
- **Text-to-Speech**: Employs advanced TTS models to convert the text into audio for accessibility purposes. It uses techniques such as prosody modelling to ensure the audio is natural and engaging.
- **Keyword Generator**: Utilizes NLP techniques to identify and suggest relevant keywords for SEO optimization. It employs techniques such as latent semantic analysis to ensure the keywords are contextually appropriate.

Content Enrichment: This stage involves further enhancing the draft with additional elements such as summaries, translations, and music. These enrichments are generated using a combination of generative AI models and rule-based systems. For example, summarization is achieved using extractive or abstractive summarization techniques, while translations are handled by neural machine translation models.

Quality Checker #2: The second Quality Checker performs a final review of the enriched content. This component uses a combination of machine learning models and rule-based systems to assess various quality metrics, such as coherence, engagement, and factual accuracy. If any issues are detected, the agentic AI system identifies specific issues and suggests revisions, ensuring the final content is of high quality.

Human Checker: Before final publication, a human checker reviews the article. This step ensures that the AI-generated content aligns with human judgment and editorial standards. The human checker may make final edits or approve the content for distribution. This step is crucial for maintaining the integrity and credibility of the news organization.

Distribution Recommender: The Distribution Recommender suggests the most effective channels for distributing the news article. This component uses machine learning models to analyse historical data on audience engagement and content performance. It employs techniques such as collaborative filtering and content-based filtering to recommend the optimal distribution channels, ensuring maximum reach and engagement.

Embargo & Publish: Once approved, the article is embargoed if necessary and then published across the recommended channels. This step is orchestrated by a workflow management system that ensures timely and coordinated publication. The system uses APIs and automation tools to facilitate seamless distribution.

Content Performance Metrics: Post-publication, the performance of the news article is tracked using various metrics. These metrics include engagement metrics (e.g., clicks, shares, comments), reach metrics (e.g., impressions, unique visitors), and conversion metrics (e.g., sign-ups, purchases). The data is collected using web analytics tools and processed using machine learning models to provide actionable insights. These insights inform future content strategies and help in continuous improvement.

Archive: Finally, the published article is archived for future reference. This is achieved using a robust data storage solution that ensures long-term accessibility and preservation of the content. The archive is indexed using metadata and tags, allowing for easy retrieval and analysis.

Illustrative Use Case – Generative AI Powered News Feature Generation

Let us take the illustrative example of generating feature content for a news network. This involves significant time and effort investment for scouting data, collating information, researching through previously produced editorial content, resulting in production of 2-3 variations of the story are drafted, before the final version is carved out and send for publication. Each story may have some basic tenets such as genre, nature of the article (example: political gossip, humorous), editorial will (example: explanation, opinion, recommendation), writing style (example: narrative, descriptive, subjective, persuasive) and tone (example: positive, negative, and neutral). The above tenants would form the determinants driving the LLM workflow and synthesizing the best prompts. System should have a feedback loop to get continuously trained to attain a certain maturity level, ideal state should be where editor can accept the generated story as it is.

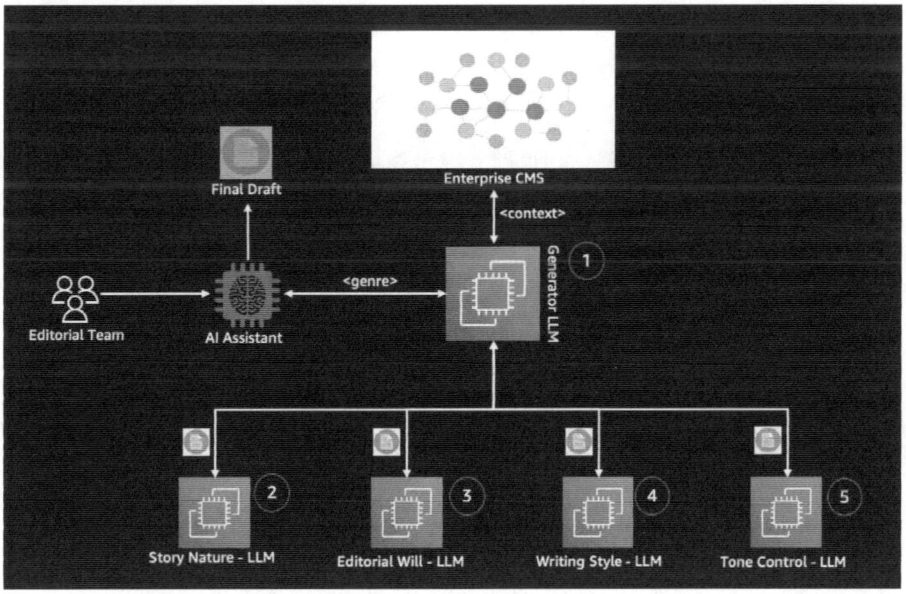

FIGURE 3: GENERATIVE AI POWERED NEWS FEATURE GENERATION

The diagram presents a sophisticated content creation workflow to streamline the editorial process as outlined above. The workflow begins with an editorial team interfacing with an AI assistant (agent), which serves as the central processing hub. This agent communicates with multiple specialized Large Language Models (LLMs), each handling specific aspects of content creation. The system is connected to the graph-styled embedding store of an enterprise content management system.

The process is broken down into five key components, each managed by specialized LLMs:

1. **Generator**: Acts as the primary content generator, taking context from the enterprise CMS
2. **Story Nature**: Determines and shapes the article's nature (political, gossip, humorous)
3. **Editorial Will**: Manages the content's purpose (explanation, opinion, recommendation)
4. **Writing Style**: Controls the narrative approach (descriptive, subjective, persuasive)
5. **Tone Control**: Ensures appropriate tone (positive, negative, neutral)

The system produces the final news draft which represents the culmination of all AI-assisted refinements while still maintaining human editorial oversight. This hybrid approach ensures both efficiency and quality control in the content creation process. It may be noted that the representation of multiple LLMs in this architecture is from a logical point of view. From an actual implementation perspective, this can either be lightweight models, finetuned with enterprise data for a specific use case; alternatively, this can be a single massive LLM trained on hundreds of billions of parameters and provides adequate performance across a range of use cases.

The table below provides a summary of the key solutioning aspects adopted here.

Solution Aspect	Description / Notes
Architectural Considerations	• Modular Design: The system's compartmentalized approach allows for independent optimization and updates of each component • Scalability: Each LLM can be scaled independently based on workload and requirements • Maintainability: Issues can be isolated and resolved without affecting the entire system • Quality Control: Multiple specialized checkpoints ensure comprehensive content refinement • Flexibility: Easy to add new specialized LLMs or modify existing ones without system overhaul
Graph-Style RAG Implementation	• The Enterprise CMS integration suggests a knowledge. graph approach to Retrieval Augmented Generation • Benefits of graph-based RAG: o Better context understanding through relationship mapping o More nuanced content generation by understanding content interconnections o Improved relevance in content retrieval o Enhanced ability to maintain consistency across related content pieces o Better handling of complex editorial guidelines and brand voice requirements
Specialized Lightweight LLMs	• Each component uses purpose-built lightweight LLMs instead of a single large model • Advantages: o Reduced computational resources and costs o Faster processing times o More precise and focused outputs for each task

	<ul><li>Easier to fine-tune for specific requirements</li><li>Lower latency in the overall system</li></ul><ul><li>Examples from the architecture:<ul><li>Story Nature LLM: Focused solely on content categorization</li><li>Tone Control LLM: Specialized in maintaining consistent voice</li><li>Writing Style LLM: Dedicated to structural elements</li></ul></li></ul>
Agentic AI Iteration Process	<ul><li>The AI Assistant acts as an orchestrator for multiple iteration cycles</li><li>Process Flow:<ul><li>Initial content generation</li><li>Sequential refinement through specialized LLMs</li><li>Continuous improvement through feedback loops</li><li>Final optimization based on editorial guidelines</li></ul></li><li>Benefits:<ul><li>Progressive refinement of content quality</li><li>Multiple validation checkpoints</li><li>Adaptive learning from editorial feedback</li><li>Consistent improvement in output quality</li></ul></li></ul>
Integration with Human Workflow	<ul><li>Editorial Team remains central to the process</li><li>AI augments rather than replaces human expertise</li><li>Feedback loop between human editors and AI system</li><li>Balanced approach to content creation and refinement</li></ul>
Performance Optimization	<ul><li>Parallel processing capabilities</li><li>Resource allocation based on task complexity</li><li>Efficient use of computational resources</li><li>Quick turnaround times for content generation</li></ul>

TABLE 1

This architecture represents a significant advancement in content creation systems, combining the efficiency of AI with the precision of specialized components and human oversight. The use of multiple lightweight LLMs, graph-based RAG, and agentic AI creates a robust, scalable, and efficient content generation pipeline that can adapt to varying editorial needs while maintaining high-quality standards.

The system's ability to iterate and refine content through multiple specialized checkpoints, while maintaining human oversight, makes it particularly valuable for enterprise-level content management. The modular nature ensures future adaptability, while the specialized LLMs provide focused expertise for each aspect of content creation.

The Way Forward

The news industry is witnessing a fundamental shift in content production and editorial workflows through advanced AI systems that promise to revolutionize how newsrooms operate while maintaining journalistic integrity and editorial standards.

Editorial Workflow Enhancement:
- Parallel Content Processing: Multiple AI agents simultaneously handle different aspects of news production - from initial story drafting to fact-checking and style editing. This allows editors to focus on high-value tasks like strategic decisions and complex editorial judgments.
- Real-time News Verification: Implementation of graph-based knowledge systems enables instant cross-referencing of facts across multiple trusted sources, significantly reducing the time needed for fact-checking while improving accuracy.
- Multimedia Content Integration: Advanced video generation capabilities allow newsrooms to create complementary visual content for breaking news, with AI agents ensuring consistency across text, images, and video elements.

Business Impact and Efficiency:
- Cost Optimization: With inference costs now at historic lows ($0.15-$0.60 per million tokens), newsrooms can automate routine content production while maintaining quality
- Resource Allocation: Specialized lightweight LLMs reduce computational overhead while maintaining high performance
- Scalable Operations: Support for both breaking news and long-form journalism through configurable workflows

Editorial Quality Control:
- Multi-stage Verification: Iterative refinement loops ensure content meets editorial standards
- Source Credibility Assessment: Automated evaluation of source reliability and cross-referencing
- Style Consistency: Automated enforcement of house style and tone across all content

This new architecture paradigm enables newsrooms to maintain high journalistic standards while significantly improving production efficiency. The system supports various content types - from breaking news to investigative pieces - while ensuring editorial oversight remains central to the process. This transformation allows news organizations to compete effectively in the digital age while maintaining their commitment to quality journalism.

Conclusion

The integration of AI technologies in newsrooms represents a pivotal moment in journalism's evolution. This transformation goes beyond mere technological adoption – it demonstrates how artificial intelligence can enhance rather than replace human editorial judgment. Through the careful implementation of multi-agent systems, specialized LLMs, and graph-based knowledge architectures, newsrooms can maintain their commitment to journalistic excellence while meeting the demands of modern news consumption. The success of this paradigm shift lies in its ability to preserve the fundamental values of journalism – accuracy, integrity, and public service – while leveraging technological innovations to better serve audiences in an increasingly digital world.

References

[1] Ng. Andrew, December 2025 article on the rise of agentic AI: https://www.deeplearning.ai/the-batch/issue-281/

[2] Tyler Thomas Procko, Omor Ochoa, IEEE paper on Graph Retrieval-Augmented Generation for large language models. Link: https://ieeexplore.ieee.org/document/10771030

[3] Kun Li, Tianhua Zhang, et. all, Decoding on Graphs: Faithful and Sound Reasoning on Knowledge Graphs through Generation of Well-Formed Chain. https://huggingface.co/papers/2410.18415

[4] Aske Plaat, Annie Wong, et. all, Reasoning with Large Language Models, a Survey. Link: https://arxiv.org/html/2407.11511v1

[5] Pei Chen, Boran Han, et. all, Collaborative multi-agent, multi-reasoning-path prompting for complex problem solving, Link: https://www.amazon.science/publications/comm-collaborative-multi-agent-multi-reasoning-path-prompting-for-complex-problem-solving

[6] Raphael Shu, Nilaksh Das, et. all, Towards effective genAI multi-agent collaboration: Design and evaluation for enterprise applications. Link: https://www.amazon.science/publications/towards-effective-genai-multi-agent-collaboration-design-and-evaluation-for-enterprise-applications

[7] Zhou Qin, Kai Yuan, et. all. Cooperative multi-agent deep reinforcement learning in content ranking optimization, Link: https://www.amazon.science/publications/cooperative-multi-agent-deep-reinforcement-learning-in-content-ranking-optimization

[8] Raphael Shu, Yi Zhang, et. all. Unlocking complex problem-solving with multi-agent collaboration on Amazon Bedrock. Link: https://aws.amazon.com/blogs/machine-learning/unlocking-complex-problem-solving-with-multi-agent-collaboration-on-amazon-bedrock/

[9] Nisar Keshavni, The Integrated Newsroom: the changing face of news journalism as we know it. Link: https://www.academia.edu/47351855/The_Integrated_Newsroom_the_changing_face_phase_of_news_journalism_as_we_know_it

Vision and Language Models for Enhanced Archive Video Management

Khalil Guetari[1], Yannis Tevissen[1], Frederic Petitpont[1]
[1] Moments Lab Research
Boulogne-Billancourt, France
khalil.guetari@momentslab.com

Abstract – Archival video collections contain a wealth of historical and cultural information. Managing and analyzing this data can be challenging due to the lack of metadata and inconsistent formatting across different sources. In particular, identifying and separating individual stories within a single archived tape is critical for efficient indexing, analysis and retrieval. However, manual segmentation is time-consuming and prone to human error. To address this challenge, we propose a novel approach that combines vision and language models to automatically detect transition frames and segment archive videos into distinct stories. A vision model is used to cluster frames of the video. Using recent robust automatic speech recognition and large language models, a transcript, a summary and a title for the story are generated. By leveraging computed features from the previous transition frames detection, we also propose a fine-grained chaptering of the segmented stories. We conducted experiments on a dataset consisting of 50 hours of archival video footage. The results demonstrated a high level of accuracy in detecting and segmenting videos into distinct stories. Specifically, we achieved a precision of 93% for an Intersection over Union threshold set at 90%. Furthermore, our approach has shown to have significant sustainability benefits as it is able to filter and remove approximately 20% of the content from the 50 hours of videos tested. This reduction in the amount of data that needs to be managed, analyzed and stored can lead to substantial cost savings and environmental benefits by reducing energy consumption and carbon emissions associated with data processing and storage.

Introduction

Video archiving is the process of storing and preserving a video file for long term access and retrieval. This field has significatively evolved in the past decade especially with the replacement of video tapes by more modern media storage. But a large portion of the world's cultural heritage has still not been digitized. For instance, UNESCO estimates that 95% of its archives have not yet been digitized [1] with an ever-growing risk of losing it due to the material degradation.

Archival is an ever-changing field that needs to quickly adapt to new technological paradigms with the risk of losing important pieces of history if not moving fast enough [2]. One of the many challenges of digitizing a video tape lies in the fact that one tape often contains various recordings without any proper pagination, index or even handmade chapters. The only thing that could help separate a specific film, report or sequence is the short introduction screen that was added before the actual footage. One tape can contain very different transition frames, with varying text, colors and patterns as illustrated on Figure 1.

In this paper, we propose a novel method to separate meaningful stories from archive tapes. This method is to the best of our knowledge the first contribution to tackle this complex video understanding

This paper is excerpted from the Proceedings of the 2025 NAB Broadcast Engineering and Information Technology (BEIT) Conference, © 2025, National Association of Broadcasters, 1 M Street SE, Washington, DC 20003 USA.

problem. We also present an automatic video chaptering approach to generate a comprehensive breakdown of each story. With these new methods we achieve better results than any state-of-the-art VLM-based approach.

FIGURE 1: EXAMPLES OF TRANSITIONS FRAMES INCLUDING SLATES, COUNTDOWNS AND SMPTE COLORS BARS

Related Work

Video indexing has always been an important field of research and even before the rise of AI. Nowadays, video content through broadcasting, streaming and social media are the first means of communication. To index, manage and retrieve such a vast amount of data, AI based systems become more and more mandatory. Archive video collections are libraries of analog devices that store video content. This content needs to be indexed accurately but the sheer volume of it makes it not practicable. Therefore, high level information (title, subject, dates of recording, celebrities) are sometimes only considered and content is retrieved using archivist expertise. This typically does not encompass the indexing of specific content (e.g., transcripts and objects) or structural data, such as a hierarchical arrangement of chapters consisting of sequences of shots [3].

In the current literature and among commercialized products [4,5], slate detection often refers to the clapper-board physical object detection which is a common pattern detection task often followed by OCR to read the written information on the clapperboard [6]. In our case, we are talking about digital slates: countdown frames, SMPTE colors bars and sometimes black frames. We regroup all of these under the appellation of “transition frames”.

Video chapter generation task requires temporally segmenting the video into chapters and generating a title. Chapters are contiguous and non-overlapping segments which completely segment a video [7]. Thus, the end of a chapter is the start of a new chapter. Unsupervised learning was mostly used in previous approaches. For efficient processing of long video datasets, shots are first detected. Then, they are represented in a feature space using low level features, clustering algorithms are used to group shots into chapters [8,9]. More recent techniques use deep learning to fuse different modalities into a trained neural network. Rotman et al. [10] uses visual and audio embeddings from frozen backbones. Embeddings are then trained in a fully connected network and fused together. Tiago et al. [11] trains an LSTM to output if a shot is a shot transition between two scenes. CSIFT visual features [12] and MFCCs [13] are passed through a CNN each before being fed to the LSTM network.

More recently, Xiao et al. [14] use transformers to generate chapters in a two stages framework where chapter localization is modeled as a binary classifier on short clips of the video. Titles are then generated using text and visual features in the location of the chapter. Yang et al. [15] manages to generate chapters’ timestamps and titles in an interleaved manner by modeling temporal modality as special tokens.

Finally, recent video understanding breakthroughs are also driven by large vision-language models (VLM) that often combine a visual encoder with a LLM to interact with a video through natural language. Among these approaches, a few recently introduced the use of time tokens to give the VLM the ability to locate objects and actions in a video timewise [16,17].

Proposed Method

Video tapes consist of a succession of different footage, news reports, interviews (called stories from now on) that are separated by transition frames. Figure 1 shows some examples of possible transition frames. The average duration of a video tape is one hour. These stories can have various durations and are not placed in a particular order. Since tapes are decaying, the video once digitized can include some static and moving noise. That's why the approach needs to be robust. To index and manage these tapes, we build a three-stage approach as pictured in Figure 2.

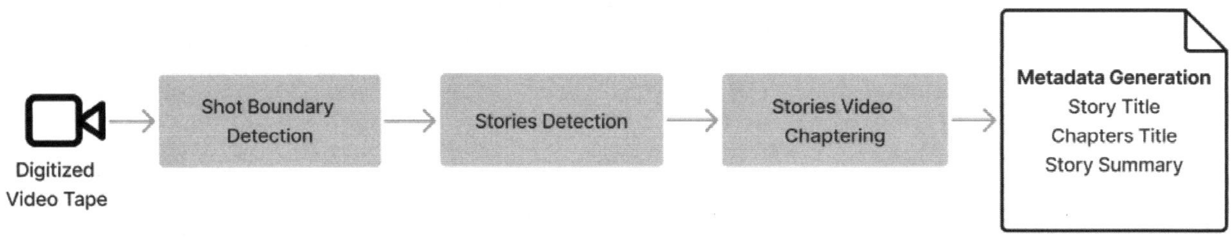

FIGURE 2: OVERVIEW OF THE PROPOSED METHOD. VIDEO TAPES ARE PROCESSED TO DETECT SHOTS AND TO EXTRACT AUDIO AND TRANSCRIPT. STORIES LOCATIONS ARE DETECTED AND A PRECISE CHAPTERING IS PROPOSED FOR EACH STORY. USING THE TRANSCRIPT AND VISUAL DESCRIPTIONS, TITLES AND A SUMMARY ARE GENERATED.

Story Detection

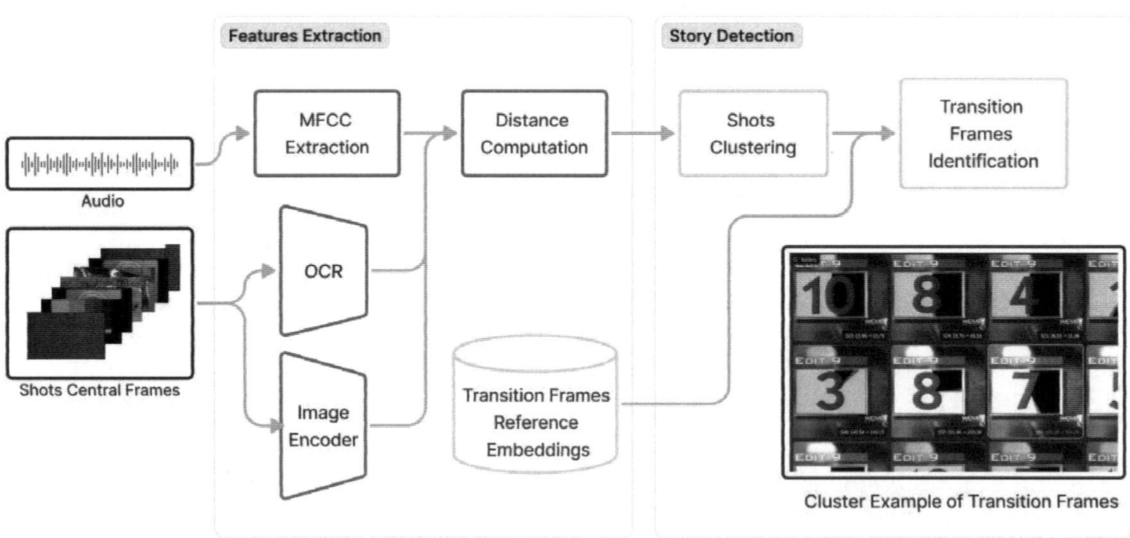

FIGURE 3: OVERVIEW OF THE STORY DETECTION PIPELINE. FEATURES ARE EXTRACTED FROM THE RAW AUDIO AND VISUAL AND TEXT FEATURES FROM SHOTS' CENTRAL FRAMES. EACH SHOT'S FEATURES ARE COMPARED USING SPECIFIC DISTANCE FUNCTIONS CREATING CLUSTERS OF SHOTS. BASED ON REFERENCE TRANSITION FRAMES, THE RIGHT CLUSTERS ARE SELECTED

First, entire stories are found by detecting transition frames between stories. We opt for an unsupervised approach because of a lack of ground truth annotations or open dataset and because of a growing number of videos as tapes are being digitized. To be more compute efficient, we decide to model the stories' timestamps detection as a shot boundary detection. Shots are detected using Pyscenedetect [18]. This enables the pipeline to process fewer frames. We extract several features from different modalities in order to cluster shots based on their similarity.

- **Visual Features**: Image embeddings are extracted from a frozen image vision transformer encoder originating from CLIP's open weights [19]. The classification token is extracted to model the visual features of the shot. The central frame of the shot is used. A cosine distance is used to compare visual representation of each shot,
- **Audio Features**. Audio is extracted using FFMPEG. From the audio, MFCCs [13] are extracted using librosa library. Audio features are aligned with shot timestamps by averaging the different MFCC values for a given shot. This gives an audio representation of a shot. A Euclidean distance is used to compare the intensities of MFCC values.
- **Optical Character Recognition**: Text is recognized on the central frame of the shot using EasyOCR. Countdown transition frames usually have the same text inside since they display the name of the channel station. A Levenshtein [20] distance is used to compute the similarity between text from different shots.

Before clustering extracted features, a simple image processing step is applied on every shot to detect black frames.

A weighted average of distances from visual, audio and text modalities is computed to cluster shots based on their global similarity. Countdowns have usually a consistent format throughout the same tape video, so they end up in the same clusters, as shown in figure 3. The last step is to select the clusters corresponding to transition frames. A simple rule used is to choose the cluster with the biggest number of shots, which is the approach later called "zero shot cluster identification". However, there can be different types of transition frames in the same tapes, so we conduct experiments on a few-shot approach to perform cluster identification by providing and comparing several reference transition frames to detected clusters. Once transition shots are identified, stories can be extracted using FFMPEG and transition shots can be erased.

Story Video Chaptering

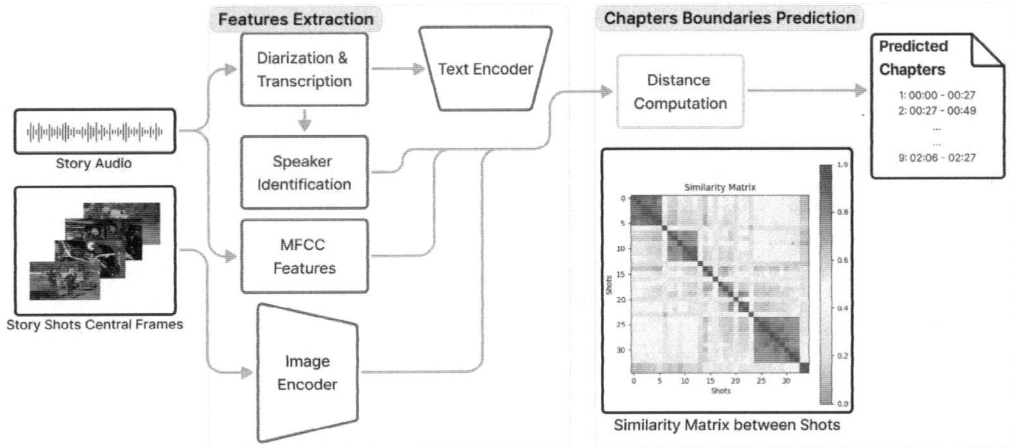

FIGURE 4: OVERVIEW OF THE VIDEO CHAPTERING PIPELINE. FEATURES ARE EXTRACTED FROM THE AUDIO, TRANSCRIPT AND SHOTS CENTRAL FRAME. EACH SHOT'S SET OF FEATURES ARE COMPARED USING SPECIFIC DISTANCE FUNCTIONS CREATING A SIMILARITY MATRIX. A SIMPLE THRESHOLD IS USED TO RETURN CHAPTERS.

The second stage of our pipeline is designed to chapter detected stories based on the content spoken and displayed inside. The approach is similar to the first stage as it consists in computing distances between shots. Visual and audio features from the story detection stage are used again here. At this point of the pipeline, ASR (Automatic Speech Recognition) is performed thanks to WhisperX [21] to produce two additional features to improve chaptering on speech context:

- **Textual Features**. Transcript segments are aligned with detected shots using timestamps. We use GTE-Large [22] to compute text embeddings on these chunks of text. To avoid having small chunks of words with not enough context, the text is not shot based but the whole transcript segment is given to a shot. Likewise for visual features, cosine distance function is used to compare shot's textual embeddings.
- **Speaker Features**. Speakers in the video are identified during the diarization step. There may be several speakers in the same shot so a simple rule to associate a speaker to a shot is to take the speaker with the maximum time of speech in the shot. Potential silences are also associated with a shot when no speaker is found. The speaker modality distance between two shots is computed by following a simple rule: the distance equals 0 if the speakers are the same and 1 if the speakers are different.

Unlike stories' detection clustering, chaptering is based by comparing shots sequentially. If the global distance between two shots is above a threshold set empirically, then it means that a chapter boundary is found at this location.

Using shots as compute entry points instead of using frames at a specific framerate bring some limitations. Interviews or press conferences are likely to be recorded as a single shot, hence creating a single chapter. Preprocessing steps are added to create "virtual" shots based on audio segments. Additionally, some videos can lack audio content, so several distance thresholds are used depending on the presence of a transcript.

Metadata Generation

Each shot is described using Idefics2 [23], a vision language model, prompted to caption the central frame of the shot. Description of shots and transcript extracts belonging to a chapter are used to generate chapter titles with LLAMA3.3 70B a state-of-the-art open-source large language model. Moreover, a title of the story and a summary are also generated by using all shot descriptions and the full transcript of the video. Some examples of generated metadata are shown in Appendix A.

Datasets

Two datasets are used to conduct experiments on stories detection and video chaptering. To our knowledge, there is no open-source dataset for the task of stories detection in archive tapes. Therefore, we build and annotate a dataset of 50 hours which consists of 1561 number of stories and 16768 number of transition shots to filter. The average duration of a story is 89.3 seconds, and the average duration of a transition shot is 2.2 seconds.

For the video chaptering task, we use FineVideo [24], a recent video understanding dataset with 43000 videos spanning on about 3400 hours of diverse content like sports, news, politics, education, or lifestyle. FineVideo consists of a rich set of video understanding annotations such as summaries, questions and answers, chapters, or time codes. A test split of about 190 hours is used to evaluate the proposed approach. As depicted on Figure 5., this test split follows the same duration distribution as the full dataset.

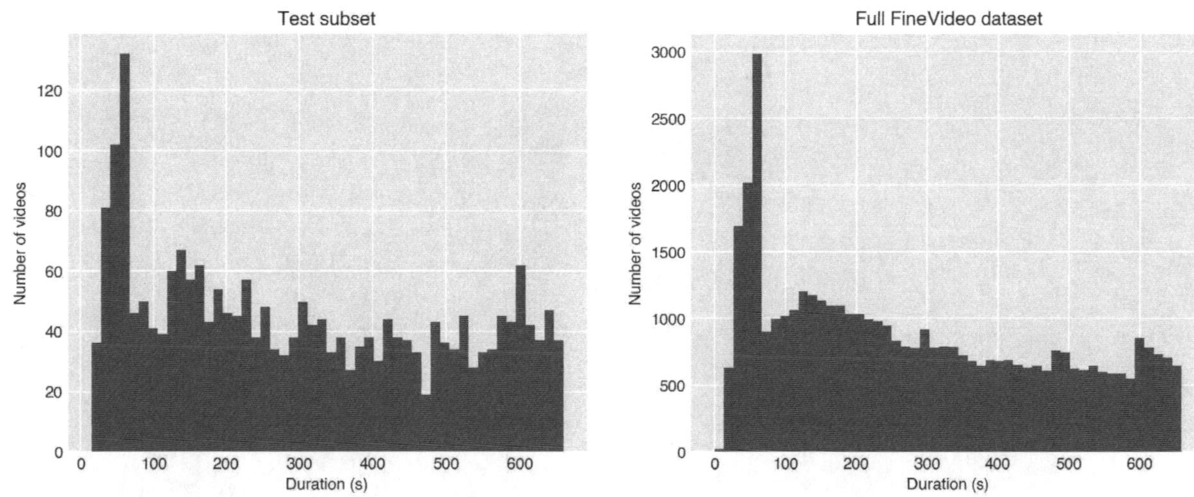

FIGURE 5: VIDEO DURATION DISTRIBUTIONS ACROSS FINEVIDEO AND THE CREATED TEST SUBSET.

Evaluation Metrics

Both tasks involve locating time codes for stories and chapters. Therefore, evaluation metrics consist of one set of metrics to assess the performance of both tasks. Located chapters are evaluated using precision (P@Ks, P@K) and recall (R@Ks, R@K) across various thresholds for both distance to the ground-truth chapter start timestamp and for the IoU between the predicted and ground-truth start and end timestamps window. F1 scores (F1@Ks, F1@K) are computed and shared in the results tables. The distance metrics are evaluated at 1, 3 and 5 seconds thresholds and the IoU based metrics are evaluated at 0.5, 0.7 and 0.9 thresholds

Results

Story Detection

We conduct experiments on the dataset of 50 hours of tapes archive on several configurations:

- Zero shot approach: all modalities are used and the cluster with the highest number of shots is selected
- Zero shot approach without the OCR modality
- Few shot approach: all modalities are used and clusters are compared to embeddings from a set of reference transition frames.
- Few shot approach without the OCR modality

Results presented in Figure 6 and Table 1 prove that using few shots learning of transition frames drastically improves story detection by about 15% for all metrics. This shows the robustness of the proposed approach since no model has been trained for this task. Using the OCR as an additional modality also shows a smaller improvement of about 1% giving an insight that extra text modality helps in clustering similar transition frames.

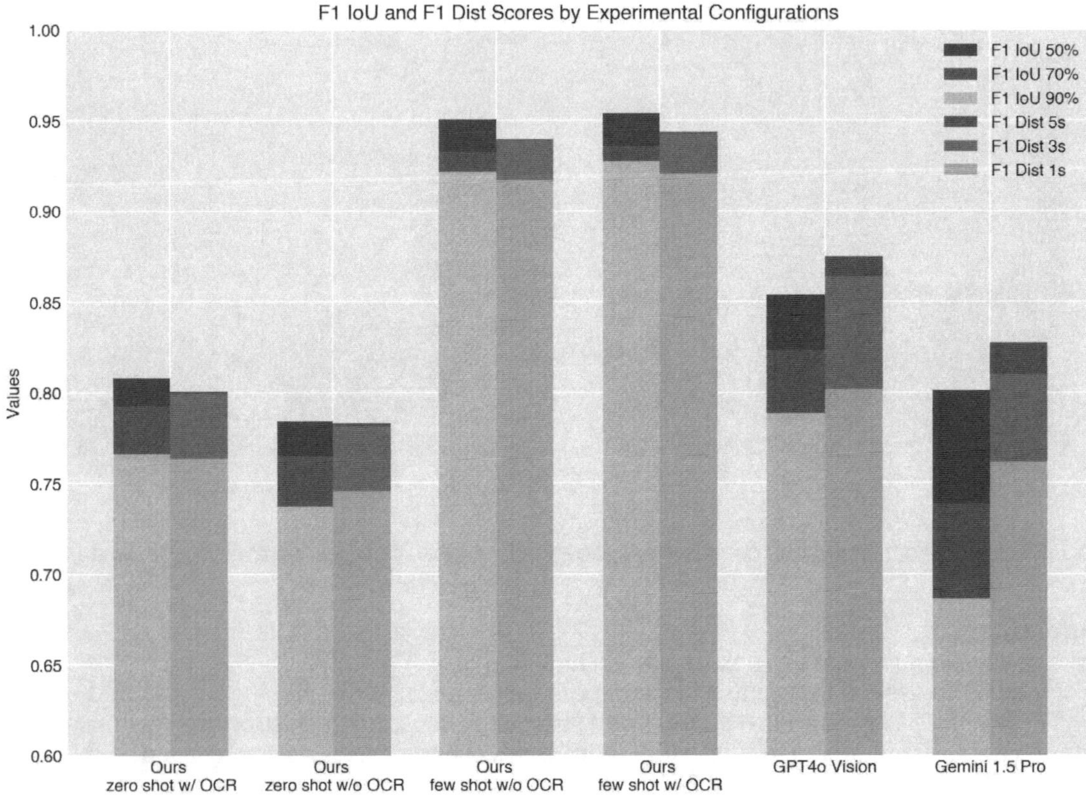

FIGURE 6: STORY DETECTION BAR CHART RESULTS SHOWING F1 IOU AND F1 TEMPORAL DISTANCES AT SEVERAL THRESHOLDS FOR SEVERAL CONFIGURATIONS AND FOUNDATIONAL LANGUAGE MODELS.

Method		F1@5s	F1@3s	F1@1s	F1@0.5	F1@0.7	F1@0.9
Gemini 1.5 Pro		82.72	80.97	76.13	80.13	73.85	68.59
GPT4o Vision		87.47	86.40	80.14	85.39	82.31	78.84
Ours Zero shot	OCR	80.06	79.93	76.35	80.79	79.26	76.64
	No OCR	78.32	78.14	74.55	78.42	76.52	73.71
Ours Few shot	No OCR	93.94	93.89	91.70	95.03	93.26	92.17
	OCR	**94.35**	**94.25**	**92.05**	**95.38**	**93.58**	**92.72**

TABLE 1: STORY DETECTION RESULTS.

Finally, we also attempt to use Gemini 1.5 PRO video understanding capabilities to assess its performances on this task. Gemini has a limit of 1 hour of input video, so we chunk video tapes above 40 minutes into two or three chunks having roughly the same duration.

Gemini is asked to study and detect stories within the video and to return them as a list of start and end timestamps which are compared with the ground truth. Prompting it with the full video ends up with very low performances. Thus, we decide to prompt Gemini with images from shots rather than chunks of video. This change leads to better results, giving insights that image analysis capabilities are better than video analysis capabilities. We also use GPT4o Vision capabilities in the same way to assess its performances. Figure 5 shows that our approach powered by few-shot learning still beats foundational closed source vision language models by a large margin. We note that GPT4o Vision performs better than Gemini 1.5 Pro.

Story Video Chaptering

Story video chaptering task is evaluated on the test split of FineVideo. We conduct experimentations on several configurations of our pipeline. We try two different image encoder models:

- CLIP image encoder, trained on COCO captions dataset [25]
- SigLIP image encoder, an iteration of CLIP where the loss function is changed [26]

Our approach was compared with Vid2Seq [15], a state-of-the-art video chaptering model, trained on VidChapters-7M [7], HowTo100M [27], and Vitt datasets [28].
Finally, we also attempted using NVILA-15B [17] and VTimeLLM [16], two generative vision language models that use time tokens to enable object and action localization in videos. But this didn't work as the two models failed at generating the multiple timecodes needed to create a chapter's breakdown.
Finally, we also assess the performances obtained with the use of the creation of "virtual shots" in videos having long duration shots.

Table 2 and Figure 7 summarize the results for the task of story video chaptering. Our approach, whatever the configuration used, drastically beats Vid2Seq, a trained transformer, by a large margin (more than 10% for every metric). It could be interesting, in future works, to train Vid2Seq on the FineVideo training set. Regarding the choice of the image encoder model, we can conclude that there is no winner since differences of performances are marginal, below 0.3%. CLIP and SigLIP were trained on the same data, so we can conclude that their vision transformers models are very similar.

Finally, regarding the use of preprocessing steps to create "virtual shots" for long shots, the idea firstly originates from press conferences and interviews with long shots. However, results show that adding the preprocessing step reduces slightly the performances between 1% to 2%. An explanation to this could be because FineVideo presents a very small number of videos with long shots. Among the 2282 videos from the test split of FineVideo, only 385 went through the preprocessing step hence making a small contribution to the overall performances for better or worse. Also, we notice, e.g. in Appendix A, that some videos appear to have only one chapter whereas having more than one chapter could be satisfactory. More generally, chaptering can depend on some specific editorial guidelines, or it can depend on specific business needs. Therefore, training a video chaptering model on FineVideo training split could be more interesting to grasp the editorial guidelines used to create FineVideo dataset. We also mention that FineVideo annotations were generated by Gemini 1.5 Pro which can present potential errors or biases.

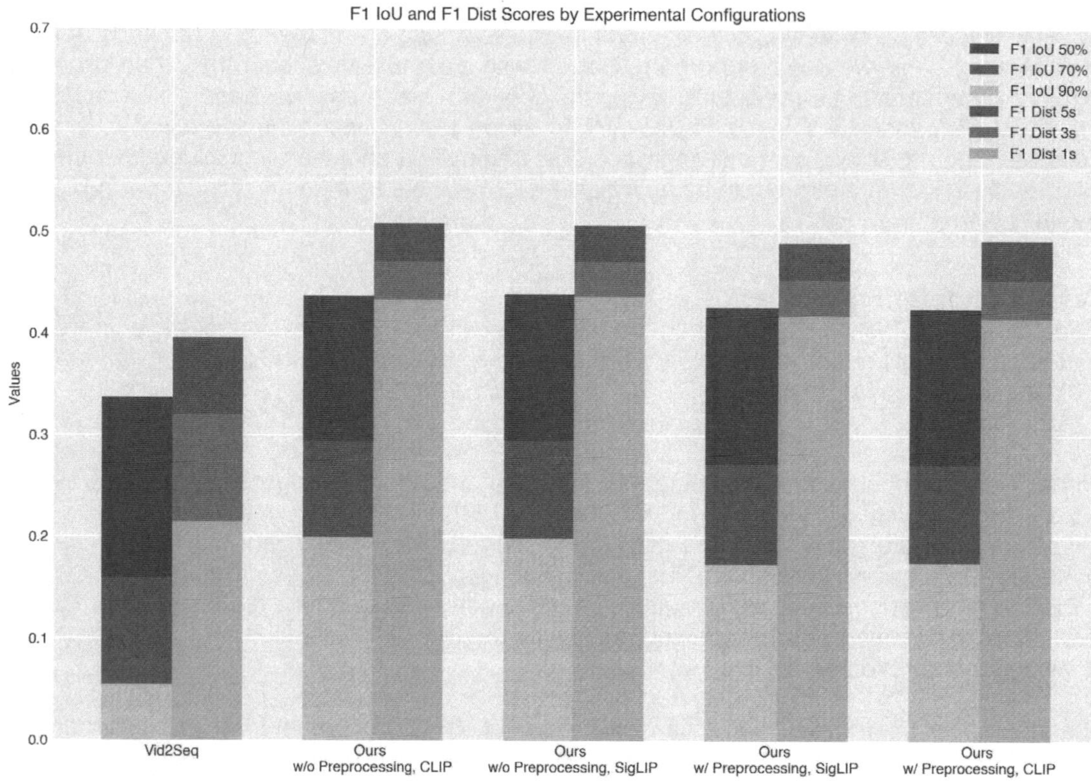

FIGURE 7: VIDEO CHAPTERING BAR CHART RESULTS SHOWING F1 IOU AND F1 TEMPORAL DISTANCES AT SEVERAL THRESHOLDS FOR SEVERAL CONFIGURATIONS

Method		F1@5s	F1@3s	F1@1s	F1@0.5	F1@0.7	F1@0.9
Vid2Seq		39.57	32.00	21.46	33.67	15.99	5.46
Ours Without Preprocessing	CLIP	**50.84**	47.08	43.37	43.70	29.44	**19.95**
	SigLIP	50.64	**47.12**	**43.66**	**43.90**	**29.51**	19.88
Ours With Preprocessing	SigLIP	48.96	45.31	41.74	42.64	27.21	17.37
	CLIP	49.20	45.32	41.51	42.45	27.16	17.50

TABLE 2: VIDEO CHAPTERING RESULTS.

Discussion

Stories detection using an unsupervised method has shown good performances on the tapes dataset, but this can be less adapted when tapes present different types of transition frames. Using a few examples of them improves performance as seen above but this method can be less robust when new formats of transition frames are presented. Also, parameters for the shot boundary detection need to be monitored as some content can present a short number of transition frames (less than one second). Therefore, we believe a trained transition frames classifier will be more suited for the task of story detection.

We also want to highlight that the video chaptering pipeline presented can be further finetuned on a labelled dataset to match specific chaptering needs. An example of this can be found in [29] where a LSTM model was trained using a late fusion of features extracted from shots.

Furthermore, our approach has shown to have significant sustainability benefits as it is able to filter and remove approximately 10 hours of transition footage from the original 50 hours of videos tested. This reduction in the amount of data that needs to be managed, analyzed and stored can lead to substantial cost savings and environmental benefits by reducing energy consumption and carbon emissions associated with data processing and storage.

Finally, regarding our failed attempt using VideoLLMs, we believe that this is due to the training data of the two benchmarked models. They were trained on video QAs with only a limited number of timecodes whereas chaptering requires generating many timecodes within a single answer. Finetuning such models of automatic chaptering data could lead to better results.

Conclusion

In this paper we proposed a new method, arguably the first in the literature, for performing transition frames detection on digitized archival tapes. We hope this method can serve as a baseline for future research and development in this area. We also introduced an automatic video chaptering technique designed at retrieving meaningful chapters by breaking down video stories extracted from the tapes. Together, these two techniques unlock a wide new range of possibilities for utilizing old video archives and restoring a key part of the world's audiovisual heritage. Going further to improve the proposed method, we envision the creation of a dedicated benchmark with human annotated data. Indeed, the task of automatic video chaptering still lacks a north star metric and a well identified evaluation dataset with a ground truth that was not semi-automatically generated by a deep learning model.

References

[1] UNESCO Archives, (n.d.). https://www.unesco.org/en/archives.

[2] F.J. Stielow, Archival Theory and the Preservation of Electronic Media: Opportunities and Standards below the Cutting Edge, The American Archivist 55 (1992) 332–343.

[3] L.A. Rowe, J.S. Boreczky, C.A. Eads, Indexes for user access to large video databases, in: C.W. Niblack, R.C. Jain (Eds.), San Jose, CA, 1994: pp. 150–161. https://doi.org/10.1117/12.171772.

[4] Automated Detection of Slates in Media Content, (n.d.). https://www.veneratech.com/automated-detection-of-slates-in-media-content/.

[5] Clapper Board Detection, (n.d.). https://learn.microsoft.com/en-us/azure/azure-video-indexer/clapper-board-insight.

[6] F. Han, Z. Meng, A Metadata Generation System with Semantic Understanding for Video Retrieval in Film Production, arXiv Preprint arXiv:2312.00104 (2023).

[7] A. Yang, A. Nagrani, I. Laptev, J. Sivic, C. Schmid, VidChapters-7M: Video Chapters at Scale, in: A. Oh, T. Naumann, A. Globerson, K. Saenko, M. Hardt, S. Levine (Eds.), Advances in Neural Information Processing Systems, Curran Associates, Inc., 2023: pp. 49428–49444. https://proceedings.neurips.cc/paper_files/paper/2023/file/9b5c3e00d6ed30aad7adac9e7a664de1-Paper-Datasets_and_Benchmarks.pdf.

[8] R. Panda, S.K. Kuanar, A.S. Chowdhury, Nyström Approximated Temporally Constrained Multisimilarity Spectral Clustering Approach for Movie Scene Detection, IEEE Transactions on Cybernetics 48 (2018) 836–847. https://doi.org/10.1109/TCYB.2017.2657692.

[9] L. Baraldi, C. Grana, R. Cucchiara, Analysis and re-use of videos in educational digital libraries with automatic scene detection, in: Digital Libraries on the Move: 11th Italian Research Conference on Digital Libraries, IRCDL 2015, Bolzano, Italy, January 29-30, 2015, Revised Selected Papers 11, Springer, 2016: pp. 155–164.

[10] D. Rotman, Y. Yaroker, E. Amrani, U. Barzelay, R. Ben-Ari, Learnable Optimal Sequential Grouping for Video Scene Detection, in: Proceedings of the 28th ACM International Conference on Multimedia, Association for Computing Machinery, New York, NY, USA, 2020: pp. 1958–1966. https://doi.org/10.1145/3394171.3413612.

[11] T.H. Trojahn, R.M. Kishi, R. Goularte, A new multimodal deep-learning model to video scene segmentation, in: Proceedings of the 24th Brazilian Symposium on Multimedia and the Web, Association for Computing Machinery, New York, NY, USA, 2018: pp. 205–212. https://doi.org/10.1145/3243082.3243108.

[12] A.E. Abdel-Hakim, A.A. Farag, CSIFT: A SIFT Descriptor with Color Invariant Characteristics, in: 2006 IEEE Computer Society Conference on Computer Vision and Pattern Recognition (CVPR'06), 2006: pp. 1978–1983. https://doi.org/10.1109/CVPR.2006.95.

[13] S. Davis, P. Mermelstein, Comparison of parametric representations for monosyllabic word recognition in continuously spoken sentences, IEEE Transactions on Acoustics, Speech, and Signal Processing 28 (1980) 357–366. https://doi.org/10.1109/TASSP.1980.1163420.

[14] X. Cao, Z. Chen, C. Le, L. Meng, Multi-modal Video Chapter Generation, (2022). https://arxiv.org/abs/2209.12694.

[15] A. Yang, A. Nagrani, P.H. Seo, A. Miech, J. Pont-Tuset, I. Laptev, J. Sivic, C. Schmid, Vid2Seq: Large-Scale Pretraining of a Visual Language Model for Dense Video Captioning, in: 2023 IEEE/CVF Conference on Computer Vision and Pattern Recognition (CVPR), IEEE, Vancouver, BC, Canada, 2023: pp. 10714–10726. https://doi.org/10.1109/CVPR52729.2023.01032.

[16] B. Huang, X. Wang, H. Chen, Z. Song, W. Zhu, VTimeLLM: Empower LLM to Grasp Video Moments, (2023). https://doi.org/10.48550/arXiv.2311.18445.

[17] Z. Liu, L. Zhu, B. Shi, Z. Zhang, Y. Lou, S. Yang, H. Xi, S. Cao, Y. Gu, D. Li, X. Li, Y. Fang, Y. Chen, C.-Y. Hsieh, D.-A. Huang, A.-C. Cheng, V. Nath, J. Hu, S. Liu, R. Krishna, D. Xu, X. Wang, P. Molchanov, J. Kautz, H. Yin, S. Han, Y. Lu, NVILA: Efficient Frontier Visual Language Models, (2024). https://arxiv.org/abs/2412.04468.

[18] B. Castellano, PySceneDetect: Video Scene Cut Detection and Analysis Tool, (2014). https://github.com/Breakthrough/PySceneDetect.

[19] A. Radford, J.W. Kim, C. Hallacy, A. Ramesh, G. Goh, S. Agarwal, G. Sastry, A. Askell, P. Mishkin, J. Clark, G. Krueger, I. Sutskever, Learning Transferable Visual Models From Natural Language Supervision, in: Proceedings of the 38 Th International Conference on Machine Learning, arXiv, 2021. http://arxiv.org/abs/2103.00020 (accessed March 5, 2024).

[20] V. Levenshtein, Binary codes capable of correcting deletions, insertions, and reversals, Proceedings of the Soviet Physics Doklady (1966).

[21] M. Bain, J. Huh, T. Han, A. Zisserman, WhisperX: Time-Accurate Speech Transcription of Long-Form Audio, INTERSPEECH 2023 (2023).

[22] Z. Li, X. Zhang, Y. Zhang, D. Long, P. Xie, M. Zhang, Towards General Text Embeddings with Multi-stage Contrastive Learning, CoRR abs/2308.03281 (2023). https://doi.org/10.48550/ARXIV.2308.03281.

[23] H. Laurençon, L. Tronchon, M. Cord, V. Sanh, What matters when building vision-language models?, (2024). https://arxiv.org/abs/2405.02246.

[24] M. Farré, A. Marafioti, L. Tunstall, L. von Werra, P. Cuenca, T. Wolf, FineVideo: Behind the Scenes, (2024). https://huggingface.co/blog/fine-video.

[25] T.-Y. Lin, M. Maire, S. Belongie, L. Bourdev, R. Girshick, J. Hays, P. Perona, D. Ramanan, C.L. Zitnick, P. Dollár, Microsoft COCO: Common Objects in Context, in: Springer, 2014. http://arxiv.org/abs/1405.0312 (accessed February 12, 2024).

[26] X. Zhai, B. Mustafa, A. Kolesnikov, L. Beyer, Sigmoid loss for language image pre-training, in: Proceedings of the IEEE/CVF International Conference on Computer Vision, 2023: pp. 11975–11986.

[27] A. Miech, D. Zhukov, J.-B. Alayrac, M. Tapaswi, I. Laptev, J. Sivic, Howto100m: Learning a text-video embedding by watching hundred million narrated video clips, in: Proceedings of the IEEE/CVF International Conference on Computer Vision, 2019: pp. 2630–2640.

[28] G. Huang, B. Pang, Z. Zhu, C. Rivera, R. Soricut, Multimodal Pretraining for Dense Video Captioning, in: K.-F. Wong, K. Knight, H. Wu (Eds.), Proceedings of the 1st Conference of the Asia-Pacific Chapter of the Association for Computational Linguistics and the 10th International Joint Conference on Natural Language Processing, Association for Computational Linguistics, Suzhou, China, 2020: pp. 470–490. https://doi.org/10.18653/v1/2020.aacl-main.48.

[29] K. Guetari, Y. Tevissen, F. Petitpont, Multimodal Chaptering for Long-Form TV Newscast Video, (2024). https://arxiv.org/abs/2406.17590.

Appendix A

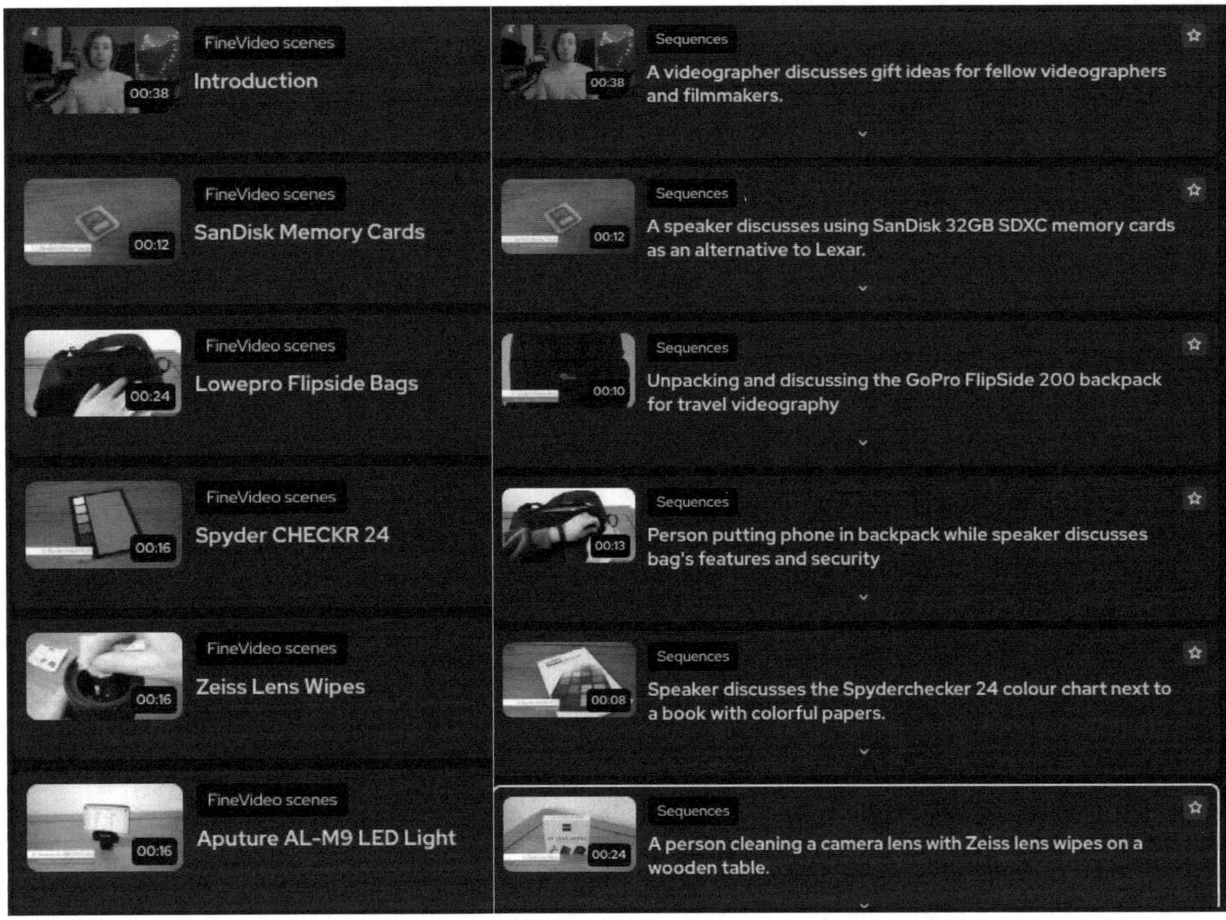

EXAMPLES OF CHAPTERING RESULTS AND GENERATED CHAPTERS METADATA. ON THE LEFT, FINEVIDEO CHAPTERS FOR COMPARISON, AND ON THE RIGHT, OUR APPROACH RESULTS

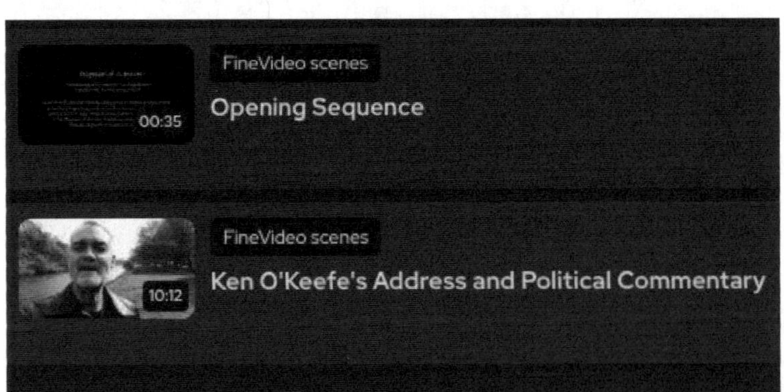

EXAMPLE OF AN ANNOTATION FROM A FINEVIDEO WITH ONLY 2 CHAPTERS:

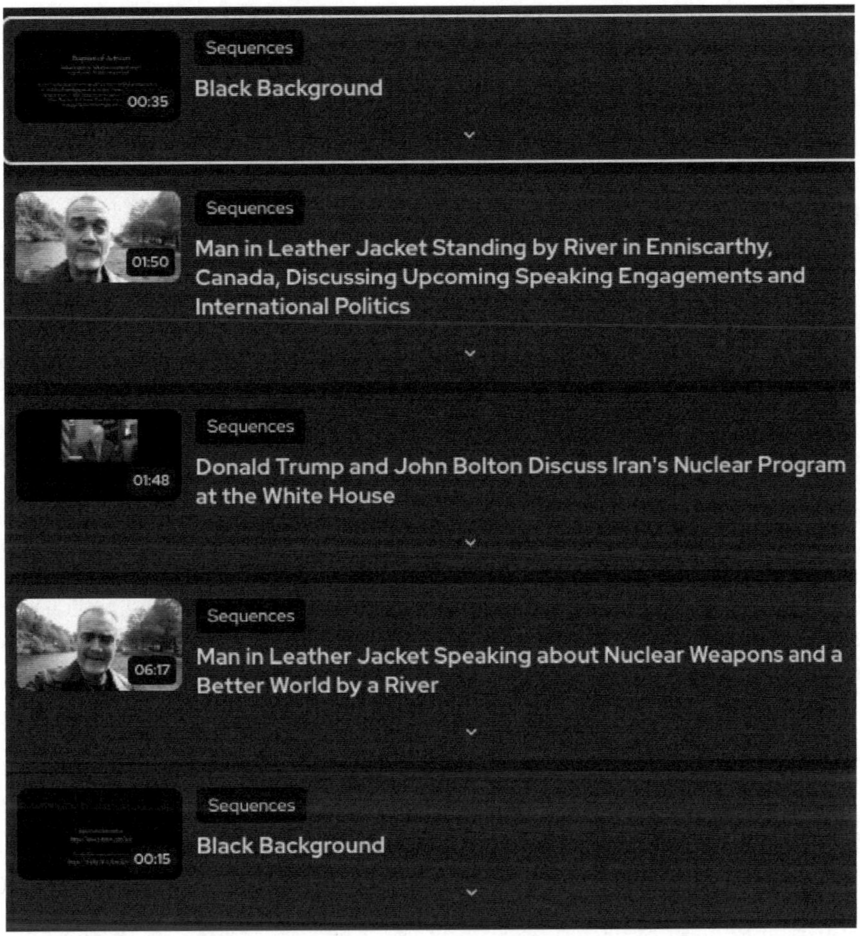

EXAMPLE OF CORRESPONDING CHAPTERS GENERATED BY OUR PIPELINE

Two-Pass Encoding for Live Video Streaming[1]

Mohammad Ghasempour, Hadi Amirpour, and Christian Timmerer
Christian Doppler Laboratory ATHENA, Alpen-Adria-Universität
Klagenfurt, Austria

Abstract – Live streaming has become increasingly important in our daily lives due to the growing demand for real-time content consumption. Traditional live video streaming typically relies on single-pass encoding due to its low latency. However, it lacks video content analysis, often resulting in inefficient compression and quality fluctuations during playback. *Constant Rate Factor* (CRF) encoding, a type of single-pass method, offers more consistent quality but suffers from unpredictable output bitrate, complicating bandwidth management. In contrast, multi-pass encoding improves compression efficiency through multiple passes. However, its added latency makes it unsuitable for live streaming. In this paper, we propose *OTPS*, an online two-pass encoding scheme that overcomes these limitations by employing fast feature extraction on a downscaled video representation and a gradient-boosting regression model to predict the optimal CRF for encoding. This approach provides consistent quality and efficient encoding while avoiding the latency introduced by traditional multi-pass techniques. Experimental results show that *OTPS* offers 3.7% higher compression efficiency than single-pass encoding and achieves up to 28.1% faster encoding than multi-pass modes. Compared to single-pass encoding, encoded videos using *OTPS* exhibit 5% less deviation from the target bitrate while delivering notably more consistent quality.

Introduction

In recent years, the demand for high-quality live streaming has increased due to the popularity of online platforms that offer real-time content, such as gaming, sports, and live events. To meet the quality expectations of the audiences while minimizing bandwidth, processing costs, and latency, efficient encoding strategies are essential. In video streaming or specifically in *HTTP Adaptive Streaming* (HAS) [1], a video is encoded into a set of bitrate and resolution pairs, referred to as bitrate ladder. This allows viewers to receive the most suitable quality representation based on their device capabilities and current network conditions. However, for encoders, the primary challenge lies in achieving the target bitrate for each video while consistently maintaining high visual quality, a task complicated by the need to adapt to varying content and network dynamics.

The rate controller of the video encoder is responsible for dynamically adjusting the encoding parameters to manage the trade-off between bitrate and visual quality. *Constant Bitrate* (CBR) encoding is a widely used approach in live streaming, where maintaining a fixed bitrate throughout the video is crucial to ensure predictable and efficient bandwidth usage. CBR encoding continuously adjusts the encoding parameters to adhere to a specified bitrate, regardless of the complexity of individual frames. This makes it advantageous for live streaming, as it simplifies network management,

[1] The financial support of the Austrian Federal Ministry for Digital and Economic Affairs, the National Foundation for Research, Technology and Development, and the Christian Doppler Research Association, is gratefully acknowledged. Christian Doppler Laboratory ATHENA: https://athena.itec.aau.at/

minimizes the risk of buffer underruns, and ensures low latency, which is essential for real-time applications like live sports broadcasts and online game streams. However, since the bitrate remains constant, high-complex frames may suffer from quality degradation due to insufficient bit allocation, while low-complex frames may be over-compressed, leading to inefficient bit usage. This results in a trade-off between achieving consistent video quality and maintaining a steady bitrate, yet CBR remains popular for its predictable nature and suitability for low-latency streaming scenarios.

Constant Rate Factor (CRF) encoding is a quality-based rate control method commonly used in video compression to maintain consistent visual quality across frames. Instead of targeting a specific bitrate, CRF provides a target quality, making it popular for scenarios where quality consistency is more important than precise control over the output bitrate. However, the main drawback of CRF encoding is the unpredictability of the final file size or bitrate, which can pose challenges for applications where bandwidth needs to be carefully managed, such as live streaming. Despite this, CRF is highly effective for offline encoding and scenarios where quality takes precedence over bitrate consistency, as it delivers a more visually pleasing experience compared to traditional single-pass or fixed/constant bitrate methods.

Multi-pass encoding is an advanced method that seeks to combine the advantages of constant bitrate and constant quality encodings by optimizing bitrate allocation to achieve consistent visual quality while adhering to a target bitrate. Unlike single-pass methods, multi-pass encoding processes the video multiple times. In the first pass, the encoder thoroughly analyzes the entire video to collect detailed information about frame complexity and motion characteristics. This data enables the encoder to make informed decisions during subsequent passes, allocating more bits to complex frames that require higher quality and fewer bits to simpler frames. By doing so, multi-pass encoding efficiently balances the trade-off between bitrate and quality, providing better compression efficiency and more consistent visual quality than single-pass CBR method. However, the primary drawback of multi-pass encoding is the increased latency introduced by the additional encoding passes. This added processing time makes it less suitable for live streaming applications where low latency is crucial, but it is highly effective for offline encoding scenarios where achieving optimal quality and bitrate efficiency is more important than encoding speed.

Numerous studies have focused on optimizing video encoding, particularly for *Video on Demand* (VOD) applications, frequently employing multi-pass encoding techniques. For instance, Que et al. [2] introduced a two-pass encoding approach where the first pass employs CBR encoding to collect key encoding statistics from the input video. These statistics are then used to determine the optimal QP for the second pass. Wang et al. [3] proposed a two-pass control algorithm that distributes the bit budget across three different levels: *Group of Pictures* (GOP), frame, and block. At the frame level, the sum of absolute transformed differences is used to enable adaptive QP selection based on the allocated coding bits. Malladi et al. [4] developed a model based on the *Rate-Distortion* (RD) characteristics of each frame, using data from the first pass to identify the best QP for second-pass encoding. Cao et al. [5] introduced a two-pass rate control scheme designed to reduce video quality fluctuations by minimizing distortion variance between GOPs. In first-pass encoding, a fixed-QP configuration is used, and a set of candidate QPs is specified. For each candidate, the corresponding rate and distortion are computed, which enables the selection of the optimal quantizer for the second pass. However, none of these schemes are suitable for live streaming.

In the past decade, machine learning techniques have made video streaming more efficient and have been successfully integrated into video streaming applications. In this study, we aim to take advantage of a lightweight machine learning technique to enable CRF encoding for live video streaming and to achieve the performance of multi-pass in a time close to single-pass encoding. To achieve this, fast feature extraction methods are used to extract information from the video content that can be used to predict the optimal CRF value based on a predefined target bitrate. In this way, the output video is encoded efficiently, minimizing quality fluctuations while closely adhering to the target bitrate.

Online Two-Pass Encoding Scheme

The proposed online two-pass encoding scheme aims to achieve efficient real-time encoding for live video streaming by predicting an optimized CRF for a given target bitrate. This section details the methodology used to predict the optimized CRF.

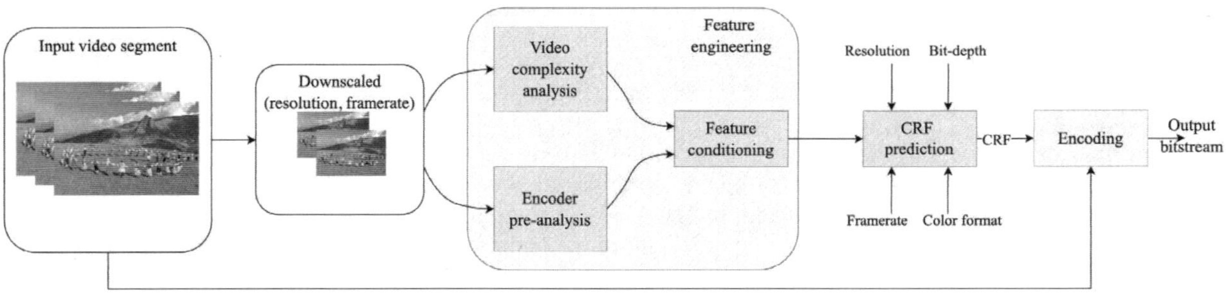

FIGURE 1. THE ARCHITECTURE OF *OTPS*

OTPS Architecture

The architecture of *OTPS* is shown in Figure 1. The process begins with extracting a set of features from a downscaled version of the input video segment. The reason to utilize downscaled video representation for feature extraction is to minimize the computational complexity of the process. Using these features, along with the original video characteristics such as video resolution, framerate, bit-depth, and color format, *OTPS* predicts an optimized CRF to guide the encoding process. The following is the explanation of each block in the *OTPS* workflow.

Feature engineering: For live streaming applications, selecting video segment features that can be extracted with low computational overhead is essential. Two feature extraction approaches are employed to capture video complexity and other relevant information for precise CRF prediction. To extract video complexity, the *Enhanced Video Complexity Analyzer* (EVCA) [6] is used, providing various complexity metrics, such as spatial and temporal complexity metrics, with minimal computational load. To further improve prediction accuracy, a pre-analysis step was added to extract compressed domain features. This step uses the libx264 ultrafast preset to encode the spatially and temporally downscaled version of the video, meeting real-time constraints, please refer to Appendix A1.

For refining the feature set, a feature conditioning block selects and normalizes the most relevant features using three feature selection algorithms: correlation-based [7], variance threshold-based, and importance-based. The correlation-based approach removes features with high inter-correlation to reduce redundancy, while the variance threshold-based eliminates features with minimal variance, assuming they contribute little to prediction. Finally, the importance-based method uses the *Least Absolute Shrinkage and Selection Operator* (Lasso) [8], a lightweight linear model, to identify the most influential features for output prediction. This selection process is performed once during training to define the final input feature set, which is listed in Table 1. The values of these features are normalized using a standard scaler to have a mean $\mu = 0$ and a standard deviation $\sigma = 1$.

CRF Prediction: The optimal CRF value that achieves the target bitrate is influenced by multiple factors beyond just the content of the video. These include the video's original resolution, framerate, bit-depth, and color format. Consequently, alongside video content features, these parameters are included as model inputs. To ensure precise prediction, a dedicated model is trained for each target bitrate. Since CRF encoding allows for floating-point values, the prediction process is structured as a regression problem to minimize the output error. To this end, a gradient-boosting regression model is utilized. This ensemble technique is known for its high accuracy and the ability to capture complex data patterns. The predicted CRF value is then applied to encode videos, enabling efficient, constant-quality encoding that meets the target bitrate requirements.

Feature	Explanation	Feature	Explanation
qpP	Average QP values of P-frames	i8d	Percentage of 8×8 blocks using DC intra prediction
sizeP	Size of P-frames in Bytes	sizeI	Size of I-frames in Bytes
mbPI16	Percentage of intra 16×16 macroblocks in P-frames	yI	Percentage of coded blocks for luma intra blocks
mbPP16	Percentage of inter 16×16 macroblocks in P-frames	SI	Average spatial information
i16v	Percentage of 16×16 blocks using vertical intra prediction	TI	Average temporal information
i16d	Percentage of 16×16 blocks using DC intra prediction	TC	Average temporal complexity (EVCA method)
uvDCP	Percentage of coded blocks for DC chroma inter blocks	E	Spatial complexity (VCA method); Aggregated using average, median, last, and maximum functions
mbskip	Number of skipped macroblocks	h	Temporal complexity (VCA method); Aggregated using average, median, last, and maximum functions
i8p	Percentage of 8×8 blocks using planar intra prediction	l	Brightness (VCA method); Aggregated using average, minimum, maximum, first, and last functions

TABLE 1. THE LIST OF SELECTED FEATURES WITH THEIR EXPLANATION.

Training Process

To train the gradient boosting model, the first step is to encode videos in the training dataset at various CRF values within a specified range from C_{min} to C_{max}. This range varies by codec; for instance, with *Advanced Video Coding* (AVC) [9], the CRF values span from 0 to 51. After encoding, the "desired CRF," is calculated, which is the CRF value that would produce an output video bitrate matching the target bitrate. Since the target bitrate often does not precisely match the bitrates of the encoded outputs, a linear interpolation is used to estimate the desired CRF. Linear interpolation is effective for cases where the CRF difference between two encodings is small, yielding a close approximation of the desired CRF. Specifically, to determine the desired CRF, two records in the dataset that target bitrate falls in between them should be identified. The bitrate and CRF of these records are denoted as B_l, B_h, C_l, and C_h. B_l and C_l are for the lower bitrate index, B_h and C_h are for the higher bitrate index. The desired CRF is then calculated as in (1), (2), and (3):

$$S = \frac{C_h - C_l}{B_h - B_l} \quad (1)$$

$$I = C_l - (S \times B_l) \quad (2)$$

$$C_{desired} = (S \times B_{target}) + I \quad (3)$$

where S and l represent the slope and intercept, respectively, simplifying the formula, and B_{target} is the target bitrate.

Experimental Setup

To assess the performance of *OTPS*, we selected videos from the Inter4K dataset [10], originally in 3840×2160 resolution at 60 fps. It should be noted that the videos contain scene-cuts. The evaluation spans four key areas: compression efficiency, encoding time, bitrate difference, and quality consistency. For compression efficiency, we used the *Bjøntegaard Delta Rate* (BD-Rate) metric [11], which quantifies bitrate savings at a consistent quality level. Results were validated with *Video Multi-method Assessment Fusion* (VMAF) [12] quality metric. Furthermore, *OTPS*'s time consumption was analyzed in comparison to existing encoding techniques as in (4):

$$T_{saving} = \frac{T_{ref} - T_{OTPS}}{T_{ref}} \times 100 \tag{4}$$

where T_{ref} is the time consumed by the existing single-pass and multi-pass encoding modes.

The bitrate difference is also calculated using the target bitrate as its reference for each video sequence as in (5):

$$B_{deviation} = \frac{|B_{target} - B_{OTPS}|}{B_{target}} \times 100 \tag{5}$$

where B_{target} and B_{OTPS} are the target bitrate and the output bitrate of encoded video, respectively.

Finally, the quality deviation is defined as the difference between the maximum and minimum provided quality for each video sequence as in (6):

$$Q_{deviation} = \frac{max(f_1, f_2, \ldots, f_n) - min(f_1, f_2, \ldots, f_n)}{max(f_1, f_2, \ldots, f_n)} \times 100 \tag{6}$$

where n is the number of frames and f_n specifies the VMAF quality of the n-th frame.

Dataset

To train the model, a diverse dataset of videos encoded with a range of CRF values is required. For this purpose, all videos from the Inter4K dataset are encoded at CRF values ranging from 16 to 51, capturing a broad spectrum of bitrate and quality variations. Additionally, the above-mentioned features are extracted from each video to provide comprehensive data points. Figure 2 shows the spatial and temporal complexity of the videos in this dataset. This extensive dataset, which has 35000 records, varied content, and a CRF range, is well-suited for tasks such as rate and quality control and cost optimization [13].

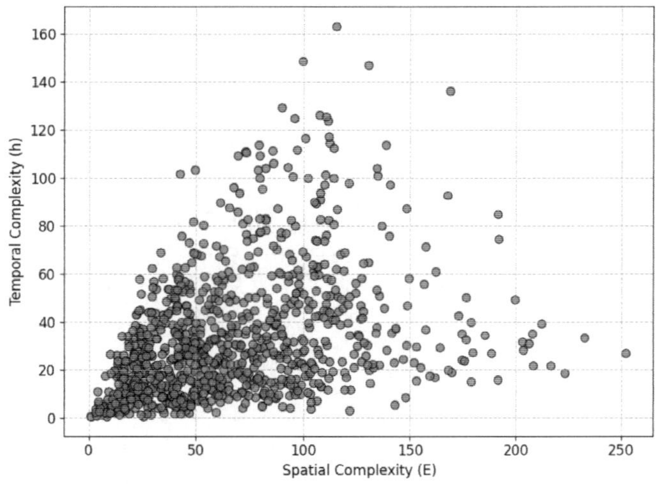

FIGURE 2. DISTRIBUTION OF SPATIAL (E) AND TEMPORAL (H) COMPLEXITIES USING EVCA FOR THE VIDEOS USED IN THIS STUDY.

Encoder Configuration

For the evaluation, we selected the cloud-based Bitmovin encoder because it provides three encoding modes: single-pass, two-pass, and three-pass. This capability allows for a comprehensive comparison with *OTPS*, ensuring a thorough evaluation of the results. These encoding modes operate by taking the target bitrate as input, while *OTPS* employs CRF encoding. In all cases, live encoding configurations are applied as shown in Table 2. The evaluation is conducted at four target bitrates: 2 Mbps, 5 Mbps, 8 Mbps, and 12 Mbps.

Parameter	Value
adaptiveQuantizationMode	VARIANCE
adaptiveQuantizationStrength	1
adaptiveSpatialTransform	TRUE
bAdaptiveStrategy	FAST
bPyramid	NORMAL
bframes	3
cabac	TRUE
encodingMode	SINGLE_PASS
fastSkipDetectionPFrames	TRUE
macroblockTreeRatecontrol	TRUE
mixedReferences	FALSE
motionEstimationMethod	HEX
mvPredictionMode	SPATIAL
mvSearchRangeMax	16
nalHrd	NONE
partitions	"I4X4,I8X8,P8X8,B8X8"
profile	HIGH
rcLookahead	20
refFrames	2
sceneCutThreshold	0
subMe	QPEL4
trellis	ENABLED_FINAL_MB

weightedPredictionBFrames	TRUE
weightedPredictionPFrames	SIMPLE

TABLE 2. LIVE ENCODING CONFIGURATION.

Experimental Results

In this section, we first evaluate the prediction accuracy of the gradient boosting regression model used in *OTPS* by applying three different metrics: *Mean Absolute Error* (MAE), *Mean Squared Error* (MSE), and the R^2 score. Next, we examine the quality deviation of each encoding mode compared to the consistency achieved by *OTPS*. Finally, we compare the compression efficiency and time savings of the proposed *OTPS* against the three encoding modes discussed.

Prediction Performance

To evaluate the gradient boosting model's performance, the video sequences in the dataset are divided into training and testing sets. Figure 3 shows the distribution of the training and testing video sequences based on spatial and temporal complexity metrics. A total of 80% of the video sequences are used for training, while the remaining 20% are used for testing to ensure that the test video sequence is not seen in the training phase. Four separate models are trained, each tailored to a specific target bitrate.

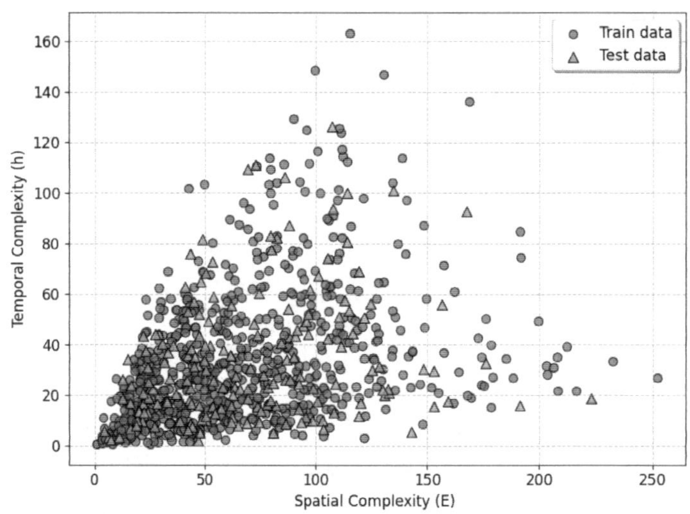

FIGURE 3. THE DISTRIBUTION OF TRAINING AND TESTING VIDEO SEQUENCES.

To assess the impact of each input feature on CRF prediction, Figure 4 displays the correlation values of individual features with the target CRF. Features such as *qpP*, *sizeP*, and *h_avg* show the highest positive correlations, indicating that temporal complexity and inter-frame information significantly impact the CRF output. In contrast, the number of skipped macroblocks (*mbskip*) and *i16v* show the strongest negative correlations, suggesting that these features inversely influence CRF prediction.

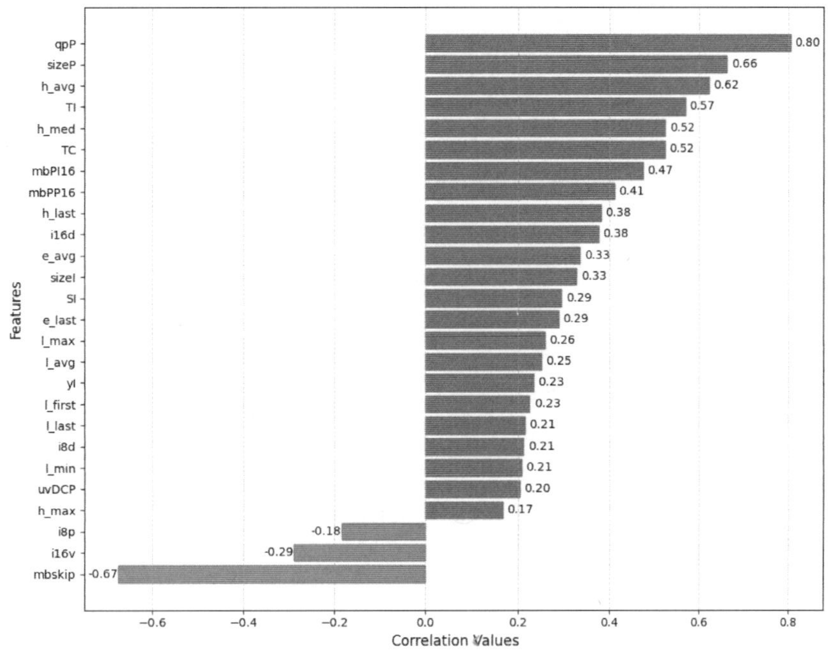

FIGURE 4. THE CORRELATION VALUES OF INPUT FEATURES TO THE TARGET VALUE (CRF).

The prediction performance results for each target bitrate are reported in Table 3. For target bitrates other than 2 Mbps, the MAE remains below or equal to 0.82 for the training set and 1.4 for the test set, with the R^2 score close to 0.8. However, for 2Mbps, the MAE for the test set increases to 3.04. This is due to the limitation of the CRF range up to 51, which restricts the bitrate to values that some test videos cannot achieve at 3840×2160 resolution and 60 fps, resulting in higher prediction errors.

Target Bitrate	Train data			Test data		
	MAE	MSE	R^2 score	MAE	MSE	R^2 score
2 Mbps	2.22	9.57	0.81	3.04	18.71	0.40
5 Mbps	0.82	1.09	0.95	1.40	3.66	0.80
8 Mbps	0.79	1.01	0.94	1.32	3.10	0.81
12 Mbps	0.75	0.92	0.93	1.22	2.65	0.82

TABLE 3. THE ACCURACY METRICS FOR TRAINING AND TESTING DATA FOR DIFFERENT BITRATE VALUES FOR CRF PREDICTION.

To illustrate the prediction error more clearly, Figure 5 presents a scatter plot of actual versus predicted CRF values for target bitrates of 12 Mbps and 2 Mbps. The dashed line represents a perfect prediction; deviations from this line indicate prediction errors. For 12 Mbps, most points cluster close to the perfect prediction line, with prediction errors generally below 1 CRF value. In contrast, for 2 Mbps, the model struggles to track increases in CRF values beyond 45 and shows similar errors for CRF values below 30, indicating limitations in predicting extreme values in either range.

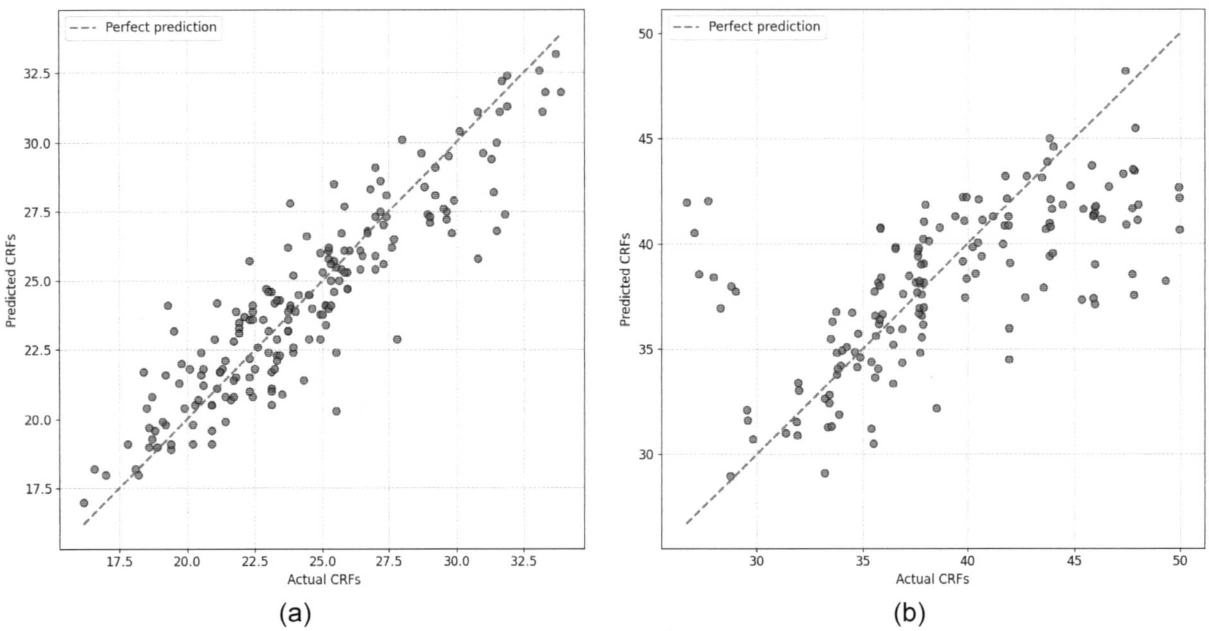

FIGURE 5. PREDICTION PERFORMANCE OF THE TRAINED MODEL FOR (A) 12 MBPS AND (B) 2 MBPS.

Quality Deviation

A key limitation of single-pass encoding in live video streaming is its inability to adjust encoding parameters effectively based on frame complexity, which results in noticeable quality fluctuations. This section evaluates quality deviation across three encoding modes, emphasizing the benefits of using CRF-based encoding in *OTPS*. In Figure 6, the per-frame quality of video sequence #453 is shown, comparing single-pass, two-pass, three-pass, and *OTPS* CRF encoding. The single-pass encoding, shown in blue, initially exhibits a sharp quality drop of around 30 VMAF points as it adjusts encoding parameters on the fly to compensate. In contrast, multi-pass encoding methods analyze the video content during the first pass, enabling them to provide more stable quality across frames. *OTPS*'s use of CRF encoding further enhances stability, maintaining the most consistent quality among all modes. Quantitatively, the quality deviation ($Q_{deviation}$) for single-, two-, three-pass, and *OTPS* are 33.7%, 11.2%, 10.3%, and 4.9%, respectively. This highlights the superior consistency and suitability of *OTPS* for live streaming applications.

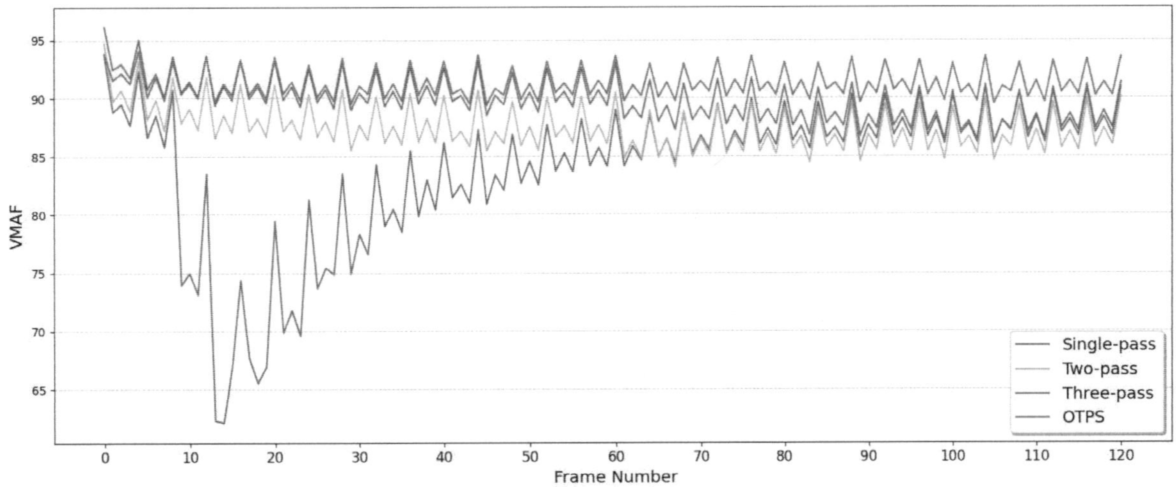

FIGURE 6. PER FRAME QUALITY OF ENCODED VIDEO WITH DIFFERENT ENCODING MODES FOR VIDEO #453.

OTPS Performance

To demonstrate the impact of prediction error on encoding results, the test videos were encoded using the predicted CRF values for all four target bitrates. Table 4 reports the compression efficiency, measured by BD-Rate, and time savings. Compared to single-pass encoding, *OTPS* achieves a 3.7% improvement in compression efficiency with nearly identical encoding time. When compared to two-pass and three-pass encoding modes, *OTPS* reduces encoding time by 18.8% and 28.1%, respectively, while maintaining comparable compression efficiency.

Encoding Mode	BD-Rate (%)	T_{saving} (%)
Single-pass	-3.70	1.84
Two-pass	-0.92	18.80
Three-pass	-0.54	28.14

TABLE 4. THE PERFORMANCE OF *OTPS* COMPARED TO SINGLE- AND MULTI-PASS ENCODING.

To have a more detailed analysis, Figure 7 presents the compression efficiency of *OTPS* compared to single-pass encoding across all test video sequences. In this scatter plot, red points indicate videos where *OTPS* achieves better compression efficiency (negative BD-Rate values), while blue points denote videos where single-pass encoding performs slightly better. The size of each point reflects the magnitude of the efficiency difference: larger red points represent significantly improved compression efficiency achieved by *OTPS*. This visualization indicates that *OTPS* performs particularly well even for complex videos with limited data available in the training set. Additionally, most blue points are quite small, suggesting that *OTPS* closely matches single-pass mode performance for those videos.

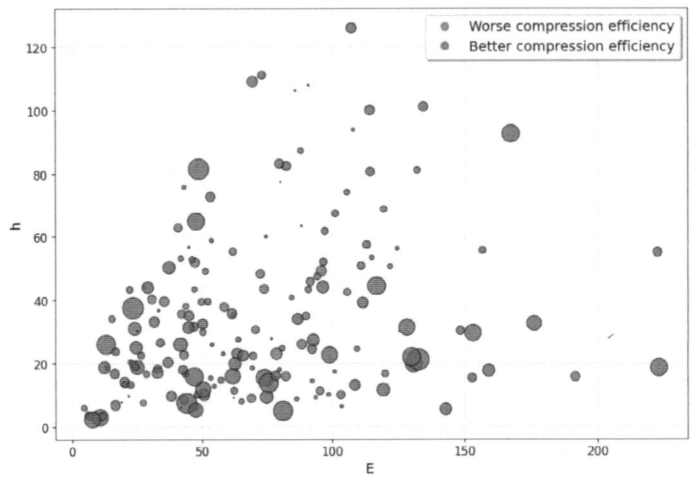

FIGURE 7. THE COMPRESSION EFFICIENCY OF *OTPS* COMPARED TO SINGLE-PASS ENCODING.

Furthermore, four videos with varying levels of spatial and temporal complexity were selected to illustrate RD performance, as shown in Figure 8. In this figure, vertical dashed lines indicate the target bitrates. Notably, *OTPS* achieves RD-curves that are very similar to those of three-pass encoding, demonstrating comparable quality across the bitrate spectrum. By accurately predicting CRF values to meet target bitrates, *OTPS* achieves higher video quality than single-pass and two-pass modes. Only in video #997 does three-pass encoding achieve slightly closer alignment with the target bitrate, though this comes with increased encoding time.

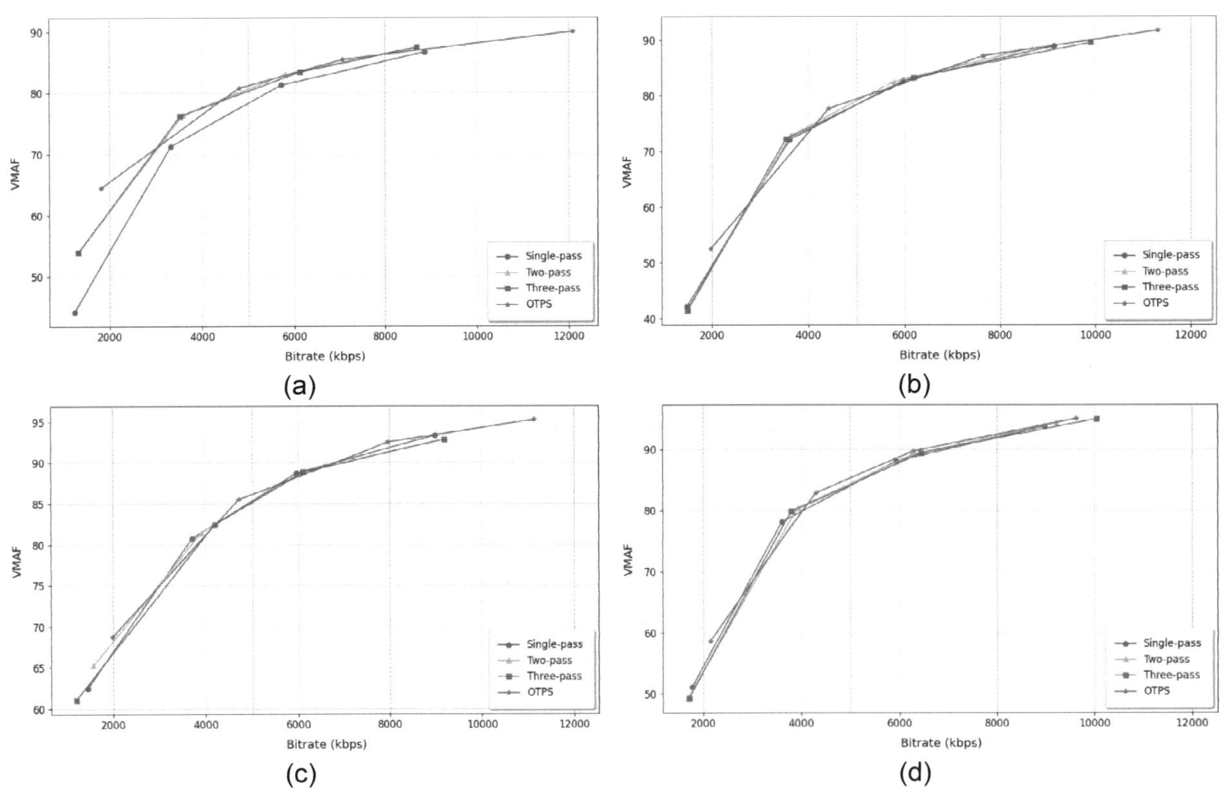

FIGURE 8. RD-CURVES FOR VIDEOS (A) #193, (B) #551, (C) #901, AND (D) #997.

Achieving a bitrate close to the target is crucial. If the output bitrate is below the target, video quality is lower; if it significantly exceeds the target, buffering issues may arise. To assess how each encoding mode performs in this regard, we calculate the bitrate deviation ($B_{deviation}$) for each mode across all four target bitrates, as shown in Table 5. The results demonstrate that *OTPS* consistently achieves a bitrate closer to the target compared to the single-pass, two-pass, and three-pass modes across all targets. On average, *OTPS* produces approximately 5% less deviation from the target bitrate, underscoring its effectiveness in balancing quality and streaming stability.

Target Bitrate	$B_{deviation}$ (%)			
	Single-pass	Two-pass	Three-pass	*OTPS*
2 Mbps	22.86	21.80	22.59	20.43
5 Mbps	23.14	21.98	23.61	16.16
8 Mbps	22.01	22.37	21.59	16.75
12 Mbps	21.89	22.51	21.28	15.72
Average	22.47	22.16	22.26	17.26

TABLE 5. THE PERCENTAGE OF DEVIATION FROM THE TARGET

Conclusions

In this paper, we proposed *OTPS*, an online two-pass encoding scheme, designed specifically for live video streaming. Traditionally, single-pass encoding is used for live-streaming applications. Live streaming relies on single-pass encoding, which, while fast, is less efficient due to its lack of video content analysis before encoding. This could also lead to quality fluctuations during playback. Multi-pass encoding, though more efficient, introduces latency that is impractical for live applications. *OTPS* addresses these limitations by leveraging efficient feature extraction techniques on a downscaled version of the video. A well-selected set of features, combined with a gradient boosting regression model, enables *OTPS* to predict the optimal CRF that aligns closely with the target bitrate in the output, providing high encoding efficiency and consistent quality. To improve prediction accuracy, a separate model is trained for each target bitrate. Given that only a limited number of bitrates are typically used in streaming, it is feasible to manage multiple lightweight models. *OTPS*'s performance is evaluated across four areas: compression efficiency, encoding time, bitrate accuracy, and quality consistency. Experimental results demonstrate that *OTPS* achieves 3.7% greater compression efficiency than single-pass encoding with comparable time consumption, thus adding no significant latency to live streaming workflows. Furthermore, *OTPS* offers time savings of 18.8% and 28.1% compared to two-pass and three-pass encoding modes, respectively, while providing similar compression efficiency. In terms of output bitrate accuracy to the target bitrate, *OTPS* maintains a deviation of around 5% from the target bitrate, outperforming other encoding modes tested. Quality consistency is also improved, with *OTPS* showing only a 4.9% quality deviation, significantly lower than the 33.7% observed with single-pass encoding. These results position *OTPS* as a fast, efficient, and suitable solution for live video streaming applications.

References

[1] Sodagar, I., "The MPEG-DASH Standard for Multimedia Streaming Over the Internet," IEEE Multimedia, vol. 18, no. 4, pp. 62–67, Apr. 2011.

[2] Que, C., Chen, G., and Liu, J., "An Efficient Two-Pass VBR Encoding Algorithm for H.264," in 2006 International Conference on Communications, Circuits and Systems, vol. 1, 2006, pp. 118–122.

[3] Wang, S., Rehman, A., Zeng, K., Wang, J., and Wang, Z., "SSIM-Motivated Two-Pass VBR Coding for HEVC," IEEE Transactions on Circuits and Systems for Video Technology, vol. 27, no. 10, pp. 2189–2203, 2017.

[4] Kumar, M. V. P., Ravi, K., and Mahapatra, S., "A Novel Two Pass Rate Control Scheme for Variable Bit Rate Video Streaming," in 2015 IEEE International Symposium on Multimedia (ISM), 2015, pp. 140–143.

[5] Cao, G., Pan, X., Zhou, Y., Li, Y., and Chen, Z., "Two-pass rate control for constant quality in high efficiency video coding," in 2018 IEEE Visual Communications and Image Processing (VCIP), 2018, pp. 1–4.

[6] Amirpour, H., Ghasempour, M., Qu, L., Hamidouche, W., and Timmerer, C., "EVCA: Enhanced Video Complexity Analyzer," in Proceedings of the 15th ACM Multimedia Systems Conference, ser. MMSys '24. New York, NY, USA: Association for Computing Machinery, 2024, p. 285–291.

[7] Hall, M., "Correlation-Based Feature Selection for Machine Learning," Department of Computer Science, vol. 19, 06 2000.

[8] Tibshirani, R., (1996). "Regression Shrinkage and Selection via the Lasso," *Journal of the Royal Statistical Society. Series B (Methodological)*, *58*(1), 267–288.

[9] Wiegand, T., Sullivan, G., Bjontegaard, G., and Luthra, A., "Overview of the H.264/AVC Video Coding Standard," IEEE Transactions on Circuits and Systems for Video Technology, vol. 13, no. 7, pp. 560–576, 2003.

[10] Stergiou, A., and Poppe R., "AdaPool: Exponential Adaptive Pooling for Information-Retaining Downsampling," IEEE Transactions on Image Processing, vol. 32, pp. 251–266, 2023.

[11] Bjontegaard, G., "Calculation of average PSNR differences between RD-curves," ITU SG16 Doc. VCEG-M33, 2001.

[12] Li, Z., Swanson, K., Bampis, C., Krasula, L., and Aaron, A., "Toward a Better Quality Metric for the Video Community," Dec. 2020.

[13] Menon, V. V., Amirpour, H., Feldmann, C., Ilangovan, A., Smole, M., Ghanbari, M., Timmerer, C., "Live-PSTR: Live Per-title Encoding for Ultra HD Adaptive Streaming," in Proc. 2022 NAB Broadcast Engineering and Information Technology Conference, Las Vegas, USA, 2022.

Appendix A1: Command-line Options

Feature extraction using X264

- ffmpeg -hide_banner -i $input.mp4 -vf "scale=640x360,select=not(mod(n\,6))" -preset ultrafast -c:v libx264 -crf 32 -vsync 0 -f null –

Bitrate calculation

- ffprobe -v info -select_streams v:0 -show_entries stream=bit_rate -of default=noprint_wrappers=1:nokey=1 $output.mp4

Quality assessment

- vmaf -r $reference.yuv -d $distorted.yuv -w $w -h $h -p $p -b $b -o quality.json --json --feature psnr -m path=$model_path

Verifying Video Signals Using Computer Vision and Machine Learning Techniques

Shekhar Madnani, Raman Kumar Gupta, Siddharth Gupta, Saurabh Jain
Interra Systems, Inc.
Cupertino, California, United States
info@interrasystems.com

Abstract – High-quality video streams pass through various processes inside media workflows, including pre-processing, transcoding, editing, post-processing, etc. The media transformation in these processes can alter the properties of the intermediate video, potentially disrupting subsequent processes or degrading the final output video quality experienced by viewers. Reliable content delivery necessitates verification of video data to ensure an acceptable quality of experience (QoE). The verification of video data is not just limited to the measurement of degradation in perceived quality on the viewing screen but also considers validation of video parameters affecting the proper functioning of media devices. For example, the Y, Cb, and Cr values are altered after lossy compression that can result in out-of-gamut RGB data and hence will lead to erroneous functioning of display devices. Similarly, parameters like light levels, black bar widths, color bar types, telecine patterns, photosensitive epilepsy (PSE) levels and patterns, field order, scan types (interlaced or progressive), etc. also need validation before distribution. This paper explores critical video properties and demonstrates how computer vision, image processing, and machine learning techniques can measure and validate these properties and detect defects. Experiments utilizing machine learning (ML) techniques to quantify the quality degradation, due to lossy compression of video data, will also be discussed. A discussion of challenges and future directions to enhance the accuracy of measurement and detection is also included here.

Introduction

The production and administration of media material have undergone a significant paradigm shift in recent years. Many diverse requirements should be met by video/audio content, such as smooth playback and transmission, high-quality standards, compatibility with different types of viewing and display devices, accessibility for editing stations, and integration with media asset management systems, among other requirements. To ensure that the content seamlessly fits into the media landscape, an automated tool that verifies its compliance with these different requirements is essential.

To execute the required measures, the automated tool should be able to examine the audio or video signals, analyze the content for flaws, and indicate mistakes without the need for human interaction. Camera-captured or tape-produced digital video and audio content are converted to digital files using a variety of digital procedures, including compression systems and editing stations. There can be a loss of data in the video content during these procedures, which could cause the video to deviate from acceptable levels, display less clearly, lose details, or behave differently than planned when replayed in front of the user, among other issues.

This paper is excerpted from the Proceedings of the 2025 NAB Broadcast Engineering and Information Technology (BEIT) Conference, © 2025, National Association of Broadcasters, 1 M Street SE, Washington, DC 20003 USA.

This paper will focus solely on the characteristics of the video. Additionally, the paper will explore more than just assessing video quality. It will also examine essential video attributes and settings that are crucial for the smooth operation of media processing workflows.

Figure 1 illustrates one such media (video) processing workflow. These workflows involve activities like capturing video streams directly from high-quality cameras or converting them from analog or digital tapes. The video stream that has been captured is then sent to the next stage of post-processing, which involves adjustments to color or brightness as part of planned editing tasks.

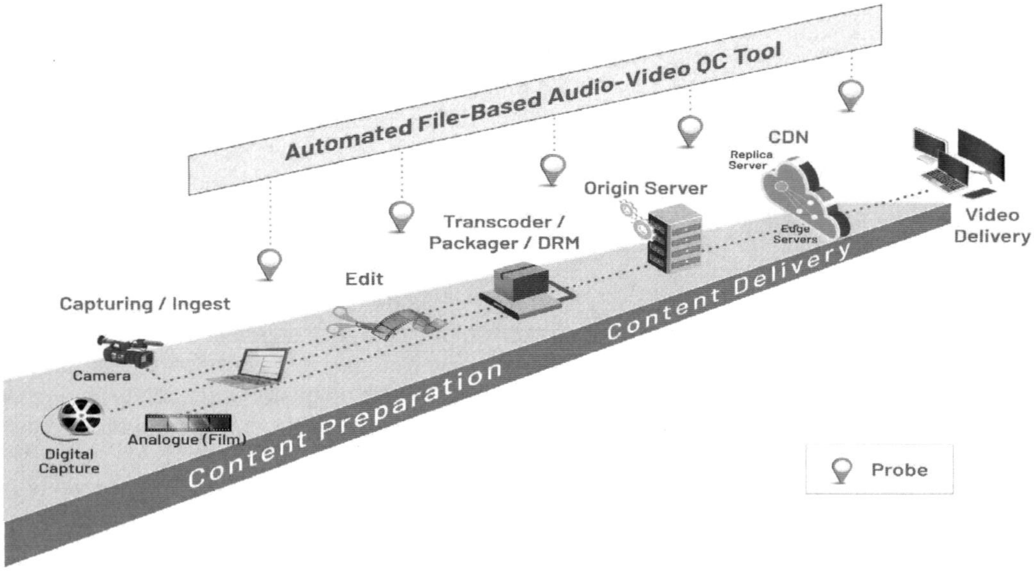

FIGURE 1: MEDIA PROCESSING WORKFLOW [1].

The next necessary stage is transcoding, which modifies factors such as frame rate, resolution, encoding format, and storage or transmission formats, among others. After transcoding, the modified streams can undergo further processing.

These intermediary steps can cause the video parameters and content to deviate from the anticipated values and behaviors. Therefore, the paper will address the tools, technologies, and methods needed to assess and analyze the discrepancies in video parameters and their final representation as video quality viewed by the audience. This study will not be confined solely to video quality assessment; it will also examine various metrics related to video parameters essential for seamless video transmission, storage, retrieval, playback, editing, and management.

Implementation of Algorithms

In general, video quality analysis can be divided into three main categories: signal measurements, adherence to legal requirements and guidelines, and perceptual quality. For measurements, every pixel value is examined to obtain video metrics. For instance, the pixel values are analyzed to determine the widths of black bars, types of color bars, high dynamic range (HDR) optical light levels, and composite signals, and to log YCbCr and RGB range values.

To meet legal requirements and guidelines, higher-level operations such as corner detection, edge detection, contour finding, connected component analysis, motion vector estimation, and various frequency analyses (including Fourier transform, discrete cosine transform, Wavelet transform, etc.), as well as denoising, are utilized to measure quantities and validate them according to the legal standards.

For example, to validate the RGB color gamut limit, the decoded video signal in YCbCr is converted to RGB using specified matrix coefficients and then compared against user-defined thresholds.

In the case of photosensitive epilepsy (PSE), numerous measurements are performed as outlined by the guidelines for final validation against conditions specified in PSE standards (ITU-R BT. 1702, Ofcom, NAB-J). When validating perceptual video quality, video artifacts arising from discontinuities in spatial and temporal information are identified. The methods used for detecting these discontinuities vary based on the specific type of video artifact involved. Along with basic edge detection and motion estimation techniques, proprietary and advanced methods are employed to model both generic and specific error behaviors in the video.

Machine learning algorithms are also applied in situations where modelling of spatial and temporal discontinuities is not feasible. Pre-existing external libraries are not utilized for the proprietary steps unique to the errors. In some instances, intricate combinations of computer vision and machine learning algorithms are implemented, resulting in significant demands on memory and processing resources. The goal is to deliver analysis results in real time. A multi-core and distributed computing approach is adopted. Each algorithm is executed across multiple cores or machines. These algorithms are designed to fully leverage CPU capabilities using internally optimized operations and efficient cache utilization.

Computer Vision and Machine Learning Techniques

This part focuses on providing a high-level overview of various computer vision and machine learning methods applicable to video analysis. A video is defined spatially by the differences in pixel values, which are referred to as edges. To identify edges, the 2D image function must be differentiated for each dimension. This can be mathematically expressed as [2, 3],

$$For\ \text{an}\ Image, \mathbf{I}(\mathbf{u}), where\ u = \begin{bmatrix} \text{x} \\ \text{y} \end{bmatrix} \in \mathbf{R}^2$$

$$Gradient\ is\ defined\ as\ \nabla\mathbf{I} = \begin{bmatrix} d\mathbf{I}/dx \\ d\mathbf{I}/dy \end{bmatrix} = \begin{bmatrix} G_x \\ G_y \end{bmatrix} \text{ which is a vector quantity having,} \quad (1)$$

$$\text{Direction, perpendicular to the edge, } is\ defined\ by\ the\ angle, \theta = tan^{-1}\left(\frac{G_y}{G_x}\right) \text{ and} \quad (2)$$

$$\text{Its edge Gradient magnitude is defined as, } |\nabla \boldsymbol{I}| = \sqrt{{G_x}^2 + {G_y}^2} \quad (3)$$

A straightforward approach to edge detection is to apply a mask to the magnitude image $|\nabla\mathbf{I}|$ using a set threshold. This threshold can be determined either statically or dynamically by the algorithm in use. However, methods based on thresholds might not consistently identify the correct edges across various types (such as low contrast or blurred edges cluttered with noise).

To address these challenges, more sophisticated techniques can be employed to identify the diverse forms of edges (including Canny edge detection, frequency-based methods, and multi-resolution analysis). Identifying corners is also essential for extracting features from images at significant points and for comparing features of neighboring regions over time for additional contextual validation. Error validation can also be accomplished using motion vector techniques like block matching, optical flow, normalized cross correlation, machine learning [6], and feature correspondence, among other advanced approaches.

These methods facilitate the measurement of linear motion; however, they struggle to accurately detect motion caused by rotation, zooming, panning, and perspective changes. To effectively identify such motion, advanced techniques must estimate the Affine matrix, which captures translation, rotation, and scaling. For the affine motion, involving the translation of $[t_x \quad t_y]^T$, rotation by an angle θ and scaling of a_x and a_y in the horizontal and vertical directions, respectively, the Affine matrix is represented as,

$$\boldsymbol{A} = \begin{bmatrix} a_x\, cos(\theta) & -a_y\, sin(\theta) & t_x \\ a_x\, sin(\theta) & a_y\, cos(\theta) & t_y \\ 0 & 0 & 1 \end{bmatrix} \tag{4}$$

These parameters are approximated using algorithms like the Scale Invariant Feature Transform (SIFT) concept [5], Fourier Domain transform, Harris-Laplace Transform and its variations [4], and combinations of these techniques. Techniques such as discrete cosine transform (DCT), wavelets, and Fourier transform are effectively employed to analyze the overall behavior of patterns present in a video frame or in any intermediate image.

Video Parameters and Quality Issues

The video illustrates a '2D+t' representation of the '3D+t' environment recorded by the camera. This camera is characterized by its ability to capture a vast number of pixels across both vertical and horizontal dimensions (resolution) as well as to capture multiple frames in a second (frame rate). Another important feature of a camera is its capacity to capture a range of brightness, contrast, and colors. When a scene is first captured by the camera, it utilizes its full potential, but this can be modified by various processing units in the media workflow.

This section will explore the different parameters that influence how the video is presented and the artifacts that may occur if these parameters are not adequately maintained. This section will also discuss another group of artifacts in the video when retrieved as digital files from either analog or digital tapes. These artifacts present as irregular or regular-shaped disruptions resulting from errors during the data capture from faulty tapes.

A crucial aspect of video production is the signal levels, which can be assessed using IRE levels, voltage levels (ranging from 0 to 700 millivolts), and pixel values (16–235 for luminance (Y) and 16–240 for chrominance (Cb, Cr) in 8 bits). The YCbCr data, once decoded, is transformed into red, green, and blue channels (RGB) for display on screens, adhering to specified limits regarding signal voltage (0-700 millivolts) or IRE levels and pixel values (0-255 with a ± 5% tolerance for 8 bits per channel).

Furthermore, the RGB color values must align with the boundaries established by the standard gamut, defined by the color primary-based triangles found in the CIE 1931 "xy" color space. Alongside these standardized parameters, video sequences must comply with regulations that limit certain patterns that could negatively impact those with photosensitive epilepsy, as outlined by the PSE guidelines ITU-R BT. 1702, Ofcom, and NAB-J. These regulations restrict the creation of spatial and temporal patterns in a video sequence that may induce visual reactions potentially leading to severe health issues for individuals with photosensitive epilepsy. This rule enforces constraints on generating spatial and temporal patterns within a video sequence that, if included, could provoke visual experiences that might result in significant health risks for those suffering from photosensitive epilepsy.

Other important metrics include analyzing black bars, calculating the widths of these black bars, checking color bars and identifying their standardized categories, and noting the presence of black frames and text to provide a comprehensive overview of the video content. The pixel values can reveal information about any potential issues within the camera. For instance, there may be defective pixels in an output video frame immediately after they are captured by the camera. These faulty pixels may appear to be stuck or dead, failing to reflect the changes occurring in the captured scene. Additionally, they do not correspond to the variations found in neighboring pixels. A single pixel or a cluster of pixels in a video sequence might be defective. Such faulty pixels can occur due to errors during data capture from an analog or digital videotape, or because of logical data loss disrupting the decoding process of encoded video, resulting in errors that manifest as irregular patches (blotches/scratches), rectangular blocks, checkerboard patterns, or misaligned blocks. Various types of noise, including film grain, patterned noise, and salt-and-pepper noise, can also impact the video content.

The final perceptual inaccuracies noted in videos result from lossy compression, which includes problems such as blockiness, blurriness, ringing, mosquito noise, banding, flickering, Moiré patterns, and a variety of other recognized artifacts. A different set of issues arises from the poor depiction of temporal continuity. These are perceived as still images or freeze frames, field judder (the reversal of the displayed field order), motion jerks like video shaking or jittering, jerks resulting from telecine, interlacing artifacts, and numerous complex situations. While the aforementioned artifacts and errors do not involve content loss, there are instances where the output video suffers from dropouts due to the loss of raw or encoded data. These dropouts manifest as scratches, blotches, sync losses, blocky dropouts, errors or loss in chroma data, displaced blocks, line repetitions, comet errors, and many other types of errors.

Performing manual inspections does not allow for efficient and precise detection, measurement, and analysis of the significant volume of video data processed at each point in the media processing workflow. There is a requirement for an automated file-based tool for media analysis and quality verification to address this necessity. This automation can be realized through a software tool that utilizes algorithms to analyze video data. These algorithms employ a combination of computer vision, image processing, pattern recognition, and machine learning techniques to measure video parameters and examine spatial and temporal discontinuities. No reference video is assumed in this entire study. The following sections will focus on techniques for measuring and analyzing video data by outlining significant use cases related to video parameters and perceptual artifacts.

Freeze Frames

Freeze frames refer to instances where video remains static without any temporal changes, meaning that it stops showing new frames and continuously displays the same frames. Errors related to freeze frames have a detrimental effect on the video's perceived quality. They disrupt the continuity of motion, leading to a frustrating viewing experience and breaking continuity. These freeze frames often arise from mistakes during video capture, problems within the encoder source buffer, or alterations made to the content. Additionally, they can stem from malfunctions in the encoder itself or within the encoded stream provided to a transcoder. The pause may occur because the expected frame is unavailable to the encoding module, or the decoding module has encountered an error at the start of the video frame being processed. In the camera, the capture process may have stopped, causing the capture buffer to repeatedly send the same data to the encoder by default.

Detecting freeze frames involves analyzing the temporal variations between consecutive frames. While two adjacent frames in a frozen video sequence may appear similar, their pixel values might not be identical. The presence of freeze frames is influenced by various types of noise, such as Gaussian noise, encoding noise, and salt and pepper noise, among others. Therefore, advanced methods are employed to evaluate motion between frames. These techniques encompass gradient analysis, dynamic thresholding, and further motion assessment using the attributes that indicate pixel-level differences between neighboring frames. There is a requirement for thorough validation of a freeze sequence, which considers very slow-motion behavior and differentiates between actual freezes and instances with negligible pixel differences.

Managing encoding noise presents a significant challenge, generating considerable differences between frames despite a lack of visible change. Figure 2 shows such a scenario. This complicates the detection of subtle motion, where larger noise-induced variations can mask small differences. Consequently, accurately identifying freeze frames is challenging, particularly in situations of subtle motion.

Frame 1 *Frame 2* *Absolute Difference*

FIGURE 2: TWO ADJOINING FRAMES ARE SHOWN ALONG WITH THEIR ABSOLUTE DIFFERENCES. FRAME 1 AND FRAME 2 ARE FREEZE FRAMES BUT DUE TO DIFFERENT COMPRESSION SCHEMES (I, P OR B), THE ABSOLUTE DIFFERENCE IS NOT ZERO AT THE EDGE BOUNDARIES.

Blockiness

Blockiness refers to a noticeable distortion characterized by visible rectangular pixel blocks in videos (Figure 3 depicts the video frame with blockiness) that have been compressed using lossy compression methods, typically those based on blocks, at high compression levels. This phenomenon primarily occurs when the video encoder struggles to match the allocated bandwidth, particularly during fast motion sequences, and it further intensifies with highly detailed texture areas. The introduction of artificial vertical and horizontal edges disrupts the perception of natural edges. The impact of blockiness worsens the perceived video quality, especially when intra-encoding is used (I, P, or B encoding), since the motion-compensated blocks also contain the blockiness pattern. Recent encoding techniques, such as H.264/AVC and H.265, incorporate in-loop deblocking filters; however, the final output still retains traces of the original blockiness.

FIGURE 3: VIDEO FRAME SHOWING BLOCKINESS IN A VIDEO FRAME.

To evaluate the degree of video quality degradation caused by blockiness, a suitable algorithm must consider all vertical and horizontal discontinuities, even if they have been softened by low pass filtering from deblocking filters and are not positioned at logical pixel locations (i.e., multiples of 4, 8, or 16, etc.). Just noticeable differences (JND) and luminance masking should be utilized to correlate human perception with the magnitude of discontinuities.

This algorithm disregards discontinuities arising from natural edges and calculates absolute pixel differences in both horizontal and vertical directions at the edges of the blocks. One major difficulty in identifying blockiness lies in distinguishing authentic compression artifacts from intrinsic content features. Certain types of content, like textured surfaces or geometric designs, may naturally exhibit block-like formations, which complicates the ability to differentiate between these and compression-induced blockiness.

Jittering/Sync Loss

In the context of video, jitter refers to two different types of artifacts related to both spatial and temporal aspects. The error in spatial information arises when horizontal and/or vertical signals required to align video lines and frames are not received properly. A loss of the horizontal signal, known as horizontal sync loss, leads to the misalignment of odd or even horizontal lines in the frame, resulting in displaced video lines. Observe the discontinuities at the left and right boundaries of the video frame shown in Figure 4 (A). Conversely, errors in the vertical signal, referred to as vertical sync loss, cause the initial pixel to be misplaced, producing a video frame that contains two adjacent fields or frames, as shown in figure 4(B).

A B

FIGURE 4: (A) HORIZONTAL SYNC LOSS AND (B) VERTICAL SYNC LOSS.

Another form of jitter occurs in the temporal domain, known as temporal jittering. This is characterized by a vertical shaking of the video, typically occurring when the camera moves during recording or due to inconsistent cropping aimed at removing the upper wide-screen signaling (WSS) lines (usually 32 pixels in 512p video). The irregular cropping contributes to a vertical jerk in the displayed information.

Horizontal Sync loss can be identified by looking for horizontal discontinuities and examining these at the vertical boundaries of the frame. Verification of Vertical sync loss can be done by checking the continuity between the top and bottom content of the current frame and the adjacent bottom and top content of the neighboring frames on the left and right.

Temporal jittering is recognized by analyzing the dense Global motion vectors between successive frames. These global motion vectors are statistically evaluated over a larger frame window to detect vertical jolts or temporal jitters. The overall evaluation of spatial jitter greatly depends on the content in question. When the content has low contrast, identifying errors becomes difficult, which could lead to false positives. In scenarios featuring complex motion scenes and low-contrast spatial data, acquiring precise global motion vectors becomes challenging, ultimately affecting the final assessment regarding the presence of temporal jittering.

Defective Pixels

Defective pixels are faulty pixels within video frames resulting from issues with the Charge Coupled Device (CCD) or complementary metal-oxide semiconductor (CMOS) sensors. These anomalies can manifest as dark spots (dead pixels), fixed-color pixels (stuck pixels), or pixels that are brighter than usual (hot pixels). Identifying and rectifying these defective pixels is crucial in various sectors, including camera manufacturing and film and television production.

The detection of defective pixels utilizes both spatial and temporal analysis to spot unusual pixel activity. Pixels that display significant spatial discrepancies are flagged as possible defects. Statistical methods are then applied to confirm these anomalies, differentiating real defects from noise or natural variations in the scene. By examining pixel activity across several frames, transient noise is distinguished from persistent defects, thus improving detection precision. More advanced techniques, such as motion-compensated co-occurrence and neighborhood edge analysis, are implemented further to reduce false positives that may arise from textures or changes in lighting. Figure 5 shows a typical case of the presence of defective pixels.

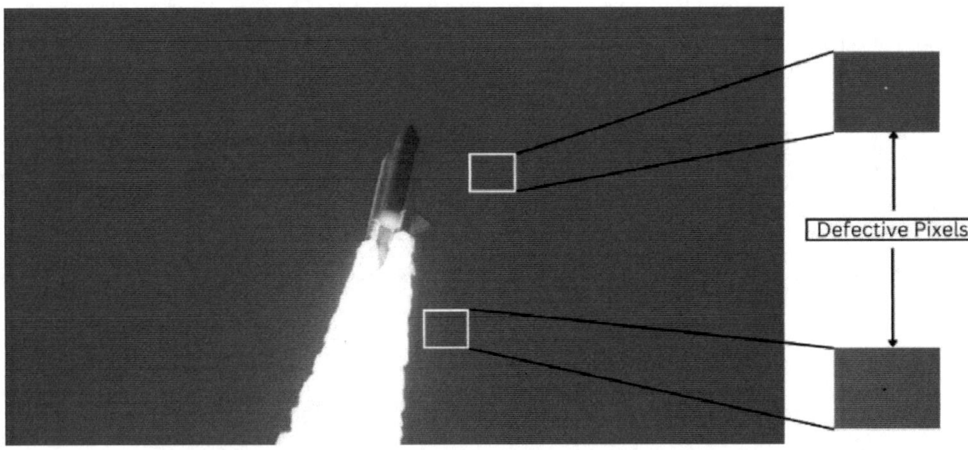

FIGURE 5: TWO LOCATIONS OF DEFECTIVE PIXELS

Existing challenges include significant distortion of pixel characteristics due to heavy compression and defective pixels that resemble their neighboring pixels over long periods. These issues complicate accurate detection while aiming for a low rate of false positives, underscoring the necessity for enhanced methods to distinguish authentic defects.

Color Banding

Color banding is a subtle and often unwanted artifact that can appear in digital images and videos. It is a type of posterization, where the smooth transition of colors is interrupted, resulting in visible bands of color. This phenomenon occurs when the color of each pixel in an image is rounded to the nearest available digital color level, causing a loss of seamless transitions between adjacent colors.

The human eye is sensitive to even slight changes in color levels, especially during sharp transitions between two nearby color areas. This sensitivity is especially noticeable in images or videos featuring gradual gradients, such as sunsets, dawns, or clear blue skies. If a camera is capable of capturing a wide spectrum of colors that nicely represent subtle color transitions but the resulting content is altered through lossy compression, or if its colors are displayed in a lower bit-depth (for example, from 12 bits to 8 bits) or using inferior color standards compared to the original capture (such as switching from ITU-R BT. 2020 to ITU-R BT. 709), banding may occur. Additionally, color banding can result from lossy image or video compression, low bit rates, camera and subject motion, de-interlacing, zooming, and super-resolution. Figure 6 shows a typical case of color banding (in the cloud and ocean regions).

The level of perception of banding is proportional to the area of the affected regions with low gradients within the image. For detection, it is essential to differentiate between areas with low and high spatial gradients. Regions with low gradients are more likely to exhibit color banding. To evaluate the level of perceived color banding, even small gradient changes are examined, focusing on the boundaries where these gradients show slight variations. These transition boundaries assist in identifying potential band contours. The identified contours are then further assessed for their smoothness. The area, gradients, and transitions at the boundaries of the contours are utilized to estimate the perceived level of color banding.

FIGURE 6: VIDEO FRAME AFFECTED BY COLOR BANDING.

Blocky Dropout

Most video encoding algorithms partition the frame into rectangular sections. During intra-frame coding of a video frame, the blocks designated for frequency-based encoding are transformed into the frequency domain using the Discrete Cosine Transform (DCT). The resulting DC and AC coefficients are encoded separately. Additionally, the motion vectors, along with the motion-compensated residual, are also encoded. Therefore, a block is represented by the encoded bits for the DC coefficient, AC coefficients, and motion vectors.

The coefficients for both AC and DC components are encoded independently. If bits representing one or more blocks are received incorrectly or lost, it becomes impossible to decode any or all the DC coefficients, AC coefficients, and motion vectors. Errors in DC encoding will result in blocks that appear quite different from their neighboring blocks. Errors in encoding AC coefficients will cause the emergence of high-frequency checkerboard-patterned blocks. In cases where motion vectors are not decoded accurately, this can lead to misplaced or stuck blocks. This issue can occur independently for both luminance and chrominance channels. Figure 7 shows these blocky errors.

To identify Blocky dropout, precise threshold-independent edge detection is essential. These detected edges facilitate the identification of blocks. A reliable method for estimating motion vectors between consecutive frames is necessary to ascertain whether the identified block is genuinely an error or an actual component of the content. The blocky dropout detection utilizes spatial and temporal analysis to recognize unusual pixel behaviors. Various edge and corner detection techniques are employed to identify blocks. Blocks that exhibit unusual or uniform brightness or have differing texture, motion, or color compared to their adjacent areas across frames are marked as possible defects.

FIGURE 7: VIDEO FRAME AFFECTED WITH BLOCKY DROPOUT DUE TO LOSS IN DCT DC AND AC COEFFICIENTS IN LUMINANCE AND CHROMINANCE CHANNELS.

Current obstacles include significant distortion in edge pixels due to excessive compression and a blurring effect that leads to inadequate edge detection. A lack of effective algorithms for tracking the affine transformation of blocks results in false positives. These issues complicate accurate detection while striving for a low false positive rate, underscoring the need for sophisticated methods to identify edges and motion vectors.

RGB/CIE Color Gamut

When transforming from YCbCr (which experiences loss due to compression) to RGB, the resultant colors must adhere to certain constraints within the RGB spectrum. Each RGB component has a valid range of [0, 255] (for 8 bits per channel). However, some colors produced during this conversion may exceed these limits (resulting in negative RGB values or values above 255), which creates what is referred to as an "out-of-gamut" situation.

Colors that fall outside the gamut must be adjusted or approximated to fit within the permissible range, which can potentially change their appearance. This adjustment can result in significant distortions in color perception, affecting the image's visual quality. An overarching detection algorithm verifies that the converted colors remain within the representable color range of the display system. This is done by evaluating each color component (R, G, B) against the gamut thresholds (0-255 +/- 5%). If any component is found to exceed the maximum or drop below the minimum, it is deemed an out-of-gamut color.

One major hurdle in detection stems from the YCbCr to RGB conversion process, which utilizes floating-point calculations. Due to rounding inaccuracies, some values might slightly surpass the [0, 255] limits, even when they should theoretically fall within the gamut. This complicates accurate detection and correction. Furthermore, user preferences must also be considered, such as identifying out-of-gamut pixels, managing black bars, and applying pre-filters before executing the gamut check. Detecting and managing out-of-gamut colors is crucial for preserving color accuracy in image processing.

On the other hand, The CIE color space (e.g., CIE 1931 or CIE Lab) serves as a device-independent representation of colors informed by human vision. When switching between color spaces (e.g., from

BT-2020 to sRGB), some colors from the source space may extend beyond the constraints of the target space. This leads to color clipping or inaccuracies when displaying images on devices with a narrower gamut. Colors created in a wider gamut may not display correctly on devices with a smaller gamut, resulting in noticeable alterations in hue, saturation, or brightness.

The analysis involves identifying the source and target color spaces while ensuring all colors are independent of the devices used. The algorithm collects 2D xy (Z) coordinates for each pixel and verifies if they are within the color space triangle defined by the associated color primaries. Users can customize the detection process by selecting source color primaries, excluding black bars, and checking whether colors lie inside or outside a designated color space. Nonetheless, recognizing out-of-gamut colors presents difficulties. CIE spaces like Lab have a non-linear structure and are computationally demanding, complicating real-time applications. The computational burden of CIE spaces and the approximations necessary for color space conversions represent substantial obstacles.

Black Bars

Aspect ratio refers to the consistent relationship between the width and height established during video recording. The pixel count in each direction of a 2D representation of a 3D scene is predetermined, and improper alteration may result in abnormal shapes within the video frame. When the display dimensions of the video do not align with those of the captured video, black bars may be introduced in one or more dimensions to preserve the aspect ratio and the standard shapes of the objects within the video. For example, when a 16:9 video is played on a 4:3 monitor, the video is reduced in size to fit the available width, leading to black bars in empty spaces. These bars aid in maintaining the original aspect ratio without causing distortion. Nonetheless, black bars can detrimentally affect the viewing experience. They consume valuable screen space, resulting in a less immersive experience. In certain instances, the overall visual coherence is affected due to the irregular distribution of black bars. Additionally, prolonged exposure to black bars on organic light-emitting diode (OLED) displays may lead to screen burn-in after a while.

An advanced detection algorithm entails extracting pixel data from every frame, pinpointing edges, and identifying dark regions. Black bars generally contain dark pixels close to (0,0,0) RGB values, although some variations may arise from different encoding methods. The detection technique should allow for customization, so users can identify various types of black bars, such as letterboxing, pillar boxing, and slanted bars, along with setting their range for black pixels.

Despite the availability of these detection methods, there are still numerous challenges. Dark frames can make it difficult to identify black bars. Text overlays or subtitles within the black bar areas can further complicate detection. Additionally, the accurate identification of black bar widths is affected by the overlapping elements or titles embedded in the video.

Identifying black bars in videos is vital for maximizing screen usage and preventing undesirable display artifacts. While current methods can recognize and categorize black bars, challenges persist when dealing with dark frames, text overlays, and embedded titles. A versatile and adaptive detection method is crucial for achieving reliable results. It is recommended not to place imported text or graphics within the areas of black bars since such elements may be disregarded by smart displays to enhance screen usage and eliminate the appearance of black bars. The automated analysis system must also identify any text included in the black bar regions. Thus, detecting text is a significant aspect of this analysis. Text detection and Optical Character Recognition (OCR) rely on techniques from machine learning.

No-Reference Video Quality Index

Assessing video quality can be quite complex, especially when videos exhibit a variety of both spatial and temporal changes. The quality of video diminishes when its inherent characteristics, represented through spatial and temporal features, are disrupted by external influences. Such external interferences can include information loss during lossy compression, editing processes, deinterlacing, transmission errors like packet loss or jitter, and several other forms of disruption.

Addressing every type of disturbance in the natural behavior of all video content presents significant challenges. Techniques from computer vision, Signal Processing, and Image Processing are utilized to gauge the overall alterations in natural statistics that lead to quality degradation. The Video Quality Index based on natural statistics is formulated by using established measurements from signal processing and computer vision on the video content. While this method has been effective in many instances, it does not consistently yield the anticipated results. This inconsistency arises from the various assumptions and simplifications made while modeling the natural statistics of video content. Recent developments in MLand Deep Learning (DL) techniques are being applied to understand the connection between degraded video content and the anticipated video quality score. Architecture utilizing Convolutional Neural Networks (CNNs) and Recurrent Neural Networks (RNNs) [6] are instrumental in representing both the spatial and temporal characteristics of videos.

A deep neural network architecture that combines CNNs and Long Short-term Memory (LSTM, an improvement over standard RNN designs) is developed to gauge the extent of degradation in video content. This assessment, expressed as a Video Quality Index, is intended to align closely with human perception. Furthermore, the machine learning approach determines video quality without relying on a reference by extracting essential visual and temporal features. Upon training with a vast amount of video data, this deep neural network architecture gains the ability to identify relevant features from the input data. The CNN elements within the network extract features that encapsulate structural details and degradation trends. LSTM functions to capture temporal relationships, tackling the inconsistencies that arise among various video frames. A nonlinear mapping function transforms the extracted features to enhance their conformity with human perception. The created and trained deep neural network is tested on a substantial dataset, exhibiting a significant correlation between the Mean Opinion Score (MOS) and the Video Quality Score generated by this model. This correlation is shown in Figure 8 for a set of streams (snapshots are as depicted) encoded with different quality settings.

There is room for enhancements in upcoming developments. The approach may encounter challenges with distortions it hasn't dealt with before, requiring further strategies to address unrecognized quality declines. While it effectively captures short-term dependencies in videos, improving its performance for extended sequences remain difficult and could benefit from advanced temporal analysis methods. Efficiency is vital as reducing computational costs without sacrificing accuracy is crucial for real-time uses. Tackling these obstacles will enhance this framework, increasing its adaptability and scalability for a broader range of applications.

Conclusion

In summary, although existing video verification techniques have improved our capability to assess video quality, they are still limited by foundational assumptions that do not consistently apply in varied real-world contexts. These constraints frequently lead to both false positives and false negatives. The heuristics developed from these assumptions might falter when faced with the intricate and unpredictable nature of spatial and temporal discontinuities in video data. This inherent bias arising from fixed assumptions is a significant limitation of the current techniques.

Moving forward, upcoming research will focus on employing advanced machine learning and deep learning approaches to address these issues. By utilizing data-driven strategies, we intend to enhance and broaden the detection power of video verification. These innovative methods will concentrate on uncovering the fundamental spatial and temporal patterns within video data. The objective is to reduce the effects of the existing methods' shortcomings, allowing for more precise detection and classification of discontinuities without being bound by restrictive assumptions. This shift in paradigm holds the promise of improving detection accuracy and resilience.

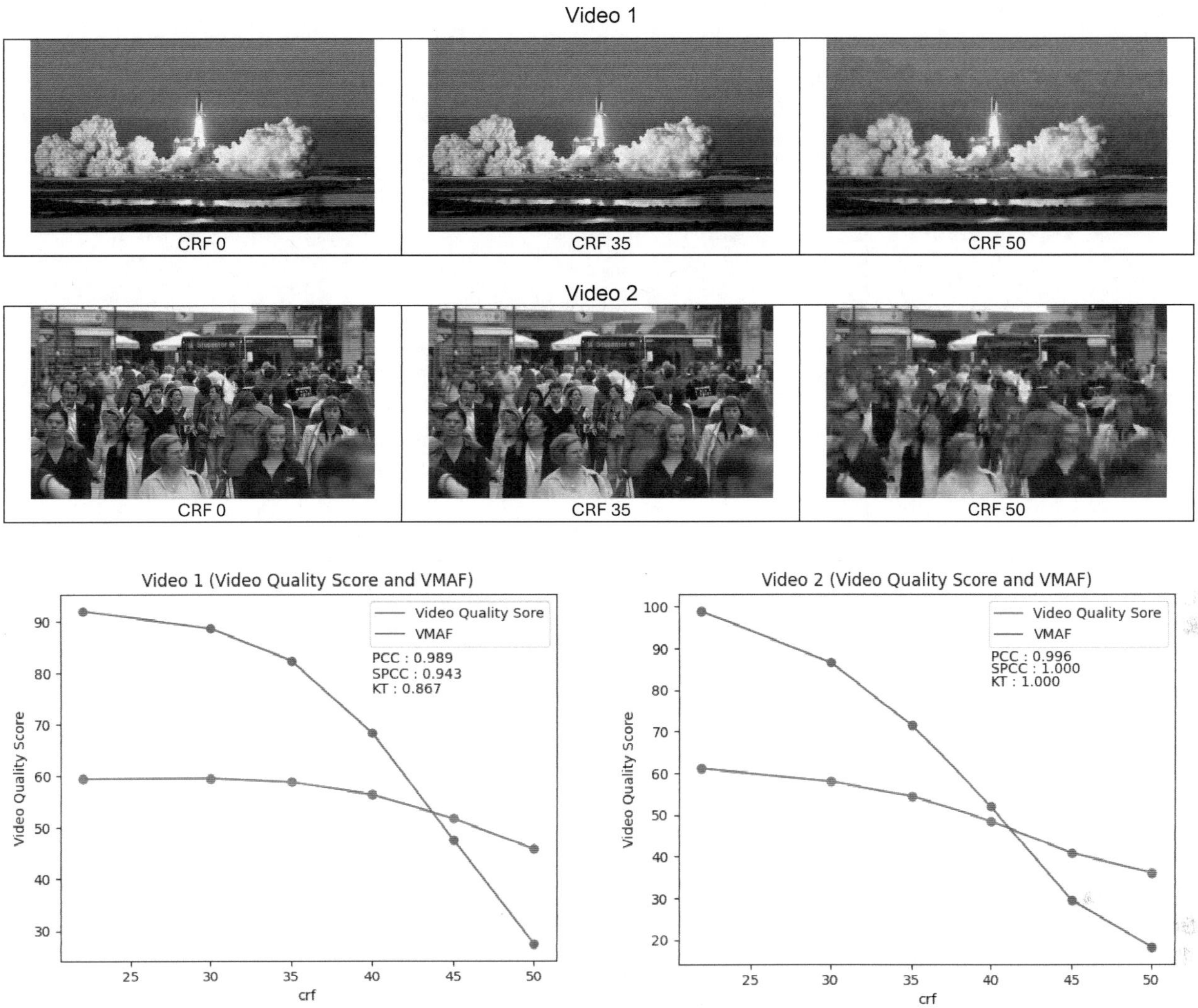

FIGURE 8: PCC: PEARSON CORRELATION COEFFICIENT; SPCC: SPEARMAN'S RANK CORRELATION COEFFICIENT; KT: KENDALL RANK CORRELATION COEFFICIENT

NOTE: Rescaling the Video Quality scores to match VMAF's minimum and maximum reveals nearly identical trends, explaining their high correlation despite differences in absolute values. VMAF scores 100 for REFERENCE-identical video and decreases as distortion increases. Our no-reference model lacks a pristine reference and thus no strict "perfect" definition but instead learns subjective quality from human evaluations. It also outputs scores from 0 to 100, yet the meaning of 100 is less definitive. Consequently, our metric is more suited for comparative assessments than for determining an absolute "ideal" score.

References

[1] Automated File-Based Video QC Software - BATON®
https://www.interrasystems.com/pdf/datasheet/baton-datasheet.pdf

[2] Szeliski, Richard.,"Computer Vision, Algorithms and Applications," 2022.

[3] Gonzalez, Rafael, C. et. al., "Digital Image Processing", Fourth Edition, 2018.

[4] Mikolajczyk, K. and Schmid, C., "Scale & affine invariant interest point detectors", IJCV, 2004. 1, 4.1

[5] Lowe D. G., "SIFT: scale invariant feature transform", Journal Computer Vision 60, 91–110.

[6] Goodfellow, Ian., et. al., "Deep learning", Vol. 1. 2016.

Measurements of AM Band RF Noise Levels and Station Signal Losses

John Kean
Cavell Mertz & Associates (a division of Capitol Airspace Group)
Alexandria, Virginia, United States
John.Kean@capiltolairspace.com

Abstract – This report covers measurements of RF noise levels on various roadway types from open interstate highways to city streets, to determine how the noise would affect AM broadcast reception. These environments reflect the current habits of AM radio listening, which is primarily in vehicles. In addition to RF noise level, RF signal levels were measured for three AM stations operating on frequencies in the lower, middle and upper portions of the AM broadcast band. These measurements provide a better understanding of how AM radio reception is affected by RF signal strength and noise in a range of roadway environments from rural to dense urban environments.

Background

AM radio broadcasters are increasingly concerned about environmental radio frequency (RF) noise, which is deteriorating reception quality and contributing to decreased listenership. To better characterize this issue, the AM Improvement Working Group (AIWG) of the NRSC's AM and FM Analog Broadcasting Subcommittee (AFAB) supported this study to help understand current signal quality degradation and identify potential areas for improvement for AM service.

This study focuses on RF noise levels on roadways, since in-vehicle listening is how most listeners receive AM radio. RF noise levels were measured on various roadway types ranging from open interstate highways to city streets.

Reception quality is a combination of desired signal strength and in-channel noise. In addition to RF noise, the study included calibrated measurements of signal strength from three AM stations operating at different points within the AM broadcast band. This comprehensive data provides insight into how AM radio reception is affected by signal strength and noise in diverse roadway environments, from rural to urban areas.

Test Procedure

Measurement System

The measurement hardware was specifically designed for use in a moving vehicle. Unlike traditional AM field strength meters used in stationary environments, this system was designed to receive signals from all directions while in motion. To support vehicular operation, a vertical monopole antenna was mounted on the vehicle's roof instead of a directional loop antenna. This monopole, like most antennas used on vehicles, effectively captures the electric field (E-field) of AM signals. The measurement vehicle with antenna is shown in Figure 1.

This paper is excerpted from the Proceedings of the 2025 NAB Broadcast Engineering and Information Technology (BEIT) Conference, © 2025, National Association of Broadcasters, 1 M Street SE, Washington, DC 20003 USA.

The base of the monopole antenna contains an impedance converter to provide a 50-ohm output for the instrumentation that follows. Voltages from the antenna were compared to field strength readings from a Potomac Instruments FIM-41 field strength meter. Comparisons were made at a cemetery in Arlington, Virginia at low, medium and high AM station frequencies. The cemetery provides an open area that is free of buildings, light poles, and power lines, which may introduce errors into the station fields. These measurements produced calibration factors across the AM band so that the mobile measurements would correspond to field strength readings taken with the FIM-41.

FIGURE 1. MEASUREMENT VEHICLE AND ANTENNA BEING CALIBRATED WITH POTOMAC INSTRUMENTS FIM-41 FIELD STRENGTH METER

A simplified diagram of the measurement system is shown in Figure 2. Signals from the monopole antenna are fed into the system. An active impedance converter at the antenna base ensures compatibility with the 50-ohm measurement equipment. To eliminate electrical noise from the vehicle's power 12-volt power line, instruments are powered through a noise filter.

A software defined receiver (SDR, model RSPdx, used in combination with SDRuno software, see Appendix A) was used to collect noise measurements on locally unused AM channels as well as field strengths from three clear-channel AM stations (one Class A and two Class B). This SDR is suited to these measurements because of high sensitivity and automatic filter preselection ahead of the analog-to-digital converter. Tests of the measurement system in the quiet environment of Arlington Cemetery found its internal equivalent noise level to be low (without station interference, approximately 0.03 mV/m at 555 kHz and 0.02 mV/m at 1625 kHz).

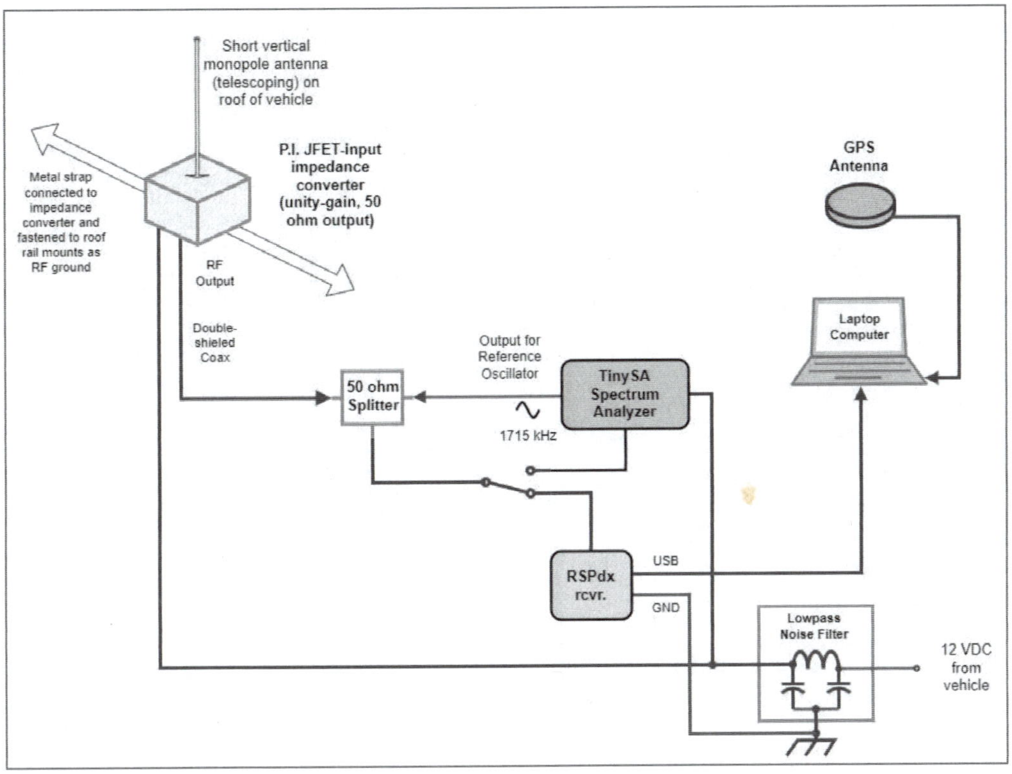

FIGURE 2. MEASUREMENT SYSTEM DIAGRAM

A combination spectrum analyzer/signal generator (model TinySA, see Appendix 1) was used to produce a fixed reference carrier at 1715 kHz to correct automatic gain control shifts in the RSPdx. A switch allowed the TinySA to be converted from a signal generator to spectrum analysis when needed to study signals from the roof antenna. A laptop computer running Windows 10 was connected to the RSPdx and a GPS antenna to store AM band voltage measurements and location data.

The RSPdx and SDRuno files allowed later playback as audio for quality assessment. Nearly three- and one-half hours of audio and data were collected for each of the three AM stations and three low-noise channels over the entire route.

Test Route Selection

Measurements were collected on March 23, 2023, between noon and 5 PM EST. The weather was cool and dry, and no lightning was detected in the region. The route covered 50 miles of roadway as shown in Figure 3, beginning near Germantown, Maryland and ending south of downtown Baltimore, Maryland. Short stops were made between route segments to store data files and restart the instrumentation. The route passed through areas that are categorized, according to building clutter density in Table 1.

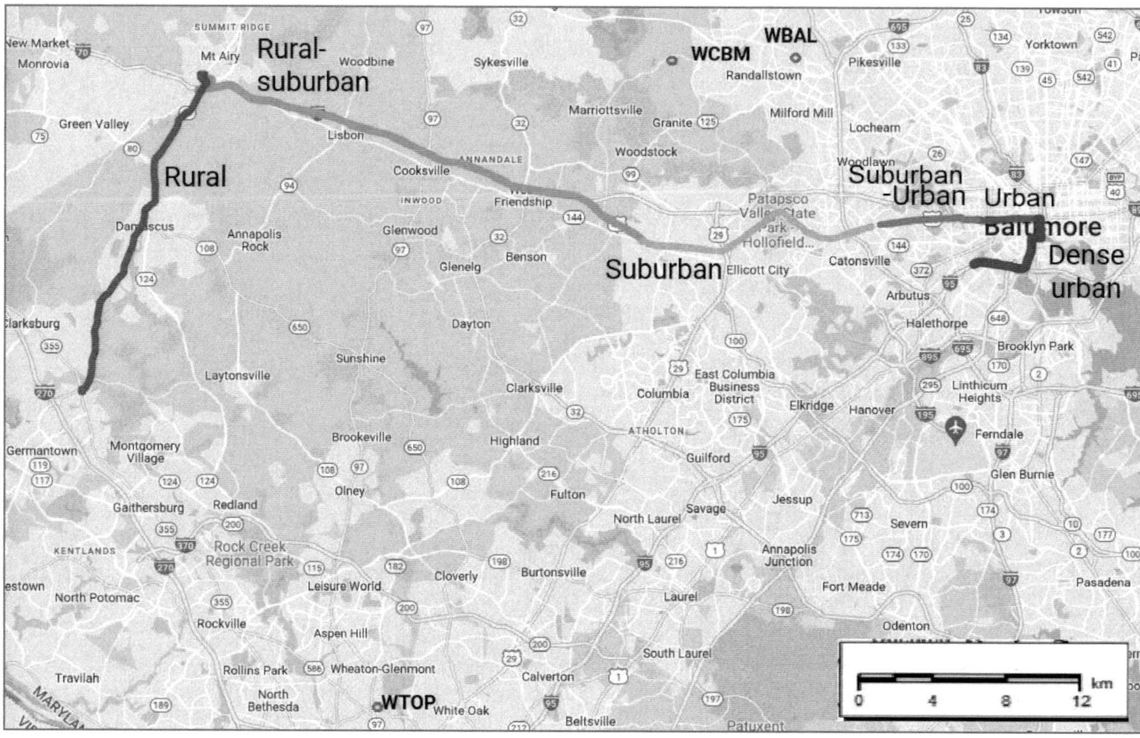

FIGURE 3. MAP SHOWING MEASUREMENT ROUTE WITH BUILD-UP AREAS SHOWN IN GRAY. COLORS REPRESENT THE GENERAL ENVIRONMENT BEING MEASURED. SEE TEXT.

This study examines whether noise levels change with building clutter density, which assumes that RF environmental noise in denser areas is degrading AM reception quality to a greater degree than in less dense areas. However, RF noise is only one factor in reception quality: the other being the strength of the desired signal. To address this critical signal factor this study collected simultaneous field strength measurements with three regional AM stations, listed in Table 2.

Environment	Description
Rural	Geographic area located outside of towns and cities, predominantly natural landscape
Rural-suburban	Transitional area blending residential, agricultural and commercial land uses
Suburban	Residential areas on the outskirts of cities, apartment complexes, commercial spaces
Suburban-Urban	Transitional area blending suburban and urban areas
Urban	Highly developed areas with a mix of low or medium rise apartments and commercial buildings and industrial use
Dense urban	High population density, tall buildings, extensive streets and public transportation systems

TABLE 1 – ENVIRONMENT CATEGORIES IN THIS STUDY

Call Sign	City	Frequency (kHz)	Class	Power kW Day	Antenna Mode Day
WCBM	Baltimore MD	680	B	50	DA
WBAL	Baltimore MD	1090	A	50	Non-D
WFED	Washington DC	1500	A	50	DA

TABLE 2. AM STATIONS USED FOR SIGNAL STRENGTH MEASUREMENTS

Station Selection and Signal Performance

The AM stations listed in Table 2 were chosen to meet several criteria:

- To span the AM band by frequency,
- Operating channels free of co- and first-adjacent channel station interference,
- Transmitter sites distant from the measurement route to avoid signal overload, and
- Provide coverage across the entire measurement area.

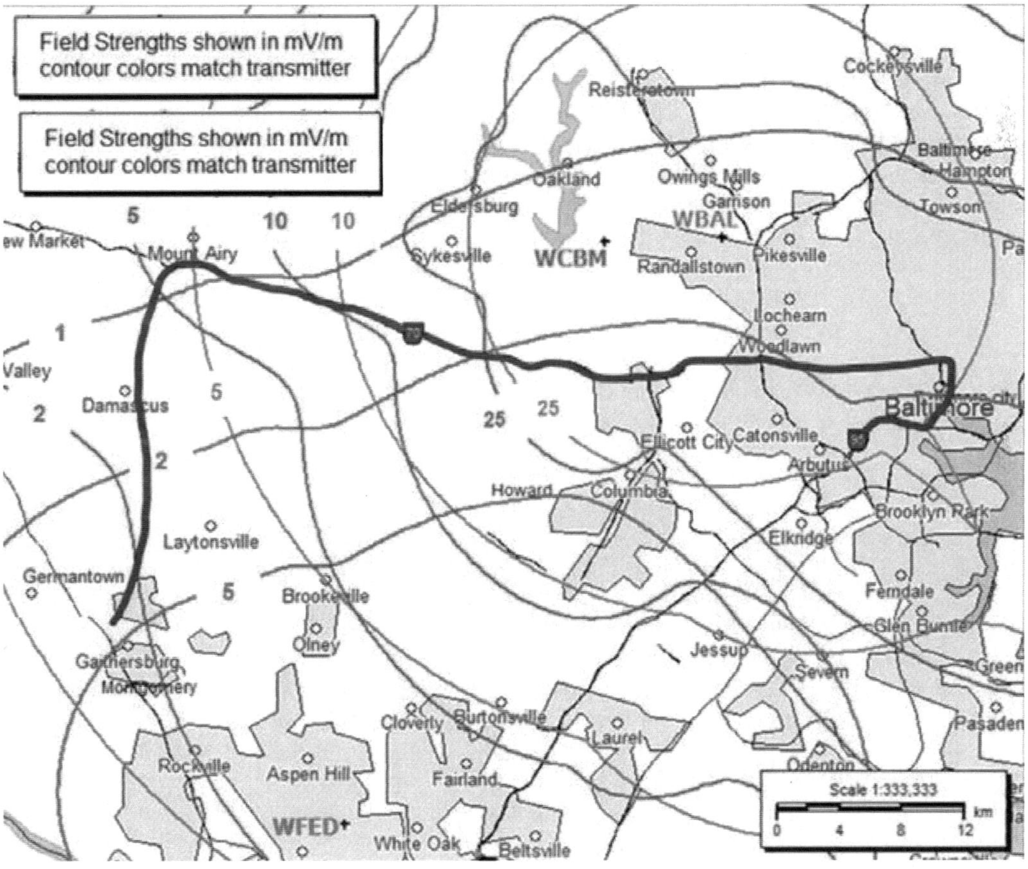

FIGURE 4. TRANSMITTER LOCATIONS AND SIGNAL CONTOURS OF WCBM (GREEN), WBAL (GRAY) AND WFED (RED)

The map of Figure 4 shows the daytime groundwave contours of the stations, color-keyed to their respective transmitter sites. Given the dynamic range capability of the RSPdx receiver, these stations provide measurable coverage over most of the drive-test route.

RF Noise Measurements

Measurement Criteria

To avoid interference from nearby AM stations, noise measurements were taken at three frequencies, selected for separation to the same and adjacent channels used for local RF noise measurements:

- 555 kHz (noise channel 1)
- 1075 kHz (noise channel 2)
- 1625 kHz (noise channel 3)

The RSPdx receiver captured the entire AM radio spectrum (approximately 2 MHz) at a 14-bit depth. The in-phase (I) and quadrature (Q) components of the signal were stored as left and right channels in a WAV file format. A custom OCTAVE program extracted signal strength and RF channel noise data from these raw WAV files and converted them into numerical CSV files.

Noise measurements were taken within 1 kHz bandwidths centered 5 kHz away from each of the three noise channel center frequencies. This frequency offset helped to minimize interference from distant radio stations. To process the data, noise measurements were extracted in 2-second blocks. For each block, the peak and root mean square (RMS) noise values were calculated and saved in the CSV file.

The noise measurements used the same antenna system and RSPdx receiver as the station signal measurements, making it possible to convert the noise data into standard values such as microvolts per meter. However, collecting noise data in a moving vehicle complicates the calibrated reference techniques traditionally used in human-caused radio noise measurements. Mobile measurements are also less comparable to fixed, time-averaged measurements, which are beyond the scope of this study. Therefore, the noise measurements are presented as relative values, using the same horizontal-axis scales for comparison.

This study aimed to compare noise levels across five different environments as discussed in Section 3.2:

- Rural
- Rural-suburban (transition area)
- Suburban
- Urban
- Dense urban

The goal was to understand how these types of environments impact AM radio reception, both in terms of signal strength and RF noise conditions. Excluding interference from other radio stations, reception quality is a function of both radio signal strength and prevailing RF noise. Station interference is regulated by the FCC's allocation rules and is primarily an issue in fringe areas of a desired station (usually less than the station's 2 mV/m daytime groundwave contour).[1] Figure 4 illustrates that the study area is primarily within this contour for all three test stations, the notable exception being parts of the rural and rural-suburban environments for WFED which fall outside of the 2 mV/m contour.

Processing of RF Environmental Noise

Figure 5 is an example of how RF noise is presented on the three measurement channels. The red trace shows the RMS RF noise level in mV/m in a 6 kHz bandwidth around 555 kHz, the lowest "quiet" test frequency. This sample is for the rural-designated route segment between Germantown and Mount Airy, Maryland. The horizontal scale indicates the sample time in seconds.

[1] 47 CFR § 73.182, Engineering standards of allocation, subsection (d) states that "The groundwave signal strength required to render primary service is 2 mV/m for communities with populations of 2,500 or more and 0.5 mV/m for communities with populations of less than 2,500."

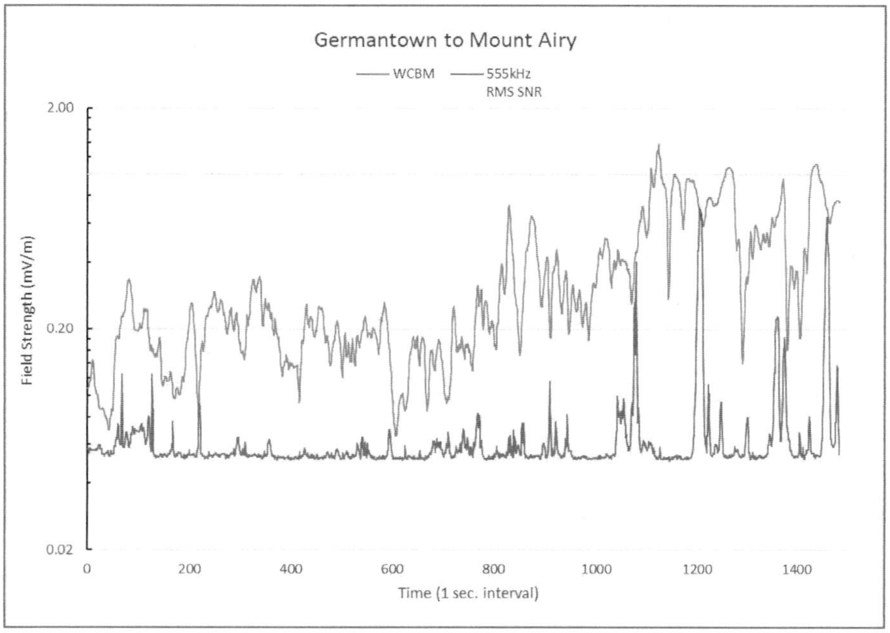

FIGURE 5. CHART SHOWING RMS NOISE LEVEL AT 555 KHZ ON THE RURAL ROUTE SEGMENT WITH THE SIGNAL FROM WCBM ON 680 KHZ

Figure 5 illustrates WCBM's signal reception in green along the route, contrasting it with measured background noise levels in red. While an audio signal-to-noise ratio (SNR) along the route would offer a deeper understanding of reception quality, this metric is influenced by a variety of factors such as audio bandwidth, noise duration, noise frequency distribution, and station program level. These factors vary across stations and receiver models, making a simple audio SNR a limited representation of perceived AM reception quality. Therefore, this report presents a combination of measured field strength and RMS noise level. Although not a direct measure of quality, the vertical difference between the two can provide some indication of reception quality.

While field strength and RMS noise levels can offer insights into reception quality, a benchmark for minimum AM reception quality has traditionally been a 25 dB audio signal-to-noise ratio (SNR). However, modern car radios often have narrow audio passbands, which can make a lower SNR acceptable for listening (at the expense of poor audio fidelity). Considering this trend, a more practical ratio between field strength and measured noise in quiet channels might be 20 dB, equivalent to a 10:1 voltage ratio on the chart. For instance, a field strength of 1 mV/m would require noise levels below 0.1 mV/m at the same moment. This generalization would apply to other station field strengths. WCBM's signal consistently meets this 20 dB signal to RF noise ratio criteria in only the last quarter of this route, and even then, there are several moments when noise peaks sharply drop that ratio.

Noise analysis in various environments, including urban and rural areas, reveals a common pattern: frequent, low-level background noise often near the measurement system's noise floor, is punctuated by intermittent noise bursts. In the rural settings measured in this project, these bursts are primarily caused by power lines crossing the road, resulting in spikes in the RMS noise graphs seen on the graphs.

Passing beneath highway overpasses has little impact on received noise levels. This is because these locations are not inherently more likely to have noise sources than the adjacent road segments. However, sharp signal drops may occur under overpasses and can trigger rapid responses from AM receivers' automatic gain control (AGC) systems, amplifying any ambient RF noise during these moments.

Another measurement on the "quiet" channels was noise peaks, which make "pops" in the received audio. The value of the highest noise peak per second was measured, relative to the RMS noise (in field strength) in that second. The number of noise peaks at values in each second of time was then counted. Peak sensing was normalized to the RMS noise in the block second, thus the peak noise values are treated as dB relative (dBr) measurements. What is of most interest is the distribution of peak values versus the frequency of occurrence. Peaks that frequently extend to higher values are an indication of noisy and unpleasant reception.

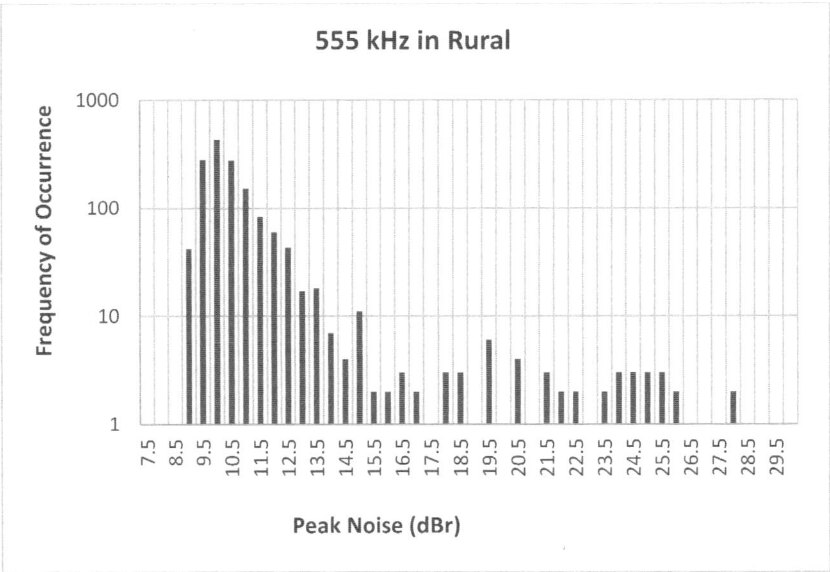

FIGURE 6. SAMPLE CHART SHOWING THE IMPUSLE NOISE HISTOGRAM ON A ROUTE SEGMENT

The count for each threshold is displayed in a histogram, with the horizontal axis representing the threshold levels and the vertical axis representing the frequency of occurrence for the route segment. Figure 6 illustrates the noise behavior observed on the 555 kHz channel on the Rural route segment, demonstrating that the frequency of impulses decreases as the peak amplitudes increase. In this case, however, higher level (and louder) noise peaks extend to field strength levels up to 20 dB greater than the frequently occurring peaks. This distribution can vary widely with frequency and locale, as seen in subsequent charts.

Field Measurement of Station Signals and RF Environmental Noise

Germantown to Mount Airy (Rural) Segment

The maps in Figure 7 show the first route segment (driven from south to north) with a color-coded line to represent field strength in mV/m.

This 13-mile route, primarily a two-lane road (Maryland route 27), passes through a mix of farmland and residential areas set back from the road. The route goes through Damascus, Maryland, a town with small stores and two schools (high school and elementary school) located roughly halfway along the route. A 12.6 kV power line runs parallel to most of the route, and there are numerous low-voltage AC service lines crossing the road.

Comparing the measured field strengths to the predicted groundwave contours for each station in Figure 4, we observe that the measured values are significantly lower than predicted. For example, WCBM's predicted field strengths on this segment range from 2 to 5 mV/m, but the measured values are only about 0.2 to 0.7 mV/m.

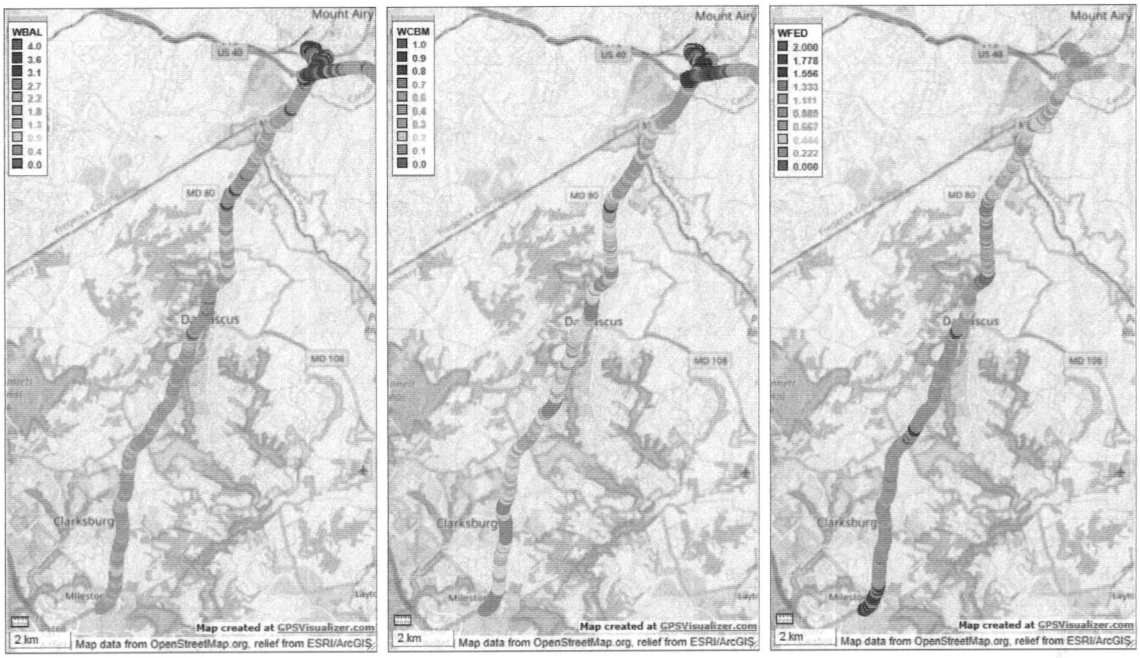

FIGURE 7. MEASURED FIELD STRENGTH OF WBAL, WCBM, AND WFED ALONG THE RURAL SEGMENT. THE LEGEND IN UPPER LEFT SHOWS FIELD STRENGTHS IN MV/M ACCORDING TO COLOR

WFED's predicted groundwave field strength ranges from 4 mV/m at the southern end to 1 mV/m at the northern end. However, the measured field strengths along this route are between 0.5 and 0.2 mV/m. The reasons for these large discrepancies are uncertain, but they could be attributed to factors such as low ground conductivity within the region, changes in road elevation relative to the surrounding terrain, local building obstructions, and other environmental factors.

For comparison of signal levels along the roadway on the Germantown to Mount Airy (rural) route, Figure 8 shows the field strengths of WCBM, WBAL and WFED. This is graphed over 1500 seconds (25 minutes) along this route segment. WCBM and WBAL have somewhat parallel traces at first, but later show a difference in the field strength generally in a ratio of 10:1. However, the groundwave field strength contours of the two stations in Figure 4 (WCBM in green, WBAL in gray) predicts both signals in the range of 2 to 5 mV/m and generally closer in ratio.

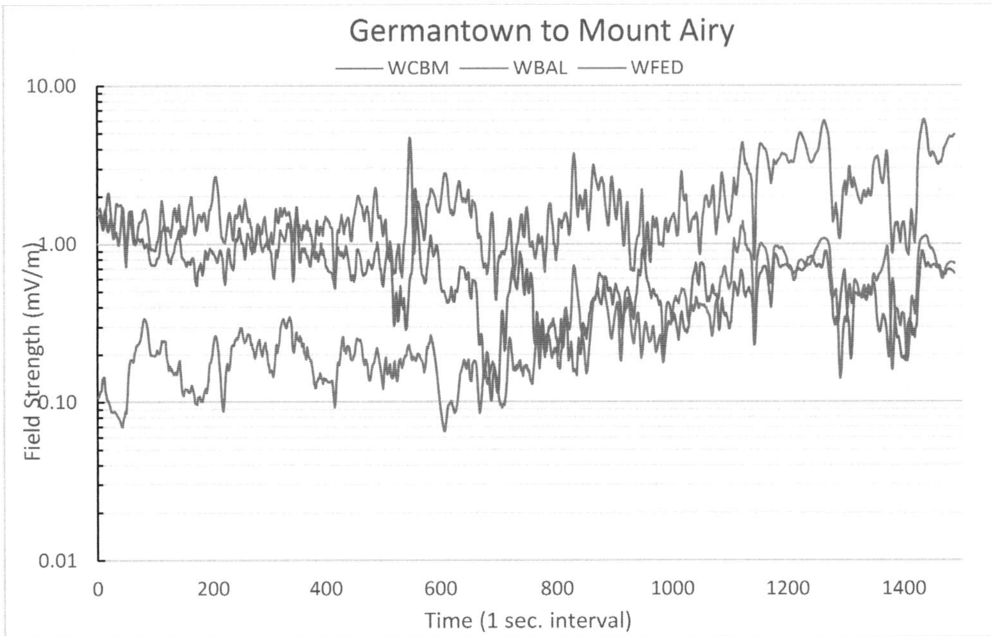

FIGURE 8. FIELD STRENGTHS OF THE THREE AM STATIONS FOR THE RURAL SEGMENT SHOWN IN FIGURE 7

The transmitter sites of WCBM and WBAL are both northeast of this route, while WFED's transmitter is south-southeast. The observed WFED field strength decreases with distance from its transmitter and its predicted field is expected to decrease from approximately 5 mV/m to 1 mV/m. Like WCBM and WBAL, WFED's measured field strength starts near 2 mV/m and drops to around 0.5 mV/m. The differences between measured and predicted measured fields are notable, although investigating their cause is beyond the scope of this study. It has been suggested by expert reviewers of this report that such differences are not unusual at large receiving distances and may be due to errors in the FCC ground conductivity data. Others point out that the E field measurements could be adversely affected by clutter and terrain height near the roadways.

The other part of this investigation determined the RF environmental noise levels along with field strengths. As discussed above, three "quiet" channels were selected, each being near in frequency to one of the test stations. For comparison, the RF noise power in the test channel was converted to a field strength value for comparison with the associated AM station. The data were graphed separately for the three station and noise pairs on all route segments for both RMS (averaged) and peak values.

While this approach could be viewed as a "signal to noise" ratio (SNR), there are several factors that govern the perceptual measure of SNR, including audio content type and modulation level, channel bandwidth, and duration of noise. Given this caution, one can view the momentary ratio between the field strength and noise level for a general sense of the quality of reception: a ratio of 10:1 (20 dB voltage) could be a marginally unacceptable condition. (Audio recordings of the received station signals were collected for the three stations on the full route, which provides an opportunity for a reader to make their own judgement of the audio reception quality. These recordings will be posted on the nrscstandards.org website for downloading.)

Figure 9 illustrates the measured field strength for WCBM, plotted alongside the RMS noise level on this rural route segment. Significant decreases in field strength are evident, primarily due to overhead obstructions like highway overpasses. While these obstructions do not directly increase RMS noise, they can potentially amplify background noise on the desired channel because of receiver Automatic Gain Control (AGC) adjustments.

The noise peaks observed on the bottom line are attributed to the presence of overhead power lines or noisy electrical equipment near the road. These factors, however, have a minimal impact on WCBM signal strength. Their influence on perceived noise levels is contingent on the strength of the station's signal at the specific moment the noise source is encountered.

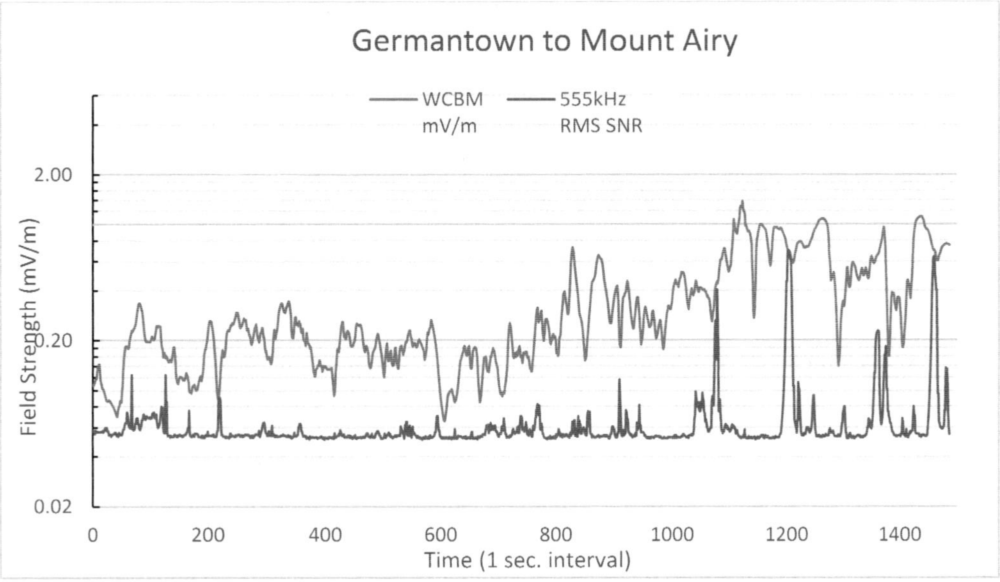

FIGURE 9. WCBM FIELD STRENGTH (GREEN) AND 555 KHZ RMS NOISE MEASUREMENT (RED)

The graphs for WBAL and WFED in the rural route segment are show in Figure 10 and Figure 11. Color coding is the same as WCBM. Baseline RMS noise at 1075 kHz and 1625 kHz are similar to 555 kHz but the number of peaks in the noise has reduced significantly. With the exception of a couple of short bursts, WBAL's signal would produce acceptable reception quality across the entire route. WFED's reception quality is good until its field strength drops below about 1 mV/m, about 500 seconds from the start.

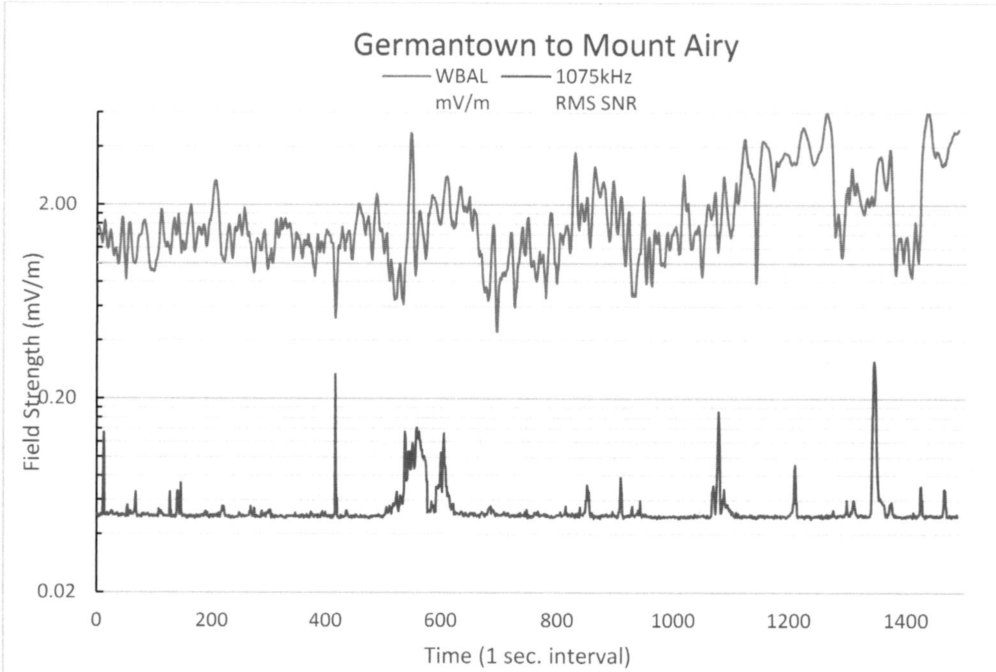

FIGURE 10. WBAL FIELD STRENGTH (GREEN) AND 1075 KHz RMS NOISE MEASUREMENT (RED)

It is notable that the RMS noise at around 550 seconds appears at 1075 kHz and 1625 kHz but is not detected at 555 kHz. This means that RF environmental noise can be frequency-dependent, according to how the noise was generated. For example, broadband noise, such as arcing contacts in a large motor, could be frequency-shaped by cable inductance and distributed capacitance in its wiring.

"Peak Noise" in this study is calculated as the ratio of the maximum instantaneous noise voltage in a "quiet" noise channel compared to the channel's average noise level (RMS). Listeners would perceive this noise as a sudden pop or crack that is significantly louder than the background hiss.

"Buzzing" noises are primarily measured as contributors to the RMS noise level rather than as a series of distinct peaks. The frequency (or number of occurrences) of these events per measurement second is calculated and displayed below as histograms. The charts in Figure 12 illustrate the distribution of noise peaks for each noise channel along the rural segment.

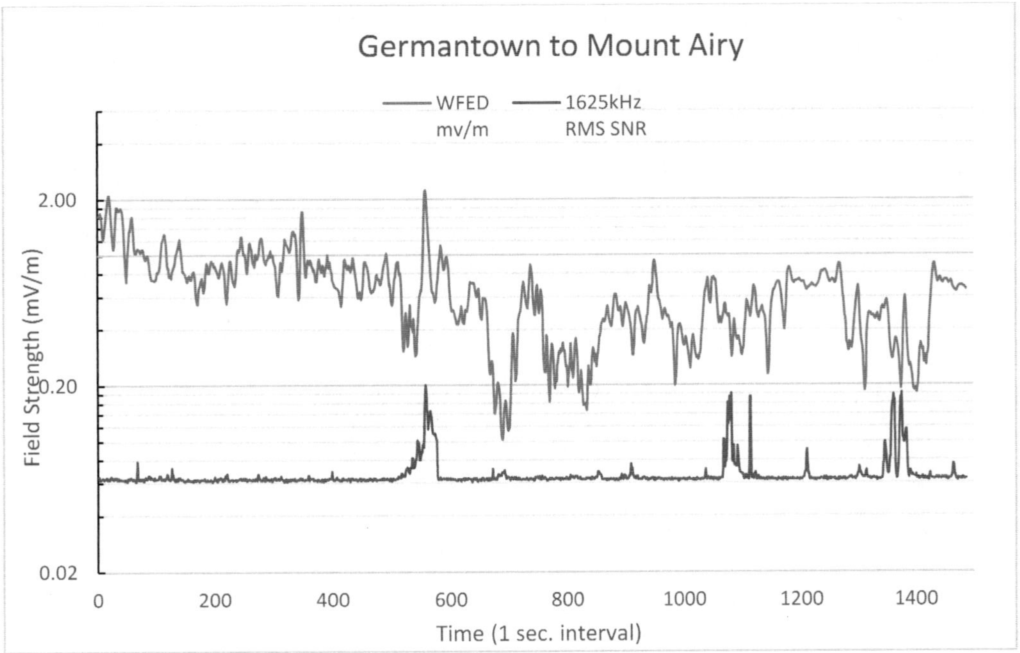

FIGURE 11. WFED FIELD STRENGTH (GREEN) AND 1625 KHZ RMS NOISE MEASUREMENT (RED)

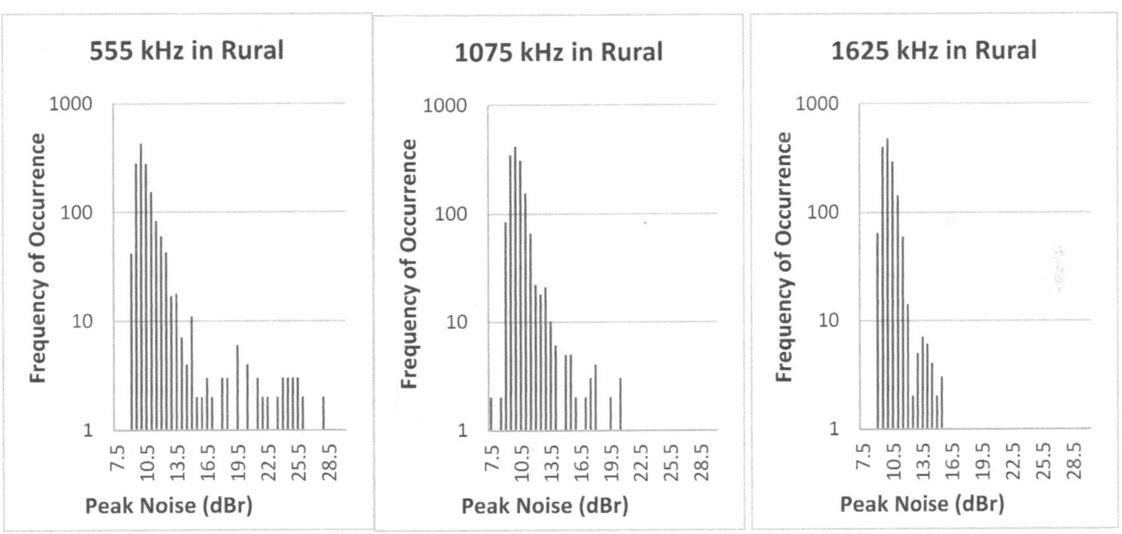

FIGURE 12. DISTRIBUTION OF NOISE PEAKS FOR EACH NOISE CHANNEL ALONG THE RURAL ROUTE SEGMENT

The number of noise peaks was almost always greatest on the lower frequency channel (555 kHz) compared to the middle channel (1075 kHz), and the highest frequency channel (1625 kHz). This can be seen by the height and density of vertical lines on the histograms. Again, by a noticeable margin, the lower frequency channel also had a greater number of peaks at far higher amplitudes than the other two channels. The 1625 kHz channel above shows noise peaks ending at 15 dBr, while the 555 kHz channel peaks extend to 28 dB. Listeners to stations on lower channels can be expected to hear occasional pops and crackles that are noticeably louder than on the middle and higher frequency channels at similar station field strengths.

This observation aligns with research showing that the amplitude of human-caused noise sources like power lines and distant lightning events decrease as the frequency increases. Therefore, listeners on the higher end of the AM band would experience less impulsive noise, although the groundwave signal propagation is generally weaker at those frequencies.

Mount Airy to Ellicott City (Rural-Suburban)

The maps in Figure 13 show the rural-suburban segment (driven from west to east) with a color-coded line to represent field strength in mV/m. This route begins in a mixed rural and suburban setting on Interstate 70, a wide, open roadway environment that cuts over to US Route 40, a four-lane divided highway much like I-70.

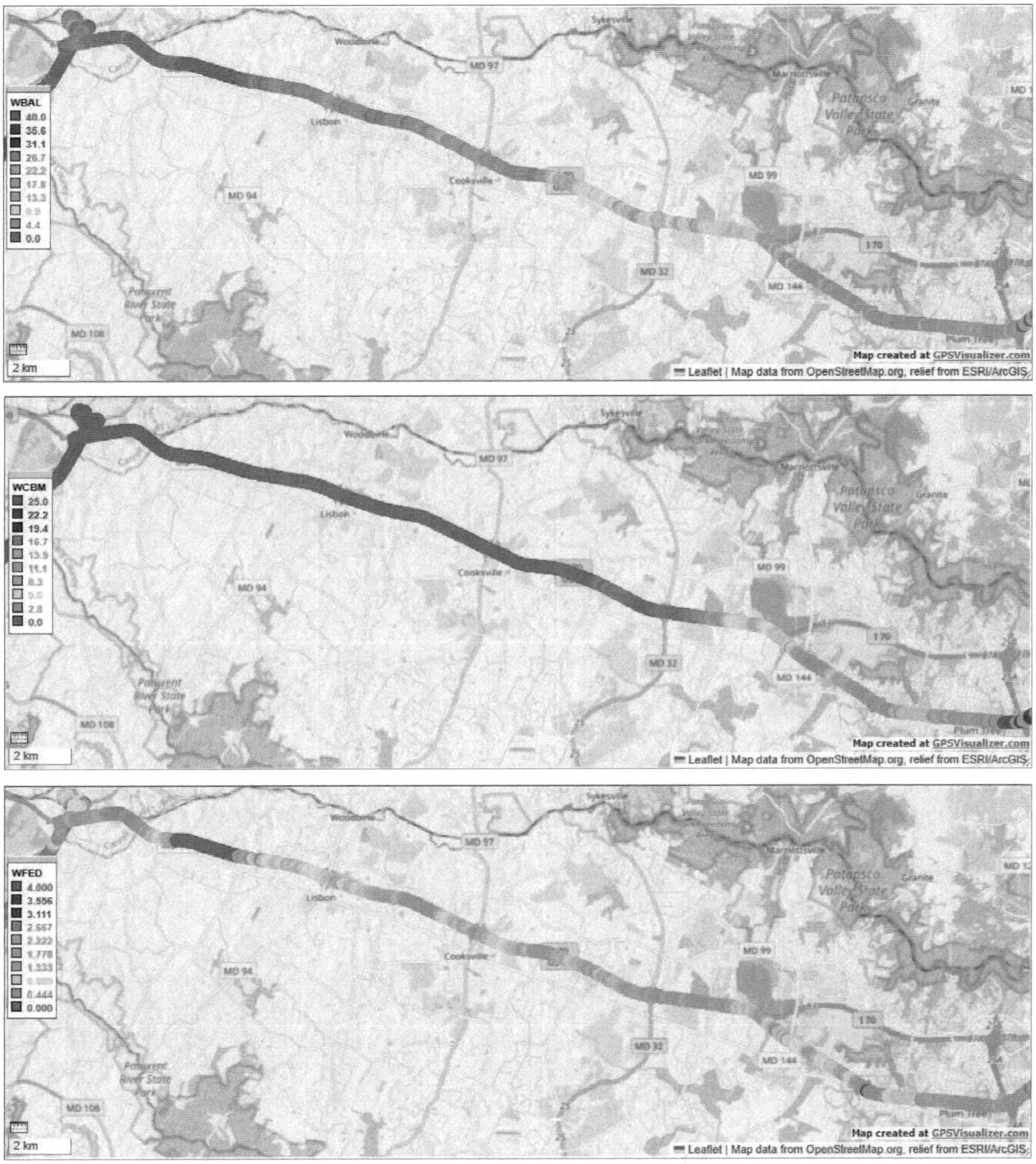

FIGURE 13. MEASURED FIELD STRENGTHS OF WBAL, WCBM, AND WFED ALONG RURAL-SUBURBAN SEGMENT. LEGEND DEPICTS FIELD STRENGTH COLORS IN MV/M

This segment generally has stronger signal strengths compared to nearby arterial roads, which may present building obstructions, electrical power lines, and other factors that can scatter and weaken radio signals.

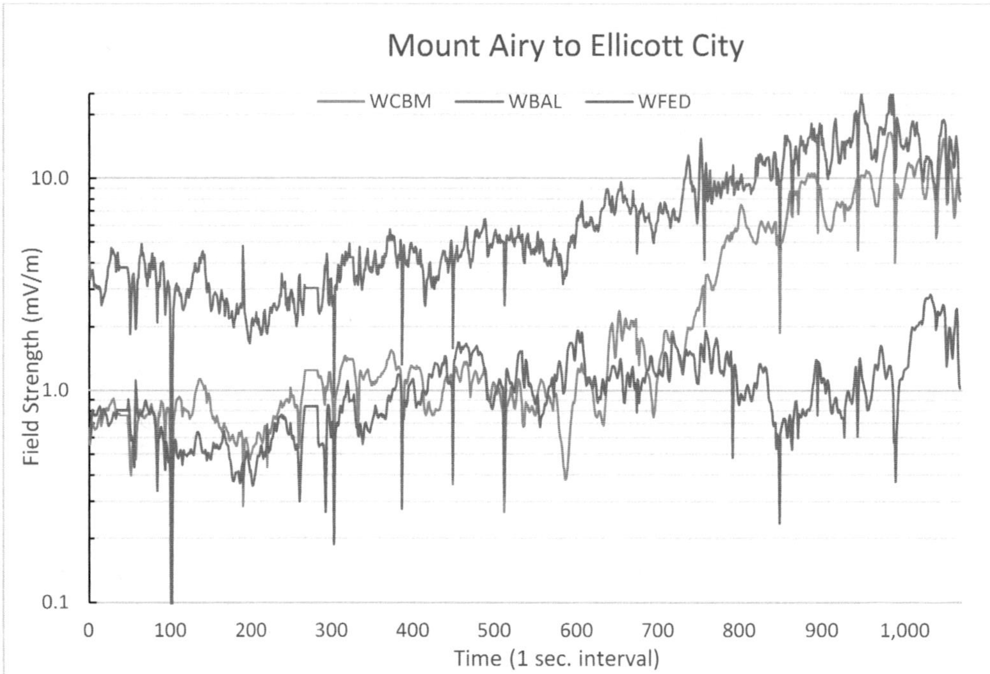

FIGURE 14. FIELD STRENGTHS ON THE RURAL-SUBURBAN SEGMENT (25 TO 0.1 MV/M SCALE)

Figure 14 shows the field strength data of the three stations shown in Figure 13 but plotted as a function of time. WBAL's signal along the rural-suburban route is significantly stronger than those of WCBM and WFED. The three stations share a low-signal area between Mount Airy and Lisbon (100-300 seconds). After the split from I-70 to US-40 (around 750 seconds), WCBM's signal nearly catches up to WBAL. Interestingly, WFED's signal drops in nearly the same area that WCBM rises. The cause is not clear. A notable feature of this area is that the interstate passes through embankments of approximately twenty feet on one or both sides. The terrain elevation continues to decrease in this route section. These factors may be creating apertures that attenuate the AM signal from some directions.

The signals shown in Figure 14 show a striking similarity in their downward spikes along the route. The largest spike, located on the far left, occurred at a large overpass. The other downward spikes occurred at smaller, two-lane overpasses typical of state roads, which the measurement vehicle passed under more quickly. The signal fades were prolonged enough to significantly reduce the field strengths and, in the case of WCBM and WFED, to substantially lower their signal-to-noise ratio.

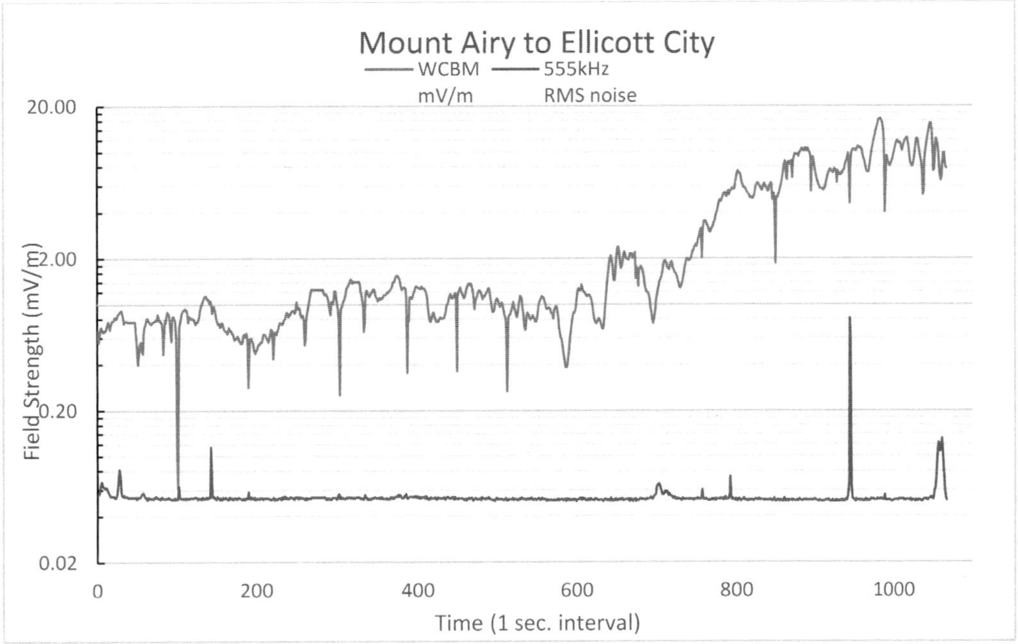

FIGURE 15. WCBM FIELD STRENGTH (GREEN) AND 555 KHZ RMS NOISE MEASUREMENT (RED)

Figure 15 adds the RMS measurement on 555 kHz for comparison to WCBM's field strength. It is apparent that noise is unaffected by the downward signal drops discussed above. There is also no connection between the three noise spikes in red and the field strength measurements. The first two, at approximately 143 seconds and 943 seconds, are very brief. This is because they were physically small sources of noise, in contrast to power line noise, which was found to stretch for longer periods of time, and were passed quickly at highway speeds.

The last noise blip at about 1060 seconds was a little long because the measurement car had pulled off the highway and slowed down. Given WCBM's high field strength at this point the noise was unnoticeable.

Figure 15 also illustrates how low RF noise can be in the AM band along this highway route – essentially at the RMS noise floor of the instrumentation (approximately 40 to 60 µV/m, depending on frequency). Open surroundings on this open highway place it far away from electrical noise emitters such as power lines, traffic signals and electrical equipment. Even at field strengths of 1 mV/m the station signals provide a listenable and comfortably quiet reception.

The charts in Figure 16 and Figure 17 illustrate the levels of RMS noise for the mid-band and high-band channels along the route segment. Common to other route segments, they decrease with frequency.

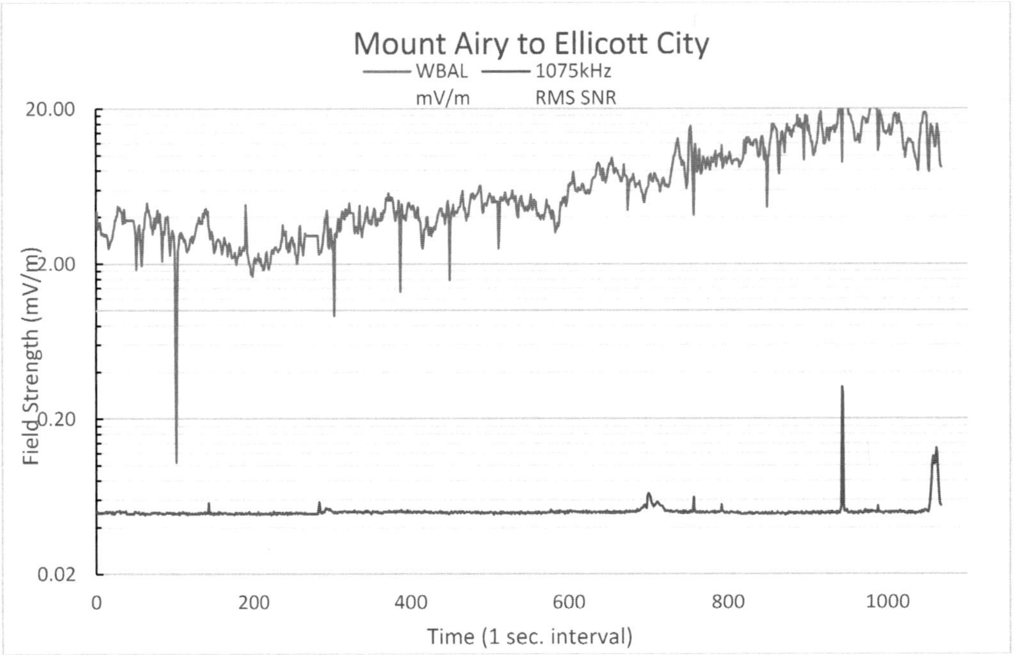

FIGURE 16. WBAL FIELD STRENGTH (GREEN) AND 555 KHZ RMS NOISE MEASUREMENT (RED)

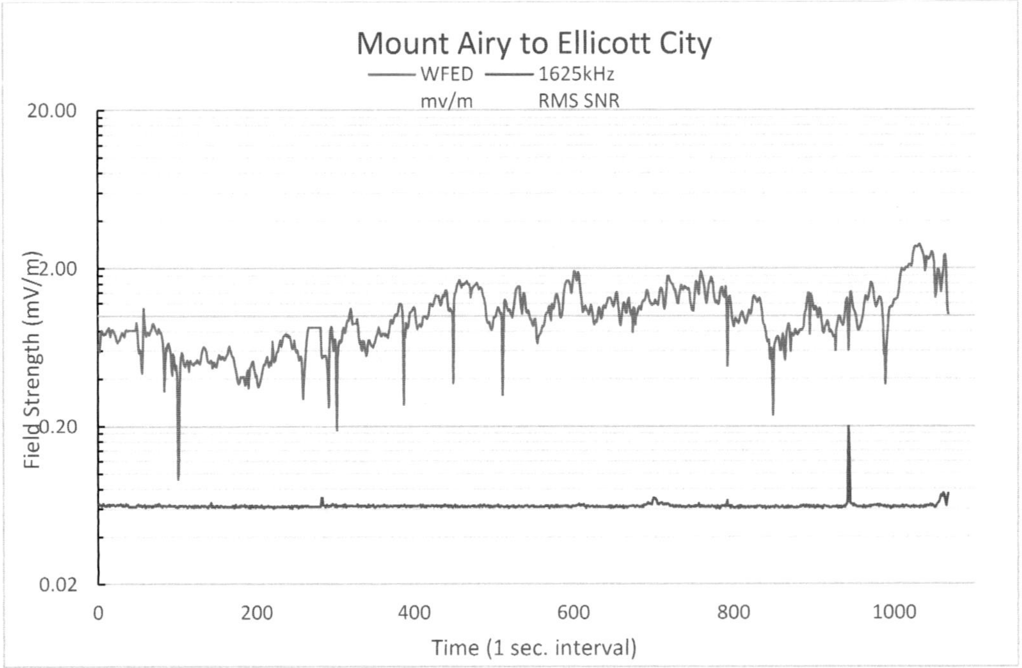

FIGURE 17. WFED FIELD STRENGTH (GREEN) AND 555 KHZ RMS NOISE MEASUREMENT (RED)

The distributions of peak noise occurrences are displayed in Figure 18 for all three channels on this interstate highway segment. Like the RMS noise measurements, this interstate highway exhibited the lowest peak noise occurrences among all the route segments.

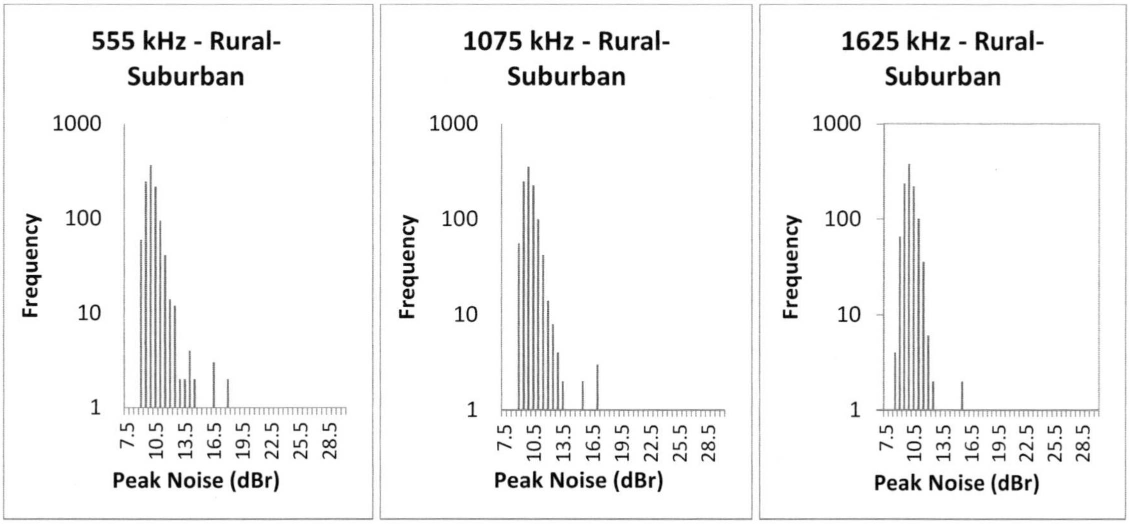

FIGURE 18. DISTRIBUTION OF NOISE PEAKS FOR EACH NOISE CHANNEL ALONG THE RURAL-SUBURBAN ROUTE SEGMENT

Ellicott City to Catonsville (Suburban)

The maps in Figure 19 show the mostly suburban segment (driven from west to east) with a color-coded line to represent field strength in mV/m. This route segment is US Route 40, a four-lane divided highway which transitions east of the state part (green area) to a low-speed suburban highway, flanked by open shopping centers and interspersed with stop lights.

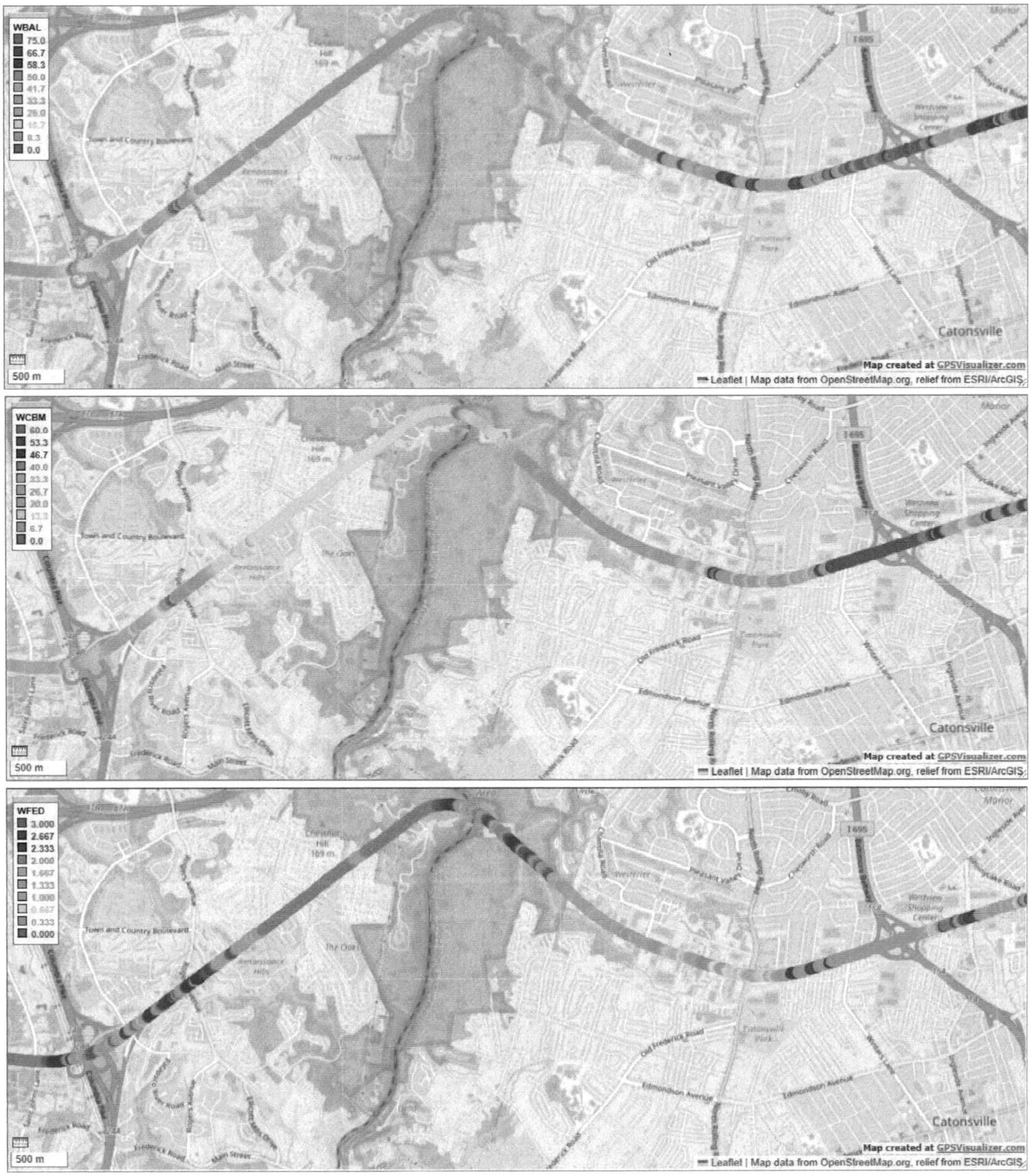

FIGURE 19. MEASURED FIELD STRENGTHS OF WBAL, WCBM, AND WFED ALONG SUBURBAN SEGMENT. COLOR LEGEND DEPICTS FIELD STRENGTH IN MV/M

The maps in Figure 19 show the mostly suburban segment (driven from west to east) with a color-coded line to represent field strength in mV/m. This route segment is US Route 40, a four-lane divided highway, which transitions east of the state part (green area) to a low-speed suburban highway, flanked by open shopping centers and interspersed with stop lights. Field strengths climb from single digits to nearly 60 mV/m for WCBM and 75 mV/m for WBAL. WFED remains around 2 mV/m in the eastern half and shows some apparent clutter loss effects in the business areas in the eastern half of the route segment.

The time-series field strengths of the suburban segment shown in Figure 20 shows the gradual climb, reaching or exceeding 100 mV/m for WCBM and WBAL. WFED's signal stays mostly between 1 and 2 mV/m and is less affected by RMS noise and signal dropouts under overpasses as shown in Figure 23.

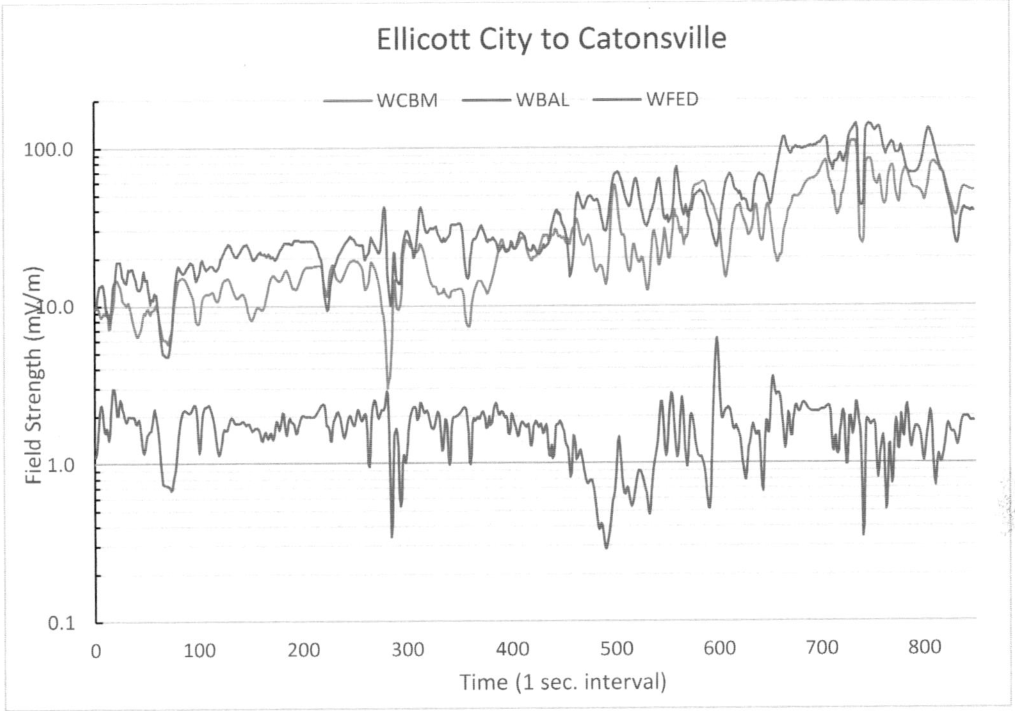

FIGURE 20. FIELD STRENGTHS ALONG THE SUBURBAN SEGMENT

On Figure 21 this suburban-classified route the RMS noise levels begin to rise as the measurements proceed east. This is evident in the red line in the right half of the route.

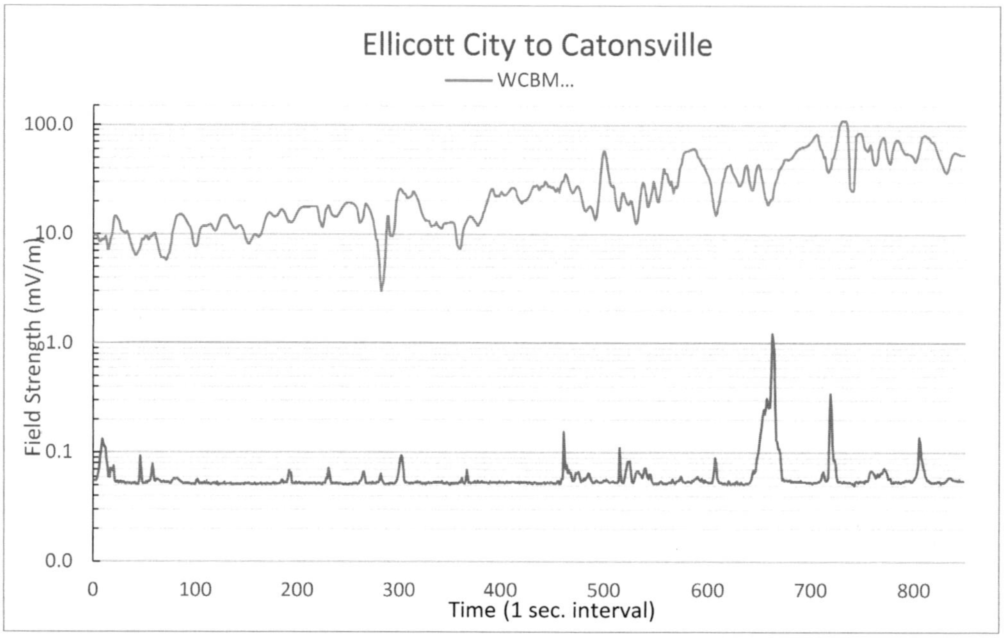

FIGURE 21. WCBM FIELD STRENGTH (GREEN) AND 555 KHZ RMS NOISE MEASUREMENT (RED).

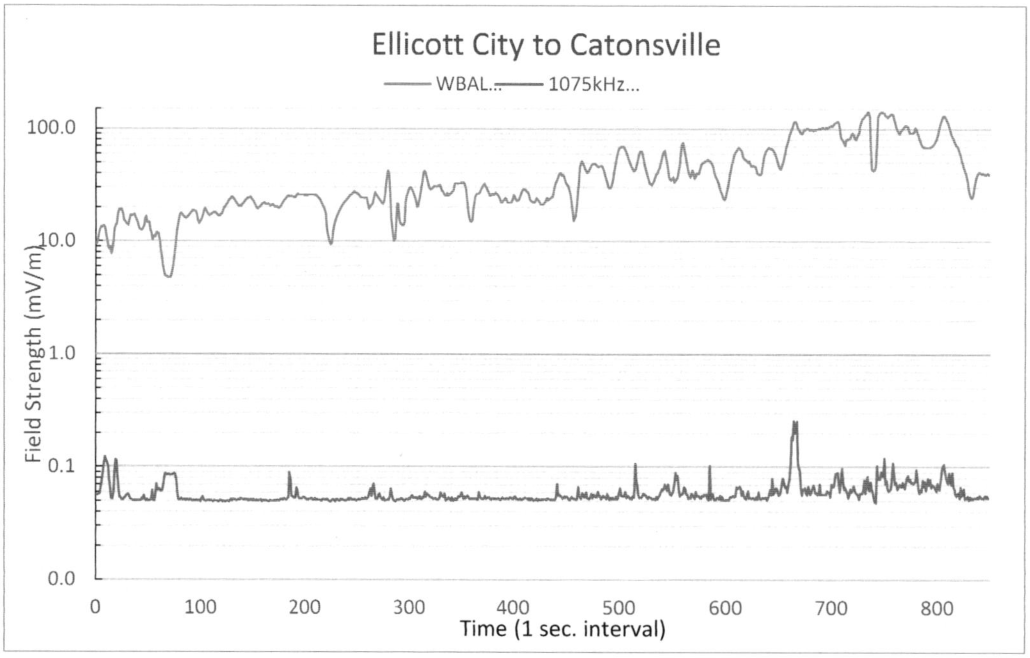

FIGURE 22. WBAL FIELD STRENGTH (GREEN) AND 1075 KHZ RMS NOISE MEASUREMENT (RED)

Figures 21-23 show the expected reduction in RMS noise as the channel frequencies increase. WFED's measured field strength, nearly 2 mV/m, is close to the predicted groundwave field strength. This results in a usable, but somewhat noisy reception, indicating that a consistent 25 dB (approximately 18:1) ratio of signal to noise is needed for quiet reception.

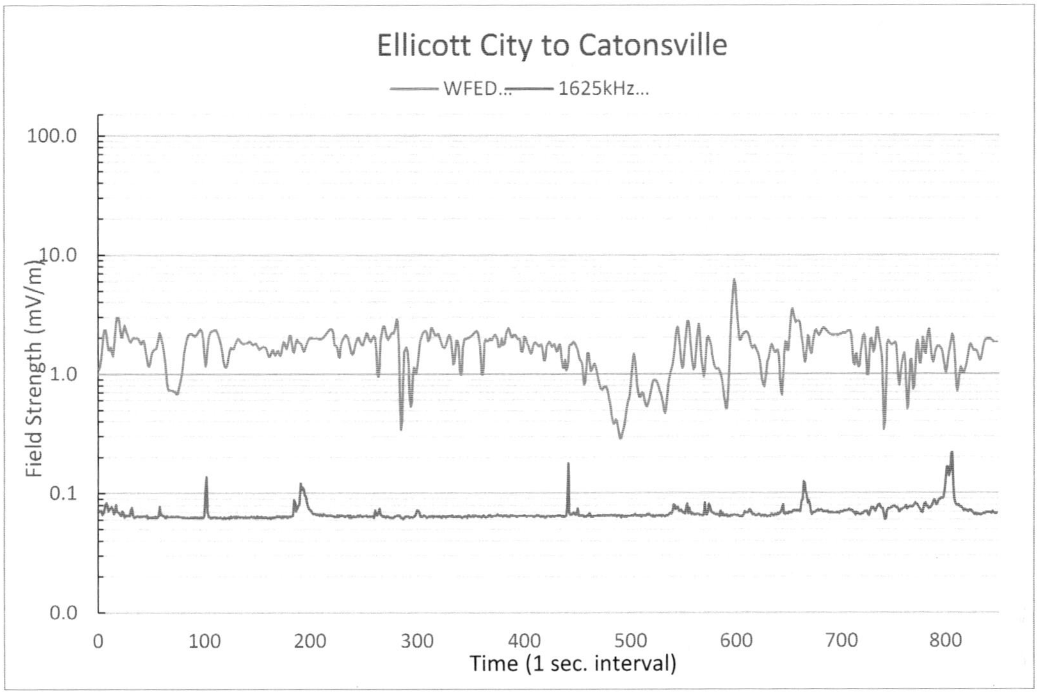

FIGURE 23. WFED FIELD STRENGTH (GREEN) AND 1625 KHZ RMS NOISE MEASUREMENT (RED)

The charts in Figure 24 illustrate the distribution of noise peaks for each noise channel along the suburban segment. The histograms for this segment of the route show little peak noise on 555 and 1625 kHz, while 1075 kHz alone has some added noise occurrences.

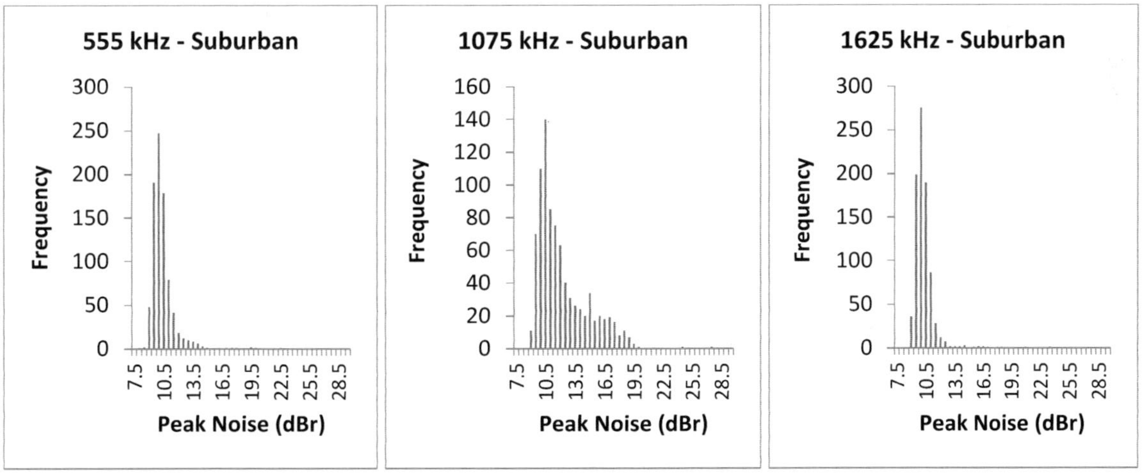

FIGURE 24. DISTRIBUTION OF NOISE PEAKS FOR EACH NOISE CHANNEL ALONG THE SUBURBAN ROUTE SEGMENT

The audio tracks for the noise channels shown in Figure 25 indicate that most of the increased noise at 1075 kHz was produced by a burst of noise with line-frequency related "buzz" characteristic.

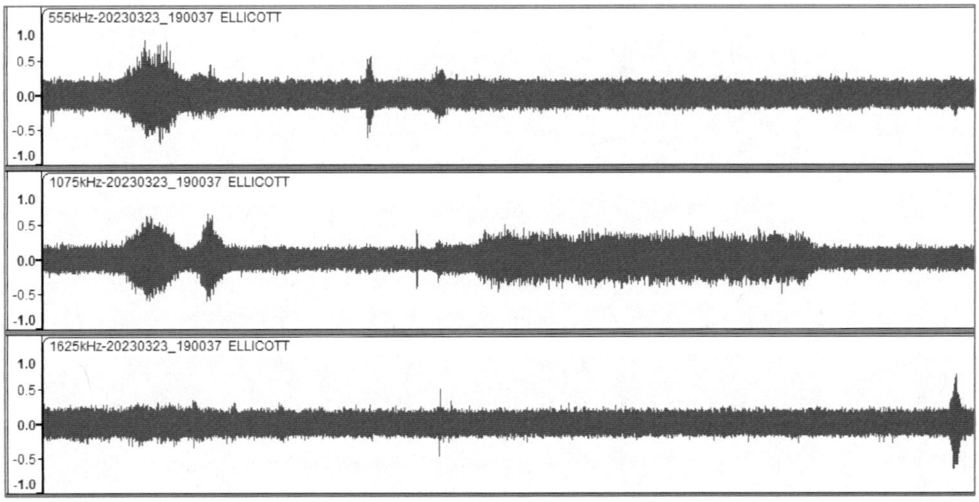

FIGURE 25. NOISE MEASUREMENT OF 555 KHZ (TOP), 1075 KHZ (CENTER) AND 1625 KHZ (BOTTOM) ALONG THE SUBURBAN ROUTE

The audio waveforms of the three noise channels in the first 2.6 minutes of the suburban route show the noise burst beginning midway through this sample and lasting for more than a minute. The noise channels at 555 kHz and 1625 kHz were not affected by the RF noise on 1075 kHz.

The differences in noise by frequency is clear from Figure 25: some noise can be limited mostly to one frequency or two frequencies, but rarely on all three frequencies. The frequency restriction may be due to inductive and capacitive characteristics of the electrical source (presumably power lines), which may form a resonance, or a low-pass or high-pass filter.

Catonsville to West Baltimore (Suburban-Urban)

The maps in Figure 26 show the transition to a suburban-urban segment (driven from west to east) with a color-coded line to represent field strength in mV/m.

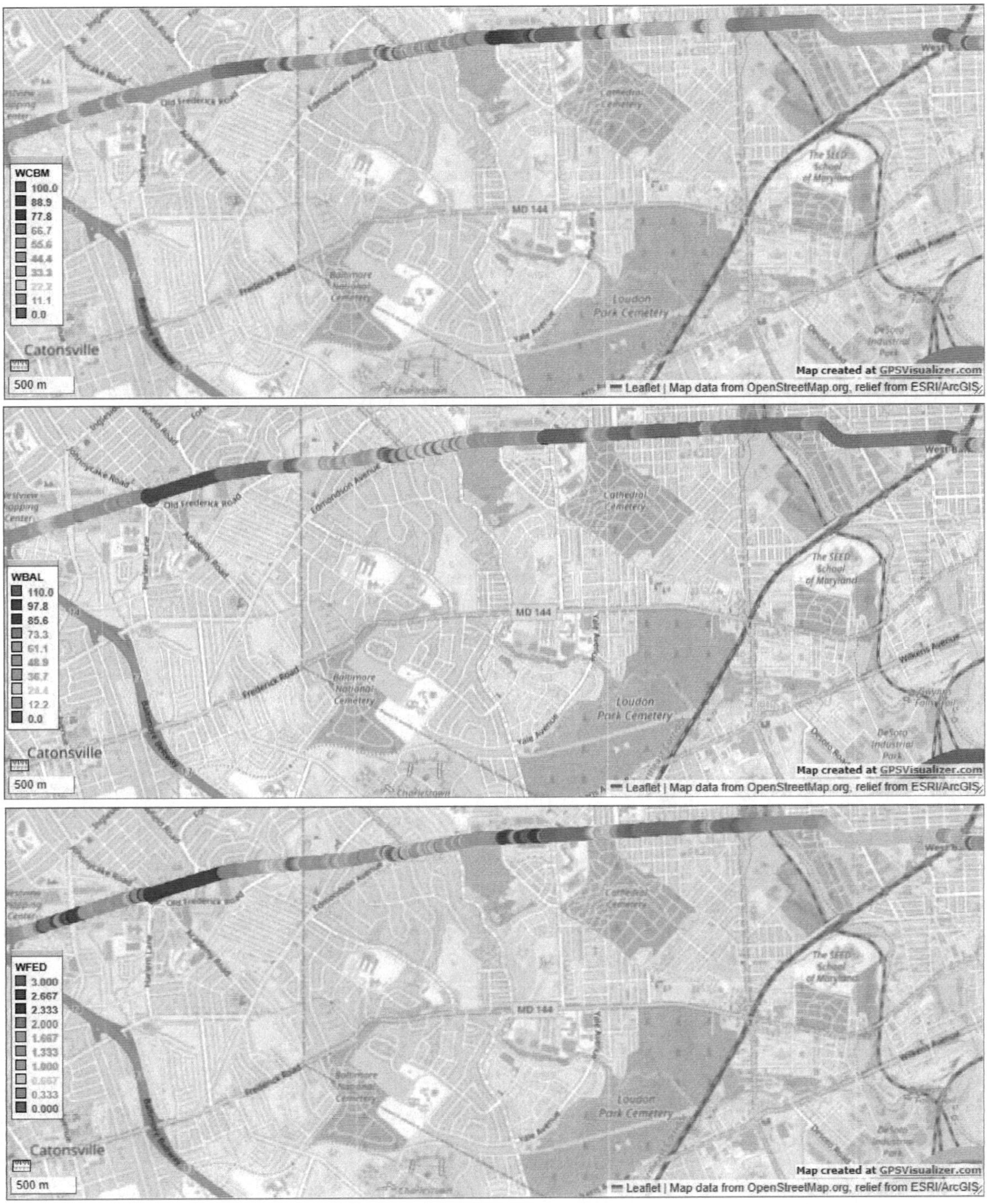

FIGURE 26. MEASURED FIELD STRENGTHS OF WBAL, WCBM, AND WFED ALONG SUBURBAN-URBAN SEGMENT. LEGEND DEPICTS FIELD STRENGTH COLORS IN MV/M.

One thing that is striking is the intensity of the WCBM and WBAL signals, which reach maximums of 100 mV/m and 110 mV/m (shown in violet). It is notable that WCBM is located farther northwest, 11 miles from the location of the maximum, while WBAL is located north of the maximum at a distance of 6 miles, yet the signal peaks are reversed in location.

The path ray from WCBM to its peak on US Route 40 appears to be in line with a forested area and a creek (Gwynns Falls/Leakin Park), which may improve ground conductivity. There is nothing apparent that would be responsible for the location of WBAL's peak field strength; earlier parts of the previous route segment, north of Ellicott City, are closer to the transmitter site than the location of the observed peak, which was northeast of Catonsville.

Field strengths gradually decline off their peaks from the suburban route segment as shown in Figure 27, settling to approximately 40 mV/m for WCBM and 20 mV/m for WBAL. WFED's signal remains within 1 and 2 mV/m.

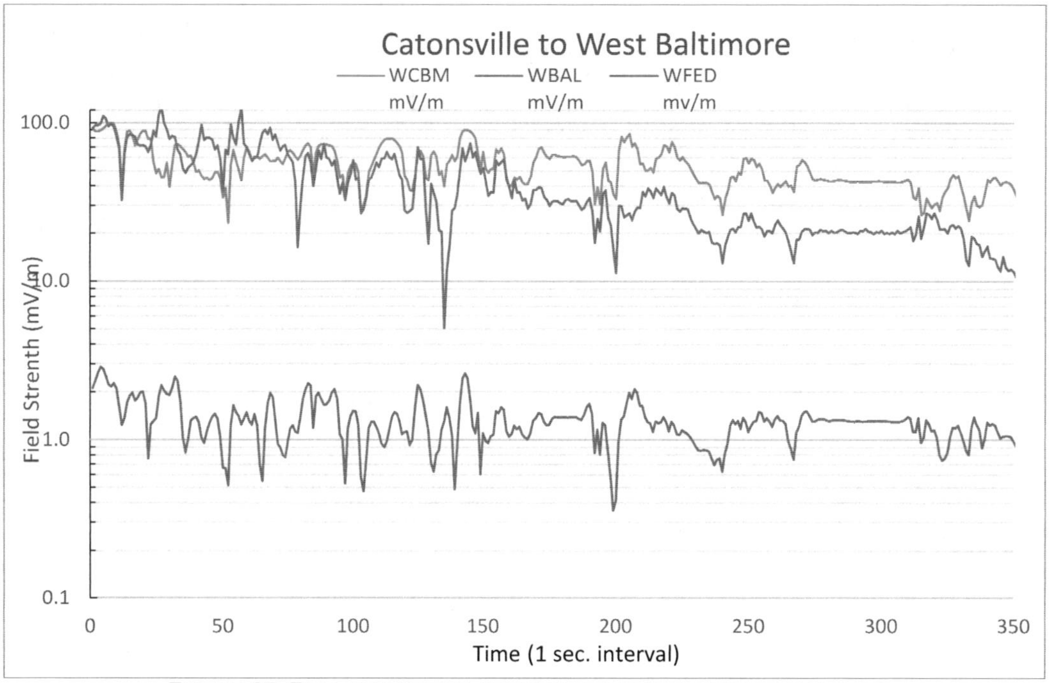

FIGURE 27. FIELD STRENGTHS ALONG THE SUBURBAN-URBAN SEGMENT

The relative uniformity in station signals along the suburban-urban route segment is likely due to two factors. First, this section of US Route 40 (becoming West Franklin Street to the east) is a wide 6-land divided roadway with few nearby obstructions. Second, much of the West Baltimore area has neighborhoods comprised of apartments and homes that are no more than two stories high. This building clutter environment has a minimal effect of groundwave signal propagation, particularly from the open roadway.

The charts in Figure 28 to Figure 30 illustrate the distribution of noise peaks for each noise channel along this route segment. Peak RF noise levels on the test frequencies are relatively low due to the significant separation from power lines, traffic signals, and buildings on US Route 40 and West Franklin Street, which minimize interference from these kinds of noise sources.

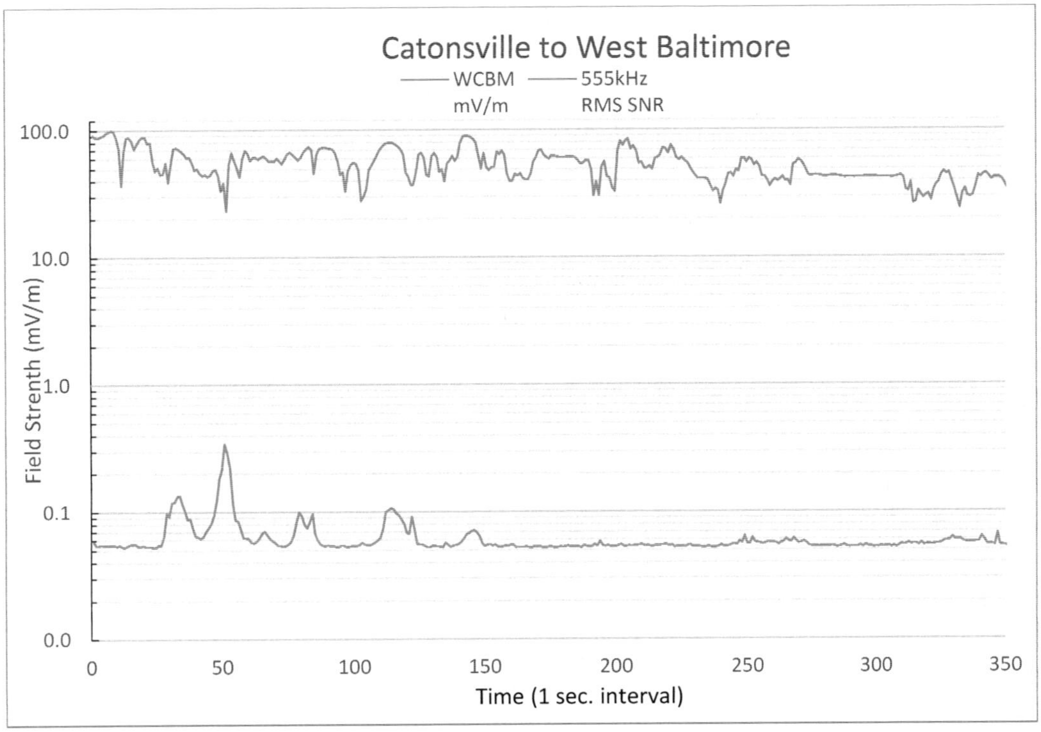

FIGURE 28. WCBM FIELD STRENGTH (GREEN) AND 555 KHz RMS NOISE MEASUREMENT (RED)

The lowest test frequency, for 555 kHz shows some scattered occurrences at higher noise levels, while 1075 and 1625 kHz have tighter distributions at the lower noise levels.

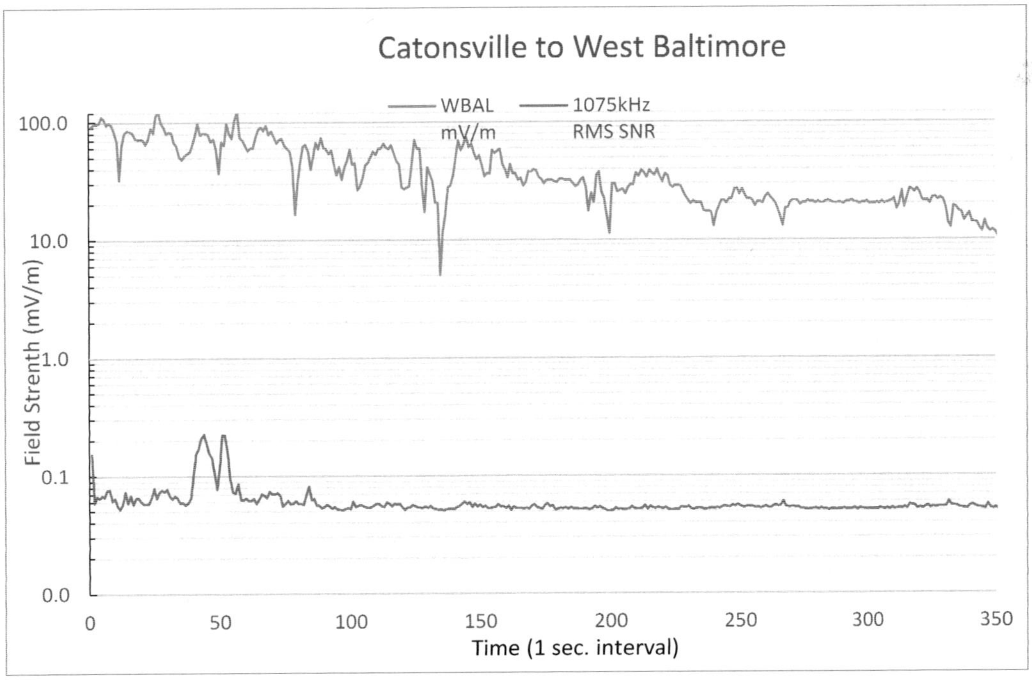

FIGURE 29. WBAL FIELD STRENGTH (GREEN) AND 1075 KHz RMS NOISE MEASUREMENT (RED)

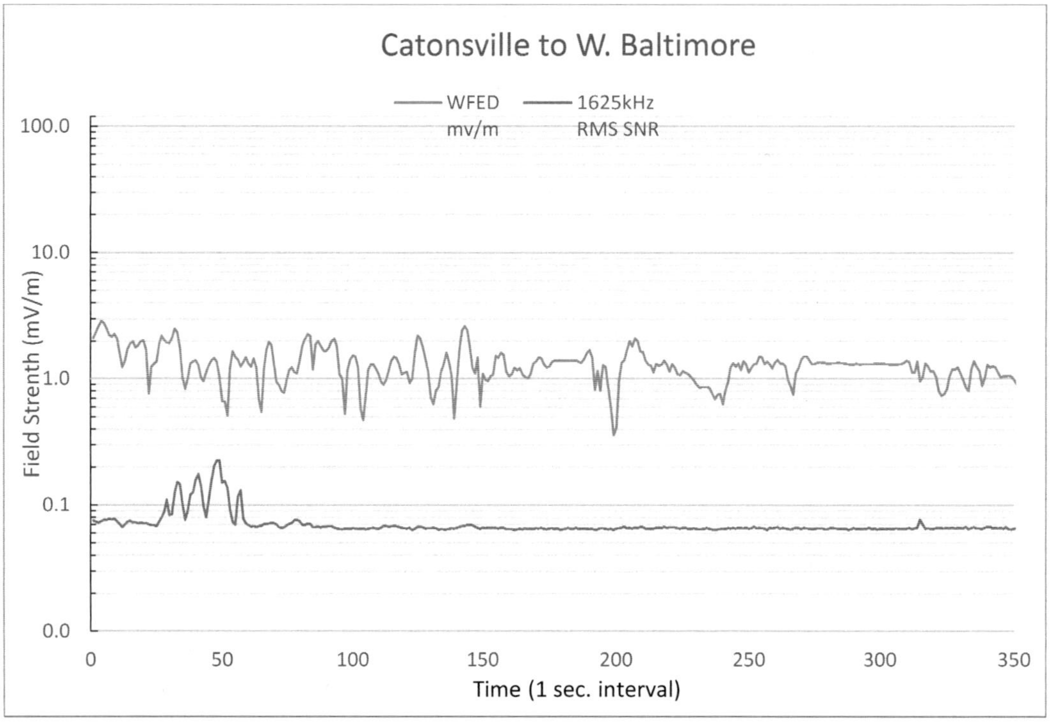

FIGURE 30. WFED FIELD STRENGTH (GREEN) AND 1625 KHZ RMS NOISE MEASUREMENT (RED)

The charts in Figure 31 illustrate the distribution of noise peaks for each noise channel along the suburban-urban segment.

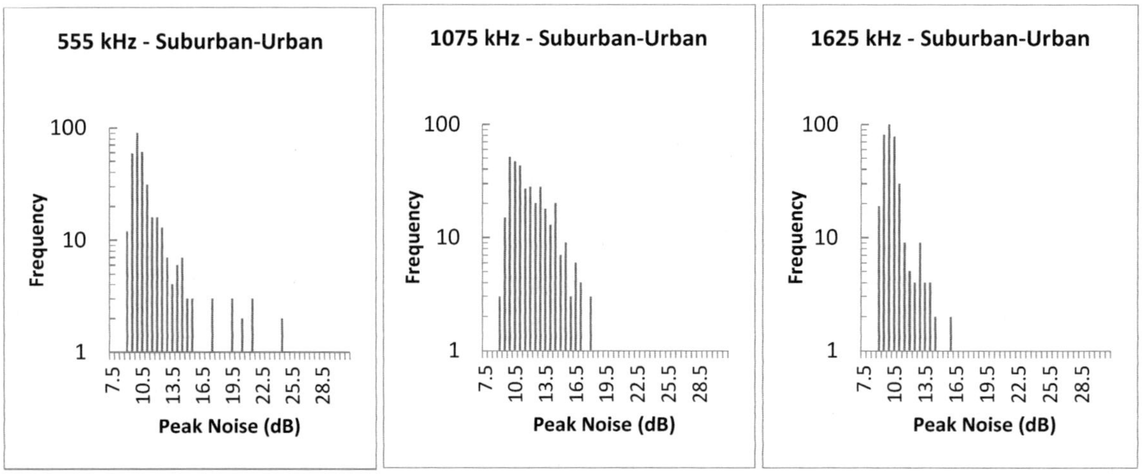

FIGURE 31. DISTRIBUTION OF NOISE PEAKS FOR EACH NOISE CHANNEL ALONG THE SUBURBAN-URBAN ROUTE SEGMENT

West Franklin to West Mulberry Streets (Urban)

The maps in Figure 32 show the urban segment (driven from west to east) with a color-coded line to represent field strength in mV/m.

FIGURE 32. MEASURED FIELD STRENGTHS OF WBAL, WCBM, AND WFED ALONG URBAN SEGMENT. LEGEND DEPICTS FIELD STRENGTH COLORS IN MV/M

Field strengths from WCBM and WBAL again reach high levels, sharing the 100 mV/m scale (see Figure 33). WFED shows a remarkably similar track of field strengths, but on a scale of 3 mV/m maximum. West Mulberry Street comprises much of this route segment and is part of US-40, a fast four-lane divided road.

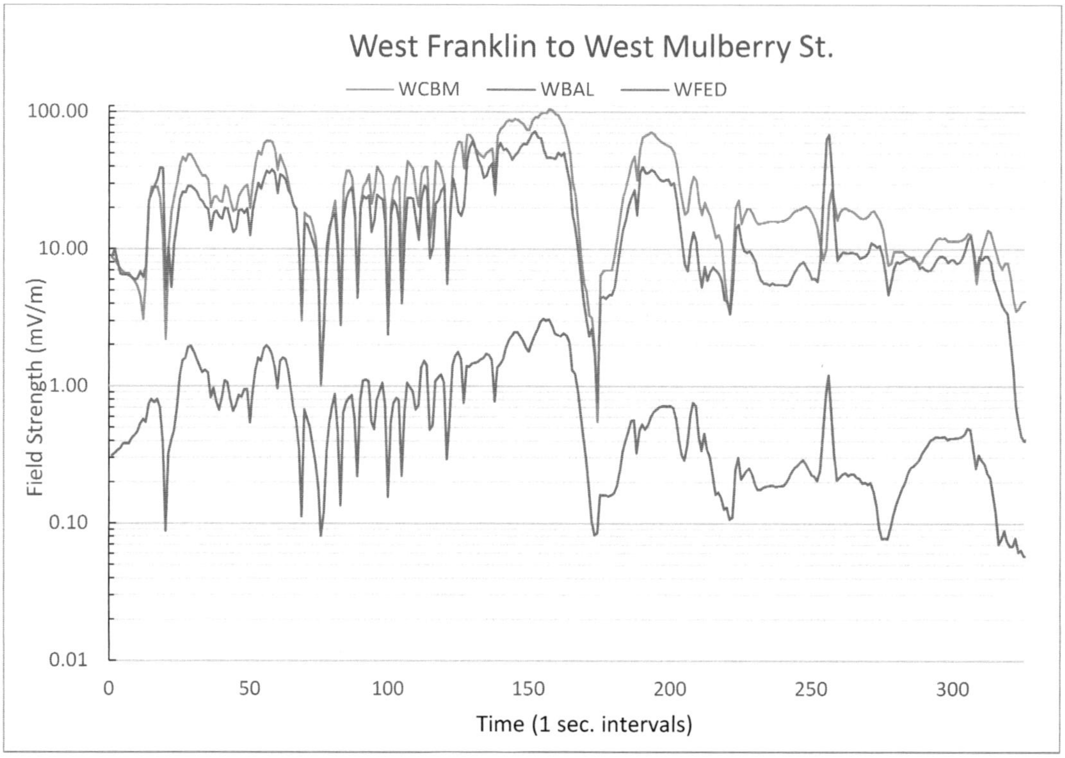

FIGURE 33. FIELD STRENGTHS ALONG THE URBAN SEGMENT

Field strengths in the open section of this route remain relatively high but display a regular pattern of signal rise and fall. In the middle of blocks the signals dip because of clutter attenuation. The signals reach maximums near the crossing of MD Route 129, which is an open area that is distant from buildings. The three signals drop in the last half mile to the east, where it turns into a city street, flanked by two- to three-story buildings.

The cyclical effect on signals in passing through city blocks is clear in these charts. Driving under the large Metro West Garage caused a major dip in signals, shown in the middle. Continuing east, signals decline in the dense low-rise business district.

Figure 34 shows a major jump in noise around 255 seconds from the segment's start, crossing North Howard Street in Baltimore. The environment in this area is densely packed two story buildings, and nothing appears out of the ordinary until one notices the electric streetcar lines overhead. The 440-volt AC streetcar lines radiate noise that is manifest as a loud "buzz" in the station audio reception.

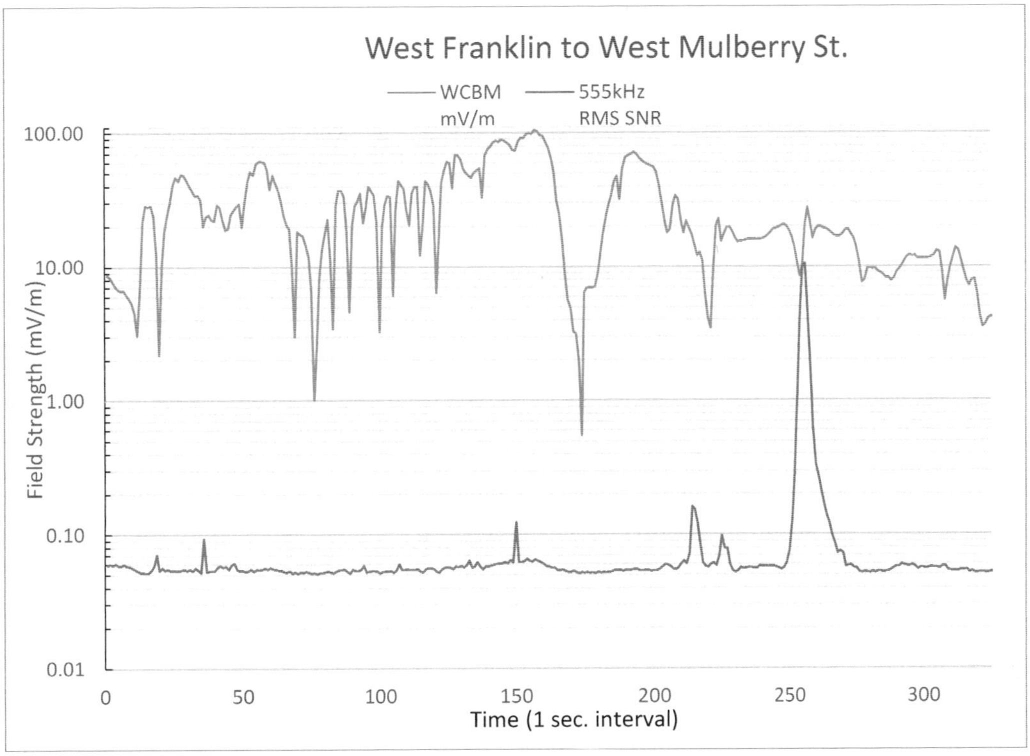

FIGURE 34. WCBM FIELD STRENGTH (GREEN) AND 555 KHZ RMS NOISE MEASUREMENT (RED)

North Howard is a north-south route for the Light RailLink line, shown in Figure 35. This line can be seen in the map of Figure 32. Although there was no trolley nearby at the time, the electric lines, less than 25 feet over the road, appear to be energized continuously and radiate high levels of RF noise. It is notable that the field strength of these emissions decrease with frequency, by comparing Figure 34, Figure 36 and Figure 37.

FIGURE 35. BALTIMORE LIGHT RAILLINK.

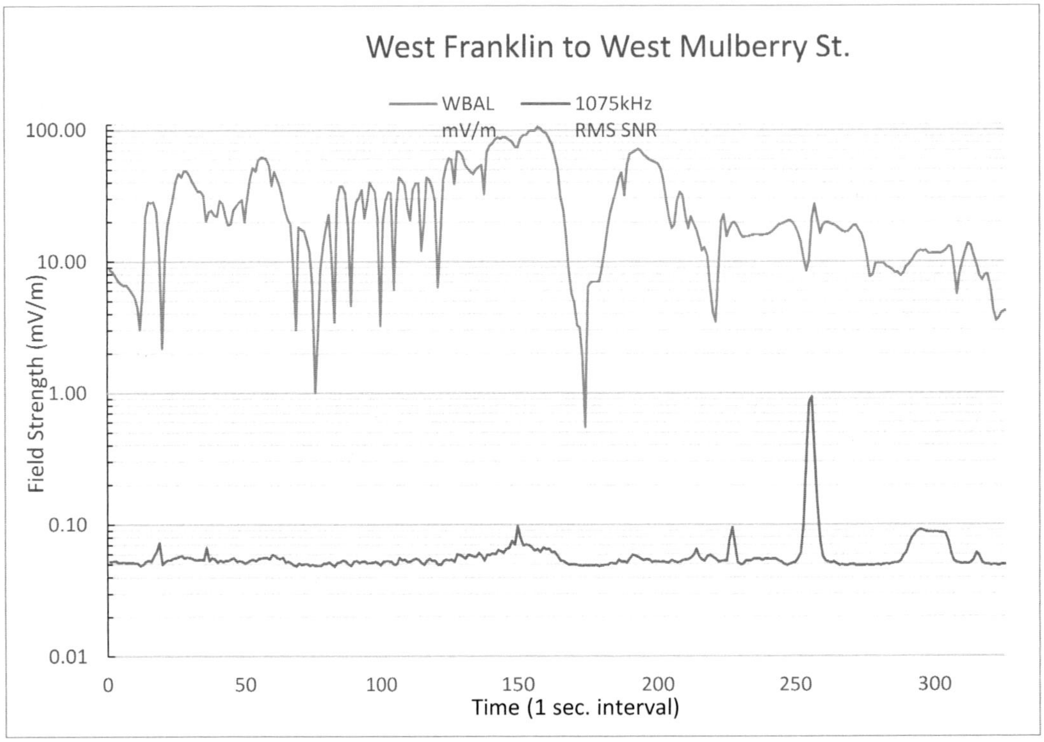

FIGURE 36. WBAL FIELD STRENGTH (GREEN) AND 1075 KHZ RMS NOISE MEASUREMENT (RED)

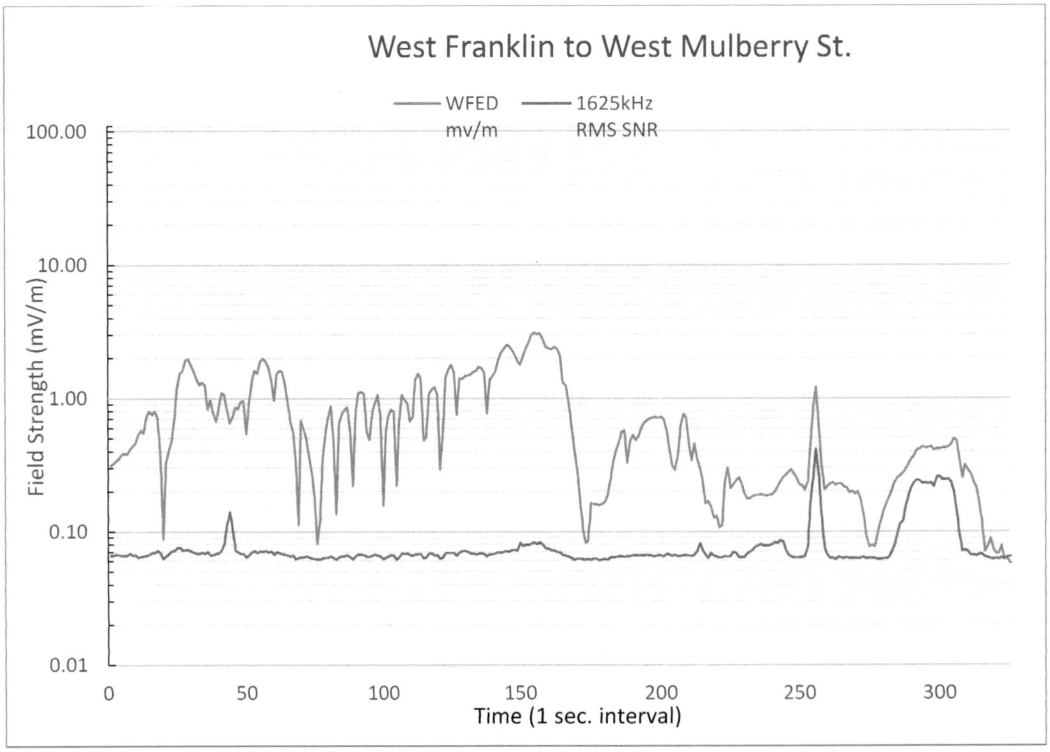

FIGURE 37. WFED FIELD STRENGTH (GREEN) AND 1625 KHZ RMS NOISE MEASUREMENT (RED)

The charts in Figure 38 illustrate the distribution of noise peaks for each noise channel along the urban segment. Due to the relatively open space around most of this route the occurrence of noise peaks is reduced. The 1625 kHz test frequency shows slightly higher peaks than usual.

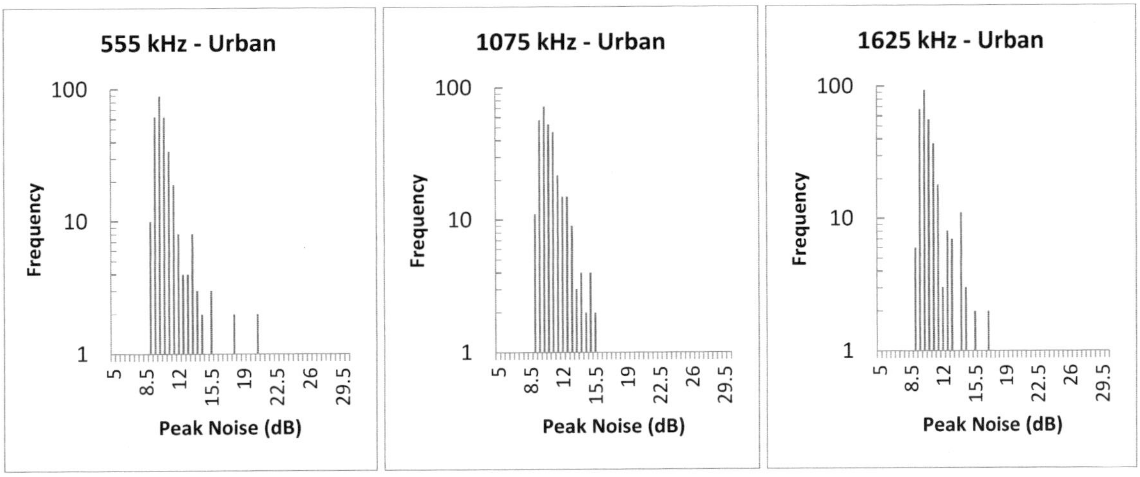

FIGURE 38. DISTRIBUTION OF NOISE PEAKS FOR EACH NOISE CHANNEL ALONG THE URBAN ROUTE SEGMENT

Listeners to WCBM and WBAL should receive low noise signals until the end of this route. The measurement includes a turn around the corner to Saint Paul Street, which shows a rapid fall in field strengths and a rise in noise-limited audio.

West Mulberry Street Through Downtown Baltimore (Dense Urban)

The maps in Figure 39 show the Dense Urban segment (driven from north to south) with a color-coded line to represent field strength in mV/m.

FIGURE 39. MEASURED FIELD STRENGTH OF WCBM, WBAL, AND WFED ALONG DENSE URBAN SEGMENT. LEGEND DEPICTS FIELD STRENGTH COLORS IN MV/M

The final segment of this route passes through Baltimore's central business district, starting at West Mulberry Street and turning onto Saint Paul Street (aka Light Street). Due to the city's numerous high-rise buildings, including at least five exceeding 35 stories, the radio signals from nearby transmitters exhibit varying levels of attenuation.

Field strengths for this route are shown in Figure 40. WBAL's signal, for example, begins at 20 mV/m at the corner of Mulberry and Saint Paul Streets but quickly declines as one heads south. Beyond the harbor, the signal drops below 0.5 mV/m, a significant reduction for a 50-kW transmitter just 10 miles away.

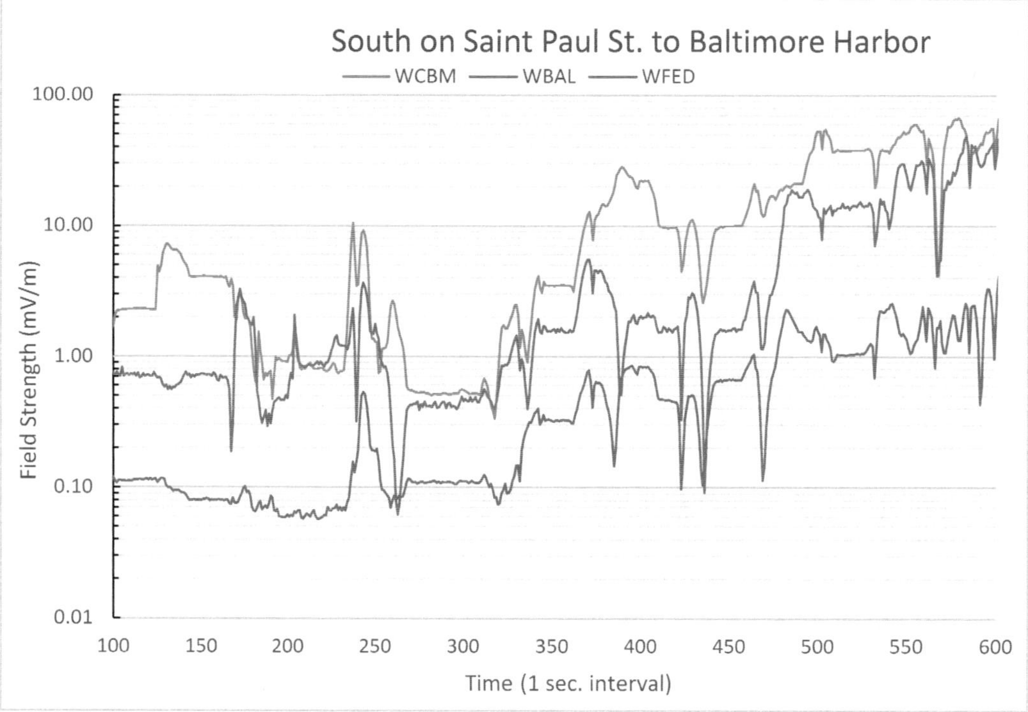

FIGURE 40. FIELD STRENGTHS ALONG THE DENSE URBAN SEGMENT

In contrast, WCBM's signal performs similarly through the high-rise district, dropping to 0.6 mV/m. Both signals rise again out of the shadow of the high-rise area, rising to 20 mV/m for WBAL and 55 mV/m for WCBM on part of Conway Street, heading toward Camden Yards stadium. One can realize the devastating impact of urban clutter by observing that the field strengths of these two stations were nearly 100 mV/m on Mulberry Street, less than a mile away!

WFED's signal, arriving from the southwest, shows the reverse pattern. Its signal weakens on the north side of downtown, rarely exceeding 0.1 mV/m along Saint Paul and Mulberry Streets.

The "urban canyon" on Saint Paul Street weakens the station signals to as low as 0.5 V/m, but conversely, Figure 41, Figure 42 and Figure 43 indicate that noise levels are for the most part low. As shown in Figure 41, the field strength of RMS noise on 555 kHz is around 50 to 60 mV/m.

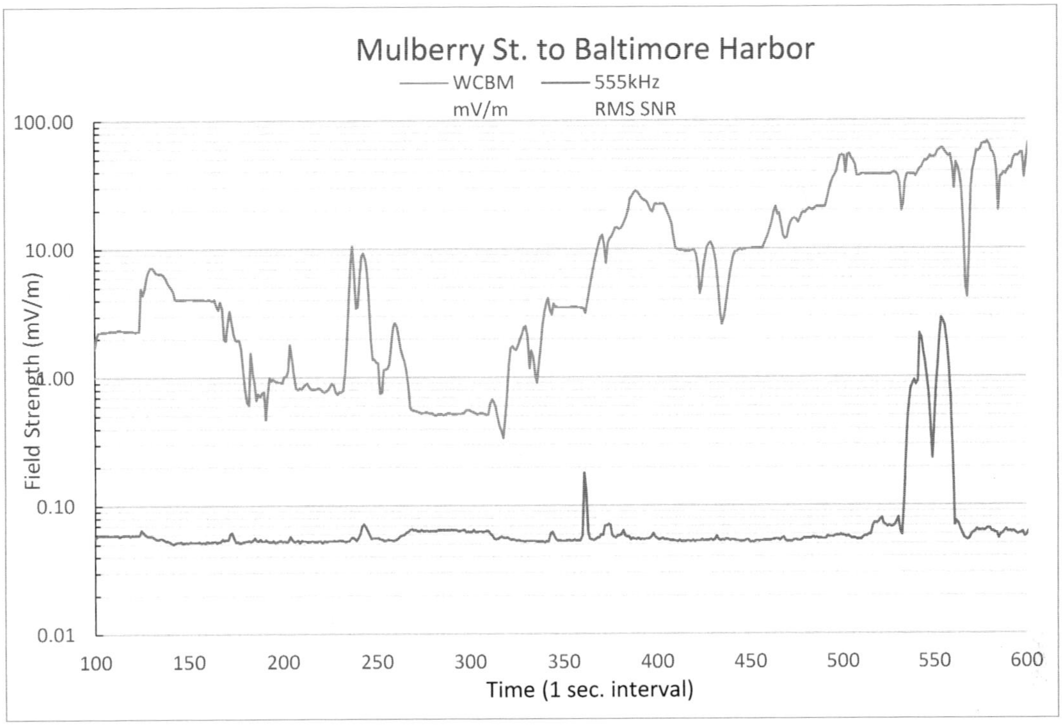

FIGURE 41. WCBM FIELD STRENGTH (GREEN) AND 555 KHZ RMS NOISE MEASUREMENT (RED)

While passing through the urban canyon in the first half of St. Paul Street the reception is weak and noisy, but once the measurements drove south of the skyscrapers, and turned west on Conway Street the field strengths returned. However, there are two closely spaced occasions where the RMS noise rises enormously, near the end of this route.

Close examination of the map found that this happened at the last (left) turn to Cal Ripken Way, across from the Camden Yards baseball stadium. Cal Ripken Way is South Howard Street, just two blocks north. These high-noise points occur at Camden Station, a depot for the Baltimore Light RailLink, and the same trolley line that causes the observed noise burst on Mulberry Street.

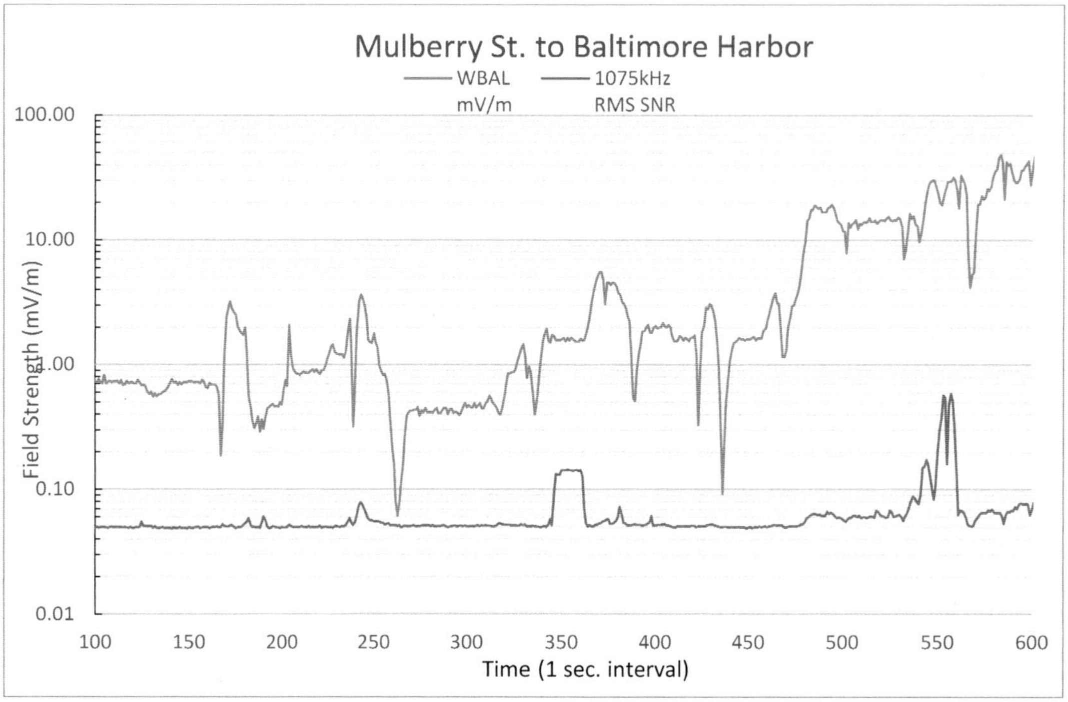

FIGURE 42. WBAL FIELD STRENGTH (GREEN) AND 1075 KHZ RMS NOISE MEASUREMENT (RED)

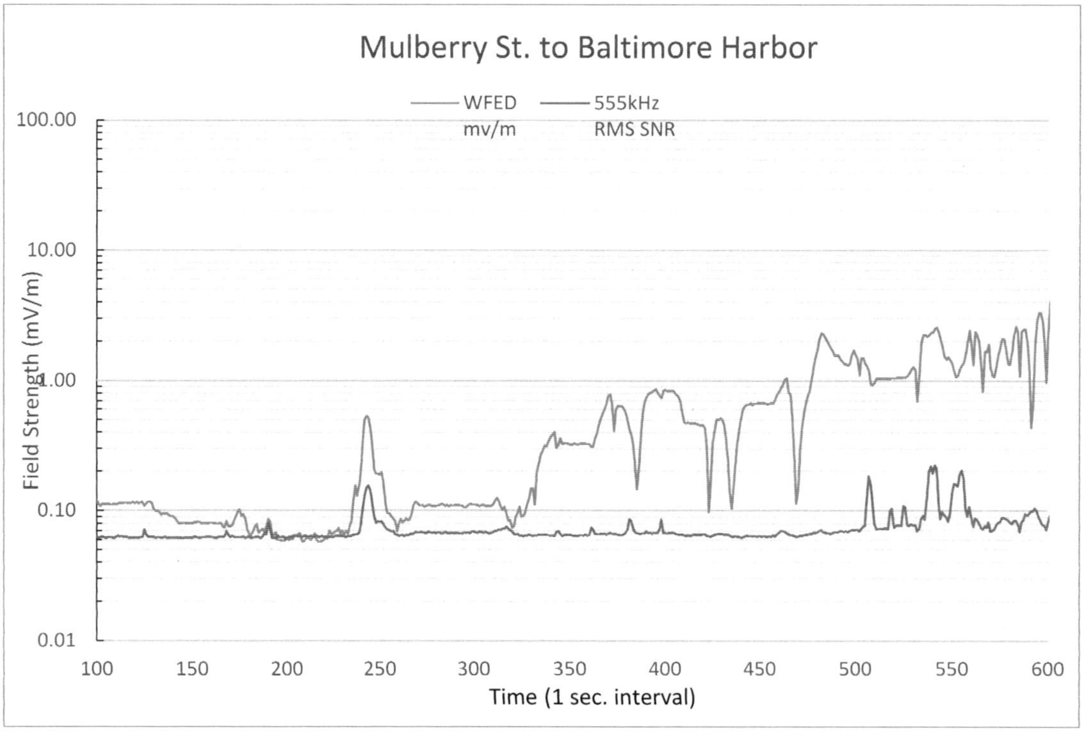

FIGURE 43. WFED FIELD STRENGTH (GREEN) AND 1625 KHZ RMS NOISE MEASUREMENT (RED)

The charts in Figure 44 illustrate the distribution of noise peaks for each noise channel along the route segment. This peak noise was surprisingly low, like the RMS noise measurements. Despite the drops in station signals discussed above, listening tests confirmed that that the noise increases were less of a "crackle" and more like swishing noises.

Perhaps contrary to what one would expect, the noise levels in Baltimore's downtown area are not high, aside from the intense RF noise near the light rail lines. If AM station signals were not severely weakened by building clutter loss and shadowing, the low urban RF noise levels would result in service quality that was found in suburban areas, far outside the city.

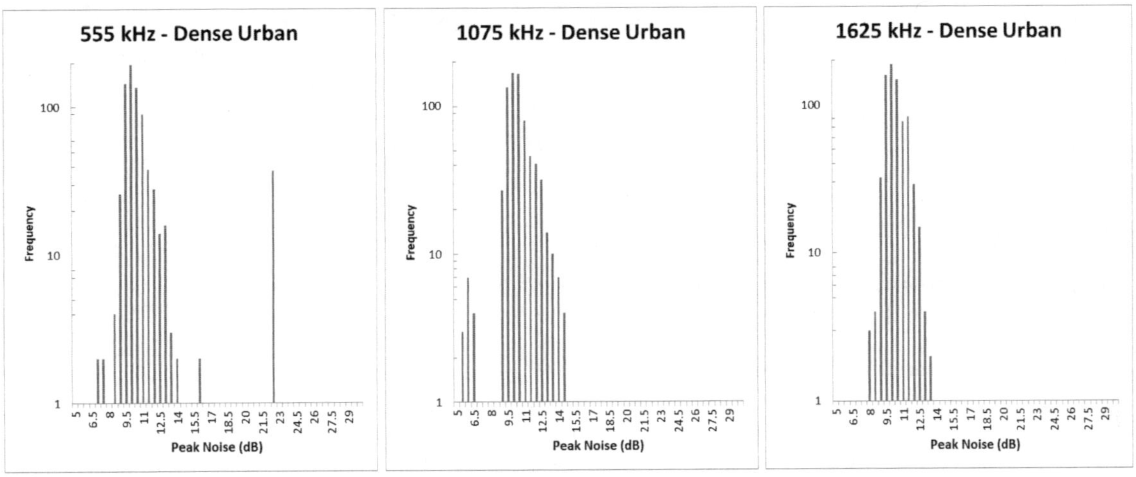

FIGURE 44. DISTRIBUTION OF NOISE PEAKS FOR EACH NOISE CHANNEL ALONG THE DENSE URBAN ROUTE SEGMENT

Conclusions

This study examined the reception quality of large-class AM radio stations in various environments, including rural, suburban, and urban areas. While these stations boast wide-area coverage, audio quality can be affected by factors such as RF noise and field strength.

Rural Environments

In rural areas, field strengths and reception quality often fell short of predicted levels, as measured from a vehicle on the roadways. This discrepancy can likely be attributed to factors including poor ground conductivity, rough terrain, vegetation, and power line re-radiation. Despite average field strengths of 1.5 mV/m, which should theoretically provide satisfactory reception, noise fluctuations and occasional noise peaks can disrupt listening experiences.

Suburban Environments

Suburban areas, characterized by a mix of residential and commercial zones, offered a more stable reception environment compared to rural areas. However, electrical noise from traffic, local businesses, and power lines could still impact signal quality. High field strengths from powerful stations like WCBM and WBAL helped to mitigate these effects.

Urban Environments

Downtown Baltimore presented the most challenging environment for AM radio reception. Densely populated areas with tall buildings significantly attenuated signal strength, leading to fading, noise, and occasional loss of signal. This underscores the importance of strategic transmitter placement to ensure adequate coverage in urban centers.

Key Findings

Field strength variations: Field strengths often deviated from predicted levels likely for two principal reasons: (1) predicted fields from stations based on traditional ground-wave propagation models may be substantially less than the actual field strengths due to inaccurate conductivity data, and, (2) building clutter can reduce field strengths by a factor of up to 100 to 1 (40 dB), neither of which are accounted for in signal coverage maps.

Noise sources: Power lines, traffic, and nearby electrical equipment introduce noise into the AM band, but signal-to-RMS RF noise levels are generally good for mobile listening at field strengths as low as 3 to 5 mV/m.

Urban challenges: Densely built-up areas can significantly attenuate AM signals that effectively result in coverage 'holes' where AM reception is unacceptable. These are of course areas of population concentration, which can result in large losses of service to a station's service population.

Frequency-specific noise: Noise is often frequency-dependent, affecting certain channels more than others.

Recommendations

Strategic transmitter placement: Consider locating AM transmitters to ensure adequate coverage in built-up areas, to overcome urban clutter loss.

Deploy Single Frequency Networks: Relocation of primary transmitter sites near downtown areas may be prohibitively costly, but a synchronous booster transmitter (requiring FCC approval) can fill in urban signal loss, restoring thousands of potential listeners. The cost of a booster transmitter on a commercial building may be economically feasible, depending upon the population that may be served.

Receiver design: Improve car AM antenna efficiency, which has been lost over time through miniaturization and for aesthetic reasons. Add receiver noise-reduction capabilities to enhance audio performance in challenging environments.

By addressing these factors, the AM radio industry can strive to provide a more consistent and reliable listening experience for audiences in diverse settings.

Appendix A – Information on Devices Used in Measurement

Measurement Antenna

The mobile measurement antenna (shown below) is an active E-field type using a telescopic whip, strapped to the roof of the vehicle. The telescopic whip antenna was extended to 28 inches, which balanced antenna gain and avoidance of overload from strong nearby AM stations.

FIGURE

The antenna is connected to an integrated amplifier, providing unity gain across the AM band. The output impedance is approximately 50 ohms to drive LMR-200 cable. A schematic of the impedance converter is shown in the figure below, comprising a J-FET input and a balanced bipolar transistor output.

The amplifier case is enclosed in a styrofoam box on all sides, except the bottom, for support and stability at highway speeds. The 12 VDC power cable and RF coax were routed through the window to the instrumentation in the vehicle.

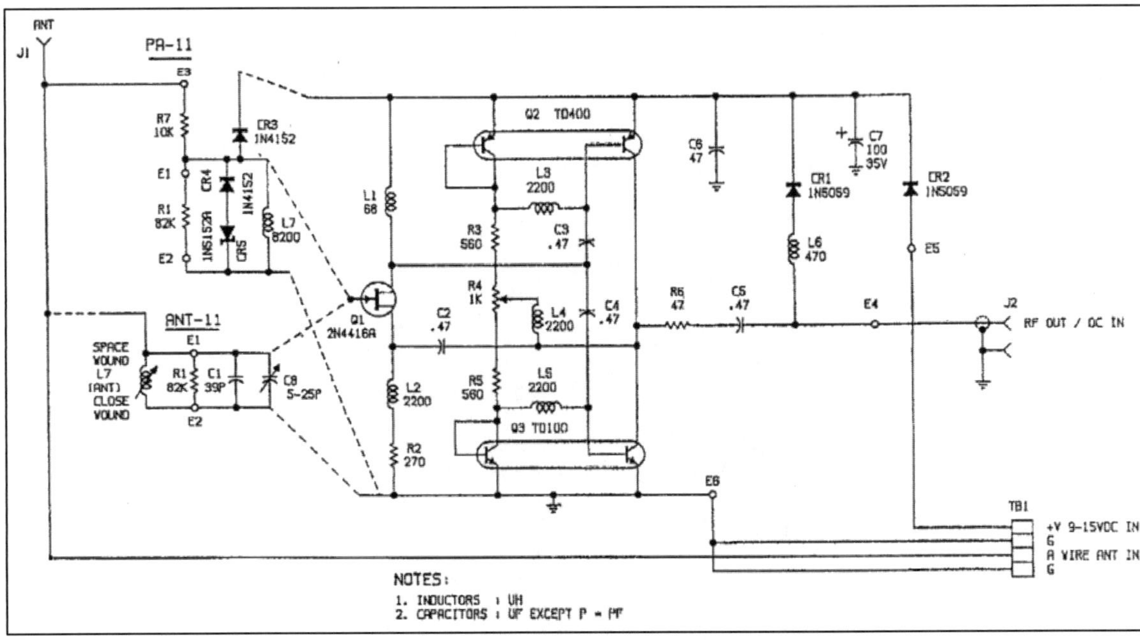

POTOMAC INSTRUMENTS PI-11 IMPEDANCE CONVERTER

To ensure the 12-volt power to the instrumentation was free of car electrical noise, a low pass filter was used, as shown in the schematic and photo here. The filter's case was tied to a chassis bolt and the dash 12-volt socket, and effectively removed alternator ripple as well as high frequency noise.

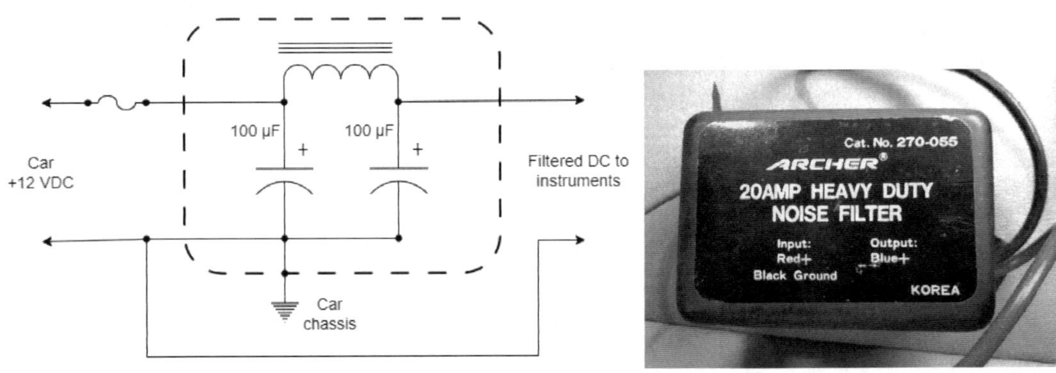

FIGURE

Receiver Hardware

The measurements were collected with an SDRplay model RSPdx® "software defined receiver" (SDR, shown at right) capable of monitoring radio frequencies from 1 kHz to 2 GHz at 14-bit resolution. With the supplied SDRuno® software it can analyze and store the entire AM broadcast band continuously. A Hewlett Packard Pavilion laptop running Windows 10 controlled the SDR and recorded data.

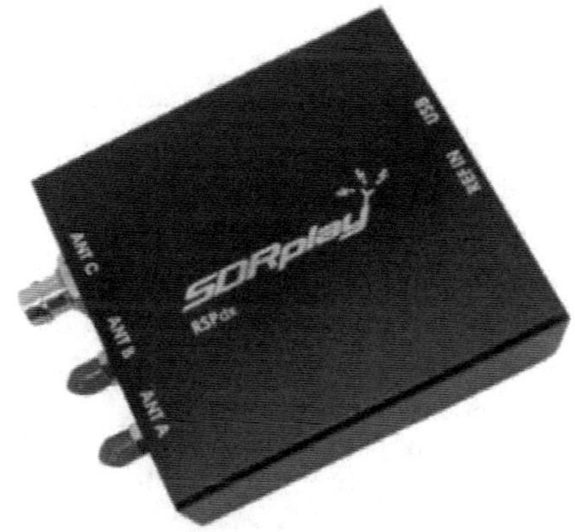

FIGURE

The RSPdx ensures a high dynamic range by activating a 2 MHz low pass filter for the AM band measurements. This ensured that out-of-band signals would not degrade performance.

The whole-band spectrum recordings are stored on the computer as WAV format files, except the I and Q data are stored in what would be left and right channels for audio. The data was processed later to convert the IQ data into audio files in FLAC format. The times on the audio files match the graphs, so readers can observe the measurements while they hear the reception on the three “quiet” channels and the three AM stations.

The SDRplay’s measurements and controls are displayed continuously during operation, providing a real-time display, like spectrum analyzers. However, it offers some unique features during live operation. Shown on page A-6 is a screenshot of the unit in operation, displaying the full AM band and dozens of AM signals. The center portion displays a frequency range of 500 to 1750 kHz, including the carrier reference pilot at 1720 kHz. The lower portion of the display is a “waterfall” chart of the signal intensity and bandwidth over time.

A data sheet and features list for the SDRplay are provided below.

SDRplay

RSPdx
Multi-antenna port 14-bit SDR

The SDRplay RSPdx is a wideband full-featured 14-bit SDR which covers the entire RF spectrum from 1kHz to 2GHz. Combined with the power of readily available SDR receiver software (including 'SDRuno' for Windows and Multi-Platform 'SDRconnect' supplied by SDRplay) you can monitor up to 10MHz spectrum at a time. The RSPdx provides three software selectable antenna inputs, and an external clock input. All it needs is a computer and an antenna to provide excellent communications receiver functionality. A documented API allows developers to create new demodulators or applications around the platform.

KEY BENEFITS & FEATURES

- Covers all frequencies from 1kHz through VLF, LF, MW, HF, VHF, UHF and L-band to 2GHz, with no gaps
- Receive, monitor and record up to 10MHz of spectrum at a time
- Performance below 2MHz substantially enhanced – improved dynamic range and selectivity
- Software selectable choice of 3 antenna ports
- Enhanced ability to cope with extremely strong signals
- External clock input for synchronisation purposes, or connection to GPS reference clock for extra frequency accuracy
- Excellent dynamic range for challenging reception conditions
- Free use of windows-based SDRuno software which provides an ever-increasing feature-set
- Strong and growing software support network
- Calibrated S meter/ RF power and SNR measurement with SDRuno (including datalogging to .CSV file capability)
- Documented API provided to allow demodulator or application development on multiple platforms

FIGURE

SDRplay

RSPdx
Multi-antenna port 14-bit SDR

SDRuno™ for Windows FEATURES

- High Dynamic Range mode ("HDR") for RSPdx use below 2MHz
- Highly integrated native Windows support for the SDRplay family
- Multiple 'virtual receivers' for simultaneous reception and demodulation of different types of signals within the same receiver bandwidth
- An integrated frequency scanner (for frequency ranges and stored memory panel lists)
- A selectivity filter with an ultimate rejection greater than 140dB.
- A unique distortion-free double stage AGC with fully adjustable parameters
- AFC for FM signals
- Multiple notch filters with BW adjustable to 1Hz + Notch Lock feature
- A unique synchronous AM mode with selectable/adjustable sidebands, dedicated PLL input filter, & selectable PLL time constants
- SNR (stereo noise reduction), featuring a proprietary noise reduction algorithm for stereo broadcast
- Powerful wideband noise filter for addressing common sources of RFI (e.g. power supplies, internet over DSL etc.)
- Calibration for receiver frequency errors
- RDS support optimised for low signal environment
- Active Noise cancelling
- CAT and Omnirig control
- Calibrated RF Power Meter with > 100dB of usable range
- Calibrated S-Meter supporting IARU S-Meter Standard
- The ability to save power (dBm) and SNR (dB)
- measurements over time, to a CSV file for future analysis
- IQ output accessible for 3rd party applications

CONNECTIONS

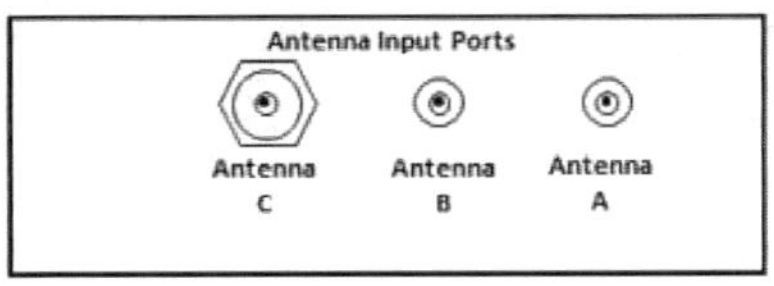

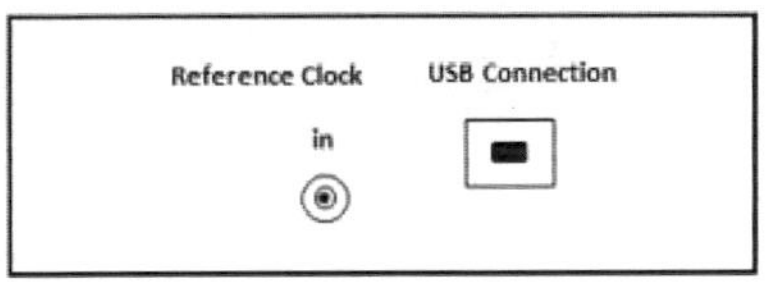

SPECIFICATIONS

General
- Weight 315g
- Size: 113mm x 94mm x 35mm
- Low current consumption:
  - 190mA @ >60MHz (excl Bias T)
  - 120mA @ <60MHz (excl Bias T)

Connectivity
- USB 2.0 (high speed) type B socket

Frequency Range
- Continuous coverage 1kHz – 2GHz

Antenna A Port Characteristics
- 1kHz – 2GHz operation
- 50Ω input impedance
- SMA female connector

Antenna B Port Characteristics
- 1kHz – 2GHz operation
- 50Ω input impedance
- SMA female connector
- Selectable 4.7V DC out (see Bias T)

Antenna C Port Characteristics
- 1kHz – 200MHz operation
- 50Ω input impedance
- BNC female connector

Reference Clock Input
- MCX female connector

Bias T (Antenna B Port only)
- Software selectable 4.7V @ 100mA

IF Modes
- Zero IF, All IF bandwidths
- Low IF, IF bandwidths ≤ 1.536MHz

IF Bandwidths (3dB)
- 200kHz
- 300kHz
- 600kHz
- 1.536MHz
- 5.0MHz
- 6.0MHz
- 7.0MHz
- 8.0MHz

ADC Characteristics
- Sample frequency 2 – 10.66MSPS
- 14-bit native ADC (2 – 6.048MSPS)
- 12-bit (6.048- 8.064 MSPS)
- 10-bit (8.064- 9.216MSPS)
- 8-bit (> 9.216 MSPS)

Maximum recommended input power
- 0dBm continuous
- 10dBm for short periods

Reference
- High temp stability 0.5PPM TCXO
- In-field trimmable to 0.01ppm.

External Reference Clock
- Plug in the external clock before power-up. Auto-detect will switch to the external reference.
- Frequency 24MHz sine/square wave
- 1V Pk-Pk Min
- 3.3V Pk-Pk Max

Typical Noise Figures
- 33dB @ 300kHz
- 20dB @ 2MHz
- 17dB @ 12MHz
- 15dB @ 25MHz
- 15dB @ 40MHz
- 2.6dB @ 100MHz
- 2.1dB @ 200MHz
- 6.0dB @ 340MHz
- 3.1dB @ 660MHz
- 4.4dB @ 1500MHz
- 5.0dB @ 1800MHz

Notch Filters
- FM Notch Filter:
  >30dB 77 – 115MHz
  >50dB 85 – 107MHz
  >4dB 144 – 148MHz
- MW Notch Filter:
  >15dB 400 – 1650kHz
  >30dB 500 – 1530kHz
  >40dB 540 – 1490kHz
- DAB Notch Filter:
  >20dB 155 – 235MHz
  >30dB 160 – 230MHz

Note: The notch filters above are software selectable and remove specific broadcast bands.

Front End Filtering

Low Pass
- 500kHz
- 2MHz

Band Pass
- 2-12MHz
- 12-30MHz
- 30-60MHz
- 60-120MHz
- 120-250MHz
- 250-300MHz
- 300-380MHz
- 380-420MHz
- 420-1000MHz

High Pass
- 1000MHz

FIGURE

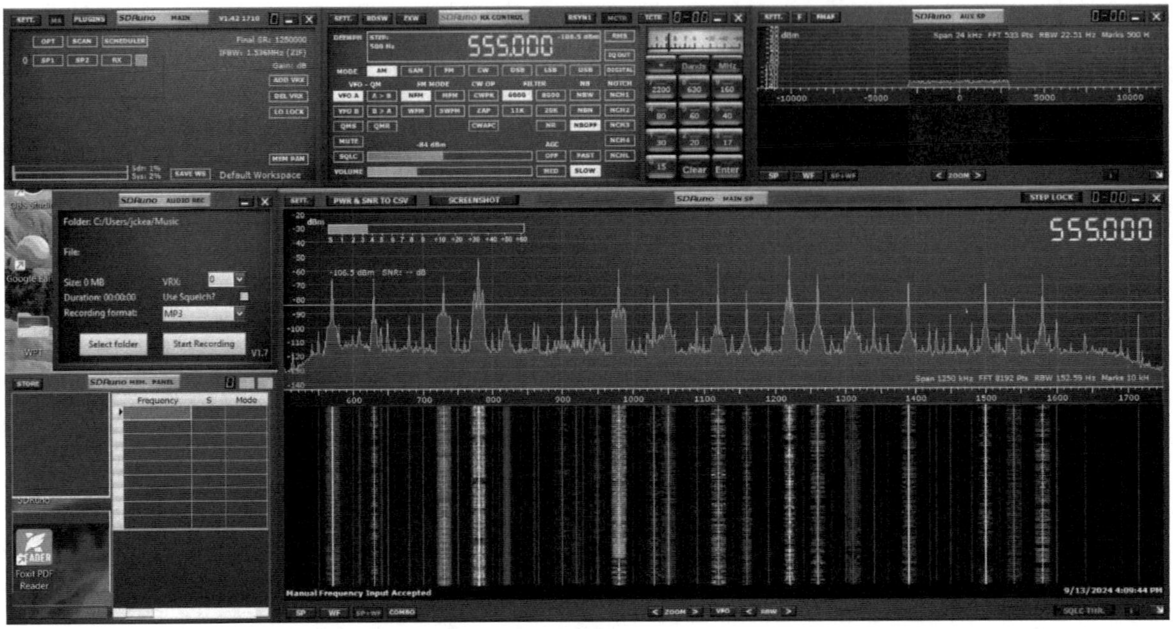

FIGURE : RSPDX SCREEN DISPLAY DURING OPERATION.

Tiny SA Spectrum Analyzer and Signal Generator

The TinySA is a combination spectrum analyzer and signal generator with a screen size of 2.8 inches (shown in photo below). In addition to signal testing and viewing, the unit includes a low noise and low distortion signal generator, which supplied the pilot reference carrier for the software-defined receiver.

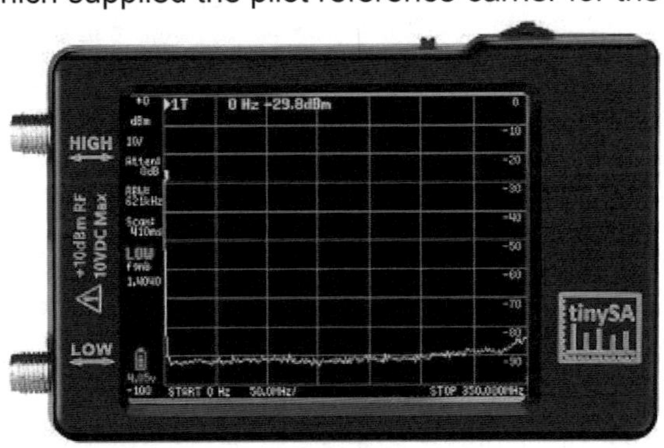

FIGURE

User Interface:

- Display resolution 320*240 pixels
- Screen diagonal 2.8"
- 16 bits per RGB pixels
- Resistive touch control
- Jog switch control
- USB serial port control
- Linear power supply to avoid switching noise.

Low Input Mode Spec:

- Input frequency range from 100kHz to 350MHz (with some limitations down to 10kHz)
- Input impedance 50 ohm when input attenuation is set to 10dB or more.

- Selectable manual and automatic input attenuation between 0dB and 31dB in 1 dB steps
- Absolute maximum input level of +10dBm with 0dB internal attenuation
- Absolute maximum short term peak input power of +20dBm with 30dB internal attenuation
- Suggested maximum input power of +0dBm with internal attenuation in automatic mode
- Input Intercept Point of third order modulation products (IIP3) of +15dBm with 0dB internal attenuation
- 1dB compression point at -1dBm with 0dB internal attenuation
- Power detector resolution of 0.5dB and linearity versus frequency of +/-2dB
- Absolute power level accuracy after power level calibration of +/- 2dB
- Lowest discernible signal at 30MHz using a resolution bandwidth of 30kHz of -102dBm
- Frequency accuracy equal to the selected resolution bandwidth
- Phase noise at 30MHz of -90dB/Hz at 100kHz offset and -120dB/Hz at 1MHz offset
- Spur free dynamic range when using a 30kHz resolution bandwidth of 70dB
- Manually selectable resolution filters with a width of 3, 10, 30, 100, 300, 600kHz. Automatic selection of one of the 57 resolution filters.
- On screen resolution of 51, 101, 145 or 290 measurement points.
- Scanning speed of over 1000 points/second using largest resolution filters.
- Automatic optimization of actual scanning points to ensure coverage of the whole scan range regardless of the chosen resolution bandwidth
- Spur suppression option for assessing if certain signals are internally generated or present in the input signal

High Input Mode Spec:

- Input frequency range from 240MHz to 960MHz
- Input impedance is frequency dependent and deviates from 50 ohm
- Absolute maximum input level without attenuation of +10dBm
- Input Intercept Point of third order modulation products (IIP3) of -5dBm with no internal attenuation
- 1dB compression point at -6dBm with no internal attenuation
- Power detector resolution of 0.5dB and linearity versus frequency of +/-2dB
- Absolute power level accuracy after power level calibration of +/- 2dB
- Lowest discernible signal using a resolution bandwidth of 30kHz of -115dBm
- Frequency accuracy equal to the selected resolution bandwidth
- Spur free dynamic range when using a 30kHz resolution bandwidth of 50dB
- Manually selectable resolution filters of 3, 10, 30, 100, 300, 600kHz. Automatic selection of one of the 57 resolution filters
- Optional 25dB to 40dB frequency dependent input attenuator. The power level error with this attenuator activated increases to +/- 10dB
- On screen resolution of 51, 101, 145 or 290 measurement points.
- Scanning speed of over 1000 points/second using largest resolution filters.
- Automatic optimization of actual scanning points to ensure coverage of the whole scan range regardless of the chosen resolution bandwidth

Low Output Mode Spec:

- Sine wave output with harmonics below -40dB of fundamental
- Output frequency range from 100kHz to 350MHz
- Level accuracy +/- 2dB over the whole output frequency range
- Output frequency resolution either 156Hz below 47MHz output or 312Hz above 47MHz output
- Output level selectable in 1dB steps between -76dBm and -6dBm
- Optional AM, narrow FM and wide FM modulation with frequencies between 50Hz and 5kHz or slow sweep over selectable frequency span
- Optional output level sweep over maximum the entire output level range

High Output Mode Spec:

Reference Generator Spec:

- Optional square wave output with fundamental at -26dBm connected to high input/output
- Frequency can be set to 1MHz, 2MHz, 4MHz, 10MHz, 15MHz or 30MHz

Measurements of Radio Frequency Emissions from Electric Vehicles and Electric Vehicle Charging Systems in the AM Broadcast Band

Robert D. Weller, P.E., David H. Layer
National Association of Broadcasters
Washington, District of Columbia, United States

Abstract – This paper describes RF emission measurements conducted near two wireless electric vehicle charging facilities in Detroit, Michigan. The purpose of the measurements was to assess whether harmonic emissions from the charging facilities are likely to coincide with or fall near frequencies within the AM band. Audio recordings of AM broadcast reception were taken both while the charging facilities were operating and idle, with findings from these recordings to be detailed in a subsequent report.

Introduction and Objective

Engineers from the National Association of Broadcasters conducted measurements of radio frequency (RF) electromagnetic fields near two wireless electric vehicle (EV) charging facilities in Detroit, Michigan operated by the Michigan Department of Transportation (MDOT), Michigan Central (MC) and supported by Electreon Wireless Ltd. One facility was embedded in the pavement at a bus stop (for stationary charging) and the other facility was embedded in a one-quarter mile stretch of roadway, allowing for charging of the vehicle while it was in motion.

The purpose of the measurements was to determine whether harmonic emissions from the charging facilities are likely to have a common or close frequency to the AM band. Audio recordings were also made of AM broadcast reception, with the charging facilities both active and idle. A deeper analysis of these recordings will be presented and discussed by NAB in a subsequent paper. Measurements and observations of the RF emissions generated by EVs and their wireless charging systems under static and dynamic conditions can help evaluate potential effects on AM broadcast reception, but the limited testing described herein is not intended to be comprehensive. Further measurement data are desired to indicate whether any potential interaction with AM reception is likely at varying distances from the vehicle being charged.

Background Information

AM Broadcast

In North America, AM broadcasting provides news and entertainment to the public using amplitude modulation in the frequency range 535–1705 kHz. Frequency assignments are made on a 10 kHz raster from 540 to 1700 kHz (*i.e.*, 540, 550, 560 … 1700 kHz) for a total of 118 channels.[1] Typical

[1] 47 CFR § 2.106 and §§ 73.25-73.30.

This paper is excerpted from the Proceedings of the 2025 NAB Broadcast Engineering and Information Technology (BEIT) Conference, © 2025, National Association of Broadcasters, 1 M Street SE, Washington, DC 20003 USA.

minimum signal levels required for satisfactory reception of AM signals are in the range 0.1 to 1 mV/m (40 to 60 dBµV/m).[2] Technical rules for the AM broadcasting service in the United States are established by the Federal Communications Commission (FCC) as described in 47 CFR Part 73 Subpart A.

WPT-EV

Wireless power transfer to electric vehicles, aka "wireless vehicle charging" or "WPT-EV," is a technology under study in the U.S. that allows convenient charging of EV batteries without a need to plug into a charging station. Some proposed WPT-EV systems would use RF energy in the band 79–90 kHz at power levels up to 15 kilowatts for consumer EV applications.

The coupling mechanism between the charger and the vehicle is typically inductive (including resonant inductive coupling) and involves a pair of coils (a primary "transmit" coil located on or below the roadway, and a secondary "receive" coil attached to the underside of the vehicle). Both static charging systems (a transmit coil or coils that charge vehicles while stopped or parked at a fixed location) and dynamic charging systems (a continuous array of primary charging coils along a roadway that can charge vehicles while in motion) are under consideration.

For these tests, NAB was provided access to a wireless charging roadway installed in Detroit by a partnership of Michigan Central, the City of Detroit and MDOT. WPT coils were installed in a 1/4 mile stretch of 14th Street in Detroit, adjacent to the Newlab at Michigan Central facility. Additional coils were installed in the roadway at a bus stop on 15th Street. Figure 1 is a Google Earth image of the test area. Figure 2 is a photo taken looking South on 14th Street by the dynamic measurement location.

NAB's RF emission tests were conducted in accordance with the normal operating schedule for the wireless charging vehicle, which was typically 3 times per week for 4 hours at a time (Monday, Wednesday, and Friday). Data were collected on Wednesday October 23 and Friday, October 25 at both static and dynamic measurement locations as shown in Figure 1.

FIGURE 1. GOOGLE EARTH IMAGE OF WIRELESS CHARGING ROADWAY AND BUS STOP. THIS IMAGE PRE-DATES THE ACTUAL INSTALLATION AND WAS MADE WHEN MICHIGAN CENTRAL WAS BEING RENOVATED.

[2] 47 CFR § 73.182(a).

FIGURE 2. PHOTO OF 14TH STREET SHOWING CHARGING LANE.

Concerns About AM Broadcast Interference from WPT-EV

Various WPT systems are presently in use throughout the world, most commonly at low power levels (below 25 watts) and used to charge small consumer devices such as mobile phones and smart watches. There have been some reports of certain WPT systems being associated with interference to AM broadcast reception at short distances (such as when a WPT charger and an AM receiver are placed next to each other on a bedside table).[3]

Systems for wireless charging of electric vehicles (WPT-EV), which operate at much higher power levels, are currently in experimental or developmental phases in the U.S., but have already been deployed elsewhere.[4] Harmonic emissions at integer multiples of the fundamental frequency from WPT-EV systems operating in the band 79–90 kHz are of particular interest to broadcasters because

---

[3] See, *e.g.*, Ranulph Poole, "Qi Charging Devices and AM Interference Levels," BBC Research & Development White Paper WHP 344, August 2019.

[4] https://electreon.com/projects (downloaded 11/4/2024).

operation in that band is of principal interest to the WPT-EV industry. Harmonic emissions are a natural byproduct of power transfer systems, in part because purely sinusoidal signals are impractical or impossible to generate, and such harmonics can interfere with the reception broadcast signals if not adequately controlled.[5] This testing did not determine the precise source of any observed harmonic emissions. Such emissions may originate from different sources such as: the coupling coils, the electronics required to maintain resonance, or from the circuitry involved in converting alternate current to direct current for battery charging (affixed under the vehicle).

A recent ITU resolution asks for provisional studies to identify possible impacts of WPT (including WPT-EV) on radiocommunication services, which includes AM broadcasting.[6] The measurements taken for this project could supplement existing ITU and other reports.[7]

Scope

Measurements of RF electric and magnetic field emissions from an EV wireless charging system were conducted at two different locations (see Figure 1) during different wireless charging modes and conditions, at distances of 2 to 10 meters from the charging coils, and listener observations also were made using consumer AM receivers at the same and greater distances. The measurements and observations included:

- Measurement of electric and magnetic fields at various frequencies with particular focus on frequencies harmonically related to the fundamental frequency of the charging system, in this case approximately 85 kHz.
- Measurement and observation of emissions during different charging configurations (*i.e.*, static and dynamic) and operating conditions as were available (*i.e.*, vehicle idle on the static charging pad, and vehicle cruising, accelerating, decelerating, and braking along the dynamic charging track).
- Measurement of emissions at different distances from the vehicle on the static pad.
- Listener observations while tuned to an AM station.

Equipment Used

The following equipment was used to observe and document emissions from the WPT-EV systems.

- RF Spectrum Analyzer: For measuring, analyzing, and capturing the frequency spectrum of RF emissions. (Rohde & Schwarz Model FSV, Serial No. 101614, Cal. 2021-12-06).
- Monopole Antenna: For calibrated measurement of electric fields in the range 79 kHz to approximately 2 MHz. (A.H. Systems Model SAS-550-1B, Serial No. 742, Cal. 2024-05-20).
- Loop Antenna: For calibrated measurement of magnetic fields in the range 79 kHz to approximately 2 MHz. (A.H. Systems Model SAS-560, Serial No. 716, Cal. 2024-05-20).
- Field Strength Meter: For calibrated measurement of AM station fields (note that this meter uses a loop antenna but reports in equivalent electric field units). (Potomac Instruments Model PI4100, Serial No. 284, Cal. 2021-12-13).
- Rangefinder: To determine distances, e.g., from the vehicle under test to the measurement antenna (Bosch Model GLM-100).
- Portable AM Receiver: To provide demodulated audio at various frequencies in the AM band. (GE Super Radio and C Crane Skywave with Tascam digital audio recorder).

---

[5] Extreme limits on harmonics of wireless charging systems can also reduce system efficiency because of increased filtering losses. See e.g., Comments from Prodrive Technologies in Outcome of the public consultation of draft ECC Report 289 on "Wireless Power Transmission (WPT) systems for electrical vehicles (EV) operating within 79-90 kHz band," CEPT ECC Doc. SE(19)012, 7 December 2018.

[6] ITU Resolution 910 (WRC-23), "Studies on the possible [frequency bands] for [non-beam and beam] wireless power transmission (WPT) to avoid harmful interference to the radiocommunication services caused by WPT."

[7] ITU-R Report SM.2451-1 (2022), "Assessment of impact on radiocommunication services from wireless power transmission for electric vehicle operating below 30 MHz."

- Automotive AM Receiver: To provide demodulated audio at various frequencies in the AM band (OEM auto receiver in Chevrolet Suburban rental vehicle)

Test Procedure

Measurements of electromagnetic fields generally followed the following procedure.

Record Antenna Calibration Data

Calibration data for the electric and magnetic field measurement antennas were obtained from the manufacturer and are tabulated in Appendix 1. The electric field (monopole) antenna was integrated with an active preamplifier and matching system that resulted in correction factors within ±0.07 dB over the frequency range of interest. Hence, no calibration adjustments were applied to the electric field measurements.

The magnetic field (loop) antenna had correction factors ranging from 22.8 to 22.4 dB over the frequency range of interest. The sparse calibration data from the manufacturer were interpolated to obtain precise values every 5 kHz over the frequency range of interest as shown in the "SAS -200/560 Loop – Interpolated Calibration Data Used in Analysis" graph in Appendix 1. The amplitude accuracy of the spectrum analyzer was spot-checked using a calibrated source upon its return to NAB and was found to be within 0.5 dB over the frequency range of interest.

Inspect Test Vehicle

The test vehicle was a Ford Transit van (shown in Figure 3), modified to include wireless charging capability. A charging coil and related components were observed under the vehicle but were not investigated in detail.

FIGURE 3. TEST VEHICLE PARKED OVER STATIC CHARGING PAD. THE ELECTREON LOGO ( ) CAN BE SEEN UNDER THE VEHICLE JUST IN FRONT OF THE REAR WHEEL, MARKING THE APPROXIMATE LOCATION OF THE CHARGING COIL.

Inspect Static Charging System

The static charging pad consisted of a rectangular primary (transmission) coil installed below the surface of the road in the "triangle" between the Michigan Central building and the Newlab building. The precise location of the coil could not be determined visually since it was below the asphalt surface but was believed to be at the approximate location of the symbol as shown to the left in Figure 4. A representative primary coil was on display inside the Newlab at Michigan Central building and is shown in Figure 5.

FIGURE 4. ENGINEERS STANDING NEAR THE STATIC CHARGING PAD.

FIGURE 5. EXAMPLE PRIMARY CHARGING COIL ON DISPLAY IN NEWLAB BUILDING.

Set Up Equipment for Static System Measurements

Durable marking tape was placed on the ground at distances of approximately 2, 4, 8, and 10 meters horizontally distant from the primary coil. Measurements were conducted with measurement antennas placed above the tape markings at a height of about 1.1 meters as shown in Figure 6.

FIGURE 6. ENGINEERS ALONGSIDE ILLUSTRATIVE SET-UP OF MEASUREMENT EQUIPMENT SET UP AT DYNAMIC MEASUREMENT LOCATION (MONOPOLE AND SPECTRUM ANALYZER SHOWN; THE LOOP ANTENNA ON THE GROUND PLANE IS SHOWN FOR SCALE).

Conduct Baseline Noise and Signal Measurements

RF levels of existing AM broadcast signals and background noise were recorded over the frequency range of interest at the 10-meter measurement location with the WPT-EV system off using the PI4100, and the monopole and loop antennas with the spectrum analyzer.[8]

Repeat E-field and H-field Measurements with Vehicle Charging System in Operation

RF levels of were recorded over the frequency range of interest at the 10-meter measurement location with the WPT-EV system operating at approximately 14.5 kilowatts (as reported by Electreon) using the monopole and loop antennas with the spectrum analyzer.

Measurement Results – Static Charging

AM Station Baseline Field Strengths

[8] It is noted that environmental (background) noise levels were not specifically assessed and may vary considerably depending upon the area (urban, suburban, rural, etc.). Such noise levels may be substantial and serve to mask interference.

Field strength measurements of several usable AM broadcast stations were taken at various times during the measurement campaign. A representative set of measurements were taken on the morning of October 24 using the PI4100 and are plotted in Figure 7. The measurements were taken at the 10-meter measurement location near the static charging pad, with no EV charging occurring during the measurements.

The stations indicated represent the stations judged to be "listenable" by the engineers present. Signals from other (weaker) stations were also present and may be usable but were ignored for purposes of these tests. These field strength values are believed to be representative of values present throughout the entire measurement period. The stations observed include a wide range of signal levels, ranging from usable (46.8 dBμV/m, for WEOL) to very strong (99.3 dBμV/m, for WJR).

The integer harmonic frequencies of the 85 kHz static charging system were calculated and compared with the assigned carrier frequencies of the AM stations as shown in Table 1. The harmonic frequency and harmonic number were noted for each AM station when the frequency difference is equal to or less than 5 kHz as shown in the third column of Table 1.

Typical AM broadcast receivers have an audio frequency response that is flat from about 70 to 2500 Hz, with lower and higher frequencies being rolled off. Beat frequencies due to harmonics offset by 5 kHz (noted in the table at 765, 935, 1105, 1275, and 1445 kHz) would be expected to be attenuated by 18–40 dB in the receiver but may still be audible.[9]

[9] NPR Labs, "Consumer Testing of AM Broadcast Transmission Bandwidth and Audio Performance -- Measurements of Broadcast AM Receivers," Sept. 8, 2006.

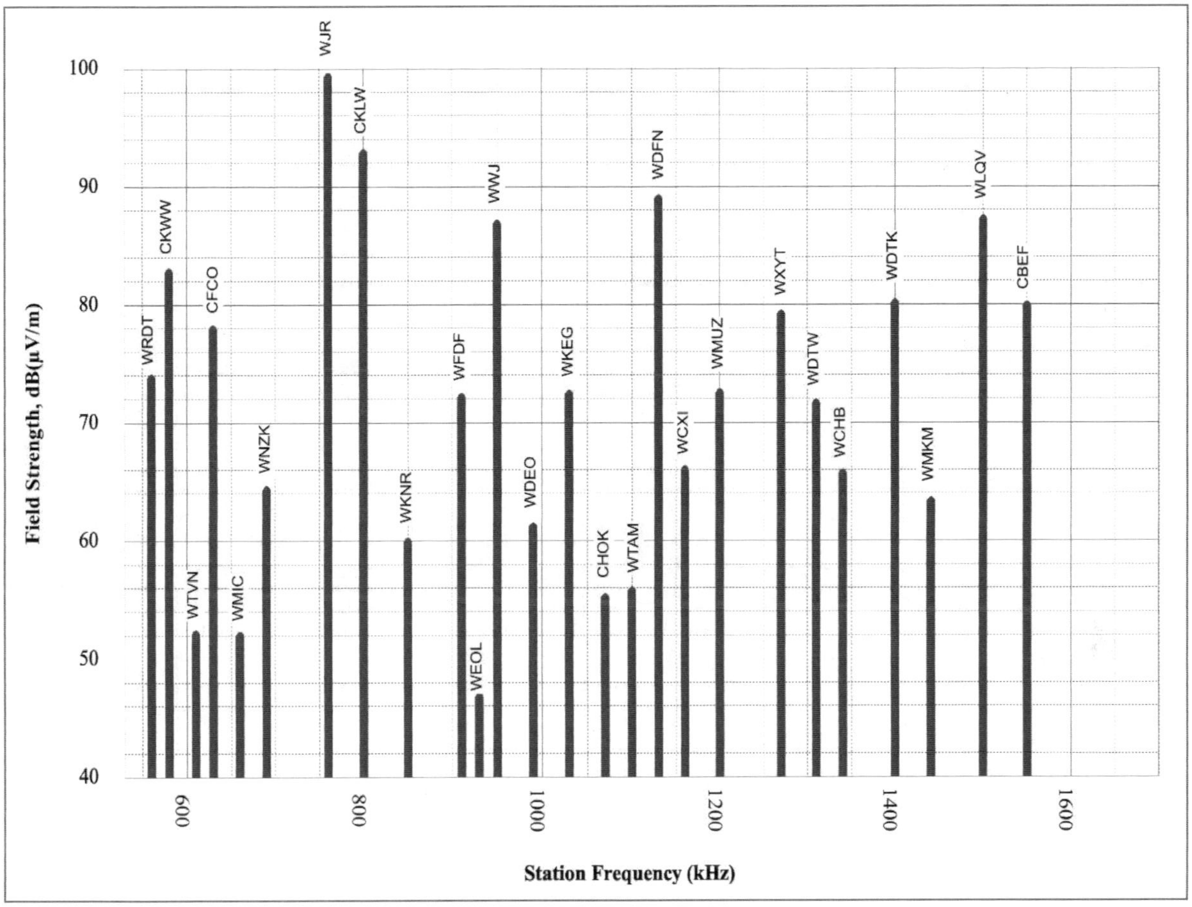

FIGURE 7. MEASURED FIELD STRENGTHS OF VARIOUS AM BROADCAST STATIONS NEAR STATIC CHARGING PAD.

Call sign	Frequency, kHz	Nearest Harmonic of 85 kHz	Field Strength, mV/m	Field Strength, dBµV/m	Equivalent dBµA/m	City of License	Licensed Power, kW
WRDT	560		4.89	73.8	22.3	Monroe, MI	0.5
CKWW	580		13.80	82.8	31.3	Windsor, ON	0.5
WTVN	610		0.41	52.1	0.6	Columbus, OH	5
CFCO	630		7.91	78.0	26.5	Chatham, ON	10
WMIC	660		0.40	52.0	0.5	Sandusky, MI	1
WNZK	690		1.65	64.3	12.8	Dearborn Heights, MI	2.5
WJR	760	765 (9)	92.20	99.3	47.8	Detroit, MI	50
CKLW	800		44.10	92.9	41.4	Windsor, ON	50
WKNR	850	850 (10)	1.00	60.0	8.5	Cleveland, OH	50
WFDF	910		4.06	72.2	20.7	Farmington Hills, MI	50
WEOL	930	935 (11)	0.22	46.8	-4.7	Elyria, OH	1
WWJ	950		22.10	86.9	35.4	Detroit, MI	50
WDEO	990		1.15	61.2	9.7	Ypsilanti, MI	9.2
WKEG	1030		4.19	72.5	21.0	Sterling Heights, MI	5
CHOK	1070		0.58	55.2	3.7	Sarnia, ON	10
WTAM	1100	1105 (13)	0.62	55.8	4.3	Cleveland, OH	50

Call sign	Frequency, kHz	Nearest Harmonic of 85 kHz	Field Strength, mV/m	Field Strength, dBµV/m	Equivalent dBµA/m	City of License	Licensed Power, kW
WDFN	1130		27.90	88.9	37.4	Detroit, MI	50
WCXI	1160		2.01	66.1	14.6	Fenton, MI	15
WMUZ	1200		4.23	72.5	21.0	Taylor, MI	50
WXYT	1270	1275 (15)	9.10	79.2	27.7	Detroit, MI	50
WDTW	1310		3.83	71.7	20.2	Dearborn, MI	5
WCHB	1340		1.94	65.7	14.2	Royal Oak, MI	1
WDTK	1400		10.20	80.1	28.6	Detroit, MI	1
WMKM	1440	1445 (17)	1.46	63.3	11.8	Inkster, MI	1
WLQV	1500		23.00	87.2	35.7	Detroit, MI	50
CBEF	1550		9.93	79.9	28.4	Windsor, ON	2.5

TABLE 1. MEASURED FIELD STRENGTH VALUES OF VARIOUS AM STATIONS NEAR THE EV STATIC CHARGING PAD WITH HARMONICS OF 85 KHZ INDICATED (COLUMN 3).

The PI4100 meter uses an integrated calibrated loop antenna that responds to the magnetic field of the station being measured but reports in electric field units (*e.g.*, mV/m or dBµV/m) to reflect standard practice and FCC specifications of field strength. In Table 1, the equivalent (far-field) magnetic field values in dBµA/m were calculated from the indicated dBµV/m values reported by the instrument by subtracting 51.5 dB from the electric field value.[10]

WPT-EV Emission Field Strengths

Electric and magnetic field strength measurements of the WPT-EV static charging system were taken at various distances from the vehicle under test using the FSV spectrum analyzer. Extrapolation of these measurement data at other distances should be done with caution as all of the data were collected in the reactive near-field zone of the primary coil.[11]

For an electrically small loop antenna, the magnetic field is maximum in the plane of the loop (along the Earth's surface in this case) and zero along the axis of the loop (directly above the center of the loop in this case).[12] The electric field will be orthogonal to the magnetic field (perpendicular to the Earth's surface in this case). At these small distances from the primary coil, the magnetic field would be expected to dominate but both electric and magnetic field measurements were taken.

Measured Emission Levels vs. Harmonic Number

Measurements were taken of both the electric (using the monopole antenna) and magnetic (using the loop antenna) field strengths at horizontal distances of approximately 2, 4, 8, and 10 meters from the source. Figure 8 shows the measured electric field strengths at the 85 kHz fundamental and its harmonics up to 2000 kHz at each measurement distance.

It is seen that the level of each harmonic generally decreases with increasing harmonic number.[13] Overall, the relative level of the electric field harmonics appears to decrease approximately linearly with harmonic number (calculated trend $1/n^{0.7}$ to $1/n^{1.7}$). This behavior may be due to a measurement artifact or case-specific complexities in the reactive near-field.

---

[10] (376.7Ω) = 51.5 dBΩ

[11] The boundary of the reactive near-field is taken to be 2π, corresponding to a range of 561 meters at the fundamental frequency (85 kHz) to 33 meters at the 17th harmonic (1445 kHz).

[12] Warren L. Stutzman and Gary A. Thiele, Antenna Theory and Design, (John Wiley & Sons, 1981) p. 244.

[13] The data also suggest that emissions may have relative maxima at regular intervals (harmonic numbers 5, 9, 13, 17, 21) and similar relative minima (harmonic numbers 3, 7, 11, 15, 19). This may be a measurement artifact or case-by-case complex behavior in the reactive near-field.

Figure 9 shows the measured magnetic field strengths at the 85 kHz fundamental and its harmonics up to 2000 kHz at each measurement distance. It is seen that the level of each harmonic generally decreases with increasing harmonic number. The data also suggest that emissions have relative maxima at odd harmonics (3, 5, 7, etc.) and relative minima at even harmonics (2, 4, 6, etc.).

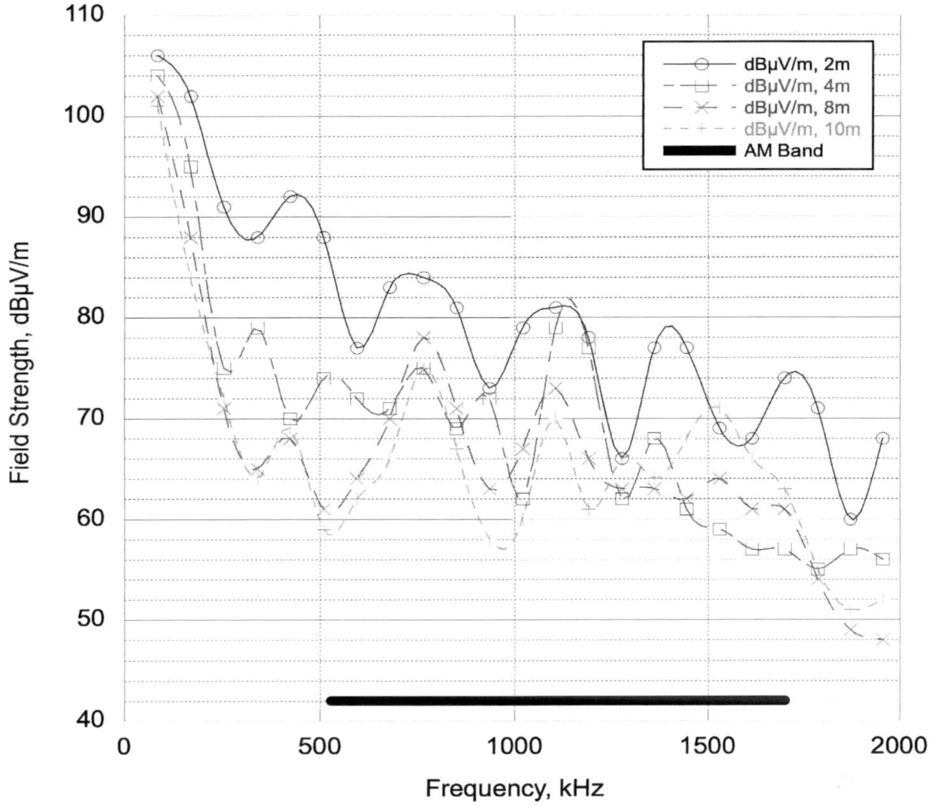

FIGURE 8. ELECTRIC FIELD STRENGTHS FROM EV CHARGING SYSTEM AS A FUNCTION OF HARMONIC NUMBER (FREQUENCY). THE FUNDAMENTAL FREQUENCY IS 85 KHZ. MEASURED DATA WERE FITTED TO ILLUSTRATE APPARENT VARIATION WITH HARMONIC NUMBER.

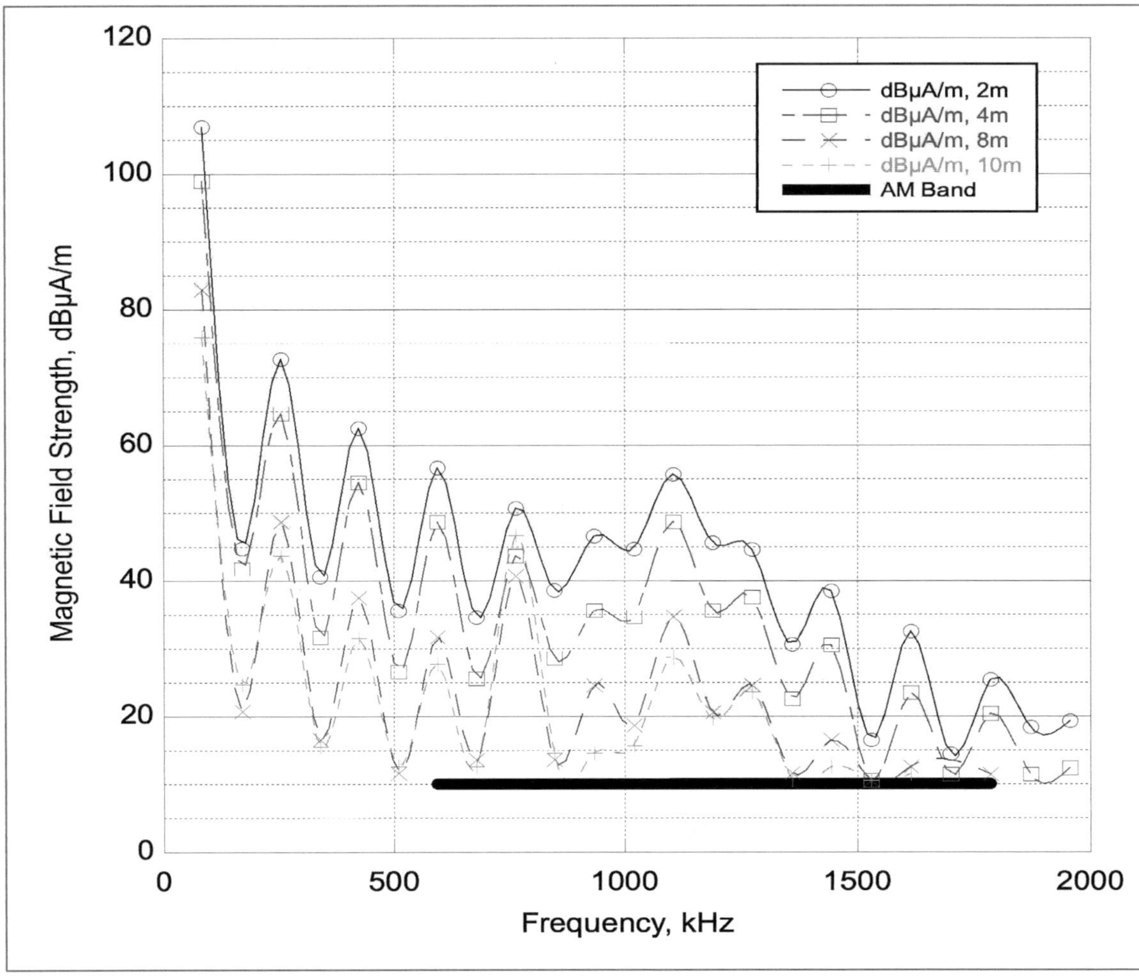

FIGURE 9. MAGNETIC FIELD STRENGTHS FROM EV CHARGING SYSTEM AS A FUNCTION OF FREQUENCY. THE FUNDAMENTAL FREQUENCY IS 85 KHZ. MEASURED DATA WERE FITTED TO ILLUSTRATE APPARENT VARIATION WITH HARMONIC NUMBER. NOTE THAT THE NOISE FLOOR OF THE SPECTRUM ANALYZER LIMITS ACCURATE MAGNETIC FIELD MEASUREMENTS IN THE AM BAND TO LEVELS GREATER THAN ABOUT 13 DBμA/M.

Dominance of odd-order harmonics is common in power systems having half-wave symmetry (*i.e.*, when the positive and negative halves of a waveform are identical but opposite). Note that the noise floor of the spectrum analyzer limits accurate magnetic field measurements in the AM band to levels greater than about 13 dBμA/m and measurements below that value were suppressed (including, potentially, unwanted signals as well). Overall, the relative level of the magnetic field harmonics appears to decrease approximately as the square of the harmonic number (calculated trend $1/n^{1.7}$ to $1/n^{2.3}$).

Emission Levels vs. Distance

Measurements were taken of both the electric and magnetic field strengths at horizontal distances of approximately 2, 4, 8, and 10 meters from the static charging pad using the FSV spectrum analyzer. Figure 10 shows the measured electric field strengths at the 85 kHz fundamental frequency and at the harmonics falling in the AM broadcast band at each measurement distance. It is seen that the levels of all emissions generally decrease with distance as expected.

Figure 11 shows the measured magnetic field strengths at the 85 kHz fundamental and the harmonics within the AM broadcast band at each measurement distance (again, using the FSV spectrum analyzer). Field strength values less than 13 dBuA/m were omitted due to proximity to the noise floor of the measurement equipment. It is seen that the levels of all emissions generally decrease with distance as expected. It is also seen that the magnetic field strengths fall off more rapidly than the electric fields, as would be expected for a small loop.[14]

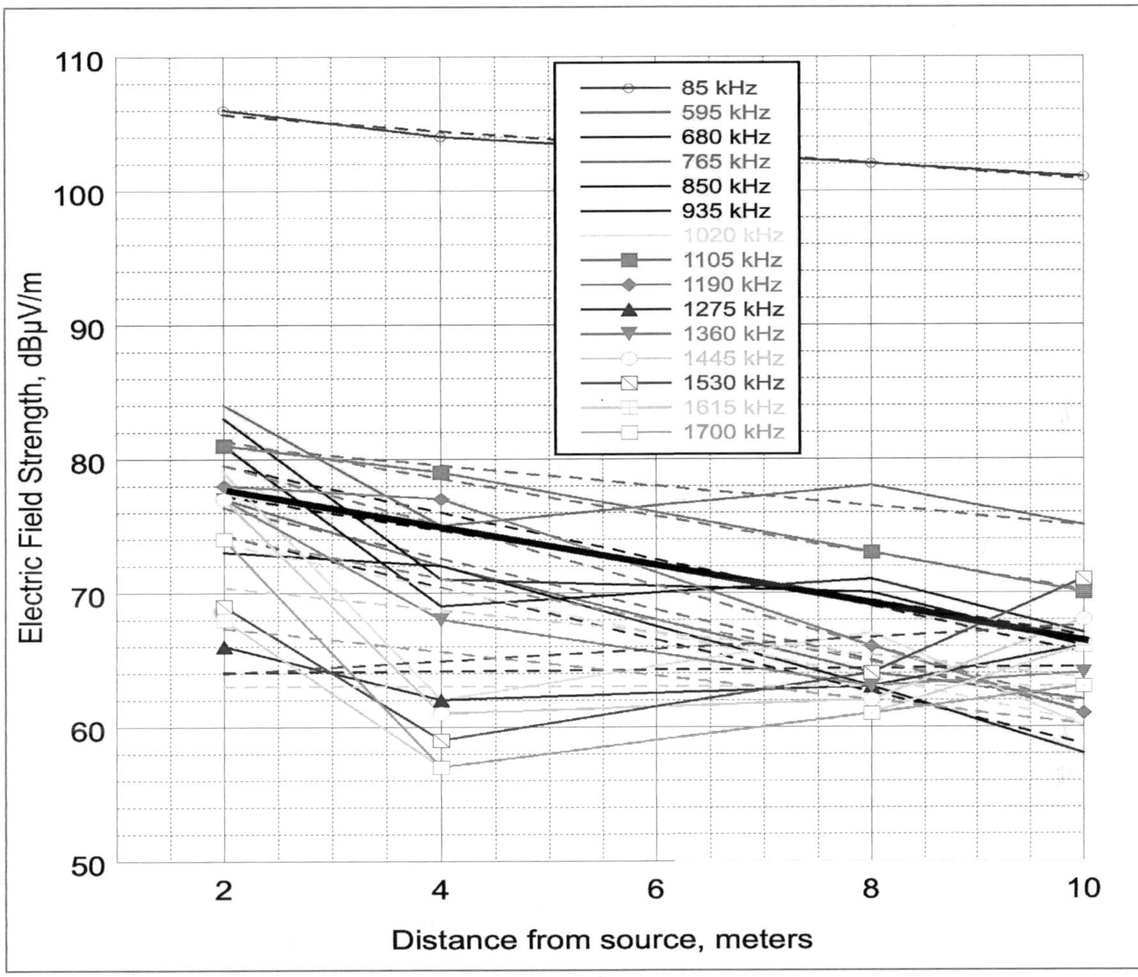

FIGURE 10. ELECTRIC FIELD STRENGTHS FROM EV CHARGING SYSTEM HARMONICS FALLING IN THE AM BROADCAST BAND AS A FUNCTION OF DISTANCE. THE FUNDAMENTAL FREQUENCY IS 85 KHZ. DASHED LINES ARE LINEAR TRENDS. THE HEAVY BLACK LINE IS THE DB-AVERAGE TREND OF THE VARIOUS HARMONICS.

---

[14] Ampere's law gives the magnetic field as $H= 1\mu o\times A$ which for a small loop reduces to $1r2$ dependance, while Faraday's law gives the electric field as $E= 1j\omega\varepsilon\times H$ which for a small loop reduces to $1r$ dependance. ITU-R Report SM.2451-1, "Assessment of impact on radiocommunication services from wireless power transmission for electric vehicle operating below 30 MHz," notes in Section 4.4 that a conversion of 60 dB per decade of distance is often applied when converting magnetic field strengths between measurement distances in the near field. 60 dB is equivalent to $1r3$.

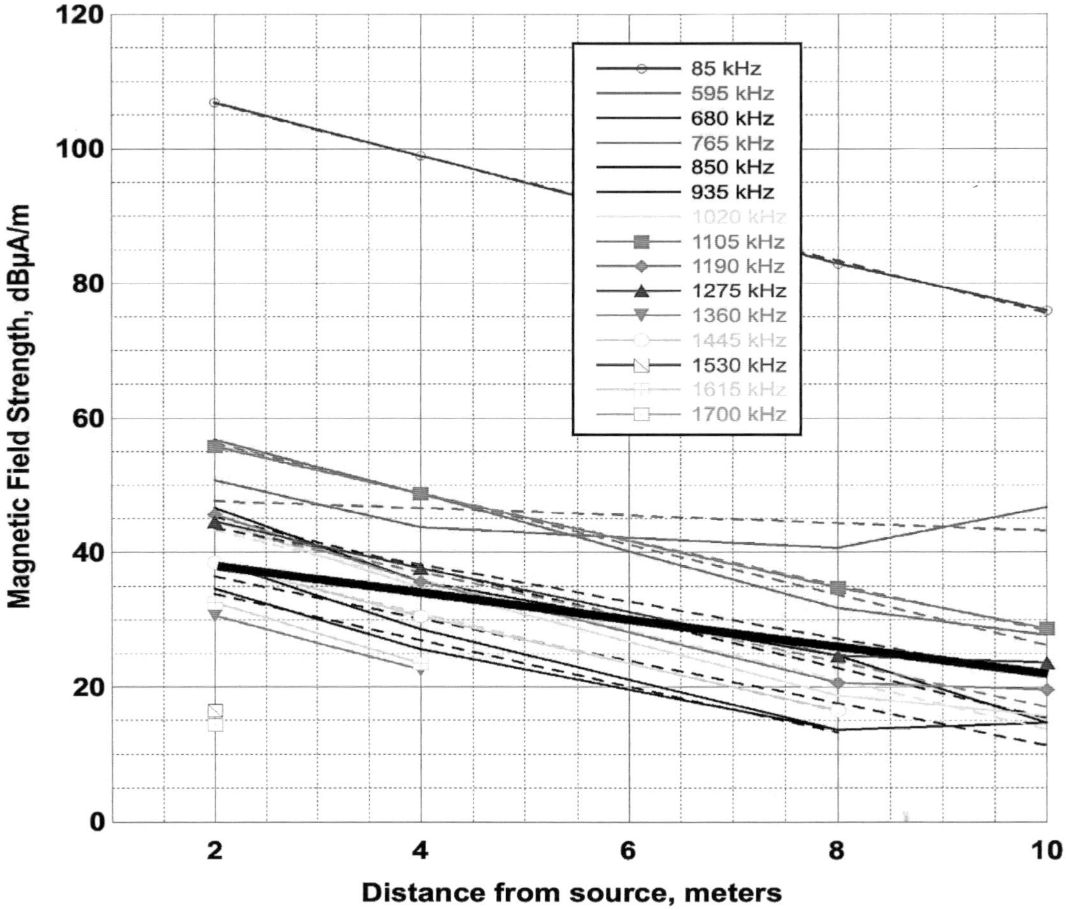

FIGURE 11. MAGNETIC FIELD STRENGTHS FROM EV CHARGING SYSTEM HARMONICS FALLING IN THE AM BROADCAST BAND AS A FUNCTION OF DISTANCE. THE FUNDAMENTAL FREQUENCY IS 85 KHZ. DASHED LINES ARE LINEAR TRENDS. THE HEAVY BLACK LINE IS THE DB-AVERAGE TREND OF THE VARIOUS HARMONICS.

Measurement data from the dynamic test track as well as audio recordings are still being analyzed and may be the subject of a subsequent report.

Notably, Electreon reports that these measurements were conducted on an early generation system. Since then, new generation systems have been deployed featuring advancements and optimizations. Electreon reports that it will conduct additional internal testing on its new-generation system in the coming months and that the authors will be invited to retest and evaluate this new version, with further assessments planned to ensure a comprehensive analysis.

Acknowledgements

The authors wish to thank Stephen Lockwood, Mike Pappas, and Nick Straka for their on-site assistance during the measurement period. We especially wish to thank Electreon Wireless Ltd. and the Michigan Department of Transportation for their assistance and support with this project.

Appendix 1 – Antenna Calibration Data

A.H. Systems, Inc.
9710 Cozycroft Ave.
Chatsworth, CA 91311

Tel: (818) 998-0223 ◆ sales@AHSystems.com
Fax: (818) 998-6892 ◆ www.AHSystems.com

Calibration, Active Monopole Antenna with 1.04 Meter Rod Height
Model Number: SAS200/550-1 SN: 742 Date: 20-May-24

Frequency	Antenna Factor (dB)	Frequency	Antenna Factor (dB)
9 KHz	1.943	95 KHz	-0.060
9.5 KHz	1.754	100 KHz	-0.059
10 KHz	1.586	110 KHz	-0.057
11 KHz	1.302	120 KHz	-0.052
12 KHz	1.087	130 KHz	-0.050
13 KHz	0.912	140 KHz	-0.047
14 KHz	0.768	150 KHz	-0.044
15 KHz	0.655	160 KHz	-0.042
16 KHz	0.563	170 KHz	-0.042
17 KHz	0.479	180 KHz	-0.038
18 KHz	0.414	190 KHz	-0.034
19 KHz	0.357	200 KHz	-0.035
20 KHz	0.305	210 KHz	-0.034
21 KHz	0.266	220 KHz	-0.034
22 KHz	0.228	230 KHz	-0.033
23 KHz	0.197	240 KHz	-0.032
24 KHz	0.171	250 KHz	-0.032
25 KHz	0.149	260 KHz	-0.031
26 KHz	0.124	270 KHz	-0.029
27 KHz	0.106	280 KHz	-0.027
28 KHz	0.090	290 KHz	-0.028
29 KHz	0.076	300 KHz	-0.026
30 KHz	0.064	320 KHz	-0.025
31 KHz	0.051	340 KHz	-0.024
32 KHz	0.039	360 KHz	-0.024
33KHz	0.030	380 KHz	-0.024
34 KHz	0.022	400 KHz	-0.024
35 KHz	0.015	420 KHz	-0.025
36 KHz	0.008	440 KHz	-0.024
37 KHz	0.002	460 KHz	-0.024
38 KHz	-0.004	480 KHz	-0.024
39 KHz	-0.008	500 KHz	-0.023
40 KHz	-0.012	550 KHz	-0.027
41 KHz	-0.017	600 KHz	-0.028
42 KHz	-0.022	650 KHz	-0.029
43 KHz	-0.025	700 KHz	-0.030
44 KHz	-0.028	750 KHz	-0.032
45 KHz	-0.031	800 KHz	-0.034
46 KHz	-0.034	850 KHz	-0.036
47 KHz	-0.037	900 KHz	-0.036
48 KHz	-0.040	950 KHz	-0.038
49 KHz	-0.041	1 MHz	-0.040
50 KHz	-0.042	1.1 MHz	-0.041
55 KHz	-0.049	1.2 MHz	-0.046
60 KHz	-0.053	1.3 MHz	-0.047
65 KHz	-0.055	1.4 MHz	-0.051
70 KHz	-0.056	1.5 MHz	-0.054
75 KHz	-0.055	1.6 MHz	-0.059
80 KHz	-0.055	1.7 MHz	-0.060
85 KHz	-0.052	1.8 MHz	-0.064
90 KHz	-0.054	1.9 MHz	-0.066

A.H.Systems Inc.
9710 Cozycroft Ave. Chatsworth, CA 91311
Phone (818) 998-0223 Fax (818) 998-6892
E-mail: sales@AHSystems.com
Web site: http://www.AHSystems.com

Calibration, Loop Emission

Model: SAS-200/560 Serial Number: 716 Date: 20-May-24

Frequency (KHz)	50 Ohm Load (dBpT/uV)	1 M Ohm Load (dBpT/uV)
0.02	85.6	84.1
0.03	82.0	80.4
0.04	79.8	78.2
0.05	77.5	75.9
0.06	76.2	74.4
0.07	74.5	73.2
0.08	73.8	71.7
0.09	72.6	71.0
0.1	71.5	69.8
0.25	63.9	62.2
0.5	57.7	55.9
0.75	54.1	52.4
1	51.6	50.0
2.5	44.0	42.2
5	37.9	36.3
7.5	34.2	32.6
10	32.4	30.1
20	27.5	24.2
30	25.3	20.6
40	24.2	17.9
50	23.6	16.3
60	23.3	14.4
70	23.0	12.9
80	23.3	12.3
90	22.7	11.0
100	23.0	10.2
200	22.7	
300	22.7	
400	22.5	
500	22.6	
600	22.7	
700	22.6	
800	22.7	
900	22.5	
1000	22.7	
2000	22.3	

Conversion Formulas: **dBpT= dBuV + dBpT/uV +Cable Loss**
dBuV/m = dBpT + 49.5 dB

SAS -200/560 Loop – Interpolated Calibration Data Used in Analysis

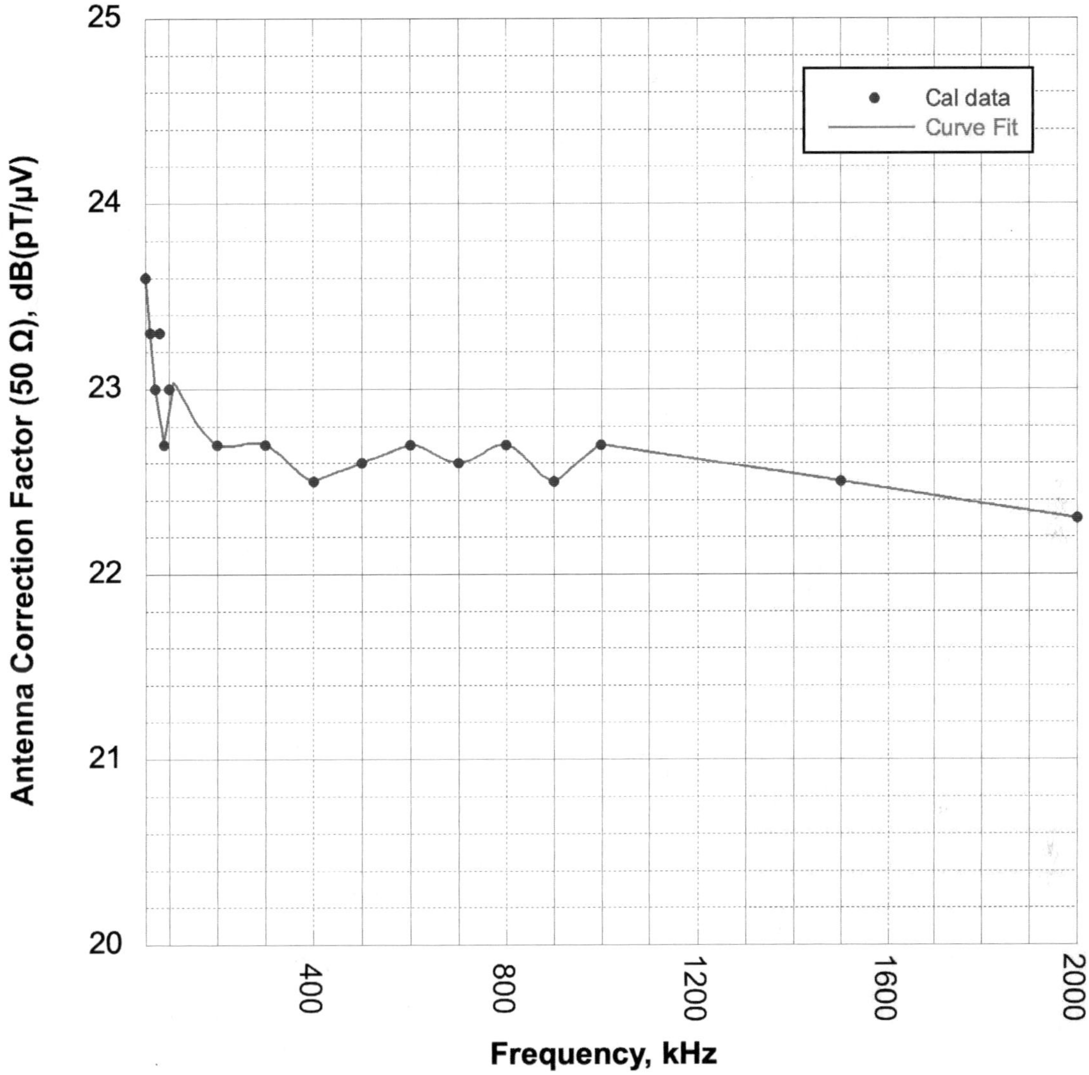

Proving the HEBA Antenna

David Maxson
Isotrope, LLC
Boston, Massachusetts, United States
david@isotrope.im

Abstract – The HEBA (High Efficiency Broadband Antenna) has been limited to daytime operation for 7 years. Recent NEC modeling efforts were successful in proving the vertical radiation pattern. The FCC granted nighttime approval in September 2024. Because the HEBA's 72-foot height makes it a "short antenna," the FCC rules for nighttime approval are difficult to satisfy. The HEBA also uses a novel two-port design to drive two active elements in the antenna system, while the antenna elements are stacked above a 40-foot square elevated ground plane. There are no ground radials. The HEBA is immune to seasonal tuning variations experienced by many conventional AM antenna systems. This paper explores the antenna design, provides measurements and uses NEC modeling to illustrate its performance.

Introduction

A novel AM broadcast antenna design has achieved FCC approval for both daytime and nighttime operation. The HEBA (high efficiency broadband antenna – pronounced *HEE-buh*) is in the class of electrically short broadcast antennas (<<¼ wavelength). It has a small footprint, requires no ground radial system, is reasonably efficient for its size, and is immune to seasonal changes in ground conductivity.

The HEBA design evolved from its predecessor, the controversial crossed-field antenna ("CFA"). They have similar physical components. They are optimized differently, and their behavior is described differently. The CFA was designed around the controversial premise that "independent" magnetic and electric fields could be "crossed" to produce a propagating electromagnetic wave. The HEBA evolved to use the basic architecture of the CFA with the introduction of pragmatic AM broadcast engineering principles. The HEBA therefore has an unconventional design, with two driven elements: 1) a cylindrical horn-shaped vertical frame positioned above 2) a large capacitive plate parallel to the ground plane below it. See Figure 1. The former is called the "E-cylinder" and the latter is the "D-plate," names inherited from its predecessor. See Figure 2.

The recently licensed [1] HEBA is 72 ft (22 m) high, occupying a small (40 ft [12 m] square) footprint. There is a table-like structure supporting the active elements. The table surface is an elevated ground plane (20 ft [6 m] AGL). The two active elements are driven by separate feeds from an antenna tuning unit ("ATU"). While its design concepts are inherited from the CFA, the HEBA operating principles are firmly rooted in physics as confirmed by numerical modeling (NEC-5) and field measurement. The D-plate and E-cylinder are adjacent but not electrically connected. The E-Cylinder is series-fed from the bottom of the cylinder and is insulated from ground. The D-Plate just below the E-Cylinder is fed from the other output of the ATU.

This paper describes the HEBA's operational characteristics and permitting history. The HEBA radiation characteristics are compared to the station's prior 1/6-wavelength series-fed tower with conventional ground system. While daytime approval was straightforward, nighttime approval required electromagnetic modeling and considerable deliberation by Federal Communications Commission ("FCC") engineers. Further research will include field measurement of the vertical radiation pattern to corroborate the NEC-5 calculations. Value engineering is ongoing to further simplify its design.

FIGURE 1 HEBA E-CYLINDER VISIBLE ABOVE 20-FOOT-HIGH GROUND PLANE STRUCTURE

Development History

WQVR is a 1 kW (daytime) non-directional station on 940 kHz. The HEBA was constructed at the site of WQVR (formerly WGFP), Webster, Massachusetts. According to Worldwide Antenna Systems representatives, initial experimentation began in early 2011 using a small wooden platform and an arrangement of elements built at the station's tower site. The initial design was based upon the CFA built on The Isle of Man. After initial testing and modifications, an application for experimental operation in the expanded band at 1640 kHz was granted by the FCC in 2015, callsign WX1CFA. When the experimental work resulted in success at this higher frequency, the design was scaled up in size to work on a lower frequency (940 kHz). By mid-2016, a new, even larger antenna was constructed from the ground up at the present location near the transmitter building. Final testing was completed in 2017 and the license with daytime authorization was issued in 2018.

Continuing work on evaluating the vertical pattern of the HEBA struck several procedural dead ends until NEC-5 modeling in 2022 led to FCC nighttime approval in 2024. The nighttime power is quite low (4 W), not because of the HEBA design, but because the station is protecting a co-channel 50 kW clear-channel station in nearby Montreal, Canada from skywave interference at the Canadian border. The Canadian station is about 400 km (248 mi) from WQVR and about 48 km (30 mi) from the border. The skywave-departure elevation angle required to protect the station is 28.5-degrees. The HEBA is licensed for the same nighttime power as the previous antenna on site. Regardless of the ultimate nighttime power authorized, the effort to prove the vertical pattern to the satisfaction of the FCC still had to be rigorous.

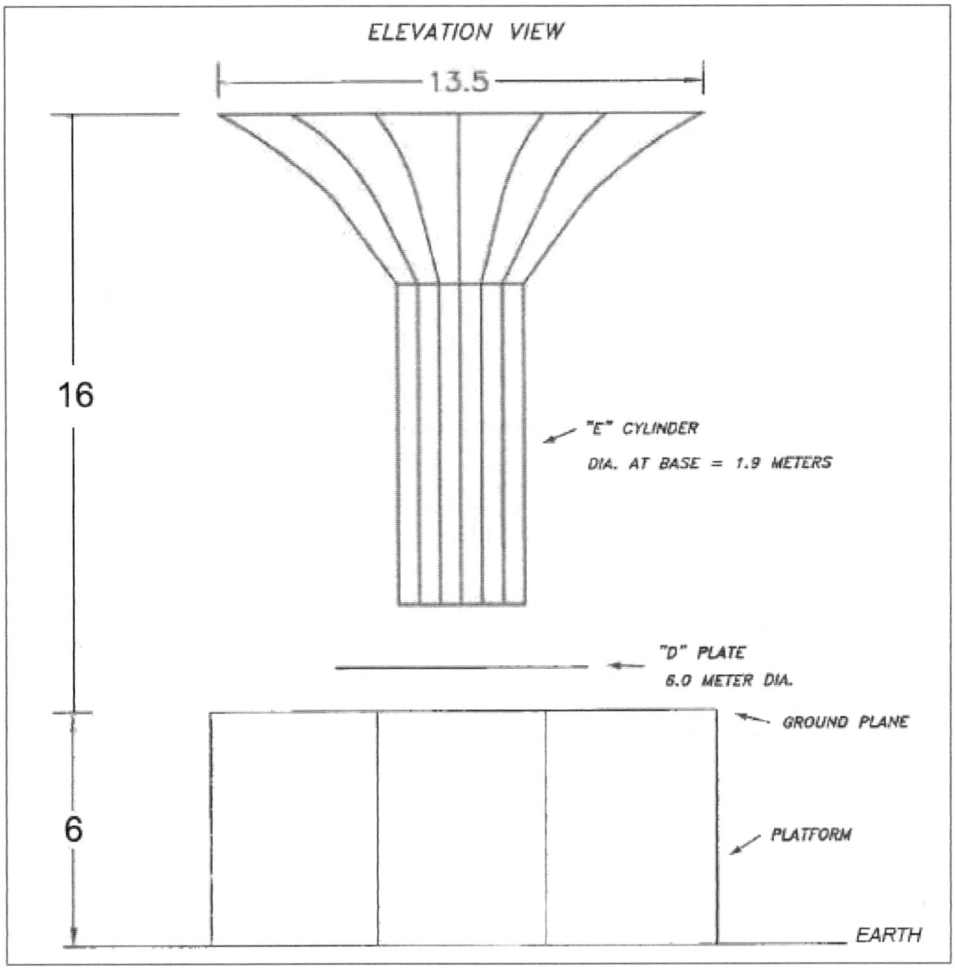

FIGURE 2 - HEBA ELEVATION DRAWING (MEASUREMENTS IN METERS)

Daytime

First and foremost, the HEBA had to satisfy the FCC criteria for efficiency. With persistence, Kurt Gorman of Phasetek developed a design for the ATU and carefully walked in the setup to maximize transfer of power. The resulting rms efficiency was 263.4 mV/m/km, which is 91% of the original licensed value (289.7 mV/m/km) for the 1/6-wavelength tower. The last proof of performance of the tower system, in 2010, showed a less-than-licensed operational efficiency of 261.4 mV/m/km. In other words, the HEBA is a bit better than the decades-old tower and ground system it replaced.

The HEBA location on site is offset approximately 60 m southeast of the base of the former tower. The tower was removed before any measurements of the HEBA were made. Initially, the center point of the tower ground system was connected by a 4-inch strap to the HEBA ground. This was removed early in the testing and made no difference in the HEBA's coverage. It stood to reason at the time that there might be some eccentricity of the HEBA omnidirectional coverage pattern caused by the abandoned ground radial system. If so, one could expect the eccentricity to favor the northwest where the ground radial system lies with respect to the HEBA. This proved not to be the case.

The coverage plots in Figure 3 show two key facts. First, it is the tower that had an eccentricity in its omnidirectional pattern. This suggests that there was a favorable anomaly in the ground conductivity that caused the tower coverage pattern to have a bulge to the southwest. The second fact is that the HEBA coverage is about as circular as one could expect. The HEBA radiation is implicitly omnidirectional, regardless of whatever conductivity issues were distorting the tower's coverage.

This information serves to reinforce some hunches about the HEBA's unique ability to set up a radiating signal without being overly coupled to and dependent on the earth ground near it. The NEC modeling discussed in the next section might provide some clues to the physics of this phenomenon.

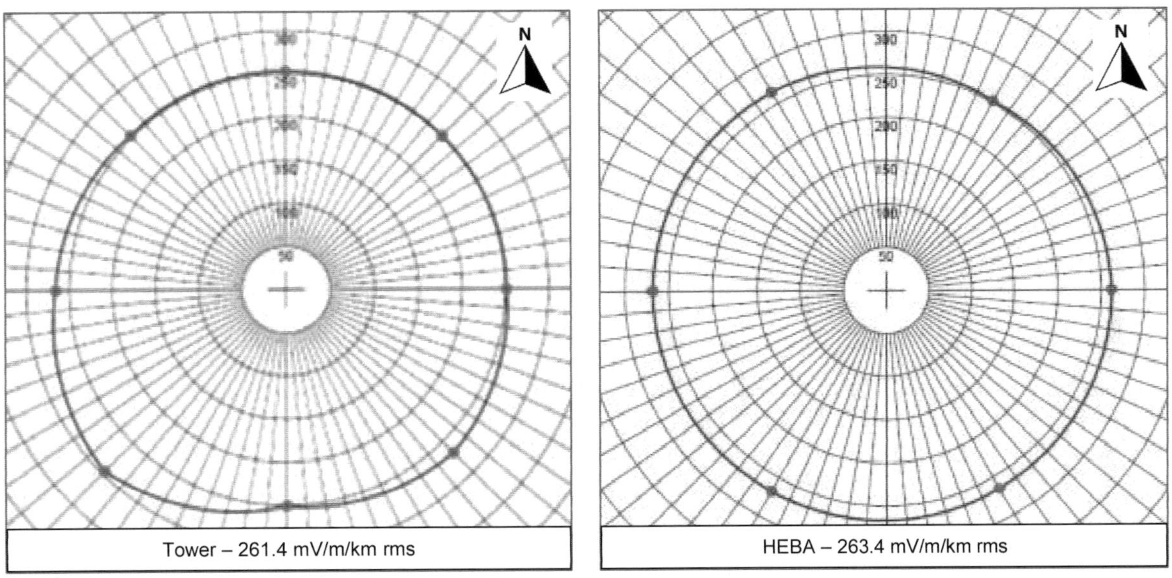

FIGURE 3 – COVERAGE PATTERN OF THE ORIGINAL TOWER AND THE HEBA, SIGNAL STRENGTH BY AZIMUTH

Nighttime Conundrum

The Rules

The FCC process for approving an antenna for nighttime operation has been almost unchanged since the 1930s when the AM propagation curves and radiation standards were first published. For a conventional (not electrically short) broadcast tower there is an equation that the FCC relies on to calculate the vertical plane radiation pattern (hereafter, "vertical pattern"). The equation takes as its input the estimated electrical height of the tower. Found in 47 CFR 73.160(b),[1] the equation predicts the vertical pattern of a thin-wire monopole (an idealized representation of a tower). To provide the equation its input variable, the electrical height must be estimated. For conventional-height towers, there is a process by which the electrical height is estimated using a series of current-distribution measurements up the tower. The shape of the current distribution curve varies depending on the effective electrical height of the tower. However, short radiators do not provide much insight to their effective electrical heights because of their relatively uniform current distributions.

Short-Antenna History

In 2003, the FCC accepted the thin-wire equation for the Valcom electrically short AM antennas,[2] citing an analysis by Ronald Chase of the FCC Office of Engineering and Technology [2]. The Chase analysis studied the question of using modeling to predict AM radiation characteristics. Chase concluded in part, "In many cases, and particularly that of the Valcom proposal, antenna analysis using NEC modeling will provide data in sufficient detail for the construction of formulas characterizing vertical plane radiation."

The longstanding thin-wire-equation method of estimating vertical patterns, while a good general guide, is imperfect. For example, in his analysis supporting an application for FCC approval of the KinStar[3] electrically short antennas two years later, Thomas King noted that even conventional-height towers that were not ideal slender cylindrical forms had vertical patterns that differed from their predictions using the 73.160(b) formulas.[4]

In other words, the FCC method, which had been relied upon for decades to validate the vertical patterns of tall AM towers, included a margin of error that was deemed tolerable for the purpose. Examples of such towers with larger errors are self-supporting towers, which are widest at the base, and the vaunted Blaw-Knox halfwave tower, that has a wide waist and tapers to narrow cross-sections at the top and bottom.

Ronald Rackley noted this analysis "demonstrates that the departure of the Kinstar [short] antenna's performance from the ideal thin-wire current distribution model assumed for AM antenna analysis is within the range typical of tower antennas that have been routinely authorized by the FCC for decades and that are presently in common use" [6]. Thus, the error in estimating the vertical pattern of the KinStar short antenna was no worse than the error in estimating the patterns of full-size antennas that have "large cross-section geometries."

King also supported the notion that modeling was indeed more accurate than the thin-wire monopole equations of 73.160(b), "The NEC-4.1 calculation accounts for more terms, including effects of the relatively wide wire spacing in the [Kinstar] antenna on the phase velocity, and thus produces a more accurate result than either of the other methods, which are based on mathematical approximations" [5].

Nevertheless, instead of relying on modeling every new Kinstar antenna, Rackley opted to recommend the physical height of the short KinStar antenna as a proxy for its electrical height. KinStar could seek approval for its class of towers based on the 73.160(b) equation. This avoided having to develop new equations for the design on every frequency. The KinStar vertical pattern was allowed to be imprecisely

[1] Section 73.160(b) contains several equations depending on the geometry of the vertical radiator: monopole, monopole with top hat, and sectionalized monopole. The focus here is on the fundamental equation for a monopole.
[2] "We recommend that the formula given in Section 73.160(b) of FCC Rules for a typical tower which is not top-loaded or sectionalized should be used to represent the vertical plane radiation characteristics of the electrically short antennas manufactured by Valcom, Ltd. in the AM broadcast band. Our recommendation is based on a thorough study of the factors affecting radiation in the vertical plane of electrically short antennas in general and the Valcom, Ltd, Antenna in particular." [3].
[3] "The KinStar antenna consists of a cage of vertical wires (usually four), symmetrically arranged around a central support. The vertical wires extend to a height of approximately 0.08 wavelength (75 feet at a frequency of 1000 kHz). Each vertical wire is connected to a horizontal top-loading wire extending to a radial distance of approximately 0.17 wavelength (169 feet at 1000 kHz). The KinStar antenna requires use of the standard 120-radial, one-quarter wave, buried ground system." [4]
[4] "All of these [tall] antennas show a deviation between the 73.160 calculated elevation pattern and the NEC calculated pattern similar to that seen with the KinStar, with some showing errors larger than seen with the KinStar." [5]

predicted using its physical height as a proxy for the electrical height. The conclusion was based on the "more accurate" verification using NEC modeling of the prototype.

The HEBA's Distinction

Despite the success of both these antenna initiatives (Valcom and KinStar), the HEBA design was just enough different to give the FCC reviewers pause. The HEBA's predecessor was touted as using unconventional physical principles that were thought to produce unconventional results. Moreover, the HEBA's shape and method of excitation were not analogous to regular series-fed towers (short or tall). These features naturally fostered skepticism on whether the 73.160(b) equation for the ideal thin-wire monopole could be relied upon to predict the HEBA vertical pattern. This meant that the HEBA effort was unable to simply apply the approach taken by Rackley *et al* with Kinstar and Valcom.

Instead, the FCC pointed to clause 73.160(c). It says that the applicant who cannot use 73.160(b) must provide a well-documented "formula" that describes the vertical pattern of the antenna. The HEBA development team had to find a way of evaluating the vertical pattern and converting it to a formula. 73.160(c) also makes it clear that simply submitting a table of values is not sufficient.

The HEBA development team attempted to produce an equation based on drone measurements of the vertical pattern. One challenge with field measurements is to keep outside the near field of the antenna. A set of measurements was made, with a degree of near-field uncertainty. The second challenge, converting the measurements to an equation, was daunting. The equation would be based on a limited set of measured data rather than any discovered physical principles.

When this effort proved unsuccessful in satisfying the FCC, the HEBA development team connected with this writer. We learned of the history and the problems encountered. Our opinion was that the most likely solution would be by going back to first-principles by using computer modeling. NEC-5 (Numerical Electromagnetics Code, version 5.0) is the fifth revision of the modeling application published by Lawrence Livermore National Laboratory. It had recently been released. NEC-5 includes a new feature that allows for modeling planar surfaces, such as is required of the elevated ground plane and the D-plate. Previous versions required the modeler to simulate such surfaces with numerous intersecting line segments, which imposes an unreasonably heavy computational burden.

Modeling

Physical and electrical measurements were taken on the HEBA. The ensuing computer model of the HEBA's structure, electrical connections and tuning components was programmed and yielded good results. The computer model behaved like the measurements of the HEBA. As is often the case with models, there might be ways to improve the model's description of the real-world installation. Particularly, the connections to earth and the behavior of the transmission lines operating into challenging impedances are likely more complex than the model anticipates. Nevertheless, the model is a very good approximation.

Figure 4 is a heat map of the relatively uniform current density of the HEBA model. Figure 5 shows a moment in the sinusoidal cycle of generating a radiating signal depicting the magnetic field. A video of the full RF cycle is available at this hyperlink.[5] Note the dense field lines concentrated around and particularly under the ground plane. The elevated ground plane appears to isolate these dense gradients in the near-field return path from the losses that would be incurred in the earth around a typical tower base. The active element of the D-Plate might provide further impetus for the near-field lines to concentrate on the ground plane rather than diffusing to nearby earth. It is postulated that these

[5] https://www.loudandclean.com/dl/HEBA_EandH.mp4

two features help the system to be immune to seasonal variations in ground conductivity while obtaining respectable efficiency for a short antenna.

From the model, a vertical pattern was generated. When graphed, its shape was like that of the thin-wire model used in 73.160(b). On a hunch, the 73.160(b) equation was iteratively processed with a series of electrical height values. Each electrical height produces a slightly different curve. Data points on each curve were calculated at 2-degree intervals and compared to the results of the NEC model.

The electrical height of 32.9 degrees at 940 kHz showed the best match between 73.160(b) and the NEC model. Figure 6 shows the convergence of the successive approximations on the 32.9-degree value. As the series of electrical heights converges on 32.9 degrees, the error reaches a minimum. The match between the best 73.160(b) curve and the NEC-5 model is as close to perfect as one could hope for. The differences in directivity per sampled elevation angle are within 0.004% of the maximum directivity.[6] This is visualized in the Figure 7 overlay of the NEC-5 vertical pattern on the 73.160(b) pattern based on the 32.9-degree electrical length.

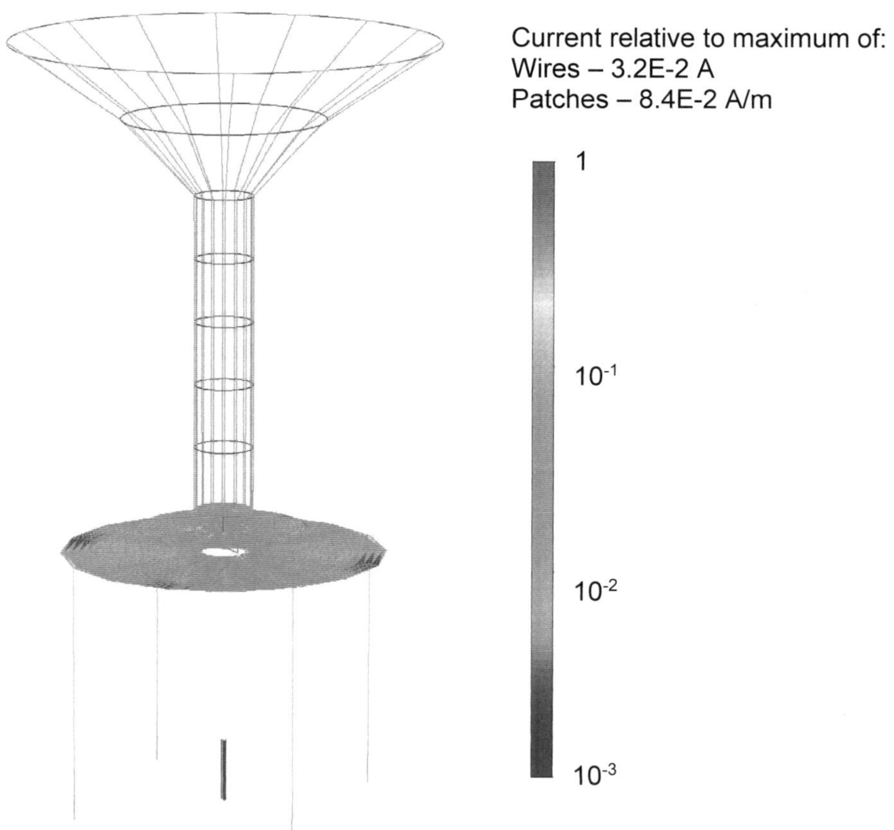

FIGURE 4 - CURRENT DISTRIBUTION IN HEBA CONDUCTORS

[6] Absolute error is used instead of percent variance to keep the results normalized to the reference directivity.

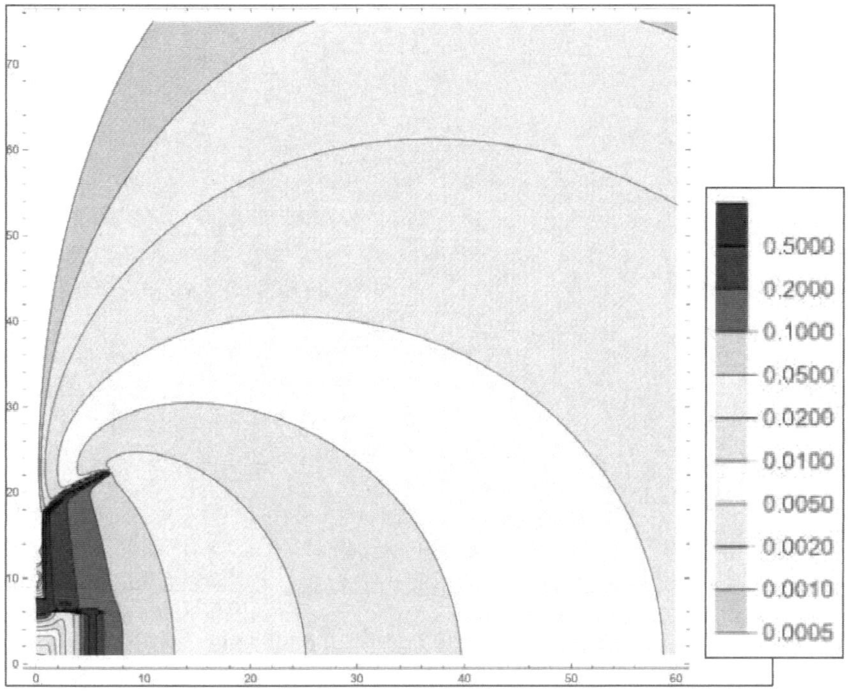

FIGURE 5 - FREEZE-FRAME OF CYCLICAL VIDEO OF UNDULATING MAGNETIC FIELD IN THE HEBA NEAR FIELD (A/M)

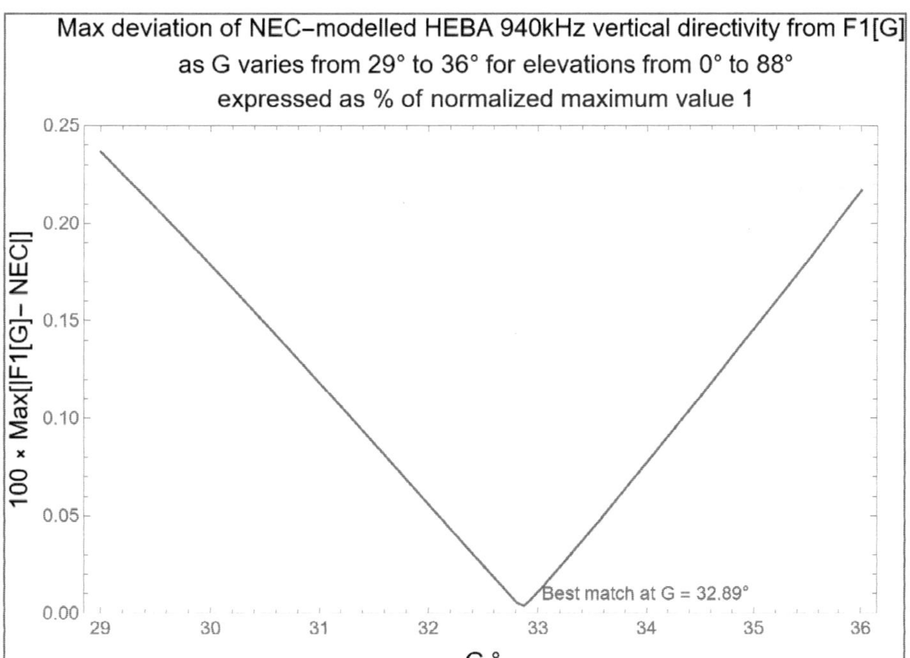

NOTE- The function $F_1(G)$ is the section 73.160(b) equation in which G is the presumed electrical height

FIGURE 6 - SUCCESSIVE APPROXIMATIONS OF PATTERN ERROR BY ELECTRICAL HEIGHT IDENTIFYING BEST MATCH WITH NEC MODEL

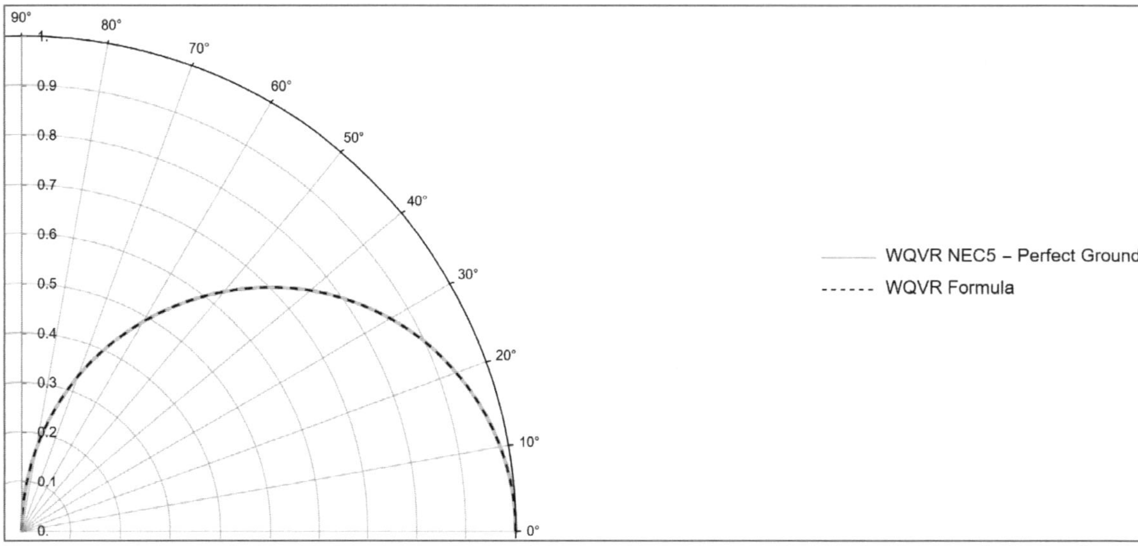

FIGURE 7 - VERTICAL RADIATION PATTERNS OF FCC FORMULA (USING 32.9° ELECTRICAL HEIGHT) AND NEC MODEL

In short, rather than estimate the electrical height and plug it into the 73.160(b) equation to obtain an approximated pattern, it was done the other way around. A series of electrical heights were plugged into the 73.160(b) equation until the result matched the computer model. By this approach, an equation describing the NEC model pattern was obtained. It was submitted as the required 73.160(c) "formula" supporting the application.

It was difficult for some to grasp this inside-out approach to using the equation in 73.160(b) as the "formula" required by 73.160(c). The team was obligated to not use 73.160(b) to generate a pattern based on an estimated electrical height. The HEBA was understandably suspected as being too unconventional to trust the FCC thin-wire model. On cursory review, it seemed like cheating – using the equation when prohibited from using the equation. However, with much explaining and head-scratching, it became clear that the NEC model was the reference vertical pattern, just as Rackley and King demonstrated, and the successive approximations iterating the 73.160(b) equation with a series of electrical heights were used to derive the required "formula." The 32.9-degree electrical height figure was a byproduct of the process rather than an input to it.

At 940 kHz, 319 m wavelength in free space, a 32.9-degree electrical height is 0.091 wavelength, or 29 m. The derived electrical height is 180% of the physical height of the active portion of the HEBA above its ground plane. Compared to the overall height above ground of the HEBA, the electrical height is 130% of that. The design of the HEBA clearly contributes to increasing the effective height of the radiator.

Theory of Operation

The guiding principle for the design of the HEBA's predecessor [7] was the hypothesis that a predominantly electric field could be "crossed" with a separately generated predominantly magnetic field to produce a radiating electromagnetic field. First, it is generally accepted that there is no way to generate a purely electric field and a purely magnetic field with alternating current sources. In conductive media, varying magnetic and electric fields produce varying electric and magnetic fields, respectively. At best, a CFA would need to use a conductor that generates a *mostly* electric external field paired with a conductor that generates a *mostly* magnetic external field.

However, the principle of superposition in electromagnetic fields challenges the literal interpretation of the crossed-field concept. Hately *et al* suggest, "Two separately controlled fields stimulated as radio frequency electric field E and an independent magnetic field H, driven by power from the same source but time phased so that across the interaction zone around the antenna there is E X H synchronism and Poynting vector synthesis occurs."

In contrast, superposition holds that *fields* emanating from one source do not interact with *fields* emanating from another source. Rather, they merely sum linearly at each point in space that they are observed. Only if those fields jointly interact with a common conductor is it anticipated that interaction of the superimposed fields will *appear* to occur. At this point, it is the interaction of independently sourced fields on a surface with a common set of moving electric charges that could yield more or less radiation than was already present. The hypothesis that separately generated magnetic and electric fields would interact in free space to create a radiating electromagnetic field seems to conflict with the superposition principle.

For example, at a point in free space where any two electromagnetic waves intersect, they overlap and continue unabated in their respective directions of propagation. By inserting a conductive surface, the sum of the two fields' energy is received (superposition). Or, if they are not propagating but overlapping (as in an evanescent field), neither field influences the other unless they are mutually coupled to a common conductor. Simply put, mutual coupling occurs when the moving charges on one excited element are additionally influenced by the fields coming from a nearby element. The movement of the charges, not the intersection of the fields themselves, is necessary to produce a radiating field.

Fortunately, the two excited elements of the HEBA are positioned next to each other and directly above a ground plane. This implies that the fields generated by each element will be mutually coupled in a way that could be constructive. The actual behavior of a system consisting of two adjacent components will be much more complex than simply combining idealized electric and magnetic fields in free space. The NEC modeling seems to bear this out.

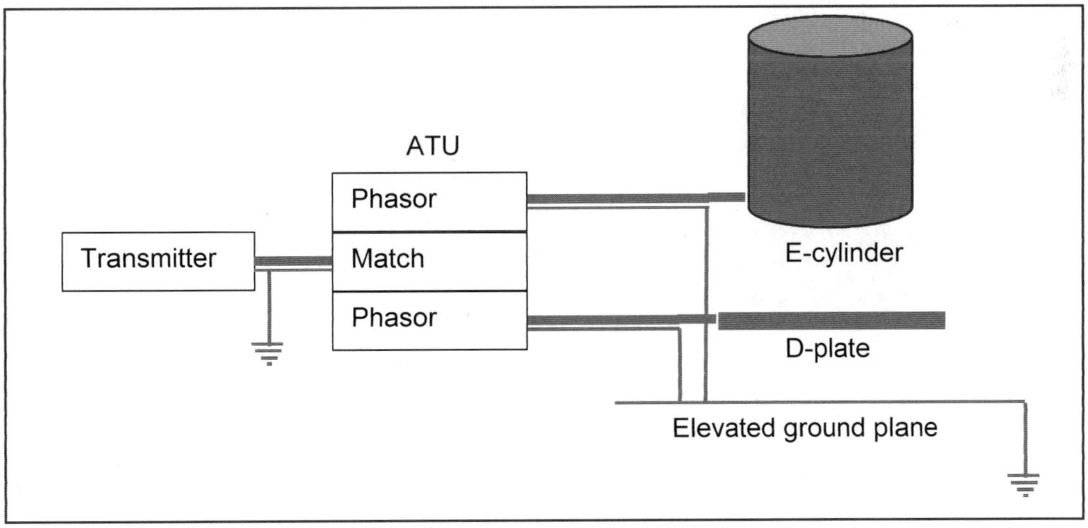

FIGURE 8 - BLOCK DIAGRAM OF HEBA ANTENNA SYSTEM

To energize the two active elements, the ATU has three sections that are conceptually like the sections of a phasor for energizing an AM directional array. (Figure 8) The first is a matching network for the transmitter. The output of the matching network branches to two phasor units. One is connected to the

E-cylinder while the other is connected to the D-plate. Being a capacitor connected to a ground plane while the ground plane is immersed in the electric field of the E-cylinder, it is apparent that the D-plate would present a challenging impedance. It took a diligent tuning effort by Mr. Gorman to maximize power transfer to the system. Once set, however, it has been stable and in need of no adjustment for years. A US patent on a novel HEBA ATU system design [8] lists Mr. Gorman as inventor and Worldwide Antenna Systems as the assignee.

The theory of operation of the HEBA therefore remains open for further conjecture. NEC modeling confirms the behavior seen with the working unit. Its modeled performance is consistent with that expected of a short antenna. The fact that the system has been immune to seasonal ground conductivity variations (and has not been affected in nine seasons of testing and licensed operation with snow/ice accumulation) indicates the novel feed method favors the system's elevated ground plane over imperfect earth for completing the circuit around the vertical radiator. It is postulated that, somewhat like a counterpoise, the elevated ground plane separates the dense magnetic and electric field lines from nearby ground losses imposed by an earth-based ground system. The benefits of the HEBA design include what appears to be greater efficiency than what might be expected of a simple ground-radial-based radiator of the same size.

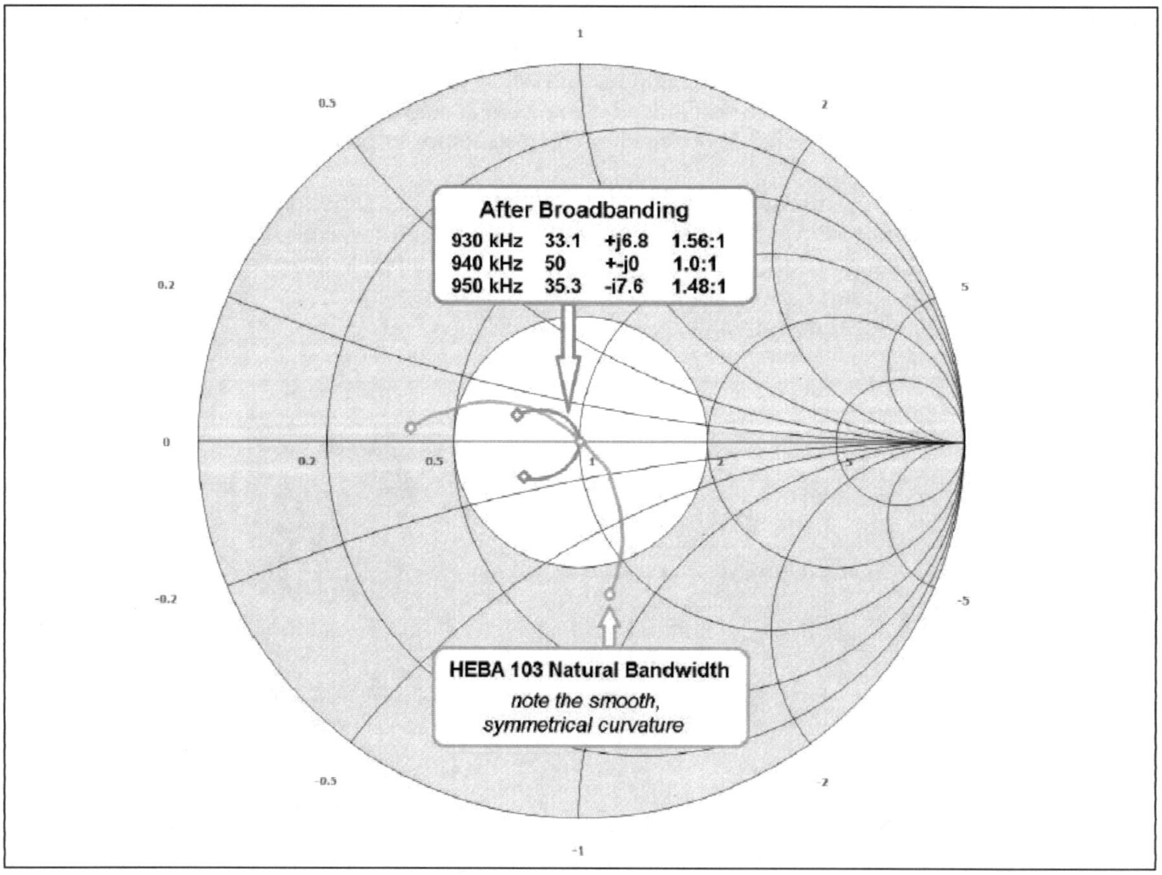

FIGURE 9 - SMITH CHART OF THE HEBA

In addition, because gain is dependent not only on the radiation pattern of the antenna (directivity) but also the resistive losses in the system, the HEBA gain is perhaps enhanced by the resulting reduction in near-the-tower ground losses over systems requiring the earth to complete the circuit. Further study of the vertical plane radiation characteristics is ongoing. Field measurements will be compared with the NEC model.

Bandwidth

Using basic tuning unit components and design, the HEBA has a bandwidth that is consistent with short antenna performance and is capable of being matched for analog and digital signal bandwidth requirements. Using a relatively conventional ATU design, the HEBA behaves like other electrically short radiators – it can handle the bandwidth of an analog signal (measured performance, green trace in Figure 9). Mr. Gorman has developed a broadbanded ATU design, but it has not yet been constructed and tested (calculated performance, orange trace). It simply has a higher parts count than the analog ATU. This more sophisticated ATU design provides the Hermitian Symmetry required by hybrid HD Radio™ transmissions [9].

Conclusion

In summary, while the HEBA's predecessor was developed based on a controversial interpretation of physical principles, the HEBA inherited some novel features that obey the laws of physics. These features offer benefits not seen with other short AM broadcast antennas. The novel dual-feed arrangement appears to enhance the electrical height as well as cooperate with the elevated ground plane to reduce near-field ground losses. The lack of a ground radial system reduces the footprint to 144 m^2 (~1600 square feet). Moreover, the overall height (22 m or 72 ft) reduces the environmental impact and maintenance burdens compared to conventional-height towers with ground radials. The radiation efficiency is comparable to that of an aged-in-place standard series-fed tower with ground radial system.

The FCC has approved the Webster, Massachusetts HEBA for daytime and nighttime operation. The next HEBAs to be built are on different frequencies and may have modified dimensions. This will require each to be modeled separately for FCC nighttime approval. As the designs evolve, it will come to a point that the HEBA can be standardized and authorized by calculation without modeling each design.

Assisting in the preparation of this paper, we gratefully acknowledge the support of the Worldwide Antenna Systems organization, and the talented and generous guidance of Grady Moates, Loud and Clean Broadcast Science, and Peter Zollman, Chartered Engineer.

References

[1] FCC AM station license, file number 243394, August 16, 2024.

[2] Chase, R., "The Electrically Short Vertical Monopole used for AM Broadcast – Engineering Analysis using NEC-MOM Software, Study Report," FCC Office of Engineering and Technology, May 1, 2003.

[3] Bromery, R., FCC Memorandum, May 1, 2003.

[4] FCC Public Notice – "MEDIA BUREAU ADOPTS SIMPLIFIED APPLICATION PROCEDURES FOR AM NONDIRECTIONAL KINSTAR ANTENNAS," October 25, 2005.

[5] Jacobs, M. W., King, T. F., "ENGINEERING REPORT FOR EXPERIMENTAL STATION WS2XTR AND REQUEST FOR APPLICATION OF 47 CFR 73.160(b)(2) FOR THE KINSTAR AM TRANSMITTING ANTENNA FOR GENERAL USE BY AM RADIO STATIONS IN THE UNITED STATES," Appendix 2 "Elevation Pattern Ratio Comparison Between NEC-4.1 And 73.160 Calculation Formula For Selected Licensed AM Broadcasting Antennas," July 30, 2004.

[6] Rackley, R., Cover letter to Peter Doyle, Chief Audio Division, Media Bureau, FCC, July 30, 2004.

[7] Hately & Kabbary, Patent WO 1989007348, August 10, 1989.

[8] Gorman, K., Patent US 10135143B2, November 20, 2018.

[9] Maxson, D., The IBOC Handbook – Understanding HD Radio Technology, Ch. 12 "AM Considerations," Focal Press, Boston, 2007.

Enhancing Resilience: An Emergency Backup Communication System with Cyber Communications Integration for Broadcasters

Matthew Straeb
ALERT FM/Global Security Systems LLC
Lafayette, Louisiana, United States
mstraeb@gssnet.us

Abstract - Broadcasting has long been a critical backbone for emergency communications, particularly during catastrophic events. However, increasing cyber threats against communication infrastructure necessitate a dual-resilient system that withstands both physical and digital disruptions. This paper introduces FM-Based Cyber Communications, a hybrid solution integrating FM radio infrastructure with advanced cybersecurity layers to create a fail-safe emergency broadcast network. By leveraging FM Radio Data System (RDS) technology, satellite uplinks, and air-gapped failover mechanisms, this system ensures encrypted, redundant, and uninterrupted information flow even when cellular networks, IP-based alerting protocols, and traditional Emergency Alert Systems (EAS) are compromised. Field testing under simulated disaster conditions demonstrates superior resilience, minimal transmission latency, and rapid failover capabilities, making FM-Based Cyber Communications an essential addition to next-generation emergency broadcasting infrastructure.

Introduction

The broadcast industry plays a pivotal role in public safety, particularly during crises where information dissemination is critical. Recent cyberattacks against public communication systems have demonstrated the fragility of internet-based emergency platforms, underscoring the need for an offline, infrastructure-independent failover system. FM-Based Cyber Communications leverages existing FM broadcast infrastructure to provide a secure and resilient emergency alerting mechanism.

Key benefits include:

- Cyber-Resilient Communication: Operates independently of traditional telecom networks, ensuring reliable messaging even during a total cyber shutdown.
- Satellite-Backed Redundancy: Uses FM-RDS and satellite downlinks to maintain emergency broadcasts when terrestrial networks fail.
- Automated Threat Mitigation: AI-driven anomaly detection identifies and isolates malicious signal injection attempts, ensuring message authenticity.
- Hybrid Multi-Layer Failover Model: Integrates high-power FM, encrypted FM-RDS data transmission, localized receiver networks, and satellite relays to ensure end-to-end operational continuity.

System Architecture & Technical Overview

High-power FM broadcast towers in the US (50 kW – 100 kW equivalent radiated power, ERP), taken as a group, ensure nationwide signal reach, exceeding the coverage of cellular and IP-based networks. Redundant low-power FM (LPFM) nodes serve as localized backup stations in case of primary

transmission failure. The FM-based alert system utilizes a hybrid satellite and terrestrial network to ensure uninterrupted emergency messaging across wide geographic areas. **Proven Infrastructure**
Wireless broadcast, including FM radio, is the best medium to quickly send content to many people. This fact is best reinforced by the FCC mandate requiring broadcast station owners to carry traditional EAS signals and maintain EAS equipment. No viable alternative exists to supplant this basic infrastructure.

For most of its history, the broadcast industry benefited from the fact that it was one of the only media capable of providing adequate and reliable signal coverage over a large area. Although many wireless networks now coexist with FM broadcast, they succumb to nodal vulnerability (Figure 1) due to a lack of overlapping signals.

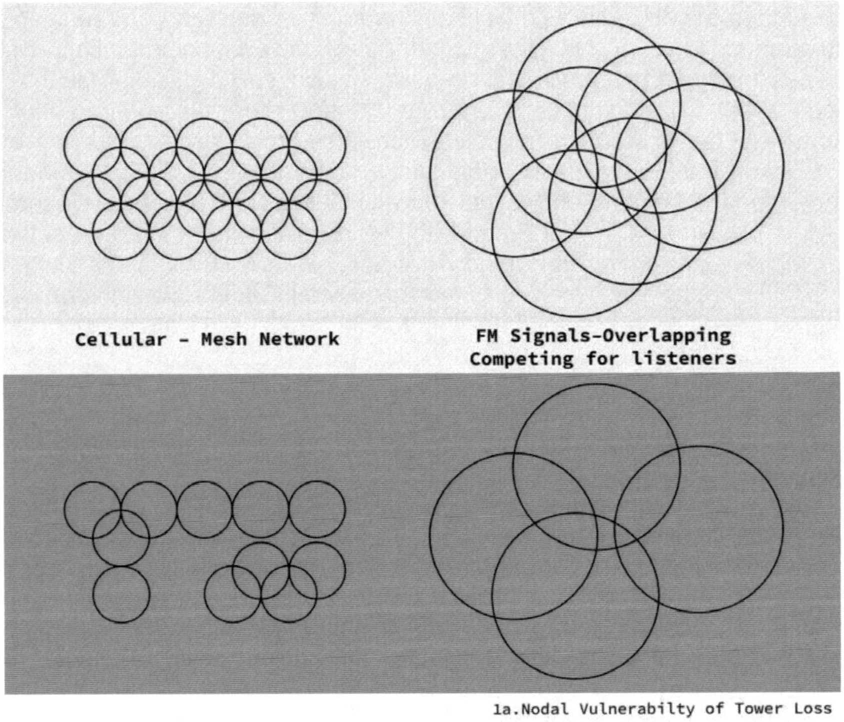

FIGURE 1: NODAL VULNERABILITY OF TOWER LOSS.

Overlapping signals are not economically feasible when building a telco/data network; however, it is the only economic model for a radio network competing in a market for listeners. This has always been the primary factor motivating the author to advocate for advancement, support, and adoption of data distribution using FM radio. Specifically, FM/RDS cyber communications systems utilizes the FM-RDS subcarrier. RDS is a digital FM subcarrier dedicated to sending data packets with information such as alphanumeric messaging.

Priority

The Internet or any internet-based protocol is not a broadcast medium. The internet is a distributed network with a hierarchical structure and multitude of connections. Internet service providers are comprised of telecom (wireline and/or wireless), cable, and satellite distribution all reliant on one another to connect server and client. This world wide web, comprised of providers and consumers, cannot prioritize the delivery of one data type over another. This is the essence of "net neutrality."

Often, this network is extremely fast and can process vast amounts of data. We rarely encounter a "traffic jam" when requesting something in our web browser or mobile apps; nevertheless, attend a large gathering at a major sports venue to get a glimpse of network capacity. Things slow down, messages aren't received, and the venue offers you free WIFI likely sponsored by your favorite cellular carrier. Every smartphone or computer requires a constant connection for requesting and receiving. Now, attempt to alert 100,000 fans or 1,000,000 citizens of imminent danger. It may work or it may not, due to network topology.

FM/RDS cyber communications systems receivers use standard alkaline batteries with useful capacity measured in months. Smartphones are feature-rich devices and critical to our daily lives, but when daily life deviates from the norm, 12-24 hours of battery life is not enough. FM/RDS cyber communications systems offers a complement to these devices and a respite from cumbersome weather radios reliant on a single regional tower.

The Space and Terrestrial Combo

A satellite-connected FM radio network (see Figure 2) provides a perfect solution for entities that require economical and reliable audio and/or high-speed data delivery to multiple locations. Such a system uses a one-way satellite network to deliver common alerting protocol (CAP)-based text and audio (if required).

FIGURE 2: TYPICAL FM/RDS CYBER COMMUNICATIONS SYSTEMS WORKFLOW.

EAS Messaging to Radio, TV & Cable Stations

This satellite data delivery occurs much quicker than traditional delivery using daisy chains to various broadcast stations. CAP-EAS message origination and system administration is handled through the Satellite-connected FM radio network Alert Studio, a secure web-based application. Paired with terrestrial internet, satellite-connected FM radio network satellite data delivery provides redundant CAP-EAS message data delivery for both message origination and delivery to the broadcast stations.

A satellite-connected FM radio network uses an approximately 1-meter satellite receiving dish (assuming Ku-band satellite links) with a digital receiver at the broadcast transmitter site. CAP-EAS messages are then passed to an EAS encoder-decoder (ENDEC) for broadcast over the air. The system features the ability to provide large amounts of information and a combination of various forms of audio and data. It is also fully scalable so bandwidth upgrades at the system level can be accomplished in minutes. Bottomline, this system digitizes EAS as a backup in case that PEP stations fails. The system also sends automated NOAA weather severe warnings to those individuals who "opt in" to receive them on FM/RDS cyber communications systems receivers. If a severe weather event is occurring, satellite-connected FM radio network will fire off the signal to all FM/RDS cyber communications systems towers in that warning area. Any receiver in that area will wake-up and alert the user.

Cyber Resilience of FM/RDS Cyber Communications Systems

FM/RDS cyber communications systems is designed with robust security measures to ensure its resilience against cyber-attacks, leveraging the strengths of high-power FM transmitters and a sophisticated system of secure identifiers. These features collectively make it nearly impossible for unauthorized entities to take over the FM/RDS cyber communications systems network.

High-Power FM Transmitters

The backbone of the FM/RDS cyber communications systems is its network of high-power FM transmitters. Unlike traditional communication methods that rely on internet or cellular networks, FM transmitters are inherently more resistant to cyber intrusions. These transmitters broadcast over a wide area, making physical tampering difficult and reducing the risk of cyber-attacks that typically target network infrastructure.

Secure, Random FM/RDS Cyber Communications Systems Identifier

Each FM/RDS cyber communications systems transmitter broadcasts a secure, randomly generated system identifier. FM/RDS cyber communications systems receivers are programmed to listen exclusively for this identifier, ensuring that only authorized signals are received and processed. This unique identifier acts as a digital fingerprint, making it extremely difficult for malicious actors to replicate or spoof the signal.

Building an FM/RDS Cyber Communications System Network

To establish a robust FM-based Alert Distribution System (using RDS), the following key components must be integrated:

- Infrastructure requirements - FM transmission network:
  - Identify primary FM stations with extensive regional coverage (50 kW – 100 kW ERP).
  - Establish secondary LPFM backup stations (10 W – 250 W) to maintain localized resilience.
  - Implement RDS encoders at each FM station to transmit alert data over the 57 kHz RDS digital subcarrier.
  - Deploy emergency power backups (generators and battery banks) at FM transmission sites.
- Infrastructure requirements - satellite integration:
  - Implement an uplink system at a central broadcast operations hub to transmit emergency messages to geostationary and low-earth orbit (LEO) satellites.
  - Utilize DVB-S2 modulation to ensure spectral efficiency and robust signal integrity under adverse conditions.
  - Deploy receiver stations at each FM transmitter site to receive satellite-fed alert messages during network disruptions.
- Signal processing and data transmission - RDS data encoding & encryption:
  - Utilize IEC 62106-compliant RDS encoders to inject digital emergency messages into the FM subcarrier.
  - Implement AES-256 encryption for FM-RDS emergency messaging to prevent unauthorized signal injection.
  - Design message authentication procedures using blockchain technology for verification integrity.
- Signal processing and data transmission - alert processing hub:
  - Deploy a cloud-based or on-premises alert management server to coordinate emergency message origination.

- Utilize AI-driven analytics to monitor network health, detect interference, and prevent unauthorized signal transmission.
- Enable geographic targeting capabilities within the alert system, allowing messages to be broadcast only in affected regions.

- Receiver Network Deployment- Public and Emergency Service Receivers:
  - Deploy fixed-location receivers in critical infrastructure facilities such as hospitals, emergency response centers, and law enforcement agencies.
  - Provide battery-powered portable receivers to first responders and emergency personnel.
  - Integrate FM-RDS receiver modules into consumer mobile devices via smartphone applications and embedded radio chipsets.
- Receiver Network Deployment - End-User Alert Devices: (see Figure 3)
  - Implement dedicated FM-based alert radios with LCD displays for text-based alerts.
  - Develop vehicle-integrated alert receivers, ensuring mobile users receive emergency notifications even when traveling.
  - Enable "wake-up" functionality in emergency receivers, ensuring alerts are received even when devices are powered off or in standby mode.

FIGURE 3: TYPICAL ALERT FM RECEIVING DEVICE.

- Failover and Redundancy Planning - Automated Network Failover Mechanisms:
  - Implement AI-driven failover switching between terrestrial FM transmission and satellite-fed RDS alerts.
  - Establish redundancy across multiple broadcast stations, ensuring continuous alert propagation even if primary stations are compromised.
- Failover and Redundancy Planning - Cybersecurity and Threat Mitigation:
  - Develop intrusion detection mechanisms to monitor FM transmission integrity and identify unauthorized broadcast attempts.
  - Establish a dedicated security operations center (SOC) to monitor and respond to potential cyber threats.

Real-World Use Cases

Some real-world use cases for FM-based Cyber Communications include the following:

- **Shake Alert Earthquake Early Warning System** – Provides rapid earthquake warnings to the West Coast [1].
- **Chemical Stockpile Emergency Preparedness Program (CSEPP)** - Kentucky – Disseminates real-time alerts regarding chemical stockpile incidents [2].

- **New Orleans Terrorist Attack** - January 1 – Informed the public and coordinated emergency response efforts [3].
- **Colonial Pipeline Ransomware Attack (2021)** – A cyberattack severely disrupted fuel distribution across the East Coast, causing panic and logistical crises. While digital communications were compromised, FM radio stations continued to broadcast emergency updates and fuel availability information to the public [4].
- **Hawaii False Missile Alert (2018)** – An accidental emergency alert was sent via cellular and internet-based systems, causing mass panic. FM and AM radio stations played a crucial role in dispelling misinformation and providing official government updates [5].
- **Ukraine Cyberattacks (2022)** – Large-scale cyberattacks targeted critical infrastructure, disrupting power grids and telecommunications. FM radio remained one of the most reliable sources of communication, providing war-related updates and emergency broadcasts in real-time [6].

Future Roadmap

The next phase of FM-Based Cyber Communications development will focus on:

- **Artificial Intelligence-Enhanced Signal Monitoring:** AI-driven analytics to detect and mitigate signal interference, unauthorized transmissions, and potential cyber threats in real-time.
- **Blockchain Authentication for Message Integrity:** Implementing blockchain technology to provide a decentralized, tamper-proof verification system for emergency alert transmissions.
- **Integration of Dynamic Frequency Hopping:** Utilizing adaptive frequency management to counteract jamming threats and improve FM-RDS message delivery reliability.
- **Expansion of Multilingual Alerting Capabilities:** Enhancing FM-RDS transmission to support multiple languages simultaneously, improving emergency communication for diverse populations.
- **Enhanced Power-Efficient FM Receiver Design:** Developing ultra-low-power FM receivers with solar or kinetic charging options to ensure long-term functionality in extreme disaster scenarios.
- **Network Expansion for First Responder Use:** Enabling FM-RDS messaging to function as a secure alternative to compromised first responder communication networks, providing encrypted dispatch messaging and priority overrides during emergencies.

Summary

FM-Based Cyber Communications is a game-changing approach to emergency alerting, ensuring the resilience of national communication systems against both cyber and physical threats. By integrating FM-RDS technology, satellite redundancy, and AI-driven threat detection, this system offers a superior alternative to traditional infrastructure-dependent alerting mechanisms, ensuring compliance with international broadcast standards, NRSC guidelines, and FCC emergency broadcast mandates.

References

[1] US Geological Survey (USGS), “ShakeAlert: Earthquake Early Warning for the West Coast,” Available: https://www.shakealert.org.

[2] Federal Emergency Management Agency (FEMA), “Chemical Stockpile Emergency Preparedness Program (CSEPP),” Available: https://www.cseppportal.net/

[3] New Orleans Office of Homeland Security and Emergency Preparedness, “After-Action Report: New Orleans Terrorist Attack,” 2025.

[4] Cybersecurity and Infrastructure Security Agency (CISA), “Colonial Pipeline Cyberattack Incident Report,” 2021, Available: https://www.cisa.gov/news-events/news/attack-colonial-pipeline-what-weve-learned-what-weve-done-over-past-two-years.

[5] Federal Communications Commission (FCC), “Hawaii False Missile Alert: Investigation and Recommendations,” 2018, Available: https://docs.fcc.gov/public/attachments/DOC-350119A1.pdf.

[6] Ukraine Government Communication Agency, “Cyberattacks and Infrastructure Resilience During Wartime,” 2022.

Shielding Truth: A Strategic Defense in Depth Approach to Deepfake Detection for Media Professionals

Ryan Ofman, Rijul Gupta
Deep Media AI
Oakland, California, United States
rijul@deepmedia.ai

Abstract – The detection of Deepfakes presents critical challenges to media integrity, necessitating robust, scalable solutions. This paper introduces a comprehensive Defense in Depth strategy, integrating advanced AI techniques alongside human expertise. Central to this strategy is the use of diverse datasets to train detection models, ensuring broader applicability and reduced bias. Furthermore, it emphasizes the importance of ongoing education and skills development for media professionals, equipping them to leverage detection technology effectively. This approach not only enhances current Deepfake identification capabilities but also aligns with broader industry initiatives focused on innovation and workforce development. By fostering interdisciplinary collaboration, we aim to fortify the media landscape against evolving synthetic media threats. The paper showcases real-world case studies and offers strategic recommendations, underscoring the necessity of continuous adaptation and cooperation within the broadcasting sector to maintain public trust and media authenticity

Deepfake Challenges and the Role of Broadcast Media

The proliferation of Deepfake technology poses significant challenges to the integrity of broadcast media, demanding advanced solutions to maintain public trust. As Deepfakes become more sophisticated, their potential to distort information escalates, making it imperative for broadcasters to adopt resilient strategies to discern truth from falsehood. This section outlines our comprehensive Defense in Depth strategy, emphasizing the crucial role that broadcasters play in deploying effective countermeasures against synthetic media.

In today's rapidly evolving media landscape, broadcasters have long been at the forefront of addressing misinformation. Their experience managing these issues uniquely positions them as pivotal partners in the fight against Deepfakes. By integrating advanced detection methodologies with their deep understanding of content verification, broadcasters can enhance their capacity to authenticate media. This collaboration not only mitigates the risk of deception but also reinforces the public's trust in legitimate media sources.

Our Defense in Depth Strategy Includes the Following Elements:

- Verification Techniques: Employ advanced cryptographic and metadata analysis tools to ensure content authenticity.
- AI-Based Detection: Utilize machine learning models trained on diverse datasets to identify Deepfake anomalies across varied media types.
- Strategic Responses: Develop rapid response protocols for addressing confirmed Deepfake content, bolstering public communication efforts.

These elements collectively form a robust framework for tackling Deepfake threats. With broadcasters playing a central role, this strategy ensures a multilayered approach, safeguarding media authenticity and strengthening the industry's resilience against evolving synthetic media threats.

Technological Foundations for Deepfake Detection

The accelerating capabilities of Deepfake technologies stem from the strategic advancements within artificial intelligence, particularly fueled by intricate architectures such as Generative Adversarial Networks (GANs) and Variational Autoencoders (VAEs). These AI developments enable the crafting of hyper-realistic synthetic media, heightening risks to media integrity across platforms. Increasingly, humans have become much less effective at correctly identifying Deepfakes, with humans rapidly reaching a threshold in which they will be unable to differentiate fake from real content.

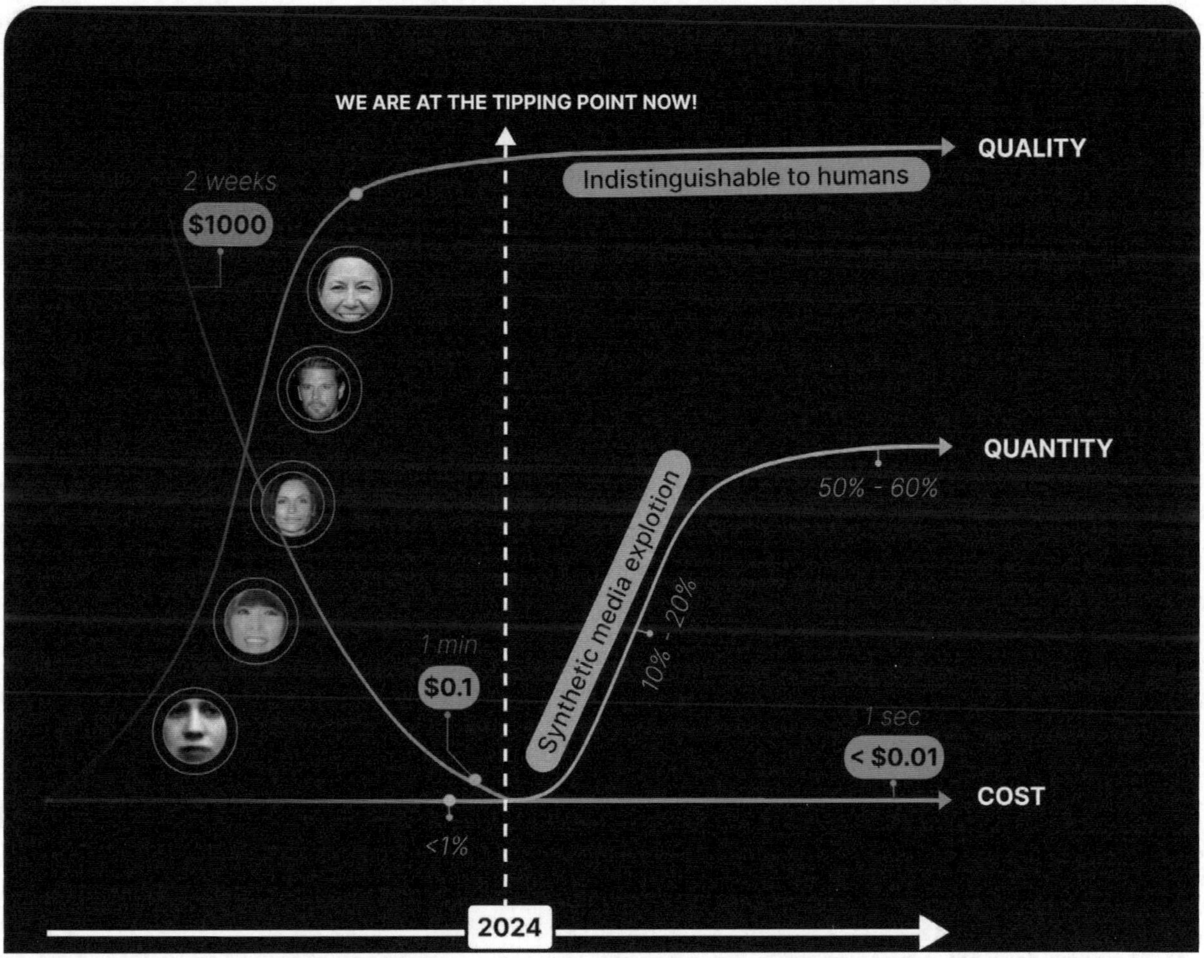

FIGURE 1: DEMONSTRATING THE INCREASINGLY LOW COST TO GENERATE AI GENERATED CONTENT, AS WELL AS THAT WE ARE RAPIDLY APPROACHING DEEPFAKES BEING INDISTINGUISHABLE FOR HUMANS.

To counteract these evolving threats, media personnel are uniquely positioned to harness AI advancements for detection and verification processes. By integrating machine learning models trained on comprehensive and representative datasets, they can adeptly identify intricate anomalies that betray synthetic manipulations. This integration underscores the necessity for a diverse approach in detecting Deepfakes, ensuring models account for various demographic nuances and reduce bias.

The symbiosis between AI engineers, media experts, cybersecurity professionals, and ethicists forms an interdisciplinary collaboration essential for developing robust detection ecosystems. This collaboration encourages the design of technologically adept and ethically grounded solutions, ensuring that media integrity defenses are both innovative and aligned with societal values. The resultant tools empower media professionals to secure content authenticity and uphold public trust.

Moreover, interoperating these technologies with existing media workflows fosters resilience against Deepfake propagation. By cultivating a comprehensive understanding of AI's capabilities and limitations, media personnel can enhance defenses, strategically fortifying their platforms against the encroaching threat of synthetic media.

Implementing a Multi-Layered Defense in Depth Strategy

Addressing the sophisticated and adaptive nature of Deepfake threats requires a comprehensive, multi-layered Defense in Depth strategy tailored to the diverse operational landscapes of media organizations. This strategy integrates multiple defensive components, forming a cohesive and adaptive framework that safeguards content authenticity across various stages. At the core of this strategy is the verification layer, which employs a range of advanced techniques to confirm content provenance and integrity. Metadata analysis forms the foundational aspect of this defense, utilizing tools like ExifTool or MediaInfo to extract valuable information embedded within digital files. This includes inspecting Exif data such as camera specifics and geolocation, XMP metadata detailing editing history and copyright information, and file format data indicating processing origins. These metadata details are meticulously parsed and analyzed through custom scripts to detect anomalies or indicative patterns, and the results are stored within structured databases for efficient cross-referencing against known Deepfake profiles, making it a crucial first line of defense.

In parallel, digital watermarking enhances security by embedding imperceptible identifiers within media files. This process involves spatial domain methods like Least Significant Bit modification and frequency domain strategies such as Discrete Cosine Transform, as well as keypoint-based techniques targeting specific features. Each watermark serves as an embedded signature that can be detected through specialized extraction methods and is secured by robust key management systems, ensuring that media integrity is preserved without perceptible tampering. Cryptographic hashing, another vital component, contributes to forensic analysis by generating secure digital fingerprints of media files. Utilizing advanced algorithms like SHA-256 or Blake2, cryptographic hashing creates fixed-size, collision-resistant hashes that validate media authenticity. Any deviation from the original hash suggests potential manipulation, enabling rapid identification of tampered media.

Further bolstering this multi-faceted approach, provenance tracking incorporates digital signatures, watermarking, and blockchain technologies to establish an unbroken chain of custody for media files. This transparent and auditable journey enhances credibility assessments and builds user trust in digital content. The integration of cryptographic methods and watermarking within this framework further increases its dependability, building an interconnected defense system that media personnel can rely upon to counteract the propagation of synthetic media.

The AI detection layer is another critical component, leveraging advanced models like transformers and Vision Transformers (ViTs) to identify subtle inconsistencies within media artifacts that are often undetectable to the human eye. These AI models monitor and analyze data streams for Deepfake anomalies, implementing real-time detection and verification processes that safeguard media outputs. By incorporating robust AI frameworks, media professionals enhance their capacity to rapidly identify manipulated content, thereby preventing the dissemination of false information.

The response layer completes this defensive structure by enacting strategic operational protocols for identified threats, streamlining communication efforts to mitigate the impact of misinformation. Media personnel deploy these protocols swiftly upon detection of synthetic media, ensuring accurate public information through thoughtful communication strategies that reinforce trust and maintain organizational transparency. This layer ensures that every incident detected is responded to efficiently and effectively, thereby protecting the integrity of the media landscape.

Together, these layers provide a comprehensive defense mechanism that empowers media professionals to anticipate and neutralize Deepfake threats, ensuring holistic protection and alignment with the evolving dynamics of digital media ecosystems.

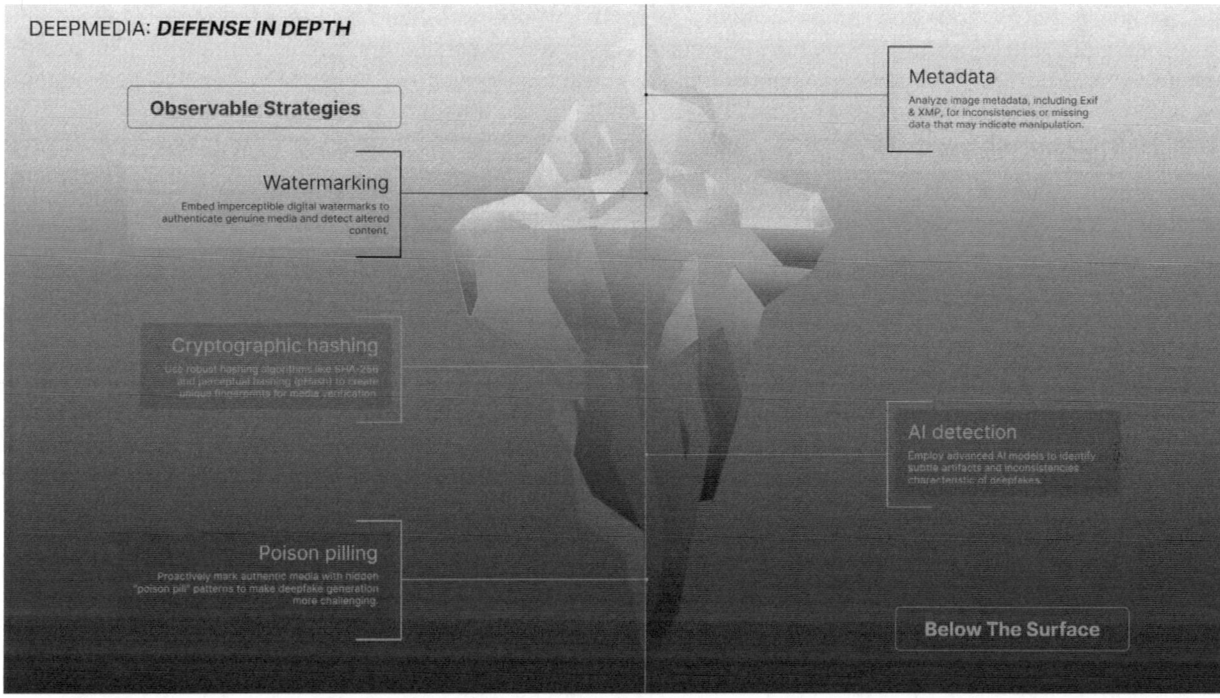

FIGURE 2: A VISUAL REPRESENTATION OF THE VARIOUS LAYERS TO A DEFENSE IN DEPTH DEEPFAKE STRATEGY. MANY LAYERS APPEAR BELOW THE SURFACE, INVISIBLE TO THE VIEWER, WHILE OTHERS HEAVILY INVOLVE THE VIEWER'S OBSERVATION.

Strategic Implications and Preparing for Future Threats

As Deepfake technologies continue to evolve, reshaping media environments with unprecedented speed and complexity, the need for dynamic and forward-thinking strategies becomes increasingly critical. Media personnel, including broadcasters, must remain agile and proactive, embracing both current technological advancements and anticipating future challenges to effectively combat synthetic media threats. A cornerstone of robust preparation lies in the continuous education and upskilling of media professionals. By integrating media verification tools and AI competencies within education programs, media organizations cultivate a workforce that not only understands the complexities of modern media ecosystems but is also skilled at identifying and countering Deepfake tactics. This commitment to ongoing training elevates individual proficiency, strengthening overall organizational resilience against these evolving threats.

Moreover, the proactive development of standardized ethical guidelines and robust policy frameworks is essential for managing and regulating Deepfake content. In collaboration with regulatory bodies, media personnel are pivotal in establishing these standards, fostering an environment of accountability and integrity within digital media. Such guidelines ensure that organizations can confidently navigate ethical challenges, safeguard content authenticity, and maintain public trust. Furthermore, fostering a culture of interdisciplinary collaboration amplifies innovation in Deepfake detection by leveraging expertise from diverse fields such as technology, media studies, and policy development. Strategic alliances enable the creation of solutions tailored to address the multifaceted nature of Deepfake threats.

By working together, media professionals enhance their capacity to devise adaptable strategies that defend against the sophisticated nature of synthetic media. Through these strategic initiatives, including a focus on training, ethical standards, and collaborative innovation, media personnel can ensure the enduring integrity of media and uphold public trust in an era characterized by rapid technological disruption. Continually refining these strategies ensures that the media landscape remains resilient and prepared to meet the challenges and opportunities brought by tomorrow's technological advancements.

Conclusion and Call to Action

In summation, the digital media landscape faces formidable challenges from Deepfake technologies, demanding a responsive and layered Deepfake Detection strategy. By integrating advanced AI detection techniques with human expertise, media personnel are uniquely equipped to defend against these threats. This strategy not only addresses the technical complexities of Deepfake detection with innovative solutions but also emphasizes the critical role of ongoing education, ethical standards, and strategic collaboration across the industry.

Media professionals are at the forefront of maintaining media integrity, mandated to stay agile amidst evolving technological landscapes. The commitment to continuous professional development ensures they are well-prepared to implement detection technologies effectively, safeguarding public trust and media authenticity. Sharing these insights and methodologies fosters a culture of resilience and innovation, vital for adapting to future technological disruptions.

Engagement and Collaboration

- Media personnel and organizations are urged to remain vigilant and proactive, not only in implementing these strategies but also in contributing to the broader discourse on digital ethics and innovation.
- By fostering a cooperative culture that spans technology developers, policy-makers, and educators, the media industry can create a robust ecosystem. This ecosystem is essential for the continuous refinement of detection capabilities and the development of new solutions against synthetic media threats.
- Attendees and readers are encouraged to take these insights forward into practice, advocating for standardization of ethical guidelines and participating in ongoing research and collaboration efforts.

In engaging with these strategies and fostering interdisciplinary collaboration, we ensure a fortified digital media environment capable of confronting current and future challenges posed by Deepfakes. By leveraging both technological and human resources, media personnel can secure the future of trustworthy media communications.

References

[1] Diel, A., Lalgi, T., Schröter, I. C., MacDorman, K. F., Teufel, M., & Bäuerle, A., "Human Performance in Detecting Deepfakes: A Systematic Review and Meta-Analysis of 56 Papers," Computers in Human Behavior Reports, Vol. 16, 2024, p. 100538. https://doi.org/10.1016/j.chbr.2024.100538.

[2] Byman, Daniel, et al. Deepfakes and International Conflict, www.brookings.edu/wp-content/uploads/2023/01/FP_20230105_deepfakes_international_conflict.pdf. Accessed 20 Feb. 2025.

[3] Pei, Gan, et al. “Deepfake Generation and Detection: A Benchmark and Survey.” arXiv.Org, 16 May 2024, arxiv.org/abs/2403.17881.

[4] Sontakke, Nikhil, et al. “Comparative Analysis of Deep-Fake Algorithms.” arXiv.Org, 6 Sept. 2023, arxiv.org/abs/2309.03295.

Tower Site Safety: A Comprehensive Approach to Risk Management

Clark Lindstrom
American Tower Corporation
Cary, North Carolina, United States

Kathy Stieler
NATE: The Communications Infrastructure Contractors Association
Watertown, South Dakota, United States

Abstract – Ensuring tower site safety is critical for preventing accidents and protecting workers from hazards associated with tower climbing, RF exposure, and structural failures. This paper outlines essential safety requirements, referencing OSHA, NFPA, and ANSI standards to reinforce best practices. Key topics include personal protective equipment (PPE), fall protection, RF hazard management, emergency response, and site maintenance.

Introduction

The telecommunications industry relies on tower sites for broadcasting and communication. However, these sites present significant risks, including falls, RF exposure, and hazardous materials. Compliance with safety standards is essential to protect workers and ensure operational integrity. This paper will discuss the critical safety aspects of tower site operations, emphasizing compliance with OSHA, NFPA, and ANSI standards to mitigate risks effectively.

General Safety Requirements

OSHA's General Duty Clause (29 U.S.C. § 654, 5(a)(1)) mandates that employers provide a workplace free from recognized hazards. This includes ensuring all personnel receive proper training and have access to PPE as outlined in OSHA 29 CFR 1910.132. Workers must wear hard hats, full-body harnesses, and lanyards when working at height. Clear safety signage must be posted, in accordance with ANSI Z535.2, to warn of site-specific dangers.

Site Access and Security

Uncontrolled site access can lead to trespassing and unauthorized activity. OSHA 29 CFR 1910.37 outlines emergency exit access requirements, while NFPA 730 provides guidelines on site security and surveillance. Perimeter fencing, signage, and CCTV monitoring should be utilized to ensure restricted access and prevent unauthorized entry.

RF Hazard Management

Exposure to high levels of radiofrequency (RF) radiation poses health risks, including burns and tissue damage. The FCC's Maximum Permissible Exposure (MPE) limits, as referenced in OSHA 29 CFR 1910.97, should be strictly followed. Workers must use personal RF monitors and coordinate power-down procedures with antenna owners to minimize exposure. ANSI/IEEE C95.1-2019 provides further guidance on safe RF exposure limits.

This paper is excerpted from the Proceedings of the 2025 NAB Broadcast Engineering and Information Technology (BEIT) Conference, © 2025, National Association of Broadcasters, 1 M Street SE, Washington, DC 20003 USA.

Fall Protection
Falls are the leading cause of fatalities in tower work, making fall protection a critical safety component. OSHA 29 CFR 1910.268(g) mandates the use of fall protection for telecommunications workers, requiring continuous fall protection when working at height. Additionally, ANSI Z359.2 outlines managed fall protection programs, ensuring that safety climb systems and anchor points are regularly inspected.

Emergency Response Procedures
Rapid response to emergencies such as tower collapse, medical incidents, or hazardous material exposure is essential. OSHA's 29 CFR 1910.151 mandates that first aid supplies be readily available. Emergency contacts must be listed at each site, and workers should be trained in emergency evacuation procedures. In the event of a tower collapse, the NFPA 1561 Standard on Emergency Services Incident Management System should be followed to coordinate rescue operations.

Hazardous Materials Management
Encountering hazardous materials, such as asbestos or lead, during site maintenance requires immediate action. OSHA 29 CFR 1910.1001 sets strict guidelines for asbestos exposure, requiring specialized handling and disposal procedures. Workers should cease operations and notify safety personnel if hazardous materials are discovered.

Site Maintenance and Inspections
Routine inspections help identify potential safety hazards before they become critical. OSHA 29 CFR 1910.66 mandates regular inspection and maintenance of personal fall arrest systems. Additionally, ANSI/TIA-222 provides guidance on structural maintenance for telecommunications towers, ensuring compliance with load-bearing and environmental requirements.

Conclusion

Safety at tower sites is a shared responsibility that requires strict adherence to industry regulations and continuous improvement in safety practices. By following OSHA, NFPA, and ANSI standards, organizations can mitigate risks, protect workers, and maintain operational efficiency. Safety culture should be reinforced through training, regular inspections, and incident reporting to ensure a proactive approach to workplace safety.

References

[1] American National Standards Institute (ANSI). (2019). *ANSI Z359.2 – Minimum Requirements for a Comprehensive Managed Fall Protection Program*. ANSI.

[2] Federal Communications Commission (FCC). (2019). *Guidelines for Evaluating the Environmental Effects of Radiofrequency Radiation*. FCC.

[3] National Fire Protection Association (NFPA). (2022). *NFPA 1561 – Standard on Emergency Services Incident Management System*. NFPA.

[4] Occupational Safety and Health Administration (OSHA). (2021). *29 CFR 1910 – Occupational Safety and Health Standards*. U.S. Department of Labor.

[5] Telecommunications Industry Association (TIA). (2018). *ANSI/TIA-222 – Structural Standard for Antenna Supporting Structures and Antennas*. TIA.

The UHD HDR Host Broadcast Vision Engineering Workflow of the Olympic Games Revealed

Geert Heirbaut
Olympic Broadcasting Services
Madrid, Spain
gheirbaut@obs.tv

Abstract – This paper offers a unique and insightful behind-the-scenes look at the design, implementation, and future of the Ultra-High-Definition and High-Dynamic-Range Vision Engineering Workflow by Olympic Broadcasting Services (OBS) for the Host Broadcast of the Olympic Games. It provides unprecedented details, including diagrams, schematics, and data that have never been publicly shared, showcasing OBS's commitment to serving both broadcasters and athletes as a neutral and unbiased organization.

Introduction

Olympic Broadcasting Services (OBS), established by the International Olympic Committee (IOC) to eliminate the need to rebuild broadcast operations for each edition of the Games, produces the live television, radio, and digital coverage of the Olympic and Paralympic Games. This coverage remains neutral, favoring no country or athlete, and includes both sports competitions and the Opening and Closing Ceremonies.

In addition to delivering coverage to broadcasters worldwide, OBS designs, builds, and operates the International Broadcast Center (IBC). OBS assists broadcasters in tailoring their coverage for their home audiences and represents the needs of Media Rights-Holders (MRHs).

OBS ensures that the high standards of Olympic broadcasting are consistently maintained from one edition of the Games to the next. As part of this mission, OBS leverages state-of-the-art broadcasting technologies to continuously enhance service quality, setting industry benchmarks and driving future innovations.

One of the most significant advancements in recent years has been the transition to Ultra-High-Definition (UHD) and High-Dynamic-Range (HDR) image capture and display. Committed to delivering the highest possible quality to broadcasters, OBS fully embraced this transition – despite the immense challenges presented by the scale of the Olympic Games. With more than 1,000 broadcast system cameras deployed during a single edition, OBS faced the monumental task of transforming its Vision Engineering Workflow.

Over the past decade, OBS has collaborated with key MRHs, manufacturers, and trusted partners worldwide through extensive research sessions, lab tests, and test events to develop what is now known as the OBS Single-Layer HDR Workflow. This innovative approach has so far enabled the production of more than 15,000 hours of native UHD HDR live multilateral footage, distributed and viewed by billions of people worldwide through broadcasters' networks.

This paper is excerpted from the Proceedings of the 2025 NAB Broadcast Engineering and Information Technology (BEIT) Conference, © 2025, National Association of Broadcasters, 1 M Street SE, Washington, DC 20003 USA.

Workflow History (2012-2018)

At the Olympic Games London 2012, OBS conducted its first-ever live 8K trial, marking a significant step toward higher-resolution sports broadcasting. While the Games were primarily produced and broadcast in HD (1080i50), OBS partnered with key industry players to explore the future of ultra-high-definition production in a sports environment.

By 2015, the development of HDR standards was well underway in the industry, though adoption remained limited. Many broadcasters were still transitioning to High Definition (HD) and Ultra High Definition (UHD), each presenting its own challenges. As a result, HDR adoption was considered premature at the time. The early adopters of HDR were primarily broadcasters involved in developing the Hybrid Log-Gamma (HLG) standard, pioneered by BBC (national broadcaster of the UK) and NHK (national broadcaster of Japan), which later became part of ITU-R BT.2100 (2016) [1] – the global standard for HDR television production and program exchange.

The Olympic Games Rio 2016 marked the first time OBS produced a selection of live events in 4K UHD, following the UHDTV-1 (UHD-1) standard. This initiative aimed to support broadcasters interested in testing UHD workflows. OBS deployed a dedicated roaming Outside Broadcast Vehicle (OBV) alongside the Host Feed Production at seven different venues. This UHD feed was transmitted to the IBC in both SDR and HDR.

Beyond UHD resolution, OBS used this opportunity to analyze the feasibility of native HDR production, particularly its ability to handle high-contrast scenes such as outdoor sports under strong sunlight. The production utilized the S-Log3 HDR Opto-Electrical Transfer Function (OETF) in an ITU-R BT.2020 color space [2], which was then converted downstream inside the OBV to Perceptual Quantization (PQ) and SDR. This conversion was performed both parametrically using dedicated hardware and through publicly available Lookup Tables (LUTs) at the time. While these experiments were not part of the main production feed offered to MRHs, they played a crucial role in shaping OBS's HDR strategy and its future Vision Engineering Workflow.

PHOTO 1: RIO 2016 SUMMER OLYMPIC GAMES, BEACH VOLLEYBALL ARENA

The Olympic Winter Games PyeongChang 2018 marked the first Olympic Games where OBS covered all venues in UHD, with HDR available at five different sports. OBS continued its long-standing collaboration with NHK, particularly in cutting-edge broadcast technology such as Super Hi-Vision (SHV), a partnership dating back to 2012. The HDR coverage in PyeongChang was the result of a joint effort, with HLG chosen as the Transfer Function [3] for HDR image capture in a BT.2020 color space. This decision was strongly supported by broadcasters and MRHs, as HLG's robustness to different video processing pipelines, broad camera manufacturer support, and lack of a requirement for metadata made it an ideal choice.

PHOTO 2: PYEONGCHANG 2018 WINTER OLYMPIC GAMES, SHV (8K) CAMERA AT FIGURE SKATING

During this first six-year phase (2012–2018), the feasibility of producing HDR and SDR in parallel was rigorously examined. To move forward in a technically, logistically, and financially viable way, OBS explored the possibility of using a single OBV to produce both UHD HDR and HD SDR feeds – the two primary house formats of OBS.

However, with extremely high camera counts – up to 80 UHD sources entering the vision switcher at certain Olympic events – a Dual-Layer Workflow (where HDR and SDR sources are processed separately) was ruled out due to broadcast hardware limitations at the time. Implementing multiple vision switcher mainframes within existing OBVs proved to be both complex and impractical, introducing an additional level of risk that was deemed unacceptable for an event of the Olympic Games' scale.

Workflow Phase I (2018-2022)

The post-PyeongChang era, beginning in late 2018 and leading up to the Olympic Games Tokyo 2020 (postponed to 2021 due to the COVID-19 pandemic [4]), was a pivotal period for the solidification of OBS's Vision Engineering Workflow for the future.

By early 2019, OBS had finalized its decision to adopt a Single-Layer Workflow, marking the start of an extensive research and development phase. With clear objectives in place, OBS collaborated with external partners, broadcasters, and manufacturers to address key components and prerequisites – all of which were defined and refined through years of testing and findings.

Single-Layer

Establishing a Single-Layer Workflow was one of the key takeaways from previous years of testing, primarily due to the complexity and technical limitations of broadcast hardware when scaled to the size of an Olympic production. By implementing this approach, OBS successfully reduced infrastructure complexity while ensuring deterministic and consistent HDR and SDR availability across all required points – all within a single pipeline.

Additionally, this approach provided financial advantages, as it required less equipment compared to a Dual-Layer Workflow, leading to cost savings in both hardware and operational resources.

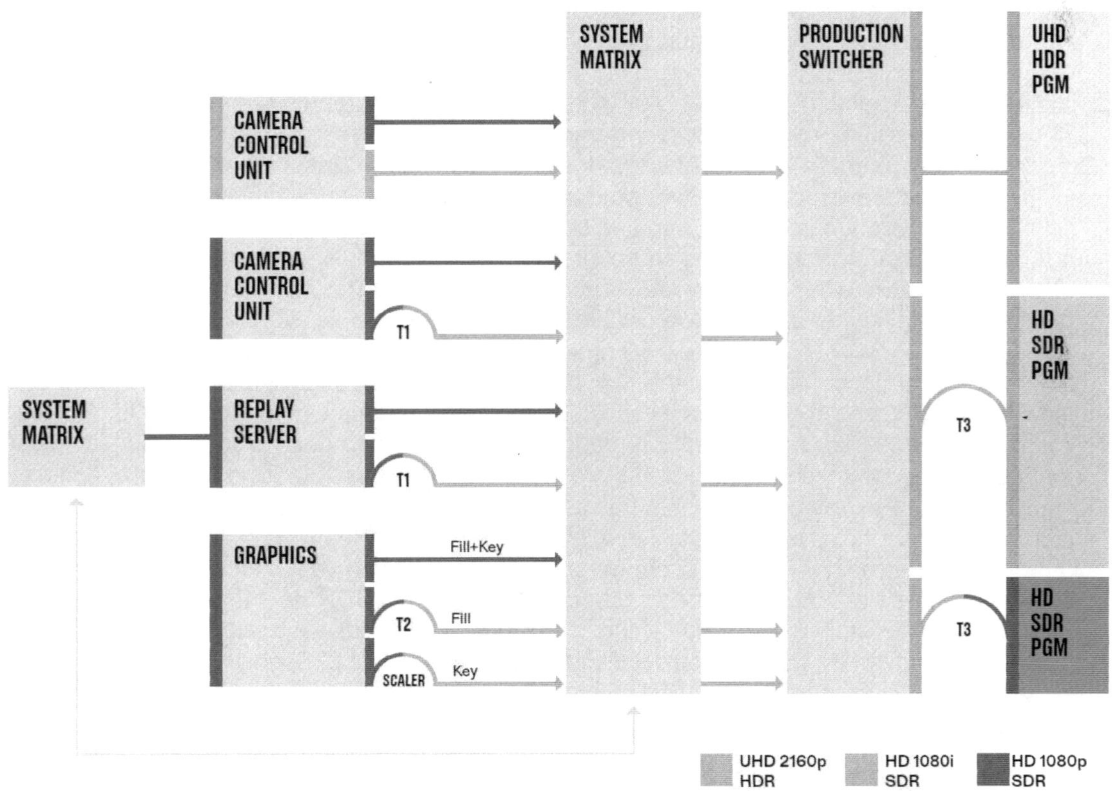

IMAGE 1: SIMPLIFIED DIAGRAM OF THE VISION ENGINEERING WORKFLOW AS USED IN TOKYO 2020 AND BEIJING 2022 SUPERSEDED BY THE WORKFLOW PHASE II WITH 'CLOSED-LOOP SHADING' FROM PARIS 2024 ONWARDS

Static Conversions

One of the key principles of a Single-Layer (HDR) Workflow is that the SDR signal should be derived from the HDR source. However, at the time of the workflow's design in 2019, dynamic conversions between different Transfer Functions and color spaces were still in their infancy. OBS carefully evaluated the feasibility of such conversions but quickly concluded that the available solutions – implemented in only a limited number of broadcast conversion devices using academic research-based algorithms – were incapable of accurately detecting graphics embedded in a composited "dirty" program signal. As a result, the idea of dynamic conversions was abandoned.

For OBS, it was crucial that colors and relative tones, particularly those of graphics and national flags, remained consistent throughout every stage of the image pipeline.

A static LUT processing pipeline was chosen due to its predictability, repeatability, and low risk – especially when deployed across multiple OBVs and fly-away systems (53 in Tokyo 2020, 26 in Beijing 2022 [5][6]). This approach also ensured that broadcasters could apply the same type of conversions while maintaining creative intent and consistent results, which was essential for international program exchange as the Host Broadcaster.

OBS LUT Package v2

The fact that OBS contributed only a "Dirty" multilateral signal – including both the underlying camera images and overlaying graphics – played a significant role in the LUT selection process. At the time, the open-source and commercially available LUTs on the market were limited, subject to uncontrolled updates, and did not fully meet OBS' specific technical and creative requirements.

Through collaboration with external partners, MRHs, and the HDR Project Group at OBS, a proprietary set of LUTs was developed to meet the following prerequisites:

- **Standards Compliance:** The LUTs were designed to be fully compliant with the existing HDR and SDR-related standards available at the time, such as ITU-R BT.2100 and ITU-R BT.2408 [7]. As the Host Broadcaster, ensuring this compliance was crucial for the continued success of our MRHs. OBS prioritized keeping complexity to a minimum by limiting the number of different LUTs. The decision to support only HLG and SDR as transfer functions was made in earlier project stages, following consultations with the MRHs.
- **Clean SDR-HDR-SDR Roundtrip:** OBS strictly adhered to internationally defined standards for RGB values of national flags, ensuring that colors and relative tones remained faithful after an SDR-HDR-SDR conversion process. While some round-trip loss was expected – especially given the choice to use two different up-mapping LUTs and only one down-mapping LUT – OBS prioritized the Graphics up-mapper to maintain the cleanest possible round-trip conversion.
- **Enhanced SDR Performance:** Within the Single-Layer Workflow, OBS aimed to take full advantage of the extra dynamic range available in HDR, ensuring it was optimally mapped within the SDR domain. The default direct tone-mapping of 75% luminance in HLG to 100% in SDR was adjusted to 90% luminance instead, resulting in an SDR down-mapped image that was superior to a native SDR signal. Even in cases where super-whites (100–109%) might be clipped due to downstream signal processing, the adjusted mapping ensured a better overall SDR output.
- **Shading in SDR:** With nearly 300 Vision Operators (commonly called "Shaders") deployed by OBS during a Summer Olympic Games operation, it was critical to maintain shading in the SDR domain. After carefully evaluating available market solutions, OBS determined that deploying more than 1,000 conversion channels to derive an SDR shading signal from HDR was neither operationally nor technically viable. Instead, OBS developed LUTs that were compatible with, and matchable to, the SDR outputs from the camera base stations – a process later referred to as "parametric replication." While this approach introduced its own challenges, extensive testing – including test events attended by key MRHs – confirmed its effectiveness. This methodology ultimately became the foundation for what is now widely known in the industry as "closed-loop shading," which is further detailed later in this document.

The OBS LUT Package v2 was developed in 2019 using a conversion software that enabled the parametric creation of LUTs while ensuring they remained mathematically invertible. The process incorporated a two-stage knee, a three-step conversion workflow, and additional tools that provided OBS with the necessary control to meet all broadcast requirements.

The package included two up-mapping LUTs for SDR to HLG conversions and one down-mapping LUT for HLG to SDR, both available in Type A and Type B (later renamed to Type I and Type III, following a more widely recognized nomenclature). The LUTs featured the following tone-mapping characteristics:

SDR	0	40	75	90	100	109
HLG	0	38	68.6	73.5	80	89.3

TABLE 1: OBS LUT PACKAGE V2, SDR TO HLG FOR CAMERA SOURCES.

SDR	0	40	75	90	100	109
HLG	0	38	68.8	75	82	89.3

TABLE 2: OBS LUT PACKAGE V2, SDR TO HLG FOR GRAPHICS SOURCES.

HLG	0	38	68.8	75	82	89.3
SDR	0	40	75	90	100	109

TABLE 3: OBS LUT PACKAGE V2, HLG TO SDR FOR DIRTY MULTILATERAL SOURCES.

OBS recognized the challenges associated with parametric replication, as it required a highly precise preparation and operational process by the Vision Engineering team at each venue. With the support of the industry's leading system camera manufacturers and the OBS HDR Project Team, extensive research was conducted to develop a corresponding set of camera settings that aligned almost imperceptibly with the OBS LUTs. This effort proved to be a significant success.

Although the application of these parameters was occasionally restrictive, feedback from Vision Operators, the visual results on-screen, and responses from Media Rights-Holders (MRHs) strongly validated this approach. In total, more than 1,000 camera systems were deployed during the Olympic Games Tokyo 2020, contributing to the production of over 3,800 hours of live television over 19 days of competition (17 days of official events plus two additional days before the Opening Ceremony) [5].

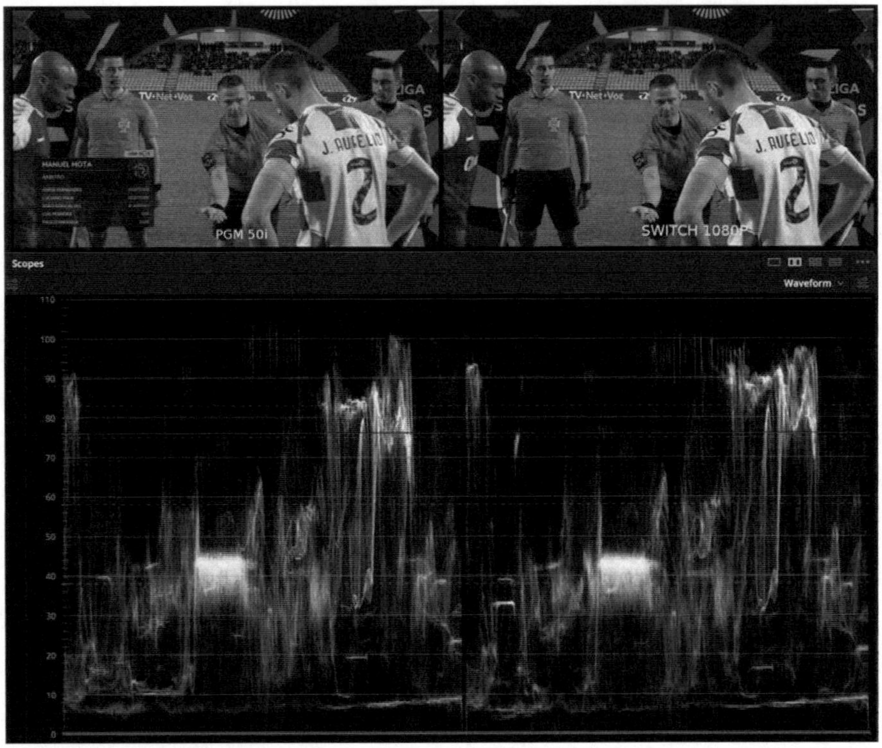

IMAGE 2: EXAMPLE OF PARAMETRIC REPLICATION DURING AN OBS UHD HDR EXERCISE IN 2019
LEFT: PGM HLG>SDR VIA DOWN-MAPPER V2 (ROLL-OFF BENEFITS), RIGHT: SDR OUTPUT CCU.
ANALYSIS © OLYMPIC BROADCASTING SERVICES. ALL RIGHTS RESERVED
FOOTAGE © LIGA NOS 2019

It is worth noting that the same LUT authoring software used to create the OBS LUTs was later utilized for the development of the NBCU Peacock LUTs [8], shortly after the release of the OBS LUT Package v2. At that time, more advanced parameters – such as a MaxRGB function – became available and were successfully implemented.

Due to the postponement of Tokyo 2020 (held in 2021) and the short turnaround before the start of the Olympic Winter Games Beijing 2022, OBS decided to maintain the existing Single-Layer Workflow and LUT Package v2, as both had proven highly effective in Tokyo. OBS postponed further evaluation of the workflow and LUTs until after Beijing 2022. This decision was well received by the MRHs, who faced significant challenges during this unique period in Olympic broadcast history.

Approved Convertors

The support for custom 3D-LUT conversions in broadcast equipment was increasing at the time the initial workflow was designed, but most manufacturers were only supporting standard color space conversions for direct, up, and down-mapping, with exposed parametric controls at best. If LUT support was available, the implementation of the LUT pipeline often resulted in inconsistent results between different devices. Common errors stemmed from poor conversion implementations between color space representations (YCbCr and RGB), color-matrix compensation errors due to differences in primary coordinates in BT.709 and BT.2020, or the lack of tetrahedral interpolation, which could result in interpolation deficiencies. Additionally, on the resolution-scaling front, there were strict requirements, as the HD multilateral signal had to be derived from the UHD source.

OBS conducted thorough research on the available products on the market that could meet all the requirements. This led to a list of OBS-approved converters and the identification of a single device responsible for creating all HD multilaterals within each Production Unit (PU) and at the IBC. Although most of the 'approved' converters could use LUTs, some devices were selected based on the availability of mapping parameters that matched the behavior of the OBS LUTs. Dedicated OBS software versions and settings packages were created and distributed to ensure the process could be deployed in all PUs. Since HDR support was not yet available for all camera sources (especially mini- and super-slow-motion cameras) and the replay environment inside the PU was still SDR, the total number of conversion channels during Tokyo 2020 was well above 1,000. The same approach was used during Beijing 2022.

Education

The transition to a Single-Layer Workflow and the introduction of HDR represent one of the most significant advancements in broadcast technology since the shift from analog to digital or SD to HD resolution. With nearly 400 Vision Operators set to join the operations temporarily in Tokyo, OBS needed to ensure that sufficient training was available to educate Games-time Vision Engineering personnel on these new technologies. To address this, OBS planned two editions of the 'OBS UHD HDR Seminar': one in Spain for EMEA-based Engineers and another in Beijing for participants from North America (NA), Latin America (LATAM), and the Asia-Pacific (APAC) regions.

In late 2019, nearly 100 representatives from OBS' PU vendors attended the Madrid seminar, where they participated in an intensive two-day program featuring lectures and hands-on training to gain first-hand experience with HDR workflows. The event received overwhelmingly positive feedback, as many of the engineers had never worked with HDR technology before. However, due to the COVID-19 pandemic, the second seminar in Beijing was canceled at the last minute, requiring OBS to explore alternative training methods.

For an extended period – including the lead-up to Beijing 2022 – physical gatherings were discouraged or impossible for many countries. While online-based training and induction had long been part of OBS's educational initiatives, the HDR Project Team took this opportunity to elevate the eLearning concept to the next level. OBS developed an extensive UHD HDR online course, covering both technical and operational aspects of the workflow. All Vision Engineering team members received secure access to the platform ahead of the Games, allowing them to complete the training anytime, anywhere.

The OBS eLearning system, built as a Learning Management System (LMS) framework with embedded content, was platform-independent and could be updated in real time to reflect any new or corrected information. To accommodate the large team of Chinese Vision Engineers working for OBS during Beijing 2022, the entire UHD HDR course was also translated into Simplified Chinese.

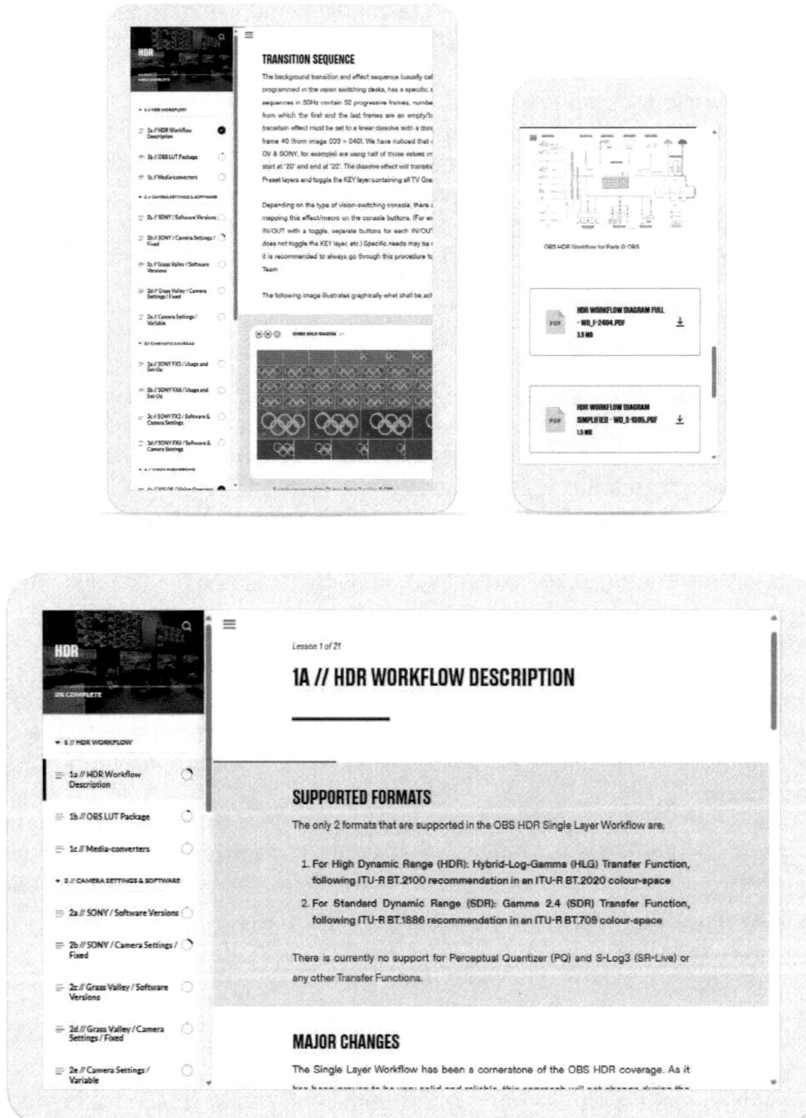

IMAGE 3, 4 & 5: UHD HDR COURSE ON THE OBS ELEARNING PLATFORM, DEVICE INDEPENDENT

In addition to the online courses, select members of the Vision Engineering team were invited to the IBC in Tokyo and Beijing for a hands-on training session the day before their official start date. A replica of the "Vision In Charge" (VIC) position inside a PU was set up, complete with multiple cameras from the leading manufacturers in the industry. Due to the staggered arrival of the VICs in the host city, these hands-on sessions were conducted over a period of approximately 10 to 15 days.

Workflow Phase II (2022-2026)

The period following the conclusion of Beijing 2022 marked the beginning of the second phase in the development of the Vision Engineering workflow. Since the time span between a Winter and a Summer Games is longer than that between a Summer and a Winter Games, OBS had a valuable opportunity to assess the workflow's past performance and identify areas for improvement ahead of future events.

By organizing multiple feedback sessions with MRHs that adopted HDR, OBS gathered essential insights to evaluate the workflow's strengths and weaknesses and develop a strategic plan leading up to the Olympic Games Paris 2024.

One of the key advancements enabling further refinement of the workflow was the wider availability of high-density conversion devices in the broadcast market. This development allowed OBS to fully implement the closed-loop shading [9] approach using the OBS LUT Package, rather than relying on parametric replication. As a result, OBS could ensure a 100% match between what the Vision Operators saw and the SDR multilateral signal derived from the HLG version. This approach provided greater creative flexibility, as it reduced the number of mandatory parameters that needed to be adjusted – an enhancement highly appreciated by both the Production and Technical teams at the venues.

As more equipment began to support and enhance HLG as the chosen transfer function, OBS progressively transitioned all remaining SDR elements into the HDR domain. By Paris 2024, the replay environment, graphics, and the majority of (H)SSM (High-Super-Slow-Motion) cameras were natively integrated into the vision switcher in (UHD) HDR.

From a deliverable perspective, only HLG signals were contributed from the PU to the TOC. Every SDR version of the multilateral feed provided to MRHs downstream was created at the IBC.

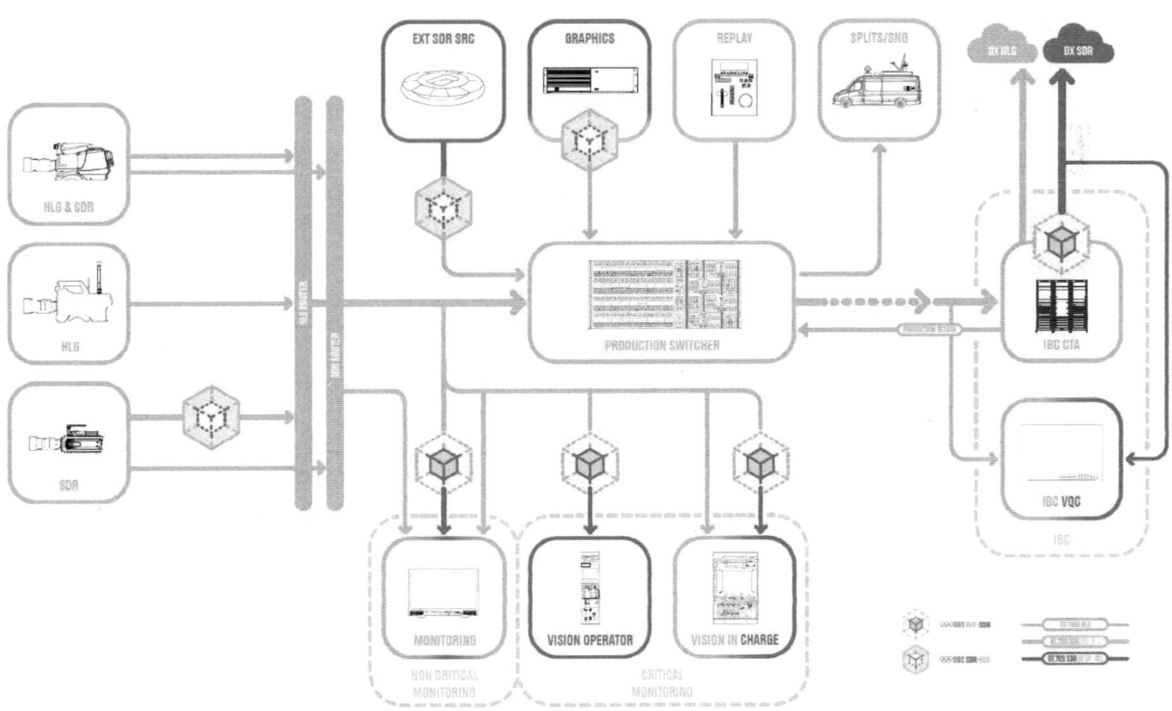

IMAGE 6: THE END-TO-END VISION ENGINEERING WORKFLOW PHASE 2 WITH CLOSED-LOOP SHADING

OBS LUT Package v4

The second phase of the workflow provided a valuable opportunity to review and enhance the OBS LUT Package. The implementation of closed-loop shading enabled a comprehensive redesign of both the up-mapper and, most importantly, the down-mapper, without losing the unique tone-mapping characteristics of the previous version successfully used in Tokyo and Beijing. With new features like gamma compensation and MaxRGB becoming available in the LUT authoring software, OBS improved the tone-mapping and roll-off without affecting the diffuse white anchor point of 75% HLG / 90% SDR. Since the v4 LUTs were fully display-referred, the up-mapper was further simplified, reducing the need for multiple versions. The LUTs featured the following tone-mapping characteristics:

SDR	-7	0	10	20	30	40	43	50	60	70	80	90	100	109
HLG	-6.5	0	9.6	17.7	25.7	34.7	37.8	45	55.1	63	69.5	75.8	82.1	91.9

HLG	-7	0	10	20	30	38	40	50	60	70	75	80	83	90	96.1	100	109
SDR	-6.4	0	10.4	23.2	35.2	43.2	45.1	54.7	65.9	80.8	89.9	97.3	100	103.5	105	105.6	106.5

SDR	-7	0	10	20	30	40	43	50	60	70	80	90	100	109
SDR (RT)	-6.4	0	9.8	20.1	30.3	40	42.9	50	60.2	70.1	80.1	91.3	99.3	104

IMAGE 7: OBS LUT PACKAGE V4.1 LUMINANCE MAPPING TABLE

In addition to standard 33³ lattice LUTs in the traditional Adobe CUBE format [10], OBS also provided several other versions for specific NLE support, such as the CLF format [11]. Up until today, OBS encouraged standards bodies to further enhance and improve the use of metadata inside LUT files to enable hardware and software to be configured in a common and automated manner. This is particularly important, as misconfigurations related to the particularities of each LUT are among the most common errors encountered when setting up large mixed-format workflows.

OBS provided extensive documentation to both MRHs and technical providers to ensure the correct implementation of LUTs throughout the entire signal-chain – from production to contribution, distribution, and transmission. The use of standardized test patterns, such as the ITU-R BT.2111 HDR [12] and SMPTE ST 219 SDR color bars [13], helped all parties verify that devices were set up correctly. Some broadcast manufacturers were receptive to implementing specific features (gadgets) at OBS's request, enabling downstream users to identify HDR-specific test patterns that had been down-mapped by the OBS LUT – an approach with which they were previously unfamiliar.

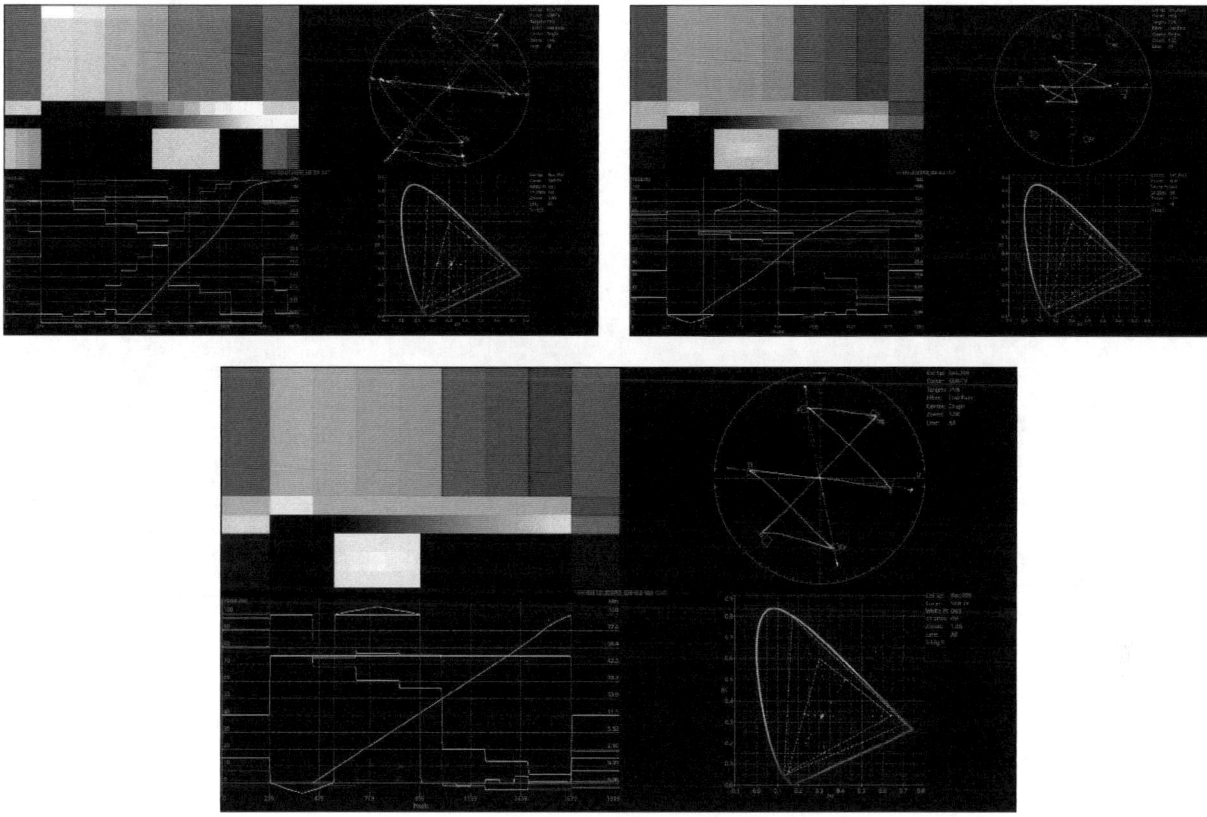

IMAGE 8, 9, 10:
TOP LEFT: ST2110 TEST PATTERN AFTER HLG>SDR DOWN-MAPPER V4.1
TOP RIGHT: ST219 TEST PATTERN AFTER SDR>HLG UP-MAPPER V4.1
BOTTOM: ST219 TEST PATTERN AFTER SDR>HLG>SDR ROUNDTRIP V4.1

By organizing another series of HDR exercises, in which different LUT candidates were tested under various conditions with multiple camera brands and models, OBS ensured that nothing was left to chance for a full deployment during Games-time. Hundreds of hours of test footage were captured across multiple events and lab sessions, both in and outside of Europe, in collaboration with some of OBS's most trusted partners. Paris 2024 marked the culmination of an intensive yet successful period for the HDR Project team at OBS, with the OBS LUT Package serving as a foundational element of this achievement.

Vision Database

After the decision to implement closed-loop shading and during the creation of the OBS LUT Package v4, the HDR Project team was able to focus extensively on refining its internal knowledge database of the various broadcast systems available on the market. By collaborating with the R&D teams of leading camera manufacturers, OBS successfully cataloged over 250 recordings of both a standardized HDR color chart and a live-action scene, captured using pre-defined camera setting iterations.

In addition to the HDR plates, OBS also concentrated on measuring the dynamic ranges (latitudes) of different camera sensors. This was achieved using specialized dynamic range test charts from a well-known industry brand, enabling the archiving of each individual transfer function mapping – not only HLG but also PQ and S-Log3 – for future reference.

This sub-project allowed OBS to build a comprehensive comparison matrix, facilitating informed decisions on camera settings before the start of the Games. Additionally, during Games time, the VQC could refer to this database to provide guidance and technical support on Vision Engineering topics raised by both the PUs and certain MRHs.

The ongoing collaboration with camera manufacturers remains a key priority for OBS, as it plays an essential role in ensuring the success of the Games and guarantees that MRHs receive the highest possible quality from the Host Broadcaster.

PHOTO 3 & 4: ONE OF THE VISION DATABASE EXERCISES BY OBS 2023, 2024

Cinematic Cameras

For the first time in Olympic history, OBS deployed several 35mm full-frame single-sensor cinematic cameras at the Paris 2024 venues. These cameras provide a unique shallow depth-of-field effect, closely resembling the look and feel of modern cinematic images. This approach offers viewers a more immersive and detailed perspective of the events, bringing them closer to the action.

By design, cinematic cameras have a vastly different image pipeline compared to traditional broadcast system cameras. To ensure visual consistency, OBS collaborated extensively with the R&D teams of the selected manufacturer to develop an optimal settings package that could be pre-configured before deployment. Additionally, OBS provided the Vision Engineering team and Cinematic Camera Operators with comprehensive training and detailed guidelines to ensure the expected results during the Games.

One key consideration was the use of the exposure triangle, which consists of aperture, shutter speed, and ISO. These three settings work together to regulate the amount of light entering the lens (aperture and shutter speed) and the sensor's sensitivity to light (ISO), ensuring optimal image quality under varying lighting conditions.

- **Aperture**
  - Controls the amount of light entering the lens.
  - A lower f-stop allows more light, creating a shallow depth-of-field.
  - A higher f-stop allows less light, keeping more of the scene in focus.
- **Shutter Speed**
  - Determines how long the camera's sensor is exposed to light.
  - A fast shutter speed freezes motion.
  - A slow shutter speed allows motion blur and is used in low-light conditions.
- **ISO**
  - Controls the camera sensor's sensitivity to light.
  - A lower ISO results in less noise but requires more light.
  - A higher ISO makes the image brighter but can introduce digital noise.

The following graphics were provided through the OBS eLearning platform, as a visual guide for both Shaders and Camera Operators.

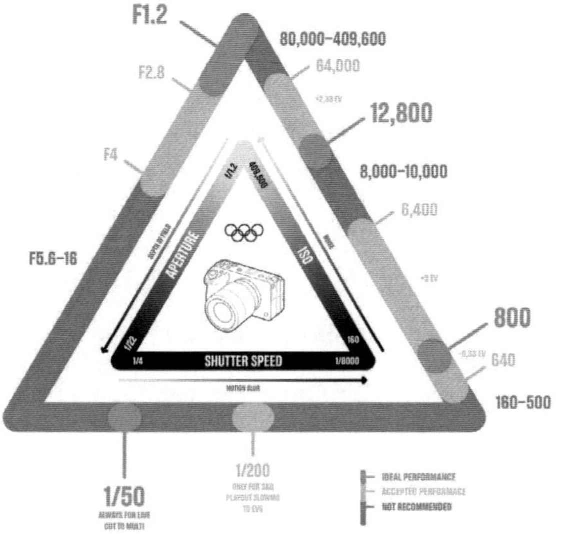

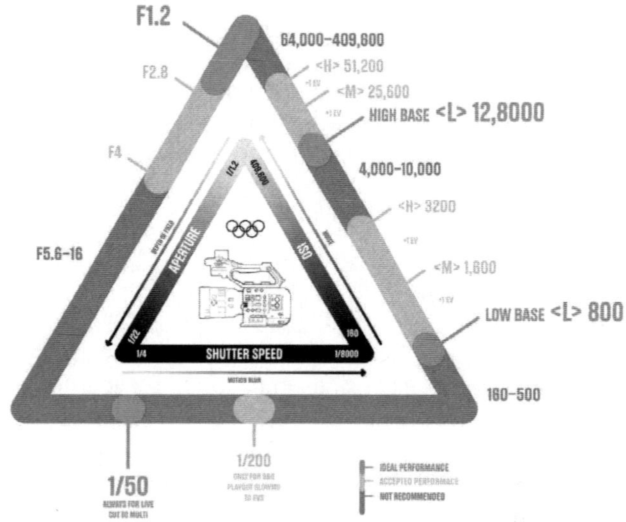

IMAGE 11 & 12: OBS RECOMMENDED EXPOSURE TRIANGLE VALUES FOR TWO COMMON CINEMATIC CAMERAS

Games-Time Operations

OBS operations during Games time result from extensive planning and coordination. On the Vision Engineering front, this is when years of preparation are put to the test in a live environment. The entire team gathers in the host city to oversee thousands of hours of live television, ensuring seamless execution and top broadcast quality.

Since the large-scale introduction of UHD HDR in Tokyo, OBS has taken the necessary measures to ensure that all critical aspects of the Vision Engineering workflow function optimally. To maintain consistency, new roles, areas, and workflows were introduced, focusing on color accuracy, tone-mapping, and real-time monitoring. Below, we highlight the key innovations that played a crucial role in refining and optimizing the workflow.

Vision In Charge

With the introduction of HDR into the Vision Engineering Workflow and OBS's decision to maintain camera shading in SDR, an additional technical role was required within the PU. As a result, the Vision In Charge (VIC) position was introduced for the first time during the Olympic Games Tokyo 2020 and has been an essential part of the workflow ever since.

The VIC is part of the Engineering Team inside the PU and works closely with the Engineer In Charge (EIC) and the Vision Operators (VIS OPs) from the Production Team. However, the VIC does not actively participate in camera shading. Instead, their primary responsibilities include:

- **Deploying baseline camera settings** to ensure the VIS OPs can work effectively.
- **Assisting in the setup of HDR devices** or HDR processes in the PU together with the EIC.
- **Guiding the team of Vision Operators** who will effectively be shading all camera sources.
- **Guiding, assisting, and making corrections** where necessary to maintain consistency and uniformity across all cameras.
- **Managing HDR-exclusive parameters**, which are not visible to the VIS OPs, as camera shading is performed in SDR.

The VIC position is typically equipped with the following materials:

- **UHD HDR and HD SDR monitors** following specifications for HLG, SDR and BT.2020, BT.709
- **Dedicated waveform monitors** and vectorscopes for precise signal analysis
- **Router panels** to send signals from source to destination as needed
- **A central camera control panel** to manage and adjust all cameras simultaneously. This is typically referred to as an MCP (Master Control Panel) or MSU (Master Setup Unit), which may be available as either a physical device or software interface.
- **A Multiviewer** to monitor multiple sources simultaneously
- **An Intercom panel** to allow for communication with engineers in the PU or in the IBC

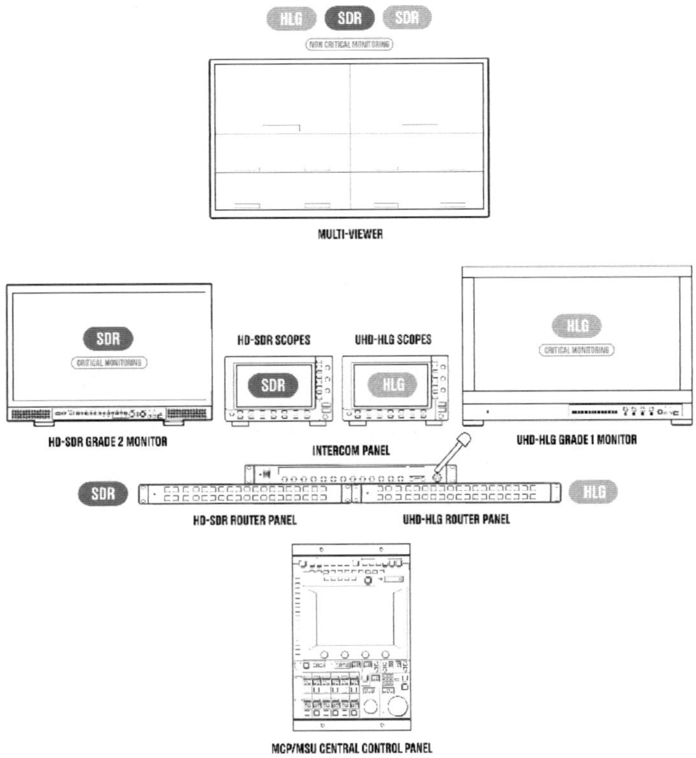

IMAGE 13: A TYPICAL MONITORING STATION FOR A VIC POSITION IN A PRODUCTION UNIT

OBS takes great pride in equipping the Vision Engineering team with the necessary information and tools to create an optimal working environment. The VIC position operates in a mixed viewing environment and is expected to feature a Grade 1 monitor for HLG monitoring, following EBU Tech 3320 [15].

HLG is a scene-referred curve that utilizes a variable Opto-Optical Transfer Function (OOTF) system gamma. This system gamma is determined based on two key variables:

- **Lsurround**: The luminance of the surround viewing environment in cd/m^2
- **Lw**: The peak luminance of the monitor in cd/m^2

Using the formula defined in ITU-R BT.2390-11 [3], the appropriate system gamma for the monitor can be calculated to ensure accurate HLG image reproduction, considering the adaptation state of the human eye.

The diagram below illustrates the HLG OOTF system gamma for the two most common panel peak luminance values – 1000 nits and 600 nits. Most Grade 1 monitors are placed in low-light environments, where ambient luminance typically ranges from 2 cd/m^2 to 10 cd/m^2. This range corresponds to conditions from a dark shading position without strip lighting to a mildly illuminated environment with low diffuse lighting.

$L_{surround}$

Luminance of surround viewing environment in cd/m2

L_W Nominal peak luminance of the display in cd/m2

UHD HDR HLG Grade 1 Monitor

A HLG OOTF System Gamma
Rep. ITU-R BT.2390-11 | Page 28

$$\gamma = 1.2 \cdot 1.111^{log_2\left(\frac{L_W}{1000\ cd/m^2}\right)} \cdot 0.98^{log_2\left(\frac{L_{surround}}{5\ cd/m^3}\right)}$$

B

	Dark			Low light		Bright	
	Pitch Black	Dark MCR	Dark Shading	Reference VQC	Shading with lights	Windows or lighting	Outside Viewing
	0.05 cd/m²	1 cd/m²	2 cd/m²	5 cd/m²	10 cd/m²	100 cd/m²	500 cd/m²
600 nits	1.26	1.16	1.14	1.11	1.09	1.01	0.96
1000 nits	1.35	1.25	1.23	1.20	1.18	1.10	1.05

Common viewing environments found in OBs

IMAGE 14: A TYPICAL MONITORING STATION FOR A VIC POSITION IN A PRODUCTION UNIT

Vision Quality Control

With the introduction of UHD and HDR, OBS implemented an advanced Vision Quality Control (VQC) room in the IBC. The VQC serves as the heart of the Vision Engineering Workflow, staffed by a team of seven experienced VQC Supervisors and Operators, who are available 24/7 to handle all Vision Engineering-related tasks.

Within the VQC, all contributed signals from the venues are received via the IBC CDU (Contribution, Distribution, Unilateral). Supervisors assign incoming feeds and tasks to Operators, who perform line-up procedures and quality checks to ensure consistency and uniformity before handing over the feeds to Production Quality Control (PQC). At peak times, the VQC simultaneously monitors more than 100 different signals.

- **VQC is responsible** for the image quality, conformity, uniformity, consistency and overall look and color appearance of all multilateral signals throughout the Games, both in HLG and SDR.
- **VQC coordinates** and provides guidance for all the VIC positions at each venue.
- **VQC guarantees** and conducts a correct line-up procedure with each PU at every venue.
- **VQC assists** in Vision Engineering troubleshooting and problem-solving whenever required.

During the Games, only the multilateral Dirty Program in UHD HDR is contributed from each venue to the IBC. Since Workflow Phase II, this means the VQC has direct visibility only of the HDR Program being produced in the PU. At the IBC, the multilateral feed is converted to SDR using the OBS HLG to SDR down-mapper, a 3D-LUT-based process identical to what occurs inside the PUs at the venues, at the VIC positions and every closed-loop VIS OP position.

PHOTO 5 & 6: THE VQC IN THE IBC DURING THE OLYMPIC GAMES PARIS 2024

Line-Up Process

At least two hours before the start of any rehearsal or transmission, the VQC team conducts a Line-Up procedure. During this process, the VQC receives the contribution signal from the CDU, after which a series of checks is performed between the VQC Operator and the VIC in the PU. These checks provide OBS with a level of assurance that basic settings, functions, and effects are properly configured, allowing the feed to be released to Production.

Such procedures are critical, particularly in dynamic environments where Field of Play (FOP) conditions frequently change, or when different disciplines or sports rotate within the same venue. To ensure consistency, all VIC operators are trained on this process through OBS eLearning modules and hands-on sessions at the IBC

The VQC team utilizes various tools, including waveform monitors, vectorscopes, and a line-up management system that enables post-event analysis. All actions are meticulously logged, allowing for continuous monitoring and follow-up across multiple shifts and broadcast days.

The following sequence of checks is performed, prioritized by importance:

- **Multilateral:** ITU-R BT.2111 color bars [12] live through the vision switcher
- **Replay:** Recorded and replayed ITU-R BT.2111 color bars [12]
- **ORT/PRT (Olympic/Paralympic Replay Transition):** Levels, effect, keyed on black & camera
- **CMGS (Core Media Graphics System):** Proprietary test pattern for levels, color & alpha
- **Native UHD HDR cameras:** A set of main cameras used in the coverage
- **Cinematic cameras:** Exposure, shallow-depth-of-field effect and color
- **Non-native HDR:** Any Up-mapping processes through the OBS up-mapper
- **Non-native UHD:** Any Up-scaling processes that occur in the PU
- **Additional Effects:** Any sport-specific effects in the vision switcher, (looping) backgrounds

Since VQC is only one part of the larger signal flow between the PU and the IBC, the Line-Up procedure follows a strict communication protocol between various operational teams. To ensure smooth handovers between entities, OBS employs a standardized nomenclature, guaranteeing that every feed undergoes the necessary VQC evaluation while avoiding delays in delivery to Production.

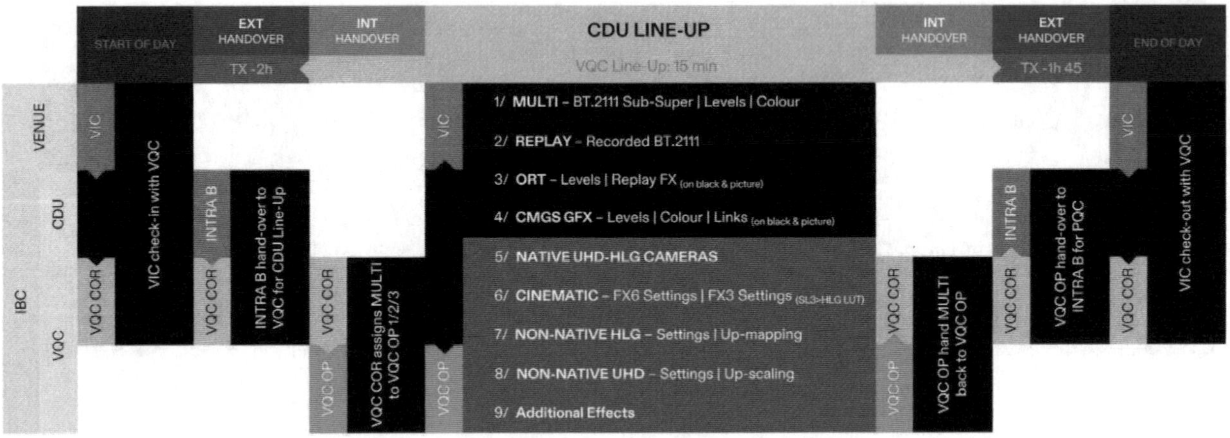

IMAGE 15: A GRAPHIC REPRESENTATION OF THE DIFFERENT HANDOVERS OF A LINE-UP PROCEDURE

Many of the Olympic sports and disciplines during the Games take place in similar FOPs and under consistent broadcast lighting conditions. The same branding, known as the 'Look of the Games', is applied by the local Organizing Committee across all venues, featuring a distinct color scheme.

It is crucial for OBS to maintain a consistent look and feel across its various multilateral feeds. This uniformity is especially important for MRHs that transmit recaps or distribute multi-channel services to end users.

To achieve this, OBS provides exposure guidelines for all multi-FOP sports – such as football, hockey, and tennis – through the OBS eLearning platform. These guidelines are available to VIC and VIS OPs and specify exposure levels in Y IRE/% for both HDR and SDR, aligned with the OBS LUT framework.

Ensuring that VIS OPs adhere to these values is an integral part of the daily Line-Up procedure, which is performed to verify and maintain consistency in the broadcast image quality.

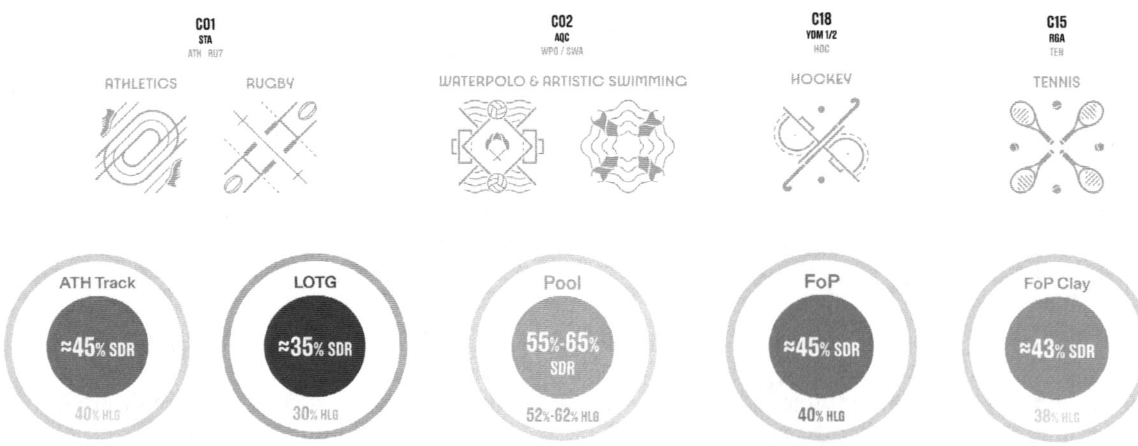

IMAGE 16: EXPOSURE GUIDELINES FOR A FEW EXAMPLE SPORTS IN PARIS 2024

Future Developments

OBS consistently strives to push the boundaries of advanced broadcasting technologies, ensuring that it remains at the forefront of innovation, efficiency, and high-quality content delivery. OBS is committed to exploring, testing, and implementing cutting-edge solutions that enhance both the production workflow and the viewing experience for audiences worldwide.

By continuously investing in emerging technologies, such as UHD HDR, next-generation IP-based production, cloud-based workflows, immersive audio, and artificial intelligence-driven automation, OBS ensures that it stays ahead of industry trends. Collaborating with leading technology partners, broadcasters, and research institutions, OBS plays a pivotal role in shaping the future of live sports broadcasting.

Furthermore, OBS not only adopts new technologies but also actively drives their development and standardization, contributing to industry-wide advancements that benefit both MRHs and the viewers at home. Through rigorous testing, pilot programs, and large-scale implementations during the Olympic Games, OBS consistently sets new benchmarks in scalability, resilience, and sustainability.

The following sections illustrate some of the fields that are being investigated around OBS's view on Vision Engineering.

Advanced Gamut-Mapping

Gamut-mapping is the process of converting colors from one color gamut (range of reproducible colors) to another while preserving visual accuracy as much as possible. It is essential in situations where the target display or medium has a smaller or different color gamut than the source. When a color from the source gamut does not exist in the target gamut, gamut-mapping ensures that the colors are adjusted in a way that maintains natural appearance and avoids issues like color clipping (where out-of-gamut colors are simply replaced with the nearest possible color).

There are different techniques used for gamut-mapping, depending on the priority:

- **Clipping:** Simply replaces out-of-gamut colors with the nearest boundary color of the target gamut. This is fast but can cause loss of detail in highly saturated areas.
- **Compression:** Scales the entire source gamut into the target gamut to maintain color relationships, avoiding sudden shifts. This is useful for smooth transitions.
- **Perceptual Mapping:** Optimizes the appearance of colors based on human vision to ensure natural-looking images.
- **Hue-Preserving Mapping:** Adjusts brightness and saturation while keeping the hue as close as possible to the original.

OBS is currently exploring ways to optimize the existing gamut-mapping in the OBS LUT Package v4.1 using advanced mapping algorithms, without modifying the tone-mapping (luminance preservation). This enhancement could potentially prevent colors in the SDR post-down-mapper from clipping, allowing them to be smoothly rolled off instead, thereby preserving the perceived color and relative tones in the image.

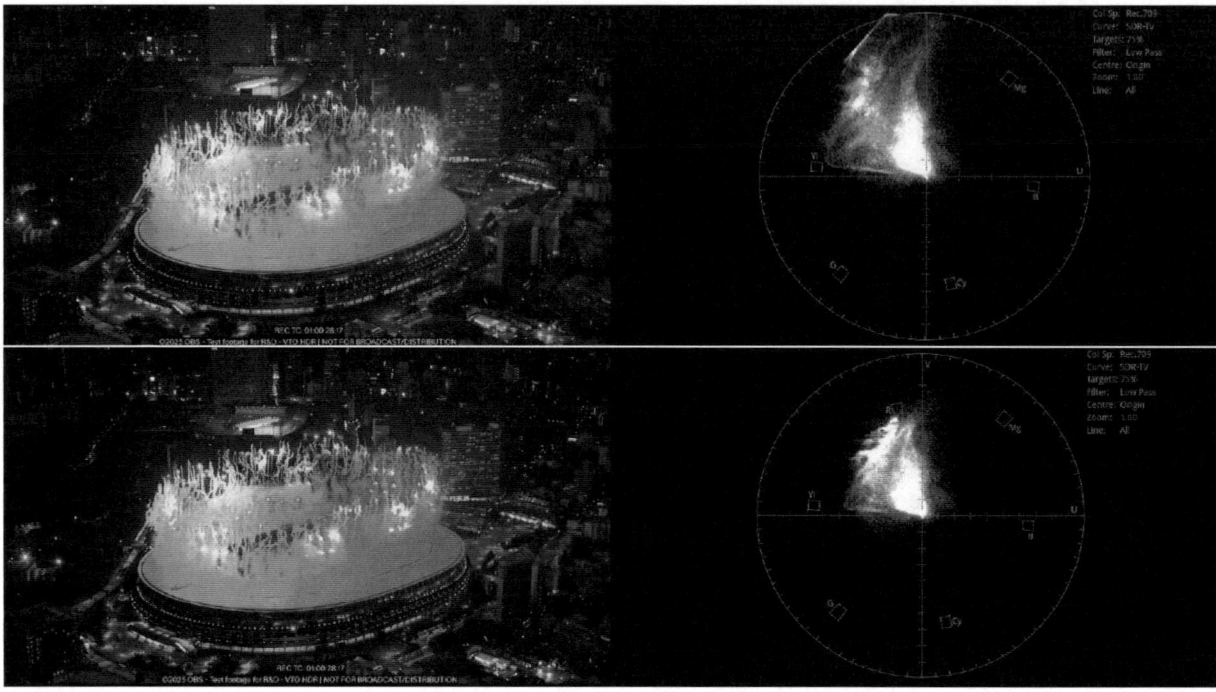

IMAGE 17: SDR EXAMPLE OF ADVANCED HLG>SDR GAMUT-MAPPING WITHOUT ADJUSTING THE INTENDED TONE-MAPPING
TOP: ORIGINAL OBS V4.1 HLG>SDR DOWN-MAPPER
BOTTOM: ADVANCED GAMUT-MAPPED DOWN-MAPPER

GPS and AI-Powered Conversions

Outside Races – such as road cycling and marathons – are among the most challenging events to cover at each Summer Olympics. This complexity arises not only from the demanding Radio Frequency (RF) transmission technologies but also from the intricacies of the Vision Engineering Workflow.

Camera feeds transmitted from motorbike-mounted cameras are classified as long-range RF signals, which inherently introduce higher latency compared to wired cameras due to the nature of wireless transmission. While camera operators control the iris settings locally, this transmission delay often makes it difficult for Vision Operators to adjust exposure and color correction in real time. The challenge becomes even greater when motorbikes move through rapidly changing lighting conditions – such as transitions between sunlight and shadow, tunnels, or other obstructions – where quick adjustments to exposure and color are necessary but can sometimes be suboptimal due to latency constraints.

Through extensive research, OBS has found that dynamic color and exposure conversions – specifically within the HDR domain – can help mitigate these issues. Advanced AI-based dynamic conversion models leverage historical data, allowing for more deterministic behavior, meaning adjustments can be made more intelligently and accurately. These frame-by-frame adjustments smooth out sudden lighting changes, ensuring a more consistent visual presentation.

To maintain uniformity in multilateral feeds, dynamic conversions can be applied to clean camera sources before they enter the Vision Switcher hardware. This ensures that outdoor race footage maintains a consistent look and feel, ultimately improving the overall viewer experience.

However, the potential of advanced RF-based setups goes even further. These systems can store, transmit, or record GPS coordinates for each source, embedding location data alongside a precise timestamp. By integrating this GPS data into the dynamic conversion algorithm, the AI model can anticipate lighting conditions at specific locations, allowing for more proactive exposure and color adjustments. Additionally, incorporating advanced weather models can further enhance the predictability of these adjustments, refining the conversion process and ensuring optimal visual consistency.

PHOTO 7 & 8:
LEFT: HELICOPTER FLYING OVER ODAIBA MARINE PARK, TOKYO 2020
RIGHT: MOTORBIKE CHASING CYCLIST AT INVALIDES, PARIS 2024

Over-Range Signals

In the analog era, when only SDR existed, over-range signals (commonly known as "super-whites") were not explicitly defined but were inherently present due to signal variations and processing headroom. The industry later formalized video signal code levels 64–940 (in a 10-bit environment) as the legal range. However, many professional cameras and workflows continued to allow headroom up to code value 1019 to prevent highlight clipping.

HDR standards inherently encode a much wider luminance range, eliminating the need for the 100–109% SDR headroom, as HDR systems can natively store much higher brightness values. However, due to the characteristics of the HLG curve, utilizing this additional 9% headroom could extend the available dynamic range.

With the increasing availability of professional broadcast monitors capable of handling and displaying peak brightness values beyond (or below) the technical definitions of HDR transfer functions, a growing variety of approaches have emerged regarding how these signals are represented on-screen. Additionally, the advantages and disadvantages of allowing such values in broadcast signals have not been thoroughly researched in recent years by the broader industry, and minimal documentation is available for review.

These factors indirectly make the work of the Host Broadcaster more challenging, as OBS strives to adhere to industry standards while also meeting the diverse needs of MRHs worldwide.

OBS encourages standards bodies to continue researching the use, display, and distribution of over-range signals and to review the existing documentation on recommended video signal tolerance levels [14] and best practices.

HDR Shading

As production units continue to evolve and broadcast monitors increasingly support native HDR signals, a natural progression for the Vision Engineering Workflow would be to transition to native shading in

HLG. However, given the high number of shaders required during the Games – typically between 300 and 400 for a Summer Olympics – this shift would present significant challenges due to the steep learning curve for production teams from around the world.

Shading in HLG poses several difficulties for shaders accustomed to SDR workflows. One major challenge is exposure management, as HLG's wider dynamic range requires a different approach to balancing highlights and midtones. Retaining highlight details is also more complex, as HLG retains more highlight information rather than abruptly clipping them like SDR. Contrast and black levels behave differently, necessitating precise adjustments to avoid crushing shadows or lifting blacks. Additionally, HLG's BT.2020 color gamut can lead to oversaturation if not managed correctly.

OBS recognizes the value of mixed-viewing environments, where either SDR is the master and HLG follows or vice versa. However, space constraints inside production units and the high number of sources requiring shading make large-scale implementation of this approach impractical.

To address these challenges, OBS has begun exploring the feasibility of implementing native HLG shading for select sports in future Games. The success of this initiative will largely depend on industry advancements over the next five to ten years, as well as the growing experience of engineers with HLG shading during regular sports competitions. Training and education efforts are already underway, as OBS aims to serve as a catalyst for vision engineering advancements and remain at the forefront of broadcast technology.

References

[1] ITU, "Recommendation ITU-R BT.2100-2, Image parameter values for high dynamic range television for use in production and international programme exchange", https://www.itu.int/rec/R-REC-BT.2100

[2] ITU, "Recommendation ITU-R BT.2020-2, Parameter values for ultra-high definition television systems for production and international programme exchange", https://www.itu.int/dms_pubrec/itu-r/rec/bt/r-rec-bt.2020-2-201510-i!!pdf-e.pdf

[3] ITU, "Report ITU-R BT.2390-8, High dynamic range television for production and international programme exchange", https://www.itu.int/dms_pub/itu-r/opb/rep/R-REP-BT.2390-8-2020-PDF-E.pdf

[4] IOC, "Tokyo 2020 Olympic and Paralympic Games postponed to 2021", https://www.olympics.com/en/news/tokyo-olympic-games-postponed-ioc

[5] OBS, "Media Guide Olympic Games Tokyo 2020", https://library.olympics.com/Default/doc/SYRACUSE/735123/media-guide-olympic-games-tokyo-2020-olympic-broadcasting-services

[6] OBS, "Media Guide Olympic Winter Games Beijing 2022", https://library.olympics.com/Default/doc/SYRACUSE/1568145/media-guide-olympic-winter-games-beijing-2022-olympic-broadcasting-services

[7] ITU, "Report ITU-R BT.2408-7, Guidance for operational practices in HDR television production", https://www.itu.int/dms_pub/itu-r/opb/rep/R-REP-BT.2408-7-2023-PDF-E.pdf

[8] NBCUniversal, "NBCU UHD-HDR-SDR "Single-Master" Production Workflow Recommendation & LUTS for Public Distribution", https://github.com/digitaltvguy/NBCUniversal-UHD-HDR-SDR-Single-Master-Production-Workflow-Recommendation-LUTs/

[9] EBU, “Shining More Light On HDR Production”, https://tech.ebu.ch/news/2022/08/shining-more-light-on-hdr-production

[10] Adobe, “Cube LUT File Specification 1.0”, https://kono.phpage.fr/images/a/a1/Adobe-cube-lut-specification-1.0.pdf

[11] ACES, “Specification S-2014-006 Common LUT Format (CLF)”, https://community.acescentral.com/uploads/short-url/iHX8xsDczlEg7l7OtIbJrbPvm4C.pdf

[12] ITU, “Recommendation ITU-R BT.2111-2, Specification of colour bar test pattern for high dynamic range television systems”, https://www.itu.int/rec/R-REC-BT.2111/en

[13] SMPTE, “SMPTE RP 219-1:2014, High-Definition, Standard-Definition Compatible Color Bar Signal”, https://pub.smpte.org/doc/rp219-1/20140714-pub/

[14] EBU, “R 103, Video Signal Tolerance In Digital Television Systems”, https://tech.ebu.ch/docs/r/r103.pdf

[15] EBU, “User Requirements For Video Monitors In Television Production”, https://tech.ebu.ch/docs/tech/tech3320.pdf

Optimizing Dynamic Ad Insertion for ATSC 3.0 in Low Broadband Access Markets

Liam Power
ONE Media Technologies
Hunt Valley, Maryland, United States
lpower@ONEMediaLLC.com

Abstract – This paper builds on previous work presented at the 2024 NAB Broadcast Engineering and Information Technology (BEIT) conference, which explored Dynamic Ad Insertion (DAI) within the ATSC 3.0 framework using MPEG Media Transport (MMT) [1]. The current study extends this research by developing a robust broadcast-only transmission solution within encoder/packager systems to enable targeted ad delivery. The implementation supports precise control over ad breaks and allows for real-time event tracking by leveraging broadcaster applications, NRT data distribution, and DASH EventStream technologies. Additionally, this architecture integrates with mobile devices featuring local application storage, allowing for preloading and personalized selection of advertisements based on individual user preferences and service viewing history. Designed with the India D2M (Direct-to-Mobile) Project in mind, this paper examines the unique requirements and solutions developed to address an environment in which all ad distribution and decision logic must be completed in a broadcast-only system, with no guarantee of broadband access.

Introduction and Summary

In recent years, one of the key advantages for streaming video has been the ability for streaming services to insert advertising on a viewer-by-viewer basis, increasing the value of each avail by matching the profile of the viewer to the most relevant ad. Linear broadcast ads, on the other hand, have been limited to a 'one size fits all' method of delivery for the most part. It was therefore important for the ATSC 3.0 standard to meet or exceed this capability for broadcast television. This was particularly challenging for the implementation for India that is part of ONE Media Technologies' Direct-to-Mobile(D2M) project, where we're working to implement a broadcast offload system to alleviate the immense cellular congestion in the market, as traditional internet-based methods are not viable.

Over the course of this process, refinements were made not only to the broadcast workflow, but also to the base broadband methodology. This paper outlines the decision points, and the solutions developed:

- **Section 1** presents an overview of DAI and the benefits to broadcasters.
- **Section 2** looks at various options for implementing DAI within ATSC 3.0.
- **Section 3** provides a description of the chosen workflow.
- **Section 4** examines the limitations imposed by a broadcast-only model.
- **Section 5** describes the solutions developed to handle the broadcast-only implementation.
- **Section 6** lays out a series of future-facing optimizations to improve both broadband and broadcast DAI.

This paper is excerpted from the Proceedings of the 2025 NAB Broadcast Engineering and Information Technology (BEIT) Conference, © 2025, National Association of Broadcasters, 1 M Street SE, Washington, DC 20003 USA.

Section 1: DAI Overview and Benefits

Dynamic Ad Insertion (DAI) is a well-known concept, but this section will seek to familiarize the reader with the basics, as well as why it is relevant to a broadcaster. In a traditional linear ad sales model (depicted in Figure 1), ads are sold ahead of time in varying categories, which establishes a set of rules on what ads need to be aired at what time, in what order, and next to what content or ads. These rules are then used by the broadcaster's traffic department to assemble the programming logs for each day, normally set out the day before. This results in a fairly static set of spots, though programming variances on live shows can sometimes cause more or fewer spots to be aired than planned. These variances are in turn often handled by a series of rules, with replacement spot or spots' cutting priority being laid out in advance, though some broadcasters, particularly cable sports broadcasters, have been known to simply provide the dollar value of each spot in the logs to allow the operator to make rapid judgments in the moment. Regardless of this, each spot is sold on and shown to all viewers, with some exceptions as noted below.

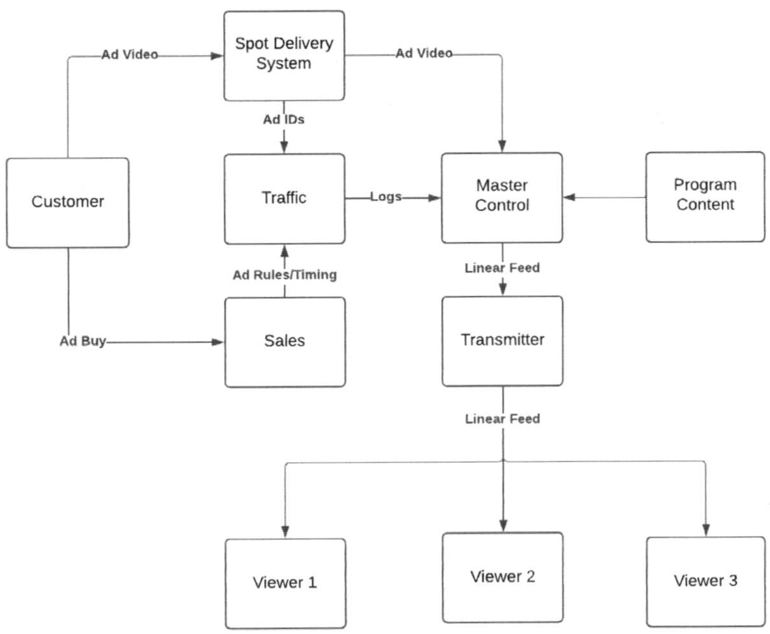

FIGURE 1: THE TRADITIONAL AD ASSEMBLY PROCESS FOR BROADCAST TELEVISION.

By contrast, dynamic ads on streaming video services are generally sold in the moment, with an 'instant auction' being held to determine which spot should air. This is often handled by an external marketplace, such as Google Ads, Magnite, or The Trade Desk to name a few. This is an almost fully automated system, with advertisers selecting budgets and audiences, then allowing the ad platform to handle the rest.

In this method, depicted in Figure 2, the stream contains an indicator of when an ad is available. These can take many forms, and some will be explored in the next section. Regardless of method, it allows the client, generally controlled by the streamer, to determine when an avail begins and ends. When this information is received, the application, be it a website or native app, reaches out to the ad server to request an ad, generally giving information on the viewer, the avail location, and the duration. The server in turn offers the block up on an ad exchange. The Demand Side Platforms (DSP) contain the rules for airing the ad, the advertiser's budget for the campaign, and the ad content and metadata. The DSP uses this information to place bids for the block.

Once a winner is determined, the exchange then hands the ad back to the ad server, which in turn tells the client which ad to play. This whole process happens in a matter of milliseconds, ensuring a decision is made rapidly with no interruption to the viewer. [2]

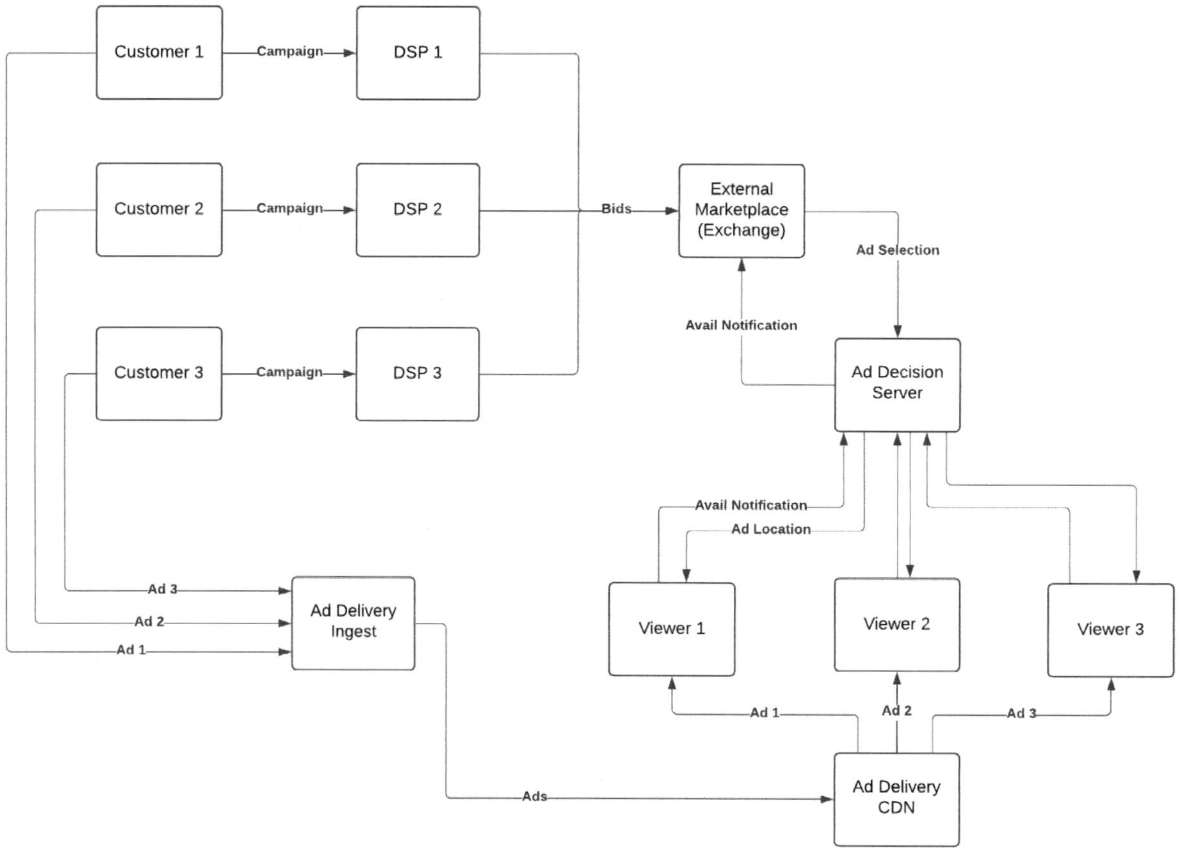

FIGURE 2: THE AD ASSEMBLY PROCESS FOR PROGRAMMATIC SYSTEMS.

While this is a drastically different approach from traditional broadcast sales, many broadcasters are already familiar with these methods. Digital, referring to website, social media presence, and other internet-based content from stations, has been rapidly growing across the industry, and is likely to continue doing so. Rather than linear feeds delivered in a unidirectional format, these are fully integrated content delivery systems with bidirectional feedback mechanisms. This has led to most broadcasters implementing some form of ad insertion system, particularly for first-party owned content not normally covered by broadcast ad sales deals.

One other crossover point that must be noted is cable headends. While not fully targeted on an individual basis, these have long been used to do ad insertion on a geographic basis, at varying resolutions. This allows a few key workflows:

- **Local Weather:** National channels like The Weather Channel will often insert local weather information in their graphics via a keyer at the cable headend, allowing the viewer to see information relevant to their specific area.
- **Local News:** While this practice has declined, national cable news networks have been known to splice in local news hits in partnership with stations in the area, similar to cut-ins on broadcast network news.
- **Cable Ad Separation:** Some MVPDs prefer to air different ads for their customers compared to non-customer viewers. This allows them to offer deals only to new customers, while advertising,

for example, service upgrades to their current customers. This can happen at the station level, where the station handles the ad insertion and passes a separate feed to the MVPD, or in the MVPD infrastructure, where the station simply provides markers to allow the ad replacement.

Despite the broader brush, many of the concepts used for the MVPD insertion mechanism can be reused in a broadcast insertion method, as will be explored in the next section. Indeed, vMVPDs such as YouTube TV have begun rolling out ad insertion on linear feeds to enable these streaming ad advantages on a more traditional content model.

Section 2: DAI Options in ATSC 3.0

The ATSC 3.0 standard provides a few options for handling ad insertion. There are distinct pros and cons to each, and so it is important to match the correct solution to a given use case. This section will provide an overview of some of the potential systems that can be used. These cases will focus solely on ROUTE/DASH streams.

XML Linking Language (XLink)

Historically, XLinks have seen the most discussion when it comes to ATSC 3.0 ad insertion solutions. In this mechanism, the broadcaster generates a DASH stream with an xlink:href attribute, generally assigned to a period. This is normally done at the beginning of an ad avail, with the encoder splicing the last segment before the avail to ensure a smooth transition. This creates the layout depicted in the sample media presentation description (MPD, acts like a playlist) in Figure 3.

```
<Period
  xlink:href="https://example.site/sample/xlinkperiod.period"
  xlink:actuate="onLoad"
  xmlns:xlink="http://www.w3.org/1999/xlink"
></Period>
```

FIGURE 3: AN EXAMPLE OF A PERIOD USING AN XLINK.

There are two options when the end device receives this MPD as shown in Figure 4. In the event the xlink:href is pointing to some https location, the receiver can simply reach out as normal under the DASH spec [3] and retrieve the correct content to insert into the MPD at that point. If it has any other URI scheme, it is instead passed to a BA (Broadcaster Application) that has subscribed to the XLink notifications. [4] The BA then determines what content, either specific text or a full MPD, should be inserted at that location, and passes that information back to the receiver. This allows both online and offline ad insertion.

Regardless of which mechanism is utilized, the result is that the receiver is given a response with a new set of text. This will contain the playback information for the specific ad chosen for the client to air, essentially splicing in the period for the ad to the main MPD. The receiver then proceeds to continue through the timeline as normal, returning to the original broadcast content when it reaches the end of the ad period and hits the next linear broadcast period.

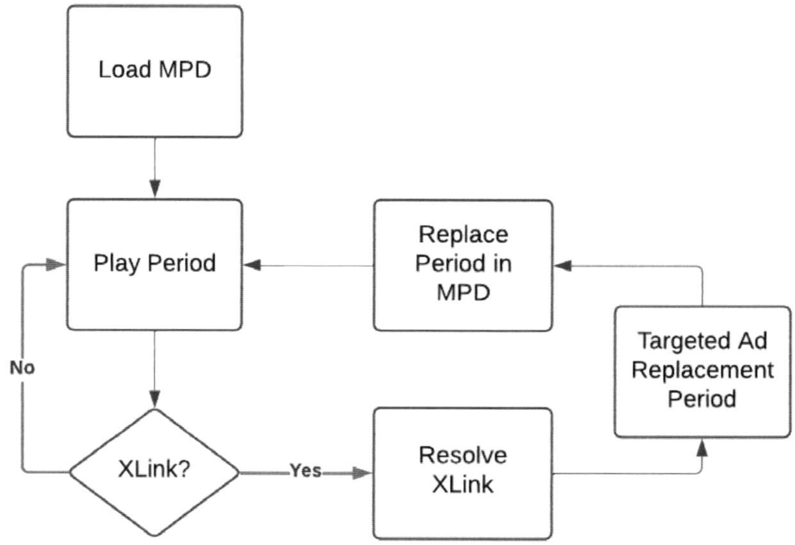

FIGURE 4: THE XLINK WORKFLOW.

One major point in favor of XLinks is the ability for the receiver to resolve them locally, without BA involvement, by using https-based XLinks. This simplifies the process from the broadcaster perspective and means that if a receiver does not support the interactive environment, ad insertion still works. However, XLinks are not as flexible as Events (see DASH Events), require more complex receiver action, and most importantly, are in the process of being removed.

Out of Band Broadcaster Application Insertion

In this method, the broadcaster plays an ad via the BA at a specific time via the Application Media Player (AMP). This is the least elegant of the options described here, as the timing is virtually impossible to align due to the varying nature of reception. Receiver-side delays, such as different player implementations and segment reception times, coupled with delays in the airchain, mean receivers will generally be off by at least several seconds from each other.

However, the method is worth noting as it eliminates any dependency on interaction with the receiver aside from implementing the interactive environment.

DASH Events

The DASH specification defines an EventStream element [5], which essentially form the DASH version of the SCTE [6] markers common to the Serial Digital Interface (SDI) and Transport Stream (TS) worlds. Events signal the time and duration of various data to the receiver. The use cases for events are quite broad; for ad insertion, they contain the full set of information from a SCTE marker, as well as the relative timing within the MPD timeline.

This workflow will be explored more fully in the next section, but one key item is the use of the AMP vs the Receiver Media Player (RMP). Because the AMP is controlled by the BA, it is very difficult to synchronize the insertion with the actual timeline on the receiver, despite the event notification containing the current and event times. This is due to variances in processing time causing potential offsets thus reducing the chance for a frame accurate insertion.

The RMP method, on the other hand, uses time marks relative to the RMP timeline. Assuming the receiver has correctly implemented the relevant APIs, it can seamlessly jump to the ad and back without misplacing the ad in either direction. This also allows the ad to take full advantage of the RMP's playback hardware, as not all receivers provide the same decode options to the AMP as they do to the RMP. For this reason, the preference is towards the RMP for ad insertion.

Overall, the Event workflow allows for the best accuracy in insertion with the least complexity on the receiver side. It also maintains the flexibility of SCTE markers, which is advantageous for non-insertion use cases. The spec is fully fleshed out, and well implemented by many receivers, as will be explored in Section 6. The primary downside is that it requires the BA to handle the insertion logic, which means the receiver must implement the interactive environment and the relevant APIs.

Section 3: Connected EventStream Workflow

The best path forward, therefore, is to handle ad insertion with a combination of EventStreams and the RMP workflow. The following outlines this implementation in a connected device environment as depicted in Figure 5. This will form the basis for the implementation of the more complex broadcast implementation covered in section 5.

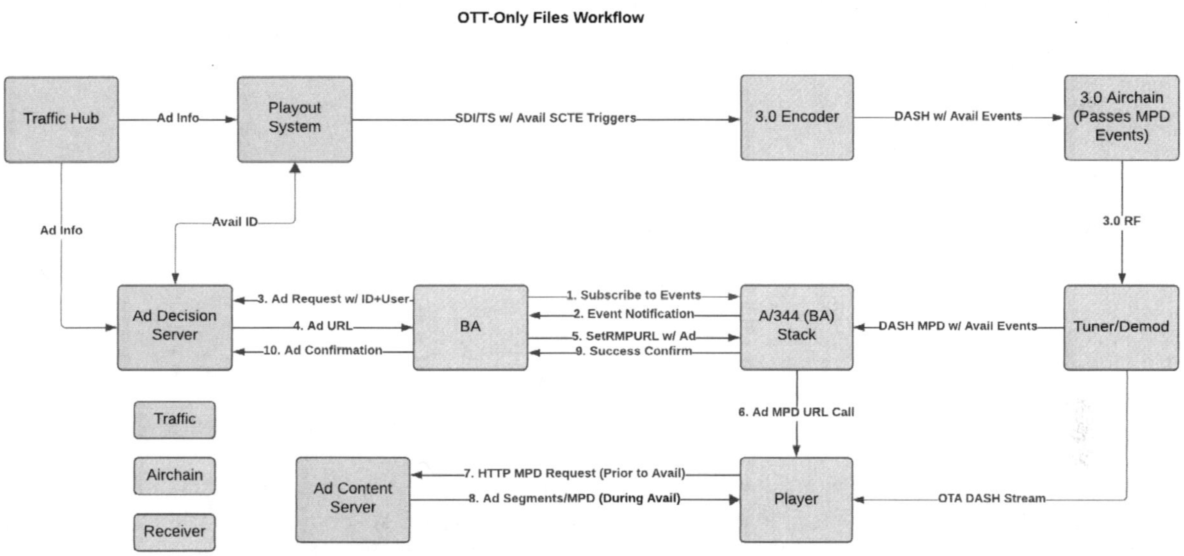

FIGURE 5: THE CONNECTED AD INSERTION WORKFLOW.

Transmission Requirements

The first step in any insertion process is to figure out when the ads can be inserted. This is best accomplished at the playout/automation stage, as the master control automation can generate the markers at the precise time the spot begins or ends. This allows the broadcaster to tag each break with the time of the break, the duration of the break, and an ID to allow the ad server to associate the break with a request on the receiver side. The automation system then adds this information, along with other optional functionality, to a SCTE 35 or 104 marker [7], depending on whether the video is being carried via a TS [8] (TS) or SDI [9] transport.

In ATSC 1.0, the SCTE marker would be carried unmodified into the TS stream used for the actual broadcast. However, ATSC 3.0 utilizes more advanced transports in the form of ROUTE/DASH and MMTP, so the markers must be translated into an appropriate format. This paper is focused solely on

ROUTE/DASH-based DAI, and so will not discuss the MMTP format, but more detail on this can be found in the paper *Dynamic Ad Insertion Using a Data Distribution as a Service Platform and MPEG Media Transport* [10] from the 2024 NAB BEIT Conference.

As mentioned earlier, the DASH spec contains an element called "EventStream." [5] This comes in two forms: inband, and MPD-based events. Inband events can be found in the emsg box, with an InbandEventStream element in the MPD to indicate which representation contains the emsg box, while MPD-based events are located fully within the EventStream element in a Period of an MPD. Inband events are best used for unexpected events that require immediate action, such as rolling a news cut-in during a live network program and bringing the BA up for the duration of that cut-in.

For ad insertion, the receiver needs enough time to buffer the ad media before the break to ensure a smooth and frame-accurate transition in and out of the inserted ad. MPD-based events are therefore easier to execute in this situation. To achieve this, the encoder doing the DASH packaging must read the SCTE markers on the input, noting the time on each one to ensure the time is maintained relative to the new DASH timeline. It must then splice the segment at the indicated time and generate a new period with a new timeline beginning with the second half of the spliced segment. This ensures a complete Group of Pictures (GOP) at the start of each Period, which is critical to allowing the player to switch between two distinct streams with no interruptions. Without this, it would need to wait for the next I-frame when resuming the live broadcast after an ad, which would lead to some amount of black video. Figure 6 shows an example of segment splicing for event periods.

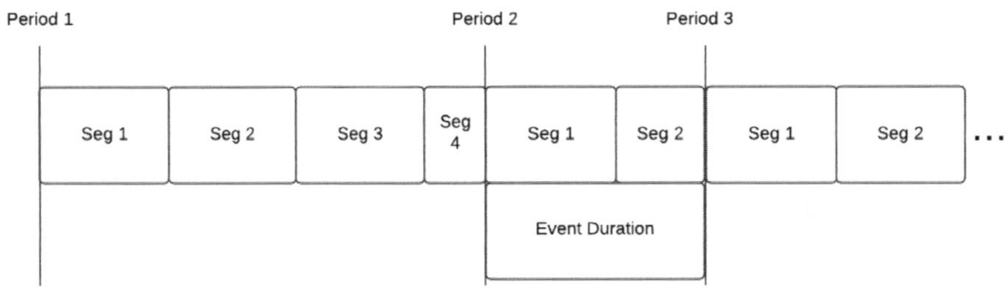

FIGURE 6: AN EXAMPLE OF SEGMENT SPLICING FOR EVENT PERIODS.

Once the splicing is completed, the packager must then generate the corresponding MPD for these segments. Each new avail, indicated in the source feed by the SCTE splice_insert markers, generates a new period in the MPD. So, in a workflow where the feed is going program-break-program, with the break listed as one large avail, the MPD would initially have a single period. Around three to ten seconds before the break, the input would receive the first of the SCTE markers. This could either be an open-ended avail with no duration signaled, indicating no specific time to return, as is sometimes seen in live events, or a fixed duration avail, which is common in a broadcast station running fixed ad breaks. In either case, the packager would generate an early available period in the MPD [11]. This is a period that has no segments but indicates that there will be a period in the future. In our case, this period also contains the EventStream element, allowing the receiver to begin processing the event before it comes up in the timeline.

This element has several key attributes:

- **presentationTimeOffset:** Present in the individual events (non-offset) and the EventStream (offset), this indicates the time within the period that the event occurs. For example, if the event has a PTO of 1100, and the EventStream's PT is 1000, then the event would occur 100 timescale units into the period.
- **schemeIdUri:** This identifies the scheme used for the events. The majority of events will be urn:scte:scte35:2014:xml+bin or urn:scte:scte35:2014:xml+bin, but there is a provision in the ATSC spec for the use of custom URIs [12].

- **value:** This optional attribute allows the receiver to distinguish between events when the BA subscribes to specific values, as described in the BA workflow later in this section.

The EventStream element in turn has several child elements, named Event, which identify the individual events within the element. These events again have a series of attributes to enable the timing:

- **presentationTime:** This is used as described in the PTO section of EventStream.
- **duration:** This is optional and not present in open-ended avails. It indicates the expected time of the avail to allow the ad decision server to put together a playlist of appropriate length. This can be modified in later MPD updates if, for example, the program needs to come back early.
- **id:** This indicates an identifier within the URI and value. The id is most useful as a transfer from the SCTE marker. In this way, the ad logic on the receiver side can determine which ad break is upcoming, as it has a record of the IDs and their corresponding breaks available.
- **Data:** Within the Event element, the packager can insert arbitrary data in XML form. In the urn:scte:scte35:2014:xml+bin scheme, this is utilized to place the full body of the SCTE marker in base64 encoding within the event, giving 1:1 parity on SCTE features to DASH events.

At this point, the DASH stream now has a properly spliced set of representations, along with events to indicate the timing and reasoning for each splice. The transmit side must now feed the DASH stream into the ROUTE encapsulator, add the appropriate signaling, and bundle it all into an ATSC 3.0 transmission. Everything after the DASH packager is simply passing along the stream unmodified.

Receiver Requirements

The receiver must now process the essence and signaling, then communicate to and from the BA using the standard interactive content APIs. The core function revolves around two sets of APIs: those pertaining to the events, and those pertaining to changing the RMP source.

When receiving a DASH service, the receiver is expected to monitor the MPDs for new events whenever the MPD version changes. The new events can be supplied not only by the DASH items described above, but also by methods like video watermarking [13] or out-of-band delivery. MPD-based DASH events are the only ones relevant for this DAI workflow (see Figure 7).

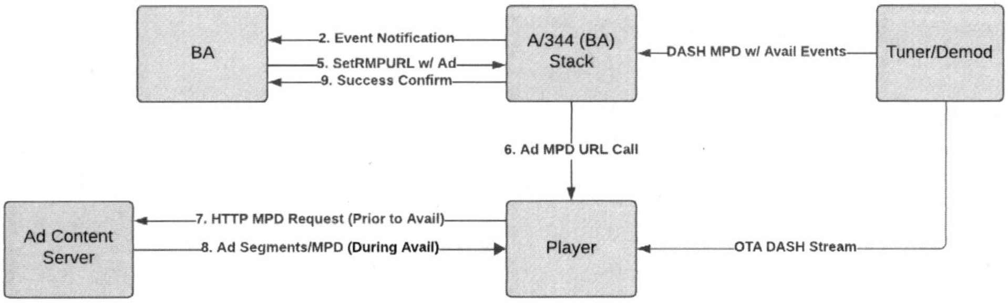

FIGURE 7: THE RECEIVER SECTION OF THE WORKFLOW.

When the receiver spots an event, it notes the listed attributes and calculates the current time and the time the event will occur relative to the current media presentation timeline. It then sends a notification to any BA subscribed to events with a matching schemeIdUri and optionally a matching value. The notification contains the currentTime and the eventTime. The BA can now calculate the time until the event and tell the receiver to execute an action relative to the eventTime with a high degree of precision. It also provides the id and duration attributes, and any data contained within the element.

The BA will then process this notification, as explored in the next subsection. At some point between the notification and event, if the BA chooses to insert an ad, it will make a Set RMP URL call to the receiver. There are several operations allowed in this call, but for the purposes of ad insertion, only startRmp and resumeService are necessary. In the initial call, the BA will utilize startRmp, with rmpSyncTime set to the eventTime from the prior notification. This tells the receiver to, at the time the event is set for, switch the Receiver Media Player (RMP) to an alternative MPD with a given URI. This is the critical component for frame accuracy, as the event is placed at the precise time on the timeline where the splice occurs. This provides a dramatic improvement over systems that utilize wall-clock time, as the time remains consistently expressed in terms of the timeline on the player, regardless of how far off the internal time may be. It also means that precise timing on the BA call is unnecessary, as the RMP change is set to a fixed time on the timeline, rather than one relative to the current time.

Ideally, the receiver begins buffering the MPD ahead of the eventTime to ensure a smooth transition with no black sections. If the MPD has not been buffered, it can cause brief interruptions while the receiver acquires the MPD and segments. This can lead to a viewer missing the beginning of the next program block, an unacceptable result for all parties. In the event the receiver does not buffer, however, there is an alternative approach that is explored in Section 6.

In a normal situation, the receiver would play through the presentation referred to by the new MPD, and upon reaching the end, return to the primary MPD by default. However, breaks may end early or otherwise be interrupted. In this scenario, the BA may choose to cut out of the ad early rather than cover programming with a spot. To do so, the BA makes a Set RMP URL call, but instead of specifying a URI and using the startRmp operation, it uses the resumeService operation with no rmpurl. The time is either left empty to immediately resume, or the time is specified to resume based on the time in the event indicating the break is ending early.

The receiver must also supply information on the device and user and confirm an ad has successfully run. The former is accomplished using the Query Device Info API, which provides the deviceId and advertisingId of the receiver to the BA. This allows the BA to associate the receiver with a given profile of a viewer for ad decisioning.

The confirmation that an ad has run is handled using the RMP Media Time Change Notification. When the BA is subscribed, it receives a notification any time the player time changes. This occurs when the Set RMP URL API is used, as the timeline in the ad will be different to that of the main service. The BA knows the notification is caused by the player beginning playback of the ad, and later resuming the main service on completion, because of the 'source' section of the API.

Broadcaster Application Requirements

In the model described in this section, where an internet connection is available, the BA has a lighter workload, as many of the responsibilities described in the next two sections are offloaded to remote servers.

When the BA launches via the HELD upon the user selecting the relevant service, the first thing it must do is subscribe to the relevant notifications: events and RMP media time changes, both described above. It should also query the device info to retrieve the two relevant IDs to reduce the delay when it comes time to request an ad from the decision server (see Figure 8). With these tasks accomplished, it can then wait for an event to come through.

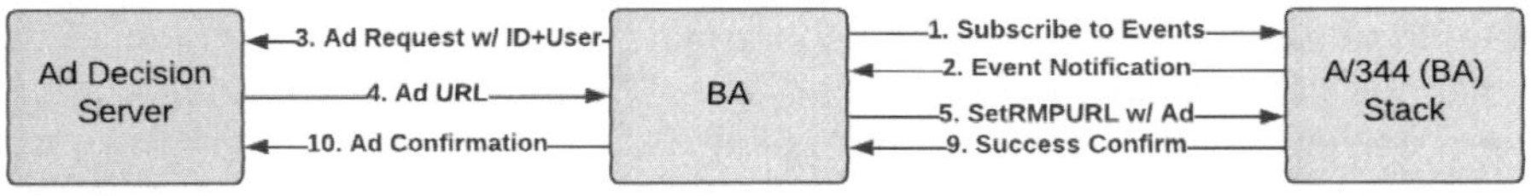

FIGURE 8: THE BA COMPONENT OF THE SYSTEM.

When an event indicating an avail does come through, the BA should immediately hand off the advertisingId, avail ID, and duration to the ad decision server to request an ad. The server uses the avail ID to determine what rules should be applied based on the surrounding content. This avoids situations like duplicate spots airing adjacent to each other. The advertisingId, meanwhile, is associated with prior data gathered on the user to enhance the ad selection process. Based on these three items, the server puts together the ad or ads to be aired during the avail, and hands the URL(s) back to the BA, potentially including a callback URL to indicate whether the ad successfully aired. The BA in turn makes the calls noted in the preceding section to begin playback of these ads.

The receiver section covered the case of a single ad, but as noted above, there can be multiple ads in a single block, particularly if breaks are being signaled as one large break. Luckily, this is handled through a slightly different usage of the SetRMPURL API. Rather than setting the rmpSyncTime to nothing or a specific time, it can instead be set to -1.0, which tells the receiver to execute the action upon completion of the current media presentation. Only one call can be queued at a time, however, so it is important to wait until the preceding presentation has begun before calling the next startRmp. This is achieved using the time change notification mentioned earlier, as it triggers just as easily going between ad presentations, as it does going from program to ad and back. The sequence of events can be seen in Figure 9.

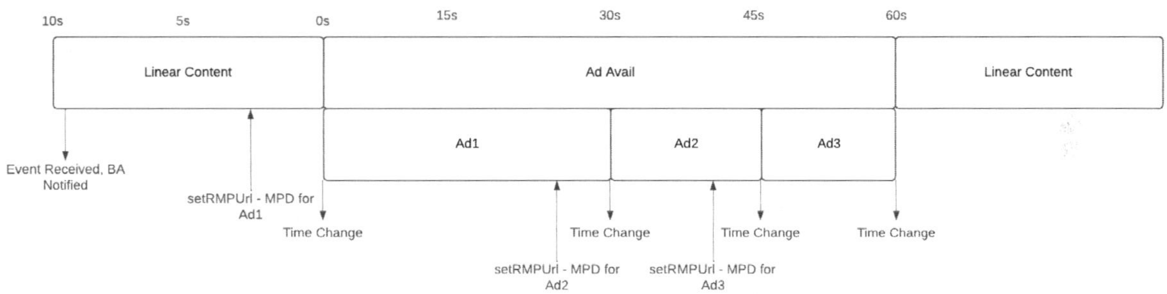

FIGURE 9: THE SEQUENCE OF TIME CHANGE NOTIFICATIONS AND SETRMP CALLS.

Once the receiver has handed off the URL(s) to the receivers, it listens for the time change notifications and notifies the ad decision server's API whether the ad has successfully run. And with that, there is a fully functional connected device insertion.

Section 4: Broadcast-Only Reasons and Restrictions

While the combination of functions is relatively new, the system described above is fairly simple to put together with standard-based "building blocks," leaning primarily on the existing ad infrastructure used in streaming. This works well in markets like the US or Korea, where broadband access and connected devices are common. In a market such as India, however, this gets more complicated. One of the primary reasons for the push towards ATSC 3.0 in India is the lack of reliable internet access, with many users reliant on mobile data to connect. The availability of mobile data in particular varies wildly in standards, speed, and access. Over 20% of mobile phone users in India have feature phones, and of those, over 75% are still 2G based [14].

As part of our overall Direct-to-Mobile(D2M) effort in India, one of the core features was linear services on mobile devices with ad insertion and minimal internet usage. The goal is to increase efficiency by offloading as much common data as possible to broadcast delivery, while maintaining a minimal internet backchannel that does not require constant availability.

This results in the following restrictions compared to the connected device scenario:

- Ads cannot be retrieved from an external server, and so must be delivered via broadcast
- Ad decision logic must be local to the receiver
- No immediate feedback mechanism for ad reporting is available due to inconsistent internet availability

Section 5: Broadcast-Only Solutions

This section will cover each of the restrictions individually, and explore the solutions devised for each of them.

Locally Sourced Ad Media

The ad media is the most internet intensive component of the broadband solution, as the receiver is effectively streaming the ad for the duration of the spot. This is due to the individualized nature of targeted advertising, which in a US-style broadband environment, makes it preferable to save the broadcast bits for other items. However, when broadband is less reliably present, that equation shifts back towards broadcast.

Other solutions have explored the usage of parallel advertising, in which multiple ads are transmitted simultaneously during a given ad break, with the receiver switching between multiple MPDs to choose the preferred ad for the viewer. This flow can be seen in Figure 10. While this makes synchronization easier, it negatively affects broadcast efficiency for two reasons.

First, if an ad is going to be reused, it is sent multiple times, once in each break. In the first airing, it requires the same number of bits as a Non-Real Time (NRT) solution. However, each subsequent break will double, then triple etc. the number of bits required by the parallel solution. The receiver could cache the ads after they're received, but that loses the timing advantage over the NRT solution.

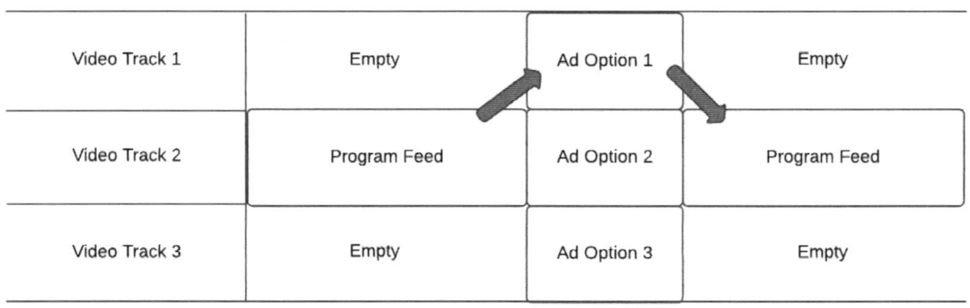

FIGURE 10: THE SEQUENCE FOR THE PARALLEL AD WORKFLOW.

Second, broadcasts have a fixed number of bits available in a time unit. Therefore, when real time delivery is required, the transmission of the ad media can't simply be averaged over a long period. Instead, it must utilize the live bitrate of the media. Broadcasters max out their PLP payloads, so there isn't normally bitrate available for the additional video bitrate necessitated by the ad. Workarounds like running the ads at a lower bitrate or using a dynamic spectrum allocation tool [15] run into issues if multiple services go to a break simultaneously.

Instead, the best option is to deliver the ads as NRT files. This means sending the media in a bundle in advance, ideally during non-peak hours when more spectrum is available. Because this media is not critical to the user experience, as the service can always fall back to the linear feed, it does not need to be sent 24/7, which reaps significant savings in bit consumption over the parallel approach. The impact of the instantaneous and cumulative bitrate usage of the NRT file solution compared to the parallel advertising solution can be seen in Figure 11.

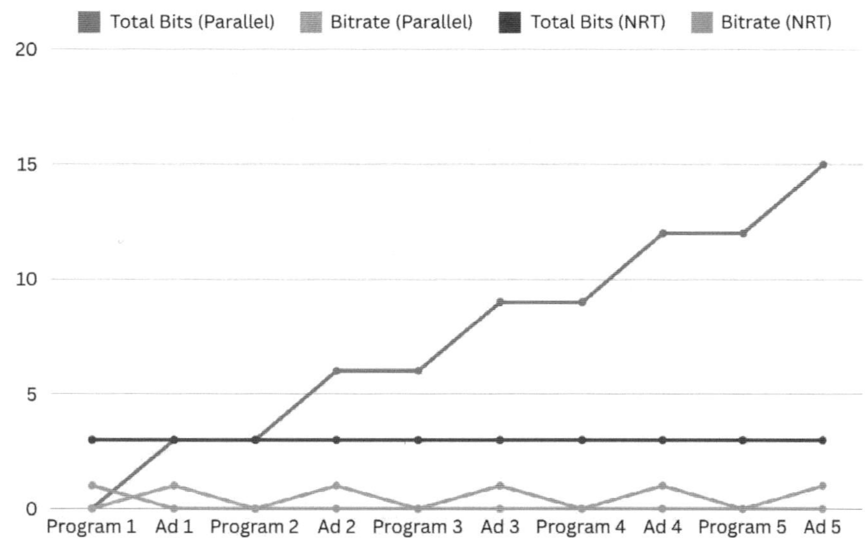

FIGURE 11: A COMPARISON OF RESOURCE USAGE BETWEEN THE TWO DELIVERY SOLUTIONS.

One downside, however, is storage usage. Caching every possible ad can get quite unwieldy, particularly in a model where the phone is designed to act as a nano-CDN for other applications, which means local storage can become a premium. Luckily, there are a few workarounds to avoid this:

First, proper signaling. The ATSC 3.0 spec includes an optional 'validUntil' [16] attribute for individual files within a package. This enables the receiver to discard the files when no longer needed, reducing the cache load. For example, if the broadcaster knows an ad campaign will only run through a given date, they can signal the validUntil for that date.

Second, the use of filter codes [17]. These are a set of identifiers unique within a single appContextId which can be used to *filter* files by relevancy. Once the application has built a user profile, it requests the receiver to only retrieve files matching the filter codes, which correspond to ads relevant to the viewer. For example, if the viewer consistently watches cooking shows, cricket matches, and soap operas, the BA selects the filter codes corresponding to kitchen tools, sports memorabilia, and soap opera promos. Filter codes are 32-bit unsigned integers, so it is easy to get as granular as desired in the selection of ads. These workarounds ensure a slim cache while keeping relevant ads available, all with a minimum of spectrum usage.

Scheduling is also key, as a tuner shouldn't constantly remain tuned to receive ad media, particularly on battery-dependent mobile devices where every watt counts. Fortunately, the Distribution Window Description (DWD) table within the Service Layer Signaling (SLS) contains the start date, end date and time for each file transmission, as well as a label to distinguish duplicates, the AppContextId and filter codes for each file. The DWD is analogous to the Electronic Service Guide (ESG) but for file delivery [18]. Using this table, the receiver can tune to the signal at the scheduled time and cease tuning once the file is received. The filter codes ensures only relevant files are received.

Offline Ad Decision Logic

The ad decision logic is the next piece of the puzzle. We can run the logic wholly within a lightweight BA using the typical ad insertion workflow described in Section 3. Our goal for the pilot in India was to prove the concept, so the actual user data and ad categories were limited, as were the rules for airing the spots. However, there is no reason this same methodology would not apply to a full production system.

We initially explored using filter codes to communicate all of a file's metadata, but this became unwieldy as we began to add more detail to each piece of ad media. Instead, we created a separate ad manifest containing the metadata for each piece of content available on the broadcast. An example of this can be seen in Figure 12. This allowed the logic engine to determine which files should be downloaded off the air and to build ad playlists using the rules described in the manifest.

Some key attributes are as follows:

- **advertiserId:** Identifies the advertiser, e.g. Bob's Discount Cars, or Coca-Pepsi.
- **advertisementNo:** A unique identifier for an individual spot.
- **duration:** Length in seconds of spot.
- **languageID:** Identifies the language used in the ad to ensure the viewer can understand it.
- **genre:** One or more genres the advertisement is relevant too, e.g. news, movies, music, sports, travel, shopping, or finance.
- **presentationImpressionNumber:** Indicates the maximum number of times an ad can be played on a given device, with 0 indicating no limit.
- **forceDeliver:** Overrides all other rules to air a spot for a given genre, with the repeat number indicating how many times.

The file is transmitted as part of the BA and updated with new ads via the validFrom field to indicate when a new version is available. Once the BA has the manifest file, it calls the relevant APIs to set the filter codes, then checks for upcoming media via the DWD.


```
"serialNo": 1,
"data": [
    {
        "advertiserId": 2000000001,
        "advertisementNo": 3000000001,
        "duration": 1005000010,
        "categoryID": 5,
        "languageId": [1000003001],
        "advtAgeId": [1000002999],
        "genre": [1000001101, 1000001102, 1000001103],
        "forceDeliverGenre": 0,
        "forceDeliverRepeatNumber": 0,
        "presentationImpressionNumber": 0,
        "isGenreUnique": false,
        "playInLoop": false
    },
    {
        "advertiserId": 2000000001,
        "advertisementNo": 3000000002,
        "duration": 1005000010,
        "categoryID": 5,
        "languageId": [1000003001],
        "advtAgeId": [1000002999],
        "genre": [1000001104, 1000001105, 1000001106],
        "forceDeliverGenre": 0,
        "forceDeliverRepeatNumber": 0,
        "presentationImpressionNumber": 3,
        "isGenreUnique": false,
        "playInLoop": false
    },
    {
        "advertiserId": 2000000001,
        "advertisementNo": 3000000003,
        "duration": 1005000010,
        "categoryID": 5,
        "languageId": [1000003001],
        "advtAgeId": [1000002999],
        "genre": [1000001107, 1000001108, 1000001109],
        "forceDeliverGenre": 0,
        "forceDeliverRepeatNumber": 0,
        "presentationImpressionNumber": 0,
        "isGenreUnique": false,
        "playInLoop": false
    },
```


FIGURE 12: AN EXCERPT FROM A SAMPLE METADATA FILE FROM THE PILOT.

The workflow for the event processing is then virtually identical to the connected method (see Figure 13). Some key differences are as follows:

- The rmpUrl points to an MPD inside the Application Context Cache, rather than an internet one, corresponding to the chosen ad.

- The BA must check what ads are available in the cache before choosing one, as receivers can discard files from the cache at will.
- The decision logic is done according to the manifest rules, rather than calling the decision server API.
- Precaching, explored in Section 6, is unnecessary, as the files are already in the cache.

Inconsistent Feedback Mechanism

The whole purpose of dynamic ad insertion is to increase the value of each spot. However, much like a tree in the forest, if a targeted ad airs but no one knows about it, how does the broadcaster get paid? This is the problem with the inconsistent return channel and the lack of internet-delivered ad media. With a connected device, the BA can send a message to the ad server to indicate an ad was successfully run, and the advertiser knows a device accessed the ad from their server at a specific time. With a disconnected device, both of those options are gone. The solution was to accumulate a record of the ad airings and send them in bulk the next time the device connects to the internet. This, of course, has high potential for fraud, so this component needs the most additional work, as will be seen in the next section.

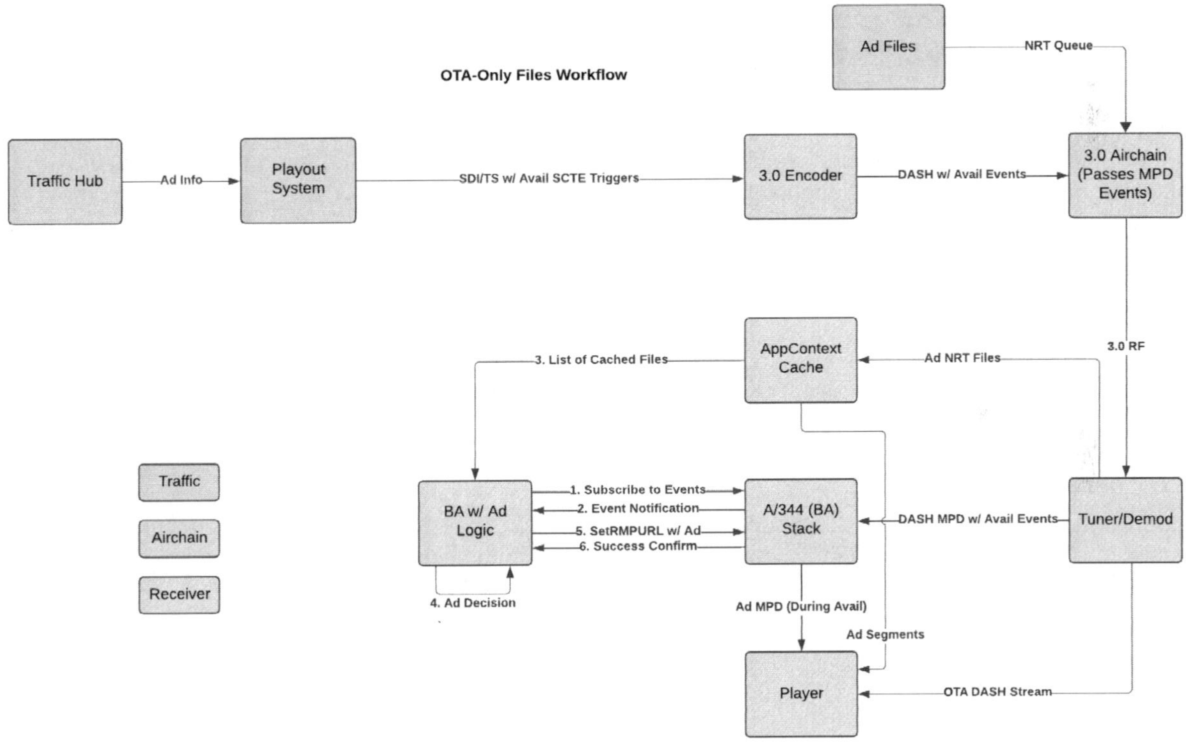

FIGURE 13: THE WORKFLOW FOR BROADCAST-ONLY AD INSERTION.

Section 6: Future Plans and Optimizations

Now that we've proven out the core functions of this methodology, for both connected and low-connectivity markets, we can begin to optimize and advance the system with the following refinements:

Preloading Content

In the connected model, there is a danger the receiver may wait until the syncTime to begin buffering the segments. This would result in delays entering and exiting the avail, causing black at the start and overlap at the end. Ideally, receivers would simply begin buffering upon receiving the Set RMP call, but this cannot be guaranteed. Luckily, the cache request API can be used specifically for this situation. The API allows the BA to cache the necessary segments from a DASH MPD.

Under this model, the BA processes the event like normal, but instead of directly setting the URL in the Set RMP call, it calls the cache request API repeatedly until it confirms that all files are in cache. Once this is received, the BA would call Set RMP and point to the local MPD instead of the remote one. This should enable near perfect frame accuracy regardless of the receiver's buffer model, as it will instantly have the full MPD available.

Common Data Services

Currently, files intended for a BA are transmitted alongside each service. This leads to inefficiencies in distribution, as multiple services will likely be consuming the same ad media. Unfortunately, no default tune service for files exists the way it does for service information via the ESG. The new Data Service category fulfills the role well for private file distribution, but it's specifically intended to be ignored by receivers that do not know the global service identifier (GSID). A "common service" intended for files consumed by multiple services would address this. The Common Data Service would eliminate duplicate files, with backwards compatibility maintained via signaling the file transmissions in each service for those receivers that don't update to the new category.

Ad Skipping

One potential danger of providing a receiver with each ad's start and end times is it enables DVRs to easily skip past all the ads in a recorded broadcast. While this is a narrow case, particularly as most DVRs are very capable when it comes to automatic commercial detection, it is a topic worth exploring in future modifications. There may be some form of obfuscation that can be used to raise the bar above the lowest hanging fruit.

Receiver Support

While the APIs in question are part of the NextGenTV logo suite, that does not necessarily guarantee all receivers will behave the same way. Initial testing has been done to validate the presence of the APIs and the viability of the workflow, as can be seen in Table 1, with the manufacturer names altered for confidentiality reasons.

Receiver	Multiperiod	Event Subscribe	Event Notification	Time Change	startRMP	resumeService	Device Info
Receiver 1	Y	Y	Y[1]	Y	Y	Y	Y
Receiver 2	Y	Y	Y[1]	Y	Y	Y	Y
Receiver 3	Y	Y	Y	Y	Y	Y	Y
Receiver 4	Y	N/A[2]	N/A[2]	N/A[2]	N/A[2]	N/A[2]	N/A[2]
Receiver 5	N	Y	N[3]	Y	Y	Y	Y
Receiver 6	Y	Y	Y	Y	Y	Y	Y
Receiver 7	Y	N/A[4]	N/A[4]	N/A[4]	N/A[4]	N/A[4]	N/A[4]
Receiver 8	Y	N/A[4]	N/A[4]	N/A[4]	N/A[4]	N/A[4]	N/A[4]

TABLE 1: RESULTS OF OUR TESTING OF RECEIVER SUPPORT FOR DAI.

Additionally, we've validated the timing possibilities with our in-house receiver stack, using a test system with a series of countdown timers, as shown in the sequence in Figure 14.

[1] The core event notification functionality is present, but with some bugs that require adaptations on the transmit side.
[2] The BA fails to run the Javascript, instead only displaying the HTML, which causes the other tests to fail. This appears to be due to a BAAppear implementation.
[3] Event notifications are unable to be tested without multi-period support in our implementation, making this an automatic fail.
[4] Receiver does not implement A/344.

FIGURE 14: AN EXAMPLE OF THE COUNTDOWN TIMERS SEQUENCE.

While not all receivers are fully up-to-snuff, the testing has given us confidence that the average receiver should be able to achieve this. Luckily, failure simply means the insertion does not occur and the linear feed will play as normal. The only exception is Receiver 5, which does not support multi-period video, and so will require a fix before deployment.

Codecs are another concern as not all RMPs support the same codecs, including many common ones used in streaming. Audio has been a particularly mixed bag historically. The ingest workflow for ads will be key to ensure the viewer does not experience silent audio or video due to poor media choice. This, however, is a user-by-user issue, so codec requirements can be set in the BA on a per-model basis, allowing the BA to choose not to air an ad with an unsupported codec. Fortunately, this is a situation that has improved over the years as Table 2 illustrates, showing the results of various codecs in the RMPs of common receivers.

Receiver	HEVC	AVC	AC-4	EAC-3	AC-3	LC-AAC
Receiver 1	Y	Y	Y	Y	Y	Y
Receiver 2	Y	Y	Y	Y	Y	Y
Receiver 3	Y	Y	Y	Y	Y	Y
Receiver 5	Y	Y	Y	Y	Y	Y
Receiver 7	Y	Y	Y	Y	Y	Y

TABLE 2: RESULTS OF OUR TESTING OF RECEIVER SUPPORT FOR RMP CODECS.

Conclusion

We believe this solution is the most viable method for both connected and broadcast-only ad insertion. It avoids problems discovered in previous solutions, while adding additional functionality, including for non-content replacement-based use cases. It also makes use of long-established standards and APIs that are well-supported on all but a few receivers. We plan to continue testing out each aspect of this system to ensure full viability, both in our lab and at interoperability events throughout the year.

References

[1] Kim, S. “Dynamic Ad Insertion through [Data Distribution as a Service System (DDaaS) – MMT Protocol – Broadcast Application] without Internet Connection,” *BEITC Proceedings*, No. 2024.

[2] Yuan, Shuai. Wang, Jun. Zhao, Xiaoxue. “Real-time Bidding for Online Advertising: Measurement and Analysis,” *ADKDD ’13: Proceedings of the Seventh International Workshop on Data Mining for Online Advertising*, No. 3, August 11, 2013, pp. 1-8.

[3] “Information technology – Dynamic adaptive streaming over HTTP (DASH),” *ISO-IEC 23009-1:2022(E),* p.108-110.

[4] “ATSC Standard: ATSC 3.0 Interactive Content,” *A/344:2024-04*, 3 April 2024, pp. 162-167.

[5] "Information technology – Dynamic adaptive streaming over HTTP (DASH)," *ISO-IEC 23009-1:2022(E),* p.135-146.

[6] "Digital Program Insertion Cueing Message," *ANSI/SCTE 35 2023r1.*

[7] "Automation System to Compression System Communications Applications Program Interface (API)," *ANSI/SCTE 104 2023.*

[8] "Information technology – Generic coding of moving pictures and associated audio information – Part 1: Systems," *ISO/IEC DIS 13818-1.*

[9] "3 Gb/s Signal/Data Serial Interface," *SMPTE 424M-2006.*

[10] "MPEG media transport (MMT)," *ISO/IEC 23008-1:2023.*

[11] "Dynamic adaptive streaming over HTTP (DASH)," *ISO-IEC 23009-1:2022(E),* p.34.

[12] "ATSC Standard: Application Event Delivery," *A/337:2024-04,* 3 April 2024, p. 5.

[13] "ATSC Standard: Video Watermark Emission," *A/335:2024-04,* 3 April 2024.

[14] Counterpoint Research, "India Smartphone Market Share: Quarterly," 25 Nov 2024.

[15] Hottinger, N. "Optimizing ATSC 3.0 Spectrum Utilization with Dynamic Resource Allocation and Management," Proceedings of the 2025 NAB Broadcast Engineering and Information Technology Conference, April 2025

[16] "ATSC Standard: ATSC 3.0 Interactive Content," *A/344:2024-04*, 3 April 2024, pp. 23-24.

[17] "ATSC Standard: Signaling, Delivery, Synchronization, and Error Protection," *A/331:2024-04,* pp. 155-156.

[18] "ATSC Standard: Signaling, Delivery, Synchronization, and Error Protection," *A/331:2024-04,* pp. 73-77.

Acknowledgments

- Nick Hottinger, Sangsu Kim, and the ONE Media Lab for their support and advice
- Viktor Matiash and the Middleware group for their able work on the proof-of-concept receiver
- Sanjay Yadav and Saankhya Labs for their efforts in the D2M project
- Mike Dolan of Pearl for his assistance with alternate content replacement methods

Off-piste 5G in the Broadcast Auxiliary Service Band

Douglas G. Allan, Samuel R. Yoffe†, Kenneth W. Barlee, Dani Anderson, Iain C. Chalmers, Malcolm R. Brew, Cameron A. Speirs, Robert W. Stewart
Neutral Wireless and University of Strathclyde
Glasgow, Scotland
†Corresponding author: sam.yoffe@neutralwireless.com

Nicolas Breant, Jeremy Tastet, Sebastien Roques, Bastien Chague
AW2S
Bordeaux, France

Abstract – 5G New Radio (NR) can be used to provide flexible, high-capacity and low-latency networks suitable for broadcast content acquisition or delivery, but access to suitable spectrum can be challenging. One of the enablers for private network deployments is shared spectrum licensing, such as the upper n77 band (3.8–4.2 GHz) available in the UK and elsewhere in Europe. The Third Generation Partnership Project (3GPP) was created to develop mobile standards for WCDMA and TD-SCDMA and their respective core networks, and has continued to publish standards as radio access technologies have progressed to 4G and 5G. These standards define frequency bands, numerologies, duplex models and messaging (among many other things). While software-defined radio (SDR) is emerging as a viable and highly flexible solution for core and radio access network (RAN) functions, user equipment (UE) typically remain hardware based with modems that implement the 3GPP standards to ensure device compatibility. The flexibility of SDR RAN allows for wireless radio networks based on 5G NR to be built in non-3GPP defined spectrum bands, but there are no compatible devices to connect. In the USA, broadcasters have access to spectrum in the Broadcast Auxiliary Service (BAS) band (2025–2110 MHz), which coincides with the programme-making and special events (PMSE) band used in the UK and Europe. This allows for rapid licensing of 10/12 MHz channels for traditional wireless camera systems, such as COFDM, that could instead be used to license low-to-medium power private 5G NR-based networks capable of supporting multiple cameras and other IP-based workflows. This paper discusses the development of a flexible software-defined UE capable of connecting to non-3GPP 5G NR networks in BAS/PMSE spectrum.

Introduction

All wireless communication relies on radio frequency (RF) resources to transport a modulated signal. Different frequencies are used by different devices and for different purposes. There are some unlicensed frequency bands, such as 2.4–2.5 GHz for Wi-Fi, which are available for anyone to use. However, these can become unusable when many people are trying to use them at the same time. Different devices or even networks can be competing for the same resources and interfere with one another. Other frequency bands, like n78 (3.3–3.8 GHz) in the C-band, are instead licensed to a user such as a public mobile network operator (MNO) to run their commercial networks. Figure 1 shows cellular spectrum allocation and usage at a location in Glasgow, UK.

This paper is excerpted from the Proceedings of the 2025 NAB Broadcast Engineering and Information Technology (BEIT) Conference, © 2025, National Association of Broadcasters, 1 M Street SE, Washington, DC 20003 USA.

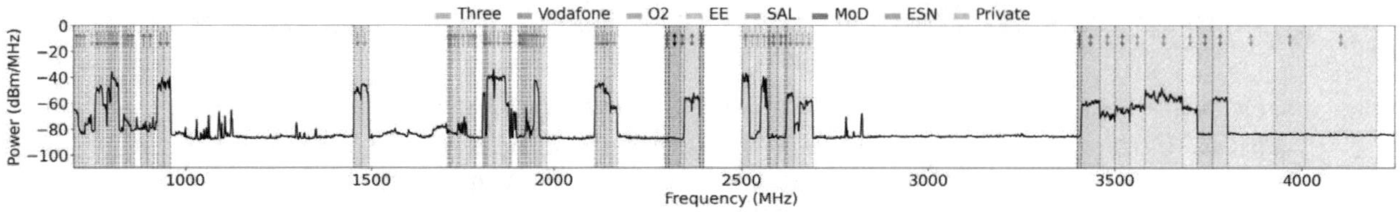

FIGURE 1: CELLULAR SPECTRUM ALLOCATION AND USAGE AT A LOCATION IN GLASGOW, UK.

5G New Radio (NR) can be used to provide flexible, high-capacity and low-latency networks suitable for broadcast content acquisition or delivery, but access to suitable spectrum can be challenging. One of the enablers for private network deployments is shared spectrum licensing, such as the upper n77 band (3.8–4.2 GHz) available in the UK and elsewhere in Europe. In the USA, the Citizens Broadband Radio Service (CBRS) band provides shared access to 150 MHz of radio spectrum in the n78 band in areas where the incumbent user (the U.S. Department of Defense) is not operating.

In the USA, the Broadcast Auxiliary Service (BAS) bands are a set of radio frequencies that are available for broadcasting operations, including video and audio transmission between field locations and production facilities for applications such as electronic newsgathering (ENG) and coverage of major sporting and entertainment events in stadia, arenas and outdoor locations. The BAS mainly operates in ultra-high frequency (UHF) and microwave spectrum, including allocations in the 2 GHz, 7 GHz, 13 GHz and 17 GHz bands. The 2 GHz BAS band coincides with the programme-making and special events (PMSE) spectrum between 2025–2110 MHz available in the UK and across Europe for wireless video contribution, mainly using the coded orthogonal frequency division multiplexing (COFDM) digital video transmission standard.

In recent years, the major rollout of 4G/5G public networks has led to a significant reduction in the availability of dedicated spectrum for broadcasting applications (including ENG). Since the broadcasting use case is uplink intensive and public networks can be unpredictable, this has led to the emergence of technologies such as bonded-cellular that simultaneously utilize multiple 4G or 5G network connections to transmit video. This reduces the required resources on each network and allows the device to adapt to network conditions on each path, facilitating robust video delivery using IP-based protocols with forward error correction (FEC) and packet retransmission. Despite the reduction in resources required on each individual connection, broadcasters typically use target bitrates as low as 5 Mbps for interlaced HEVC video feeds. Moreover, the bonding over multiple paths, recombination, and packet retransmission all need time, such that bonded-cellular contributions typically operate with end-to-end latency between 1 and 2 seconds. This is acceptable for average quality remote contribution feeds.

The need for multiple cellular connections for a single device is often caused by a lack of control over the quality of service (QoS) provided by public 4G and 5G networks, especially in high demand density (HDD) environments. This makes bonded-cellular a less attractive solution than traditional COFDM links for major sporting events or festivals, where there are likely to be many thousands of concurrent users competing for the same network resources.

Despite this, the evolution to IP-native video transmission over 5G has numerous potential advantages, such as removing the need for on-site production facilities, and bi-directional connectivity for services such as camera control, tally, talkback and return video using a single spectrum allocation. There are two major solutions for improving the QoS provided by 5G networks: network slicing and private (non-public) networks.

In network slicing, a portion of the physical resources of the (public) network, such as bandwidth, is reserved for a particular use or user(s). Currently, network slicing is not widely deployed, which means that broadcasters may be unable to access a slice in every location that they are operating. In addition, the slice is usually limited and costly because the Mobile Network Operators (MNOs) cannot afford to substantially reduce the QoS for their main customer base. As a result, the user of the slice is still competing for resources with other network users and does not have operational control over the network parameters and QoS. While there have been several successful demonstrations of public slicing [1,2,3], they have often required the MNO to deploy additional hardware to support the slice.

In private (or non-public) networks, a dedicated 5G network including radio access network (RAN) and core is deployed at the broadcast location using licensed spectrum. The private network is based on the standalone (SA) architecture, whereas many public networks use non-standalone (NSA) that relies on existing 4G infrastructure. Shared spectrum refers to 5G bands that cannot be exclusively licensed by the public MNOs, such as the upper n77 band extending from 3.8-4.2 GHz in the UK. The private 5G network is owned and operated by the broadcaster or contracted service provider, and gives them full control of all network parameters, such as the time division duplexing (TDD) frame structure. This allows them to deploy a network configuration that is tailored exclusively for the broadcast application – to maximize uplink capacity and minimize end-to-end latency. One of the key enabling technologies of private networks is virtualized RAN (vRAN), which refers to a fully software-based implementation of the 5G RAN or gNodeB (gNB) running on a commercial off-the-shelf (COTS) Linux server. This permits a high degree of flexibility in the configuration of the 5G network and choice of compute form factor.

Even with the introduction of shared spectrum, there still remains a lack of harmonization [4] between countries. It is also subject to challenge from public MNOs, which creates a potential barrier to greater adoption of 5G networks by broadcasters. Broadcasters (like all other interested parties) must still apply for a spectrum license for the shared spectrum band from the in-country regulator. An application does not automatically guarantee a license will be offered as it is subject to whether other network operators hold licenses in the same channel or location. Furthermore, in the UK for example, licenses must be applied for well in advance of the deployment date, which may not be possible when reacting to major news events.

Private 5G networks are still dependent on the use of COTS user equipment (UEs) from manufacturers such as Qualcomm, which are based on fixed hardware implementations and are strictly adherent to the 3GPP-defined 5G NR bands. In this paper, we describe a prototype private 5G network and UE that can operate between 2025–2100 MHz within the BAS band. The benefit of this system approach is that it allows for IP-native video transmission using spectrum already dedicated for broadcast applications. The use of the BAS band precludes the need to compete with the MNOs for spectrum and allows broadcasters to license deployments as they typically would for their COFDM transmitters.

In such a system, the broadcaster can exploit the inherent advantages of video-over-IP technology while also having full control of the QoS, which is of paramount importance for high-quality low-latency video contribution. A major innovation of this system is the development of a software-defined UE, which can operate "off-piste" (also known as "backcountry skiing" in the USA) in non-3GPP spectrum. The prototype demonstrates the possibility of deploying private 5G networks in *any* spectrum.

Spectrum Regulation

In the BAS spectrum, the 2 GHz band is available for radio links for broadcast video contribution. The overall spectrum allocation extends between 2025–2110 MHz, which is flanked by 4G LTE bands B1 and B34, as illustrated in Figure 2. This is licensed as seven 12 MHz channels described in Table 1.

Channel	**1**	**2**	**3**	**4**	**5**	**6**	**7**
Center freq. (MHz)	2031.5	2043.5	2055.5	2067.5	2079.5	2091.5	2103.5
NR-ARFCN	406300	408700	411100	413500	415900	418300	420700

TABLE 1: CHANNELS IN THE 2 GHZ BAS BAND.

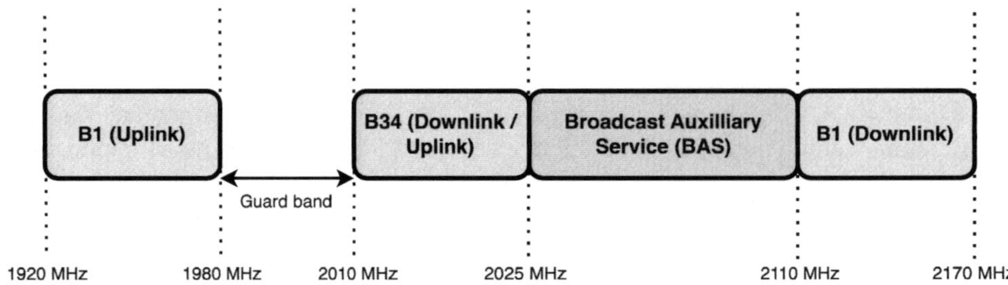

FIGURE 2: ILLUSTRATION OF 2 GHZ BAS BAND AND ADJACENT 4G LTE BANDS.

The LTE band B1 is a frequency division duplexing (FDD) band, where different channels are used for downlink and uplink. The downlink is usually the higher of the two frequencies. In this case, the duplex spacing is 130 MHz. LTE B34 is a time division duplexing (TDD) band, where the downlink and uplink share the same frequency with resources allocated in different time slots. As can be observed, it is located between the B1 downlink and uplink channels from 2010–2025 MHz. The BAS band is sandwiched between B34 and the B1 downlink channels with no guard band. Adjacent channel leakage could raise the noise floor for the bordering BAS channels. The 5G NR bands n1 and n34 utilize the same spectrum as their LTE counterparts, however 5G NSA network services are typically deployed in so-called “midband” spectrum at 3.5 GHz in the lower n77 (or n78) band.

In most countries, including the US, the MNOs have exclusive rights to use the B1 and B34 spectrum for their commercial services, so these cannot be used by a private network operator. Just like in the UK and elsewhere, the broadcasters can use technology such as bonded-cellular for IP video transmission to cope with the loss of spectrum access, but they have minimal control over the network performance and QoS in HDD environments such as large-scale sporting events.

In terms of shared spectrum, a common framework for private 5G networks is the Citizens Broadband Radio Service (CBRS), which comprises 150 MHz of spectrum in the 3.5 GHz band. However, unlike the Shared Access License (SAL) framework in the UK, access to this spectrum is based on priority levels with protection for incumbent users such as U.S. Navy radar systems. This makes obtaining a license and operating in certain environments very challenging for secondary users of the spectrum. There are a few technical challenges that we believe limit its suitability for critical broadcast connectivity. The relatively high permitted transmit powers pose a severe risk of interference to uplink-biased networks, while matching the standard downlink-biased TDD pattern offers limited uplink capacity in the modest (10-40 MHz) channels available. Furthermore, with the potential for many users running in adjacent channels and dynamic licensing, it is very difficult to ensure a clean RF environment, or to isolate and take measures to mitigate any issues encountered. The ability of users to operate “opportunistically” using unused spectrum assigned to another licensee increases the risk of interference in congested areas. Finally, public networks are allowed to access spectrum in the CBRS band, reducing availability in HDD environments where it is potentially needed by broadcasters most.

Just like the CBRS band, the BAS band is a shared spectrum band with different rules for priority access. However, unlike CBRS, individual television stations and large broadcaster networks such as ABC and NBC are the incumbent users, which have pre-existing licenses for this band. There is also a second co-primary user of the BAS band—the Department of Defense. An emerging condition on the use of the BAS band precludes the hidden node problem, where two unidentifiable transmitters operating in the same spectrum can cause interference at a receiver, thereby preventing either signal from being decoded. Unfortunately (but hopefully not surprisingly), COFDM camera links fall into this category. Therefore, we propose that one approach to maintaining use of the BAS band for broadcast video transmission is to deploy private 5G networks in the BAS band. Single channel (12 MHz) carriers could potentially support multiple cameras simultaneously, or several channels could be combined to deploy even larger carriers. The main barrier stopping this is the availability of user equipment—the end user device that connects to the 5G network. The COTS 5G UEs that are used in bonded-cellular devices only support 3GPP bands, such as n1, n34 or n77; they cannot be used in the BAS band.

A bespoke UE implementation is needed that can operate “off-piste” in non-3GPP bands. This novel approach can be realized through software-defined radio (SDR), where the majority of radio functionality is implemented in software running on a general-purpose compute. The CPU could be based on RISC or CISC instruction sets from manufacturers such as ARM, Intel or AMD. The inherent flexibility of SDR allows the 5G UE to operate in non-3GPP bands and to be configured specifically for the broadcast use case. Note that SDR 5G gNB based on vRAN already allows the base station to operate off-piste and with flexible network configuration, enabling high uplink capacity, low latency, and fine-tuned QoS for the broadcast application. In the next section, we propose a custom 5G band in BAS spectrum to lay the groundwork for the SDR UE implementation that follows.

Beyond 3GPP (Going Off-piste)

The Third Generation Partnership Project (3GPP) was created to develop mobile standards for WCDMA and TD-SCDMA and their respective core networks, and has continued to publish standards as radio access technologies have progressed to 4G and 5G. These standards define frequency bands, numerologies, duplex models, and messaging (among many other things). While software-defined radio (SDR) is emerging as a viable and highly flexible solution for core and RAN functions, user equipment (UE) typically remains hardware-based with modems that implement the 3GPP standards to ensure device compatibility. The flexibility of SDR RAN allows for wireless radio networks based on 5G NR to be built in non-3GPP defined spectrum bands, but there are no compatible devices to connect.

In this section, we propose a new 85 MHz TDD band called “n250” operating within the BAS band between 2025–2110 MHz. TDD is employed to ensure that the spectrum can be flexibly used to efficiently support different uplink/downlink use cases. FDD requires separate channels for downlink and uplink. The channel uses the global frequency raster of 5 kHz that applies to all 5G bands operating up to 3 GHz. In addition, a 100 kHz frequency raster is used to define the spacing between potential center frequencies within the overall band. Each discrete frequency is represented by an absolute radio frequency channel number (ARFCN), which is simply an index for each center frequency. The lowest and highest NR-ARFCN in the new *n250* band is

$$\text{NR-ARFCN}_{\text{min}} = \frac{2025\ \text{MHz}}{5\ \text{kHz}} = 405000 \quad \text{and} \quad \text{NR-ARFCN}_{\text{max}} = \frac{2110\ \text{MHz}}{5\ \text{kHz}} = 422000. \tag{1}$$

The center frequency must also be an integer multiple of 100 kHz, so ARFCNs that are integer multiples of 20 between 405000–422000 are acceptable as center frequencies. This allows for 851 discrete center frequencies, although care must be taken to avoid intentional emissions outside the defined band. The custom “n250” band is illustrated in Figure 3. The existing 12 MHz BAS channels are presented in Table 1, and to begin we propose 10 MHz 5G NR carriers be deployed within these channels to provide a small guard band, minimize licensing disruption and allow business-as-usual where possible. Larger 5G NR carriers (20/30/40/50 MHz) should span adjacent BAS channels, and non-3GPP bandwidths (such as 12 MHz and 24 MHz) can be achieved using physical resource block masking (see footnote 7 in [5]). Regarding regulatory concerns, n250 could be reduced to allow guard bands with B34 below and B1 (downlink) above, and bandpass filters incorporated to isolate n250.

The 5G synchronization signal block (SSB) is used for the initial cell search process before the UE establishes a connection to the network. It operates using the global frequency raster and global synchronization channel number (GSCN). This is a larger frequency raster used to speed up cell search. In the prototype system, the SSB frequency is chosen as the lowest possible GSCN in the carrier bandwidth, although other implementations may use a different scheme. Currently, the SDR UE does not perform cell search but rather the center frequency of the cell must be set manually.

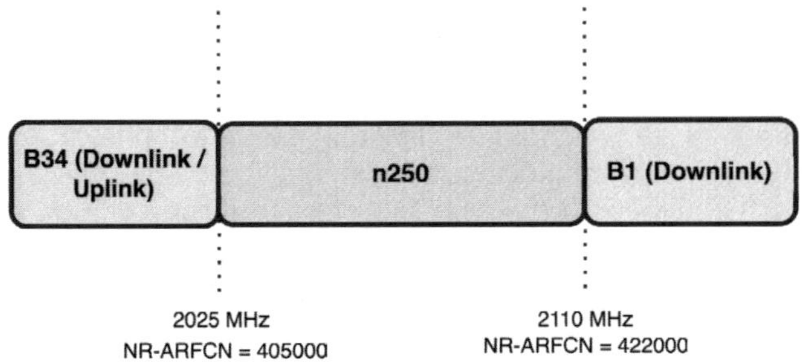

FIGURE 3: ILLUSTRATION OF THE CUSTOM N250 BAND IN THE BAS SPECTRUM.

There are some important advantages to running a fully SDR solution and removing the reliance on COTS hardware manufacturers and 3GPP specification. The first major advantage is upgradability. The SDR network and UE developed here started their life as an LTE system, before being updated to the release 16 specification of the 3GPP. Since then, it became release 17 compliant and is now at release 18. This is simply not possible with fixed hardware solutions (such as ASIC), and we can start to benefit from rapid development cycles. Secondly, since we are *not constrained* to the specification, we can, for example, make use of the 120 kHz numerology reserved for frequency range 2 (FR2: 24.25–71 GHz) when operating networks in frequency range 1 (FR1: 0.41–7.125 GHz) spectrum. This has some potential implications for latency that are interesting to explore.

Off-piste 5G NR in the Broadcast Auxiliary Service Band

Having defined the custom TDD band, this section describes the private 5G network and SDR UE implementation and discuss its performance. The off-piste 5G architecture is illustrated in Figure 4.

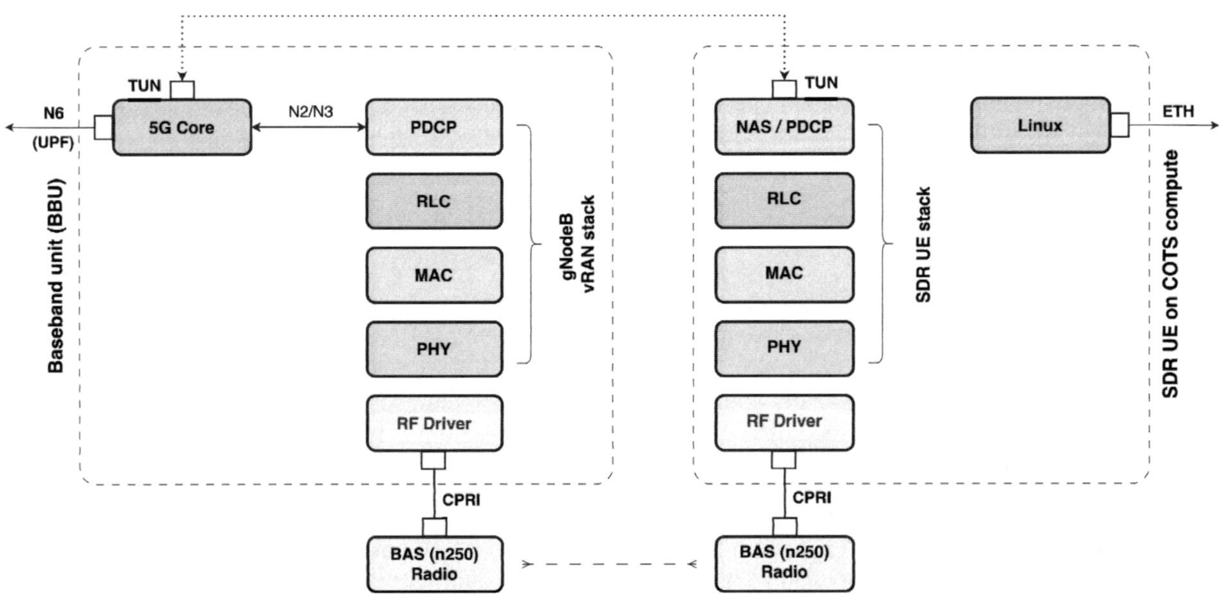

FIGURE 4: OVERVIEW OF THE SDR OFF-PISTE 5G SA NETWORK (LEFT) AND UE (RIGHT) ARCHITECTURE.

The gNB vRAN stack and 5G core shown in Figure 4 (left) are implemented purely in software running on the baseband unit (BBU) server. The gNB exchanges baseband I/Q samples with the radio over the common public radio interface (CPRI) fronthaul connection. The 2 GHz BAS radio is a low power indoor unit with a small form factor capable of supporting 4x4 multiple-input multiple-output (MIMO) configuration and up to 50 MHz instantaneous bandwidth. In the tests carried out for this paper, we configured single layer (single-input single-output (SISO)) cells with 10/20/30/40/50 MHz bandwidths centered at 2067.5 MHz, corresponding to channel 4 of the band. The radio can transmit a maximum power of 20 dBm (100 mW) and uses digital pre-distortion (DPD) to compensate for non-linearities in the power amplifiers, thus minimizing adjacent channel leakage. This ensures the radio surpasses the required spectral mask and allows the network to co-exist harmoniously with other spectrum users.

The SDR UE stack uses a similar architecture as shown in Figure 4 (right). As is the case for the gNB, the entire UE stack is implemented in software running on a COTS Intel or AMD compute. The SDR UE also exchanges baseband I/Q samples with the 2 GHz radio using the CPRI protocol. The UE is configured to operate at the same center frequency of 2067.5 MHz (no cell search), decodes the SSB, and sends a physical random access channel (PRACH) signal to initiate the network connection.

The SDR UE currently uses the same indoor 2 GHz radio unit as the gNB, which means that it can also benefit from high quality power amplification, DPD, and optimized front-end filtering for the band of interest. This leads to a much higher quality uplink signal than is possible with multi-band COTS UEs. The gNB reports maximum SNRs above 40 dB, which allows 256QAM modulation to be used in the uplink, with stable and high modulation and coding scheme (MCS) logged by the gNB. An adaptive MCS loop can be used to optimize the cell capacity based on the target and instantaneous block error rates. Moreover, 1024QAM could be used where RF channel conditions allow to increase channel capacity in both uplink and downlink.

The network must be able to provide sufficient uplink capacity and low end-to-end latency to support broadcast quality video contribution. In order to compete with existing broadcast transmission standards such as COFDM, several network configuration parameters must be optimized. Detailed discussion of 5G network configuration for uplink-biased broadcast applications [5] and low latency optimization [6] have been given elsewhere. These discussions and optimizations remain relevant for network configuration in the BAS band. Since n250 has been proposed as a TDD band to maximize spectral efficiency and flexibility, narrow channel bandwidths require the TDD frame structure to be chosen to meet the requirements of the use case. As a "broadcast" band, we recommend an uplink-biased TDD pattern such as SUUU be considered as the standard for n250 in order to support both low latency and uplink-biased broadcast workflows. Downlink MIMO can be used to increase downlink throughput if needed [5]. While the SDR UE developed here is capable of running 4x4 MIMO for both downlink and uplink, we caution the use of uplink MIMO to increase capacity compared to using receive diversity to increase channel robustness.

Since RF propagation at lower frequencies (such as 2 GHz) out-performs higher frequencies, we can typically expect lower pathloss than we experience using, for example, UK shared spectrum in upper n77, and significantly less than mmWave. At the center of the BAS band, f_c = 2067.5 MHz, we find the free-space distance for a pathloss of 75 dB to be 65 m, compared to 33.5 m for f_c = 4 GHz (see equation (3) in [5]). It should be noted that uplink-biased networks tend to be limited by UE uplink power class or license conditions [5]. In this case, with the same radio front-end being used on base station and UE, this is not the case, and we can run with a symmetric link power budget. The effective (isotropic) radiated power (ERP or EIRP) should be carefully considered to provide robust RF performance to deliver the use case while being considerate of other licensees and spectrum reuse density, particularly if operating with a downlink-biased TDD pattern.

The first iteration in the development of a SDR UE used low power Ettus USRP B210 SDR boards for the radio link. A narrow LTE FDD carrier was demonstrated in the BAS band at the 2023 NABShow, as shown in Figure 5 (left). The link was used to transport an ultra-low latency (~40 ms) HEVC 1080p50 UDP video stream from a prototype FPGA-based video encoder built in collaboration with BBC R&D to its counterpart decoder over the tabletop. A return video feed was sent from the decoder back to the encoder, and camera control of a Grass Valley camera using a Grass Valley remote control panel (RCP) and nameserver. The link was so fragile that the plastic sign could be used to disrupt the video.

FIGURE 5: EVOLUTION OF THE SDR UE. (LEFT) DESKTOP SDR CARDS AT NABSHOW 2023. (CENTER) LOW-POWER SDR CARDS AT IBC 2023. (RIGHT) "PORTABLE" UE AT NABSHOW 2024.

A second iteration of the prototype SDR UE was demonstrated with BBC, Zixi and BT Media and Broadcast later that year at IBC 2023. The system used internal Amarisoft SDR PCIe cards with a slightly higher transmit power than the USRP boards. The BBC R&D prototype ultra-low latency video codec was used to encode and decode the video stream, with the Zixi transport protocol used to protect the UDP video stream for an end-to-end latency around 100 ms. Camera control was this time demonstrated using Sony camera and RCP equipment. The configuration is shown in Figure 5 (center) with the Intel NUC running the base station and a small form factor custom-built AMD computer mounted on the tripod leg running the SDR UE. The live video was transmitted a few meters over the air using PMSE spectrum licensed from the Dutch spectrum regulator. A 10 MHz TDD 5G SA carrier was broadcast in a single PMSE channel. (As an aside, the video was then bonded over Starlink and OneWeb low-Earth orbit (LEO) connections to BT Tower in the UK then returned to Amsterdam over the BT Vena fiber network with a latency of around 1 second.)

It was clear that to cover any meaningful area a proper radio front-end was required. A custom-made low-power indoor radio head based on the AMD/Xilinx RFSoC was developed with custom filters to operate in the new n250 band. The radio was capable of up to 50 MHz carrier bandwidth in the range 2025–2100 MHz (not quite the full n250 band). Meanwhile, the RF driver and UE software stack were developed to make use of the new radio hardware. Figure 5 (right) shows the SDR UE and new BAS (n250) radio packaged together with a battery power supply into a rucksack. An omni-directional 2 GHz antenna was mounted above head height. The SDR gNB was located behind the LED wall on the AMD booth at NABShow 2024, with a small sector antenna protruding above the LED wall. The same Intel NUC was used for the SDR gNB to generate a 10 MHz 5G SA carrier in channel 4 in the center of the BAS band (Table 1), and the SDR UE was used as a gateway for an iPhone connected by Ethernet. The iPhone used the Zixi OnAir mobile application to stream a 16 Mbps video (with 100 ms Zixi transport latency) to a decoder and displayed on the LED wall. The end-to-end latency was less than 500 ms, with the extra latency in the processing driving the LED wall. This system was sensitive enough for the "mobile" SDR UE to be taken elsewhere in the hall and still deliver stable video.

Conclusions

All wireless communications rely on RF spectrum to transport information. Spectrum is a finite resource, and access to radio spectrum needs to be controlled. The emergence of shared spectrum models has accelerated the development and uptake of private 5G networks in a number of industries, including live broadcast, but accessing spectrum can be challenge that varies across the World. The UK spectrum regulator, Ofcom, has designated the upper portion of n77 (3.8–4.2 GHz) as shared access spectrum for use by low- to medium-power non-public networks. There is movement towards harmonization of this band across Europe [4], but the current license processing times are not conducive to many broadcast applications.

Dynamic access to spectrum is used by broadcasters to deploy wireless camera links using COFDM technology, and suitable spectrum is available to broadcasters (PMSE in UK/Europe and BAS in the USA). It is of interest to explore the deployment of private 5G networks to support broadcast use cases using this spectrum. Software-defined radio systems are highly flexible and have been used to demonstrate the suitability of private 5G to the broadcast industry at high profile international events. However, most COTS devices are based on hardware multi-band modems from companies such as Qualcomm, and implement a subset of the 3GPP specification to ensure compatibility. Broadcaster spectrum is not part of the specification, so these devices cannot operate in spectrum that broadcasters have access to. While we can create SDR networks at 2 GHz, there are no UEs to connect.

A SDR UE solution has been developed with a focus on the 2025–2110 MHz spectrum available as PMSE and BAS to broadcasters. A new 5G NR TDD band named *n250* has been discussed and a dedicated RFSoC-based radio head developed to function in this band. This can be used to build functioning private 5G SA networks with Release 18 UEs in broadcast spectrum. The SDR nature of the solution means that the gNB and UE are essentially frequency agnostic, and other non-3GPP bands can be explored in a similar manner with the development of suitable radio front-ends. The BAS/PMSE system developed currently uses the same radio for the network cell and UE, which can create very clean carriers and provides excellent uplink performance with SNRs above 40 dB recorded. The prototype system remains rather bulky for mobile UEs. We hope to continue development and to reduce the size of the UE. Perhaps COTS multi-band modems will one day allow users to go off-piste.

Acknowledgments

The authors gratefully acknowledge the support and expertise of the wider Neutral Wireless and StrathSDR (University of Strathclyde) group. In addition, we are grateful to the BBC, BT Media and Broadcast, Zixi, and AMD for their interest in exploring this concept with us. We are indebted to Bob Weller at NAB for their guidance and support navigating the spectrum landscape in the USA. We are grateful for the support and expertise of our partners AW2S and Amarisoft. This project was supported by the EPSRC Federated Telecoms Hub 6G Research Partnership Project (THRPF), and a part of HASC (Future Communications Hub in All-Spectrum Connectivity) led by University of Oxford in a project titled "Spectrum Sharing and Sensing in non-3GPP Bands for 5G/6G".

References

[1] Ericsson, "A slice fit for a King; how the British King's Coronation was broadcast using 5G and network slicing", (26/06/2023).

[2] Mobile Europe, "Deutsche Telekom uses Live TV via 5G at football" (24/06/2024).

[3] A. Stewart, "5G slicing on public networks: field results, observations and roadmap to ubiquitous 5G access for professional media", IBC Technical Papers (2024).

[4] CEPT ECC, "ECC Decision (24)01: Harmonised technical conditions for the shared use of the 3800-4200 MHz frequency band by low/medium power terrestrial wireless broadband systems (WBB LMP) providing local-area network connectivity", approved (08/11/2024).

[5] S. R. Yoffe *et al.*, "Low latency wireless broadcast production over 5G", submitted to NAB BEITC (2025).

[6] M. B. Waddell *et al.*, "Optimising 5G for low latency broadcast production", IBC Technical Papers (2024).

Deploying 5G Broadcast in UHF Spectrum

Ayan Sengupta, Javier Rodriguez Fernandez, Alberto Rico Alvarino
Qualcomm Technologies Incorporated
San Diego, California, United States

Thomas Stockhammer
Qualcomm CDMA Technologies GmbH
Munich, Germany

Abstract – We describe how to deploy 5G Broadcast—a technology built on the LTE air-interface backbone—in the broadcast UHF spectrum, with a different channelization from cellular systems. LTE-based systems have classically had channelization in segments of 1.4, 3, 5, 10, 15 and 20 MHz, none of which are an exact match for channels in the broadcast UHF spectrum, which have typical channelization in segments of 6, 7 or 8 MHz. We first describe how new supportable channel bandwidths for the physical multicast channel (PMCH) were added to the 5G Broadcast standards, while minimizing the changes necessary to the 5G Broadcast synchronization signals and the bandwidths associated with these. Specifically, we describe how a small, backwards-compatible bandwidth for the synchronization signals (transmitted in the Cell Acquisition Subframes, CASs) were leveraged to indicate a larger, UHF-compliant bandwidth for the PMCH. We then describe the physical layer signals and parameters—such as the reference signals (RSs) and Transport Block Sizes (TBS)—that were adapted in accordance with the new PMCH bandwidths, followed by a discussion on higher-layer signaling via Radio Resource Control (RRC) that was necessary to configure these new PMCH bandwidths. We then highlight the subsequent addition of the broadcast UHF bands (with respective band numbers) to the 3GPP RAN4 specifications, that were crucial in facilitating broadcasters to deploy 5G Broadcast in their allocated spectrum.

Introduction

In recent years, 5G Broadcast has emerged as an attractive broadcasting technology that can enable broadcasters to deliver content directly to mobile devices. This is facilitated by the cellular modem-friendly design of 5G Broadcast, which leverages key building blocks of 3GPP-compliant cellular modems—such as those present in our smartphones—to facilitate broadcast reception without requiring additional dedicated hardware for this purpose.

While 5G Broadcast presents a unique opportunity for broadcasters to expand their reach to smartphones, certain key bridges between the world of traditional broadcasting and that of cellular systems need to be built along the way, to take full advantage of this opportunity. One such bridge, that we address in this paper, is to enable 5G Broadcast to be seamlessly deployed in the frequency bands designated for broadcast systems in varied geographies across the world.

Since 5G Broadcast targets broadcasters—as opposed to cellular operators—the most important target spectrum for this technology is the portion of UHF spectrum allocated to broadcast systems (a subset of ~470 - ~694/698MHz, depending on the region). The channelization used within this spectrum can

This paper is excerpted from the Proceedings of the 2025 NAB Broadcast Engineering and Information Technology (BEIT) Conference, © 2025, National Association of Broadcasters, 1 M Street SE, Washington, DC 20003 USA.

vary between 6, 7 and 8 MHz in bandwidth, depending on the geography (such as those defined by different ITU regions).

While 3GPP specifications in Release 14 and 16 introduced features for 5G Broadcast in the Radio Access Network (RAN), which—together with the corresponding enhancements in the core network—enabled the deployment of a downlink-only dedicated broadcast network using 3GPP technologies, the channelization was inherited from cellular LTE—i.e., only bandwidths of 1.4, 3, 5, 10, 15 or 20 MHz were supported. As a result, Release 16 specifications for 5G Broadcast did not natively support a seamless deployment on UHF spectrum for broadcast systems that use 6, 7 or 8 MHz channel bandwidths.

To address the above issue, in Release 17, 3GPP set out to adapt 5G Broadcast to the UHF spectrum, while minimizing the changes required to the specifications in the process. In this paper, we describe how this was accomplished.

First, we describe the physical layer design principles that were used as the backbone to support physical multicast channels (PMCHs) with bandwidths different from legacy LTE. Next, we discuss the impact on reference signal (RS) mapping and Transport Block Sizes (TBSs), on account of supporting the new PMCH bandwidths. Thereafter, the higher layer signaling needed to facilitate the new bandwidths are outlined. We end the paper by describing the addition of broadcast UHF bands to the 3GPP RAN4 specifications, which—in conjunction with the enhancements at the physical (and higher) layers—enable broadcasters to deploy 5G broadcast in UHF spectrum.

Physical Layer Design to Accommodate 6, 7, 8 MHz Channel Bandwidths

Design Overview—Legacy CAS Bandwidth with New PMCH Bandwidths

The design to support new bandwidths (with respect to those in legacy LTE standards) leverages the fact that there are LTE bandwidths smaller than the broadcast UHF system bandwidths—namely, 3 and 5 MHz—that can be embedded centrally (in frequency), within a larger 6, 7 or 8 MHz UHF channel, and used for the transmission of “always-on” signals (i.e., the Cell Acquisition Subframes (CAS), comprising synchronization signals, the Master Information Block (MIB) and the System Information Block, SIB), associated with the multimedia broadcast multicast service single frequency network (MBSFN) Area(s) served by the UHF channel.

Such an embedding ensures that no changes need to be made to the synchronization signals and MIB (which occupy a central bandwidth of 1.08 MHz), both from a transmission as well as a reception point-of-view.

Once the User Equipment (UE) decodes the MIB (transmitted via the PBCH), it determines from the MIB payload whether a 3 MHz or a 5 MHz bandwidth is employed for the CAS, which enables the UE to decode the SIB within the CAS. The SIB, in turn, indicates to the UE whether there exist MBSFN Area(s) with a larger bandwidth than that of the CAS—i.e., a 6, 7 or 8 MHz bandwidth—over which the UE can expect to receive the Physical Multicast Channel (PMCH) that carries the eventual broadcast content.

The process described above is depicted schematically in Figure 1.

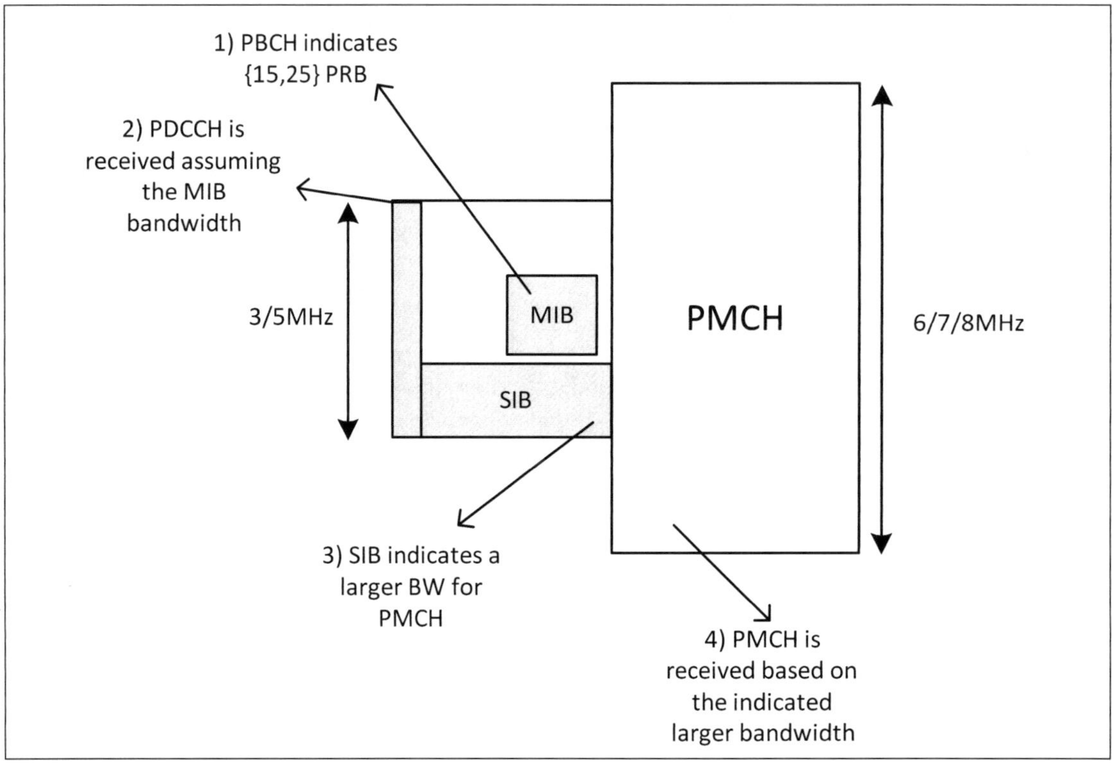

FIGURE 1: CAS WITH MIB-INDICATED LEGACY LTE BANDWIDTHS OF 3 MHZ (15 PHYSICAL RESOURCE BLOCKS, PRBS) OR 5 MHZ (25 PRBS), WITH SIB SUBSEQUENTLY INDICATING A NEW, LARGER PMCH BANDWIDTH OF 6, 7 OR 8 MHZ.

Physical Layer Signals and Parameters for New PMCH Channel Bandwidths

Owing to the new values of the number of resource blocks (RBs) in the downlink for PMCH—namely, 30, 35 and 40 RBs, for 6, 7 and 8 MHz respectively—the frequency-domain span of the reference signals associated with the PMCH (termed MBSFN RS) were updated, to cover these bandwidths. Further, to determine the Transport Block Size (TBS) for these PMCHs, the physical layer frequency resources would now take into consideration the new PMCH bandwidths, when mapping a MCS/TBS index to the corresponding TBS. This is detailed in Section 11.1 of [1], by using the higher layer parameter *pmch-Bandwidth*, which is defined in [2]. Additionally, to keep UE reporting simple, it was decided that for all the new values of the PMCH bandwidths, a UE would assume a 10 MHz bandwidth when reporting the receive-only mode “interest indication” to the eNodeB.

Higher Layer RRC Configurations to Support New PMCH Bandwidths

Within the system information block configuring MBSFN Areas for broadcast transmission, a new list of MBSFN Areas (defined by *MBSFN-AreaInfoList-r17* in [2]) was added in Release 17, which was designed to facilitate 5G Broadcast deployments in the UHF band with the requisite channel bandwidths. The reason for adding a new list of MBSFN Areas was to maintain backwards compatibility with legacy services and receivers, which may be scheduled on legacy LTE channel bandwidths and targeted to UEs that would not be able to interpret the Release 17 enhancements on supporting the new PMCH bandwidths.

For each MBSFN Area within this new list mentioned above, an MBSFN Area-specific field for PMCH bandwidth was introduced, which could indicate from among three values (30 RBs for 6 MHz, 35 RBs for 7 MHz, and 40 RBs for 8 MHz), the PMCH bandwidth used in the corresponding MBSFN Area.

Adding Broadcast UHF Bands to 3GPP Specifications

After completion of the physical (and higher) layer designs in Release 17, enabling 6, 7 and 8 MHz PMCHs to be supported, in Release 18, broadcast UHF bands (with band numbers characterized by the carrier frequency and associated channel bandwidths) were added to the 3GPP RAN4 specifications. These can be found in Sections 5.5H and 5.6H of [3].

These RAN4 specifications for the UHF bands, in conjunction with the Release 17 work described above, now allow broadcasters to deploy 5G Broadcast on UHF bands with 6, 7 or 8 MHz channel bandwidths.

References

[1] TS 36.213: "Evolved Universal Terrestrial Radio Access (E-UTRA); Physical layer procedures".

[2] TS 36.331, "Evolved Universal Terrestrial Radio Access (E-UTRA); Radio Resource Control (RRC) Protocol specification"

[3] TS 36.101: "Evolved Universal Terrestrial Radio Access (E-UTRA); User Equipment (UE) radio transmission and reception".

Open-Source Low-Complexity Perceptual Video Quality Measurement with pVMAF

Jan De Cock, Axel De Decker and Sangar Sivashanmugam
Synamedia
Kortrijk, Belgium
jdecock@synamedia.com

Abstract – With the rise of digital video services, viewers expect high-quality visuals, making Quality of Experience (QoE) a priority for providers. However, poor video processing can degrade visual quality, leading to detail loss and visible artifacts. Thus, accurately measuring perceptual quality is essential for monitoring QoE in digital video services.

While viewer opinions are the most reliable measure of video quality, subjective testing is impractical due to its time, cost, and logistical demands. As a result, objective video quality metrics are commonly used to assess perceived quality. These models evaluate a distorted video and predict how viewers might perceive its quality. Metrics that compare the distorted video to the original source, known as full-reference (FR) metrics, are regarded as the most accurate approach.

Traditional quality metrics like Sum of Absolute Differences (SAD), Sum of Squared Differences (SSD), and Peak Signal-to-Noise Ratio (PSNR) are computationally lightweight and commonly used within encoders for Video Quality Measurement (VQM) and other encoder optimization tasks. However, methods that simply measure pixel-wise differences often lack alignment with human perception as they do not account for the complex intricacies of the Human Visual System (HVS).

In recent years, more advanced metrics have been developed to better reflect human perception by incorporating HVS characteristics. Among these, Video Multi-method Assessment Fusion (VMAF) has become a widely accepted industry standard for evaluating video quality due to its high correlation with subjective opinions.

However, the high computational demand of VMAF and similar perception-based metrics limits their suitability for real-time VQM. Consequently, encoders primarily offer only PSNR and Structural Similarity Index Measure (SSIM) for full-frame quality monitoring during encoding. While not the most accurate, these metrics are the only options that can be efficiently deployed during live encoding, as more advanced VQM approaches would consume too much processing resources needed for real-time encoding.

To address these limitations, we introduced predictive VMAF (pVMAF), a novel video quality metric that achieves similar predictive accuracy to VMAF at a fraction of the computational cost, making it suitable for real-time applications.

pVMAF relies on three categories of low-complexity features: (i) bitstream features, (ii) pixel features, and (iii) elementary metrics. Bitstream features include encoding parameters like the quantization parameter (QP), which provide insights into compression. Pixel features are computed on either the original or reconstructed frames to capture video attributes relevant to human perception, such as blurriness and motion. Finally, elementary metrics, such as PSNR, contribute additional distortion information.

These features are extracted during encoding and fed into a regression model that predicts frame-by-frame VMAF scores. Our regression model, a shallow feed-forward neural network, is trained to replicate VMAF scores based on these input features.

Initially designed for H.264/AVC, we extended pVMAF's applicability to more recent compression standards such as HEVC and AV1. In this paper, we explain how we developed and retrained pVMAF for x264 and SVT-AV1. Experimental results indicate that pVMAF effectively replicates VMAF predictions with high accuracy while maintaining high computational efficiency, making it well-suited for real-time quality measurement.

Video Quality Measurement: A Brief Overview

In recent decades, video quality measurement (VQM) has been a heavily researched topic. VQM is used in various applications such as comparing video quality, configuring and benchmarking encoders, 24/7 quality monitoring, A/B testing, and standardization. There are different types of VQM, and based on the availability of the source signal, it can be classified into full-reference VQM and no-reference VQM.

Full-Reference VQM

Full-reference VQM (FR-VQM, Figure 1a) uses pixel values from both the receiver side (after decoding) and the source/input signal side. By comparing these values, an accurate evaluation of the received signal can be obtained. Many FR-VQM metrics have been proposed over the years, as detailed in the following sections.

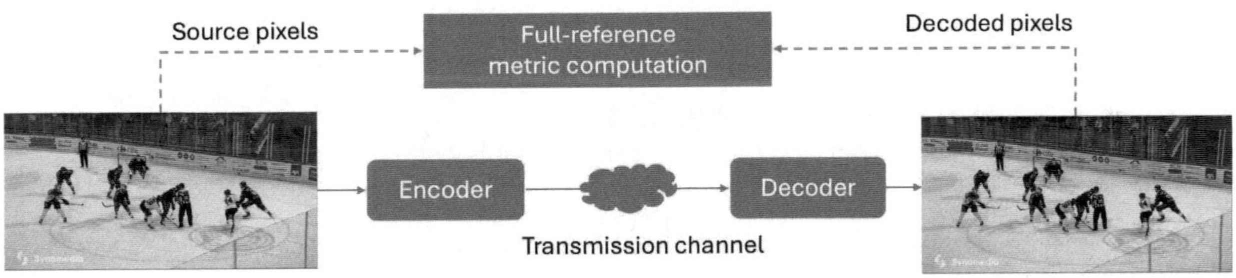

FIGURE 1A: FULL-REFERENCE VQ COMPARISON AND METRIC COMPUTATION: COMPARING THE DECODED FILE TO ITS SOURCE SIGNAL.

No-Reference VQM

No-reference VQM (NR-VQM, Figure 1b) does not require access to the source signal. A video quality score can be calculated at different points during distribution, based on an overall assessment of video quality without referring to the original video. While this method increases flexibility and allows for VQ scoring regardless of the source quality, NR-VQM metrics are generally less accurate than FR-VQM metrics.

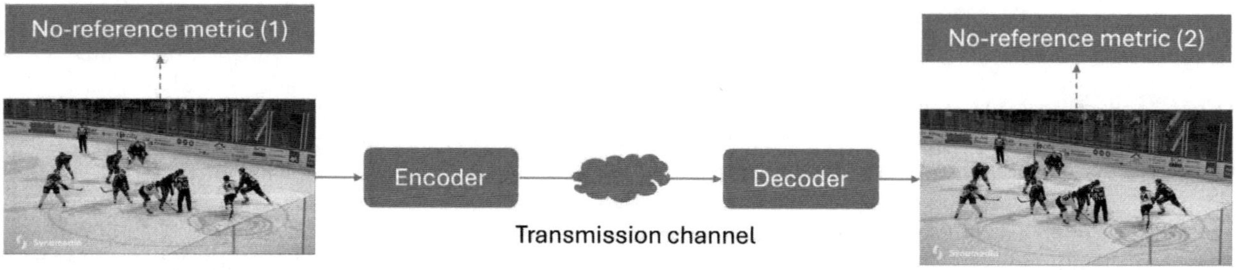

FIGURE 1B: NO-REFERENCE VQM COMPUTATION AT DIFFERENT POINTS IN THE DISTRIBUTION CHAIN.

Several NR metrics have been proposed, each offering varying degrees of accuracy. Examples include BRISQUE, NIQE, and NR-VMAF [1]. However, NR-VQM remains a challenging area, and the accuracy of these metrics often depends on the specific application or type of distortion being measured [2].

Traditional VQM Metrics: PSNR and SSIM

In many applications, traditional L2-norm-based metrics such as mean squared error (MSE) and peak signal-to-noise ratio (PSNR) are still in use. These metrics are easy to calculate and provide a rough indication of quality differences. However, their lower accuracy limits their applicability in modern video quality assessment [3].

A popular metric with higher accuracy is Structural Similarity (SSIM) [4], which computes and combines luminance, contrast, and structural similarity across local neighborhoods in the video frames. SSIM was later extended into multiscale SSIM (MS-SSIM), which calculates SSIM at several resolutions to improve accuracy, though this also increases computational complexity [5]. A comprehensive overview of SSIM, MS-SSIM, their implementations, and recommended practices is provided in [6].
Other metrics based on human visual system models have been proposed, such as the Detail Loss Measure (DLM) [7]. Combined with natural scene statistics, DLM led to the development of the Visual Information Fidelity (VIF) criterion [8].

The Emergence of VMAF: A Fusion of Multiple Metrics

In 2016, the strengths of multiple metrics were combined into the Video Multimethod Assessment Fusion (VMAF) metric, introduced by Netflix [9]. VMAF produces quality scores by taking into account both quantization artifacts (such as blockiness) and scaling artifacts (such as blurriness from upscaling). This makes VMAF particularly well-suited for comparing video quality across multiple ABR renditions and optimizing ABR ladders.

VMAF uses a scale from 0 to 100, which is easy to interpret and maps intuitively to Mean Opinion Scores (MOS), ranging from poor to excellent video quality. Due to its advantages and open-source availability [10], VMAF has become a de facto industry standard for VQM in video-on-demand environments.

2a. VMAF= 96.7

2b. VMAF= 81.0

2c. VMAF= 62.1

2d. VMAF= 42.1

FIGURES 2A-D: VARIOUS VMAF SCORES ILLUSTRATING DIFFERENCES IN VIDEO QUALITY ACROSS AVC ENCODES.

Enhancements and Extensions of VMAF

Since its introduction, several VMAF extensions, improvements [11], and approximations have been developed to increase its utility. VMAF has been deployed in encoder optimization, shot-based encoding [12], and even in no-reference VQM [1]. One key improvement is the "no enhancement gain" model (VMAF-NEG), which accounts for the potential effects of sharpening or image manipulation [13].

Despite its strengths, VMAF has several limitations. For instance, it does not consider color (chrominance) channels, its temporal features are relatively weak, and no publicly available model exists for high dynamic range (HDR) video. To address banding artifacts, Netflix developed the CAMBI detector, which complements VMAF by assigning a score to regions affected by banding [14].

VMAF's Computational Complexity in Live Applications

One of the most significant challenges with VMAF, particularly for live video or real-time applications, is its computational complexity. Certain underlying features, such as VIF, are especially time-consuming to compute. While approaches based on deep neural networks (DNNs) offer high accuracy, their extreme complexity makes them impractical for live environments.

In recent years, work by Meta and other researchers has focused on simplifying and unifying VQM features. For example, the FUNQUE metric [15][16] offers high accuracy at lower computational complexity. Additionally, the XPSNR metric [17] has emerged as a low-complexity alternative for high-resolution video quality assessment.

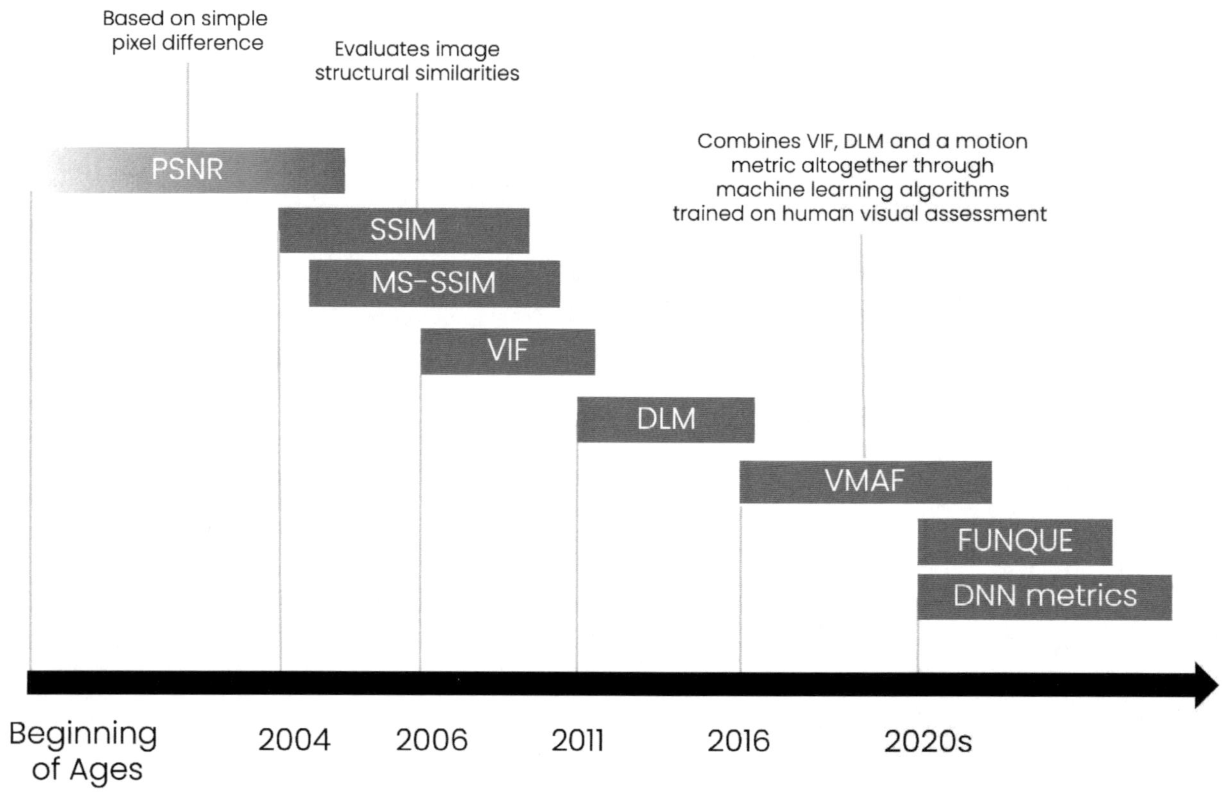

FIGURE 3: OVERVIEW OF MILESTONES IN FR-VQM METRIC DEVELOPMENT OVER THE PAST DECADES.

Although both VMAF and FUNQUE have merits, the computational cost of VQM remains substantial — sometimes even comparable to video compression itself. For most video-on-demand applications, this CPU and financial cost is acceptable, but in live environments where cost and CPU cycles are constrained, more efficient approaches are necessary.

This is why we introduced **pVMAF**, a VMAF predictor specifically designed for live video encoding applications. In the remainder of this paper, we dive deeper into pVMAF, exploring its accuracy and how it significantly reduces computational requirements for real-time video quality assessments.

Predicting VMAF

Real-time video quality measurement (VQM) is a persistent challenge in the streaming and broadcast industry. Above we highlighted the limitations of current methods: many either lack the speed required for real-time analysis or fail to accurately capture the nuances of the Human Visual System (HVS) when assessing video quality.

What if we could combine the predictive accuracy of a metric like VMAF with the computational efficiency of a simpler method like PSNR? To satisfy these constraints we designed pVMAF, a VQ metric designed to deliver real-time, accurate video quality measurement with minimal computational overhead. pVMAF operates within the encoding loop, leveraging key encoding parameters and pre-analysis statistics to achieve VMAF-like precision, but without the heavy computational load.

How Does pVMAF Work?

Feature extraction

pVMAF's success in balancing accuracy and efficiency lies in its **smart feature extraction**. During video encoding, parameters like the quantization parameters (QPs) are already calculated to control the bitrate of the produced bitstream. These parameters also contain valuable information for assessing quality degradation — essentially offering quality-aware features "for free" since the encoder would compute them anyway. By repurposing these parameters, pVMAF avoids adding any significant computational load.

Another valuable source of quality information comes from **pre-analysis statistics** calculated on the pixels of original video frames. These statistics help optimize the encoding process and ensure the best quality-to-bitrate trade-off. Unlike PSNR, which only measures pixel-level differences, pVMAF takes into account how viewers perceive quality by factoring in measures for texture, brightness, and content masking — making it more closely aligned with human perception.

Additionally, pVMAF integrates **PSNR** as a core feature to capture distortion, while leveraging various **encoding parameters** that directly influence visual quality. These parameters provide a solid basis for assessing distortions in the bitstream. In parallel, the **pre-analysis statistics** gathered from the original video frames capture the nuanced characteristics of the HVS, especially regarding how perceptible visual artifacts are in different types of content, based on textures, brightness, and other visual characteristics. This combined feature set — distortion data from encoding parameters and PSNR, along with perceptual insights from pre-analysis statistics — allows pVMAF to make highly accurate predictions that closely align with human quality perception.

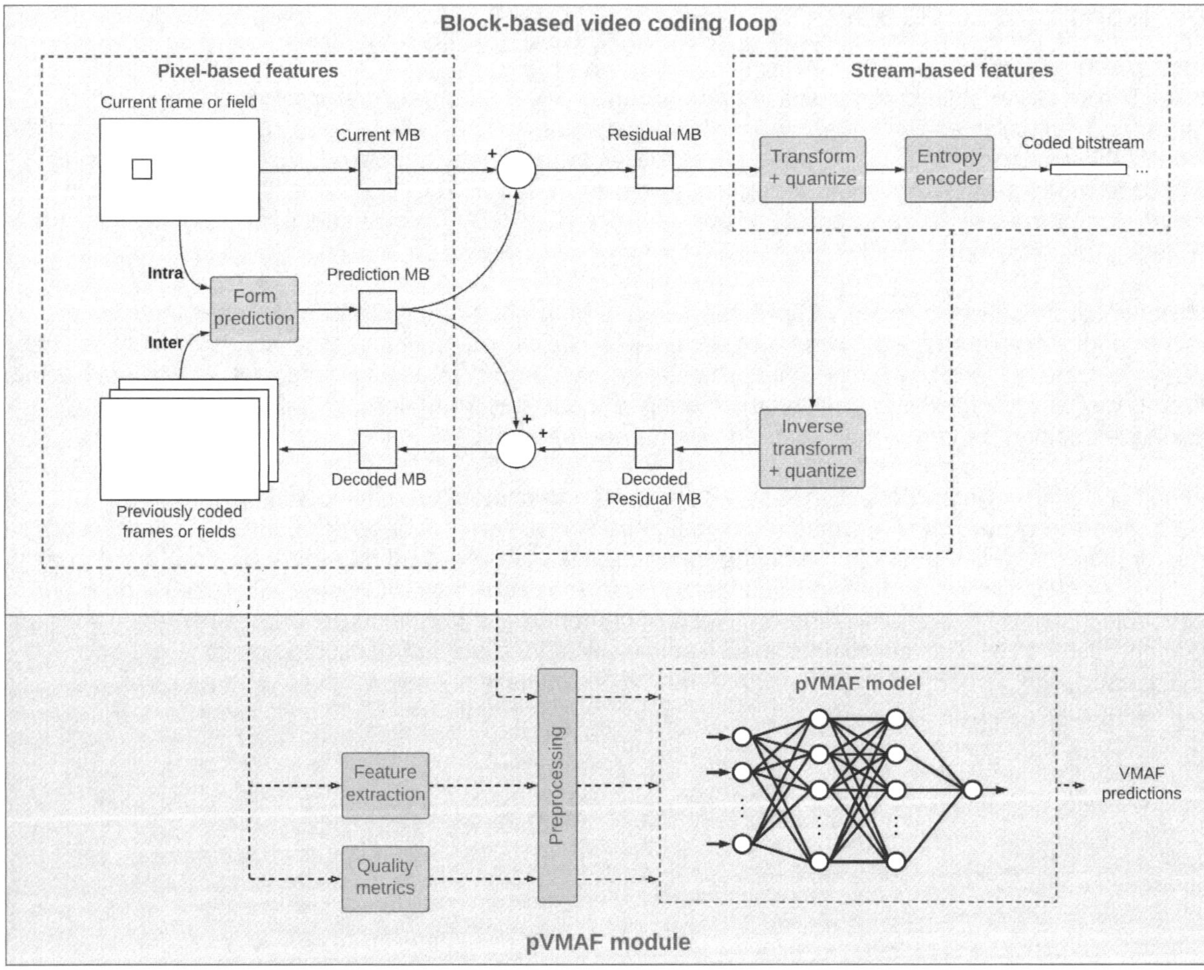

FIGURE 4: HIGH-LEVEL OVERVIEW OF PVMAF'S INTEGRATION WITHIN THE ENCODING LOOP. THIS DIAGRAM ILLUSTRATES HOW PVMAF ACCUMULATES STREAM-BASED FEATURES FROM THE ENCODING PROCESS, TOGETHER WITH PRE-ANALYSIS STATISTICS AND PSNR CALCULATIONS, TO GENERATE REAL-TIME QUALITY PREDICTIONS.

Inference

Once these features are extracted, **inference** – the process of transforming input features into a quality score – is handled by a lightweight **shallow neural network**. This architecture includes only 1-2 hidden layers, ensuring minimal computational overhead. Furthermore, by implementing Single Instruction Multiple Data (SIMD) instructions, pVMAF's efficiency is boosted further, making it highly suitable for real-time applications.

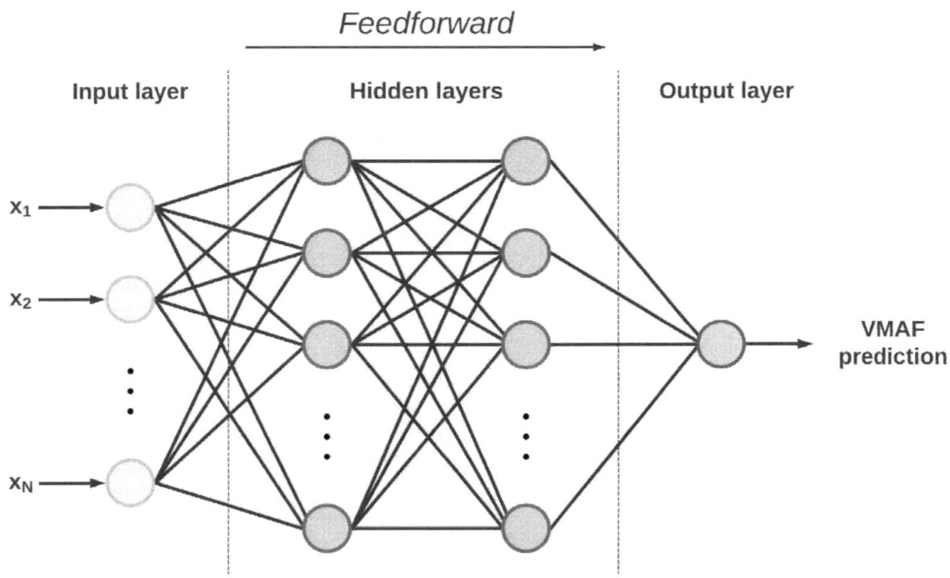

FIGURE 5: PVMAF MODEL ARCHITECTURE, CONSISTING OF A SHALLOW FEED-FORWARD NEURAL NETWORK ARCHITECTURE.

pVMAF Performance Metrics

pVMAF has been trained to closely replicate the quality predictions of VMAF, which is renowned for its accuracy but is too compute-intensive for real-time applications. When tested on a diverse dataset, pVMAF demonstrated a high correlation with VMAF scores, as seen in the performance numbers in Table 1. We report the Spearman Rank Order Correlation Coefficient (SROCC) and the Pearson Linear Correlation Coefficient (PLCC), which measure the correlation between VMAF and pVMAF, as well as the Mean Absolute Error (MAE) and the Root Mean Squared Error (RMSE) which measure the average prediction error between pVMAF scores and true VMAF scores.

Performance Metric	Frame-level	Sequence-level
SROCC	0.941	0.988
PLCC	0.947	0.985
MAE	2.75	1.34
RMSE	4.51	2.20

TABLE 1: CORRELATION COEFFICIENTS (SROCC, PLCC) AND PREDICTION ERROR MEASURES (MAE, RMSE) OF PVMAF WHEN EVALUATED AT BOTH THE FRAME-LEVEL AND SEQUENCE-LEVEL

These results highlight pVMAF's ability to deliver highly accurate VQM with only a negligible increase in CPU usage (~0.06% increase in CPU cycles for FHD encoding on a medium encoding preset) — making it ideal for real-time video quality assessment.

Use Cases

pVMAF opens the door to efficient, real-time video quality measurement during encoding, delivering VMAF-level accuracy with minimal computational overhead. This versatility makes it ideal for a range of practical applications:

- **In-depth video quality analysis**: pVMAF's frame-by-frame evaluations reveal precisely which video segments are more challenging to encode and where visual quality degradation occurs. This insight helps diagnose and troubleshoot specific encoding issues.

- **Live encoding monitoring**: pVMAF serves as a real-time monitoring tool, capable of raising alerts when video quality falls below a defined threshold. Automating quality checks reduces the need for human oversight, freeing up resources and improving operational efficiency during live broadcasts.
- **Proactive rate control**: pVMAF can also play an active role in rate control, acting as a feedback mechanism during constant-quality encoding. It informs the rate controller if the encoding process is overshooting or undershooting the target quality. This functionality is already integrated into Synamedia's **QC-VBR (Quality-Controlled Variable Bitrate)** rate control algorithm, ensuring that the target quality is consistently met without sacrificing efficiency.

Open-Sourcing pVMAF for x264

In the previous paragraphs, we introduced pVMAF, which has been integrated in Synamedia's in-house encoders. We've also adapted pVMAF for the widely used x264 encoder and made it available open-source as x264-pVMAF. In the remainder of this section, we describe its usage, performance, and future potential.

How to Use x264-pVMAF

Our customized x264 encoder (available via Github [18]) incorporates pVMAF seamlessly as an optional quality metric. Our integration was designed to keep x264's original functionality intact while adding an advanced, real-time quality measurement tool. Currently, pVMAF supports video quality measurement (VQM) for Full High-Definition (FHD) progressive video encoding with 4:2:0 chroma sampling on x264's medium preset without "tune" options enabled. By providing VMAF-like quality predictions directly within x264, this setup allows users to monitor and optimize video quality during encoding with minimal setup.

Enabling VQM with x264-pVMAF

To enable pVMAF-based quality measurement during encoding, add the --pvmaf option to the x264 command. For detailed frame-level scores, use this option along with –verbose (or -v) and –log-level debug, which will display pVMAF metrics alongside other enabled metrics. This provides real-time insights into video quality throughout the encoding process. Below is an example command:

./x264 --input-res 1920x1080 --crf 30 --input-csp i420 --fps 30 -o output.264 input.y4m --threads 10 **--pvmaf** --preset medium --verbose --log-level debug

```
x264 [debug]: frame= 286 QP=38.03 NAL=0 Slice:B Poc:70  I:44   P:3048 SKIP:5068 size=4435 bytes PSNR Y:36.14 U:42.24 V:42.84 pVMAF:78.64
x264 [debug]: frame= 287 QP=35.15 NAL=2 Slice:P Poc:80  I:1596 P:4037 SKIP:2527 size=18003 bytes PSNR Y:36.74 U:42.28 V:43.00 pVMAF:85.45
x264 [debug]: frame= 288 QP=37.10 NAL=2 Slice:B Poc:76  I:133  P:3756 SKIP:4271 size=7971 bytes PSNR Y:36.46 U:42.31 V:42.99 pVMAF:80.52
x264 [debug]: frame= 289 QP=38.24 NAL=0 Slice:B Poc:74  I:69   P:3106 SKIP:4985 size=4698 bytes PSNR Y:36.11 U:42.25 V:42.91 pVMAF:78.40
x264 [debug]: frame= 290 QP=38.14 NAL=0 Slice:B Poc:78  I:49   P:3040 SKIP:5071 size=4501 bytes PSNR Y:36.27 U:42.23 V:42.97 pVMAF:78.84
x264 [debug]: frame= 291 QP=35.45 NAL=2 Slice:P Poc:88  I:1642 P:3816 SKIP:2702 size=17000 bytes PSNR Y:36.79 U:42.30 V:42.94 pVMAF:85.05
x264 [debug]: frame= 292 QP=36.83 NAL=2 Slice:B Poc:84  I:168  P:3643 SKIP:4349 size=7751 bytes PSNR Y:36.55 U:42.33 V:42.92 pVMAF:80.49
x264 [debug]: frame= 293 QP=38.01 NAL=0 Slice:B Poc:82  I:79   P:3031 SKIP:5050 size=4672 bytes PSNR Y:36.19 U:42.24 V:42.90 pVMAF:78.28
x264 [debug]: frame= 294 QP=37.74 NAL=0 Slice:B Poc:86  I:51   P:3005 SKIP:5104 size=4299 bytes PSNR Y:36.32 U:42.31 V:42.94 pVMAF:78.37
x264 [debug]: frame= 295 QP=36.41 NAL=2 Slice:P Poc:96  I:1395 P:3783 SKIP:2982 size=15705 bytes PSNR Y:36.27 U:42.05 V:42.74 pVMAF:82.88
x264 [debug]: frame= 296 QP=36.40 NAL=2 Slice:B Poc:92  I:185  P:3778 SKIP:4197 size=7840 bytes PSNR Y:36.47 U:42.22 V:42.93 pVMAF:80.56
x264 [debug]: frame= 297 QP=37.70 NAL=0 Slice:B Poc:90  I:86   P:2914 SKIP:5160 size=4389 bytes PSNR Y:36.24 U:42.24 V:42.90 pVMAF:78.35
x264 [debug]: frame= 298 QP=37.71 NAL=0 Slice:B Poc:94  I:29   P:3214 SKIP:4917 size=4419 bytes PSNR Y:36.09 U:42.10 V:42.70 pVMAF:77.77
x264 [debug]: frame= 299 QP=38.38 NAL=2 Slice:P Poc:100 I:730  P:3252 SKIP:4178 size=9707 bytes PSNR Y:35.55 U:41.83 V:42.42 pVMAF:78.28
x264 [debug]: frame= 300 QP=37.78 NAL=0 Slice:B Poc:98  I:26   P:3250 SKIP:4884 size=4673 bytes PSNR Y:35.79 U:41.94 V:42.55 pVMAF:76.58
x264 [info]: frame I:2     Avg QP:32.28  size: 39425 pVMAF Mean:82.67  PSNR Mean Y:39.64 U:44.14 V:45.26 Avg:40.76 Global:40.64
x264 [info]: frame P:76    Avg QP:34.78  size: 15759 pVMAF Mean:81.71  PSNR Mean Y:38.21 U:43.71 V:44.63 Avg:39.45 Global:39.28
x264 [info]: frame B:223   Avg QP:36.84  size:  4331 pVMAF Mean:78.28  PSNR Mean Y:37.93 U:43.78 V:44.67 Avg:39.20 Global:39.04
x264 [info]: consecutive B-frames:  1.0%  0.7%  0.0% 98.3%
x264 [info]: mb I  I16..4: 29.3% 64.5%  6.2%
x264 [info]: mb P  I16..4:  4.7%  8.1%  0.2%  P16..4: 42.6%  4.8%  1.3%  0.0%  0.0%    skip:38.4%
x264 [info]: mb B  I16..4:  0.1%  0.1%  0.0%  B16..8: 35.1%  1.1%  0.1%  direct: 0.1%  skip:63.3%  L0:38.4% L1:61.0% BI: 0.6%
x264 [info]: 8x8 transform intra:62.4% inter:95.0%
x264 [info]: coded y,uvDC,uvAC intra: 28.3% 32.1% 4.3% inter: 4.1% 2.3% 0.0%
x264 [info]: i16 v,h,dc,p: 25% 19%  6% 50%
x264 [info]: i8 v,h,dc,ddl,ddr,vr,hd,vl,hu: 23% 11% 20%  7%  8% 10%  7% 10%  5%
x264 [info]: i4 v,h,dc,ddl,ddr,vr,hd,vl,hu: 28% 12% 15%  7% 10% 10%  7%  7%  3%
x264 [info]: i8c dc,h,v,p: 77%  7% 14%  3%
x264 [info]: Weighted P-Frames: Y:0.0% UV:0.0%
x264 [info]: ref P L0: 61.4% 17.7% 17.1%  3.8%
x264 [info]: ref B L0: 96.1%  3.2%  0.7%
x264 [info]: ref B L1: 98.9%  1.1%
x264 [info]: pVMAF Mean :79.17
x264 [info]: PSNR Mean Y:38.012 U:43.760 V:44.665 Avg:39.276 Global:39.107 kb/s:3575.75
```

FIGURE 6: ENCODING WITH PVMAF ENABLED, DISPLAYING FRAME-LEVEL PVMAF SCORES DURING ENCODING AND A QUALITY SUMMARY POST-ENCODE.

In this example, the pVMAF scores generally fall within the high 70s, which aligns with the expected quality for Quantization Parameter (QP) values in the high 30s. Along with frame-level scores, x264-pVMAF also produces an overall VQM summary at the end of encoding.

Obtain the pVMAF Log File

To generate a CSV log file that captures frame-level properties such as display picture number, QP, frame type, and pVMAF score for each frame, add the -l option in combination with –pVMAF. This log file can be particularly useful for detailed post-analysis. Here's an example command:

./x264 --input-res 1920x1080 --crf 20 --input-csp i420 --fps 30 -l pVMAF_score_log.csv -o output.264 input.y4m --threads 10 --pvmaf --preset medium --verbose --log-level debug

Creating a Comprehensive Feature Log

To output a full log of all features used by pVMAF during quality measurement, use the -g option. This works well in combination with –pvmaf and –psnr, allowing you to capture an extensive feature set for in-depth quality assessment. This detailed feature log is designed to support ongoing research, inviting exploration that may further enhance and optimize pVMAF.

Here's an example command:
./x264 –input-res 1920×1080 –crf 30 –input-csp i420 –fps 30 -g feature_file.csv -o output.264 input.y4m –threads 10 –pvmaf –psnr –preset medium –verbose –log-level debug

x264-pVMAF in Numbers

Prediction Accuracy

x264-pVMAF provides real-time visual quality assessment with VMAF-like accuracy. Trained to emulate the Full High-Definition VMAF model, x264-pVMAF achieves this precision at a significantly reduced computational cost. Table 1 demonstrates the prediction accuracy, tested across a broad and varied dataset. The performance metrics include the Spearman Rank Order Correlation Coefficient (SROCC) and the Pearson Linear Correlation Coefficient (PLCC), which indicate the correlation between x264-pVMAF and VMAF, alongside the Root Mean Squared Error (RMSE) and Mean Absolute Error (MAE), which reflect average prediction error between pVMAF scores and actual VMAF scores. The results show a strong correlation with VMAF and minimal prediction errors, underscoring the precision of pVMAF as a reliable, low-cost alternative for visual quality measurement.

Performance metric	Frame-level	Sequence-level
SROCC	0.991	0.996
PLCC	0.993	0.997
RMSE	3.7	2.48
MAE	2.51	1.65

TABLE 1: PERFORMANCE METRICS FOR X264-PVMAF REPLICATING VMAF, WITH EVALUATIONS CONDUCTED AT BOTH THE FRAME AND SEQUENCE LEVELS ACROSS A LARGE-SCALE TEST DATASET.

The scatter plot in Figure 7 further illustrates x264-pVMAF's ability to mirror VMAF accurately across a wide quality spectrum. Each dot represents a unique distorted video, with VMAF scores on the X-axis and pVMAF scores on the Y-axis, color coded by source.

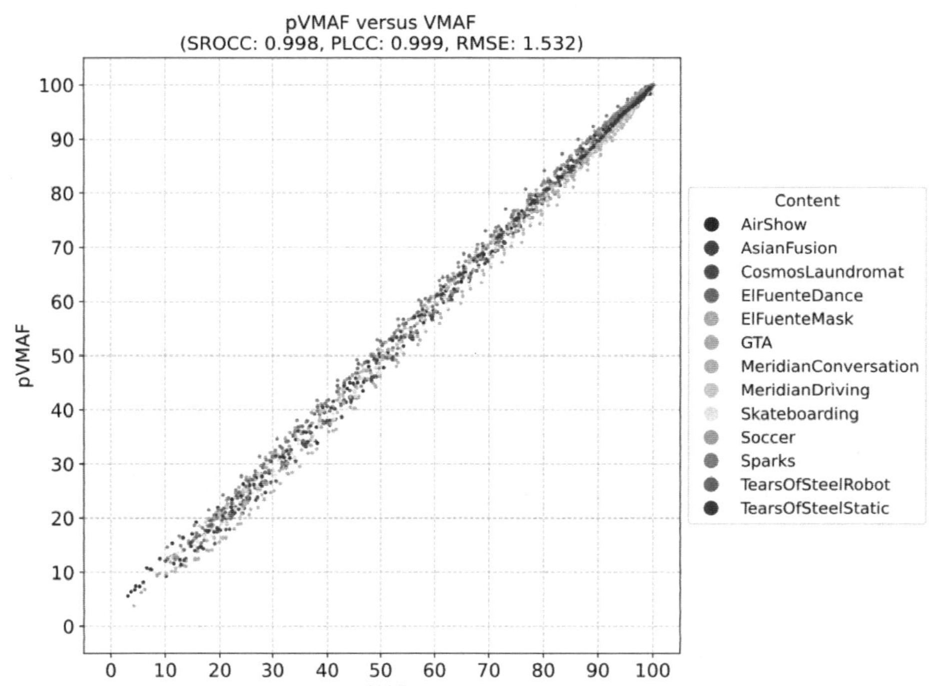

FIGURE 7: SCATTER PLOT COMPARING PVMAF AND VMAF PREDICTIONS ON THE LIVE NFLX PLUS TEST FOLD.

Computational Efficiency

Leveraging efficient feature extraction, x264-pVMAF integrates encoder parameters and lightweight pixel-based features, including PSNR on the luma component, to maintain computational efficiency. While less efficient than Synamedia's in-house pVMAF models due to x264's lack of pre-analysis statistics, x264-pVMAF can still be deployed in real time. Table 2 shows the CPU impact per FHD frame at medium preset, compared to other metrics available in x264:

VQ Metric	Increase in CPU time per FHD frame (ms)	Increase in CPU cycles per FHD frame (%)
PSNR-Y	0.54	0.43
SSIM	0.98	1.55
pVMAF	3.17	3.93

TABLE 2: CPU OVERHEAD FOR VQM METRICS IN X264, MEASURED ON THE MEDIUM PRESET.

For broader comparison, Table 3 highlights runtime per FHD frame of various metrics available in FFmpeg, including our reference metric VMAF, underscoring pVMAF's strong efficiency in comparison:

Metric	Runtime per FHD frame [ms]
PSNR	0.77
PSNR-HVS	63.8
SSIM	31.19
MS-SSIM	528.39
VMAF	112.84
pVMAF	3.17

TABLE 3: RUNTIME ANALYSIS OF VQM METRICS AVAILABLE IN FFMPEG, IN COMPARISON TO PVMAF.

The efficiency of x264-pVMAF, illustrated in Figure 8 as a scatter plot of runtime (on a logarithmic scale) versus prediction accuracy, shows how the metric offers an optimal trade-off: it's over 35 times faster than VMAF, yet provides quality predictions with a VMAF-level accuracy. Though not the absolute fastest metric, x264-pVMAF occupies a unique position by balancing speed with perceptual accuracy, making it ideal for live workflows that need accurate, real-time video quality monitoring.

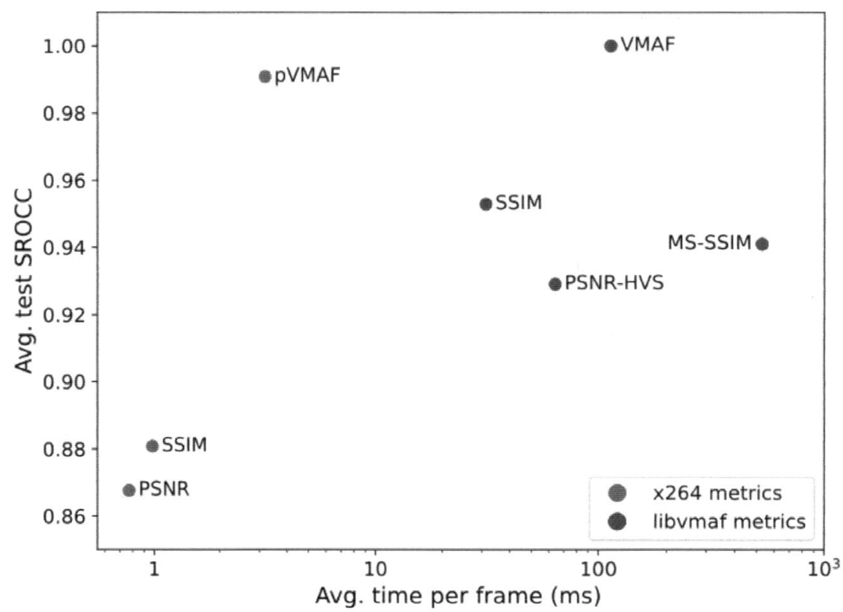

FIGURE 8: ACCURACY VERSUS RUNTIME TRADE-OFF ACROSS METRICS, WITH ACCURACY MEASURED BY FRAME-LEVEL SROCC CORRELATION TO VMAF.

Quality Tracking: Moving Beyond PSNR

While metrics like PSNR are frequently used for real-time monitoring and rate control, they don't fully capture viewer-perceived quality. As illustrated in Figure 9, where we compare frame-level PSNR, VMAF, and pVMAF scores for a distorted video (CrossWalk scene, 2048×1080, CRF 35), VMAF detects frequent quality fluctuations, which PSNR misses. pVMAF, however, closely follows VMAF's frame-level predictions, detecting subtle quality changes. This responsiveness could make pVMAF invaluable in rate control, enabling it to steer encoding quality more effectively.

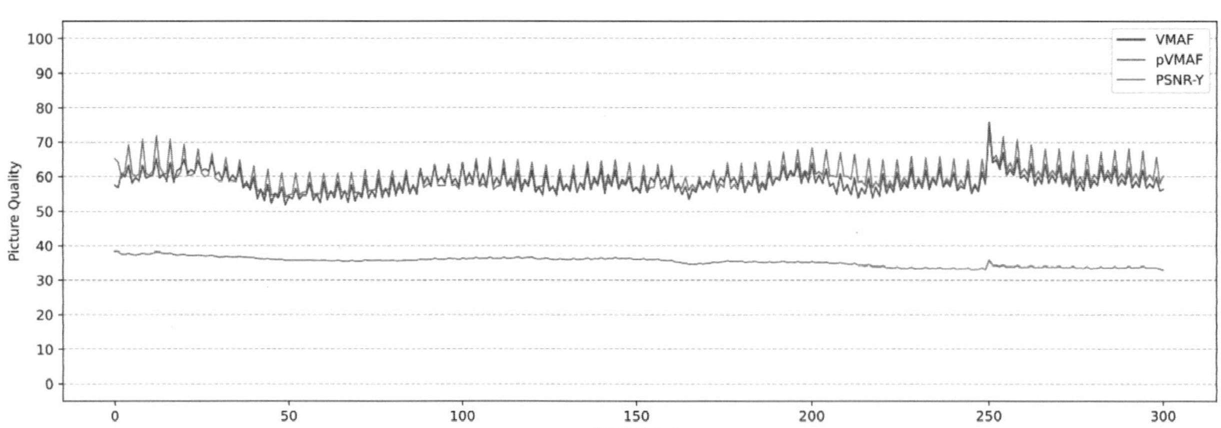

FIGURE 9: FRAME-LEVEL QUALITY SCORES FOR VMAF, PVMAF, AND PSNR-Y ON A VIDEO ENCODED WITH X264, SHOWING FLUCTUATIONS IN PERCEIVED QUALITY ACROSS FRAMES.

pVMAF for SVT-AV1: First Results

In this last section, we present the introduction of pVMAF for AV1 live streaming. Our encoder of choice is the open-source SVT-AV1 encoder, which offers a good balance between compression performance and encoder optimization. The SVT-AV1 project was initially founded by Intel in partnership with Netflix and was then adopted by the Alliance of Open Media (AOM) Software Implementation Working Group (SIWG) [19].

We applied the same methodology as described above to identify relevant features, fuse them in a shallow network, and predict VMAF scores for AV1 encoding. First results indicate that we can achieve a high correlation for pVMAF, at similar computational cost as for x264. This is illustrated in Figure 10, highlighting the strong PLCC and SROCC correlation values for a wide variety of test clips.

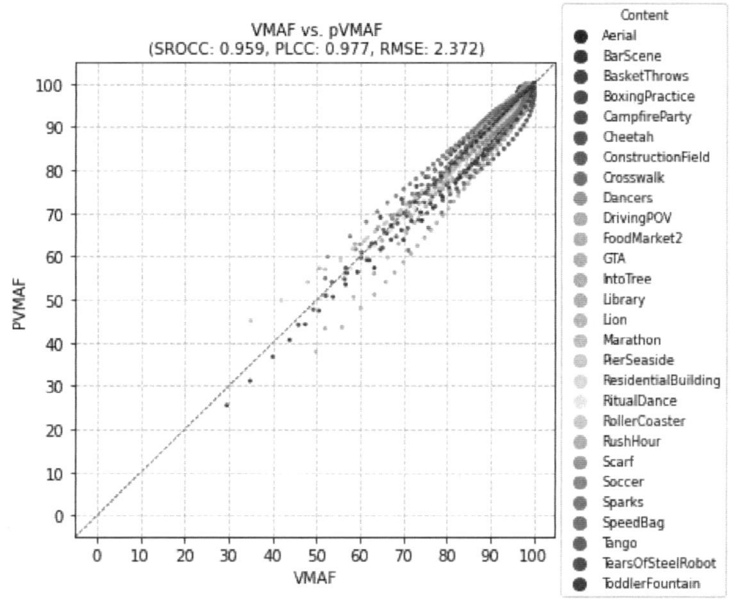

FIGURE 10: SCATTER PLOT COMPARING PVMAF AND VMAF PREDICTIONS ON A WIDE VARIETY OF TEST CONTENT.

In terms of computational complexity, we evaluated a range of SVT-AV1 presets that offer fast enough encoding for live streaming (presets 8-10). In this range, we measured an increase between 2.4% and 6.1% when enabling pVMAF. Interestingly, the overhead for calculating pVMAF is 7x lower than the cost of PSNR and SSIM calculation, which is offered as an option during SVT-AV1 encoding (by using "--enable-stat-report"). Similar as for x264 (cf. Figure 7), we are obtaining higher correlation than other metrics at a much lower computational cost.

Preset	Metric	Time increase per frame (ms)	% increase in encode time per frame
8	PSNR + SSIM	22.40	17.14%
	pVMAF	3.14	2.39%
9	PSNR + SSIM	23.90	28.88%
	pVMAF	3.75	4.52%
10	PSNR + SSIM	24.20	38.39%
	pVMAF	3.84	6.10%

TABLE 4: CPU OVERHEAD FOR VQM METRICS IN SVT-AV1, MEASURED ON DIFFERENT PRESETS.

Conclusions

In this paper, we have given a brief overview of VQ measurement, highlighting the difficult balance between accuracy of VQ metrics and their complexity.
By introducing pVMAF inside the encoding loop, we've reached a better sweet spot than most available metrics, making it possible to approximate VMAF with high correlation for real-time applications.
We illustrated the strengths of pVMAF for both x264 and SVT-AV1, and have made x264-pVMAF available open-source to encourage further research in this direction. Stay tuned for further announcements around other code base implementations.

References

[1] A. De Decker, J. De Cock, P. Lambert and G. V. Wallendael, "No-Reference VMAF: A Deep Neural Network-Based Approach to Blind Video Quality Assessment," in IEEE Transactions on Broadcasting, vol. 70, no. 3, pp. 844-861, Sept. 2024.

[2] M. H. Pinson, "Why No Reference Metrics for Image and Video Quality Lack Accuracy and Reproducibility," in IEEE Transactions on Broadcasting, vol. 69, no. 1, pp. 97-117, March 2023.

[3] Z. Wang and A. C. Bovik, "Mean squared error: Love it or leave it? A new look at Signal Fidelity Measures," in IEEE Signal Processing Magazine, vol. 26, no. 1, pp. 98-117, Jan. 2009.

[4] Zhou Wang, A. C. Bovik, H. R. Sheikh and E. P. Simoncelli, "Image quality assessment: from error visibility to structural similarity," in IEEE Transactions on Image Processing, vol. 13, no. 4, pp. 600-612, April 2004.

[5] Z. Wang, E. P. Simoncelli and A. C. Bovik, "Multiscale structural similarity for image quality assessment," The Thrity-Seventh Asilomar Conference on Signals, Systems & Computers, 2003, Pacific Grove, CA, USA, 2003, pp. 1398-1402 Vol.2.

[6] A. K. Venkataramanan, C. Wu, A. C. Bovik, I. Katsavounidis and Z. Shahid, "A Hitchhiker's Guide to Structural Similarity," in IEEE Access, vol. 9, pp. 28872-28896, 2021.

[7] S. Li, F. Zhang, L. Ma and K. N. Ngan, "Image Quality Assessment by Separately Evaluating Detail Losses and Additive Impairments," in IEEE Transactions on Multimedia, vol. 13, no. 5, pp. 935-949, Oct. 2011.

[8] H. R. Sheikh and A. C. Bovik, "Image information and visual quality," in IEEE Transactions on Image Processing, vol. 15, no. 2, pp. 430-444, Feb. 2006.

[9] Zhi Li, Anne Aaron, Ioannis Katsavounidis, Anush Moorthy and Megha Manohara, "Toward A Practical Perceptual Video Quality Metric", Netflix Technology Blog, June 2016.

[10] Source code for VMAF – Video Multi-Method Assessment Fusion, available through https://github.com/Netflix/vmaf.

[11] F. Zhang, A. Katsenou, C. Bampis, L. Krasula, Z. Li and D. Bull, "Enhancing VMAF through New Feature Integration and Model Combination," 2021 Picture Coding Symposium (PCS), Bristol, United Kingdom, 2021, pp. 1-5.

[12] Megha Manohara, Anush Moorthy, Jan De Cock, Ioannis Katsavounidis and Anne Aaron, "Optimized shot-based encodes: Now Streaming!", Netflix Technology Blog, March 2018.

[13] Zhi Li, Kyle Swanson, Christos Bampis, Lukáš Krasula and Anne Aaron, "Toward a Better Quality Metric for the Video Community", Netflix Technology Blog, December 2020.

[14] Joel Sole, Mariana Afonso, Lukas Krasula, Zhi Li, and Pulkit Tandon, "CAMBI, a banding artifact detector", Netflix Technology Blog, October 2021

[15] K. Venkataramanan, C. Stejerean and A. C. Bovik, "FUNQUE: Fusion of Unified Quality Evaluators," 2022 IEEE International Conference on Image Processing (ICIP), Bordeaux, France, 2022, pp. 2147-2151.

[16] A. K. Venkataramanan, C. Stejerean, I. Katsavounidis and A. C. Bovik, "One Transform to Compute Them All: Efficient Fusion-Based Full-Reference Video Quality Assessment," in IEEE Transactions on Image Processing, vol. 33, pp. 509-524, 2024.

[17] C. R. Helmrich, M. Siekmann, S. Becker, S. Bosse, D. Marpe and T. Wiegand, "Xpsnr: A Low-Complexity Extension of The Perceptually Weighted Peak Signal-To-Noise Ratio For High-Resolution Video Quality Assessment," 2020 IEEE International Conference on Acoustics, Speech and Signal Processing (ICASSP), pp. 2727-2731.

[18] x264-pVMAF Github repository, available at https://github.com/quortex/x264-pVMAF.

[19] SVT-AV1 Github repository, available at https://gitlab.com/AOMediaCodec/SVT-AV1.

The Liability of Elasticity

John Guntenaar, Daniel Murphy, Jorge Llano
NEP Group
Pittsburgh, Pennsylvania, United States

Abstract – The shift to software-driven cloud infrastructure in the media and entertainment industry offers powerful scalability but introduces complex security challenges. Dynamic scaling capabilities—essential for handling variable demand—expand potential attack surfaces and create risks in tenant isolation, data segregation, and cross-tenant security. Traditional, static security approaches fall short in this fluid environment, necessitating innovative solutions that anticipate inevitable breaches and focus on minimizing the blast radius.

This paper examines critical vulnerabilities that can drive up costs by exploiting elasticity and emphasizes the need for fast detection, segregation of duties, technical standards, and response mechanisms. By adopting lessons from tech sectors and implementing robust, responsive security frameworks, companies can harness elasticity without compromising operational integrity or security.

Introduction

This paper explores the primary risks associated with elastic infrastructures which can exploit scaling features to trigger lateral expansion, resulting in unanticipated operational costs and potential service disruptions. A key focus will be on securing connectivity and controlling the "blast radius," minimizing the scope of impact from potential breaches by implementing strict isolation and containment strategies within and between tenants. Additionally, we discuss the unique requirements for effective incident detection and response within an elastic environment, emphasizing the importance of fast response times, thorough auditing, and continuous monitoring.

Elastic architectures demand new approaches to cybersecurity that adapt to their inherent dynamism. Traditional installations relied on physical segregation and infrequent updates, yet cloud-based systems require a mindset shift toward anticipating inevitable failures and attacks. We advocate for a comprehensive security framework including supplier assessments, as well as adopting best practices from industries like fintech and e-commerce, which have pioneered robust responses to cloud vulnerabilities. By focusing on modular incident response training, playbook development, and automated alert systems, companies can protect themselves in a landscape where threats evolve as rapidly as the infrastructure.

Ultimately, "The Liability of Elasticity" calls for a new cybersecurity paradigm, one that balances elasticity with robust security protocols, tenant isolation, and rapid response mechanisms. We aim to provide a blueprint for broadcasters and media companies navigating the challenges and opportunities of elastic cloud environments. This includes actionable insights into reducing exposure to cross-tenant risks, developing strong governance over dynamically deployed assets, and ensuring that security measures scale in parallel with elasticity, safeguarding both operations and reputations.

Challenges in Tenant Isolation

As broadcast organizations shift toward elastic and cloud-based infrastructures to enhance flexibility, rapid deployment, and dynamic scaling, the need for robust isolation becomes ever more critical. Traditional setups relied on physically segregated hardware to prevent unauthorized data access or accidental cross-contamination, but today's environments typically involve logically segmented resources that may be ephemeral and dynamically allocated. This can introduce an array of isolation-related challenges, from inadvertent data leakage to threats like side-channel attacks and workload interference. In this section, we examine the unique security, compliance, and operational hurdles that arise when isolation depends on virtual boundaries rather than physical ones, illustrating why careful segmentation strategies and proactive security controls are critical for modern broadcast environments.

Data Leakage Risks

The adoption of elastic production infrastructures sees the shift from physically isolated broadcast environments to multi-tenant architectures, where resources are shared across multiple productions, clients, and even external partners. This shift introduces complex challenges in tenant isolation, where logical separation must be enforced between different users and production teams operating within the same infrastructure. The separation of the hardware from the users creates an immediate trust barrier where the responsibility is on the infrastructure provider to ensure an even greater level of security and assurance than currently is standard for much of the broadcast industry. Without robust segmentation mechanisms, media assets, metadata, and real-time processing workloads risk data leakage, cross-tenant access violations, and security breaches.

In traditional broadcast environments, tenant isolation was largely achieved through physical separation, with dedicated equipment, networks, and storage assigned to specific productions. The move to cloud-based and elastic media infrastructures, whether private on-premise or publicly hosted, has made logical isolation the primary method of tenant segregation. However, misconfigurations in identity management, resource allocation, and access policies can result in unintentional data exposure. Studies in cloud security have identified that improper identity and access management (IAM) configurations are among the leading causes of data leaks in multi-tenant environments [18]. In an elastic broadcast environment, where resources such as compute power, video processing nodes, and storage are dynamically allocated, ensuring strong tenant isolation is critical to prevent unauthorized access to sensitive production data.

One of the main challenges in tenant isolation is cross-tenant data leakage due to misconfigured access controls and improperly segmented storage environments. In a cloud-based media infrastructure, tenants often share virtualized compute and storage resources, and if proper isolation mechanisms are not in place, a production or client may gain unauthorized access to another tenant's content, raw footage, editing projects, transcoded assets, or proprietary metadata. This issue is particularly concerning in media post-production workflows, where multiple stakeholders—including production companies, post-production houses, and third-party editors—collaborate within the same environment. Studies on multi-tenant security in cloud computing have shown that insufficient role-based access control (RBAC) policies and weak identity segmentation can lead to data exposure across tenants, increasing the risk of intellectual property theft and unauthorized content distribution [12].

Another significant risk factor in tenant isolation failures is side-channel attacks, where an adversary within a shared infrastructure can infer or extract information about another tenant's workload. In media production environments, this could lead to unauthorized insights into high-profile productions, pre-release content leaks, or unauthorized monitoring of editing and rendering workflows. While traditional IT security measures often focus on network segmentation and access controls, modern tenant isolation strategies must also address resource-level threats, such as CPU cache side-channel attacks, memory-based inference attacks, and metadata exfiltration risks.

Inadequate isolation of processing workloads presents another serious challenge in elastic broadcast infrastructures. In dynamic cloud environments, media encoding, AI-driven content analysis, and real-time graphics rendering often run on shared compute nodes. If sandboxing mechanisms are not properly enforced, one tenant's workloads could impact or interact with another tenant's processes, leading to performance degradation, unauthorized data exposure, or workload interference. The risks are further amplified when public cloud resources are integrated into broadcast environments, as cloud-based AI models and GPU-intensive workloads must operate alongside other tenants' media processing tasks, increasing the need for secure execution environments [1].

Compliance Requirements

A thorough comprehension of the security and operation of cloud services is necessary to fully understand the compliance issues for tenant isolation in cloud infrastructures, especially in multi-tenant environments.

Preventing data leaking between tenants is the main goal of tenant isolation. This entails using advanced access control methods that specify who can access what data, putting encryption solutions into place that guarantee data cannot be read by other tenants, and making sure shared resources like caches and snapshots are managed securely.

All actions made by any administrator or tenant within the cloud environment must be recorded to create safe and thorough audit trails. To offer a clear trail for forensic and compliance purposes, these logs need to be time-stamped, unchangeable, and securely stored. Prompt identification and response to possible security problems are facilitated by efficient logging and monitoring systems.

The General Data Protection Regulation, or GDPR, places stringent standards on data protection and privacy for businesses that operate in or offer services to clients in the European Union. One important aspect of tenant isolation is taking precautions to guarantee that data is not accessed or used by unauthorized parties.

Establishing an information security management system (ISMS) based on the international standard ISO/IEC 27001 can allow organizations to evaluate and manage information security threats. ISO27001 covers topics that are essential for tenant separation for cloud providers, such as data encryption, access control, and security procedures.

Leveraging Immutable Cloud Technology

As modern broadcasting and media operations increasingly shift to the cloud—or adopt cloud-native methodologies—embracing immutability has emerged as a transformative approach to managing infrastructure at scale. By deploying fresh instances for each software update, rather than patching or updating existing servers, organizations can significantly streamline version management, reduce configuration drift, and enhance overall resilience. This section examines how creating and relying on "golden images" helps teams quickly spin up, tear down, and audit systems in fast-moving, elastic environments, and highlights the advantages of short-lived instances through the "cattle vs. pets" analogy. Additionally, we explore how Infrastructure as Code (IaC) intertwines with these principles to automate deployments, minimize manual errors, and enable consistent security practices. While these methods unlock new levels of flexibility and efficiency, they also bring challenges, such as heightened build complexity and rigorous testing requirements. The following sections delve into both the opportunities and considerations that make immutable, code-driven infrastructure a centerpiece of next-generation media workflows.

Immutable infrastructure

When using immutable infrastructure, one creates new servers or computing instances with each deployment of software, rather than modifying ("mutating") existing ones. Once an image (or template) is defined (for instance, a virtual machine image or a container), it is deployed "as is". Any required updates or changes occur by creating a new image from an updated base, then "spinning up" fresh instances while "destroying" old ones. With an immutable image-based deployment, using virtual machines or containers, rolling back a system to a known good image is simpler when compared to patching a live system, done through downgrading of software, which could result in complex downgrades procedures and management of system dependencies.

This methodology of frequently replacing infrastructure uses software tools (Infrastructure as Code) to automate and codify changes. This ensures version control and repeatability of infrastructure, changes and deployments, and minimizes "configuration drift", reducing the likelihood that outdated servers remain [2].

However, immutable infrastructure has risks and challenges associated with it when not handled correctly. While each deployment of infrastructure is considered "clean", it increases build complexity. Teams must maintain build pipelines, testing suites, and orchestration logic. When tests are not conducted properly, it can lead to large-scale impact where new instances inherit configuration faults that have slipped into the image that then propagates widely [3]. As instances are intended to only be short-lived, the extra effort to retain historical logs at a centralized facility needs to be considered. Frequent instance turnover can make it harder to maintain continuous logs and track system state over time [4].

Additional focus needs to be put in the base images used, often referred to as "golden images" and make sure they are fully up-to-date and patched. Any vulnerability in the base image is multiplied across the entire infrastructure [5]. Regular scanning of an environment using vulnerability scans becomes less practical. Because instances are short-lived, the benefit of doing regular scans on these instances is limited, making the process of patch management and tracking security advisories in the golden images crucial.

The mindset of development has evolved hand in hand with the shift towards elastic, cloud-based environments, fundamentally changing how systems are built, deployed, and maintained. Immutable deployments, whether using container platforms like Docker or virtual machine templates, reduce the risk of lingering misconfigurations by discarding old instances rather than patching or upgrading them in place. When combined with container or virtual machine isolation, each ephemeral instance operates in a stateless fashion, limiting the "blast radius" of any single vulnerability or misconfiguration. This approach not only simplifies rollback procedures—since teams can revert to a previously verified image instead of orchestrating complex software downgrades—but also streamlines scaling by allowing new instances to be spun up in response to fluctuating demand. Short-lived instances align well with security best practices.

However, this rapid churn of resources also creates new challenges, such as the need for centralized logging and rigorous golden image management, where every updated base image must undergo thorough scanning and testing before it is propagated across production environments. Despite these complexities, the resulting agility drives a shift in how broadcast and media organizations can build and operate their systems in an increasingly dynamic infrastructure landscape.

Infrastructure as Code (IaC)

Infrastructure as Code (IaC) is the practice of provisioning and managing computing resources through machine-readable configuration files rather than manual processes. By treating infrastructure like software, where every change is versioned in a source code repository, teams can implement automated build pipelines and peer reviews [6]. Through IaC, organizations minimize configuration drift and reduce the chance of human error, resulting in faster deployments, greater standardization, and improved collaboration.

```
terraform {
```

```
  required_version = ">= 1.0.0"
  required_providers {
    aws = {
      source  = "hashicorp/aws"
      version = "~> 4.0"
    }
  }
}

provider "aws" {
  region  = "us-east-1"
  profile = "default"
}

data "aws_vpc" "default" {
  default = true
}

resource "aws_default_vpc" "default" {}

resource "aws_security_group" "web_sg" {
  name        = "short-web-sg"
  vpc_id      = aws_default_vpc.default.id
  description = "Allow inbound HTTP"

  ingress {
    from_port   = 80
    to_port     = 80
    protocol    = "tcp"
    cidr_blocks = ["0.0.0.0/0"]
  }

  egress {
    from_port   = 0
    to_port     = 0
    protocol    = "-1"
    cidr_blocks = ["0.0.0.0/0"]
  }

  tags = { Name = "ExampleSG" }
}

resource "aws_instance" "web_server" {
  ami                    = "ami-08c40ec9ead489470"
  instance_type          = "t2.micro"
  vpc_security_group_ids = [aws_security_group.web_sg.id]

  tags = { Name = "TestServer" }

  user_data = <<-EOF
    #!/bin/bash
    yum update -y && yum install httpd -y && service httpd start
    echo "Hello World! I should use HTTPS instead of HTTP!" > /var/www/html/index.html
    EOF
}
```

FIGURE 1: SIMPLE INFRASTRUCTURE AS CODE EXAMPLE USING TERRAFORM

One of the most significant advantages IaC brings is repeatability. Manually spinning up servers introduces inconsistencies in operating system versions, security settings, or patch levels, limiting scalability and increasing potential security risks. By contrast, standardized templates enable organizations to deploy consistent infrastructure across different environments or clouds [7]. Because the entire configuration is stored as code, automated testing and security scans can be integrated into CI/CD pipelines, enabling a “shift-left” security strategy [3].

Despite its benefits, IaC demands discipline to avoid widespread misconfigurations. A single error can propagate rapidly when infrastructure is rebuilt from a shared template [3]. To mitigate this risk, teams should incorporate code reviews, validation tools (e.g. Terraform Sentinel, Open Policy Agent), and rigorous testing into every deployment pipeline.

Additionally, secret management becomes critical. Storing credentials in version-controlled infrastructure files can unintentionally expose them to unauthorized parties [5]. Using a secure vault (e.g., HashiCorp Vault, AWS Secrets Manager) and automating secret rotation are essential for minimizing vulnerabilities, limiting the attack surface, and confidently relying on IaC to deliver a highly available, on-demand infrastructure.

Tenant Isolation with Elasticity (or, Elastic Tenant Isolation)

As broadcasting environments grow increasingly elastic, the traditional boundaries that once separated tenants and productions are replaced with shared infrastructure, rapidly spun-up compute resources, and dynamically allocated network paths. This shift creates opportunities for on-demand scalability, centralized resource pools, and global collaboration. Yet it also opens the door to security concerns. In this section, we explore how the nature of virtualized and containerized workloads, the flexible allocation of memory and bandwidth, and the evolving requirements for data isolation each influence the new realities of tenant isolation. By highlighting both the vulnerabilities that arise when resources are provisioned at the click of a button and the strategies required to maintain tight logical boundaries, we aim to illustrate why tenant isolation must remain a central pillar of any resilient, future-ready broadcast infrastructure.

Dynamic Resource Allocation

Elastic infrastructure introduced unprecedented flexibility, enabling centralized and remote production models to scale efficiently across multiple facilities, data centers, and cloud infrastructures. Traditional centralized production or REMI facilities benefit from utilization increases when a central pool of equipment can be "checked out" to different productions at different times. The ability to dynamically create workloads from low-level resources, like compute, memory, and bandwidth, and to burst capacity into other public or private cloud-connected datacenters, allows virtually limitless scaling to occur.

While this model significantly enhances resource efficiency and operational resilience, it also introduces substantial security risks that must be carefully mitigated to ensure the availability, integrity, and confidentiality of live and on-demand broadcasts.

One of the primary security challenges in elastic media workflows is compute resource exploitation. Unlike traditional production environments, where dedicated hardware is pre-allocated, dynamic allocation relies on virtualized and containerized workloads that are assigned on demand. Without proper authentication and workload validation, adversaries may hijack compute resources for unauthorized workloads, leading to resource exhaustion, cryptojacking, or covert data exfiltration. For example, malicious actors may deploy rogue virtual machines within the resource pool, consuming CPU and GPU cycles needed for live encoding, graphics rendering, or signal processing. These unauthorized workloads not only degrade performance but can also introduce malicious code into the broadcast chain, potentially compromising the integrity of live production feeds [8]. To mitigate these risks, robust role-based access control (RBAC) and least-privilege access policies must be enforced to ensure that only authenticated and authorized workloads are executed. Additionally, hardware-assisted trusted execution environments (TEE), can be utilized to isolate critical workloads from unauthorized processes, ensuring that dynamic resource allocation does not introduce new vulnerabilities.

Memory security is another significant concern in dynamic broadcast infrastructures. The on-the-fly provisioning of shared memory pools for video buffering, transcoding metadata, and low-latency processing can expose sensitive information if memory isolation is not strictly enforced. In conventional systems, dedicated memory pools per production ensured clear separation between workloads. However, in an elastic environment, dynamically allocated memory can be reused across multiple productions, increasing the risk of data leakage and unauthorized memory access. Threats such as side-channel attacks and memory remanence become particularly relevant in multi-tenant environments, where one production might inadvertently access residual data from a previously allocated memory segment. To mitigate these risks, automated memory zeroization must be implemented, ensuring that allocated memory is securely erased before being reassigned. Additionally, real-time memory encryption and hardware-enforced memory segmentation should be employed to prevent unauthorized cross-process memory access [18].

The dynamic allocation of network bandwidth in elastic broadcast environments also presents unique security challenges. Remote production workflows rely on high-bandwidth, low-latency transmission of SMPTE ST 2110 uncompressed video and compressed streaming protocols such as SRT, RIST, and Zixi. When bandwidth allocation is elastic, improper management can lead to network congestion, starvation of critical real-time traffic, and potential denial-of-service (DoS) conditions. Malicious actors could exploit dynamic bandwidth provisioning by requesting excessive bandwidth resources, either as a direct attack or through misconfigured automation scripts, leading to service degradation for legitimate productions. Additionally, unauthorized access to dynamic bandwidth provisioning systems could allow an attacker to prioritize non-critical traffic over live broadcast feeds, disrupting high-profile productions. To mitigate these risks, software-defined networking (SDN) policies should be employed to ensure that bandwidth quotas and priority queues are dynamically enforced. Furthermore, real-time network telemetry and anomaly detection should be implemented to identify unusual bandwidth consumption patterns that may indicate an ongoing attack [9].

The ephemeral nature of dynamically allocated resources necessitates a rethinking of disaster recovery (DR) strategies in elastic broadcast infrastructures. Traditional DR models were designed around statically provisioned failover sites and backup servers, ensuring predefined redundancy in case of failure. However, in a highly dynamic environment, where resources are spun up and deallocated on demand, DR strategies must incorporate real-time provisioning and failover automation. One of the key challenges is ensuring that failed compute, memory, or network resources can be seamlessly replaced without disrupting live production workflows. Inadequate DR implementation may result in orphaned workloads, desynchronized failover processes, or prolonged production outages. To address this, resources can be pre-provisioned for immediate failover. However, the best practice architecture supports n+x redundancy, where parallel nodes process tasks and the outputs can be seamlessly consumed by downstream processes in the workflow. Guidance to these High Availability (HA) architectures should be taken from other industries where protocols such as Equal Cost Multi-Path (ECMP) and technologies like RDMA over Converged Ethernet (RoCE) are frequently used. Additionally, multi-cloud redundancy architectures should be leveraged to enable automatic failover between on-premises data centers and cloud-based infrastructure, ensuring high availability even in cases of large-scale disruptions [10].

Beyond disaster recovery, securing the integrity of elastic resource allocation requires the implementation of comprehensive monitoring and governance frameworks. Real-time monitoring systems must track resource utilization, access patterns, and workload behaviors to detect anomalous activities that may indicate a security breach. For instance, unusual spikes in compute requests, memory reallocations, or bandwidth consumption could be indicative of cryptojacking, unauthorized AI model training, or DDoS amplification attacks. By integrating AI-driven anomaly detection with automated response mechanisms, security teams can proactively mitigate potential threats before they impact live production environments. Additionally, immutable logging and blockchain-based integrity verification can be used to ensure that resource allocation records remain tamper-proof, providing a verifiable audit trail for forensic investigations in the event of a security incident [11].

To further enhance security, confidential computing environments should be employed for handling highly sensitive production workloads. Technologies such as secure enclaves and hardware root of trust mechanisms can prevent unauthorized modifications to dynamically allocated compute resources, ensuring that critical rendering, transcoding, and encoding processes remain protected from external manipulation. Additionally, automated workload attestation should be enforced to verify the authenticity of software images before they are dynamically instantiated, reducing the risk of supply chain attacks where maliciously altered workloads are injected into the broadcast infrastructure.

Network Isolation

Network isolation has traditionally been a cornerstone of broadcast infrastructure security, with air-gapped networks providing a straightforward means of segmentation. This model ensures that different operational domains—such as media asset management, storage, real-time broadcast streaming (e.g., SMPTE ST 2110), compressed streaming (e.g., SRT), playout systems, and cloud interfaces—remain physically and logically distinct. By isolating critical workflows, the blast radius of potential security incidents can be effectively contained, simplifying administration and reducing the risk of cross-system compromise.

However, the shift toward elastic architectures fundamentally challenges this static approach [12]. Elastic infrastructures are designed to dynamically scale resources up or down based on demand, necessitating the continuous creation and destruction of networked environments. While traditional air-gapped networks provide strong security guarantees, they are inherently rigid, requiring extensive manual intervention, physical hardware reconfiguration, and ongoing documentation updates to reflect infrastructure changes [13].

This rigidity poses both financial and operational challenges. Maintaining dedicated physical hardware for each environment—such as separate networks for control rooms, studios, and remote production trucks—quickly becomes cost-prohibitive and operationally inefficient. As elasticity drives an increase in the number of dynamically provisioned resources, network configurations must be fluid yet secure, a contradiction that legacy network isolation models struggle to accommodate.

Furthermore, the expanding network footprint created by static air-gapping introduces significant security risks. A sprawling, manually managed infrastructure becomes increasingly difficult to monitor, secure, and maintain, leading to blind spots in network visibility, outdated documentation, and misconfigured access controls. Without adaptive segmentation strategies, the very controls intended to enhance security can, paradoxically, increase the attack surface, exposing the organization to insider threats, misconfigurations, and lateral movement of malicious actors [13].

In response, elastic environments require a shift from physical to logical isolation models. Technologies such as zero-trust networking (ZTN), software-defined networking (SDN), and network segmentation through micro-segmentation and identity-based policies offer more scalable alternatives. These approaches enable on-demand segmentation, automated enforcement of access policies, and continuous monitoring to detect and mitigate potential threats as they emerge [14].

The challenge, therefore, is not just achieving isolation but doing so in a way that aligns with the fluid, software-defined nature of elastic architectures. A modernized approach to network security must balance dynamic scalability with robust segmentation controls, ensuring that elasticity does not become an avenue for increased exposure.

An additional complexity in network isolation is the difference between on-premises cloud environments and public cloud deployments. In an on-premises environment, network controls are typically more direct and customizable, with administrators having full control over routing, firewall rules, and physical segmentation. However, when extending into a public cloud, network isolation must be approached differently due to the unavoidable need for internet exposure.

Even with direct cloud connectivity options—such as AWS Direct Connect or Azure ExpressRoute—public cloud deployments often require some level of internet access. This is especially true for licensing services, API calls to third-party applications and software updates. Unlike on-premises environments, where internet connectivity can be entirely restricted, public cloud infrastructure necessitates a structured approach to how and where internet access is allowed.

The best practice in public cloud isolation is to isolate networks with logical segmentation, ensuring that internet access is provided to hosts and workloads only where necessary. This follows the principle of least privilege, where:

1. Direct internet access is blocked by default, only permitted as an exception.
2. Internet-facing services are tightly controlled, using dedicated networks with strict ingress and egress rules.
3. Outbound internet traffic is limited to only approved endpoints, ensuring that software repositories, licensing services, and critical dependencies can function while blocking unnecessary exposure.
4. Traffic inspection and logging are enforced, monitoring all internet-bound requests for anomalies or unauthorized activity.

For organizations relying on public repositories and software dependencies, controlled proxying or private repository mirroring can help reduce direct internet exposure while ensuring that software updates remain available when needed, known as Software Supply Chain Security [15].

One last consideration in isolation is dealing with multi-tenant or multi-production environments. Traditionally, creating a new project or production environment involved assembling a team, provisioning dedicated infrastructure, and isolating it for the duration of the project. Once the project concluded, the system could either be decommissioned, repurposed, or reassigned to another client. This process ensured natural physical separation between projects, limiting the risk of cross-client data exposure or network conflicts. However, in an elastic infrastructure, where environments can be dynamically created and scaled at the press of a button, the traditional approach to network isolation is no longer viable.

As multi-tenant and multi-production workflows move toward shared, software-defined infrastructure, network segmentation must evolve to accommodate rapid provisioning and decommissioning. A critical consideration in this model is defining which types of traffic can safely coexist on the same physical or virtual network. If multiple clients or productions share the same underlying infrastructure, logical separation must be enforced at the network layer, ensuring that tenant traffic remains isolated and protected, even when operating over shared physical connections [16].

To achieve this, network isolation in multi-tenant environments must address several key challenges:

1. Traffic Segmentation: Ensuring that traffic from one tenant never inadvertently crosses into another's domain, even when operating on shared hardware or virtual networks. This requires strong VLAN separation, VRFs (Virtual Routing and Forwarding), or software-defined overlays to isolate data paths.
2. Policy-Driven Access Controls: Manual network configurations introduce human error, making automated, software-defined perimeters (SDP) essential. These allow access policies to be enforced dynamically, granting tenants the ability to share only what they explicitly intend to share while keeping all private resources isolated. User interfaces should allow authorized users themselves should ideally be able to control access to their traffic [17].
3. Security at the Edge: As multi-tenant environments increasingly span across on-premises data centers and public cloud infrastructure, security policies must be consistent across hybrid deployments. Secure tunnels, identity-based access, and encrypted overlays help maintain end-to-end isolation, even across disparate locations.
4. Dynamic Isolation Rules: Unlike static air-gapped networks, modern architectures require real-time segmentation adjustments. This means network isolation policies must be software-driven, with APIs that allow for dynamic rule creation as tenants come and go, minimizing attack surfaces while maintaining operational flexibility.

5. Minimal Exposure During Transit: Traffic traversing the network—whether moving between cloud regions or across private backbones—must be minimized in scope. This includes limiting direct internet exposure, enforcing ingress/egress filtering, and ensuring cross-tenant communication is explicitly permitted, rather than assumed.

Securing multi-tenant network isolation in an elastic architecture requires real-time enforcement of access policies, automated response mechanisms, and clear governance over shared resources. Without these controls, the benefits of elasticity can be quickly outweighed by the risks of cross-tenant vulnerabilities, service disruptions, and security breaches.

Ultimately, network isolation in elastic environments must evolve beyond physical boundaries, integrating dynamic, policy-driven security controls that adapt to changing infrastructure needs. Whether on-premises or in the public cloud, the key challenge is maintaining strict segmentation without sacrificing the scalability and flexibility that elasticity provides.

Data Isolation

The transition of the media and entertainment industry to elastic, cloud-based infrastructures have introduced significant challenges in ensuring data isolation. Traditionally, broadcast environments relied on dedicated hardware and localized storage, which provided inherent segregation of assets and minimized the risk of unauthorized access. However, as media organizations increasingly adopt cloud-native architectures, the dynamic nature of elastic infrastructures presents new security risks, particularly regarding data leakage, cross-tenant exposure, and performance degradation [12]. Unlike physical storage systems, which enforce isolation through strict hardware boundaries, cloud-based environments require software-defined controls to manage access, visibility, and segmentation of assets.

One of the primary concerns in elastic media workflows is the management of shared storage and dynamic provisioning. In conventional environments, PAM and MAM, media archives, and production storage were housed in isolated Network Attached Storage (NAS) or Storage Area Network (SAN) systems, ensuring that only authorized personnel could access specific files. Typically, these are static environments that take significant administration to set up and manage and are intimately linked to workflows that don't change. In these environments, scaling occurs vertically, where you add more storage, but the management and infrastructure itself evolve from the original setup.

In contrast, elastic infrastructures utilize cloud-based object storage services, such as Amazon S3, Azure Blob Storage, and Google Cloud Storage, which scale automatically based on demand [18]. While this scalability enhances efficiency, it also increases the risk of misconfigured access controls, potentially exposing critical production assets to unauthorized users. The inherent nature of shared cloud resources means that tenants operating within the same environment may inadvertently gain access to data belonging to other productions if isolation policies are not meticulously implemented.

Cross-tenant data exposure is particularly concerning in multi-production broadcast environments, where multiple teams work on concurrent projects using shared infrastructure. Traditionally, media organizations maintained distinct physical infrastructure for each production to ensure absolute segregation. In an elastic architecture, however, multiple productions often share virtualized resources, requiring sophisticated access control policies to prevent unintended data sharing. Failure to implement proper segmentation can result in cross-production interference, leading to unauthorized access, accidental overwrites, or even content leaks [18]. Moreover, as cloud-based environments are increasingly used for live broadcasting, latency considerations further complicate data isolation strategies. The constant migration of data across cloud storage layers—dictated by elastic scaling—can introduce delays in content retrieval, inconsistencies in versioning, and unexpected service disruptions if not properly managed [19].

Another critical factor in data isolation is content integrity and versioning. Modern post-production workflows require frequent file versioning, collaborative editing, and automated transcoding, necessitating robust data governance strategies. Without immutable storage policies, critical assets risk being inadvertently overwritten or lost due to misconfigurations or unauthorized access [11]. To address these risks, media asset management systems (MAMs) integrated within cloud infrastructures must enforce role-based access controls (RBAC) and attribute-based access controls (ABAC) on the infrastructure itself, to dynamically adjust permissions based on project status, production stage, and user roles.

Data lifecycle management is another key component of secure data isolation. Moving from an environment where the location of the storage physically is readily known, to an elastic world where software provisions storage in a system and administrators do not know the location of the data requires additional diligence to ensure integrity, redundancy, disaster recovery and eventual disposure of critical data. Elastic storage infrastructures require automated policies to control data retention, expiration, and archival strategies, ensuring that obsolete content does not accumulate unchecked. Cloud providers offer tiered storage strategies, such as hot, warm, and cold storage, which allow organizations to balance performance with cost efficiency. However, improper lifecycle management can lead to unexpected content deletion, data fragmentation, and excessive storage costs, necessitating automated backup consistency checks and real-time replication across multiple cloud regions [19].

Ultimately, ensuring robust data isolation in elastic broadcast environments demands a shift from hardware-defined security to software-enforced policies. Unlike static, on-premises architectures, which inherently limit access to physical infrastructure, elastic workloads require continuous monitoring, dynamic access enforcement, and encrypted storage mechanisms to prevent unauthorized access and mitigate cross-tenant data risks. By adopting Zero Trust security models, integrating multi-layered access control mechanisms, and leveraging immutable data storage, media organizations can maintain a secure, scalable, and efficient data infrastructure even as their workloads expand dynamically.

Enhancing Security with Immutable Cloud Technology

Auditability

In cloud computing environments, audibility is essential for bolstering security postures, especially when improved by immutable cloud technologies. Systems where data cannot be changed or removed once it has been written, are referred to as immutable cloud technology. This feature has the potential to greatly improve data security and integrity. When used with unchangeable technology, audibility can improve security in several ways. Improving Integrity of Data, there is no guarantee that the data has been altered after the fact, auditors can depend on the completeness and accuracy of historical data when there are immutable records.

Organizations can improve their incident response and security monitoring capabilities with immutable logs. Malicious actors cannot remove their traces since the logs cannot be altered or removed, which is frequently difficult in breach situations. Future defenses can be strengthened by auditors and security teams doing more precise forensic studies to comprehend the extent and methodology of an attack.

Systems that cannot be changed lower the dangers posed by insider threats. Logs cannot be changed or removed by administrators or staff who have access to critical information to conceal malicious or illegal activity. This provides a powerful deterrent against abuse of data access privileges by guaranteeing that all actions are documented and auditable.

An organization is better prepared for future legal issues or inquiries when it has auditable and unchangeable logs. Access to unaltered historical data can be crucial in certain situations to support a claim or show due diligence. Legal non-compliance or litigation risks can be reduced by this preparedness.

Immutable Containers

Immutable containers are a natural extension of the "cattle vs. pets" mindset, where infrastructure resources are treated as disposable and uniformly configured. Each container runs from a predefined image in this model, ensuring all instances share the same operating system layers and application libraries [3]. When updates are needed (due to a change in the application or an update to the underlying base image) teams create a new container image rather than manually patching or upgrading existing instances. This approach reduces the risk of "configuration drift", particularly important in large environments where small misconfigurations can multiply rapidly.

A key advantage of immutable containers is streamlined version management. While a new container image can represent fresh application code, it may also solely address a security patch or base-image update. Thus, teams can increment container versions (even if the application itself remains unchanged) to incorporate operating system layer or library fixes. By consistently building containers from a tested baseline, administrators can easily track which version of the underlying image is running at any given time.

Compared to legacy systems that rely on manual OS patching and ad hoc upgrades, immutable containers offer a simpler and more secure operational model. Traditional infrastructures often grow heterogeneous over time, as administrators implement one-off fixes. By contrast, container-based deployments systematically replace old images with new, removing guesswork around configurations and reducing human error. In highly scalable environments, uniformity is crucial, and by maintaining consistency at every layer, organizations leveraging immutable containers can respond swiftly to emerging vulnerabilities while minimizing downtime.

Regular Validation

Maintaining and improving the overall security posture of cloud infrastructures depends heavily on regular validation in the context of tenant isolation and cloud security. Organizations can guarantee the efficacy and integrity of their security measures by carrying out comprehensive and regular validations. Regular validation helps to improve security in several ways.
Organizations can learn more about the efficacy and performance of their security controls by conducting routine validation. This makes it possible to allocate and optimize resources more effectively, whether that means increasing funding for under-protected areas or reducing overperforming measures that are wasting money.

Regular audits, penetration tests, and security assessments help businesses find weaknesses in their cloud infrastructure that may not be noticeable during initial security settings. Recognizing and addressing security vulnerabilities through frequent validation makes it easier to find defects or weaknesses in the tenant isolation methods, guaranteeing that vulnerabilities are fixed before malevolent actors may take advantage of them 20. Ensuring adherence to security standards and policies: Frequent validation verifies that security controls adhere to established guidelines and industry requirements. This involves confirming adherence to regulatory and industry frameworks such as GDPR, ISO27001, and SOC. 2. Validation guarantees that the protections that have been put in place to secure data and properly isolate tenants are not only there but also operating as intended.

Configuration Drift

Configuration drift is the phenomenon whereby environment configurations evolve without influencing one another. Development, testing, and production environments may become inconsistent because of these modifications, which could result in unexpected behaviors, security flaws, and system failures. Immutable cloud technology raises several configuration drift-related issues that must be addressed when boosting security.

Immutable environments encourage the development of new instances instead of updating preexisting ones by design [20]. If the creation operations are not closely supervised and controlled, there is still a chance that the configuration will vary between deployment cycles [21] causing disparities in deployments:

Different configurations and application code versions may be deployed throughout the cloud infrastructure if improperly controlled. If vulnerabilities in older versions are absent from more recent versions, this could result in security flaws caused by a lack of version controls. Even with immutable configurations, configuration drift can make it difficult to maintain compliance with industry norms and laws [22]. New instances must follow compliance requirements, and if configuration changes—no matter how small—are not thoroughly examined and tested, they may result in non-compliance [23].

Immutable infrastructures frequently use automated scaling strategies to handle demand variations. Each new instance created during scaling must follow the same configuration as the original; if the automated operations are not precisely synced, configuration drift could happen.

In immutable systems, patches, and security updates need to be incorporated into new configurations or images that replace outdated ones. If these settings are not kept up to date, unpatched and vulnerable systems may be deployed unintentionally.

Mitigating Configuration Drift in Immutable Cloud Technology

To avoid unintentional reuse and lower infrastructure complexity, actively decommission old images and configurations decommission Old Configurations. Implement CI/CD pipelines that incorporate automated testing, security checks, and compliance audits to guarantee that all deployments are safe and consistent across the development and production phases.

Use immutable artifacts for deployments where a new artifact must be created for each modification. This guarantees that each instance is compatible with its source configuration and prevents ad hoc changes. Perform routine configuration audits and employ monitoring technologies to identify and notify users of any departures from the cloud environment's typical state.

Conclusion

The Liability of Elasticity looks at the cybersecurity issues that arise from cloud infrastructures' capacity for dynamic scalability, especially in the media and entertainment sector. This study highlights how moving to software-driven cloud infrastructure improves scalability but also brings with it new vulnerabilities, such as larger attack surfaces and more complicated security management problems.

This research promotes creative security measures that foresee intrusions and lessen their effects. It highlights the significance of prompt incident reaction and ongoing monitoring and recommends implementing strong security frameworks from industries like finance and e-commerce. This paper discusses the difficulties in maintaining data segregation and tenant isolation in multi-tenant settings, emphasizing the need for strong access control measures and the dangers of cross-tenant data leakage. Also discussed are the benefits of immutable cloud technology in terms of improving security and compliance requirements for tenant isolation in cloud infrastructures.

To safeguard media organizations in cloud environments, the study advocates for a new cybersecurity paradigm that strikes a compromise between elasticity and thorough security standards. As the media and entertainment industry embrace cloud-based and elastic infrastructures, both on-premises and inside public hyperscalers, new cybersecurity and operational challenges emerge. This shift promises unparalleled scalability and flexibility yet also introduces significant vulnerabilities that must be carefully managed. The elasticity of cloud infrastructure allows for dynamic scaling, which, while advantageous for handling fluctuating demands, brings heightened risks, including increased attack surfaces and the complexities of managing tenant isolation and data segregation in multi-tenant environments.

Traditional security models often prove insufficient in addressing these new concerns, as elastic systems respond dynamically to both genuine demand and potential threats.

References

[1] Saif, M. A. N., Niranjan, S. K., & Al-ariki, H. D. E. (2021). Efficient autonomic and elastic resource management techniques in cloud environment: Taxonomy and analysis. Wireless Networks, 27(4), 2829–2866

[2] Netflix Tech Blog. (2016). Netflix Tech Blog. Retrieved from https://netflixtechblog.com/ [JOHN UPDATE]

[3] Kratzke, N., & Peinl, R. (2016). Lightweight virtualization on cloud infrastructures: A state-of-the-art survey. Journal of Cloud Computing, 5(1), 1–22. https://doi.org/10.1186/s13677-016-0053-9

[4] Nunn, B., & Shakarian, P. (2022). Using ephemeral containers to improve cybersecurity posture. ACM Digital Library

[5] Turnbull, J. (2014). The Docker Book: Containerization is the new virtualization. Turnbull Press.

[6] Morris, K. (2016). Infrastructure as Code: Managing Servers in the Cloud. O'Reilly Media.

[7] Brikman, Y. (2019). Terraform: Up & Running (2nd ed.). O'Reilly Media.

[8] Hajjem, L., Benabdallah, S., & Ben Abdelaziz, F. (2010). A dynamic resource allocation decision model for IT security. 2010 Second International Conference on Engineering System Management and Applications, 1-6

[9] Murphy, D. (2023). Redefining the control plane. Proceedings of the 2023 NAB Broadcast Engineering and Information Technology Conference. National Association of Broadcasters.

[10] AWS. (n.d.). What is Elastic Disaster Recovery? Retrieved from https://docs.aws.amazon.com/drs/latest/userguide/what-is-drs.html

[11] Zhang, Y., & Zhang, X. (2021). Research on data security in big data cloud computing environment. In Proceedings of the 2021 IEEE International Conference on Computer Science, Electronic Information Engineering and Intelligent Control Technology (CEI) (pp. 939–942)

[12] [Bazm, M.-M., Lacoste, M., Südholt, M., & Menaud, J.-M. (2019). Isolation in cloud computing infrastructures: new security challenges. Annals of Telecommunications, 74(3-4), 197–209

[13] Riedel, M. (2022). Mind the Gap: An Updated Assessment of the Air-Gap Network Security Concept (Master's thesis). The Pennsylvania State University

[14] Ahmadi, S. (2024). Zero Trust Architecture in Cloud Networks: Application, Challenges and Future Opportunities. Journal of Engineering Research and Reports, 26(2), 215–228.

[15] M. Mounesan, H. Siadati and S. Jafarikhah, "Exploring the Threat of Software Supply Chain Attacks on Containerized Applications," 2023 16th International Conference on Security of Information and Networks (SIN), Jaipur, India, 2023, pp. 1-8

[16] B. Medeiros, M. A. Simplicio and E. R. Andrade, "Designing and Assessing Multi-tenant Isolation Strategies for Cloud Networks," 2019 22nd Conference on Innovation in Clouds, Internet and Networks and Workshops (ICIN), Paris, France, 2019, pp. 214-221

[17] F. Pizzato, D. Bringhenti, R. Sisto and F. Valenza, "An intent-based solution for network isolation in Kubernetes," 2024 IEEE 10th International Conference on Network Softwarization (NetSoft), Saint Louis, MO, USA, 2024, pp. 381-386

[18] Ratnam, K. V., & Yasani, R. R. (2021). Multi-tenant data isolation techniques in public clouds: Assessing the effectiveness of isolation mechanisms. World Journal of Advanced Research and Reviews, 12(1), 529–539

[19] Saif, M. A. N., Niranjan, S. K., & Al-ariki, H. D. E. (2021). Efficient autonomic and elastic resource management techniques in cloud environment: Taxonomy and analysis. Wireless Networks, 27(4), 2829–2866

[20] Bafana, M., & Abdulaziz, A. (2024). Immutable Infrastructure in Practice: A Comprehensive Guide to AWS Deployment. Asian American Research Letters Journal, 1(1)

[21] Odukoya, O. (2024, May). The Transformative Impact of Cloud Computing on Small and Medium-sized Enterprises (SMEs): A Comprehensive Analysis. In 2024 International Conference on Smart Applications, Communications and Networking (SmartNets) (pp. 1-5). IEEE

[22] Malaiyappan, J. N. A., Prakash, S., Bayani, S. V., & Devan, M. (2024). Enhancing cloud compliance: A machine learning approach. *AIJMR-Advanced International Journal of Multidisciplinary Research*, *2*(2)

[23] Goswami, A., Patel, R., Mavani, C., & Mistry, H. K. (2024). Secure Cloud Collaboration in Data Centric Security. International Journal on Recent and Innovation Trends in Computing and Communication, 12(2), 539-47

Downtime Management in Multi-CDN Steering Systems

Gwendal Simon
Synamedia
Rennes, France
gsimon@synamedia.com

Abstract – Managing CDN failures in multi-CDN streaming environments requires a careful balance between maintaining Quality of Experience (QoE) and ensuring timely detection of CDN recovery. Traditional methods rely on external probes or client-based monitoring, both of which have limitations in accuracy or feasibility. This paper explores an alternative approach that strategically assigns a small subset of users to a failing CDN while dynamically adjusting their Time-To-Live (TTL) based on buffer length information. By leveraging buffer-aware content steering, the system ensures that only users with sufficient buffer capacity are temporarily assigned to the faulty CDN, minimizing rebuffering events while maintaining continuous monitoring of the CDN's recovery status.

Through simulations, we evaluate the trade-offs between different user assignment strategies and demonstrate that a Rotating Sacrifice with Buffer-Based TTL approach provides an effective balance. This method achieves rapid recovery detection, typically within seconds, while keeping QoE degradation at levels comparable to a baseline approach where no monitoring is performed. The findings highlight the benefits of incorporating buffer length data into the content steering process, leading to a fairer and more efficient multi-CDN orchestration. We advocate for the inclusion of buffer-level reporting as a standard parameter in content steering systems to improve resilience and service continuity in large-scale streaming operations.

Introduction

The rapid growth of online video consumption has posed significant challenges for content providers seeking to deliver high-quality streaming experiences at scale. Content Delivery Networks (CDNs) have become essential in this process, leveraging distributed edge caching to bring content closer to end-users and reduce latency. However, as traffic volumes surge and networks expand across diverse regions, relying on a single CDN often proves insufficient to handle the load effectively.

To address these limitations, content providers have embraced multi-CDN strategies, distributing traffic across multiple providers to enhance reliability and performance. Despite the clear advantages, multi-CDN management remains largely empirical, relying on heuristics rather than systematic optimization. The core enabler of multi-CDN orchestration is content steering, a mechanism that dynamically assigns users to different CDNs based on real-time performance metrics. In this model, video players continuously communicate with a centralized steering server, which evaluates CDN conditions and makes routing decisions accordingly. This dynamic redirection ensures seamless transitions between CDNs, particularly in cases of failure or degradation.

The effectiveness of a content steering system is directly tied to the accuracy of its CDN performance monitoring. Typically, steering decisions are based on Quality of Experience (QoE) reports gathered from video players, either through direct feedback mechanisms like Common Media Client Data

(CMCD) or via third-party QoE analytics services such as Mux, Conviva, and Bitmovin Analytics. While these data sources enable quick detection of CDN failures, a critical challenge remains: how can the system confirm that a previously failed CDN has recovered if no users are actively streaming from it?

CDN failure management in content steering systems presents a complex optimization problem. The goal is twofold: reduce the delay in detecting a CDN's recovery while preventing unnecessary QoE degradation for users. This dilemma arises because assigning no users to an unhealthy CDN ensures a smooth experience but leaves the system unaware of when the CDN is operational again. Conversely, assigning users to a potentially faulty CDN risks poor playback performance.

This paper explores multiple algorithms designed to tackle this trade-off within a multi-CDN content steering framework. Through empirical evaluation in realistic conditions, we demonstrate that simple yet effective randomized strategies can strike an excellent balance between timely recovery detection and user QoE preservation. Additionally, we highlight the benefits of incorporating real-time buffer length reporting into the steering process, which significantly enhances the system's ability to maintain a high-quality streaming experience during CDN failures.

Related Work

CDN failures in large-scale multi-CDN streaming systems are common. The architecture of HTTP Live Streaming (HLS) [3] and Dynamic Adaptive Streaming over HTTP (DASH) [6] specifies that video clients should follow a predefined content steering mechanism. According to these standards, when multiple CDNs are available, a video player must first attempt to stream from the primary CDN and only switch to an alternative if an error, such as an HTTP 404 response, occurs. However, complete CDN failures are rare. More often, a CDN remains operational but with reduced performance, returning HTTP 200 responses while serving content slowly. This situation requires the steering server to ensure that users are directed to a functioning CDN while also monitoring the performance of others.

If no users are assigned to a failing CDN, the steering server does not receive performance data and cannot determine when the CDN has recovered. Three main approaches exist to address this issue.

External Probes

One approach is to deploy external probe machines in data centers that continuously request content from the failing CDN. While this method does not impact real users, it has limitations. Probes do not fully represent user environments and cannot detect network congestion or ISP-related issues that affect actual playback quality.

Client-Based Probing

Another approach, proposed by the Streaming Video Technology Alliance (SVTA) QoE working group, involves using end-users to periodically probe multiple CDNs. This method provides real-world performance data from diverse networks but increases bandwidth consumption. Streaming already requires significant bandwidth, and adding extra probing may affect overall quality. Additionally, this approach is not included in DASH or HLS standards and is not currently implemented in video players.

End-User Assignment

A third approach involves assigning a small fraction of users to the failing CDN to gather real-time QoE data. This provides direct feedback on the CDN's recovery status. However, affected users experience degraded performance, which may lead to dissatisfaction and service abandonment.

Multi-CDN Research

Multi-CDN management has been a subject of research, including studies on Netflix's streaming infrastructure [2]. Netflix initially used a multi-CDN strategy but later switched to a single-CDN model [4] to improve control over delivery quality. Research on multi-path delivery [7] explores distributing traffic across multiple CDNs to reduce failure risks, but implementation remains complex. Many streaming services assign each user to a single CDN per video segment, making traffic distribution difficult. Even recent standardization efforts [1] have not been widely adopted.

CDN failure management remains an open challenge. Current methods either lack full visibility, increase bandwidth use, or negatively impact some users. This paper explores alternative algorithms that aim to minimize detection delays while maintaining QoE. By improving steering mechanisms and user assignment strategies, we seek to enhance multi-CDN resilience and ensure stable content delivery.

Algorithms

This paper examines a practical approach that adheres to content steering standards without requiring modifications to video players. The goal is to implement a strategy that enables monitoring of a failing CDN while minimizing Quality of Experience (QoE) degradation for end-users.

Available Information at the Steering Server

The steering server receives periodic QoE reports from clients when they request new segments. These reports include measured throughput, as specified in DASH and HLS standards [3,6], and additional insights can be obtained from Common Media Client Data (CMCD).

A key contribution of this paper is demonstrating that buffer length information, reported through the "bl" key in CMCD [5], is valuable for improving multi-CDN orchestration. By leveraging buffer length, the steering server can make more informed decisions on TTL values, dynamically adjusting how long a client remains on a particular CDN.

Selection of Monitored End-Users

To monitor CDN performance, a subset of users must continue receiving data from the failing CDN. A target of 10% of the total user base is maintained on the faulty CDN, providing real-time performance insights while limiting the overall impact on service quality.

The following algorithms define how end-users are selected for assignment to the failing CDN:

- **Baseline (No Sacrifice):** All users are redirected to healthy CDNs immediately, preventing performance monitoring of the failing CDN. This serves as a lower-bound reference for evaluating recovery detection efficiency.
- **Unlucky Sacrifice:** The number of clients on the failing CDN is gradually reduced until 10% remain. Users who arrive earlier are switched to a healthy CDN, while those who arrive later remain on the failing CDN. This results in a subset of users experiencing longer durations of degraded QoE.
- **Rotating Sacrifice with Buffer-Based TTL:** A fixed portion (10%) of clients is always assigned to the failing CDN. Instead of a fixed TTL, the steering server dynamically adjusts TTL values based on each user's buffer length. Clients with higher buffer levels are assigned a longer TTL before returning to the steering server, while those with lower buffer levels return sooner. This ensures that users are not exposed to prolonged rebuffering while still allowing the steering server to monitor the CDN's status.

Example of Controlled Buffer-Aware Process

This section presents a complete example illustrating the dynamic behavior of a content steering system using DASH Content Steering and CMCD buffer length data.

Step 1: Initial State (Normal Operation)
At the beginning of the streaming session, both CDN1 and CDN2 are fully operational. The steering server assigns users to either CDN1 or CDN2 based on load balancing. The default TTL for all users is set to *30 seconds*, ensuring that each client remains on the assigned CDN for a stable duration before rechecking with the steering server.

```
{
  "VERSION": 1,
  "TTL": 30,
  "RELOAD-URI": "https://steering.example.com/api/steering?session=xyz",
  "PATHWAY-PRIORITY": ["cdn1", "cdn2"]
}
```

Step 2: CDN1 Failure Detected
In this scenario, the steering server suddenly receives multiple reports of degraded throughput and increased buffering events from users streaming from CDN1. Based on these reports, it determines that CDN1 is failing. To prevent further QoE degradation, the steering server immediately redirects all users to CDN2 and sets their TTL back to *30 seconds* to maintain a stable connection.

```
{
  "VERSION": 1,
  "TTL": 30,
  "PATHWAY-PRIORITY": ["cdn2"]
}
```

Step 3: Controlled Monitoring of CDN1 Recovery
To determine when CDN1 recovers, the steering server assigns **10% of users** back to CDN1. However, these users are selected based on their buffer length to minimize the risk of rebuffering. The TTL for these users is set to be *slightly lower than their current buffer length*, ensuring they return to the steering server before experiencing playback issues.
For example, if a user reports a buffer length (bl) of **10 seconds**, the TTL is set to **9 seconds**. The steering manifest response for monitored users is:

```
{
  "VERSION": 1,
  "TTL": 9,
  "PATHWAY-PRIORITY": ["cdn1", "cdn2"]
}
```

Meanwhile, the remaining *90% of users* continue to stream from CDN2 with a TTL of 30 seconds, ensuring stable playback. Here is an example of a CMCD report sent by a user assigned to CDN1

```
{
  "bl": 10000,
  "mtp": 4500,
  "ot": "v"
}
```

Step 4: Users Return to CDN2 and New Users are Selected for CDN1
Once the monitoring users' TTL expires, they return to CDN2 with a TTL reset to *30 seconds*, preventing prolonged exposure to potential CDN1 failures. At the same time, the steering server selects another *10% of users* to be reassigned to CDN1, continuing the monitoring process. The steering manifest response for returning users is as follows:

```
{
  "VERSION": 1,
  "TTL": 30,
  "PATHWAY-PRIORITY": ["cdn2"]
}
```

Meanwhile, the steering manifest response for the newly assigned users to CDN1 is:

```
{
  "VERSION": 1,
```

```
  "TTL": 8,
  "PATHWAY-PRIORITY": ["cdn1", "cdn2"]
}
```

This process repeats periodically until the steering server detects that CDN1 has fully recovered. At that point, normal traffic distribution resumes, restoring the original TTL of *30 seconds* for all users across both CDNs.

Step 5: CDN1 Recovery and Full Traffic Redistribution

Once the steering server observes sustained improvements in CDN1 performance through CMCD reports, it rebalances the traffic and reinstates CDN1 as a primary pathway. Users are now assigned evenly between CDN1 and CDN2 with *TTL set back to 30 seconds*.

The final steering manifest response after CDN1 recovery is thus:

```
{
  "VERSION": 1,
  "TTL": 30,
  "PATHWAY-PRIORITY": ["cdn1", "cdn2"]
}
```

Summary

We summarize the process with these five steps:

1. **Normal operation:** Users are balanced between CDN1 and CDN2 with TTL = 30s.
2. **CDN1 failure:** All users are switched to CDN2 with TTL = 30s.
3. **Controlled monitoring:** 10% of users are assigned to CDN1 with a TTL based on their buffer length.
4. **Rotation mechanism:** Monitoring users return to CDN2, while a new group of users is selected for CDN1.
5. **CDN1 recovery detected:** Traffic is gradually restored to CDN1 with TTL = 30s.

This method leverages buffer length information to optimize the monitoring process, ensuring CDN failures are detected and handled with minimal QoE impact while efficiently orchestrating traffic distribution in a multi-CDN environment.

Simulations and Analysis

We have developed a set of analysis related to these algorithms in a recent conference paper [13]. We will not dive into all details of the simulations in the current paper. We mainly focus on the analysis in the following paragraphs.

The performance metrics shown in [13] include key indicators such as recovery detection delay and the number of rebuffering events. Additional insights into user behavior and CDN switching events can also be found.

Baseline Approach

The Baseline approach serves as a reference case, as it does not attempt to detect CDN recovery. As expected, it ensures the lowest number of rebuffering events since users are only moved away from the failing CDN. However, because no users remain on the failed CDN, the steering server lacks the necessary data to determine when it has recovered. Consequently, recovery detection is impossible, and CDN1 remains unused even after returning to a healthy state.

Unlucky Sacrifice Approach

The Unlucky Sacrifice approach assigns a fixed 10% of users to the failing CDN, exposing them to potential QoE degradation. The users assigned to the faulty CDN frequently experience rebuffering events. Since these users report performance frequently, the recovery detection delay is minimal—almost immediate in the buffer-aware version. However, this comes at the cost of a highly uneven distribution of QoE degradation. A small group of users experiences a disproportionate number of rebuffering events, making it unlikely that they would continue their session. Additionally, the frequent reporting from these users increases the load on the steering server, leading to higher signaling overhead.

Rotating Sacrifice with Buffer-Based TTL Approach

The Rotating Sacrifice approach provides a balanced trade-off between QoE degradation and recovery detection efficiency. By dynamically selecting 10% of users for reassignment to the failing CDN, and adjusting their TTL based on buffer length, the algorithm ensures that only users with sufficient buffer levels are mapped to the failed CDN. This minimizes the number of rebuffering events while maintaining continuous monitoring of CDN1. Recovery detection occurs in under 10 seconds, comparable to the Unlucky Sacrifice approach but with significantly lower QoE degradation.

Furthermore, the number of CDN switch events remains lower than in the Unlucky Sacrifice approach, indicating a more stable user experience. The buffer-based TTL mechanism ensures that users transition back to a healthy CDN before exhausting their buffer, preventing playback stalls. While some switch events are inevitable, they are kept within an acceptable range, making this approach practical for real-world deployment.

Simulation Analysis Conclusion

Among the evaluated approaches, the Baseline strategy minimizes QoE degradation but completely prevents recovery detection. The Unlucky Sacrifice approach enables fast recovery detection but at the cost of a highly concentrated QoE impact. The Rotating Sacrifice with Buffer-Based TTL approach achieves a reasonable balance, ensuring rapid recovery detection while minimizing user disruptions.

Conclusion

This paper examined the problem of CDN failure management in multi-CDN systems. The central challenge arises from the need to balance two conflicting objectives: ensuring end-users are not assigned to a faulty CDN to maintain QoE while also maintaining a subset of users on the failing CDN to monitor its recovery status. The subset of users assigned to the faulty CDN is referred to as "sacrificed" users, as they provide essential data at the cost of potential QoE degradation.

Existing approaches in the community rely on external probing, but these solutions either lack sufficient accuracy or require modifications to video players that are unlikely to be adopted in the near term. Instead, we investigated whether it is possible to minimize QoE degradation while still assigning some users to the failing CDN. Our results indicate that this is indeed achievable.

We demonstrated that simple assignment strategies based on randomized processes, even without explicit tracking of the number of users on the failing CDN, can achieve effective recovery detection while minimizing QoE impact. The resulting degradation, measured in terms of rebuffering events, remains close to that of a strategy where no users are assigned to the failing CDN—though such an approach fails to detect recovery. By distributing the assignments dynamically, these strategies allow user buffers to absorb short periods of degraded service, leading to a transparent experience for most users while enabling fast recovery detection, typically within seconds.

Furthermore, our findings highlight the benefits of incorporating buffer length information into the steering decision-making process. This information, already available in the Common Media Client Data (CMCD) standard, allows the steering server to make more informed decisions, ensuring that users with lower buffer levels spend less time on a failing CDN, thereby reducing the risk of playback interruptions. We advocate for the inclusion of buffer level reporting in the content steering standard, as it enables a more efficient and fair multi-CDN orchestration strategy.

These insights contribute to the ongoing development of multi-CDN steering techniques by offering a practical approach that balances service continuity, QoE preservation, and rapid recovery detection without requiring complex or intrusive modifications to existing systems.

References

[1] Coded Multisource Media Format (CMMF) for Content Distribution and Delivery. ETSI TS 103 973 V1.1.1.

[2] Vijay Kumar Adhikari, Yang Guo, Fang Hao, Matteo Varvello, Volker Hilt, Moritz Steiner, and Zhi-Li Zhang. 2012. Unreeling netflix: Understanding and improving multi-CDN movie delivery. In Proceedings of the IEEE INFOCOM, IEEE, 1620–1628. https://doi.org/10.1109/INFCOM.2012.6195531

[3] Apple. 2021. HLS Content Steering Specification. [Online] Available: https://developer.apple.com/streaming/HLSContentSteeringSpecification.pdf

[4] Timm Böttger, Felix Cuadrado, Gareth Tyson, Ignacio Castro, and Steve Uhlig. 2018. Open connect everywhere: A glimpse at the internet ecosystem through the lens of the netflix cdn. ACM SIGCOMM Computer Communication Review 48,1 (2018), 28–34.

[5] Consumer Technology Association. 2020. Web Application Video Ecosystem – Common Media Client Data (CMCD). [Online] Available: https://shop.cta.tech/collections/standards/products/web-application-videoecosystem-common-media-client-data-cta-5004

[6] DASH-IF. 2024. Content Steering for DASH. [Online] Available: https://www.etsi.org/deliver/etsi_ts/103900_103999/103998/01.01.01_60/ts_103998v010101p.pdf

[7] Ali Hodroj, Marc Ibrahim, and Yassine Hadjadj-Aoul. 2021. A survey on video streaming in multipath and multihomed overlay networks. IEEE Access 9 (2021), 66816–66828.

[8] Burak Kara and Gwendal Simon. 2024. Power Efficient Multi-CDN Communication over Content Steering Server. In ACM Proceedings of the 15th ACM Multimedia Systems Conference. https://doi.org/10.1145/3625468.3652196

[9] Hongzi Mao, Ravi Netravali, and Mohammad Alizadeh. 2017. Neural Adaptive Video Streaming with Pensieve. In Proceedings of the Conference of the ACM Special Interest Group on Data Communication. 197–210. https://doi.org/10.1145/3098822.3098843

[10] Yuriy Reznik, Guillem Cabrera, Daniel Silhavy, Stefan Pham, Alex Giladi, Alex Balk, Ali C. Begen, and Will Law. 2024. Content steering: a standard for multi-CDN streaming. In Proceedings of the 3rd Mile-High Video Conference. https://doi.org/10.1145/3638036.3640293

[11] Naoki Satake and Masaki Bandai. 2013. Dynamic QoE-aware live streaming with clustering clients. IEICE Communications Express 2, 12 (2013), 518–523.

[12] Rachee Singh, Arun Dunna, and Phillipa Gill. 2018. Characterizing the deployment and performance of multi-CDNs. In Proceedings of the Internet Measurement Conference 2018. 168–174.

[13] Burak Kara and Gwendal Simon. 2025. Resurrection of a CDN: Briefing Steering Server on CDN Recovery. *ACM Mile-High Video (MHV)*, 2025.

Securing Hybrid Media and Entertainment Workflows Practical Strategies for Protecting Intellectual Property and Critical Assets

Jonathan Solomon
Technicall
Columbia, Maryland, United States
technicall@thesolomonhouse.com

Abstract – The media and entertainment industry has undergone a significant shift towards hybrid and cloud-based workflows. As organizations leverage a growing ecosystem of Software as a Service (SaaS) solutions and multi-vendor integrations, new security challenges have emerged. These hybrid environments, which often involve on-premises storage and processing coupled with cloud-based services and remote users, present potential compromise vectors for sensitive data and assets. This paper explores practical strategies to address security threats and safeguard intellectual property, pre-release assets, and other critical resources within hybrid media and entertainment workflows. It will examine the diverse threat vectors malicious actors can exploit, with a focus on vulnerabilities introduced by SaaS solutions and the integration of bespoke vendor offerings.

Introduction

The Media and Entertainment (M&E) industry's shift toward hybrid and cloud-based workflows presents challenges related to Software as a Service (SaaS) adoption and multi-vendor integrations. Security is not just about protection—it extends to safeguarding applications and users.

The phrase **"content is king"** continues to drive revenue for content owners, making the protection of intellectual property (IP) essential, particularly when working with third-party tools, operators, and providers. As new content is created and archived content is repurposed for monetization and personalization, the industry continues to adopt best-of-breed solutions across SaaS and self-deployed infrastructures, both on-premises and in the cloud.

Historically, broadcasters and other content creators maintained internal systems for content creation, processing, and distribution. These siloed systems, operated within segregated computer networks with limited access to third-party tools. Consoles, workstations, and user access were managed within a closed network. However, these systems often contained small, controlled firewall exceptions—known as pinholes—for specific external connections for content ingest, distribution, administrative functions, or custom user access.

Today's hybrid environment requires integrating formerly closed systems with external platforms to leverage cloud capabilities and support remote workforces. Even with dedicated networks and virtual private networks (VPNs), security risks persist.

Content owners, including studios and networks, must meet growing consumer demand while increasingly relying on the cloud for storage, processing, and distribution. Hybrid media workflows, which combine on-premises infrastructure with third-party and cloud-based services, have become the industry standard. In the past, security was often an afterthought, with weak credential policies, open network ports, and broad user access permissions. In today's interconnected landscape, where IP traverses public networks, security must be a top priority. Protecting both on-premises and third-party environments is critical.

The shift from on-premises solutions to SaaS, coupled with multi-vendor integrations, introduces new vectors for IP compromise. Hybrid cloud infrastructures, on-premises workloads, and remote operators create additional risks.

Consider a customer with a hybrid environment that includes on-premises storage and processing, cloud-based services, and multiple SaaS providers. Users operate both on-premises and remotely. A cloud orchestration service facilitates interactions between SaaS platforms and on-premises storage, allowing on-premises users to access cloud services and vice versa. The customer is concerned about unauthorized access.

The organization seeks a solution to prevent or detect such threats within its network.

NOTE: Companies and products mentioned in this paper are provided as examples. The author and publisher are not endorsing any single solution.

Why This Matters

Traditional on-premises media workloads—whether base-band or file-based—historically operated in closed networks with tightly controlled access and data flows. The industry's transition to cloud-based and SaaS driven models introduces new security challenges. While enterprise IT has established access control mechanisms, media environments often follow different access patterns that require tailored security strategies.

Previously, organizations treated their infrastructure like a fortress. Access was granted sparingly, often through physical key cards or specific firewall pinholes linked to designated network ports or addresses.

As media workflows evolved, organizations realized the benefits of broader access. This shift opened the castle doors, necessitating a shift from perimeter-based security to identity-driven access control. Rather than assuming anyone should have access, modern security approaches require users and systems to continuously prove their identity.

This paper introduces vulnerabilities at the network, application, and user levels, highlighting mechanisms for proactive risk mitigation. It covers common IT security solutions for reactive monitoring and detection while introducing proactive security measures tailored to M&E workflows.

Threat Landscape in Hybrid M&E Workflows

Key Security Challenges

Hybrid workloads require access to traditionally protected infrastructure by previously unauthorized entities, particularly third parties. A simple example involves processing services such as transcoding, quality control, or AI-driven metadata enrichment, which require access to on-premises storage that contains valuable IP.

The proliferation of SaaS vendors introduces additional concerns. SaaS vendor operations often occur in a shared environment, even when data handling occurs in a more isolated or controlled manner.

The growing number of distributed work teams—including freelancers, consultants, and remote employees—has expanded network access to entities previously restricted. Network access can be controlled at the physical layer through established policies and Virtual Private Networks (VPNs). In cases where cloud usage has grown, direct connections between customers and cloud environments are now possible.

However, a critical security concern arises from credential-based threats. Entities—including programmatic users, machines, and physical users—require credentials for connectivity. Credentials may include usernames and passwords, passkeys, Single Sign-On (SSO), API keys, or cross-account roles based on policies. In the hands of a bad actor, any of these can become a threat vector.

A major challenge content owners face is balancing security and usability. Overly restrictive policies can hinder productivity, while loose controls increase risks. Access should be seamless and friction-free for legitimate users while maintaining strict security controls over network and content access. For example, anomaly detection might identify a false positive, mistakenly locking out a legitimate user. Organizations must have clear policies and rapid resolution mechanisms to minimize productivity disruptions.

The key to securing hybrid workflows lies in identifying potential attack vectors while supporting bespoke and remote access requirements.

Threat Vectors

In both cases, lateral movement is the primary threat. "Blast radius," refers to the extent of damage caused by a failure, in this case a security breach. When credentials are compromised, containing the blast radius is crucial.

For example, consider a quality control (QC) operator responsible for reviewing media content. This operator needs read-only access to specific proxies at designated times. In some cases, they may also need access to high-resolution or original content. Implementing just-in-time (JIT) access ensures that their permissions are granted only when needed and revoked once the task is complete. This significantly reduces the potential blast radius of credential compromise.

For a SaaS vendor, the challenge is more complex. Many SaaS services require broad access to content. For instance, if a vendor is transcoding a media library, it will need full read access to the original content and write access to the destination folder. If a SaaS vendor's credentials are compromised, an attacker could gain access to all the content that the vendor has been permitted to process.

Furthermore, in environments where entities have lateral access across systems, the risks increase. If a manager or administrator has cross-silo or cross-network access, a compromised credential could allow an attacker to explore the network, traverse between systems, and cause widespread disruptions.

The methods used by attackers to obtain credentials—such as phishing, malware, or social engineering—are beyond the scope of this paper. However, these topics are covered extensively in this Cisco Talos blog [1] and MITRE ATT&CK Techniques [2]. In today's threat environment, the question is not if credentials will be compromised, but when. Organizations must proactively plan for this inevitability by carefully designing access roles, security policies, and credential rotation strategies before deploying hybrid workflows. Regular security reviews are essential to maintaining robust defenses.

Real-World Examples

As companies adopt hybrid workloads, three primary scenarios emerge: cloud-based processing, cloud-based production, and cloud-first operations.

In Cloud-Based Processing, content is sent to the cloud for processing and then returned. If this workflow is machine-only (i.e., no user interaction), the risk of credential misuse is lower. However, key rotation and access logging remain critical.

With Cloud-Based Production, operators (editors, VFX artists) access content in the cloud while most assets remain on-premises. This introduces increased risk because many operators are freelancers or part-time employees who may not follow the same security standards as full-time staff. Operators often work with multiple clients and may use weak local security practices for storing credentials. In this case, more granular access control is required to limit exposure based on the user's role, location, and duration of need.

Cloud-First Operations presents the highest security risk and requires the strongest security controls, including rigorous access management (e.g., role-based access control, zero-trust principles), continuous monitoring and anomaly detection, and strict credential policies (e.g., rotating API keys, limiting long-term access tokens)

Cloud-first organizations must define and maintain high levels of security discipline.

Security Strategies for Hybrid Workflows

Organizations must balance security, usability, and operational efficiency while proactively mitigating risks related to credential theft, lateral movement, and SaaS vulnerabilities. Implementing robust security frameworks, continuous monitoring, and proactive controls, helps content owners safeguard their intellectual property and reduce exposure to modern cyber threats.

Beyond following standard IT best practices for networking and user security, it is essential to apply the principle of least privilege when granting entities access to content and resources. In addition, proactive anomaly detection can help identify activity that deviates from normal behavior. While such security measures may introduce some friction for users, proper monitoring and resolution can mitigate their impact.

The impact of a business-to-business (B2B) entity's access to prerelease or proprietary content differs from that of business-to-consumer (B2C) or direct-to-consumer (D2C) systems. For consumer-facing content, it may be preferable to assume access while validating authentication, terminating access if authentication fails. The revenue impact of denying a consumer access to content they are not entitled to is minimal, while the customer's experience is improved. Conversely, in a B2B system—whether machine-to-machine, programmatic, or user-based—it is preferable to prevent access until the entity's authorization is verified. This approach ensures that content remains restricted until appropriate access is granted, reinforcing the principle of least privilege.

Note: These strategies are foundational guidance. Security landscapes continuously evolve with new methodologies, vendors, software, and attack profiles. Use these strategies as foundational guidance, but consult your IT and security teams regularly to review and update security models and strategies.

Zero Trust Architecture

Zero Trust is a security model based on the principle of "never trust, always verify." It assumes no entity is inherently trustworthy, even within the network perimeter, and requires authentication and authorization for every access request. Given the prevalence of compromised credentials, whether through human error or programmatic discovery, organizations must assume that any access attempt could be illegitimate.

By enforcing continuous verification organizations can minimize the blast radius of an incident. When an entity is compromised, attackers are restricted to only the resources explicitly authorized for that entity, preventing lateral movement and limiting potential damage. Implementing granular access controls based on device security posture and context for access significantly reduces unauthorized access risks.

Zero Trust frameworks center around network security and identity management. For networking, this may include restricting ports and network addresses. For identity, it means granting access only when necessary and with the least privilege required. However, organizations must balance security with user experience and infrastructure flexibility. Typically, Zero Trust begins with centralized single sign-on (SSO), enabling users to access systems with a unified login, while enabling administrators to block a user across systems as needed.

In M&E environments, Zero Trust is a relatively new concept that requires a strategic implementation plan. Achieving Zero Trust across workflows and systems may take months or years, and requires collaboration with knowledgeable security personnel and vendor support.

Anomaly Detection

Anomaly detection and behavioral analytics use machine learning to identify unusual patterns in system activity that may indicate security threats. Unlike traditional rule-based security systems, these approaches learn normal behavior and flag deviations.

Proactive anomaly detection enhances security beyond reactive monitoring methods such as log analysis and access reviews. Behavioral analysis systems detect deviations from standard activity, such as unusual API calls or excessive elevated permission usage, which may signal a security breach. Software-as-a-Service (SaaS) solutions should have minimal behavioral deviation, whereas compromised credentials often result in significant anomalies.

Organizations can implement different anomaly detection approaches to balance security and user experience. For instance, advanced users requiring restricted access may use a self-assertion system that logs access attempts with justifications, generating security alerts if needed. In contrast, users with limited access may be blocked from unauthorized systems and prompted to request access, ensuring security oversight while maintaining workflow efficiency.

Mitigation Strategies

Historically, M&E infrastructure and systems relied on assumed trust. Connectivity such as SDI and AES67 are by nature secure. However, with the adoption of commodity IT networking, organizations must adopt mitigation strategies similar to those in traditional IT environments.

To mitigate security risks, organizations must establish network isolation and trusted zones to segregate critical systems, reducing exposure in the event of a breach. By segmenting networks, unauthorized access to core systems and sensitive content is minimized, ensuring that compromised devices or users cannot move laterally across environments. Explicit access grants should be enforced using least privilege principles and role-based permissions, ensuring that users and applications only have access to the resources they need. Additionally, secure communication channels, such as private fiber links or private connections within the cloud, should be used to protect data in transit and prevent unauthorized interception of sensitive media assets.

Managing user access effectively is critical to maintaining a secure environment while minimizing operational disruptions. Just-in-time (JIT) access provisioning should be implemented to grant temporary permissions only when required, reducing the risk of persistent elevated privileges being misused or compromised. Multi-Factor Authentication (MFA) must be enforced as part of a centralized authentication process to verify user identities and prevent unauthorized access due to stolen credentials. Regular access reviews are essential for auditing denied access events and privileged accounts, allowing security teams to identify anomalies, detect potential insider threats, and close security gaps before they are exploited. Organizations should also enforce separate credentials and roles for different security zones, preventing attackers from using compromised accounts to gain access to sensitive systems across multiple environments.

Proactive security monitoring is a fundamental component of a robust security strategy. User Behavior Analytics (UBA) should be integrated into security frameworks to detect abnormal activity and identify compromised accounts before they can cause damage. By continuously analyzing user behavior, organizations can spot deviations from normal patterns, such as unusual access times, aggressive permission escalations, or unexpected API calls, which may indicate unauthorized access attempts. Security teams should leverage automated monitoring tools and Security Information and Event Management (SIEM) solutions to correlate access logs, flag suspicious activity, and trigger real-time alerts for potential threats. By combining anomaly detection with access control mechanisms, organizations can enhance their security posture while minimizing disruptions to legitimate users.

Adopting these strategies, M&E companies can modernize their security frameworks to align with best practices from traditional IT while addressing the unique challenges of media production, distribution, and collaboration.

Vendor-Oriented Solutions

Organizations often opt for vendor-provided solutions to leverage expert knowledge and dedicated security resources. Many security vendors offer off-the-shelf solutions for monitoring, access control, and threat detection.

Vendors play a crucial role at different layers of the security stack, particularly in SaaS environments. However, SaaS providers may not always be security experts, so organizations must work with them to implement best practices. For example, using cross-account role sharing instead of embedding credentials in applications. Regularly updating or rotating security keys reduces usability from exposure. Where possible, configure dedicated network endpoints to secure connections.

In M&E, orchestration solutions often integrate multiple third-party software tools across vendors, facilities, and customers. Organizations must assess potential attack vectors and implement connectivity and access controls to safeguard intellectual property and proprietary systems. It is essential to maintain the ability to disconnect from vendors when necessary to ensure both vendor and customer security.

Challenges and Considerations

The Media and Entertainment industry faces distinct security challenges due to the high value of its content and the complexity of its workflows. Protecting media assets—including content, metadata, and production systems—requires a mix of technical controls, user access policies, and secure communications. Historically, media systems have struggled to align with standardized IT security practices, often prioritizing workflow efficiency over security. The shift toward global production further complicates security, as media professionals need specialized applications and interfaces that differ from traditional IT environments. These challenges are compounded by the limitations of legacy security models, necessitating a transition to modern frameworks like Zero Trust, cloud security best practices, and hybrid security models. These frameworks provide continuous threat detection and robust access controls, but successful adoption requires industry-wide collaboration between media companies and technology vendors to balance security with operational flexibility.

Industry-Specific Challenges

Media security is essential to protect assets such as content, metadata, and systems from unauthorized access, use, modification, or disruption. This involves technical measures, content access policies, and access request procedures to ensure the protection, integrity, and availability of assets. However, media systems have struggled to align with standardized IT and networking practices. The era of open systems and brute-force connectivity "to make it work" must evolve, requiring a proactive approach to protecting media—especially prerelease content.

Given the global nature of production, anomaly detection may occasionally impact users, but using effective out-of-band validation resources can minimize disruption, particularly during atypical working hours. Unlike traditional IT users, media professionals require unique applications and interfaces. Despite these differences, industry stakeholders—including customers and vendors—must collaborate to overcome these challenges and adopt security-first models like Zero Trust.

Limitations of Traditional Security Models

Traditional security models in the M&E industry are often reactive, responding to threats only after damage has occurred. These legacy approaches, relying on outdated standard operating procedures and expected user access, challenge the implementation of stronger security frameworks like Zero Trust. Cloud security practices safeguard data and applications in cloud environments, addressing challenges such as shared responsibility, data sovereignty, and access control. Best practices like strong access management, data encryption, and regular security assessments help mitigate risks and enhance protection.

Hybrid cloud security extends protection across on-premises infrastructure, private clouds, and public clouds—often integrated with SaaS applications. This requires a unified approach to security management and policy enforcement. A well-designed hybrid cloud security strategy ensures consistent security posture and minimizes vulnerabilities from integrating disparate systems.

Adapting modern security models is challenging, especially due to user access limitations, training, and understanding. Industry-wide collaboration with vendors is essential to address vendor-specific constraints and advance best practices that enhance security without impacting workflows.

Continual Threat Assessment and Adaptation

As the M&E industry evolves with new technologies for content creation and consumption, so do the threat vectors for access security. A proactive security framework requires ongoing awareness of cybersecurity threats, vulnerabilities, and attack techniques. Whether managed internally or with a security provider, monitoring the threat landscape, analyzing attack patterns, and assessing emerging risks is crucial.

Regular information sharing among security peers strengthens collective defenses. Programs such as Common Vulnerabilities and Exposures (CVE) [3] provide vital information on known vulnerabilities, while industry-specific groups, such as the Financial Services Information Sharing and Analysis Center (FS-ISAC) [4], focus on sector-specific vulnerabilities. Proactive monitoring, sharing, and action on security intelligence are crucial to safeguarding assets and operations.

Conclusion

The security landscape within the M&E industry is evolving, driven by the growth of hybrid and cloud-based workflows. Security strategies like Zero Trust, anomaly detection, and mitigation strategies are essential tools for proactive risk mitigation. Industry reports highlighting security incidents involving credential compromise underscore the need for robust security frameworks across cloud-based and hybrid processing, production, and operations.

A proactive, multi-layered security approach is essential, even if it requires a shift for legacy lines of business. Organizations must move beyond reactive measures, embracing modern security frameworks, monitoring, and anomaly detection. Mitigation strategies such as network segmentation, least privilege access, and multi-factor authentication are crucial for minimizing vulnerabilities.

M&E professionals should advocate for these proactive security measures to protect valuable intellectual property and ensure business continuity. Ongoing threat assessment and adaptation are necessary, as the threat landscape is constantly changing. Industry collaboration and knowledge-sharing are vital for staying ahead of emerging threats and developing best practices. By adopting these principles, the M&E industry can navigate the complexities of hybrid workflows while safeguarding its assets, contributing to a more secure and resilient industry.

References

[1] Cisco Talos Blog: https://blog.talosintelligence.com/how-are-user-credentials-stolen-and-used-by-threat-actors/

[2] MITRE ATT&CK Techniques (valid accounts): https://attack.mitre.org/techniques/T1078/

[3] Common Vulnerabilities and Exposures: https://www.cve.org/

[4] Financial Services Information Sharing and Analysis Center: https://www.fsisac.com/

Transforming Team Collaboration with Avatars: Enhancing Productivity and Content Creation in Broadcasting

Ira Sharma, Kaushal Dadi, Anesh Madapoosi, Shyam Kapur
TipTop Technologies
Sunnyvale, California, United States
ira@feeltiptop.com

Abstract – In the fast-paced world of broadcast and media, teams must collaborate efficiently and create content quickly to remain competitive. Avatar technology offers an innovative solution, enabling team members to stay connected even when they are unable to be physically present. By stepping in to summarize past meetings and capture key insights, avatars bridge communication gaps and ensure continuity, allowing teams to resume their work without the need for lengthy catchups. This approach enhances decision-making and streamlines workflows, keeping teams aligned and productive. In addition to avatars, the integration of intuitive tools for video editing, content creation, and subtitling empowers teams to produce high-quality content without specialized skills. These tools support multiple languages, enabling broadcasters to reach a diverse, global audience. With simplified video clipping, merging, and subtitling processes, teams can adapt and release content more quickly, making their workflows more efficient and responsive to industry demands. This combination of avatar-driven collaboration and user-friendly content tools optimizes production time, enhances engagement, and ensures a smooth workflow, even when team schedules do not align. It allows broadcasters to work smarter, integrating technology into the creative process. This approach empowers teams to create exceptional content, collaborate seamlessly, and meet the growing demands of today's dynamic media landscape.

Introduction

The media industry increasingly relies on digital collaboration tools such as Slack, Zoom, and newsroom automation systems. However, traditional tools struggle with asynchronous collaboration challenges, causing workflow inefficiencies. AI-driven avatars offer a solution by acting as intelligent assistants capable of summarizing meetings, retrieving contextual media content, and generating subtitles in multiple languages. This paper explores the role of avatars in enhancing teamwork and production efficiency in broadcast environments. The increasing adoption of digital avatars in professional environments presents new opportunities for team collaboration, broadcast media workflows, and content management [1]. Understanding these dynamics is crucial for developers and designers aiming to create virtual agents that effectively motivate and engage users. By carefully considering avatar design and the transparency of their AI nature, it is possible to enhance user experiences and outcomes in virtual interactions [2].

This paper is excerpted from the Proceedings of the 2025 NAB Broadcast Engineering and Information Technology (BEIT) Conference, © 2025, National Association of Broadcasters, 1 M Street SE, Washington, DC 20003 USA.

Technical Framework

The Avatar System is designed with flexibility and scalability in mind, using a modular architecture that connects all the necessary components, including the user interface, backend processing, collaboration tools, and data management. Together, these elements create a seamless experience for users, enabling real-time interactions, efficient content processing, and smooth collaboration. This section breaks down how each part of the system works together to enhance the user experience, streamline teamwork, and support fast, effective content production.

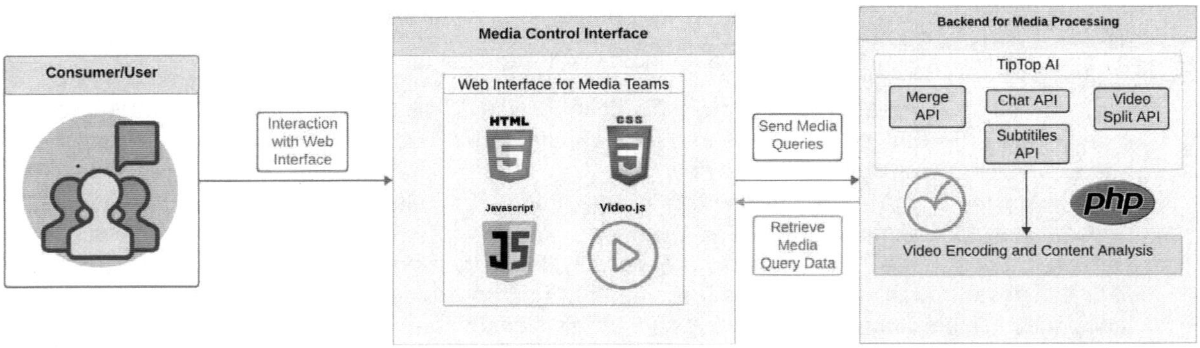

FIGURE 1: FRONTEND AND BACKEND OF AVATAR ARCHITECTURE DIAGRAM.

Media Control Frontend Layer

As shown in Figure 1, the Frontend Layer is the main interface between users and the Avatar System, providing an interactive space for querying avatars, managing video content, and viewing multimedia. The frontend is designed to be responsive, ensuring smooth interaction across a variety of devices. Users can input queries to retrieve meeting summaries, speaker-specific insights, or video clips, making it easy to access relevant information quickly. With the integration of Video.js, the system allows users to clip, merge, and customize video content directly within the platform, streamlining the process of content creation. This flexibility helps teams extract specific moments from longer meetings or presentations.

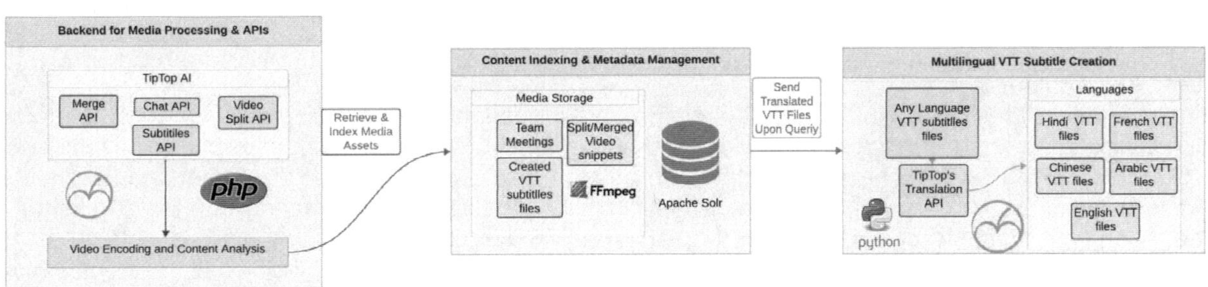

FIGURE 2: BACKEND, PROCESSING, AND DATABASE OF AVATAR ARCHITECTURE DIAGRAM.

Backend for Media Processing

The Backend Layer is responsible for processing user requests, generating personalized responses, and managing the logic behind all interactions. It ensures that all data necessary for avatar responses, video content management, and real-time user interactions is efficiently handled and served without delay.

TipTop AI offers a suite of powerful tools designed to enhance media production workflows and facilitate seamless team collaboration. These tools include the following:

- **Chat API**: This API helps process user queries, pulling relevant meeting summaries, action items, and speaker details. It allows users to ask avatars for specific information, like a summary of past discussions or video clips from particular topics, ensuring responses are quick and on point.
- **Video Split API**: This component lets users extract key video clips using FFmpeg from larger recordings based on their queries. It's especially helpful for pulling out specific moments, like an important discussion or decision, making it easier to access exactly what's needed. This eliminates the need to watch entire videos.
- **Merge API**: The Merge API takes multiple video clips and combines them into one cohesive video file using FFmpeg, which is great for collaboration. This tool allows team members to merge their individual contributions into a single video that has all the relevant content in one file and it is easy to share as well as review.
- **Subtitles API**: This API generates real-time multilingual subtitles, making the system accessible to users from different regions. A Python-based solution was developed to automate the conversion of subtitle files and video transcripts. By integrating TipTop's Translation Language API, this system enables seamless translation of content from English into a variety of languages. This automation greatly speeds up the localization workflow, allowing broadcasters and media teams to quickly adapt content for global audiences. The integration not only optimizes content production but also improves accessibility by offering multilingual support, ensuring a broader and more diverse reach for media and broadcast content.

Content Analysis Processing Layer

As seen in Figure 2, processing and data layer is responsible for turning raw information into useful insights. It processes user queries and ensures fast, accurate responses in real-time. The Load Balancer makes sure data requests are handled efficiently by spreading the workload across different processing engines. This helps keep the system responsive even when multiple users are querying at the same time. The Processing Engine organizes and summarizes meeting transcripts and recordings, allowing the system to pull up relevant information quickly. The Decision Logic layer then takes this processed data and figures out which pieces of information are most important to answer the user's query. This makes sure that our system delivers concise and actionable insights without delay.

Database Server

The Database and File Server layer plays a crucial role in managing and storing different types of data, such as recorded team meetings, video files, and processed content like video snippets and subtitles as illustrated in Figure 2. It ensures that data can be retrieved quickly and that the system can scale to handle large volumes of information, especially when multiple users are interacting with it at the same time. At its core, data storage is centralized meaning all meeting videos, subtitles, and associated metadata are stored in one place. This data is then indexed using an Apache Solr-based system, which makes it easy to search and retrieve relevant content. Data storage in solr helps power the search feature allowing users to find specific video clips or meeting summaries based on a variety of criteria including any combination of speaker, timestamp and topic. The database is tightly integrated with other components, like the Video Split API, Merge API, and Subtitles API, ensuring that video content and subtitles are managed efficiently even when they are in several different languages.

Avatar Interfaces in Media Production

The avatar interface in media production acts as the bridge between users and the system, offering an intuitive, easy-to-use space for managing content and collaborating with team members. Through this interface, users can interact with avatars, which act as virtual assistants, to quickly retrieve important information such as meeting summaries, key speaker insights, or specific video clips. This makes it much easier to find and share relevant content without having to scroll through hours of footage. The avatar interface also allows users to perform tasks like clipping and merging video segments, giving teams the flexibility to create the right content faster. It adds multilingual subtitles, so content is accessible to a wider, global audience. With its customizability and smooth integration of various media tools, this interface helps teams stay aligned and focused, enabling them to work more efficiently and deliver content quickly in today's fast-paced media environment.

Interactive Query System with Dynamic Speaker Selection

The avatar interface, as seen in Figure 3, includes an Interactive Query System allowing users to interact with the system through an easy-to-use chat box. It is fully customizable. Users can adjust the number of responses they get, with options to choose from 10, 25, 50, or even 100 responses depending on how much information they need. The Dynamic Speaker Selection allows users to easily retrieve and display a list of team members helping to streamline collaboration in large, data-driven teams. The lists of team members can be organized by role as well as location. This feature enhances communication making it especially valuable for teams working across various departments and locations. The system is set up to ensure that everyone remains aligned and decision-making is smooth and efficient across each group and also the entire organization.

FIGURE 3: QUERY SYSTEM WITH SPEAKER SELECTION.

Insights with Video Management and Playback

When users query the system for specific information, the summarization feature automatically highlights key parts of past discussions as seen in Figure 4, making it easy to locate important details without having to sift through long videos. This is especially beneficial for media teams operating under tight deadlines. The system integrates with Video.js to provide smooth video playback and automatically generates multilingual subtitles in languages such as English, French, Arabic, Chinese, and Hindi as seen in Figure 3. Additionally, videos are automatically segmented, with important topics extracted and categorized. These segments are akin to chapters, making it easier for users to navigate to relevant portions of the content. When users query the system, it retrieves the most relevant video clips and displays them with dynamic subtitles, ensuring the content is accessible to diverse, multilingual teams. This combination of automated segmentation, summarization, and subtitle integration helps teams make decisions faster, collaborate more effectively, and create content quickly, all while supporting a global audience and improving efficiency across different regions and languages.

FIGURE 4: QUERY RESULTS AND SUMMARIZATION.

Content Clipping and Merging for Seamless Collaboration

The avatar interface makes video management easier with two key features, content clipping and content merging. Content clipping lets users quickly extract the most relevant video segments that address their queries, thereby saving time by focusing only on key parts of the conversation. The user can also choose to include or exclude subtitles, as illustrated in Figure 5, depending on the project's needs giving them more flexibility. This feature is perfect for pinpointing important moments in discussions and sharing them efficiently with other team members. The platform offers content merging which lets users select multiple clips, arrange them in any desired order as seen in Figure 5, and then combine these video clips into one seamless video. This is especially useful for creating summary videos or curating content for presentations and meetings. By simplifying the editing process, content merging helps teams quickly put together videos that capture the most important points of their discussions, thus saving time and boosting productivity. Together, these features make collaboration smoother and more efficient helping teams share exactly what they need and when they need it.

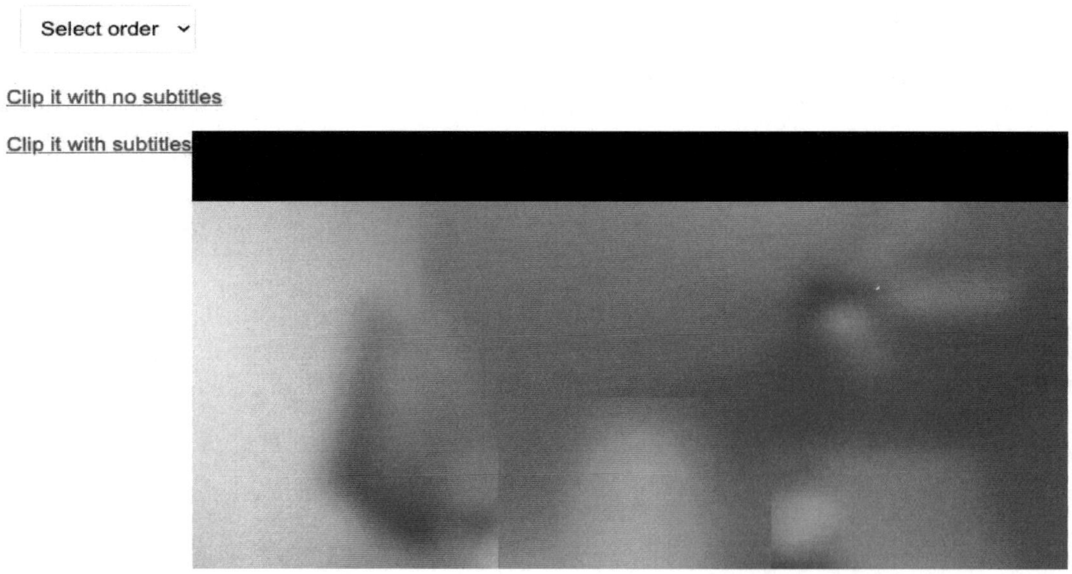

FIGURE 5: QUERY RESULTS FOR VIDEO PLAYBACK WITH CONTENT CLIPPING AND MERGING.

Subtitles Integration

The avatar interface also supports Subtitles Integration, which syncs subtitles with video playback using a WebVTT parser. This system automatically generates subtitles in multiple languages, including English, Hindi, Spanish, French, Arabic, and Chinese. The ability to create and display subtitles makes content more accessible, allowing teams from around the world to communicate effectively. By providing synchronized subtitles that offer real-time context, this feature breaks down language barriers, helping diverse teams collaborate more efficiently and ensuring that everyone can follow along, regardless of which language they are comfortable with.

Integration with Broadcast & Media Tools

Our Avatar System is designed to integrate seamlessly with widely used collaboration platforms allowing media and broadcast teams to access, share, and analyze information directly within their existing workflows as seen in Figure 6. By connecting with communication tools like Slack and Zoom, the system streamlines communication, saving valuable time and ensuring that teams stay focused on more creative tasks such as content creation and decision-making instead of searching for footage or for meeting notes.

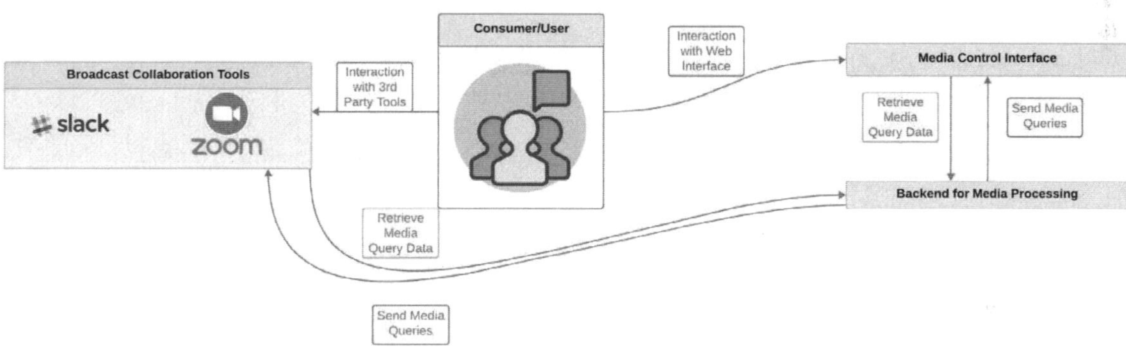

FIGURE 6: INTEGRATION WITH BROADCAST AND MEDIA TOOLS.

Slack Integration

The Slack integration is a game-changer for media and broadcast teams that need to maintain continuous communication while managing and reviewing large volumes of content. As illustrated in Figure 7, users can tag the avatar bot and specify the name of the team member whose avatar they wish to query. The bot then provides relevant results, including the title, segment text, and a video link that directly corresponds to the part of the conversation where the team member discussed the topic. This functionality ensures that the system extracts and plays only the relevant portion of the video, eliminating the need to watch the entire recording. This streamlined process helps teams save time and focus on the specific content they need, enhancing productivity and collaboration.

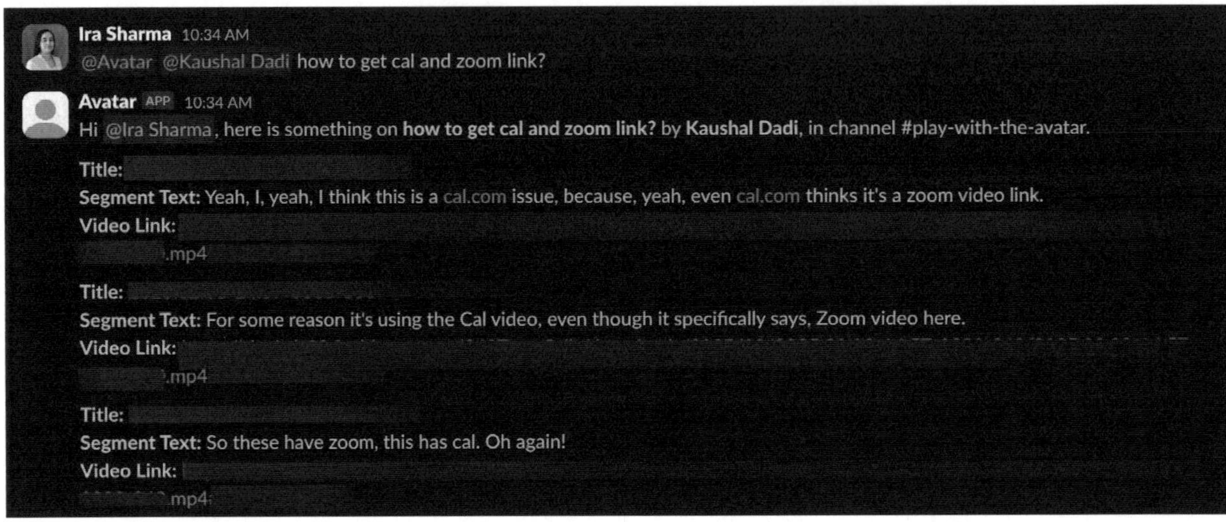

FIGURE 7: AVATAR SLACKBOT.

Zoom Integration

In addition to Slack, the Avatar System integrates with Zoom, enhancing collaboration especially in post-production or live event debriefs. By analyzing Zoom recordings and transcripts, the avatar extracts key information such as speaker contributions, decisions made, and action items, which can be particularly useful for media teams reviewing complex discussions or production meetings.

Enhancing Content Production & Management

The integration of avatar technology in content production and management provides a transformative approach to automating repetitive tasks and significantly improving workflow efficiency. By leveraging avatars as virtual assistants, many time-consuming and lower-value tasks such as content categorization can be reduced. This allows media teams to focus more on the creative and strategic aspects of content creation. These avatars can also act as digital proxies for team members who are unavailable, thereby ensuring seamless communication and collaboration across different time zones. This feature is particularly crucial for global teams working in remote or hybrid environments where maintaining continuity in discussions and decision-making can often be a challenge. Additionally, avatars offer unparalleled flexibility by enabling real-time multilingual content adaptation, ensuring that content can be quickly localized and personalized for diverse audiences. This combination of automation, communication facilitation, and data analytics not only saves time and resources but also optimizes the entire content creation and distribution process. Ultimately, this technology enhances productivity by eliminating bottlenecks and inefficiencies, empowering media teams to produce, manage, and distribute content more effectively, while maintaining a high level of user engagement and accessibility [3].

Impact on Media Workflows

The integration of avatars and virtual environments into media workflows has a significant impact on improving collaboration, communication, and overall efficiency. By using avatars as virtual stand-ins for absent team members, media teams can maintain seamless communication across time zones, thus ensuring that projects continue to progress without delays. These avatars facilitate interaction, allowing team members to query information, share insights, and collaborate on content production in a more dynamic and engaging way. Additionally, virtual environments enable teams to work in immersive spaces where they can collectively analyze, edit, and manage media content. This reduces the need for physical meetings and streamlines decision-making. This makes workflows more agile. Furthermore, the application of universal design principles in these environments ensures that all members, regardless of their cognitive or physical abilities, can access and engage with the content. The combination of these tools enhances productivity by eliminating bottlenecks, accelerating content creation, and improving the quality of collaboration, ultimately transforming the media production process [4].

Benefits and Competitive Advantage

Avatar-based innovation in virtual worlds offers a wealth of advantages for content production and management. By fostering interactive and immersive environments, companies can tap into a global reservoir of creativity, with consumers represented as avatars, engaging across every stage of product development, from ideation to prototyping. This direct collaboration ensures that media content is precisely tailored to meet real customer preferences, thereby enhancing its relevance and appeal. Virtual spaces, with their flexibility and global accessibility, enable businesses to stay agile and competitive in a rapidly evolving market [5]. Additionally, by eliminating the need for travel, companies can reduce costs and time, all the while broadening access to diverse, global talent. The use of avatars further enriches these interactions, providing immersive, real-time feedback from participants across different locations [6]. Moreover, these virtual platforms support rapid prototyping and testing, streamlining the development process and improving flexibility. As these technologies advance, they will allow for the simulation of varying user behaviors and preferences, thus driving even more personalized, customer-centric content creation.

In addition to these operational advantages, avatar-based innovation offers companies a distinct competitive edge by enabling them to develop advanced, customer-driven content. The ability to rapidly innovate combined with cost-effective processes allows businesses to outperform competitors in the fast-moving media industry [5]. By harnessing the diverse expertise and creativity of global teams, companies can craft content that resonates with a wider audience, thus standing out in a crowded marketplace [6]. The flexibility of virtual collaboration accelerates content iteration, enabling quicker refinement and adaptation to meet audience demands. This constant adaptability ensures that media companies can maintain a continuous cycle of innovation, thereby allowing them to respond effectively to unexpected challenges or market shifts [6].

Performance Evaluation

The Avatar System's performance was tested in scenarios simulating real-world asynchronous and hybrid collaboration, focusing on key functionalities like summarizing discussions, retrieving video content, and enabling real-time interactions. As shown in Figure 8, the results were impressive across several critical metrics. For summarization, the system delivered 86% accuracy, effectively extracting important points and action items from long discussions. When it came to video interactions such as indexing and retrieving relevant video clips, the system achieved 92.96% accuracy. This confirmed its ability to quickly pinpoint and manage the right content. The interface responsiveness also stood out, with users highlighting its ease of use, seamless integration with tools like Slack and Zoom, and features like real-time subtitles and dynamic speaker selection, which made collaboration smoother and more efficient. All in all, the Avatar System proved to be a powerful tool for enhancing teamwork, simplifying content retrieval, and improving communication in a fast-paced, multi-location work environment.

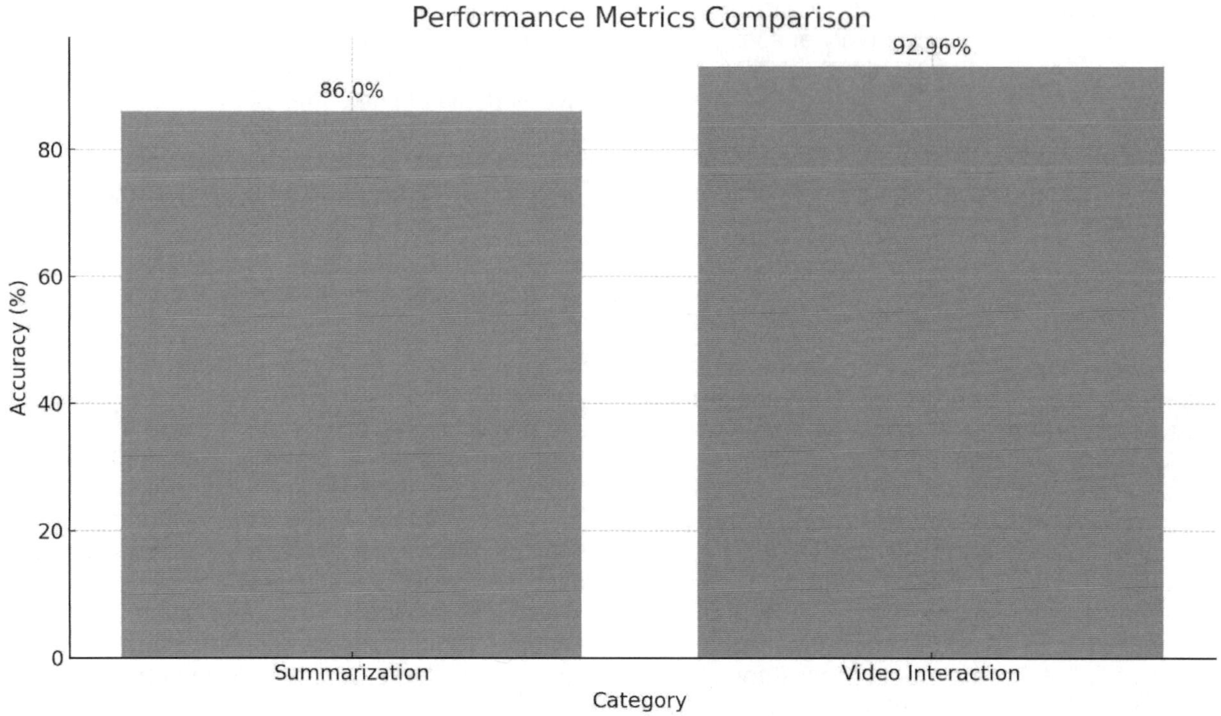

FIGURE 8: PERFORMANCE EVALUATION.

Industry Impact

The use of avatars in the media and broadcasting industry is set to revolutionize how content is created, presented, and consumed. With avatars available around the clock, broadcasters will no longer be tied to traditional human schedules, making it possible to produce and broadcast content without interruptions. This means that news outlets can provide a constant stream of content, something that was difficult to achieve with human anchors or presenters [7]. As AI-generated avatars and automated systems become more integrated into broadcasting, they will make content production more efficient and accessible. This will allow news organizations to deliver more localized, diverse, and timely content, reaching a wider audience and meeting the needs of different viewers [8].

Conclusion

The use of avatars in media and broadcasting has completely transformed the industry, opening up new possibilities for content creation and collaboration. These avatars allow teams to work together seamlessly, no matter where they are in the world, without being limited by time zones or traditional work hours. By taking care of repetitive tasks, avatars give teams more time to focus on the creative and strategic aspects of their work, which ultimately leads to better content and increased productivity. Plus, avatars can generate real-time, localized, and multilingual content, allowing media organizations to reach and connect with a diverse range of audiences, making their content more inclusive and globally accessible.

As virtual worlds continue to grow, avatars will likely play an even bigger role in product development and innovation, helping companies stay ahead in an increasingly digital and connected world [5]. For broadcasters, this means a constant flow of content, the ability to break through geographic and time barriers, and the opportunity to create media that speaks to a broader, more diverse audience. As avatars become more integrated into media workflows, they'll not only improve the way content is delivered but also change how we experience and consume media in the digital age.

References

[1] M. Korban and X. Li, "A Survey on Applications of Digital Human Avatars toward Virtual Co-presence," *arXiv (Cornell University)*, 2022. [Online]. Available: https://doi.org/10.48550/arxiv.2201.04168.

[2] B. Visser, P. van der Putten, and A. Zohrehvand, "The Impacts of AI Avatar Appearance and Disclosure on User Motivation," *arXiv*, 2024. [Online]. Available: https://doi.org/10.48550/arxiv.2407.21521.

[3] A. Stoicu and D. -G. Ionica, "Social Media Avatar: My Dear Virtual Assistant," in *IEEE 16th International Conference on Embedded and Ubiquitous Computing (EUC)*, Bucharest, Romania, 2018, pp. 117–122. [Online]. Available: https://doi.org/10.1109/EUC.2018.00024.

[4] N. Gregg, Y. Chang, and R. Todd, "Social Media, Avatars, and Virtual Worlds: Re-imagine an Inclusive Learning Environment for Adolescents and Adults with Literacy Barriers," *Procedia Computer Science*, vol. 14, pp. 336–342, 2012. [Online]. Available: https://doi.org/10.1016/j.procs.2012.10.038.

[5] T. Kohler, K. Matzler, and J. Füller, "Avatar-based innovation: Using virtual worlds for real-world innovation," *Technovation*, vol. 29, no. 6, pp. 395–407, 2009. [Online]. Available: https://doi.org/10.1016/j.technovation.2008.11.004.

[6] R. M. Löllgen, J. Berger-Estilita, L. A. Rössler, and L. P. Mileder, "Avatar and distance simulation as a learning tool - virtual simulation technology as a facilitator or barrier? A questionnaire-based study on behalf of Netzwerk Kindersimulation e.V.," *Frontiers in Pediatrics*, vol. 10, p. 853243, 2022. [Online]. Available: https://doi.org/10.3389/fped.2022.853243.

[7] L. Chi, "Research on the Impact and Application Strategies of AI in Virtual Streamer Based on the Media Industry," *Highlights in Business, Economics and Management*, vol. 41, pp. 144–149, 2024. [Online]. Available: https://doi.org/10.54097/gfc28x72.

[8] C. S. Owsley, "Understanding the impact of Artificial Intelligence on newsroom social culture and journalistic performative roles: a qualitative case study of AI as an emerging digital innovative technology in newsrooms," 2023. [Online]. Available: https://doi.org/10.32469/10355/96115.

Hidden Depths: Disguise's Integration of Depth and Volumetric Capture Workflows for Virtual Production

Chris Nash, Nathan Butt, Andrea Loriedo, Robin Spooner, Taegyun Ha, Philip Coulam-Jones, James Bentley
Disguise
London, United Kingdom
chris.nash@disguise.one, philip.coulam-jones@disguise.one

Aljosa Smolic
Lucerne University of Applied Arts and Sciences
Lucerne, Switzerland

Abstract – The ability to capture a volumetric representation of performers in a production environment would enable a multitude of novel on-set and post-production workflows. Current methods are impractical due to their reliance on large numbers of cameras and consistent lighting conditions. We propose a framework for creating 2.5D assets from a single monocular video, allowing digitised performers to be viewed from a range of angles with the appearance of depth. An application processes the video offline, using depth and segmentation AI models to create a packaged 2.5D asset. This is then loaded into Disguise Designer for pre-visualisation of the performers within the virtual stage. Analysis of state-of-the-art depth inference models, using videos captured to represent the challenges of production environments, shows that it is possible to obtain coherent video depth maps in these conditions. However, metric models do not always identify absolute depth values accurately, and it is necessary to use models specifically tailored for video to ensure temporal consistency in the result. This work is intended to act as a foundation for more comprehensive 3D volumetric capture of performers in real production environments.

Introduction

Volumetric capture and reconstruction are emerging technologies that are rapidly gaining interest for their implementation in production workflows. The ability to digitise, reconstruct and manipulate 3D representations of real performers and environments promises to reshape the production landscape as crews can use these digital assets in a variety of new and exciting ways. Volumetric capture will enable revolutionary new pre-visualisation methodologies, placing the movements of performers into a simulation of the real space to gain an understanding of how they will interact with complex sets and props. It could also reduce the need to reshoot scenes by enabling digitised performers to be recoloured, relit or recorded from new camera angles, saving resources and cutting production costs.

In this paper we describe a new framework for combining state-of-the-art AI models into a pipeline for capturing and playing back volumetric representations of performers from a single monocular camera capture. The pipeline consists of an application which combines depth and segmentation models to convert the video into a 2.5D asset, and new functionality within the Disguise Designer software to allow these assets to be played back for pre-visualisation purposes.

This paper is excerpted from the Proceedings of the 2025 NAB Broadcast Engineering and Information Technology (BEIT) Conference, © 2025, National Association of Broadcasters, 1 M Street SE, Washington, DC 20003 USA.

This work has been carried out under the pan-European consortium EMERALD [1] and the joint funded UK/Switzerland project Fast Volumetric Reconstruction (FaVoRe) [2], building off work begun in the MAX-R research initiative [3]. As part of these projects, we have been working with partners at multiple European academic and business institutions to determine the best ways to enable practical volumetric capture workflows in a production environment.

Background

The Disguise Platform

Disguise is an industry-leading platform powering cutting edge visual experiences around the world, operating across various industries including live events, fixed visual installations, and virtual production for film, broadcast and extended reality (xR) studios [4]. We produce hardware and software solutions for sequencing and playing back video and generative content in the most demanding environments.

At the centre of many of our workflows is the Designer application. Using this software, studio operators can set up a digital representation of the physical elements of their production such as screens, projectors, lights and cameras, then sequence video or real-time content which can be pre-visualised within this virtual setup. The same software then runs on our servers during the production itself, connecting with external systems such as LED processors, tracking devices and lighting desks to drive a fully interactive and flexible production environment.

Motivation

While Designer allows for accurate pre-visualisation of the hardware and sequenced content used in a production, it is difficult to get a complete overview of the final performance without being able to see the live performers. Our intention is to use volumetric capture to fill this final missing piece by digitising performers in a rehearsal environment and inserting their virtual representations into a pre-visualisation of the production in Designer. Furthermore, by capturing the performers during the performance itself, we will enable a multitude of new workflows for post-production or spatial and interactive playback opportunities.

While the field of volumetric capture has progressed significantly in recent years, many of the existing solutions are built for captures taken in tightly controlled conditions. Our solution needs to be robust enough to work in a real-world production environment and should take account of the technical and commercial constraints in such a setting. Notable requirements for our intended solution include:

- The capture must be taken with a small (<10) number of cameras mounted in unobtrusive positions
- The capture should work in conditions with varying lighting
- The solution should be able to capture people and props
- The capture can be processed offline, but must be achievable in a reasonable timeframe on non-specialist hardware
- The capture must be played back in real-time
- Any dependencies should be licensable for commercial use

Current State of the Art

There are many potential use cases for a volumetric capture solution which can capture 3D representations of people, objects and backgrounds. However, no such general solution is currently available which doesn't have specific requirements or limitations. There have been many recent developments in capturing static scenes, using volumetric representations such as NERFs [5] [6] [7] and Gaussian splats [8] [9] [10]. However, these solutions generally require a camera to be moved around a scene, capturing images from hundreds of poses, so are not suitable for dynamic capture of time-varying scenes. Dynamic capture has been shown to work with large, regular arrays of cameras [11], or by making assumptions such as capturing humans only [12]. Our research partners in the

FaVoRe project have reviewed current approaches [13], concluding that existing methods are not fully suited to a dynamic, sparse-camera setup. They recommended a pipeline for GPS-Gaussian using video depth as a foundation [14] and are working on modifications to make it more suitable for our use-case.

AI is a rapidly advancing field, with new neural models constantly being released with ever-improving fidelity. Of particular interest for volumetric workflows is depth inference, where an image or video from a single camera is converted into a depth map - a single-channel 2D image encoding the estimated depth from the camera to the objects in the scene. The MiDaS model [15] represented a large step forward in accuracy of AI generated depth maps for images. Since then, further improvements in accuracy have been shown by Depth Anything [16] [17], and Depth Pro [18], which apply transformers to estimate the depth map directly from the input image. Marigold [19] takes an alternative diffusion-based approach, based on the Stable Diffusion image generation model [20]. While these image-based depth estimation models can be applied to videos by processing each frame individually, they can suffer from temporal inconsistency issues where object depths appear to flicker between frames. Recent models aimed at video depth estimation have improved this significantly, such as DepthCrafter [21], RollingDepth [22] and Video Depth Anything [23].

Image segmentation models generate masks for individual objects in an image or video based on user prompts, allowing the selected objects to be separated from their background. Previously this has been achieved by extending models for object detection such as YOLO [24] and Mask R-CNN [25], or semantic segmentation such as DeepLabV3+ [26]. However, recently Segment Anything [27] [28] has become the dominant choice for generating zero-shot segmentation masks based on user-supplied prompt points and bounding boxes. As of V2 [28], it can propagate selections across video frames to keep tracking the selected objects, which was previously only achievable using extensions such as Track Anything [29].

Virtual production studios have historically used 2D video plates placed behind performers. This limits the amount of camera movement that can be achieved before the lack of parallax in the background becomes obvious. More recently, studios have used game engines such as Unreal Engine or Unity to create detailed 3D scenes which can be viewed from a much greater range of camera positions. However, creating such scenes can be time-consuming and expensive, and it is difficult to achieve the same level of realism as video footage. Recently at Disguise, we have implemented a new 2.5D workflow [30]. This works similarly to the multiplane camera used in traditional animation [31], by stacking 2D plates at different depths to produce a parallax effect when the camera moves. By adding depth to the plates, we enable an even more realistic volumetric effect. We have integrated with Cuebric [32], which uses generative AI to generate 2.5D assets for virtual production. However, our current 2.5D implementation only supports static depth maps. This work extends the 2.5D framework to support video plates with video depth maps.

Based on our study of the state of the art, we have concluded that the fastest route to achieving a volumetric representation of performers within Designer is to leverage our existing 2.5D infrastructure. Using depth and segmentation AI models we can create a digitised representation of the performers from footage captured by a single camera, which can be viewed from a range of angles. This representation will be packaged as a 2.5D asset with segmented video content and video depth maps. We aim to use this representation to investigate the ways in which a volumetric capture of performers can be used by productions. As the field advances, we hope to use this as a starting point for building more complete volumetric representations, by fusing captures from multiple cameras surrounding the performers.

Technical Solution

In this section we describe our technical solution for capturing performers and props from monocular video and reconstructing them as 2.5D volumetric assets. First, we give an overview of the whole end-to-end volumetric capture and playback pipeline. Then we describe the application developed for offline processing of video into 2.5D assets. Finally, we discuss how these assets are integrated for pre-visualisation within Disguise Designer.

Volumetric Capture Pipeline Overview

Our monocular volumetric capture and reconstruction pipeline is designed to process input media (either images or videos) and output static or dynamic 2.5D assets suitable for pre-visualisation and other production needs within Disguise Designer. At the core of the workflow is an offline application that processes footage selected by the user, converting raw video into digital assets enhanced with depth using AI techniques. The application leverages a suite of state-of-the-art models to generate depth maps and segmentation masks that capture the nuanced geometry of designated subjects within the scene aided by user-supplied prompts. The results from depth inference and segmentation are combined with spatial metadata into a 2.5D asset with a custom *.2p5d* file format [30]. The resulting asset is loaded and interpreted by the 2.5D framework within Designer, where it is rendered on a virtual stage. Figure 1 presents the different stages of the pipeline broken down into a block diagram:

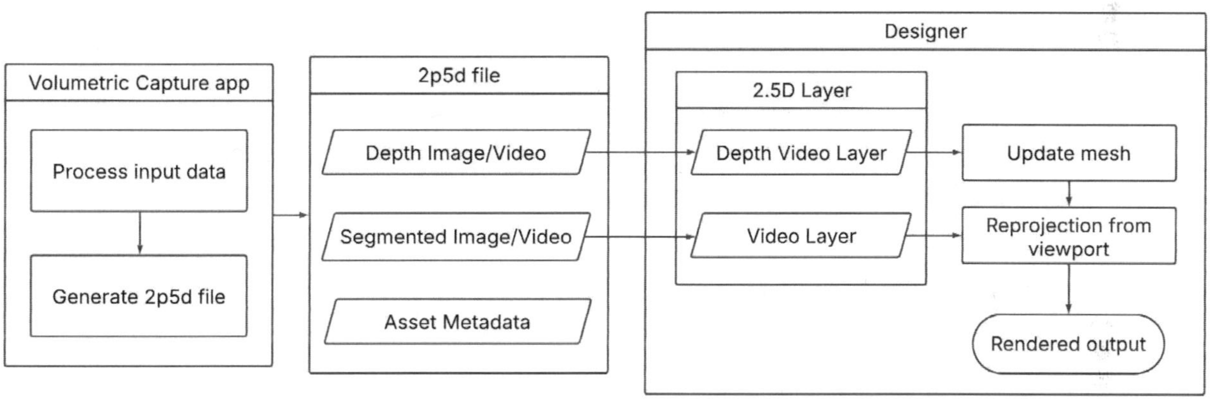

FIGURE 1: OVERVIEW OF THE VOLUMETRIC CAPTURE PIPELINE.

Volumetric Capture Application

The application comprises a Python backend and an Electron-based frontend, providing the user with flexible control over depth inference and segmentation model configurations through a graphical user interface (pictured in Figure 2). It offers cross-platform support and can run on multiple operating systems using non-specialist hardware, making it accessible to a wide range of users in production environments.

The backend processes the input media according to the configuration data received from the frontend, handling computationally intensive tasks such as depth estimation and segmentation by leveraging CUDA-enabled GPU processing. It then generates a *.2p5d* file and returns a preview of the depth inference and segmentation results as Base64-encoded data, which the UI displays. Although not yet available through the UI, batch processing is supported via the command line. Users can provide a configuration file that adheres to the defined schema, configuring multiple jobs by specifying parameters for each input media as JSON objects within a list.

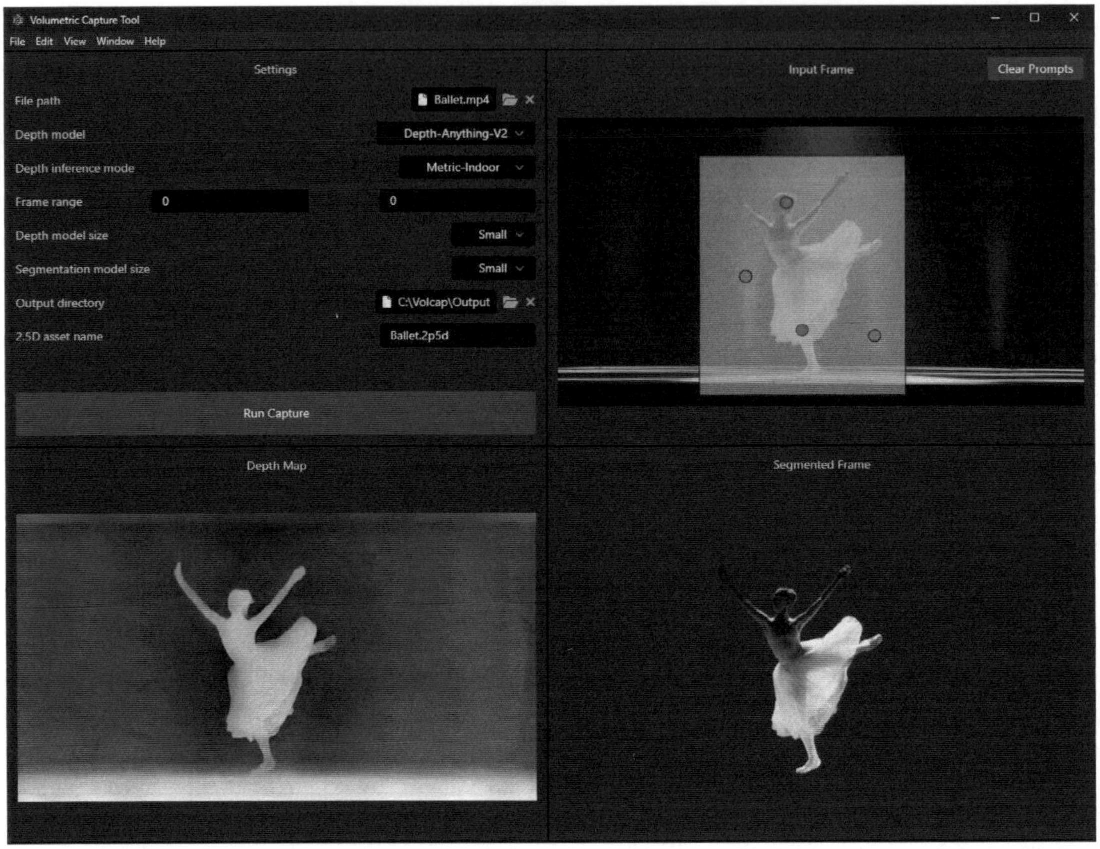

FIGURE 2: GRAPHICAL USER INTERFACE FOR THE VOLUMETRIC CAPTURE APPLICATION.

The processing pipeline within the application consists of the following stages, depicted in Figure 3:

1. **Input media selection**: The tool accepts either still images or video files as input. For video input, each frame is processed either individually or using a batched "sliding window" approach depending on the model used, to perform depth estimation and segmentation. Users can specify a range of frames to process.
2. **Segmentation and depth inference**: The tool provides a framework for cutting-edge AI models to generate depth maps and segmentation masks from the input media. The model choice and parameters such as checkpoint sizes can be selected by the user.
    a. **Segmentation**: Currently the only segmentation model implemented is Segment Anything V2 (SAM2) [28]. Users can provide prompts (either points or bounding boxes) to isolate regions of interest in the scene. Point prompts can be labelled as *positive* or *negative*, to help the segmentation model to distinguish subjects from the scene's background. The tool's graphical interface allows users to manually draw and refine prompts on the media canvas. These prompts are processed into segmentation masks that separate the selected subjects or props from the scene. The resulting masks are applied to the original footage to generate the segmented output. The top right corner of Figure 2 illustrates the segmentation UI in action, where *positive* and *negative* point prompts are depicted as green and red dots, respectively, while bounding boxes enable a coarser subject selection. The bottom right corner of the figure shows the segmented output, generated by applying the masks from SAM2 [28] to the original input media.

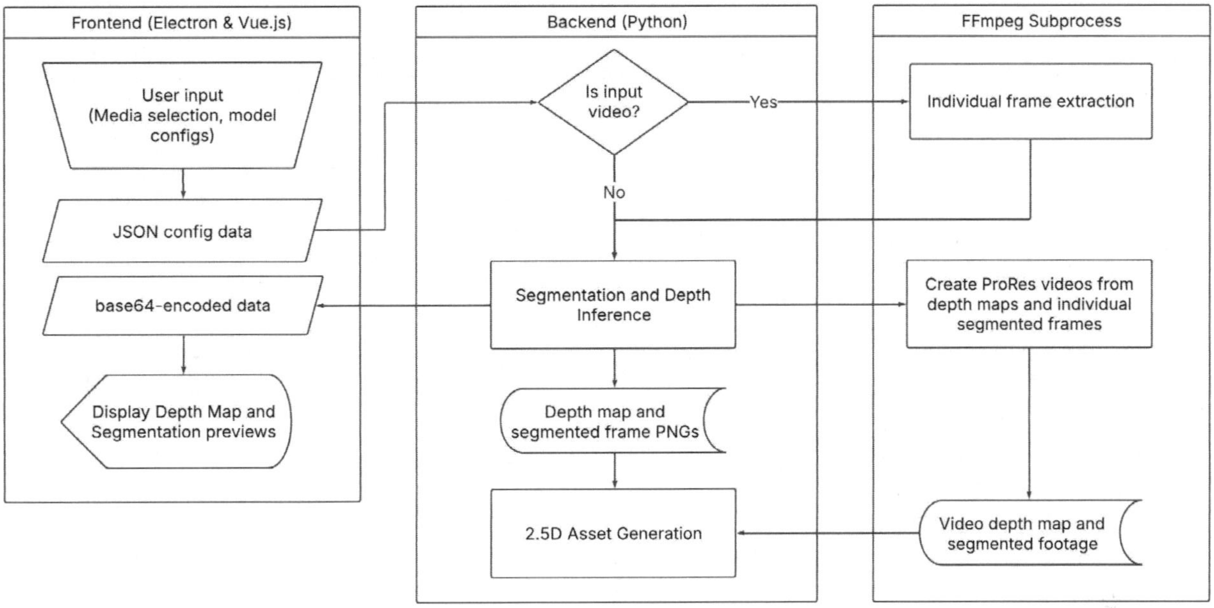

FIGURE 3: SYSTEM BLOCK DIAGRAM FOR THE MONOCULAR DEPTH RECONSTRUCTION APP.

b. **Depth inference**: Three depth inference models are currently implemented in the tool: Depth Anything V2 [17], Video Depth Anything [23] and Depth Pro [18]. Depth estimation is carried out per frame to create grayscale depth maps. An example depth map is shown in the bottom left of Figure 2. These single-channel images encode the relative distances of elements in the scene, with lighter pixels representing closer objects and darker pixels indicating objects farther away. Some models return 'metric' depth, i.e. absolute depth in metres, whereas others return normalised depth, requiring the user to provide maximum and minimum depth values.

3. **2.5D asset generation**: The segmentation masks and depth maps are used to generate 2.5D assets that Designer can natively interpret and display in its visualiser. The assets are encoded in a *.2p5d* format [30], embedding the video depth maps and segmentation output for playback within a 2.5D layer. The resulting file also stores spatial metadata and depth information, enabling realistic reconstruction of the selected objects from the original scene.

Integration With Designer 2.5D Workflows

The existing 2.5D framework within Disguise Designer allows a series of plates to be rendered with static depth maps, providing a realistic parallax effect as the camera perspective shifts. To support both static and dynamic depth maps, we extended this workflow by adding the ability to process depth videos. This allows the assets processed in the volumetric capture app to be viewed within Designer, expanding the creative possibilities for on-set and post-production workflows.

Video depth maps are rendered using a dedicated mesh specialisation for depth map rendering, the 'Depth Map Mesh'. This is controlled by a new 'Depth Video' layer on the timeline that interprets depth information from grayscale video textures. Configurable blur and dilation are applied to smooth out inconsistencies in the depth maps and reduce edge effects. Each pixel is then interpreted as inverse normalised depth and used to distort the mesh and render dynamic depth changes in real time. Figure 4 shows how the Depth Map Mesh appears within the Designer visualiser.

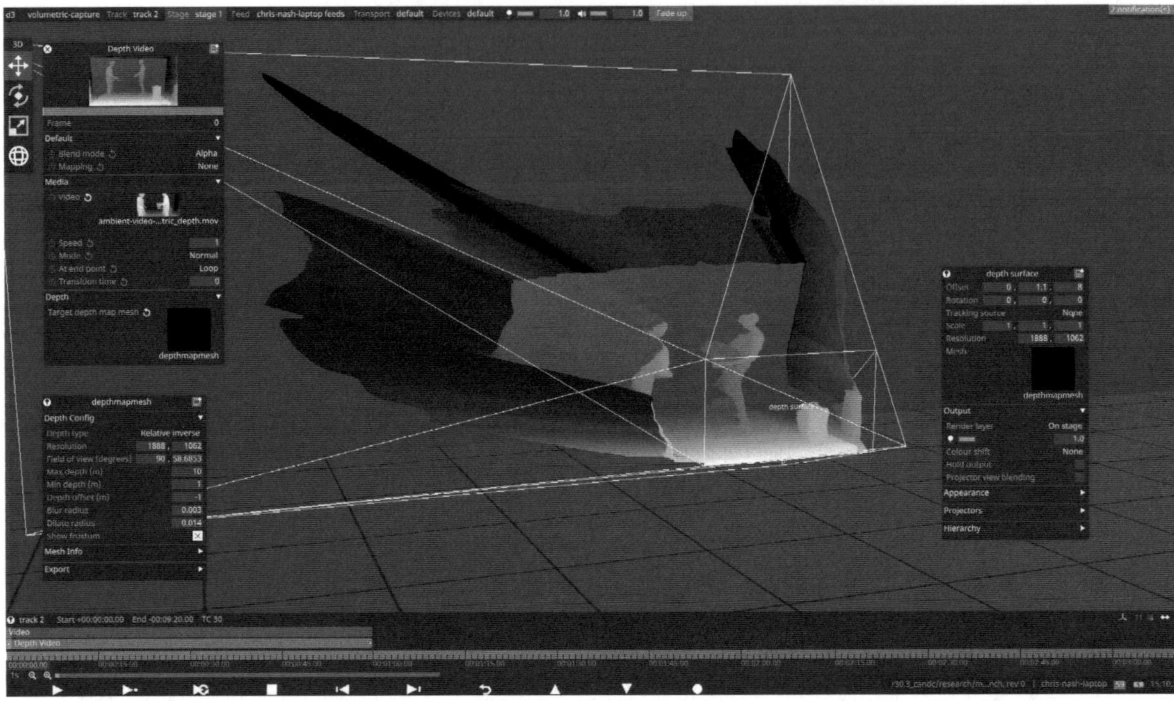

FIGURE 4: RENDERING A DEPTH MAP MESH IN THE DESIGNER VISUALISER.

The new video depth map mesh and layers are integrated as part of the existing 2.5D infrastructure, which loads assets into Designer as a series of 2.5D plates. As illustrated in the block diagram in Figure 1, the 2.5D plate now contains a depth video layer. Upon parsing the 2.5D asset, if present, the video depth map is loaded within the depth video layer and is used to distort the plate's mesh. The video layer loads the main video content, with any segmentation masks applied to it, and renders it directly onto the distorted surface. This produces a dynamic depth effect which can be viewed from several angles as shown in Figures 4 and 5.

2.5D assets and plates contain options to adjust the viewing frustum of meshes distorted by video depth, including the field-of-view of the frustum and the minimum and maximum depth values. These define the range over which depth values are normalised, ensuring that the mesh accurately reflects the intended spatial dimensions of the scene. The resulting 2.5D plates are rendered within the Designer visualiser to reconstruct the spatial layout of actors, props, and other scene elements. In addition, performer-dependant real-time effects can be pre-visualised. Figure 5 illustrates an example workflow, where a colour layer is used to generate the yellow shadow effect rendered on the wall behind the 2.5D representation of the performer.

Depth Model Evaluation

A virtual production environment is a complex and dynamic space containing multiple light sources and props with a wide spectrum of different materials. This introduces a whole range of potential complexities that any depth inference model must account for. For the proposed pipeline to be useful, it must be able to produce a temporally stable output that accurately maps the captured environment. Any form of noise or inaccuracy in the sequence will present as observable artefacts in the final volumetric representation, diminishing its visual quality. While it is possible to mitigate some issues with the application of image filters, doing so may fail to eliminate all artefacts.

FIGURE 5: VISUALISATION OF 2.5D ASSET RENDERED WITH VIDEO DEPTH ON DESIGNER STAGE.

The monocular depth estimation application is designed as a framework which allows depth models to be used interchangeably. We have used this framework to compare three state-of-the-art depth inference models: Depth Anything V2 [17], Depth Pro [18] and Video Depth Anything [23]. We carried out a brief study to assess the suitability of these models for virtual production environments, capturing videos with a range of objects and lighting conditions and comparing the video depth maps estimated by each model. This study is not intended to be a thorough investigation into the relative accuracy of different depth models against a ground truth, which has been done already elsewhere [17] [18] [23]. The aim is to provide simple quantitative and qualitative assessments of the performance of the models in a production setting and highlight some of the difficulties involved.

Test Scenario Video Capture

To assess the various depth models, we captured a series of video sequences for different test scenarios under a range of environmental conditions. Video sequences were taken from a representative small-scale VP production environment consisting of INFiLED LED wall and floor panels, driven by a Brompton Tessera S8 LED processor and a Disguise VX4 media server. Lighting was provided by a Rush Par-2 RGBW spotlight and fixed ambient ceiling lights located around the stage.

Each sequence is roughly 10 seconds in length and was captured using a Red Komodo 6k camera. This camera was equipped with a Samyang XP 10mm F3.5 lens, capturing at 1920x1080p resolution, 50Hz frame rate with ISO400 configuration, 1/50 shutter speed, f/8 aperture, 5948K white balance using a Rec. 709 colour space. These camera settings were unchanged between all sequences.

On the stage we set up a shelf containing a range of objects representing a wide spectrum of materials from microfacet to smooth specular surfaces, designed to be representative of some of the props that may be used as part of a shoot. Distances of all objects within the frame as well as near and far points in the scene were measured using a Bosch Zamo III laser measure. An example frame from one of the captured sequences is shown in Figure 6.

FIGURE 6: SAMPLE FRAME TAKEN FROM ONE OF THE CAPTURED SEQUENCES.

Sequences were captured for the following set of lighting conditions:

- **Unlit**: No fixed light sources with only minimal indirect lighting from the surrounding environment.
- **Ambient**: Lighting from ceiling lights placed both in front of and behind the Wall LED panel:
    - **Uniform**: All lights switched on.
    - **Backlit**: Only the ceiling light behind the Wall LED panel switched on.
- **LED Panels**: Sequences were shot recording a combination of both wall and floor screens emitting light and each screen independently with the following permutations:
    - **Fixed**: Screen emits white at full brightness.
    - **Variable**: Screen displays a generative chevron pattern comprised of several primary colours.

  For each of these permutations, sequences were shot both with no ambient ceiling lighting and with full ambient lighting.
- **Spotlights**: Sequences were shot with the spotlight colour being rotated between its 4 primary colours: Red, Green, Blue and White.

One sequence was shot for each of the described lighting conditions and permutations, giving a total of 19 sequences.

Model Benchmarking Configurations

For benchmarking, all sequence footage was processed using depth models with the following configurations:

- **Depth Anything V2 (DAV2)** [17]: The metric-indoor configuration was chosen as it was best suited for this use case, with both the small and large checkpoints being tested. Note that the large model is not available for commercial use.
- **Depth Pro** [18]: No further configuration required. This is a metric model by default.
- **Video Depth Anything (VDA)** [23]: This does not provide a metric model, so a relative model was used. The large model was chosen for direct comparison of the best possible results against Depth Anything V2, although this is also unavailable for commercial use.

Temporal Consistency Analysis

Temporal consistency is an important metric affecting the visual fidelity of the depth maps. When processing a video with multiple frames, the depths of static objects should be the same in each frame, and moving objects should not exhibit any unrealistic jumps in depth. Temporal consistency can be quantified for each pixel by calculating the standard deviation in depth across all frames of a video. A video of a static scene was used for testing, so the expected standard deviation is zero over the entire image.

The calculated standard deviations for all models are shown in Figure 7 for three representative lighting conditions. Unsurprisingly, the three models which are not specifically set up for video processing exhibited much higher variance than VDA. This was observed in the rendered results, with flickering seen between frames, compared with the consistent depth maps seen for VDA. DAV2 Small is the least consistent of the models. DAV2 Large slightly outperforms Depth Pro, although it struggles with the reflective surface of the toaster under ambient lighting.

The lighting conditions had a clear impact on temporal consistency across all models. Consistency was better with a fixed colour on the LED wall than with solely ambient lighting; this is likely to be because it allowed the models to distinguish the props from the background more easily. The dynamic LED pattern proved difficult for many of the models, in particular DAV2 Small and Depth Pro where a large level of variance is seen across the LED wall itself. VDA still deals with this case well, although there are larger errors around the edges of the props which may require some processing to remove edge effects. Overall, it is encouraging that by using a depth inference model targeted for video processing, it is possible to get consistent results even in the sort of dynamic lighting conditions which may be present in a production environment.

FIGURE 7: TEMPORAL VARIANCE WITH DIFFERENT DEPTH MODELS AND LIGHTING CONDITIONS.

Depth Accuracy Analysis

To evaluate the spatial accuracy of our depth captures we performed a comparison of the measured depths of the objects within our static scene against the respective depth estimates produced by the set of metric depth models that were benchmarked. Estimates for each model were extracted from regions in the frame contained within several of the objects in the scene. This region roughly corresponds to the location on the prop where the measurement was originally taken. The final depth estimate value was obtained by taking a median of all the estimates within the defined region. Depth estimates are shown in Table 1, with cells coloured by the distance from the ground truth.

It is clear from Table 1 that none of the metric models can provide accurate absolute depths across all conditions. Errors in the estimated values are significant, up to 1 m difference, with the models tending to underestimate the depths of the props in the scene. In addition to the absolute errors, the depth order of some props is not always inferred correctly, especially for objects which were located close together.

Of the models presented, DAV2 Small is the least accurate across all conditions. DAV2 Large is the most accurate under ambient lighting, estimating most object depths to within 10 cm of the ground truth, although the reflective surface of the toaster appears to have caused it confusion. With a fixed colour on the LED wall, Depth Pro provides the most accurate estimates, which may indicate differences in how the two models distinguish objects from the background. With variable lighting on the LED wall, estimation errors are similar for DAV2 Large and Depth Pro, with all models performing poorly. The results show that metric depth models cannot be relied upon to provide accurate absolute depth estimates in all production conditions. Improved accuracy may be achievable by calibrating the depth map against measured ground truth values within the scene.

	LED Wall	Big Case	Corkboard	Book	Toaster	Left Cabinet	Small Case
Ground Truth	3.538	2.532	2.480	2.470	2.425	2.400	2.388
Ambient Lighting							
DAV2 Small	3.626	1.597	1.588	1.777	1.822	1.682	1.778
DAV2 Large	3.714	2.433	2.387	2.435	2.837	2.394	2.449
Depth Pro	2.401	1.810	1.776	1.823	1.907	1.786	1.829
Wall LED Screen Fixed							
DAV2 Small	2.911	1.469	1.468	1.476	1.487	1.488	1.486
DAV2 Large	3.431	2.089	2.031	2.05	2.063	2.045	2.052
Depth Pro	4.181	2.405	2.372	2.326	2.488	2.395	2.385
Wall LED Screen Variable							
DAV2 Small	3.159	1.304	1.299	1.345	1.345	1.321	1.326
DAV2 Large	2.962	2.138	2.085	2.104	2.110	2.102	2.099
Depth Pro	3.244	1.909	1.880	1.931	1.948	1.900	1.901

TABLE 1: DEPTH ESTIMATES (IN METRES) FOR OBJECTS WITHIN THE TEST SCENE.

Conclusions

We have built a new framework for combining depth and segmentation AI models to produce a 2.5D asset which can be used to visualise the dynamic movements of performers and props. While this is not a full 3D volumetric representation, it can be viewed from a range of angles and give a useful overview of the performance. The visual quality is certainly good enough for pre-visualisation purposes; other use-cases in production and post-production may require higher visual fidelity that we hope future work will bring.

Comparison of state-of-the-art AI depth models has shown that temporal consistency can be an issue, resulting in flickering artifacts in the results. Models such as Video Depth Anything [23] which are specifically aimed at video workflows significantly improve this, giving smoothly varying depth maps where static objects remain stationary, even under dynamic lighting conditions.

Metric depth inference models can provide an estimate of absolute depth in metres, but our results have shown that these are not always accurate across a range of production lighting conditions. Obtaining accurate absolute depth values may require calibration against known reference measurements in the captured video. Alternatively, solutions involving additional hardware such as depth cameras or multi-camera setups may provide improved accuracy.

Further Work

We have shown that monocular video can be processed to produce a depth-enhanced 2.5D asset which can be viewed from a range of angles. As a next step we would like to expand the workflow to multi-camera setups, to create a more complete volumetric representation. This could follow the GPS-Gaussian approach of our research partners in the FaVoRe project at HSLU [13] [14], or alternative methods for fusing depth cameras into volumetric representations [33] [34] [35].

In addition to depth maps and segmentation masks, AI models are available for extracting other physical-based rendering (PBR properties) from video, such as normal maps, albedo, and roughness [36] [37]. We would like to investigate how these properties could be extracted and packaged into 2.5D assets to enable more advanced rendering workflows such as relighting. If performers and props can be captured in sufficient detail, this could result in huge benefits for post-production workflows, by allowing scenes to be reshot virtually without requiring additional time on physical sets.

One further potential implementation for this work is for streaming live events into virtual worlds, building a volumetric avatar of the performer in the digital environment. A version of this was investigated by our partners at the BBC as part of the MAX-R project [38] but rejected for their use case in favour of alternative methods due to the lower fidelity of depth inference models available at the time. We have not yet begun to investigate the implementation of this within our Designer ecosystem, but would like to explore this as a potential long-term implementation goal of this development initiative.

References

[1] Universitat Pompeu Fabra, "Emerald consortium homepage," 2024. https://www.upf.edu/web/emerald.

[2] Smolic, A. "FaVoRe - Fast Volumetric Reconstruction for Media and Video Communication," 2024. https://www.hslu.ch/de-ch/hochschule-luzern/forschung/projekte/detail/?pid=6705.

[3] Universitat Pompeu Fabra, "MAX-R: Mixed Augmented and Extended Reality Media Pipeline," 2023. https://www.upf.edu/web/max-r.

[4] Disguise, "Disguise homepage," 2025.https://www.disguise.one/.

[5] Verbin, D., Hedman, P., Mildenhall, B., Zickler, T., Barron, J. T. and Srinivasan, P. P., "Ref-NeRF: Structured view-dependent appearance for neural radiance fields," *arXiv:2112.03907,* 2021.

[6] Barron, J. T., Mildenhall, B., Verbin, D., Srinivasan, P. P., and Hedman, P., "Mip-NeRF 360: Unbounded anti-aliased neural radiance fields," *Proceedings of the IEEE/CVF Conference on Computer Vision and Pattern Recognition (CVPR)*, 2022.

[7] Wang, F., Rakotosaona, M.-J., Niemeyer, M., Szeliski, R., Pollefeys, M. and Tombari, F., "UniSDF: Unifying neural representations for high-fidelity 3D reconstruction of complex scenes with reflections.," *arXiv:2312.13285,* 2023.

[8] Kheradmand, S., Rebain, D., Sharma, G., Sun, W., Tseng, J., Isack, H., Kar, A., Tagliasacchi, A. and Yi, K. M., "3D Gaussian Splatting as Markov Chain Monte Carlo," *arXiv:2404.09591,* 2024.

[9] Charatan, D., Li, S., Tagliasacchi, A. and Sitzmann, V., "pixelSplat: 3D Gaussian Splats from Image Pairs for Scalable Generalizable 3D Reconstruction," *Proceedings of the IEEE/CVF Conference on Computer Vision and Pattern Recognition (CVPR)*, 2024.

[10] Lee, J. C., Rho, D., Sun, X., Ko, J. H. and Park, E., "Compact 3D Gaussian Representation for Radiance Field," *Proceedings of the IEEE/CVF Conference on Computer Vision and Pattern Recognition (CVPR)*, 2024.

[11] Sun, J., Jiao, H., Li, G., Zhang, Z., Zhao, L. and Xing, W., "3DGStream: On-the-Fly Training of 3D Gaussians for Efficient Streaming of Photo-Realistic Free-Viewpoint Videos," *Proceedings of the IEEE/CVF Conference on Computer Vision and Pattern Recognition (CVPR)*, 2024.

[12] Kocabas, M., Chang, J.-H. R., Gabriel, J., Tuzel, O. and Ranjan, A., "HUGS: Human Gaussian Splatting," *Proceedings of the IEEE/CVF Conference on Computer Vision and Pattern Recognition (CVPR)*, 2024.

[13] Croci, S., Charisoudis, A., Haslbauer, P., Yung, L. K. and Smolic, A., "Reconstruction Principles," *Fast Volumetric Reconstruction: Deliverable D3.1,* 2024.

[14] Zheng, S., Zhou, B., Shao, R., Liu, B., Zhang, S., Nie, L. and Liu, Y., "Generalizable pixel-wise 3D Gaussian splatting for real-time human novel view synthesis," *Proceedings of the IEEE/CVF Conference on Computer Vision and Pattern Recognition*, 2024.

[15] Birkl, R., Wofk, D. and Müller, M., "MiDaS v3.1 - A Model Zoo for Robust Monocular Relative Depth Estimation," *arXiv:2307.14460*, 2023.

[16] Yang, L., Kang, B., Huang, Z., Xu, X., Feng, J. and Zhao, H., "Depth Anything: Unleashing the Power of Large-Scale Unlabeled Data," *Proceedings of the IEEE/CVF Conference on Computer Vision and Pattern Recognition (CVPR)*, 2024.

[17] Yang, L., Kang, B., Huang, Z., Zhao, Z., Xu, X., Feng, J. and Zhao, H., "Depth Anything V2," *arXiv:2406.09414*, 2024.

[18] Bochkovskii, A., Delaunoy, A., Germain, H., Santos, M., Zhou, Y., Richter, S. R. and Koltun, V., "Depth Pro: Sharp Monocular Metric Depth Less Than a Second," *arXiv:2410.02073*, 2024.

[19] Ke, B., Obukhov, A., Huang, S., Metzger, N., Daud, R. C. and Schindler, K., "Repurposing Diffusion-Based Image Generators for Monocular Depth Estimation," *Proceedings of the IEEE/CVF Conference on Computer Vision and Pattern Recognition (CVPR)*, 2024.

[20] Rombach, R., Blattmann, A., Lorenz, D., Esser, P. and Ommer, B., "High-Resolution Image Synthesis with Latent Diffusion Models," *arXiv:2112.10752*, 2021.

[21] Hu, W., Gao, X., Li, X., Zhao, S., Cun, X., Zhang, Y., Quan, L. and Shan, Y., "DepthCrafter: Generating Consistent Long Depth Sequences for Open-world Videos," *arXiv:2409.02095*, 2024.

[22] Ke, B., Narnhofer, D., Huang, S., Ke, L., Peters, T., Fragkiadaki, K., Obukhov, A. and Schindler, K., "Video Depth without Video Models," *arXiv:2411.19189*, 2024.

[23] Chen, S., Guo, H., Zhu, S., Zhang, F., Huang, Z., Feng, J. and Kang, B., "Video Depth Anything: Consistent Depth Estimation for Super-Long Videos," *arXiv:2501.12375*, 2025.

[24] Redmon, J. and Farhadi, A., "YOLOv3: An Incremental Improvement," *arXiv:1804.02767*, 2018.

[25] Abdulla, W., "Mask R-CNN for object detection and instance segmentation on Keras and TensorFlow," 2017. https://github.com/matterport/Mask_RCNN.

[26] Chen, L.-C., Zhu, Y., Papandreou, G., Schroff, F. and Adam, H., "Encoder-Decoder with Atrous Separable Convolution for Semantic Image Segmentation," *arXiv:1802.02611*, 2018.

[27] Kirillov, A., Mintun, E., Ravi, N., Mao, H., Rolland, C., Gustafson, L., Xiao, T., Whitehead, S., Berg, A. C., Lo, W.-Y., Dollar, P., and Girshick, R., "Segment Anything," *arXiv:2304.02643*, 2023.

[28] Ravi, N., Gabeur, V., Hu, Y.-T., Hu, R., Ryali, C., Ma, T., Khedr, H., Radle, R., Rolland, C., Gustafson, L., Mintun, E., Pan, J., Alwala, K., Vasudev, Carion, N., Wu, C.-Y. and Girshick, R., "SAM 2: Segment Anything in Images and Videos," *arXiv:2408.00714*, 2024.

[29] Yang, J., Gao, M., Li, Z., Gao, S., Wang, F. and Zheng, F., "Track Anything: Segment Anything Meets Videos," *arXiv:2304.11968*, 2023.

[30] Disguise, "2.5D format specification," 2024. https://developer.disguise.one/formats/2p5d/.

[31] Telotte, J. P., "Ub Iwerks' (Multi)Plain Cinema," *Animation*, vol. 1, no. 1, 2006, pp. 9-24.

[32] Cuebric, "Cuebric homepage," 2025. https://cuebric.com/.

[33] Orts-Escolano, S., Rhemann, C., Fanello, S., Chang, W., Kowdle, A., Degtyarev, Y., Kim, D., Davidson, P. L., Khamis, S. and Dou, M., "Holoportation: Virtual 3D Teleportation in Real-time," *Proceedings of the 29th annual symposium on user interface software and technology*, 2016.

[34] Weder, S., Schonberger, J. L., Pollefeys, M. and Oswald, M. R., "NeuralFusion: Online depth fusion in latent space," *Proceedings of the IEEE/CVF Conference on Computer Vision and Pattern Recognition (CVPR)*, 2021.

[35] Azinovic, D., Martin-Brualla, R., Goldman, D. B., Niessner, M. and Thies, J., "Neural RGB-D surface reconstruction," *Proceedings of the IEEE/CVF Conference on Computer Vision and Pattern Recognition (CVPR)*, 2022.

[36] Zeng, Z., Deschaintre, V., Georgiev, I., Hold-Geoffroy, Y., Hu, Y., Luan, F., Yan, L.-Q. and Hasan, M., "RGB↔X: Image decomposition and synthesis using material- and lighting-aware diffusion models," *ACM SIGGRAPH 2024 Conference Papers*, 2024.

[37] Liang, R., Gojcic, Z., Ling, H., Munkberg, J., Hasselgren, J., Lin, Z.-H., Gao, J., Keller, A., Vijaykumar, N., Fidler, S. and Wang, Z., "DiffusionRenderer: Neural Inverse and Forward Rendering with Video Diffusion Models," *arXiv:2501.18590*, 2025.

[38] Thomas, G. A., Rivera, F. M., Kelso, L., Weir, B., Rich, P. and Moolan-Feroze, O., "Live Music in Immersive Virtual Spaces," *International Broadcasting Conversion (IBC) Technical Papers*, 2024.

TSENet Video Super Resolution for Broadcast Television

Surbhi Madan
Intel Corp
San Diego, California, United States
surbhi.madan@intel.com

Onur Barut
Berlin, Massachusetts, United States
onurbarut@windowslive.com

Anand V Bodas
Intel Corp
Bangalore, India
anand.v.bodas@intel.com

Christopher A Bird
Intel Corp
Chandler, Arizona, United States
christopher.a.bird@intel.com

Jerry Dong
Intel Corp
Beijing, China
jerry.dong@intel.com

Lin Xie
Intel Corp
Beijing, China
lin.xie@intel.com

Abstract – The emergence of Video Super Resolution (VSR) has advanced the media industry. It holds great potential for enhancing broadcast and streaming, improving visual quality, and boosting user engagement. While there are benefits, applying VSR technology to broadcast presents challenges, as it requires a high-quality solution that maintains consistent quality across diverse broadcast standards, handles live content with minimal latency, and ensures compatibility with existing broadcast infrastructure. This demands sophisticated AI models, often needing high-performance GPUs, which can increase costs. In this paper, we introduce a method to upscale low-resolution, compressed video frames based on an enhanced version of Equivalent Transformation and Dual Stream Network (ETDS)[1], called a Temporally Stabilized ETDS Network (TSENet) that performs equivalent or better compared to more compute extensive solutions. This paper examines various VSR models, emphasizing the key performance indicators identified by the AIM2024 Challenge for Efficient VSR[2]. The focus is on deploying these models in workflows, considering visual quality through both subjective and objective analyses, compression artifact reduction, and real-time processing capabilities.

Introduction

Super-resolution is a technique to scale lower-resolution images or videos to higher resolutions improving its visual quality. Utilizing sophisticated algorithms, including those driven by artificial intelligence (AI), super-resolution can smartly upscale and improve visual quality (VQ), offering a sharper and more detailed viewing experience. This technology benefits those managing low-resolution video content to improve the user experience, whether dealing with standard definition (HD) videos or 1080p high definition (Full HD) footage, super-resolution can significantly upgrade the content to 2160p (Ultra HD) or even 8K resolution. This technique can enable the broadcast of content on UHD/4K displays without the costs associated with upgrading production equipment, facilitates the revitalization of archival footage, and provides cost-effective methodologies to support Free Ad-Supported Streaming TV (FAST) channels. A solution addressing this was presented at MHV 2024[5]. The high demands of broadcast television necessitate a scalable solution that delivers superior quality while maintaining consistent standards across diverse broadcast formats. This solution must handle live content with minimal latency and ensure compatibility with existing devices and broadcast infrastructure, including dealing with noise, compression artifacts, etc. This requires elegant AI models capable of enhancing the quality while operating on widely available, non-specialized computational resources, such as x86 architecture-based CPUs and low-cost GPUs from Intel, to ensure economic feasibility for deployment while offering flexibility to adapt the improvements in the industry. Advancements in developing efficient

Video Super-Resolution (VSR) technologies can democratize access to high-quality video enhancement for broadcast television, ensuring a superior viewing experience across all platforms.

While there is a clear value and a goal to invest in VSR for broadcast television, there are challenges with this technology that limit the deployment of AI models. These include the lack of real-world datasets to train on, biases due to techniques used in creating training datasets, as well as biases caused by the loss functions used during training. Elaborating on this further, many state-of-the-art super-resolution models[3] [6] are usually trained on image datasets but are applied to videos. This mismatch results in the issue of maintaining temporal coherency across frames, creating motion artifacts. The model starts lacking robustness to handle compression artifacts and textures as often the training dataset leverages non-real world videos like animation or pristine stock content that lack compression and are downscaled using a specific algorithm to create Low Resolution (LR) and High Resolution (HR) pairs for the dataset. Such algorithms achieve high accuracy on benchmark datasets but fail in the real-world where there is varying compression and artifacts. In addition to the dataset problem, biases are introduced when the loss functions used during training, like Peak Signal to Noise Ratio (PSNR), Mean Square Error (MSE), and Visual Information Fidelity (VIF) are the same metrics used as Key Performance Indicators (KPI) to evaluate the model's effectiveness. This results in a biased model trained to produce videos with higher objective metrics but not visually pleasing to human observers, making it unsuitable for real-world scenarios.

This paper details the TSENet model, developed to address the challenges described above. TSENet is a robust solution designed to enhance visual quality (VQ) and mitigate compression artifacts while upscaling low-resolution videos, all while keeping computational costs low. In section 3, we will dive into the details of evaluation methodology mimicking real-world scenarios including publishing visual quality metrics of the compressed upscaled videos.

TSENet Architecture

The TSENet model architecture builds upon the foundation of the Equivalent Transformation and Dual Stream (ETDS) model, which proposes a dual-stream approach for learning higher-frequency(HF) and lower-frequency(LF) components of the input image during the training phase. This architecture is extended to handle video super-resolution tasks by adding temporal alignment layers before the stream is split into two branches of LF-HF to learn respective components, see Figure 1 for details.

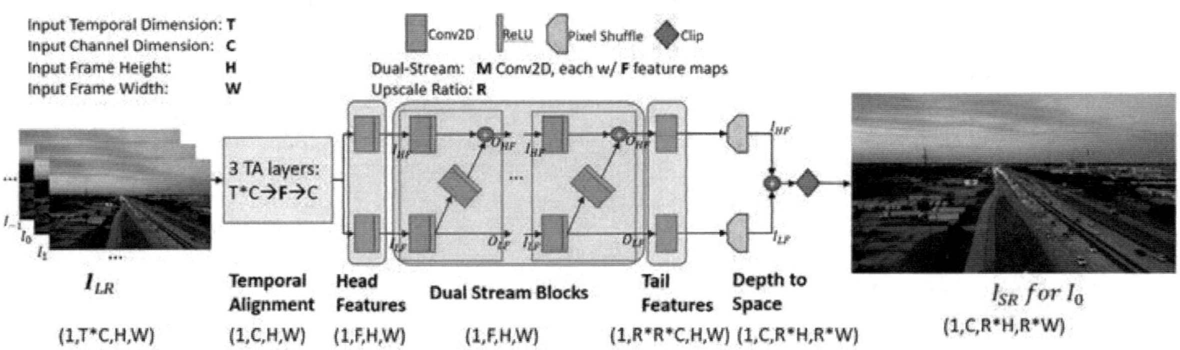

FIGURE 1: TSENET ARCHITECTURE IS CONFIGURABLE IN TERMS OF NUMBER OF INPUT FRAMES (T), INPUT IMAGE CHANNEL SIZE(C), UPSCALING RATIO(R), NUMBER OF DUAL STREAM BLOCKS(M), AND NUMBER OF FEATURE MAPS(F).

Each branch is designed to learn different components of the video frames, with the LF branch focusing on low-frequency details and the HF branch on high-frequency details. The information that passes from LF to HF branch is controlled with M number of Dual-Stream (DS) blocks, each containing convolutions followed by Rectified Linear Unit (ReLU) activation to introduce non-linear learning capabilities. In the HF branch, the output of each DS block is computed by combining the convolutional output from the HF branch with the convolved output from the LF branch. This process enhances high-frequency details by incorporating information from the LF branch. The LF branch output is calculated solely based on its own convolutional operations and ReLU activation, without any additional processing from the HF branch. After passing through the DS blocks, each branch undergoes a final convolution operation followed by a depth-to-space conversion. This conversion helps in obtaining the high-frequency and low-frequency components separately. The final output, known as the Super-Resolved Stream, is constructed by combining the HF and LF components. The components are summed and clipped to ensure that the final output remains within the desired range.

$$
\begin{gathered}
0_{HF} = \mathrm{ReLU}(Conv_{\mathrm{HF}}(I_{HF}) + Conv_{FL2HF}(Conv_{LF}(I_{LF}))) \\
0_{LF} = ReLU\big(Conv_{LF}(I_{LF})\big) \\
I_{SR} = Clip(I_{HF} + I_{LF})
\end{gathered}
\tag{1}
$$

The model design takes three input frames to generate one frame with 2x upscaling, using 7 Data Stream blocks with a feature map size of 48. To train the model, a comprehensive dataset of low-resolution video sequences paired with their corresponding high-resolution counterparts is created. The dataset consists of a diverse range of video content spanning various scenes, lighting conditions, and motion dynamics along with different levels of video compression, to ensure the model's generalization capability across real-world scenarios.

Data Preprocessing and Augmentation

Before training, the video sequences are preprocessed to standardize them in the same format. As the quality and characteristics of the training dataset influence the quality of AI model, various augmentation techniques with random selections are employed to augment the dataset and improve the model's robustness including such as:

- Channel shuffling and rotating to simulate different viewing angles and color independence
- Horizontal and vertical flipping to introduce variations in orientation
- Cropping to 128x128 patches
- Creating LR videos by randomly picking the down-scaling algorithm among bicubic, bilinear, area, or Lanczos
- Sharpening HR reference videos using FFmpeg's unsharp filter with luma_amount=0.5
- Randomly compressing LR videos between CRF 15-30 using the SVT-AV1 encoder preset 10

In the final training dataset, varying degree of compression between light to medium compression is applied to learn encoding artifacts. The sub-patches are extracted from the input videos, a little over 275k patches are obtained which are sufficient to train the model with high accuracy.

Optimization Algorithm

The Adam optimization algorithm is utilized to minimize a hybrid loss(L) function, which combines reconstruction loss (Charbonnier) and perceptual loss (VGG) to enhance high-frequency reconstruction. Reconstruction loss measures how well the model's output matches the original high-resolution image

$$
\begin{gathered}
L = \alpha * L_{reconstruction} + (1-\alpha) * L_{perceptual} \\
L_{reconstruction} = L_{charbonnier}(I_{HR}, I_{SR}) + \beta * L_{charbonnier}(I_{HR}, I_{LF})
\end{gathered}
\tag{2}
$$

On the other hand, perceptual loss focuses on preserving the perceptual and semantic quality of the image by comparing high-level features extracted from a pre-trained VGG model. Together this approach better preserves perceptual and semantic understanding by focusing on high-level features, resulting in a more visually pleasing generation. The algorithm adjusts the model's parameters iteratively based on the gradient of the hybrid loss function, ensuring convergence toward the optimal solution.

Results

To quantify the performance of the models, objective metrics such as Peak Signal-to-Noise Ratio (PSNR), Structural Similarity Index (SSIM), and Video Multi-method Assessment Fusion (VMAF) scores are computed using libvmaf and ffmpeg on the benchmark test set. Additionally, qualitative evaluations are conducted using different low-resolution clips without high-resolution references to assess visual quality. Last, each model is run on the test system to measure out of box performance to assess the computational complexity of the models for possible real-time performance.

Evaluation Dataset

The evaluation dataset comprises video streams from Netflix Open Content that consist of movies, shows, animation, and close-up scenes. To simulate real-world scenarios, videos in 4K and 1080p are saved as HR reference, then are downscaled by 2x to create LR clips. In this case we used four different downscaling algorithms (area, bicubic, bilinear, lanczos) to remove any chance of bias towards a particular algorithm. Each LR input is encoded at a Constant Rate Factor (CRF) ranging from 23, 31, 38 for 1080p.

$$\begin{gathered} ffmpeg - y - i\ - y\ - i\ < inputp.mp4 > \ -vf\ format = yuv420p, \\ scale = \frac{iw}{2}:\frac{ih}{2}: flags =< downscale\ alg > -c\!:v\ libsvtav1\ - svtav1 - params\ preset = 10: \\ lookahead = 0: keyint = -1: pred - struct = 1 - crf\ \ < crf\ value >< \ output.mp4 > \end{gathered} \tag{3}$$

In total, 19 LR test clips of 1080p are upscaled using Lanczos (a common interpolation algorithm), Enhanced RAISR[5] (a machine learning approach), two state-of-the-art models EDSR (Enhanced Deep Residual Networks)[4], and Real-ESRGAN (Real Enhanced Super Resolution Generative Adversarial Networks)[6] and the TSENet model. The upscaled output is encoded at lossless quality, using "-qp 0" during encoding for the logistic reason to store and inspect data. Both qualitative and quantitative evaluations are conducted to assess the quality and computational complexity of the models.

$$\begin{gathered} ffmpeg\ \ - i\ < distorted\ clip > \ -i\ < reference\ clip > \ -lavfi\ [0\!:v]setpts = PTS - STARTPTS[main]; \\ [1\!:v]setpts = PTS - STARTPTS[ref];\ [main][ref]libvmaf = 'model = version = \\ vmaf_{v0.6.1}\!: name = vmaf\!: feature = name = psnr|\ name = float_{ssim}|name = float_{ms_{ssim}}: \\ log_{path} =< quality_{log} >\!: n_{threads} = 64'\ - f\ null\ - \end{gathered} \tag{4}$$

Subjective Results

Figure 2 presents a comparative visual analysis of the 1080p to 4k upscaling from the previously selected models. The images chosen are from various clips, each representing unique and distinctive characteristics that are crucial for evaluating the models. Before delving into the results, it is important to note that the output of the Lanczos algorithm is included as a baseline for reference, serving as a minimum threshold for these models. Overall, the outputs of Lanczos algorithm generates blurred output with compression artifacts, making it unappealing. Consequently, the focus of the discussion is on comparing the AI based models rather than the Lanczos algorithm.

While Raisr delivers strong quality results versus Lanczos, it may be outshined by some of the other models. Image 2 shows a ringing artifact around the metal pipes which only Raisr is creating. EDSR could be the biggest disappointment here since it is the slowest of all algorithms tested and doesn't appear to offer much improvement in quality. Real-ESRGAN offers a pleasant output in many cases and seems to modify the image more than any other tested model. In some places it offers the best sharpness and clarity, but we also observe a general issue with it smoothing too much of the grains and textures present in the input, most noticeable in the skin and clothing areas of the below images. On occasion it negatively modifies the image and adds blackness to the man's teeth in Figure 1 and twists the word "Mexico" in Figure 3. Sometimes resolution is added non-uniformly like in Figure 3 where the word "Pancho" is showing much bolder than the word "Rosales".

TSENet also demonstrates detailed resolution versus Lanczos and appears to fare quite well in this lineup by preserving textures and adding sharpness.

1080P -> 4k Upscales (zoomed at 200%, inputs encoded with CRF31)

FIGURE 2 VISUAL COMPARISON OF VSR OUTPUT.

Objective Results

Among all the algorithms evaluated, Lanczos outperforms in PSNR and SSIM metrics compared to all AI models across all the encoder compression levels while it scores lowest in the VMAF metric. This aligns with the observation of the subjective evaluation where lanczos performed poorly, validating the VMAF metric is more closely aligned with human visual perception. For the streams with light to medium compression (i.e. CRF 23, 31), Real-ESRGAN exhibits the lowest score across all VQ metrics and performs better for higher compressed streams. This may be attributed to high texture loss seen with the model, which is more pronounced in lightly to moderately compressed streams. When comparing metrics of the Enhanced RAISR, EDSR, and TSENet across all compression ratios, TSENet consistently achieves the highest VQ metric for VMAF, followed by RAISR and EDSR respectively. This data provides confidence to companies and users who are using VMAF as their automated metrics for the deployment decisions.

Algorithm	Params (K)	MACs (G)	PSNR Y	SSIM	VMAF	PSNR Y	SSIM	VMAF	PSNR Y	SSIM	VMAF
	Compute		CRF23			CRF31			CRF38		
Lanczos	*	*	**40.02**	**0.997**	88.30	39.02	**0.995**	83.79	**37.88**	**0.991**	77.33
Enhanced RAISR	104	50	38.88	0.996	94.02	38.12	0.994	89.72	37.21	**0.991**	83.18
EDSR	40730	21115	39.16	0.996	89.58	38.28	0.994	84.96	37.28	**0.991**	78.36
Real-ESRGAN	16703	2324	35.02	0.991	87.30	34.47	0.989	84.04	33.77	0.985	79.34
TSENet	178	92	38.24	0.996	**94.02**	37.63	0.994	**89.82**	36.86	**0.991**	**83.35**

TABLE 2: OBJECTIVE COMPARISON OF VSR MODELS AVERAGED OVER N VIDEO STREAMS ENCODED WITH VARYING COMPRESSION RATES UPSCALED TO 2160P (HIGHEST SCORES IN EACH METRIC CATEGORY ARE IN BOLD).

While objective VQ metrics provide valuable insight, it is important to recognize these metrics are not specifically designed for video enhancement. Consequently, it would be biased to deduce the best solution solely based on VMAF. It is important to factor subjective visual quality inspection as shared in Fig 2 along with compute cost. Therefore, the comparison in Table 1 also includes computational information of the AI model architectures as it is a critical factor in the context of deploying AI models for video upscaling. Enhanced RAISR stands out as the fastest and least computationally intensive option for real-time upscaling. However, for improved quality enhanced by AI, TSENet emerges as the best choice. TSENet delivers superior visual quality, as confirmed both visual inspection and quantitative metrics, while maintaining a significantly lower compute cost, < 1% of that required by competitive models such as EDSR. This makes the solution viable to run efficiently on Intel® Xeon® Scalable processors deployed commonly in datacenters as these platforms have two AI engines since 4th generation processors, called Intel® Advanced Matrix Instructions (AMX) and Intel® Deep Learning Boost (DL Boost). These engines enhance AI model performance by optimizing convolution and matrix multiplication operations. Together, AI acceleration for video pre-processing and software encoders on CPU provides an efficient solution that is optimized for both cost and quality on Intel Xeon platforms.

Conclusion

As the TSENet model demonstrates both economic and performance viability for deployment, it is crucial to facilitate its integration into the FFmpeg framework to be used as a pre-processor for video workflows. To streamline and ease the deployment of the AI models, Intel developed the iVSR plugin which is integrated into FFmpeg dnn_processing, serving as a common plugin to run AI models as part of the FFmpeg framework. Under this plugin, TSENet model is supported and available in open source, supporting seamless integration for media applications.

Acknowledgments

The authors would like to thank Tahani Trigui (Intel Corp) for her guidance on objective visual metrics people and Kevin Cone (Intel Corp) for reviewing the paper. The work supporting this paper was done while Onur Barut was employed by Intel Corp.

References

[1] Jiahao Chao, Zhou Zhou, Hongfan Gao, Jiali Gong, Zhengfeng Yang, Zhenbing Zeng, and Lydia Dehbi1. 2023. “Equivalent Transformation and Dual Stream Network Construction for Mobile Image Super-Resolution”(CVPR’23). https://ieeexplore.ieee.org/document/10203599

[2] Marcos V. Conde, Zhijun Lei, Wen Li, Christos Bampis, Ioannis Katsavounidis, and Radu Timofte, “AIM 2024 Challenge on Efficient Video Super-Resolution for AV1 Compressed Content,” 2024 https://arxiv.org/pdf/2409.17256v1

[3] Chao Dong, Chen Change Loy, Kaiming He, and Xiaoou Tang, “Image Super-Resolution Using Deep Convolutional Networks,” 2015 https://arxiv.org/pdf/1501.00092

[4] Bee Lim, Sanghyun Son, Heewon Kim, Seungjun Nah, and Kyoung Mu Lee,“Enhanced Deep Residual Networks for single-image super-resolution” 2022 https://arxiv.org/abs/1707.02921

[5] Carlos Salazar, Surbhi Madan, Anand Bodas, Arturo Velasco, Christopher A Bird, Onur Barut, Tahani Trigui, and Xiaoxia Liang, “AWS Compute Video SuperResolution powered by the Intel® Library for Video Super Resolution,” 2024 https://dl.acm.org/doi/pdf/10.1145/3638036.3640290

[6] Xintao Wang, Liangbin Xie, Chao Dong, and Ying Shan, “Real-ESRGAN: Training Real-World Blind Super-Resolution with Pure Synthetic Data, 2021 https://arxiv. org/pdf/2107.10833

Innovative Internet Protocol Remote Production Devices Using Open Standards

Takaya Omuro
Japan Broadcasting Corporation
Shibuya-ku, Tokyo, Japan
oomuro.t-hm@nhk.or.jp

Abstract – Growing demand for remote Internet Protocol (IP) production has led to an increase in demand for IP devices. Although it is possible to transmit audio signals using the SMPTE ST2110 standard, detailed control, such as adjusting audio levels and matrix control, is not allowed. Therefore, this study introduces innovative IP remote production devices that use open standards, Ember+, and investigates the use of an open protocol to handle control signals during remote IP production.

Additionally, using open standards for control signals, a device that converts the ST2110 standard and Dante—the major standard in the audio industry—for IP remote production, including control signals, is developed.

By using this converter with ST2110 compatible devices and Dante-compatible devices, we demonstrated its usefulness for IP remote production of the converter.

Introduction

Recently, the television industry has experienced a considerable increase in Internet Protocol (IP) live production. The Japan Broadcasting Corporation has been actively promoting live IP production across various TV programs with the aim of realizing more diverse workflows. By promoting live IP production, we aim to develop the broadcasting industry while considering work-style reforms to establish a system that improves personnel efficiency.

For example, in March 2023, we successfully established a comprehensive IP studio production system in Hiroshima based on the SMPTE ST2110 standard. This studio serves as a production hub for nationwide programs, including the National Men's Ekiden, a long-distance road relay, and the Peace Memorial Ceremony held in August. While developing the system, we built a studio production system with remote production capabilities. This system uses a broadcast controller and considers the reformation of work and production methods.

Evidently, we are working to promote IP remote production. However, in promoting IP remote production, we have realized that although IP remote production is possible for audio signals using the ST2110 standard, there are challenges with control signals.

The Advanced Media Workflow Association (AMWA) Networked Media Open Specifications (NMOS) has been standardized as a control protocol; however, it only supports controls such as device discovery and connection [1]. Vendor-specific protocols—such as adjusting the audio levels and matrix control—are often used for detailed control. Therefore, when using devices from different manufacturers in IP remote production between the subcontrol room and remote location, communication often fails, making the system design difficult.

To explore the possibility of remote production that can maintain compatibility among different vendors, the Japan Broadcasting Corporation developed a tool that uses international standards for simple control—such as device discovery and connection—and an open standard control protocol for detailed control.

This study introduces the efforts made to realize remote IP production—including control—using open standard protocols with the aim of further promoting remote IP production.

To investigate the usefulness of the devices for IP remote production, we used an audio mixing console that is compatible with ST2110 and audio devices that are compatible with Dante.

Open Standards for Device Control Protocol

In IP-based systems, audio and video transmissions are standardized according to the SMPTE ST2110 and AMWA NMOS standard, which has been widely employed and device control —such as device or signal connections are allowed, however, parameter control—has not been completely standardized. Parameter control depends on the manufacturer's protocol. In addition, the NMOS IS-08 specification for audio channel mapping (i.e., audio signal routing) has not been widely used, although the specifications have already been established and published. Consequently, depending on a manufacturer's closed protocol strategy, system vendor lock-in can occur.

This study focused on "Ember+," a publicly available open-source control protocol, as a control signal. Its specification has been published in GitHub [2], and it is gradually being adopted among broadcast equipment developers. Ember+ does not define the content of the control data itself but defines the procedure to communicate the data structure of the control parameters, as illustrated in **Figure 1**. This renders the protocol versatile, thereby enabling the protocol to be adopted in broadcast equipment and aiding the protocol to become the "de-facto standard."

Here, "Ember+" was used to develop a tool that could achieve detailed control—such as the input/output unit control of the microphone head amp gain and on/off control of the phantom power. The results demonstrate that this is a useful control protocol for remote environments. Based on this, a tool to promote remote production was developed.

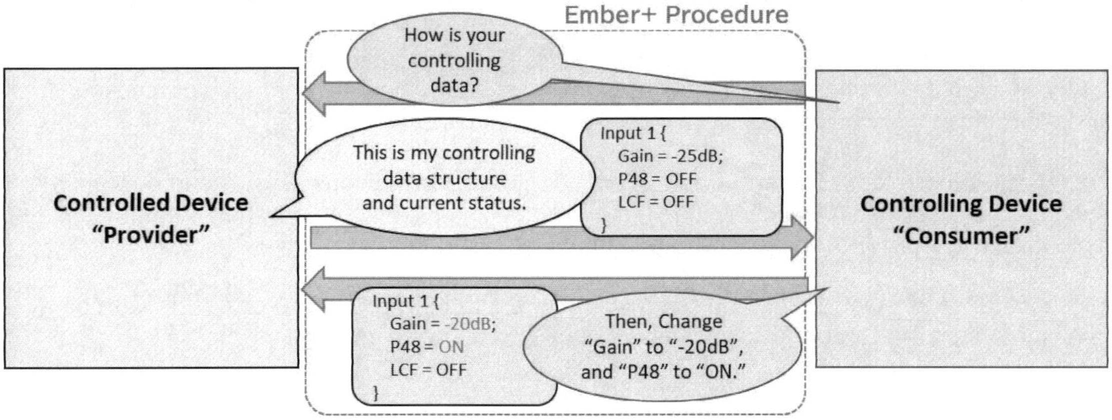

FIGURE 1: HOW "EMBER+" CONTROLS THE DEVICE PARAMETERS.

Interconversion for IP Remote Production

This study also focused on the Dante standard, which has a large share of audio IP standards in the audio sector. Although equipment exist that can convert Dante products used in short-distance networks into (international standard) ST2110-compatible devices for use in remote production, two problems made it difficult to use them in remote production.

The first problem was related to control; although products existed that could convert audio signals between the Dante and ST2110 standards, they did not support control signals.

The second problem was related to transmission delays. Because Dante is a standard developed for local networks, it is unsuitable for long-distance transmissions that involve large delays, and considerable effort is required to establish a system to synchronize the bases.

Many of broadcasting companies use Dante equipment. Therefore, this study developed an Audio over Internet Protocol (AoIP) converter that can convert audio signals between the Dante and ST2110 standards including parameter control. To achieve this, we converted Dante control signals into Ember+, which is useful in remote environments, making it possible to control audio levels and matrices. Additionally, a reclocking mechanism, which is like a sampling rate converter (SRC), was installed in the converter to facilitate synchronization and bridge the ST2110 signals, thereby reducing the amount of work required in the system setup. (**Figure. 2**)

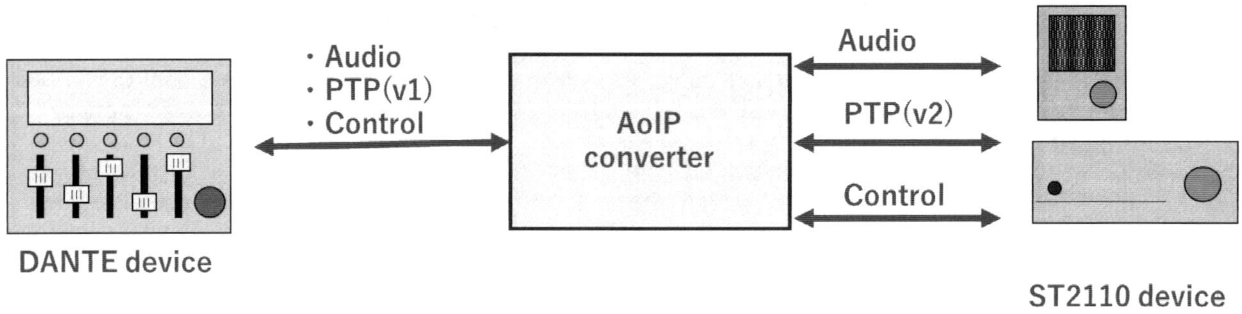

FIGURE 2: MECHANISM OF THE INTERCONVERSION BETWEEN DANTE AND ST2110.

To evaluate the converter, we used an audio mixing console that is compatible with DANTE and audio device that is compatible with ST2110 which are for consumers. We can transmit audio signals and control the audio devices parameter such as shown at fig.1 interactively.
Until recently, system design has been a time consuming process; however, the use of the AoIP converter developed in this project has streamlined the system design process.

We showed that "Ember+" is useful for remote production, because various signals can be transmitted for controlling remote devices. Moreover, the Dante protocol, which is used for short-range networks, can be used for remote production using an open standard protocol.

This study successfully converted the audio signal with the Dante and ST2110 protocols, and as a control, the signal from the Dante protocol was converted to an open protocol.

Future Outlook

Using the open protocol as a control signal, we can use Dante devices that were previously difficult to incorporate into remote production systems, thereby broadening the range of remote production.

We are currently working on other initiatives to promote remote production. In particular, we aim to reduce the number of personnel and make system construction easier by developing various devices.

The first involves developing a tool to remotely control devices that are not intended for use in remote environments by converting Ember+ into a general-purpose input output. For example, we designed a cough box that supports remote control such that comments can be recorded by bringing a microphone and the cough box to a remote location. This equipment can improve work productivity and efficiency in remote locations.

The second involves developing a tool to remotely transmit the speaker's voice back to the speaker in a remote environment. Typically, a staff member and system construction are required to be in a remote environment for the sending back system with low latency. Therefore, developing such a tool is expected to reduce labor costs and make system construction easier.

The Japan Broadcasting Corporation plans to continue developing equipment to promote remote production, while considering the needs of program production.

Acknowledgments

The author would like to thank Mr. Okano, Mr. Kuramata and Mr. Imai for suggesting the topics addressed in this paper. I would also like to thank Hanaoka Musen Denki Corporation for their technical assistance with the experiments. This study was supported by the Japan Broadcasting Corporation.

References

[1] EBU, The TECHNOLOGY PYRAMID FOR MEDIA NODES, Tech 3371, Version 3.0, April 2023, pp.10-11.

[2] https://github.com/Lawo/ember-plus

How the Eurovision Song Contest 2024 Leveraged the Benefits of ST 2110 and Transitioned Away from Baseband Video Formats

Scott Blair, Joe Bleasdale
Megapixel VR
Los Angeles, California, United States
scott@megapixelvr.com, jbleasdale@megapixelvr.com

Abstract – This paper explores the challenges associated with baseband video formats in large-scale live productions, emphasizing the advantages introduced by SMPTE ST 2110 [1]. By analyzing conventional point-to-point video transmission against IP-based systems, key benefits such as enhanced metadata management, streamlined infrastructure, and increased adaptability are highlighted. A case study of the Eurovision Song Contest 2024 demonstrates how these technologies were applied to improve performance and reliability in a demanding live environment.

Introduction

The choice of video transmission format plays a crucial role in live event production and broadcasting, influencing quality, efficiency, and reliability. Traditional baseband video formats, including high-definition multimedia interface (HDMI), serial digital interface (SDI), and DisplayPort, have long been industry standards due to their seamless integration with graphics processing units (GPUs) and existing infrastructure. However, as production requirements expand and demand for scalability increases, these legacy formats present significant limitations, particularly in terms of bandwidth, distance constraints, and system flexibility.

Technical Limitations of Baseband Video Formats

Bandwidth Challenges

Baseband video formats like HDMI, SDI, and DisplayPort facilitate high-quality video transmission via point-to-point connections. However, as live productions increasingly demand higher resolutions and frame rates, these formats face significant bandwidth constraints [2]. For example, while HDMI 2.1 supports data rates up to 48 Gbps, it is restricted by cable length and signal integrity, making it impractical for large venue applications requiring extended distances.

Cable Length Constraints

One of the most notable limitations of baseband video formats is cable length. HDMI cables, for instance, perform optimally only within short distances—typically under 15 meters for 1080p and even less for 4K signals. Although SDI allows for longer transmission distances, it too has limitations. This challenge necessitates strategic equipment placement, which adds complexity to large-scale event setups.

This paper is excerpted from the Proceedings of the 2025 NAB Broadcast Engineering and Information Technology (BEIT) Conference, © 2025, National Association of Broadcasters, 1 M Street SE, Washington, DC 20003 USA.

Signal Distribution Complexity
Baseband video infrastructures require dedicated cabling for each video feed, resulting in an intricate network of connections, particularly in high-profile events. Each source must be individually linked to its destination, often requiring multiple converters and splitters, which introduce latency and synchronization concerns.

Scalability Challenges
Expanding a baseband video system to accommodate additional sources or displays is both costly and technically demanding. More inputs require additional SDI, HDMI, or DP ports, which, in turn, require extra cabling, converters, and support hardware. The increased system density makes troubleshooting difficult and raises the likelihood of signal degradation or failure.

Interoperability Issues
Baseband video formats, despite adhering to standards, often face interoperability challenges due to variations in connectors and protocols. This necessitates frequent use of adapters and converters, increasing system complexity and potential failure points.

Advantages of SMPTE ST 2110 in Live Event Production

The shift from baseband video formats to SMPTE ST 2110 introduces several key advantages, particularly in terms of efficiency, scalability, and infrastructure simplification [3]. Unlike traditional point-to-point connections, ST 2110 utilizes an IP-based framework, allowing seamless integration of new video and audio streams without requiring additional cabling.

Additionally, ST 2110 streamlines infrastructure by consolidating multiple media streams over a single network. This approach significantly reduces the amount of physical cabling required and minimizes the number of hardware components necessary for signal distribution. By eliminating traditional routers, amplifiers, and signal converters, large productions benefit from a reduced system footprint and a more efficient workflow.

Case Study: Eurovision 2024 and the HELIOS LED Processing Platform

Redundant System Design
To ensure seamless operation, Eurovision 2024 employed two independent but fully redundant network systems, "Red" and "Blue" (see Figure 1). These networks operated in parallel, providing an automatic failover mechanism to eliminate downtime in the event of a system failure. Central to this architecture were redundant Panasonic Kairos KC2000S1 units, which managed media server output switching, ensuring continuous video feed availability.

Figure 1 shows the overall building layout in relation to the network topography. Crucially, most equipment was kept backstage making more space available at Front of House for critical control system equipment. Thanks to the network-based nature of the deployment, it was easy to monitor and control the system from multiple locations within the facility.

Figure 2, a high-level network overview, shows how the 200/100/25Gb networks coexisted with each other. Feeds from the media servers and image processing gateways flowed through two Artisa 7060CX switches before being routed to the corresponding HELIOS for processing and output to the LED network.

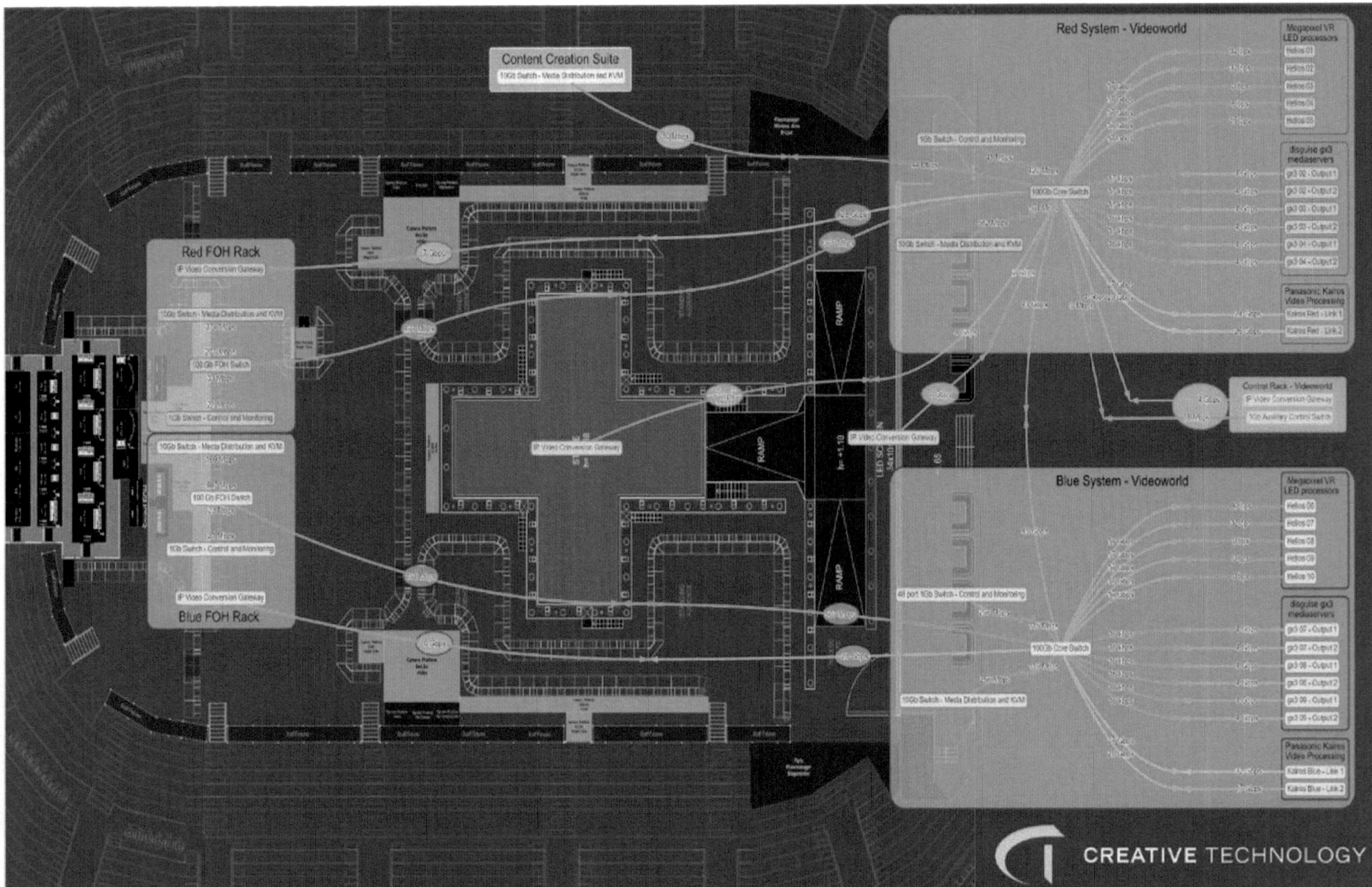

FIGURE 1: RED & BLUE NETWORK OVERVIEW IMAGE.

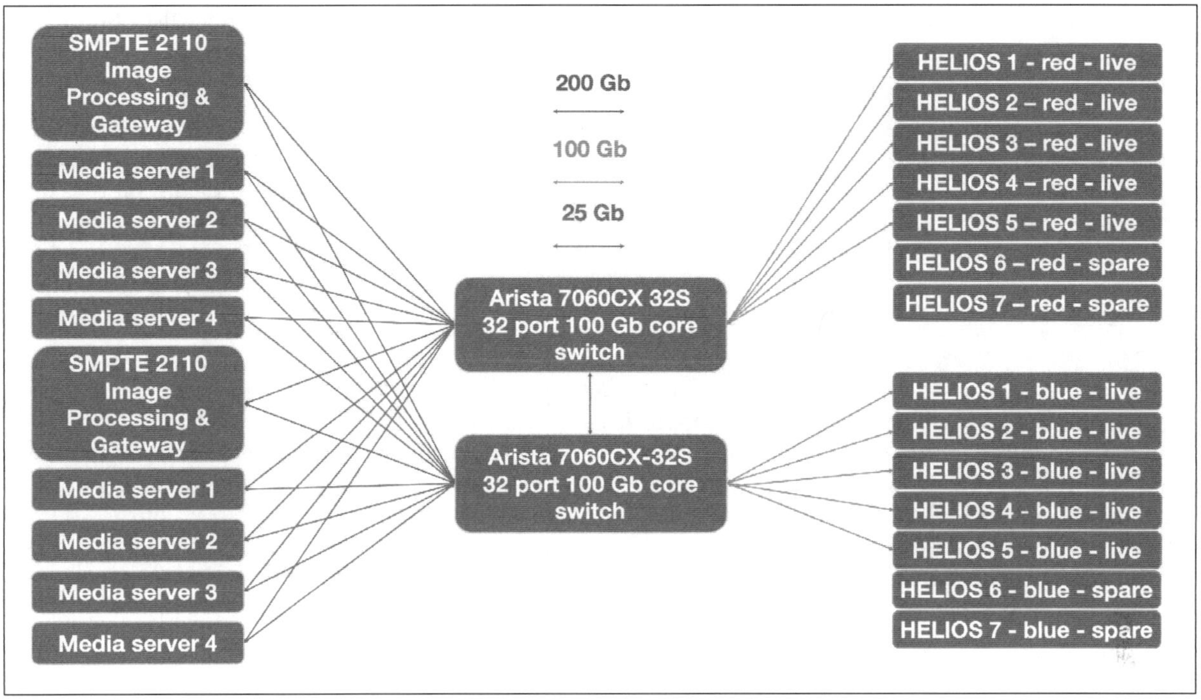

FIGURE 2: OVERVIEW OF 200GB, 100GB AND 25GB FEEDS WITHIN THE NETWORK.

Implementation of HELIOS and ST 2110

The HELIOS LED processing platform [4] was a key component of the Eurovision 2024 video infrastructure. Designed to process large-format LED content, HELIOS featured native support for ST 2110, allowing seamless IP-based video integration. The adoption of 100G ST 2110 facilitated high-resolution, low-latency video handling, ensuring synchronized content delivery across all display elements.

Network Routing and Management

Once processed, media streams were distributed using a network of strategically placed switches. The Ethernet-based infrastructure allowed for flexible routing, enabling real-time system adjustments as production demands evolved.

Overcoming Challenges

One of the primary challenges of Eurovision 2024 was managing the high volume of video data while maintaining system reliability. The IP-based approach streamlined this process, with the parallel network design ensuring uninterrupted performance. Additionally, the inherent flexibility of network-based routing simplified the handling of bandwidth-intensive video feeds.

Key Benefits Achieved During Eurovision 2024

Seamless Integration and Scalability

The integration of HELIOS within the Eurovision 2024 setup allowed the production team to seamlessly manage many video sources and LED displays across the venue. The IP-based infrastructure, supported by ST 2110, provided the flexibility to adjust the system in real-time, responding quickly to evolving production needs without the need for significant reconfiguration. This scalability was particularly important in an event of this magnitude, where last-minute changes and dynamic content adjustments are common.

Low Latency Performance

Low-latency performance was a critical factor in ensuring the synchronization of live video feeds, audio tracks, and lighting cues. The HELIOS LED processing platform was able to handle multiple high-bandwidth video streams with zero delay, preserving the integrity of real-time production elements. Given the rapid transitions between shots and frame-accurate content delivery needed in Eurovision's fast-paced environment, the low-latency processing offered by the IP-based system was essential to maintaining the show's visual and audio alignment for both the in-venue audience and live broadcast viewers.

Enhanced Redundancy and System Reliability

The implementation of the dual-network (Red and Blue) system design provided critical redundancy throughout the event. Using ST 2110, the production team was able to ensure that any disruption in one network would immediately trigger a seamless failover to the backup network, with no impact on the broadcast. The robustness of the IP network infrastructure ensured high reliability, reducing potential points of failure and increasing overall system resilience [5]. This redundancy was a key requirement in maintaining uninterrupted video feeds and providing peace of mind during such a high-profile event.

Reduction in Equipment and Power Consumption

By transitioning to an IP-based system using ST 2110, the Eurovision production team significantly reduced the amount of physical equipment needed. Traditional baseband setups typically require separate routers, distribution amplifiers, and extensive cabling to manage video feeds, but the network-based solution consolidated many of these functions. This not only simplified the setup but also reduced the overall power consumption, which is a growing concern in large-scale events. The compact design of the system also eased logistical challenges, minimizing the amount of space needed for video racks and lowering the complexity of troubleshooting.

Conclusion

The transition from baseband video formats to SMPTE ST 2110 represents a transformative shift in live event production. While traditional formats have served the industry well, they are increasingly unable to meet the evolving demands of large-scale productions.

By offering enhanced metadata management, streamlined infrastructure, and improved redundancy, ST 2110 presents a compelling alternative. The Eurovision 2024 case study exemplifies how these advantages translate into tangible improvements in live broadcasting. As the industry continues to evolve, IP-based technologies like ST 2110 will become the new standard, paving the way for more efficient and scalable production workflows.

References

[1] SMPTE ST 2110 Professional Media Over Managed IP networks suite, available at https://www.smpte.org/standards/st2110.

[2] B. Ferguson, "Cable considerations for AV over IP," 02/11/2021. Available: https://www.belden.com/blogs/smart-building/cable-considerations-for-av-over-ip

[3] B. Kovacs, "Is SMPTE ST 2110 the future of your facility?," 08/02/2024. Available: https://www.tvtechnology.com/features/is-smpte-st-2110-the-future-of-your-facility

[4] Megapixel HELIOS LED Processing Platform https://megapixelvr.com/helios/

[5] Arista Networks, "High-speed networking for digital media creation, post production and centralized content management," 2015. https://www.arista.com/en/solutions/high-speed-networking

Network Distribution and the Internet Snake! - Transcoding Anywhere

David Edwards, Adam Nilsson, Pierre Le Fevre, Jonathan Smith
Net Insight
Stockholm, Sweden
david.edwards@netinsight.net, adam.nilsson@netinsight.net, pierre.lefevre@netinsight.net, jonathan.smith@netinsight.net

Abstract – Video content distribution faces challenges and conflicts, particularly in balancing high-quality delivery with technical and commercial constraints. Different network endpoints have varying requirements, such as bandwidth limitations or specific codec needs, making efficient distribution complex. While live transcoding can help, traditional solutions often rely on centralized data centers, leading to high processing costs and dependency on strong connectivity. This paper explores an alternative approach that decentralizes live transcoding, leveraging distributed edge-transcode technologies to optimize network utilization, reduce cloud OPEX costs, and enable scalable, cost-efficient content delivery.

Network Distribution Needs

The core function of network distribution is to share content with many receiving entities. Ensuring reliable media delivery to multiple takers, across multiple locations. As our industry becomes more globalized, often multiple locations are spread across a wide geographical area.

Frequently, with a large geographic spread, the needs of the takers can have different requirements. A need for content personalization for a particular region or demographic. Sometimes a need for different video formats or different compression formats, or different video quality levels or profiles to fulfill varying local platform needs. In a world where media is increasingly being handed off to devices in IP formats we find ourselves with a cross-product of consumer behavior and the number of delivery platforms putting ever more pressure on the processing of streams.

The growing need to distribute and hand-off content in multiple formats presents challenges to the distribution operator in finding the most operationally efficient and cost-efficient solution for fulfilling the taker's needs. Capital expense (CAPEX) costs and operating expense (OPEX0 costs need to be balanced within an overall and often tightening budget.

The Business of Risk

The business of broadcast is changing rapidly, with focus being firmly on content creation and the monetization opportunities for that content. In the past, the business was about reliable delivery to a mostly captive consumer base. Massive investments in distribution networks, whether over the air or through terrestrial means would be amortized over years or decades. A distribution network operator, broadcaster or programmer would invest appropriately in program making to give the competitive advantage over the small number of other players in a region with the same channel variants.

This paper is excerpted from the Proceedings of the 2025 NAB Broadcast Engineering and Information Technology (BEIT) Conference, © 2025, National Association of Broadcasters, 1 M Street SE, Washington, DC 20003 USA.

Now, consumers are untethered with freedom to easily move between platforms, to subscribe and unsubscribe with immediate effect. The new generation of consumers can be far more fickle about the media they consume and demand higher levels of engagement to retain their business.

With this change in consumer behavior comes the need to do more in content creation. Alternative angles, data driven feeds, player point-of-view (PoV) cameras all exist to engage and retain consumers, to build interest in a particular genre and ultimately keep eyes on content long enough to consume revenue-building commercials.

With all this extra work being done, content creators must reach new markets to try and squeeze every last drop of potential in order to capitalize on the creation investment and develop the market further. This need cannot be approached in the traditional network distribution approach. Expensive connectivity, long-term contracts and extended time-to-market are the enemies of the scale fast, fail fast mentality needed to tap new opportunities today.

Evolution of Network Distribution

Historically, primary network distribution has leveraged satellite connectivity. The global geographic reach of satellite, combined with its "five nines" reliability has been a key factor in fulfilling service provision needs.

But distribution architectures are changing, and business budgets are evolving. IP connectivity has now become near-ubiquitous and provides promise in the normalization of IP transport protocol from head to tail. Many core media sites have guaranteed fiber connectivity and other installations closer to the network edge have evolved to acquire high speed connectivity to the unmanaged internet.

Following the application of automatic repeat request (ARQ) IP techniques for media and using media encapsulation protocols such as secure reliable transport (SRT) and reliable internet stream transport (RIST), it is now possible to deliver content with data reliability and geographical coverage approaching that of satellite.

The cost profile of content distribution is changing, too. Satellite transponder costs can reach up to $1m per transponder per year with typical link budgets allowing 90 Mbit/s delivery utilizing DVB-S2X (example parameters and cost based on 50 Mbit/s shown in Table 1).

Transmission Standard	Modulation	FEC	Symbol Rate	Bit Rate	Number of Services	Typical Cost per Service
DVB-S2X	8PSK	5/9	30 MSym/s	49.8 Mbit/s	10	$100k per year

TABLE 1: TYPICAL SATELLITE MODULATION PARAMETERS AND COSTS FOR A DISTRIBUTION SYSTEM.

IP delivery over the unmanaged internet has a different cost profile. Available data rates are frequently greater than satellite. Charges in IP delivery architectures are applied per destination location. While costs can range from country to country, a point of reference is $160 per month for one destination per internet stream (excluding cloud processing or cloud egress charges) or $1920 per year. That could therefore lead to a break-even equivalent between satellite and IP delivered services of 1x IP stream delivered to 520 destinations, or 10x IP delivered services to 52 destinations for the cost of a yearly satellite lease. This example demonstrates one of the reasons why the cost dynamics of IP content delivery are driving change into Broadcaster's distribution models.

Onwards to the IP-Native World

The ability to deploy IP-native distribution systems has been driven by the efficiency and pricing models that data centers offer. Their scale, global reach from rapid growth and ability to dynamically flex capacity can offer many benefits. The ability to format and compress video for distribution in cloud environments has enabled some content owners to offload on-premises solutions to cloud architectures and re-balance their expenditure profiles.

But cloud processing is not a panacea for all. Many content distribution systems are 24/7/365 operations. Cloud charging schemes need to be carefully examined and calculated to look at how best to balance the cost profile for these less dynamic distribution systems. With Cloud processing offering the ability to provide some stream customization to tailor outgoing services to individual taker's needs, the cost profile of the distribution system needs to be managed to balance stream customization and cloud costs.

IP is Not Always Low Cost

Cloud has a cost. A cost for video processing instances but also for stream egress. For distribution systems serving multiple takers, stream egress from cloud systems has the potential to become a significant part of distribution system costs. Charges in the region of $250 to $400 per stream per month are not uncommon.

Taking into account cloud egress costs, there is an onus on the system design to strike a balance between the number of stream egress points, scaling of the network and customization of the video services to individuals or groups of takers.

The Internet Snake

Data centers are surrounded by high-speed gigabit fiber connectivity. Internet-delivered media content has many permissible paths from the head of the media network hosted within a data center. Closer to the tail, at the network edge, speeds reduce, latency increases, and connection robustness can decrease. Content distribution takers at the network edge may not be so fortunate in having high quality connectivity. The result being that takers at the network edge may need to have different stream properties.

Network architecture designs need to take account of stream requirement properties for takers at the network edge and where the stream is originated. Modern distribution systems can provide capabilities to manage bit rate restrictions that may occur closer to the network edge. Capabilities exist to transcode the video service to match any bit rate restrictions. The costs of doing so and how any stream customizations are required is a balance that comes from optimization of multiple taker's needs.

An Alternate Strategy – Customization at the Edge

While it may not be commercially or practically viable to customize content distribution streams for each and every taker, having made the transition from uniform, satellite distribution to IP distribution, service provision may be best served not through a centralized data center model but through a hybrid approach.

Through a hybrid, distributed transcode architecture, the most appropriate video format, video quality and stream data rate can be originated in the most appropriate location. This architecture can help to ensure that service provision can be optimized for the largest number of takers. Cloud processing, egress costs and network transport to the edge can also be optimized – including for the outliers.

Hybrid Distribution - Flexible Pipelines, Optimized Per Output

Through a hybrid approach (shown in Figure 1), it is possible to optimize the distribution pipeline. To put processing intensive tasks in a location where they can be best served – perhaps in the cloud. And to move other processing functionality closer to the edge.

By moving processing out towards the network edge, the distribution system may be optimized. Processes that are less intensive, processes that must be applied to a video source, processes that need to be targeted to a limited number of takers may be more efficiently applied closer to the edge of the network.

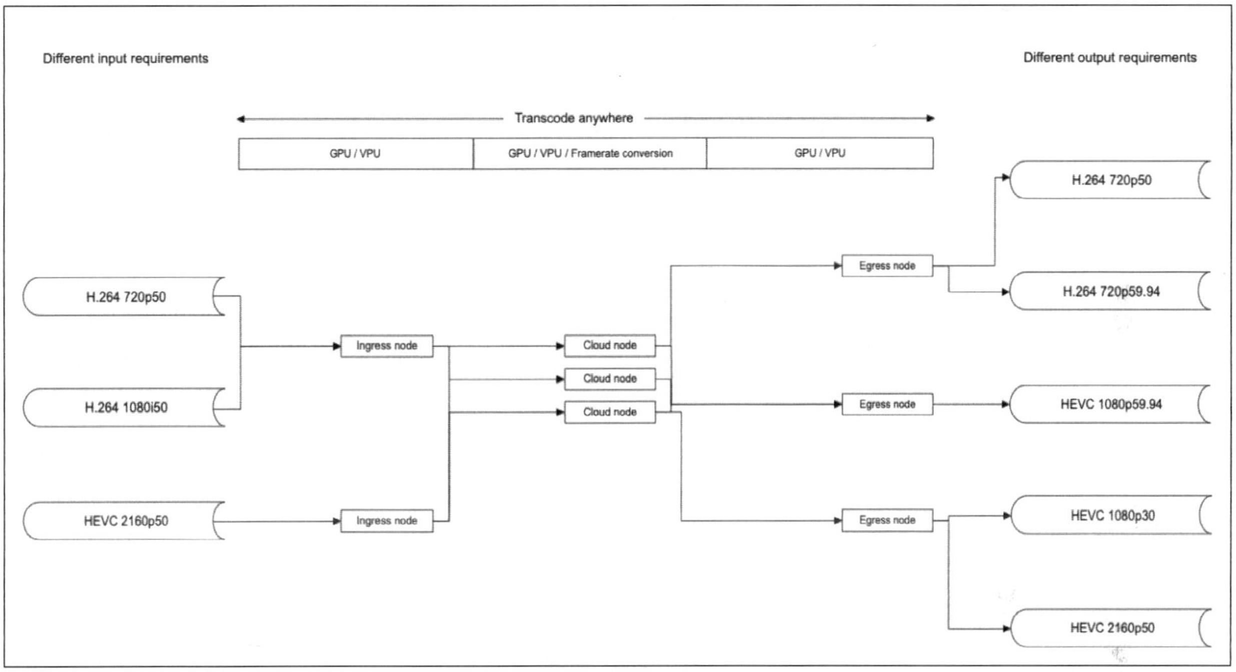

FIGURE 1: CLOUD AND COTS HYBRID DISTRIBUTION SYSTEM.

Performing video processing at the network edge can be implemented in a "Video Region" processing node – a server geographically positioned to originate or terminate ARQ connectivity to the broadcaster/distributor or taker.

The processing power of the video region can be scaled to match the number of streams passing through that segment of the video network. The processing power can also be scaled to apply video processing functionality. Video regions on content ingress may be suitable for applying functionality such as motion compensated frame rate conversion, useful perhaps for originating content distribution between global regions such as the Americas and Europe where frame rates are different.

When distributing content to multiple takers, there may be the need to address certain endpoints that are situated far from the network core, where network bandwidth is low, where connectivity is less reliable. In these situations, where connectivity to a very remote taker is marginal, then it may prove most optimal to provide a stream – not routed directly from the hub of the cloud network, but through a remote video region, a region that can condition the stream appropriately for the most remote takers.

Addressing the most remote and marginal takers through a video region can save on egress costs from the core cloud hub. A single service can egress from the cloud, at single service egress costs and be adapted close to takers for their individual needs. For example, a service can be transcoded to a different CODEC or lower bit rate or cross-conversion / down-conversion applied to reduce the resolution. The result can provide the ability to address takers closer to the network edge without incurring ongoing OPEX egress costs in an affordable manner with localized edge processing in a video region.

By deploying stream processing closer to the edge, it becomes possible to reduce the round-trip time. Any lost data requiring a re-transmission can originate from a server closer to the destination, allowing takers on more marginal network connections to achieve a lower latency service. In order to scale the processing of video servers within a video region, the server can be equipped with a graphics processing unit (GPU) or vision processing unit (VPU) as appropriate.

Comparing Service Provision Costs Between Cloud and COTS

In designing a network architecture, evaluations need to be made on infrastructure costs, where to locate processing functions and which platform to build them on. Information for cloud platform pricing is readily available, an example is shown in Figure 2.[1] Analysis shows that on-demand pricing is high. Pre-paid pricing is lower and available for multiple years of service. For attributing costs to service planning, pre-paid pricing can be thought of as being similar to a CAPEX cost.

Price per Location

Costs and pricing for Amazon Elastic Compute Cloud (EC2) instance type `g6.xlarge` in AWS locations in which the instance type is available.

Location				Costs per Hour		Costs per Month					
Code	Name	Continent	Type	On-Demand	Spot	On-Demand	Spot	1Y RI (No)	1Y RI (All)	3Y RI (No)	3Y RI (All)
us-east-1	US East (N. Virginia)	North America	Region	$0.8048	$0.2664	$587.5	$194.47	$382.46	$357	$269.66	$234.69
us-east-2	US East (Ohio)	North America	Region	$0.8048	$0.3301	$587.5	$240.97	$382.46	$357	$269.66	$234.69
us-west-2	US West (Oregon)	North America	Region	$0.8048	$0.542	$587.5	$395.66	$382.46	$357	$269.66	$234.69
eu-south-2	EU (Spain)	Europe	Region	$0.848	$0.2423	$619.04	$176.88	$403	$376.17	$284.14	$247.31
eu-north-1	EU (Stockholm)	Europe	Region	$0.8536	$0.2996	$623.13	$218.71	$405.65	$378.58	$286.01	$248.94
ca-central-1	Canada (Central)	North America	Region	$0.8936	$0.3245	$652.33	$236.89	$424.66	$396.33	$299.42	$260.61
ap-south-1	Asia Pacific (Mumbai)	Asia Pacific	Region	$0.9664	$0.3267	$705.47	$238.49	$459.26	$428.67	$323.81	$281.83
ap-northeast-2	Asia Pacific (Seoul)	Asia Pacific	Region	$0.9896	$0.3216	$722.41	$234.77	$470.29	$438.92	$331.59	$288.61
eu-central-1	EU (Frankfurt)	Europe	Region	$1.0064	$0.3235	$734.67	$236.16	$478.27	$446.42	$337.22	$293.5
ap-southeast-5	Asia Pacific (Malaysia)	Asia Pacific	Region	$1.0138	$0.468	$740.07	$341.64	$481.79	$449.67	$339.69	$295.67
us-gov-west-1	AWS GovCloud (US)	North America	Region	$1.0144	N/A	$740.51	N/A	$482.07	$449.92	$339.9	$295.83
eu-west-2	EU (London)	Europe	Region	$1.0216	$0.2837	$745.77	$207.1	$485.49	$453.17	$342.3	$297.94
eu-west-3	EU (Paris)	Europe	Region	$1.0216	$0.3026	$745.77	$220.9	$485.49	$453.17	$342.3	$297.94
ap-southeast-2	Asia Pacific (Sydney)	Asia Pacific	Region	$1.0464	$0.368	$763.87	$268.64	$497.28	$464.17	$350.62	$305.17
eu-central-2	EU (Zurich)	Europe	Region	$1.085	$0.337	$792.05	$246.01	$515.63	$481.25	$363.55	$316.42
ap-northeast-1	Asia Pacific (Tokyo)	Asia Pacific	Region	$1.1672	$0.4935	$852.06	$360.25	$554.69	$517.75	$391.09	$340.39
sa-east-1	South America (Sao Paulo)	South America	Region	$1.368	$0.1368	$998.64	$99.86	$650.12	$606.75	$458.37	$398.94

The accuracy of the data is not guaranteed. Please report issues you see. Portions of this webapp are modifications based on work created and shared by Amazon Web Services and used according to terms described in the Creative Commons 4.0 Attribution-ShareAlike License.

Last Update: Fri Jan 31 04:57:42 2025 (GMT) · Imprint

FIGURE 2: EXAMPLE CLOUD PROCESSING COSTS FOR G6.XLARGE PROCESSING FUNCTION.

As discussed, conditioning of media streams for takers at the edge of the network with processing such as transcoding, transrating or format conversion may be implemented centrally in the cloud, regionally in the cloud or close to the network edge in a COTS-based video region processing device.

When designing the network architecture, evaluating how to achieve an optimum cost profile, not only may it be optimum to analyze multi-year cloud provision but also to consider the geographical location

[1] Also see g6.xlarge - Amazon EC2 Instance Type suitable for Transcode or deinterlacing functionality.

of that provision. It should be noted that cloud deployment in locations further removed from continental US or central Europe can have an elevated cost. And for regionalized media processing, cloud costs may be highest where they are needed most critically.

It is, however, more common for distribution platforms to source a cloud *service* rather than simply leverage solely an underlying processing *instance*. Pricing for a complete service, such as transcoding, is bundled to give more attractive pricing.

Using readily available published information for AWS MediaLive, as an example, a single service distributed to 10 takers involving a HEVC to MPEG-4 AVC transcode can be calculated (Table 2).

AWS MediaLive				
Location	Monthly Cost	3-Year Cost	Number of Streams	3-Year Cost per Stream
US N. Virginia	$ 2,810.50	$ 101,178.00	10	$ 10,117.80

TABLE 2: EXAMPLE PRICING FOR TRANSCODE CAPABILITY AS A CLOUD SERVICE.

To allow a comparison, a software solution is additionally required to complete the COTS based distribution platform (Table 3).

AWS MediaLive				
Location	Monthly Cost	3-Year Cost	Number of Streams	3-Year Cost per Stream
US N. Virginia	$ 2,810.50	$ 101,178.00	10	$ 10,117.80

COTS Implementation					
Server Cost	VPU Cost	Total CAPEX Cost	3-Year Software Service Cost	Number of Streams	3-Year Cost per Stream
$ 3,500.00	$ 1,500.00	$ 5,000.00	$ 30,000.00	10	$ 3,500.00

TABLE 3: COST COMPARISON OF A CLOUD TRANSCODE SERVICE VS. A COTS TRANSCODE SERVICE.

By moving some functionality closer to the edge, operational costs may be lowered by reducing the number of streams egressing from cloud domains and incurring additional service charges. Or reducing costs by moving a function into video region COTS-based edge devices, that where a CAPEX charging element may give a better cost profile than an on-going OPEX charge.

Optimized Stream Processing

With software processing advancing and enabling a broader range of video processing functionality, distribution architectures can be optimized and consolidated, delivering greater operational simplicity and allowing broadcasters to respond to the pressure of doing more for less. Designers of distribution systems now have a toolset of functionality such as transcoding, watermarking, audio shuffling/PID remapping, framerate conversion and many more.

Having integrated video processing building blocks that were previously implemented as stand-alone technology to optimize signal flow and reduce costs, it becomes possible to automate the flow architecture to further optimize the architecture – and reduce stream processing costs.

With automated pipeline optimization (see Figure 6) it becomes possible to remove process and workflow duplication, delivering network simplicity, reducing process utilization, increasing efficiency of processing power and reducing utilization charges.

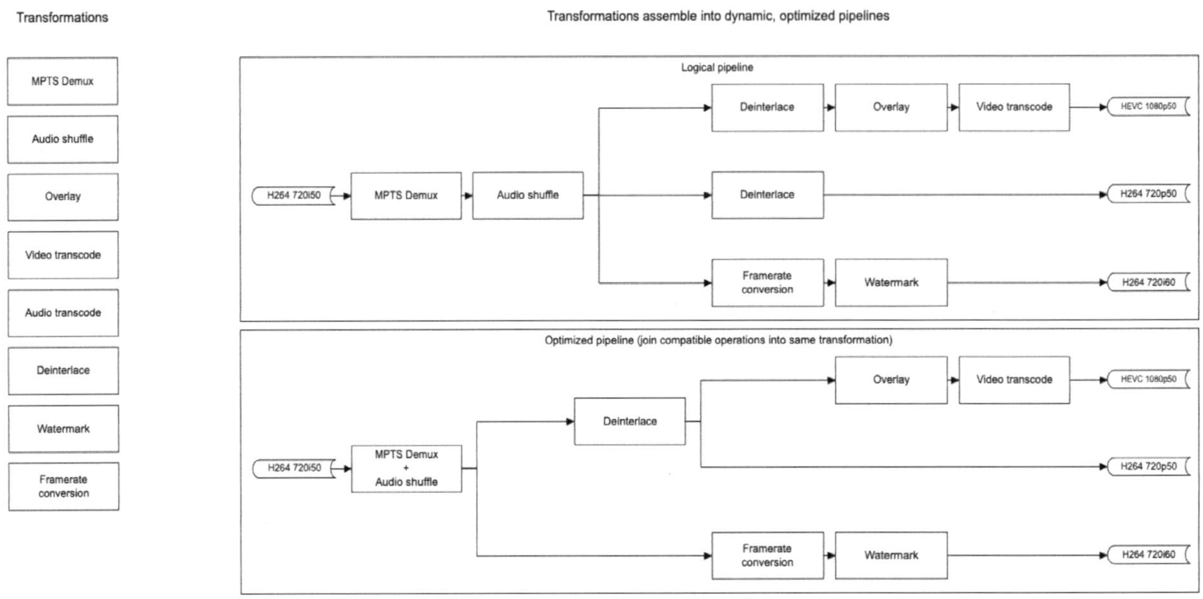

FIGURE 6: PIPELINES OPTIMIZED PER OUTPUT.

Further, by partitioning the processing workflow throughout the network topology, it becomes possible to optimize the distribution network across cloud and video region domains ensuring that stream processing is deployed at the best position within the entirety of the video network where it is most beneficial.

Compatibility with Multiple Accelerator Vendors, OS, Virtualization Methods

In creating a complete content distribution system that leverages the benefits of cloud and edge computing to give the most optimal architecture, it can be beneficial for all the processing elements to interoperate with minimal issues and be monitored and managed through a system that gives a comprehensive overview.

In order to facilitate these operational efficiencies, it can be beneficial for the video processing functionality to be portable between centralized cloud and network edge implementation. In such a system configuration, the edge implementation could be performed in a regional cloud location or on a COTS server.

By implementing the video processing in a way that is portable, the distribution service operator can benefit from the flexibility of moving from a cloud-based service to a ground-based / COTS implementation as their business evolves with minimal impact in service interfacing and system control and management. Such methodologies allow distribution operators to launch a service rapidly in the cloud and confirm the assumptions in their business plan and then, solidify the service provision in a way that can be more permanent, and perhaps more cost optimized than a full cloud implementation.

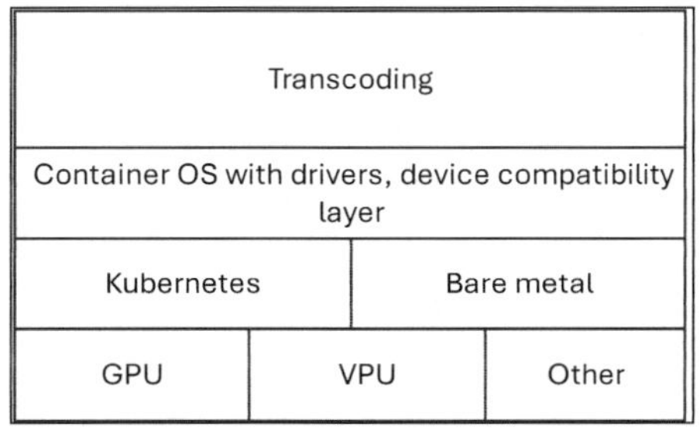

FIGURE 7: DEVICE SUPPORT ACHIEVED THROUGH A LAYERED MODEL.

Conclusion

This paper has outlined how latest, IP-based distribution systems can be optimized by using a hybrid architecture of both core cloud processing and COTS processing in a video region close to the network edge.

By implementing a hybrid architecture, the network topology can better support providing video services that are more targeted at the differing needs of takers. Customization can be made to accommodate regional video format needs and CODEC requirements. Customization can also better accommodate takers who may be at the very edge of the network where data rates and network robustness may be more marginal.

Through partitioning the video processing functionality throughout the hybrid network, operational costs and total system costs can be reduced to more optimally manage cloud and COTS costs. Costs and processing instances can be further optimized by leveraging intelligent stream and processing-path algorithms to ensure that functional processes are not overly duplicated.

Finally, this paper describes how video processing functionality can be made portable between cloud and ground-based COTS platforms, so that as the distribution network evolves, key network functional building blocks can be easily migrated from one type of processing host to another without disruptive re-integration tasks.

By taking into account the sum of these distribution new enhancements, an IP distribution system can be optimized across the media network from the distribution head of the network through to the tail at the very edge of the network – at the end of the internet snake.

Solving the Multiview Problem

Rob Koenen and Ray van Brandenburg
Tiledmedia
Rotterdam, The Netherlands
rob@tiledmedia.com, ray@tiledmedia.com

Abstract – As streaming services evolve, viewer demand for new and innovative ways to consume content is making multiview an essential feature. There are several ways to provide multiview experiences on end-user devices including encoding composite feeds in desired permutations ("Many Encodes"), spawning multiple independent players on the user device ("Many Players"), or using cloud encoding. These approaches that are currently used in the market all have downsides.

Single-Player Multiview, an alternative to these approaches, is flexible, responsive and scalable. With full knowledge of everything that is happening on the screen and the network combined in a single player, that player can adapt its adaptive bitrate (ABR) decisions and segment retrieval strategy accordingly. Single-Player Multiview is also the only approach that can ensure reliable sync between multiple feeds.

Multiview – What Is It and Why Use It?

We refer to "multiview streaming" when a consumer can track multiple independent video feeds on a single display (an example is shown in Figure 1). These videos they represent can be related, such as when a specific event is captured by multiple cameras that the user can choose from. These cameras may capture the same content from a different angle, e.g., with multiple cameras following the same ball in a "single-ball sport" like football. They may also capture different locations for the same event, such as different golf holes.

FIGURE 1: MULTIVIEW EXAMPLE.

Arguably the strongest case for multiview streaming is in sports where the action is distributed, and the director is forced to make choices. *Multi-camera* examples include all forms of motor racing, road cycling, golf, track and field, and gymnastics. Services already exist where a user can *change* the camera, but fans will lose the director feed and the storyline if they do. Sometimes they also lose the commentary. True multiview will allow the user to follow the director cut while *adding* their own story to that of the director, for example the onboard camera of their favorite driver in a race. Thy may even be able to mix audio feeds.

Multiview streaming is also useful – and indeed deployed – for *multi-game* days. YouTube allows NFL fans to follow multiple games at the same time on Sunday and NBC Universal deployed multiview for the Paris Olympics when many events took place at the same time.

A further use case for multiview is for *multi-channel* video providers, who can let their users keep an eye on two or even three channels, e.g., using Picture-in-Picture display (See Figure 2).

Multiview streaming can additionally be useful for professionals working with video, e.g., first responders that might have access to multiple security cameras as an emergency develops.

This paper focuses on scalable solutions for entertainment use cases with large audiences. We will look at streaming efficiency, ease of implementation and the options for making a great user experience. We will also consider the seamlessness of feed switching and cross-feed synchronization, both of which are especially important in multi-camera events.

FIGURE 2: MULTI-CHANNEL EXAMPLE.

Approaches to Tackling Multiview

There are several ways to tackle multiview. While variations exist, all current multiview deployments are a form of these four basic approaches:

1. Many Encodes
2. Many Players
3. Single-Player Multiview
4. Single-User Cloud Transcoding

In the last approach each viewer has a dedicated edge/cloud transcoder like what's used for cloud gaming and for Synamedia's Senza service [1]. It should be obvious that this is very costly to deploy at scale to millions of users if used for more than a brief period, and we are not aware of any large-scale multiview streaming deployments. Therefore, we won't discuss the cloud transcoding solution further in this paper.

We'll now describe the two basic approaches that are used in the market today and then explain why we believe that a third approach ("*Single-Player Multiview*") provides the best performance and scalability.

Many Encodes

Server-side encoding of multiple layouts is perhaps the simplest way to deliver a multiview experience. This method involves creating several streams with different layouts and allowing viewers to select their preferred layout (see Figure 3). It leverages existing infrastructure: regular players and transcoders. This method is currently used by YouTube, and NBC Universal used it for the Paris Olympics.

It has the advantage of being easy to support on many different types of devices. But the method has significant disadvantages as well. Every combination of streams requires a unique transcode. This solution is practical for basic services with up to, say, four feeds, such as a with 2×1, 2×2, or 3×1 grids. And even that has limitations as has been expressed by YouTube users that complain about the limited options in the NFL multiview offering.

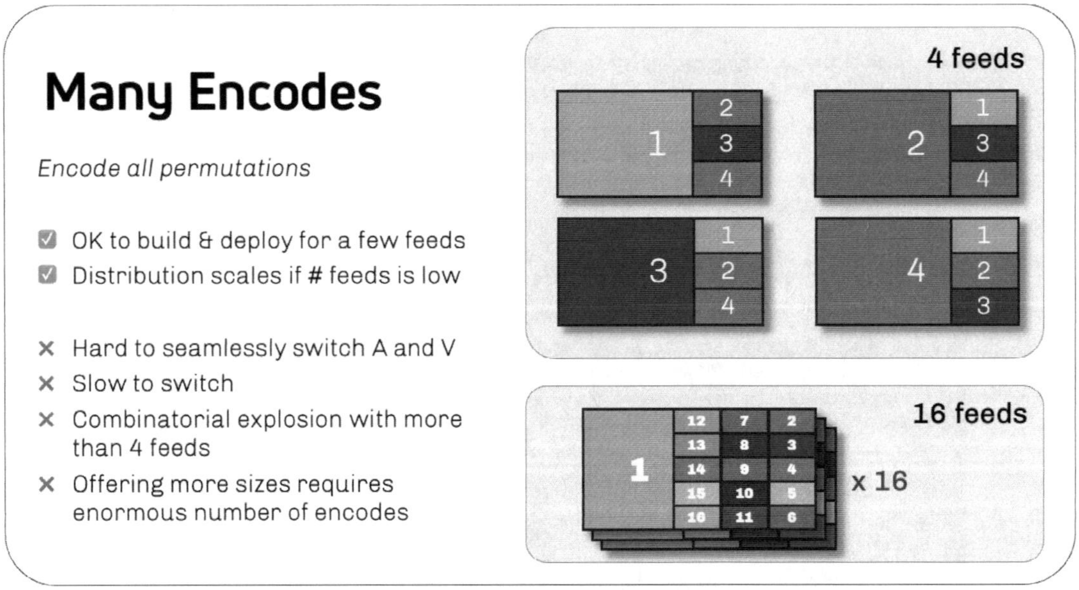

FIGURE 2: MANY ENCODES.

But let's say we want to offer 10 streams in a motorsport race with some layouts. For instance, we want to offer 2×2, 2×1 and 10×1 layouts. Offering all possible combinations requires encoding ABR ladders for 375 different streams. And if we wanted to give full flexibility, where users can arrange streams in any order on screen, that would require close to 6,000 ladders.

Aside from this "combinatorial explosion," switching between streams can be sluggish because the frame buffer is emptied at every switch to a different layout. Users are likely to see the video stall while the new layout is retrieved. There will also be a brief silence. Or, if we keep the "old" video playing while the new layout is loading in parallel, the switch will take some time to complete. Either way, the switch usually results in a timeline discontinuity – a jump back or ahead in time. This makes the experience feel sluggish and glitchy, and it creates FOMO – the fear of missing out – on important moments in an event. So while server-side encoding offers a relatively easy entry point into multiview, it is not a viable solution for a future-proof, scalable, seamless, enjoyable multiview experience.

(Note that in theory the distinct transcodes could be omitted by doing a set of HEVC tiled encodes. These encodes could be merged by a packager into a single stream. A separate packaging step is then required for every single lay-out, and the combinatorial explosion remains – it's only been moved from the encoding to the packaging. Or one could do real-time packaging, which will require a dedicated packager instance per user – akin to cloud encoding per user and hardly a scalable solution either.)

Many Players

The second multiview solution deployed today entails using a separate player for every feed on the screen (see Figure 3). Most platforms support spawning multiple players in parallel, and this allows for the reuse of existing player and transcoding infrastructure. This approach enables flexible client-side interaction and feed positioning. It supports existing ABR ladders, digital rights management (DRM), and dynamic ad insertion (DAI) mechanisms, so it would seem a natural evolution from conventional, single-feed streaming. Like in the single-stream world, most players will use the platform-native player stack to do the actual content streaming (ExoPlayer for Android, AVPlayer for iOS and MSE for Web).

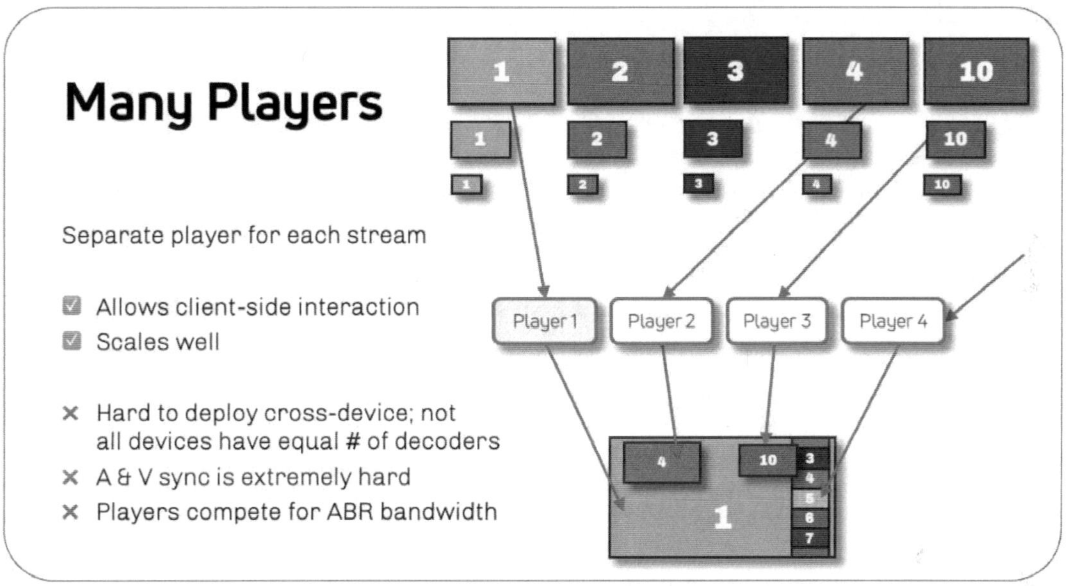

FIGURE 3: MANY PLAYERS.

Multiview offerings from Apple and FuboTV take this approach, but it has its own challenges. It's difficult enough to control the behavior of a single native platform player, and it's harder still to manage several players running in parallel. Some platforms don't allow spawning multiple players, and even if they do, their number varies. Smart TVs and devices connected to TVs are frequently constrained, supporting only one or two players running simultaneously. Some platforms allow time-multiplexing for decoding multiple streams, but certainly not all. And multi-player behavior has platform-specific quirks, making cross-platform multiview a very tough nut to crack. It is virtually impossible to sync multiple feeds between uncorrelated players running in their own sandbox.

Adaptive bitrate and buffer management are particularly hard to get right. Assume we have a multiview scene with four players running in parallel. Each player lives in its own sandbox and downloads segments for its own stream. In Figure 5 below, each rectangle is a segment. All segments have the same content length, say 2 seconds.

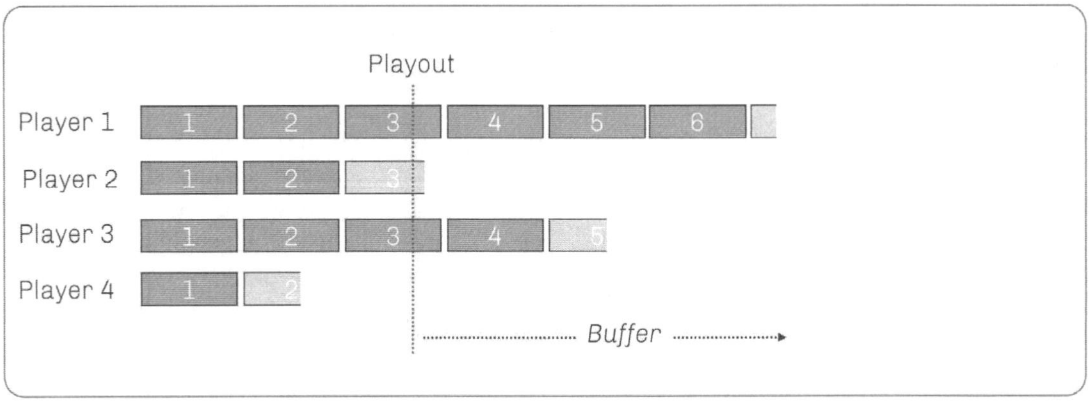

FIGURE 4: SEGMENT MANAGEMENT WITH MANY PLAYERS.

Because all players are independent and unaware of each other's existence, they will run their own segment download strategy and ABR decision engines. Player 1 is not aware of Players 2, 3, and 4, so it will greedily start filling its buffer. In doing so, it will compete for the same bandwidth that Players 2, 3 and 4 are using. Due to the way transmission control protocol (TCP) works, it's very unlikely for all players to fill their buffers at the same rate. One of them will invariably move faster than the others. But even when Player 1 has enough data to start playing, it won't stop to give its colleagues extra room to fill their buffers. Instead, the "faster" Player 1 might already start downloading segment 3 while Player 4 might still struggle to retrieve segment 1.

For end-users, this means that the multiview experience is unnecessarily slow to load. This problem is further exacerbated each time the user adds, removes or switches any of the multiview feeds. A newly spawned player will be at a disadvantage, starting with an empty buffer, while the other players are blissfully unaware and will continue filling their already well-filled buffers. The user will experience even more buffering.

Higher-than-necessary load times are inconvenient, but there are more pitfalls with the Many Players solution. Most video players base their ABR decision logic on a combination of buffer size and download rates. They calculate download rates by simply timing the download of a segment of a given size. When players are not aware of each other's existence, this strategy causes major problems. One moment, a Player 1 might be downloading a segment at the same time as Player 2 and conclude that the effective available bandwidth is half the actually available bandwidth. A few moments later, it might be downloading a segment when the other players are not requesting segments, and it will think available bandwidth has just doubled. A little later still, all 4 players may be retrieving segments, and Player 1 will draw the conclusion that bandwidth has dropped by a factor of 4. The result is four independent, unstable, and untrustworthy ABR decisions, with unnecessary buffering and annoying quality fluctuations for the user.

To demonstrate this effect, we created a simple test app that shows this behavior when spawning four AVPlayers in iPadOS. Figure 6 provides a screenshot. Each player streams a 60-fps clock that counts seconds (the large numbers in the circles) and frames ("xx/60" in the circles). In the 4-player solution, there is no simple coordination in the playback timing, and there is no coordination in the segment retrieval strategies either.

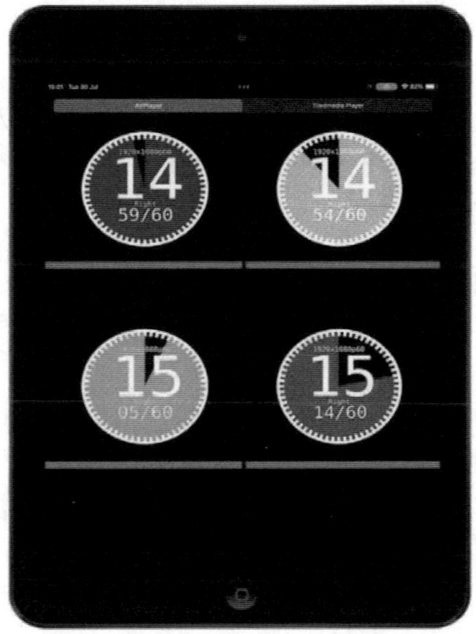

FIGURE 5: MULTIVIEW PLAYERS GETTING OUT OF SYNC.

Single Player Multiview

The third approach to doing multiview is using a single, multi-stream player (See Figure 7). The heart of this player is an engine that has full knowledge of all videos on the screen and the sizes of these videos. It knows which videos to retrieve at which ABR levels. A single engine controls the network interface and manages segment retrieval and the buffer fullness for all visible feeds. Assume a user switches a small PiP video ("A") with the main video ("B"). The player will immediately start requesting video A at a higher resolution and ABR level, and do the opposite for feed B. While this is happening, the application can upscale feed A and downscale feed B. As soon as the new ABR levels arrive, the player starts decoding and displaying these. No new players needed to be spawned, and the two switches are completely seamless for the user without discontinuities or buffering.

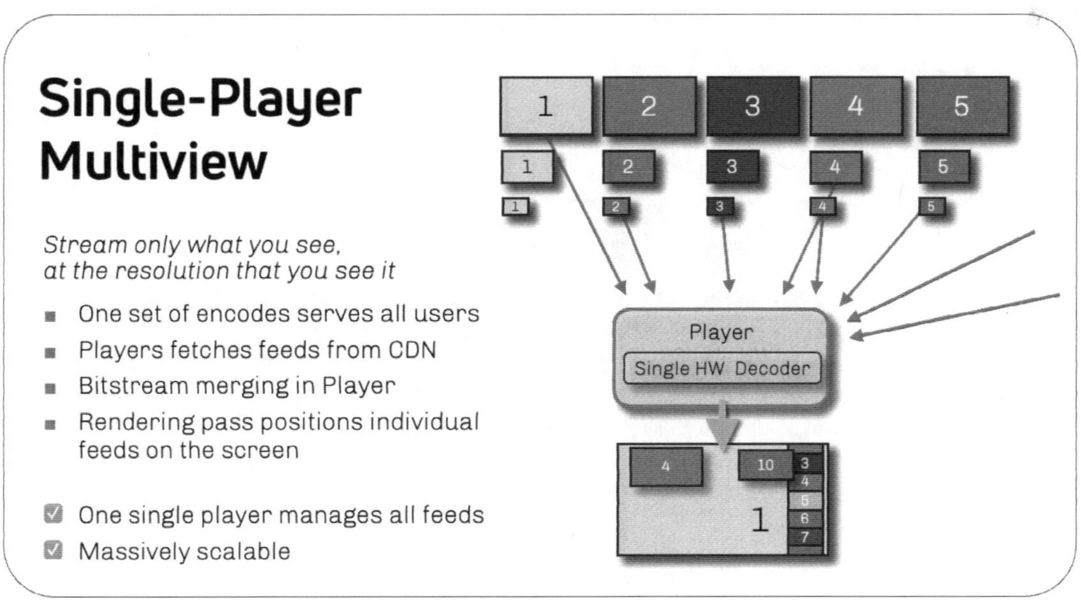

FIGURE 6: SINGLE-PLAYER MULTIVIEW.

When network bandwidth decreases, it can make an intelligent decision, across all visible feeds, about where to spend bits. It can adjust the ABR levels of these feeds in a coordinated fashion. In a pinch, it might even decide to, e.g., switch to still images for small (thumbnail) video feeds to optimize the quality of the main video. The player also knows the buffer fullness for all videos and has full control over the decoding and rendering chain, so it can guarantee frame-accurate sync between all feeds.

These trade-offs and decisions can only be made well if a single engine has both *full knowledge* of network, buffer and display state, and *full control* over retrieval and playback of all feeds. This combination of full knowledge and full control makes the single-player solution superior in efficiency, switching speed, ABR, and synchronization. It is also the most scalable solution: it doesn't require additional encodes or cloud processing.

In its most advanced form, this method may leverage streams encoded in a tiled fashion. This is a bit like how 4K content is often encoded as four HD tiles by 4 separate encoders, and then streamed and displayed as a single feed on the screen. This option uses the tiling feature included in the HEVC coding standard [2]. There is one difference with tiled multiview: in the 4K case, there is only one stream with 4 tiles. In tiled multiview streaming, the player retrieves individual feeds as required (there could be 4, but also many more, or less) and then the multi-stream player merges these bitstreams into a single bitstream before giving it to the decoder – the hardware device decoder.

We implemented these mechanisms in our natively multi-stream Tiledmedia Player; see Figure 8 for its high-level architecture. Since platform-native players don't provide these features, we were forced to build our multi-stream player engine from the ground up. (The player evolved from our work on tiled viewport-adaptive VR streaming which required us to build a player from scratch; see e.g., the IBC paper on providing groundbreaking live 8K VR180 at the Beijing 2022 winter games [3].)

While our multi-stream player contains very advanced stream management logic, it relies on standard streaming formats and simple http streaming. That makes our Single Player Multiview approach compatible, out of the box, with DRM, ad insertion solutions (server-side and client-side), quality metrics and error reporting frameworks, and other client-side tooling. It can be used with existing transcoding chains, where a few straightforward encoder settings unlock the most advanced form of multiview that relies on tiling as described above. There are no special requirements on the content delivery network (CDN); what works for conventional http streaming also works for multiview steaming.

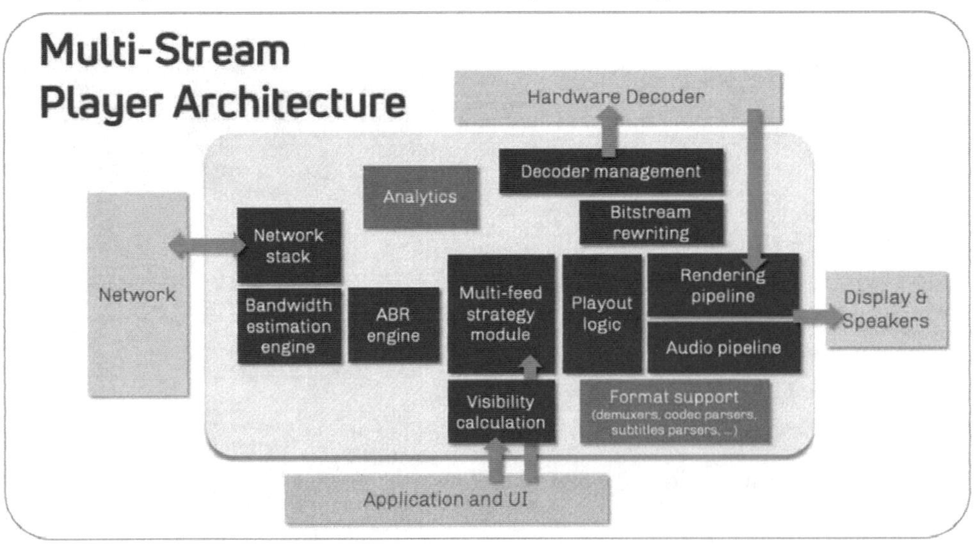

FIGURE 7: HIGH-LEVEL MULTI-STREAM PLAYER ARCHITECTURE

In this paper we have focused on streaming behavior. A single-player multi-steam approach has other benefits as well. Here is a brief summary:

- **Unlimited stream views:** There is no device-imposed limit on the number of feeds that can be displayed simultaneously. With HEVC bitstream rewriting, many streams can be shown and multiview can be supported even on devices that only expose a single decoder.
- **Full layout freedom**: Both app designers and individual users can have complete control over the layout, where the app designer determines which degrees of freedom are presented to the user. (Examples: number of simultaneous feeds, options to place feeds, affordances to drag them around, etc.)
- **Instant switching with continuous audio**: Because all feeds are handled by a single player, stream switching is seamless without any audio interruptions, drops or discontinuities.
- **Frame-accurate synchronization**: Streams always maintain frame-accurate sync.
- **Personalization and scalability**: the number of feeds shown in a multiview experience is only limited by the user interface and what makes sense to display at the same time in an app. Theoretically, the decoder capacity and available bandwidth play a role as well, but in practice the UI limits kick in before hitting any of these limits. Modern devices can easily handle 25+ streams, and indeed our player will shortly be used in an OTT service that has more than 20 simultaneous feeds.
- **Bandwidth efficiency**: a multi-stream player will only retrieve the steams that are visible, and only at the resolution that is required for the size of the feed on the display. Other solutions, for example, sometimes retrieve 4 HD stream for a 4-feed multiview, regardless of the size on the display.
- **Optimized ABR**: As explained above, a single ABR engine has full knowledge of the network and what is visible on the screen. The ABR engine can make trade-offs across all feeds and their buffers, ensuring the most efficient retrieval and the least amount of buffering.
- **Universal compatibility**: A single set of ABR ladders serves all users and devices across all platforms. We typically recommend encoding all individual feeds as regular HLS ladders that will play in any player. When bitstream merging is used, the HEVC encoders need to be synchronized, and a few parameters need to be configured to enable tile merging in the player. While the exact details are beyond this paper, these parameters broadly pertain to tile sizes, GOP structures and motion vectors.
- **Multiview QoS reporting**: a single player can provide coherent reporting across all feeds in a multiview session. This is also possible with the Many Encodes approach, but it will be very hard with the Many Players solution.

Conclusion

We listed four approaches for providing multiview services, of which we examined three in detail. We concluded that compared to the “Many Players” and “Many Encodes” approaches, the Single-Player Multiview” solution is superior, with significant advantages in flexibility, responsiveness and scalability.

At the time this paper was authored, a major OTT provider of sports streaming services was preparing to roll out a Single-Player Multiview service, and we anticipate that it will be live and public by NAB 2025.

References

[1] Synamedia, Senza product page, https://www.synamedia.com/product/senza/, last accessed on 30 January 2025.

[2] ISO/IEC, Information technology — “High efficiency coding and media delivery in heterogeneous environments (MPEG-H) Part 2: High Efficiency Video Coding”, ISO/IEC 23008-2:2023, 2023.

[3] Koenen, R., Lorenceau, F., Umansky, J., Poolman, D., Van Eck, M. Velhal, R., Willock, C., "Trailblazing With 8K Live VR At Beijing 2022", *IBC Conference September 2022*, available at https://www.tiledmedia.com/wp-content/uploads/2022/11/230020robkoenenapprovedversion_538655.pdf.

Low Latency Wireless Broadcast Production Over 5G

Samuel R. Yoffe†, Douglas G. Allan, Kenneth W. Barlee, Dani Anderson, Damien Muir, Malcolm R. Brew, Cameron Speirs and Robert W. Stewart
Neutral Wireless and University of Strathclyde
Glasgow, United Kingdom
†Corresponding author: sam.yoffe@neutralwireless.com

Mark B. Waddell‡ and Jonas Kröger-Mayes
BBC R&D and BBC Scotland
United Kingdom
‡Visiting Professor, University of Strathclyde, Glasgow, United Kingdom

Giulio Stante
RAI CRITS
Torino, Italy

Abstract – Wireless camera feeds are an integral source of content for programme making, and typically utilize licensed point-to-point radio links or "bonded-cellular" devices. Cellular bonding using public 4G and 5G networks has become a mainstay for electronic newsgathering and remote contribution feeds. These contributions can tolerate latencies up to several seconds. However, such latencies are far too long for broadcast production, where wireless cameras are cut in with cabled systems, or where remote camera control, tally and return video are required. Since 5G is a native IP technology, it can support bi-directional connectivity and facilitate additional services alongside ultra-low latency video. This paper explores the use of (private) 5G to support full low-latency wireless production workflows, discusses how 5G connectivity can augment existing wireless systems, and gives practical advice for configuring camera control systems over 5G.

Introduction

Wireless camera feeds are commonly used in live broadcasting applications that can be broadly separated into contribution and production workflows. Broadcasters have invested heavily in cellular bonding, which has become the dominant technology for remote contribution feeds, replacing satellite links for day-to-day electronic newsgathering and on-location reporting. Bonded-cellular devices simultaneously connect to a number of 4G/5G public mobile networks and aggregate the capacity. The encoded video traffic is split across multiple public networks and the bitrate of the encoder is adapted according to the network conditions on each path. These devices require no specific radio frequency (RF) licensing and are straightforward to deploy. Remote contribution feeds using this topology typically achieve an end-to-end latency of between 1 and 2 seconds.

The use of private 5G to augment public networks and support remote contribution workflows in high demand density (HDD) environments has been well documented, such as the coronation of King Charles III [1,2]; but typical workflow latencies are too high for live broadcast production where wireless cameras are cut alongside cabled camera feeds. Camera racking also becomes impractical when the

This paper is excerpted from the Proceedings of the 2025 NAB Broadcast Engineering and Information Technology (BEIT) Conference, © 2025, National Association of Broadcasters, 1 M Street SE, Washington, DC 20003 USA.

video latency exceeds around 300 ms [3]. To achieve the required latency, specialist point-to-point RF links based on coded orthogonal frequency division multiplexing (COFDM) technology are deployed in dedicated radio spectrum referred to programme-making and special events (PMSE) band in Europe, or the Broadcast Auxiliary Service (BAS) band in the USA. These links can be robust and support low latency video acquisition, but typically only accommodate a single camera per channel. They are low latency because they use one-way unacknowledged transmitters with dedicated receivers, and do not support retransmissions[1], power control or adaptive modulation and coding scheme (MCS) loops that can dynamically adjust the modulation to maintain target error rates and achieve improved spectrum efficiency according to the propagation conditions.

This paper discusses the readiness of (private) 5G to support low-latency production workflows and the advantages it can offer in modern production workflows. Unlike traditional one-way RF video links, 5G is a native IP technology, providing bi-directional connectivity to devices. This allows the same network to concurrently support many devices and services, with quality of service (QoS) mechanisms to satisfy the requirements of the application and control device or data priority. A single network can support multiple video and audio contributions from dedicated encoder devices alongside return connectivity for services such as camera control, tally and intercom, but also support mobile handsets, point-of-sale systems, and emergency services connectivity.

Since the 5G standard is defined by the 3GPP, many compatible commercial off-the-shelf (COTS) user equipment (UE) are available for use on the network, with no need for specialist or proprietary hardware. Spectrum allocated to a COFDM RF video link is reserved for that camera, whether it is being used or not. In contrast, the 5G scheduler allows multiple devices to share radio resources as they need them, increasing spectral efficiency. As an example, over 60 devices were used at the coronation of King Charles III in a total of 80 MHz spectrum – a fraction of the spectrum that would have been required for 60 individual RF video links.

The deployment of 5G standalone hardware by public mobile network operators (MNOs) is opening up some exciting possibilities. Perhaps the most eagerly awaited is network slicing, where a portion of the network resources (resource blocks) can be reserved or given priority for a particular subscriber. This offers a very compelling solution for remote contribution feeds, guaranteeing throughput even in crowded environments where networks can become congested. However, their cost and viability are not yet clear. Moreover, the network configuration used by public networks is not optimized for high uplink capacity, so there is a limit to how many slices an operator would be able to simultaneously support while ensuring reasonable service for their paying customers.

One less obvious benefit of standalone technology is that it allows operators to deploy additional user planes (where data exits the 5G network) at the network edge.[2] This can significantly improve latency and jitter experienced by devices accessing particular resources. An edge user plane could provide direct on-premises breakout to video decoders, facilitating ultra-low latency video workflows not possible when breaking out onto public Internet. Again, the cost and viability are not yet clear.

As it stands, most public networks are not able to support ultra-low latency broadcast workflows. This paper will therefore focus on the use of flexible software-defined radio (SDR) private (non-public) 5G standalone networks. 5G public networks are generally optimized to maximize downlink throughput, rather than to support low-latency uplink-biased use cases. SDR can support the considerable optimization required for live production. We begin with a discussion of network configuration and some advice for deploying networks for broadcast production (rather than content distribution). Following this, results from testing three COTS ultra-low latency vendor solutions in a controlled studio environment are presented, before real-world deployments in stadia and wide-area environments are discussed.

[1] COFDM can support forward error correction (FEC) and time/frequency interleaving to introduce resilience to some transmission errors.
[2] This was introduced in LTE-A as control user plane separation (CUPS) and was available with 5G non-standalone (NSA) where uplink remained LTE, but is potentially of more interest in full 5G standalone due to the lower latency and increased capacity with mmWave bands.

Network Configuration

5G technology is often cited as providing high capacity and low latency wireless connectivity. While 5G is certainly capable of delivering high capacity and has significantly improved latency over previous radio access technologies (RATs), as with everything in life the reality is more of a compromise. To achieve reliable ultra-low latency transmission, various optimizations to the radio access network (RAN) can be made, but these often come accompanied by a reduction in the network cell capacity. Moreover, there is no one-size-fits-all configuration, and an optimum solution for downlink-biased applications will not be suitable for uplink-biased applications, and *vice versa*. In this section we discuss some of the primary network properties and their impact on suitability for uplink-biased low latency broadcast production workflows.

Transmit Power and Cell Coverage

One of the most obvious network parameters is the transmit power of the network cell. This will usually be specified by the spectrum license and is measured in Watts or dBm. In the UK, public mobile networks are licensed to use effective isotropic[3] radiated powers (EIRPs) such as 60 dBm/5 MHz. That's a staggering 1 kW/5 MHz or 20 kW into a 100 MHz channel. Operators optimize their deployments according to the target downlink cell size, the proximity to their other masts, and the power limit for the specified band as set by the spectrum regulator. Whereas, shared access licenses (SALs) offered by the UK regulator, Ofcom, in the shared access band 3.8–4.2 GHz can be low power (up to 24 dBm = 0.25 W)[4] or medium power (up to 42 dBm = 16 W)[5] [4], with the license tied to a transmitter at a particular geographical location.

Downlink transmit power has a direct impact on coverage and cell size. The total power radiated in the downlink will depend on network utilization, but the power of the reference signal used for network synchronization and channel estimation is known and always constant. The reference signal received power (RSRP) is used by the user equipment (UE) to estimate the channel path loss, and RSRP measurement provides a useful measure of cell coverage.

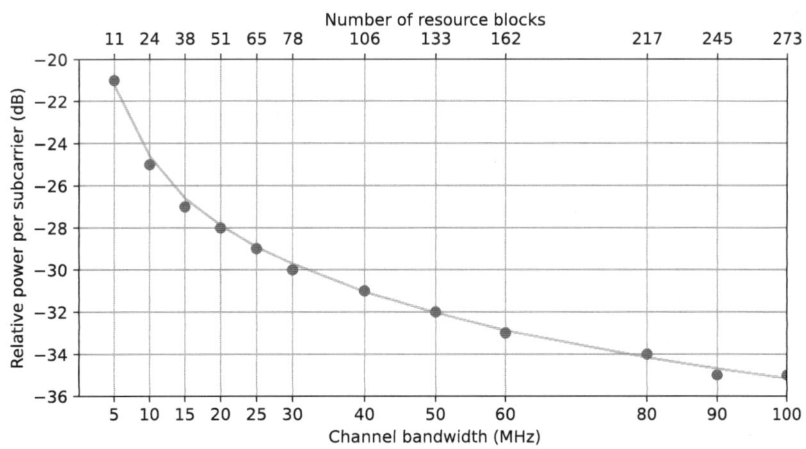

FIGURE 1: RELATIVE POWER PER SUB-CARRIER FOR DIFFERENT CHANNEL BANDWIDTHS.

Figure 1 shows the variation of the relative power per sub-carrier for channels with different bandwidths. Each of the channel bandwidths contain a number of resource blocks (RBs), each of which is comprised of 12 sub-carriers. The relative power per sub-carrier is then expressed as

---

[3] This paper will discuss EIRP rather than effective radiated power (ERP). The conversion is EIRP = ERP + 2.15 dB.

[4] Note that this has recently been increased to 27 dBm for carriers ≤ 20 MHz, or 21 dBm/5 MHz for carriers > 20 MHz – see Table 1 and disregard the value specified in Figure 2 presented in [4].

[5] Medium power SAL specifies up to 42 dBm for carriers ≤ 20 MHz, or 36 dBm/5 MHz for carriers > 20 MHz – see Table 9 presented in [4].

$$P_{\text{subcarrier}} = P_{\text{Tx}} - 10\log_{10}(12N), \quad (1)$$

where N is the number of RBs in the channel. The curve in Figure 1 indicates the second term of this equation (in blue), while the dots represent the integer values assumed for each bandwidth. For example, under the low power license mentioned above, transmitting a 20 MHz channel at 24 dBm is delivering 24 dBm – 28 dB = -4 dBm (0.4 mW) per sub-carrier, while the same power into a 100 MHz provides 24 dBm – 35 dB = -11 dBm (0.08 mW) per sub-carrier.

Measurement of the RSRP on a UE provides the measured power of the reference signal in dBm. If the UE reports a value of -75 dBm and the reference signal was transmitted at -4 dBm (*e.g.* the low power 20 MHz channel above) then the path loss is estimated to be the difference between the two, in this case 71 dB. The free-space path loss (FSPL) model[6] is often used to estimate distances and sanity check RSRP measurements:

$$FSPL = 20\log_{10}\left(\frac{4\pi df}{c}\right), \quad (2)$$

where d is separation of the cell and UE (in m), f is the frequency of the carrier (in Hz), and c is the speed of light in vacuum (in m/s). This can be rearranged to give an estimate of distance based on the measured path loss,

$$d_{\text{FS}} = \frac{10^{\frac{PL}{20}}c}{4\pi f}. \quad (3)$$

Using this expression, the equivalent free-space distance for the path loss of 71 dB for a reference signal at 4 GHz is d_{FS} = 21.2 m. If we define the cell edge to be where the measured RSRP is -100 dBm, then this gives an approximate cell radius of about 375 m for the low power 20 MHz cell and 168 m for the low power 100 MHz cell discussed above.

Turning our attention to the medium power SAL with a maximum EIRP of 42 dBm [4], the same analysis as above gives the cell radius as 2.99 km for the 20 MHz medium power cell and 1.34 km for the medium power 100 MHz cell. It might, therefore, seem like a good idea to transmit at as high power as possible to provide the best possible coverage for UEs; but this is all in the *downlink* – transmission from the base station to the UE.

Mobile terminals (UEs) are limited to transmit at a maximum power depending on their power class. The default, power class 3, limits uplink transmission to 23 dBm (0.2 W). Higher power is available in some bands using power class 2 (26 dBm = 0.4 W) or power class 1 (up to 31 dBm = 1.26 W) devices, but the spectrum license in use may also specify maximum UE powers for static and mobile terminals that must be adhered to. High gain receive antennas can help, but also raise the noise floor. For the uplink-biased broadcast production use case, it does not matter if the UE downlink performs adequately at a kilometer if the baseband unit cannot sufficiently decode the lower-power physical uplink shared channel (PUSCH)[7] transmissions from the UE. For these uplink-biased use cases, we suggest that high network transmission power should actually be avoided, as it does not increase the uplink performance nor distance from which a UE uplink will function. Instead, the high cell transmission power and increased downlink propagation could become a source of interference for neighboring cells or (private) networks trying to coexist nearby, or reduce potential spectrum reuse and cell density.

Finally, Figure 1 provides the number of RBs available for each of the defined channel bandwidths. We note that there are more RBs available in one 100 MHz channel than there are for five 20 MHz channels. It is therefore more spectrally efficient to share a 100 MHz cell with quality of service (QoS) to ensure equity of resources (such as network slicing) than to run five independent cells (with adjacent channel leakage). However, the sub-carrier power and cell radius should also be considered.

---

[6] FSPL can include antenna gain, in which case the gain of the base station and UE antennas should be *subtracted* from this path loss in (2).
[7] Physical uplink control channel (PUCCH) can continue to be adequately decoded at very low SNR.

Latency and Jitter

Of critical importance for low-latency broadcast production workflows are the latency and jitter of packets transported over the 5G connection. Moreover, it is not the often-quoted mean round-trip time (RTT) that determines how quickly video or audio can be transported over the network. Instead, we are limited by the *maximum* packet delay over the link. An ultra-low latency workflow can only function at a latency that provides sufficient time for the encode and decode processes plus the maximum packet delay from encoder to decoder. Anything less and there will be dropped packets that can cause unacceptable artifacts in the feed. In many applications, additional buffering is configured at the video decoder to allow for application layer retransmissions supported by some media transport protocols.

There are a significant number of factors that determine end-to-end latency of a 5G network, some of which can be optimized to reduce network latency and jitter. We refer the reader to our IBC 2024 Technical Paper [3] for a dedicated discussion on latency optimization.

Frame Structure and Synchronization

The move from LTE to 5G New Radio (NR) allowed for higher numerologies, such as the increase to 30 kHz sub-carriers for sub-6 GHz frequencies, but it also supports new flexibility in the frame structure definition. In time-domain duplexing (TDD), the same frequency resources are shared between uplink and downlink in time. Network traffic is either transmitted to (downlink) or received from (uplink) the UE. Public mobile networks all operate using the same downlink-uplink pattern to minimize interference with each other and preserve compatibility with legacy LTE networks. For this to be effective, reference time synchronization to atomic standards is required, and is achieved using either 1 pulse per second (1PPS) from a local global positioning system (GPS) receiver or by precision time protocol (PTP). We encourage the use of reference time synchronization for all private network deployments.

The TDD frame is comprised of ten 1 ms *subframes*, each of which contains two 0.5 ms *slots* assuming 30 kHz numerology in frequency range 1 (FR1: 410-7125 MHz). The slot is the basic transmission time interval (TTI) in both downlink and uplink. Each slot comprises 14 OFDM symbols in 5G NR.

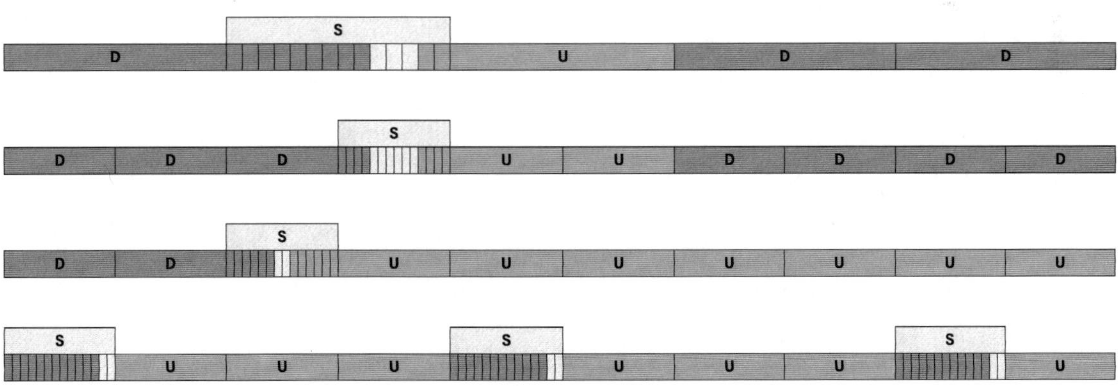

FIGURE 2: EXAMPLES OF DOWNLINK- AND UPLINK-BIASED TDD PATTERNS.

Figure 2 illustrates 10 slots for the four different TDD patterns. The top row presents the 3:1 downlink-biased TD-LTE frame configuration 2 (with special subframe config. 6) used by public LTE and 5G non-standalone (NSA) networks, and the second row gives the 5G NR equivalent. This pattern consists of 7 downlink slots and 2 uplink slots (which we refer to as 7:2), separated by a special slot that defines 4 downlink symbols, 6 gap symbols, and 4 uplink symbols and is denoted S=(4,6,4). The number of gap symbols restricts the maximum size of the cell.[8]

[8] A gap period (GP) of 2 symbols allows for cells up to 10.7 km, while 4 and 6 symbols allow for 21.4 km and 32.1 km cells, respectively [5].

The 3:1 (LTE) and 7:2 (5G NR) patterns provide more resources (capacity) to downlink traffic, which is ideal for public networks with large numbers of customers consuming content. In contrast, broadcast content acquisition (as opposed to distribution to end users) is inherently uplink heavy, and the use of this "standard" frame structure is spectrally inefficient and inappropriate. In order to achieve the uplink capacity required, networks using the standard DDDSUUDDDD pattern must use larger channel bandwidths, with the larger amount of downlink resources potentially going to waste.

Uplink-biased use cases such as broadcast production benefit from alternative frame structures such as the third row in Figure 2, which illustrates the 2:7 uplink-biased pattern DDSUUUUUUU with S=(6,2,6). Significantly more resources are dedicated to uplink, allowing for higher uplink capacity. For comparison, indicative cell capacity measurements at modulation and coding scheme (MCS) 25 in a 40 MHz channel in n40 support an uplink capacity of around 40 Mbps (1 b/Hz) when using the standard pattern DDDSUUDDDD; reconfiguring the TDD pattern to use the 2:7 uplink-biased pattern DDSUUUUUUU with the same system increases the uplink capacity to 150 Mbps (3.75 b/Hz).

The last row in Figure 2 illustrates the SUUU pattern with the downlink resources provided by S=(12,2,0) and a shorter TDD period (four slots = 2 ms). Note that there must be an integer number of complete TDD pattern repetitions in a full 10 ms radio frame; in this case, there are five. A discussion on the use of shorter TDD periods and how they can reduce network latency is given in [3]. We note that uplink throughput for DDSUUUUUUU and SUUU is approximately the same, as they both provide the same 1:3 (DL:UL) resource allocation.

As a final comment on cell capacity, the uplink-biasing of networks to support uplink-heavy use cases might seem like a huge compromise on downlink resources, and there are many workflows that need to make use of both. In this case, downlink capacity can often be increased by spatial diversity using more downlink layers. Most UE support 2x2 or even 4x4 downlink MIMO (multi-input multi-output), which can help significantly increase channel throughput. However, there are relatively few devices that support uplink MIMO, and instead the user is encouraged to explore receive diversity with maximum ratio combining (MRC) for improved signal-to-noise ratio (SNR) rather than adding uplink layers.

Networks running uplink-biased frame structures are susceptible to interference from downlink-biased networks, since the high-power downlink transmit occurs when the uplink-biased network is receiving from low power user equipment. For the 2:7 uplink-biased pattern, we see from Figure 2 that five of the seven uplink slots (plus the special slot) coincide with downlink on the 7:2 downlink-biased pattern. Since the base station will (usually) have a significantly higher transmit power (kW in the case of public networks compared to 0.2 W for a standard UE), this downlink signal can be substantially higher than the UE uplink, leading to poor receive sensitivity and interference. The poor channel and high error rate on these slots will cause the network performance and capacity to be dramatically reduced. The reciprocal interference on the downlink-biased network is not practically observed, particularly for low- to medium-power uplink-biased networks. This supports the previous conclusion that to minimize interference and maximize coexistence, network cell transmit power should be considered and reduced where possible while still facilitating the requirements of the use case.

Finally, Figure 2 highlights the importance of time synchronization. Without synchronization, TDD patterns are not aligned at slot 0, and even networks running the same TDD pattern will suffer interference as high power downlink overpowers low power UE uplink. Even when not matching the TDD pattern to another network, time synchronization ensures consistency and repeatability.

Indoor (studio) Applications

The performance of commercial off-the-shelf (COTS) equipment operating on a private 5G standalone network in a studio environment was explored at Glasgow Pacific Quay Studio A: a large studio (576 m^2) operated by BBC Scotland. This studio is typically used for light entertainment shows, quiz programs and other TV productions requiring space for a studio audience. Wireless cameras are of interest both for mobility but also health and safety considerations for extended cable runs. Camera back encoders intended for low-latency operation from three manufacturers were evaluated and the stability of video streaming was assessed.

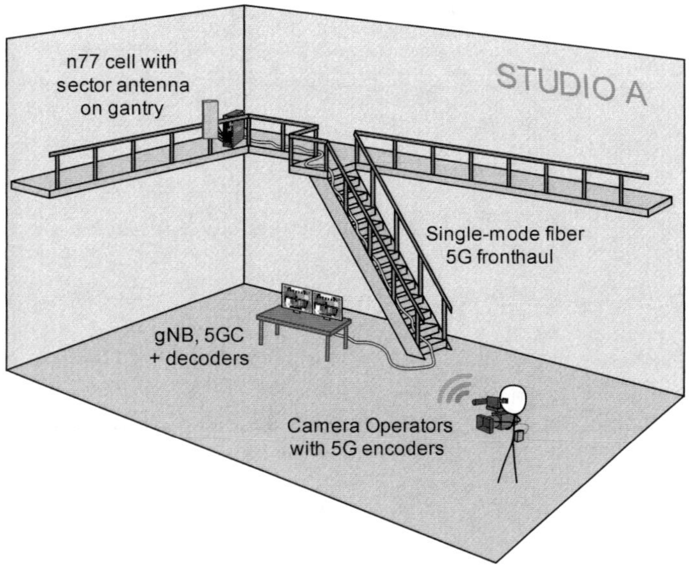

FIGURE 3: INDOOR (STUDIO) PERFORMANCE TESTS IN STUDIO A AT BBC SCOTLAND.

As illustrated in Figure 3, radio and antenna equipment were located up on the gantry in one corner of the studio, with a 7 dBi gain sector antenna positioned to provide coverage over the studio floor. The private 5G core (5GC) and gNodeB (gNB) were located on the studio floor along with the video decoding and monitoring equipment, connected by single-mode fiber to the radio head.

Several spectrum licenses were available for the tests to allow the propagation characteristics of different bands to be explored. The BBC holds a Shared Access Licence at 3865 MHz with a permitted bandwidth of 100 MHz and a transmit EIRP of 18 dBm/5 MHz (maximum 31 dBm = 1.26 W) into a 100 MHz carrier). This license is within the 3GPP n77-upper band (3.8–4.2 GHz) and was used for the majority of the video streaming tests. In addition, an Ofcom Innovation and Trial license [6] for a 50 MHz bandwidth centred at 2325 MHz was obtained with an EIRP 33 dBm/5 MHz (42 dBm = 15.8 W into a 40 MHz carrier[9]). This license is in the 3GPP n40 band and potentially offers superior propagation characteristics. The University of Strathclyde has a Glasgow-wide license (700 km^2 around George Square) for a 100 MHz channel centred at 3967 MHz, subject to a low power limit of 27 dBm (0.5 W); this was briefly used to determine if low power operation could give satisfactory performance in a large studio space but requires attenuation on the transmit ports, so the BBC SAL was preferred.

Coverage

The radio coverage was assessed by taking spot measurements of the RSRP of the downlink signal using an Anritsu MS2090 spectrum analyzer fitted with an omni-directional Linx antenna that has been used extensively by the BBC and Neutral Wireless on 5G projects and has an antenna gain of approximately 0 dBi. The following results were obtained at the n77 test frequency (3865 MHz) with the cell operating at the licensed power of 31 dBm EIRP.

[9] A 40 MHz bandwidth was used for the n40 tests because most COTS mobile handsets do not support 50 MHz carriers. This can be overcome by using a larger supported carrier with physical resource block (PRB) masking or blanking. To the UE, the cell appears to be the larger supported bandwidth; but the scheduler never schedules PRBs outside the desired range, preventing out-of-band (OOB) transmissions.

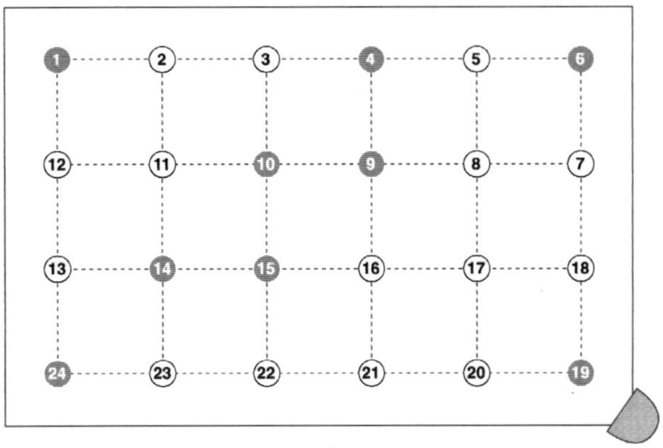

Test Point	RSRP (dBm)	d_{FS} (m)
1	-75	21.9
4	-75	21.9
6	-77	27.6
9	-75	21.9
10	-70	12.3
14	-76	24.6
15	-75	21.9
19	-66	7.8
24	-72	15.5

FIGURE 4: STUDIO A COVERAGE MEASUREMENTS. MEASUREMENT TEST GRID 5M SEPARATION.

Figure 4 (left) illustrates the test point grid and relative position from the transmitting antenna, with the table (right) providing measurements taken at the points highlighted in green. Note that the corresponding transmitted RSRP for a cell operating at 31 dBm is -4 dBm for a 100 MHz carrier (see Figure 1). The above results indicate propagation path loss measurements between 73 dB and 62 dB, which are consistent with free-space path loss values at distances of 25 m and 8 m [see (2)]. This is consistent with the studio floor area of 27 m x 21 m and the height of the antenna on the gantry.

Antenna Performance

Commercial 5G-enabled video encoders typically use small, low gain, internal multi-band antenna arrays for ruggedness and simplicity for the user, but for uplink-heavy use cases they are not ideal.

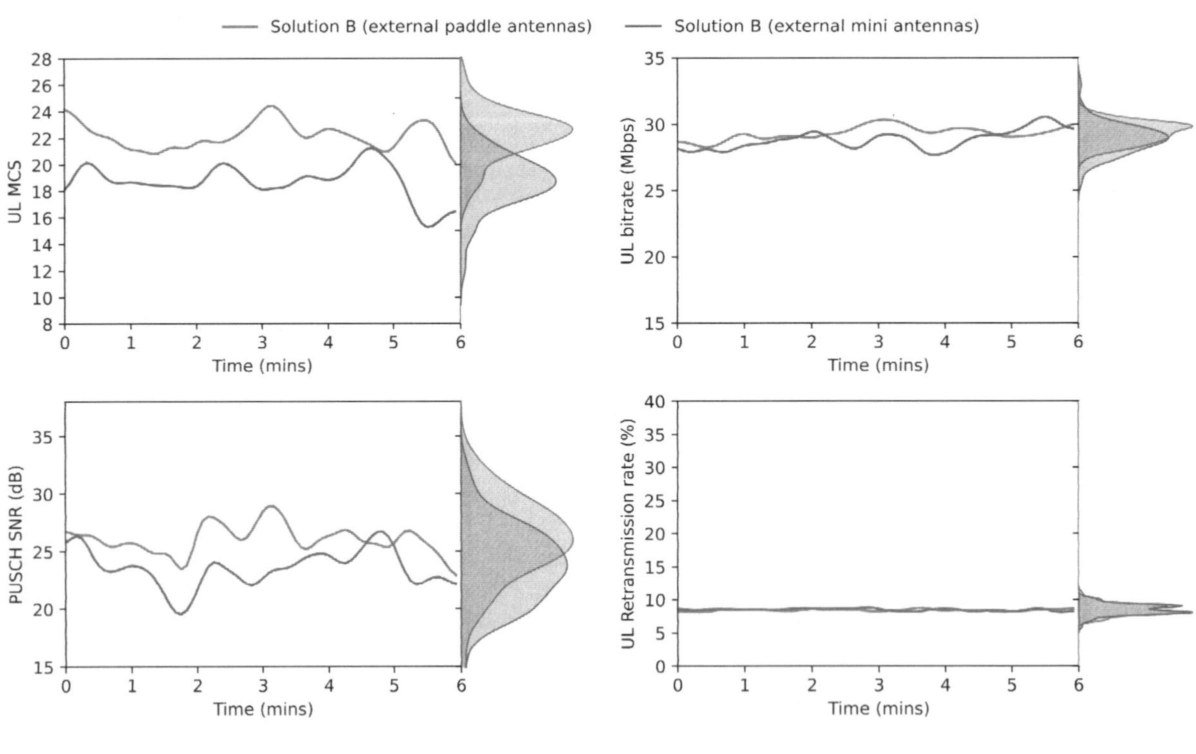

FIGURE 5: 5G-ENABLED VIDEO ENCODER PERFORMANCE USING DIFFERENT EXTERNAL ANTENNA CONFIGURATIONS.

The imbalance between high power downlink transmission and low power uplink transmission (with devices usually limited to 23 dBm) and the impact on effective cell size was discussed above, and antenna systems with negative gain further add to the challenge of reliable uplink transmission. This does appear to have been recognized, with several devices from well-known encoder manufacturers now coming to market with external antenna connectors (in some cases in addition to an internal array).

Figure 5 (above) shows the performance of one vendor solution configured to deliver a 20 Mbps video stream while the device was walked around the studio floor. It is common for devices to be fitted with small, wideband antennas suitable for many mobile bands, but the trade-off is often poorer performance at higher frequencies such as upper n77, where they function with negative effective gain. The use of such small antennas (purple) is compared to 0 dBi paddle antennas (green). The distribution (using kernel density estimation) for each of the time series is plotted to the right. The panel in the lower-left shows how the external paddle antennas provide an increased uplink signal-to-noise ratio (SNR) of around 3 dB, while the upper-left shows that a higher MCS was sustained during the walk test. The higher MCS allows for more data to be transported per symbol, so fewer radio resources were required to transport the video stream. As expected, the use of higher-gain antennas on the uplink transmitter has a notable difference in uplink channel performance. The additional bitrate observed in the top-right panel includes both the network retransmissions (due to around 8% block error rate, lower-right panel) and transport stream overheads such as forward error correction.

Receive Diversity

Spatial multiplexing can be used to increase cell throughput by increasing the number of data layers in multiple-input multiple-output (MIMO) systems. While the use of MIMO for downlink transmission is common and many UE devices are compatible with multiple downlink layers, the same is not true for uplink and most COTS devices are only single-input single-output (SISO) for uplink.

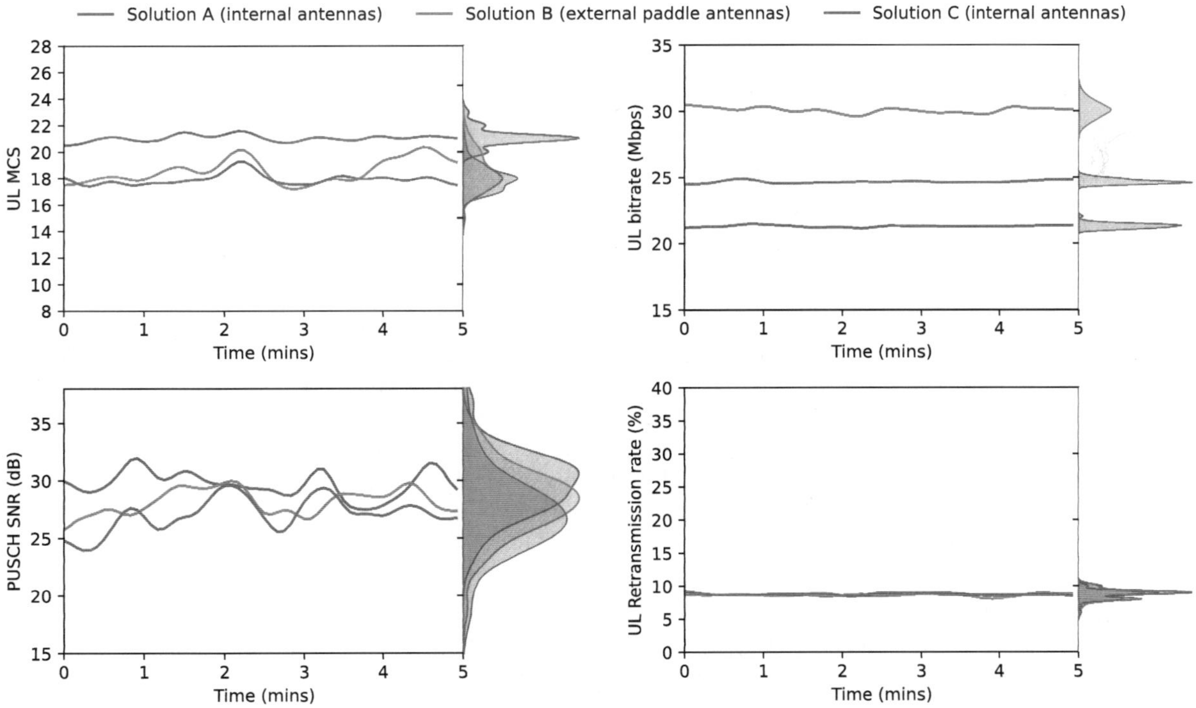

FIGURE 6: STUDIO WALK TEST FOR THREE VENDOR SOLUTIONS OPERATING WITH A SINGLE UPLINK LAYER (SISO).

Figure 6 presents a comparison of three COTS vendor solutions operating in the n77 (upper) band. The walk test was performed concurrently, with all three solutions mounted to the camera and transmitting at the same time. The video encoders were configured to send a 20 Mbps HEVC video stream over the 5G network at the lowest stable latency the solution could sustain (80-200 ms). With a SISO uplink configuration, all the devices were able to sustain their streams with similar retransmission rate. Note the significant difference in network bitrate despite the same 20 Mbps video configuration.

Instead of uplink MIMO, multiple receive antennas can be used to all receive the same single uplink layer with spatial diversity and maximum ratio combining (MRC) used to increase the effective SNR of the signal. We refer to this as receive diversity (RxD).

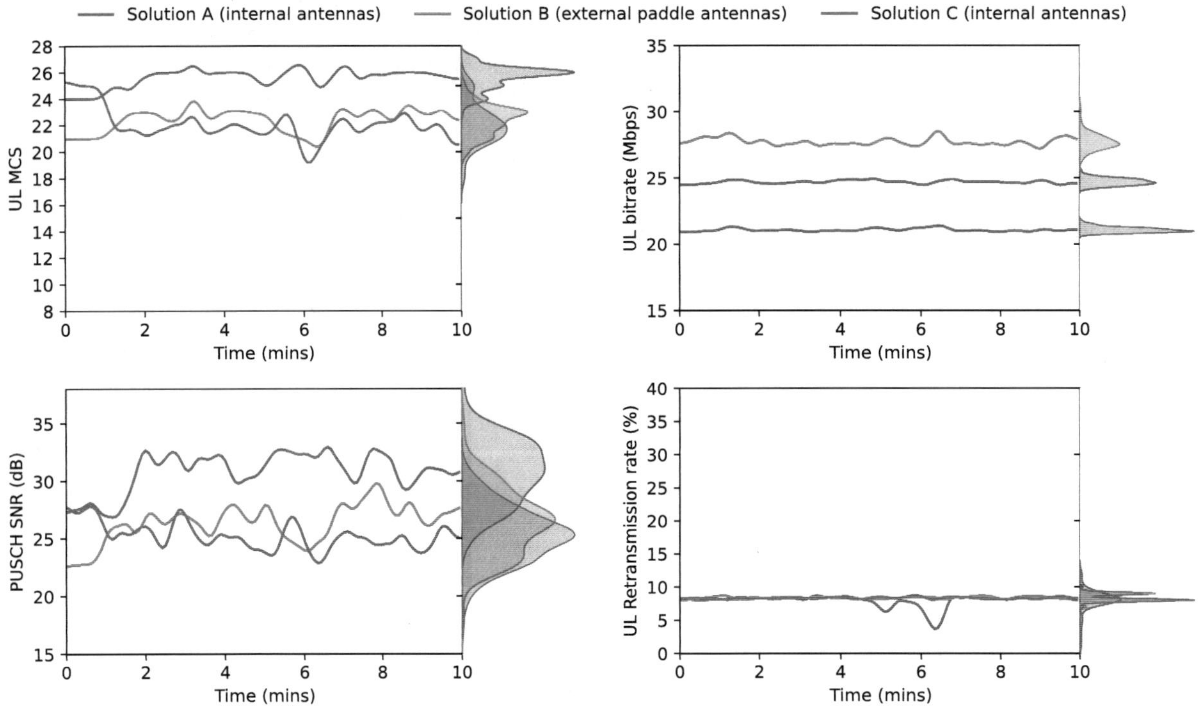

FIGURE 7: STUDIO WALK TEST FOR THREE VENDOR SOLUTIONS OPERATING WITH DUAL RECEIVE DIVERSITY (2RXD).

Figure 7 shows the walk test with the same three vendor solutions repeated using receive diversity with two receive antenna paths (2 RxD). This allows for opposite polarizations to be received and combined and can be very effective in environments with variable UE orientation or large amounts of multipath propagation. While SISO operation supported adequate uplink performance, uplink receive diversity is potentially protecting the uplink signal from flat fading that is a characteristic of indoor propagation with short duration multipath. The use of uplink RxD is seen to lead to a significant increase in sustained MCS, and we highly recommend the use of MRC receive diversity if available.

Performance at 2 GHz

The results discussed and presented above were obtained up near 4 GHz, where propagation properties typically require direct line of sight. Propagation can be significantly enhanced by moving to lower frequencies such as 2 GHz, where many broadcasters have dynamic (PMSE-style) access to spectrum for point-to-point wireless (COFDM) cameras links. The n40 SAL obtained by the BBC was used to compare performance at 2 GHz and 4 GHz.

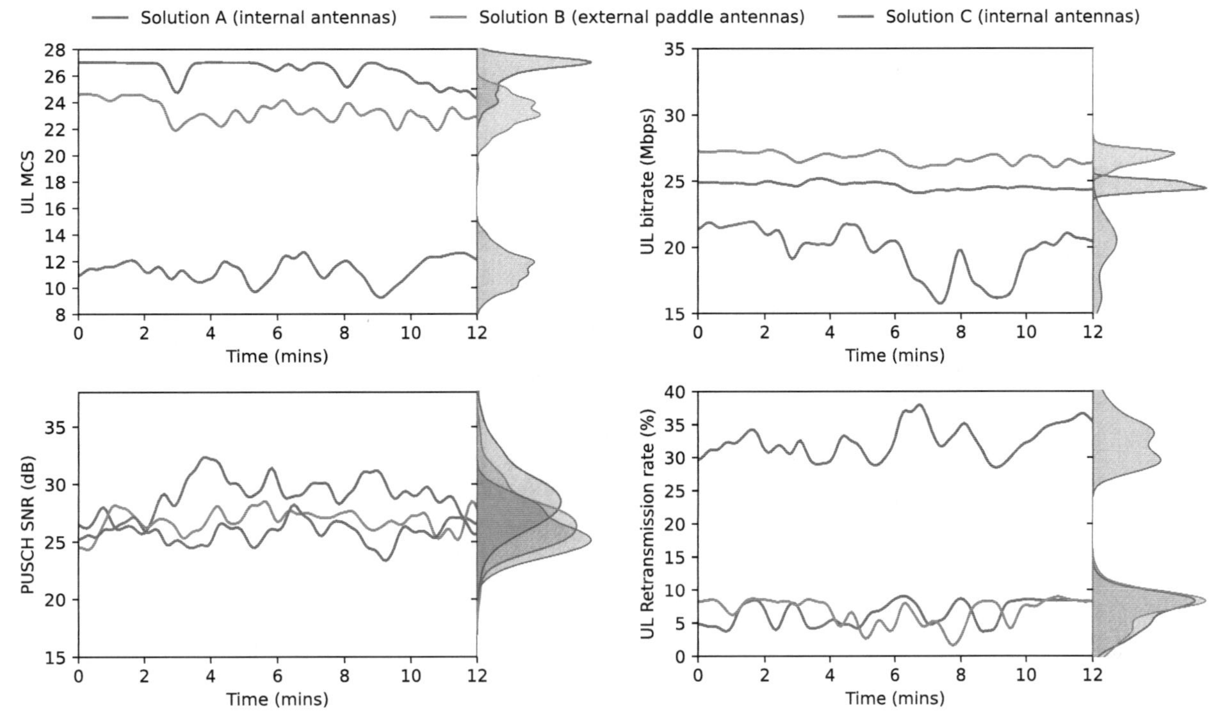

FIGURE 8: WALK TEST FOR THE THREE VENDOR SOLUTIONS OPERATING AT 2 GHZ.

Figure 8 shows the walk test with the same three vendor solutions repeated using a 40 MHz carrier centered at 2325 MHz and operating at 39 dBm (7.9 W) EIRP. Extended periods of transmission at MCS 27 (the maximum for the 256QAM table in use) were observed for Solution A, with increased performance also observed for Solution B. However, Solution C appeared to struggle in n40, with low MCS and high block error rate preventing the solution from maintaining its target bitrate. The video feed received using Solution C was in this case unusable, with significant disturbance to the feed. This could have been due to the particular internal antenna configuration in the 5G device.

Summary

To summarize, the performance of several encoder solutions over private 5G standalone networks operating in UK shared spectrum at 4 GHz and 2 GHz has been investigated, and their suitability to deliver low-latency broadcast production workflows evaluated. We found that a single network cell was sufficient to provide comprehensive coverage throughout the studio, with receive diversity increasing uplink performance and potentially offering protection from flat fades. All three vendor solutions performed well at 4 GHz. At 2 GHz, improved performance was observed for two solutions. Camera control of the Sony FX9 camera using a Sony RCP-1500 was performed directly through Solution A, or via a virtual private network (VPN) using a mobile handset for Solutions B and C. The lowest latency achieved was 80 ms from SDI input-to-output, but at this latency we were able to perform multiple handovers between cells operating in n77 and n40 with no packet loss or impact on the video stream.

Real-world Deployments

While the previous section discussed and compared several solutions and configurations operating in a controlled studio environment, this section presents some real-world deployments over the last year.

Stadium coverage

A private 5G standalone network was deployed at a large stadium in Glasgow to explore low-latency workflows in a stadium, as well as coverage and performance in a HDD environment.

The network cell was located towards the east corner of the Main (South) Stand, with a 7 dBi sector antenna mounted to an unused scaffolding tower. The University of Strathclyde's Glasgow-wide license was used for a 100 MHz carrier centered at 3967 MHz, with an increased maximum transmit power of 33 dBm EIRP approved by the regulator, Ofcom. The cell was operated at 32 dBm (1.58 W), with a transmitted reference signal power of -3 dBm.

FIGURE 9: CELL LOCATION AND COVERAGE IN A STADIUM ENVIRONMENT.

Figure 9 shows that excellent RSRP between -80 and -91 dBm was measured inside the stadium using a Samsung S24 Ultra mobile handset. Outside the stadium, RSRP dropped to around -120 dBm in most places, but increased to -106 dBm directly outside the stadium in the corner nearest to the antenna. This was due to an open passageway directly into the stadium allowing the rear lobe of the antenna to escape the confines of the stadium. Outside the North Stand, RSRP as low as -136 dBm were measured and the handset even lost connectivity completely for a period. These data provide useful insight on the propagation characteristics at 4 GHz in a stadium environment, and how an understanding of this can help plan coverage and cell placement. While a single cell can provide adequate coverage inside the stadium, devices outside may connect but will struggle to perform any useful uplink activity. The metalwork and construction of the stadium also introduces the potential for multi-path propagation, and receive diversity is recommended to flatten the radio channel.

Stadium Low-Latency Multi-Camera Production

As part of the *Tay5G Challenge*, a private 5G standalone network was deployed at Dens Park football (soccer) stadium for the Dundee *vs.* Aberdeen fixture with the production company QTV. For the event, a UK Innovation and Trial license [6] was approved by Ofcom for a 100 MHz carrier centered at 3950 MHz with a maximum transmit power of 38.7 dBm (7.4 W). A 100 MHz cell was deployed inside the stadium on a scaffolding tower towards the northeast corner of the stadium. A 5 dBi omni-directional antenna was used for a transmit power of 34 dBm (2.5 W) EIRP, but with 2 downlink layers (often referred to as 2x2 DL MIMO) for an effective total power of 37 dBm (5 W) EIRP. The adjacent spectrum was monitored with a spectrum analyzer and found to be clear. The network ran using uplink-biased TDD pattern DDSUUUUUUU to increase uplink capacity, and SISO uplink with 2 RxD.

The radio head inside the stadium was connected to the baseband unit located in a secondary 5G OB van by SMPTE cable for fiber and power. The Haivision Streamhub decoder and a Blackmagic ATEM Television Studio HD8 ISO video switcher were located on the 5G user plane, with local monitoring for the camera feeds and an Internet connection back to the QTV master control room (MCR).

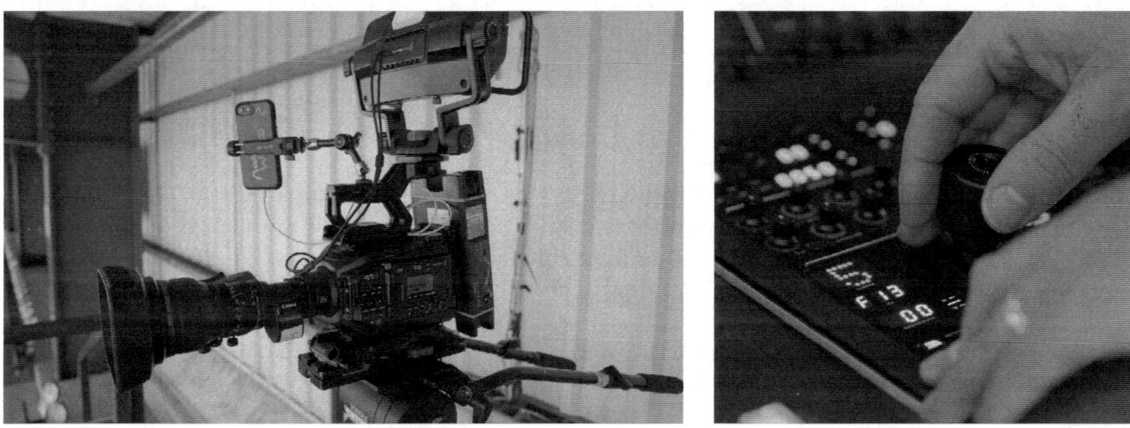

FIGURE 10: CAMERA DEPLOYMENT WITH 5G-ENABLED VIDEO ENCODER AND IPHONE.

Before the game, four Blackmagic URSA Broadcast G2 cameras were deployed in camera positions across the stadium, with Haivision Pro460 encoders providing an ultra-low latency (100 ms) 20 Mbps 1080p50 HEVC video feed from each camera to the production vehicle. In addition, each URSA Broadcast G2 camera was connected to an iPhone SE, providing a 5G connection to the camera itself. The camera rig is shown in Figure 10 (left). A secondary 10 Mbps H.264 RTMP stream was sent directly to the ATEM TVS HD8 switcher, which features built-in Streaming Bridge to directly receive compressed IP streams. While the Streaming Bridge can support SRT at around 200 ms and RTMP at around 500 ms, at the time of testing the ATEM TVS HD8 did not support receiving SRT streams. The RTMP connection establishes a return path from the ATEM switcher to the camera, allowing for full camera control and tally functionality. The iPhones were also used for low-latency talkback using the Unity Intercom application, with a local server on the 5G user plane. This was integrated using Dante with the main OB intercom system, allowing seamless connectivity between the OB vehicles and camera operators, as well as back to the QTV MCR. In summary, four ultra-low latency (100 ms) streams and four RTMP (500 ms) streams were transmitted simultaneously, with full camera control, return video, tally and talkback integration.

During the football match itself, the six fixed camera positions deployed by QTV were shadowed using the private 5G network – as well as the standard SMPTE connection, an SDI feed from each camera was encoded by a Haivision Pro460 video encoder and transmitted over the private 5G network to the Streamhub located in the OB van. The production used interlaced 1080i50 video, preventing ultra-low latency use. The standard broadcast SST transport protocol was used with a latency of 500 ms, but this was unstable with the interlaced input and was increased to 800 ms. The standard broadcast SST profile allowed video feeds to be monitored locally as well as passed on to a second Streamhub at the QTV MCR (with a latency of 500 ms). This enabled the production gallery to have both the cabled feeds and 5G feeds. Three of the URSA Broadcast G2 cameras were set up next to the production cameras and configured with a 10 Mbps RTMP stream to the ATEM switcher.

FIGURE 11: 5G MULTIVIEWER AND REMOTE FEED MONITORING DURING THE MATCH.

Figure 11 (left) shows the nine 5G video feeds on the ATEM multiviewer in the 5G OB van. The Pro460 feeds from the six production cameras can be seen along with the three RTMP feeds from the Blackmagic cameras, for a sustained uplink network load of around 190 Mbps (6 x 25 Mbps for the Pro460 streams plus 3 x 12 Mbps for the RTMP streams). Both the local Streamhub and QTV MCR Streamhub were configured to have SRT outputs available, which allowed for remote monitoring of the feeds by devices (such as tablets) on the private 5G network. Figure 11 (right) shows a 2x2 multiview being monitored on an iPad at the pitch side just before kick-off. Total latency on the pitch-side feed was about 1 second. Providing wireless monitoring or return video feeds to camera operators is a reasonable use of the available downlink resources.

Of primary interest was the video quality of the compressed HEVC video streams when compared with the lossless compression of the existing system, as well as synchronization and drift. The video feeds were independently evaluated, and the feedback was excellent – the quality, synchronization and drift were deemed to be more than sufficient. The ability to send encrypted return video streams directly to wireless devices on the pitch side (or even on to the pitch itself direct to the referee) is attractive. Since the connection between the OB vehicles and the QTV MCR appears as a flat network, a Blackmagic RCP at QTV in Glasgow (62 miles as the crow flies) was used to remotely rack the cameras. While this successfully demonstrated the principle, the end-to-and latency to the MCR of 1.3 s was not ideal, but could be severely reduced by using the low latency SST profile to land progressive video streams directly at QTV in around 100 ms.

FIGURE 12: PRIVATE 5G DEPLOYMENTS FOR LOW-LATENCY PRODUCTION IN STADIA.

Finally, Figure 12 (left) shows a private 5G cell deployed in Stade de France (Paris) and (right) in use at Inalpi Arena (Turin) to support ultra-low latency broadcast production workflows.

Outdoor performance for winter sports

While 5G propagation and performance in a stadium is expected to be quite different to a studio they are still confined areas, and the above examples demonstrate that ultra-low latency broadcast production is feasible using (private) 5G for bi-directional wireless camera connectivity in these environments. However, an alpine ski resort is a completely different environment.

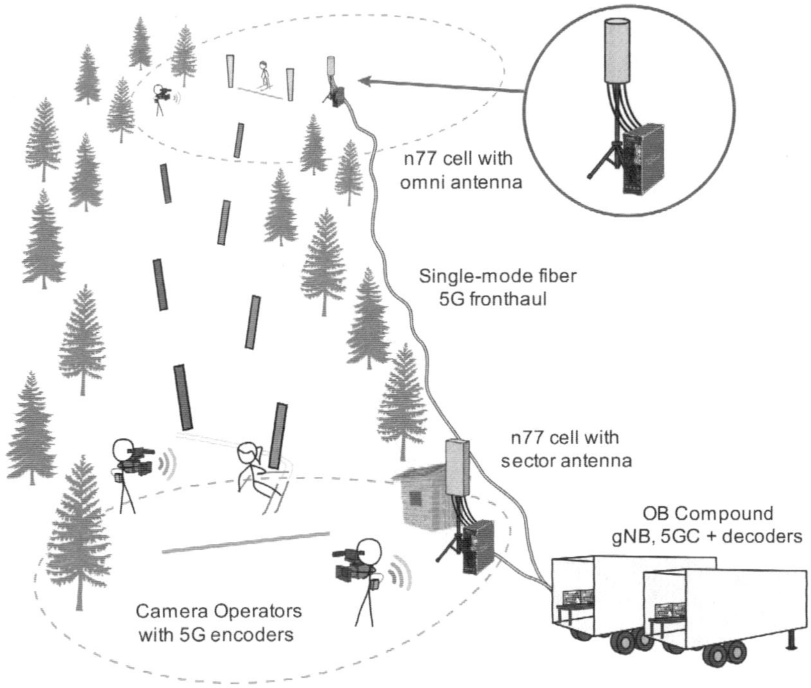

FIGURE 13: ILLUSTRATION OF THE TWO-CELL NETWORK DEPLOYED IN BARDONECCHIA.

Italian public service broadcaster RAI (Italy) deployed a two-cell private 5G network at the Bardonecchia ski area for testing ultra-low latency broadcast solutions and workflows during the FISU University Winter Games. Figure 13 illustrates the network layout, with cells providing coverage for wireless cameras at the top and bottom of the piste. The two cells were connected back to the baseband unit located in the OB compound, along with the decoders and monitoring equipment. Both cells used 100 MHz carriers centered at 3960 MHz in n77 spectrum licensed to RAI. The network used the uplink-biased frame structure DDSUUUUUUU with low-latency optimizations [3] and was used to support four low-latency camera feeds along with additional contribution feeds from mobile handsets.

A spectrum analyzer was used to verify that the spectrum was clear at both cell sites before transmission, and there were no issues running the uplink-biased frame structure in close proximity to a public mobile network as there was sufficient spectral separation between the networks.

Figure 14 (left) and (center) shows the lower cell located next to the timing cabin and using a 17.5 dBi sector antenna directed downhill towards the bottom of the piste, providing coverage over the end of the run and among the athletes and spectators gathered at the base. The top cell (right) instead used a 10 dBi omni-directional antenna inclined with its plane along the gradient of the mountain to provide coverage for cameras around the race start point. Both cells used receive diversity on two antenna ports.

FIGURE 14: NETWORK CELLS PROVIDING COVERAGE AT THE BOTTOM (LEFT, CENTER) AND TOP (RIGHT) OF THE RUN.

The coverage provided by the cells was measured using a Sony PDT-FP1 mobile handset logging RSRP data. This was done around both cell locations, but also for the duration of the chairlift and through the village of Melezet.

FIGURE 15: COVERAGE (RSRP) AND HANDOVER LOCATION (GREEN) MEASURED AROUND THE TWO CELLS (BLUE).

Figure 15 presents the measured RSRP data along with the cell locations (indicated by blue arrows). Good coverage was observed around both cells, including on the back lobe of the lower cell (towards the left). Walk tests with video streaming confirmed that low latency video (150 ms) was possible around the base of the run, but also all the way back to the village itself where line of sight (LoS) was maintained. At the top, video streaming was interrupted when passing behind the restaurant (non-LoS) but was otherwise excellent. When travelling on the chairlift from the top to the bottom, devices handed over from the top cell to the bottom cell as soon at the chairlift dipped below the plateau and LoS to the top cell was lost. This position is illustrated by the green arrow. The mobile handset handed over (it did not lose connection and reconnect) at a distance of 1.26 km on the back lobe of the lower cell sector antenna, which was unexpected. However, signal strength was very low, and no meaningful bitrate could be sustained until the UE was closer and RSRP had reached around -100 dBm. Live video was successfully captured from the chairlift for periods at the top and bottom.

FIGURE 16: CONTENT CAPTURED OVER THE PRIVATE 5G NETWORK.

Figure 16 highlights some examples of the content that was captured over the private 5G network during the testing, from pieces to camera (left) to contributions from the piste itself (right). This included ultra-low latency video feeds using codecs from Haivision (Cam2) and Sony (Cam3/ME1 in center image), but also contribution feeds from mobile handsets. The MojoPro application was used to capture live content from chairlifts and the piste as a colleague from RAI made their way down on skis (Cam1). Note that in the center screenshot from the multiviewer, the iPhone streaming the MojoPro feed and camera with the Sony encoder are filming each other. The potential for cameras to deliver new content from new perspectives and locations (even from the athletes themselves) opens up a host of new angles and opportunities for storytelling, bringing audiences closer to the athletes and action.

Discussion

The use of 5G technology to provide increased wireless connectivity at live events and to support live broadcast continues to increase. Recently, at the Super Bowl LIX, attendees were advised not to use the stadium Wi-Fi but instead make use of the massive extra capacity installed by Verizon and AT&T. Verizon is reported to have installed over 700 additional antennas (including beam forming antennas), while AT&T installed 34 high-power and 255 low-power mmWave radios [7]. This is a huge amount of hardware in a single venue. There is substantial interest in mmWave as there is a lot of capacity available due to the amount of spectrum and large supported channel bandwidths. A recent proof-of-concept [8] demonstrated four low latency[10] video feeds and a drone connected over a public 5G standalone network using 20 MHz spectrum in n78 but also 800 MHz in mmWave (n258). The reduced propagation performance of mmWave presents some challenges for widespread deployment – for example, 75 dB path loss at 26 GHz occurs at just 5 m using the free-space model (2), compared to 34 m at 4 GHz.

While the Citizens Broadband Radio Service (CBRS) spectrum available in the USA for private networks is a great resource, it presents a few technical challenges that we believe limit its suitability for critical broadcast connectivity. The relatively high permitted transmit powers pose a severe risk of interference to uplink-biased networks, while matching the standard downlink-biased pattern offers

[10] Actual video latency achieved was not specified.

limited uplink capacity in the modest (10-40 MHz) channels available. Furthermore, with the potential for many users running in adjacent channels and dynamic licensing, it is very difficult to ensure a clean RF environment, or to isolate and take measures to mitigate any issues encountered. The ability of users to operate "opportunistically" using unused spectrum assigned to another licensee increases the risk of interference in congested areas. Moreover, public networks are allowed to access CBRS spectrum, reducing availability in high demand environments where it is potentially needed by broadcasters most.

There is interest in the use of (private) 5G for wireless production in studio environments. Whether this is to replace or augment traditional wireless camera links, the ultra-low latency requirement is present for camera control, audio synchronization, and integration among cabled cameras. Although latency is (currently) higher than that of commercial COFDM systems, it is still very much suitable for live TV production. The TV2 breakfast studio in Copenhagen has successfully utilized a private 5G standalone network with low latency 5G-attached cameras. Feedback from production staff (including sound engineers, directors, and the Technical Operation Manager) has been positive, with no noticeable degradation in performance.

The studio test results presented here demonstrate that good coverage could be obtained in the studio using just a single antenna panel located on the gantry in the corner of the studio. Measurements of the RSRP indicated good signal strength across the entire studio floor, varying between -67 dBm and -75 dBm. Using an uplink-biased TDD pattern, a throughput of over 400 Mbps could be sustained in a 100 MHz channel. It would be interesting to assess how an omni-directional antenna instead suspended above the center of the studio might perform, as well as repeat tests with a complete set and audience. We note that Studio A at BBC Scotland is lined on the inside with an open wire mesh, which acts like a Faraday cage for 4 GHz, resulting in a very clean RF environment.

The COTS radio backs varied somewhat in performance. The best implementation achieved a video latency of 80 ms, with stable operation across the entire studio floor and direct camera control through the encoder itself. This was verified using walk tests and monitoring of the video decoder and RF performance metrics. Another vendor solution appeared unstable operating below a latency target of 200 ms but was otherwise satisfactory. The third solution potentially offered the lowest latency down to 65 ms but was unable to perform reliably at this latency. The radio metrics allowed the antenna performance of the encoders to be assessed. Devices with external antennas tend to operate with the best radio margins. Tests with mobile handsets demonstrated similar reductions in the link margin, confirming that internal patch antennas cannot match the performance of resonant external antennas. All devices were tested in both n40 and n77 (upper) bands. One vendor solution with internal antennas tended to operate with reduced margin in the n40 band, indicating that its antenna system is not optimized for lower frequency operation.

The majority of the testing at BBC Scotland was carried out using the shared access license, allowing transmission up to 31 dBm (1.26 W). Operation proved perfectly possible in the University of Strathclyde's Glasgow-wide low power license with transmit power limited to 27 dBm (0.5 W). It should be noted that the tests were made in an empty studio without any sets or audience seating. It would be desirable to repeat some of the low power measurements in a studio rigged for a production.

Camera-back encoders such as the Haivision Pro460 can create IP tunnels between the encoder and decoder, allowing devices on the user plane to be able to communicate with the camera. This can be used to enable camera control. The encoder needs to have the tunnel activated and act as a gateway with a distinct subnet on which the camera is then connected. The appropriate IP route is often added automatically, but if not then a rule to route the camera subnet through the tunnel should be added on the decoder, and the IP address of the decoder used as the gateway for remote control panel (RCP) units. Some other vendors also have tunnels to facilitate communication with the camera, but if not then it can be achieved quite simply using low-cost VPN-enabled hardware. The homemade system used here consisted of a MikroTik hAP ac lite router located on the user plane as a Wireguard server and a

GL.iNet GL-AR300M16 as a Wireguard client and serving the camera subnet. The MikroTik router had a rule added to route traffic for the camera subnet via the GL.iNet VPN address. The GL.iNet was connected to the 5G network using a tethered mobile handset and RCPs configured to use the MikroTik as their gateway. This was quick to connect and proved to be reliable over extended periods.
A series of real-world deployments that used low latency production workflows were discussed, highlighting that the right (private) 5G configuration is certainly capable of delivering ultra-low latency video with camera control, tally, return video, and intercom. For stadium deployments, it is important to understand how cell coverage behaves, and we have found receive diversity to be important in assisting with multipath. Once again, comprehensive coverage can be achieved using a small number of cells with modest transmit power, since the use case is predominantly limited by uplink power. This can be helped by using devices with decent external antennas – while an increase in network cell downlink transmit power does not help with uplink sensitivity, an increase to the effective uplink transmit power *will* increase usable cell size and capacity.

The deployment at Dens Park stadium was crucial for showing that multiple ultra-low latency feeds could be maintained over an extended period. Quality and synchronization comparisons to lossless SDI-over-fiber feeds showed excellent performance, more than sufficient for the broadcast. The deployment also showed how mobile handsets could be used for a push-to-talk intercom system that integrated seamlessly with the Dante-based audio system used by the OB and MCR. Finally, camera control and tally were straightforward with the Blackmagic equipment, and was connected when the URSA Broadcast G2 camera was configured to send an RTMP video stream to the ATEM TVS HD8 switcher. For a "data only" connection, the camera can be configured to stream a very low bitrate. The URSA camera was easily made 5G-enabled by tethering a mobile handset by USB. The camera was instantly able to create the RTMP stream and establish the camera control and tally link. The only issue we experienced was with the streaming keys on the ATEM switcher changing, requiring us to recreate stream profiles and reload onto each camera. Hopefully this will be addressed in future switcher and camera firmware. Camera control was responsive, and the camera could even be remotely racked from the production MCR located in another city.

Deployment for testing at a winter sports competition confirmed that private 5G could support ultra-low latency video workflows from both Haivision and Sony, and across larger outdoor areas. There is strong potential to capture new content (from chairlifts or the piste). The individual cell performance was very good, with extensive coverage probably helped by propagation over snow being like propagation over water. Handover between cells (which was unexpected at the distance) showed that multi-cell networks could provide continuous coverage along the field of play for small wireless cameras such as mobile handsets or drones. Encoders would again benefit from external antennas to maximize uplink budget.

Conclusions

When configuring 5G standalone networks to best support low latency uplink-heavy broadcast production workflows, care is required to assess the necessary transmit power and to select the most appropriate frame structure. Uplink-biased TDD patterns can provide a significant increase in uplink capacity but are susceptible to interference from downlink-biased networks. When trying to operate using an uplink-biased frame structure in a location surrounded by high-power downlink-biased networks, it may be necessary to use bandpass filters to reduce interference from adjacent channels. We suspect that transmit powers above 30 dBm (1 W) are unnecessary for uplink-biased use cases due to the limited uplink transmission power available from the user equipment. Where system configuration allows, there are a number of optimizations that can be made to reduce network latency and jitter, and better support ultra-low latency workflows [3].

Extensive studio tests were undertaken at BBC Scotland, with three commercial encoder solutions evaluated using spectrum in upper n77 and n40. A single sector antenna was sufficient to provide comprehensive coverage throughout the studio. Ultra-low latency video with 80 ms latency from SDI

input to SDI output was sustained with camera control. All three solutions performed well in upper n77, with one solution performing exceptionally well in n40. Receive diversity using maximum ratio combining was demonstrated to have a positive impact on uplink performance, and we recommend the use of receive diversity over additional uplink layers (uplink MIMO).
Finally, a selection of recent private 5G deployments supporting ultra-low latency broadcast production workflows were discussed. The deployments demonstrate how private 5G can be successfully used in very different environments to provide wireless connectivity.

5G technology is now mature and ready for critical video production applications. Initially, productions are likely to experiment by using private 5G to augment their existing wireless systems, rather than replace them altogether. Use of the network for camera control, tally and other auxiliary services could save the plethora of additional licenses and transceivers required to complement point-to-point RF links. In Bardonecchia, the live-to-air piece-to-camera was simultaneously transmitted over private 5G and a traditional RF link, as was done for a premiership rugby match back in April 2022 [9]. Alternatively, private 5G could be used to increase creative freedom and bring new perspectives or camera angles to a production, particularly as cameras on mobile handsets continue to get better. 5G remains an attractive technology for future wireless connectivity and integrates naturally into modern IP workflows using cloud technology.

Acknowledgments

The authors gratefully acknowledge the support and expertise of the wider Neutral Wireless (NW) and StrathSDR (UoS) group. In addition, we are grateful to BBC Scotland for support with access to Studio A, as well as BBC colleagues Ian Wagdin, Simon Eley and Purminder Gandhu. We would also like to thank Peter VanDall from Celtic F.C.; Gareth Gordon, Seth Edwards, David Lowe, Julie Robinson and the team at QTV; Luca Vignaroli, Federico Pandolfi and Alessandro Lucco Castello from RAI CRITS; as well as Blackmagic Design, Sony, Haivision and Teradek for making their hardware available to us on multiple occasions. UoS, NW and the BBC acknowledge support provided by UK Government Department for Science, Innovation and Technology (DSIT) co-funding for the Open Networks Shared Spectrum Innovation Environment (ONSIDE) project (October 2023 – March 2025). UoS and NW also gratefully acknowledge the financial support provided by the *Tay5G Challenge Fund*.

References

[1] M. B. Waddell *et al.*, "5G standalone non-public networks: modernising wireless production", IBC Technical Papers (2023).

[2] S. R. Yoffe *et al.*, "Using a private 5G network to support the international broadcast of the coronation of HM King Charles III", NAB BEITC (2024).

[3] M. B. Waddell *et al.*, "Optimising 5G for low latency broadcast production", IBC Technical Papers (2024).

[4] Ofcom, "Shared Access Licence: Guidance Document" (2025).

[5] GMSA, "5G TDD Synchronisation: Guidelines and Recommendations for the Coexistence of TDD Networks in the 3.5 GHz Range" (2020).

[6] Ofcom, "Innovation and Trial licensing: Guidance notes for applicants" (2018).

[7] Light Reading, "Why Verizon swapped Wi-Fi for 5G at Super Bowl LIX" (11/02/2025).

[8] Ericsson Press Release, "Ericsson, 3 Denmark, TV 2, and Sony kick off new era of live sports broadcasting" (13/06/2024).

[9] Sports Video Group, "BT in talks to commercialise use of 5G non-public networks" (11/11/2022).